MARKET

A Global
Perspective

Bronis Verhage

Professor of Marketing
Georgia State University
Atlanta, Georgia

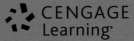

CENGAGE
Learning®

Australia • Brazil • Japan • Korea • Mexico • Singapore • Spain • United Kingdom • United States

Marketing: A Global Perspective
Bronis Verhage

Publishing Director: Linden Harris

Publisher: Andrew Ashwin

Development Editor: Felix Rowe

Production Editor: Beverley Copland

Senior Manufacturing Buyer: Eyvett Davis

Marketing Manager: Vicky Fielding

Typesetter: Integra Software Services
    Pvt. Ltd.

Cover design: Adam Renvoize

Text design: Design Deluxe

For product information and technology assistance,
contact **emea.info@cengage.com**.
For permission to use material from this text or product,
and for permission queries,
email **emea.permissions@cengage.com**.

British Library Cataloguing-in-Publication Data
A catalogue record for this book is available from the British Library.

ISBN: 978-1-4080-6490-0

Cengage Learning EMEA
Cheriton House, North Way, Andover, Hampshire, SP10 5BE
United Kingdom

Cengage Learning products are represented in Canada by Nelson Education Ltd.

For your lifelong learning solutions, visit
www.cengage.co.uk

Purchase your next print book, e-book or e-chapter at
www.cengagebrain.com

Printed in China by RR Donnelley
1 2 3 4 5 6 7 8 9 10 – 15 14 13

To the memory of
Ed Cundiff
Mentor and long-time friend

BRIEF CONTENTS

CONTENTS

PART 1 INSIGHT INTO MARKETING   3

PART 3 PRODUCT DECISIONS   259

7   Product strategy and services marketing   260

PART 4 PROMOTION DECISIONS 355

PART 6 DISTRIBUTION DECISIONS 563

13 Distribution 564

PREFACE

INTRODUCTION

We live in an exciting period of rapid changes and major challenges. In order to compete successfully, firms must continue to launch better products and services. Marketing strategies considered excellent a few years ago, might not suffice in today's dynamic markets. A company must systematically differentiate its brands and pursue an effective marketing strategy.

Never before in the history of marketing have changes in the business environment occurred so quickly and relentlessly. The corporate world has become more global and competitive. Companies have succeeded in cutting development and launch time for new products in half. Their products and services are not only of high quality, but also carefully tailored to the needs and wants of the target market. As a result of numerous innovations, distribution costs have been slashed, while customer service continues to be improved. This tremendous progress in the marketing of goods and services has been accomplished by replacing outdated business practices with new marketing insights and techniques. In executing their strategies, for example, many managers now rely on social media, guerrilla marketing and other communication methods that make effective use of the Internet. The Internet also gives small start-up companies access to the international market. By systematically applying contemporary marketing fundamentals and techniques in this progressive new domain, any firm can improve its competitive position.

REASONS FOR WRITING THIS BOOK

An important goal of those who work in higher education is to help students gain useful insights and skills, preparing them for leadership positions in organizations around the world. This is a demanding task for educators. Traditional American concepts that dominate most marketing books may not be adequate in today's global market. Neither are the domestic examples and voluminous lists of definitions that comprise many US textbooks.

To be prepared for successful careers and the 21st century challenges they will face as managers in the global economy, students should not only be familiar with the principles of marketing, but must also be able to develop and implement effective marketing strategies *abroad*. Helping to equip students with a professional *attitude,* as well as the knowledge and practical skills required to take advantage of international marketing opportunities, was the driving force behind the introduction of *Marketing: A Global Perspective*. Future managers must be able to use their skills in organizations that market in countries and cultures other than their own.

Global companies are increasingly interested in recruiting a new generation of managers who apply the marketing fundamentals in creative ways and have acquired hands-on skills. Ideally, they are ambitious yet realistic team players, who operate as flexible but results-driven managers and can work independently in innovative and customer-focused ways.

Today's students are tomorrow's marketers and leaders who have learned to anticipate change in a turbulent global environment and to think in an analytical, multi-disciplinary fashion. *Marketing: A Global Perspective* makes a significant contribution to cultivating this *mindset*. The book will prepare students for the challenges ahead by engaging and motivating them to learn about marketing management and by encouraging them – through international marketing examples, cases and insightful perspectives – to practice making sound marketing decisions.

POSITIONING

This contemporary text was developed to introduce students to the fundamentals, practices and analytic techniques of marketing. It is comprehensive in scope and managerial in orientation. The book is designed to facilitate student learning from individual reading and independent study, which is increasingly important in marketing education. The main objective is to help students deepen their understanding of marketing and develop the skills to become successful, market-oriented managers, who are able to satisfy their customers – no matter where they live – in this era of cut-throat competition.

How does Verhage's *Marketing: A Global Perspective* differ from other English-language marketing text books used in universities, colleges and business schools around the world? The book features powerful ideas and insightful, provocative opinions on key issues in marketing management by esteemed professors and executives based in Europe, Africa, the Middle East and the United States, embedded in a global context. With its key marketing concepts tailored to fit the international framework of the text – such as management's strategic viewpoint and focus on social responsibility, ethical and sustainability concerns – the book incorporates a teaching style and marketing curriculum preferred in prestigious, internationally-oriented business schools.

Each of the book's 15 chapters includes five mini-cases and professional perspectives. Featured companies include Heinz, Philips, L'Oreal, BMW, Google, Zara, Ikea and many others. The book also analyzes marketing strategies used in the global hotel industry, music business and by a soccer club such as Manchester United Football Club.

PEDAGOGICAL APPROACH

The book's engaging, lively writing style enhances student learning. The use of 'easy reading' language especially appeals to non-native speakers of English. Its up-to-date, comprehensive coverage of marketing concepts and best practices helps to broaden the scope of marketing beyond the traditional marketing management paradigm, which has long dominated the field.

Marketing: A Global Perspective offers a contemporary review of new priorities in marketing, as illustrated by a fascinating selection of analyses of world-class companies' customer-focused strategies. These memorable and often provocative examples of marketing practices include large and small companies, working in both business-to-business and consumer marketing of products or services. Their strategies and performance make clear that marketing is a universal function, essential to any company that wants to achieve outstanding results in the marketplace.

STRUCTURE OF THE TEXT

Marketing: A Global Perspective's clear structure and managerial approach are identical to the Dutch-language version, *Grondslagen van de Marketing* (8th edition). This book – the market leader in the Netherlands for three decades – has created a great deal of enthusiasm about marketing among the hundreds of thousands of students who have used it.

The topics are arranged in a logical manner. The book begins with a discussion of foundation concepts, strategy development and major changes in the marketing environment, including an overview of ethical and social responsibility issues affecting marketing. It also highlights strategic planning, organizing the marketing efforts and developing a marketing plan. The next three chapters take an in-depth look at buyer behaviour and two important marketing tools: marketing research and market segmentation. It emphasizes the need for effective relationship marketing, targeting and positioning strategies.

The remaining chapters of the book address the elements of the marketing mix: product, promotion, pricing and place (including online marketing), all from a decision-making perspective. The final chapter (Chapter 15) tackles the challenges of plotting and implementing a global marketing strategy. Today, global competititon is so intense that, to remain competitive, every manager should try to identify international marketing trends and opportunities promptly. Therefore, cutting edge techniques as well as intriguing cases and illustrations of successful global marketing strategies are integrated throughout the text.

KEY FEATURES

Marketing: A Global Perspective features up-to-date content and dozens of mini-cases that capture the excitement of marketing. Each chapter opens with a brief statement of *learning goals*, an eye-opening introduction and an inspiring *Marketing-in-Action* vignette – based on a real-world business problem – to show students how theory and principles relate to marketing as it is actually practiced. Since these vignettes are thought-provoking, they stimulate student interest in marketing and can be effectively used to start class discussion.

Other boxed features include a range of pan-European and global examples – both successes (*Marketing Toppers*) and failures (*Marketing Mistakes*) in business – encompassing the entire field of marketing. This includes services marketing, B2B and green marketing.

The *Professor's Perspectives* and the *Practitioner's Perspectives* (featuring executives discussing their companies' strategies) in every chapter offer powerful ideas and insightful opinions on key issues in marketing management. They help bring the marketing fundamentals to life in a global context. Through these concise box features, students are able to reflect on current marketing challenges and techniques, making them better prepared to apply the tools they explore in the book.

Each chapter ends with a clearly presented *summary* and a set of review and *discussion questions* that reinforce the major concepts presented. The text, in other words, sticks to the time-tested pedagogical formula of 'tell them what you're going to tell them, tell them, then tell them what you've told them.'

ONLINE RESOURCES

The book is autopackaged with access to Cengage's premium platform offering students a range of resources from cases and videos, to crosswords, flashcards and multiple choice questions to help students prepare for exams. It also includes *Verhage's Glossary*, which defines the more than one thousand bold-faced marketing terms in the book.

This glossary – both organized by order of appearance of the key terms in each chapter and, comprehensively, in alphabetical order – will help students build a solid marketing vocabulary. It is also available as *flashcards*, making it easy for students to check their understanding of marketing terms. Since these concepts are commonly used terminology in business when developing strategies or evaluating marketing plans, the book and its support package remain a great reference resource for managers and marketing practitioners.

The lecturers' companion *website* contains various teaching and learning tools to support instructors. The online platform complements the text with 15 *PowerPoint* presentations for lecturers and offers relevant articles and useful links to videos. For more information on access, please see the 'About the Digital Resources' page.

ACKNOWLEDGEMENTS

Like most textbooks in this era of benchmarking, *Marketing: A Global Perspective* reflects the ideas of many competent researchers, professors, writers and practitioners who have contributed to the development of the marketing discipline. As an author, I appreciate the opportunity to include and recognize their efforts in this book. I would especially like to thank my colleagues and former students of Georgia State University and the Rotterdam School of Management at Erasmus University who used the book in their marketing curriculum, and of The University of Texas at Austin for their many contributions. In particular Ken Bernhardt, Bill Cunningham and my mentor and long-time friend Ed Cundiff – who, regrettably, passed away recently – were a source of inspiration in completing and revising this book. I am grateful for their valuable insights and advice.

I also want to recognize and thank my colleague Wes Johnston and his Center for Business and Industrial Marketing at Georgia State University for their support, as well as my graduate research assistants Jeff Foreman, J.P. Kill and Michael Ellers. In addition, special thanks go to Andrew Ashwin, Publisher, Felix Rowe, Development Editor, and the other talented publishing, editing and marketing professionals at Cengage Learning EMEA who have made this book a reality. Their dedication and hard work are admirable.

Last but not least, I would like to thank my wife Eveline and our daughters Tiffany, Georgianna and Emily for their patience during this 'transatlantic mission'. They were a source of inspiration on both sides of the ocean. This book could not have been written without their support.

Atlanta/Haamstede, 2013
Bronis J. Verhage

Publisher Acknowledgements

The publishers would like to thank the following individuals and companies for their invaluable contributions to this book:

Elmira Bogoviyeva (KIMEP University, Kazakhstan)
David Chalcraft (University of Westminster, UK)
Andy Cropper (Sheffield Hallam University, UK)
Carla Fourie (*Twenty3 Media*, South Africa)
Julian Glover (*6x6 Creative Ltd*, UK)
Simon Groves and Kathryn Ranger (*PRG Ltd*, UK)
Paul Johnston (Sheffield Hallam University, UK)
Mihalis Kavaratzis (University of Leicester, UK)
Simon Kelly (*Cohesion*, UK)
Jessica Lichy (*IDRAC Research*, France)
Farah Mihoubi (USA)
Laetitia Radder (Nelson Mandela Metropolitan University, South Africa)
Peter Spier (SKEMA, France)
Madéle Tait (Nelson Mandela Metropolitan University, South Africa)
Marcus Thompson (*Contract Marketers* and University of Stirling, UK)
Uchenna Uzo (Pan-African University, Nigeria)
Andrew Weir (*ZenithOptimedia Worldwide*, UK)
Lisa Williams (*BHP Information Solutions Ltd*, UK)
Media Select International
Noordhoff Uitgevers bv

ABOUT THE AUTHOR

DR BRONIS VERHAGE is Professor of Marketing at Georgia State University's Robinson College of Business in Atlanta. He holds degrees from the University of Oregon, Texas Tech University and the University of Texas at Austin, where he received his PhD.

Verhage's primary research interests are in global marketing and cross-cultural consumer behaviour. He has authored over a hundred articles in scholarly journals, conference proceedings and various business publications. His research has been published in leading academic journals, including the *Journal of Consumer Research*, *International Journal of Research in Marketing* and *Journal of the Academy of Marketing Science*. He has written several bestselling marketing text books in the Netherlands and benefited from the feedback of many of its users, a group that exceeds a quarter of a million students. His industry experience – prior to entering academia – includes a marketing management position at a multinational corporation, based in Holland. Being actively involved in global business, he has served as a marketing consultant for numerous non-profit organizations and companies, both in B2B and fast moving consumer goods.

Professor Verhage, formerly on the faculty of Erasmus University and the Rotterdam School of Management in the Netherlands, has been active in Georgia State University's Executive MBA, Flexible MBA and Global MBA programmes for three decades and enjoys teaching International Marketing, Marketing Principles and Marketing Management at the Robinson College of Business. With programmes on five continents and students from about 100 countries, the College is worldwide and world-class. The Georgia State University MBA-programme is ranked among the best by *Bloomberg Businessweek* and *US News & World Report*, and its Executive MBA is on the *Financial Times* list of the world's best EMBA programmes. Verhage has also held visiting appointments and taught marketing at United Arab Emirates University in Abu Dhabi, Nyenrode Business Universiteit in the Netherlands and other European business schools.

As a Dutch national and an American resident, Bronis Verhage commutes frequently between the United States and Europe, where his wife and three daughters live on the Dutch North Sea coast. As a global citizen, he is a keen observer of the latest developments in marketing and in business education on several continents. Many of his observations find their way into his teaching and his regularly updated marketing textbooks.

Steve Thackston (Georgia State University)

WALK THROUGH TOUR

Part openers **explain the structure of each part of the book.**

Marketing-in-Action **vignettes based on real-world examples show students how theory and principles relate to marketing as it is actually practiced, stimulating class discussion.**

Learning goals **clearly set out the content and coverage of each chapter.**

Marketing Toppers **boxed features, encompassing the entire field of marketing, including services marketing, B2B and green marketing, highlight successes in business.**

Marketing Mistake **boxed features include a range of pan-European and global examples, highlighting failures in business.**

Summary **and at the end of each chapter, clearly presents the themes and concepts discussed.**

Professor's Perspectives **and** Practitioner's Perspectives **offer powerful ideas and insightful opinions on key issues in marketing management.**

Discussion questions **at the end of each chapter reinforce the major concepts presented.**

DIGITAL RESOURCES

Dedicated Instructor Resources

To discover the dedicated instructor online support
resources accompanying this textbook, instructors
should register here for access:
http://login.cengage.com

Resources include:

- Solutions Manual
- ExamView Testbank
- PowerPoint slides

Instructor access
Instructors can access the online student platform by registering at
http://login.cengage.com or by speaking to their
local Cengage Learning EMEA representative.

Instructor resources
Instructors can use the integrated Engagement Tracker to track students' preparation and
engagement. The tracking tool can be used to monitor progress of the class as a whole,
or for individual students.

Student access
Students can access the online platform using the unique personal access card included in
the front of the book.

Student resources
The platform offers a range of interactive learning tools tailored to the first edition of
Marketing: *A Global Perspective*, including:

- Quizzes and self-test questions
- Interactive eBook
- Games
- Media cases
- Glossary
- Flashcards
- Links to useful websites
- Extra case studies

PART ONE
INSIGHT INTO MARKETING

Anticipating and satisfying the needs and wants of the buyer and making a profit in the process is the essence of marketing set out in Part 1 of this book. The first part of *Marketing: A Global Perspective* offers insight into the marketing discipline and profession and defines the scope of this book. Three fundamental questions will be considered. What exactly *is* marketing? How do successful companies plan their marketing and develop their marketing strategies? And finally, why – and to what extent – is marketing strategy influenced by external factors? In other words, we will be looking at what, how and why.

Part 1 establishes the framework for the material presented in the rest of this book. We will see that the marketing discipline presents the manager with both meaningful theoretical insights and practical techniques that enable a company to successfully compete in the market. Marketing is an intriguing field of study because, beyond its value to business operations, it explains how organizations influence us as consumers.

1 What is marketing?

2 Strategy development and marketing planning

3 The marketing environment

CHAPTER 1
WHAT IS MARKETING?

LEARNING GOALS

After studying this chapter you will be able to:

1 **Explain what marketing means**

2 **Compare macromarketing, mesomarketing and micromarketing**

3 **Discuss which management philosophies dominated in business over time and how they influenced the production and marketing of goods and services**

4 **Describe the marketing concept and how it can be used in practice**

5 **Explain the strategic importance of a company's sound reputation and its ongoing relationships with customers**

6 **Understand different forms of marketing and how the marketing fundamentals are applied in those situations**

1.1 The meaning of marketing
1.2 Levels of marketing systems
1.3 Development of the marketing mindset
1.4 The marketing concept
1.5 Tasks of marketing in a company
1.6 Marketing applications and preview of the text

LA BIOSTHETIQUE®
PARIS

The first decade of the 21st century will be remembered as a time of economic upheaval unlike any since the Great Depression. As nations struggle to recover from this crisis, the business community is left to contemplate what can be expected in the years to come. The market is changing drastically, and there is considerable uncertainty about the future. Use of the Internet and e-commerce is on the rise, creating informed and demanding consumers worldwide. While consumers in Europe continue to worry about the impact of the eurozone crisis on their future, their buying power is stagnating, resulting in an increased concern with value in their purchase decisions.

Competition is steadily increasing within Europe, as well as from outside the EU. And, while the new rules in the business sector may vary from one industry or company to another, one thing is certain. In the face of extensive and rapid change, the implementation of an effective marketing strategy is more essential than ever before.

Consumers and other buyers always want higher quality, lower prices and better service. Aggressive competitors try to increase their market share through constant innovation and product improvement, and by satisfying their customers' needs and wants as effectively as possible on all fronts. To survive and to operate profitably all organizations must practise marketing, and they must adapt their marketing strategies to keep pace with market changes. Chapter 1 provides the basis for this challenge.

MARKETING IN ACTION
L'Oréal's Global Marketing Strategies

L'Oréal has been the world's largest cosmetics and beauty products seller for over a century, marketing more than 20 global brands in 130 countries. For decades, this company built its growth on a strategy of intensive *market penetration*, targeting a limited number of consumers mainly in Western Europe and North America. Today, however, the European beauty giant is eyeing one billion new consumers in emerging markets – which L'Oréal calls 'New Markets' – such as India, China and Brazil. The emergence of these new foreign markets, including those in Eastern Europe, Africa and the Middle East, creates exciting marketing opportunities to reach huge numbers of potential buyers.

While the emerging markets have already overtaken L'Oréal's sales in Western Europe and North America, they will account for more than half of overall sales before the end of the decade. This will fundamentally change the company's marketing history. The spectacular rate of growth also represents a major shift in the global cosmetic market. The immense number of potential buyers in emerging markets will open up new marketing opportunities for many companies worldwide.

> ## L'Oreal is well positioned to gain one billion new consumers in emerging markets.

'Our objective is to win the loyalty of one billion new consumers in these countries over the next ten years, so doubling the number of men and women across the planet using our brands and our products', according to a L'Oréal spokesperson. In India, for example, L'Oréal plans to increase market share by focusing on territory held by competitors such as Hindustan Unilever and Procter & Gamble in product categories like hair and skin care. The company is aiming for a 'leadership position' in India and intends to increase its buyers from 30 to 150 million before 2020, according to Vismay Sharma, director of L'Oréal's consumer products division. L'Oréal is well positioned to achieve its goal of gaining one billion new consumers in emerging markets through a customer-oriented marketing strategy that includes the following components:

Marketing Research: Listening to consumers

Every year, country managers and marketers personally visit consumer homes to better understand consumer needs across the world. 'You have to stay close to consumers, always,' says Sharma. Marketing research has enabled L'Oréal to successfully launch innovative skin-lightening products, some of them targeted to men. Its research centres create the most effective formulas to meet consumer needs on each continent.

Product: Brands that meet customers' needs

By staying close to consumers, L'Oréal is able to develop the right products for each country and tailor its product ranges to meet customers' expectations. Its new products generate hundreds of patents a year. Over 60 000 employees are committed to carrying out L'Oréal's mission 'to make beauty universal in a sustainable and responsible way'.

Promotion: Communication strategies that reflect lifestyles

By communicating the benefits that are important to consumers in target markets with different needs, the company is maximizing customer satisfaction and creating an attractive global brand image.

Price: Offering affordable products

By not always passing on the increasing costs of raw materials, packaging and transportation to buyers, L'Oréal is making aspirational brands affordable to the mass market. Its pricing and other marketing strategies reflect the lifestyles of less affluent consumers. In India, L'Oréal sells tubes of skincare cream for 25 rupees (€0.39) and inexpensive sachets of shampoo for those with limited access to running water. 'We offer smaller packs for consumers who want high-quality products but do not have much money to spend,' explains Sharma. 'We realized we needed to adapt to local needs.'

Distribution: Getting the products into the buyers' hands

In India alone, L'Oréal has increased the number of outlets from 250 000 to over a million. And although it is facing different trends in Africa and the Middle East as well as major challenges in South Africa, Turkey, Lebanon and Morocco, it is still growing fast in these nations. Sharma: 'As we develop new products to meet customers' wants and needs, we are also creating distribution networks to reach them.'

In conclusion, L'Oréal's marketing strategies represent a phenomenal business opportunity for long-term growth and profitability in its new markets. Its market share and sales are growing across the world. L'Oréal China's sales revenues, for instance, now exceed one billion euros, making this the company's number three cosmetics subsidiary. L'Oréal's customer-oriented managers have developed a global vision and have clearly identified many lucrative international marketing opportunities.[1]

The very nature of marketing is often misinterpreted. Some think that marketing is a modern form of *selling*, or that it is simply another word for *advertising*. Selling and advertising are indeed important marketing functions, but marketing involves much more. It includes a great number of other activities that enhance an organization's ability to satisfy the needs and wants of its customers effectively, thereby strengthening its position within the market. These other activities include market research and product development. *Market research* is conducted to identify the desires of (potential) customers, for example, or to size up the competition. *Product development* is the process of developing and launching attractive products based on an accurate insight into the market.

In all of this, one thing is clear. Marketing is not an 'exact' science that offers a standard solution to each problem. On the other hand, one cannot rely solely on intuition or business instinct. To make effective marketing decisions, we must be familiar with the principles and techniques of marketing that we will be exploring in this book.

In this chapter we start by examining the nature of marketing and the role it plays in society and in the business sector. We also look at the marketing concept and the main tasks involved in marketing. Throughout this chapter and the remainder of the book, important marketing terms are highlighted in green and listed in the glossary section. Nearly a thousand of these concisely defined key marketing terms are compiled at the back of the book. You will be able to review this glossary on the premium digital platform that accompanies this book (details are available on the 'about the digital resources' page). They are also published online with each chapter as *flashcards* to help you prepare for exams and learn the marketing vocabulary.

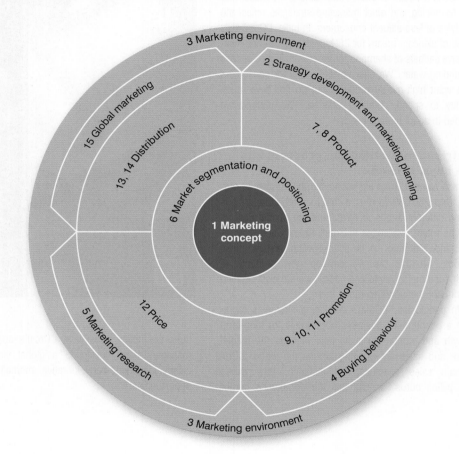

1.1 THE MEANING OF MARKETING

Marketing is a broad subject. It includes all the activities that bring buyers and sellers together. To gain an insight into the meaning of marketing, we begin by looking at the differences between marketing and selling. Then we examine a definition of marketing, the so-called marketing mix and the exchange process between the buyer and the seller.

1.1.1 Differences between selling and marketing

Broadly speaking, companies do two things: they make products (or they provide services) and they put them on the market. In other words, they *produce* something and they are involved in *marketing*. Not long ago we would have said that they produce and 'sell' something. The difference between marketing and selling is the difference between a society in which consumers can *choose* from products and services designed to meet their specific needs and wants, and a society in which people have very little, if any, choice.

The main purpose of marketing-oriented companies is to anticipate and satisfy the needs and wants of the customer. Rather than focusing first and foremost on the product, managers of these companies constantly seek to identify with their customers. They have become accustomed to thinking from the point of view of the consumer. Furthermore, they are convinced that this is the only right way to do business. When surveyed, this is what four senior managers had to say about the role that marketing plays in their organizations:

→ 'Nothing has more influence on the success of this company than marketing. Our rapid growth is primarily due to a well-developed marketing strategy.'

→ 'Market research and marketing are indispensable in this industry, particularly since the buying behaviour of customers is constantly changing.'

→ 'We are known as a dynamic and progressive company. Our international expansion was the result of a pure marketing decision. Marketing is central in our planning.'

→ 'When I talk about marketing planning, I am talking about the selection of the right markets and products, in other words, the most fundamental, strategic choices our company has to make.'

Marketing builds a bridge between production and consumption. The types of products available in the stores and the quality of those products are both determined by the preference of the consumer. In short, *selling* is 'trying to get rid of what you have on the shelves', while *marketing* is 'making sure that what you have on the shelves is what the customer wants'.

Essentially the objective of marketing is to make selling – in the sense of 'putting pressure on others' – unnecessary. The purpose of marketing is to get to know and understand the customer so well that the product is precisely what the customer wants. Then the product will sell itself. In fact, the need to be familiar with the desires of customers and to establish an ongoing relationship with them is part of our definition of marketing.

1.1.2 *A definition of marketing*

Thanks to the marketing function in the business sector, the development of products and services is linked to specific markets. In other words, supply is precisely tailored to meet demand. Think of *Heineken* for example, which markets not only lager, but also bock beer, white beer, low-calorie and other types of beer – with brand names such as Murphy's, Wieckse Witte and Amstel Light, so consumers can always drink their favourite beer at home and in bars. The brewery conducts marketing research to find out which outlets sell its products and what kinds of beer different groups of consumers prefer. As a marketing-oriented company Heineken also makes sure that its many products are sold in the right stores, that the prices are neither too high nor too low and that potential buyers know what kinds of specialty beers are available at different times of the year.

So marketing requires not only an appropriate product, but also the right type of distribution, the right price and the right kind of promotion. Together these factors make up the so-called *marketing mix*. If any of these four elements is lacking, a product will not achieve the sales and profit objectives as listed in its annual plan or marketing plan. Not only will the company fail to maximize sales and profits, the *target market* (the potential buyers for whom

© Nitr / Shutterstock

the product was intended) will probably be left with unsatisfied needs and wants. With this example in mind, let us now look at the – formal – definition of marketing:

> *Marketing is the process of developing, pricing, promoting and distributing products, services or ideas that are tailored to the market; it includes all other activities that create value and systematically lead to increased sales or another desired response, establish a good reputation and ongoing relationships with customers, so that all stakeholders achieve their objectives.*

We will come back to this definition shortly. In the meantime it is clear that marketers are not only involved in advertising and selling, but, on the basis of marketing research, marketers also decide which products are developed, for whom the products are intended and how they are introduced. By providing information about the needs and wants of both potential and current customers, marketers influence the decision making process at the very inception of the product or service. So our definition immediately dispels the misconception that marketing is a kind of 'superior selling' that starts at the end of the production line.

1.1.3 The marketing mix

An effective marketing strategy consists of a clever combination of four marketing instruments that are used to tackle the market. These marketing tools are often referred to as the **marketing mix** or the four Ps. The marketing mix variables are closely related to one another. If we change one of them, this may have consequences for the other three; essentially it creates an entirely new mix. Since each of the four Ps will be covered extensively later on in this book, we now only briefly review the main questions and decisions with respect to the marketing mix.

Product

Product: goods, services or ideas that meet the wants and needs of the customer.

Besides the physical product, this P includes other factors that determine which brand a person buys, such as the warranty, packaging, brand image, product range and customer service. Hence, product strategy is concerned with, among other things, the development of new products and services, the refinement of existing products and the decision to take products off the market when they no longer satisfy a need.

Price

Price: the amount of money exchanged for a product or service.

When developing a price strategy a company will consider not only the product's manufacturing cost, but also the prices being charged by its competitors and how an increase or reduction in the selling price is likely to affect demand. If the price is too high it will deter customers, but if the price is too low, revenues will suffer. When determining the price, several questions need to be addressed. Should pricing generate a profit in the short term or in the long term? Is a discount necessary? Are some buyers prepared to pay a higher price for a more refined product, and who are they?

Place

Place ('Distribution'): how the company gets its product into the buyers' hands.

How a product is distributed often matters more in determining its success than the product itself. Because of their contacts with the retail trade, companies such as Philips and Unilever often stand a better chance of achieving success than do smaller companies, when bringing new products onto the market.

Distribution strategy is concerned with decisions about which distribution channels and intermediaries (the wholesale and retail trade) should be used, the number of sales outlets, the necessary stock levels and best forms of transportation (physical distribution). An efficient distribution system ensures that the right products are on sale in the right place at the right time.

Promotion

Promotion: the supplier's activities to communicate with the market and to promote sales.

Very few products sell themselves. Potential buyers first have to be made aware of the product and its benefits. Effective communication is needed to inform, persuade or – in the case of established brands – remind them of a product.

Promotion or marketing communication includes advertising, sponsorship, sales promotion (such as free gifts, contests and product demonstrations), direct marketing, and personal selling and public relations activities, including free publicity. Developing a promotional strategy requires various decisions, such as establishing communication objectives, determining the advertising budget and selecting the best combination of promotional instruments and media, including social media. Other decisions involve using displays efficiently, offering special discounts, attending trade fairs and, finally, assessing the effect of these promotional activities.

1.1.4 Target market selection and the process of exchange

A well thought-out marketing mix increases the chance of success. However, because it is impossible to devise and implement a marketing strategy satisfying the needs of *all* consumers, companies must concentrate on the desires of a specific group of potential buyers, as illustrated in Figure 1.1. This group of consumers is known as the **target market**, the part of the market that an organization concentrates on and wants to turn into customers. *Customers*, after all, are loyal consumers who will make repeat purchases. Once a company has divided the market into '*market segments*' on the basis of certain criteria, it will then select one or more target

FIGURE 1.1 The marketing mix

markets. With these groups the organization tries to bring about an *exchange*, in which the two parties agree to exchange *something* of value so that both parties' needs are met.

This exchange transaction underlies all marketing activities. In fact, organizations develop a marketing strategy to stimulate this process of exchange. Exchange objects are items of worth. Often they are products that are exchanged for money, but they can also be something less tangible, such as a *service*, an *idea*, *labour* or even *status* (see Figure 1.2). For instance, in exchange for their tuition fees and perseverance, students get a meaningful education; in exchange for voting for a political party, voters are given certain promises by the party leader regarding the policy to be pursued. So the process of exchange is also a process that creates, communicates and delivers value. Both parties involved in the transaction gain something of value in exchange for something they are prepared to part with and – because their needs are satisfied – as a result of the transaction they are better off.

1.2 LEVELS OF MARKETING SYSTEMS

The origins of marketing date back to the era of bartering, when goods were exchanged for other goods. This practice was widespread in primitive societies. Bartering was an exchange 'in kind'. That is to say, no money changed hands, and those involved in the exchange were only interested in products they wanted. Bartering remained popular even when currency, travelling salesmen and shops simplified the process of exchange. In the 21st century

FIGURE 1.2 Exchange process between buyer and seller

bartering is still an important form of (international) trade in many countries and one that calls for a market-oriented approach.

Marketing can be conducted and studied on different levels. If we are considering those who make the marketing decisions in a company, we are referring to *micromarketing*. However, because marketing at the societal level and at the *sector* or branch of industry level offers important leads for marketers in an organization, we will first consider macromarketing and mesomarketing.

1.2.1 Macromarketing

If, rather than looking at marketing from the point of view of the individual company, we see it – at a broader level – as a *process* that must function effectively for a society as a whole to realize its economic objectives, we are talking about macromarketing. At this level the role of marketing is described only in general terms. After all, when it comes to macromarketing, we are primarily interested in the system that a society has developed to arrange the exchange of goods and services to ensure that its scarce resources will meet its needs as effectively as possible. Today, because of new media, satellite connections and means of transport, marketing functions are implemented more efficiently than ever. Improved communication systems, transaction possibilities (the Internet) and methods of distribution simplify the marketing process at a macro level. Yet these tools and techniques are also important for marketers, for the less they cost, the more efficient the organization's marketing strategy.

1.2.2 Mesomarketing

So far we have distinguished two different approaches to the study of marketing: macromarketing and – what is commonly referred to as – micromarketing. *Mesomarketing* occurs at a level that lies between the two. This form of marketing is best analyzed within the framework of the supply chain.

The supply chain

Historically, people produced things largely to meet their own needs. This system of 'direct production' was later replaced by a more efficient approach in line with the *economic principle*. Division of labour, specialization and the principle of exchange gave rise to a system of production and trade in which different parties within society were dependent on one another. We can depict this system by referring to the supply chain: the series of persons and organizations – from the original manufacturer to the consumer – involved in the production, distribution and consumption of products and services. If these individuals and organizations in the supply chain organize marketing activities, they do so at the level of *mesomarketing*.

Figure 1.3 shows – in a simplified form – the elements that make up a supply chain. This marketing system consists of various horizontal sections or 'links'. One such link, which is made up of companies that perform the same function in the production or trade of a certain product, is known as a sector. Within such a sector, a group of organizations that is similar in its production techniques and end products is known as a branch of industry. The book industry within the graphic sector is one example. The food industry within the retail sector is another.

In Figure 1.3 we can see two different 'flows'. The product moves from the manufacturer – via intermediaries who distribute the product – to the consumer (with the aid of advertising

FIGURE 1.3 Simplified supply chain for consumer products

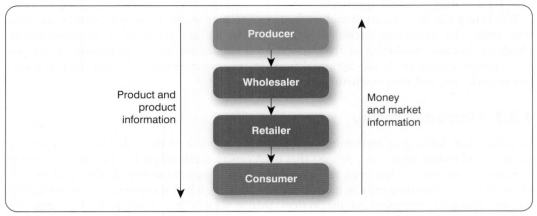

and other promotional activities). The money flows in the other direction together with an *information flow* that moves from the buyer to the manufacturer. Because retailers and wholesalers are in proximity to the consumer, they are able to give the producer an accurate insight into the needs and wants of the market and the reactions of the customers.

In practice, each link adds value to the products or services. If the *added value* that a certain link contributes is too small, it will eventually lose its function in the chain. Wholesalers, for instance, are constantly threatened with the prospect of losing their place in the chain. The party that adds the least value is also the weakest link in the chain.

Sometimes a product will skip some of the links in the supply chain. In some distribution channels the manufacturer (or importer) delivers products directly to the consumer, as is the case in purchases made via the Internet. We will return to the subject of the supply chain in paragraph 3.2.

Definition of mesomarketing   Marketing activities – designed to meet a certain need – which parties in the supply chain carry out jointly fall within the domain of mesomarketing. One example is the collective advertising campaign for milk, which is financed by organizations operating at different levels in the supply chain, united within a branch organization. In other words, mesomarketing is generally confined to a certain sector of society.

We can now define mesomarketing as 'all activities developed by several collaborating organizations within a supply chain or sector to match supply and demand and meet a certain need, in order to realize their shared marketing objectives'. The term 'mesomarketing' can be used for the collective activities of organizations in a specific sector (such as insurance companies) or of companies with a common interest (such as retailers in the same shopping centre). It is also used to refer to the collective marketing of certain types of products (such as flowers or meat).

1.2.3 Micromarketing

While macromarketing refers to society as a whole and mesomarketing refers to collaborating organizations in the supply chain, the focus of **micromarketing** is the *individual firm*. What we are concerned with in this book is *marketing management* – in the sense that we will be analyzing problems from the point of view of the manager who makes the decisions.

MARKETING MISTAKE
The French Wine Industry's Cherished 'Terroir'

France is a country famed for its rich cultural heritage, as the birthplace of a wealth of fine art and literature. This is coupled with a proud gastronomic tradition spanning many centuries, which includes one of France's greatest exports – wine. Historically, French wines have been identified by the region from which they originated, for example Champagne, Bordeaux or Médoc. However, today's marketing trend in the wine industry is to identify a wine by its grape type (such as Merlot), rather than its region of origin. For French winemakers, it seems that changing their marketing strategy in the global marketplace is a challenge, involving a complex tradition of *appellation* that accentuates 'terroir.'

Terroir is a French concept that refers to the unique features of a terrain, including its geology, geography, climate and soil type. These factors impact the wine's taste. It implies that even if all conditions of the grape-growing process are perfectly reproduced elsewhere on the globe, the wine still cannot be duplicated. Some French winemakers even argue that their main role is to *facilitate* the ability of a wine to express its unique 'terroir.'

For a long time, regional characteristics in France were important to help distinguish the produce of one particular province from that of neighbouring ones, especially when selling wines in other regions. The tradition of naming wines by region of production also stems from

an emotional connection invoking issues of identity and loyalty: a 'badge of pride and honour.' To a wine connoisseur, this may be important. In the words of Philippe Chaumont, a merchant from Toulouse, 'When I'm drinking a Tuscan wine, I don't want it to taste like a Beaujolais.'

The typical foreign consumer has no clue of the meaning of a region or vineyard

Returning to the changing global market, since the average consumer looking for a decent but affordable wine is not a wine connoisseur, there needs to be a way that they can differentiate between a €10 and a €50 bottle of wine. The current marketing trend to identify wine by grape type ('varietal wine') and even brand name (e.g. Mondavi) helps to accomplish this. Winemakers in other nations, including South Africa, Chile, Australia and the United States usually market their 'New World' wines as Chardonnay, Merlot, Malbec, Cabernet Sauvignon, etc., reflecting the types of grape used to produce the wine. French winemakers, however, have traditionally left the grape type off their labels altogether.

Why does this even matter, when France and the French wine industry enjoy a long-standing favourable impression among numerous wine consumers? The answer is simple: the changing global marketplace. In the last 25 years, sales of New World wines rose dramatically, from 3 per cent to 30 per cent of the global market. Now, research shows that the majority of wine importers in Europe, Asia and North America expect a further increase in demand for *varietal wines*.

It is understandable why French wine producers may not want to betray their heritage. Yet, by failing to adapt to changing preferences and buying behaviour of today's wine drinkers (who are less preoccupied with regional distinctions or the merits of specific vineyards), France may be missing out on a huge marketing opportunity. In the words of the president of the Confederation of French Wine Cooperatives, Denis Verdier, 'I think France was sleeping on the laurels of its past success.' This statement is especially troubling, now that France has recently been overtaken by Italy as the world's largest producer of wine.

Fortunately, a new generation of French winemakers is beginning to recognize the need for a shift in marketing strategy, by looking at fresh and innovative ways to sell wines. Some are poking fun at old traditions, while breaking down notions of elitism and snobbery. Successful French exports now include the rock-and-roll-inspired 'Rhôning Stones' and 'Le Freak Shiraz-Viognier'. Meanwhile, the cheekily-named 'Arrogant Frog', from Domaine Paul Mas, sells a million bottles per year in Australia, suggesting that important lessons have been learnt.

Wine purists might look at these changes in horror, arguing that this represents a 'dumbing-down' in the wine industry. However, approaching the issue from a marketing perspective, it is unwise to ignore key shifts in the wine marketplace. Especially where it concerns the need to boost flagging wine sales in a globalized market, in which more marketing-oriented winemakers must appeal to a growing segment of young, less wine-savvy customers.[2]

Marketing management is the analysis, planning, implementation and constant evaluation of all activities designed to ensure that the products and services produced and provided by an organization are tailored to meet the needs and wants of potential customers as effectively as possible. In practice this means formulating and implementing a product, promotion, price and distribution strategy that enables the company to approach the market successfully and accomplish its marketing objectives.

A marketing manager always tries to see their company from the viewpoint of their customers. They begin by conducting market research to identify the needs, wants and ideas of potential buyers, which, in turn, helps them develop products and services that meet the desires of the target group. Then, ensuring that the target audience is well informed by promotion, they can offer these products and services to the target market for the right price and through the best sales channels. Finally they stay in touch with their customers to make sure that they are indeed satisfied. This process of strategy development and business decision-making, which does not always occur in this order, should be based on the *marketing concept*. We will come back to this in section 1.4.

1.3 DEVELOPMENT OF THE MARKETING MINDSET

Focusing on the customer when developing a strategy seems so logical that we might wonder why companies ever did anything else. Until shortly after the Second World War, however, most products were so scarce that there was no major competition. So there was no real incentive to adapt products to the wants of the consumer. Most manufacturers sold everything they were able to make and put forth no effort to offer products that the consumer might prefer.

The shift to a marketing orientation in the business sector in Europe was stimulated by several multinationals, such as Unilever, that were exposed to marketing in the United States. The American 'invasion' of the European market in the sixties simply accelerated this development, because American organizations brought their own market research

FIGURE 1.4 The evolution of marketing

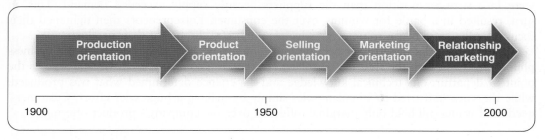

bureaus and advertising agencies with them. This led many European companies to become increasingly interested in marketing.

In fact, since the industrial revolution, most sectors have gone through a series of *phases*. Figure 1.4 shows the main orientation in each stage. Over time emphasis has shifted from production, to the product, to selling, to marketing. Still, many companies have not yet reached the last phase of marketing-oriented management with its emphasis on relationship marketing.

Manufacturers of consumer products were the pioneers in this process. Producers of industrial goods, service providers, retailers and not-for-profit organizations – roughly in that order – followed them. Unfortunately, some organizations are still production-oriented or selling-oriented. However, an increasing number of managers are clearly aware of the importance of a *market-oriented* approach. They now think in terms of markets and people, rather than seeing the product as the point of departure. Before exploring this mindset, let's examine the management philosophies that originally dominated the business sector: a production- or product-orientation and a selling-orientation.

1.3.1 Production- and product-oriented companies

A production-oriented company does everything possible to make its production process highly efficient. At the beginning of the 20th century, when the consumer's disposable income was low and mass production technology still in its infancy, the production concept was the most common business philosophy. By concentrating on mechanizing and increasing production, entrepreneurs were able to greatly reduce the cost of their products. They reasoned that if a product was inexpensive and widely available, it was bound to sell.

In the aftermath of World War II, with an acute shortage of raw materials, machinery and production facilities, there was little change in the managerial mindset. Production and distribution of reasonably priced, mass-produced goods was still the priority. One difference, though, was that manufacturers shifted their attention from the production process to the product itself. Once the product concept was adopted in this era, the main objective became to improve quality. Managers assumed that 'a good product will sell itself' and regarded marketing as a superfluous activity.

Despite this *product-oriented* market approach, sales flourished, primarily because demand exceeded the limited supply. It was a typical sellers' market, in which the suppliers or sellers had the upper hand – to the detriment of the customers.

1.3.2 Selling-oriented companies

In most industries the production- and product-oriented phases of management philosophy lasted only for a brief period after World War II. With technological progress and huge investment in the post-war economy, production capacity grew so fast that products were no longer in short supply. Greater prosperity gave rise to a **buyers' market**, in which the buyers were in a stronger position than the suppliers because supply exceeded demand. This, in turn, resulted in a battle for winning over the consumer. Entrepreneurs then tightened their focus on selling and began to use aggressive techniques to dispose of their products.

Although the sales department became more important, little else changed in the business philosophy. Even with the shift to the **selling concept**, the company itself was still seen as the point of departure. Its technical knowledge and experience determined what was produced, while the sales staff tried to stimulate sales simply by making a huge sales effort. Customers' needs and wants still held only marginal influence over the company's product offerings.

1.3.3 Marketing-oriented companies

Faced with greater consumer **buying power** and greater competition, companies finally learned that they had to tailor their products and services to meet the needs and wants of the buyers more effectively. And, with prospects of amassing a glut of unsaleable products looming on the horizon, managers adopted a *customer-oriented* mode of thought and put the marketing concept – the basic idea of marketing – into practice. In short, they started implementing a market-oriented approach.

Market orientation

More than ever before, the business sector is characterized by a high degree of **market orientation**. Market-oriented companies consider not only customers, but also intermediaries and competitors, in making business decisions at all levels of the organization. This is the crucial distinction between a market-oriented and a product- or selling-oriented market approach. As we can see in Figure 1.5, a product-oriented approach (and also a

FIGURE 1.5 Comparison of a product and a market orientation

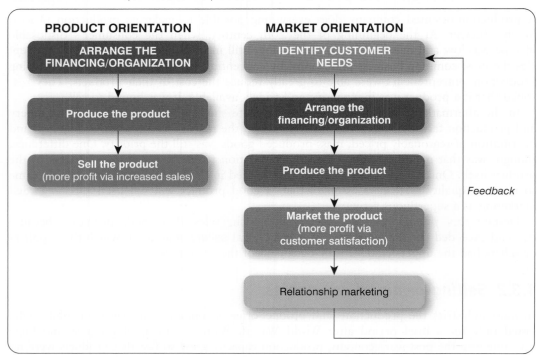

selling-oriented approach) consists of three stages: setting up the financing and organization, making the product and selling the product.

A market-oriented entrepreneur, on the other hand, starts by conducting marketing research to identify the needs of the buyers (within the context of products offered by competitors). This enables them to select a target market on which to concentrate. Only then do they contemplate the organization and financing, the development of products or services that meet the needs and, of course, the marketing of those products or services. They are also well aware that increases in profits are closely tied to their customers' level of satisfaction – so they prefer to concentrate on customer satisfaction instead of sheer sales efforts.

Note that we are referring to *marketing* the product rather than selling the product. The difference between the two is that marketing entails an *integrated plan*. Selling is but a component of this overall marketing plan. Other elements of the marketing plan encompass the product, distribution, communication and pricing strategy. Finally, a firm practicing the marketing concept continually monitors the market and seeks *feedback*, to determine not only how well the product is selling in different market segments, but also to learn the degree to which it satisfies the needs and wants of the customers. This allows the firm to quickly develop new or improved products that are in line with new trends and customer preferences. Also, this approach helps the marketer establish and maintain an ongoing relationship with their customers, and thus to engage in *relationship marketing*. Figure 1.6 summarizes the main differences between selling- and marketing-oriented organizations.[3]

The societal marketing concept

Widespread concern about the undesirable side effects of marketing for third parties has recently led to a renewed interest in *macromarketing* (in the sense of socially responsible marketing). The increasing preoccupation with the long-term interest of society has led to an extension of the marketing concept known as the **societal marketing concept**. The underlying principle is that, since the production and marketing of certain products (for example,

FIGURE 1.6 Differences between a selling and a marketing orientation

	What is the organization's focus?	What business are we in?	Who are we targeting?	What is our primary goal?	How do we intend to achieve our goal?
Selling orientation	Inward on the company's problems	Selling the products we make	Everybody	Profit through maximizing sales volume	Mainly through intensive selling and promotion
Marketing orientation	Outward on the customers' needs and wants	Satisfying the needs and wants of the target market and delivering superior value	Specific groups of buyers	Profit through satisfying customers and building relationships with them	Through integrated marketing and cooperation with other departments

© Green Peace

packaging) may – in the *long* term – have damaging consequences (such as deforestation) for society as a whole, every effort must be made to prevent harming the interests of buyers *and* non-buyers.[4]

Marketers should balance the interests of the consumer, the producer and society. As is illustrated in Figure 1.7, consumers are often driven by their needs and wants in the short term, while companies are driven by their objective to make a profit. However, society as a whole has to consider human wellbeing in the long run and must make it a priority. When developing a societal marketing-oriented strategy, firms with a sense of responsibility consider the impact of marketing activities on various groups within society (including children), social issues such as environmental protection and, often, the views of activists like the Amsterdam-based Greenpeace organization. The combined efforts of consumers and corporations have resulted in positive trends in the development and acceptance of safer products, including environmentally friendly detergents and hybrid cars.

FIGURE 1.7 The societal marketing concept: balanced interests

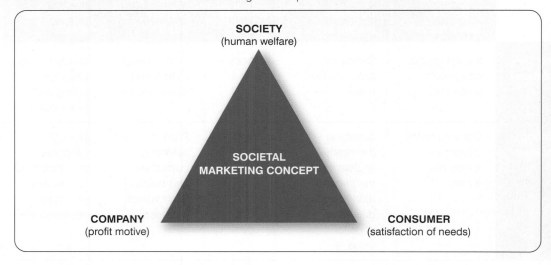

1.3.4 Relationship marketing

One of the most recent developments in the changing orientation of companies is the rise in relationship marketing. A need to retain valued customers has driven an increasing number of firms to take customer-orientation one step further, to actively cultivate good customer relationships. Similarly, companies are working to strengthen long-term relationships with suppliers.

Relationship marketing involves a strategy completely different from simply creating an exchange process between the supplier and the buyer. The emphasis is on developing long-term relationships with customers and suppliers who add value to the collaboration for all parties involved. Therefore we are also seeing more and more *strategic alliances* and other forms of cooperation within the market.

Table 1.1 clarifies the differences between transaction-oriented marketing and relationship marketing.[5] Although in relationship marketing each transaction is only one of the links in the chain between the company and its customers, this can considerably strengthen the relationship between the two parties. This underlines the need for a systematic and well thought-out strategy when it comes to implementing the marketing concept.

TABLE 1.1 Transactional marketing versus relationship marketing

Transactional marketing	Relationship marketing
1 Emphasis on getting new customers	1 Emphasis on keeping customers as well as getting new ones
2 Short-term orientation	2 Long-term orientation
3 Interest in making a single sale	3 Interest in repeat purchases and ongoing relationships
4 Limited commitment to customers	4 High level of customer involvement
5 Success means making a sale	5 Success means customer loyalty, word-of-mouth communication and low customer turnover
6 Quality is a production concern	6 Quality is every employee's concern
7 Limited customer service	7 High degree of service commitment

1.4 THE MARKETING CONCEPT

In the final analysis the marketing concept is a business philosophy. It is an attitude or *mindset* in which the needs and wants of customers are factored into virtually every decision. This market-oriented management style should be actively supported by senior management. The chief executive officer (CEO) does not necessarily need much marketing expertise or need to be a marketing professional, however they must understand the importance of marketing to the organization. If senior management focuses solely on the product or operational considerations, overlooking customer needs, the marketing concept will be very difficult to implement.

What are the main features of the marketing concept? As illustrated in Figure 1.8, the marketing concept is based on six principles.

PRACTITIONER'S PERSPECTIVE
Jim Stengel (Procter & Gamble)

Jim Stengel is the former Global Marketing Officer of Procter & Gamble, the world's largest brand manufacturer, where he oversaw an $8 billion advertising budget. He is now President/CEO of the Jim Stengel Company – both think tank and consultancy – and Adjunct Professor at the UCLA Anderson School of Management.

When asked about the secret of Procter & Gamble's marketing strategy, Jim Stengel gives a sobering answer: 'Focusing on the consumer. That's all. The consumer is our boss. And while I would be the first to admit that the phrase has become something of a cliché, what I say still stands. Because every time we focused on the consumer, we were successful. And every time we took a different approach, we were much less successful.

I demand passion from my staff. I want them to have both feet in society. I want them to work together with consumers, to observe, to show dedication. Only then does brand development result in magic. If we really want to achieve something in this market, if we have ambitions for the future, that is the only way. Not dreaming things up in an ivory tower. Not producing products simply because we are able to make them, but because they *satisfy* a huge need.

The consumer is our boss

The danger of being a market leader is becoming arrogant. And that is something we cannot afford. We have to listen to our customers as much as possible. It might seem simple. But putting theory into practice is far from simple. We operate all over the world and there are great *cultural* differences.

When I visit P&G employees abroad, no matter in what country, I always start by visiting them at home and by going to a few shops. That immediately changes the nature of the meeting. It makes my visit less formal, and as a result, people are less concerned about what they should say to Jim Stengel. At the same time I also get straight to the crux of the matter. Why is that particular product there, how is it used, how is the kitchen set up, what products do you have in the bathroom, how do those who live in the house use the different rooms and what kinds of problems do they experience? And above all, what can Procter & Gamble do to make improvements?'.[6]

1.4.1 *Customer satisfaction*

The customer is always right. The firm must be dedicated to satisfying customer needs. If maximizing profit is the ultimate goal, a company will not prosper *in the long run*. A customer-orientation is crucial in decision-making, with the objective of developing ongoing relationships. This line of thought should be followed not only by the marketing department, but by all individuals in the organization.

To make sure that customers are satisfied, we have to make *choices*. Given that no company can be all things to all people, it must choose between offering a very wide range of products, and concentrating on certain groups of customers. There may be consumers, for instance, that a company would prefer *not* to have as customers. An upscale restaurant that

FIGURE 1.8 The marketing concept

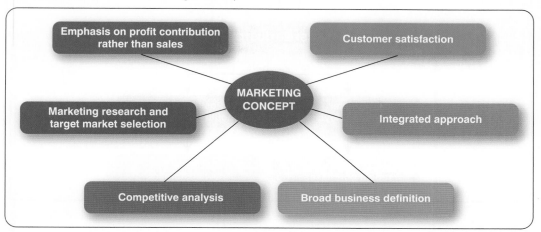

appeals primarily to business people would rather not reserve tables for a noisy soccer team, out of fear it will lose regular customers. In such cases a strategy of *demarketing* (which we will come back to later) may be the solution.

Marketing-oriented companies make sure that they provide great customer service and that they handle customer complaints well. They pay as much attention to *customer affairs* (another term for customer service) as they do, for example, to public relations.

What does customer affairs involve beyond a 'money back' guarantee or a polite letter in response to a complaint? It is everything an organization does to maintain good relations with its customers. The customer affairs or customer service department should:

→ Anticipate the wants and needs of customers.

→ Provide useful information about the products and services.

→ Assure that the product or service is easy for customers to use.

→ Determine how satisfied customers are with their purchases.

→ Maintain contact and develop relationships with buyers.

→ Deal with complaints and solve customer problems in the best possible way.

Because customer service is the external face of the company's quality standards, it is often regarded as one of the most important marketing instruments. The essence of great customer service is that each customer is taken seriously and must be satisfied. The importance of customer satisfaction in the fight for market share is shown in Figure 1.9.

1.4.2 Integrated approach

The difference between a product- and a marketing-oriented approach is the extent to which the various activities are systematically *integrated* into the overall marketing policy. In a product-oriented company most activities are performed in isolation. The production manager, for example, keeps the machines running, the engineer improves the quality of the products, the accountant calculates the selling prices and the sales representatives try to secure lucrative orders. The departments operate independently from one another, without paying attention to the interest of the company as a whole. Coordination is lacking and the customer is no more than a minor consideration. This compartmentalized approach is illustrated in Figure 1.10A.

FIGURE 1.9 Importance of customer satisfaction

FIGURE 1.10 Organizations with different management philosophies

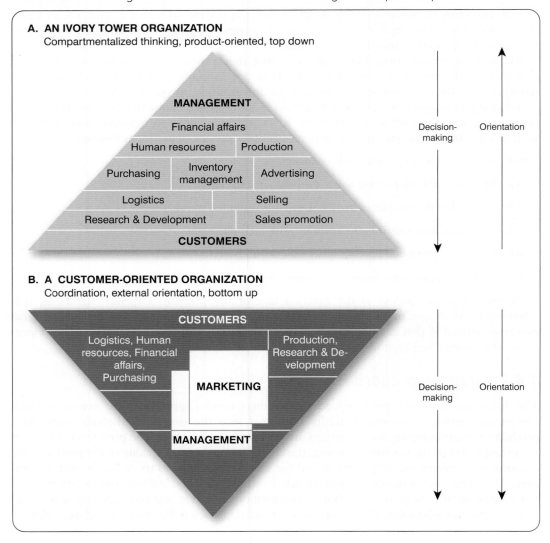

A marketing-oriented company follows a different approach. Its strategy is highly dependent on the needs and wants of customers identified through market research. The departments still exist, but their tasks are partly defined by incorporating measures designed to create customer satisfaction. The organization operates as a unified *system* driven by the marketing concept. Although some departments are primarily concerned with internal affairs and others with external affairs, their decision-making process centres on the customer. Figure 1.10B illustrates the coordinating role of the marketing department in a customer-oriented organization. Marketers are actively involved in decisions about production strategy, stock planning and service policy – or anything else where customer satisfaction is at stake. Thus, marketing is integrated in nearly every aspect of management.

To stimulate this kind of collaboration in the company, management should not just focus on stakeholders outside of the firm, but also be committed to internal marketing. Regardless of their departmental assignments, all employees – including the receptionist and cashiers – have to be well-trained and motivated to satisfy the customers. It goes without saying that effective internal communication is required to coordinate these activities.

1.4.3 *Broad business definition*

Companies that do *not* implement the marketing concept tend to describe their business in terms of the products they make ('we produce laptops' or 'we make frames for glasses'). Such self-limiting definitions can lead to marketing myopia. What these companies fail to recognize is that their cherished products may fall out of favour (in this case as a result of the increased use of tablets and contact lenses).

To facilitate a rapid adjustment to the changing needs of the market, many companies now choose to formulate a *business definition* as well as a mission (the role and ambitions of the organization within its chosen field of activity) in broad, customer-oriented terms. Marketing-oriented companies describe their activities comprehensively – focusing on the *needs* of their customers. They also like to describe their *role* in their chosen field of activity in ambitious terms. The founder of Revlon once described the mission of the company in this way; 'In the factory we make cosmetics, in the drugstore we sell hope!' Companies like Shell and Texaco also use need-oriented descriptions of what they do. They no longer define themselves as oil companies, but instead, as energy companies. Accordingly, they are now heavily invested in the development of alternative sources of energy, including wind, nuclear and solar energy systems. This emphasis on energy rather

Every woman has a story
It's not how you tell it
It's how you live it

REVLON

Image courtesy of The Advertising Archives

than simply on oil will galvanize companies to change as society changes, to prevent overreliance on a single energy source and to remain leading energy suppliers even after the last oil well has run dry.

1.4.4 Competitive analysis

A firm adopting the marketing concept understands that even its most successful product – and often an entire product category – will someday be obsolete. For example, cotton diapers, LPs and video recorders have been replaced by disposable diapers, MP3 players and on-demand Internet streaming. Hopefully, the company itself, rather than a competitor, is able to develop an alternative product or service that replaces the existing products. In any event, the company needs to keep an eye on its **competitors** – even if only to adopt or improve on their good ideas.

Successful managers constantly monitor the competition when identifying the opportunities and threats in the market and when examining the strengths and weaknesses of their own companies. Regular analysis of the competition is indispensible if a company is to gain and develop **competitive advantages**. In practice, competition often has a stimulating influence on product improvement and innovation through the whole branch. Occasionally, it also leads to meaningful agreements and collaboration between businesses.

1.4.5 Marketing research and target market selection

When making decisions managers need useful – and usable – information. They can obtain some of this information by consciously observing the environment. For example, marketers employed by Heineken go into the stores, along with sales representatives, at least twice a quarter to assess the retail climate and meet customers. This is a good idea, but on its own it is not enough. Well-organized gathering and *systematic* analysis of all relevant marketing information is essential.

Marketing research forms the basis of marketing. By collecting, analyzing and interpreting the right data, a market-oriented company can find out, among other things, who the buyers are and which product features are most important to them. Of course, not everyone has the same desires. The 'average' consumer does not exist. So the company first has to analyze and then *segment* the market. In other words, it divides the market up into smaller groups of customers who have the same needs and preferences, or the same buying behaviour. The company then selects segments on which to concentrate. It regards these groups as its *target markets* and develops products and marketing strategies especially for them. The more useful information the marketer has at their disposal, the more able they are to differentiate their products and services.

1.4.6 Profit contribution

Marketers sometimes say 'It is better to own a market than a factory.' By this they mean that *demand* for their products is more important in assuring the continuity of the company than the *possession* of a building and machinery. For if demand stagnates (and with it *sales*), the factory that takes care of the supply is superfluous.

We can take this line of reasoning a step further. In evaluating a business, it is not *how many* sales a product generates that is important but *how much profit* those sales contribute to the enterprise. Increased sales do not assure increased profits. If a firm cannot make a profit, the question of whether it is satisfying a customer or societal need is immaterial because the firm will not survive. In this sense, profit is not so much an objective as it is a constraint.

MARKETING TOPPER
Levi's versus the Dutch Consumers' Association

At first sight the results of a jeans test conducted by a leading consumer organization appeared to be devastating for the most famous jeans brand in the world. The two most expensive pairs of jeans in the test, both made by *Levi's*, were bottom of the list and were described as 'average/reasonable'.

'We produce poor quality jeans, because that's what young people ask for'

'We are very happy with the results of the test,' was the surprisingly laconic reaction of Jan Keijzer, Managing Director of Levi Strauss Benelux. As far as he was concerned, the test was not relevant to the Levi's target market. Furthermore, it showed a fundamental misunderstanding of the *buying motives* of young people – Levi's primary target market. 'The Consumers' Association assesses physical product quality, but that doesn't matter that much to young people. They are more concerned with what the jeans look like. We deliberately produce poor quality jeans, because that is what they ask for. They want worn-in, stonewashed or faded jeans.

When the consumer test report says that the finish of the buttonholes "unfortunately leaves a lot to be desired", it is showing that its assessment is not based on *market research*, for the frayed look is what young people want. Blue Ridge, the house brand of *We International*, was top of the list. But this was hardly surprising given that this retailer targets buyers aged thirty or more, who want beautifully finished jeans that will last for at least a year. We on the other hand stonewash and tear our jeans to meet our customers' preferences.'

Levi's market research shows that the young target market agrees with Jan Keijzer: Many of them said: 'The

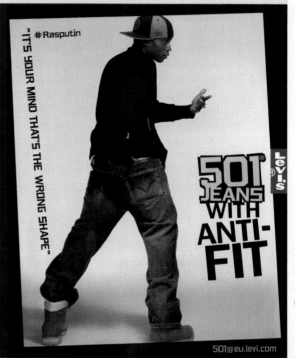

Image courtesy of The Advertising Archives

Consumers' Association doesn't know what it's talking about. We want Levi's….' And they get Levi's: Levi's 501 red-tab jeans are targeted at 15 to 25-year-olds and sell for about 100 euros. Europe accounts for about 1 billion euros of San Francisco-based Levi's annual sales that are estimated at over 4 billion euros.

Levi's aims to stay one step ahead of its competitors (brands such as Lee, Pepe Jeans, Wrangler and Diesel). The market leader is not afraid of these rivals. 'To stay out there in front we need strong competitors. That keeps jeans popular and inspires us to be better than the others,' said Kenny Wilson, Marketing President of Levi's Europe. 'Ultimately we have something that no one else can copy: we invented the jeans market. Levi's is the first brand. And we still offer a product that is precisely what our customers want. That is a solid marketing proposition.'[7]

Since *profit contribution* is a more important criterion than turnover, the firm may be forced to abandon a product that contributes to overall sales but not to profits. Hence, every company has to strive, for example by building brand equity, to make a profit in the long term.

1.5 TASKS OF MARKETING IN A COMPANY

It is often said that the marketer's job is to create more demand. But this is a widespread misconception. Many marketing-oriented organizations actually implement a demarketing policy to *discourage* demand for their products among certain groups of buyers. European telecom companies like T-Mobile and Vodafone are implementing a demarketing strategy by no longer targeting 'pay as you go' customers (with prepaid phone cards) in their advertising campaigns for mobile phones. Instead, they are focusing on consumers that make more calls and use other services, such as text messaging. Their objective in this nearly saturated market is to gain the loyalty of the most profitable subscribers.

In fact, the task of marketing involves much more than influencing demand. To ensure that buyers are satisfied, a marketer also devotes considerable attention to customer service, the handling of complaints, communicating with recent buyers and after-sales services. That's also how they strengthen the *reputation* of their company and develop a good *relationship* with the buyers, hoping that they are converted into regular customers who will *respond* positively to future offers and new products of the company. We will come back to these three Rs (reputation, relationship and response) later in this chapter.

1.5.1 Marketing's first task

The first task of marketing is to anticipate and identify the needs and wants of the market. To do this, companies conduct marketing research among potential buyers to gain insight into their ideas about the kinds of 'ideal' products and services that meet their desires. This simplifies the selection of target markets. At the same time, the expressed ideas are the basis for developing the right products or services and the marketing strategy for the selected market segment. This first task of marketing is illustrated in Figure 1.11.

Before the marketer can develop an effective marketing strategy geared to *consumer behaviour* and the potential *demand* for new products, they first have to conduct marketing research to discover the *needs* and *wants* of future buyers. What is the relationship between these terms?

Needs

Before there can be demand for a product or service, the consumer first has to be aware of their needs. Needs have to do with a shortage of something and with a person's strong – almost instinctive – inclination to relieve this shortage. There is little, if anything, a company can do to influence such fundamental behavioural stimuli. In other words, marketers do *not* create needs! This is true of physical (innate) needs (such as thirst) as well as psychological needs (such as the need for recognition). Psychological needs are greatly influenced by culture. For instance, affluent Western societies devote more attention to needs relating to physical health and mental wellbeing than other cultures.

Wants

Needs can be satisfied by more than one product. Once a consumer becomes aware of a need and considers the available alternatives, they will usually develop a *preference* for a certain product. This is the product they *want*.

FIGURE 1.11 Marketing's first task: anticipating and identifying needs and wants

In choosing between similar products, the consumer will consider factors such as time, place and money. They have to decide when and where they will buy the product and how much they are willing to spend on it. In this stage, advertising and other marketing efforts can influence their wants. Wants are also referred to as *desires* or *preferences*.

Consumer behaviour and demand

As soon as the consumer starts acting based on their needs and wants, *consumer behaviour* comes into play. Consumer behaviour generally takes three different forms: communication (the *search* for information and products prior to making a choice), the *purchase* (everything that relates to the transaction) and the *use* or consumption of the product. The purchase marks a turning point in this process: from then on, there is an actual demand. We define demand as the quantity of goods or services purchased on the basis of certain wants in order to satisfy a need.

So needs, wants and demand are closely related to one another. They are essentially a sequence of phases that consumers go through. Once needs have turned into certain desires and the consumer visibly responds to internal stimuli, this process is regarded as consumer behaviour. The relationship between needs, wants, consumer behaviour and demand is illustrated in Figure 1.12.

1.5.2 Marketing's second task

Although the purchase of a product is an important step in consumer behaviour, and certainly one that marketers try to bring about, it is usually not the only goal. The purchase indicates that the marketer has carried out his first task – discovering needs and wants – well and has successfully tailored the four Ps of the marketing mix to suit the buyer. According to 'traditional' marketing theory, this is the marketer's primary objective.

FIGURE 1.12 Relationship between needs, wants, demand and consumer behaviour

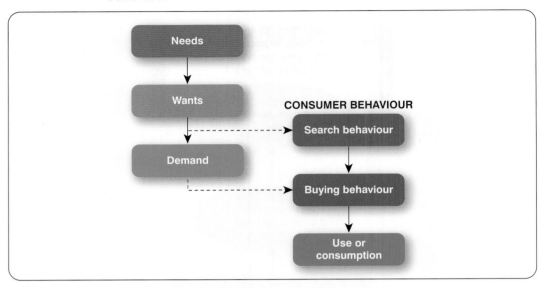

However, as competition increases many products become universally available, all the while becoming more and more similar in terms of quality and price level. At this point, product, price and distribution have become less important as marketing instruments. Some companies try to stand out from their competitors through a creative promotional campaign. But even then, it is increasingly difficult to build a leading position. In short, the four Ps are necessary as marketing instruments, but have become less important as 'weapons' in the fierce competitive battle.

What then are the new priorities in the field of marketing? We already listed them in our definition of marketing at the beginning of this chapter. As you recall, we defined *marketing* as 'the process of developing, pricing, promoting and distributing products, services or ideas that are tailored to the market; it includes all other activities that create value, and systematically

→   lead to increased sales or another desired **R**esponse,

→   establish a good **R**eputation and

→   ongoing **R**elationships with customers,

so that all stakeholders achieve their objectives.

The four Ps and the three Rs are all key elements in the second task of marketing – the implementation of a sound marketing strategy to satisfy the wants and needs and help create demand. This is illustrated in Figure 1.13.

1.5.3 The three Rs

To avoid getting entangled in the downward spiral of tactical competition, marketing managers – who are responsible for the marketing activities in their organization – concentrate on more than just 'transaction-oriented' marketing instruments (the four Ps). When plotting the strategy, experienced marketers also focus on the company's *reputation* (or brand image), on the *relationship* with customers and on the desired *response* in the exchange process. Let's further explore these three Rs.

FIGURE 1.13 Marketing's second task: catering to demand with the four Ps and three Rs

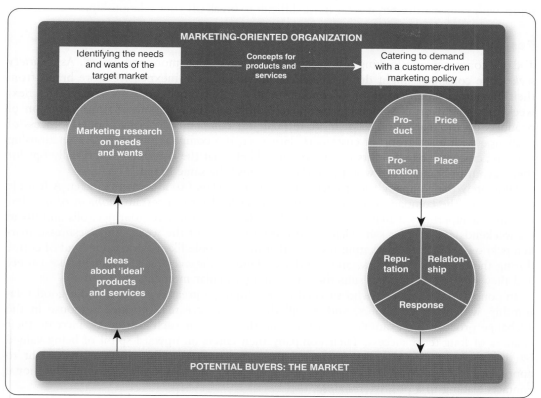

Reputation

An organization develops a certain *reputation* – the image that buyers have of the organization and its products or brands – through what it does in comparison with competitors. To make a positive impression on the consumer, a company has to do more than simply sell quality products. It also has to offer buyers excellent service in the long run. Once customers are not only satisfied, but also enthusiastic, they will most likely favour the organization. That is how a company creates a great reputation.

Just as a doctor is valued by a patient when they give them a prescription and then calls two days later to see how the patient is doing, the company has to do everything it can – through sponsorships, publicity, campaigns or personal contact – to reassure the customer that their confidence in the company is well placed. Appreciation is the basis of a good reputation and creates the climate for a good relationship between the two parties.

Relationship

If most brands of a particular product are equally good, the key question for the buyer is not so much, 'Which brand do I buy?' but, 'Where should I buy it?' So marketers have to 'come out from behind their stand' to show the customer who they really are. What kind of company and what kinds of people are behind the product? Ongoing *interaction* with the customer, which eventually creates a certain loyalty, is indispensable when developing a **relationship**. An interactive website, direct mail with a freepost address and a customer service line are all effective instruments in creating a customer loyalty system.

To create a bond with their customers, firms try to expand and deepen their communication with the customer. This increases loyalty. If you are able, for instance, to discuss many different topics with your hairdresser, it is far more difficult to break off your relationship.

Response

Today's consumers are looking for variety; they always want 'more and better'. As a *variety seeker,* the consumer might drink Heineken on Monday, the inexpensive store brand from their favourite supermarket on Wednesday and Grolsch bock beer on Friday. The next week they might drink something completely different. This response to the profusion of products on the market makes it more difficult for companies to bring about a process of exchange with a set group of customers. However, if a company has created a relationship with the customer based on its reputation, it is likely that the consumer will usually opt for their favourite brand. They won't just *always* choose the same brand.

Ultimately the company tries to get consumers to *respond* to a marketing offer. A feasible objective for the company is to become the market leader for a certain *moment of use*. For example, a supermarket may try to do this by offering a variety of gourmet rolls and bread on weekends and regular sandwich bread during the rest of the week. And Nespresso marketers know from their marketing research that many people like to drink one kind of coffee during the day, while at work, and a different kind in the evening. Consumers like variety and they simply choose what suits them best at a particular moment.

In conclusion, marketers who succeed in developing a great reputation and a good relationship with their customers, and do all they can to create a positive response in the exchange process (for example by customizing the offer for each customer), increase their chances of long-term success. Their company then enters an upward spiral of being valued by the customer as a supplier (*reputation*), confirmation that the customer was right to appreciate the company (*relationship*) and enhancing the relationship through additional contacts leading to a positive *response*.

Of course, the creation and exchange of value must be consistent with what the customer expects from the supplier. A butcher might give their customers a small bottle of liqueur as a gift, but this will do little to strengthen their reputation as an excellent butcher. A better idea would be to give customers a piece of superb sausage. Whatever the situation may be, through strategic use of the three Rs, a company can stand out from its less marketing-oriented competitors.

for a fresher world ★ **Heineken**

Image courtesy of The Advertising Archives

1.5.4 *Customer equity*

Some companies are determined to increase their sales and profit as quickly as possible. In order to grow, they constantly try to acquire new customers, and end up devoting less time to their existing customers. This weakens their position in the long run. To find the right balance in short-term versus long-term performance and in new customer acquisitions versus attention paid to existing customers, managers should consider the idea of systematically building customer equity.

Customer equity is the financial value of the relationships the company maintains with its customers. This includes both the profits from first-time customers and the expected profits from future sales to these new and to existing customers. Customer equity can be increased by:

→ Reducing the cost of getting new customers

→ Retaining more customers longer

→ Increasing profits from retained customers by selling them more products at higher margins and with lower marketing costs.[8]

A company's customer equity is the total *lifetime value* of all customers. The lifetime value of an individual customer is the present value of the profits derived from this customer's future purchases from the company. This profit contribution of a loyal customer from repeat sales may be increased – as a result of their recommendations and referrals – by the revenue stream from purchases made by others. One study has estimated that the lifetime value of a loyal pizza customer can be 7000 euros and of a loyal Mercedes owner, in excess of 300 000 euros. Facing these numbers, more and more managers realize that losing a customer may result in a far greater loss than the value of a single transaction. Hence, they are trying to develop ongoing relationships with customers, because this leads to customer loyalty and a greater customer retention rate.

The relationship between marketing strategy and customer loyalty on the one hand and sales, profitability and customer equity on the other is illustrated in Figure 1.14. Loyal customers contribute to increased sales growth and profits because they buy more over time. Also, gaining new customers from their referrals tends to substantially lower the customer acquisition costs. From this perspective, customer equity may be a better measure of a company's marketing performance than its current sales or market share.

Customer *complaints* need to be dealt with properly to satisfy the buyers' needs and to build a good reputation for the company. Unfortunately, many firms underestimate the importance of complaint handling as a marketing tool. The first reaction of those in charge of dealing with complaints is often defensive. What happened? Who was to blame? What should I do about it? In other words, they immediately concentrate on the *business* side and don't consider the emotional aspects of the problem.

FIGURE 1.14 Increasing customer equity

PROFESSOR'S PERSPECTIVE
Laetitia Radder (Nelson Mandela Metropolitan University, South Africa)

Laetitia Radder, Professor in Marketing Management at the Nelson Mandela Metropolitan University, South Africa, has published numerous articles on marketing and consumer-related topics in the services, hospitality and tourism industries. Her teaching career in South Africa and – as a visiting professor – in Germany, spans over 20 years.

© Heather Stevens

One of the most exciting developments in global marketing in the next ten years is the rise of the African consumer. Research by McKinsey's Africa Consumer Insights Center portrays the emerging African consumers as young, *brand conscious* innovators, who like to find information online, seek a modern, formal shopping environment and are loyal to products and stores with the right image. The retail, banking, telecommunications and tourism sectors in particular benefit from targeting these African consumers who demand high quality and reasonable prices.

This decade will be characterized by the rise of the African consumer

Entrepreneurs and companies that are new to marketing in Africa can learn from recent South African success stories. For example, *Woolworths'* marketing success can largely be attributed to 'being a customer–centric business'. The retail chain's increase in market share is the result of its management appealing to customers' needs and wants as defined by lifestyle segments; being brand-driven; building profitable customer relationships; and taking a leading role in multichannel retailing and communication. The channels on which the company relies include a state-of-the-art Internet shopping site and social commerce platforms that integrate social media marketing for the convenience of its customers.

The success of *Pick 'n Pay*, South Africa's first food discounter, can be ascribed to its marketing principles of offering the best quality, decent prices, good service, appropriate store formats and distribution channels that meet customers' expectations and evolving needs. Pick 'n Pay is also building strong customer relationships through its Smartshopper rewards programme. This direct marketing programme provides the retail chain with easy access to cardholders by SMS or email, and allows it to obtain direct feedback from customers. The two-way interaction helps the company to get to know and understand its customers, communicate with them in an engaging manner, tailor-make its product ranges and effectively serve its customers.

MTN, one of the leaders in the South African telecommunication industry, provides voice, data and telemetry services to its 20 million domestic customers. Innovation has put MTN at the forefront. For example, the company was the first one to pioneer the pre-paid customer solution and to launch the highly acclaimed MTN Zone, a dynamic tariff billing system. The company also offers the right products and services that are marketed to well-defined customer categories. In addition, it systematically engages in societal marketing through an extensive greening initiative that reduces its energy consumption; sponsorship of sport and music events; and its involvement in community development programmes.

What is the common denominator in the success of these organizations? They know that successful marketing starts with the marketing concept. They do not equate marketing with selling or advertising, but implement marketing as an integrated process of developing, pricing, promoting and distributing products, services and experiences tailored to the changing needs of consumers, in a socially responsible and sustainable manner. Finally, they conduct marketing research to make sure that what they offer, and how they do so, satisfies their customers' needs and wants.

Successful marketers, however, go beyond offering the products, services and experiences consumers want at prices and locations that appeal to them. They also build long-term relationships with their clients, realizing that servicing an existing customer is much more cost effective than trying to find new ones. A customer-centric approach is at the heart of transforming customer interactions into long-term relationships. To this effect, successful marketers know their customers well, regularly obtain and act upon customer feedback, minimize customer attrition, build emotional bonds with their customers and turn them into advocates for the company. This is exactly what companies wanting to capitalize on the potential of the rising market in Africa have to do as well.[9]

But a complaint usually has a deep *emotional* element. And that needs to be addressed first. So start by showing a sense of *commitment*. 'Oh, how awful for you! Tell me more about what happened.' Then explore a possible solution with the customer that is not only clearly in their interest, but also underscores the *relationship* with the customer. 'What would *you* prefer? As one of our valued customers, would you be happy if we...?'

A complaint is a negative reaction that, with the right marketing strategy, can be transformed into a positive experience. This is illustrated by the Chinese sign for 'crisis', which is made up of two symbols – one means 'threat' and the other 'opportunity'. A complaint is an opportunity; if handled properly in a customer-friendly manner, it will lead to greater customer loyalty.

1.6 MARKETING APPLICATIONS AND PREVIEW OF THE TEXT

As we saw earlier, companies making everyday consumer products were the first to apply the marketing concept. In this book, too, we will focus mostly on the marketing of fast moving consumer goods, such as food products that consumers buy regularly. But the success of consumer marketing (in which the supplier concentrates its efforts on the 'end user') showed that marketing also has a great deal to offer for other types of organizations. So in this section we take a brief look at different applications of the marketing concept.

1.6.1 Applications

The fundamental idea behind marketing is universal. In trying to stimulate the exchange process, the key is to start with the market and think backwards, and to always work in a customer-oriented way. This not only applies to consumer marketing, which focuses on private individuals, but also to a target market made up of other companies. This is referred to as business-to-business marketing, and sometimes as *industrial* or *organizational marketing*. B2B-marketing is discussed in paragraph 4.6.

Because the influence of retailers has increased enormously, many manufacturers now develop a marketing strategy specially geared to retailers that is known as trade marketing. The marketing strategy of the retail company itself (such as Ikea), which sells to the consumer, is referred to as retail marketing. Both of these subjects will also be covered in more detail later on in this book.

Other important applications of the principles of marketing are:

→ *Services marketing*: the marketing strategy of a supplier of intangible services, such as a bank or an insurance company.

→ *International marketing*: marketing activities that are planned domestically and aimed at customers outside of the domestic market.

→ *Direct marketing*: a form of marketing in which the supplier not only wants a transaction, but also tries to develop – based on what they know about potential buyers – an ongoing relationship with them, through direct communication (direct mail, telephone or the Internet) tailored to the individual customer, often followed by direct delivery.

→ *Database marketing*: a form of (direct) marketing in which a firm systematically collects and analyzes information about customers (for example, about their ordering and buying behaviour) and uses this information, which is stored in a *database*, to tailor marketing activities and campaigns to individual customers.

→ *Demarketing*: a marketing strategy designed to reduce the overall demand ('general demarketing') or the demand of a specific group of customers ('selective demarketing') for a certain product either temporarily or permanently, for example to avoid increasing production capacity, when working with scarce resources (like tropical hardwood) or to prevent environmental pollution (use of cars).

→ *Internal marketing*: marketing activities aimed at part of a company's own organization, for instance because certain business units do business with each other, or because management wishes to communicate to its own workforce what it is trying to achieve 'externally' and what it is promising customers.

→ *Non-profit marketing*: the marketing strategy of organizations without profit objectives (also known as *not-for-profit marketing*).

All but the last application make sense in terms of for-profit businesses, but what does marketing have to offer non-profit organizations?

1.6.2 *Non-profit marketing*

Although marketing is usually associated with business activities, organizations without a profit motive – such as educational institutions, libraries, museums, hospitals, religious groups and charities – can also apply the principles of marketing to their advantage. Just like corporations, they also need money and other resources to achieve their goals and survive in a competitive market. Their long-term success is not measured by profits, but by the benefits they provide as well as by the support they get from donors and volunteers.

Unfortunately, recent scandals have undermined the consumer's faith in some good causes. At the same time, government subsidies have decreased. Their declining income has prompted charitable organizations to engage in non-profit marketing. They develop professional consumer campaigns or tap new donors through *corporate sponsorship*.

Quite a few charities have turned to the business sector to find interested companies to support them. For instance, ING sponsors the Museum of Modern Art in New York as well as Amsterdam's Rijksmuseum, while Essent sponsors the WWF (World Wildlife Fund) Netherlands. Through this alliance, the WWF is not only boosting its financial resources, but also trying to influence corporate strategy, in this case by promoting, together with Essent, the use of green energy.

This kind of cooperation can also be profitable for the sponsoring company. Research shows that consumers see a collaborative partnership with a charitable organization as evidence of corporate social responsibility. They often turn this approval into action by purchasing the company's products. Because many consumers are also prepared to penalize a lack of corporate social responsibility by boy-cotting products or by negative word-of-mouth, the added value of corporate social responsibility is significant.

However, not all collaboration between a company or brand and a charitable organization is fruitful. For a good fit, both organizations should have the same supporters or target market. If a company wants to win the hearts and gain the confidence of a certain group of consumers, it has to tie in with the ideals of the people in this market segment. And we know what their ideals are if we know what charities they support. For example, the target market of Renault and the *Amnesty International* supporters appear to form a good *match*.

If a charity knows what products its supporters use and how they perceive certain brands, it can deliberately approach a company that stands to gain most added value from such an alliance – and may therefore be willing to invest more (or to make more concessions in terms of its strategy). This can also work the other way around. If a company is aware of what charities its target market supports, it can plan its *corporate sponsorship* accordingly, thereby making its marketing efforts a noble pursuit.

© Marco Secchi / Alamy

Not-for-profit organizations other than char-ities benefit from applying the marketing concept as well. Simply being devoted to 'a good cause' in an idealistic way will not generate income. Any highly competitive market needs to be analyzed on a regular basis – through marketing research – to identify market segments and learn about the attitudes, needs and behaviour of consumers. The 'product' that the organi-zation offers – possibly in different versions – must tie in closely with the characteristics of the selected target markets. We also need to decide whether each target market warrants a sepa-rate marketing and communication strategy. Think for example of colleges and universities that offer different courses for full-time and evening students. So, just like profit seeking companies, all non-profit organizations have to be marketing-driven to survive and, among competitors, to expand their market share.

1.6.3 *The need to study marketing*

Marketing is a fascinating subject that affects everybody, but unfortunately, almost everybody also seems to think that they know a lot about it. Although marketing skills, now more than ever, are in high demand, few people have a clear understanding of the real nature of marketing.

Reprinted with permission from Dixons Retail plc

There are plenty of good reasons to take the study of the subject of marketing seriously. First of all, more and more organizations are adopting a marketing-oriented approach. This trend in corporate culture provides many interesting *career opportunities* for (future) marketing managers. But even those who do not work in marketing-related positions are likely to interact with marketers involved in, for example, product planning, marketing research, advertising or distribution. Therefore, it is essential to be aware of the principles of marketing. Furthermore, almost everyone who works in an organization has to deal with demanding *customers*. This is another sound argument for being familiar with marketing fundamentals and for adopting the mindset of a marketing-oriented manager. Knowing about the theory of marketing is like having a driver's licence: you have to get one, but after that you have to put the knowledge into practice in order to realize its full benefits.

Since, as *consumers*, we interact daily with the marketplace, it is important to understand both the market system and what individual firms are trying to accomplish. For example, does it make sense to put off buying a tablet, now these products are becoming increasingly advanced and their prices are dropping? As consumers, are we better off cutting out the middleman by buying directly from the manufacturer through the Internet? If a retailer is not responding to our complaints, how do we exercise our rights? By exploring these and many other questions in the chapters to come, we will hopefully become more informed and intelligent consumers.

1.6.4 *A preview of the text*

Although by now we have a general idea of what marketing is all about, we cannot immediately start deciding on how to best use the marketing instruments. In reality, managers first figure out which market segments to target and establish their objectives in each submarket. Since these decisions are based on both the corporate strategy and information about the market – including the competition and customers' buying behaviour – we need to cover these subjects before we proceed. Only then can we work out the marketing mix.

The sequence in which subjects are discussed in *Marketing: A Global Perspective* is generally the same order in which marketing managers address them on the job. Figure 1.15 shows which subjects are covered in which chapters.

FIGURE 1.15 How the various components of marketing fit together

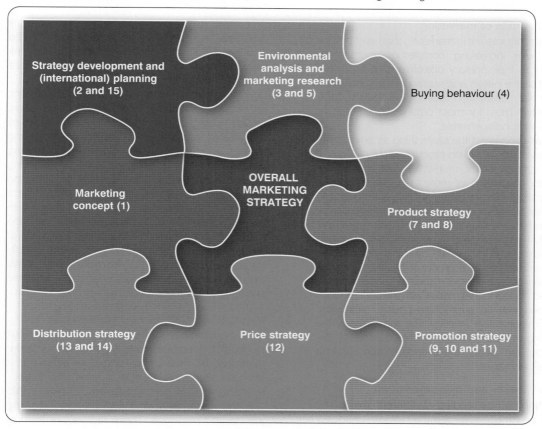

The remaining chapters in Part 1 look at an effective system of marketing planning and strategy development. We will then consider the environment – at the meso and macro levels – in which the firm operates. These include environmental forces beyond the control of the marketing manager, as well as situations that can be influenced in order to market products and services profitably.

Part 2 discusses the analysis of the market. We will explore the buying behaviour of customers in the consumer and in the business-to-business market, and compare the most widely used methods of marketing research. Chapter 6 offers advice on how to segment the market, how to select the right target market and how to develop a successful product positioning strategy.

The next four parts examine the key marketing ingredients: product, promotion, pricing and distribution. Here, we will also look at recent developments in marketing and at techniques that companies apply to plot their marketing strategies. Finally, Chapter 15 investigates international marketing planning, the global marketing environment and strategies to enter foreign markets.

SUMMARY

1   Fundamentals of marketing

There is more interest in marketing than ever before. Faced with increasing competition, companies realize that their primary objective is to *anticipate and satisfy the needs and wants* of their customers. If they fail, unsatisfied buyers will switch to a competitor. Thus, for most organizations, effective marketing is indispensable.

Marketing is not the same thing as advertising, or a 'clever' way of selling products. Advertising and selling are important marketing instruments, but marketing involves a lot more than that. It includes virtually all of the activities that bring the buyer and the seller closer together in the exchange process. Many individuals in an organization contribute to this goal. For instance, one of the main tasks in marketing is to find a 'gap in the market', by identifying unfulfilled needs and wants of a group of buyers. Once the marketer knows the *target market's* precise interests, they can appeal to that market with the right product, combined with an appropriate pricing, distribution and communication strategy. The more closely the *marketing mix* is tailored to the desires of the customer, the greater the chance of success in a competitive market.

2   Macro-, meso- and micromarketing

Marketing can be studied at different levels. The macro and meso level are the domain of *society* and the *business sector* respectively. In this book we will be concentrating on micromarketing: the marketing strategy of an organization, from the point of view of a manager who has to make effective decisions. This is also known as the *marketing management* approach.

3   Historical development of marketing thought

The development of marketing thought was preceded by the *production-*, *product-* and *selling-orientation*: management philosophies that most industries embraced during the 20th century. Under a *marketing* orientation, business decisions are based on the customer, rather than on the company and its products. The company has to satisfy the needs and wants of its customers as effectively as possible. This fundamental idea of marketing is known as the marketing concept.

4   The marketing concept

Under the *marketing concept*, the primary aim of a company is to discover and satisfy the needs and wants of the buyer, developing an ongoing relationship and helping to solve the customer's problems in a profitable way. Marketing is therefore a demand- or *consumer-oriented* activity, which makes it necessary to 'think backwards from the market', and requires extensive marketing research.

In implementing this philosophy of management, rather than being carried out in isolation, promotion, pricing, distribution and other marketing activities are treated as part of an integrated marketing strategy and are discussed as such in a *marketing plan*. All marketing functions – from marketing research and product development to analyzing the competition and evaluating the customer's reaction to the product range – are *aligned* with one another. Finally, implementation of the marketing concept requires a broad definition of the firm's mission, expressed in terms of *needs*, rather than products. This will make it more likely that the company will regularly adapt to meet the changing preferences in the market.

5   Reputation, relationship and response

Most organizations are finding it increasingly difficult to develop a unique marketing mix that is better than that of their competitors. Nevertheless, a firm can stand out on the basis of the three – overlapping – Rs: its *reputation*, its *relationship* with the customer(s) and systematically creating the desired *response*. These factors are the key to success in the marketing strategy of the 21st century. However, the selection of the right target market and a constant analysis of unfulfilled needs, wants and demand are equally important. In short, a shrewd and consistent implementation of the *four Ps* and the *three Rs* makes it possible to carefully tailor corporate policy to the market – to the advantage of suppliers *and* customers alike.

6   Marketing in practice

Marketers spend a great deal of time identifying and analyzing the needs and wants of their customers and prospects. Armed with this information they are able to develop and – with the right strategy – market attractive products, in line with the attitudes and the behaviour of the target market. This increases their market share.

As pointed out in Chapter 1, this approach is not only essential for companies that are competing with others, but also offers helpful leads for *non-profit* organizations. Therefore, it's crucial to have a clear insight into the *fundamentals of marketing*.

Note: A thousand definitions at a glance

All of the terms highlighted in green in this book are listed alphabetically and defined in the glossary at the back of the book as well as on the online platform (see the 'about the digital resources' page for more information). You can also find these marketing definitions online as 'flashcards' and crossword puzzles by individual chapter. This interactive tool will help you prepare for exams and master the vocabulary of marketing.

DISCUSSION QUESTIONS

1 How would you explain the nature of marketing to someone who is not familiar with the subject?

2 Many people do not know exactly what marketing involves. This is clear from the following statements:

Marketing is simply another word for selling.

The main objective of marketing is to get people to buy products they don't really want or need.

Marketing only makes sense if supply exceeds demand.

Marketing is less important than the company's other activities.

If you were talking to someone who made such a comment, how would you respond?

3 How – in the context of the societal marketing concept – could a business that makes soft drinks achieve (for example in its packaging) an optimal balance between the interests of the consumer, society and its own continued existence?

4 **a.** During the course of the 20th century what were the factors that influenced the shift in emphasis from a production-orientation to a selling-orientation?
b. Many companies were once production-oriented, and even at the start of the 21st

century there are still some organizations that do not adopt a marketing-oriented approach. How would you explain this?

5 List some of the arguments you would use to convince the executives of a company that does not adopt a marketing-oriented approach that the marketing concept is essential for sound management.

6 Why, despite the implementation of the marketing concept, are there still so many unsuccessful products?

7 What do you think is the most innovative development in marketing in recent years, and why?

8 Has the institute at which you are studying adopted a marketing-oriented approach? Describe the four marketing instruments of this organization.

9 The Internet is not only a new medium; it is also regarded as a new marketing instrument. How can the Internet play an important role in marketing? Give some examples.

10 Make a short questionnaire (of approximately five questions) to measure the extent to which a company succeeds in satisfying its customers.

CHAPTER 2
STRATEGY DEVELOPMENT AND MARKETING PLANNING

LEARNING GOALS

After studying this chapter you will be able to:

1 **Understand why a sound marketing strategy is essential for any company**

2 **Explain what information a mission statement should include**

3 **Conduct a SWOT analysis for an organization**

4 **Describe how to formulate useful objectives**

5 **Discuss portfolio analysis as well as generic and growth strategies**

6 **Explain how the marketing organization may influence performance**

7 **Develop an effective marketing plan**

8 **Recognize how the marketing plan can help in controlling the marketing effort**

2.1 Marketing planning
2.2 Business definition and mission statement
2.3 SWOT analysis
2.4 Determining marketing objectives
2.5 Developing the marketing strategy
2.6 The marketing plan
2.7 Implementation and control

Image Asset Management

Managers are paid to make important, often difficult decisions. They must select a lucrative target market and launch a range of attractive products and services using the best distribution channels, while successfully communicating product and service benefits to customers. And all this must be accomplished within the allocated marketing budget, bearing in mind that resources are limited. Factor in cut-throat competition and the problem of incomplete market information, and it becomes evident that the latest marketing knowledge and skills are absolutely indispensable.

Although there are no cookbook recipes for marketing, a systematic marketing approach greatly increases the chances of success. Rather than concentrating *internally* on their products and costs, successful managers focus *externally* on their customers and competitors. Their challenge is to develop an effective, decision-oriented marketing plan that helps anticipate future events, and develop marketing strategies for achieving the organizational objectives. Meeting that challenge is what we will be exploring in Chapter 2.

MARKETING IN ACTION
McDonald's Global 'Plan to Win'

Image Asset Management

McDonald's, with its 33 000 restaurants across the globe, is doing quite well. Ever since Jim Skinner was appointed CEO, the company has grown at an annual rate of 5 per cent, with global sales topping €60 billion and same-store sales – a closely watched industry-metric – climbing each year. In fact, McDonald's sales revenues exceed those of Burger King, Pizza Hut, KFC, Subway and Starbucks collectively. Skinner's no-nonsense leadership and focus on the positioning and performance of the fast food chain has resulted in a 'Golden Age for the Golden Arches'.

Those who haven't ventured into a Macdonald's restaurant recently might attribute the chain's success to a recession in which consumers prefer an inexpensive fast food place over an upscale restaurant. A closer look, however, would reveal that Jim Skinner has developed a strategy that continues to draw McDonald's customers who come in for a hamburger, French fries and a shake, but also brings in new guests who are craving for a Premium Southwest Salad with Grilled Chicken and a Wild Berry Real Fruit Smoothie, or an Angus Mushroom and Swiss Snack Wrap with a Fruit 'N Yogurt Parfait, along with a delicious cappuccino. The updated menu has definitely increased the average sales volume of McDonald's restaurants.

> 'By addressing the needs of our on-the-go customers, we are keeping our brand relevant and in demand'

Today, the average restaurant's sales volume is close to €2 million, nearly twice as high as ten years ago. Some of the biggest increases were gained in McDonald's European

restaurants and in its Pacific, Middle East and Africa division, where same-store sales recently climbed 11 per cent over the previous year – the most in ten years. 'Our strategic focus on building the McDonald's business by being *better*, not just bigger, and our global *Plan to Win* have combined to create enduring business momentum,' CEO Jim Skinner said. 'By offering menu innovations and everyday conveniences that address the *needs* of our on-the-go customers, we are keeping our brand relevant and in demand.'

For a restaurant chain, success on a global scale does not come easy. Taking into account past failures such as the doomed 'McPizza', McDonald's cooks have to come up with the right recipes to be tested by the kitchen crew; management must select companies that can supply the ingredients in large enough quantities; the behind-the-counter crews need to be trained to cook the new menu items; and marketers have to develop effective strategies to persuade consumers across the world to try out the new products. They also have to deal with the nutrition-minded 'food police' that monitor the calories, saturated fat and sodium content as well as portion sizes of the new menu items. 'Better to improve the diets of many than to seek perfection for the few,' says

Dr. Adam Drewnowski, Director of the University of Washington Center for Obesity Research. Luckily for McDonald's, Skinner has turned the restaurant giant into a well-oiled marketing machine, guided by a passion for satisfying customers and insisting on strategic planning and accountability throughout the organization.

For years, Skinner worked in McDonald's international business, opening up restaurants in over fifty new markets throughout Europe and Africa, in addition to the Middle East. When he returned to the Illinois headquarters, McDonald's priority was to continue to expand by opening up at least twenty new restaurants per week. Unfortunately, this rapid expansion came at the expense of food and service quality. To remedy the situation, Skinner developed the 'Plan to Win', a back-to-the-core marketing strategy that emphasized growth through increasing sales volume at McDonald's current restaurants (*market penetration*) instead of growth through starting new restaurants (*market development*).

A proven strategy, developed to stimulate customers to order more food and come back to the restaurant more often, was to think in terms of *platforms* instead of one-hit wonders. A popular platform, for example, is chicken, while a best-selling product is Chicken McNuggets. Another example: McCafé is the company's beverage platform (its most successful launch in the past four decades), while freshly made smoothies and coffee products are part of it. This platform is responsible for additional sales of over €100 000 per restaurant. It is clear that innovations continue to be important for the restaurant chain. And in today's global market, overseas divisions are exchanging new product ideas worldwide. To illustrate, both McCafé and Chicken McBites were originally developed in Australia, but are now available across the globe.

Although today's menu includes more than one hundred products, Jim Skinner's strategies reflect the importance of McDonald's core business, which is all about hamburgers. To not get distracted from that, the CEO divested of McDonald's stakes in *Chipotle* – a Mexican grill restaurant chain that it had diversified into. As a former McDonald's executive pointed out, just because you're doing a great job selling burgers doesn't mean that you can be equally successful in the rental car, IT or pizza business. McDonald's got rid of the Golden Arch hotels it had opened in Switzerland for the same reason: they were not helping the hamburger business that it should be focusing on.

These days, the company's marketing-oriented managers systematically decide what new products will be the best addition to the restaurants' menu. Before any product is added to the menu board, it is first analyzed in terms of potential return on investment, profit contribution and ease of being rolled out in the domestic and international market. Right now, the company is developing or test marketing about forty different products. For some of them, such as the Angus Burger, a period of at least four years is needed to develop a perfect product and to decide if its introduction would create incremental sales, rather than *cannibalizing* (or stealing sales from) the current products.

An example of a sound marketing strategy involves the Snack Wrap, introduced right after sales volume of Chicken Selects, the crispy chicken strips, had peaked. McDonald's *value delivery network* – its executive chef, food scientists, suppliers, franchisees and advertising agency – jointly developed the product and pricing strategy. Hundreds of consumers in focus groups assessed the new Snack Wrap. A one-month operational test in restaurants showed to what extent the cooking equipment or crew positioning should be changed. McDonald's menu-development team knew everything about the bun, but now had to make important tactical decisions about the Snack Wrap's main component: the tortilla. For example, how hot and how flexible should it be when served, and what packaging is best for the customer?

Within a record-breaking period of a year and a half after the idea was first discussed, McDonald's launched the Snack Wrap. Its introduction met two of the company's *marketing objectives*: to reach another price point on the menu and to create a new product that would stimulate repeat business. In addition, it allowed management to get the most out of the *snacking market* – the increasing number of people who are longing for a bite between meals – and an opportunity to increase *traffic* (the number of customers) at slow times, such as between lunch time and dinner. The new product development team then used its tortilla expertise to develop the new McSkillet Burrito, a breakfast item popular in the US. An added bonus is that the two items are made with the same tortilla, eliminating the need for an additional ingredient in the kitchen.

Although McDonald's loves to develop profitable products, you may not see new major hits any time soon. To maintain the current rate of growth, management will likely focus on successfully executing the strategy and increasing the efficiency of the global infrastructure that supports the restaurants. After all, the restaurants, of which 80 per cent are operated by independent owners, are the only places where the money is made. The executives in Illinois may develop great ideas, but if the kitchen crew can't handle the preparation of a new product, it's bound to fail. To illustrate, McDonald's headquarters once cooked up the idea of adding deli sandwiches to its product line. Guess what? It turned out to be impossible to prepare the sandwiches within a minute. And while managers often talk about the importance of hospitality and relationship marketing, consumers are increasingly rushed for time, according to Skinner. Does anyone have the patience today to sit in a drive-through and wait for several minutes after ordering a turkey sandwich? Probably not. But then again, that does not necessarily apply to all of the 65 million consumers per day who eat at one of the McDonald's restaurants in 120 different countries. This makes developing a sound global marketing strategy quite a challenge![1]

Developing a successful marketing strategy is of key importance to marketing executives. Marketing strategy must be in line with overall corporate strategy, and therefore we must understand how an effective corporate strategy is designed. To get a better grasp of this procedure, we will look at a model that maps out the entire marketing planning process. We will see that before we can draw up and implement meaningful *plans*, we need to conduct an *analysis* of the situation – not only an internal analysis of the organization, but also an external analysis of the environment in which it operates. By combining the results of the internal and external analyses, we can plot an effective marketing strategy. In other words, we can put our objectives down on paper, strategize for the future and develop concrete

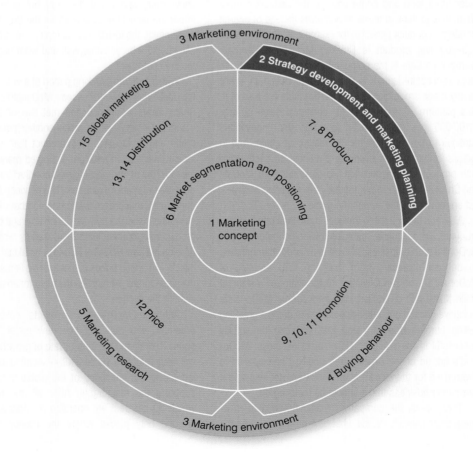

plans for the years to come. The development and systematic *implementation* of a carefully considered marketing action plan is the key to success.

2.1 MARKETING PLANNING

In addition to leading other people in the organization, a manager is also responsible for planning the work and seeing that it is carried out. In fact, managers are basically concerned with four things: the *analysis*, *planning*, *implementation* and *control* of the company's activities. These tasks – essential for effective *marketing management* – can be seen in Figure 2.1.

The diagram shows the four basic tasks of marketing management in logical order. Having completed various *analyses*, a manager then makes *plans* and *implements* them. To maintain the necessary *control*, work is constantly monitored during and after the implementation to ensure that it is being carried out as planned. This usually leads to new analyses, corrective action and adjustments of the plans.

In Chapter 2 we focus on the analysis and planning of the activities; the other marketing tasks are covered elsewhere in this book. In the next paragraph we look at the differences between strategic and tactical planning and the different levels at which strategy is developed.

2.1.1 Differences between strategic and tactical planning

Many companies operate without any formal plan. Their managers do not schedule time to formulate ideas for the future. And if managers do make time, the plan is often short sighted, projecting only a single year in advance.

Planning should not be confined to the short term. Rather than concentrating on the day-to-day business operation, which is relatively easy to oversee, we need to anticipate significant future opportunities and challenges. Hence, we need to prepare for both the long term and the short term, with a well thought-out strategy that includes tactics. Strategy and tactics combined form the company's *policy*.

The long-term plan sets out the strategy. A strategic marketing plan defines the marketing goals (such as increased market share and revenue) for a period of two to five years and indicates *how* (in which markets and with what products) those goals can be realized. This long-term plan is based on certain assumptions, estimates and scenarios. Although these are not always accurate, the plan establishes the 'thread' by clarifying the connection between all of the strategic decisions that affect the company's survival and success. Of course the marketing strategy must also be carefully aligned with the previously formulated *corporate* strategy. Only then can the marketing strategy help the company to achieve its overall corporate objectives.

A short-term plan (or 'annual plan'), on the other hand, is more *operational* in that it describes the tactics the company will implement to achieve its short-term objectives. An operational

FIGURE 2.1 The four basic tasks of marketing management

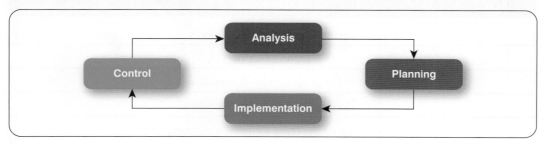

© Zurijeta / Shutterstock

marketing plan for a period of one year is quite common. This kind of elaboration of the marketing mix can relate to an individual product or brand, a product line or the company as a whole. If the operational marketing plan is for the entire company, it will set out all of the marketing objectives and the company's full marketing strategy, including the budgets and action plans per **product-market combination**. It is possible to go into such detail because the analyses that serve as the groundwork for the marketing tactics are based far more on 'hard' facts, and therefore involve less uncertainty than analyses for projecting a longer time span.

Figure 2.2 summarizes the characteristics of the strategic marketing plan. By now the differences between marketing strategy and marketing tactics should be clear. While a company sets out its main objectives and the methods (strategies) it will use to achieve them in its strategic marketing plan, the company's tactics explain in detail how it intends to implement the strategy. For example, if a company's marketing objective is to increase its market share by 20 per cent over the next three years, an appropriate *strategy* may be to expand its range of products to tap new segments of price-conscious customers. The *tactics* that the company will employ to implement the marketing strategy will determine the new products and their corresponding prices, as well as the best distribution techniques and promotional means to employ in launching the products successfully and selling them to the target market.

As Harvard Business School professor and management guru Michael Porter said recently at a strategy seminar conducted for European managers, it is not so much the economy that creates problems in the business sector, but wrongly chosen or implemented *strategies*. In the last decade many companies have been concentrating on large takeovers and mergers. This has led to sweeping reorganizations and cutbacks of marketing budgets.

Porter points out that a more lucrative long-term strategy is to develop and exploit a *competitive advantage*. Too many companies have very similar offerings. This puts pressure

FIGURE 2.2 Characteristics of the strategic marketing plan

Strategic Plan
Typically long to medium range
Broad in scope
Focus on overall objectives
Top management responsibility
Serves as the basis for tactical planning

on prices and leads to narrow margins. To avoid this, a company should select the right target market and try to market something better or different.[2]

2.1.2 Three levels of strategy development

No marketing department is autonomous. Like their colleagues elsewhere in the organization, marketers are bound by the objectives and guidelines established by top management. Just as the production manager cannot independently determine which products to make, the marketing manager cannot independently decide which markets to enter.

In fact, it is the business plan that determines how much room marketers have to manoeuvre. When making decisions, senior management will, of course, take the plans and priorities of the marketing department into consideration. Because of this interaction, many marketing and product managers get involved in strategic planning at higher levels. This enables them to align their operational marketing or product plan with the business plan, which sets out the *business strategy*. One level higher in the hierarchy of a large organization, the marketing strategy described in the business plan must, in turn, be optimally aligned with the overall *corporate strategy*. Therefore, marketers also need to know how the strategy and objectives are established at the top echelon of the organization.

As can be seen in Figure 2.3, strategy development occurs at three levels in a company. A person's function within the organization determines the (strategic or tactical) plans with which they are most concerned, and we make a distinction between corporate strategy, business strategy and marketing strategy.

Corporate strategy

The *corporate strategy* is developed at the uppermost levels of the organization. A concern or parent company is usually comprised of various **Strategic Business Units** (SBUs). Each of these SBUs is a division of the organization that operates more or less independently; it sells a range of products to a certain group of customers and – among clearly defined competitors – is responsible for the development and implementation of the strategy.

An SBU can vary from a single product line or production facility to one or more divisions, or even a whole market. In any event, these kinds of organizational units are regarded as 'decentralized *profit centres*': independent firms with their own management. Hence the CEO of a corporation will assess each of the SBUs individually, using criteria such as profit contribution, sales, quality of the strategic plan and the investments proposed in that plan.

An organization can be divided into Strategic Business Units in different ways. A good starting point is to determine how the corporate activities fundamentally differ. Sometimes these correspond to the strategic variables that are already being used to divide the market into segments, or *target markets* that are each approached with a different strategy. For example, a multinational might set up its SBUs based on *geographical location*. This makes sense if its foreign markets are all totally different. Other organizations establish their SBUs around identical *products* or around products that satisfy the same customer *needs*. Finally, *customers* and the *distribution channels* to reach them can also serve as a basis for forming SBUs, as the following example illustrates:

'Royal Philips Electronics of the Netherlands is a diversified Health and Well-being company, focused on improving people's lives through timely innovations. As a world leader in healthcare, lifestyle and lighting, Philips integrates technologies and design into people-centric solutions, based on fundamental customer insights and the brand promise of "sense and simplicity"'. At Philips, the SBUs are based on product-market combinations. This reflects the market-oriented approach of the head office in Amsterdam. At one time, the company created a separate business unit for Hewlett Packard, a client that purchased large quantities of components and monitors. 'The customer is more important than the product

FIGURE 2.3 The three levels of strategy development

POSITION IN THE ORGANIZATION	LEVEL OF STRATEGY DEVELOPMENT	PLANNING FOCUSED ON THE DEVELOPMENT OF:	TYPICAL MARKETING QUESTIONS
Top management	Concern level: CORPORATE STRATEGY SBU 1 ↔ SBU 2 SBU 4 ↔ SBU 3	Corporate plan	– What is our mission? – What business are we in? – What is the best way to organize the corporation?
Middle management (subsidiaries)	SBU level: BUSINESS STRATEGY Marketing ↔ Production Human resources ↔ Financial affairs	Business plan per strategic business unit (division or product)	– What growth strategy are we pursuing? – What is our core competence? – How do we compete?
Supervisory or functional-level management (marketing/ product manager)	Product/market level: MARKETING STRATEGY Product ↔ Price Promotion ↔ Distribution	Operational plans for implementing tactics	– How do we support the business-level strategy? – What do our customers value? – What are our weekly plans and tasks?

division', said a Philips board member. 'Thanks to this management model our head office can now better concentrate on monitoring the strategy.'[3]

Strategic planning at the highest organizational level is best visualized as the 'big picture' drawn by the head office to assure a profitable future for the corporation. These broad outlines are also known as the strategic profile. By determining resources to which the SBUs have access (the so-called *allocation of resources*), management also influences the SBUs' investments. This, in turn, affects in which markets the SBU competes and the activities it undertakes to bridge possible gaps between the stated objectives and the anticipated results.

Business strategy

The divisions, subsidiaries or SBUs of the corporation conduct the second level of planning. The *chief executive officer* or CEO of such an operational unit develops a business strategy. This involves more than the marketing strategy. The CEO also distributes the resources – for instance, money, manpower and production capacity – made available to the SBU among its various activities (such as the product lines) in a way that will achieve the best results.

The steps in this planning process are about the same as those at the corporate level, even though they deal with different issues. Here again, strategy development starts with the *strategic profile*. This can be established in a brief description of the company, its products and the markets in which it operates, including the market of suppliers, the financial market, the labour market and, of course, the customers. Although product managers (who usually work at a lower level in the hierarchy) often play a key role in describing the products and markets as well as the marketing strategies, the financial viability of their ideas is assessed at the SBU level.

In a small firm that sells only a limited number of products in one target market, the corporate level and the business level coincide, and management only has to plot the business strategy discussed here. The same principle applies to start-up companies.

Since, in the real world, product lines and markets tend to overlap, product lines are frequently used to describe a market in marketing plans. For example, a manager may refer to the 'mountain bike market'. But a market is more than a product line; hence, it is better (as clarified in Chapter 6) to view a market as groups of (potential) customers with certain needs, particularly since the strategy of an SBU is tailored to these customers.

Marketing strategy

The third level at which strategy development occurs, is the level of a product, brand or product line. This is usually called *marketing planning*. Marketing planning is the marketing managers' or product managers' responsibility. They develop a product-, price-, promotion- and distribution strategy in order to achieve the objectives of their product-market combination. With this goal in mind, they analyze information about the size of the market, their target markets and the profit contribution per product. In this sense, marketing and product managers are concerned with both strategic and operational management tasks. Thus, in many organizations they are part of *middle management*. The information they include in the individual marketing plans is ultimately integrated into the corporate marketing plan.

2.1.3 *Building blocks of success*

Research has shown that several components of a *marketing strategy* contribute to an effective business strategy. The more the various *business units* or divisions succeed in achieving their marketing objectives, the greater the chance that the *corporation* – or the organization as a whole – will be able to compete successfully. In this respect, we can view the organization as a pyramid made up of various building blocks. Figure 2.4 shows the main building blocks of success.[4]

The four cornerstones of a marketing strategy are:

1 *Brand image*, to make products and services recognizable and attractive in the customers' eyes;

2 *Quality*, which must meet customers' expectations about the products' performance;

3 *Innovation*, to create new and unique benefits in using the product;

4 *Ongoing customer relationship*, to be able to meet customers' needs as well as possible.

Sometimes a structural improvement in one of these factors is achieved at the expense of the other building blocks. Hence, an important challenge for an organization is finding the right balance in setting priorities with regard to these key factors for success.

2.1.4 *A marketing planning and management model*

Strategy development is usually considered at *business unit* level (with corporate strategy as a logical point of departure). The cornerstone of this business unit strategy is the marketing

FIGURE 2.4 Building blocks of a successful strategy

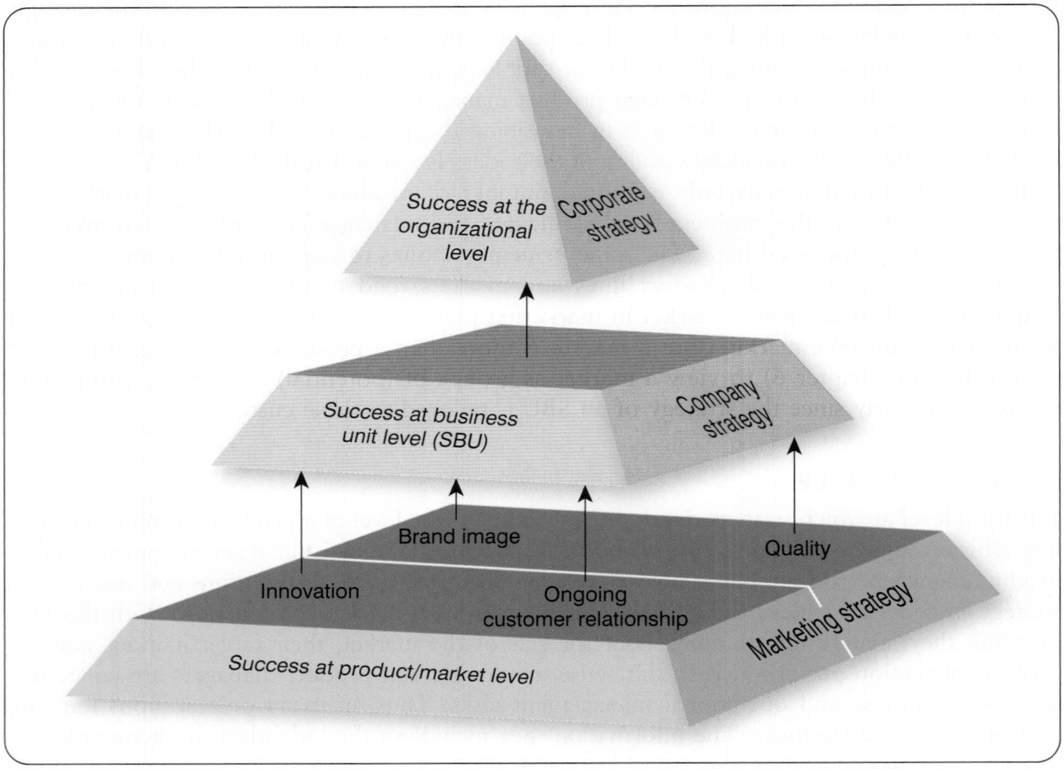

strategy, which in turn often serves as the basis for the strategies of other departments or functional areas. The combination and integration of *all* functional strategies constitutes the strategy of the business unit.

The company's chief executive officer sets guidelines for the planning procedure and the values that should dominate each plan. Senior managers are expected to have analytical skills, to be persistent, to be capable of assessing situations rapidly, to dare to take the initiative, to turn setbacks into opportunities and to link creativity to practical solutions. Most importantly, marketing is a mindset for these managers. They focus on customers and other stakeholders rather than on the company's products and services.

In a marketing-oriented company marketing planning begins with the *customers*. Their needs and wants – within the firm's business definition – should be carefully analyzed in order to satisfy them successfully. Figure 2.5 shows the importance of the customers – they are positioned at the top of the model that maps out the process of *marketing planning* and *marketing management*. This model is divided up into three phases: *analysis*, *marketing strategizing* (strategy development, planning and marketing control) and *implementation* of the strategy (execution and control).

As we can see, the marketing planning and management process involves activities related to each of the four basic tasks of management mentioned earlier: analysis, planning, implementation and control. In this section we examine the individual components of the model. For the remainder of the chapter, we will explore these activities in more detail.

FIGURE 2.5 A model of the marketing planning and marketing management process

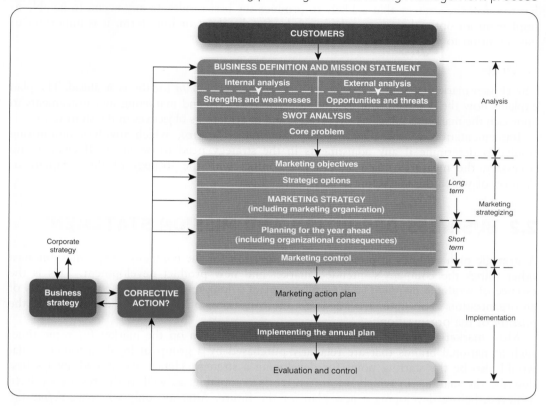

Analysis

A company striving to satisfy its customers has to make *choices*. Obviously, a single company cannot meet all of the needs and wants in the market. It has to focus on a certain target market. This principle applies in *consumer marketing* (*Business-to-Consumer marketing*, or B2C), as well as in *Business-to-Business marketing* (B2B).

The most effective strategy is largely dependent on the main step in the analysis part of the marketing planning process: the so-called *SWOT analysis* (SWOT stands for Strengths, Weaknesses, Opportunities and Threats). As we will see shortly, a feasible plan is based on an analysis of the company's strengths and weaknesses (the *internal* analysis) as well as of the opportunities and threats it is likely to encounter in the environment (the *external* analysis).

Planning and implementation

In the marketing planning process the strategy development phase begins with the formulation of *marketing objectives* in light of the results of the analysis. One marketing objective might be 'to increase the company's market share held by current products in currently serviced markets by 5 per cent by the end of the year'.

The next step in developing an effective strategy is to define and evaluate *strategic options*. A feasible strategy to achieve the stated objective might be to sell more of the existing product range to current customers, increasing sales by offering 'buy two, get one free'. Another strategic option is to find new customers within the target market, such as younger users, or buyers of other brands. Because the organization's resources are limited, it has to *select* the strategy that is likely to produce the best results. In any event, to be able to implement an optimal strategy, whether it be for the short or long term, it is important to pay attention to *planning* for the year ahead.

Control

The chosen marketing strategy results in a *marketing action plan* for the year ahead. The plan explains how the company will use the available resources and marketing mix instruments to approach the market as effectively as possible and to achieve its objectives in the short term.

Implementation of the plan requires continuous *control*, which involves monitoring results to determine if any adjustments in the strategy need to be made. If changes are necessary, the measures taken should not conflict with the strategy of the company or division of which the marketing department is a part.

2.2 BUSINESS DEFINITION AND MISSION STATEMENT

A strategic plan outlines in broad terms the *direction* for the company. It specifies amongst other things the company's intended market and new product development. This is the essence of **strategic planning**: the development of a long-term plan to use the resources of an organization in an optimal way, within the constraints of the business definition and the *mission* of the organization.

Most marketing plans focus on products that have been on the market for some time, such as national brands that are regularly purchased by a group of loyal customers. That would also be the starting point for developing a strategy. Hence, we should always first describe the markets in which we are currently competing, as well as the results we have achieved, before developing a new plan for the future. After all, only when we *define* the market correctly can we calculate our market share, conduct the right market analyses and plot out a course that will lead to further growth.

2.2.1 *Formulating the business definition*

Companies used to define their business in terms of the *product* ('we make glasses frames that last') and the materials or *technology* used ('we work in the plastic processing industry'). Nowadays however, rather than using a product- or production-oriented definition, companies tend to define what they do in relation to a target market, usually focusing on the *needs* of these customers. That is because products and technologies have a limited lifespan (and may become obsolete), while needs – and therefore markets – are constant.

To illustrate, a company that 'makes glasses' will see its sales decline as an increasing number of young people start wearing contact lenses or choose to have laser eye surgery. It would be better for this company to define its *business* as 'satisfying the consumers' need for optical products and services'. It could then easily expand its range of products with, for example, sunglasses, binoculars and contact lenses. The firm might also consider developing new activities, such as acting as an intermediary for LASIK surgery, or supplying telescopes for stargazers and microscopes for nature lovers or other target markets.

Auping, the European bed manufacturer, is a specific example. The company has been in business for more than 100 years and has evolved from producing spring mattresses through supplying completely furnished bedrooms, to providing consumers with an 'experience' while continuing to expand its business. 'We no longer see ourselves as supplying fully-fitted bedrooms, but as a firm delivering a peaceful environment and good night's sleep,'

MARKETING MISTAKE
Working Without a Strategic Plan

In most companies there are countless ideas and plans for the future floating around. Unfortunately, many of these ideas are never converted into activities, and many plans never become anything more than plans. Research shows that small and medium-sized companies often do not even go through the trouble of trying to put a *strategic plan* down on paper!

Too many managers simply allow the future to run its course. They are stuck in their old ways of thinking and tend to concentrate on internal *operational problems* or side issues. Acting more like supervisors who are always putting out fires, they lose sight of their primary role as strategically thinking executives. Also, because they lack much needed insight into markets, technologies and competitors, their work may be based on inaccurate assumptions. Given this mindset, strategic alternatives (such as entering a new market or adopting more innovative ways of approaching the current market) are rarely considered. Without a sound strategy, managers fail to detect or respond to the opportunities and threats that their company faces.

Why do managers make decisions without a sound business plan? There are six major reasons for a lack of strategic planning:

1 *Inability to stand back*
Some managers never view the market and their company with any degree of abstraction. As a result, a deliberate choice of target markets and a critical analysis of the products offered never get off the ground. Even the company's mission and business definition may not be clear.

2 *Too operationally oriented*
Day-to-day operations come first. Everything revolves around sales, even at the expense of developing and implementing a long-term strategy.

3 *Lack of self-criticism*
Because some managers do not allow themselves to be critical and open-minded, they rarely exchange views or ideas. Comments about the company's weaknesses are taken personally.

4 *No vision*
Since management lacks a clear vision of the future, the company responds to every trend in the market – under the guise of 'flexibility'. This kind of drifting benefits neither growth nor profitability.

5 *Reluctance to make choices*
A common question is: 'How can we implement a strategy when the market keeps changing?' Yet, particularly in turbulent times, it is crucial to develop a long-term plan to determine which developments are most relevant for the firm. Unfortunately, some managers lack the confidence, courage and decisiveness to make strategic choices.

6 *Insufficient time*
If a company does not allocate time to make a strategic plan, it probably does not consider strategy development as a top priority. Or, perhaps its management does not *know how* to develop and implement strategy.

Market leaders excel in three things: they focus, simplify and adapt

Research among executives in Europe, Asia and the US shows that market leaders consistently do three things better than their competition: they *focus*, they *simplify* and they *adapt*. Top performing companies, for example, typically try to increase speed-to-market, simplify communications between the boardroom and the 'front lines' and constantly adapt their business model. 'The findings show a fundamental shift in the nature of strategy and competitive advantage,' concluded James Allen of global consultancy Bain & Company. 'Most executives say that strategy is now more about their ability to *sense and adapt*, and they expect to deal with different key *competitors* within five years. They also spend more time with key *customers* to understand their emerging needs and wants. Today's speed of change and need for immediate responsive actions is remarkable.'[5]

according to Marketing Communication Manager Steven Koster. 'We are also expanding our target market by appealing to a younger age group.'[6] The choices they make for the company are closely related to the question, *What is our business definition?*

The Abell model

The business definition specifies the company's (potential) activities. It indicates the sphere or limits of the organization's field of activity, leaving enough room to develop new, additional products and services.

At the core of the business definition is the *business domain* or business scope: the extent of the firm's current activities. To describe a company's broader business definition, we often use three dimensions, which also form the basis of the Abell model. These three dimensions are:

→ *Customers*: which groups of customers or market segments do we distinguish, and what target market do we single out (what type of customer)?

→ *Needs*: what product features or benefits are customers looking for in order to satisfy their needs (what 'customer functions' should we fulfil)?

→ *Technologies*: how can we satisfy the identified needs (with which products and services)?

The *market* consists of the first factor (the customers we focus on), while the *product* is largely determined by the last two factors (customers' needs and technologies). That's why we also refer to business units defined in this way as *product-market combinations*, or as product-market-technology combinations. An analysis based on these dimensions is not only useful for describing the business definition, but also for developing the company's strategy. It not only provides insight into the market in which the firm operates, but also clarifies the firm's (potential) position in that market, relative to the competition. Finally, it helps us identify alternative strategies to approach the market segments that we have selected.

An application of the Abell model

An example of how the Abell model can be used to define the *business domain* is shown in Figure 2.6. This company sells fast food products. The target market's *lifestyle* is described in marketing research as 'carefree convenience seekers'. The customer need that the company satisfies is 'convenience' and the technology used is 'deep-frying'. The orange-coloured floating block in the diagram represents the business domain.

If this company wants to expand its activities, it can focus on other groups of customers identified by the marketing research study (such as 'health conscious connoisseurs'). It can also develop a product range to meet certain needs (such as a greater emphasis on health), and it can use a better technology to prepare healthy food (such as a steam oven).

FIGURE 2.6 Abell model for a company that makes fast food products

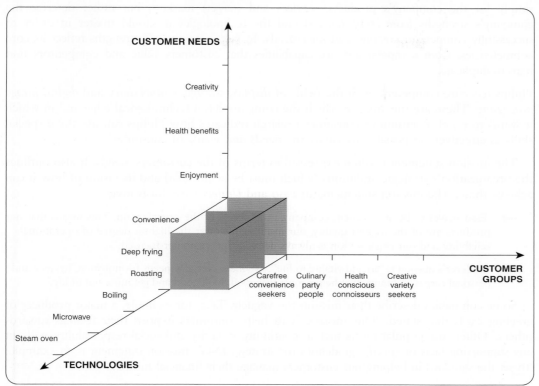

We can now define any 'business' by referring to the intersection of the three dimensions. The organization can expand its business domain or scope by entering other cells. The strategic decision to do so will often be made on the basis of a SWOT analysis. We will discuss that later. First, let's consider the role of the mission statement in strategy development.

2.2.2 Defining the company's mission

Like the business definition, the mission is usually defined once top management – in its strategy development efforts – has considered what kind of company it is (or should be) running, what markets it should focus on, and how it can – profitably – beat the competition. Addressing these issues is not a useless exercise. If you never think about the company's mission and spell it out, you run the risk of making the wrong strategic decisions. The company, for example, may change its course and get involved in activities that are counterproductive to its growth. Without a clear mission, the company may also overlook marketing opportunities and may not be able to take advantage of them.

Mission statement

The *mission statement* spells out the company's strategic vision, including its corporate philosophy, the overall goals, top management's values and priorities and the strategies it pursues. A good *mission statement* addresses questions such as: What are our core activities or, in other words, what business are we in? What kind of company are we and would we like to become? Who are our customers and what are their needs and wants?

A **mission statement** is the formal description of an organization's mission. It should not simply list the company's products, services and (target) markets, but rather describe the company's strengths (*core competencies*) and the technologies it should master in order to successfully compete in meeting customer needs. In fact, a company's strengths reflect its core competencies. **Core competencies** are capabilities that customers value and competitors find hard to duplicate.

Philips has core competencies in the fields of *display, storage, connectivity* and *digital image processing*. These are the areas in which the company has a technological edge and in which it wants to excel. Continuous consumer research indicates how Philips can use these special skills as effectively as possible to satisfy the needs and wants of consumers.

The mission statement is often expressed in terms of the customers' needs. It also outlines the organization's strategic ambitions (which must be achievable) and its vision of how it can achieve these. The mission statements of *Esso* and *Unilever* are illustrative:

→ 'Esso strives to be an excellent company, at all levels of the organization. This means that our products are of the highest quality, our installations offer the highest degree of operational reliability and our organization is always decisive and customer-focused.'

→ 'Unilever's mission is "to add vitality to life". We meet everyday needs for nutrition, hygiene and personal care with brands that help people feel good, look good and get more out of life.'

Some companies describe their mission too vaguely. Take, for example, a major producer of greeting cards that stated: 'Our mission is to help consumers express their feelings towards others.' Others use popular terms such as continuity, integrity and social responsibility, without any supporting facts or specific guidelines for strategy. ING's mission statement is an example: 'to set the standard in helping our customers manage their financial future'.

Functions of the mission statement

A mission statement has both an external function and an internal function. The *external* function of the mission statement – when published in the annual report or in promotional material – is to emphasize the distinctive features of the company. It may outline the organization's *raison d'être* (the essential purpose that differentiates the company from others) and the underlying philosophy of its operations (its attitude towards society, its employees and its shareholders). In other words, the mission statement describes the nature of the company, what it does and what it stands for. It is often supplemented with several shorter **vision** statements about what the company wants to achieve in the future. These reflect the ambitions of its management in terms of, for instance, the type of products the company supplies, its markets of concentration and the **image** it wishes to project. At the same time the mission statement often describes how the company perceives itself, the importance of growth or profit for its continuity and the needs of its customers.

Internally the mission statement's function is to motivate the employees and to get them – particularly managers – to reflect on the strategy. Because it helps to create a positive mindset (What business are we in and what do we really want?), the time devoted to defining the company's mission is well spent. After all, in trying to find just the right words, several strategic options are taken into consideration. By exchanging ideas about these alternative strategies, managers gain a clear insight into the course they need to follow.

Above all, the mission statement's key function is to *direct* the growth of the company or of the SBUs, using the corporate mission statement as a point of departure. Therefore, the mission should not be formulated either too broadly or too narrowly. If it is too broad and vague, it will not serve as a 'compass'. If, on the other hand, it is formulated too narrowly, it will unnecessarily restrict management's vision and the company's future expansion. Ultimately, the art of defining the mission is to find the right balance.

PROFESSOR'S PERSPECTIVE
Michael Porter (Harvard Business School, USA)

Michael Porter is a professor at Harvard Business School. The most famous business professor in the world is tired of hearing senior managers say that sticking to a long-term strategy makes no sense when everything is changing so rapidly. According to Michael Porter, strategy development has never been more important!

'I am determined to get business strategy back at the top of the agenda in industry. Strategy development has been neglected in recent years. Too many managers just focus on fighting competition. Of course, they don't admit this and claim to have a sound strategic vision. But in fact they are simply trying to make decent quality products at the lowest possible cost. That's not a strategy, that's applying *best practices*.

One reason why strategy development has fallen out of favour is that the world is changing quickly. Managers who insist that only speed matters, that companies must remain flexible enough to continually adapt, do not spend enough time on reflection. They see strategies as rigid, inflexible and outdated before they can be implemented. But that doesn't make sense. Successful companies are built on a sound strategic vision.

There is a fundamental difference between strategy development and efficient tactical management. Developing a strategy involves making conscious *choices* to differentiate the company. In day-to-day operations, those choices don't exist. You simply have to do what is best. Influenced by books about *just-in-time*, *total quality* and *re-engineering*, managers have become fixated on efficiency in managing daily operations. They probably still think of Japanese companies that have become more competitive by becoming more efficient.

A company without a strategy is inclined to try everything

However, since a sustainable competitive advantage can only be created through a long-term strategy, the Japanese obsession with 'back-to-basics' has become a problem. The essence of a strategy is setting limits to what you intend to do. A company without a strategy is inclined to try everything. If you copy your rivals who are also focusing on efficiency, you won't be very successful. It may even create a kind of rivalry that is destructive for both parties. If everyone does the same thing, customers will look for the lowest price. That has led to recent price erosion. Yet, in every industry there are plenty of opportunities for lucrative strategic diversification.

A sound strategy begins with setting clear profit objectives. If you fail to do that, you may be tempted to act in ways that undermine the strategy. If your goal is, for instance, to be big, to grow fast or to be a technological leader, you may run into problems. A strategy also has to establish continuity. It cannot constantly be reinvented. Strategic thinking involves both your company's *basic principles* – that you would also like to communicate to your customers – and the selection of *target markets*.

Over the years, strategy development has become more complicated. Twenty years ago you could simply determine the direction in which the company needed to go and then set off in that direction at your own pace. Today you first have to determine how to stand out. But simply making strategic choices is not enough to survive. You also have to use all available resources to improve your performance. Companies sometimes seem to act inconsistently by maintaining their long-term strategy while at the same time always trying to excel. Ultimately, they have to find the right balance between *continuity* and *change*.

Continuity should be present in strategy and in making improvements. The two are fully compatible and actually reinforce each another. If there is continuity at the top level, it is easier for a company to keep changing effectively. If, for example, you have spent ten years striving to be the best in a particular field, you will find it easier to apply new technologies.

The essence of strategy development is making tough *choices*. That's difficult, as even winners rarely do everything right from the start. But you don't need to have all of the answers at the outset. Most successful companies make sure that they're initially doing a great job on two or three things, and then they refine their strategy as they go along. In any case, it is essential to define the *core* strategy.

The CEO, as the leading strategist, must also make sure that everyone understands the strategy. After all, the fundamental goal of a strategy is to ensure that the thousands of things that need to be done in an organization are all moving in the same direction. If employees do not understand how the company wants to *stand out*, how on earth can they make the choices they're facing every day? In successful firms strategy is seen as something worth fighting for. Therefore, every co-worker needs to know what the company stands for!'[7]

2.3 SWOT ANALYSIS

A company that wants to grow sets ambitious objectives and creates a plan to achieve them. In doing so it should not lose sight of reality. A feasible plan must be based both on an analysis of the company's strengths and weaknesses (*internal analysis*) and of the opportunities and threats in the environment (*external analysis*). Together these two analyses are known as the 'situation analysis'. By inserting the results of these analyses in a *SWOT analysis* and combining them in a confrontation matrix, we can evaluate the company's fulfilment of its basic mission and systematically come up with guidelines for strategy development and future management actions.

2.3.1 Internal analysis

The internal element of a *situation analysis* addresses factors that the company itself can influence – at least in the long term. These *controllable factors* include the resources needed to achieve the company's objectives – such as the capital required for investments, the production technology, the employees' know-how, the nature of the product mix and the company's reputation among its customers.

The internal analysis should provide insight into the company's *strengths and weaknesses*. These apply to the organization as a whole and therefore go beyond the marketing function. For example, a strong market position may be the result of a customer-friendly product design, an efficient, low cost production system and the selling efforts by well-trained sales representatives. These come under the responsibility of the marketing, R&D, production and human resources departments. Therefore, all of these departments (or, in a small company, the individuals responsible) need to be included in the internal analysis. Only then can the company fully assess its strengths and weaknesses and effectively support the activities of those who contribute to the execution of the strategy. To illustrate an internal analysis, Table 2.1 lists a number of Unilever's strengths and weaknesses.[8]

2.3.2 External analysis

Some managers skip the external analysis when making plans. They are too busy with their own organization to systematically examine what is going on outside the company. But this lack of regard for external factors can lead to problems in a rapidly changing environment.

TABLE 2.1 An analysis of Unilever's perceived strengths and weaknesses

Strengths	Weaknesses
1 Effective communication to the customer.	1 Takes few risks when tackling the market.
2 Subsidiaries with strong national brands.	2 Lacks a decisive marketing strategy.
3 Expertise in developing production processes.	3 Inflexible, dated organization.
4 Technological know-how converted into new product concepts.	4 Heavy overheads reduce competitiveness.
5 Well-trained marketing managers.	5 High turnover of talented young managers.

To obtain a realistic picture of the company's situation, we must identify and consider all relevant **environmental factors** and eventually tailor the marketing strategy to those factors. The marketing environment consists of external variables that the company is unable to influence: the so-called *non-controllable factors*. Consumers' increasing use of social media is an obvious example. Trends or events that have an impact on the market are difficult to ignore. They are important in strategy development, but may require large investments for an appropriate response by the company. External analysis will help to determine the extent to which these trends represent *opportunities* or *threats*, and to identify those which are irrelevant for the company. This analysis may well influence the decisions to enter or avoid certain markets.

The external analysis should be conducted in a decision-oriented way to avoid wasting time by gathering irrelevant information. Identifying both opportunities and threats is key in simplifying the choice between strategic options. An *opportunity* is a trend or incident that, with an appropriate response, may lead to an increase in sales or profit. A *threat*, on the other hand, is a trend or incident that, if we fail to strategically respond to it, may result in sales or profit reduction.

Identifying significant opportunities and threats works best when a company has a clearly defined mission, creating a lens through which the external environment is seen. Management should also predict the likelihood of special events taking place. It will then be aware of what is likely to happen, when and which consequences this may have for the firm.

The most interesting opportunities to look for in the external environment are those that have not yet been exploited by others. *Threats*, too, need to be identified, because they often create opportunities for launching new products and services. For example, the decreasing consumption of high-cholesterol products because of health concerns – a threat for a company such as Lay's – creates lucrative opportunities for the introduction of low-fat snacks, if the manufacturer has the right production technology (an internal factor) as one of its strengths. Obviously, strategic decisions should be based on both an external analysis and an internal analysis.

Basically, strategy development is influenced by four categories of external factors. These are *market* trends (including customer behaviour), *competitors'* strategies, developments in the *industry* or broader environment and trends and shifts in power in *distribution channels*.[9]

2.3.3 Situation analysis

To structure the information collected during the analysis phase, we can put it in a framework that supports strategy development. The internal analysis gives us an overview of the company's *strengths and weaknesses*. **Strengths** are the capabilities that may help a

TABLE 2.2 SWOT analysis, including key questions

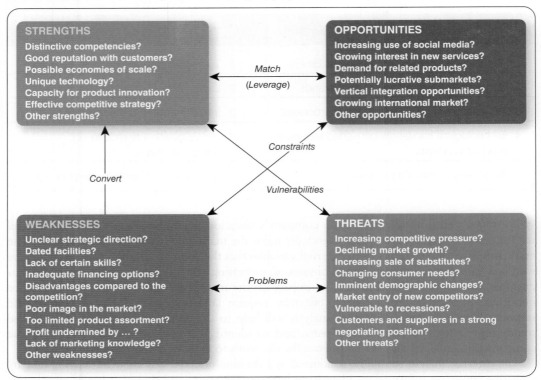

firm achieve its goals, whereas **weaknesses** are constraints that could obstruct a firm's ability to reach its goals. The external analysis provides us with a list of the *opportunities and threats* in the environment. **Opportunities** are circumstances that a firm could possibly exploit to its advantage, whereas **threats** are either current or developing circumstances that could negatively affect the firm's performance. We can now link these two sets of results by combining them in a **SWOT analysis**, which is a widely used tool for conducting or presenting a situation analysis. Table 2.2 shows the type of questions that may be asked in this analysis.

A crucial element of the SWOT analysis is assessing the implications for the company's strategy. Do any findings call for strategic changes? To decide, we must include all components of the analysis in our evaluation. For example, to identify the areas in which we enjoy *competitive advantages*, we should consider our strengths not only in light of opportunities in the environment, but also in light of the competitors' strengths and weaknesses.

The arrows in Table 2.2 clarify this part of the SWOT analysis. For example, matching an internal strength with an external opportunity, results in so-called *leverage* for the organization. At the same time, companies face a *problem* when threats in the environment (such as changing consumer needs) attack their own weaknesses (such as lack of marketing knowledge and a narrow product assortment). Managers may anticipate *constraints* when internal weaknesses or limitations (such as inadequate financing options) make it difficult for the company to take advantage of opportunities (such as a growing international market). Finally, these internal weaknesses can create *vulnerabilities* for the company if particular threats (such as the entry of new competitors) affect the company's strengths (such as its unique technology and distinctive competencies).

TABLE 2.3 The confrontation matrix: SWOT combinations and strategies

External	Internal	
	Strengths	Weaknesses
Opportunities	Exploit Grow	Improve Turn into strengths
Threats	Defend Compete with strengths	Avoid or withdraw Seek to collaborate

2.3.4 Confrontation matrix

A helpful tool to identify possible strategies, based on the SWOT analysis, is the **confrontation matrix**. As Table 2.3 illustrates, the matrix combines (internal) strengths and weaknesses with (external) opportunities and threats and suggests several preferred strategies for each quadrant. Whether – depending on the company's available resources and mission – these strategies are feasible and desirable can be decided whenever the strategic options are evaluated.

When outlining preferred strategies, of the four cells in the matrix, the first (top left) one usually gets most attention. For example, a *strength* (such as a great reputation) enabling us to effectively respond to an *opportunity* (such as entering a new market) is a combination that we should exploit. With the right strategy this may result in rapid growth. Dealing with *weaknesses* – while keeping in mind the *opportunities* we have identified – we can develop strategies to improve these or even turn them into strengths. The best way to do this may be through a strategic alliance or merger with another company.

We can arm and defend ourselves against a *threat* (such as the increasing use of substitutes) by emphasizing the relative *strengths* of our own products in our marketing communication. This will also increase **brand equity**. It may even be possible, by an aggressive response, to turn the threat into an opportunity, for example by investing in product innovation!

Unfortunately, a combination of *weaknesses* and *threats* offers little hope. Although confrontation may be an option (possibly in cooperation with others in the industry), it might make more sense to focus on different market segments. Whatever strategy seems best, the SWOT analysis should provide a foundation for the next stages in marketing planning.

2.4 DETERMINING MARKETING OBJECTIVES

The model of the marketing planning process in Figure 2.5 showed that – depending on the situation to which the model is applied – the analysis stage may be completed by defining the company's *core problem*. Although the confrontation matrix offers important clues, it is not always easy to identify the main problem we are facing. In any event, we need to make a distinction between the main issues and secondary issues, and between the core problem and its *symptoms*. For example, declining profits could be symptomatic of any number of problems, including a defective product, demotivated sales force, weak distribution strategy or increasing competition in the company's market segment. Regardless of the symptoms, the core problem should be expressed in such a way that it reveals the real causes, so that they can be addressed *effectively* in strategy development.

MARKETING TOPPER
Spar's Retail Strategy to Beat Aldi

Although just about all large companies conduct SWOT analyses in their strategy development, smaller firms can benefit from these analyses as well. German entrepreneur Dieter Niemerszein, who owns a Spar store in Hamburg, Germany, did just that with remarkable results. His 900 square metre retail store on Oststrasse was doing pretty well when he learned that the large discount chain Aldi was planning to open an 800 square metre discount supermarket right next to him. He had heard plenty of horror stories from fellow retailers who lost out in fierce battles with the discount chain and had gone out of business, because they were unable to compete with its low prices. He was determined that this would not happen to him. Dieter was convinced that a great supermarket could prosper next to a discount store, as long it knows its strengths and competes on the basis of its core competencies. He was confident that a SWOT analysis would enable him to develop the right strategy.

© mkimages / Alamy

A supermarket can prosper next to a discount store by knowing its strengths and competing on its core competencies

The SWOT analysis revealed that Aldi's main strength was its low price level. Other than that, the discounter was at a disadvantage; its weaknesses presented quite a few strategic marketing opportunities for Dieter. To accentuate the differences between the two stores and leverage Spar's strengths, he first purchased another 300 square metres of retail space. Shortly after that, he acquired eighty parking spaces to provide an additional service for his customers.

Next, he invested in the store itself – starting with his employees. After all, he reasoned, as long as the basics were good, everything else would fall into place. From now on, his employees were expected to work with a smile, since he remembered from his internship that, while a smile does not cost anything, it goes a long way. He himself made a point of setting a good example whenever he was interacting with customers. In addition, he arranged motivational training for his staff in order to instil a customer-oriented mindset. Since speed of service was one of Aldi's weaknesses, Dieter shortened the checkout lines in his Spar store. Guided by his motto 'customers come first', he introduced a new policy of opening another checkout whenever there were more than three people waiting in line.

Then, Dieter changed the store's layout and product assortment. He lowered the shelves so customers could see the whole store, which resulted in a better shopping experience. To capitalize on the identified marketing opportunities, he reduced the number of non-perishable items, setting aside a larger part of the store for freshly prepared and ready-to-eat products, local delicacies and organic products. Market research studies indicated that this should help to broaden his target market. The new fresh foods department – which offered pre-cut vegetables and top quality fruit – was profitable right from the start. Orange juice sold for €2.25 per bottle, with a profit margin of 50 per cent. Dieter purchased his steak and other meat products from local farmers and printed details about the background and history of their farms on the packaging. The exact locations of the farms that supplied the meat were conspicuously displayed on the walls of the meat department. At the same time, Dieter invested in a five metre-long salad bar and a unique antipasto bar. All of this enabled him to differentiate his store from Aldi and other competitors.

Finally, Dieter started using the well-known Spar store brand to compete on price. Spar products were highlighted in advertising, which also emphasized the fact that the prices of 300 national brand items sold in the Spar store were only 5 per cent higher than the prices charged by Aldi, and that, given the obvious advantages offered by the Spar brand, he was happy to leave the decision as to where to shop to the discerning consumer.

As a result of Dieter's new strategy, sales of fruit and vegetables increased considerably and now accounted for 15 per cent of total revenues. More than a quarter of the store's turnover was spent on lucrative ready-to-eat products. Labour costs were relatively high, but thanks to the greater emphasis on efficiency, they were actually only 1 per cent higher than they were before Dieter made the changes. The bottom line? Sales went up by more than 60 per cent and gross profits increased by 1½ per cent. Not bad for a retailer that has Aldi as a neighbour! It certainly proves that small companies, too, can achieve a significant increase in sales and profits by conducting a SWOT analysis and pursuing a customer-oriented strategy, based on their relative strengths and competitive advantage.[10]

A well-defined mission statement and a clear description of the core problem create the best possible starting point for plotting a marketing strategy. Strategy development, in turn, begins with formulating *marketing objectives*. Ultimately, we can only describe our intended results in detail when we agree on the company's business definition and mission, and after the SWOT analysis has provided us with a critical view of the organization's internal and external environments and a clear sense of the firm's ability to accomplish its mission.

The lower in the organization these *objectives* are set, the more specific they are. But even at higher organizational levels they are expressed in quantitative terms to allow measurement of the extent to which they are being realized. Of course, the description of the objectives must meet certain requirements. These are discussed in the next paragraph. We will also look at how the marketing objectives should conform to the corporate goals.

2.4.1 *How to formulate objectives*

To motivate executives and managers who are involved in a strategy's implementation, objectives must be *ambitious*, but *realistic*. They need to be *specific* in terms of numbers or percentages and in determining the time periods for the intended achievements, so that they direct future strategy and are also *measurable*. Vague goals, such as 'to increase sales', are useless. In addition, different goals should be *consistent* with one another. Finally, it must be clear which of the strategy objectives receive *priority*.

Table 2.4 shows several examples of both well and poorly formulated objectives. In addition, a distinction is made between strategic, long-term goals (essential for the company to still be successful in three to five years time) and short-term goals. These short-term objectives enable management periodically to monitor progress made in attaining the long-term goals.

Realistic

Objectives that are not realistic or feasible, fail to establish a sense of direction for strategy development and the employees' efforts. For instance, a firm with limited resources and strong competitors that wants 'to obtain a market share of 90 per cent within six months' will not stand a chance.

TABLE 2.4 Examples of good and bad objectives

Examples of badly formulated objectives	Examples of well formulated objectives
Long term	Long term
Our goal is to occupy a leading position in product development in the European Union.	Our goal is to increase our market share to 35 per cent between 2014 and 2016.
Short term	Short term
Our objective is to increase sales and maximize profits in 2014.	Our objective is to increase our market share from 21 to 25 per cent in 2014 by opening two new shops and increasing our advertising budget by 15 per cent.

Measurable

The objectives must be specific and measurable in order to monitor any progress made in achieving them. A goal such as 'to maximize profit' or 'to increase market share' is neither specific nor measurable. The subsequent phases in the planning process would then be useless. One marketing consultant put it this way, 'If you don't know where you're going, any road will take you there and once you think you're there, you'll stop trying.' A quantitatively expressed goal with a specific timeframe – such as 'to increase the average profit margin on freshly prepared food products to 12 per cent within one-and-a-half years' – *is* measurable and, therefore, preferable.

Consistent

Different goals should be consistent with one another. It is impossible, for instance, to 'maximize both sales and profits' or 'to develop the very best products in the shortest period of time'. A company cannot do everything simultaneously.

Prioritizing

Companies have priorities, and their objectives should reflect this. A company can clarify its priorities by ranking objectives in order of importance. This clear *hierarchy* of objectives makes it easier to decide where the most time or money should be allocated to achieve certain goals. It also clarifies who is accountable for which results.

2.4.2 *Hierarchy of objectives*

If objectives are ranked in order of importance, they reflect the company's priorities. In fact, its **hierarchy of objectives** implies that the broader organizational objectives – concerning market share, return-on-investment and others – have been 'translated' into objectives for specific departments and individuals. Thus, the corporate objectives provide guidelines for the entire organization.

Objectives are formulated at the corporate, business unit and operational levels. At the lowest level, they are typically concrete, functional (in this case, marketing) objectives, such as projected sales results. These lower level objectives help to attain goals set at the higher levels. Usually, the lower-level objectives are the most specific.

FIGURE 2.7 Translating corporate objectives into marketing objectives

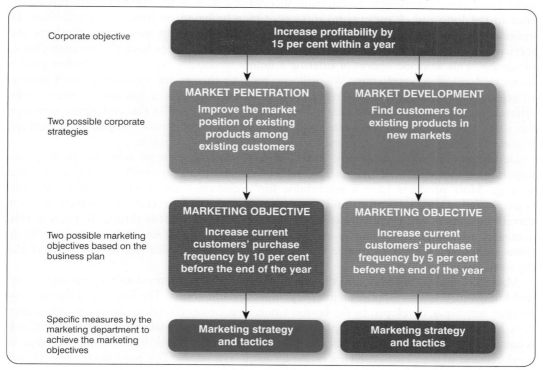

Let's assume that an organization has a *corporate objective* of increasing profitability by 15 per cent within a year. Although there might be various strategies to achieve this goal, the company decides to pursue a *strategy* of 'market development'. As explained later in more detail, *market development* involves finding new customers in new market segments for a company's existing products. To express this goal, the marketing manager might set a *marketing objective* of increasing market share by 5 per cent by the end of the year by tapping new export markets for the company's products. This would be consistent with both the corporate objective and the corporate strategy. Figure 2.7 shows how this corporate objective may be translated into parallel strategies and marketing objectives.

In many companies, marketing objectives are ultimately expressed in terms of sales. Generally, the more objectives are worked out in detail, the more those objectives are concerned with marketing tactics. Of course, it only makes sense to formulate tactical or operational objectives after everyone involved has agreed on the strategy to be pursued.

2.5 DEVELOPING THE MARKETING STRATEGY

In any market-oriented company, careful planning of marketing strategies is vital. To identify the best way to attain the stated objectives, we should first spell out the *strategic options*. These are our options in strategy development, generally derived from the – combined – external and internal analyses. The results of the situation analysis, as presented in the confrontation matrix, can be worked out as potential strategies. While critically evaluating these alternatives, we establish our priorities. We then select the most promising strategy to compete in the market.

In developing an effective competitive strategy a firm has to decide how it intends to *differ* from other companies. To compete successfully, it must be able to sustain this difference in the long run. A meaningful difference may be based on lower *costs* (enabling the option of selling a similar product at a *lower price*), although in most cases, products and services with unique benefits that offer more value to customers have the greatest chance of success. This strategic option of offering a unique product – typically for a higher price – is referred to as *differentiation*. We will get back to this as we examine Porter's generic strategies. The differences between the two strategic options – a low-cost strategy versus differentiation – can be traced back to how the company handles the underlying activities: the *value* that these activities create is the foundation of the firm's *competitive advantage*. In the end, either strategic option may lead to greater sales and profits.

Developing ambitious long-term and short-term *plans* to increase sales and profits is an important responsibility of marketers. These plans should always spell out a goal-oriented strategy. Most products have a predictable life cycle: once the market is saturated, sales begin to fall. Companies that limit themselves to selling their current products to their current customers will eventually see their market share and profits shrink. To prevent this, managers use *analytical techniques* and *models* to help them plot successful strategies. While these techniques are no guarantee for success, they are practical tools that support the decision-making process.

Marketers apply – in addition to the model of generic strategies previously mentioned — two well-known methods to support their strategy development efforts. The first one is the portfolio analysis technique, developed by the Boston Consulting Group (BCG), an American consultancy firm. Marketing managers rely on the '*market share/market growth matrix*' (or *Boston matrix*, as it is commonly called in Europe) to evaluate their organization's strategic business units (or range of products) and to get a bird's eye view of the company as a whole. This portfolio framework also provides them with well-founded supporting arguments for their investment plans.

The second technique discussed here is the *product/market expansion matrix* or *Ansoff model*, as it is known in European countries. As the name implies, this, too, is drawn up as a matrix. This type of analysis is especially useful for companies seeking to implement *growth*-oriented strategies, usually in the hope of benefiting from *economies of scale*. However, let's first explore portfolio analysis as a useful marketing planning tool.

2.5.1 *Portfolio analysis*

Probably the most effective way to assure long-term profitability, a major business goal, is to obtain a large market share. Objectives and strategies that result in a larger share of a particular market segment are at the top of many marketers' priority lists. After all, a growing market share essentially guarantees lower costs per item. In fact, each time production doubles, in many industries the cost per item falls by 20 to 30 per cent. This is due to economies of scale (greater efficiency) as well as to the effect of the learning curve or experience curve (meaning that, with experience, companies learn to operate more efficiently).

Lower costs enable a firm to charge a lower selling price, which stimulates sales. This, in turn, initiates another cycle of lower production and marketing costs, lower prices and higher sales and profits. A company that increases its market share in this way (especially when the market is still growing!) and invests a substantial portion of its profits in R&D, product development and marketing, builds a strong competitive position.

With sound financial management, a relatively high profit also results in a large cash flow. Hence, there is a positive correlation between market share and cash flow. Conversely, there is a negative correlation between *market growth* and cash flow: in a growing market, the company has to invest much more money in production (new equipment), marketing (larger sales force) and operating capital to keep up with the expanding market, and grow at the same rate. In portfolio analysis we use these two dimensions – *market share* and *market growth* – to determine the profit potential of different products or SBUs.

The objective of the BCG portfolio analysis – given the large differences between SBUs in terms of the revenues or the need for financing – is to establish a balance between the various activities in the 'portfolio', allowing some SBUs to be financed with the cash flow generated by the company's other SBUs. A portfolio model such as the Boston matrix is a diagnostic tool for identifying SBUs with the greatest and the least potential, to help a company set priorities and to move financial resources from one part of its organization to another (*resource allocation*).

2.5.2 Boston matrix

The Boston matrix (known in American marketing literature as the *market share/market growth matrix*) places SBUs in a four-quadrant chart that plots market share – the percentage of a market that a firm controls – against market growth. The position of an SBU along the vertical axis indicates the annual growth rate of the market. As we see in Figure 2.8, the axis

FIGURE 2.8 The Boston matrix (market share/market growth matrix)

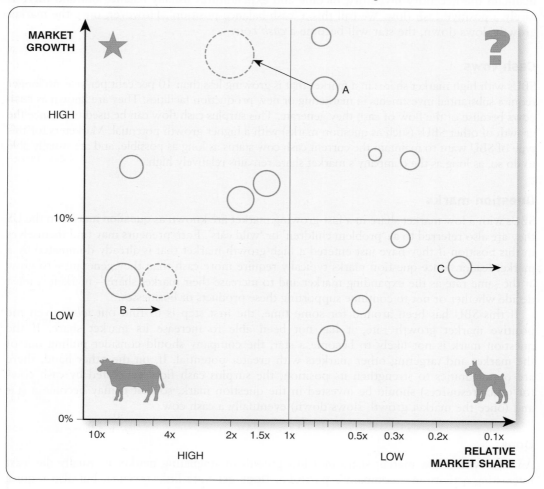

is divided into two parts: more and less than 10 per cent growth per year. Market growth, of course, is a major factor that determines how attractive the market is in the long run.

The horizontal axis, on the other hand, shows the Strategic Business Unit's *relative market share*. This is calculated by dividing a firm's own market share by that of its largest competitor in the industry. Here the axis ranges from 0.1 to 10, with a middle value of 1. For example, a relative market share of 0.2 means that the company's market share is equivalent to just 20 per cent of the market share of its main competitor. On the other hand, a relative market share of 1.9 means that the company's SBU is the market leader, with a market share almost twice the size of the next strongest company. We can now situate each SBU – indicated by a circle, the diameter of which is proportional to the size of its revenues in euros (or another currency) – in its appropriate place in the matrix, depending on its relative market share and the growth rate of the market. The four cells are labelled stars, cash cows, question marks and dogs.

Stars

A star is an SBU with a large market share in a high-growth market. As the market leader, this attractive SBU will generate considerable income, but it will also have to spend a great deal on R&D and marketing to protect its market share and to finance further growth. Since significant investments are required to increase production and sales while continuing to maintain the necessary inventory, income and expenditures usually balance out and there is rarely a positive cash flow. We call this a 'cash-balance position'. However, once the market growth slows down, the star will become a *cash cow*.

Cash cows

SBUs with high market shares in a market that is growing less than 10 per cent per year no longer require substantial investments in marketing or new production facilities. They are known as cash cows because of the flow of cash they generate. This surplus cash flow can be used to finance the growth of other SBUs (such as question marks) with a higher growth potential. Marketers for this type of SBU want to maintain the current cash cow status as long as possible, and are usually able to do so, as long as the company's market share remains relatively high.

Question marks

SBUs with a low market share in a fast-growing market are known as question marks. In the US they are also referred to as 'problem children' or 'wild cats'. Entrepreneurs may find themselves in this position if they have just entered a high-growth market that is already dominated by a market leader. Since question marks typically require more cash than they generate – to grow at the same rate as the expanding market and to increase their market share – marketers must decide whether or not to continue supporting these products or businesses.

If this SBU has been around for some time, the first step is to find out *why*, given the positive market growth rate, it has not been able to increase its market share. If the question mark is not likely to become a star, the company should consider pulling out of the market and targeting other markets with greater potential. If, on the other hand, there are opportunities to strengthen its position, the surplus cash flow generated by cash cows (or other resources) should be invested in the question mark, so that it may become a star and (once the market growth slows down) eventually a cash cow.

Dogs

An SBU with a low market share in a low-growth or stagnating market is usually the least interesting activity in a company's portfolio. Dogs generate little revenue, but also require little investment. They are like stars in the sense that their income and expenditure generally balance out. Some dogs, however, produce a significant profit contribution for years, which makes them reasonably attractive activities or divisions of the company.

Because quite a few markets are saturated and the number of market leaders is, by definition, limited, numerous brands are in this category. There may be good reasons to maintain dogs if there is a loyal group of customers or if management expects changes in the market growth rate or market share. However, if future prospects are poor, marketers should recommend selling the brand or product line and disposing of the SBU.

2.5.3 *Strategic implications*

A portfolio analysis is usually conducted at the corporate level, when deciding on corporate investments and strategies (including SBU objectives). However, this type of analysis also makes sense at the SBU level. Here, too, we need to decide how much should be invested in certain product lines or brands and what SBU strategies and marketing objectives are most appropriate. In this case we assess the growth of the *market segment* (rather than the growth of the market as a whole) and the position of the product line or the *brand* within that segment (rather than the position of the SBU in the overall market).

Regardless of the level at which the analysis is conducted, the SBUs must be considered not only individually but also relative to each other. After all, the company would like to create a balanced 'portfolio' of activities in different stages of their life cycles, with, for example, one or more *cash cows* to generate a strong cash flow, one or more *stars* that will become cash cows in the future and one or more *question marks* that have potential to become stars and eventually cash cows if the company invests enough in them. A successful product or business usually begins as a question mark, then becomes a star and eventually turns into a cash cow. At the end of its life cycle, it may ultimately become a dog. If there are too many *dogs* or question marks and too few stars or cash cows, the company must take action. This calls for a well-planned comprehensive strategy.

Possible strategies

How can portfolio analysis be used to develop or modify a marketing strategy? Of the two dimensions in the Boston matrix, one (*market growth*) usually cannot be influenced by the marketer. That leaves only the desired *market share* as a possible outcome of a *strategic option*.

A good starting point is to assess the direction in which each of the SBUs in the matrix is likely to move if the strategy remains unchanged. We can draw these anticipated positions in the cells of the matrix, using dotted lines, as demonstrated with SBUs A and B in Figure 2.8. This schematic representation allows us to compare an SBU's current position with anticipated future positions. It also enables us to determine which investment strategies should be pursued for the SBUs in order to create an ideal portfolio. Depending on the company's objectives, there are at least four alternative investment strategies: to build, hold, harvest or divest.

→ **Build strategy**: this is an aggressive growth strategy to increase market share, for example by going after new target markets. This may come at the expense of short-term profit, but it is a good way of turning *question marks* into stars.

→ **Hold strategy**: the goal of this investment strategy is to maintain the SBU's current (relative) market share by defending its market position. A company may pursue this defensive strategy of *milking* its investments for its lucrative *cash cows*.

→ **Harvest strategy**: investments in marketing are kept to a minimum in order to maximize cash flow. This kind of 'milking' may lead to a reduced market share. A harvest strategy is appropriate for cash cows with dubious prospects, as well as for question marks and dogs.

→ **Divest strategy**: sometimes the best strategy is to withdraw – by liquidating or selling off SBUs like dogs and question marks – if the proceeds from the sale will generate a higher return on investment elsewhere. This is the primary reason that Philips has stopped making computers and mobile phones; more recently, it also moved its television arm into a joint venture with monitor maker TPV to allow an increased portfolio focus in health and well-being.

Advantages and limitations of portfolio analysis

The main *advantage* of portfolio analysis is that management, in a relatively simple way, acquires an overview or 'helicopter's view' of corporate activities. This is a useful analytical tool when the company must decide which SBUs or products might be suited to further investment for future growth, or which ones it should consider candidates for a strategy of disinvesting or withdrawing.

A portfolio analysis recently proved quite helpful for a medium-sized Amsterdam-based company with liquidity problems. By turning one of its *dogs* into an independent unit, discontinuing the production of two other *dogs* and selling a *cash cow* that was losing market share, the company was able (as a result of the cost savings and the profit it made on the sale) to invest heavily in new products with a greater profit potential: the stars and cash cows of the future. Clearly, even for small and medium-sized firms, the Boston matrix is a useful planning tool to help determine the most appropriate strategies for the entire product line.

A significant limitation of portfolio analysis and management is that it is based on the principle of the *experience curve*: higher production leads to lower costs and therefore to greater profits. However, in some industries – such as in the labour-intensive services sector – a higher market share does not automatically lead to lower costs per unit. Thus, the Boston matrix is less relevant in some industries.

A second limitation has to do with the simplicity of the model. For instance, when making strategic decisions, a company should always consider the *synergy* between SBUs, and portfolio analysis does not allow for this. Furthermore, a firm's competitive position is dependent on more variables than its 'relative market share', just as the attractiveness of a market depends on factors other than simply the rate at which this market is growing. Therefore, many companies prefer to use portfolio models that include a greater number of factors in the analysis, such as the GE/McKinsey-matrix in the General Electric portfolio analysis.

Professor C.K. Prahalad, who was a consultant to Philips for many years, believed that the current market share, market growth and even profit contribution should not be the dominant criteria when critically evaluating a company's activities. 'It is more important to figure out what the company's *core competencies* are. Having identified these strengths, management can then determine in which areas it should develop new, profitable activities.'

A second challenge for companies, according to Dr. Prahalad, is to pursue an effective marketing strategy in rapidly changing markets. 'Because it is increasingly difficult to predict how much of a particular product you will be able to sell, the firm must be *flexible* enough to increase or reduce production and develop new products at short notice. This works best if your factories – with clever product-development and production methods – are able to work for more than one business unit.'[11] Thus, a situation analysis (to determine the core activities) and a market-oriented, flexible organization are prerequisites for a company to keep growing.

2.5.4 *Generic strategies*

A company's profitability is correlated to the profitability of the industry in which it operates. But equally important is its position within that industry. Even if an industry, as a whole, is not highly profitable, a company that is optimally positioned within that industry can still generate high returns. A company positions itself by leveraging its strengths. Research shows that companies bold enough to make strategic choices (through which they distinguish themselves from competitors) and adhere to them are more successful than companies that act impulsively on any opportunity they encounter.

Harvard Business School professor Michael Porter suggests that – from a strategic perspective – the most basic choices a company makes are the size and composition of the markets that it will serve (*target market* or *competitive scope*) and how – based on its core competency or strategic strength – the company will compete in the selected markets (*source of competitive advantage*). By applying its strength in either a broad or narrow scope, three possible generic strategies result. These strategies are applied at the business unit level.

They are called generic strategies because they may be pursued by any company – regardless of which industry it belongs to or products it sells – to gain a *competitive advantage* among similar business units in the same industry. Porter contends that a company's strength ultimately falls into one of two categories: cost advantage or product uniqueness. As Figure 2.9 illustrates, the strategies that companies can undertake to attain competitive advantage – or the most advantageous position in the industry – are cost leadership, differentiation and focus (a market segmentation strategy).

In essence, the profit of a firm is the difference between its revenues and costs. Thus, high profitability can be attained through achieving the lowest costs (cost leadership) or the highest prices relative to the competition ('price premium') by differentiating products and services from those of competitors. Also, companies can try to cover virtually the entire market, (broad market scope) or they can focus on a few particular market segments (narrow market scope).

Cost leadership strategy

The first generic strategy to gain a competitive advantage is a cost-leadership strategy. With this strategy, a firm concentrates on cutting expenses and reducing prices of its standardized products, while appealing to a wide range of market segments. Being in a cost-leadership position does not necessarily mean that the firm's products have the lowest price. Instead, a company employing this strategy is able to operate at a lower cost than its rivals, allowing cost reduction in every activity in the *value chain* (the steps a business performs to design, produce, market, deliver and service a product). The company is then able to offer the lowest *price to value ratio* (price compared to what buyers receive) or to reinvest the extra profits into the business.

FIGURE 2.9 Porter's Generic Strategies

	Source of competitive advantage	
Target Market Scope	Low Cost	Product uniqueness
Broad Market Scope (Industry Wide)	Cost leadership	Differentiation
Narrow Market Scope (Market Segment)	Focus strategy	

Using a cost-leadership strategy, the company can gain market share by appealing to cost-conscious or price-sensitive consumers. Dell, for example, has been able to become a cost leader by outsourcing production to low-wage countries and simultaneously investing in sophisticated equipment to slash distribution costs. This is an effective strategy, especially in markets where the company can attain economies of scale. Other examples of companies with a cost leadership strategy are Aldi and Tesco in retailing and Hyundai in the automobile market.

Differentiation strategy

A differentiation strategy calls for charging premium prices for unique services or superior quality products with an attractive brand image, that are valued by customers and that they perceive to be better than those of competitors. The company may, for instance, offer better product performance, premium or 'green' packaging, faster delivery or other features that provide more convenience compared to the competitors' existing products. The value added by the unique attributes of the product or service will allow the company to charge a higher price for it.

A differentiation strategy may require significant investments. These investments often assume the form of increased advertising to promote a differentiated brand image for the product. To illustrate, McDonald's – in a very competitive and saturated market – is differentiated by its very brand name and brand images of Big Mac and Ronald McDonald. The resulting brand loyalty lowers customers' sensitivity to price. In other industries, a differentiation strategy is only feasible for companies that are highly innovative and have unique capabilities (such as technical expertise) or resources (for example talented engineers or patents) to satisfy customer needs in ways that are difficult for competitors to copy. Here, too, the company is targeting a broad array of market segments (as TomTom does in globally marketing its portable GPS car navigation systems, or Apple in selling its iPad). Even if the physical product is similar to that of competitors, effective customer relationships or brand management may result in perceived uniqueness. To a great extent, this explains the substantial market share obtained by companies such as Starbucks and Nike.

Focus strategy

A firm appealing to just one target market or a narrow range of market segments may choose one of two possible generic strategies. Both 'focus' strategies involve creating products or services that completely meet the needs of a limited group of buyers in the market (a *niche*), often where there is the least amount of competition. Therefore, a focus strategy is sometimes called a *niche strategy*. The premise is that, by focusing entirely on the needs of a narrow market segment, that segment can be better serviced.

The first option in this category is a cost focus strategy with low product prices, made possible by a cost advantage in the target segment through reduced expenses. Examples are discount airlines such as Ryanair and easyJet. The alternative is a differentiation focus strategy, involving products or services that are significantly different from those that competitors offer (such as an automobile manufacturer's attempt to tap an upscale market with an electric car). Bentley and Aston Martin are classis examples of niche players in the automobile industry. The high degree of customer loyalty in the market segment discourages other companies from competing directly.

A focus strategy is especially popular among small and medium-sized firms. To be successful, companies choosing one of these strategies must be able to tailor a broad range of strengths in new product development and marketing to a narrow target market that they know inside out. Also, for the target market to be lucrative, the overall market should be sufficiently large and diverse. The obvious risk associated with this strategy is that the niche may gradually disappear as the marketing environment and buyer preferences change over time.

Stuck in the middle?

If a company does not choose and continually focus on one of these generic strategies, it may drift and get 'stuck in the middle'. By trying to implement all of the strategies concurrently, management will not realize a competitive advantage, and will likely see a substantially reduced return on investment. For example, if a company tries to differentiate itself by offering premium quality products, it risks undermining that quality if it also strives to become a cost leader.

Corporations succeeding with multiple strategies tend to be those that establish separate business units for each generic strategy. When all is said and done, the company is less likely to become stuck in the middle if it separates the strategies into different SBUs having different policies and corporate cultures.

2.5.5 *Ansoff model*

When developing strategies that will result in a higher market share – so-called (intensive) growth strategies – we should first examine whether our existing products and the markets in which we currently operate, offer any potential for increasing sales. If not, we may have to launch new products or enter new markets. In fact, there are four possible routes for expansion: (market) penetration, market development, product development and diversification. As Figure 2.10 illustrates, these are the four product-market strategies in *Ansoff's product-market expansion matrix*.

Penetration strategy

With a penetration strategy, we continue catering to current customer needs by selling our existing products to existing markets (the market segments on which we are already focused). However, we do make a move to increase our market share. For example, we may be able to sell more of our present range of products to current customers by selling larger package sizes or by encouraging them to increase their usage and purchase frequency. This is a classic strategy of *market penetration*. Another approach – known as *market expansion* – involves attracting new customers within the currently serviced market; these may be users of competitive brands, or nonusers of the product category.

To increase our market share through a strategy of market penetration, we will probably have to adjust our promotion, distribution and price strategies. We may develop a new social media campaign that really appeals to the target market, advertise more frequently, create a more attractive website, negotiate a better shelf position, run special offers in the stores and organize other sales promotion activities or reduce our prices, either temporarily or permanently.

FIGURE 2.10 Ansoff's product-market expansion matrix

Market	Product	
	Existing products	*New products*
Existing markets	1 (Market) penetration	3 Product development
New markets	2 Market development	4 Diversification

Market development strategy

A second strategic option in Ansoff's product-market expansion matrix is *market development* – finding new markets or new uses for our current products. This market development strategy can be implemented without changing the existing product mix; we simply target new market segments. Some possibilities include tapping new demographic target markets (such as teenagers), geographical markets (through exporting) and institutional markets (such as nursing homes) that we have not yet approached.

To achieve the best results we may have to enlist the services of new distribution outlets (such as discount stores or boutiques) and intermediaries (such as trading companies). To suggest new ways in which the product can be used, we might develop an effective promotion campaign involving a combination of marketing communication instruments, such as sport sponsorship, television commercials, social media and websites.

Product development strategy

If we improve the product substantially or introduce an entirely new one, we are pursuing a product development strategy. By improving the product quality or launching a new model, we may reach groups of buyers in the market (that we are already serving) who previously showed no interest.

Improvements or modifications could take the form of designing contemporary packaging, introducing a new flavour or even changing the brand name, to cite but a few methods. Another way to grow is by creating a simplified and less expensive version of a product for the mass market.

Diversification strategy

Finally, a diversification strategy involves introducing new products to reach entirely new markets or satisfy new consumer needs. To gain the necessary (marketing) knowledge or experience and expand our product mix instantaneously, we may acquire or merge with an existing firm. This will also reduce the number of competitors (by at least one) and increase our market share at the same time. Other reasons for diversification are entry into a lucrative growth market, thereby increasing profits, and spreading risks, for example by reducing the effects of seasonal and cyclical patterns.

Research on the kinds of growth strategies pursued by European firms indicates that regardless of their size or the industry in which they operate, two-thirds of the companies follow a *market penetration strategy*, with *product development* being the second most widely adopted approach. Thus, most companies somehow try to increase sales in their existing market. Overall, less than 10 per cent of companies are systematically pursuing market development and diversification strategies.

2.6 THE MARKETING ORGANIZATION

Not every company with a marketing strategy is guaranteed success. The strategy itself may be flawed, or attempts to implement it may not be effective. Problems with the strategy's implementation are often related to the *internal* organization of the company's marketing activities, such as the lack of effective leadership. In some instances, companies have assumed that a manager's experience in a specific marketing function, such as advertising, or in a marketing related department, such as the in-house export department, will prepare them to be thrust into the role of the marketing department manager.

PRACTITIONER'S PERSPECTIVE
Marcus Thompson (Contract Marketers, Scotland, UK)

Marcus Thompson – who wrote this perspective with Shona Sinclair – is a visiting academic who teaches marketing and strategy at several Scottish universities. As an academic practitioner – and co-author of Creating sustainable social enterprises *– he is continually testing the value of marketing theory by working with fast growth companies and non-profit organizations. He is also developing content for a UK affiliated degree in customer relationship marketing and in entrepreneurship for educational programmes in Botswana and South Africa.*

© TerryM / Shutterstock

Non-profit organizations, including charities, face many opportunities and threats in today's economic climate. With decreasing public sector funding, they are forced to generate new types of income and adopt the strategic thinking and planning approaches that are usually associated with larger multinational corporations.

A non-profit organization must be innovative, develop a clear brand reputation and build long-term customer relationships

The key question is: what value does *strategy* have for small social enterprises? Understand that a *social enterprise* is a hybrid organization – a type of third sector Strategic Business Unit. Just like a private company, it seeks new market opportunities to generate income. However, it distributes any surplus back to its *stakeholders* rather than to shareholders. To raise money, a social enterprise may sell products and services to a group of end-user customers, while still maintaining the social values of its stakeholders. Like any corporation in a competitive market, it must be innovative, develop a clear brand reputation and build long-term customer relationships.

Social enterprises also need to have a clear understanding of their business's *scope*. They must know who their customers are and what technologies and processes should be used to satisfy their needs, while generating income. All of this has to be done competitively; in other words, the service offering must be *distinctive*. This presents a strategic challenge – how to be opportunity and profit seeking, yet still maintain social values.

This is where the *mission statement* comes in. A charity, for example, should clearly define its mission and deliberately cultivate its *core competencies*. This can be challenging enough for a private sector organization but is more difficult for a social organization where stakeholders often have conflicting views.

When it comes to developing a *marketing strategy*, using the Boston matrix can help managers to identify a portfolio of income streams and to distinguish today's business from tomorrow's stars. But these are tools of analysis rather than formulation of choices. A social enterprise can become too dependent on a substantial income stream from one customer group, making the business model not sustainable. Multiple income streams from multiple customers will ensure a balanced flow to grow the organization. Ideally, most of these should come from independent sources.

So what kind of organization does this leave? Can a social enterprise be 'market orientated' and especially 'customer focused'? This is where the strategic approach needs to *adapted*. 'Customers' for a social enterprise come in three forms. The primary customer stakeholder is a group of *clients* who often face special economic or social problems that require specialized support: the 'inward facing' dimension. A second stakeholder group might be funding agencies that expect a different form of service delivery than those using the service. They will be challenged around the principle of the business 'making profit'. The third and newest group of stakeholders are customers who 'buy' services directly at market rates that they can afford, creating pricing challenges. Using *corporate social responsibility* as a Unique Selling Proposition (USP) can be a market advantage, but how do you demonstrate quality outputs?

To illustrate, SKS (Scotland) creates work opportunities for people with long term (health) conditions. It '*provides services to charities, third sector and private organizations to help develop their long-term sustainability*'. And '*as a social firm, money generated stays within the social economy and helps SKS provide employment to people with long term conditions*'.

With support from the Long Term Conditions Alliance (LTCAS), SKS has created *Work4ME* as a cooperative employability initiative – an umbrella framework that gives its members (people living with long term health problems) access to self-managed, self-employment opportunities within a supported online environment.

After developing a new business model and positioning strategy, SKS is now extending its services to new communities. The plan is to develop 'cells' that are membership-owned and responsive to local employment needs as well as opportunities. With little or no corporate planning from the centre, the aim is to create sustainable business networks and multiple income streams. So this is not a normal charity – the business vision has a bigger scope than that.

As Shona Sinclair, the founder of SKS says:

'*This organization has the potential to challenge current perceptions on an international scale. The perceptions surround the capacity and capability of people living with long term conditions and about doing "good business" successfully. In other words: to be competitive and quality driven but with clear social benefits delivering a sustainable business model which empowers people to succeed.*'

Clearly, a social enterprise needs a strategy because it has different customer groups with different needs. And it does not matter whether this is an organization supporting the parents of young autistic children, a group that engages people living in areas of high unemployment and deprivation, a mental health charity or Work4ME. Strategy formulation is challenging. Moreover, the implementation and evaluation of strategies are often more demanding in non-profit organizations than in corporations. Therefore, the third sector offers countless career opportunities for well-educated, dedicated and customer-focused managers around the world.[12]

While marketing's influence varies across companies, it plays a key role in most organizations. Marketers collect, analyze and interpret data needed to assess the present situation, identify important trends in the marketing environment and evaluate the impact of these emerging currents. Such information is critical to develop a sound strategic plan. And, by helping everyone in a company focus on customers and markets, marketers stimulate organizations to be marketing-driven, rather than product- or selling-oriented. Today, marketing's influence in the strategic planning process is gaining status as an increasing number of firms push the responsibility for strategic planning to lower levels of the organization.

2.6.1 Organizational framework

People, as individuals and as members of groups, do the actual work of marketing. To make sure marketing work gets done efficiently, we must assemble the best organizational framework and, in particular, the best marketing organization. After all, an organization is the mechanism through which a managerial philosophy is translated into action. As conditions change, organizational goals are revised and the organization itself may be altered. This includes the marketing organization, which is part of the company's link with the market. In essence, the marketing organization is the vehicle for making decisions about the marketing mix and implementing them.

There is no best way to organize the marketing functions critical to the success of an enterprise. However, management must design a marketing organization that allows the company to pursue marketing strategies that provide a competitive advantage in delivering value to the target market. In a small firm, most marketing activities, such as market research, selling and promotion, may all be carried out by just one person. But, as the firm grows and the need for such activities as customer service and product development mounts, a marketing department or unit is needed to develop and carry out the company's plans.

The structure of the marketing unit, including the lines of authority and relationships between people within the firm, significantly influences the company's marketing activities as well as management's attitude toward those activities. A marketing-oriented company will focus on customers' requirements when determining the marketing mix, rather than emphasizing new product development and gambling that they will find buyers. If a customer orientation serves as a firm's guiding philosophy, the marketing activities become meshed with other functional areas or departments, such as R&D, manufacturing, human resources and finance. In sum, a company's success in maximizing customer satisfaction depends not only on how well the marketing department performs its work, but also on how well the various departments coordinate their activities to deliver value to all customers.

The organizational structure of the company and marketing unit also determines who is responsible for making certain decisions and performing specific activities. In a traditional centralized organization, most marketing decisions are made by top-level managers who delegate little decision-making authority down the chain of command. In a decentralized organization, on the other hand, much of the decision-making authority is delegated to lower levels in the hierarchy. For instance, an assistant brand manager who is able to decide on promotional matters, is expected to actually make those decisions. This gives the firm more flexibility and speed in responding to changing conditions and customer needs. Thus, the decision to centralize or decentralize the organization may directly impact a firm's marketing effectiveness.

2.6.2 The marketing department

Operating in a market-oriented way not only requires an effective overall organization, but also carefully structured marketing activities. After all, the marketing organization is an essential link between the company and its markets. There are several approaches to organizing a marketing unit or marketing department. As we will see, each works best for a particular type of business. Let's look at the four most common types of marketing organization, and especially the product management system.

Functional organization

For a relatively small firm, or for a large company selling a limited line of products to one market, a *functional organization* is effective. In this type of organization, the firm's key functions – purchasing, manufacturing and marketing – are performed in separate departments. Using the marketing department as an example, the functional specialists – marketing research, sales, advertising, product development and customer-service managers – supervise their own functional areas. They then report directly to the top-level marketing executive, usually the chief marketing officer (CMO) or marketing vice-president.

Although this structure is common in companies with centralized marketing operations, one problem with the functional organization is that it tends to generate specialized sub-units that may establish goals of their own that conflict with those of the CMO. Proper coordination can only be achieved if the CMO or marketing vice-president, who is heavily outnumbered by the functional managers, has direct staff assistance as well as a sufficiently strong personality to ensure that the specialists conform to the company's overall marketing plan.

Geographic organization

A firm that operates nationwide or that markets products internationally often organizes its marketing activities by geographic regions. In a *geographic organization*, functional specialists are assigned to specific regions or countries and report to a regional marketing manager. The regional marketing managers then report directly to the marketing vice-president or CMO.

This organizational framework works well for a company catering to customers whose needs and characteristics vary from region to region. A geographic organization especially improves the sales force's effectiveness; the sales professionals or account managers can adapt their selling methods more closely to the needs and customs of local markets and are able to build long-term customer relationships. In addition, there is little travel required of the sales force.

Market management organization

A third way to organize a firm's marketing unit is on the basis of the types of customers or markets it serves. When a firm serves several highly diverse markets (such as the consumer, the institutional and the service sectors), it may be most appropriate to organize the marketing unit on the basis of the types of customers or markets it serves. This works especially well in situations where customer needs and preferences or the marketing channels used vary considerably.

As an example, a manufacturer of food refrigeration equipment may market its products to consumers, hospitals and restaurants. These markets need somewhat different products but, more to the point, they require completely different marketing strategies. In particular, each market may be serviced through a separate distribution channel, different media may be used to reach the buyers in each market and the customers may purchase the products for different reasons. Thus, it is essential that the company recognizes the unique characteristics of each of its markets.

In a market management organization, the responsibility for developing marketing strategies and plans for specific customers or markets rests with each market manager. If the market is large enough, the market manager may have the assistance of several functional specialists. By effectively communicating and coordinating the efforts of the firm, marketers make sure that work is not duplicated between markets.

Product management organization

Often, a company's products dictate the organization of its marketing unit, notably when it offers a wide range of products and brands. The more product lines, the more difficult it is for the firm to manage each one effectively. For instance, a promotion or pricing strategy that works well for one product may not be effective for another type of product, even if it's aimed at the same consumer market. Organizing by products or product lines gives the company sufficient flexibility to develop an optimal marketing strategy and programme for each product.

A product management organization is quite common in the *fast-moving consumer goods* industry. In many companies, the width of the overall product line is such that a separate manager is needed for each product. The product management system was pioneered by Procter & Gamble, a company divided into numerous brand groups, each headed by a *brand manager* or product manager. This individual develops and implements the strategic and annual plans for a product or group of related products, and assigns each of the assistant product managers one or more areas of responsibility for that product. The product manager, however, remains responsible for coordinating all aspects of the product's market strategy. It is also up to the product manager to convince senior management of the merits of the product's marketing programme. After the plan has been approved the product manager works with corporate specialists on the product's media planning, advertising copy, sales promotion, package design, marketing research and sales forecasting.

A product manager closely monitors their product's sales pattern in order to evaluate and recommend modifications in the product's promotional and sales programmes or other aspects of the marketing programme. To illustrate, if the members of a brand group for a fragrance wanted to change the package design, they would work with the art and package design departments. Then the sales department would help evaluate how the new package would affect shelf space, stacking, special displays and trade reaction. Marketing research would run tests to assess consumer reaction to the new package, while the production department would develop cost data for producing the new package.

The product management system has both drawbacks and benefits. Although product managers have a great deal of responsibility (including the profit-and-loss responsibility for the performance of the product line), they have relatively little authority to see that the product is marketed according to the original plan. No one in the product management hierarchy – including the group product manager or director of product management – has any control over the functional areas of marketing. This situation may create frustration and conflict in the organization, as the product manager tries to direct people who do not work in the product hierarchy to do what is best for the product. To achieve the product's goals and effectively coordinate all marketing activities, product managers must rely on sound arguments and the powers of persuasion.

The real key to success for a product management system is that the company's top management is dedicated to the concept that one person is primarily responsible for each of the firm's products. Without vigorous support, the product manager will not have enough clout to gain the necessary cooperation from people in various functions both inside the organization (such as R&D, finance and quality control) and outside (such as a public relations firm, independent research agencies, distributors and major buyers).

2.7 WRITING THE MARKETING PLAN

A company's marketing plan is one of its most important annual managerial documents. Some consider it a creative coup; others, a Herculean task; and most, a bit of both. But just about everyone is looking for the best approach to this yearly ritual.

Planning is the basis for sound decision-making, but not every plan should be the same. Many business and marketing plans are written every year, but they are individually crafted for diverse organizations and at various levels: for entire corporations, business units, specific markets,

product lines, products and brands. Government agencies and non-profit organizations, too, must develop marketing plans in order to be market-oriented and effective.

Developing a clear, concise marketing plan is no easy task. A substantial investment of time and effort is required to outline and explain – in a systematic and decision-oriented manner – the marketing strategy and those activities necessary to attain the marketing objectives. But it is time well spent, given the reasons for writing a marketing plan.

2.7.1 Why write a marketing plan?

The **marketing plan** is a detailed document that describes the context and scope of an organization's marketing effort, specifying how it will allocate available resources and use various marketing tools to achieve its formulated objectives within a particular time period. The plan also portrays the expected return for the organization. Because of its systematic structure, the plan allows management to evaluate whether the marketing activities are properly coordinated and makes sure that all parties involved work toward common goals. One of the critical roles of the marketing plan is to keep every employee focused on the activities that contribute to achieving corporate objectives.

Since the marketing plan specifies the assignment of tasks and responsibilities – including schedules for implementation – it provides a basis for internal communication and guides employees in achieving the objectives. It also helps managers monitor and assess the company's marketing performance. In short, the marketing plan is essential to:

→ Assess the *feasibility* of the proposed marketing objectives and strategies.

→ Enumerate essential *tasks* and specify who is responsible for executing them.

→ Provide a rationale for obtaining financing by calculating the monetary requirements and other *resources* needed to implement the plan.

→ Provide insight into the anticipated *results*.

→ Serve as a standard against which the company's progress can be measured and evaluated, in order to make any necessary *adjustments*.

This feedback also generates useful information for creating a new plan in the next planning cycle.

Good preparation is half the work, in particular when devising the marketing plan. Solid plans are based on facts gathered from marketing research, realistic assumptions and managerial expertise. Marketers may also ask colleagues, suppliers and customers for input and ideas. Since collecting this input will take some time, preparations for the marketing plan must be started well in advance (often as early as ten months prior to being submitted for approval).

2.7.2 Marketing plan components

Companies use different formats when developing marketing plans. The optimal format is determined by both the time frame for the plan (an annual marketing plan differs from a longer term plan with a three-year planning horizon) and the organizational level for which the plan is developed. A business or *company marketing plan* has a broader scope than a product or brand marketing plan. It addresses issues such as how the marketing department is organized, the marketing research required, the type of markets in which the company operates and the relationship between the corporate goals and product strategy. Such a plan goes far beyond uniting the marketing plans for each product or brand. It also explains the correlation between these plans and establishes managerial priorities. In effect, the company marketing plan sets out the marketing strategy for the entire organization.

The structure of the marketing plan for an individual *product* or *brand* is, in many ways, similar to that of the company marketing plan, but is restricted to information relevant to that specific product. It describes the marketing programme for each target market, the company resources needed (on a quarterly or monthly basis) and the expected results in terms of sales volume, profit and such measures as the degree of customer satisfaction. The plan may also include controls (such as a comparison of actual sales against anticipated sales) that help identify and avert potential problems. Information other than the marketing objectives and strategy is covered only briefly. After all, the objective is not to inform management of every interesting detail, but to improve its ability to make sound decisions about the product or brand. Therefore, many product managers do not include the company's strategy, objectives and strategic options in a short-term marketing plan focusing on a single product or brand.

Although its format and content depend on the organization's needs, a marketing plan should always be easily read and clearly organized. This may be achieved by following a plan outline like the one shown in Figure 2.11.

While every marketing plan has different content – depending on the organization, its goals and marketing strategies – all marketing plans cover basically the same topics and questions. Keep in mind, however, that because every marketing plan is unique, there is no single best format or order of presentation. Thus, the overall structure of the plan should not be regarded as a predetermined sequence of planning steps. Some components of the marketing plan are decided on in combination with each other, or simultaneously.

Ultimately, a marketing plan – as a decision-making tool and road map for getting from point A to point B – is only as good as the information it contains and the effort invested in its development. Most marketing plans are between 15 and 30 pages long (excluding appendices), depending on whether they are written for an existing brand or a more complicated new business venture. We will now examine each component of a typical marketing plan.

Title page

A title page that is poorly laid out, contains spelling errors or is incomplete creates the impression that the entire report has been carelessly written. A professional appearance, on the other hand, will communicate a positive first impression. In fact, how the marketing

FIGURE 2.11 Elements of a marketing plan

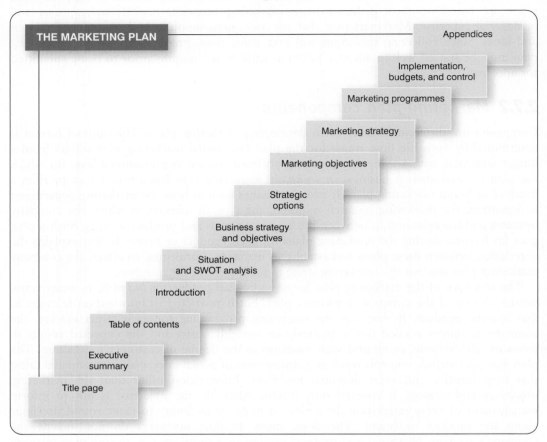

plan – including the title page – is written and presented not only conveys the substance of the marketing effort, but also its author's professionalism. An effective title page is well designed and provides the following information:

→ The name of the organization or product for which the report is written (e.g. Marketing Plan for Old Amsterdam).

→ The time period covered by the plan (2015).

→ The name and title of the author (Developed by David Mills, product manager).

→ The person or department receiving the marketing plan (Submitted to Shona MacIntosh, marketing manager).

→ The date on which the final plan is submitted (September 29, 2014).

Executive summary

An *executive summary* is a one or two page synopsis of the plan's key points and recommendations. Its main purpose is to provide senior management, or other readers not directly involved in the plan's approval or implementation, with a clear and concise overview. Although the executive summary is the first component of the marketing plan, it should be written last, as it is an abstract of the entire plan.

A good executive summary includes an introduction, usually with a recap of the product's performance during the prior year, the objectives of the plan, a brief explanation of the marketing opportunities and a list of activities proposed to meet the company's objectives. It typically includes an overview of the resources or budgets (for market research and promotion) required to support the plan, sales forecasts and benchmarks for evaluating the results (such as market share and profits). This important section of the plan should provide the organization with answers to the *who, what, where, when, why* and *how* questions.

Table of contents

For readers who need more information than is presented in the executive summary, the table of contents provides quick access to the topics in the marketing plan. Therefore, it immediately follows the summary. It may also include a list of graphs and tables with their titles and page numbers.

Introduction

Not all marketing plans require an introduction section. But if the plan is written for a brand new product, the introduction will state the product concept and provide information about the market and the competition. It should also explain how the new product fits within the company's mission and current strategy and why the product is expected to succeed. This will pique the interest of investors and make the venture more appealing to managers who administer the budgets. Additionally, the introduction serves as a guide for the rest of the report, explaining the plan's purpose, its structure and the topics to be discussed in each section.

Situation and SWOT analysis

The situation analysis begins with a systematic assessment of the firm's operating environment or, depending on the type of plan, of the brand's current status in the marketplace. The analysis includes the most relevant trends in the industry and their impact on the company, information about the distribution channels and competition, and the firm's marketing strategy with respect to the brand. It may also include a critical review of the previous year's activities, such as a comparison of the actual sales results to the stated objectives.

Quite a few managers like to organize the information gathered in a situation analysis into the four categories of a SWOT analysis (strengths, weaknesses, opportunities and threats). The *external analysis* considers the changing *marketing environment* – the economic, technological, sociocultural and political-legal forces that impact the way a company formulates and implements its marketing strategy. The analysis provides a detailed breakdown of factors related to the industry, current and prospective competitors and customers (categorized by segments or the type of buying situation) that influence the firm's marketing opportunities. The author might also indicate what information was not available when the plan was written to help the reader assess the risks facing the company. An overview of the main *opportunities and threats* (resulting from environmental factors and trends that are favourable or unfavourable to the company) is an appropriate summary of the external analysis. It will help management anticipate developments that may potentially affect the company and its marketing strategies.

The *internal analysis* evaluates the company's strengths and weaknesses to provide a foundation for identifying subsequent actions in the marketing plan. Important developments may be presented through graphs, as illustrated in Figure 2.12.

FIGURE 2.12 Recent product performance data

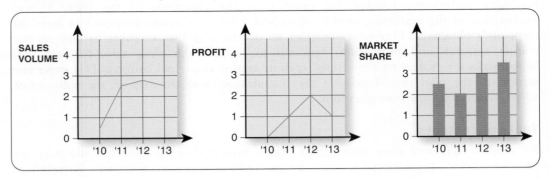

The three graphs show that sales volume peaked in 2012 and subsequently declined. Profits fell by as much as 50 per cent in 2013. Despite this development, the company's market share has steadily risen since 2011. The overall impression is that of a company willing to sacrifice sales volume and profit to increase its market share.

The internal analysis provides insight into the firm's controllable factors. These include the resources needed to realize the company's objectives, such as the available production capacity, management experience, product mix and brand image. The plan may also indicate what measures were taken to minimize the negative effects of the company's weaknesses.

A critical step following the SWOT analysis is assessing the implications for the company's strategy. Combining the firm's primary strengths and weaknesses with the opportunities and threats in its marketing environment – as is done in a *confrontation matrix* – will help management identify its competitive advantage and determine appropriate future objectives along with feasible strategies to achieve them.

Business strategy and objectives

Effective marketing planning is possible only with a clear understanding of the business strategy and objectives. In a company marketing plan, the objectives might be formulated in terms of desired annual growth in sales volume, profit as a percentage of sales or return on investment (ROI). Well-developed objectives must be 'SMART' – Specific, Measurable, Achievable, Relevant and Time-bound. They should also focus on the outcome of a measure, instead of the measure itself. Rather than stating an objective broadly, it is preferable to formulate the objective in much more precise terms. 'To lower prices' is better stated as 'to increase the company's market share in 2015 from 32 to 40 per cent, by taking various measures including lowering the price level of the entire product line on the European market by an average of 10 per cent'.

Strategic options

To discover a marketing opportunity or decide on the firm's objectives and strategies, we must first identify and assess its strategic options. One method for developing strategic alternatives is to use Ansoff's *product-market matrix* (also called 'strategic opportunity matrix'). Selecting which options to pursue – such as market penetration, market development or product development – often depends on how soon management seeks a return on its investment. Although increasing market share and profitability are compatible long-term goals, many firms either pursue profits immediately, or strive to maximize market share, with the expectation of future profits, but at the expense of short-term profitability.

In explaining the company's choices, we should make reference to the assumptions made in the situation analysis. This results in an overview of forces beyond our control or too difficult to predict. A clear understanding of these influences helps management modify the company's strategy immediately, should it fall behind schedule.

Marketing objectives

The *marketing objectives* component of the plan – a statement (and constant reminder) of *what* management wants to accomplish through its marketing activities – is the most fundamental. Without marketing objectives there is no standard for measuring the success of the firm's marketing programme. The objectives on which the marketing plan is based must be consistent with the organization's mission statement, as well as the outcome of the situation analysis and company objectives. This does not, however, mean that an organization cannot have different marketing objectives (such as increasing versus reducing market share) for various brands.

Marketing objectives may be expressed as absolute numbers (such as sales revenues in euros) or as percentages. Examples of marketing objectives are: launching at least four new services before 2016, achieving 75 per cent brand awareness in the premium brand segment in 2015, gaining a rating of 87 per cent or higher on the annual customer satisfaction survey and retaining at least 90 per cent of the 2014 customers as repeat buyers in 2015.

Marketing strategies

The marketing strategy describes *how* the company will achieve its marketing objectives. The strategies prescribed by a marketing plan are geared towards achieving *a sustainable competitive advantage*. They address issues such as selecting target markets fitting for the firm's products or services, using the right marketing mix to satisfy the needs and desires of the target markets and determining the best positioning campaign to clearly and simply communicate distinguishing characteristics of the firm's products or services to prospective buyers. This information should be covered in the plan along with arguments supporting the recommended course of action.

In practice, the primary goal for many companies is to maximize profits and, from that perspective, to identify the best options to do so. They consider various ways to increase sales, cut costs or to do both at the same time. Managers using Ansoff's product-market expansion matrix may consider the riskiest option for growth, a *product diversification* strategy. Each product-market strategy necessitates specifying the steps that should be taken, for example, to enter new distribution channels, increase consumers' purchasing frequency, or lower costs. The desired outcome might be to increase production levels in order to gain economies of scale or *experience curve* effects. Management may also consider a strategy to increase salespeople's effectiveness by providing education and training in the techniques for building long-term relationships with major clients.

By and large, marketing objectives are best met through a combination of measures. This requires marketers to formulate an overall marketing strategy. The marketing manager may use a variety of tools and models in creating a marketing plan, including the Boston Consulting Group's portfolio analysis and Porter's Generic Strategies model. Ultimately, the marketing plan must shed light on the market and market segments, the nature of competition, the target market and customers' requirements and buying behaviour. This allows the organization to develop products or services with features that customers value and to introduce them through effective strategies.

Marketing programmes

The broadly formulated marketing strategy is now translated into specific marketing programmes or marketing tactics. The best approach is to base these programmes on the *marketing mix* – a blend of product, promotion, price and distribution policies resulting in a mutually satisfying exchange with the target market. By detailing *which* measures must be taken *when* to meet the short-term objectives, as well as *how much* they will cost and *who* will be responsible for them, the firm creates an 'action plan' or *action programme* for the year ahead.

Developing an optimal *product* policy entails closely examining not only the physical product but also its packaging, warranty, value, after-sale service and brand image. Ultimately, consumers buy some products and services not only for what they do (concrete benefits), but also for what they mean to them in terms of perceived status, prestige or reputation. Given the product's position in its life cycle, we analyze the differential advantage: what does the product or service offer customers that the competition does not, and what role does this play in their buying decisions? These insights are extremely beneficial in positioning the product.

A good *promotion* mix can significantly increase sales. The marketing plan will describe the proposed *push* and *pull* efforts (including personal selling, sales promotion, publicity and use of interactive media) that are key elements of the company's integrated marketing communications programme. It should also include a description of the advertising themes and, if available, copies of advertisements demonstrating the themes' roles in the positioning strategy.

The third variable in the marketing mix is *price*, a major competitive weapon. This section of the marketing plan should clarify the company's price point as well as its price position compared to potential product substitutes. It may address such issues as the mark up chain in the channel, buyers' price sensitivity and, if space permits, demand and cost analyses. Here, too, the marketing strategy is translated into operational decisions. To increase profitability, for example, the firm might decide to selectively raise prices of products that are in highest demand and to discontinue other items with low profit margins.

Finally, the company's target market coverage, selected channel members and online marketing activities are components of its *distribution* policy. This section of the plan also covers the marketing activities to be conducted in each distribution channel – including the intermediaries' roles in providing customer service – and the most important challenges in marketing logistics, including those in foreign markets.

Each of these key decisions is discussed in the plan's section on marketing programmes. To achieve maximum effectiveness, the four marketing mix variables must be carefully developed and blended. The marketing mix is, like the proverbial chain, only as strong as its weakest link: an outstanding and attractively priced product – even when extensively promoted – is likely to fail with a poor distribution strategy. To achieve optimal results, this part of the plan or an appendix usually includes a time schedule to specify when certain activities must be conducted or fine-tuned to better satisfy the customers' needs and gain advantages over the firm's competitors.

Implementation, budgets and control

Strategies are meaningless unless they can be implemented. Therefore, the final component of the marketing plan is concerned with implementing the marketing tactics to carry out the strategy. In this phase, management's ideas and decisions are transferred into actions that move the organization forward. Since the marketing plan also presents information about the investments needed for its execution, supporting budgets should be provided. In fact, any well-documented marketing plan includes detailed budgets (for such activities as market research, product development, sales and promotion) and a system for measuring and evaluating the plan's success, as well as its shortcomings. This calls for performance standards, financial controls and monitoring procedures (such as a marketing audit).

Top management relies on this section of the report for comparison to the other submitted plans, focusing on the expected return on investment (Is it in line with company standards?), the anticipated risk (Is it acceptable?) and the implementation schedule (Is the timing right?). It may also provide the basis for approval of the plan or subsequent negotiations between senior management and the developer of the plan. Chances to obtain funding for the plan are greater if the financial analysis shows a positive ROI in a strategically relevant business at the corporate level.

The *budget* (which is really a projected profit-and-loss statement showing the expected revenues, costs and profit) is more than the basis for the plan's approval by top management. It also plays a crucial role in monitoring the plan's success or failure, or exercising marketing control. In a nutshell, marketing control is a four-step process of setting specific marketing goals (or other standards for performance), measuring progress toward realizing these goals, comparing the results (actual performance) with the goals (expected performance) and taking corrective action when necessary. Thus, management wants to ensure that it achieves the sales volume, cash flow, ROI and other goals outlined in the budget section of the plan. In order to accurately evaluate the causes of discrepancies between the established standards of performance set out in the plan and the actual performance, the goals and budgets are often broken down by territory (e.g. the northern part of the country), distribution channel (Internet), product type (model X) and time period (quarter).

The control procedures and performance standards used to monitor progress must be clearly spelled out. The benchmarks to be used depend on the company's objectives. If, for example, the firm wants to increase its market share by 10 per cent within a year by launching a new service, it can monitor its progress monthly or quarterly based on Nielsen data collected in retail stores. Such control procedures keep the marketing plan on course and facilitate making any necessary adjustments to the strategy or marketing plan.

Appendices

The marketing control procedure is most effective when the company – while identifying and assessing its strategic options – has developed contingency plans for alternative actions. Contingency plans usually appear at the end of the plan as appendices.

A contingency plan provides an alternative to the primary marketing plan in the event of threats or opportunities that were thought to have a low probability of occurring at the time the main plan was prepared. The contingency plan deals not with unforeseen events, but with events that are considered unlikely to occur, such as the launch of a competing product. But it can also outline an alternative strategy for an unexpected *favourable* development. Take, for example, a company's options if the demand for a new product grows much faster than predicted, with sales exceeding forecasts by more than 25 per cent. Four possible responses to this scenario might be to initiate round-the-clock production in shifts, to rapidly add production capacity, to temporarily suspend accepting new orders or to raise prices. If the firm has also drawn up contingency plans for price wars and other market disruptions, it will be prepared to act on short notice. Therefore, contingency plans are a valuable addition to any marketing plan.

Finally, Figure 2.13 presents several questions that can be asked to help evaluate the strengths and weaknesses of a marketing plan as a starting point for improving it.

FIGURE 2.13 Ten questions for evaluating a marketing plan

1	To what extent will the company's position in the market be compromised, if the assumptions underlying the marketing plan prove to be incorrect?
2	Is the required information available, and is the market research of high quality?
3	Do the marketing objectives and strategy follow logically from the results of the situation analysis?
4	Is the marketing plan consistent with the business strategy and objectives, and what impact will it have on the company's profits and market share?
5	Can the marketing plan be executed, and are the necessary resources available?
6	Are the marketing mix variables properly aligned and consistent with the rest of the plan?
7	Will implementing the plan evoke negative reactions from competitors, and if so, how will we respond to that eventuality?
8	Is the marketing strategy's primary goal to attract new customers or to increase consumption among existing customers?
9	Does the marketing strategy contribute to increasing brand equity and brand preference?
10	Will the marketing plan lead not only to short-term success, but also strengthen the company's profitable market position long term?

2.7.3 *Focus of marketing plans*

Among the countless marketing plans developed each year, there are both good ones and bad ones. Bad marketing plans include those in which the customers' needs and wants are an afterthought; a marketing plan is, by definition, a plan for identifying, acquiring and retaining clients. A marketing plan may also be considered inadequate if it is virtually identical to the previous year's plan, devoid of innovative ideas or does not consider various strategic options. So, when writing a marketing plan, the best approach is generally to put the old one aside and start from scratch. Another questionable type of plan is one that proposes radical measures – such as drastic changes to the marketing mix or strategy – without a sound rationale or adequate substantiation.

Although there are many reasons for writing a marketing plan, its initial function is to prompt internal discussion. If management – after assessing its feasibility or likely outcome – does not approve the first draft, some sections will have to be rewritten or negotiated. The marketing plan is an ideal tool for this purpose because it provides a summary of both the expected *results* and the *resources* required for implementation. From this perspective, the plan has a *communicative* function: it gives executives who control the allocation of financial resources a clear understanding of the proposed activities as well as the vision on which they are based.

The art of writing a good marketing plan is much like preparing a good dinner; it calls for selecting, measuring out and ideally presenting the best ingredients. The main ingredients of a marketing plan are: analysis, vision, activities and outcome. Which, then,

FIGURE 2.14 Four ingredients of a marketing plan

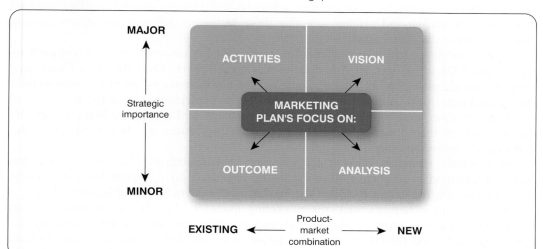

of these elements should we emphasize in the plan? As Figure 2.14 illustrates, that depends on whether the product or business unit presented in the plan is of major or minor *strategic importance* to the company. The second factor influencing which elements of a marketing plan are emphasized is whether the plan is a *new* or an *existing* product-market combination: how much do we know about the product and the target market's needs or purchasing habits?

It all boils down to four options. In planning for a new product-market combination that is of major strategic importance, you – as the plan's author – must have a clear *vision* of how to create a lucrative market position within a given time frame. The key point of the marketing plan, then, is validation of the underlying management vision.

In the case of a commercially important, but existing product-market combination – one that the firm has already actively pursued – the emphasis of the marketing plan will be placed on *activities* to be carried out in the coming year that will extend and strengthen the company's position. Because the company's executives are already familiar with the market as well as with the – hopefully consistent – ideas of the plan's author, their vision does not require much elaboration.

If the company is launching a new product or enters a new market that is not yet of great strategic significance, the focus shifts to a thorough *analysis* of the market. In this case, the marketing plan will primarily examine the market characteristics and developments in order to justify the manager's vision and recommendations.

Finally, for existing product-market combinations that are of minor strategic importance, the key question becomes whether the expected *outcome* is still worthwhile for the company. This is often a key consideration for executives in the allocation of resources. It is clear that the ideal structure and focus may differ from one marketing plan to another.

2.8 IMPLEMENTATION AND CONTROL

No matter how well written a marketing plan may be, it remains a sterile document with limited usefulness, if the strategies it describes fail to activate the organization. The process of implementation entails converting the plan into action through marketing action plans.

More specifically, it involves translating the marketing plan into descriptions of activities, detailed job assignments, budgets and time schedules to be communicated to those involved in the implementation and making sure that these marketing action plans are executed in order to achieve the stated goals.

A systematic approach in implementation and control is essential, as made apparent by the words of David Maister, an American management expert. 'Over the years I have seen a lot of strategic plans, but in practice, some just do not measure up when it comes to their implementation. In the end, what really matters is the implementation of the strategy – to get done whatever must be done. This requires courage and discipline. Many companies do not stick to their long-term objectives. Instead, they focus on short-term gains. But that's disastrous for any plan's implementation.'[13]

Unfortunately, strategies can fall apart during implementation. Therefore, after it has been implemented, a marketing plan should be evaluated on a regular basis. Evaluation refers to assessing the extent to which the marketing objectives are being accomplished.

Once the plan is implemented, the marketing manager is in charge of monitoring its effectiveness. Control provides the formal and informal mechanisms for evaluating the marketing results and for taking corrective action to ensure that the objectives are attained in the most efficient way, i.e. within the restraints of the specified budgets and time schedules. The marketer who has written the marketing plan is usually also responsible for the implementation, evaluation and control of the marketing efforts. We will examine this process more closely in the final part of this chapter.

2.8.1 Evaluation and control

The essence of planning the marketing effort is the development of marketing objectives and the determination of how best to meet these objectives. *Control* is concerned with determining – through measuring and evaluating the results – whether satisfactory progress is being made toward achieving the stated objectives. When proper control procedures exist, the company is able to act quickly to improve its performance. The process of adjusting the marketing effort in response to changing conditions is critical for the success of the firm, since very few marketing efforts unfold according to plan.

If the marketing plan is well structured, it allows management to assess the interaction between the marketing mix variables and to determine how they should be effectively integrated under varying circumstances. Consider the following example. A company intends to launch an attractive new, low-priced product with a national advertising campaign. However, middlemen in the distribution channel are not prepared to deal with the volume. This mix could generate huge demand, but would also lead to stock shortages, a wasted advertising budget and upset consumers. A well-informed marketer would prefer to implement a more effective and integrated marketing mix; one, for instance, with a higher price level and fewer promotional efforts. Such an approach would limit consumer demand until the distribution capacity could be increased.

The information in a *marketing action plan* must be detailed enough to clarify exactly what should be done when, and with which resources. If the marketing objective is to launch a new product by March 1, the plan should include all necessary information about deadlines, the production schedule, the introductory campaign, promotional support and any necessary sales and service training for employees. The marketing plan's financial implications, budgets and cash flow should also be spelled out. Finally, the marketing plan should describe which measures and criteria are used, at regular intervals, to determine if the objectives are achieved.

FIGURE 2.15 A step-by-step approach to marketing control

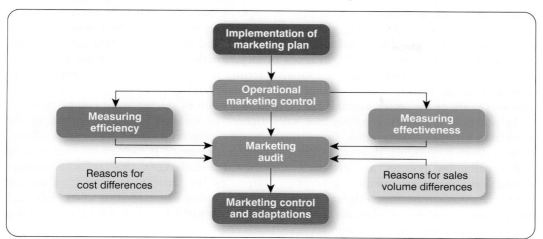

Figure 2.15 illustrates the last phase in strategy development and marketing planning: a step-by-step approach of the evaluation and control process. *Control* involves comparing the company's actual performance (achieved results) with the expectations (anticipated results) presented in the plan, for example in terms of monthly sales or other intended outcomes of the marketing strategy. These comparisons will show the extent to which current activities are moving the firm toward its objectives. Since there is usually a discrepancy between the firm's actual and projected performance, measuring and evaluating the results should begin at the very first stages of the marketing plan implementation. From that moment on, the marketing plan serves not only as a blueprint for action but also as a control mechanism. Of course, management will not adjust the marketing strategy until any discrepancies have been carefully analyzed and evaluated.

The sooner we identify any differences between the actual and the planned results, the more time we have to examine the causes and take any necessary action. Reasons for not achieving the marketing objectives may be ineffective strategies, unrealistic objectives, poor implementation or unexpected changes in the marketing environment. Therefore, the appropriate corrective action can take on various forms. Sometimes we may have to adapt the *marketing strategy* and put new measures in place to achieve the formulated marketing objectives. We may, for instance, improve customer service to increase customer loyalty or introduce a new product to attract new buyers. In other cases (such as during an economic downturn) we may need to adjust the *marketing objectives* themselves, if they have proven unrealistic. Each of these measures is a form of *operational marketing control* (or 'annual plan control'). Companies also rely on *strategic marketing control* to determine whether their strategy is still optimally tailored to current market developments and opportunities. As we shall see, the marketing audit is a useful instrument for that purpose.

2.8.2 *Operational marketing control*

A great deal of this book has been devoted to the planning and execution of the marketing effort. No less important, however, is the need to continuously identify problems in the business operations and resolve them before they spiral out of control. This type of operational control consists of two steps: the first one is formulating parameters for the marketing strategy – including acceptable deviations – to determine when we should take action. The second step is measuring and evaluating the attained results in order to examine what has been accomplished and how, as managers, we evaluate those accomplishments.

Benchmarks for the marketing strategy

Marketers use many different benchmarks to appraise both the strategy's effectiveness (to what extent are the targets being met?) and its efficiency (the cost of the resources utilized relative to the results). The standards are usually derived from the existing corporate and marketing objectives (for example, in terms of target market coverage or brand awareness). If expressed in operational and quantitative terms, they can also serve as performance standards. If the objectives are not stated operationally and quantitatively, the results from previous years or the sector average can be used as a point of reference for comparison.

In practice, managers generally use sales figures to measure the effectiveness of the marketing strategy. Many track fluctuations in the company's sales and market shares, broken down by product, district or type of client, to determine if their promotion, pricing and distribution policies are effective. Or they use indicators that reflect customer satisfaction, including quality perception, attitudes or repeat purchases. Common parameters used to measure efficiency include manufacturing and marketing costs. Table 2.5 shows some examples of objective and subjective benchmarks for evaluating the marketing strategy's effectiveness and efficiency.

TABLE 2.5 Possible measures for the effectiveness and efficiency of marketing strategy

Marketing activity	Objective measures	Subjective measures
Product strategy	– Stage in the product life-cycle – Profit contribution per product	– Customer satisfaction with the quality – Brand preference
Advertising	– Cost per thousand – Medium reach	– Unaided awareness – Communication capability
Sales promotion	– Number of sweepstake entrants – Cost per customer	– Consumers' buying intention – Retailers' willingness to participate
Personal selling	– Number of new customers per year – Expenses as a percentage of sales increase or decrease	– Ability to develop new ideas – Extent to which the sales force communicates the corporate image
Pricing decisions	– Correlation between turnover and price changes – Gross profit margin	– Customers' reactions to prices – Tailoring the price strategy to the target market
Distribution	– Level of distribution intensity – Number of on time deliveries	– Retailers' attitudes toward merchandisers – Complaints about damaged products
Market research	– Expenditure as a percentage of sales – Cost of data collection	– Training of research personnel – Quality of the recommendations
Marketing management	– Ratio of managerial / non-managerial personnel – Administrative overhead as a percentage of sales	– Ability of the management to motivate – Conflicts of interest

Corrective measures are not needed for all deviations from the norm or for each marketing objective that is not met. Some deviations are acceptable. Therefore, we need to establish in advance the discrepancy between the actual and planned market share, sales or cost level that warrants an intervention. This preparatory work guarantees that we spend our time only on the most urgent problems.

Evaluating the results

Managers in market-oriented companies regularly check the booked results against the objectives stated in the marketing plan. Whether this is a weekly, monthly or quarterly task depends not only on the product's purchase frequency, but also on the marketing instrument being evaluated. For example, the impact of a theme-based advertising campaign will take longer to assess than the effect of a price promotion. The time between measurements must be sufficiently long to generate useful data for measurement, but not so long that the opportunity to take corrective action will be lost. The analysis of the differences between the planned and the actual sales (or cost) is easier if we systematically record the results, as shown in Figure 2.16.

The cause of stagnating sales, underfunded budgets or other deviations from the numbers in the marketing plan can only be identified with complete information, including facts about the efforts of the advertising agency or the firm's own marketing department. That data can often be obtained through market research or the *marketing information system*. A closer look could show that the results aren't particularly bad, but that the forecast was unrealistically ambitious. That is why it is important to make sure that correct information is available before deciding to adjust the marketing strategy or an objective.

2.8.3 *Strategic marketing control*

One of management's important tasks is to periodically assess the effectiveness of the marketing strategy. This is usually done by conducting a marketing audit. We will first examine what an evaluation of the overall marketing strategy involves. Then we look at an effective process for conducting a marketing audit.

FIGURE 2.16 Differences between the expected and actual sales

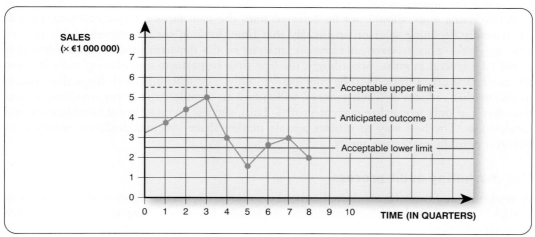

Marketing audit

A marketing audit is a systematic, critical, impartial review and appraisal of the total marketing operation: of the basic objectives and policies of the operation and the assumptions which underlie them, as well as of the methods, procedures, personnel and organization employed to implement the policies and achieve the objectives. The audit's primary purpose is to help marketers formulate specific recommendations for improving the marketing strategy and its implementation.

Many companies periodically monitor certain aspects of their marketing activities; a typical evaluation is limited in scope. The management team might analyze the effectiveness of the advertising program, product development efforts or sales organization. However, because each of these elements of the evaluation is approached separately, without an overall, coherent plan, these types of analyses are *functional audits* rather than a comprehensive and integrated analysis of the overall marketing operation. Additionally, these separate marketing evaluations are concerned primarily with performance evaluation, both of functions and personnel, rather than with the validity of the fundamental objectives of the marketing program.

A marketing audit, on the other hand, is not only concerned with performance evaluation, but is also an assessment of:

→   the long-term and short-term objectives on which the policy is based.

→   the size and nature of the various market segments and the company's relative position in each segment.

→   the company's strengths and weaknesses in fighting for market share in each of the segments.

Because such an in-depth study must be conducted objectively, the marketing audit is usually performed by an independent consulting firm.

When should the audit take place?

Often, executives invest more time in solving current problems than in identifying and analyzing emerging issues that may cause problems or present opportunities for the company in the future. These executives are at a loss, when it comes to making timely and necessary adjustments. Those missed opportunities can be avoided by conducting a marketing audit. Because a marketing audit is both a *diagnosis* and a *prognosis*, it examines past, current and future conditions. In this sense, an audit is as much a search for problems as a search for opportunities.

A marketing audit should not be deferred until the firm faces a major problem, such as dramatically declining sales or profits. By that time, looking for an immediate, short-term cure may take priority over an extensive analysis of the department's major problem that could take several months. Accordingly, the best time to perform a marketing audit is when the marketing effort appears to be running smoothly. The reason behind this is that success in the market reduces decision makers' willingness to abandon the status quo, out of fear that they can only jeopardize current profits. Thus, success tends to breed complacency and carelessness. The best way to protect against market share loss and declining profits is to perform periodic marketing audits.

The marketing audit process

A marketing audit can be conducted either by a marketing manager's own staff or by third-parties. External *auditors* are preferable, especially for small companies without much auditing experience.

In order to obtain the desired information, the audit should be carefully prepared. Prior agreement must be reached with the firm's management about the audit's scope and objectives, the time it will take, the people to be interviewed and how the analysis and recommendations will be reported. Who, for example, must be consulted about the auditor's recommendations on adapting the product assortment, expanding online activities or changing the organizational structure?

A marketing audit encompasses the marketing environment, strategy and organization, as well as the marketing mix variables. Of course, not all issues are equally important or relevant to each audit. The auditors typically interview not only company officials, but also clients, suppliers, distributors and others from outside the company. Sometimes they also collect secondary data (from annual reports, competitors' websites and relevant marketing research studies) about the products, services and markets in order to analyze them. It is always important for auditors to work professionally and tactfully, especially when broaching controversial issues and asking sensitive questions.

The marketing audit gives marketers better insight into the competitive situation, customers' needs, the best positioning of their products or services and the effectiveness of the marketing mix. At the end of the day, the marketing audit yields plenty of information that is useful to the marketing department's future strategic and operational plans.

2.8.4 *Integrated marketing*

In addition to being used for determining if the marketing strategy, marketing objectives and marketing mix need to be adjusted, the marketing audit also assesses the company's overall performance. A company's performance tends to be closely related to the quality of cooperation and partnership between the marketing department and other departments in the organization.

In their efforts to apply the marketing concept, some managers come into conflict with other departments that put their own interests before those of the organization as a whole. This lack of cooperation between departments that results in less than the best possible outcome is known as *departmental management or* sub-optimization. Many disputes over setting budgets are rooted in differences of opinion about the company's priorities or similar conflicts of interest.

The integration of the marketing function is one of the cornerstones of the marketing concept: the marketing department not only leaves its mark on the policies of other departments, but its effectiveness is dependent on other departments as well. An otherwise sound marketing policy can be hindered if, for example, the production department advocates larger series and fewer models, the credit department wants to lower credit limits for customers and the shipping department believes it is best to use less expensive but slower transportation modes. The resulting conflicts may well hurt the organization's performance as a unified system.

Table 2.6 illustrates the main conflicts that may arise between the marketing department and other units in an organization.[14] Although some conflicts of interest are difficult to avoid, the marketing manager should maintain good relationships with other departments and deliberately seek cooperation, so that they can encourage a customer-oriented approach in decision-making at strategic moments. An experienced, professional marketer realizes that, like any investment, marketing requires patience, perseverance and commitment if it is to bear fruit.

TABLE 2.6 Conflicts of interest between the marketing department and other departments

Department	Departmental preferences	Marketing preferences
Product development	– Technically and functionally perfect products – Development time as long as necessary – Basic model with few options	– Products preferred by customers – Short design and development time – Many models, customized to meet buyer needs and wants
Purchasing	– Standard parts – Narrow product assortment – Most economical inventory quantity – Most efficient order size and delivery time	– Parts adapted to customer requirements – Deep product assortment – Large inventory to avoid stock shortages – Delivery soon after customers place orders
Manufacturing	– Large series with few product models – Easy to produce	– Launch a new model as soon as buyers are interested – Attractive looking products
Finance	– Fixed budgets – Fixed conditions – Pricing policy that covers costs – Low credit risk and strict debt collection procedure	– Flexible budgeting to address changing needs and wants – Conditions depending on type of customer – Pricing policy adapted to desired market development – Easy credit and non-aggressive debt collection procedure

SUMMARY

1 Marketing management and marketing planning

Anyone who works for an organization needs to structure their thoughts and plan their activities. Systematic planning forces us to analyze the company's situation, quantify its goals, consider and select strategic options for the long term and develop an action plan for the next year. In marketing planning, the focus is on developing effective marketing strategies and plans to achieve the marketing objectives.

For top executives as well as middle-level managers – including sales managers – it is essential to think and act strategically. *Strategic thinking* includes the ability to anticipate long-term threats and opportunities in the marketing environment and respond appropriately. *Strategic action* is converting strategies into various activities and implementing them. Putting this all together, executives and managers are responsible for four basic tasks: *analysis*, *planning*, *implementation* and *control* of the company's activities.

Planning and strategy development take place at several levels in the organization. A distinction is made between *corporate strategy* (the parent company), *business strategy* (the division or SBU) and *marketing strategy* (for a product line or brand). Most large organizations consist of different *Strategic Business Units*: divisions that operate independently and – with their own management and resources – are responsible for developing and implementing their own strategies. These divisions not only have their own management and strategies, but also the resources to meet the needs of their target markets.

Strategic planning is complemented by tactical planning, which guides the implementation of activities outlined in the strategic plan. Unlike strategic plans, tactical plans typically focus on shorter-term (current and near-future) activities – typically involving the marketing mix – which a company must carry out to implement its strategies. These activities often involve working on the firm's brand image, quality, innovation and relationships with its customers, which were also described as the four cornerstones of a successful strategy.

2 Market definition and mission

The first step in the marketing planning process is to come up with the *business definition* and the organization's mission statement. The company's business definition can be expressed in terms of the customer segments, customers' needs and technologies. Using these three dimensions helps management address the question, 'What business are we in?' and eventually in defining the company's mission.

The corporate mission describes the nature of the company, its core activities and what it stands for. The formal description of the corporate mission – the *mission statement* – typically defines the market in which the company wants to compete and its long-term objectives, as well as management's vision of how it will achieve these objectives. By assessing how alternative strategies (strategic options) fit in with the corporate mission, management uses the mission statement to influence the company's future growth.

3 The SWOT analysis

For a plan to be feasible, it must be based on a *SWOT analysis*: an analysis of the company's strengths and weaknesses (internal analysis) and the opportunities and threats in the environment (external analysis). Most trends and other factors in the external environment are outside of the firm's control, yet, these uncontrollable variables do have an impact on the results. Hence, given the importance and urgency of the most relevant factors, management must assess, in a situation analysis, the extent to which the identified developments are potential opportunities or threats to the company. In addition, by using a confrontation matrix, it can decide what the right objectives and preferred strategies should be.

4 SMART PC objectives

Objectives need to meet certain requirements. The acronym SMART PC is an easy way of remembering these requirements. Well-formulated objectives are Specific, Measurable, Attainable, Realistic and Time-bound. They are listed in order of importance (Priority) to create a clear hierarchy of objectives. They also should be Consistent with each other.

5 Strategy development

An important part of strategic planning is spelling out the *strategic options* with which the company can reach its objectives. Typically, a company's competitive position improves as its market share increases. To make sure it chooses the right options, management first positions its Strategic Business Units in the *Boston matrix*, based on their relative market share and the market growth rate. The matrix offers an overview of the optimal combination of activities – particularly in terms of cash flow. A balanced portfolio contains at least a *cash cow* to generate a surplus cash flow, a *star* that will become a cash cow once the market growth slows down and a *question mark* that may become a star if we invest enough in it.

A second widely used model in strategy development was developed by Michael Porter. He argues that the two most essential choices a company faces are the scope of the markets that it will serve (broad or narrow) and – based on its competitive advantage – how the company will position itself to compete in this target market. In order not to get 'stuck in the middle', management must select one of three possible generic strategies: a cost leadership strategy, a differentiation strategy or a focus strategy.

Ansoff's product-market expansion matrix is a third analytical tool to help management select and develop appropriate strategies. This model categorizes four growth strategies that may all lead to higher profits: market penetration, market development, product development and diversification.

6 Organizing marketing activities

In organizing marketing departments, most firms begin with the functional approach, since it is the simplest to implement. In a functional organization, however, it is difficult to effectively plan and coordinate the marketing activities, since none of the functional specialists is directly responsible for a particular market segment or specific product. Therefore, a large company is usually better off with a market management organization (whereby its marketing unit is structured according to types of markets or customers) or a product management organization. Using this approach, a single person – the product manager – is responsible for developing and implementing a marketing strategy for their product and for coordinating all required activities to manage it successfully. The product management system enables the company to respond to market developments more quickly. Unfortunately, most product managers shoulder major responsibility, but have little direct authority. Their effectiveness therefore relies heavily on the decisions of others in the organization.

7 The marketing plan

Planning is a responsibility for every manager, and the *marketing plan* for the forthcoming year(s) is perhaps the most important document a marketing or product manager drafts. This plan establishes the framework for executing the marketing activities and serves as a blueprint for action. It also serves a multitude of other purposes. The marketing plan allows the reader to assess the reasoning behind and the feasibility of the marketing objectives and strategies, describes the tasks to be delegated and determines the required resources. It also provides insight into the expected results and facilitates timely strategy modifications. Although there are many ways to structure a marketing plan, it should always include the following components: executive summary, situation and SWOT analysis, business strategy and objectives, strategic options, marketing objectives and strategies, a description of the marketing mix and, finally, a section on the budgets, implementation and control of the marketing activities.

The marketing plan is also an effective instrument for internal deliberation, discussion and communication. Depending on the strategic or commercial significance of the product-market combination and the extent to which top management is familiar with the product and markets, the plan's focus should be on the manager's vision of how to create a lucrative market position, the activities to be carried out, a thorough analysis of the market or the expected outcome of the plan.

8 Marketing control

Great marketing plans are doomed to fail if they are not implemented well. Therefore, the very last key tasks in the marketing planning and management process are implementation and marketing control. Marketing control refers to the activities concerned with determining whether the firm is making satisfactory progress toward the achievement of its stated marketing objectives. Both objective and subjective measures provide insight into the effectiveness and efficiency of the company's marketing programme.

Unfortunately, strategies can fall apart during implementation. For this reason, companies – in addition to conducting operational marketing control – also periodically assess the effectiveness of their marketing strategy, especially when deviations from the standards defined in the marketing plan are significant. Through a marketing audit – a comprehensive survey and analysis of the entire marketing function – management tries to identify the causes of any problems before beginning to make any strategy adjustments. A marketing audit is, after all, both a search for problems and a search for opportunities and threats. In implementing the recommended changes in the firm's marketing policies, it is crucial to avoid internal conflicts between marketers and managers of other departments that would hurt the overall organization's effectiveness.

Marketing is a dynamic, future-oriented activity that requires careful planning. Plans must be comprehensive and flexible to allow management to consider the marketing opportunities and threats in the environment. But they must also be specific enough to permit measurement and control of the company's performance.

DISCUSSION QUESTIONS

1   Some people claim that marketing is too important to be left to the company's marketing department. What do you think they mean by this?

2   Can a company be successful without a strategic marketing plan? Give reasons for your answer.

3   An organization's strategic planning culminates in both a long-term and a short-term marketing plan. Explain the relationship between these plans and give examples of strategic and operational decisions.

4   Some people consider the corporate mission a 'meaningless PR sentence' and believe that the time spent formulating the mission statement is wasted. Do you agree or disagree? Why?

5   Which do you think is more important in developing a marketing plan: the internal or the external analysis? Why?

6   How can a company find out if it has a competitive advantage? And, how does it know whether this is likely to become greater or smaller?

7   What are the advantages and disadvantages of market leadership? Illustrate with an example.

8   **a.** What are the risks of applying the Boston Consulting Group's portfolio analysis methods too rigidly in strategy development?
    b. Give some examples of strengths that allow a company to pursue a cost leadership strategy. What are the risks of pursuing such a strategy?

9   What should a company do first in plotting its marketing strategy: define the target market, develop a product or formulate the objectives? Why?

10 If you were the marketing manager of a company that markets sophisticated audio equipment, how would you respond with your strategy to demographic developments and major trends in the marketing environment?

CHAPTER 3
THE MARKETING ENVIRONMENT

LEARNING GOALS

After studying this chapter you will be able to:

1 Explain the difference between the internal and external marketing environment

2 Identify the individuals and groups a manager interacts with in the mesoenvironment

3 Describe significant developments in the macroenvironment

4 Appreciate the importance of ethical and socially responsible decisions in marketing

3.1 The marketing environment
3.2 Mesoenvironment
3.3 Macroenvironment
3.4 Marketing ethics and social responsibility

We live in an exciting period of rapid change and major challenges. Companies recognize the rapid pace of environmental change and realize they must anticipate change and respond quickly to remain competitive. Many have adapted by cutting development and launch time for new products by half, while improving quality and more closely tailoring products and services to the needs and wants of the target market. Their customers are making an increasing number of purchases through the Internet. In the meantime, other innovations have slashed distribution costs, while competitive pressure has led to continuous improvements in service levels.

While keeping track of societal change and innovations in business, a marketing-driven manager realizes that their own company must continually advance the development of better products and services to keep growing. Something that was outstanding a few years ago, may not be good enough today. To be a successful competitor in the global market, a company has to excel in creating and implementing an effective marketing strategy. This chapter examines why a systematic analysis of the environment is a crucial part of this process. We will explore the most important environmental factors that need to be considered when developing strategies.

MARKETING IN ACTION
How Nestlé Fights High Commodity Prices

The world's largest food and beverage company, Nestlé, is a big spender on supplies to keep its production process going. It purchases at least €25 billion worth of raw materials per year. This includes not only 300 000 tons of cacao and twelve million tons of milk, but also more than 10 per cent of the world's annual supply of coffee beans. As a buyer, Nestlé's key problem is that the costs of the ingredients it needs – sugar, milk, grain and other commodities – have been fluctuating, but have also doubled within a few years. According to the IMF, global food prices will continue to rise for years, at least until the global agricultural production will go up enough to make prices fall again. This year, though, Nestlé expects to pay at least €2.5 billion more for the same amount of raw materials that it bought across the globe last year.

Nestlé has pursued several strategies to increase control over its environment and to cope with the volatility in food and raw material costs. First of all, the company's CEO Paul Burcke – who was born in Belgium – is doing whatever he can within the organization to lower operational costs. To illustrate, in order to reduce the impact of a 25 per cent PET plastic price increase, Nestlé has decreased the amount of plastic it needs for the production of a spring water bottle by over 30 per cent in the past four years. By limiting its use of other packaging materials as well, the company is saving more than €1.2 billion per year. Hence, it has already managed to offset about half of the recent increase in its raw materials costs.

At the same time, management is gradually raising consumer prices of its products, irrespective of whether the costs of its ingredients are going up or down. Still, in order to better predict future commodity price changes, Nestlé keeps in touch with more than half a million farms from which it buys corn, wheat, sugar and other ingredients to make products such as Purina Pet food, Nesquik milk and Nescafé coffee. Nestlé's management realizes that the developing countries' growing population and expanding economies will continue to contribute to the rising prices of raw materials. The Swiss company has therefore decided to start raising wholesale prices of its products before its competitors raise theirs. As the chief executive officer points out, if you wait until other big food companies have announced their price increases, retailers are less likely to accept your higher prices.

Perhaps the most effective marketing strategy to reduce the effect of increasing food commodity costs is to continue to launch higher-margin brands in which raw material costs account for a smaller portion of the retail price. Nestlé, for example, has turned its Nespresso brand into a €2.5 billion global business that grows at a rate of 20 per cent per year, generating significant profits. No wonder, since the consumer price of its high-quality coffee offered in single-serve capsules is – per cup – about ten times higher than regular coffee beans sold by competitors.

Nespresso. What else?

www.nespresso.com

NESPRESSO
Café, cuerpo y alma

Similarly, in Europe Nestlé is selling Mövenpick – an upscale brand of ice cream – in small containers for a price that works out to over €12 per litre. Even Nestlé's high-margin bottled water, Pure Life – already the world's best-selling water brand – is gaining market share in many countries, including Pakistan and other emerging markets.

Another strategy to adapt to the constantly changing environment is to transform Nestlé from a food company (known for its chocolate, sugary snacks and ice cream) into a leading health, nutrition and wellness firm. To illustrate, the global market for *functional foods* – food products that have been intentionally modified and improved by manufacturers to provide health benefits – now exceeds €100 billion and is growing much faster than overall food sales. This shift in emphasis towards health and nutrition will help convert Nestlé from a supplier of low-margin, commoditized foodstuffs into a provider of high-margin products and services. Nestlé expects that incorporating healthier ingredients into its products – such as live bacteria in yogurt and sterols (plant fat) that reduce blood cholesterol – will help increase sales in rich countries, but also win over hearts and minds in emerging markets.

To cut raw material costs, Nestlé is educating farmers in Africa on techniques to boost crop yields

The ultimate strategy that Nestlé uses successfully to combat high raw material costs is to educate and help farmers across the globe on how to boost crop yields. This is more complicated than you might think. Cocoa, for example, is primarily produced in West Africa, and passes through a long supply chain before it reaches manufacturers of chocolate products. Today, major chocolate companies – including Nestlé, Hershey, Mars and Kraft – try to control their supply chain by taking responsibility for every link in it and by cooperating with the World Cocoa Foundation. In this organization, global chocolate companies work closely together with cocoa-producing farmers and governments. Of course, large companies are in business for profits and growth, goals that are not always compatible with small farmers' well-being in foreign nations. However, since all parties benefit from higher cocoa production, and thus share an interest in *sustainable* cocoa production, the chocolate companies in this highly competitive industry have made a commitment to work together in assisting farmers.

Global chocolate companies not only help farmers by encouraging them to participate in training programmes to boost cocoa production, but also monitor *environmental* threats to cocoa yields. Every year, over 30 per cent of the crop is lost to various diseases and pests. By setting up research centres in West Africa and sending farmers with cellphones useful data on pest control and weather conditions by SMS, they are able to double crop yields within two or three years. For one thing, this will help meet the increasing consumer demand for chocolate, coffee and other luxury products in countries like China and India. Eventually, it will also put a dent in global food commodity and food prices, which will benefit consumers around the world.

Osita Ogbu, an economics professor at the *University of Nigeria* and a fellow with the *Brookings Africa Growth Initiative*, welcomes any effort made to increase cocoa farmers' productivity and income. But he strongly feels that the best way to create sustainability is to actually produce chocolate in nations with equatorial climates where cocoa growing is possible. This move would certainly create more jobs and higher profits for West Africans. His dream is to see the children of cocoa farmers in Africa not follow in their fathers' footsteps, but to become well-paid employees in chocolate factories in their own countries. Ultimately, producing chocolate in Africa would jumpstart the creation of a truly sustainable chocolate bar.[1]

Managers can stimulate strategy changes, or they can slow a company's response to developments in the environment. 'Unfortunately, many senior managers are against any type of change', says well-known organization expert Gary Hamel. 'The people at the top of the organization are typically those with the most experience. But experience doesn't count for much when the environment keeps changing as fast as it does today. Ongoing technological progress, globalization and social change mean that much of senior management's experience is now worthless'.[2]

Yet, for today's skilled, well-trained managers, the prospects are boundless. For one thing, they realize that changes in the marketing environment could be viewed as a *threat* to the company, but may, at the same time lead to lucrative marketing *opportunities*. Although we cannot actually influence most changes in the environment, the uncontrollable environment should still be taken into account when pursuing strategies. In fact, anticipating and responding decisively to a dynamic environment is one of the marketer's most important tasks, and the key to a successful marketing strategy.

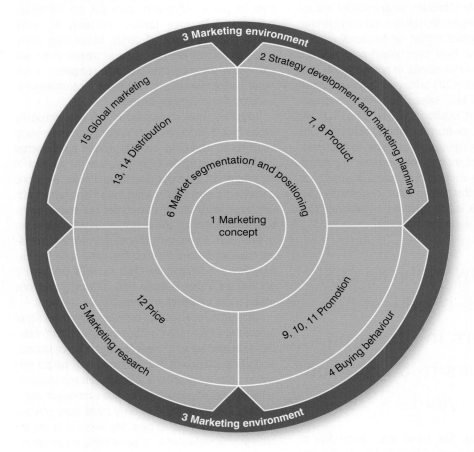

Companies in all industries – and ultimately a country's competitive position in the global market – will reap the benefits of a new generation of young managers with innovative ideas about strategic options who use their leadership skills to motivate others to become actively involved in developing and implementing new strategies. If they systematically *analyze* the marketing environment, draw meaningful conclusions and *integrate* the findings into the strategies they develop, they have a decided advantage over others who have not yet mastered these marketing fundamentals in a strategic framework.

In this chapter we will examine the impact of major environmental factors in more detail. We will explore all components of the internal and external environment that influence strategy development and implementation. And, finally, we will consider a company's social responsibility.

3.1 THE MARKETING ENVIRONMENT

A company does not operate in a vacuum, but in a complex environment that includes consumers, competitors, distributors and other organizations. In order to come up with a marketing-oriented approach, we need to have clear insight into this environment. From the company's perspective, the environment is everything that is not part of its own organization.

Exactly how the environment will be described often depends on the job title and point of view of the person who develops the strategic plan requiring environmental analysis. For example, rather than considering the environment from the perspective of the overall organization, marketing managers typically focus on their own department's marketing function, and thereby analyze the so-called *marketing environment* in which the company operates. As illustrated in Figure 3.1, here, we make a distinction between the internal and the external environment: both internal and external analyses are required to assess each of these environments' respective influences.

The *internal environment* is also known as the *microenvironment*. Microenvironmental factors are departments (such as production and Research & Development) and resources (financial and technical resources) that are part of the organization, but outside of the marketing department. They are essentially controllable, at least at the upper management level. For example, by analyzing the organization's strengths and weaknesses, top management can evaluate resources available for implementing a particular strategy and, if necessary, acquire additional resources. All environmental factors not classified as *microenvironmental* are, by definition, part of the *external environment*. Because the external marketing environment is most important for marketers, this chapter will primarily focus on that environment.

While companies have control over the marketing mix and the internal environment, they cannot possibly influence external environmental factors. Therefore, they must adapt to these trends or events. Many managers rely on a *marketing information system* to help them keep track of these occurrences. Ultimately, changes in environmental factors can represent opportunities (such as for new products) as well as threats. The sooner we know what these changes mean for the company, the more effective our marketing strategy will be.

FIGURE 3.1 The marketing environment

3.1.1 *Internal environment*

When developing a marketing strategy, the manager must consider the company's internal capabilities and limitations. If, for example, they discover a marketing opportunity for a reasonably priced navigation system for motor-scooters, but the production department cannot make the new product, or the company does not have sufficient financial resources to finance its introduction, the plan for the new product launch is unlikely to succeed. These kinds of limitations are internal, because they are imposed by the organization itself.

As shown in Figure 3.1, the internal environment consists of the resources available to implement the strategic plan and the various departments of functional areas ('operational functions') in the company. It also includes the corporate culture. Next, we will look at these functional areas and the resources the organization can use to achieve its objectives.

Functional areas

When developing a strategy, the marketing department considers the business strategy and objectives established by top management. The marketing strategy should also be aligned with the strategies of the other departments in the organization, such as production, R&D, human resources and purchasing. Each of these operational functions has specific interests, agendas and responsibilities.

Conflicts between functional areas within a company are unavoidable, if the various departments focus more on achieving their own objectives than on helping the company to achieve its overall business objectives. How well a company manages this conflict depends on how the marketing function is organized within the company and to what extent its employees apply the marketing concept. As discussed earlier, the more customer-oriented the company is in conducting its business, the less likely the different departments are to clash.

Although in theory, the internal or microenvironmental factors are *controllable*, this usually only applies to the company's top management. For example, the marketing manager may be able to generally control the marketing strategy, but they can probably only *influence* the other operational activities. To be able to implement the marketing plan successfully, they need to make sure that all of their colleagues involved agree on the company's objectives and business strategy.

Available resources

Regardless of their size, organizations have only limited resources to accomplish their objectives. Their primary resources are:

→ *Financial resources.* These include the firm's liquid assets and any loans it has taken out to finance the necessary investments.

→ *Commercial resources.* The available knowledge and experience in targeting specific customer segments is often crucial in the company's ability to realize its goals.

→ *Technical resources.* Technical know-how and expertise in production methods determine which products the company is able to develop and produce.

→ *Natural resources.* The organization must have the necessary raw and auxiliary materials – of the desired quality level – to ensure efficient production.

→ *Human resources.* Experienced managers, as well as skilled and motivated employees, are essential to run a successful business.

A company's management team should assess the available resources on a regular basis. One way to determine available resources is to analyze the company's *strengths* and *weaknesses*. Not only is this analysis important for strategy development, but it will also reveal areas in which the company is better than – or not as good as – its competitors. An analysis of the external environment provides more essential information and can help identify *trends* that represent opportunities and threats. In practice, the evaluation of the company's strengths and weaknesses is usually linked – in a SWOT analysis – to an assessment of the company's external environment.

3.1.2 External environment

The external environment involves all of the *uncontrollable* influences and groups that originate outside the organization. However, in an environmental analysis (the monitoring and evaluation of the external environment to determine the source of a company's opportunities and threats) we only consider *relevant* environmental forces, in other words, those that influence the company's performance and, ultimately, its results. After all, those forces are the only ones important in strategy development. Relevant external elements may be people (such as customers), organizations (such as competitors), circumstances (such as the expansion of the European Union) and developments (such as the aging of the population).

When exploring the external environment, European analysts and managers often make a distinction between influences that stem from the *immediate* external environment (the *mesoenvironment*) and those that stem from the *macroenvironment*. In the United States – and in most American-oriented marketing books – a distinction is made only between the microenvironment and the macroenvironment. The (external) mesoenvironment is then considered to be part of the microenvironment. As can be seen in Figure 3.1, *mesoenvironmental factors* include customers, suppliers, intermediaries or middlemen, competitors and other stakeholders, such as creditors.

The first step in environmental scanning – the process of collecting information about the elements of a company's environment – is to determine the *need for information* for strategy development. Managers can simply define their need for information as follows: 'What questions do we really need to answer to support our strategic decision-making?' In the end, these questions are selected based on two criteria: the importance and the urgency of the situation.

The *importance* of a situation relates to the possible consequences of a set of circumstances or certain trend for the company's financial performance. Here, we have to estimate how serious the threats are or how lucrative the opportunities, relative to this environmental force.

The second selection criterion is the *urgency* of the situation. Urgency is determined by the likelihood of the circumstance actually occurring, when that might be and how much time we will have to respond appropriately.

The assessment of available data plays a major role in marketing decision making based on the environmental diagnosis, an evaluation of the significance of the opportunities and threats disclosed by the environmental analysis. In this process, a multi-functional team of experts (such as a marketing manager, R&D specialist, production planner, marketing research expert and a financial controller) weigh the facts, taking into consideration the market conditions and alternatives available to their customers.

Other than the importance and urgency of a situation, there are additional criteria to bear in mind when analyzing the environment. A company must consider the cost of additional analysis relative to its potential benefit. An exact *cost-benefit analysis* may not be possible, but if, for example, it will cost us €5 000 to collect the information, and a better decision based on the analysis will generate, at most, an extra €3 000 long-term, it makes more sense to ignore this particular environmental force. Unfortunately, it is easier to predict the cost of gathering and analyzing information than it is to predict its usefulness, if this can even be expressed in monetary terms. Still, a rough estimate is better than no estimate at all. Just as we should avoid postponing a decision indefinitely due to lack of information, we should not persist in analyzing information without ever making a decision.[3]

We will now explore some major external environmental forces. In doing so, we make a distinction between influences stemming from the immediate environment (the mesoenvironment) and from the macroenvironment.

MARKETING MISTAKE
Nokia's Downfall

It's hard to imagine now, but Europe's most successful company of the 1990s was located in a town called Oulu, Finland. Its name may ring a bell: Nokia. After introducing the first handset in 1992, the Finnish manufacturer soon controlled the mobile phone market, particularly in emerging markets. It also built one of the most successful mobile phone brands in the world. Within six years, Nokia became the largest mobile phone producer on the globe, and by 2005, it had sold more than one billion handsets.

Since Nokia failed to adapt to the changing marketing environment, its market share plunged

Politicians considered Nokia an ideal model of a European company that captured a new market and defined the industry. As Romano Prodi, the European Commission's president, noted, Nokia's example proved that European regions were capable of developing new, high-tech centres of innovation. Today, however, Nokia has lost its position of leadership and – by many critics – has been written off as the most disappointing corporation of the 2000s. Why? Its management did not succeed in predicting and assessing key changes in the company's marketing environment – including globalization – and failed to benefit from technological breakthroughs and social developments. As a result, Nokia's stock price tumbled. In 2012, Nokia was pushed out of the top-100 ranking of global brands; a substantial fall for a corporation that a few years earlier still held a top-ten position. Its market share has been reduced to less than 25 per cent. Although that still amounts to a huge number of cellphone sales, Nokia's market position is 'stuck in the middle', as it fell off the list of the top five smartphone makers in the world. Samsung is the market leader in terms of consumer handset sales, while Apple – since the iPhone's introduction in 2007 – is the undisputed frontrunner in upscale smartphone sales.

In spite of attempts to make a comeback through the Windows 8 phone and its partnership with Microsoft, Nokia still appears outmoded and firmly past its prime in the highly competitive market. What are the most important lessons here? First of all, management misinterpreted the significance of the alliance between the social media, computing and mobile phone industries. After becoming market leader, Nokia became *complacent*. The lesson is that managers should never stop monitoring the environment in order to anticipate and identify important developments and influences. In addition, the company suffered from *marketing myopia* and quit aggressively pursuing new marketing opportunities. Nokia assumed that consumers would continue to buy mobile phones just to receive and make phone calls. Management did not understand – until it was too late – that most people also wanted to read their email, see what their Facebook friends were up to, find their way around town and order products or services online, all through their mobile phone.

Image courtesy of Nokia

Maybe the most fundamental cause of Nokia's failure to adapt its marketing strategy in time is the company's *location* in Finland. Located in the periphery of Europe, it was isolated from more innovative rivals, online marketing giants and other producers of high-tech products for consumer markets. Similar to Sweden's Ericsson in Stockholm, Nokia's managers were not forced to continuously and critically assess their approaches to solving business problems and addressing new marketing opportunities and challenges in global markets.

Most companies take advantage of their geographical closeness to customer-focused rivals, attracting experienced, well-trained employees and exposing themselves to fresh ideas. It is no coincidence, for example, that Europe's major pharmaceutical companies are primarily located in geographic hubs such as Britain's south east and Basel (Switzerland), investment banks and other financial institutions in London, and upscale car makers in Munich and Stuttgart (Germany). Of course, there are occasional exceptions to this rule, as illustrated by the success of the aircraft manufacturer Airbus SAS, located in Toulouse, France. But for the majority of managers and leading companies in fast changing industries, being isolated from the pack is a big disadvantage.

Should Nokia have moved to Silicon Valley or another California location in the 1990s, when it was still dominating the industry? Would relocating to an area thriving with Internet, music and movie businesses have helped the Finnish company to better keep up with technological and other crucial developments in the mobile phone industry? Would it have enabled its managers to be more innovative in new product development and more effective in global brand management, instead of desperately trying to maintain its market share while losing it to computer companies that weren't even very successful at the time?

The unfortunate reality, as some commentators have noted, is that Nokia 'took its eye off the ball'. It lost pole position in the smartphone market to Apple's iPhone, Google's Android and others. By failing to understand key market changes, not focusing on innovation and remaining geographically removed, the mobile phone maker ceded control to its competitors. Hopefully, other European firms will spend time analyzing Nokia's failed strategies so they'll learn to avoid making the same blunders. After all, Europe can't afford to lose any more companies with once leading global brands.[4]

3.2 MESOENVIRONMENT

The mesoenvironment is essentially the (branch of) industry or market in which the company operates. It is the immediate environment in which the marketer and firm interact with customers, suppliers, intermediaries such as distributors, competitors and public groups or stakeholders. The organization usually maintains contact with some of these groups and is at least familiar with the others. Although these mesoenvironmental factors are external in nature and therefore uncontrollable, they can, as players in the firm's own market, certainly be influenced to some degree.

3.2.1 *The supply chain*

Usually, several organizations are involved in the stages that a product goes through from production to consumption. Together, these parties make up the *supply chain*: the connected chain of all of the business entities, both internal and external to the company, which perform or support various functions in the production process. As illustrated in Figure 3.2, the supply chain stretches from raw materials to semi-manufactured goods (or components) to final products that are marketed to the ultimate consumers.

The *supply chain* originates with both the raw material suppliers and, importantly, those supplying semi-manufactured goods. Various *intermediaries*, such as trading companies, deliver these materials or goods to the manufacturer for final processing or assembly. The finished product then enters the distribution phase and is eventually consumed by the *final user* or *ultimate consumer*. From this perspective, flower auctions describe their goods flow

FIGURE 3.2 Supply chain

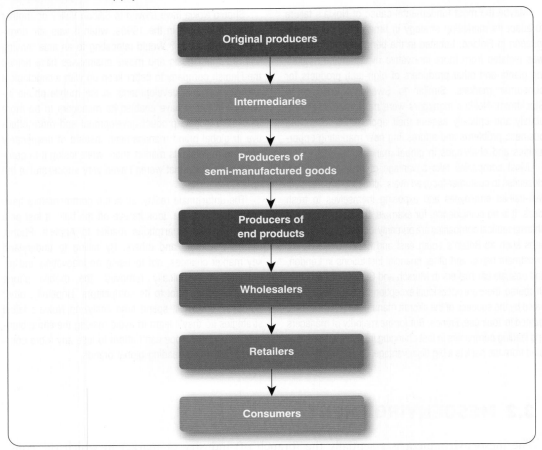

as being 'from the field to the vase', while gin distilleries are part of a supply chain that stretches 'from the grain to the glass'.

Some corporations – such as those in the oil industry – control all links in the supply chain, from raw materials acquisition through ultimate consumption. However, in most industries independent intermediaries (such as wholesalers, agents and storage and transport companies) perform some of these activities.

Each link or 'horizontal section' in the supply chain is known as a *sector* (for example the wholesale sector). It is made up of organizations that perform the same function in the production of a certain product. This is also the level at which we analyze the mesoenvironment in which the company operates. From this viewpoint, a *sector analysis* offers insights into both the attractiveness of the market and the opportunities and threats for a company.

Within these sectors, a group of organizations that have certain similarities in their production techniques or the products they make, is known as a *branch of industry*. The food industry within the retail sector is one example, while the book industry within the graphic sector is another.

Today, companies rely on *supply chain management* to coordinate and integrate all the activities of the supply chain members – from the source to the point of consumption – into an efficient process. Whereas in the era of mass production, manufacturers made standardized products that were pushed down through the pipeline to consumers, in today's competitive market, products and services are being driven by demanding customers who expect to be able to buy exactly what they need and want.

3.2.2 Customers

Customers play a key role in a company's mesoenvironment. After all, developing ongoing relationships with **customers** and satisfying their needs, so that both parties achieve their objectives, is really the essence of marketing. Therefore, the company must have clear insight into the needs and wants of its customers and their buying behaviour. The company should also know the size and the importance of various categories of *current* and *potential* customers.

In business, markets are sometimes described in terms of the type of customers that make up the market. Essentially, there are four types of *customer markets*:

→ The *consumer market*: the market for products and services purchased or rented by individuals, families or households for their own consumption or use. Consumers and their behaviour are discussed in Chapter 4 of this book.

→ The *industrial market*: also called the *organizational* market, it is the market for goods sold to and purchased by businesses for use in their own production of other goods and services, which they then sell or supply to other businesses at a profit. Organizational customers' behaviour is discussed in Chapter 4, section 4.6, which covers business-to-business marketing.

→ The *intermediary market*: the market consisting of organizations that buy products and resell them without any further processing, with the objective of making a profit. The importance of these intermediaries or **resellers** is explained in Chapters 13 and 14 about the wholesale and retail trade.

→ The *institutional market*: the market consisting of large-scale users (such as nursing homes, schools and hospital cafeterias), government agencies and other non-profit organizations. Their buying behaviour is similar to that of industrial customers.

In environmental scanning, we collect information about key factors for each of the firm's active markets (or those the firm might want to enter). For example, how many competitors are there? Who, exactly, are the customers? How great is the overall demand? And, what is our market share? We also describe the most relevant developments within the market.

© Monkey Business Images / Shutterstock

Next, we try to identify possible market segments in the four customer markets outlined above. These are groups of customers with common characteristics, such as age category in the case of consumers, or size in the case of companies. If we discover that customers in one of these segments have needs and wants that are not being met by our competitors, we have identified a marketing opportunity. We could then develop an effective marketing strategy to satisfy the unmet needs and wants of that part of the market.

3.2.3 Suppliers

If a company does not have the necessary materials and manpower, it cannot produce or market anything. In this sense, it is dependent on its suppliers, both in terms of the availability and the price and quality levels of the raw materials, goods and services that it needs to buy.

Yet, most manufacturers spend little time systematically analyzing their suppliers. Supplier marketing (or *procurement marketing*) is in its infancy. Many business transactions are still initiated by vendors, which use their representatives or websites to inform potential buyers of the products and services available and the terms and conditions of delivery. This traditional system, by which firms typically negotiate to obtain lower prices, tends to encourage a passive attitude on the part of the buyer.

Any company that lacks sufficient insight into the supplier market may be unpleasantly surprised by unforeseen price increases or delivery problems, and is often unaware of other options for obtaining supplies. Fortunately, more and more managers are beginning to realize that purchasing is an important business function, which, on average, makes up more than half the value of the company's sales turnover. By making relatively small cost savings in purchasing, firms can increase their profitability substantially. However, this calls for a proactive approach in all stages of the purchasing process by buyers who use the purchasing function to strategically manage suppliers in order to reduce the total cost of products and services.

Of course, a company can reduce its dependency on suppliers, as well as its costs, by buying from several suppliers. This strategy is known as multiple sourcing. Participation in a purchasing consortium, developing long-term relationships with vendors and *backward integration* (acquiring one or more of the company's suppliers or developing in-house supply capability) are other methods companies use to increase profits or gain more control of supply. Philips, for example, has managed to negotiate lower prices by having different departments combine their purchasing and by conducting business with a limited number of suppliers. Through cost reductions of more than 10 per cent in its purchases of raw materials, supplies and components, Philips is saving hundreds of millions of euros per year.

3.2.4 Intermediaries

In marketing their products, most manufacturers rely on intermediaries. These are companies that operate as a link between producers and consumers or, as middlemen, specialize in providing services to facilitate transactions between suppliers and customers. Examples of intermediaries are distributors (wholesalers and retailers), marketing research agencies and transportation and storage companies.

Most distributors and agents are companies that – sometimes at their own risk – help suppliers find customers and sell products. These intermediaries are involved because they are able to perform certain marketing tasks more efficiently than producers. In other words, in moving products from the factory to the customer, these channel partners are able to add more value to the products at lower costs. The costs that intermediaries add are offset by the *utilities* they create; utility is a measure of the extent to which a product or service satisfies the needs and wants of a consumer or organization.

Usually, there is a wide separation between the production and the consumption of a product. The intermediaries' task is to add value by bridging the differences created by this market separation. These include:

→ Differences in *quantity*.
Although products are made and shipped in large numbers – allowing for economies of scale – the individual consumer only needs a small amount. This 'quantity difference' is bridged by splitting up the large quantities packaged by the manufacturer into smaller unit sizes.

→ Differences in *time*.
Production and consumption almost never occur simultaneously (except in the marketing of services). Because, for example, some vegetables are only grown in summer and skis only sold in winter, both types of products are characterized by a *temporal* market separation. Intermediaries who store agricultural products in refrigerated warehouses create time utility by making the product available to the consumer when it is needed. The same applies to skis, which are produced year-round but typically sold in winter.

→ Differences in *place*.
Production (for example in China) and consumption (at the consumer's home) rarely occur in the same place, leading to *spatial* market separation. Through transportation, manufacturers and dealers create place utility by making the product available wherever consumers want it.

→ Differences in *product assortment*.
Consumers like to choose from a wide range of products that is more varied than that which individual manufacturers offer. Wholesalers and retailers who offer a customer-oriented merchandise mix by combining the product lines of several manufacturers bridge this market separation.

Retail organizations were once little more than an 'extension' of manufacturers, and largely under their control, but have since become powerful forces in the distribution channel. Many retail chains have developed a unique store image and ambience that cultivates customer loyalty. Other intermediaries that play key roles in a company's success in implementing its marketing strategies (such as sales agents, marketing consultants and advertising agencies) are also indispensable middlemen in the mesoenvironment with whom relationships should be built. In conclusion, productive partnerships with selected trading partners are fundamental for marketing-oriented firms.

3.2.5 *Competitors*

A company is usually not the only supplier in the market. Therefore, in its external analysis, it should pay attention to its *competition*. This includes all companies that sell products and services that meet the same – or similar – needs of customers in its target market. More broadly defined, the competitive environment consists of all the organizations that try to serve similar customers.

Shrewd, successful executives keep as close an eye on their competitors as they do on their customers. This is essential, as the availability of up-to-date information and advanced technologies has led to intensified competition and products quickly becoming obsolete. No wonder so many companies use a systematic approach to help them identify their competitors, evaluate their strengths and weaknesses, estimate their costs and profit numbers and monitor their activities in the market. This detailed competitive analysis enables them to anticipate competitive moves. Nevertheless, for many firms the primary question remains, 'Who is our real competition?'

Forms of competition

When discussing their competition, some managers tend to focus on the price and quality of competing brands, or the delivery time of other firms in the industry. Others are so preoccupied with their own products that they don't even take the competition seriously or simply overlook it. These are dangerous shortcomings, since a company's market position is largely determined by how its management perceives the competitive situation. The point to keep in mind is that competition is not limited to comparable brands.

There are actually four different kinds of competition. The most direct form is **brand competition**. This comes from other brands of the same type of product, which are more or less substitutes because they are very similar; *Grolsch* and *Heineken* beers are a good example.

The next level at which companies face competition is called **product competition**. This form of competition is between different types of products within a particular product category. To illustrate, this is the competition that occurs between different types of beer, such as lager, malt beer, white beer and bock beer. Product competition is also known as product-type or product-form competition.

Both brand competition and product competition occur within a sector, so they are described as *in-sector competition*. But companies outside the sector are also actively competing for customers. This competition is known as *cross-sector competition*, and it takes two forms: generic competition and need competition.

Generic competition occurs between alternative product lines that are able to satisfy the same consumer need (such as the competition between beer, wine and whisky). **Need competition** is

Courtesy of Image Asset Management

the competition between the different kinds of needs for which the consumer is willing to pay. For example, a consumer might choose to spend money on eating out on a regular basis – as a form of relaxation. On the other hand, they might decide to save up for an extended holiday in an exotic destination, or to remodel their home. Because these products and services are competing for the same budget – as this is essentially a battle for the consumer's money – need competition is also known as (total) *budget competition*.

The different forms of competition – brand, product, generic and need competition – are illustrated in Figure 3.3. The same diagram identifies the types of decisions consumers are facing at these four levels of competition, in terms of choosing between different brands, product types, product classes and needs or wants. In any external analysis preceding the development of effective marketing strategies, these four different levels at which the company is competing should be taken into account.

Competitive analysis

Too frequently, competitive analysis emphasizes only numbers – the number of competitors, the market shares of the three leading rivals, competitors' advertising budgets or their estimated profit margins. Focusing on the *dynamics* of the market, however, is a far more productive approach to competitive analysis. Companies should ask questions such as: Which competitor is developing a more cost-effective production method? Who is working on an improved product development system? Who is testing a new distribution strategy that is more closely aligned with changing consumer behaviour? If such issues are key factors in the competitive battle, the answers to these questions will provide more insight into the competitive situation than, for example, a list of market shares. It is, without question, less important to know a competitor's current market share than to know which company has seen the greatest change in its market share, and why.

A useful competitive analysis begins with the identification of current *and* potential competitors. If there are many rivals in the marketplace, we need to divide them into *categories*. Some managers simply make a distinction between *primary competition* (between brands) and *secondary competition* (between products). But many also consider other forms of competition (for example, generic competition and need competition, as shown in Figure 3.3) in their analysis and marketing planning.

FIGURE 3.3 Different levels at which competition occurs

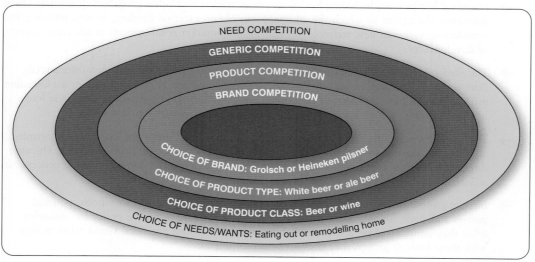

It may be helpful to divide competitors into strategic groups with common strategic features (such as size, location and quality level), identical strengths (distribution intensity, product development and product mix) and similar strategies (market segmentation, positioning and growth strategies). This type of analysis does not have to be limited to the marketing strategy – it may also include other functional areas or elements in the micro- or mesoenvironment, including management expertise or alliances with suppliers.

Analyzing the policies and performance of companies in a strategic group is particularly useful for benchmarking. Benchmarking is a comparison of a firm's own business processes and performance in various activities (such as production and marketing communication) with those of other organizations (within or outside of the sector or industry). These cross-company comparisons often focus on purchasing procedures, product development cycles, inventory management, recruitment or training practices and overall performance (for example, in terms of customer satisfaction) in a range of marketing activities. Here, the key question is, 'Why is a competitor doing better than we are?'

Benchmarking is especially helpful when trying to anticipate rival strategies in the process of planning one's own strategy. This approach to competitive analysis is used because organizations focusing on the same markets, selling similar products or using identical distribution channels (in other words, companies that are in the same *strategic group*) also tend to respond to changes in the environment in similar ways. Therefore, an awareness of the similarities and differences in companies' strategies and their performance offers valuable insights for the strategy development process.

3.2.6 Public groups

A company's results are not only dependent on its customers, suppliers, intermediaries and competitors, but also on a fifth party in the mesoenvironment, public groups. These are individuals, companies and other organizations that influence, and are affected by, the way in which a firm achieves its objectives.

Because this influence can be both positive and negative, companies strive to develop and maintain good relations with their public groups. Usually, the company's public relations department (or firm) is in charge of creating goodwill and improving the company's image. But actually, all managers should be aware of the motives and needs of the company's public groups in order to foster good relationships with them. The main public groups are:

→ *Financial institutions*, including banks, securities traders and other providers of capital. These determine the extent to which the company can obtain external funding, in turn allowing the company to invest in new technologies and product-market combinations at the early stages of development.

→ The *media*, including the Internet, newspapers, magazines, radio and television infomercials. Both the press and audiovisual media influence public opinion. A critical article or a misleading programme can have a disastrous effect on a company's image. Experienced marketers know how to generate positive publicity by satisfying journalists' need for timely 'news'.

→ The *government*, particularly local and regional authorities. They issue licences and permits, authorize expansion and maintain the infrastructure that makes the firm accessible. Through direct contact (*lobbying*) a company may be able to influence the decision-making process, or at least limit the potential damage for the organization.

→ *Interest groups*, including environmental organizations, consumers' associations, political parties and trade unions. Some of these organizations try to influence policy by criticizing what they consider to be unacceptable business activities and practices. Good relationships with these interest groups may prevent future problems.

MARKETING TOPPER
Going Green Makes Good Business Sense

The concept of *sustainability* implies that businesses responsibly attempt to satisfy consumers' wants and needs without impairing future generations' ability to do the same. Once a mere trendy buzzword for developing greener products or trying to reduce pollution in the manufacturing process, 'green' social responsibility is now becoming more and more part of the very 'DNA' of global corporations worldwide. No longer just a necessary 'should' in boardrooms across the world, or a mere stepchild to the company's core operations, there are real and tangible bottom-line benefits for embedding an environmentally-focused view into the very fabric of a company's operations. In the past, sustainability efforts have been viewed with suspicion, as taking costly actions that may have potential long-term benefits did little to comfort shareholders of the time. Nowadays, with stricter environmental regulations around the world, green thinking is becoming essential to global companies that wish to remain competitive.

Image courtesy of BP p.l.c.

Green corporations are more likely to successfully compete in today's global markets

For starters, there are considerable cost savings to be gained by introducing innovative measures to make products and production processes more 'green'. Walmart, for example, instituted fuel efficiency measures to the tune of $200 million a year in lowered fuel costs, and reduced packaging to the tune of $3.4 billion a year, making the already-lean retailer all that much more competitive. A leading potato chip maker in England adopted an interesting strategy by encouraging its potato growers to water their potatoes less frequently, thereby making the potatoes less expensive to transport, and even faster to bake. A win on all fronts: a cost saving in growing and shipping the product, an environmentally-friendly reduction in water consumption and, besides, a streamlining of the company's production process.

In addition, global companies are finding that adopting a 'green' perspective is a crucial part of a marketing strategy to gain competitive advantage. For example, *Max Burgers* (a top Swedish burger chain) found that reducing waste in children's meals resulted in an increase in sales of these. Other similar measures found the chain nearly doubling its market share in Sweden. Increased competitiveness remains a compelling reason for companies to adopt environmentally-sound practices.

Furthermore, creating new markets in industrialized countries is proving less effective than seeking out new markets in developing countries. For Unilever, these fast-growing emerging markets already generate over 40 per cent of the company's current sales. When Unilever in Brazil helps poor consumers by facilitating free laundry services, or its efforts in India help grow women-owned micro-businesses, or its markets in Bangladesh enjoy free health care from floating clinics or potential consumers in Ghana enjoy clean water, this also becomes a part of the company's marketing strategy to gain a sustainable competitive advantage in developing countries.

Managers worldwide now see various other benefits from pursuing sustainability strategies. Such strategies may help avert environmental catastrophes, as companies such as Shell in Nigeria or BP on the US Gulf Coast had to deal with. Others see a benefit in relations with foreign governments; GlaxoSmithKline found that their efforts in introducing low-priced drugs for developing markets had the parallel benefit of having those governments become more cooperative in protecting the company's *patents* there. And in this fast-moving information age, where information about company environmental practices travels the Internet, blogs and social media channels like wildfire, both watchdog groups and consumers (who are increasingly voting with their wallets) are expecting *transparency* about company environmentally-focused practices. No longer viewed as a luxury or a topic for abstract discussion, companies now ignore social responsibility 'at their own peril'. Analysts often point at the relationship between sustainability practices and management quality, arguing that *green* corporations are more likely to successfully compete in today's global markets.

Global companies are also finding that long-term investments in the infrastructure of emerging markets will help in growing future consumers. Philips Electronics recognizes that within the next 25 years, more than 80 per cent of its consumers will live in emerging markets with insufficient resources and infrastructure to meet health care needs. Philips is launching mobile medical care services that utilize satellite connections to connect physicians from far-away urban hospitals for needed medical care. It has also introduced affordable means for providing clean water for developing countries as well as a revolutionary smoke-free, wood-burning stove that cuts air pollution, saving millions of lives of people relying on wood to cook their daily meals who – before this product's introduction – were suffering from serious pulmonary illnesses. For Philips, sustainability is a necessary component of its global strategy development. Perhaps, in the short run, these worthy initiatives may not guarantee a company a high ROI; in the long run, however, they are very likely to significantly save companies money and create more loyal customers than any other business strategy.[5]

Not only should companies be concerned with the possible impact of the stakeholders' actions, but also with the corporate image among the general *public*, their contacts with **trade organizations** and their relationships with *internal groups* (such as employees and the board of directors). All of these groups can leave marks on the company's results. Therefore, it is essential to respect their ideas and, if possible, to consider their needs when determining strategies.

3.3 THE MACROENVIRONMENT

A company's performance is influenced by factors within the company itself (the microenvironment) and by its sector or industry (the mesoenvironment). The conditions and developments a company faces in society as a whole – the *macroenvironment* – also guide its approach to the market and help determine its profitability. **Macroenvironmental factors** differ from the rest of the marketing environment in that a company can neither control nor influence them. The economic climate in which a business operates is an obvious example of such an uncontrollable variable.

Not all developments in society may be significant for a company. In fact, they are only relevant to the firm if they influence its performance, and they may then be perceived as either an *opportunity* or a *threat*. Identifying – based on their importance and urgency – the most relevant macroenvironmental trends that should be taken into account in strategy development is an important task for managers. We can only intelligently plan for the future and respond to influences in the environment, if we have monitored and analyzed these environmental forces in advance. In environmental scanning, we make a distinction between events that affect the *market* as a whole and those that specifically affect the company.

Some developments in the macroenvironment have a direct impact on the market – they may make it grow or even create an entirely new market. For example, population growth combined with increased purchasing power and lower interest rates can lead to a greater number of people buying cars. In addition to these demographic and economic factors, sociocultural trends – such as the increasing number of single working women – also influence purchase decisions in an industry. This creates lucrative marketing opportunities for companies that are able to respond decisively.

Macroenvironmental factors may also present opportunities and threats, because they have a direct impact on the organization's *business activities*. Within a company they affect not only the marketing strategy, but also other functional areas or departments (such as production and purchasing). For instance, the introduction of the *Smart* fortwo coupe cdi and the subcompact Mercedes A 160 CDI BlueEFFICIENCY that boasts a fuel consumption of 4.5 l/100km, was a reaction to economic and political developments that call for energy-efficient cars, legislation requiring small cars to be safer and technological advances that have reduced the time it takes to design and produce new models.

Clearly, marketers can only make effective strategic decisions if they fully understand what is happening in the external environment. Changes that some perceive as threats, may – in the long run – be lucrative opportunities for informed marketers who respond early, based on a sound analysis of these forces. In the next few paragraphs we will look at the demographic, economic, political-legal, ecological, technological and sociocultural environment – though we should keep in mind that those influences cannot always be considered in isolation. Still, we will now explore each one of the six macroenvironmental factors shown in Figure 3.4.

3.3.1 Demographic factors

Demography literally means the study and measurement of human populations. A population may be described by various demographic factors or characteristics, such as its size (the number of residents in an area), birth rate and composition (for example in terms of the number of households and most prevalent nationalities). Keeping track of demographic changes helps reveal the likely future demand for certain types of products and services. Examples of commonly used demographic variables are age, gender, education, race, consumer income and family size, as well as the population's age distribution and the degree of

FIGURE 3.4 Macroenvironmental factors

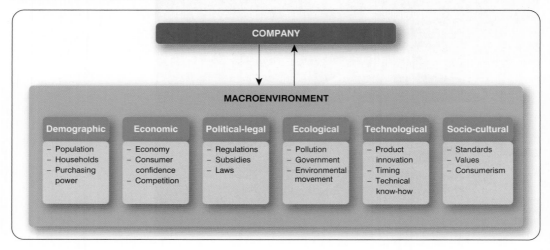

urbanization (the percentage living in cities). The demographic characteristics most important to marketers in some way relate to purchasing behaviour, since consumers from different cultures, countries, age categories or household arrangements usually exhibit different buying behaviours in the marketplace.

Population

Marketers cannot simply focus on the average consumer (someone 40 years old with an average income) or the 'typical' family (married couples with children living at home). They must also be aware of the age distribution. An interesting current trend is the *aging* of the population in many countries, in which the percentage of older people increases while the percentage of young people (up to the age of 20) simultaneously decreases. This demographic shift has important implications for marketers in countries like Japan, Great Britain, The Netherlands, Italy and the United States. After all, mature consumers have different needs, attitudes and purchasing habits than do younger consumers.

Slowly, we are changing from a society dominated by young people, with their emphasis on discovery, consumption, steady change, starting families and developing careers, to a society characterized by retirement and scaling down. In many European countries, by 2015 the number of people celebrating their 65th birthday will exceed those celebrating their 20th.[6] The disappearance of the dominant youth culture will unavoidably change the romance of youth that we have always had in our society, but will, at the same time, also create marketing opportunities. There will be, for example, expanding markets for new products and services – anything from well-built stepladders and home exercise equipment, to organized trips – that satisfy the needs and wants of senior citizens with their relatively high purchasing power.

Households

Markets are people. However, when marketing their products and services (such as cars and vacation destinations), many marketers focus on households rather than on individual consumers. Throughout most of Europe the growth rate of households has exceeded the growth of the population. This is due to the declining average household size, stemming from the rising number of single-parent households, households without children, households of one person and other non-traditional households. Marketing-oriented companies are developing products that reflect the changing structure of households, such as Pickwick 'Tea for One'. The increasing number of smaller households also results in a greater demand for housing, home furnishing products, personal entertainment and travel, especially since smaller households usually have more per capita income than larger households.

Education and purchasing power

Education levels among consumers are rapidly increasing. For managers, too, lifelong learning has become essential, since market globalization and technological advancements take place continuously. The combination of increased education and emancipation (a sociocultural development) has resulted in a working population that now includes a growing number of women. In fact, there are already more dual incomes than sole incomes among traditional households. For marketers, the trend toward increased education is significant because more highly educated consumers are more sophisticated in evaluating product offerings, more willing to accept new products and more demanding of quality and performance.

Because of the *greater purchasing power* of families with two working partners, the demand for luxury goods is increasing. In those households, products – like appliances – and services designed to save time and provide convenience have become virtual necessities. There is also rising interest among dual income couples for *one-stop shopping* stores that offer their customers food products, clothing and electronics, as well as services such as vision care and pharmaceutical care. It is clear that demographic shifts present both challenges and market opportunities for companies.

3.3.2 *Economic factors*

Although consumers' occupations and incomes are significant demographic variables, consumer spending is also affected by the economic environment. *Consumer buying power*, for example, is largely determined by macroeconomic factors such as employment, productivity (an estimate of output per labour hour), distribution of income, inflation and interest rates. In business, these economic variables present a wide range of uncertainties. In fact, if there is one rule of thumb with respect to the economy, it is that it is constantly changing. Therefore, economic factors play an important role in evaluating a company's strategic options and in developing its strategy.

Generally, a healthy economy is good for consumers and marketers alike. Consumers are able to buy more products and services, while companies can make higher profits. Because many firms operate internationally, they keep a close eye on worldwide economic developments and compare competitive environments in different countries. For instance, they keep track of the general economic climate, inflation, the interest rate, exports, unemployment, the retail price index and consumer purchasing power.

Companies also monitor consumer confidence. Recently, consumer confidence reached an all-time low, which, combined with a decrease in disposable personal income (a consumer's total after-tax income available for spending and savings), had a negative impact on the purchase of consumer durables. In times of recession, some producers of *fast moving consumer goods* may also suffer, as the market share of inexpensive store brands and *discount grocery chains* increases. Hence, in business, economic factors present both marketing opportunities (such as for home improvement stores) and threats (such as for the home furnishing industry).

In the long run, slower economic growth means that a company will no longer have the easy option of increasing sales by taking advantage of growth in the overall market. Rather, it must grow by increasing its market share, that is, by taking sales away from its competitors. Thus price, product and cost decisions will become even more important. From this perspective, any firm should maintain acceptable profit margins on its products and services, which may mean pricing ahead of anticipated cost changes, as well as eliminating products that cannot be sold at a profit. Also, new products should be carefully analyzed to ensure that they have a good chance of meeting the firm's profit objectives. Finally, the firm should consider adopting stringent cost control measures to increase profitability. Quite a few companies have adopted *zero-based budgeting*, which forces every unit within the organization to justify all future funding requests.

3.3.3 *Political-legal factors*

No matter what or where a firm markets, it is subject to the rapidly changing political-legal environment, consisting of the governmental policies, laws and regulations that affect marketing practice. These rules and restrictions may limit a company's options in strategy development and, therefore, affect managers' decision-making. Political-legal factors are closely tied to the economic and social environments. For instance, *economic* issues (such as a recession or high unemployment) and *social* problems (such as air pollution or health concerns) usually lead to political decisions or laws intended to improve the situation. These may be designed to regulate companies or an industry, maintain competition or protect the consumer. Regardless, managers need to understand and stay informed of any legislation, court rulings and regulations that may affect the company.

When analyzing political-legal factors and considering national laws in European nations, we should bear in mind rulings by the European Commission, as well as regulations at provincial and local levels (regarding, for example, available business locations or permits). These too, can affect a company's business strategy and pose a threat. However, they may also create opportunities and reasons to revise strategies and to take advantage, for instance, of new subsidies or to exploit the expansion of the European Union, which has increased the size of the market.

Some government measures affect all of the companies in the market. Think, for example, of legislation to restrain the growth in wages, stimulate employment or increase tax rates. Other political or legal decisions mostly affect marketing strategies.

Influences on marketing strategy

Governmental decisions may have major consequences for a company's marketing strategy. Therefore, marketers should monitor laws and regulations governing, among other things, product safety, product labelling, packaging, communication with customers, transportation or trade restrictions. New import restrictions or a ban on the use of certain raw materials (such as tropical hardwood), for example, can lead to declining demand for particular products, and increased demand for alternatives (such as PVC window frames). This change in the competitive situation may well call for a change in marketing strategies. Hence, when developing product, promotion, price or distribution strategies, companies need to be aware of laws and regulations that curb or regulate the use of certain marketing instruments. Here, too, each change in these laws and regulations can be considered an opportunity – or a threat.

The Danish company that makes Stimorol chewing gum tried to introduce a new package that was very similar to that of its competitor Sportlife. Although the name Stimorol was prominently displayed on the packaging, it was printed in a diagonal strip – just like on a pack of Sportlife chewing gum. The floating pieces of gum around the brand name and the colours used in the design were also quite similar. Sportlife took legal action, claiming that its trademark rights had been violated. The court ruled that, because the two products looked *confusingly similar*, Sportlife's trademark rights had indeed been *infringed*. Stimorol was given four days to withdraw all of their new packages of chewing gum from all stores. Trying to look a lot like the market leader turned out to be a brief and expensive adventure for the Danish chewing gum manufacturer.[7]

Lobbying

Companies sometimes try to influence government decisions. Through lobbying they attempt to persuade politicians to consider their interests by enacting, defeating or changing particular laws. Small firms often collaborate with other companies in their industry in a joint lobbying effort to provide the necessary facts, figures and background to legislators. If, for example, a new law forces the packaging industry to reduce its use of disposable packaging, the industry can lobby in an attempt to tone down the law, or to gain more time by getting the government to gradually phase in new regulations.

© Picstive / Shutterstock

'Ultimately, lobbying is about coming up with the right arguments,' says Sjoerd Keilholz, who lobbies for Unilever in Brussels, 'preferably as early as possible, when the European Commission is just starting to develop policy. At that stage, officials are still interested in relevant input. If you act quickly, you're at a real advantage. As long as your argument holds water, that is. You can't come up with something like, "we are against it because we're against it, and because jobs will be lost". If you do, next time you try to contact that official, they will always be in a meeting.'[8]

3.3.4 Ecological factors

Ecology is the study of the relationship between living things and their surroundings. Worldwide, there is growing interest in preserving the natural environment. Publicity generated by social activists and the environmental movement, along with stricter governmental controls and initiatives by individual companies, has increased public awareness of maintaining the ecological balance. Many people are concerned about the depletion of natural resources, clear-cutting of rain forest and pollution of the environment by the release of non-biodegradable waste or toxic substances into the atmosphere, ground and water supply. The BP Deepwater Horizon oil spill in the Gulf of Mexico serves as a stark reminder of the high level of responsibility many major corporations shoulder in protecting and preserving the natural environment.

Today, when developing strategy, companies are more likely than ever to weigh the impact of their actions on the natural surroundings, taking into consideration what are known as ecological or physical factors. Frequently, a manager's performance is evaluated, in part, on their handling of environmental issues. On one hand, this environmental consciousness is driven by a company's need to protect its own interests. No firm wants to be associated with irresponsible use of scarce natural resources, or with noise, air, water and soil pollution. Furthermore, companies cannot pass on to their customers the rising cost of materials that are harmful to the environment or the cost of waste disposal, if the resulting price increases would undermine their *competitive position*. Increasingly accurate *measurement methods* make it easier to assess the effect of potentially harmful business activities on the natural environment. Therefore, many managers closely monitor ecological factors.

Green marketing

Despite many companies' sincere intent to be more socially responsible with respect to the environment – often referred to as a green marketing strategy or going 'green' – it is not always clear what action is best. *McDonald's* decision to stop using polystyrene foam containers for packaging its hamburgers and to use paper containers instead was based on evidence that chemicals used in producing polystyrene harmed the environment. However, recent studies have suggested that deforestation to obtain raw materials for paper production is potentially more destructive to the environment, and that use of foam containers may be less damaging than using paper containers. Still, McDonald's, citing its commitment to recycling, will stick with paper.

Some banks, such as HSBC and ABN Amro, study the environmental impact of projects they help finance. Another company espousing such a proactive policy is *Body Shop*. This global retailer of cosmetics and hair care products displays information about environmental issues – such as rainforest destruction and ozone depletion – in all of its stores and allows employees to spend five days a year engaging in environmental activism and other work in the community.[9] Firms in all kinds of industries invest heavily in the development of alternative raw materials, energy-efficient production processes or environmentally friendly products.

Image Asset Management

Environmental movement

Greenpeace and other organizations involved in the environmental movement have done much to raise awareness of environmental issues. Not only do these activists identify problems, but they also try to educate the public about social responsibility in corporate decision-making. In recent years, these organizations have been less inclined to appeal to the government, and choose, instead, to focus directly on the polluter. Businesses, ranging from major corporations to small enterprises, are seeking ways to provide for today's needs and wants without depleting valuable resources required by future generations. Marketing decision makers understand that they can make a difference.

While pressure to conform to safer and more sustainable production practices limits certain opportunities, it opens up new avenues for product and services innovation. Energy-efficient appliances, recyclable products and environmentally friendly packaging have all been developed in response to ecological concerns.

3.3.5 Technological factors

Rapid technological advancement in recent years has helped generate many innovations. New products and services – such as sophisticated smart phones, tablet computers and ever increasing Internet use – have changed consumers' lifestyles forever. And, in the business sector, high-performance software, telecommunications connections and robots have enabled organizations to increase their efficiency and effectiveness in producing and marketing new products by leaps and bounds.

When a better product or procedure is found, it is called *innovation*. Although innovations are facilitated by technology, the two terms have different meanings. *Technology*, by definition, is a country's or industry's accumulated competence to provide goods and services for people; in other words, it is the *application* of knowledge and new methods that makes it possible to develop new products, solve problems and perform tasks more efficiently. Therefore, when analyzing technological factors or the technological environment, we don't just consider product technology, but also the extent to which the existing infrastructure (including the availability of trained employees) allows us to apply technology, for example in streamlining the production process.

Technology and marketing

Our society is characterized by steady technological changes. These can fundamentally transform the customer's consumption pattern. More than any other force in the external environment, technological breakthroughs may bring about revolutionary changes in an industry, leaving many companies stranded. In the end, a company's market share and profitability are closely related to its efforts to stay abreast of new developments in technology and to use them at an early stage to strengthen its competitive position.

From a marketing perspective, new technologies can lead to:

→ New *production methods* (such as robots in the automobile industry), allowing for the production of smaller series and lower retail prices.

→ *Improvement* of existing products (such as portable GPS car navigation systems).

→ The development of *new products* (mobile phones with extra functions, such as touch screen and GPRS).

→ Better *services* (telephone calls made over the Internet).

→ *Efficient distribution systems* (automated inventory management and ordering procedures – thanks to barcodes and scanning equipment – in retailing).

→ New *markets* (biotechnology) and improved marketing techniques (such as *database marketing*).

Timing is everything

There are two types of motives to develop completely new products. With a demand-pull or market-pull strategy, the customers' needs – and the attempts to satisfy them – activate the search for a technological innovation that will lead to better products. Automobile manufacturers have developed clean, energy-efficient (hybrid car) engines because of market demand. The opposite approach is a technology push strategy, in which breakthroughs in technology (such as those made for space exploration) motivate product developers to look for a suitable application in the consumer market. This is how mobile phones came about. Usually, *market-oriented* technological innovation processes – which are initiated by unmet customer needs and wants – are most likely to succeed.

Either way, innovation enables companies to overcome competitive barriers to entering new markets and to compete successfully by offering buyers a better solution to their problems. Thanks to improved technology, marketers can now, faster than ever, give customers what they are looking for, often customized to their unique requirements. Speed of service, high quality and a customer-oriented approach are increasingly valued and expected by consumers, now that the cost of technology is rapidly falling and price becomes less of an issue. Thus even established products are constantly improved, as in the case of cars now offered with GPS navigation systems that use satellite technology to help drivers locate their destinations.

We live in a period of spectacular technological change. As managers, in monitoring the technological environment, we begin by identifying relevant technologies that are close to the end of their *life cycles*. At the same time we try to predict which new technological developments – inside and outside of our industry – will significantly affect society, the market or our company and in what way. This will help us to weigh the benefits of a new technology against the costs of converting to it.

The right *timing* is essential in this assessment. Since new technologies are often **substitutes** for existing ones, the 'old' (and possibly improved) technology will continue to be used for some time. It will certainly be used as long as the new technology is not yet widely available, or innovations are showing 'teething troubles'. In practice, however, a successful technological breakthrough quickly brings other technologies and innovations within reach. This reduces the life span of product innovations, so investments must be recovered rapidly. Hence, companies should not unnecessarily delay the application of new technologies.

We should not only apply promising new technologies as soon as possible, but also outline strategies to seize marketing opportunities and deal with threats (such as the introduction of substitutes). The real challenge is to make every innovation *user-friendly* from the start, so potential buyers will readily accept it.

3.3.6 *Sociocultural factors*

The last range of influences we consider in a macroenvironmental analysis is that of **sociocultural factors**. These consist of people and their customs, values and behavioural norms that are learned and shared in society, as well as its institutions. Of course, they vary from one country to another, but always influence consumers' life style and consumption habits.

The social component of the social-cultural factors partly portrays the characteristics of a certain society, such as its educational levels, size, age distribution, birth rate and migration patterns of the population, as summarized in this chapter's section on the demographic environment. The cultural element, to which we will turn our focus first, involves people's values and norms of behaviour. Both social and cultural influences strongly affect marketing decisions, because they determine what is desirable and set limits for what is considered acceptable in a society.

Behavioural norms and values

The standards and values of a society are deeply rooted in its culture, and have considerable impact on its citizens' attitudes and behaviour. People's **values** include not only their beliefs, likes and dislikes, but also prejudices that influence their world view. When analyzing these influences to assess their effect on marketing strategies, we make a distinction between primary and secondary cultural values.

Primary cultural values influence people's attitudes towards marriage, sexuality, children, religion and work ethic. These social standards and values are relatively stable. They change, but only in the long term. An example is the trend that men, particularly in dual-income families with young children, are becoming more active in running the household. When it comes to caretaking, working and studying, the male and female roles are converging. Marketers are responding to this development by defining new market segments and targeting them with special advertising campaigns. They understand the importance of values as a justification for purchases and use those values as a basis for effective marketing communication.

Secondary cultural values change much faster. These values directly influence how consumers view brands, and what products and services they use. They are expressed through clothing choices, how leisure time is spent and eating habits. Here, too, the culture or subculture sets a standard for how people should behave. Marketing research can offer useful leads to help companies respond with effective marketing strategies.

A *subculture* is a separate group within a particular society that preserves its own unique values and lifestyle. Their norms and values are often referred to as *ethnic patterns*. Ethnic groups or subcultures may be based on nationality, race, religion or region. In many European countries Turkish, Moroccan and other ethnic minorities are subcultures with a strong presence. For marketers, these are potentially interesting target markets.

Consumers' behaviour and lifestyle are influenced not only by cultural, but also by *social factors*. For instance, many purchase decisions are influenced by family members, friends, neighbours, colleagues and *reference groups*; these are groups with which the consumer identifies or feels associated. There is also a relationship between consumption patterns and *social class* – although this correlation is not as clear as in the past. Analyzing the role of social class may provide useful clues for strategy development. We will come back to this in the next chapter, which discusses consumer behaviour.

Consumerism

The growing power of corporations in an affluent society, with an increasingly complex and impersonal marketplace, has led to a consumer reaction called consumerism. Consumer organizations are an important part of this movement to help consumers and protect them from business practices that infringe upon their rights. They empower the consumer and make the market more transparent. Consumer organizations also lobby the government for legislation to strengthen the consumer's position.

Marketers' reactions to consumerism vary considerably. Some companies regard it as a threat that calls for opposition. Others ignore it, hoping it will disappear. A third group views consumerism as an indication that they need to improve their relationships with customers. This positive interpretation makes sense. After all, since the objective of marketing is to stimulate exchange processes so that all parties achieve their objectives, both sellers and buyers may take the initiative in maximizing customer satisfaction.

Market-oriented managers should respond positively and proactively to feedback from the market. They should strive to make environmentally friendly products, help educate the customer, provide clear labelling and instructions, offer understandable sales contracts, create excellent service and have an effective complaint handling system. All in all, a thorough analysis of the environment can help a company to enhance and refine its customer orientation.

3.4 MARKETING ETHICS AND SOCIAL RESPONSIBILITY

Marketing-oriented managers not only adapt their strategies to the external environment, but should also gauge the impact of their decisions on the world around them. To avoid any obstacles, they should consider existing legislation, as well as ethics and social responsibility in decision-making.

In this section, we start by looking at how ethics and legislation differ from *and* complement each other. We then explore the role of ethics in decision-making and the forces influencing this process. We also examine the possible tension between 'moral choices' and a firm's business objectives. Finally, we analyze an organization's social responsibility.

PRACTITIONER'S PERSPECTIVE
Andrew Weir (ZenithOptimedia Worldwide, UK)

Andrew Weir is a Director at ZenithOptimedia Worldwide – *one of the world's leading global media agency networks. He has a global strategic planning role working with some of the company's largest clients. Previously he spent 15 years at* Saatchi & Saatchi *in London and Hong Kong working with clients such as* P&G, Mars *and* British Airways. *He can be found regularly at Heathrow Terminal 5 and occasionally on his blog (Brand Experience Matters).*

Designing Brand Experiences that Build Sustainable Brand Success
Not long ago building a successful brand was relatively straightforward: Take a good product or service and follow the four Ps of marketing. Key factors were:

→ Get your product on shelf at the right price

→ Make a great TV ad

→ Spend a decent amount on media

…then sit back and watch the sales come in.

Okay, maybe this oversimplifies things a little but the reality is that life for a brand marketer used to be a lot easier in the past than it is today.

Technology has changed the game for marketers in a number of ways. For a start it has evaporated production *barriers to entry* (cost and time) so brands can easily be copied. This makes it hard for brands to build sustainable differentiation. It has also powered the development of the *Internet* which, among other things, has given consumers an influential voice online, so if they love or hate a brand they can talk about it online. Social media like *Twitter* have turbo-charged the speed and scale at which good and particularly bad stories are spread (see the *Marketing Topper* feature in Chapter 5 for more examples).

To survive and thrive in this new world, winning brands have to recognize that they need to deliver more than just good products; they have to build a *service* around their brands in a way that their competitors will find hard to copy. It's about building a brand organization capable of consistently delivering winning *brand experience* that delights and excites the consumer. To do this requires understanding of some key questions about the marketing environment inside and outside the *brand organization*.

Brand experiences that delight drive loyalty and advocacy

Firstly it is important to define what a winning brand experience looks and feels like from the *consumers'* point of view. *Outside* questions include: What types of experiences do consumers expect? How does this differ between the various stages of a consumer's journey through the relationship with the brand (from first becoming aware of it, to purchasing and to ongoing usage of it)? What types of brand experiences should we deliver that will exceed consumer expectations? What do we need to drive *advocacy* – so that delighted consumers will tell others good stories about our brand (powered by social media)? What is the competition doing?

Secondly it is important to design an approach that ensures that the *whole organization* is delivering a consistent brand experience through every touchpoint. *Inside* questions include: What are the brand vision and values? How do we ensure that our brand promise is delivered (ideally over-delivered) at every touchpoint by all internal stakeholders – from the packaging, to the online website to the customer care line? How do we use technology and consumer information (data) to improve relationship management?

There are some brand organizations – off- and online – that do all this really well. An offline brand example in the UK is *The John Lewis Partnership*: a store group that comes top of most customer service rankings and that consistently outperforms the rest of the high street when it comes to financial results. This is due to a number of factors, but key is their strategy, based on interdependent objectives that include Partner satisfaction (it is a co-owned enterprise, so profit is shared) and a focus on the recruitment and retention of loyal customers (through trust, value honesty and behaving like good citizens). Shopping in *John Lewis* is a joy. I shop there occasionally and am always quietly delighted by the shopping experience, aided by the honesty and knowledge of their staff. Their 'bricks and mortar' business success is starting to be very effectively delivered online.

A great online brand example is *Amazon*. They consistently deliver powerful brand experiences online that are second to none. I bought my wife a *Kindle* for Christmas. Six months later it broke. I went online, clicked on the relevant button and got a phone call from them immediately. The person knew who I was, had my history to hand and efficiently arranged to send an instant replacement. *Amazon*'s vision is to be Earth's most *customer-centric* company; to build a place where people can come to find and discover anything they might want to buy online. They deliver this by being committed to great service and through smart use of consumer data.

The benefit of delivering brand experiences that delight is that it drives loyalty and advocacy. It isn't complicated. Happy consumers tend to buy again and maybe even tell their friends – a powerful combination that all brand marketers should strive for.[10]

3.4.1 Legislation versus ethics

Among the many people in commercial professions, there is a handful that disregards the laws and codes of conduct that apply to marketing. Unfortunately, because this minority receives a lot of press coverage, it significantly influences public opinion about marketing and marketing research.

Governments worldwide have enacted laws that help put an end to abuse in marketing practices. This has led to tighter controls on business and greater protection of consumers' rights. However, we must make a distinction between the law and ethics, because the two are far from synonymous. As an illustration, activists may claim (rightly or wrongly) that some corporate decisions are socially unacceptable, antisocial or unethical – yet, these decisions could be completely lawful.

Ethics can be defined as the personal standards, values and (moral) principles that affect a person's actions and decisions. Or, more loosely, as someone's deeply rooted sense of what is right and wrong. When facing a moral dilemma, ethics provide guidelines for making a fair decision.

Legislation is not inherently ethical, and not all ethical conduct is described in laws. In fact, chances of engaging in dubious practices are likely to increase if people believe that they are (morally) entitled to base their actions on legal loopholes. Ethics (beliefs about what is right and wrong) transcend legislation, and they are especially important for issues that are *not* regulated in detail by the law. Therefore, an ethical code of conduct can offer valuable guidelines for decision-makers. In addition to an industry's self-regulation, monitoring by independent professional organizations helps ensure that companies regularly assess their marketing policies in light of both legal and ethical criteria. We will first qualify our definition of ethics in a global and corporate context and then take a specific look at *marketing ethics*.

3.4.2 Ethics and marketing

Making a profit may be the primary goal in business, but discussions of right and wrong are increasingly common in firms – from the boardroom to the shop floor – as well as in higher education. Often, these philosophical debates quickly turn to the ethical aspects of business decisions.

An action can only be considered ethical if it is in line not only with the prevailing *legislation* and *social* standards (not laid down by law), but also with a person's own *ethical* principles. This last assessment is important, because a country's laws only cover the most basic ethical issues and societal interests that can be enforced by the courts. Ethics, on the other hand, are moral principles and values held by an individual, although they can also apply to an organization.

Conflicts about ethics

Conflicts about ethics arise not only as a result of differences of opinion, but also – internationally – because of different culturally inspired interpretations in various countries. Because ethics are relative, not absolute, what might be considered acceptable behaviour in, for instance, Japan (such as offering monetary incentives to an intermediary to have them distribute your product) is inappropriate or even illegal in other countries. Thus, the perception of what constitutes ethical behaviour partly depends on the generally accepted norms of a particular society.

Conflicts about ethics may also occur between a manager and the *organization* for which they work. Moral principles and standards are personal, but they can also apply, based on a particular agreement, to a *group* (such as a board of directors or a certain industry). An employee's personal convictions as to what is ethical may differ from the company's view. For example, a manager may tell one of their sales representatives to lie about the delivery date of a product to a customer on the phone. Conflicts about ethics are, indeed, prevalent at all levels in an organization.

Marketing ethics

Although conflicts about ethics are common in all professions, here we are primarily concerned with marketing ethics. Marketing ethics are the principles and ethical standards that establish guidelines for decision-making and acceptable behaviour in marketing. We will look into the perception of 'acceptable' behaviour as well as the factors that influence this behaviour.

If we must make a decision and are not certain whether to follow our own ethical standards or those of the firm, we are faced with an *ethical conflict*. Research shows that the norms and values of the organization tend to have a greater impact on marketing decisions than an employee's personal convictions.

Ethics are a hot topic in business and are discussed regularly in the marketing literature. Its very nature makes marketing a field charged with ethical issues. This can be attributed to the fact that marketing is inextricably linked with public opinion – marketers are responsible for communicating with stakeholders, as well as for informing and persuading potential customers. Because the subject of marketing is widely misunderstood, it has become a target for social critics who see fit to condemn business ethics. Therefore, it is important for every marketer to have extensive insight into ethical behaviour.

3.4.3 Insight into ethical behaviour

In business, marketers often face *ethical dilemmas*, situations in which they must choose between options that, although not easy to assess, are not equally ethical. Conflicting interests may complicate the evaluation process and the ultimate choice. The importance of greater profits or greater market share can, for example, pressure the marketer to prematurely launch a product that has not been fully tested or found to be totally safe. A moral

© szefei / Shutterstock

choice – doing the right thing – often costs the company money and may be at odds with its short-term business objectives. Ethics extend beyond marketing and may involve a wide range of issues from insider trading or age discrimination, to tax evasion and air pollution.

One of Shell's top executives, Jean-Marie van Engelshoven, was once faced with an ethical dilemma when a large oil field was discovered in the rainforest of Gabon – a relatively poor country, at least by Western standards. 'It was impossible to get to the oil without disturbing the rainforest. But we could limit the number of trees to be cut down to a minimum and replant the forest. Nevertheless, some folks protest against any loss of the rainforest. Considering the benefits of developing the oil field – not only for Shell, but also for Gabon, which gets 87 per cent of the proceeds – you wonder if this kind of purist attitude is really ethical.'[11]

Figure 3.5 illustrates that a manager's ethical behaviour and moral principles are influenced by three factors: the overall culture and norms of society, the industry practices in a country's business sector and the corporate culture and expectations of the company or employer.[12]

Society

As will be discussed in the next chapter, a *culture* is the set of standards, values, ideas and attitudes transmitted from one generation to the next. Culture not only influences the

FIGURE 3.5 Influences on ethical behaviour

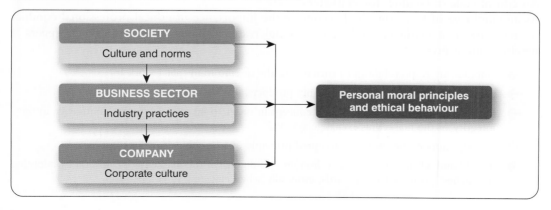

relationships between individuals, groups and (business) organizations in a society, but also dictates what is morally right or wrong. Hence, an individual's moral standards are shaped by the society's culture and norms. This also explains why people in different cultures have different attitudes towards marketing practices.

One example is the unauthorized use of legally protected brand names, patents and copyrights in countries like Korea, Mexico and Taiwan. Because of an unwritten rule in the Korean culture that 'everyone is free to take advantage of other people's ideas', virtually no one is prosecuted for infringing these rights. This unauthorized and illegal use of intellectual property results in estimated losses of more than 40 billion euros per year to American companies in the music, software and movie industries alone!

The business sector

Anyone working in a particular country is guided by the generally accepted rules of business, which – as *codes of conduct* in an industry – determine the boundaries between competitive and unethical behaviour.[13] To gain a sense of what is morally acceptable in global business, we must look at the rules of the game through the 'cultural lens' of each particular country, because perceptions and customs in business vary widely from one nation to another.

For example, in international trade, particularly in high-tech industries, it is not uncommon for companies to rely on economic espionage, illegally obtaining trade secrets or confidential information about competitors. They may also resort to bribing government officials to get them to issue permits without delay. These bribes (just like kickbacks in business-to-business marketing to win or retain business) are usually disguised as consultant fees or business gifts. The less economically developed a country is and the more intense the competition in an industry, the greater the likelihood of unethical behaviour.

The company

A third influence on the ethical behaviour of managers is the company's **corporate culture**: the norms, ideas and values that the members of an organization share, which influence their attitudes as individuals and their behaviour in a group context. Corporate culture is expressed in the way that people think and communicate, in the relationships they maintain and in the style of management. And, it includes norms for ethical behaviour for all managers and co-workers.

To influence the standards and expectations for ethical behaviour of employees, companies may develop a *code of conduct* (also called *code of ethics*). In the United States nine out of every ten large companies have such a formal statement of ethical principles and rules of conduct, a formal code of conduct that defines this aspect of their corporate culture. An example of a possible code of ethics for marketers is shown below.

An ethical code of conduct for marketers

As an employee of Company X, I recognize the importance of ethical professional conduct in my work as a marketer, and of my special responsibilities to society and my peers. I hereby commit myself to:

→ embrace my responsibilities to society and the organization that I work for;

→ paint a clear and honest picture of my products, services and ideas;

→ improve insight into the marketing concept in order to increase consumer confidence in the integrity of the marketing exchange system;

→ actively support the generally accepted principle of free choice for the consumer;

→ uphold and advance the integrity, honour and dignity of the marketing profession by adopting the highest professional standards, especially when engaging in competition.

PROFESSOR'S PERSPECTIVE
Ronald Jeurissen (Nyenrode Business Universiteit, the Netherlands)

At first glance it looks like the recent recession has pushed the subject of corporate social responsibility off the boardroom agenda. But according to Professor Ronald Jeurissen, who teaches business ethics at Nyenrode Business Universiteit in the Netherlands, nothing could be further from the truth. He tells companies that don't take it seriously to address the issue soon, or they'll be in real trouble...

When the economy starts to wane, many companies focus on two priorities: increasing sales and cutting costs. But they also pay attention to corporate social responsibility. 'It may not be their number one priority, but many companies still have it on their top ten list,' says Ronald Jeurissen. 'Every time a corporate scandal makes headlines, we are all reminded of the importance of corporate social responsibility.

With the negative publicity on child labour and sweat shops in developing countries, companies have become more careful about choosing their suppliers. Executives realize that the socially responsible image they want to project extends beyond the gates of their own factory or firm.

Although many companies try to be socially responsible, relatively little progress is being made. Businesses primarily want to avoid a negative image, instead of creating an organization that systematically employs corporate social responsibility as a strategic marketing instrument. Rather than positioning themselves as pioneers in this field, organizations are concerned that such an approach will hurt their image by making them look 'soft' and vulnerable.

Jeurissen admits that corporate social responsibility is not exactly consistent with the traditional image of business. 'Creating a new perception may add an emotional dimension to the brand, in terms of how it is experienced. But companies need to consider whether this new image is appropriate. For example, many retail organizations are great in assuming corporate social responsibility, but are not eager to emphasize this in their marketing communication, because it may not fit in with their image as a straightforward and inexpensive retailer. On the other hand, other companies, like banks, try to outdo each other in portraying themselves as socially responsible, fearing that they may lose their *Unique Selling Proposition* with their target market.'

Companies should help the customer make a logical connection between their corporate social responsibility and the product attributes

The real breakthrough will come when *consumers* start considering the manufacturer's track record in corporate social responsibility when making buying decisions. 'Social responsibility is usually not a key factor in wanting to buy a certain product. You buy a lipstick because it enhances your appearance. Positive and negative associations – such as whether or not it has been tested on animals – play a role, but only a minor one. The trick is to link the intrinsic product attributes to corporate social responsibility in the company's communication. We now see marketers looking for effective ways to incorporate this value in their *branding*, like *Kuyichi* does in marketing its clothing. So when you sell coffee, it is not enough to say that the coffee is delicious and that the coffee bean farmers have been paid a fair price. No. You have to stress that this particular coffee is especially delicious because the farmers have been able to devote a lot more time to it. In other words, you help the customer make a *logical connection* between your corporate social responsibility and the product attributes.'

Having said that, Jeurissen also acknowledges that many consumers don't care whether products have been produced in a socially and environmentally responsible way. 'Some people are just not interested; they simply want the lowest price. Then there is a substantial group of consumers who do consider it in most of their purchasing decisions, because they perceive social responsibility as being consistent with their self-image. One reason the Toyota Prius is doing well as a hybrid car is that it *combines* reliability with protecting the environment. There are many consumers for whom this product is completely consistent with their self-image. But this approach did not work for marketing gasoline. Shell Pura did not sell; V-Power does. So green gasoline did not fly, but it seems that many drivers are clearly willing to pay more money for fast gasoline.'

Companies that want to become more socially responsible should be aware of the pitfalls. 'A common mistake is to start putting it into people's faces, how responsible they are, before everything has even been put into motion. That can get you into trouble real fast,' says Jeurissen. 'The point is that the outside world is always setting higher standards. Take Body Shop, for example. There are journalists who seem to enjoy bringing a company like that down, and they make it their mission to do so. So if you stick out your neck and put the spotlights on yourself you can win, but you can also lose.'

In spite of the risks that the marketing environment brings along with it, Professor Jeurissen is convinced that sooner or later, all companies will have to be socially responsible. 'Today, companies can still make a USP out of it. But it won't be long before it is a *dissatisfier* – if you don't act responsibly, you stand out in a negative way. And that will happen before you know it!'[14]

No one can tell someone else what does or does not qualify as ethical behaviour. Ultimately, people are individually responsible for decisions that involve ethical issues. Ethical dilemmas may arise unexpectedly during a meeting or negotiation process. The only way to prepare for this is to consciously determine our own ethical boundaries ahead of time.

3.4.4 *Social responsibility*

Compelled by public opinion, companies are now paying more attention than ever before to ethical behaviour and corporate social responsibility. Although the concepts of business ethics and social responsibility are sometimes used interchangeably, they have distinct meanings.

As already established, the term ethics refers to someone's attitudes and behaviour in individual or group decisions that require the right choice. Hence, ethics involve – usually individually based – judgments about what is right or wrong in a specific decision-making context (often a dilemma). *Social responsibility* on the other hand is a broader concept. It is concerned with the (marketing) decisions of an organization and the effects of those decisions on society. As was discussed in Chapter 1, as a management philosophy this is also known as the *societal marketing concept*. This means that, in addition to implementing the marketing concept, the company also considers the side effects of its exchange processes and activities in the long term.

In marketing, social responsibility refers to an organization's obligation to maximize its positive impact and minimize its negative impact on society. The best way of doing this is to pay *equal* attention to the concerns of all of its stakeholders.

© Nolte Lourens / Shutterstock

Four dimensions of social responsibility

A company's social responsibility is made up of four dimensions. These are the economic, legal, ethical and philanthropic aspects of doing business. Figure 3.6 shows these dimensions in the so-called pyramid of corporate social responsibility.[15]

The *economic* dimension – as the foundation of business – states that a company must strive to be profitable. The company can then provide a return on investment to its owners and shareholders, create jobs for the community, and contribute products and services to the economy. The *legal* dimension dictates that marketers are expected to obey laws and regulations. They simply must play by the rules of the game.

While the economic and legal responsibilities are well accepted in business, ethical and philanthropic issues have only recently been gaining more recognition. The *ethical*

FIGURE 3.6 The pyramid of corporate social responsibility

dimension embraces the concept that companies are obligated to avoid harm and should do what is right, just and fair. Ethical marketing decisions create trust and help build long-term marketing relationships. Finally, at the top of the corporate pyramid are *philanthropic* social responsibilities, which go beyond marketing ethics. Although these are not required of a company, they do promote human welfare and, as long as they are done subtly, they generate goodwill among customers.

Many companies take a strategic approach to corporate philanthropy and link their products and services to a specific social cause. This is known as cause-related marketing. For example, Shell has set up a charitable institution (the *Shell Foundation*) that donates money to humanitarian projects, such as constructing hospitals and schools in developing countries, reducing air pollution in large cities in Latin America and building greenhouses for poor farmers in China. By working to improve people's lives, this Anglo-Dutch multinational seeks to position itself as a socially responsible corporation.

Importance of social responsibility for marketing

In many organizations, it is the marketer's responsibility to carefully define the company's relationships, functions and obligations with respect to society. As externally oriented managers, they recognize that the long-term value of doing business in a socially responsible manner far outweighs short-term costs. It may also increase the company's competitive advantage. Research has shown that when quality, service and price are equal among competitors; most consumers prefer to buy from the company with the best reputation for social responsibility. And if consumers *boycott* certain products, it is often because the company is suspected of dubious practices.[16]

Society is made up of various groups with diverse, oftentimes opposing, interests. This makes it impossible to determine what society as a whole wants. Moreover, from a financial perspective, it is simply not feasible to meet all identified needs, since many of society's demands impose costs. For instance, society wants a cleaner environment and wants to protect nature, but it also wants low-priced products. Some companies are able to satisfy the wants and needs of environmentally conscious consumers with *green marketing*, which involves developing and marketing 'green' products that do not harm the natural environment. Think of the efforts of Toyota, Honda and Ford to develop hybrid vehicles that use partly electric motors to improve fuel economy without reducing power.

The fact remains that demand for ecologically friendly products comes largely from consumers in a relatively small, environmentally conscious segment. Hence, most marketers perform the necessary analyses before they decide to target this segment. They have to evaluate the extent to which consumers are willing to pay for what they want. All in all, making socially responsible decisions is a real challenge for the marketer who, at the same time, is expected to help the company achieve its other objectives.

SUMMARY

1   Internal versus external environment

Experienced marketers know that market-driven and other environmental forces influence how successful their company will be in the marketplace. They also realize that their marketing strategies must be carried out in an ever-changing marketing environment. Anticipating important developments in this environment and responding to them effectively is one of the marketer's key tasks. This is quite a challenging task, since the marketing environment is very complex. It is made up of an internal and an external environment.

The marketing manager's *internal environment* is the 'rest' of the organization – departments or functional areas other than marketing (such as production, purchasing and R&D) as well as the available (financial, technical and human) re-sources. This internal environment can be con-trolled to a great extent by top management and can at least be influenced by the marketer. To avoid conflicts in the organization, the marketing strategies must be aligned with those of the other departments – all of which have their own interests and responsibilities. Of course, any strategy should also be implemented within the constraints of the limited available resources.

The *external environment* involves the major forces of society, originating outside of the organization. These elements are uncontrollable, yet have a great impact on the company's performance. The marketer's external environ-ment includes various groups (such as custo-mers, suppliers and competitors) in the immedi-ate or *mesoenvironment*, as well as relevant (demographic, economic and technological) developments in the *macroenvironment*. In an environmental analysis and diagnosis we decide which of the most relevant forces (depending on their importance and urgency) represent oppor-tunities or threats.

2   Players in the mesoenvironment

The immediate or mesoenvironment is made up of several parties in the *sector* in which the firm operates. In this part of the external environment there are five players with which the company interacts. First of all, any marketing-oriented organization nurtures an ongoing relationship with its *customers*. These may be customers in consumer and industrial markets, but also in intermediary and institutional markets.

When it comes to the quality, price and availa-bility of the goods and materials it needs to purchase, the firm is dependent on its *suppliers*. For buying these supplies, as well as for marketing its products and services, it may use *intermediaries* who create utility by bridging the differences in quantity, time, place and product assortment between production and consumption.

Competitors are the fourth party in the mesoen-vironment. A comprehensive competitive analysis not only focuses on competing brands and products, but also identifies generic and need competition. Finally, financial institutions, the media, government institutions, special interest groups and other *stakeholders* also influence how the company is run. Therefore, management should maintain an excellent relationship with these groups.

3   Macroenvironmental variables

Usually, macroenvironmental factors cannot be con-trolled or influenced. In strategy development, a com-pany should consider *demographic* forces (such as the increasing number of households), *economic* circumstances (consumer confidence, competition), *political-legal* factors (subsidies, legislation) and the *ecological* environment (pollution, the environmental movement).

Technological developments (such as wide availability of the Internet) and *social-cultural* factors (behavioural norms and values) also affect a firm's strategy. Opportunities and threats may be the result of macroenvironmental influences on the entire market (an economic expansion making the market grow) or just on the company itself (such as a new law that affects the company's exports).

4   Marketing ethics and social responsibility

Besides assessing how macroenvironmental factors will affect strategy, managers must also consider the impact of their decisions on the world around them. This is particularly important in the case of *ethical dilemmas* and issues that are not completely addressed by a country's laws. Managers will then have to base their decisions on their own ethical standards and values, on a personal conviction of what is right and wrong. In practice, a person's moral philosophy and ethical behaviour are influenced by *society*, by the industry practices and codes of conduct of the *business sector* and by the *corporate culture* of the company for which they work. Ethical behaviour is in the eye of the beholder, but it is usually behaviour that meets generally accepted norms of a society.

An organization cannot avoid its social respon-sibility. In addition to the widely acknowledged economic and legal principles, the pyramid of *corporate social responsibility* also includes an ethical dimension and philanthropic activities. In the long run, the benefits of ethical and socially responsible decisions far outweigh the short-term costs.

DISCUSSION QUESTIONS

1 How would you explain some companies' conservative approach in a dynamic environment, and how can this problem be solved?

2 How does the concept of the 'internal environment' conflict with the underlying ideas of the marketing concept?

3 Why is the consumer not considered to be part of the supply chain?

4 Comment on the following statement: 'By systematically gathering information about the meso- and macroenvironment, by also including generic competition in competitive analyses and, if necessary, by adapting its strategy to the marketing environment, a company assures itself long-term success.'

5 Why are demographic shifts in society important for business?

6 Consumers are increasingly concerned about the environment. In light of this trend, what suggestions – in terms of strategy development – would you offer a producer of plastic shopping bags selling these products to chain stores?

7 Give a few examples of technological innovations that have had huge benefits for marketers. Also give an example of the negative impact of a technological breakthrough.

8 What are the most important criteria for a company to consider when deciding whether or not to switch to a new technology in its production process?

9 A recent Gallup Poll study showed that, as a profession, marketing is perceived as being relatively low on the 'ethical ladder'. How would you explain this?

10 Explain the concept of corporate culture and how it may influence decisions made in a company.

PART TWO
ANALYZING THE MARKET

In Part 1 of this book we learned about marketing and a customer-oriented approach. Now, we turn our attention to the market itself. Identifying and systematically analyzing the market to be served is one of the manager's main tasks in creating any marketing program. The bottom line is that a manager can only develop a successful strategy – no matter in what area of marketing – with a thorough understanding of buyer behaviour.

Chapter 4 focuses on the customer. Here we ask what really motivates consumers and how we can influence their buying decisions. We will also examine how companies focusing on other firms – as business-to-business marketers – analyze their customers' behaviour before developing a strategy. Because the best marketing decisions are always based on reliable information, in Chapter 5 we examine the role of marketing research in planning and strategy development. Finally, in Chapter 6, we study the process of dividing the market into segments, selecting a suitable target market and developing an effective positioning strategy.

4 Buying behaviour

5 Marketing research and marketing information

6 Market segmentation and positioning

CHAPTER 4
BUYING BEHAVIOUR

LEARNING GOALS

After studying this chapter you will be able to:

1 **Outline the stages in the purchase decision process**

2 **Identify the types of orientation and buying behaviour used by the consumer**

3 **Understand how a person's lifestyle and other personal characteristics affect his behaviour as a consumer**

4 **Describe which psychological factors influence purchase decisions**

5 **Explain the importance of culture, family, friends and other social forces affecting buying decisions**

6 **Recognize how consumers and organizations are similar and different in their buying behaviours**

4.1 The purchase decision process
4.2 Types of orientation and buying behaviour
4.3 Impact of personal circumstances
4.4 Psychological influences on consumer decisions
4.5 Social influences on consumer behaviour
4.6 Business-to-business marketing

FIGURE 4.1 The black box model of decision-making

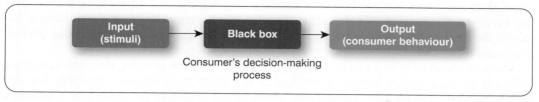

It is seldom possible to know, with certainty, what underlies an individual's behaviour, but we can infer a consumer's motives from their observable activities. If the buying decision process is not further explored through marketing research, a **black box** model may be used. This model simply indicates that something unperceivable, such as the consumer's mental processing, is occurring in a 'black box'. As can be seen in Figure 4.1, the only variables in this (not very informative) model are the – often visible – stimuli on the *input* side (such as the websites that are consulted) and the consumer's explicit or measurable behavioural response (such as a purchase) on the *output* side.[2] In this chapter, however, by drawing on the various disciplines that can be used to analyze and explain consumer behaviour, we will also shed light on the inside of the black box. Finally, we take a close look at the best ways for companies to approach other organizations – as buyers of their products and services – and how consumer marketing and *business-to-business marketing* differ from each other.

4.1 THE PURCHASE DECISION PROCESS

We begin our analysis of **consumer behaviour** by examining the *purchase decision process*, or series of stages the consumer goes through when deciding to buy a product or use a service. As Figure 4.2 illustrates, it is a five-stage process consisting of problem recognition, information gathering, alternative evaluation, the purchase decision and post-purchase evaluation.

The consumer's decision-making process begins long before they decide to buy something, and it continues after the purchase. Needless to say, the decision process does not always result in a purchase. The consumer can interrupt the process at any point, in which case there will be fewer than five stages. Either way, the very first step is recognizing a need, desire or problem.

4.1.1 Problem recognition

The purchase decision process begins when the consumer experiences a need, a want or a problem. This problem recognition phase may be initiated by *marketing efforts* – such as advertisements, in-store demonstrations or attractive offers on websites. In other cases a physiological stimulus (such as thirst), or envy – the desire to have something that someone else

FIGURE 4.2 The consumer purchase decision process

has – may be the decisive factor. For example, a person may feel that it is time to get a new car if their neighbour has just bought a dazzling new Porsche 911 Turbo S, or if their own car keeps breaking down. Whatever the stimulus, perceiving a *problem* – a difference between the ideal and the actual state of affairs – may well trigger the decision-making process that leads to a purchase.

Problem recognition is a crucial step in the decision-making process, since the consumer will only proceed if they identify a problem or if a latent need becomes manifest. For this reason, successful marketers continuously research the problems or needs that consumers experience to determine what will stimulate them to look for information about possible solutions (such as the purchase of a better product).

4.1.2 Information gathering

The consumer does not always know exactly what products will satisfy their needs and wants – or even if those products exist. This is something they have to find out. They may deliberately search for information about available brands, how much they cost, how they differ from each other and where to buy them. Even the warranty conditions may be of interest.

This information-seeking stage begins with a cognitive internal search – the consumer scans their memory to see what they already knows about the product or service. Consumers are rarely even aware that they go through this process, especially for frequently used products like shampoo. If this internal search does not yield sufficient information on which to base a purchase decision, an external search is required. A more extensive search is particularly likely if consumers have little experience with a product, if making the wrong decision involves considerable risk and if the cost of collecting information (for instance through the Internet) is low. There are four broad sources of external information:

1 *Personal sources*, such as family members, friends and colleagues – people whom the consumer trusts. Although this information may not be accurate, it often confirms the consumer's inclination or preference.

2 *Public sources*, such as information issued by the government, unbiased articles in magazines and objective product tests conducted by consumer organizations.

3 *Commercial sources*, including advertisements, labels, advice given by sales people, displays in stores and (corporate) websites. Marketers try to make information from these sources as convincing and easily available as possible.

4 *Experiential sources*. The consumer's own experience of examining, handling or actually using the product (such as during a test drive) is often a critical factor for the remainder of the decision process.

Marketers should find out what information sources the prospects in the target market are most likely to use and the type of information that most interests them.

4.1.3 Alternative evaluation

Keeping in mind the credibility of each source of information, the consumer must decide which criteria are best for product evaluation. These are called the evaluative criteria or choice criteria. Actually, there is some overlap between this stage and the information search, because the consumer also tends to evaluate the information while they are searching for it. Hence some of the available information may be rejected, put into perspective or even misinterpreted as alternative evaluation takes place.

The evaluation phase starts off with the evoked set, or the brands that someone actually considers when making a purchase decision. Often, the evoked set is limited to only three or four brands, even if the consumer is aware of more brand names or exposed to them in the store.

The consumer will usually place the brands in the *evoked set* in a particular order. To determine the ranking within the evoked set – and, in particular, which brand should be at the top of the list – the potential buyer must first identify product features or attributes to be used in assessing the alternatives, then determine the importance of each of these criteria in the specific situation. In considering a car purchase, for example, the selection criteria may include the price, size, design and fuel consumption. When choosing a brand of beer, the selection criteria may be the taste, brand image, price and alcohol percentage.

For most purchase decisions, consumers rarely develop a formal list of criteria, ranked in order of importance. For the most part, this happens almost subconsciously. Nevertheless, consumers are still guided by a set of criteria, no matter how informally they may be compiled and ranked.

The marketer's task is to determine which criteria the consumer will use in a particular purchase decision. Will the customer even consider buying their brand? Does the brand meet the consumer's choice criteria? The company may have to develop an advertising campaign that influences the criteria used to evaluate the various purchase alternatives. An informative website or a hands-on trial can also help consumers evaluate alternatives.

4.1.4 *Purchase decision*

During the purchase decision stage the consumer makes up their mind whether or not to buy. If they do decide to buy, they also *choose* the product and brand, typically the top-rated alternative in the evaluation phase. This decision reflects their *buying intention*, or their intention to purchase the product in the near future. At this point the consumer will make additional decisions. If, for instance, they are buying a car, they will need to decide what options they want, which dealer to buy from and the payment method (leasing, payment in cash, or, when financing, the terms of the loan).

© wandee007 / Shutterstock

Situational influences – such as in the physical and social surroundings of the buyer – may, at this point, have an impact on the final choice. For example, when buying a mountain bike, the customer's preferred brand may be out of stock, in which case, rather than buying a Specialized bike, they may, based on a friend's advice in the store, consider getting a Giant – their second ranked alternative. However, if on closer inspection that brand fails to live up to their expectations, another *response* may be not to buy at all, to postpone the purchase, to go to another store or to consider lesser-known brands.

The order in which these decisions are made and the time spent on them will vary from one consumer or product to another. But the more the marketer knows about the weight of these decisions and how they relate to one another (for example, exactly *when* in the process does the buyer choose the brand and the supplier?), the better able they are to influence them.

4.1.5 *Post-purchase evaluation*

After the purchase, the buyer begins to use and evaluate the product. They determine if it, in fact, meets the *need* that prompted them to make the purchase and if the product performs well. In other words, they decide if the product or service lives up to their *expectations*.

Now, the marketer needs to determine if the customer is satisfied or dissatisfied, and why. The Customer Service department or the *call centre* can help to provide this information. Every year more than a quarter of a million consumers call Unilever with various questions and (sometimes) complaints. The dozens of nutritionists, laundry experts, beauticians and other telephone support staff offer beneficial advice. 'We look at Customer Service as a sophisticated marketing tool that is primarily concerned with *customer loyalty*,' according to an executive in charge of the Unilever Consumer Care Centre in Rotterdam.[3]

There may be several reasons why a customer is dissatisfied with a purchase. If the product is unsatisfactory, it may have to be adapted. If on the other hand, the customer's expectations were too high, as a result of the advertising campaign or an overenthusiastic sales pitch, then a revision should be made to the marketing strategy.

Cognitive dissonance

After making an important purchase, the consumer sometimes experiences *buyer's remorse* or **cognitive dissonance**: an unpleasant feeling of doubt or anxiety after making a difficult, irreversible decision. The consumer may even regret their brand choice. They are most likely to experience this feeling of post-purchase anxiety if the product was relatively expensive and if there were many similar alternatives available. This increases the risk of making a regrettable decision. Cognitive dissonance is most common if the product is conspicuous (meaning that the consumer has to 'justify' their purchase of, for example, a sports car) and if it reflects the consumer's *lifestyle* (as in the case of designer label clothing).

Implications for marketing strategy

Most consumers try to reduce or eliminate their cognitive dissonance through **rationalization**. They will emphasize the merits of the product and dismiss its drawbacks, or even ignore their own unfulfilled needs. Marketers can help recent buyers resolve cognitive dissonance in a number of ways. A portion of the promotion budget can be set aside for communicating with customers who have just bought the product. Many consumers, in fact, read more advertising about a product after buying it than they did prior to the purchase! This is because appealing pictures and statements made in the ads about a product they now own helps to reassure them that they have made the right choice.

Other firms alleviate post purchase doubt by contacting recent buyers, or by creating special toll-free telephone numbers and website links for those with questions and complaints. Finally, marketers should never make exaggerated claims about a product. By *overselling*, they simply crank up the customer's expectations and increase the likelihood of cognitive dissonance. A more sensible strategy is to ensure that the product's performance exceeds the claims made in their advertisements or by the sales staff. Liberal warranties, return policies and exceptional after-sales service can also help to demonstrate a firm's commitment to its customers. This is crucial, because an unsatisfied customer may decide to return the product, to shop elsewhere in the future or to discuss their negative experience with other potential buyers, whereas a satisfied customer usually generates positive **word-of-mouth** communication. In the long run, reducing cognitive dissonance not only increases sales, but also leads to customer loyalty.

4.2 TYPES OF ORIENTATION AND BUYING BEHAVIOUR

Consumer behaviour is a difficult topic to master. Marketers who want to predict or influence buying behaviour examine not only how consumers make choices – the essence of *buying behaviour* – but also their *information seeking* and *communication behaviour* (the preferred sources of information) and even *usage behaviour* (how they use and later dispose of the product).

Whether or not a consumer goes through each step in the purchase decision process or whether they skip or minimize one or more stages – such as searching for information and evaluating the alternatives – depends on the product and how familiar they are with it. Obviously, when buying a soft drink the consumer is less *involved* with the product than when choosing a new tablet.

As discussed in this, *Howard* and *Sheth* identify three kinds of consumer orientation and buying behaviour: **extensive problem solving, limited problem solving** and **routine problem solving**.[4] Which type of behaviour consumers engage in depends on four key variables: the product's price, the perceived risk, the purchase frequency and the degree of consumer involvement. This has implications for two other key factors: how much information they gather and how many brands they consider. *Extensive problem solving* is typical for the purchase of expensive products with a high perceived risk that are not frequently bought but quite important to buyers. On the other hand, *routine problem solving* is characteristic for frequently bought, low-priced products with a limited consumer involvement and a low perceived risk; without collecting any information, the buyer may consider only one brand. Finally, *limited problem solving* is somewhere in between these two forms of orientation and buying behaviour.

4.2.1 Extensive problem solving

If the consumer does not frequently buy a certain product or service, or has little experience with it, they will go through each step of the purchase decision process. For example, when remodelling the kitchen or buying a new car, they may want to analyze as much information as possible. This is known as **extensive problem solving**.

The customer has to explore the market to find products and brands that meet or exceed their requirements. In doing so, they also develops the choice criteria to evaluate the alternatives in their *evoked set*. They are willing to spend considerable time and effort on their complex buying process.

This **high involvement** decision-making is typical when buying *high-involvement products* – expensive items that the consumer considers personally important. The purchase (of a house, for example) involves a great deal of risk, or the product (such as jewellery) helps to express the consumer's self-image or *self-concept*. Marketers can simplify the learning process for customers in this situation by providing information about the product's main features and its benefits, as compared to competitive brands.

4.2.2 *Limited problem solving*

If the buyer already has some experience with the product and is familiar with the product category, limited problem solving will be sufficient. It is estimated that consumers make 40 per cent of purchase decisions spending limited time and effort on researching options. A limited problem solving process is often applied to frequently purchased products and services such as restaurant meals, household appliances, garden tools and furniture.

In such instances, the consumer does not have to go through all steps in the decision-making process. Typically, several brands might be evaluated using a limited number of attributes. To reduce the risk of making the wrong decision, the consumer might seek some information about unknown brands or rely on a friend to help evaluate the available options. The marketer's task is to meet the need for information and to create or enhance confidence in the brand through informative advertising or other means of communication.

4.2.3 *Routine problem solving*

At least half of the things that consumers buy are bought out of a habit, developed as a result of their experience with the product or brand. This kind of purchase decision is referred to as routine problem solving (or *routinized response behaviour*). The consumer no longer needs to think about the purchase, since they have already made up their mind about it. They believe that the various alternatives (such as different brands of fuel for their car) are very similar or they have developed a distinct preference for a certain brand (such as Red Bull energy drinks). Although they act virtually out of habit, they may sometimes try another brand for a change or may respond to a special offer.

© Tyler Olson / Shutterstock

MARKETING TOPPER
A Diamond is Forever

There are few slogans as famous as the slogan 'A Diamond is Forever'. And there are few companies that have as much hold over a market as the company that 'owns' the slogan – De Beers. 'The marketing campaign for diamonds is the best campaign that there has ever been for a commercial product,' says marketing author Jack Trout. 'De Beers took the word "forever" and turned it into a synonym for "diamond".'

During the economic crisis in the twentieth century, with falling prices and decreasing demand, things looked bleak for the diamond business. So, in 1938, De Beers launched a huge advertising effort in the United States, and commissioned Dali and Picasso to produce inspiring paintings for the campaign. The paintings had to evoke emotion – they had to portray diamonds as valuable masterpieces created by nature. But the artwork alone did not create much demand.

Something else was needed to convince consumers that a diamond was not a luxury, but an essential symbol of romance and love. The slogan 'A Diamond is Forever' (first used in 1948) associated the idea of *everlasting love* with the *enduring* quality of the diamond. 'May your happiness last as long as your diamond', read the accompanying line in 1950 – the year in which the number of marriages peaked. In 1963 De Beers was delighted to discover that 80 per cent of American brides had been given an engagement diamond.

Later campaigns focused on other memorable events, such as wedding anniversaries and the birth of a child, with diamonds as a symbol of everlasting love. They also tried to promote the diamond as a gift from a woman to a man, and as an expression of success, with the message, 'Let your wife show your success. Give her a diamond'.

Two words. One lifetime.

DE BEERS
Because a diamond is forever

OLD BOND STREET · ROYAL EXCHANGE · HARRODS · WESTFIELD
www.debeers.com 020 7758 9700

Image courtesy of The Advertising Archives

> ## Two months' salary may seem a lot ... until you divide it by forever

Another component of the marketing strategy focused on *education* of future buyers. To illustrate, the De Beers advertisements suggested that the buyer should expect to spend quite a lot of money on a diamond. 'Two months' salary may seem a lot...', begins one American advertisement, '...until you divide it by *forever*.' This strategy had the desired effect. Marketing research showed that those who were familiar with the 'two-months' salary' guideline spent an average of 60 per cent more on diamond jewellery (more than two thousand dollars) than customers who were not familiar with the slogan.

For each country De Beers developed a specially tailored marketing strategy designed to influence consumer behaviour. For example, in The Netherlands the diamond company used the slogan, 'How else do you get one month's pay to last a lifetime?' 'This kind of campaign, which tells people how much they are supposed to spend on a diamond, doesn't work as well in The Netherlands,' says advertising executive Jan Wouters, who has been the head of the *Netherlands Diamond Information Centre* for years. Yet, he has seen an increase in the acceptance of diamonds by the Dutch, who are traditionally known for their thriftiness. One in three women over the age of 16 now owns a diamond, compared with one in five 20 years ago.

De Beers made only one attempt to change its positioning strategy in the past 50 years. During the seventies, when traditional institutions such as marriage were under attack, the company introduced a slogan that said *'A Diamond is for Now,'* in an attempt to make the diamond a symbol of non-conformity. But the campaign misfired and was quickly transferred to the mausoleum of marketing failures. De Beers revived its tried and tested slogan, and has remained faithful to it ever since. Who knows? De Beers may well stick to it *forever…*[5]

The consumer buys these products without a thorough decision-making process. Some of these unplanned purchases are known as **impulse purchases**. Impulse products are typically bought on the spur of the moment, without advance planning or serious consideration, often right after the consumer notices the product on a display in the store or through some form of *Point of Sale* (POS) promotion.

Routine problem solving typifies **low-involvement** decision making. Most *fast moving consumer goods* fall in the category of *low-involvement* products. They include milk, candy and other low-priced, frequently purchased items. Marketers of these products must make sure to keep their current customers satisfied – by offering consistent quality, wide availability and good service. Having done so, they can then work on expanding the firm's customer base by improving these products and by offering them through eye-catching promotions.

4.3 IMPACT OF PERSONAL CIRCUMSTANCES

So far we have looked at the five steps in the consumer decision-making process and at different kinds of orientation and buying behaviour. Now we turn our attention to a number of factors that *influence* consumer behaviour. As can be seen in the top part of Figure 4.3, these influences involve personal circumstances, psychological factors and social factors.

FIGURE 4.3 A model of consumer behaviour

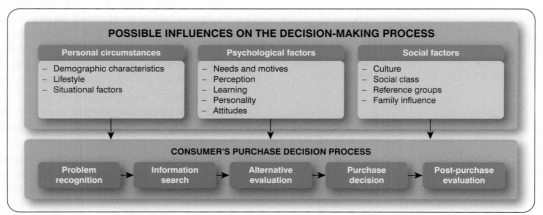

Although each individual's personal circumstances are unique, all consumer behaviour is influenced by personal circumstances, including demographic characteristics, the consumer's *lifestyle* and situational factors. These factors may well determine which products and services consumers buy.

4.3.1 Demographic characteristics

The buying process is influenced by a person's age, gender, race, marital status and religion. Other demographic characteristics, such as educational level, profession, income and family size also affect decision making. For instance, the consumer's age partly determines their thinking on certain topics, their social network and their general interests. Income can also be a major factor in certain purchases. Consumers with limited financial resources may have to go through a more extensive problem-solving process to make the best choice than buyers with a relatively high income, who can simply choose the highest quality.

4.3.2 Lifestyle

Lifestyle is a way of living characterized by consumers'

→ *Activities* – how they spend time and money.

→ *Interests* – what they consider important in the environment.

→ *Opinions* – what they think of themselves and the world around them.

In consumer research, an individual's *Activities* (such as work, hobbies and sports), *Interests* (for example, in family, society and fashion) and *Opinions* (about politics, culture and the future, among other topics) – all of which identify their lifestyle – are known as the AIO variables.

Usually, a person's lifestyle will reflect their *self-image* or self-concept; how they see themself and how they believe other people perceive them. Here, we make a distinction between a person's self-image in terms of how they actually are (real self concept or *actual self*) and their self-image in terms of how they would *like* to be viewed (ideal self concept). To a great extent, people determine their own lifestyles, although their choices are obviously influenced by their unique *personalities* and their demographic characteristics (such as their age and income).

An analysis of people's lifestyles, called *psychographics*, provides marketers with valuable insights into consumer behaviour. Psychographics (literally, 'describing the mind') combines psychology, demographics and lifestyle to reveal a person's motivations for buying and using certain products and services. From psychographics we know that the consumer's lifestyle will affect their brand choices and the rest of the purchase decision process. After all, someone's lifestyle will influence their needs and wants, and their preference for certain media or other sources of information, as well as the types of stores they like to frequent or websites they enjoy visiting.

4.3.3 Situational influences

A consumer's specific buying situation – where, when and how they shop – will also affect their behaviour and choices. These situational influences include such factors as the point of sale (the store's ambience) and the time of day (for example, grocery shopping right before dinner). Situational factors or influences are typically more related to the place and time frame of a consumer's behaviour than to characteristics of the product or the buyer themself.

But they definitely have an impact on their purchase decision process. For example, if someone gets a flat tyre while on holiday in Italy and urgently needs a new one, they will handle the situation differently than if they are replacing their tyres every 40 000 kilometres in their home town.

There are five *situational influences* on the purchase decision process:[6]

1 *Reason for the purchase*
   The reason for the purchase (or *purchase task*) affects how the consumer searches for information and evaluates alternatives. For example, consumers approach a purchase made for their personal or household use (in which price and durability may be the main criteria) differently from buying a gift (for which brand image and an attractive design are more important).

2 *Physical environment*
   The geographical location and weather, the size of the crowd in the store, lighting, decor, background music and even the scent of a retail store all affect consumer behaviour.

3 *Social surroundings*
   The presence of other persons – including their characteristics, role and comments – may influence what is bought.

4 *Time*
   The consumer's buying behaviour and choice are affected by the season, the time of day and the available time to make a decision.

5 *Coincidences*
   The amount of cash on hand and a person's mood at a particular moment (do they feel happy, tired, sad or bored?) tend to influence consumer purchase decisions. Yet, these so-called antecedent states or 'momentary conditions' are hard for anyone to predict, making them typical situational influences.

If a buyer allows themself to be driven by spontaneous reactions that reflect the mood of the moment, they are referred to as a *moment consumer* because their behaviour is essentially a succession of momentary responses.

4.4 PSYCHOLOGICAL INFLUENCES ON CONSUMER DECISIONS

Much of what we know about consumer behaviour is based on research and insights gleaned from psychology, the study of individual behaviour. Psychological factors are also known as *internal factors*, because their influences are felt *within* the individual. The effect of psychological factors cannot be observed, but can only be inferred from what a person does or says.

Often, consumers themselves do not even know why they behave in a particular way. Or they may know, but are not willing to share the underlying reasons for their behaviour with researchers. This makes it difficult to assess the exact influence of various psychological factors on consumer behaviour. Still, a consumer's decisions are influenced by their needs, motives, perception, learning, personality and attitudes.

4.4.1 Needs and motives

Needs and motives are closely related concepts. The two are sometimes even viewed as identical, as the 'why' of human behaviour. In actuality, needs are the basic forces that motivate a person to act.

PROFESSOR'S PERSPECTIVE
Ken Bernhardt (Georgia State University, USA)

Ken Bernhardt, Regents Professor of Marketing Emeritus at Georgia State University, has published numerous books and articles on marketing and consumer behaviour. He is former chairman of the American Marketing Association and former president of the Association for Consumer Research. He has consulted for many businesses, including Kimberly-Clark and UPS.

© Singapore Airlines

'When I discuss with executives issues related to *customer service* and service quality, I ask them to name companies that have truly outstanding customer service. Their response is usually silence at first, followed by a few executives mentioning just a small number of companies. These companies typically include American Express, Ritz-Carlton, Neiman Marcus, Fidelity, Lexus, UPS, FedEx, Dell and Singapore Airlines.

What do companies like these actually do that sets them apart from their competitors? First, they understand their customer and that customer's expectations. How? They make sure that executives spend time *interacting* with customers; conduct regular marketing research and pay attention to the results; identify what customers' experiences have been and what the satisfiers and dissatisfiers are; ensure that customer contact personnel have access to upward communications – they often know what should be done to improve customers' *experience* with an organization.

Doing it right the first time is a powerful competitive advantage

Second, these companies are truly committed to improving their customer service, service quality and customer satisfaction – and set *goals* related to each of these. They measure their progress against these goals and recognize and reward those who achieve and exceed them. They invest in technology to support these goals. Interestingly, these companies are rarely satisfied with their performance and are always seeking to improve on these measures. I once asked Holst Schultze, the CEO of Ritz-Carlton, to rate its service quality on a one to ten scale. His response: "About a four; we need to be much better."

Third, they choose their *employees* (or "team members") carefully and treat them well. As Bill Marriott has said, "Tell me how a company treats its employees, and I will tell you how the employees treat customers." These companies ensure that their employees are empowered to do what they know needs to be done. Some time ago I had the opportunity to hear Stanley Marcus (founder of Neiman Marcus) speak. He was asked what training the company did to produce such a high level of customer service in his department stores. He said, "You don't train people, you train dogs and seals. If you tried to train people in all that they would need to know, the training manuals would fill a whole shelf and no one would pay attention. So what we do is *educate* our people in our values, and then they will always do the right thing." Ritz-Carlton's "we are ladies and gentlemen serving ladies and gentlemen" philosophy is similar.

Finally, when these companies do make a mistake (which is inevitable, at least occasionally), they engage in extraordinary *service recovery* activity. For example, Lexus early on had a product recall. They called owners and asked when it would be convenient to pick up the car, and when they returned it, the gas tank was full and it had been washed. Doing it right the first time, combined with terrific service recovery, is a powerful competitive advantage.'[7]

Human motives sometimes originate with biological needs. When someone's physical or emotional balance is disrupted, they feel – consciously or subconsciously – a deprivation or need. If they are not aware of the need, it is considered *latent*. Once they are aware of the need, it becomes *manifest*; a problem the person will strive to solve. The consumer is now 'motivated' to take action. Needs are more basic than wants. If the consumer is aware of a need (for example, being thirsty) and starts thinking in terms of time, place and money to satisfy it (for instance, going to the local bar for a beer), the need becomes a *want*. As we saw earlier, this often sets off the purchase decision process.

A latent need usually becomes manifest once the sense of deprivation or lack reaches a certain level of intensity, or when a new product is introduced that would satisfy this need. Before the DVD recorder was introduced, there was already a latent need for better picture and sound quality than could be obtained with a videocassette recorder. Philips and its competitors succeeded in catering to this need before losing market share to streaming media.

When a person's needs are not satisfied, a certain urge or drive may be felt. A **drive** is a strong stimulus that encourages action or *motivates* the consumer to reduce a need. People are unique in that they are driven by many needs. Some of these are **basic needs**, relating to conditions essential for survival, such as the availability of food, water and shelter.

If marketers could simply cater to physiological needs ('drives' or instincts, such as hunger, thirst, sex and sleep) their work would be far easier, because these basic needs never change. However, human behaviour is highly complex and is also motivated by other ('secondary') needs that are more difficult to identify. To meet these needs, marketing-oriented companies rely on marketing research as a basis for developing the right products and services, as well as effective promotion strategies.

Motivation

A *motive* is an inner urge (essentially a stimulus) that compels a person to satisfy a need. This energizing force (also called motivation) prompts a specific behaviour intended to achieve a particular goal. For the marketer the key question is, 'What motivates people to buy my product? Are they, for example, driven by rational or by emotional motives?'

A person's needs are boundless. Besides being driven by motives that are inborn or based on basic needs, people also have learned needs, acquired at an early age. One example of this kind of *conditioned* **reflex** is the urge to belong to a group. This type of *psychological need* is something consumers assimilate from their social environments.

Research into **purchasing motivation** shows that buyers' motives can be rooted in *negative* motivation (such as avoiding or solving problems) or *positive* motivation (perhaps an intellectual stimulus or the desire for 'sensory' gratification). Another useful distinction – particularly when it comes to stimulating needs – is the difference between primary and selective buying motives. *Primary buying motives* relate to a particular product category (for instance, LED televisions), while *selective buying motives* lead to the choice of a particular brand (such as JVC) within that product category. Both are usually *specific to a given situation*. If an electronics manufacturer knows, for example, that television sales typically increase by 15 per cent right before the FIFA World Cup, the company might launch an advertising campaign for its new products featuring this event. Identifying and analyzing the buyer's motivation provides the basis for developing effective marketing strategies.

A hierarchy of needs

The consumer is driven by many needs. According to the well-known psychologist *Abraham Maslow*, when analyzing human motivation we should make a distinction between five fundamental types of needs. As illustrated in Figure 4.4, human needs can be classified into a hierarchy of needs, from the most pressing to the least pressing. In order of importance, these are physiological needs, safety needs, social needs, personal needs (also called: esteem needs or ego needs) and self-actualization needs.

If a person's basic needs – shown at the bottom of the pyramid – are not met, these needs will monopolize their attention and they will not be affected by higher-level needs; those are then either minimized or forgotten. For example, a hungry person is more interested in eating than in peer approval. Only when their essential needs have been met, will they experience higher-order needs and try to satisfy those. Based on this model of needs we never reach a state of complete satisfaction.

FIGURE 4.4 Maslow's hierarchy of needs

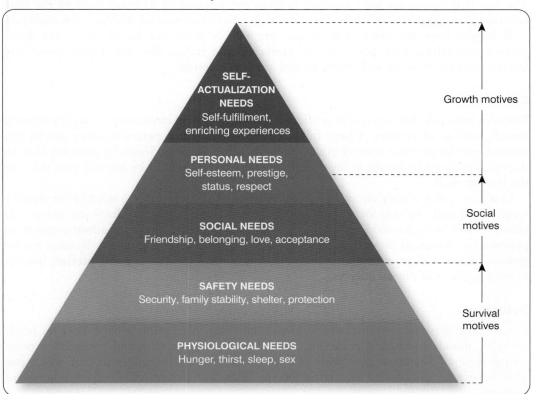

The boundaries between different categories of need are not as clear as the pyramid suggests. Most of the products we buy satisfy various needs at several levels. Similarly, a single, specific need may be satisfied by any number of products or behaviours, depending on how the consumer in a particular culture perceives them. This may create lucrative opportunities for marketers.

In the corporate world, Maslow's hierarchy of needs is used to present or **position** a product so that it will be most appealing to prospective customers. For instance, many cars, rather than being advertised as a safe and reliable means of basic transportation (a safety need), are positioned as a status product that will bring about social recognition and other people's respect (social and esteem needs) – a leap of no less than two levels in the hierarchy of needs!

4.4.2 *Perception*

A motivated person is ready to take action. But how they act is influenced by a personal view or perception of the situation. **Perception** is the process whereby people gather (through any of their five senses), organize and interpret information, so that it gives meaning to the world around them. Perception has three basic characteristics: it is subjective, cumulative and selective.

Subjective

No two individuals perceive the same object or situation in the same way. Each individual perceives reality through their own 'filter', and interprets what they see based on their own experience, preconceptions and associations. This makes each perception *subjective* and unique. The fact that consumers with identical motives can respond in different ways to the same advertising campaign makes the development of an effective promotion strategy a real challenge.

If buyers have no perception of the product or have not heard of it, the firm's promotional efforts have been wasted. Marketers can reduce this risk if they know how human perception works and which factors affect perception.

Cumulative

Research indicates that perception is affected by both personal circumstances and by external stimuli, such as advertising. A large full-colour advertisement is perceived more quickly and remembered longer than a small black-and-white advertisement. Similarly, products that are displayed at shoulder height in the supermarket are more likely to be noticed than those on the bottom shelf.

Our perception is also summative or *cumulative*. The more often a stimulus or signal is received – ideally by way of varying communication channels or media – the greater the chance it will be understood and correctly interpreted. This is why most advertisements are published or broadcast more than once and why suppliers in the business-to-business market provide buyers with product information not only by mail and through the Internet, but also in person, via sales representatives.

Selective

Exactly how personal circumstances influence individual perception is dependent on needs, attitudes, moods and past experiences. The human brain organizes and interprets external stimuli through a *selective perception* process. It filters the information so that only a part of it is noticed, understood and remembered. Thus, our perception is *selective* in several respects.

Marketers have to allow for **selective exposure**, because consumers do not expose themselves to all stimuli, as is the case in media consumption. Those who never watch television will not see television commercials. Similarly, consumers who close pop-up ads on websites without even looking at them will not be exposed to the ad. People tend only to pay attention to messages that interest them and that are consistent with their beliefs and attitudes; they ignore messages that are inconsistent with what they already believe.

Even if consumers do see advertisements, marketers still have to cope with **selective attention**. Research shows that mass media bombard the average consumer with more than 1 500 commercial messages every day, many of which go unnoticed. Because our brains simply cannot process so many stimuli, most of these messages are screened out; we are not even conscious of them. For example, we may only notice bicycle advertisements, if we are planning to buy a bicycle. Due to selective perception, advertisers who want to maximize reach should carefully select media and make sure that their messages relate to their prospects' needs.

Additionally, people tend to see only what they want to see and to hear what they want to hear. This is known as **selective distortion** or *selective interpretation*. Many consumers form a brand *image* in their minds, an image they carry forward in their buying behaviour. They see the brand in terms of the (perceived) advantages they ascribe to it. Therefore, they keep buying the same brand (out of brand loyalty), even if they know they can get a better quality product at a lower price. Not until their dissatisfaction or frustration reaches a certain threshold will they look for alternatives and start noticing advertisements.

Generally, consumers who have seen an advertisement only remember – even minutes after being exposed to the information – what they want to remember, those facts that are relevant to their problem or decision or in line with their own beliefs and attitudes. This is known as **selective retention**. Marketers may, in trying to appeal to a wide range of viewpoints, be tempted to include multiple messages in their advertisements. However, if an ad contains too many messages, consumers will probably not remember even one. It is, therefore, important that a company develops a clever communication strategy, taking into consideration that the consumer's perception (exposure, attention, distortion and retention) is selective.

4.4.3 *Learning*

Almost all consumer behaviour is learned. *Learning* is a process through which a person – as a result of information processing, reasoning and (repeated) experiences – acquires knowledge, and by which a pattern of behaviour and attitudes is established or modified. As this relates to marketing, if a consumer is pleased with a new product, this positive experience will lead them to rate the brand highly, and they will probably buy it again when they need to replace the product.

So how do consumers 'learn' to change their behaviours, and what is the best way for companies, if necessary, to stimulate this process? There are two primary theories as to how the learning process works: stimulus-response theory and cognitive theory.

Stimulus-response model

The **stimulus-response** model is based on the famous experiments of Russian psychologist *Ivan Pavlov*. In these experiments Pavlov rang a bell immediately before feeding a dog (a stimulus that caused the dog to respond by salivating). Eventually the dog, associating the sound of the bell (a neutral stimulus) with the arrival of dinner, learned to salivate when the bell was rung regardless of whether food was supplied. As a result, Pavlov concluded that learning is largely an *associative* (or 'reflexive') process.

Psychologists have further developed and refined this theory. The stimulus-response model states that as humans, we also learn primarily through experience, and that our learning is based on certain stimuli, such as brand names or packaging. These experiences cause us to develop certain habits in our behaviour or response. For example, certain buying habits can be explained by the fact that the consumer associates a national brand with 'high quality', an open-air market with 'value for money' and a large supermarket with 'good atmosphere and service'. The stimulus-response theory outlines four stages in the learning process:

→ *Drive*: Drive is a strong internal stimulus that moves an individual to action. It may be innate, such as hunger, thirst or sex, or it may be learned, such as the need for status.

→ *Cue*: The cue is a weak stimulus or symbol in the environment (such as a product, sign or advertisement) that determines when, where and how the person responds to the drive. If someone is thirsty (a basic drive), a Coca-Cola commercial may encourage them to suppress that drive by going to the refrigerator or vending machine for a Coke Zero.

→ *Response*: The reaction to the stimulus or *cue* is the *response*, such as a purchase. Everyone reacts differently to cues based on how rewarding their past responses have been.

→ *Reinforcement*: If the response is rewarding and positive, the person is likely to react in the same way to the cue every time it appears. The strength of the ensuing habit depends on the number of situations in which the particular response has been reinforced. Therefore, a consumer who has been satisfied with a particular brand will likely continue buying that brand as long as the cue pattern remains the same. The habit diminishes when the response is not reinforced.[8]

The stimulus-response model has two important implications for marketers. The first is that when introducing a new product, the company initially must break the consumer's existing buying habits and brand preferences before trying to form new buying habits. This calls for strong cues (like free samples distributed door-to-door) rather than a relatively weak cue (such as a television commercial, after which the consumer still has to go out and buy the product in a store in order to try it). Whatever cue is chosen, it should clearly appeal

Image courtesy of The Advertising Archives

to certain *drives* and their related emotions experienced by the consumer. In marketing food, a company might appeal to the consumer's drive for 'good health', for promoting safety belts, 'fear' and for jewellery (as a gift), 'love'.

The second implication for marketing is that because people are conditioned through repetition and reinforcement, a single cue, such as a television commercial, may not be sufficient to penetrate the consumers' consciousness. Therefore, it is necessary to repeat the commercial several times. Through repetition consumers learn to respond to stimuli in a certain way. Repetition also helps to ensure that they do not forget (or 'unlearn') the learned response. Finally, marketers should bear in mind that the likelihood of a repeat purchase of the same brand increases if the consumer is satisfied with (= rewarded for) their last purchase, and decreases if they are disappointed (= punished).

Cognitive learning

The second major learning theory rejects the idea that all learning is of a stimulus-response nature. Cognitive learning theory views people as problem solvers with complex mental processes, who do more than passively react to associations between stimuli. Consumers also learn through cognition, through reasoning, insight and mental problem solving without any direct experience. This theory about learning – the cognitive approach – stresses that many habits are formed by analytical *thinking* and processing *information* while solving problems. By purposefully gathering and analyzing information, buyers gain enough *insight* into the problem to weigh certain alternatives and make deliberate choices. This is typical of high-involvement decision making, such as that used in formulating the decision to buy a computer.

The cognitive learning theory also has several implications for marketing. For example, when designing a promotional strategy, a firm cannot assume that the consumer will buy the product simply because of previous satisfaction with the brand and company. An existing business relationship will help the firm, but consumers may also consider competitors' offerings and compare products with which they are less familiar. Therefore, in situations that normally involve cognitive learning, marketers need to develop a campaign with a logical presentation that helps the potential buyer to evaluate the product in a favourable light, for example by allowing consumers to observe the benefits of using their products.

4.4.4 *Personality*

We are all unique individuals, with distinct personalities. Personality is the sum total of experience and psychological and behavioural characteristics that make a person unique and distinguishable, leading to a consistent pattern of responses in coping with perceived reality.

Marketing research firms are always trying to get a better insight into the personality traits or characteristics of groups of people. It is these characteristics – and the resulting consistency in the responses to the stimuli in the environment – that allow marketers to type potential buyers as, for example, ambitious, self-confident, conservative, aggressive, introverted, innovative, materialistic or independent.

Most marketers assume a correlation between someone's personality traits and their buying behaviour. They take for granted that a person's favourite brands of beer, clothing, watches, cars or cosmetics reflect certain aspects of their personality, and they address this in their advertising campaigns. However, experienced managers always try to link information about personality to other variables, such as the demographic characteristics and attitudes of the prospects in the target market. Ultimately, using a *combination* of these data provides the best chance of successfully influencing buying behaviour.

4.4.5 *Attitudes*

Insight into customers' attitudes is a great advantage when trying to predict or influence their behaviour, because attitudes and behaviour are closely related. This is apparent from our definition, which describes an **attitude** as a learned tendency to respond in a consistently favourable or unfavourable way to a certain idea or other **attitude object**, such as a product, service, brand, company, store or person. Over time, consumers develop a positive or negative attitude toward a brand (for example, 'McDonald's has the best French fries') and toward more general consumption-related behaviour ('French fries and other high-fat foods are not part of a healthy diet'). Clearly, an attitude is a strong feeling that exists at a deeper level than someone's opinion or perception.

Because attitudes are good predictors of consumer behaviour, marketers spend a lot of time and money studying and influencing consumer attitudes. They know that attitudes are learned, and therefore, in the long run, can be changed. Since attitudes may influence a person's intention to buy, as well as their preference for a certain brand or store, marketers develop strategies that target consumers' attitudes. Through advertising, they deliberately try to influence **attitude formation**. An example is the Philips' 'sense and simplicity' campaign designed to create a customer-focused, no-nonsense image for the brand.

Those who measure people's attitudes in **attitude research** are careful to include the relevant dimensions. For example, a potential SUV buyer may have a positive attitude toward a Jeep, but may decide – for financial reasons – to be satisfied with a Korean-built Hyundai ix35. Thus, marketing researchers measure not only the consumer's attitude towards the Jeep as a brand (possibly positive), but also their willingness to actually purchase the vehicle (possibly negative).

Components of attitudes

Attitudes are complex. They consist of three components: cognition (the *knowing* component), affect (the *feeling* component) and behaviour (the *doing* component). While attitudes cannot be changed easily after they have been formed, the best way to accomplish this is initially to focus on changing one of these three components:

→ The **cognitive component**: a person's *knowledge* and beliefs about a product or another object. Obviously, this is the person's perception of the characteristics or attributes of a product or service. Reasoning about whether or not to buy the product would involve questions such as, 'Is it expensive? Is the quality level satisfactory? Would it be an appropriate gift for Uncle John?' Marketers can try to change consumers' beliefs by providing new information about the product (for example, about the power or gas mileage of a car equipped with a diesel engine) or by repositioning the product.

→ The **affective component**: a person's emotions and feelings about an object. This dimension is the core of someone's attitude. An emotional evaluation of the positive and negative aspects of a certain brand would lead the consumer to ask such questions as whether the brand is good or bad, if it is attractive or if they will regret the purchase. With the affective component of attitude in mind, countries like Croatia and Greece have tried to attract tourists by presenting themselves in advertising campaigns as fun destinations.

→ The *behavioural* or **conative component**: a person's intended (and actual) *behaviour* with respect to an object. This involves a person's tendency to act in a certain way and raises questions such as, 'Should I buy this product? And if so, should I get my favourite brand?' To stimulate consumers to take action such as trying a new product, marketers may distribute discount coupons, free samples or other incentives. In the case of a new energy drink, a consumer may, on the basis of limited information, act first – buy the product and drink it – and then evaluate it afterwards.

FIGURE 4.5 Two views on attitudes

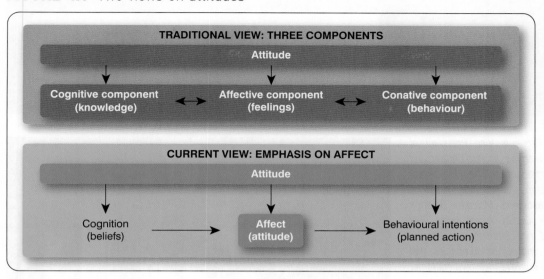

The three components of a person's attitude usually reinforce one another. For instance, if a person believes that a product or service has all of the features they are interested in, they will probably have positive feelings toward it and is more likely to actually purchase it. The cognitive, affective and behavioural components, which form the basis of the traditional theory about attitudes, are shown in the top part of Figure 4.5.

Current view on attitudes

Theories about attitudes are changing. Today, many practitioners and researchers use the word 'attitude' to refer only to the affective component (emotions and feelings). The cognitive or conative processes are still important, but they are no longer considered to be parts of an attitude, as the bottom part of Figure 4.5 illustrates.

Although someone's knowledge and beliefs about a brand – which are part of the cognitive dimension – are multidimensional (based on various product features and presumed advantages and disadvantages), the affective component only has one dimension. This means that a person's attitude towards a brand can be measured on a single scale, which ranges from positive or very good to negative or very bad. In addition, a person's affect (attitude) can be expressed in terms of *direction* (is the respondent for or against Turkey joining the European Union?), *degree* (how harsh or smooth does Ketel One vodka taste?) and *intensity* (how strongly is the consumer convinced of their feelings?).

4.5 SOCIAL INFLUENCES ON CONSUMER BEHAVIOUR

Whereas psychological factors are internal, social factors are *external* – they originate outside of the individual. And while the effect of psychological factors differs from person to person, many people in a society are exposed to the same *social influences* (such as a culture). Other social factors impacting consumer behaviour are *social class*, *reference groups* and *family influences*. Figure 4.6 illustrates the relationship between these social factors and how they relate to the individual.[10]

PRACTITIONER'S PERSPECTIVE
Diana Oreck (The Ritz-Carlton Hotel Co.)

© Chin Kit Sen / Shutterstock

Diana Oreck is Vice President of global learning at Ritz-Carlton and vice president of The Ritz-Carlton Leadership Center. After receiving the prestigious Malcolm Baldrige National Quality Award twice, Ritz opened this centre to share its expertise with other companies that want to improve their own customer service and satisfaction levels. Here, Oreck shares the most important customer service lessons that she teaches Ritz's 30 000 employees.

The great news is that we have totally simplified customer service. Legendary service is really three things: It's common sense, it's common courtesy and it's treating every customer as if they are a guest in your home. The other thing to remember: if you only have a satisfied guest, that's not enough because that just means you're competent and have met their needs. There's not a 'wow' here. What you are looking for is an *engaged* customer; there's one step between satisfied and engaged and that's the heart. You have to make an *emotional connection* in service. An engaged customer means you have exceeded those expectations, not just met them.

Our 'Radar On – Antenna Up' concept means that in service, you have to keep your eyes and your ears open. You can't be on auto-pilot to give great service. It all revolves around knowing the difference between a customer's expressed and unexpressed wishes and needs. I'll give you an example of both. An expressed wish is, 'Diana, I'm very thirsty.' So I bring the guest a bottle of water, pour it for them, make eye contact and say, 'Enjoy.' That's nice, but the guest told me exactly what they needed. An unexpressed wish looks like: I'm the housekeeper in the guest's room. I notice there's a loose button on the desk, and I put two and two together because there's a jacket hanging on the chair at the desk without the button and I sew it up'. That's the 'wow' – an emotional connection – and that's what we teach.

To make sure these lessons are executed by every employee at every hotel, we have something called the gold standard. It's a pocket card and has five components. It has a *credo*, which is our promise to our guests of the consistently high level of service that they see, whether they're in Dubai, Cairo or New York. We've got the *motto*: 'We're ladies and gentlemen serving ladies and gentlemen.' We've got the three *steps of service*, which are a warm welcome, anticipation and fulfilling of needs and a fond farewell. We have the employee *promise*, where we're promising our employees that they're going to work in an environment of trust, honesty, respect, integrity and commitment. And then we have twelve *service values*: These are twelve little instructions to live by, such as, 'I own and immediately resolve guest problems', 'I take pride in my appearance, language and behaviour', and 'I am *empowered* to create unique, memorable and personal experiences for our guests.'

We also practise systems behind the smiles and realign back to those gold standards 365 days a year. There are 16 elements on that gold standards card and we revert back to one of them – with examples of 'wow' stories – every 16 days, so this creates consistency. This so-called *daily lineup* is the golden thread that weaves our global company together.

Legendary service is a mindset, and doesn't have much to do with money

No matter what industry, you should never treat your customers in a transactional fashion. So if you're in a bank, it shouldn't be just another deposit or withdrawal. If you are in a hospital, you're not just another procedure. Let's take little Susie, who is six-years-old, in the bank. Don't you, as the banking institution, want to be the bank she chooses to open her first savings account with, and then as she gets older, her checking account, and as she gets her home, her mortgage account and then her retirement account? It's customers for life; it's not just transactional. But you can't execute this by telling your employees, 'Go out and give legendary service.' You need a written service strategy, such as: Greet them, give them what they want, thank them…We teach our housekeepers, 'Yes, your function is cleaning toilets, but your purpose is you are making a home away from home for our guests.' So that puts your mindset into a totally different realm of pride and we reinforce this every single day. Legendary service is actually a *mindset*; it doesn't have much to do with money at all.

A strong *corporate culture* is not a part of the game; it *is* the game and you should be reinforcing your culture every day, just the way we do with our daily lineup. The most important thing around service is that *consistency* is the foundation of service and that attention to *detail* is crucial. We have all heard that expression, 'Don't sweat the small stuff.' In service, it's all small stuff – and everything matters.[9]

FIGURE 4.6 Social influences on the individual

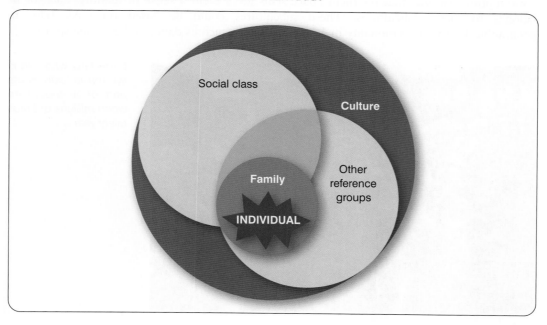

4.5.1 *Culture*

Because we absorb our cultural background while we are quite young, we have very little sense of how much the culture in which we are born influences our behaviour – not just our buying behaviour, but our entire lifestyle. The various components of a culture (such as the prevailing values, habits, beliefs and morals) are closely related to each other and all affect our lives.

By definition, culture is the set of values, customs, ideas, beliefs, attitudes and symbols that the members of a community have developed to shape their behaviour and way of life. These elements are shared by all who are part of a particular society, and they help distinguish this society from other communities.

Culture is not inborn but a *learned* response, and it is transmitted from one generation to the next. This applies both to its material elements (such as architecture and art) and its intangible elements (such as table manners and laws). As they are raised – a process through which a culture is transmitted – children tend to accept most rules of conduct without question. This incorporation or absorption of the culture is known as socialization. A child learns their culture from many sources, including family, teachers and peers, and even from sports heroes and celebrities. Since marketing-oriented firms try to connect to various trends in the culture, advertising tends to confirm and reinforce many of the previously established rules and role patterns, thus contributing to cultural learning.

Culture characteristically exists to satisfy *needs* within society. Not until young people feel that the values and standards passed on to them by their parents leave them ill-equipped to deal with their own situations – a phenomenon referred to as a *generation gap* – will they be critical of that part of their culture. As a result of these conflicts, some values and ideas are no longer transmitted and slowly, but surely, are eliminated from the culture. Thus culture is dynamic, changing and adaptive. The implication for business is that the cultural environment must be monitored closely to ensure that products and services are consistent with the changing needs, values and behavioural patterns in society.

A culture consists of various subcultures. The members of a subculture subscribe to many of the cultural mores of the overall society, yet they also share beliefs, values, customs and consumption patterns that set them apart. This gives them a sense of identity. Each of us belongs to many subcultures. These subcultures could be based on race, religion, geographical location, nationality or leisure activities, such as dance and extreme sports.

Loyal fans who attend live music festivals are part of a subculture worth millions of Euros every year

© R.W. Rowe

4.5.2 Social class

Consumers can be categorized into a hierarchy of social classes. A social class determination is made not only by income but also by a combination of other factors, such as education, occupation, sources of income, possessions, personal achievements, social interaction, values and attitudes.

Social class is therefore a *multidimensional* concept. A wealthy person is only accepted as an equal by members of the upper class if they also exhibit socially approved behaviour. Only then will they enjoy equal social status or social prestige. Experience, age, roles, knowledge or skills are all factors potentially contributing to class acceptance. A social class can be defined as a relatively permanent and homogenous group of individuals or families sharing similar values, interests, lifestyles and behaviour; the differences between the various categories are based on their social status and esteem.

Social classes exist within a *hierarchy* (as is illustrated in Table 4.1, which shows five distinct social classes); people usually position their social group either above or below other groups. Although there is some mobility within the social class structure – with people moving up or down the social class hierarchy over time – most people choose their friends based on a similar level of education, professional status and common interests. Hence, there are relatively few intensive contacts between people from different social class levels, especially with regard to social functions.

Research has clearly documented how social class influences consumer behaviour. Members of different social classes often prefer different types of *media*, *shop* in different stores, spend their *leisure time* differently (field hockey as opposed to soccer) and *buy* different products (cognac as opposed to beer). Therefore, social class can be a useful variable in segmenting the market for specific types of products and services.

4.5.3 Reference groups

A reference group is a group of people having a substantial influence over an individual's attitudes and behaviour. The individual feels associated with the people in the group or compares themself to them and wants to please or imitate them. For marketers, reference groups are important because they influence product and brand decisions made by consumers and, therefore, the effectiveness of promotion strategies.

Types of reference groups

There are four distinct types of reference groups: membership groups, automatic groups, aspiration groups and dissociative groups. Some have an indirect and others a direct, face-to-face influence on consumers' behaviour.

TABLE 4.1 Social classes in the Netherlands

Class	Description
A	Upper class (for instance CEOs of large companies, high government officials)
B1	Upper middle class (senior business executives, professionals)
B2	Lower middle class (middle management, small business owners)
C	Upper lower class (office staff, construction workers)
D	Lower lower class (unskilled labourers, poorly educated, unemployed people living on benefits)

Membership reference groups are those in which the consumer participates. They may be as small as the immediate family or co-workers (**primary groups**, with whom a person interacts frequently and informally) or as large as a trade union, church or professional organization (**secondary groups**, which are formal groups that involve less interaction). Even large organizations, in which the individual's role is minor, may influence personal attitudes as well as their members' purchase decisions.

Consumers automatically belong to particular reference groups based on their age, marital status, gender, nationality and economic classification (such as being a student). Membership in these *automatic groups* is often loose, and identification among members quite low. Yet, the influence of these groups should not be underestimated. For example, many students (or other groups of young people) dress alike. The dominating influence in automatic reference groups comes from consumers' perceptions of what society expects them to do in certain circumstances; this obviously affects the types of products that they buy.

An **aspiration group** is a reference group of which a person is not a member, but to which they aspire to belong. For young people, rock groups may be aspiration groups, while students – as future managers – may identify with a professional society. The hope to join an aspiration group often leads to **anticipatory socialization**, in which a person already adopts the values, standards, and consumption pattern of the group they wish to join. Aspiration groups especially influence purchases involving clothes, cars and entertainment. If someone looks at a person, rather than a group, as a basis for self-appraisal or as a 'point of reference' in determining their own preferences, beliefs and behaviour, that individual is called a **reference person**. This could be a movie star, athlete or even a close friend. Such a person will – as an **opinion leader** – have a great deal of influence on purchases and may informally offer information or advice about how a product should be used and which brand is best.

A *dissociative group* (also known as a *negative reference group*) is the opposite of an aspiration group. It is a group that a person shuns. They reject the group's values and behaviour and may take deliberate steps to dissociate themself from it. Politicians, bureaucrats in three-piece suits and skinheads are all examples of dissociative reference groups for many people.

Not every group that a person belongs to serves as a reference group. For example, someone may be a member of the European Marketing Academy (EMAC) or another professional association because of their career, without this having any influence on their attitudes, behaviour and lifestyle. Reference groups are also *specific to a particular situation*: for example, a political party may serve as a reference group prior to an election, but no longer play a role after the political campaign, and may not even influence that person to vote.

Reference groups and consumer behaviour

Many researchers have studied the relationship between reference groups and consumer behaviour. In determining why a person buys a certain brand of clothing or beer, or drives a certain make of car, researchers will commonly look at reference groups. The answer often lies in the influence that friends, athletes, actors, pop stars and other reference persons have over the individual's brand choice. This applies primarily to product categories that are socially conspicuous or visible; thus, the influence is greater on brands of blue jeans and watches than on microwave ovens or canned peaches.

What does this mean for marketers? If a product's purchase is strongly influenced by reference groups, the *brand image* is usually more important than the quality, price or other objective product features. Marketers of products that are particularly similar to competing brands – such as perfume, vodka or beer – invest a great deal of time and money to create images of the type of people who use their products. In this case *what* is said about a product is not as important as *who* says it (or simply shows it). Therefore, many companies hire celebrities, experts or even members of the public – as 'average consumers' – to endorse the brand or talk about their own positive experiences with the product in advertisements. This is known as **testimonial advertising**.

4.5.4 *Family influences*

Three out of every four consumers live with other **family** members under the same roof. As an independent unit of two or more people, together they form a household. They gather for meals on a regular basis and sleep in the same home. It makes sense, then, that the family – as a kind of reference group – has a substantial impact on many purchase and consumption decisions, and that quite a few of these decisions are made jointly, rather than by one person. Because the decision-making roles may differ per product and per target market, companies need to know how buying decisions are made for their specific products or services and who in the family makes the purchase or plays another role in the buying process. This will influence which family members (husband, wife or children) should be addressed in advertising.

Let's further explore how the family situation may influence consumption patterns. We will first consider the *family life cycle*, which describes the typical phases a family goes through from formation to retirement. Then, we will examine the *roles* played by family members in making purchase decisions.

Family life cycle

Household consumption is shaped by the family structure. Today, less than a third of European households are classified as traditional families – married couples with children under 18. The rest includes unmarried couples, single parents, gay couples and never-married, divorced or widowed individuals. Marketers, of course, know that these non-traditional households have different purchasing behaviours. The consumption pattern of a family of five (two parents and three children) will differ from that of a single parent and two children. Even families or households with the same number of people and purchasing power can buy completely different products and services. This is often related to the stage the family has reached in the **family life cycle**.

The family life cycle describes the phases through which a traditional family progresses, from moving in together or getting married to the death of one of the partners. Critical life events such as childbirth, teenagers leaving home, retirement and other transitions or milestones bring about dramatic changes in the family's needs, priorities and buying preferences. Companies that are well informed of these changing purchasing behaviours – whether they sell prepared foods, furniture, electronic equipment, recreational services or life insurance – will benefit from these insights, if they segment the market accordingly and meet the needs of a carefully selected target market.

Family purchasing roles

In most traditional households wives tend to make most of the purchasing decisions regarding clothing, groceries and children's toys. Husbands have more influence in car maintenance decisions. But research also shows that joint decision making of husband and wife is common for products and services like houses, cars, home appliances, electronics and vacations.[11] In general, the better educated the wife and husband are, the more decisions are made jointly. Finally, children are increasingly influential in many family purchases. Often, the decision makers are not involved in the actual purchasing process. Therefore, marketers should familiarize themselves with the family member who buys the product, the decision maker(s) and with each person's role in the process.

FIGURE 4.7 Roles of family members in purchase decisions

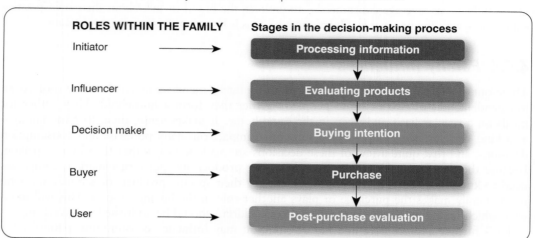

As is illustrated in Figure 4.7, family members can play different roles in the various steps of the decision-making process. The *initiator* is the person who first suggests the idea of a purchase. Often, they act as an information gatherer as well, collecting and evaluating information and (selectively) passing it on to the other members of the family. Because not all information may be shared with all family members, this person – who controls the information flow – is also the *gatekeeper*.

The *influencer* determines which criteria will be used to evaluate and compare the various brands. The *decision maker* is the person who has the final say in the choice of product and brand and, from this perspective, holds a position of power in the household. The actual purchase is made by the buyer. Sometimes, the *buyer* also determines in which store the purchase is made. And lastly there is the *user*, who is the actual consumer of the product. Because they also evaluate the product and probably have a decisive say in the brand choice of any subsequent purchase, the user – from a strategic point of view – may even be more important to the marketer than the buyer or anyone else in the household.

Of course, family members may assume different roles for the purchase of different products and services. Since many buying decisions are made jointly, focusing on just one person – such as the buyer – might make the marketing strategy ineffective. Hence, marketing research is indispensable in gaining sufficient insight into the roles and influence of family members on purchases of products and services.

4.6 BUSINESS-TO-BUSINESS MARKETING (B2B)

When we think of companies such as Philips, Heineken or Unilever, we probably think of them as important *suppliers* in the market; companies that *sell* their widescreen televisions, detergents, energy drinks and other products to consumers. This view is correct, but there are two additional points to keep in mind. One is that these companies first have to sell the majority of their products to other firms (intermediaries, such as wholesalers and chain stores) before a retailer can sell them to the consumer. Secondly, these corporations are also important *buyers* – every year they spend billions of euros on products, parts and services supplied to them by other organizations.

MARKETING MISTAKE
The B2B Sales Experience

When it comes to building valuable relationships with customers in the business-to-business (B2B) market, sales representatives are critical players on the front lines. But are they getting the basics right? Customers want to be contacted just enough, not bombarded. Sales representatives should know their products or services intimately and know how their offerings compare with those of their competitors. Customers need information on exactly how a product or service will make a difference to their businesses. And while they may say price is one of their biggest concerns, a *satisfying sales experience* is ultimately more important.

These were the key findings of a survey McKinsey conducted of more than 1 200 purchasing decision makers in small, medium and large companies throughout the United States and Western Europe who are responsible for buying high-tech products and services. The insights were consistent across simple to complex products and apply readily to most business-to-business (B2B) industries, which also have complex, multi-touch point sales processes involving both end users and purchasing professionals.

The McKinsey study found a big difference between what customers said was important and what actually drove their behaviour. Customers insisted price and product aspects were the dominant factors that influenced their opinions of a supplier's performance and, as a result, their purchasing decisions. Yet, when the researchers examined what actually determined how customers rated a vendor's overall performance, the most important factors were product or service features and the overall sales experience. The upside of getting these two elements right is significant: a primary supplier seen as having a high-performing sales force can boost its share of a customer's business by an average of 12 percentage points.

That makes the next finding all the more important. Of the many habits that undermine the sales experience, two that are relatively easy to remedy accounted for 55 per cent of the behaviour customers described as 'most

destructive' – failing to have adequate product knowledge and contacting customers too frequently. Only 3 per cent of the respondents said they weren't contacted enough, suggesting customers are open to fewer, more meaningful interactions.

Customers are open to fewer, more meaningful interactions

Fortunately, both damaging habits can be fixed. Companies can address a lack of product knowledge by centralizing content development to guarantee a uniform message and creation of compelling value propositions for customers. And to ensure deep understanding, sales representatives can receive experiential training and on-the-job coaching, preferably side by side with the content-development team. Finally, sales representatives don't need to know everything. When it comes to specifics, the study found that customers were more than happy to use online tools and selectively tap specialist support for the most complex situations.

Striking the right balance between contacting customers too much and too little requires understanding of their stated and actual needs. There should be a clear strategy for reaching out to customers based on needs and profit potential, with schedules dictating frequency. The best contact calendars centre on events that create value for customers, such as semi-annual business reviews, which provide an opportunity to assess customer needs and ensure satisfaction. The key is to recognize that customers are also looking to lower their interaction costs, so any contact with them must be meaningful.

In general, B2B customers say they care most about product and price, but what they really want is a great sales experience. For sales professionals, that means getting the basics right. Companies should examine exactly how they are performing by asking the following questions, 'What are the most influential drivers of the sales experience?' 'What things are your sellers doing that could damage relationships?' and 'How does the perception your customers have of your sales force compare to how they view your competitors?' It is only by knowing and understanding the answers to these questions that companies can begin to identify and pursue corrective action.[12]

So far, in studying buying behaviour, we have concentrated on the end consumer and on *consumer marketing* – as seen from the point of view of a producer or other supplier. However, consumers are obviously not the only buyers. There are also many *organizational* or *industrial buyers*. Customers in this market think of marketers as *suppliers*. From these suppliers or vendors, companies purchase products (such as raw materials) used to manufacture their own products or – as in the case of government agencies or banks – to provide various services.

Purchasing of industrial products, such as machinery, raw materials, semi-manufactured goods, packaging materials and industrial services, is complex and differs from the buying process of consumers in several ways. This distinction has led to a specialization in the field known as *industrial marketing*, *organizational marketing* or *business-to-business marketing*, often abbreviated to B2B. Products sold to organizational customers vary from basic office supplies to complicated telecommunication systems. All in all, the business-to-business market is quite fascinating and huge in size.

Chain stores and other *retailers*, too, purchase tens of thousands of items from manufacturers and from intermediaries (importers or wholesalers) and resell them to the consumer. Other products find their way to the end user via *institutions* such as hospitals, school cafeterias and government agencies. Products are often sold and resold three times or more before they ever reach the final consumer. This means that the marketing efforts of many organizations are not aimed at the ultimate consumer, but at other companies and their purchasing agents. In the last part of this chapter we will explore how the business market differs from the consumer market and how purchase decisions are made by organizations in several types of buying situations.

4.6.1 *Differences with consumer marketing*

There are many differences between business-to-business marketing and consumer marketing. The primary distinction between the two is that in B2B marketing, sales of products and services are conducted between organizations, rather than between a business and an end-user. The objective of the buyer in a B2B transaction is not to consume these products, but to use them in their own production process or to resell them. Although the organizational or business market includes all buyers who are not the ultimate consumers, there are actually four types of organizational markets:

→ The *industrial market*, consisting of businesses that buy goods and services to use directly or indirectly in producing other goods and services (such as Original Equipment Manufacturers (OEMs), construction firms, insurers and transportation companies).

→ The commercial or *reseller market*, serving wholesalers and retailers that buy products for resale to others (such as car dealers, department stores, supermarket chains and online merchants).

→ The *government* market, made up of federal, regional, local and foreign government agencies that buy a wide variety of goods and services (from trucks and software to security and cleaning services), mostly to serve their citizens.

→ The *institutional* market, composed of schools, hospitals, churches, prisons, charities, libraries, museums and other institutions that purchase products and services ranging from furniture and beverages to natural gas and telephone services.

While consumers are spread out across the country, industrial customers are typically *geographically concentrated*. These companies are located near raw materials, labour pools, transportation hubs or customers. Industrial areas such as the Europoort region (in Holland) or the Ruhr region (in Germany) are clear examples. At the same time, the *number* of buyers in the business market is limited; in fact, the number of businesses is only a fraction (less than 10 per cent) of the number of households in most countries.

The part (or sector) of the organizational market in which a company operates is usually limited, too. For many firms, it is a 'small world' in which almost everybody knows everybody else – including the competitors. The contacts between suppliers and buyers are more direct, both before and after a transaction. And, although women are playing an increasingly important role in business, most purchasing decisions in companies are still made by *men* – in contrast to the consumer market, where women are the primary decision makers in their households.

Whereas demand for consumer products is affected by price and availability, as well as by consumers' preferences, demand for organizational products is derived. **Derived demand** means that the need for industrial products is driven by, or derived from, the demand for related consumer products. Demand for sheet steel by car manufacturers is, for example, based on consumer demand for cars. Derived demand is based on expectations of future consumer demand, which can change quickly and unpredictably. For this reason, sheet steel producers monitor the consumer demand for cars in order to better estimate their own sales, as well as their future need for iron ore and other raw materials.

Finally, organizational products are more complex and more difficult to describe than consumer products. Many organizations expect products to be tailored to their precise technical specifications, and they are often willing to be actively involved in product development. Purchases are made after carefully weighing alternatives, based on rational criteria. The products' attractiveness to the customer largely depends on the added value. Documentation material, financing options, warranties, demonstrations, technical support during installation, delivery time, post-purchase service and maintenance may all be crucial. Customer satisfaction is usually dependent on the combined efforts of several departments in both the supplier's and customer's organization. Teamwork is essential.

4.6.2 *Organizational buying behaviour*

Just as most organizational products differ from consumer products, organizational customers differ from consumers – particularly in terms of their buying behaviour. Of course, in both markets the objective of a purchase is the same, to solve a problem or to satisfy a need. However, as a rule, a company's business objectives and strategy have a major influence on its decision-making. Organizational customers typically make much larger purchases than consumers. Transactions involving millions of euros for a single purchase – such as for sophisticated production equipment or for recurring purchases of raw materials in large quantities – are commonplace.

Organizational purchasing agents are usually technically qualified and well-informed professionals who follow established purchasing policies and procedures. Consequently, they are in a strong position to negotiate with vendors. To avoid possible shortages, professional buyers often identify several potential supply sources. Although long-term **relationship building** between suppliers and customers is increasingly common (partly because of the high number of repeat purchases), technical or economic criteria – including product quality, price and delivery time – are often the decisive factors in purchase decisions. Impulse purchases are rare.

Organizational buyers are frequently involved in time-consuming decision procedures. Some decisions can take months, or even years. Identifying a need is often difficult and may require lengthy consultation with suppliers. Before an order can be placed, the buyer must develop specifications, identify and evaluate qualified suppliers (known as **vendor rating**), arrange financing and evaluate products made by potential suppliers. Furthermore, both parties – often working together – have to figure out how the product can best be used or integrated in the production process.

Finally, buyers are usually part of an official *committee* – a **Decision Making Unit (DMU)** – which decides on the purchase. The Decision Making Unit is a temporary or permanent group of people from different departments of the organization who participate in the buying process. They share the responsibility for large transactions that may involve millions of euros per year. The wide-ranging expertise in the buying centre reduces the risk of making the wrong decision.

Just as in the case of consumer purchases, organizational buying involves several stages, each of which calls for a decision. Table 4.2 describes the most important steps in the organizational buying process.[13] In reality, a firm may not always go through all of these steps in the same order, whereas some stages will take place simultaneously.

4.6.3 *Roles in the buying centre*

In many businesses, several people work closely together to reach a buying decision. Depending on what will be bought, the participants may be engineers, production workers, financial officers, secretaries, supervisors or other individuals with specific know-how or a shared interest in the purchase. Together, this cross-functional team of decision makers is called the *buying centre* or *Decision Making Unit*.

Each member of the DMU may play one or more roles while participating in the organizational buying process. A marketer should find out what these roles are and how they have been assigned. This will enable them to better meet the needs and expectations of the various group members in their sales presentation or other business contacts. There are at least seven roles that a person in a buying centre can play:

→ The **initiator** sets off the buying process by being the first one to recognize that the company needs to make a purchase. This is often someone who uses the product (such as a secretary asking to replace a worn-out laser printer) or a manager who wants to improve the organization's efficiency. The marketer must make sure that the initiator is aware of all of the (new) products their company carries.

→ The **influencer** affects the purchase decision by helping to define the technical specifications for what should be bought or by providing useful information for evaluating the alternatives. For example, an information systems manager would be a credible influencer in the purchase of new computers. Other co-workers – such as engineers, R&D managers or quality control personnel – may be *unofficial* influencers by sharing their opinions about certain suppliers. When buying technically complicated products, a company may hire an external consultant as an **advisor** – offering the company more alternatives to choose from or facilitating the decision process in some other way. A marketer should identify key influencers in the DMU and try to convince them that their products are superior.

TABLE 4.2 Stages in the organizational buying process

Stage	Example
1 Problem recognition	A company's management needs new high-speed packaging equipment to support a new product introduction.
2 General description of need	The production manager – in cooperation with the purchasing manager - determines the features needed in the new packaging machines, which involves formulating the functional specifications.
3 Product specifications	An experienced production manager helps the purchasing manager determine the technical specifications, including a detailed description (in qualitative terms) of the requirements and standards the equipment should meet. The budgets, (internal) lines of communication and ordering procedures are also agreed on in the organization.
4 Supplier search	The purchasing manager, in cooperation with the production manager or other members of the DMU, draws up a 'short list' of possible suppliers that could satisfy the formulated requirements.
5 Acquisition and analysis of proposals	Selected suppliers are invited to submit a proposal based on a detailed briefing. These proposals are analyzed and compared – using technical, financial and commercial criteria – while the suppliers are evaluated in a vendor rating.
6 Negotiations and supplier selection	Negotiations – primarily based on functional specifications – are conducted with the two finalists and include issues such as the price, terms of payment, delivery, installation, service and maintenance. A supplier is chosen (or, in the case of dual or multiple sourcing, the DMU will decide to do business with two or more suppliers).
7 Drafting the purchase agreement	The delivery date and other details are established during the completion of the negotiation process. In a long-term contract, purchasing guidelines (such as the required quantity per order and expected time of delivery) are agreed on in principle, but may be adapted at a later date.
8 Monitoring and performance review	The purchasing manager monitors the supplier's production process to make sure that the packaging machines will be delivered on time. After the equipment is installed, both the performance of the machines and the service support provided by the supplier are evaluated. The supplier is given feedback to prevent future errors and to lay the basis for follow-up orders.

→ The **gatekeeper** is the contact person (such as a purchasing agent) who controls the flow of information to other buying centre members. Even a secretary who books appointments can help or prevent sales representatives from reaching other DMU members. Marketers and salespeople should try to build close working relationships with gatekeepers, so they can actually present their products to the buying centre.

→ The **decider** is the person who ultimately selects the product or service to be bought, even though someone else in the organization is formally authorized to determine the vendor with which the company signs a contract. For routine purchases – also known as *straight* *re-buys* – the decider may be the purchasing manager, while for complex purchases or *new-task* situations, it could be someone from the R&D, quality control or engineering department. To further complicate the marketing challenge, the decider might also be the company's CEO or a high ranking engineer who may have come up with specifications that only one supplier can meet. However, since the decider plays a crucial role, the marketer should try to identify that powerful member of the buying centre early on in the selling process.

→ The **buyer** is authorized to select a supplier and is officially responsible for the outcome, although they may ask one of their superiors to take over and negotiate the contract. Their main task, then, is to attend to details, such as getting competitive bids and setting up delivery and payment schedules after the supplier has been selected. For the marketer, providing excellent service is essential in getting repeat business.

→ The **user** is one of the most important people in the buying process, because they end up working with the new product. Marketers must show users the product's benefits and realize that their feedback will play a key role in future sales.

A typical buying centre has at least five participants, but it could easily involve dozens of people. In some purchases the same person may perform multiple roles, especially in small companies that do not have a full-time buyer on the payroll. In large companies, on the other hand, new members may be temporarily added to the Decision Making Unit in different stages of the buying process. A financial manager, for instance, may be asked to evaluate the terms of a contract just prior to its signing. Therefore, marketers need to find out exactly which members are involved in the purchase decision, how they might influence the outcome and what criteria these participants are most likely to use in their evaluation of suppliers and their products or services.

4.6.4 *Types of buying situations*

In today's global and competitive marketplace, many suppliers and their sales representatives are inclined to use price as their primary marketing weapon. Some may overlook, however, that while most companies need to reduce their (overall) purchasing costs, they do not necessarily want to drive down the price of all products and services they buy to an absolute minimum. Research makes it clear that they also have other priorities and criteria in selecting their vendors. Figure 4.8 shows the five most important criteria used by firms to evaluate suppliers in the business market.[14]

FIGURE 4.8 Common criteria used to evaluate suppliers in the business market

To make sure that their suppliers keep their promises, remain customer-focused, provide excellent service and offer consistent quality at an acceptable price, buyers strive to develop long-term relationships with suppliers. But whether or not they make a supplier a real partner in a strategic alliance also depends on the specific buying situation. Companies can purchase a particular product in different ways, depending on how experienced they are in buying it, how frequently it will be bought in the future, the number of co-workers involved and the time available to make the purchase. In fact, these variables in the buying situation may have a greater impact on the decision-making process than the complexity of the product. Depending on how much effort the buying procedure takes, and on the level within the organization where the purchase decision is made, we distinguish three types of buying situations or *buy classes*: the *new task*, *modified re-buy* and *straight re-buy*.

New task

In a new task buying situation, the organization is either a first-time buyer of a product or faces a unique purchase situation. Since there is considerable uncertainty and risk (especially in case of a large investment), the buying centre is often enlarged to include more participants who have a stake in the new purchase. Without any previous experience on which to base a decision, it takes considerable effort to collect and analyze information about qualified suppliers, as well as about the prices, quality and service levels they offer. The more suppliers are involved, the more complex the decision-making process will be.

In many ways, new task buying is similar to the *extensive problem-solving* orientation and buying behaviour of consumers shopping for a product that they have not bought before. Here, too, the DMU members do not have specific criteria yet to compare products or suppliers, nor do they have a preference for a particular solution or brand. Hence, making a decision is time-consuming.

In a new task situation, a proven strategy for a potential supplier is to create a competitive advantage by becoming actively involved in the first few steps of the buying process. For example, the marketer could collect information to help identify the customer's problem, offer assistance in developing the technical product specifications and then come up with a tailored proposal to satisfy the needs. This may also lay the groundwork for a formal presentation or detailed written proposal to be submitted later.

Suppliers who have previously conducted business with a particular company are in the best possible position to anticipate its changing needs. They are already familiar with the corporate culture and know what types of problems the organization is facing. Hence, they are more likely to develop effective solutions. On the other hand, a new task situation may also offer excellent opportunities for new suppliers. After all, the buyer has not yet established firm relationships with vendors of the needed products or services and the specifications may still be flexible. This means that the buying centre may be open to interesting proposals submitted by new suppliers.

Modified re-buy

If a company has bought a product before but now wants to shop around for potential suppliers offering higher quality, lower prices or better delivery times, or if it intends to modify the product specifications, the situation is called a modified re-buy. This re-evaluation of available options may be driven by internal considerations – such as the need to cut costs or improve quality – or external factors, such as a new competitor entering the market with better products or services. A modified re-buy is most likely if an organization is dissatisfied with the products or services provided by its current suppliers.

The decision-making process is somewhat similar to the *limited problem-solving* behaviour of consumers, for example when buying a second computer. The buyers have clear purchase criteria and can probably name several potential suppliers, but are not sure yet which of these suppliers or which products will best meet their needs. In any event, the decision will be made faster than in a new task buying situation.

A new supplier's best strategy is to find out what exactly has led to the modified re-buy situation. They can then act accordingly, for example (in case of price competition) by offering a guaranteed price per product or no price increases in the upcoming year. The current supplier's most effective reaction is to inquire about how they are falling short and then to immediately satisfy the customer's unmet needs and wants. If they succeed in this, they may still be able to persuade the decider to go for a *straight re-buy*.

Straight re-buy

A straight re-buy is the routine purchase of products that a company needs on a regular basis. For example, when office supplies are low or maintenance services are needed again, the purchasing department simply orders them from a supplier on its 'approved list', probably without even checking with any users or influencers from the production, engineering or quality control departments. After all, the company has bought the same products many times before and does not want to spend more time than necessary on reordering them from one of its current vendors. Obviously, a straight re-buy closely resembles *routine problem solving* by consumers.

The company's current vendor will retain their 'preferred supplier' status as long as they maintain a good working relationship with the customer, continue to meet the client's expectations and are flexible enough to satisfy any new needs and wants. On the other hand, an 'out-supplier' must offer something new and better, and convince the buyer that they will benefit by changing their routine. Unless the buyer is dissatisfied with its current supplier, making inroads is not easy because companies will usually consider it risky to switch to suppliers with whom they are less familiar. If the results are disappointing, the company may hold the buyer responsible. Still, new suppliers sometimes get a foot in the door by offering better conditions than their competitors, and subsequently try to get more business over time. Then again, current suppliers often encourage automatic reordering systems (for instance, through their websites) to save the buyer time, while continuously building long-term relationships with their best customers. Ultimately, repeat purchases keep suppliers' selling costs down and their sales volume up, translating into higher profits.

SUMMARY

1   Consumer purchase decision process

Marketers are constantly analyzing consumer buying behaviour. In keeping with the marketing concept, an organization should concentrate on satisfying the customers' needs and wants as the best way of achieving its own objectives. We must really understand the customers' buying motives and behaviour in order to develop effective marketing strategies that lead to satisfied customers. As we saw in this chapter, there are various models and theories that we can draw on to help us create satisfied consumers.

Consumers go through a five-step decision procedure when buying a product or service: problem recognition (the start of the purchase decision process), information search (for brands, prices and resellers), evaluating alternatives (based on various criteria), the purchase decision itself and post-purchase evaluation. In this last step the consumer determines if the product indeed satisfies their needs and meets their expectations.

After making a difficult purchase decision, consumers often experience buyer's remorse or *cognitive dissonance*, a feeling of anxiety about making the right decision and uncertainty about the merits of a recently purchased product. Companies deliberately try to eliminate this post-purchase doubt through, among other methods, advertising campaigns that emphasize the benefits of the product or service.

2   Problem solving variations

The model of the purchase decision process in this chapter is simply a conceptual outline that shows the steps that the consumer *might* take. He will often skip one or more stages. Also, the model does not indicate how much time will be involved. That depends on the buying situation. We compared three different kinds of orientation and buying behaviour.

Extensive problem solving is typical when consumers buy relatively expensive products that they don't purchase very often and with which they are not very familiar. High-involvement decision making is the rule here. *Limited problem solving* is most common when the consumer is buying a product in a category with which they are familiar, but they would like to get more information about unknown brands to make the right choice. Finally, the consumer relies on *routine problem solving* when obtaining fre-quently purchased, low-cost products. They do not spend much time on evaluating and comparing brands. This is characteristic of impulse purchases.

3   The influence of personal circumstances on consumer behaviour

Consumer behaviour is influenced by many *personal circumstances*. For example, someone's age and other demographic characteristics will strongly determine how this individual thinks, with whom they socialize and what they buy. A person's major **a**ctivities, **i**nterests and **o**pinions – the so-called AIO variables that characterize their *lifestyle* – also affect their buying behaviour. Whether or not the purchase eventually takes place partly depends on *situational* influences, such as the reason for the purchase, the physical environment, social surroundings, time-related factors and coincidences.

4   The influence of psychological factors

The purchase decision process is driven by many psychological factors as well, such as a consumer's *needs* and motives. The inner – and energizing – urge to satisfy a need is known as *motivation*. Maslow's hierarchy of needs motivation model ranks human needs according to the order in which they must be satisfied – from biological and instinctive on the primary level to social and spiritual on the highest levels.

A motivated person is ready to take action, but how they act is influenced by their perception, learning experiences, personality and attitudes. *Perception* is the process by which people gather (through their five senses), organize and interpret information from the world around them. Perception is subjective, cumulative and selective. It is a significant concept in marketing, in that how consumers perceive a product's benefits is generally more important than its actual features and strengths: 'perception overrules reality'.

Learning can be approached from two perspectives. The *stimulus-response learning model* has four basic principles: drive, cue, response and reinforcement. On the other hand, *cognitive theory* suggests that habits are mostly acquired by insight, thinking and problem solving. Finally, a person's *personality characteristics* and *attitudes* – which link their beliefs or feelings and their behaviour – also affect their buying intention and brand preference. Attitudes were traditionally thought to be made up of three – closely related – dimensions: cognitive, affective and conative components. However, today the word 'attitude' often simply refers to the affective component, a person's feelings toward a product, service, brand or company.

5 Social influences on consumer behaviour

Besides being influenced by personal circumstances and psychological factors, consumer behaviour is also affected by social influences such as culture, social class, reference groups and family situation. *Culture* is a society's set of behaviour-shaping values, ideas and symbols that people have created. For an element of culture to be passed from one generation to the next, it must satisfy a real need. Subcultures are distinct cultural groups within society. Their members often purchase different types of products for reasons different from the rest of society. Subcultures can be based on nationality, race, religion or geographical location.

A *social class* is a more or less permanent and homogenous group of people with similar lifestyles, interests and behaviour. Social class influences people's communication skills, their choice of where to shop, their leisure activities and their saving and spending habits.

A *reference group* is any group within society that influences the behaviour of an individual. There are membership, automatic, aspiration and dissociative reference groups that have been shown to influence both product and brand decisions. Studies of family decision-making show who purchases products and who decides which products are to be bought. These days, many couples make purchase decisions jointly or are influenced by other members of the *family* who play the roles of initiator, gatekeeper, buyer and user.

6 Business-to-business marketing

Finally, in this chapter we explored the buying behaviour of organizations and the role of the buying centre. Although there are numerous similarities between the consumer buying process and that of organizations, we noted that professional buyers usually know more about the technical aspects of products than consumers and that rational considerations are the decisive factor in purchases. Many companies use committees (Decision Making Units) to manage the purchasing of products and services, especially if they are dealing with a 'new task' or a 'modified re-buy' situation. After this brief look at business-to-business marketing, in the remainder of this book we will again focus on consumer marketing.

DISCUSSION QUESTIONS

1 Why should a marketing manager have an insight into what motivates customers to make purchase decisions?

2 Why do we consider 'post-purchase evaluation' a part of the purchase decision process? How relevant is this stage for marketers?

3 Have you ever experienced a feeling of cognitive dissonance? If so, what did you do to reduce this 'buyer's remorse'?

4 Is there a link between consumers' personal circumstances – such as their age, income, lifestyle and family situation – and their perceived importance of the various stages of the purchase decision process? Consider each of the personal factors listed above separately.

5 Some people believe that the behaviour of the often unpredictable and fast changing consumer will make the 'lifestyle' models that marketers and advertising agencies have used for years, obsolete. Why? How would you respond to this new situation if you were responsible for strategy development?

6 Define the type of orientation and buying behaviour when a consumer buys:
   a. a cup of coffee in the cafeteria.
   b. a new pair of skates.
   c. a candy bar from a vending machine.
   d. a new kitchen.
   e. a new iPad to replace an older model.

7 Classify each of the following products in Maslow's hierarchy of needs:
   a. a yoga course.
   b. an Audi TT.
   c. a skiing holiday.
   d. health insurance.
   e. cocktail snacks.
   f. temporary government housing after a major flood.

8 Which theory makes most sense if a marketer needs to explain how people learn: the stimulus-response theory or cognitive theory?

9   Are you a member of any subcultures? If so, how does this influence you in buying products and services?

10   HAK – a European company that markets preserved fruit and vegetables – has introduced a new product line known as HAK Extra, which is positioned between its traditional vegetables in glass jars and its ready-made meals. HAK Extra Brown Beans in Vegetable and Tomato Sauce is a typical example. Consumers can make chilli con carne seasoned to suit their own taste simply by adding ground beef. To what trends in consumer behaviour is the company responding with this type of product? Assess – or offer suggestions for – the brand's marketing strategy.

CHAPTER 5
MARKETING RESEARCH AND MARKETING INFORMATION

LEARNING GOALS

After studying this chapter you will be able to:

1	**Explain the objectives of marketing research**
2	**Identify the stages of the marketing research process and different methods of data collection**
3	**Describe how a marketing information system works**
4	**Discuss the underlying principles of test marketing**

5.1 Role of marketing research
5.2 The marketing research process
5.3 Marketing information system
5.4 Test marketing

The environment is changing so fast that an organization's ability to make timely changes is, in itself, a competitive advantage. This certainly applies to marketing. To keep the marketing strategy and its implementation effective, we must thoroughly understand the major developments that affect our customers, intermediaries, suppliers and competitors.

High-quality marketing decisions are made on the basis of up-to-date information about the market. The competitive battle between today's marketers is based less on material business assets than on having the kind of information that allows the organization to adapt to its environment and to be among the first to anticipate new trends, needs and preferences. Often, it is fairly easy for a firm to imitate a competitor's product and to copy its production methods. But in order to maintain a leading position long term in a rapidly changing market, companies need a continuous flow of useful data about that market. That database is the company's intellectual capital, an intangible asset that cannot be used or duplicated by competitors. This chapter explains how we can obtain the kind of information that allows us to develop successful marketing strategies.

MARKETING IN ACTION
How the Internet Changed the Music Business

The American band *OK Go* practically invented the viral video and, with well over 125 million views on *YouTube* alone, has successfully gained global attention through the Internet. OK Go's frontman, Damian Kulash – the undisputed master of viral Web success – recognizes the important role of music videos in the band's marketing strategy. OK Go is known for investing at least as much time and energy into making its buzz-creating videos as in writing and recording new songs. Some critics wonder if creating free online videos is a worthwile investment of the band's time, who have sold a respectable yet relatively modest 600 000 CDs over the years. But Kulash isn't worried. At the end of the day, he argues, online statistics have a much greater impact on the band members' income than their CD sales.

In fact, OK Go's income is higher than before, when it was largely dependent on how much money and time its record company, *EMI*, was investing in the band. Since discontinuing their relationship with the major label, the group has been generating substantial revenues straight from its fans as well as from sponsorships and licencing fees. Besides, the band members can do whatever they want without any restrictons on creativity, which – in their profession – is a huge advantage.

It's been more than ten years now since the Internet fundamentally changed the traditional music industry forever. Regardless, as Kulash asserts, there's no doubt that music will always be around to enjoy, even if it is no longer created or consumed in the same formats traditionally cherished. Just because one particular model was once appropriate for the market does not necessarily mean that this will continue to be the case indefinitely. Throughout the second half of the 20th century, record companies defined music – in essence a short-lived and subjective experience – as 'recorded music' that was meant to be sold. As a medium, records and CDs enabled musicians to reach out to their fans. In fact the medium itself even helped to shape the creative process; an album's length, for example, was literally dictated by

© OK Go

the amount of music that could be fitted on a vinyl record, or a tape cassette or a CD; the concept of a 'B-side' song literally stemming from the format of old vinyl singles that contained the 'hit' on one side, and another track on the other side.

> Bands must try out new methods of marketing themselves in the digital age

The arrival of the Internet changed all that. Since music can now – in a few seconds – be downloaded and distributed for free across the globe, sales of recorded music have dropped off significantly. To most consumers, music has changed from a physical product – a CD sold in record stores – into an experience enjoyed by downloading it, or streaming online through services like

Spotify. From a marketing perspective, this has turned the traditional music industry on its head. Bands like OK Go have harnessed the combination of the web and corporate sponsorship to great effect. The band gets the money and resources to do what it wants creatively. At the same time, the sponsors benefit through being aligned with a fashionable or 'hip' phenomenon, quantified tangibly by traffic to their website generated by direct 'click-throughs' from the band's latest video. In today's tough economy, you can't beat a win-win situation like that!

The Internet is not just a valuable tool for promoting and drawing revenue from a 'product' *after* it has been created, whether this product is a new video, single or album. It is also valuable in the *creative development* stage, such as in raising capital directly from fans. Increasingly, more established bands are shunning the traditional model, in favour of 'fan-funded' enterprises; countless services such as 'Kickstarter' are widely available on the Internet to artists and bands, whatever stage they may be at in their career. In recent years, *Patrick Wolf*, *Ben Folds Five* and *Amanda Palmer* (who raised a record-breaking $1.2 million to invest into her album) have used this new model to great effect.

It is largely the rise of social media enabling more direct contact between artists and fans that has made this possible, helping musicians reach out to a huge audience and get feedback simultaneously. Eager fans will invest anything from €10 upwards in advance for a 'stake' in the album. Their investment is rewarded with exclusive freebies, ranging from rare signed merchandise and track downloads, to priority pre-sale gig tickets. Yet it's worth noting that the above bands had already received investment from major labels before going it alone. Arguably it's much easier to entice the public to invest their own money when the artist in question is already a well-established act with an existing loyal fan base.

Some critics argue that it is only through this initial investment in raising their profile that these acts have enjoyed the freedom to branch out alone. To them it is a flawed and unsustainable model, and they claim that it is much harder for start-up bands to follow this approach. The fan funding model also raises an interesting *ethical* debate – to what extent is it morally acceptable to utilize fans as a means of raising capital? Is it wrong to prey upon their good nature and support to fund an enterprise, and where should the line be drawn? Some have gone so far as to call it 'fan exploitation'. Amanda Palmer does not think so; she has argued on the contrary that it puts the power into the hands of the fans, who get a greater connection to the creative process and their favourite artists as a result.

The digital landscape is forever changing and evolving. Communication tools such as *Facebook* and *Twitter*, which didn't even exist just a few years ago, have become multi-billion dollar companies that now dominate the global consciousness on a scale that not too long ago would have been simply inconceivable. Artists are now enjoying unprecedented power to market themselves and reach out to their audience in exciting new ways. Yet at the same time, the removing of traditional barriers has led to greater saturation and less quality control, requiring music fans to seek out what they desire. It is not certain what the model of the future will be, or if indeed one model will dominate ever again as it did in the past. It *is* clear, however, that bands and artists must continue to try out new methods of marketing themselves in this digital age.[1]

Marketing research, often referred to as market research, is one of the most important, but least understood parts of marketing. It is critical to the implementation of the marketing concept. In order to serve its customers well, a firm must know a great deal about the market. Through marketing research, it can determine such things as the product features most appreciated by customers, the total size of the market and how that market can be broken down into separate market segments. It can also assess consumers' responsiveness to pricing and promotional strategies, the demographic and psychographic make-up of the target market, and the sales potential of new products and services. Since this information is vital to the development of effective marketing strategies, all companies should be willing to invest in *marketing research*.

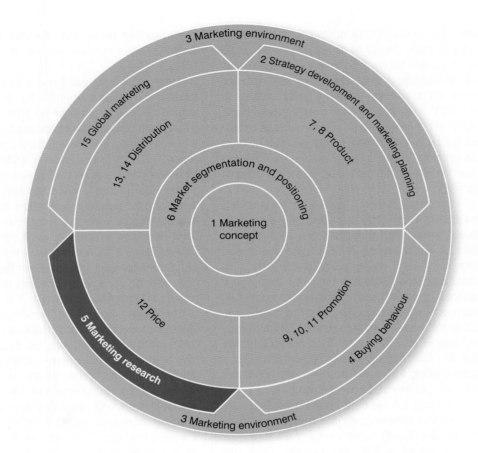

In this chapter we will find out what marketing research is all about. We will explore the various steps in the marketing research process – identifying the problem, deciding on the research plan, gathering secondary data, conducting exploratory research, developing and conducting surveys and utilizing alternative methods of data collection. We will also examine how an organization's marketing information system provides managers with the exact information they need to make better decisions. Finally, we will consider the role of test marketing in evaluating the effectiveness of marketing strategies.

For those who want additional information about marketing research, the accompanying *website* to this book contains sections on omnibus and panel research, the use of samples in collecting data, and the most common types of product, price, promotion and distribution research in strategy development.

5.1 ROLE OF MARKETING RESEARCH

How do marketers come up with ambitious marketing goals, decide which particular target market to pursue, and develop effective product, promotion, price and distribution strategies? The key to success often lies in the company's ability to act on accurate, up-to-date information collected through marketing research and organized through a marketing information system. As we will see, marketing research is one of the cornerstones of a marketing information system

(MIS). To understand its role in the firm's marketing programme, we start by defining marketing research and examining what conditions must be met for the data to be useful. We also consider the objectives of marketing research.

5.1.1 What is marketing research?

Marketers not only analyze and solve a company's current marketing problems, but should also anticipate, define and, if possible, avoid problems that the company may face in the future. To obtain the information needed for this analysis and decision-making, they rely on marketing research. So what exactly is marketing research?

Marketing research is the systematic and objective gathering, analyzing and interpreting of data that help marketers explore opportunities and make better marketing decisions. This is deliberately a broad definition, since the information that companies collect in their market research relates to a wide range of issues. Research may be used to:

→ Identify and analyze marketing opportunities.

→ Define and solve marketing problems.

→ Develop and evaluate marketing programmes.

→ Monitor and assess the results of marketing strategies.

Globally, companies spend over 15 billion euros per year on marketing research, enabling them to stay in touch with their customers and society as a whole. It is clear that marketing research is a crucial support function for developing and implementing marketing strategies.

Marketing research data must be collected and analyzed *systematically*, consistent with a previously developed research plan. A **market research plan** describes the methods and techniques that will be used to ensure that the research is carried out *objectively*, or in an unbiased and unemotional manner. Only then can it provide a realistic analysis of, for example, the firm's target market and the customers' needs or level of satisfaction. For this reason, marketing research activities are typically not the responsibility of the marketing or product manager, since they are usually too emotionally involved with a particular product or problem. Instead, companies often hire marketing research agencies to conduct their research for them. The project is still supervised internally – especially in large companies – by an experienced market researcher. This person performs various *tasks*. For instance, they will describe the exact information the company needs to make the necessary decisions, outline the data collection methods, coordinate the field work and may even analyze the results themself. Finally, they will make sure that the conclusions and implications of the marketing research are communicated clearly to the firm's decision-makers.

5.1.2 Objective of marketing research

Today's managers increasingly rely on marketing research. Studies indicate that the majority of companies *systematically* use marketing research data when developing their strategies. For large companies (employing more than 50 people) the number even exceeds 90 per cent. The two dominant reasons for conducting marketing research are the need to identify and analyze new *markets* and to improve the *image* of the company or its brands. Other common objectives are to obtain information about *competitors'* activities and to find effective ways to *increase sales*.[2]

Although all of these are commercially inspired motives, approximately one quarter of the total amount spent on marketing research comes from not-for-profit organizations (including governments). Thus, marketing researchers also help organizations in the non-profit sector to systematically analyze the effectiveness of their strategies and tactics in the market.

All in all, marketing researchers spend a great deal of time systematically gathering and analyzing relevant information. Note that 'relevant' is not the same as 'interesting' information. Many of the reports that managers get on their desks or computer screens are loaded with interesting ('nice-to-know') information. But what they really need is *relevant* information that empowers them to make *better decisions* when planning and implementing their marketing strategies. That brings us to the primary objective of marketing research, which is to reduce decision risk by providing management with relevant, timely and accurate information.

At Philips marketing research data are primarily requested by the product development and marketing departments. 'The product development people already know which products are selling today, but would really like to find out what products will be *hot* three

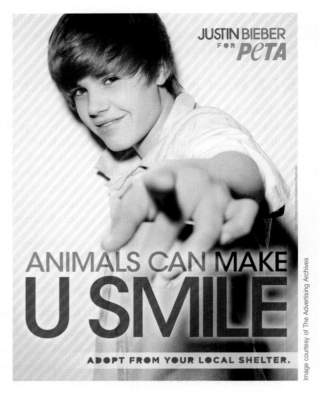

years from now,' says Randy Emond, a market research manager at Philips. 'And the marketers are always complaining about their tight budgets. They just want to make sure that every euro invested in a marketing campaign is a euro well spent. They want to make better decisions.'[3]

Of course, marketing research can *reduce*, but not *eliminate*, the risk of making the wrong decisions. There are at least two reasons for this. First, human beings are extremely complex, and even the most powerful psychological tools can only help us understand a small part of human behaviour. Consequently, marketing researchers sometimes reach the wrong conclusions in predicting what consumers will do in a particular purchase situation. The second reason why marketing research cannot provide perfect answers or eliminate decision risk entirely is that a sudden change in the environment, whether economic, political, legal, social or technological in nature, may make the results of a market study no longer relevant.

Nevertheless, decisions based on marketing research findings tend to be better than those based on intuition or groundless assumptions. The use of the so-called *scientific method* in marketing research means that every idea is meticulously and systematically tested before assuming that it is valid. For example, we cannot simply assume that, if we reduce the price of a product by 20 per cent, consumers will buy more of it. We might intuitively suppose that this would be the case, but this is really only a **hypothesis**, which describes what we expect to happen, or the kind of relationship that we *assume* exists between two variables. Before making any final decision, this hypothesis – or educated guess – needs to be tested to *verify* the expected relationship. In this example we can test the hypothesis by reducing the price by 20 per cent in a *test market* (a number of stores in a certain area) to see if this will indeed lead to increased sales. Only if this appears to be true, may we decide to reduce the price. The principles of the scientific method (systematic observation, hypothesis development, forecasting and testing) reduce the uncertainty of management decisions. Regardless, it is essential that the researcher points out the limitations of a study as well as the risks involved in the recommended decision options.

PRACTITIONER'S PERSPECTIVE
Finbarr O'Neill (J.D. Power and Associates)

Finbarr O'Neill is president of J.D. Power and Associates, a global marketing research firm based in California. As former president and CEO of Hyundai Motor America, he played a key role in the Korean brand's global turnaround.

© P. Cox / Alamy

'The focus in my career has always been on the customer. Whether it is a product like a car or a service such as legal advice, you must see the world through the customer's eyes. Can your product meet, or better yet, exceed the customer's expectations? Does your service address their pain points, solve their problems or enhance their experience?

At Hyundai, we relied on *external* marketing research to provide actionable insights from the unfiltered voice of the customer. In any company, there is always the risk that you will see the customers as you want them to be, not as they are. Accordingly, your insights – and, ultimately, the decisions that you make – are filtered through your own preconceived notions of the desired outcome.

The key to putting customer research to use is to be *willing* to accept the voice of the customer. A car navigation system may be elegantly designed and superbly engineered, but if the customer finds it counterintuitive and difficult to use, you have a problem. Moreover, you cannot rely on just your own research. Internal research can be biased – either in the compilation, the analysis or the reporting. Independent research, *unfiltered* by internal corporate prejudices or politics, is a critical *reality check*.

Social media contain a wealth of unsolicited information about consumer perceptions and attitudes

The future of customer satisfaction measurement lies in accessing customer feedback in all of the various ways that consumers communicate. At J.D. Power, we describe this as *"asking, watching and listening."* Today, the predominant ways of contacting consumers to ask for their feedback are surveys delivered online or to mobile devices and tablet computers.

Watching *trends* in consumer behaviour and "listening" to opinions expressed through *social media* are two types of customer satisfaction research that will continue to be shaped by advances in technology. Through *click-stream analysis* and by gathering operational metrics data, we can learn about consumers' actual behavioural patterns. Social media contain a wealth of unsolicited information about consumer perceptions and attitudes. As social media networks and *online communities* continue to grow, listening to feedback expressed in these forms will become even more essential.'[4]

5.2 THE MARKETING RESEARCH PROCESS

Some managers may not give enough thought to the precise information they need for making important decisions. They collect seemingly relevant information they come across, hoping to find the right answer. They seek solutions without understanding the nature of the problem. And they do research without knowing exactly what marketing decisions have to be made. Such a hit-or-miss approach is usually a waste of time and money. To avoid this mistake, we will look at a systematic (and scientifically justified) method of marketing research, involving a number of steps. In practice, there may be some overlap between the activities in each of these stages. Still, the whole process should be carried out as systematically as possible. As can be seen in Figure 5.1, the very first step in the **marketing research process** is to define the nature of the problem and the research objectives.

FIGURE 5.1 The marketing research process

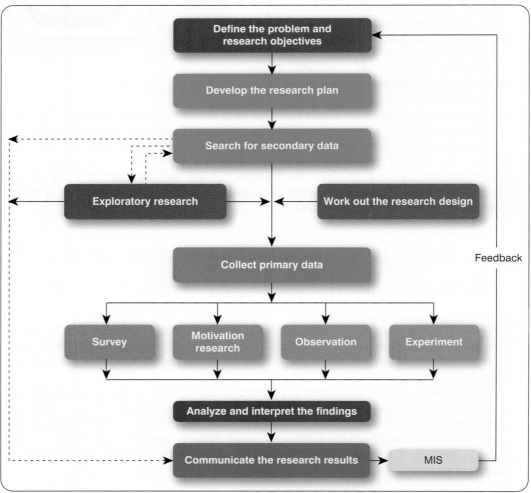

5.2.1 Problem definition and research objectives

Before we can decide what information research should provide, we have to identify and define the *research problem*. The word 'problem' here does not mean that something is wrong. It refers instead to the overall questions requiring answers. Unless the research problem is clearly defined, the marketing research agency or department may design an excellent research study, but one that will be useless to management. Failure to spell out the problem is responsible for more errors in marketing research than any other single factor. Hence, correctly defining the problem is half the battle and probably the most difficult step in the process. It is not unusual to come back to this challenge after more information has become available in one of the subsequent steps and, based on those insights, redefine the problem.

If we are planning for an external agency to conduct the research, we should have the problem clearly defined before we can *brief* the agency. In fact, defining the problem will help us formulate the assignment for the agency. Therefore, some managers, from the outset, define the problem in the form of a briefing. Whatever approach is taken, the ultimate goal of the problem definition stage is to develop the *research objectives*, which are really the 'research questions' to which the research should provide answers (for example, 'Should we introduce a new model next year?').

Even if we are clear about the issue from a marketing management perspective (for instance, 'If we spend more on advertising, will that increase sales?') and have already incorporated it into, for instance, the marketing plan for the purpose of conducting marketing research, the question should be reworded as a research problem. This problem statement should include a description of the objectives and the design of the research. Unfortunately, defining the problem is often complicated. A major challenge is differentiating between *symptoms* and *problems*. We should not confuse the real problem with a *symptom* of the problem. For example, a sore throat is a symptom. The cause of the pain – possibly a throat infection – is the real problem.

In marketing, declining sales and increasing competition are common symptoms. But they are not the nature (or the 'definition') of the problem. We must ask ourselves if these developments (such as declining sales) indicate that, quite simply, part of the *marketing mix* is not working properly (for example, the price may be too high, or the brand awareness too low), or are they the result of a *more extensive* underlying problem (such as a bad location decision or a poorly motivated sales force), which calls for more extreme measures? Marketers should carefully examine the facts surrounding an issue to identify and isolate the actual problem. Among other things, they should analyze the information the firm collects from the marketplace, including customer feedback.

Since marketing problems do not occur in a vacuum, we always have to look at the context of the current situation. For instance, which products are most lucrative? Does the public perceive our brand image as positive? What are the opportunities and threats in the environment? And who are the most dangerous competitors in the market? Addressing questions like these helps us define our situation and restrict the research to areas that will provide useful data for a meaningful and informed decision.

The more intensive the collaboration between the market researcher and the manager responsible for making the marketing decisions, the more accurate problem identification and specification of research objectives become. When in doubt, the problem should – at least, initially – be described in relatively broad terms. Then, when additional information becomes available to place the problem in the context of the company's situation, the research can be further structured. It is essential to spend enough time on this, because the problem definition (which, in the end, should neither be too narrow or too broad) determines the *information need*, which data will be collected and thus the nature and direction of the research.

A poor problem definition often results in wasted time and money, or even worse, no solution to the actual problem. To illustrate, a producer of chocolate bars recently conducted marketing research to find out whether it would be best to advertise in magazines and newspapers or on television. The company hoped to increase its shrinking market share by spending its advertising budget more effectively. Although the research was carried out perfectly, the research report that focused on marketing communication options ended up in someone's desk drawer because it was practically worthless. The real problem, as later discovered, was that the consumer's taste had changed and many customers had started buying competitors' candy bars because they were sweeter. Hence, in this case the shrinking market share was a symptom of a larger concern: a gradual change in consumer preference. More extensive analysis and advance deliberation would have led to a better – more broadly formulated – definition of the problem and useful market research.

5.2.2 Developing the research plan

Now that the problem has been defined and the research objectives have been set, the next step in the marketing research process is to develop the research plan. After all, a marketing research project is a planned search for information. This master plan outlines the **research design**, or how the research will be conducted. In this written proposal, we determine what data we need for the marketing decision, how these data will be collected (which research instrument, what sample) and our constraints while conducting the study.

In identifying the necessary data, we are essentially translating the research objectives into specific *information needs*. For instance, if we are considering the introduction of a new model, we might want to collect data on the demographic and psychographic characteristics of the present users, their preferences (in terms of the product features and usage of the product) and their perception of the price. We may also want to get input from resellers, as well as a sales forecast, in order to assess the chances of a successful introduction.

Most likely, **secondary data** (pre-existing data) will not be sufficient, and we will need to plan *field work* to gather *primary data* for our specific research objective. In this case, we need to decide on the:

→ *Research approach,* or the best way to collect data (by means of a survey, motivation research, observation, an experiment or other methods).

→ *Sampling plan* (who exactly will be surveyed, how the respondents will be selected and how large the sample should be).

→ *Contact method* (an online survey, for example, or a telephone interview).

→ *Constraints* or restrictions on the marketing research study (including the available budget and deadlines – specific dates by which the research findings should be collected, analyzed or presented to management).

Many of these decisions hinge on the question of how detailed the results need to be. Depending on the research objectives and information need, several types of research may be considered.

Exploratory research is appropriate when the research question has not been defined yet and is used to gather preliminary information on which to base the hypotheses. We will come back to this research approach shortly. A more formal research process is required for *descriptive* research. We may use descriptive research when we are seeking general information about the market. This form of research can answer such questions as: How much market share do the three leading brands have? How many hours per week, on average, do our customers in different income categories spend using the Internet? What are their demographic characteristics, purchasing preferences, choice criteria and satisfaction levels? This is known as

descriptive research because it describes existing situations (such as quantity, frequency and time) without considering possible relationships between different factors.

A third type of research is *experimental* or **causal research**, which does examine cause-and-effect relationships. Often, the marketer may have an idea about the relationship between two or more variables and will formulate a research *hypothesis* that can be tested through causal research. For example, would a 10 per cent higher advertising budget increase sales enough to compensate for the additional promotional cost? When formulating hypotheses, the researcher translates the problem defined in the first step of the research process into a number of specific research questions, which are formally worded as propositions that can be tested. Many times, a researcher will conduct exploratory research before they engage in descriptive or causal research.

5.2.3 Secondary data research

Researchers should always first find out what information is readily available on the topic being researched; nobody wants to 'reinvent the wheel'. Therefore, they start with **desk research**. *Secondary* data – existing data collected for another purpose at an earlier time – can be derived from **internal sources** as well as external sources. A good start is to determine what information is on file within the company. This will help to ensure that costly research is not duplicated. Examples of *internal* secondary data include previous studies conducted by the marketing research department, in-house accounting information, customer letters, sales call reports and sales analyses produced by the sales department. The type and quality of internal secondary data will vary from company to company.

If the internal data fail to provide the necessary information, we can search for *external data*, which originate from outside the organization. Annual reports, trade journals and reports sold by companies like Nielsen and Yankelovich (providing market-related information, such as retail sales figures and lifestyle trends) are all examples of **external sources**. Many of these are available through the Internet. Chambers of Commerce and Industry, and various professional and government organizations also issue valuable information. By using search engines (such as Google and Yahoo), metasearch engines (such as Dogpile), which search multiple search engines simultaneously or commercial *online databases* (using ProQuest, LexisNexis, Dialog or other general database services), researchers can discover useful sources of secondary data.

Secondary data have both advantages and disadvantages. Some of these are listed in Table 5.1. Occasionally, secondary data are all we need to answer our research questions (note in Figure 5.1 the dashed line which connects 'secondary data' with 'results'); more commonly, they are not sufficient. If the drawbacks of the secondary data are insurmountable or if we cannot find what we are looking for, *field research* will be necessary. This means that we will need to collect specific data ourselves for the project we're working on, or have someone else do it for us. These data are known as **primary data.**

TABLE 5.1 Advantages and disadvantages of secondary data

Advantages	Disadvantages
– Saves time (especially when using an online database)	– Questionable validity (collected and analyzed in an objective, systematic and unbiased manner?)
– Inexpensive (the cost of collecting the data was borne by someone else)	– Often dated, incomplete or not specific enough (data may not be usable for our problem)

5.2.4 *Exploratory research*

At the end of the secondary data phase, we may still lack sufficient understanding of the problem to draw firm conclusions or to proceed with a full-scale research investigation. In this situation, we may decide to conduct **exploratory research**. This is a small-scale study, designed to come up with a tentative explanation of the problem or to identify additional problems for investigation. Exploratory research can also be used to test the research approach, in which case it is described as a preliminary study, a *pilot study* or – if it involves testing a questionnaire – a **pilot survey**.

On average, only about a tenth of all marketing research is *qualitative* research, which does not seek yes or no answers but in-depth, open-ended responses in which people share their thoughts on the topic at hand. Because so little is known yet about the problem at this stage, exploratory research – which is usually **qualitative research** – is characterized by flexibility; if necessary, the questionnaire may be adapted even *during* the preliminary study. The insights or conclusions drawn from an exploratory study are usually formulated as hypotheses. The results of any exploratory research are no more than indications that cannot be generalized and quantified. However, they can be verified by later testing them by more scientific (quantitative) research methods.

A frequently used form of exploratory research is **expert research**, also known as an *expert opinion* or *experience survey*. Its objective is to tap the knowledge and opinions of people who are – often professionally – familiar with the problem under investigation. These individuals may range from company executives and business associates (such as distributors) who have solved similar problems in the past, to people not associated with the firm but who have some special understanding of the issue (such as marketing consultants).

The most extensive form of expert research is the **Delphi method**, in which experts on the subject offer their opinions independently of each other in a number of rounds. The researchers try to get a consensus by showing each expert the opinions, estimates and forecasts of the other experts at the end of every round and allowing them to revise or refine their opinion, if they wish to do so. This method of data collection is sometimes used to gain insight into very uncertain market developments. In practice however, the regular experience survey is used more often than the Delphi method. In either case, researchers should try to draw on many people, representing as many different backgrounds and views as possible.

Sometimes, if a decision is impending and the company cannot afford to wait for the results of more comprehensive research, it will base its decision on the exploratory research findings (even if these do not provide a definitive answer to the research question). Usually, however, exploratory research leads to additional secondary research or the development of a full-scale scientific research project. Such studies should be carefully and thoughtfully designed.

5.2.5 *Refining the research design*

With good secondary data and insights from exploratory research, we are now able to work out the research design that was proposed at an earlier stage, when the research plan was developed. The **research design** specifies the research questions to be answered, the data collection method and the manner in which responses will be analyzed to provide meaningful information.

To start off, we can list the unanswered research questions, rank them and determine what information is needed to answer them. In specifying how the data should be collected and processed, we need to focus on two decisions:

a. *sample selection* – as presented in the 'sampling plan' and

b. *data analysis* – the statistical techniques to be applied to the data.

The methods of *data analysis* must be determined before we develop the questionnaire or another research instrument. The statistical technique applied will have consequences, not only for the required *number* of observations (sample size) but also in terms of how the data should be measured (for example, with what scales).

For the *sample selection*, we should first determine the population, which is defined as all the individuals who share the particular characteristics in which the researcher is interested and therefore are part of the group that is studied. For example, a population might be all home-owners in Brussels, all Swedish women over the age of 21 or everyone in Munich who drives a 2014 BMW. Questioning everyone in the population would constitute a *census*. Most of the time, it is simply unnecessary and too expensive or time-consuming to contact an entire popula-tion. Instead, a sample of the population is drawn. The objective in sample selection is to choose a group of people in such a way that the results of the research on that group can be accurately generalized to the entire population. In that case, the sample is *representative*.

The procedure for selecting a sample is critical to the validity of the research. In a random sample, everyone in the population has an equal chance of being selected. A stratified random sample breaks the population down into strata (for example, male and female students), and then the respondents from each stratum are selected randomly in proportion to their percentage of the population. This procedure ensures that the sample is proportion-ate to the population on a vital characteristic in the study, which enables us to generalize about the individual strata as well as about the population.

More information on sampling is presented on the website accompanying this book. We now look at the next step in the marketing research process, which is to collect primary data through a survey, motivational research, observation or an experiment. We'll start with the best-known method of gathering primary data, the survey.

The fact that representativeness is one of the essential factors in research and that it cannot be assured simply by increasing the size of the sample has been an expensive lesson in the history of market research. In 1936 the Literary Digest in the United States conducted an election survey. It sent out *ten million* questionnaires, of which two million were returned. Yet the researchers failed to predict Franklin D. Roosevelt's *landslide* victory because the sample included a large proportion of people in higher income brackets. George Gallup con-ducted an election survey among 5 000 people. Although his sample was only a fraction of the size of the Literary Digest sample, he managed to predict the election outcome because his sample was far more differentiated.

Yet in 1948, Gallup made the same mistake as the Literary Digest, when he predicted a clear victory for presidential candidate Thomas Dewey. The last interviews conducted as part of the survey were completed ten days before the election took place. However, the mood among the voters changed in the last week, and it was Harry Truman who became the 33rd president of the United States. Bad timing of the market research can, as in this case, undermine the representativeness of a sample.[5]

5.2.6 *Collecting primary data: survey methods*

Bill Gates, one of the world's most successful businessmen, once commented, 'Your most un-happy customers are your greatest source of learning'. Many companies agree with this opinion, and survey their customers frequently to find out how they can improve their pro-ducts or services to increase customer satisfaction. Therefore, it is safe to say that most of us have been surveyed at least once in our lives. In fact, surveys are the most widespread form of marketing research. A survey is a systematic effort to gather – primarily quantitative – information by asking a group of people a series of questions. Consumers are asked about

PROFESSOR'S PERSPECTIVE
Jessica Lichy (IDRAC Research, France)

© Gts / Shutterstock

Jessica Lichy has a PhD in the field of online consumer behaviour in a cross-cultural context. She is enseignant chercheur (research professor) at IDRAC Research and Erasmus visiting professor at St Petersburg State Polytechnic University (Russia), Satakunta University (Finland), UCLan and Chester University (UK). Based within IDRAC, Dr. Lichy's current focus of research concerns ICT and business models, while her other disciplines of interest include cross-cultural management, social media and research methodology. In this perspective, she elaborates on the difficulty of acquiring reliable data.

In today's global online business environment, managers should have a broad understanding of Internet user behaviour. They need this information for monitoring their marketing efforts, segmenting markets, repositioning products or services, identifying emerging customer needs and so on. However, the methods used to gather and present data on Internet usage are often ambiguous. The various ways of collecting data on Internet usage are sometimes weak and, as we will see, can be challenged on several points.

First of all, Internet statistics are inaccurate when researchers use *sales* of computer hardware and software to gauge the number of Internet users. Telecommunication companies report the increasing popularity of triple-play offers (free national phone calls, digital TV and unlimited Internet access). However, subscribing to such an offer does not guarantee that the consumer will (or can) access the Internet. In France, for example, many consumers who sign up for triple-play only have access to digital TV reception and free national phone calls because the country lacks the infrastructure for broadband Internet access. Still, they are included in the statistics as active Internet users since they subscribe to an ISP (Internet service provider).

The second weakness concerns the practice of 'circular citation' and *replication* of data among sites. Internet usage statistics circulated on *Internet World Stats* are often drawn from Nielsen//NetRatings, the International Telecommunications Union (ITU), the CIA, local ISPs and 'other reliable sources'. The French-language *Journal du Net* website largely quotes the same data. Thus overall trends consistent across many sites may simply be the cumulative effect of this tendency to use each other's figures.

Thirdly, analysts use different survey methods and definitions of *Internet access*. Some companies begin counting Internet users at age two, and others at 16 or 18. Some studies include users who have accessed the Internet only within the past month, while others include people who have access but do not use the Internet. Definitions of *active users* also vary from one market research firm to another. To illustrate, while certain companies only count Internet users over 15 years old who surf the web at least once every two weeks for any amount of time, others include casual surfers, email browsers or even the number of customers who purchase computer hardware.

Fourthly, much research into Internet usage has been driven by the concerns of *commercial interest* seeking to understand the demographics of online audiences, in much the same way as research is done on other media. Measures of web page 'hits' and domain name growth give an indication of the Internet's shape – but such measures say little about Internet use. For example, measuring the number of domain names registered says nothing about the uses to which those domain names are put. Commercial Internet users gather domain names and often do not use them. It is a form of trade-marking; McDonald's not only reserves mcdonalds.com but also hamburger.com, ronald.com and so on. Tracking search engine key-words, therefore, does not properly reflect the ever-changing trends of Internet usage, nor does it indicate the evolution of the Internet itself. Users looking for a particular site via a search engine may follow several links before finding the site they want to look at (or they may lose the train of thought and end up on a completely different website). Typing errors mean that individuals sometimes call up a website that is then not consulted. Users without high-speed Internet access may avoid looking at some sites that take too long to load. Moreover, certain servers block access to some sites.

Fifth, there are *weaknesses* in the methods used to obtain data on Internet traffic. Sites that make traffic statistics publicly available are not a representative sample of Internet use. Data is often collected from publicly available sources such as 'routers' which forward data along networks. 'Log files' are collected from sites that make them available showing a history of activities performed by the server. Many sites cease updating their traffic records due to intermittent problems, maintenance or changes in network architecture. This can result in actual data being lost; or sometimes a site will record a huge but incorrect traffic volume as a result of some fault.

Finally, research *funding* can skew results, especially when companies are looking for a return on investment. This bias is clear in the presentation of incomplete or, worse, inaccurate quantitative information slanted toward the perspective of the funding institution. Generally speaking, government statistics are published less frequently but more accurately than commercially-funded surveys. However, the problem with government data is that 'official statistics' are neither collected nor published in the same way. This means that direct comparisons between two or more countries may not be possible. Different organizations gather data in different ways; for example, in the UK, the National Office of Statistics records data by government office region, OFCOM collects data at the national level, while the Chambers of Commerce collect data about business use. In France, some city councils monitor Internet penetration in certain areas and industries but this is not mandatory, adding to the confusion.

In conclusion, the Internet presents a unique problem for marketers; as there is no central registry of all Internet users, completing a census or attempting to contact every Internet user is neither practical nor financially feasible. Therefore, many Internet user surveys try to answer questions about all users by selecting a subset to participate in the survey – in other words sampling – and then extrapolating this data. Internet users are spread out all over the world and it is thus difficult to select users from the entire population at random. An alternative is to post a survey online, making it available to all Internet users – but the respondents who make time and effort to complete the questions are self-selected and unlikely to reflect the whole population of Internet users. Hence, in making marketing decisions, managers should be aware of the weaknesses of the available data on Internet usage and realize that they can't always rely on these statistics.[6]

products, services, how they spend their leisure time, how they feel about political parties and many other topics in an attempt to gain insight into their opinions, attitudes and buying behaviour. The four most common ways to collect survey data are through mail questionnaires, personal interviews, telephone interviews and online.

Mail questionnaires

A mail survey is one of the most widely used information collecting methods. Mail questionnaires, which are both sent and returned by mail, are relatively inexpensive, since they eliminate the need for an interviewer. In addition to the low cost of gathering large amounts of data, another advantage is that the subjects can fill in the questionnaire whenever it suits them and that the person conducting the survey does not influence their responses. Hence, there are no interviewer effects.

Mail surveys also have significant disadvantages. For one thing, questionnaires take a long time to get back to the researcher. It is also difficult to exercise any control over *who* fills in the questionnaire. Although it is designed for and addressed to the head of the household, any member of the family may actually complete the questionnaire, if instructions are not followed. Finally, a major disadvantage is the high non-response rate in this survey method. Relatively few completed questionnaires are returned. Reasons for this low response rate include incorrect addresses, recipient refusal to participate in any survey and unwillingness or inability to answer certain questions. The low response rate undermines the *representativeness* of the survey; the sample may not adequately reflect the population as a whole if the non-respondents are systematically different from those individuals who do take part in the research. Consequently, with a high non-response rate, we have to question the *reliability* of the research results.

Personal interviews

The personal interview – in which the researcher conducts the interview *face-to-face* – usually provides the most flexibility and high-quality information. Because the interviewer is present, they can clarify difficult questions and make sure the respondents answer all of the questions in full. Another benefit of the personal interview is immediate access to data.

One disadvantage of the face-to-face interview is the *interviewer effect* in which the respondent may be more inclined to react to the interviewer ('What do they want me to say?') than to answer the questions honestly. Another disadvantage is the expense of personal interviews incurred by the interviewers' travel time and costs. In the organizational market the costs of this contact method are often high because well-trained and highly qualified interviewers are needed to conduct meaningful *executive interviews* with managers in specific fields of expertise.

Telephone interviews

Although telephone interviews are not as expensive as face-to-face interviews, their costs are rising due to the increasing number of respondents who refuse to participate. Today, most telephone surveys are conducted through computer-assisted telephone interviewing (*CATI*). The interviewer reads the questions from their computer screen and enters the respondents' answers straight into the computer. The computer automatically redials any unanswered phone number three times. Because of the rapid response and reasonable cost, telephone interviews are often used in research on buying and usage behaviour.

A major disadvantage of telephone surveys is the difficulty of asking complex questions over the telephone. For example, a respondent cannot be asked to rank in order their preference for eight shopping centres or to indicate which of four advertising appeals they think is most effective in selling a new car. As in face-to-face interviews, the interviewer must be careful not to influence the respondent. That factor aside, in organizational market research, telephone interviews appear to be as reliable as face-to-face interviews.

Online survey

Now that most households have Internet access, *online marketing research* is rapidly gaining popularity. Many companies ask visitors to their websites to fill in a questionnaire. They also contact their customers through email, and use both pop-ups and web links to collect data.

Online surveys offer numerous advantages. First of all, they are fast and inexpensive, regardless of sample size. There are no printing, postage, labour, travel or telephone costs. A second advantage is the ease of finding the type of respondents who are usually hard to reach, such as busy executives and working mothers. Furthermore, a researcher can send respondents computerized online questionnaires that allow for interactivity, so they receive questions based on the answers they gave earlier in the survey. Studies show that most respondents are more honest online than they are in personal interviews. It is also easy for the marketing researcher to show the respondents photos or other images, such as *streaming video* or *hyperlinks* to websites.

A final advantage of online surveys is the relatively high response rate, as compared to other data collection methods. The anonymity of online surveys encourages people to cooperate more than they would in personal interviews, particularly on sensitive topics that normally get a low response (for instance, questions regarding income, soft drug use and sexual orientation).

Formulating questions

Whether we use an online survey or another type of survey, we must carefully consider how to formulate the questions. Neither the questionnaire nor the individual questions can be *too long*. The questions must be worded in simple language that is *understandable* and not *ambiguous*. A question like, 'Where do you work?', which may have multiple interpretations, cannot be used. Also, the respondent has to be *willing and able* to answer the questions. They must know the answer or be reasonably capable of remembering certain facts for the question to be answerable. The questions should *not be leading* or biased ('Are you also against the excessively high defence budget?'). And, finally, the *order* of the questions is important. A questionnaire should always start with general, easy-to-answer questions and save personal and more specific questions (such as those about income and age) for the end.

It is important to pre-test the questionnaire by first conducting the survey among a limited number of respondents. Only after making any necessary improvements, do we have a useful instrument for collecting the information we need. It should be noted that the guidelines for question formulation apply to all types of surveys.

Structuring the interview

Questionnaires may include two types of questions, open-ended and closed-ended questions. The respondent can answer an **open-ended question** as they wish. Their answer is then recorded word for word. By contrast, a **closed-ended question** asks the respondent to choose between a limited number of responses. This category also includes *scale questions* designed to measure the intensity of a person's response. This type of 'structured' question is especially suitable for gathering quantitative information. The number of possible answers in closed-ended questions may be limited to two (*dichotomous questions*) or three (*trichotomous questions*). Questions with more than two options are often referred to as *multiple-choice* questions.

The type of questions we include in a questionnaire depends on how structured the interview will be. In a **structured interview** the (closed-ended) questions and the order in which they are presented, are determined in advance. The same applies to the answers, which are fixed alternatives that simply need to be ticked or circled. In a **semi-structured interview** most of the questions are open-ended. The interviewer writes down the answers as they are given. Both the order and the manner in which questions are asked are established in advance and cannot be changed. In an **unstructured interview** the interviewer has more freedom. They work from a checklist of discussion points and continue their questioning until they have sufficient insight into the respondent's motives or reasoning. This is also known as an **in-depth interview**.

5.2.7 Motivation research

'People often don't say what they'll do, or don't do what they say', is a complaint often heard from researchers. The fact remains that many areas of personal behaviour cannot be explored by direct questions, because the respondents don't know (or don't want to say) why they behave as they do, or because the researcher does not know what questions to ask. In these situations, the researcher often resorts to motivation research.

Motivation research is a form of *qualitative* research that, unlike quantitative research, is usually conducted among a small number of people, without quantifying the results. The objective is to gain subjective insight (rather than numerical certainty) into the motives and mindset of the individual. Two well-known types of motivation research are the projective technique and focus group interviews.

Projective technique

The projective technique uses visual or verbal stimuli that encourage a respondent, who is not aware of the research objectives, to project their underlying motivations, beliefs, attitudes or feelings on an ambiguous situation. When using the projective technique – also known as the *indirect questioning* technique – the researcher may show the respondent a picture (to be used in an advertisement, for example), a drawing, a description of an incident or a list of words (such as someone's shopping list). The respondent is then asked to react to the stimulus provided. As the respondent puts themselves in the particular situation, their answers give the researchers insight into their personality, values, needs and (buying) motives without them realizing it. Examples of projective techniques include:

→ **Storytelling**, in which the respondent is shown a drawing, picture or cartoon and, based on that, is asked to tell a story, elaborating on their personal experiences as a consumer.

→ **Sentence completion**, in which the respondent is given incomplete sentences and asked to complete them (for instance, 'People who drive a Jaguar are…').

→ **Word association**, in which the respondent is presented with a list of words or brand names and, after each word, is asked to say the first word that comes into their mind. (Only some of the words are test words of interest to the researcher; the rest are fillers).

"I can't wait to hear what the Youth Market thinks."

Focus group research

A second type of research designed to uncover consumer motivation is a focus group discussion. This technique relies on group interaction and discussion; typically the group consists of eight to twelve people who meet with a *moderator* to discuss a certain subject. The moderator's role is to encourage, facilitate and focus the discussion (without getting involved in it) and to explore any feelings, thoughts and ideas that develop within the group.

On many occasions, focus group research has led to the development of new product concepts that the marketing department previously had not considered. The major disadvantage of this method is cost, since the effective use of motivation research requires the presence of highly trained discussion leaders. It also takes up considerable management time, because marketers and researchers typically watch the discussion behind one-way glass, recording their own observations, rather than receiving a written research report. Additionally, it may be difficult to objectively interpret the research outcome and to establish whether the group has reached a consensus. Finally, since a researcher must evaluate the results subjectively, the findings may reflect personal bias.

5.2.8 Observation

Observing consumer behaviour in the marketplace is another important way to collect market research data. The observation method of data collection uses a passive instrument by which someone's behaviour is recorded, without questioning them and usually without them even being aware of the process. It is often used to determine how shoppers behave in supermarkets or department stores. For example, do the buyers read the package? Do they compare prices? What products do they buy first and what do they leave until last? How much influence in the purchase decision does a child have on their parents? The answers to these questions can be very useful in developing promotion strategies, in designing packages and in making store layout and shelf location decisions.

Observation instruments

The systematic observation of people is also known as *micro-observation*, since it involves observing individuals' behaviour. Observations can be recorded by people (*personal observation*), for example by someone acting as a mystery shopper. These are researchers posing as normal customers, who gather observational data about stores, such as store appearance and cleanliness or number and type of products displayed, and about how employees interact with customers, for example, the speed of service. Data can also be recorded by equipment; this is known as *mechanical observation*. Retailers frequently use scanning equipment and hidden cameras to record customers' behaviour in their stores. Similarly, research firms have developed techniques to measure which websites are being visited and by whom ('cookies').

Researchers working in a *laboratory situation* (a 'secure' room in a marketing research or advertising agency) sometimes use instruments such as an eye camera to record eye movements or a pupillometer to measure changes in the size of the eye's pupil. The more interested a consumer is in an advertisement, the more dilated their pupils become. Finally, observers (usually clients of the research agency) can watch the session and follow the discussion of a focus group, unseen, from a viewing room with a *one-way mirror*.

Advantages and disadvantages of observation research

Although observation methods are often used during the initial phase of marketing research (such as in exploratory research), it is sometimes the only reliable way of gathering information. In observation research, we don't have to rely on what respondents claim to have done

A mystery shopper tries out a laptop in an electronics store

or say that they are going to do, as we do in interviews and other *communication methods of data collection*.

The main advantage of observation is that it is the most objective procedure for collecting marketing research data, since it only records *actual* behaviour. When events are recorded as they actually occur, the researcher introduces virtually no bias to the study. In fact, the possibility of bias is limited to the data interpretation phase of the research.

A disadvantage of observation is that it is indeed limited to characteristics one can observe. It does not tell us anything about consumer attitudes, motives or plans. The researcher may know *what* the consumer does, but not *why*. In the purchase of a new car, for example, the researcher could record the customer's behaviour in the showroom, but this information does not reveal what happened before the customer visited the dealer. Were there any family discussions about the merits of different cars? Had the customer already decided on the purchase before talking to the sales person? Had they just come from a competing car dealer to make a comparison? Only further research (that involves questioning) can reveal the underlying motives. To its detriment, (direct) observation in a laboratory situation tends to be expensive, often involving the use of high-tech equipment (such as a galvanometer which measures the electrical resistance of the skin) that requires operation by qualified technicians.

5.2.9 Experiments

If we increase the retail price of a particular product, will that lead to fewer sales in the store? To discover the correlation between these factors, we may conduct an experiment, in which we gather data by manipulating certain factors under tightly controlled conditions to test cause and effect. An *experiment* involves selecting two matched groups of subjects, exposing them to different treatments – while controlling extraneous variables – and investigating whether the differences in the recorded responses are statistically significant. For example, we can change the price (or the advertising theme, package design or shelf space, to name a few) for one group, and observe the effect of that change on another variable, usually sales. If we manage to hold all other factors constant, we can then observe that the increase (or decrease) in sales is indeed the result of the change in price.

Keeping all other factors in the external environment constant is often impossible. Researchers can't control the weather, economic conditions or competitors' activities. Therefore, in experimental research we make a distinction – depending on the degree of control – between an uncontrolled and a *controlled experiment*.

If we are conducting an uncontrolled experiment (or a *quasi-experiment*) we do not intervene, but simply measure the outcome of a certain factor. This enables us to establish how independent variables (a *cause*, such as the price of our products and those of competitive brands) affect a dependent variable (the *result*, such as our sales). An example of an uncontrolled experiment is a *test market*. Here, it is obviously not possible to divide consumers up into two similar groups of potential buyers, charging one of them a lower price than the other, in order to measure any difference in their willingness to buy. To conduct such a 'natural experiment', researchers usually use a *consumer panel*. Still, not all of the conditions of an experiment are met then: we simply allow time (with its potential changes in prices, purchasing power and competition) to act as a stimulus and then measure the effect of these changes on the panel members' behaviour.

On the other hand, in a controlled experiment – probably the most scientifically valid research method – the researcher is able to control both the *treatment* and those who are exposed to it. There is an experimental group and a control group, both randomly selected. Furthermore, the influence of extraneous variables is eliminated or limited. The essence of a controlled experiment is that we manipulate at least one variable (the *experimental variable*) to study what effect this has on the *dependent variable*. Marketing researchers conduct two types of experiments: laboratory and field experiments.

Laboratory experiments

In a laboratory experiment the respondents are asked to perform some type of marketing activity in an artificial setting. The investigator controls all aspects of the experiment except for the factor under study (which relates to the marketing decision to be made). The relevant experimental variables (such as price discounts, packaging or commercials) are systematically varied in order to measure any changes in the elements that the researcher wants to examine.

In marketing, this type of experiment is often used to determine the optimal price of a product. In one study, women, in several simulated shopping trips, were shown a different assortment of soft drinks and coffee brands on each trip, then asked to choose the brand they would buy. The relative prices for the various brands were changed on each of the eight trips. Eventually the researcher was able to discover how much of a price increase would cause shoppers to switch to another brand.

Unfortunately, it may not always be possible to generalize the results of such an experiment to the marketplace. In some laboratory studies, the subjects seem to be reacting to the artificial, controlled environment as much as to the experiment itself. With such a reaction, the researchers are actually measuring something other than what they intended to measure, and the test results will not be *valid*. Hence, working with experienced marketing researchers is necessary when conducting laboratory experiments.

Field experiments

The objective of a field experiment is the same as that of a laboratory experiment; to capture cause-and-effect relationships. While there is – with the experiment conducted in the 'field' – less control, an advantage is that the subjects find themselves in a realistic situation. In most cases, they do not even realize that they are taking part in a marketing experiment.

A well-known form of field experiment is an in-store test involving, for example, twenty retail stores, all similar in terms of size, product range, sales and type of location. The stores are split up at random into an *experimental group* and a *control group* of ten stores each. For a period of three months the stores in the experimental group sell a product with a new label (the *treatment variable*), while the stores in the control group continue to sell the product with the old label. Afterwards, the researchers measure what effect the new label has had on turnover (the *dependent variable*) by comparing the sales of the two groups of stores. An example of such an experiment is ACNielsen's *Controlled Store Test,* in which the agency measures consumer acceptance of new products, packaging, prices and displays. Incidentally, most marketing researchers call an experimental study a *test*.

Field experiments are also frequently used in *media research* to test advertisements. In a split-run test the print run of a magazine is divided up into two parts, with each half carrying a different version of the same advertisement, which usually includes a reply coupon. The researcher then investigates the effect of the two advertisements, by either conducting a survey to measure recall (*recall study*), or by comparing the difference in response based on the number of returned coupons. The term *split-run* approach is also used in instances where researchers split up a sample into two parts and use a different questionnaire for each group.

5.2.10 *Analyzing, interpreting and presenting research results*

After the data have been collected, the final step in the marketing research process is the data analysis and interpretation, as well as presentation of the research findings to the decision makers who charged the researcher with the task of investigating the research question during the problem-definition stage. Market researchers use different statistical techniques to *analyze* the data they have collected in order to obtain practical information. Usually, they determine which analytical techniques to use well before they start on the field work. The best approach is to first determine what must be achieved with the desired information, and then to formulate the right questions and measurement scales to obtain the necessary data. Next we choose – based on the selected questions – the best methods of data analysis.

When analyzing and *interpreting* the results of quantitative research, we try to come up with 'numerical' conclusions. Often, companies conduct quantitative research to verify a hypothesis generated on the basis of a qualitative preliminary study. However, drawing meaningful conclusions from that is generally only possible after arranging the data in a table (to get an overview of the overall responses) and possibly cross-tabulating the answers to questions by other variables. *Cross-tabulation* involves examining the data by subgroups (such as male and female consumers) to indicate how the results vary between categories.

The final step is the *presentation* or communication of the research results to management in a timely and understandable manner. The research report should not be too 'technical' to be understood by managers who may not be familiar with complex analytical techniques. Also, the researcher must make sure that the study results are aimed at answering the questions that initiated the research. In larger companies the research results are often entered in a *marketing information system* (MIS). Exactly how and why this is done, will be discussed next.

5.3 MARKETING INFORMATION SYSTEM

Up-to-date, accurate and relevant information is the lifeblood of marketing decision making. Every company produces an ocean of fragmented data: sales call reports, customer orders and monthly balance sheets, as well as other internal reports and flows of information. Many of these must be coordinated and distributed to the appropriate parties in the right form. To make sure that, out of this continuous flow of data, the most important information relating to certain decisions makes it to the actual decision makers, many companies analyze their

MARKETING TOPPER
Monitoring Social Media Postings

Many companies have adapted and responded to the meteoric rise of social media, quickly recognizing the huge marketing potential waiting to be tapped into. *Twitter* spreads the latest trends across the globe almost instantaneously. *Facebook* has huge advertising capability; intelligent mapping personalizes specific promotions to individual users depending on demographic character traits determined by their profile settings, geographic location, search history and social groups. Understanding the 'Zeitgeist' or general consensus on a subject, event or product has never been easier.

Marketers now use sophisticated programming to gather data, identify and analyze trends, and build instant profiles on almost any subject, categorized by age, gender, and socioeconomic background. Following a major sporting or television event, many people will inevitably go online to comment upon it. Whether or not they realize it, through posting personal opinions into the public domain, the populous are inadvertently contributing to one big, continuous marketing research exercise.

As a case in point, social media analytics company *Netbase* obtained a lucrative business contract with a consumer products company worth millions of euros, through overcoming a challenge to determine why many young men have *stubble* (or 'five o'clock shadow'). The research question, submitted to over one hundred market research companies, was addressed by mining a large number of male postings on Facebook, Twitter and other social media sites. With software enabling them to examine three million sentences per hour, Netbase identified over 75 000 online references to stubble in seconds. And within an hour of analysis, they had positioned and categorized the main motives. Not surprisingly, the foremost reason for wearing stubble was a perception that it looked appealing.

The real insight from this exercise was not regarding facial hair, but rather the researchers' capability to gather and analyze a stunning amount of online information quickly and methodically; scrutinizing thousands of social media posts, then selecting the most relevant ones to help marketers identify and evaluate major trends and intelligence. As a result, the global business of collecting and decoding online chatter is growing fast.

The Internet is the world's largest instant focus group

What consumers really think about marketing-related issues remains an intriguing question for customer-focused firms. Today, corporations are spending over €800 million per year for online data to better satisfy their customers' needs. Major marketing research companies are rapidly acquiring firms that specialize in monitoring social media, providing instant insights into consumers' beliefs, attitudes and behaviour. Likewise, corporations are allocating an ever increasing part of their marketing communication budgets to advertising via social media. In the US alone, advertisers are spending over $2 billion per year to reach consumers through Facebook and similar sites.

Monitoring networks and blogs also helps to limit the damage of failed new product introductions, ineffective advertising campaigns or other marketing mistakes. After *Coca-Cola* replaced its original soft drink in the mid 1980s with a sweeter variety, *New Coke*, it received thousands of phone calls and letters from disappointed customers demanding the original flavour's return. It took several months in total to receive and process all the information, to realize the mistake then act upon it, before the original soft drink (renamed *Coca Cola Classic*) was brought back on the market. Today, consumers would have been able to voice their opinion in minutes through a Facebook posting or Tweet.

In fact, that's what happened when *Gap*, a global clothing retailer with more than 3 000 stores, recently introduced a redesigned, more contemporary logo. Immediately, the new logo was harshly criticized by many of Gap's *Facebook* fans and *Twitter* followers. Overwhelmed by the outburst of passionate criticism, management quickly responded by returning to the old design. In 2009, in protest against the talent show *The X Factor*'s annual monopoly over the UK Christmas number one single, a husband and wife created a Facebook group persuading half a million fans to download a rival song by American rockers *Rage Against the Machine*. The grassroots campaign swept the nation and led the corporation's bosses to change the release date of future X Factor winners' singles, to avoid another chart battle. Elsewhere, *Domino's Pizza* used Twitter to effectively enact an image overhaul through their 'Oh yes we did' campaign.

Conventional marketing research methods involving questionnaires or focus groups don't always capture what's on consumers' minds and may fail to bring up the topics that respondents want to discuss. Online customer comments and interaction, on the other hand, are of great value in assessing spontaneous opinions and emotions about the company, its strategy and its products. As Elaine Boxer, a marketing strategist in the healthcare sector recently asserted, 'The Internet is the world's largest instant focus group'. While managers cannot control this consumer input, they do have the option to engage in the dialogue and to promptly act in response to the customer feedback.[7]

managers' information needs and set up a *marketing information system* (MIS). A **marketing information system** involves people, computers and procedures to collect, sort, analyze, store and communicate relevant and timely information – obtained from many sources – to marketing decision makers. If the MIS is working well, it provides managers with precisely the information they need.

Knowledge is power! The underlying question is not whether a company needs an MIS, but how sophisticated the system must be and how it should be designed.

5.3.1 Sources of information

Before there is any information, there is only *data*. The term *data* refers to a number of facts that have not been processed. These individual, unprocessed data are of little use in decision-making. What managers really need is customized information, presented as clearly as possible. A marketing information system must be designed in such a way that the decision maker can get the exact information they need. For example, a sales manager might want to know the sales per product in each region, but not necessarily the effect of the company's promotion and advertising campaigns. If all of this is covered in the same report, the MIS enables the sales manager to obtain only the information that is of interest to them and inform their decision-making. This makes the marketing information system a valuable tool for any manager.

Suppose that Brussels' population increased by 6 per cent in the past three years. This lone fact will mean little to the Marriott chain in making a decision on building a new hotel in the city. The company will have to combine this fact with other data, such as a list of businesses and European Union organizations located in the area, projections of the number of flights to and from the Brussels and Charleroi airports in the near future, an overview of the existing hotels and those in the planning stage or under construction, and data relating to tourism in the region.

As illustrated in Figure 5.2, a company's marketing information system draws on four different data sources.

FIGURE 5.2 A marketing information system (MIS)

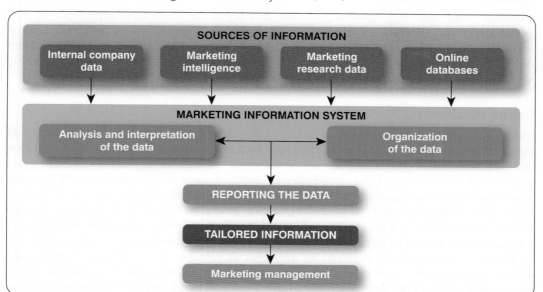

Internal company data

Internal company data originates and is stored within the company. In a well-organized firm, sales managers enter electronic data about customers and products directly into the MIS via the company intranet on a regular basis. An intranet is an internal communications network that links the company's employees, departments and databases through Internet technology. If other departments – such as the customer service department – also enter their data into the database, anyone in the company can improve the company's service to customers by having direct access to information on the customer's sales rep visits, past purchases, pricing history, production schedules, shipping dates and inventory levels. Marketing managers, too, can get weekly or monthly sales data and reports from the system to keep track of their progress in meeting their sales and market share objectives and to measure the effect of promotions and other marketing incentives.

Marketing intelligence

Information about the marketing environment is crucial for making sound marketing decisions. Therefore, a marketing intelligence system – through which external information about competitors and other relevant data in the marketing environment is gathered, processed and made available – is an important input into the MIS.

Major sources of marketing intelligence include the company's own employees who routinely interact with customers and suppliers, and various intermediaries in the industry met at trade shows. Articles in the business or financial press (such as those concerning upcoming new product launches) and, of course, the Internet, which makes government reports, trade association websites and a myriad of other information easily available, are other sources of marketing intelligence. In short, managers should not only evaluate the effectiveness of their own marketing strategies, but also monitor the actions of their competitors – including price changes, product improvements and new advertising campaigns. These observations should be entered into the marketing information system to help the company prepare for policy making in the competitive marketplace.

Marketing research data

As is clear from Figure 5.2, marketing research data is just one of the many inputs into an integrated marketing information system. While marketing intelligence data are gathered continuously to keep managers aware of events in the marketing environment, a marketing research study is only conducted when specific information is needed for a particular decision. Therefore, marketing research is indispensable in business as a source of valid marketing information.

Online databases

Much of the information needed to make marketing decisions may be obtained from (external) online databases. Thousands of these electronic databanks – computerized files of information available from online commercial sources or elsewhere through the Internet – can be accessed with any PC, notebook or other mobile device. Some of them are government databases that make economic or demographic data available at little or no cost. Companies, such as ACNielsen, Reuters, Bloomberg and Dun & Bradstreet, among others, have developed databases and sell selected data to interested buyers. Regardless of its origin, marketing researchers and managers can save a lot of money by using syndicated research as an information source for their MIS.

Although some of these organizations only provide raw data that still has to be processed and interpreted, many now offer their customers *tailored information*. They screen, select, process and interpret the data according to user needs, allowing this tailor-made information to be assimilated immediately for decision-making.

While the cost of an online *search* might appear to be high when compared to other resources, the actual costs are relatively low because of the time saved and speed with which information is compiled. For example, by spending a few hundred euros per quarter to monitor the development of the pet food market online, a company is able to save a great deal of time and money by not having to do any field work. The following examples show just how much time and money can be saved.

Example 1: A simple question
A soft drink company with plans to expand its European production and bottling operations wanted to know how the consumption of mineral water compared to the consumption of energy drinks. An online database provided immediate information about the consumption of each available type of drink on the market.
Time: Five minutes.
Cost: €10

Example 2: A more complex question
A financial planner wanted to know what percentage of household income was spent on rent versus mortgage payments in different regions. An electronic databank found statistics issued by the government and a trade association, as well as a recent article published in an economic journal and provided the required information.
Time: Ten minutes.
Cost: €20

Example 3: A shortcut to a market analysis
A supplier of computer systems for process and production automation wanted to analyze the market to obtain answers to the following questions:

→ What is the market size?

→ Which market segments can be identified and how is each segment developing?

→ To what extent are production processes in selected industries automated?

→ What is the value of the installed systems per segment?

→ Who are the main suppliers, and what are their strengths and weaknesses?

→ How is the demand developing (including marketing opportunities and threats)?

→ What technological developments – such as in the use of production robots – can be expected?

Several market surveys were traced via various electronic databases and purchased. Studies conducted by semi-government agencies and information published in trade journals made it possible to identify and analyze the competition and relevant market trends. The databank also produced a list of branch organizations that provided important information. Finally, three experts in the field of process and production automation were located and approached for telephone interviews. Within ten days, the supplier gained an insight into potentially lucrative marketing opportunities. For example, they learned which market segments were most important and which ones could be tackled later on. In short, the results provided the basis for a strategic market plan.

Time spent utilizing databanks: three hours.
Cost of utilizing databanks: €420
Time spent screening compiled material: two days.
Time spent collecting additional information: three days.

5.3.2 *Processing data*

A marketing information system makes it possible to store and efficiently retrieve all kinds of (internal and external, secondary and primary) data and information through the use of a database. Since the objective of an MIS is to enable the user to instantly call up relevant information in a clear and usable form, the data should be compiled, *processed* and stored in the best possible way. For example, Douwe Egberts – a company that values continuous research – constantly monitors the market positions of its own brands and those of competitors. Every six months the company conducts a survey to investigate the consumption habits and buying behaviour of coffee and tea drinkers. The company also conducts *ad-hoc* surveys, such as taste and acceptance tests, on a regular basis. Information obtained from these surveys is analyzed in a marketing information system and then presented to management in report form.

Analyzing and interpreting data

A major responsibility of marketing researchers is to analyze and interpret the data that have been collected. Douwe Egberts regularly uses external agencies to do its *quantitative research* – which seeks responses that can be summarized in numbers, like averages, percentages and other statistics. These agencies only provide the company with figures and tables. It is then up to the company's marketing research department to analyze and interpret the data. Using statistical techniques such as multiple regression analysis, researchers can determine if there is a correlation between the price, the advertising expenditures and sales.

If the database in an MIS is particularly large, researchers often use an analysis technique called data mining to retrieve the desired information. This allows researchers, using powerful supercomputers, to sift through terabytes of data to find certain patterns of buying behaviour among various groups of customers. These consumers can then be targeted for special offers and promotions.

Organizing the data

Suppose a marketing manager wants to know the demographic characteristics of those who have seen a certain commercial on television. The data need to be organized in a way that facilitates *presentation* of the information to management. Douwe Egbert's policy is to give external agencies conducting research for the company exact instructions specifying what they should or should not consider part of their assignment. Only in exceptional cases is an agency requested to present its findings to management.

Today, many companies improve their MIS by installing a **Marketing Decision Support System** (MDSS). This is a coordinated set of data, tools and techniques, complemented by analysis and interactive software that allows managers – using the intranet – to access MIS data and conduct their own analyses. This computerized system is easy to use, even for those who are not skilled with computers. A marketing decision support system is *interactive* (gives instructions and provides immediate feedback), *flexible* (integrates data from multiple sources, returning up-to-date statistical analysis) and *discovery-oriented* (helps managers by readily revealing trends and identifying problems).

Reporting the data

Once the collected data have been analyzed and interpreted, they are presented to management in a research report. A *research report* describes the objective of the research, how the data were gathered and the results of the analysis. Needless to say, this information should be presented in a comprehensible way – without too much technical jargon – and must clearly address the research questions. If the research does not provide information to help managers make the necessary decisions – such as choosing the target market and developing the most effective marketing strategy – the firm has wasted research time and money. Therefore, this final step has to be anticipated in each of the earlier stages in the marketing research process.

Because managers do not usually have time to study in detail how the data were collected and which statistical techniques were applied, a good research report starts with an *executive summary* of no more than two pages with a concise synopsis of the research results. If the marketing information system is working properly, it will convert data into information that marketing managers can use in marketing strategy planning and decision making.

5.4 TEST MARKETING

As is apparent from Unilever's disaster described in the *Marketing Mistake*, a fundamental task of marketing researchers is *test marketing*. This involves making the product available to the market in a limited geographical area – similar to the larger market it hopes to enter – in order to determine the product's commercial feasibility. Test marketing usually has two objectives:

→ To estimate the sales in units once the product is launched in the whole market and

→ To test the effectiveness of the product's promotional campaign or other parts of the marketing mix.

In the fierce competitive battle between new products, many managers are not as interested in how their product sells as they are in enhancing their promotional strategy. As a result, they may test market the same product in several geographic markets ('**test markets**'), varying the promotional campaign slightly in each. This approach makes it possible to evaluate the relative effectiveness of the different strategies. Test marketing can also provide information about:

→ The anticipated market share.

→ The characteristics of consumers who buy the product.

→ The characteristics of buyers who try the product, but who do not repurchase it.

→ The frequency of purchase by different consumer groups.

→ The ways in which consumers use the product.

MARKETING MISTAKE
Omo Power: Unilever's Dirty Laundry...

About two decades ago, Procter & Gamble Chairman Edwin Artzt flew from Cincinnati to Amsterdam on a highly unusual mission: to give helpful advice to top executives of major competitor Unilever, the Anglo-Dutch company that held a number two position in the European detergent market. Artzt tried to talk Unilever out of a €250 million European detergent launch of *Omo Power* (called *Persil Power* in some European countries), the brand that contained an ingredient Unilever named 'the Accelerator' because of its highly effective stain removal properties. The classic case story you are about to read illustrates the importance of testing a new product thoroughly before the promotion, distribution and price strategies are tested.

Unilever was sure that its innovation would redefine the soap powder category. Procter & Gamble (P&G) had traditionally dominated that market with its popular *Ariel* detergent that, with annual sales of €1.3 billion, had become Europe's best-selling packaged-goods brand after Coca-Cola. At the time, P&G had already beaten its rival Unilever to market with a previous big detergent innovation, the ultra-compact detergent. Now, Unilever was determined to win the latest battle with its new Power brand soap, but it would need to thoroughly test any product that had so much riding on it.

© Mike Filippo / Shutterstock

Unilever was so enthusiastic about Omo Power that it skipped formal test marketing

Before launching the Omo and Persil Power brands, Unilever missed out on one important detail: manga-

nese, the 'accelerator' ingredient, destroyed clothing! Had the company used better research, including the use of a test market, the outcome might have been completely different. However, Omo Power was introduced as planned and immediately, Procter & Gamble obtained samples of the product and tested them; it then launched an aggressive publicity campaign trying to discredit the Power products. In its advertisements, Procter & Gamble informed consumers that Omo Power not only killed stains but also killed clothing. Unilever had no choice but to admit failure for a product on which it had spent hundreds of millions of euros.

Ultimately, the Omo Power fiasco decimated Unilever's detergent market share. Within ten months of the new product's introduction, Unilever pulled the plug on the brand after wasting €20 million on promotion. The company learned the hard way that a truly new and innovative product (in this case, soap powder) can take years and tens of millions of euros to develop, with little or no guarantee of success. Time-to-market had become so important that the multinational failed to make sure the product could actually meet the expectations set by the promotional campaign.

Unilever's decision to proceed with the planned $300 million European Power roll out is a cautionary tale, accentuating the pressures global marketers face in developing products that profit internationally, while at the same time being compelled to expedite product introduction. Unilever was desperate for greater market share in Europe, and the company was so enthusiastic about Persil and Omo Power with the Accelerator, that the company skipped formal test marketing in favour of a full-blown roll out.

'It is the greatest marketing setback we've seen,' Sir Michael Perry, Unilever's former chairman, admitted of the lack of adequate marketing research. To make matters worse, samples of the harmful product had been distributed to tens of millions of European homes. Unilever moved too fast and many say the company didn't handle the crisis well. Despite the bad publicity for Omo Power in the Netherlands and Persil Power in the U.K., Unilever somehow saw fit to continue introducing the product in a dozen more countries, allowing the problem to spread across the continent!

Unilever vice-chairman Niall FitzGerald, commenting on his meeting with thirty Unilever executives after the crisis was apparent, realized where the marketing research was seriously lacking: 'I asked how many people in the room did their own laundry. Not one person raised a hand,' he said with amazement. 'There we were, trying to figure out why customers wouldn't buy our soap – and we didn't even know the first thing about how it was used.'

Unilever has learned from its marketing miss. Now, as part of its product development process, it is a standard procedure to test all new products both in the laboratory and under actual consumer usage conditions. Although Unilever claimed it spent three years testing the new Power detergent in the lab and with consumers (60 000 consumers in test markets had already bought the harmful detergent three months before the Europe-wide launch), later, independent tests costing less than €40 000 showed that the original Omo Power could leave holes in some garments after as few as twenty to thirty washes! The moral of this story is obvious. Marketing research is essential and starts with learning everything you can about your own product.[8]

So where should a company test market its products? What principles should a company apply during test marketing? And how long should a good test marketing programme last?

5.4.1 *Selecting test markets*

In deciding where to test market a product, the most important factor is to define as accurately as possible the anticipated overall market for the product. Manufacturers in relatively small countries usually distribute their products nationally. If this is the case, the test market area must be *representative* of the national market.

When determining whether a community or region is truly representative and would thus be a suitable test market, the firm initially examines the *population structure*, considering such variables as the ethnic and family make-up, social class and age of the residents. Since urban and rural areas differ in many respects, a test marketing programme is usually carried out in each of these divergent locations. Test marketers also consider factors relating to the *product* itself, the *intermediaries* and the *advertising possibilities*, such as the market share of competing (for example, regional) brands, the presence of certain types of stores and media coverage through the regional press. Most firms considering national distribution for their products test market them in several locations to achieve a more representative national sample.

5.4.2 Principles of test marketing

There are five major conditions or principles to be followed in test marketing:

1 The test market should have *representative*, or normal, distribution and advertising media channels for the product. For example, if we are planning to sell the product through department stores and specialty stores, then these types of stores must be present in the test market area. Also, the retailers should be willing to cooperate and participate in the test marketing programme.

2 The test market should be relatively *self-contained*, so that little, if any, promotional effort is wasted outside the test market area. Hence, national media such as newspapers or radio and television cannot be used in a local test market. In addition, strong outside media influences – such as widely read national newspapers – should be kept to a minimum. When such influences are present, it is difficult to evaluate the impact of the promotional effort, since consumers are then exposed to more than what is considered a normal amount of promotion. Therefore, test marketers tend to rely on free local papers distributed door-to-door, leaflets and regional editions of national newspapers.

3 The company should *not overspend* on the introductory campaign. Despite how much marketers want their products to succeed, emotions should never get the upper hand in marketing research decisions. For test market results to be meaningful, the firm cannot spend more money per prospect in the test market area than it is planning to spend in the market as a whole.

4 We should keep in mind that *potential competitors* will monitor the test market almost as closely as the company itself. Since relatively few cities meet all the criteria for a good test market, most firms watch these cities closely to see whether new products are being tested. There are even cases of competitors buying up all of the products being tested in the stores to disrupt the research, but this is not a common practice.

5 Finally, managers should be *cautious* when interpreting the test market results. While it may not be obvious in the test market, competitors rarely sit back and do nothing during a test marketing programme. For example, less than a month after Unilever launched its 'Salsa de la Casa' range in Holland, the country's largest supermarket chain Albert Heijn introduced its own store brand salsa. While Unilever failed to point out in its advertising that the product could also be used as a dip, Albert Heijn deliberately emphasized this fact. Because national brand manufacturers have to negotiate shelf space with supermarkets well before test marketing a new product, some retailers take advantage of the information they obtain when developing their own *private label* products. Therefore, in drawing conclusions from test marketing results, companies must always anticipate that competitors may introduce their own (imitation) version of a successful item – a so-called **me too product**.

5.4.3 How long to test market?

How long a test market should run depends on the objective of the test marketing effort. If, for example, the objective is simply to evaluate the market, the test market will not have to run as long as it would if the goal were to fine-tune the entire promotional strategy or to prepare for a major European product introduction.

Similarly, the length of time varies with the nature of the product. For *fast-moving consumer goods*, such as detergents and shampoo, the test market must run, at a minimum, until the first **repeat purchases** can be expected. It is one thing for a clever promotional campaign to entice people (maybe only out of curiosity) to buy a product, but it is quite another for the product to perform well enough to bring about a second purchase. It is the second purchase that shows whether or not the market accepts the product and whether consumers

© CulturalEyes-DH / Alamy

may become loyal to the brand. As a rule, the *turnover rate* of non-durable consumer goods is a good indicator of the right length of a test marketing programme. On average, non-durable consumer goods are tested for four to six months in most European countries. But, as the following example shows, a test can also run for an indefinite period of time.

Many major brand companies have opened up their own retail outlets. Some of these are mainly used as a promotional tool, as in the case of the Hugo Boss, Gucci, Nike and Adidas outlet stores. For example, Douwe Egberts, through its *Douwe Egberts Café*, is trying to encourage young people to drink more coffee. Other companies use their single-brand stores primarily to *test market* new products.

An example of such a test marketing store is the Unox *Soup Factory*. 'We are experimenting with retail because it allows us to get in touch with customers,' says marketing director Stef Gans. 'The actual sales are of minor importance. We are more interested in marketing research and trying out new products.' The bottom line is that now, Unox can determine immediately from the response in its own outlets which new flavours consumers like best. This information also helps the producer to obtain more shelf space in the supermarket.[9]

At the end of the day, many manufacturers simply launch new products nationwide without doing any kind of test marketing. Especially for durable goods, such as cars, washing machines and machine tools, the extended length of the repurchase cycle, along with the high cost of manufacturing testable products, almost forces these companies to go ahead with full-scale introduction without the safety net of test marketing. Therefore, test marketing of durable goods often involves only evaluating the effectiveness of different promotional campaigns, not the products themselves.

SUMMARY

1   The importance of marketing research

To ensure that products and services meet the needs and wants of potential buyers and that marketing programmes are effective, marketing decisions should be based on *information* obtained from the market. Marketing research generates much of the information that helps managers make better decisions, thereby reducing the risk and uncertainty they face. Marketing research provides valuable information enabling companies to identify marketing problems, discover opportunities for new products and monitor the marketing environment, including the ever-changing buyer behaviour and market structure. A company's ability to systematically gather, analyze and interpret objective data about relevant environmental changes in the market may allow it to adapt its marketing strategies faster than its rivals. And that is a major competitive advantage.

2   The marketing research process

The *marketing research process* begins with defining the problem, which involves setting the research objectives and, if feasible, identifying possible marketing actions. This first step is crucial, since it guides the entire research process. The (proposed) research design also needs to be determined early in the process. Not until we have examined the *secondary data* and the results of any *exploratory research*, can we decide how to collect and process additional data.

Primary data may be collected in several ways. The most commonly used method is surveys. Survey data can be gathered through mail questionnaires, personal interviews, telephone interviews and online.

Motivation research uses methods (such as projective techniques and focus group discussions) that offer insight into respondents' subconscious motives when making purchase decisions. The observation method of data collection is suitable, if we want to find out *what* consumers do rather than *why* they do it. Finally, laboratory and field *experiments* enable us to capture cause-and-effect relationships and trace links between certain data. The last phase of the marketing research process involves analyzing, interpreting and reporting the results.

3   Marketing information systems

Managers are paid to make decisions. The main objective of a *marketing information system* (MIS) is to reduce the risks associated with making these decisions by providing management with relevant, accurate and up-to-date information. The inputs for an MIS consist of internal company data, marketing intelligence, marketing research data and online databases.

Reliable data are crucial in decision-making. An MIS that is working properly will provide managers with tailored information. A *marketing decision support system* (MDSS) makes it even easier for managers to conduct their own analyses and, based on these results, make better decisions. Therefore, investment in gathering, analyzing and distributing information that facilitates decision-making is crucial to a company's success.

4   Test marketing

The objective of test marketing is to predict the commercial viability of a product or the success of a promotional campaign. Such evaluations are conducted on the basis of a market test in a limited geographical area. Although it is difficult to find a suitable test market in any small country, there are a number of standard test regions that are representative of the country as a whole. How long a test market should run depends on the nature of the product and the objective of the research.

DISCUSSION QUESTIONS

1   What effect has the increased interest in marketing had on market research?

2   If a property developer were considering the construction of a shopping centre along a highway and close to a new railway station, what available secondary data would help them in evaluating the market situation?

3   If you intend to conduct a survey to collect certain data, how do you decide whether to use a mail survey, a telephone survey, personal interviews or an online survey to gather the necessary research data?

4   Cite a few examples of how questionnaires for written, telephone, face-to-face and online surveys might differ from one another.

5   What criteria can a company use to determine if it is spending enough money on marketing research?

6   Suppose you are working for a candy company as a product manager. The company's CEO sends you an email saying 'Sales of our brand of liquorice have now fallen by more than 5 per cent for the third year in a row...We expect you to take immediate steps to increase sales of this product by at least 10 per cent next year.' How would you react?

7   In a competitive analysis, many firms identify not only their current competitors but also their potential rivals. What is the best way to assess the threat posed by potential competitors?

8   A tyre company is asking you to research the anticipated demand for car tyres among automobile owners in Belgium over the next five years. You know this is a difficult task, but the money that the company is willing to pay you makes all the difference. You decide to accept the assignment. Outline how you would proceed, describing the type of data you would need and your preferred data collection method.

9   When Apple entered the European market with an entirely new (and impressive looking) line of tablets, the company did not have enough insight into how prospects perceived these computers. This made it quite difficult to determine the target market for its marketing communication campaign and the type of message to convey to potential buyers. How do you think Apple should have solved this problem through proper use of marketing research? Make sure that your answer is as detailed as possible.

10   An increasing number of companies that believe the future is hard to predict, use 'scenario planning'. They develop different scenarios and assess the company's business strategy in the various market situations outlined in these scenarios. Which of the techniques discussed in this chapter or on the accompanying website do you think would be ideal for this?

CHAPTER 6
MARKET SEGMENTATION AND POSITIONING

LEARNING GOALS

After studying this chapter you will be able to:

1 Determine the size of a market

2 Explain why market segmentation is important for any organization

3 Identify the most commonly used bases to segment markets

4 Discuss the differences between three possible targeting strategies

5 Describe the role of positioning in developing a marketing strategy

6.1 Defining the market

6.2 What is market segmentation?

6.3 Bases for segmentation

6.4 Targeting strategies

6.5 Positioning strategies

There is no such thing as the average consumer. People have different needs, wants and buying habits. Managers aspiring to adopt a successful market approach keep this in mind when developing their strategies.

Wherever there is a need for something, there are opportunities for companies to satisfy this need. Marketing opportunities are plentiful, though not all are lucrative. As we will see in this chapter, we first have to identify, analyze and evaluate the marketing opportunities. Not until we have segmented the market and selected the most promising target markets can we outline marketing and positioning strategies so that we can develop a strong position in the chosen market segments.

Splitting up the market into segments – based on marketing research – and then approaching each target market separately, requires an upfront investment of management time and money, but it will pay off. In fact, market segmentation and positioning are two of the most lucrative strategies ever to have emerged from the marketing discipline!

MARKETING IN ACTION
Hotels Targeting Generation Y

The *Millennial Generation*, also known as *Generation Y*, consists of a group of young individuals between twenty and thirty-five years old, fascinated by new technology, eye-catching design and, of course, social media. With the recession largely behind it, the global hotel industry has seen this new target market of young travellers as essential to its survival. They are characterized by their iPod or iPhone, and are ready to unload their iPad upon arrival and get on Facebook. Hence, most guests in the millennial market segment consider free hotel-wide Wi-Fi Internet access to be as essential as clean towels and a comfortable bed.

In 2012, in order to keep up with the tech savvy, the Ritz Carlton introduced a mobile app incorporating QR codes (which can be scanned by smartphone to access online content) and location-based services providing guests with special promotions and experiences. As Allison Sitch, the Hotelier's head of PR noted, the introduction was designed to broaden their reach to a wider audience. This is part of a wider trend amongst hotel chains to move with the times, with technological innovation.

All the big players such as InterContinental, Marriott, Starwood and Hilton go beyond offering free Internet access to appeal to young guests. Many have given their large lobbies a facelift to resemble technology lounges, adding plush coaches, art deco furnishings and elegant bars, allowing guests to have a cocktail or a glass of wine while checking out a website or socializing with friends. Other hotels are organizing trendy social evening occasions – such as daily wine tastings and yoga sessions – to create a hospitable atmosphere. Although these events may require significant investments, hotel industry executives know that travel expenditures by the *Gen Y'ers* are growing about 20 per cent per year, so hotels ignoring Gen Y'ers are at a stark competitive disadvantage. And while these young travellers don't spend as much on travel as 'baby boomers' do, they are without doubt the fastest growing – and therefore most attractive – target market in the hotel industry.

Hotels ignoring Gen Y'ers are at a stark competitive disadvantage

Not too long ago, hotel owners were primarily targeting the *baby boomer* generation: consumers now in middle age and approaching retirement. To them, comfort is often the most important criterion in choosing between hotels. To entice baby boomers and turn them into loyal customers, hoteliers installed larger desks with brighter lights and superior quality beds. But the Millennial Generation is less interested in these types of amenities. Instead, their wish list includes unconventional features such as an *entertainment system* in to which you can plug your iPod, and – elsewhere in the hotel – a state-of-the-art *fitness* area. Since iPad-toting travellers hate to search for wall plugs under their bed and resist having to unplug lamps to charge their devices, many hotels are putting easily accessible *power consoles* in rooms. Some even place a *tablet* as a standard feature in all rooms that guests can use to read the newspaper, dim lights, turn on the air conditioning or request room service.

Much of the communication between hotels and their Generation Y target market takes place through social media and social networks. An older traveller who has an issue with, for example, room service will typically contact the hotel manager to voice their complaint. Gen Y'ers, on the other hand, are more likely to go online and post a comment on Twitter or a forum. To monitor these online comments, Starwood Hotels have created a team of two dozen people who are ultimately in charge of responding to consumer complaints, always going the extra mile to resolve any problems.

A Gen Y'er who has changed after work into a T-shirt, shorts and trainers to get some work done on a laptop in a public area may not feel comfortable in a hotel lobby with traditional oak wood panels, classic paintings and authentic Oriental rugs. Hence, quite a few hotels have remodelled their lobbies and changed them into 'great rooms'. Knowing that young travellers like to spend time in different places in the evening, hotels have added bars and restaurants with various themes that are changed throughout the week, so that guests won't have to leave their hotel to enjoy the ambience in a new setting.

One of the pioneers in creating designer hotels with hip nightclubs was Starwood with its *W* hotels and *Aloft* brand. Other brands that are targeting a market segment of younger travellers include *Indigo* (part of the InterContinental Hotels Group), *Andaz* and *Hyatt Place* (both of Hyatt Hotels Corporation) and *Yotel*. Yotel is a futuristic designer hotel with, for instance, an airport-like check-in kiosk replacing the registration counter, and reasonably priced compact rooms – inspired by an aircraft cabin – with floor-to-ceiling windows. The hotels – now located in New York, London and Amsterdam – will be expanding across the globe soon, tailoring their products and services to Generation Y travellers. As more and more hotels begin to adapt to this new market and become increasingly innovative with their designs, one thing is certain – travelling will definitely become more interesting![1]

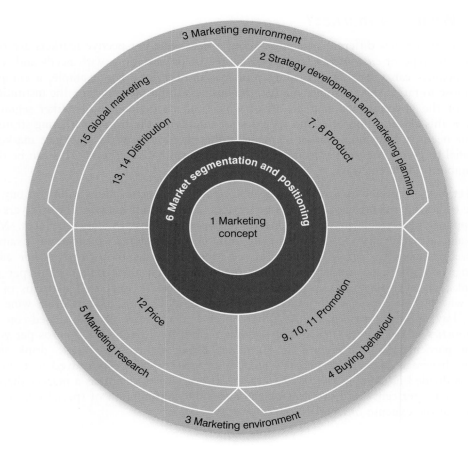

Every company must come up with the best possible strategy for approaching the market, if it wants to grow and enhance its position. Yet, healthy growth is not something that can be achieved simply by targeting as much of the market as possible. After all, different people have different needs. To be sure that we are focusing on the right target market, a strategy of *market segmentation* is essential. This boils down to developing a well-planned marketing strategy to focus on just a *part* of the total market.

In this chapter, we will analyze the concept of a market, as well as different market approach strategies. We look at why it makes sense to divide the market into segments and what techniques can be used to do so. We also examine how to select a suitable target market from the market segments we have identified. Finally, we consider the importance of an effective positioning strategy when competing in the market.

6.1 DEFINING THE MARKET

One of the manager's most important tasks is to get enough insight into the overall market to be able to identify their own market by deciding who their potential customers are. Without a realistic sense of the market size, the competition, the company's position within the market, the potential buyers and the opportunities for growth, it is impossible to develop an effective strategy. Therefore, we define the market as accurately as possible and then systematically delineate it through a strategy of target marketing. This is accomplished by selecting customer groups within the larger market and developing products and marketing programmes tailored to their specific needs and wants.

6.1.1 What is a market?

The word **market** has different meanings. From a marketing perspective markets are often identified by type of *customers* – groups of people or organizations with needs and wants that companies can satisfy by providing products and services. For example, a company may choose to target the consumer market, the business-to-business market, the institutional market or the governmental market, all of which can be divided into market segments. However, this classification offers no specifics for modifying the firm's marketing strategies to fit the needs of individual market segments, rather than those of the aggregate market. It is essential to define the market in more detail using quantitative criteria. This can be done in a number of different ways.

A market may be defined as any person, group of people or organizations willing to buy and capable of buying a company's products or services. The contacts between those buyers and the suppliers may result in transactions or business relationships between them. More specifically, a market may be described using different dimensions. Consider, for example, the beverage market. This market can be described in terms of its *size* or per capita spending: consumers in a particular country spend more than three billion euros per year on drinks, or more than 200 euros per capita. It can also be expressed in terms of the *people* who buy or consume a product: 60 per cent of all college students drink wine and usually buy it from supermarkets. Other market definitions can be based on the *characteristics* of the buyers (half of the customers earn more than 36 000 euros per year), and, in particular, on differences in *consumer behaviour* (young people drink more alcoholic beverages than older people). Finally, the market can be portrayed in terms of how it is divided up among *competitors* ('the World of Drinks chain has a market share of more than 10 per cent') and in terms of *products* ('the consumption of specialty beers has increased at the expense of lager').

It is obvious that, for the purpose of defining markets, the demand side is usually emphasized. A common view is that 'markets are people', or combinations of individual needs and wants. However, not everyone who needs a product that a company can supply belongs to its *target market*. Hence, the market first needs to be analyzed and identified or delineated in more detail.

6.1.2 *Identifying the market*

Managers often describe the market for a product in terms of the *need* or function that the product or service fulfils for the buyers. This is a meaningful perspective, because products that satisfy the same needs actually compete with each other. The companies selling these products are operating in the same market arena. Furthermore, such a broad market definition also makes it easier to link the market to the *business definition*. As we saw in Chapter 2, a company's *business* (or area of activities) is usually defined in terms of the customers' needs or the market on which it focuses. For example, marketers account for the growing liqueur market by pointing out (as revealed by marketing research) that consumers 'experience' liqueur as a *social* drink, ideal for in-home consumption. The product obviously satisfies a clear customer need, such as sharing an enjoyable occasion at home.

When defining the market in terms of satisfied needs, the needs should be broadly formulated. Companies that operate movie theatres, for example, are not simply in the film business. They actually meet consumers' *generic* (very general) *need* to relax and enjoy leisure time. From the perspective of generic need satisfaction, movie theatres are really competing with musicals, discos, restaurants and other establishments with a similar recreational function. Once their managers realize this, they are more likely to use the right marketing tools in the competitive fight and to go the extra mile to provide their customers with an enjoyable 'night on the town'.

No matter how we define the market, keep in mind that although a potential buyer or 'prospect' may have a *need* for our product or service, this does not automatically make them part of our target market. Marketing research can provide some valuable insights here. Not every person or organization has the *interest*, *purchasing power* and *willingness* to actually buy the product. As Figure 6.1 illustrates, these are meaningful criteria to start defining the market.[2]

With the generic need for the product as a starting point, the market then must be limited to a specific target group. This might be the market segment of individuals or firms that are potentially interested in buying the product and are also willing and able to pay the price for it. For retailers, the market might be further reduced to a certain geographic area.

As an example, the target market for a company that sells maternity clothing is limited to mothers-to-be who need the product. Women who are not pregnant and those who are, but are not interested in a new maternity outfit (because they still have clothing from a previous

FIGURE 6.1 A step-by-step procedure to define the market

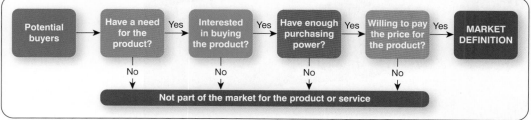

pregnancy) or are not able to afford it, fall outside of this niche. This means that only a fraction of fertile women between the ages of 15 and 45 comprise the company's target market.

6.1.3 *Analyzing market potential*

When estimating the market size, we consider not only current owners or consumers of the product, but also those who are not yet using the product. Some of the individuals or companies in this group, namely those both willing and able to purchase the product, are potential buyers. In addition, new applications for the product, as well as increased consumption levels by current users, will also affect the future size of the market. Therefore, when developing a marketing plan, we also assess the *market potential* or the **potential market**: an estimate of the maximum possible sales of a product or service in the entire market within a specified time frame with optimal marketing efforts of all suppliers.

Closely related to this somewhat theoretical measure is the difference between the effective demand and potential demand for a certain product. The **effective demand** is the total number of products currently sold (or, in the case of durable goods, products that have already been purchased). The **potential demand** is the number of products *over and above* current sales that suppliers could sell between them, assuming they have developed the optimal marketing mix. Essentially, potential demand is the demand on the part of those who are interested in the product, which is *not yet manifest*. Together, the effective demand plus the potential demand make up the market potential.

6.1.4 *Demand and market approach*

After having introduced a new product, companies that sell *fast moving consumer* goods, such as soft drinks and candy, always keep track of **repeat purchases**. With an effective promotion campaign, it is fairly easy to get consumers to make an *initial purchase* of these low priced items. But only the repeat purchases will indicate if the market has accepted the product and if consumers are becoming loyal to the brand.

For **durable consumer goods**, a market analysis is more complicated. These are products (such as high definition televisions) that consumers purchase for use over several years. Because of the relatively high price and their high involvement in the purchase, consumers typically go through an extensive decision-making – or 'problem-solving' – process when

A high definition television is an example of a durable consumer good

© Levent Konuk / Shutterstock

buying the product. Marketers of these types of goods are interested in both the level of demand and the structure or *make-up* of the demand. Thus, we distinguish three submarkets or types of demand that together form the effective demand: the initial demand, replacement demand and additional demand.

Types of demand

The **initial demand** originates with those who do not own the product and buy it for the first time. If we take a high definition television set as an example, the initial demand comes from consumers who have never purchased this product before. That group constitutes the *initial market*.

Replacement demand is the demand on the part of those who already own the product but buy a new one to replace it. These repeat buyers make up the *replacement market*. On the other hand, if those who already own the product keep it and at the same time purchase another one (such as a second high definition television for the bedroom), this qualifies as **additional demand**.

The sum total of the initial demand plus the additional demand for a particular product or brand during a certain period is known as **extended demand**. For numerous products, there is an interesting *extended market*. If we add the extended demand to the replacement demand, we arrive at the total sales or the **total demand** for the product.

Market approach strategies

The orientation and buying behaviour of consumers differs from one submarket to another. In the initial market, the crucial factor is the consumer's acceptance of the product. In the replacement market, however, sales depend on the (economic) life span of the product and on technological developments as applied to the product category. Only when we determine the composition of the total demand – enabling us to relate any increases or decreases in sales to each of the three submarkets – can we effectively influence consumer demand through tailored marketing activities.

As long as the *initial demand* continues to rise, there are plenty of growth opportunities. Because the buyers have no experience with the product and may be uncertain about brand choice, we need to provide them with information about the product and the brand. Once the initial demand starts to fall, growth stagnates and the market becomes saturated. At this point, we should stimulate both additional demand and *replacement demand* with a **product differentiation** or product innovation strategy, in order to increase market share.

Within each submarket, there are also significant differences between buyers. Not every consumer has identical needs and wants or responds to advertisements and commercials in the same way. Since most markets are *heterogeneous*, many companies pursue a strategy of market segmentation. In fact, segmentation is the key to a successful marketing strategy for many companies.

6.2 WHAT IS MARKET SEGMENTATION?

Check out any supermarket, and you will see an immense range of products. Take soft drinks for example. They come in all flavours, in regular and 'light', carbonated and non-carbonated, in cans and in bottles (either in no-return bottles or with a deposit), ranging in size from 0.15 to 2 litres. Some brands clearly target the youth market, while others appeal to price-sensitive buyers or to diet-conscious consumers who prefer sugar-free drinks.

MARKETING TOPPER
Why Philips is Targeting Poor People

As a Philips researcher, Paul van der Sluis spent many of his days perfecting a primitive wood stove. To all appearances, this was an unlikely pursuit for the company. Yet, this product incorporated high-tech components and promised to make life a little easier for millions of families in developing countries. With this unusual invention, Philips pursued a new *target market* – the poorest of the poor.

The *smokeless wood stove* is extremely clean and economical in how it burns fuel. It uses 80 per cent less wood than a three-stone campfire, slowing deforestation. It is also much healthier, producing 90 per cent less toxic emissions, which kill an estimated 1.6 million people per year!

The Chulha is in line with Philips' brand promise of Sense and Simplicity

Van der Sluis came up with the idea of developing a smokeless wood stove in his own back yard. 'I like to grill meat on a barbecue, but I also wanted something that would allow me to cook other types of food in pots or pans on charcoal outdoors. That just didn't exist.' He remembered how inefficient and time-consuming it was to cook on a traditional campfire when he was in the Rocky Mountains a few years earlier, and the penny dropped. 'Half of the world's population cooks on camp fires that are highly inefficient and inconvenient.'

Because of the huge *potential market*, Philips gave van der Sluis the necessary time, as well as a budget, to develop a wood stove. He added a fan powered by a so-called thermoelectric generator – a little unit that converts heat from the burning wood into electricity. 'A step back on the technological ladder? I don't think so. No one else had ever managed to develop a stove with a

working generator which can also power external equipment like radios and lighting.' That's good green design!

Of the 24 families in India invited to test the wood stove, most did not want to part with it. Philips saw the potential of a *market development strategy* for what is, at first sight, a low-tech product. It distributed another thousand stoves to families living in rural areas in order to *test market* the product more extensively. Andrea Ragnetti, a former Philips marketing executive, saw the stove as a good example of how the company can apply its technology and sell outside of the markets in which it currently operates. 'Consumers are willing to spend money on it because of its benefits: it will enable them to save both time and money.' Thus, the clean economical wood stove is not meant to be a scout project. It is fully consistent with other moving initiatives described in the company's annual *sustainability report*, but ultimately, Philips hopes to profit financially on this innovation.

The so-called Chulha stove ('chulhi' means stove in Hindi) is also perfectly aligned with the marketing strategy of this global company. Now that western markets are virtually saturated, the technology concern is seeking to cultivate *emerging markets*, such as India and China. The urban population in those countries is rapidly increasing its purchasing power, and Philips is trying to turn this to its advantage. But the potential market for the wood stove is much greater, since there are many more potential customers in rural areas in India and the rest of the *third world*. This is the 'base of the pyramid' that Philips and other corporations intend to explore, so they can serve all segments of the market – including those they cannot serve with their current products and through their existing distribution channels.

Philips figured out that at the base of the pyramid there are about 400 million people cooking on an open fire. Therefore, the Amsterdam-based company saw 400 million potential customers as the *target market* for its wood stove. Once the more extensive test market in India was completed, Philips decided which division would develop the appliance from that point on. Then, the company sought out local partners to handle production and distribution in India.

In deciding on a price for the new stove, marketers put themselves in the potential customer's shoes. It is estimated that in places where wood is scarce and expensive, the wood stove should pay for itself within six months. The inventor himself spent six months cooking solely on his own brainchild. That made him quite confident about the innovation. 'If we don't sell millions and millions of this product, I just won't consider it a success!'

But isn't it a bit strange when Philips, a company renowned worldwide for technological innovation, comes up with a product made of clay and concrete? 'Not at all,' says Simona Rocchi, senior director for sustainable design at Philips. 'The Chulha is completely in line with our brand promise of *Sense and Simplicity*. With the target market in mind, the stoves are definitely "designed around you" and "easy to experience" in terms of use and maintenance. And, although it may not appear so, it is definitely *advanced*. Not in a high-tech way, but because the technology is much more effective and sophisticated than the one previously available. This simple stove demonstrates that we can clearly improve the quality of many people's lives through design.'[3]

This array of choices is the result of a strategy of **market segmentation**: a demand-oriented approach that divides the total market for a product into smaller subsets of customers having similar needs or behaviour, and then modifying the firm's products and marketing strategies to fit the needs and wants of these individual, homogeneous market segments rather than those of the aggregate market.

6.2.1 Emergence of market segmentation

Originally, very few companies segmented the market. Their decision to divide the market into certain regions or groups of separately targeted customers was more of an intuitive attempt to find as many buyers as possible for their *existing* products, than it was a strategy based on a careful prior analysis of the market. In those days, most firms adopted a less customer-oriented approach to working the market and pursued alternative marketing strategies such as mass marketing and product differentiation.

Alternatives to market segmentation

Historically, most companies have followed a strategy of *mass marketing*. This approach is also known as *undifferentiated marketing* or market aggregation. The companies' business philosophies were primarily production- or product-oriented. They tried to sell as much as possible with a standard product, mass distribution and a single marketing programme – despite the fact that customers were not all the same. Operating the business efficiently was the top priority. Mass media were only used if absolutely necessary. Companies kept their costs, as well as their prices, down and they enlisted large numbers of customers – who did not have much of a choice because of the scarcity of goods – to buy their products.

If a firm did adopt a more market-oriented approach, it was usually through a strategy of *product differentiation*. To boost sales, it introduced various products that differed in terms of style, quality, price or other attributes. It did not differentiate its products in order to systematically target distinct groups of buyers, but merely reacted to buyers whose tastes were changing or who were, for whatever reasons, seeking some variety in their product use. By regularly launching larger, faster or more attractive new models, companies tried to stand out from one another. A classic example of this – in a pre-market segmentation era – is the annual introduction during the 1950s and 1960s of new models of American cars with short life cycles – often with bigger tail fins and lots of chrome. This market approach coincided with the rise of the selling concept. At that time, most companies

© Shannon Heryet / Shutterstock

still regarded their current *products*, rather than (potential) customers, as the starting point in strategy development.

Market segmentation

Since the breakthrough of the marketing concept, increasing numbers of organizations base their marketing strategies primarily on the buyers' needs and wants, as identified through market research. However, they realize that they cannot possibly appeal to all buyers in the marketplace. Therefore, they must be selective in building customer relationships.

Segmenting a market is not an exact science; its success usually depends on the manager's common sense and analytical skills. Selecting and reaching the right target segments requires a systematic approach, based on both quantitative and qualitative measures. As illustrated in Figure 6.2, this process can be divided into three steps:

1 *Segmenting* the market: dividing a larger, heterogeneous market – based on one or more meaningful and shared characteristics – into smaller, fairly homogeneous groups of people or companies that respond similarly to a marketing strategy developed especially for them. First,

FIGURE 6.2 Segmentation, Targeting and Positioning (STP)

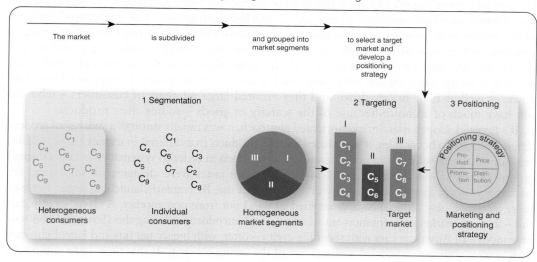

marketing research is conducted to analyze the market. This reveals different types of individual consumers, households or companies, each with different preferences. These potential buyers are then grouped into market *segments*. We will explore in paragraph 6.3 which *segmentation variables* are most useful in determining these groups.

2   *Targeting*: assessing the attractiveness of each of the identified segments that meet certain criteria, and selecting one or more of these market segments on which to concentrate when entering the market. As we will see in paragraph 6.4, there are three alternative marketing strategies in selecting the target market: undifferentiated marketing, differentiated marketing and concentrated marketing.

3   *Positioning*: finding ways to make the company (or its products) stand out – in the customer's perception – from competitors.

These three stages in the segmentation process are sometimes referred to with the abbreviation STP. The rest of this chapter covers the underlying principles and techniques of segmentation, targeting (or 'target marketing') and (product) positioning in more detail.

6.2.2 *Reasons for market segmentation*

Why do companies segment the market? An important reason for segmentation is that markets are *heterogeneous* in makeup. For example, one consumer reacts differently to advertising campaigns than another. Also, there is considerable *competition* in the market. Finally, market segmentation is consistent with the *marketing concept*. Here we look at each of these three reasons for segmentation.

Heterogeneous markets

Theoretically, a market can be subdivided into as many segments as there are people in the market who make purchase decisions. Although this extreme form of segmentation may work well when each product is made on request from the buyer (such as with custom-made clothes, or houses that are built to customer specification), it is not feasible when the product is mass-produced. On the other hand, it is impossible to attract all potential customers to one product. After all, the 'average' consumer does not exist. Different buyers simply have different needs, and they also seek to stand out from the crowd. To accommodate this heterogeneity, it makes sense to provide a variety of products. The company's goal is to locate and cultivate those market segments that are large enough to be served profitably.

A strategy of market segmentation does not necessarily mean that the firm must produce a different product for each market segment. If consumers buy a certain product for different reasons, we may leave the product as it is, and try to reach each group of buyers with a different advertising campaign built around a particular appeal. Likewise, the price and distribution strategies can be tailored to groups with different buying motives and habits.

Image Asset Management

These kinds of adaptations in marketing strategies are not just applicable to the business sector. Government agencies and non-profit organizations can increase their effectiveness in the same way.[4] For example, some politicians try to 'sell' their messages to voters by emphasizing different priorities in their speeches to union members, business leaders or the unemployed. Yet their political agenda remains the same.

Competition

Increased competition in the global market has led many companies to adopt market segmentation strategies in order to retain customers. As new firms enter the market with their own products, the company is forced to pay greater attention to the needs of prospective customers, if it wants to hold on to its market share. Marketing research usually shows how preferences differ from one market segment to another. Concentrating on a certain segment is essential to maintain dominance in the market.

The marketing concept

A final reason for using market segmentation (or *differentiated marketing*) is that this strategy is consistent with the marketing concept as a business philosophy or management orientation. Market segmentation recognizes the existence of distinct market groups, each with its own set of needs and wants.

A firm can satisfy these needs and wants with customized marketing strategies. This is the heart of the marketing concept. For example, *Pelikan* – a company that makes pens – meets the needs of left-handed people by marketing a fountain pen designed especially for this segment. With an innovative segmentation strategy, any company may become the leading supplier in the segments it targets and can even create a (temporary) monopoly position.

From a marketing perspective, market segmentation offers several other *benefits*. Since a segmentation strategy must be based on a thorough analysis of the market, it also becomes a tool for appraising competitive strengths and weaknesses. This stimulates managers to choose the right product line, determine effective advertising and sales strategies and set specific marketing objectives against which performance can be measured. Specifically, segmentation analysis helps us to:

→ Detect the first signs of trends in rapidly changing markets

→ Design products that take into account the buyers' preferences

→ Develop a distribution strategy that is adapted to the target market

→ Decide on a price level that will make the product more attractive

→ Determine the appeals in advertising that will be most effective with each market segment

→ Direct the appropriate promotional attention and funds to the most profitable market segments.

Since these decisions and measures (expressed here as the six Ds of segmentation analysis) are the foundation of successful marketing strategies for both industrial and consumer goods or services, market segmentation clearly benefits most organizations.

6.2.3 Decision criteria for effective segmentation

Not all companies decide to segment the market. If a firm does not have sufficient *financial resources*, a segmentation strategy may not be feasible. Designing special products for different segments inevitably results in higher design and production costs. After all, it costs less to make 1 000 000 units of one product than 100 000 units of ten different products, even if they only differ in a few respects. The overall costs may be excessive, even though new production techniques make it possible to take advantage of *economies of scale* at lower production levels than ever.

Also, the costs of maintaining inventory increase. With market segmentation, we have to maintain a safety stock of each product in order to be able to absorb unforeseen fluctuations in demand. This requires capital. In addition, promotion costs will increase as we create awareness of the products through different campaigns among target markets via different media. Because we cannot run a standard advertising campaign for the whole market, we miss out on media discounts.

Finally, we have to invest more in marketing research to obtain detailed market data. This information is important, since there are various ways (not all equally effective) in which a market can be segmented. There should, for example, be a correlation between the characteristics used to define buyers (such as age or attitudes) and their buying behaviours (such as brand choice) for the segmentation to make sense.

Marketing research also reduces the risk of cannibalization, which occurs when a company loses sales in its established products after introducing a new product that is seen as a substitute by buyers. This risk may be diminished with a well-planned marketing policy (unless we deliberately intend to replace, by means of cannibalization, an old product with a new one that yields a higher profit margin!). Because it is essential to choose the right market segments, VNU Business Publications, before launching a new magazine, appoints – in addition to an editor in chief – a marketing researcher and a marketing manager to supervise the product development process.

A shrewd STP (segmentation, targeting and positioning) strategy places considerable demands on decision-making. The company has to ensure that the *marketing strategy* for each of its market segments is carefully coordinated. For instance, what prices should it charge for its products? Which promotion strategy will work best? And where should the products be sold? Many firms employ *product managers* who are charged with the task of coordinating all of the activities for a particular product. Others employ *account managers* who are responsible for the sales activities aimed at important customers. Whatever system a company uses, as the number of segments it wants to reach increases, so too does the amount of time required to analyze the effect of its segmentation strategies.

In deciding whether to adopt a segmentation strategy, most companies examine four criteria: the measurability, the size and accessibility of the proposed segments and the feasibility of the segmentation strategy. These four *requirements for effective segmentation* or segmentation conditions are shown in Figure 6.3.

FIGURE 6.3 Decision criteria for successful market segmentation

Measurability of the segments

Critical to any segmentation programme is the firm's ability to identify and measure the buyer characteristics that will serve as the basis for segmenting the market. The segments themselves need to be homogeneous and sufficiently *different* from one another so that they can be isolated and targeted separately. Geographical and demographic criteria tend to present fewer problems in this respect than psychographic characteristics. If, for instance, a manufacturer of men's suits cannot measure the importance of 'status' in selecting a suit and is therefore unable to identify status buyers, then the firm cannot use that variable as a basis for segmenting the market. The condition of measurability is only met if the company is able to relate different preferences for a product to relevant, measurable characteristics of status buyers (such as income, profession and social class) which can be used to isolate a segment and develop a marketing campaign.

Size of the segments

A segment must be *large* enough and have sufficient purchasing power to be potentially profitable and interesting as a target market. For example, very tall people and very short people may well be interested in cars designed specifically for people of their height. But the potential sales revenues would be far too low to justify the expenditures of designing, producing, marketing and maintaining an inventory of these kinds of automobiles. Hence, in each case we need to assess whether the money to be made from catering to a specific homogeneous submarket will justify the additional expenditures.

Accessibility of the segments

In order to target the identified segments, we must be able to reach these segments with a focused promotion campaign and through the available distribution channels. If a segment (for example, mothers-to-be) is known to read particular magazines and to shop in certain stores, accessibility is ideal. If we have the addresses, telephone numbers or email addresses for these individuals, we can implement a direct sales approach via direct mail, personal selling or the Internet.

Feasibility of the strategy

The segment has to be *workable*. A company must have the necessary *resources* to tackle the segments it has identified as differentiated markets. Conducting marketing research, developing an effective strategy and maintaining separate stocks all require financial, production and personnel resources.

When assessing the *feasibility* of the strategy, we should also consider how *responsive* the segment will be to the organization's marketing efforts. The firm might investigate the segment's potential responsiveness through a survey or even test marketing. If the segment has a unique need and the strategy is effectively tailored to this need, there is likely to be a positive and predictable response. If, on the other hand, the marketing instruments used do not appeal to the target market, there is little point in segmenting the market in this way.

6.3 BASES FOR SEGMENTATION

Markets can be segmented in many ways. Unfortunately, a method that has proven successful for one product or market may not be effective in other situations. A person's age and social class may determine which store they prefer to shop in, but may not influence which brands they choose; instead, that may depend on their lifestyle.

PRACTITIONER'S PERSPECTIVE
Eric Paquette (Copernicus Marketing Consulting)

Eric Paquette is senior vice president of Copernicus Marketing Consulting, a company with clients such as ExxonMobil, Michelin and Procter & Gamble. He has led the firm's charge to adapt tools and solutions to all the changes in marketing communications brought on by the digital revolution.

The digital revolution has not necessarily made *market segmentation* any easier or harder, but just changes some of the things that we need to consider. We've always said you need to worry about three things with segmentation. To begin with, you must make sure that the segments are *different* in terms of their profit potential so that you can identify a clear *target* for your brands. You also want to be sure that the segments provide enough guidance on the needs, wants and *motivations* of that target so you can develop clear *positioning* and messaging strategies. Finally, you have to be able to *reach* those targets through *media*. Those criteria still hold true, but now you also need to worry about some other things.

First of all, you have to pay more attention to *brand advocates* and make sure that they are a significant part of your target segment, simply because the role of brand advocacy is much bigger now than ever before. Their scale of reach and the speed with which they can reach lots of different people has increased dramatically. Although your advocates are typically *heavy users* who, for example, eat at your restaurant every week, there are also other people who visit you on a weekly basis. So you need to know more than their usage behaviour and find out if they actually really love you.

Through *attitudinal* types of statements in a questionnaire we can measure both the intensity of their affection for the brand and their interest in telling others about the brand. We also want to know how many people they can *reach* and how quickly. How many *Facebook* friends and *Twitter* followers do they have? Are they bloggers? Somebody who loves you and only talks to a few people is less valuable than someone who loves you and talks to 1 000 people.

Second, you need to know what kind of *behaviours* your target audience members engage in when they're online. At one end of the spectrum there are *authors*, who are writing their own blogs, creating their own content or generating their own web pages. The marketing strategies that you develop for that audience in the digital environment are very different than for a group of consumers who are *connectors*, who just want to get online and be with other people like them or for *spectators* who just go online to look at the information that others are creating. Find out how your target market aligns across those behaviours so you can understand what you should be doing digitally to find them.

For a group of authors, develop digital strategies to *engage* them and try to get them to create new content. Supply the information about you that they are interested in so they can share that with others. By seeding them with *content*, you're providing them with the tools and means to post their opinions and thoughts.

Today, much of consumers' efforts to engage and learn about products is going on in YouTube

The marketing world has changed significantly, and the old advertising strategy – where you find your target and then just broadcast your message to them – is no longer adequate. Today, much of the marketing process is going on in places where consumers are trying to engage and *learn* about you. Therefore, it is critical to understand how the target group is *researching* the product category or your product, how they try to find you, what they want to *learn* and where they might be in their *purchase cycle*. Digital technologies give consumers dramatically more *control* over how

to do that – are they getting their information from you, other users, blogs, social networks or YouTube? If they're doing initial research on their computer, direct them to your website. But if they're standing at the point of purchase with an *iPhone* in their hands wanting to learn something quickly, obviously the information you provide is very different.

From a nuts-and-bolts kind of search perspective, if they are using particular *search terms*, you want to know what they are so that you can optimize your search strategies. Innovators or people in an advanced group will use different search terms than others. Having that information available so you can *tailor* your search strategies more effectively is essential in *digital segmentation*.[5]

Therefore, in planning a segmentation strategy, we should examine various demographic, geographic, psychographic and behavioural segmentation criteria in order to identify those that will be most effective in defining our markets. Some frequently used segmentation criteria are outlined in Figure 6.4, along with some examples or applications.

6.3.1 *Demographic segmentation*

Demographic data are the most commonly used basis for market segmentation. Demographic variables are relatively easy to understand and measure and have proven to be useful for segmenting many markets. In applying demographic market segmentation, the market is divided up into subgroups based on factors such as income, age, gender, ethnic and racial background, social class and education.

Income

Income level is a widely used variable for segmenting markets, because a person's income not only determines *how much* of something they can buy, but also influences their wants and thus, *what* they buy. For example, there is a correlation between consumers' buying

FIGURE 6.4 Segmentation criteria for the consumer market

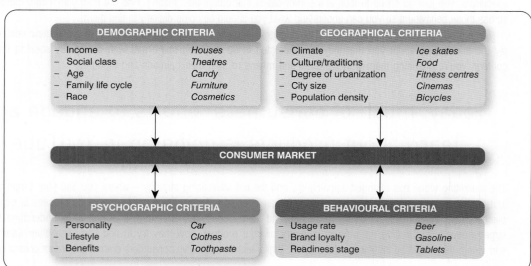

power and their purchase of a second home or a luxury yacht. The markets for automobiles and banking services have also been successfully segmented by income. Hence, many marketers deliberately focus on certain income groups.

Social class

Despite its frequent use, income is not an ideal segmentation criterion. After all, two people with the same income may have very different spending patterns. The differences can often be attributed to the *social class* to which they belong. And because people's spending habits affect their lifestyle (which is also of interest to marketers), social class is often used as a basis for market segmentation.

Automobile dealers, for instance, know that consumers in lower social classes tend to buy a used car straight from the original owner, while members of higher social classes prefer to shop for pre-owned cars at dealerships. Another example in which social class determines spending habits is in wine consumption. More than 70 per cent of consumers in the higher social classes drink wine, a much greater percentage than in lower social classes.

Age

There is a strong correlation between someone's wants and needs and their age. Whereas teenagers are heavy users of soft drinks and mobile phone services (like smartphone bundles), people in their forties are the primary buyers of reading glasses and medication.

It is important to note that age is a *dynamic* variable, always subject to change. To illustrate, since a youth magazine is read by young people who in a few years' time will cancel their subscriptions, the publisher has to constantly attract new young readers to maintain its circulation.

Stage in the family life cycle

Changes in buying behaviour often have less to do with the biological process of aging than with changes in the *family situation*. The *family life cycle* – which combines the characteristics of age, marital status, presence and age of children and survival status of the spouse – involves a predictable sequence of events, including going to school, adolescence, leaving home, getting married, having children and eventually retiring. The needs in each phase vary substantially. A 24-year-old bachelor will enjoy different activities and buy different products than a married man of the same age with three children. In fact, marital status, the size of the household and the stage in the family life cycle all account for much of what a person needs and buys. One could argue that in marketing research, more attention should be paid to the family life cycle.

Other demographic and socioeconomic factors

Besides age, household size and family life cycle, market-oriented companies use other *demographic characteristics* to segment the market. One of these is *gender*. To illustrate, men own more than 90 per cent of all motorbikes. Since many nations have become multiracial societies, *race* and **ethnic patterns** are frequently used as segmentation criteria. Ethnic groups, which often live in distinguishable regions of a country or areas of a city, are an ideal target market for companies that tailor the marketing mix to the norms, values and behavioural characteristics of this segment.

Socioeconomic variables are meaningful segmentation criteria, too. Income, profession, education, nationality and religion are all examples of socioeconomic variables. For instance, many European Catholics traditionally eat fish on Fridays, while Muslims – who generally lead temperate lives – consume neither pork nor alcohol. Marketers that regard these groups as target markets take this into consideration when developing a strategy.

6.3.2 *Geographic segmentation*

People from different countries, regions or cities buy different types of products and services to fulfil the same basic needs. Their preferences are often the result of the culture, climate, population density (*degree of urbanization*) or traditions in their environments. This explains why the demand for certain types of food, furniture, clothing, cars and recreational activities differs from one country to another.

Even regional differences *within* a country – including in small nations – lend themselves to market segmentation. In Belgium for example, different types and brands of beer are preferred in different parts of that country, whereas in the Netherlands, supermarket chains take into account that large eggs are more popular in Amsterdam than in any other Dutch city or region. Recognizing that people's preferences vary depending on where they live,

© zimmytws / Shutterstock

many companies tailor their offerings to appeal to different regions. As a result, an increasing number of marketers rely on area code or **geodemographic segmentation**, which involves a combination of geographical and demographic data. This is based on the principle that people with similar economic and cultural backgrounds and perspectives tend to cluster together.

Geographic segmentation also makes sense in business-to-business marketing, since industrial markets in most countries are much more *concentrated* than consumer markets. In the Netherlands, for example, the chemical and shipbuilding industries are all located along the main inland waterways, whereas in the US, states like New York, Illinois, Ohio, Michigan and Pennsylvania contain a disproportionately large percentage of the industrial market. For this reason, many B2B marketers focus their sales efforts on a few specific geographic areas for maximum impact on sales.

6.3.3 *Psychographic segmentation*

Another way to segment the market is through the use of consumers' *psychological* characteristics. These include the buyers' values, attitudes, interests and perceptions. **Psychographic market segmentation** is becoming increasingly popular. A company with a good understanding of the typical combinations of the attitudes, lifestyle and personality characteristics of the customers in its target markets can develop products, services and positioning strategies that appeal to those segments. If a particular group of customers could be typified as 'conservative', an investment bank could promote its services by emphasizing its 'long-standing reputation'.

Although it is often not easy to group consumers on the basis of psychographic variables, these kinds of profiles allow us to define market segments more precisely than is possible with purely demographic characteristics. Three commonly used psychographic variables are personality, lifestyle and benefit.

Personality

Personality refers to all the physical, mental and emotional characteristics of an individual as an integrated whole, especially as they are presented to others. An individual's *personality* influences the products they buy. For example, an 'aggressive' person is likely to wear different clothes and drive a different make of car than someone who tends to avoid conflict. Companies that make products such as cigarettes, liquor, cosmetics and expensive watches attempt in their advertising to create an *image* or personality for the brand that appeals to a segment with certain **personality characteristics** (such as being extroverted or ambitious).

Instead of using generalized personality traits of potential buyers in segmenting markets, marketers should develop personality measures that are

Image courtesy of The Advertising Archives

situation-specific and relate to a particular type of consumer *buying* behaviour. To illustrate, rather than looking for a general trait of self-confidence, the marketer should measure the self-confidence of the consumer in evaluating different brands within a product category. If we fail to apply these kinds of situation-bound criteria, the value of personality characteristics in segmentation research is limited.[6]

Many consumers spend a fortune on products and activities that reflect their *lifestyles*, but try to save money on items that are less important to them. They often go to extremes in both directions. They may cut back on insurance (which is, after all, an invisible service), yet vacation in The Yucatán. They routinely get their groceries from discount supermarkets like Aldi, yet buy clothes in expensive, upscale specialty stores. They don't bother to get their cars serviced regularly, yet will dine in Michelin star restaurants. They may be living in student flats, yet buy the most expensive home cinema systems on the market. They wear second-hand clothes, yet drink expensive black-label whisky. Remarkably, the contradictions in their spending behaviour to express a preferred lifestyle are countless.

Lifestyle segmentation

In the past, it was often assumed that consumer behaviour was determined by innate and unchangeable personality characteristics. We now know that environmental and situational factors also influence people's *lifestyles*, including how they spend their time and money.

Because *lifestyle* and consumption behaviour are closely related, marketers often apply lifestyle segmentation. This practice involves looking at the customer as a 'whole' person rather than as a set of isolated parts. The most widely used lifestyle dimensions are an individual's activities, interests, opinions (the *AIO variables*) and demographic characteristics. We know that consumers are willing to spend a great deal of money on products and services that emphasize their *self-concept*, but not on items that they do not consider worthwhile. Consequently, marketers have the greatest chance of succeeding if they first gain insight into the activities, interests and opinions of potential buyers and then segment the market – and position their product – accordingly.

A detailed description of potential customers in terms of lifestyle is especially useful when developing an advertising campaign that shows persons and situations with which the target market can identify. For example, Saab typically targets educated, independent thinkers. If, on the other hand, *lifestyle research* (frequently used to examine the differences between heavy users, light users and non-users of a product) indicates that members of the target group feel a strong need to be with other people, the advertisements might picture a variety of social settings showing how the product helps satisfy that need. Often, the best results are achieved if the advertising relates to the *ideal self* or to what people *want* to happen, rather than what really happens or is likely to happen.

Benefit segmentation

Another form of psychographic segmentation is benefit segmentation, also referred to as *benefits-sought* segmentation. Markets can be defined in terms of the benefits that people seek from the product, and then segmented based on consumer preference for a specific product characteristic. Although most people would like to receive as many benefits as possible from a product, research indicates that the relative importance that people attach to particular benefits varies substantially. These differences can then be used to segment and target markets.

If we link these *benefits sought* to certain potential buyers' characteristics (such as age, lifestyle and media habits, as apparent from research), we get – for each benefit segment – a unique demographic and behavioural profile. Doing so will also give us a clear idea of how the target market differs from other market segments. This information is useful for developing new products and services that satisfy certain needs, as well as for creating promotion strategies appealing to those who are interested in these products and services. Some analysts view benefit segmentation as part of behavioural segmentation, to be discussed in the next paragraph.

The market for toothpaste can be segmented in terms of various product *benefits*, which include white teeth, decay or gum disease prevention, fresh breath, flavour, product appearance and price. Research has shown that the buyers in each of these segments can be described pretty accurately.

Those consumers concerned about the brightness of their teeth are generally young women who pay a lot of attention to their appearance and who are, therefore, more interested in cosmetic benefits. These women form an excellent target market for cosmetically positioned toothpastes such as Aquafresh Natural Whitening, Macleans and Ultra Brite. 'Medicinal' toothpastes – such as Parodontax, Elmex and Zendium – are wasted on them, as are Everclean and other low-priced brands that appeal to those in the price-conscious segment. By aiming a product with specific benefits at the right target market, a company that makes toothpaste can substantially increase its market share.

The advantage of benefit segmentation is that it enables a company to develop products and marketing strategies that are designed to fit the precise needs of the market. This is more effective than trying to 'create a market' for an existing product. Also, benefit segmentation helps the firm avoid cannibalizing its existing products when introducing a new product. Because the company knows what benefits consumers are looking for, it can *position* its brands in such a way that they do not compete with one another.

6.3.4 *Behavioural segmentation*

Basing a marketing strategy on what people actually *do* rather than on what they *say* they are going to do, often involves less risk. Many people feel that consumer *behaviour* is a better segmentation variable than consumer attitudes or intentions. In behavioural segmentation, market segments are identified according to the actual behaviour of consumers in the marketplace. The market is divided into groups of customers who are similar in terms of their use of the product or their *response* to a certain product offer. For example, we may focus on the usage status (former buyers, current buyers, potential buyers) or usage situations (such as having tea for breakfast, in the afternoon or on special occasions). In broader terms, behavioural segmentation is a way of grouping people within a market on the basis of their product *usage rate*, degree of *brand loyalty* and *willingness to buy*.

Usage rate

The frequency with which consumers buy or use a product or service is called *usage rate*. Often, as few as 20 per cent of a firm's customers account for close to 80 per cent of its sales. This principle of marketing is referred to as the 80/20 rule. Applying this segmentation strategy we first divide the market, based on *usage rate*, into three categories: heavy users, light users and non-users. We then develop a different marketing strategy for each of these segments.

This approach is quite common in the organizational market. Sales representatives or account managers for industrial product companies who concentrate their efforts on a few large customers (*heavy users*) almost become external consultants to these customer firms. They know the product and service needs of the company, when orders will be placed and who in the firm makes the purchase decision. This enables a supplier to develop an optimal product mix and marketing strategy. This type of behavioural segmentation can also be effective in the consumer market. If, for example, as a result of a focused campaign, Grolsch successfully persuades consumers who drink large quantities of beer ('heavy users') to switch from Heineken to Grolsch, the resulting sales may equal the sales that would come about from winning over ten new customers (such as women) who are light users of the product.

Brand loyalty

A second behavioural segmentation criterion is the degree of brand loyalty. Some customers tend to keep buying the same brand regardless of the alternatives offered by other companies, while other buyers are more interested in variety. It pays for marketers to identify consumers who are most loyal to their brand – and the underlying reasons – and to develop marketing strategies (including some form of loyalty programme) to satisfy the needs and wants of this segment.

Readiness stage

Finally, we can often segment the market on the basis of the degree of willingness or 'readiness' to buy. Some consumers may be totally unaware of the product or not very knowledgeable about it. Others are familiar with the product offerings, but have never tried the product itself. Still others intend to buy it, have actually bought it or are already loyal users of the brand.

Each of these segments requires a different marketing strategy, likely with a different emphasis on advertising, sales promotion and personal selling. If, for example, the target market is already aware of the product, there is little point in conducting an informative advertising campaign. Instead, to reach these knowledgeable non-users of the product, it would be better to spend the budget on distributing samples, placing displays in stores, offering price discounts or other types of sales promotion designed to stimulate consumers' willingness to buy. This approach may, in fact, be the best way to increase the company's sales and profits.

6.4 TARGETING STRATEGIES

Let's assume that we have mapped out the whole market through a segmentation analysis, with the objective of dividing it up into market segments. Depending on the customer categories we have identified and the available resources, we then have to decide on our marketing strategy and the segments we should target. We now need to address three key questions:

1 Do buyers consider the products or brands on the market as identical (*homogeneous products*) or as being different from one another (*heterogeneous products*)?

2 If the products are regarded as heterogeneous, and it is possible to identify different market segments on this basis, should we target these segments with just one marketing mix or – in the context of a differentiated strategy – with different marketing propositions?

3 How many market segments should we focus on and – if we have to choose – which of the identified segments would be suitable target markets?

Once we know the answers to these questions we can choose a targeting strategy and use the market grid concept to help us select a target market.

6.4.1 Target marketing decisions

Once a market has been segmented, we have to determine which targeting strategy will be most effective to reach the potential buyers in the market. Both the nature of the products and the segments identified determine the extent to which we need to *differentiate* the

PROFESSOR'S PERSPECTIVE
V. Kumar (Georgia State University, USA)

V. Kumar ('VK') is Professor of Marketing and Executive Director of the Center for Excellence in Brand and Customer Management at Georgia State University in Atlanta. His pioneering research on customer loyalty and customer lifetime value has received attention around the globe, and has been published in premium journals such as Journal of Marketing, Harvard Business Review, Journal of Marketing Research and Marketing Science. VK was recently ranked as one of the top five scholars in marketing worldwide. He is also Chairman and CEO of his own consulting firm, Innovative Marketing Consultants. His clients include leading Fortune 500 corporations Royal Dutch Shell, ING, Coca Cola and Procter & Gamble.

'Philips Electronics proudly reports a significant increase in customer loyalty. The company's objective is to gain as many loyal customers as possible. What I want to know is, at what cost? If customer loyalty is your ultimate goal, you can retain and reward as many customers as you like, but you may not make much money on this segment.

Companies typically use three criteria in defining customer loyalty. The first is *how long* someone has been a customer. The second is the percentage of their budget for the product category that the customer spends on the company's brands, or the customer's *share of wallet*. And, the third is how profitable the customer has been for the company in the past. In my opinion, none of these three criteria is valid. Here's why.

If you've been buying Philips products regularly for the past ten years, Philips will regard you as a loyal customer, who is more profitable than someone who has only been a customer for three years. But that does not make any sense. You have to look at *what* these customers have bought in the past three or ten years and how much money they have spent. The newer customers may have purchased more high priced items such as big screen LED TVs, while long-time customers may have only been buying low priced or discounted products.

The same goes for the share of wallet criterion. If someone spends 100 per cent of their budget on products made by the same company, they would be considered more loyal than a customer who only spends 50 per cent of their budget on its products. But what do you prefer: 100 per cent of 100 euros or 50 per cent of 1000 euros? And the third criterion – profitability – simply reflects the past; it says nothing about the *future*. What you really have to look at is the *customer life cycle*. People go through stages in life that change their spending patterns. A wealthy woman may spend extravagantly on an upscale refrigerator, but after getting divorced, may only buy used appliances. On the other hand, a law student on a tight budget will start spending much more money once they get a full time job after graduation. Most companies do not take customer life cycle into account. But that's really what counts…

The value of a loyal customer is highly overrated

All of this is actually rather simple, but few managers look at customer loyalty this way. There are three reasons for this. First of all, a company needs a very good *customer database*. Secondly, a great deal of *knowledge* is required in order to develop sound predictive models. Not many companies have that kind of expertise, and buying it externally is quite expensive. It would be well worth it in the long run, but managers are often hesitant to commit to long-term projects without knowing in advance the return on investment. The third problem is the *implementation*. Customer Relationship Marketing is not just a matter of building a database. As an organization, you have to move from a product focus to a *customer focus*. Managers must learn to look at the customer life cycle, and invest in making the organization more customer-oriented.

Despite all of the CRM packages on the market, very few firms actually do this. Many companies that are split up in divisions are still sending the same customer separate mailings about products from each division. What a waste! Instead, look at the customer's purchase trend, figure out what they are likely to buy in the future and send them just *one* mailing that lists all these products. This type of strategy adjustment may involve a huge organizational change, which will cost quite a bit of money. But it is a one-time investment that will generate a great return. Most managers realize this, but don't have the vision and drive to execute such a reorganization. Unfortunately, five years from now they won't have that option any more, and I predict their profits will go down the drain.'[7]

marketing activities, or develop different *marketing propositions* (combinations of marketing instruments). In terms of the number of segments to target, there are three strategic options; these so-called targeting or target marketing strategies are undifferentiated marketing, concentrated marketing and differentiated marketing.

An *undifferentiated* marketing strategy, also called *mass marketing*, means that we develop a single marketing strategy to reach the entire market. This may be an appropriate strategy for **homogeneous products**, which are products (such as milk, sugar and bananas) that buyers consider to be identical. What matters here are not the products themselves, but how customers perceive them. From this point of view, even products that are technically different can be homogeneous. This makes product differentiation difficult, because buyers consider all brands nearly identical and believe that they offer the same use or benefit. Examples of this are the consumer markets for electricity and, to a large extent, for gasoline.

In case of **heterogeneous products** (which customers perceive as being different from one another) we can distinguish different market segments. With such a heterogeneous demand in the market, we must choose between a concentrated and a differentiated strategy. If we decide on a *concentrated* strategy, we confine ourselves to a single marketing mix and use it to target one or just a few segments. If, on the other hand, we decide on a *differentiated* strategy, we develop several marketing programmes and aim them at different segments of the market. In that case, we focus on at least two market segments. Car manufacturers are an example of companies that implement a differentiated marketing strategy.

Figure 6.5 illustrates these three targeting strategies. Of course, the more segments we tackle, the higher our marketing costs will be. Therefore, the decision as to which target marketing strategy to implement will be partly dependent on the resources at our disposal.[8]

FIGURE 6.5 Three targeting strategies

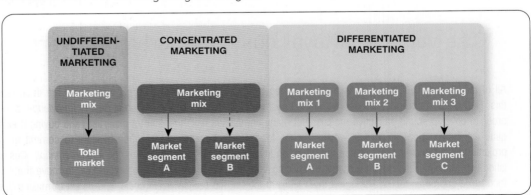

Undifferentiated marketing

Undifferentiated marketing is an appropriate strategy for markets that are homogeneous. Companies that make antifreeze, for example, concentrate on the universal need of car owners to prevent engine damage due to freezing temperatures. They know that nothing would be gained by trying to market the product to different income, geographic or lifestyle segments of the market and therefore consider a differentiated strategy unnecessary.

However, in most markets, which are heterogeneous, this is not a very marketing-oriented strategy, since companies that use it are not practicing market segmentation. They treat the market as an aggregate and focus on what consumers have in common rather than on their differences. They go after the entire market with the same product and marketing programme, hoping to achieve economies of scale and to keep costs at a minimum.

To convince the market of its product's merits, a company practicing undifferentiated marketing must have a relatively high advertising budget. If several firms adopt this approach, cut-throat competition and lower prices may result. Still, a mass marketing strategy can be effective if a new product is in the introduction stage of its life cycle, when market demand is still low and competition is minimal.

Concentrated marketing

With a strategy of either market segmentation or undifferentiated marketing, the company strives for as large a piece of the total market as possible. With concentrated marketing on the other hand, the firm aims only at a narrow portion of the market, hoping to gain a high market share and a strong position in that part of the market. Concentrating on just one market segment is called a niche strategy. If, however, the firm focuses on more than one segment, it still does so with the same marketing mix.

As with every form of market segmentation, it is important that the total market is divided up into segments *within* which there are as few differences as possible and *between* which there are as many differences as possible in the anticipated response to the marketing strategy. By concentrating on a particular target market, a firm soon gets to know its customers very well and develops a better understanding of their needs and wants than do companies competing in many market segments. Such specialization enables the firm to compete effectively and often leads to economies of scale in production, promotion and distribution, as well as an opportunity to become a market leader in the selected segment.

Rolex is a good example. With watches ranging in price from €2 000 to more than €250 000, the company clearly focuses on a limited target market and, in the words of its CEO, 'does not want everyone to wear a Rolex'. The strategy pursued by *Rolls-Royce* is another example of a concentrated strategy. The risk of concentrated marketing is that if there is a fall in demand in the market the company is targeting, or if the competition suddenly increases, this can result in sharp drops in sales. However, because of limited resources, some companies have no choice but to pursue a concentrated marketing strategy.

Differentiated marketing

In pursuing a differentiated marketing strategy, we try to reach the entire market (or at least a large part of it) by developing a unique marketing mix for each segment of the larger population. This will result in higher sales than would be possible if we simply came up with one marketing mix or focused exclusively on a single target market.

GET BETTER, FASTER.
GET FREE.

NIKE FREE'S ENGINEERED FLEXIBILITY HELPS IGNITE THE MUSCLES IN YOUR BODY FROM THE
GROUND UP FOR IMPROVED STRENGTH, BALANCE AND FLEXIBILITY – SO YOU GET EVEN MORE
FROM YOUR WORKOUT. AND WHEN COMBINED WITH ONE OF THE 90 CUSTOM BUILT WORKOUTS
FROM THE NEW NIKE TRAINING CLUB APP, YOU CAN REACH YOUR GOALS WHATEVER THEY ARE.
EVER WANTED A PERSONAL TRAINER IN YOUR POCKET? NOW YOU'VE GOT ONE.

NIKE FREE
NIKE.COM/FREE

Nike is an example of a company that produces a wide range of products for very diverse target markets. For example, golfers are quite different from amateur tennis players, while basketball players have little in common with football fans. For this reason, the company uses different logos, labels and Internet sites to promote its products for each segment, making its customers feel special.[9]

The products themselves do not necessarily have to be completely different. Often a unique brand personality or positioning strategy will be enough to get customers to perceive them as different. For example, cosmetics companies offer brands in several price categories that appeal to different segments of the market.

6.4.2 Target market selection

The segment of buyers that the company selects as its market, and for which it develops specific marketing activities, is known as the *target market*. If we are adopting either a concentrated or a differentiated marketing strategy we must first decide how to subdivide the aggregate market and then systematically evaluate the various segments in order to select the most attractive ones. In this **target market selection** process the so-called *market grid approach* can be a useful analytical tool. Under the *market grid concept*, the market is viewed as a matrix divided by relevant segmentation criteria. Since each cell within the matrix represents a smaller, more homogeneous market, this approach is also referred to as the *cell method*.

To illustrate the use of the market grid technique, assume that a real estate developer specializing in recreational property is able to build three types of second homes: simple chalets, semi-detached bungalows and single family country houses. They analyze the market of potential buyers and divides it into three groups based on stages in the family life cycle: newlyweds, married couples with children and empty nesters (older couples whose children have left home). This means that there are nine possible combinations, as can be seen in the market grid for second homes in Figure 6.6.

To decide which of these segments is likely to be the most lucrative target market, the real estate developer first has to collect information about factors such as the potential sales and profits, future growth opportunities, the estimated marketing cost per segment and the extent of the competition as well as other environmental risks they might face in each of these market segments. The best marketing opportunities can usually be found in the segment that – as is apparent from a SWOT analysis – most closely aligns with the company's strengths and involves a strategic fit with its corporate mission. For example,

FIGURE 6.6 Market grid for second homes

PRODUCTS	MARKETS		
	Newlyweds	Married with children	Empty nesters
Simple chalets			
Semi-detached bungalows			
Single-family country houses			

the property developer will only be interested in constructing single family country houses if there is sufficient demand for these homes in one of the three segments, if they have experience building such homes and if they have the necessary contacts or expertise to sell the properties. In order to define any market in as much detail as possible, we usually begin with general segmentation criteria and then proceed to apply increasingly specific criteria.

Sometimes analyzing market segments in this way leads to the development of new products for new target markets. For example, American Express focused for many years on the segment of highly paid business travellers in Europe. As a result, marketing research showed that younger consumers did not even consider applying for an American Express card. This insight led to a dramatic shift in the company's strategic thinking. 'We decided to introduce a totally new card,' said marketing manager Arthur van Essen, 'aimed at a target market of sharp young consumers between 27 and 37 years old – active Internet users, most likely into a second job and with a good income. That's how we came up with the Blue Card.'[10]

6.5 POSITIONING STRATEGIES

Once we have segmented the market, chosen a targeting strategy and identified the target markets, our next step is to develop a positioning strategy. This involves creating a clear, powerful and consistent image for our products – relative to those of competitors – that will occupy a prominent position in the customer's mind.

As the range of available products and services continues to grow, clear positioning is essential. With so many products and brands on the market, it is increasingly difficult for a company to distinguish itself from the competition on important attributes. A company can try to improve its products in each stage of the product life cycle, but competitors quickly imitate successful improvements. Therefore, product improvements have to be accompanied by a *positioning strategy,* which is something we do to the customer's mind, rather than to the product itself. Starting with the consumer's current perception, we try to find a unique position that the product can occupy in the consumer's mind.

Well-known products have usually already achieved firm positioning. For example, the brand name Volvo is associated with safety, and therefore, Volvos are thought of as safe cars. This is a strong image achieved by a consistent positioning strategy.

MARKETING MISTAKE
Tata Nano: the World's Cheapest Car

For *Tata Motors* in India, launching the world's cheapest car turned out more like a costly nightmare. In the densely-populated country, with well over a billion inhabitants, critics feared its impact on the environment, not to mention the additional congestion if motorcylists traded in their bikes for a Tata Nano. This would offset global efforts to reduce carbon emissions and to prevent global warning.

Thankfully, for the environmental activists, most of the feared harmful effects from the Tata Nano have been averted. But, for Tata Motors, the story doesn't quite have the happy ending. Even though it has been years since the first Nano was launched in this emerging market, less than 150 000 of the cars have found a home with Indian buyers.

Courtesy of Image Asset Management

Creating a new consumer market for a cheap car is a huge marketing challenge

So, in a country packed with rickshaws, mopeds, scooters, motorcycles, bicycles and pedestrians, why would a ripe market for the Tata Nano be anything but a given? What went wrong? Why would a company have to further reduce the price of a vehicle already positioned as the cheapest car on the globe, to a country with many potential first-time car buyers, in order to get consumers to buy it?

Some of the company's missteps in its marketing strategy provide at least two valuable lessons about global strategy development: (1) for consumers, there are more important considerations than price, even in

emerging markets, and (2) developing a homegrown brand while creating a new consumer market for a really cheap car is a huge marketing challenge.

Tata Motors' Nano was originally scheduled for production in a factory in the Eastern part of India (near Bangladesh), which also coincidentally happened to consist of some very fertile arable land, and which some suggested was the *most* fertile agricultural land in the region. When displaced farmers and activists protested the construction of Nano's production facility and the compensation they would receive in exchange, the car's supply chain was inconveniently disrupted. Demonstrations which became violent and required police intervention had the company abruptly shifting its operations in order to build a new plant completely on the other side of the country, on the Western side, nearer to Karachi. As a result, in order for the company to launch the Nano in 2009, as planned, management had to reduce its *production target* for the first year from a quarter of a million cars to a fifth of the original estimate.

As a result of the limited production capacity, Tata Motors was unable to build enough units to create sufficient *economies of scale* to maintain the advertised price of the car of 100 000 rupees (€1 500). Thus, the actual price of the car after taxes and other basics were included was closer to twice that, or €2 850. This new pricing level was suddenly a game-changer; the Nano would no longer be attempting to capture the non-car market; now, the Nano would be competing with other popular small cars, such as the (*Suzuki* Alto-based) Maruti 800, available for €3 500 upwards. Since the higher retail price eliminated Nano's competitive advantage, the marketing strategy's main issue appeared to be *pricing*.

This further adversely impacted the *distribution* channel as well. Even though hundreds of thousands of enthusiastic consumers had pre-ordered a Nano right after its introduction, each dealer only had one car in its showroom for the Indian consumers to view and test drive. With only a small number of cars in production, and buyers not being given permission to test drive the showroom's only unit, consumers quickly lost interest. Twelve months after the Nano's launch, less than thirty thousand cars had been sold and delivered.

Tata Motors' belated *promotion* strategy further hampered the new product introduction. Without any advertising right after the car's initial launch, consumers relied on *word of mouth*. One message making the rounds was that several new Nanos had caught on fire, even though Tata Motors claimed there were no safety issues. Regardless, by early 2011, sales to Indian consumers were no longer in the thousands, and had dropped to about 500 per month.

Soon after, Tata's first advertising campaign was rolled out, tailored toward helping create a favourable *brand image* for the vehicle. The ads primarily emphasized the car's durability, low fuel consumption and other *practical* benefits of the diminutive first-time car buyers' vehicle (which was less than three metres long, bumper to bumper), and which was billed as India's first 'car for

everyone'. However, the television spots highlighted old-fashioned middle-class traditions and values. Unfortunately, this emphasis was competing with motorcycle companies' ad campaigns, which instead chose to underline younger-adult Bollywood themes, incorporating courageous action heroes and heroines lauding the 'coolness' factor and merits of motorcycle driving instead.

Some advertising experts argue that Tata's *product positioning* strategy failed to take into account one of the Indian consumers' primary *motives* for buying their first car – namely, a desire to rise to a more glamorous life than they had previously, and to show off to their peers that they have 'arrived'. And, sales of Nanos in India reflected this aspiration: 40 per cent of those who purchased a Nano chose the *highest-priced* model with all of the available options included, while only one out of five buyers purchased the stripped-down version. Tata might have opted instead to feature influential millionaires endorsing the car, or perhaps another high-profile role model who could buy 'any car they want', but chose the Nano. Some of Tata's rivals appeared to have better understood the unique characteristics of the Indian car-buying market. *Ford*, for example, chose to stay out of the extremely low-price segment (even offering high-tech features such as Bluetooth in its low-end models for the mass market, such as the Figo).

One thing is clear: no matter what the target market is, creating brand awareness and building brand equity takes considerable time. It appears that Tata's marketers in India, where the automotive market is expected to grow more than four-fold by 2016, underestimated how *upwardly-mobile* Indian society has become. They used a positioning strategy that failed to take advantage of the rapidly-growing marketing opportunities in one of the most populated parts of the world.[11]

6.5.1 The battle for the mind

An effective positioning strategy involves three steps. The first one is to conduct marketing research to find out what customers *currently* think about the product, particularly in comparison to other brands. This link to reality (the consumer's perception of the current position) must be incorporated into any positioning message for it to be considered credible.

Next, we need to establish what we want consumers to think about the product. This is crucial for differentiating the product and creating a brand image that results in customer loyalty. However, we need to be realistic in order be effective. For example, we cannot acquire a position that is already occupied by another brand in the market. Avis only started to make a profit when it acknowledged the leading position of its competitor Hertz and played on this in its advertising. Emphasizing the theme 'We try harder', the company positioned itself in second place in the car rental business with a classic *underdog* strategy.

Finally, the marketer should determine which positioning strategy is most likely to change the company's current brand image to the intended brand image, as outlined in the previous step. In summary, the battle for the mind involves establishing (1) where we are now (our strengths and weaknesses, relative to competitors), (2) where we want to go, and (3) how we can get there.

What are some possible strategies to effectively elevate the current brand image to the desired brand image? The first option is to link our message to *existing* products or brands with which the consumer is already familiar. Heineken did this when it introduced alcohol-free beer (now available only outside of the Netherlands) with the slogan: 'Sometimes you order a beer, other times you order a Buckler.' And Slim-Fast uses the catchphrase: 'Stop dieting. Start losing weight,' in its advertising. It should be noted that positioning could also be achieved with other marketing instruments, such as packaging that reminds buyers of other products.

A second possible positioning strategy is to reposition the competition in the consumer's mind. For example, easyCar – when it first entered the Dutch market – stood out with its controversial advertising slogan, 'For the best reasons to rent a car from easyCar, visit hertz.nl.' And BMW tried to reposition Mercedes in the American market with the comparison: 'The ultimate sitting machine versus the ultimate driving machine.'

A third positioning strategy is to claim a position that no one else has claimed. Coca-Cola has succeeded in this by claiming, 'It's the real thing'. Nestlé is pursuing a similar strategy, with its 'Nespresso, What Else?' tagline.

6.5.2 *Perceptual mapping*

Because positioning is based on consumer perceptions, the best way for marketers to select a positioning strategy is to conduct marketing research and visualize the results by drawing a perceptual map. A perceptual map, also known as a *product positioning map*, is a graph indicating how consumers perceive competing brands in a product category along two or more important dimensions, usually product attributes. A positioning map might, for instance, present two different characteristics – such as price and perceived quality – and show how consumers view a product and its rivals based on these traits.

An example of a perceptual map - based on consumer perceptions of car brands - is presented in Figure 6.7. The two dimensions in this graph are price (high/low) and design (sporty/classic). Consumers in this sample consider VW to be the car with the most classic design and Porsche the highest priced sports car. Three automobile brands that are positioned close to each other in the low price, classic design quadrant of the perceptual map - Skoda, Seat and Suzuki - are apparently perceived as substitutes for each other.

The perceptual map clearly reveals how products are viewed within the market and which brands or models are most similar. It may also reveal the extent to which a brand's current position in the customer's mind differs from the intended positioning. This, in turn, may provide a useful basis for developing an effective marketing communication strategy.

6.5.3 *The art of positioning*

Like the rest of the marketing policy, developing a successful positioning strategy requires marketing research. Although the analysis of market segments and selection of target markets may have provided a lot of useful information, we must specifically identify which product attributes consumers consider most important. Only then can we decide, for example,

FIGURE 6.7 Product positioning map

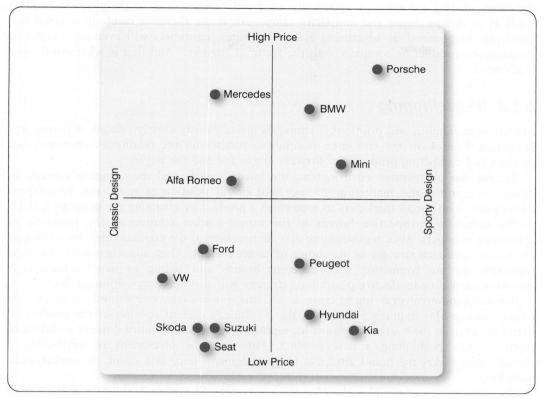

what to emphasize in our advertising. It also helps us avoid the pitfalls of *overpositioning* (a too narrowly defined, misleading image which may leave part of the target market feeling excluded) or *underpositioning* (too vague a position which does not distinguish the brand from other products).

Not all differences between brands are suitable for use in a positioning campaign. The difference should not only be clear and important in the eyes of the target market, but also – from the company's perspective – difficult to imitate by its rivals. A difference may only provide a meaningful basis for *product differentiation* if both of these conditions are met.

How do we go about making the customer aware of the differences with competing brands? A rule of thumb is that the effect of a positioning strategy decreases as the number of stated benefits increases, especially if these are difficult to comprehend. Although most consumers base product evaluations on three to five characteristics, in marketing communication it is best to concentrate on one key message. In sum, the most effective positioning is always clear and simple.

In practice, many positioning campaigns are based on instrumental product characteristics, including applied technology, brand image and design (for example, Bang & Olufsen home entertainment systems). Other companies (such as Jaguar) emphasize expressive product characteristics, such as the status and pleasure of using the product, which help express the owner's lifestyle. A major requirement of selecting an appropriate positioning theme is that it highlights the company's *competitive advantage* and ties in with what buyers consider important.

Whatever aspect we choose to focus on in our positioning strategy, the product must be presented as the leading brand in this respect – for instance, the product with the highest quality, the lowest price or the best customer service. Alternatively, it could be presented as the most reliable, attractive or technically advanced brand, if not as the simplest product (such as in Philips' Sense and Simplicity campaign). If the theme is carefully selected and constantly emphasized in advertising and on websites, customers will eventually come to associate the product or company with the featured attribute. And that is what positioning is all about.

6.5.4 *Repositioning*

Market segmentation and positioning strategies are obviously closely related. Whereas segmentation focuses on the customer, positioning focuses on the *relationship* between our product and competing products, or between the brand and the buyer.

Because the competitive environment, the buyers' needs and the company's needs all change over time, the marketing strategy and brand positioning must also be adapted periodically. This forces marketers to **reposition** a product by changing the position it holds in the minds of prospective buyers in the target market relative to the positions of competing products. Also, repositioning may be necessary if the company decides to change its market approach strategy or its choice of target market. After all, when we tackle new segments, we are competing with different brands and selling to new customers. A shrinking market or ineffective positioning strategy will also make repositioning desirable.

Repositioning involves trying to create a new image in the customer's mind for an existing brand. Because this requires a *change* in the consumer's current opinion of the product or brand (or even in their attitude toward it), repositioning is usually more difficult – and more costly – than positioning a new product. However, the investment is worthwhile if repositioning makes the brand attractive to new segments and, as a result, its market share increases.

The introduction of the Heineken *longneck* in Europe (the green 25cl bottle with a longer neck) is an example of successful repositioning. The bottle contains exactly the same beer as the standard bottle that can be returned for a deposit, but retails for one-and-a-half times the price. Young people, who had abandoned Heineken – which they viewed as a boring brand – in favour of Corona or a vodka Red Bull, drinks with a more youthful image, accepted the longneck as a trendy newcomer. This market acceptance was partly due to the striking appearance of the longneck.

Research shows that the higher price and the distribution strategy also contributed to the success of the repositioning. The product was initially only sold in trendy clubs, discotheques and beach resorts. Only after that was the longneck offered in other cafés and bars and made available in stores. Introducing a high-priced new version of a product on a small scale, initially via selected outlets, and then expanding the number of distribution channels, is a commonly used marketing strategy. The success of the Heineken campaign proved that this strategy could be equally effective when repositioning an existing brand.[12]

SUMMARY

1 Defining the market

One of the priorities in strategy development is defining the market. Are we approaching the whole market, or do we focus on just a small part of it? This decision also determines what market share we hope to obtain. A good approach is to first come up with a broad definition of the market, based on the generic needs we plan to satisfy. That way, we are less likely to overlook potential customers (and competitors!) when selecting target markets. Once we have done this, we can then confine our market to those who not only need the product, but are also interested in buying it and willing and able to pay the price for it.

When estimating the *size of the market* we are less interested in the effective demand than in the potential demand. Added together, we get the *market potential*, which gives us insight into the possible expansion of the market. In addition to the market size, the nature or *composition* of the demand should be assessed. The initial demand, replacement demand and additional demand can vary considerably. These three submarkets must be approached differently. Our strategy also depends on whether we are marketing durable or non-durable consumer goods.

2 Market segmentation

Since most markets are heterogeneous, a mass marketing and product differentiation strategy may not be effective. Buyers have different needs and also respond differently to the marketing mix. In implementing a *market segmentation* strategy we divide the market into meaningful, relatively similar and identifiable segments, then tailor marketing mixes to meet the needs of one or more selected segments. Specifically, an effective market segmentation and positioning strategy involves three steps (called 'STP'): identifying and describing market segments (*segmentation*), evaluating these segments and selecting the ones to pursue (*targeting*) and, finally, developing a product or service that satisfies the segment's needs and creating a marketing mix that will establish a competitive advantage in the minds of the prospects in the target market (*positioning*).

Market segmentation only makes sense if certain *conditions* are met. A first requirement for an effective segmentation strategy is the measurability of the segments. Meaningful segments have identifiable and measurable characteristics that are different from those in other segments. The segments should also be large enough to be profitable ('size'), and the organization must be able to reach the segments with a unique marketing mix ('accessibility'). A final decision criterion is the feasibility of the strategy, in terms of the firm's available resources and the segment's responsiveness to the marketing efforts.

3 Bases for segmentation

Markets can be segmented on the basis of various criteria, such as demographic, geographic, psychographic and behavioural criteria. Income, social class, age and the stage in the family life cycle are all commonly used *demographic* variables. *Psychographic* market segmentation, where consumers are grouped according to attitude, personality type, lifestyle or interest in the benefits that a particular product has to offer, is increasingly used. Other marketers prefer to apply *behavioural* criteria, such as the buyers' usage rate, brand loyalty or readiness stage.

4 Targeting strategies

There are three possible target marketing strategies – undifferentiated, differentiated and concentrated marketing. The first two strategies try to reach the entire market (or the greatest possible part of it), but only in pursuing a differentiated marketing strategy do we develop a unique marketing mix for each segment. If, on the other hand, we are implementing a *concentrated* marketing strategy, we confine ourselves to a single segment or a small number of segments, using the same marketing mix. The *market grid approach* can be helpful in selecting the best target market.

5 Positioning

A market segmentation strategy involves segmenting the market, selecting the target market and positioning the product or service (STP). Whereas segmentation and targeting focus on the customer, positioning centres on the *relationship* between the product and the buyer or between the product and the customer's perception of other brands. Hence, a positioning strategy helps to clarify a product relative to its competition in the minds of the intended buyers. Marketing-oriented managers use a perceptual map to identify new opportunities or to decide if repositioning of existing products is desirable.

DISCUSSION QUESTIONS

1 Market segmentation and product differentiation are two different concepts that are nevertheless related to each other. This sometimes causes confusion. Do you think that market segmentation can lead to product differentiation and that product differentiation can lead to market segmentation? Explain your answers to both questions.

2 Is the market for laundry detergents heterogeneous? Give an example of a product that is not physically changed when it is sold to two or more market segments.

3 A market segment must meet several requirements before a company can regard it as a target market. Yet in business, we often see that some market segments are targeted by one company but not by others. How do you explain this?

4 Why have demographic variables been the most commonly used basis for segmentation? Do you think that demographic segmentation criteria will continue to play as important a role in the future as they have in recent decades?

5 Do you agree with the following statement? 'Lifestyle segmentation is the best segmentation strategy developed for consumer and industrial products, because it considers the individual as a whole person.' Explain your answer.

6 There are more than one million immigrants living in a country like the Netherlands. Yet most companies fail to take this into account when developing their marketing strategies. What is market segmentation based on ethnic origin often referred to? Give three reasons why this segmentation criterion is not used to a greater extent.

7 A company may pursue an undifferentiated marketing strategy because its management believes that (a) it is impossible to identify distinct segments within the market, or (b) the cost of product differentiation would be greater than the profits generated. For each of these categories, give two examples of products that are offered with an undifferentiated marketing strategy.

8 A young, recently graduated entrepreneur argues in an interview that they are more interested in studying the behaviour of people who do not buy their products than the behaviour of their current customers. Do you agree with them?

9 Many companies try to increase sales by going after new market segments. Suggest some alternatives to this growth strategy.

10 According to Jan Sybesma, McDonald's former CEO in the Netherlands, hamburgers did not really fit in with the Dutch culture and eating habits, and the success of fast food restaurants in the Netherlands was mainly the result of a huge investment in marketing. Comment on this statement and list a number of strategic factors – as discussed in the first six chapters of this book – that will influence the marketing strategy of a small chain of fast food restaurants.

PART THREE
PRODUCT DECISIONS

We now take a close look at the marketing mix variables, starting with the *product*. As the actual exchange object, the product is the foundation of the marketing mix. In Parts 4, 5 and 6 of this book we will explore the other three Ps – promotion, price and place. Together, these are the elements of a marketing programme over which the firm has some control.

Part 3 of *Marketing: A Global Perspective* focuses on the products and services a company offers. Chapter 7 makes it clear that no matter how attractive a product or service may be, it only has a limited life span. In order to survive in the long run, it is essential for an organization to regularly devise new or improved products and services. Therefore, in Chapter 8, we will concentrate on the development and marketing of new products. Marketers look upon new product development as one of the most exciting aspects of their work.

7 Product strategy and services marketing

8 New product development

CHAPTER 7
PRODUCT STRATEGY AND SERVICES MARKETING

LEARNING GOALS

After studying this chapter you will be able to:

1	Define a product from a marketing perspective
2	Compare the characteristics of four categories of consumer products
3	Develop effective product mix strategies
4	Explain the marketing significance of the product life cycle stages
5	Recognize the importance of quality and service as key elements in marketing
6	Discuss strategies to build and increase brand equity
7	Understand the role of design and packaging in product strategy
8	Describe how services marketing differs from the marketing of products

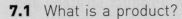

7.1 What is a product?
7.2 Types of consumer goods
7.3 Product assortment strategies
7.4 Managing the product life cycle
7.5 Product quality and customer service
7.6 Brand management
7.7 Product design and packaging
7.8 Marketing of services

Once a manager has gained good insight into the target market, one of their most important tasks is to develop an attractive marketing mix. In strategy development, marketers should look at the Product – the most visible of the four Ps – in terms of its components that provide benefits for the buyers. These include the product's quality, warranty, service, branding, design and even the packaging and labelling.

Marketing's real challenge is to develop a strong brand. Without a brand identity, products are no more than commodities, differentiated only by their prices. If customers based purchase decisions only on price, the most efficient manufacturers in the mass market would gain the highest market share. Firms trying to meet customer needs other than spending as little as possible would have a hard time surviving.

But simply branding a product is not enough. The acid test is what the brand really means to potential buyers. Does it stand for quality and service? Does it inspire confidence? Are customers willing to pay more for this brand than for products made by competitors? The answer to these questions depends on brand image as well as on other product attributes that offer added value. Since any of these attributes can tip the scales in favour of a purchase, these are the factors and decisions that we will closely examine in this chapter on product strategy and services marketing.

MARKETING IN ACTION
Manchester United's Global Brand Offensive

Manchester United is more than a popular British soccer club. It was the first club in soccer to really understand the interaction between success on the playing field and *marketing* success. This 135-year old club has turned itself into a multimillion euro marketing machine, an organization that has built a giant fan base and turned supporters' passion into persistent brand loyalty and substantial profits. Recently, Manchester United Ltd. went even more on the offensive in its mission to maximize *brand awareness* around the globe. It has been applying the same trademark attacking style used in its soccer matches to build between 90 and 100 per cent brand recognition in Europe as well as in parts of China, Latin America and Korea.

© Turkish Airlines

Unfortunately, transferring this high global brand awareness into worldwide profits has been quite a challenge. Although Manchester United is extremely successful at monetizing its popularity in Europe – where it generates most of its revenues through ticket sales and TV broadcasting rights – global markets have turned out to be more difficult to financially benefit from. The often used sports marketing motto that 'winning is the best marketing strategy' applies, but a comprehensive, systematically implemented *international* marketing plan might be United's ticket to global supremacy.

> The challenge is getting consumers to connect with a brand or organization that isn't from their home country

'A great brand is one that drives choice, builds loyalty and allows the brand to demand a price premium,' says Hugh Tallents, director of strategy at Interbrand in New York. 'The

challenge is getting consumers to connect with a brand or organization that isn't from their home country.' With that goal in mind, Manchester United has developed a portfolio of products and services that includes everything from *global media ventures* and theme restaurants to *financial services*. According to Richard Arnold, the club's commercial director, 'Manchester United is well-known for its attacking style, and it's the core principle of how the club has conducted its affairs on the pitch right from the start.' This aggressive style now also characterizes United's global branding strategy and business expansion.

To illustrate, Manchester United has its own *TV station* – MUTV – which is broadcast in more than 200 million homes. It has partnered with several companies to offer *apps* in more than a dozen countries, where subscribers can receive Manchester United content – including live broadcasts, match highlights and stats – on their mobile phones. Its *website* receives over 70 million page impressions per month; it is translated and localized into five foreign languages, including Spanish and Arabic. Its *Facebook* page has millions of fans as well. The soccer club also offers mortgages, insurance, credit cards and other financial services in the United Kingdom, Korea, Thailand, Malaysia, Indonesia and Hong Kong.

United is also capitalizing on its global brand recognition with an increasing number of all-day casual dining *restaurants*. Manchester United Food & Beverage Pte., the Singapore-based holding company, has opened restaurants across Asia and India, with several new ones located in China. They feature western cuisine and local specialties to suit the taste buds of diners across the region.

Ultimately, the power of the brand is not only measured in global recognition, but also in its ability to attract international powerhouses that view a partnership with Manchester United as a lucrative marketing opportunity. For years, the club has been sponsored by *Nike*. It also gained *sponsorships* with firms that have clout in emerging markets. Its newest sponsors include Concha y Toro, the world's fourth-largest wine producer based in Chile, the telecommunications provider MTN Group in Fairlands, South-Africa, Telekom Malaysia in Kuala Lumpur and the fourth-largest European carrier Turkish Airlines, based in a country with one of Manchester United's highest viewership ratings.

In addition, United obtained a €100 million four-year sponsorship with Aon Corp., a risk management company in Chicago. Aon saw the United jersey deal as a way to strengthen its once-fragmented marketing budget. 'We do see the opportunity to grow our business globally,' says Aon's vice-president of global public relations, David Prosperi. 'Asia is particularly compelling because the insurance market there is still in a very early stage and this is a chance to develop a strong international foothold through the sponsorship.' Within a year after the company announced its principal sponsorship agreement with Manchester United, the number of unique visitors to its website doubled to over 70 000 per week.

A long-standing Manchester United strategy to gain a global brand advantage has been the *international* tour, a chance for the team to get closer to its customers: the fans. Recently, the club travelled to North America, where it partnered for the first time with US-based Major League Soccer (MLS). The next year, the club travelled to Asia. 'Manchester United has done a tremendous job of taking their product into key international markets and doing it in such a way that when they rotate into a new market, they're building up this restrained demand over time and it just elevates the brand even more,' says Tim McGhee of IMG Consulting, a global sports, entertainment and media company.

Manchester United's roster of players is as diverse as the markets it wants to conquer. Players like Javier Hernandez from Mexico, Ji-sung Park from South Korea and Tim Howard from the United States have helped make inroads into populations of potential fans. 'The tactic of signing local players on merit is one that is very effective in building grassroots support,' says Hugh Tallents. 'The side effect is that you get notoriety and recognition in that country. They are a global brand and to have a global brand, you need global representation.' During the North American tour, the players made a point of interacting with US-based fans at the MLS All-Star Game in Houston. 'Not only did they bring the brand alive by going overseas, but they also *personalized* the brand by the way they interacted with their fans,' McGhee says. 'You know the old marketing adage: How do you build a brand? One customer at a time! Well, Manchester United has mastered it.'[1]

The product is the most tangible element in the marketing mix and possibly the most important. If the product does not meet the customer's needs and wants, it will not sell and the company will have no future. Since the customers' desires change over time, we need to reassess them on a regular basis and, if necessary, adapt the product accordingly. That way, we stay one step ahead of other companies.

Our study of product strategy and services marketing begins by looking at what is meant by 'a product'. To better understand product planning and decision making, we first examine an effective way of classifying consumer products into different categories. We also explore useful dimensions for analyzing a product range and strategies that can be used to expand it. Then, we identify the stages of the product life cycle. After all, products have a limited life span, which can only be lengthened with the right measures. Next, we evaluate several marketing tools or elements of the product mix, such as the quality, warranty and service. We consider various branding strategies as well as product design and packaging. Finally, we will explore an increasingly important issue in strategy development, the marketing of services. We now start our analysis of product strategy with a *marketing-oriented* definition of a product.

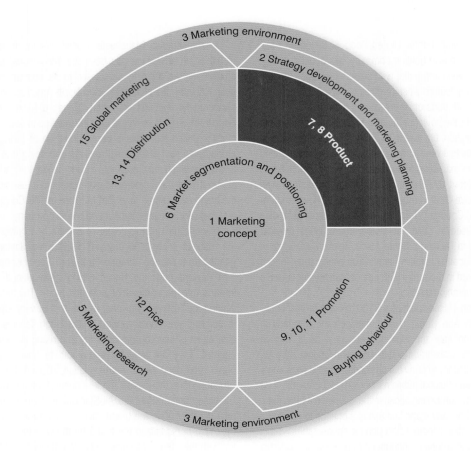

7.1 WHAT IS A PRODUCT?

If you asked an engineer and a marketer to describe their products, they would probably give you very different answers. From a marketing perspective, a product is more than a physical object or a combination of chemical and technical features. Consumers, around whom marketing revolves, are not particularly interested in the physical properties of a product. They are much more concerned with whether or not it meets their needs and wants. The product is essentially 'what it does for them', and they will only consider a purchase if it provides them with a certain degree of usefulness, pleasure or satisfaction.

From this point of view we can define a **product** as 'a combination of tangible and intangible characteristics that enable an object or a service to satisfy a customer need'. Marketers regard the product as a *bundle of benefits* to the purchaser. However, since people have different needs and preferences and some consider certain product features to be more important than others, products represent different *benefits* or levels of satisfaction to individual buyers. In order to better develop an effective product strategy, we will first analyze the product from a marketing perspective and then examine the implications for strategy development.

7.1.1 *A bundle of benefits*

Someone who buys a home theatre sound system for their 3D LED-LCD HDTV in a discount store such as Media Market pays less for it than another person who buys the same item from a traditional specialty store. Did these two consumers actually purchase the same product? It depends on how we define 'the product'. If we restrict ourselves to the *physical* product as it comes out of the box, they did indeed buy the exact same product. But this narrow view does not take into account *how* the *exchange* – or transaction – was conducted, which is the essence of marketing. The second customer probably received more personal advice and better service from the retailer than the first. Because the two customers did not experience the same 'bundle of benefits' during the transaction, from a marketing angle they clearly did *not* purchase the same product!

© Yuri Arcurs / Shutterstock

Most consumers who buy home theatre systems are less interested in the metal casing and the electronic parts (the physical attributes of the – narrowly defined – product) than the range of features and services directly or indirectly associated with the product that satisfy their particular needs and wants. For one person this may be the unusual design or unique technical capabilities of the product, the familiar brand name, the warranty conditions or the competitive price. For another person it may be the expert advice provided by a sales associate who knows all of the available brands in the extensive product line inside out, and the after sales service, including home delivery, set up and programming of the system by one of the specialty store's associates. Depending on how important these service or product attributes are to various consumers, they may view available alternatives on the market as being 'different'. Although the product's physical attributes are identical, the package of benefits provided to customers is not; thus, from a marketing perspective, the retailers are selling different products. This is expressed in our definition of the product.

7.1.2 *Product levels*

According to Philip Kotler, an American marketing scholar, we should think about a product or service on three levels, each one adding more value for the customer. These three levels or components of a product, as illustrated in Figure 7.1, are the *core product*, the *actual product* and the *augmented product*.[2]

The **core product** or 'core benefit' refers to the basic function or problem-solving *benefits* that a consumer is seeking in the exchange. At this most fundamental level, the key question is *what* the customer is really buying. For marketers, identifying the core customer needs should be the starting point in developing a new product or service. For example, the core product offered by a drill manufacturer is actually the possibility of drilling holes, allowing someone to hang works of art on the wall. In the case of a home theatre system, the core product is entertainment and the satisfaction of getting superior sound quality while watching movies conveniently and comfortably at home.

At the second level, product developers turn the core benefit into the **actual product**. Considering the buyers' expectations, they must develop the product and service *features*, *design*, *quality* level, *brand name* and *packaging* that, combined, deliver the core benefit to the customer. From a marketing mix perspective, all of these features or attributes are part of the P of *product*. Someone, for instance, who decides to buy a Panasonic home theatre system

FIGURE 7.1 The three levels of a product

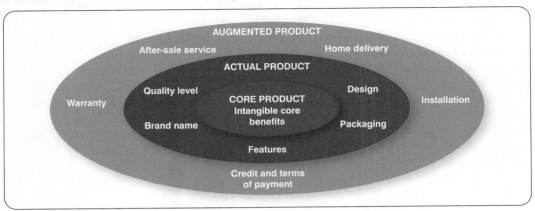

may do so because they are impressed with the reliable quality, the colour-coordinated design, the well-known brand name, the attractive packaging or the system's ease of use.

Lastly, the augmented product includes the intangible, psychological benefits and service-based features that make the total product more attractive from the customer's viewpoint. These additional features may be services that are part of the company's price strategy, distribution strategy or promotion strategy. 'Extras' such as an extended warranty, home delivery within 24 hours, free installation and comprehensive after sales service, which enhance the customer experience, are all examples of the augmented product. These are the kinds of product features that are the focus of competitive battles. If we exceed the prospects' expectations on these points, we increase our chances of securing their business.

7.1.3 *Implications for marketing*

Some managers overestimate the importance of the technical aspects (or other physical characteristics) of their products, when they should really pay more attention to the benefits that interest *customers*. In buying a home theatre system, for example, these benefits may include the user-friendliness of the equipment, the quality of the instructions in the user manual for installing the system, the level of customer service, the availability of a reasonably-priced service contract and the (perceived) reliability of the supplier. Often, these are the product attributes and (derived) characteristics that make a difference in a purchase decision or the choice between brands. It makes good sense to incorporate these in planning and implementing the marketing strategy.

Another marketing implication is that in the firm's *communication* with potential customers, instead of elaborating on the basic product, it might make sense to focus on *why* it is a good idea to purchase the product. Sensible reasons to buy a product may provide additional incentives for the consumer that can eventually increase sales. The European market for margarine products is a good example. For years, this was a stable market. With the introduction of cholesterol-lowering *Becel ProActive* and *Blue Band Culinesse*, and a promotion strategy that clearly emphasized the benefits of these relatively expensive products to consumers, Unilever managed to make the European market grow substantially again. This also inspired other companies to focus more in their advertising campaigns and on their websites on – often intangible – customer benefits, such as the product's brand image or health benefits. These derived characteristics should, in many cases, play a major role in any sales pitch or advertising campaign. As we will see in this chapter, the product components at all three levels discussed here are the building blocks of a successful product strategy.

PRACTITIONER'S PERSPECTIVE
Salmin Amin (PepsiCo)

After being President of PepsiCo United Kingdom and Ireland, A. Salman Amin recently became SVP and Global Chief Marketing Officer of PepsiCo, which generates net revenues of over $65 billion. In its global food and beverage portfolio, the company has 22 different brands that generate more than $1 billion each in annual retail sales. Amin is responsible for driving global marketing strategies and plans for PepsiCo worldwide. Earlier, he spent ten years at Procter & Gamble in various brand management positions in the US, Germany, Middle East and Asia.

We recently launched our 20th, 21st and 22nd billion-dollar brands – Diet Mountain Dew, Brisk and Starbucks ready-to-drink beverages – more than any other food and beverage company on the planet. While we are proud of this accomplishment, we believe that our experience offers useful lessons that speak to how our 21st century *global marketplace* operates. Specifically, it says what can be accomplished when a company offers great products, masters the art and science of *marketing* and leverages the interplay of new *technologies*, continuous *interactivity* and the demand for greater choice and *individuality*.

So what are the *marketing principles* behind billion-dollar brands? Fundamentally, great brands thrive (during both good and bad times) when they communicate basic *human truths* that speak to the needs and interests, concerns and dreams of the global consumer. Whether they live in New Delhi, Melbourne or Houston, consumers have far greater expectations than did previous generations. Basically, they want an ongoing and enduring relationship with their brands that is governed by a set of basic principles.

The first of these underlying principles is *authenticity*. In an era where there is so much uncertainty and cynicism, there is a strong desire for reliability. When people spend their hard-earned money, especially when it is a discretionary purchase, they want to know a brand's value proposition and they want to believe in what the *brand* stands for. They want to understand exactly what they are going to get with each purchase and want to achieve and maintain a high degree of *trust*. When it comes to food or beverages, this goes to taste, experience and ingredients and an unwavering commitment to providing exactly what is expected.

In the mid-90s, consumers interacted with a food or beverage brand in two ways: They bought the product and watched its commercials on television. Now that has all changed. People are *engaging* with brands in far many more ways. They are having conversations with brands, and Mountain Dew's DewLabs encourage a robust online conversation that solicits new ideas as to flavours and different kinds of packaging.

Consumers want brands that they can identify with

When consumers get what they want, they have the communication tools to celebrate their enjoyment and excitement. On the other hand, if they are disappointed, they will complain and make their concerns known. They also want brands that they can *identify* with – brands that are attuned to pop culture and relevant today. This is why we have been bringing *entertainment* to consumers over the past 30 years, working with such popular artists as Michael Jackson, Madonna and Ray Charles. It is why Mountain Dew's DewTour is combining the thrill of action sports with youthful creativity to connect with skateboarders and snowboarders, and why its Green Label Sound is introducing exciting new music and bands to its millions of new fans.

As time goes by, consumers will have more and more choices and will look for offerings that are clearly *distinguishable* from other options. Brands need to offer a series of unique qualities that make people stop and think about why they are preferable and superior. This is driven by people's desire to feel unique and special. They want to feel that they are in control of their own *personal branding* and they want products that reinforce this mindset.

Brand management tends to be a young profession and there is always a temptation to make dramatic changes in what the brand stands for in the offering. This kind of short-termism too often leads to mistakes because it confuses consumers and sends a message that the product may not be supported on the foundation of reliable, understandable values. Suddenly, brand loyalty starts to slip away, trust erodes and consumers look for new options. While companies need not stay glued to past realities and glories, they need to stay true to what they stand for and stay *consistent* with what made the brand great in the first place.

We have learned through the use of extensive quantitative analysis that the new global consumer has more in common with each other than one would expect. Yes, there are all kinds of subtle differences in taste – tamarind flavours in Latin America, mango flavours in Asia and lemon-lime/citrus flavours in Europe – depending where you live on the planet, but ultimately, people are living in the now and their decision making processes are in constant flux. Nevertheless, they will inevitably support brands that make a *connection* with them, care about them and help them create a more fulfilling life. This is a substantial challenge. Yet, if companies can establish such a relationship, they will be well on their way to creating powerful brands that surpass the billion-dollar mark.[3]

7.2 TYPES OF CONSUMER PRODUCTS

Depending on the use for which they are intended, products can be classified as either consumer products or business products. Consumer products or **consumer goods** are sold to individuals and their families for their personal use or consumption. These buyers are known as **ultimate consumers** or end users of the product. Television sets, cosmetics and candy are all consumer goods. On the other hand, **business products** and services or industrial goods (such as production equipment, materials, supplies, machine tools and software) are sold to organizations – including companies, government agencies and non-profit institutions – that either resell them or use them to make (semi-manufactured or final) products or to provide a service. Since the *intended customer* is the major distinction between consumer and business products, not many goods can be classified exclusively as a consumer or an industrial product. For example, the same tablet can be either a consumer or a business product, depending on whether it is purchased by a student to do their homework or a company to develop a marketing plan. The buying process and the appropriate marketing strategy are, needless to say, quite different in either case.

Marketers have classified consumer goods, depending on consumer buying attitudes and behaviour, into three classes: *convenience products*, *shopping products* and *specialty products*. Melvin Copeland, a pioneer marketing professor at the Harvard Business School, first suggested this classification, shown in Figure 7.2. He called them convenience goods, shopping goods and specialty goods. A fourth category of consumer products is called *unsought products*. The distinction between the types of consumer products is based on frequency of purchase as well as on the amount of time and effort the consumer chooses to spend on the buying decision. Since the products differ in the way they are bought, they also require different marketing strategies.

7.2.1 Convenience products

Convenience products are items the consumer buys frequently, immediately and with a minimum of shopping effort. Because most brands are fairly similar (such as soap, gasoline and milk), the consumer spends little time comparing prices and quality. They have a

FIGURE 7.2 Classification of products

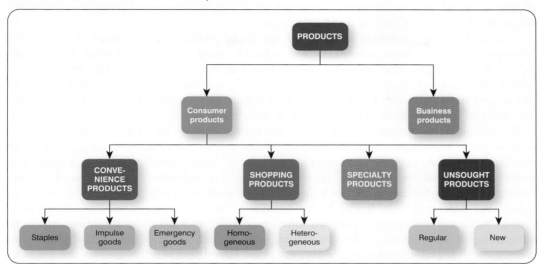

preferred brand, but will accept a substitute. Hence, manufacturers and distributors must be willing to spend a lot of money on advertising campaigns to remind the public of the existence and merits (as well the price) of a brand, in order to retain their market share. These huge advertising expenditures, in conjunction with the homogeneous nature of convenience products (all *nondurables*), often result in highly competitive conditions leading to small profit margins per unit. Many retailers claim they make little or no profit on convenience products. However, to prevent loss of sales, suppliers make sure that these products are readily available in a convenient location – for example, near the consumer's home or place of work – where the buyer expects to find them. This requires intensive distribution.

Convenience products can be further categorized into – frequently bought – staples or *fast-moving consumer goods* (for example, bread), spontaneously bought impulse goods (purchased with no pre-planning or careful decision-making, as when adding a packet of chewing gum while standing in line at the checkout in a grocery store) and emergency goods, which are purchased when the customer urgently needs the item (for example, a new umbrella bought during a downpour, even if the consumer has one at home).

Because of the narrow profit margins for the manufacturer and the retailer, convenience goods cannot be customized or even modified to fit the particular needs of any one customer. If the buyer does not like the product the way it is, they will probably try a different brand next time.

7.2.2 *Shopping products*

Shopping products are items for which the consumer normally compares the quality, price and style of a number of alternatives, often visiting several stores before making a purchase decision. Examples of shopping products include cameras, carpeting, bicycles and clothes.

Shopping products can either be *homogeneous* or *heterogeneous*. A person who assumes that all televisions with a 94cm screen are more or less the same considers these items to be *homogeneous products*. The effort in shopping for this product will be focused on finding the lowest price. However, if the consumer perceives certain product attributes to be substantially different between offerings (regardless of their similarities), the products are called *heterogeneous shopping products*. The customer may well have a *brand preference*, but is also willing to accept other brands. In the case of heterogeneous shopping goods (such as a leather sofa or a 3D LED smart TV) the price/quality ratio often determines the choice of brand. If it is difficult to compare prices, as in the case of jewellery or clothes, the style, fit and colour will be deciding factors.

The appropriate marketing strategy for shopping products differs from that used for convenience goods. Since consumers will typically shop around in several retail stores before making a purchase decision, distribution can be less intensive. The products just have to be in enough stores that the consumer will encounter the product in at least one of the several outlets visited. The higher profit margins also enable retailers to provide some adjustments in the product to fit the needs of the consumer.

Promotion is an important part of the marketing strategy for shopping products. The manufacturer and retailer must provide the shopper with information needed to make an intelligent decision. Because customers spend a lot of time shopping and going through a process of *limited* or *extensive problem solving* (as explained in Chapter 4), easy-to-comprehend information on such factors as product warranty and price is crucial to reduce the perceived risk. If this is not provided, many consumers will turn to another brand. Although salespeople play an important role in marketing shopping products, advertising in mass media, sales promotion, direct mail, point-of-purchase displays and websites with useful information are also essential. Advertising is often used to announce an upcoming sale, discounts and other special offers, while point-of-purchase displays draw the customer's attention toward unique product features and away from competing brands. All of these marketing efforts tend to influence the consumer.

7.2.3 *Specialty products*

Specialty products are items (such as parachutes) or services (such as child care) for which consumers are willing to make a special effort to acquire. The purchase is characterized by *high involvement*. A consumer may know little about the product, yet – before even feeling a need for it – knows what brand they would buy. In the buyer's perception, no reasonable substitutes exist, because of the unique features or brand image of the product. Think of the purchase of a new car. Specialty goods, however, do not necessarily have to be that expensive. For example, once the consumer has decided that only a Swatch watch will do,

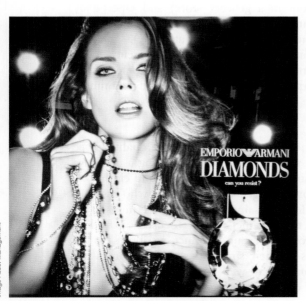

then this watch has become a specialty product for that consumer. A specialty product involves a high degree of *brand loyalty*; therefore, the effort in shopping, when it is time to purchase a watch, does not involve comparing one brand against another, but finding a store that carries the brand. Other examples of products that are specialty goods for many people are expensive cameras, designer clothing and specific restaurants. Consumers are willing to pay premium prices for these products and services.

From the company's standpoint, a product qualifies as a specialty product if a large enough group of customers has a clear preference for the brand. For example, specialty products such as competition skis are purchased on the basis of brand image, product quality and reliability. Most people who purchase an expensive specialty item are not as concerned about price as consumers who buy shopping goods. These products also have relatively high profit margins, allowing the company to customize the product to the buyer's desired specifications. Selecting the best possible retailers in a community is a critical decision for specialty goods manufacturers. These products are usually sold in a limited number of stores (sometimes only one) in any particular market. If the dealer's image or the expertise and customer-orientation of its sales staff are substandard, the manufacturer is not well represented in that market.

The defining characteristics of convenience, shopping and specialty products are summarized in Table 7.1. Because these definitions hold true only for individual buyers, it is not possible to draw a clear dividing line between the categories. Some brands of products that would normally be considered convenience products may actually be specialty products for other people. Health food products, organic vegetables and Davidoff cigarettes are all examples of products that are not sold in every supermarket. If a consumer has to go to a specific store to buy these products, they become specialty goods to them.

TABLE 7.1 Characteristics of convenience, shopping and specialty products

Characteristics	Convenience products	Shopping products	Specialty products
Product (examples)	Candy, milk, soap, gasoline	Computers, appliances, clothing, furniture	Rolex watch, perfume, fitness centre, restaurants
Price	Inexpensive but competitive, small profit margin	Relatively high, moderate profit margin	Very expensive, high profit margin
Distribution	Widespread, with convenient locations	Large number of selected stores	Limited and exclusive; few intermediaries per market
Communication	Mass communication, focus on brand name, price or standardized theme	Personal selling and advertising; focus on product differentiation	Targeted communication; emphasis on uniqueness of brand and status
Turnover	High inventory turnover, over 25 times per year	Moderate turnover, 3-24 times per year	Low turnover, less than three times per year
Flexibility	No product adjustment for buyer	Minor adjustment, good service	Often custom designed
Purchase frequency	Frequently purchased	Occasionally purchased	Infrequently purchased
Brand loyalty	Consumer has a regular brand (routine decision) but will accept a substitute	Consumer compares acceptable brands on several criteria	High brand loyalty, consumer will not settle for an alternative brand
Searching time	Little, first available acceptable product is purchased	Significant searching time during planned shopping	Considerable time spent on seeking out particular brand

7.2.4 Unsought products

Unsought products are products and services of which consumers are unaware, haven't necessarily thought of buying or discover they need in order to solve an unexpected problem. Hence, consumers do not search for unsought products until they need these products or are made aware of them. Examples of *known* or *regular unsought products* are life insurance, encyclopedias, burial plots, insurance to cover burial services, emergency car-towing services and notary services provided by a law firm to help to draw up a last will. Most consumers are inclined to postpone the decision to obtain these products and services, which presents a real marketing challenge to their suppliers.

The category of *new unsought products* includes items that have not been on the market long and are unknown until advertising and distribution increase consumer awareness. Speech recognition software (such as Dragon Naturally Speaking) – a product that few people have explored – is an example. The marketer's job is to inform the target market and to stimulate demand for the product.

Typically, prices of unsought goods vary and their distribution is limited. The purchase frequency is low, as is brand loyalty. Companies that market unsought products often fall back on persuasive advertising and aggressive personal selling. Their salesmen try to find leads to potential buyers. Since most consumers do not seek out these types of products and services, the firm must approach them directly through a salesperson, email, direct-response advertising or direct mail.

7.2.5 Other product classifications

Besides differing in terms of the effort a consumer spends on the buying decision and the frequency of purchase, products can also be categorized based on such factors as penetration ratio, gross margin and service requirements. Another, more common, classification to facilitate marketing analysis is based on durability or (in)tangibility. Using these criteria, we make a distinction between durable goods, nondurables and services.

Durable consumer goods (or *durables*) are products such as cars, e-Readers and dishwashers, which are used repeatedly over an extended period. They have relatively high profit margins. Knowledgeable salespeople and reliable service are important to customers in purchasing these products. Buyers often move slowly and deliberately through the purchasing process and need time to collect information and compare the available alternatives.

Non-durable consumer products or *nondurables* have a relatively short life cycle. Like clothing and footwear, they rarely last longer than about three years. If, like soft drinks and shampoo, these 'consumables' are consumed or used up fairly quickly, they are also known as *fast moving consumer goods* (FMCGs). Profit margins for these products are relatively small. They are usually distributed intensively and advertised heavily to create brand awareness and brand preference.

Services are products like tax preparation and bicycle repairs that are intangible and provide benefits that meet certain needs and wants. They can also be ideas, such as helping fellow citizens or naming a designated driver when drinking alcoholic beverages with friends, or activities offering emotional, intellectual or spiritual benefits. We will explore services marketing later in this chapter.

Finally, *industrial products* or 'business goods' are products that companies buy to use in their own production process. These include major capital goods (such as a factory, building, equipment or IT network), raw materials (e.g. lumber) and semi-manufactured goods (e.g. glass), and production supplies and parts that will be incorporated into the firm's final products. In addition, organizations frequently purchase maintenance, repair and operating supplies to keep the business running.

7.3 PRODUCT ASSORTMENT STRATEGIES

Successful marketing strategies are built around two fundamental decisions – the selection of markets and products. Bringing together markets of potential customers having certain needs and wants with products possessing want-satisfying capabilities is a basic tenet of marketing. Since most organizations produce and market a variety of products and services, product decisions are rarely made in isolation. In fact, one of the most important product strategy questions facing any organization is that regarding which products should be continued, introduced or phased out of the product mix. To develop an effective product assortment strategy, we must first analyze the relationship between various products.

7.3.1 What is an assortment?

To meet their needs and wants, consumers can select products from different product lines. The more we know about what makes up an optimal portfolio of products, the better we are able to compete in the overall *product class* or product category by adjusting the *product mix.*

The **product mix** is the total *assortment* of products and services that the company sells, including the various product lines, products, product types and brands. Gillette's product mix includes razors, replacement blades, shaving gels, deodorants and lighters. This mixture of products typically includes several items that are related with respect to the customers targeted, the products' end uses or the materials used to manufacture them.

A **product line** is a *group* of closely related items in the organization's assortment or product mix. For instance, all the razors Gillette sells represent one product line. These products in the same product category often meet the same need. A product line is made up of several products and product types. Soft drinks are a product line that includes *products* such as cola and fruit juice. Similarly, fruit juice is a product that includes *product types* such as apple juice and grape juice.

Looking at another industry, all of Philips' TVs are an example of a *product line*. Philips also produces other product lines, such as light bulbs and batteries. Products within a product line share some common features or technological characteristics. The relationship between them can be based on various factors, such as:

→ Production (made in the same factory, such as widescreen televisions and plasma monitors).

→ Distribution (sold in the same store or distribution channels).

→ Price (falling within a given price range).

→ Marketing (targeted at the same customer group).

→ Consumption pattern (satisfying a similar need or used together as complementary products).

Usually, the relationship between the products in a product line is based on a *combination* of these factors. Regardless, a product line calls for a coordinated marketing strategy, because a decision that affects one product may also have an effect on the other products in the same group.

A **product type** is an individual product (such as Gillette's Fusion razor) or a specific version of a service that differs from other types of the same product because of certain attributes. Ground espresso coffee is a particular type of 'coffee', which, in turn, falls within the product line of 'hot drinks'. A product type is also referred to as an article or **product item**, if it can be designated as a distinct offering within the company's products or is listed in the firm's catalogue or on its website with a specific article number. The Philips Cineos 42PF9830 Flat HDTV with a 107 centimetre plasma screen is a good example – to be a product item, the product must have a brand name, a size and, of course, a price.

Companies use different assortment strategies to realize their market share and profitability goals. Before selecting the best strategy, the product mix should be carefully analyzed. The four dimensions of a product mix that we will explore next are useful criteria to help us make sound decisions about the assortment.

7.3.2 Dimensions of the product mix

In many companies, a different marketing or product manager manages each product line. However, decisions that affect the assortment as a whole are usually made at a higher organizational level. When making these strategic decisions, top management considers four dimensions: the width, length, depth and consistency of the product mix.

Width of the assortment

The width of the assortment, or product mix width, refers to the number of product lines that a company sells. The more product lines, the wider the product mix. A specialty store sells a narrow assortment (for example, luggage only), whereas a department store sells a wide assortment (from DVDs to delicatessen products).

Length of the assortment

The length of the assortment can be expressed as the product mix length. The product mix length refers to the total number of articles that a company offers within all of its product lines, and thus is a measure of the total number of items that the company sells. A firm should manage its product mix length carefully and add articles or, more likely, drop items from each product line if this action would result in higher overall profitability.

A firm should manage its product mix length carefully and add articles or, more likely, drop items from each product line if this action would result in higher overall profitability.

Depth of the assortment

The product line depth refers to the number of product items (brands, types, models and container sizes) in a product line. The greater the number of versions offered of each product in the line, the deeper the assortment. For example, if Lipton offers only Lipton Ice Tea in Europe, and its product line consists of four flavours of this soft drink, all of which come in a large and a small bottle, the depth of the assortment is eight. A company like Unilever makes dozens of different kinds of soup, pasta sauces, spreads, margarines and other food products, so its total assortment of hundreds of brands consists of thousands of product items.

Figure 7.3 shows part of the product mix produced by Unilever. This listing is not complete, but, for the sake of the example, the matrix is made up of three product lines or categories in the product mix (Food brands, Home care brands and Personal care brands) with seven brands in each category.

The product line depth is especially an important criterion in retailing. Some specialty stores – which carry a narrow, but deep assortment – may sell fifty different types and brands of washing machines. On the other hand, a variety store at the lower end of the market may sell a wide product mix that is not very deep, while an upscale department store will carry a product assortment that is both wide and deep.

Consistency of the assortment

Some retailers try to increase their customer base by widening their product mix. However, because the product lines they add are often unrelated to the current products they carry, this is counter-productive when it comes to product mix consistency. This trend, where stores not traditionally associated with particular products offer them, is referred to as scrambled merchandising.

FIGURE 7.3 Part of the Unilever product mix

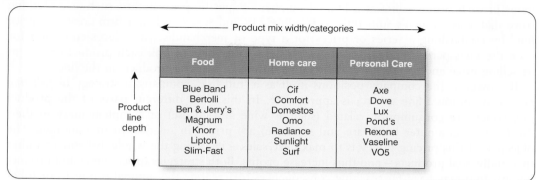

As do retailers, non-retailers also need to make sure that their product mix is consistent. This allows their customers to see a clear connection between a new product that the company has introduced and its current reputation in the industry. The *link* between product lines in a product mix characterized by consistency may be in the area of research, the production requirements or the materials used. But, as discussed earlier, the products may also be related in terms of the distribution channels in which they are sold or the customer's consumption pattern, as when the products perform the same functions, are used simultaneously, or reach the same segment of buyers. Remember Gillette's success in selling disposable Cricket lighters and Paper Mate pens in retail chains with which it already maintained a good relationship as a supplier of razors, blades and toiletries.

Finally, there is product mix consistency if the products fall within the same *price range*. This can be expressed in terms of another dimension, which European managers, in drafting their marketing plans, often refer to as the assortment height. This can also be established for each product line by calculating the average price level of the product items or brands in a line.

7.3.3 *Optimizing the product portfolio*

Exactly what product mix a firm should carry depends mainly on its marketing strategy and objectives. What wants and needs is the company trying to satisfy? Which target markets has it selected? What market share is it trying to get? How much growth does it hope to achieve? What is the best positioning strategy in the competitive global market? All of these strategic decisions will affect the firm's optimal product portfolio.

Many companies are constantly adapting their marketing strategy: they improve their products, change their prices or make other adjustments. But in doing so, they must assess the impact of each marketing decision on the rest of the product assortment and how the customers will perceive it. Does the decision fit in with the strategy that the company has been pursuing?

The product portfolio itself should be reviewed and overhauled on a regular basis. Proliferation may mean that some products do not meet the company's profit standards. If these weak items are not, for example, attracting new buyers that will become regular customers, it may be better to discontinue them – especially if the company does not have sufficient capacity to supply all of the products for which there is an increasing demand. After pruning its product lines, the company can concentrate its efforts on the most lucrative products and services.

If, on the other hand, a company is facing declining demand, it may have to expand and modernize its product mix. When developing a product mix pricing strategy – in other words, when deciding how the different products in the product lines or in the assortment should be priced to maximize profits on the total mix – there are several options that should be considered.

Some companies implement a strategy of price lining. In other words, they offer all of the items in each product line at a limited number of specific price points, such as a clothing store that sells its men's suits only at €199, €249 and €329. When a firm creates a 'price line' by establishing a series of prices for a type of merchandise, it reduces confusion for both the sales person and the customer. It helps customers to link each product's value to its selling price and to recognize the relative differences among products in the line.

If, however, the company positions itself as a 'full line' company, a strategy of *full line pricing* or product line pricing is appropriate. In this case, different parts of the product mix which are consumption related (such as wine and cheese) or complementary in their use (such as computer hardware and software) are priced in relation to one another. The objective of this pricing policy is to maximize sales – involving the whole assortment rather than individual products – and thus increase profits. Both strategies (price lining and product line pricing) may have far-reaching consequences for creating the optimal product portfolio.

An important consideration when changing the product portfolio is the 20/80 rule, which states that approximately 20 per cent of the product items offered by a company account for about 80 per cent of its total sales. This 20 per cent makes up the core assortment, consisting of those items with a high turnover rate. Because these products often form an important part of the retailers' store image and ambience, they cannot simply be removed from the merchandise mix. The remaining 80 per cent of the articles are known as the peripheral assortment. These products have a relatively low turnover rate. Their attractiveness to the firm stems from gross profit margins rather than turnover rate.

Although the percentages in the 20/80 rule are only approximate, the fact remains that quite a few of the products offered by many companies make no more than a minor contribution to their sales and profits. So when reorganizing or 'optimizing' the product portfolio, we should first evaluate the peripheral assortment. However, before we decide to discontinue any items to increase the profitability of the overall product mix, we should consider whether these products use any excess capacity, as well as how they affect the sales of the rest of the product assortment. Sometimes it is possible to increase demand simply by improving a product or by adjusting the strategy. In other cases, however, the only way to increase profits is through a carefully planned *expansion* of the product mix.

7.3.4 *Product line extensions*

In overhauling the product mix we cannot simply eliminate all of the items with low profit margins. What ultimately counts is the profit generated by the *total* product assortment, using the right marketing strategies, based on the needs and wants of the target market. To optimize their product mix, many companies turn to product line extension, which involves adding a closely related product to the current product line – developed to satisfy a somewhat different customer need – so as to compete more broadly in the industry. Let's explore four possible strategies that can be used to extend the product line: trading up, trading down (both of them forms of 'line stretching'), line filling and brand extension.

Trading up

Lengthening the product line with a higher priced, better quality product to meet the needs of the high end of the market, is known as trading up or an 'up-market stretch'. With this strategy, the product line is stretched upward beyond the original price range; therefore, it is also referred to as an *upward stretch*.

A successful trading-up strategy enables us to reach a new, quality-conscious segment at the upper end of the market. Yet selling large quantities of the more expensive, higher margin product is not our primary objective! It is much more important to improve the status or prominence of the product assortment as a whole and, in doing so, to increase the *overall* sales and profit.

A trading up-strategy is not without risks. Sometimes *consumers* have doubts about the quality of the new product. In addition, the more expensive item may not fit in with the product assortment sold by the retailers or other *intermediaries* who carry the firm's products. Finally, a *competitor* targeting the upscale market may feel so threatened that they will launch a counter attack with a new, inexpensive item. Of course, managers must anticipate these potential problems and reactions before they decide to adapt strategy.

Trading down

A second option in lengthening the product line beyond its current range is to tap a – for the company – new, price-sensitive segment at the lower end of the market, by introducing a lower priced item. This is known as a trading-down strategy or 'down-market stretch'. Its objective is for the firm to reach a larger target market. This strategy often proves successful because the new, less expensive product added to the assortment is likely to be associated with the established brand name and quality image of the existing products. The addition of the relatively small Mercedes A and B class cars, which are positioned below the original Mercedes range, is an example of a successful *downward stretch*.

Deciding to move down-market especially makes sense when demand for higher priced products is decreasing, or if the company wants to penetrate an untapped price-conscious market segment before its competitors discover its potential. However, this strategy also involves risks. First of all, the new item may *cannibalize* sales of more expensive products in the line, if it is not perceived as sufficiently different from these established products, and some buyers might switch to the lower-priced item. Secondly, there is a risk that the lower priced item will hurt the company's *brand image*. For example, the quality image of *Ronson* lighters suffered considerably when *Ronson* introduced disposable lighters. A company can reduce this risk by ensuring that the lower-priced offering, developed to penetrate the low end of the market, is a simplified, but *qualitatively equivalent* version of the existing product.

When implementing a trading-down strategy, the prices of all items in the product line must be correctly tailored to one another. If the prices are primarily based on the differences between the articles as perceived by consumers, the strategy, as discussed above, is known as *price lining*. This practice makes it easier for buyers to find the right product at a predetermined price.

Finally, there is a third form of line stretching. If a company, which is primarily serving the middle market, decides to add both a lower-priced and a higher-priced item to its current product line, it performs a so-called *two-way stretch*.

Trading down and trading up should not be confused with the concepts of 'downgrading' and 'upgrading'. In contrast to trading down, downgrading is not a product assortment strategy, but a *positioning* strategy designed to influence the customer's perception. Through quality and price modifications or by cutting back on the facilities and decor in the store, a company deliberately tries to reduce the quality and service levels of a product line or store format and ambience. When implementing a strategy of upgrading, a company does the opposite and tries to improve its image by increasing the price and the quality or by enhancing the facilities and decor in the store. These positioning measures do not necessarily go hand in hand with a change in the product mix. It should also be noted that while *downgrading* is rare, *upgrading* is fairly common.

Line filling

An alternative to *line stretching*, which, as we know, refers to lengthening the product line beyond its original range, is a strategy of line filling. This involves expanding the product line by adding more items *within* the existing range of products and prices. For example, a manufacturer of television sets with 81, 107 and 127cm flat screens may expand its product line with the addition of a television with a 94cm size screen. This may be done in response to consumers who are looking for a particular model that is currently not offered or at the request of retailers who lose customers due to missing items in the product line. Other motives to offer a full line may be related to the firm's profit objectives, excess capacity or intention to stay ahead of the competition.

When following a line filling strategy, we should make sure that it does not lead to *cannibalization* or customer confusion. Buyers should be able to see how the products differ from each other. A clear positioning strategy will help accomplish this goal.

When a new product has been well received by the target market, the company may launch other products or product items under the same brand name, possibly in new market segments. This strategy is known as **brand stretching**. A distinction is made here between line extension and brand extension.

Brand extension

The strategies discussed above to extend the product line are all forms of **line extension**: the company uses the existing brand name for new product items in *the same product line*. Examples include the introduction of *Van Melle* mints in new flavours (a 'horizontal line extension', since the new products have the same price/value ratio) and the launch of new *Alfa Romeo* models (a 'vertical line extension', because the price/value ratio of the new models differ from that of the original model).

Brand extension is a completely different strategy, since the existing, well-established brand name is now applied to a new product in a different product class or category. For example, the British entrepreneur Richard Branson has extended the brand name *Virgin* from an airline (Virgin Atlantic Airways) to activities such as retailing (Virgin Megastores), drinks, hotels, records and even space travel (Virgin Galactic). *Porsche*, too, by putting its brand name on products such as lighters and sunglasses, has successfully adopted a brand extension strategy. Today, an increasing number of companies try to avoid the risk and high cost of introducing completely new products, services and product lines that widen the product mix. Instead, the trend is toward lengthening product lines by line extension and brand extension, using brand equity to create consumer interest and build sales.

Whatever product assortment or brand strategies we choose, we can maximize sales as well as extend the life span of a product by making sure that the product design (within the limitations of the intended price range), the positioning and other aspects of the marketing strategy are based on marketing research. In addition, we should analyze the items in the product portfolio from the perspective of the product life cycle.

7.4 MANAGING THE PRODUCT LIFE CYCLE

All products, like people, have a certain length of life during which they go through predictable stages. A product's life begins with its market introduction, it then goes through a period during which its market expands rapidly, eventually it reaches market maturity, afterwards its market declines and finally its life ends. These are the typical stages of the **product life cycle**: a graphic visualization of the stages that a new product passes through over time in the marketplace, from birth to death.

Marketers take into account that their products, too, will go through a product life cycle (PLC). The life cycle is a valuable concept because it helps managers forecast product sales. They know that both sales and profits will vary significantly, depending on where a product

MARKETING TOPPER
How Mini Outperforms Smart

German car manufacturer Daimler claimed that the timing was perfect when they launched the little two-person *Smart* car, about fifteen years ago. However, while the company's executives were right to believe that the world's congested cities were ready for an upscale micro-car, unfortunately for them, a rival took full advantage of this opportunity. Competitor BMW quickly followed with the introduction of a retro model based on England's very popular Morris Mini. The *Mini* immediately outsold the Smart and gained more followers as new and slightly larger models were added to the product line.

For Daimler, the new competition turned out to be a disaster. Its losses on the Smart exceed four billion euros, while the company had to give up control of the inner-city small car market it had established. Industry analysts blame Daimler's failing *marketing* strategy for its niche product. Its managers had been too optimistic about the size of the *market* for cars seating only two people. And they did not develop a more extensive range of *models*, as its competitor BMW did for Mini.

Since Daimler, for a long time, did not launch additional models after the introduction of the *fortwo* – the tiny flagship model with which it tried to penetrate the US market – the company inevitably continued to be *defensive* about the vehicle's small size. The public's uncertainty about the Smart's safety made it necessary to keep highlighting the Smart's steel frame and other safety features, instead of emphasizing the fun of driving the unique two-seater. In contrast, Mini – today's version of the English icon of the 1960s – built its campaign around the superior *handling* of the new roadster that kept its retro *cool*, and the ecstatic *experience* of taking it for a spin.

In comparison to most small cars, the Smart's design offers many complex and high-cost standard features. For example, the *fortwo* has a turbocharged engine, semiautomatic transmission and a sophisticated electronic stability system, equipment that is not even included in many much more expensive automobiles. Still, to most car buyers, it doesn't offer enough *value*

© BMW

for *money*. In the United States – a fast growing small-car market – the Smart's *price* starts at $12 490. This is eight thousand dollars less than the top-performing Mini Cooper, but close to the price of, for example, the stylish Hyundai Accent, a much more spacious subcompact.

It is significant that Smart is now spending over $35 million on advertising in response to a more than 70 per cent drop in US sales volume over a two-year period. The campaign, believe it or not choosing the slogan 'Unbig, uncar', makes a positive feature out of the model's size.

Indeed, taking a more strategic perspective, Smart's management recognized that the main reason for the disappointing sales level in the United States – less than 10 000 cars per year – is the lack of effective marketing and *brand awareness*. Research shows that about half of consumers had never even heard of the Smart brand name; compare that to an average of only 18 per cent for other brands of cars in the non-premium segment. This lack of brand awareness made Ernst Lieb, the CEO of the US division of Mercedes, proclaim that while the Smart was a great car, it had one major problem, namely that no-one knew about it.

Because the car's small size and the limited product line are apparently crucial issues for many American consumers, Smart's product *positioning* may not be the best strategy to increase sales. Even the most skilled marketers would find it nearly impossible to sell a product that does not meet the basic *needs* of the target market. Simply put, there is not a good match between the Smart two-seater and American driving habits or preferences

Another marketing problem that may have stopped potential buyers from purchasing a Smart is the lack of an attractive *brand image*. Brand image may well be the primary reason that globally, BMW's Mini outsells Smart about three to one, and is far more profitable. The Mini brand now earns about €200 million a year on sales of 285 000 cars; compare that to Smart's annual loss of €100 million on sales of 100 000 vehicles. Mini's top

management has pointed out that what separates the car from its rivals is that Mini does not refer to a car model – as when it was launched in 1959 with an Austin or Morris nameplate – but to the very first *premium car brand* in the market *segment* of compact cars.

What made the Mini so attractive in the first place is that it is a Mini. Today's retro-Mini may not look quite like the original Austin Seven did over fifty years ago, but it continues to appeal to a global base of loyal enthusiasts. As marketers know, to most car buyers, a car is not just a vehicle to get them from one place to another, but a perceived extension of their *personality* that makes a statement to others about who they are and what they stand for.

In many consumers' perception, the Mini is the perfect car for urban individuals who are (or who feel) young, and for lighthearted folks who travel without taking anything along but a good friend, a picnic basket and a great bottle of wine. At the same time, for older buyers a big part of the car's appeal is how impressed they were in the 1960s with the classic Mini's *innovativeness*, when it was the very first car to offer front-wheel drive and a transverse engine. Adrian van Hooydonk, BMW's senior vice-president of design, realizes that millions of car buyers across the globe don't want to hear anything negative about the Mini and support it with *passion*. He proudly claims that Mini does not just have customers, but faithful *fans*. And that's probably what makes the brand stand out most.[4]

is in its cycle. Therefore, the marketing strategy must be periodically evaluated and adapted to deal with the special opportunities and challenges in each phase. What is most difficult to predict is the exact length of the stages and the shape of a product's life cycle. Those depend on many factors, including uncontrollable changes in the marketing environment. Nevertheless, with the right marketing actions, marketers may be able to influence the course of the product life cycle.

7.4.1 *Stages in the life cycle*

The 'life story' of many successful products shows that they move through five stages. As can be seen in Figure 7.4 (which includes examples of products), these stages are introduction, rapid growth, turbulence, maturity and decline. Although different-shaped curves are possible, an S-shaped curve is typical of the life cycle of innovative products.

Some authors only distinguish *four* phases in the product life cycle and create a single *growth* phase by combining the rapid growth stage (when competitors enter the market) and the turbulence stage (when, due to extreme competition, many companies leave the industry). This results in a curve with an introduction, a growth, a maturity and a decline phase.

FIGURE 7.4 The product life cycle

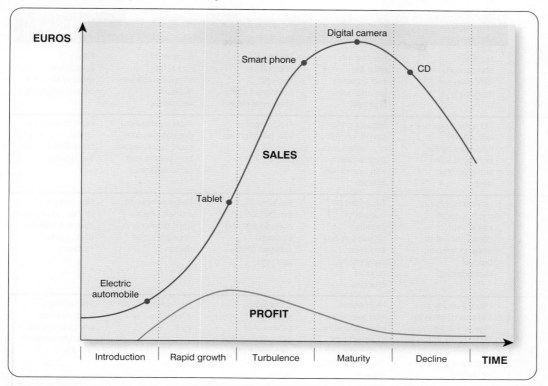

Regardless of whether we see the product life cycle as being made up of four or five phases, the pattern remains the same. At first, sales rise relatively slowly. In this market development or *introduction* stage, relatively few people, those who enjoy being 'innovators', buy the product. During the second stage – *rapid growth* – sales rise faster than at any other point in the product's life cycle; the product has caught on, and many consumers want to be among the first to purchase it. At this point, profits peak. In the third stage (*turbulence*), as new competitors take sales away from the original manufacturer, the rate of sales increase begins to decline. In the fourth phase, *maturity*, the market, without any potential for growth, becomes saturated. This stage may last for an extended period of time. Finally, a product enters the *decline* stage when many of its customers begin to switch to other products that come closer to meeting their changing needs. Eventually, because both sales and profit continue to fall, the product is taken off the market.

Let's now explore the five stages of the product life cycle and examine the extent to which this model provides practical guidelines for the marketing strategy that should be followed for the product during each of these stages. The characteristics of the five stages, including a number of policy guidelines for managing the product life cycle, are summarized in Table 7.2.

Introduction

In the introduction stage of the PLC, consumers initially are not even aware of the product and its potential uses. Hence, the company should invest in advertising and promotion to educate prospects and persuade innovators to try the new product. If there is not yet any direct competition, the firm can concentrate its communication expenditures on stimulating primary demand by convincing the target market that it should use the *type* of product, rather than

TABLE 7.2 Stages of the product life cycle: characteristics and strategy options

	Introduction	Rapid growth	Turbulence	Maturity	Decline
Competition	No direct competition, temporary monopoly	Competitors enter the market and compete for distribution channels	Fierce competition; weakest companies start leaving the market	Number of competitors stabilizes; market is clearly segmented	Fewer competitors as a result of reduced customer interest
Profits	Company makes a loss or only negligible profits; high production and marketing costs	Highest profit period; prices high while costs decline rapidly with economies of scale	Profits decline with falling prices	Profit contribution per unit low; total profit depends on cost control and sales volume	Profit remains low, unless virtually all competitors leave the industry
Product strategy	Limited number of models; better insight into consumer wants leads to frequent product modifications	Expanded number of models, targeted at new segments; constant product changes	Frequent introduction of new models and improved versions of the product	Large number of models which often differ only in appearance or design	No significant product changes; constant pruning of unprofitable models
Pricing strategy	Usually very high (skimming) price to recover R&D costs (or low penetration price that is subsequently increased)	High prices, with selective price reductions to attract new customers and enter new target markets	Competition leads to promotional campaigns (price discounts) and forces prices down	Prices stabilize at a relatively low level	Prices may rise; must maintain prices at level at which firm makes a profit
Communication strategy	Primary demand stimulation through publicity, sampling, and advertising; personal selling to distributors	Selective demand (brand preference) stimulation through positioning and awareness ('theme') communication	Promotional activities geared to intermediaries as consumer advertising gets fewer results	Creation of brand loyalty through promotion that targets consumers and distributors	Reduced communication expenditures; no discounts or dealer promotions
Distribution strategy	Limited distribution; high margins to dealers to justify their carrying and servicing the products	Expanded number of dealers despite declining margins; vital to build long-term relationships and have sufficient inventory with intermediaries	Entering new channels; margins greatly reduced; product service important	Large number of dealers; margins continue to shrink; product service critical to keep shelf space	Unprofitable distribution channels and dealers are phased out
Strategic marketing objectives	Make consumers aware of the product and stimulate trial purchases	Differentiation, optimal distribution, high profits	Large market share, product improvement and differentiation	Stimulate usage; tap new market segments	Increase productivity and efficiency; 'harvest'
	Emphasis on market penetration	**Emphasis on brand preference**	**Emphasis on brand loyalty**	**Emphasis on defending market share**	**Emphasis on 'milking' the product**

emphasizing its own brand. After all, at this early stage of the product's life cycle, any increase in the demand for all products in a particular category will largely benefit the pioneering firm with the *first mover advantage*. After establishing primary demand, the firm can focus its communication efforts on increasing selective demand, which is the demand for its own brand.

Since sales are growing slowly and are still low at the end of the introduction stage, the company must monitor its financial position closely. Although prices may be high, with considerable production and marketing costs and continuous investments in Research and Development, the company will probably lose money on the product. Many good products do not make it past the introduction stage simply because the manufacturer was unable to raise the required short-term capital to successfully launch and maintain the product.

In reality, the introduction of many products is abandoned due not only to lack of operating capital, but also because potential customers fail to see the product's unique benefits. Additionally, in considering the purchase of durable goods (such as Blu-ray Disc players), consumers may be concerned that an innovative product or technology will not catch on and, therefore, will wait to see what happens before buying it. A well thought-out marketing strategy, along with a marketing budget sufficient to make the target market aware of the product and to set up a good distribution network, is essential. Only then has a company laid the groundwork for a lucrative future for the product in the next stages of its life cycle.

Rapid growth

In the rapid growth stage sales typically grow at an increasing rate, and faster than during any other part of the product life cycle. The product 'flies' as more and more consumers buy it. Their positive *word-of-mouth communication* creates a snowball effect, which makes the market expand daily.

Although many new firms enter the market, demand is often so strong that the industry cannot supply all of the needed products. As a result, prices remain high, in spite of increased competition. For companies that have established good cost-control procedures, substantial profits are possible. During this stage, it is crucial for the firm's long-term prosperity to establish a strong dealer organization, which will help support the product when prices fall in the future. At the same time, the company needs to enter other distribution channels, tap new market segments and introduce new and improved models to retain or increase its share. Consumers, who have waited until now to buy the product, benefit from a better *price/quality ratio*.

Now that consumers have accepted the product and all of the teething troubles have been dealt with, larger corporations (which usually take fewer risks) enter the market. These competitors may challenge existing brands by offering improved versions of the product. They develop efficient production techniques and effective marketing strategies. They expand distribution to make it easier for consumers to buy the product. Their huge advertising budgets, which are needed to grab market share, lead to the explosive growth of the market. Once this growth starts to level off, the product has reached the turbulence stage.

Turbulence

In the turbulence stage of the PLC, sales continue to increase, but not as quickly as in the rapid growth stage. By now, virtually all potential buyers are aware of the product and, by the end of this stage, they will have tried or purchased it at least once. Hence, the product has reached its maximum *penetration ratio*. Increased product use by current customers is the only potential for growth.

As new competitors enter the marketplace and try to take sales away from existing suppliers, there is an intense battle for market share. Many of these competitors will simply copy the best-selling products and launch me-too products. Since the increased competition puts downward pressure on prices, profits will start to decline. Survival becomes the primary objective, and the keys to survival are good cost control procedures and a well-established dealer structure. Companies scramble to enlist distributors and to create long-term relationships. To continue building sales, firms should try to create brand loyalty by differentiating and improving their products, emphasizing their benefits and superiority, organizing sales promotion activities, adding distribution channels and – unavoidable at this point – reducing prices to combat rivals.

Meanwhile, marginal companies begin to leave the market. The remaining competitors try to strengthen their market positions, but are approaching the point at which the market reaches maturity and becomes saturated.

Maturity

At the beginning of the maturity stage, sales are still increasing slightly. Then, the sales curve peaks and starts to decline, while profits continue to fall. The company should start thinking about the future of its product.

Since market share wars are common, the primary goal in the maturity stage is to defend the firm's market share against competition. The company should monitor the market continually to determine which *product modifications* – small, but noticeable changes – would attract customers away from competitors. For example, it may make the product more user-friendly, improve the brand image or try to boost demand by suggesting new uses for the product. These efforts – as well as dealer incentives – keep intermediaries interested in the product. Since there are usually only minor differences between products in a saturated market, creative advertising is vital. At this stage of the product life cycle, an increase in market share of just a few percentage points is considered significant.

As prices and profits keep falling, there is typically a *shake out,* as the weakest competitors drop out of the market. Since high sales are essential to survival at this stage, it is difficult for any newcomers to enter the highly competitive market. Company takeovers and mergers, however, are common as the market worsens.

Decline

Finally, sales in the whole product class begin to decline rapidly. Usually, a product enters the decline stage because of changes in the environment, and not as a result of a company's ineffective strategy. In fact, common causes of falling sales are the saturated market (most households have at least one mobile phone), consumers' changing tastes or social values

Heinz Baked Beans are one example of an established, 'mature' product

Image courtesy of The Advertising Archives

(women no longer want to wear fur) and new technology (hard disk recorders have replaced video recorders, while Internet technology and email are pushing fax machines into decline).

The decrease in sales volume often leads to higher costs per unit. Thus, the primary strategic objective in the decline period is to get as much profit out of the product as possible (to 'milk' the product), while demand for it still exists. The least lucrative models or package sizes are discontinued and very little, if anything, is invested in production facilities or marketing. The strategy of retaining the product in order to meet the customers' needs, but reducing marketing costs to keep it profitable, is called a *harvest strategy*. Eventually, however, the product is withdrawn from the market.

Occasionally enough competitors will leave the market so that a firm – although it may pull out of unattractive market segments – can profitably continue to serve those customers who still want the product. This is known as a **retrenchment strategy**. In this situation, reduced competition may allow prices to rise, and the manufacturer may even feel comfortable investing in the product's future. Examples are the remaining coal mines, as well as the limited number of manufacturers of shaving brushes and of record players. Another example is Bic, which, despite the advent of the PC, continues to sell its White-Out correction fluid to companies that still use forms filled in on typewriters. A price increase is especially feasible if a group of dedicated fans is emotionally attached to the product and want to buy it before it is too late. Volkswagen, for instance, increased the price of its old Beetle Cabriolet model after announcing its intention to stop producing this classic car!

7.4.2 *Usefulness of the product life cycle*

The product life cycle is a useful tool for helping us forecast sales and plan the best marketing strategy for the product, instead of reacting defensively to past and current changes in the marketplace. However, the extent to which we can successfully manage the product by tailoring the marketing strategy to the various stages of the product life cycle depends on the *level* at which we conduct the product's sales analysis. There are three possible levels of analysis:

→ *Product category* or **product class**: all product lines in the entire industry or a group of products, such as cars, motorbikes and motor-scooters, which may be considered substitutes for each other, from which consumers may choose to meet a certain need, such as transportation.

→ *Product type* or *product form*: a variation within the product class, such as a sedan, convertible, SUV or crossover vehicle.

→ *Brand:* for example Mazda, Jeep, Suzuki or Chrysler.

Of these three levels of analysis, the *brand* is the least appropriate level at which to apply the life cycle concept. This is because a specific brand that is a market leader may be quite profitable in each stage of the product life cycle. A weaker brand, on the other hand, may, due to an ineffective marketing strategy, never reach the projected sales volume and – under competitive pressure – be taken off the market at an early stage. This is more dependent on sound management decision making than on the product's position on the bell-shaped curve. At the other end of the scale, the *product class* is too general a category for conducting a meaningful analysis. For example, automobiles have been around for over a century and could remain in the maturity stage of the life cycle almost indefinitely.

Therefore, the product life cycle concept is primarily applicable to *product forms*. Diesel engines, for example, are steadily replacing conventional gasoline engines in cars bought by European consumers, while crossover vehicles and hybrid cars are increasingly preferred over SUVs. Demand for different product forms also varies from one *segment* of the market (for example, families with young children) to another, so it could be argued that the PLC concept as an analytical tool is more applicable to this level of the market than to the overall market.

Taking the product form as an appropriate level of analysis, the life cycle – combined with marketing research – can be a helpful *guideline* to managers in creating an effective plan for developing and modifying marketing strategies, to achieve market acceptance and to maintain sales and profits. For one thing, this forces management to anticipate when competition will enter the market and to estimate or forecast the impact competitive entries will have on the product. This, in turn, prevents the need for unplanned corrective measures at a later date. Thus, as a *control* instrument, the PLC also serves as a warning sign. If, after the product is introduced, sales do not live up to expectations, the marketing plan can be modified or the forecast re-evaluated.

7.4.3 *Extending the life cycle*

When a business is evaluating the possibility of entering a new market with one of its existing products in order to maximize the return on its investment, the product's life cycle stage becomes very important. A common error that some managers make is to analyze a product early in its life cycle and then to expect the rapid increase in sales, as well as the current profit margin, to continue into the future. The fact is, however, that as more companies enter the market, prices and profit margins usually decline. Therefore, a product that appears to be quite profitable in the rapid growth stage – with a market share of, for example, 40 per cent – may prove to be only marginally profitable when it reaches the turbulence stage. By then, its market share may have shrunk considerably. We can avoid the costly error of entering new markets with overly optimistic assumptions by first determining the product's current life cycle stage and, then, forecasting how much time will elapse before it enters the next stage.

A good approach is to first define the market. To come up with a realistic assessment of the competition, the market definition should not be too narrow or too broad. We then chart the development of sales volume and gross profit margin, as well as relevant trends in the recent past, not only for our own products, but also for those of other companies in the industry. What do we know about competitors' strategies and changes in their product lines, and how have these affected their market shares? Armed with this kind of information we can then forecast the expected sales, margins, costs and profits for the next few years and position the products on the product life cycle as accurately as possible.

Many companies try to stretch out the life of a product in the maturity stage of the PLC through a series of sequential measures. This strategy is known as **market stretching**. How can a firm extend a product's life cycle? There are several actions a firm can take.[5] For instance, it can:

→ Stimulate more frequent use of the product among current users (a dairy company, for instance, may introduce new flavours of yoghurt).

→ Tap new markets (promote low-fat yoghurt as a diet product in weight-control programmes).

→ Suggest alternate uses for the product (yoghurt as a healthy breakfast item or – instead of mayonnaise – as an ingredient in dips).

If a company manages to extend the life cycle before product sales start to decline in the maturity stage, this will result in a so-called *envelope curve*, or a PLC with a *scalloped* pattern. The shape of the curve in Figure 7.5, representing the life cycle of razor blades, indicates that the company successfully improved and revitalized the product on several occasions: at points A1, B, C, D and E.

FIGURE 7.5 Extensions of the PLC of razor blades

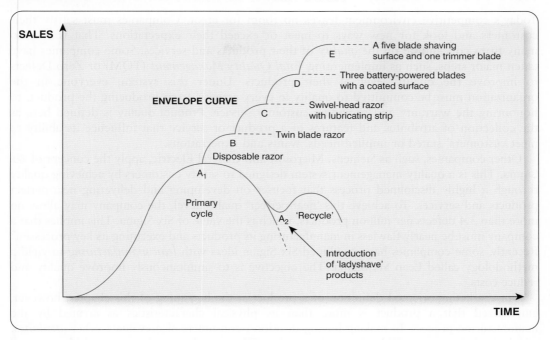

If the marketer does not succeed in prolonging the maturity stage of the cycle, sales will weaken as the product enters the decline stage. Yet even then, the company can adopt a strategy of *recycling*, as illustrated in Figure 7.5. Recycling involves innovation and heavy use of promotion to create a new life cycle for a product already in the decline stage. This results in a PLC with a so-called *cycle-recycle* pattern. Usually the second cycle, from point A2 onwards, is less pronounced and shorter in duration than the first ('primary') life cycle.

Adapting the physical *product* is one way to create sales growth for a product in the decline stage. Another option is to *reposition* the product in an extensive advertising campaign. In fact, a well thought-out repositioning strategy has saved numerous products in the decline stage from going under.

7.5 PRODUCT QUALITY AND CUSTOMER SERVICE

Just as the marketing mix is made up of the four Ps, the *product mix* consists of various product-related instruments a company can use to appeal to its target market. In the next few paragraphs we will explore the most important elements of this product mix.

Which products a consumer will buy depends on several *product attributes*, such as the prestige of the *brand name*, perception of the product's *design* and *packaging*. We will look at these elements of a marketing policy later in this chapter. Some of the product features that may determine how much buyers trust the product, or how satisfied they are with it, are intangible. Those include the manufacturer's *warranty* terms and the *service* provided by the reseller. These are also rather subjective factors; they influence the *quality* of the product as perceived by the customer. Because of their important role in the customer's decision making, we now take a closer look at a product's quality, the warranty and the service provided.

7.5.1 Product quality

Today's competitive environment leaves no room for error. Companies must satisfy their customers and look for new ways to meet or exceed their expectations. That is why so many firms concentrate on the *quality* of their products and services. Some companies have taken major steps, such as implementing *Total Quality Management* (TQM) or Zero Defects to improve the quality level of their products. Under this system, everyone in the organization must be committed to quality in every activity, from producing the product, to honouring the warranty and providing customer service. **Product quality** is defined here as the collection of attributes and features of a product or service that influence its ability to meet customers' stated or implied needs, wants and expectations.

Other companies, such as Siemens, Microsoft and General Electric, apply the concept of **Six Sigma**. This is a quality management system designed to satisfy customers by achieving quality through a highly disciplined process that focuses on developing and delivering near-perfect products and services. To achieve this 'near-perfect' quality level, the company may allow no more than 3.4 defects per million products, which is the value of Six Sigma. This implies that a company must be nearly flawless in manufacturing its products and executing its key processes.[6] Recently, some companies have combined Six Sigma ideas with *lean manufacturing* to yield a methodology called Lean Six Sigma. The objective is to simultaneously improve quality and reduce costs.

Our marketing-oriented definition of a product at the beginning of this chapter, however, emphasized that a product is more than its physical characteristics as created by the manufacturing process. In making buying decisions, consumers also evaluate other *attributes*, which, in their opinion, add value to the product. Thus, product quality is a *multidimensional* concept. Since so many factors can contribute to customer satisfaction, marketing-oriented companies focus on two dimensions when trying to improve product quality: technical quality and consumer quality.

Technical quality versus consumer quality

Technical quality – relating to a product's dependability and durability – reflects how well it performs its intended function. These functional features, such as the product's capacity or speed, its reliability, the safety of the materials used and how long it will last, can be *objectively* measured. How long a product will last is considered to be the life span (or *economic quality*) of the product. Professional and consumer organizations assess both the product's *level* of quality (as compared with other products) and the *consistency* of quality (the extent to which a product has the same level of quality over time, for instance, each time it is purchased).

Consumer quality relates to the overall, and often intangible, characteristics of a product that are important to consumers and that allow it to perform *as expected* in satisfying customer needs. The words 'as expected' are a key part of this definition, because quality typically means different things to different people. For some customers, the product's design, colour, warranty and service contract, as well as – *subjectively* determined – features such as the taste or scent signify quality. For others, the product's brand image, ease of use, ease of maintenance and ease of repair may indicate quality, and thus contribute to consumer quality.

Consumer quality perceptions are strongly influenced by the difference between consumers' expectations and their actual experience with the product. The higher the expectations, the smaller chances are that they will be met or exceeded. To avoid such disappointments, marketers should not exaggerate the product's features or performance in advertising campaigns or personal contacts with customers.

Price/quality ratio

Quality is a subjective concept not just for customers, but also for employees of the company marketing the product. One employee will be more easily satisfied than another. Therefore, firms are increasingly developing a well-planned strategy of quality management. They devote a great deal of attention to the analysis, planning, implementation and evaluation of all activities that improve the (technical) quality of their products and production processes. This kind of systematic approach is also the best way to achieve the quality standards to which the company aspires – such as the ISO 9000 standard, as determined by the International Organization for Standardization (ISO). Acquiring ISO 9000 certification for production and service facilities most likely requires some adjustments in the knowledge, attitudes and behaviour of employees at all levels of the organization.

Generally, the higher the perceived quality, the higher the price that marketers can charge for the product. But not all customers want, or are willing to pay for, the highest possible quality products. Therefore, some companies offer the same type of product in a range of qualities, at different prices. Thus, successful companies do not necessarily compete on the basis of the best quality, but on better price/quality ratio.

7.5.2 Product warranty

Most buyers see more value in a product that carries a warranty or a guarantee. A warranty is a written statement of what a seller promises to do if a product turns out to be defective or fails to perform properly within a certain period after being purchased. In the warranty, the seller spells out what they will do to compensate the buyer for any shortcoming due to production errors or faulty materials, such as repair of any defects within a reasonable time and without charge, replacement of the product or a full refund. A warranty reassures the customer about the product's quality and performance and can also help differentiate the brand from competing brands.

A guarantee, on the other hand, is the assurance that the product is as represented and that it will provide the expected performance. It is often used as a sales aid, especially in non-store retailing. In offering a guarantee, many companies pledge to refund the purchase price or replace the product if the buyer is not satisfied. A guarantee may either be *expressed* (in written form) or *implied* (suggested by statements made about the product by the seller or assumed from common practice in the industry).

Warranties and guarantees are especially important for:

→ Technically *complex* products with long life cycles (such as espresso machines), particularly if the brand is not well known.

→ Products that are sold in *packaging* that prevents a customer from inspecting the contents or the quality until after the purchase (such as PCs).

→ Products for which the manufacturer's reputation or brand name is negatively perceived (such as makes of cars with a bad quality image).

In these types of situations, a sound warranty can effectively reduce the risk for the customer and increase the prospects of a purchase.

The warranty term needs to be long enough to allow any production errors to surface and ideally should be transferable to a new owner, should the product be resold before the warranty expires. In any case, a good warranty – providing the customer with the psychological benefit of peace of mind – is part of the *augmented product*. Although the cost of providing the warranty or guarantee is incorporated in the selling price, many consumers do not mind paying more for a product bought from a company recognized for outstanding customer service of products under warranty. This makes a customer-oriented warranty policy an effective competitive tool in today's marketplace.

7.5.3 Customer service

Managers who assume that consumers dissatisfied with a purchase or shopping experience are usually forgiving are misinformed. Though it may go unnoticed, many sales are lost as a result of customer dissatisfaction. Typically, rather than complaining, these customers will switch to another brand or start shopping elsewhere. What is more, displeased customers often tell their friends, colleagues and family members about their negative experiences with a product or service, influencing others' future choice of brand and store. Consumers and business buyers generally evaluate products and their suppliers against three criteria: quality, service and price, usually in that order. Hence, being consumer-oriented and making customer service (including complaint handling) a top priority in the organization is crucial to developing an effective marketing strategy.

Evaluating service quality

Customer service is a significant part of the buyer's overall brand experience. Therefore, many firms differentiate their products by providing outstanding service, hoping to build lasting relationships and create customer loyalty. The word 'service', as used by consumers, often refers to *support services*, the extra assistance a vendor provides its customers upon delivery of the product, or after the sale. Services such as programming the channels on a newly purchased television or installing a washing machine free of charge are examples. But, from a marketing perspective, the concept of customer service entails more than product support services or after-sale service. Customer service is every form of assistance before, during and after the purchase that makes it easier for customers to buy and use the product and increases the likelihood of repeat purchases, provided by a company to differentiate its products from competitive offerings and to build long-term relationships with its clients. As is clear from the definition, we distinguish between the times at which the assistance or service is provided:

→ *Before* the purchase (for example, product demonstrations, design and budgeting assistance, trial installation).

→ *During* the purchase (technical advice, credit or finance offerings).

→ *After* the purchase (on-time delivery, installation, inspection, training, maintenance and repairs).

In the business-to-business market, as well as in marketing services and durable consumer goods (*shopping products* or *specialty products*), delivering high-quality customer service leads to positive word-of-mouth referrals. Such referrals will help the company win new buyers and retain current customers, leading to an increase in its customer base. Since the service quality is determined by the customer (who has certain expectations), and not by the marketer, a truly customer-centric firm will conduct regular marketing research to determine if the service it provides – as an important dimension of quality – meets the *expectations* of its patrons in every respect. It will measure customer satisfaction, loyalty and the quality of its relationship with customers, establish whether it is delivering enough service in the right form and ascertain how service can be improved.

Research shows that customers, in assessing service quality, use several criteria that are closely linked to employee performance. As outlined in Table 7.3, these include tangibles,

TABLE 7.3 Five critical dimensions of service quality

Dimension	What consumers are evaluating
Tangibles	What is the appearance of the facilities, service personnel, materials and equipment?
Responsiveness	Is the firm willing and able to give service when needed?
Empathy	Does the marketer provide caring attention and individualized service?
Assurance	Are the service employees knowledgeable, competent and trustworthy?
Reliability	Over time, is the firm dependable and accurate in providing service as promised?

responsiveness, empathy, assurance and reliability.[7] If the service provider does not meet customers' needs or expectations in these areas of service delivery, they may take their business elsewhere.

Marketing research and customer feedback with respect to service quality may have implications not only for the product, but also for the promotion, price and distribution strategies. In developing the *distribution strategy*, we need to make sure that the value we add to the product meets the customer's needs and wants from start to finish. The pre-purchase service provided should focus on a convenient ordering procedure and a clear description of delivery terms, while the post-purchase service should include prompt repair of any defects and a considerate, competent staff during every service encounter. To enable excellent and efficient service delivery, many companies develop vertical marketing systems at different levels in the supply chain, working together with other organizations in a professionally managed and centrally coordinated network with an agreement on customer service task responsibilities. This is, in effect, a form of *integration* in the distribution channel.

It is also essential to provide a high level of service in other areas of marketing. Even if the product is exactly what the customer needs, if they cannot find the right model, do not get a discount to which they are entitled or has difficulty contacting the supplier by phone or through the company's website, their opinion of the manufacturer or reseller will likely be negative.

Satisfiers or dissatisfiers?

In a competitive market, a company can only maintain its market share if it sells quality products at a reasonable price, offering value for money. With the widespread application of today's advanced technology most producers are able to do this. Yet technological advancement in itself makes it increasingly difficult to differentiate products. Product features that were once unique to a specific brand are now found in many *me-too products* and thus play a less important role in the competitive battle.

Companies are constantly trying to uncover which product attributes motivate buyers to choose a particular brand in a product category. These are known as satisfiers (things that cause satisfaction) in the sense that they are elements of a product that, from a customer's point of view, significantly improve its quality and are major reasons to buy the product. However, as more firms start offering these features and consumers become accustomed to them, satisfiers often turn into dissatisfiers: this feature's absence from a product will then be a reason for consumers not to choose that brand. Currently, for example, automobiles equipped with air conditioning and side airbags may provide a reason for European consumers to purchase that particular make of car. However, as more automobile manufacturers include these as standard features in all of their car models and consumers expect them, the *absence* of air conditioning and side air bags may become a reason not to buy, as the product is now perceived as having a lower quality level. What was originally a satisfier has become a dissatisfier. Marketing-driven companies not only avoid dissatisfiers (such as a very limited product warranty or the absence of help desk services for computer users) in their products, but also try to include satisfiers that motivate buyers to purchase their brand.

7.5.4 *Relationship marketing*

Twenty-first century marketers realize that their jobs go beyond providing good service and developing competitively priced quality products with desired attributes. In fact, many buyers, with such a wealth of choice in products and services, are looking for added value from their relationships with resellers. Consequently, an increasing number of companies move away from *transaction-based* marketing (which simply focuses on attracting customers and creating a deal or exchange with them) and are embracing *relationship marketing*. Their goal is to systematically build and maintain long-term relationships with individual customers, as well as with suppliers and intermediaries. Relationship marketing is primarily concerned with retaining *existing customers,* especially in stagnating markets. By reinforcing its social ties with customers and its economic or technical ties with other organizations, the firm can improve mutual understanding between these parties and develop a solid marketing network.

As illustrated in Figure 7.6, a company pursuing relationship marketing should put customers at the centre of its efforts and activities. As part of its marketing strategy, it must emphasize quality, customer service, a long-term orientation (based on the lifetime value of a customer) and frequent customer interaction. This creates benefits for both parties and leads to customer loyalty.

FIGURE 7.6 Creating a relationship marketing orientation

PROFESSOR'S PERSPECTIVE
Madéle Tait (Nelson Mandela Metropolitan University, South Africa)

Dr Madéle Tait, an expert in Services Marketing, is Head of the Department of Marketing Management at Nelson Mandela Metropolitan University, Port Elizabeth, South Africa and honorary professor at University Johannesburg, South Africa. Professor Tait's current research focuses on Customer Relationship Management (CRM).

For most of us, life without technology is unthinkable. Technology is not only wonderful, but also continuously changing, at a fast rate. Take for example a Visa card – you can use it for buying air tickets on-line, but also for making reservations for a show in the West End and paying for last-minute booked accommodation. Similarly, mobile phones are no longer only needed for telephone calls and text messaging, but for a whole new range of available services that you can choose from. At the same time, in the service industry – and specifically in financial services – Internet banking has grown tremendously.

Personal contact is crucial in the service industry

Interestingly enough, if things go wrong with your finances, you still want to see someone in person at your bank to try and solve the problems. At those times, you don't want to make use of technology to solve the problem, but rely on a traditional visit to your bank manager or customer relationship manager. Personal contact is crucial in the service industry. Besides the personal contact, you need to build a relationship with a person whom you can trust and depend on, especially at your bank. Customer Relationship Management is still a very important subject field, but is often regarded as data mining only, or keeping records of the biographic data of customers.

Customer Relationship Management includes *customer care*, which is imperative in the service industry. For customer service managers, it is important to get to know their customers. However, often businesses, such as banks, rotate their employees who deal with customer relationships or customer care. If a customer then visits the bank and asks for their specific relationship manager to solve a problem, and this particular person has moved to another department, it is difficult to start building a relationship with the new manager all over again. In marketing, it is a well-known fact that service delivery is linked to a specific person and if this person is not performing well – for example, is always late for appointments – it won't be the person as such who will suffer negative word-of-mouth, but the business they are working for. The customer will tell their friends about that particular business they need to avoid, as the service delivery is poor.

Many companies use call centres to deal with customers' questions and issues. Unfortunately, often the employees working in these call centres are not adequately equipped to solve problems. Usually, the labour turnover rate in these facilities is quite high, since continuously dealing with irritated customers and their unsolved problems takes its toll. It is important to realize, especially in the service industry, that the human element is still an imperative aspect of service delivery in general and customer relationship management in particular. Hence, customer relationship managers should be qualified and trained to deal with customers' problems and should keep themselves up to date with the latest trends in industry, but also in their particular business, in order to be able to help customers. Although technology can be a wonderful tool, the human element and personal touch are still very much needed.[8]

Creating long-term relationships with customers starts with having clear insight into who the customers really are, what they value and how they prefer to interact with organizations from which they buy. This allows the firm to create a partnership with its customers by offering them value and making sure they are satisfied. New technology is helping firms adjust products to the preferences of specific customers, differentiating these items from off-the-shelf products. Today, **mass customization** allows marketers to offer individually tailored products and services to a large number of customers cost-effectively. Examples include the automobile industry, Dell notebooks and Levi's Original Spin jeans. For a company's best customers, an even higher level of loyalty can be achieved through **one-to-one marketing**. This marketing strategy is customized to create long-term relationships with individual customers.

To provide customers with optimal service, many companies have set up *consumer affairs* or customer service departments. These departments not only deal with complaints but also provide information and technical advice, help arrange financing and leasing agreements, decide how service is to be provided (via independent dealers or internal service staff) and determine how much a customer will be charged for services rendered. Ultimately, the consumer affairs department is responsible for the service provided to all the firm's customers.

7.6 BRAND MANAGEMENT

Consumers develop a preference for certain brands at a relatively young age. Millions of school children, in fact, already prefer Coca-Cola, Nike and iPads to Pepsi, Adidas and Galaxy (or vice versa). As consumers, we are all familiar with these brand names – they 'tell us something' about the product. That is just what these companies want. Through *branding* and brand management, companies create strong identities for their products to distinguish them from similar products offered by competitors. And, since well-known brand names help sell their products, they go to great lengths to protect these brands against product *counterfeiting*, or selling low-priced copies of a popular brand not made by the original manufacturer.

A **brand** may be defined as a name, term, symbol, design or any other feature that a firm uses to identify its products or services and differentiate them from those of other sellers. A **brand name** is that part of a brand that can be spoken – including letters, words and numbers – such as HP, TomTom and mp3.com. A **brand mark** or *logo,* on the other hand, is the element of a brand that cannot be vocalized, such as McDonald's Golden Arches, the Shell emblem or the Nike Swoosh that these companies display next to the brand name or elsewhere to identify their restaurants, gas stations or products.

A **trademark** is a brand, especially one that is officially registered and protected by law, which a company or individual uses as identification on goods made or sold by them. The trademark must be legally registered – depending on the area for which protection is sought – with the Benelux Trademarks Office in The Hague or, for the EU, with the European Office for Harmonization in the Internal Market (OHIM) in Alicante (Spain). In the United States, more than a million trademarks are registered with the US Patent and Trademark Office. The ® symbol printed after many brand names indicates that these brands are registered trademarks. Thus, all trademarks are brands, but not all brands are automatically trademarks. Legal registration not only gives the owner the exclusive right to use the brand, but also may prohibit others from using brand names or brand marks so similar that they could confuse buyers.

We will now analyze the objectives of branding, as well as the differences between manufacturer and distributor brands. We also examine the characteristics of an effective brand name.

7.6.1 *Strategic objectives of branding*

In any competitive market, developing an effective branding strategy is essential and requires a great deal of management attention. A strong brand image backed by superb product quality gives a company an excellent reputation and a substantial competitive advantage. Brands have come to play a leading role in a company's marketing strategy, because the brand identity can make a huge difference to both the buyer and the seller in an exchange process.

For consumers, a brand has obvious benefits. For example, a well-known brand name will increase chances that consumers will recognize a company's products when making buying decisions. Also, a strong brand identity will contribute to customers' perceptions of product *quality* (reducing the risk of a purchase), offer *convenience* (less time spent searching, if the branded product is widely available) and give buyers the opportunity to use the brand as a form of self-expression by underscoring their values or *lifestyles*. This combination of factors also reinforces repeat purchases and *brand loyalty* – the degree to which a customer consistently buys the same brand within a product class. Thus in marketing, brand preference and brand loyalty are definitely measures of a brand's strength. Usually, the consumer's preference for a particular brand changes only if it is very difficult to find the brand, or if the price is disproportionately high.

A strong brand identity also has substantial benefits for the company that owns the brand:

→ The brand *identifies* the company's products, making it easier for customers to locate them.

→ The brand acquires a particular identity or *image* that makes it – with the right positioning strategy – appeal to a certain target market.

→ The brand, with its unique personality, enables the seller to develop a relationship with the customer, stimulating *repeat purchases*.

→ Sellers with strong brands are less dependent on retailers, making it easier for them to *launch new products*.

In the next few paragraphs we will explore the value of branding by examining these benefits.

Identification of seller

The single most important objective of branding is to identify the seller. Brands help consumers recognize the products they prefer, making it easier for them to buy the specific goods and services they know will meet their wants and needs. Brands also tell them what level of quality and service they can expect. The fact that consumers are willing to pay more for well-known brands shows how important this benefit is to them. They appreciate the fact that manufacturers of national brands make sure their products are of consistent (and often superior) quality. Needless to say, the large market shares and relatively high selling prices of branded products make a substantial contribution to healthy corporate profits.

Product image

Branding offers psychological benefits to consumers interested in buying and showing off brands with prestige images. Often, consumers are more interested in the *image* of a particular brand than in the product's objective characteristics, such as its price and ingredients. Examples of brands that convey status are Prada and Rolex. However, products don't always have to be expensive to have a desirable image. The huge demand for products with sought-after brand names, such as Nike and Levi's (despite the fact that the quality of these products is not much better than that of cheaper, lesser known brands), shows that a brand name is indispensable in creating an image that appeals to customers. These brand names, which are frequently repeated in advertising campaigns, give the product an emotional added value.

Repeat purchases

Satisfied customers tend to keep buying their old familiar brands (*brand loyalty*). By emphasizing the brand name in their advertising, companies stimulate *repeat purchases.*[9] This is how they develop a loyal customer base. At the same time, companies benefit from the fact that consumers discuss their product experiences with others (word-of-mouth communication). In short, an effective branding strategy helps the seller establish a limited form of 'monopoly' power over the customer. This provides some protection against growing competition.

New product introductions

A company with a well-established brand name, especially one denoting quality to the public, will find it much easier to introduce new products than a relatively unknown firm. When a company such as Apple, BMW or Heineken introduces a new product, it will probably get a positive response from many people who have had good experiences with its products in the past. These customers have a brand preference. The same applies to retailers: they are more likely to make space on their shelves for new products if the brand name inspires confidence.

7.6.2 *Battle of the brands*

Manufacturers and retail distributors have been competing for power in the supply chain for years. This **battle of the brands** is actually fought over control of the distribution channel, because whoever controls distribution largely controls profits. Therefore, the outcome of this battle determines who – as channel captain – will have most influence on the marketing strategies implemented by other parties in the distribution channel, the manufacturer or the *intermediaries* (wholesalers or retailers). Their main weapons in the battle of the brands are *manufacturer (owned) brands* and *distributor (owned) brands* or *private labels*. The various types of brands are shown in Figure 7.7.

FIGURE 7.7 Types of brands and strategic branding decisions

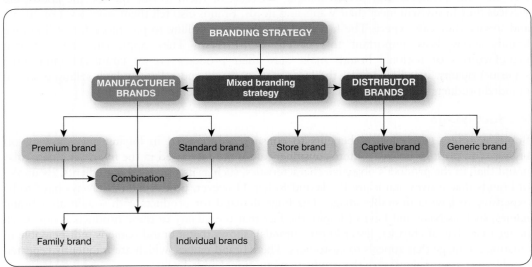

Manufacturer brands

A manufacturer brand, which is owned by the product's maker or manufacturer, is sometimes called a *national brand*, because it is often advertised nationwide. This term is not always accurate, however, because some of these products are only distributed on a regional basis, especially in large countries. Accordingly, referring to a brand as a manufacturer brand really indicates the brand's owner.

A distinction can be made between two types of manufacturer brands: premium brands and standard brands. Brands with the highest perceived quality and price level are known as premium brands. These brands (particularly in the *fast-moving consumer goods* category) have a so-called *distribution spread* or *distribution intensity* of at least 75 per cent. This ratio means that the brands can be purchased in at least three-quarters of the stores that – considering their product assortments – could carry them. Because premium brands are not only widely available, but also frequently advertised, they are fairly well known. They have relatively high market shares and, in many European countries, control approximately two-thirds of the market. Since premium brands display quality, status and confidence, they provide considerable added value to consumers. Examples of premium brands include Apple, Coca Cola, Facebook, Google and Red Bull.

Standard brands are (manufacturer owned) brands that lack at least one of the characteristics of premium brands. These products – which are still frequently purchased – may be less widely distributed (their distribution intensity is less than 75 per cent) or are advertised regionally rather than nationally. The chain stores that sell them advertise them in their brochures and other promotional materials, and ask the manufacturer to help cover the cost of this publicity. Standard brands have a limited market share. Many consumers consider the quality of standard brands to be somewhat inferior to that of premium brands. Hence, they are also sold for a slightly lower price. For example, Amstel and Bavaria are priced lower than most premium beer brands.

Many manufacturers produce both premium brands and standard brands aimed at different target markets as part of a differentiated marketing strategy. The standard brand serves to confirm the position of the premium brand and, in doing so, increases the manufacturer's profit.

Private labels

Distributor brands are owned and controlled by a retailer, wholesaler or other type of reseller. These brands are often referred to as private labels, private brands, store brands or dealer brands. They are exclusively produced for a chain store, a purchase organization or a voluntary chain. With their favourable price/quality relationship, distributor-owned brands appeal to price-conscious consumers and in many countries have a market share of more than 20 per cent. This category includes store brands, *captive brands* and generic brands.

The growth of private brands has stayed even with that of chain stores in many countries. Quite a few producers not only sell their well-known manufacturer brands to retailers, but also agree to put the store's own label on comparable products, increasing the number of options available to consumers. A *store brand* is a private brand owned by a national or regional retailer or wholesaler. Store brands include the Hema brand, Perla (sold by Albert Heijn), the George line of clothing sold by Walmart and Kenmore sold by Sears.

A spin-off of the private label is the *captive brand*, a national brand sold exclusively in the stores of a particular retail chain. Examples include Martha Stewart apparel and home furnishings available at Kmart and General Electric appliances sold at Walmart (in fact made by other producers who bought the rights to put this brand name on their small appliances). Illustrative for the high penetration of this kind of private label in the US is the fact that at Target, more than half of the merchandise at this upscale discount chain is exclusive to the store. Typically, captive brands provide even higher profit margins than private labels.

Generic brands – which were first used in 1976 by Carrefour in France – are right at the bottom of the price ladder. These products are sold in plain packaging and named only by a generic class (such as 'tea'), without a specific brand name. With the exception of pharmaceuticals, where low-cost generics are becoming increasingly popular, generic brands in most product categories and countries are not as successful as store brands, probably because retailers cannot use them in their positioning strategies. Store brands on the other hand have, for many consumers, evolved from being an inexpensive alternative to premium brands to highly valued brands in their own right.

Creating brand equity

A brand is an important marketing tool that enables many producers to maintain a hold on the market. After all, by advertising the brand on a large scale and pursuing a *pull* strategy, major manufacturers can 'force' retailers to include a product that consumers want in their product assortment. There are very few categories or markets remaining with no manufacturer owned brands (sometimes referred to as *grey markets*). Old Amsterdam, for example, is now a well-known brand of cheese in a product category in which brand names formerly played only a minor role or, in some countries, were even completely absent. To make their brand even stronger, some manufacturers use co-branding, which involves putting two (or more) brand names on their product (Dell and Intel Inside).

Retailers follow their own plans to gain market influence at the expense of producers, usually by robustly supporting their own retail brands as an important component of a positioning strategy. A retailer's advantage lies in being able to decide how the limited shelf space in a supermarket will be allocated. The store brand – which already attracts price-conscious customers – is given the best position on the shelves, while the manufacturers have to compete for the remaining shelf space. Consequently, in many industries retailers, rather than producers, are winning the battle for control of the supply chain. Although manufacturer owned brands still dominate the market, retailers are no longer simply the 'mouthpiece' or spokesperson for the manufacturer. Retail organizations try to connect to their target markets with well thought-out store formats, which include a product assortment that differs from their competitors'. The goodwill that retailers develop in customer relationships leads to store loyalty – as opposed to loyalty to premium brands. And, because the margin on private label products is relatively high, retailers' profits are higher than they would be if they only sold manufacturer owned brands.

In conclusion, both producers and distributors are trying to increase their influence by reinforcing brand equity, which is the long-term value of the brand or the value that a particular brand name adds to a product in the marketplace. High brand equity may increase a product's market share as well as the company's profits, since brand loyal buyers may be less price sensitive in purchasing the product.

Strategic options for the producer

Manufacturers of consumer goods can follow three possible strategies in terms of their production and marketing strategies:

1 *Produce only manufacturer brands.*
   A manufacturer with one or more strong brands, such as Procter & Gamble, can concentrate just on its premium and standard brands and attempt to obtain the largest possible market share.

2 *Produce only distributor brands.*
   Small or production-oriented manufacturers without their own marketing strategies may simply supply retail organizations that then sell these products as their private labels. However, because their sales are dependent on a third party, this strategy involves a great deal of uncertainty each time a contract expires.

3 *Implement a mixed-branding strategy.*
Many large producers make their own premium brand as well as distributor owned brands and supply both to resellers. Although the strategy may decrease the market share of its own brand, this is an acceptable risk if the manufacturer has excess capacity or wants to realize economies of scale. Besides, if it refuses to supply distributor owned brands, the retail chains will simply obtain their *private label* products from the company's competitors.

7.6.3 Individual or family brand name?

In addition to making the strategic branding decisions discussed above, a company must also determine whether to sell its products using an individual brand name strategy or a (blanket) family brand name strategy. A firm with an *individual brand name strategy* uses different brand names for each of its products. For instance, Unilever's margarine products are sold with brand names like Blue Band, Becel, Rama, Country Crock and Doriana.

The other branding option for a company is to use a family brand, which would involve selling most, if not all of its products in a particular product line (or even various products in different product lines) under the umbrella of a single brand name. Examples of companies that use such a family branding strategy are Philips (for light bulbs, LED TVs and medical systems) and Yamaha (motorcycles and pianos). Douwe Egberts uses a single brand for tea (DE Pickwick), coffee (DE Senseo) and tobacco (Douwe Egberts Drum). Some companies combine the use of a family name and individual brand names. This approach is common in the automobile industry where Jeep, for instance, brands its products Jeep Grand Cherokee, Jeep Compass and Jeep Wrangler.

A family brand makes it easier for a company to introduce a new product, because the new item benefits from the reputation of the existing brand. In fact, all of the products sold under the same brand name may benefit from the publicity, sponsoring, advertising (such as Philips' *Sense and Simplicity* campaign) and other marketing activities developed to increase brand awareness and stimulate sales. A *merchandise display* in a store (such as a conspicuous presentation of DE Senseo and other DE coffee products) can be used to draw attention to the entire product assortment.

Why, then, do so many firms, despite these advantages, choose to sell each of their products under a separate brand name? There are three reasons why companies opt for individual brands: to protect existing products, to increase sales through market segmentation and to stimulate internal competition.

Protecting existing products

Many consumers perceive a firm's products as essentially the same, even if they have different technical characteristics or differ considerably in price and quality. If a company uses individual brands, and one of these brands is involved in a scandal, or if a new item fails to catch on, the adverse effects are not transferred to products with different brand names made by the same company. For example, Unilever was fortunate that the frozen Iglo meals, contaminated with nitrite during transport, had a different brand name than its ice cream products shipped by the same trucks.

Companies also use individual brand names to differentiate their products from each other, especially when introducing a new, inexpensive product to the market. The objective here is to prevent the new item from 'stealing' sales of the established, more expensive product (*cannibalization*). For example, when Seiko entered the lower-priced watch market, it decided to sell its inexpensive watches under a separate brand name, Pulsar. Had it used the name Seiko, many price-conscious shoppers who were unable to see any quality difference between the watches in the store, might have selected the inexpensive watch. One way to avoid such 'trading down' is to use individual brands.

Increasing sales through market segmentation

Seiko's branding strategy also illustrates a second advantage of using individual brands: the possibility of *market segmentation*. The company was able to sell similar products under different brand names and via different (competing) distribution channels to different target markets. This strategy made it possible for the company to expand rapidly.

Stimulating internal competition

A third reason to adopt an individual branding strategy is to stimulate competition among product managers within the organization. To illustrate, in the highly competitive laundry soap business, each of the Unilever brands stands alone in the market and, in effect, competes against the products marketed by Henkel, Procter & Gamble and Colgate-Palmolive as well as – internally – against the other detergents made by Unilever sold under different brand names, such as Omo, Robijn and Sunil. This strategy keeps the marketing department on its toes. Especially with cut-throat competition, a new brand name can be a key element in a marketing strategy to get the product accepted by both channel intermediaries and consumers. For instance, Mars managed to increase its share of the snack foods market considerably by using individual brand names for confectionery products, including Mars, Milky Way, M&M's and Snickers.

7.6.4 *What makes a brand name good?*

Selecting a strong brand name is an important marketing decision, since ideally, the name should grab the buyer's attention, help create a desirable brand image and result in product trial. In choosing the actual brand name, three guidelines must be considered:

1   The brand name must be distinctive and easy to recognize (Xerox, Philips and TomTom).

2   The name should be appropriate for the product (fit the image the firm is trying to project) and possibly suggest something about the product's major benefit (Senseo, Glassex, Ketel One).

3   The name should be easy to pronounce (also in other languages), short, positive and memorable (Amstel, Mentos, Uncle Ben's).

If a brand name is used internationally, the firm should make sure that it does not evoke the wrong associations. For instance, in the British market, Fiat changed the name of its Fiat *Ritmo* to Fiat Strada, because in the UK Ritmo was a popular brand of condom. Additional blunders in choosing brand names are described in the *Marketing Mistake* in this chapter. Of course, it is increasingly difficult to think up a new brand name that meets these guidelines, while also being distinctive enough to ensure that the name – through trademark registration – can be legally protected in the countries where the product is sold.

7.6.5 *Legally protecting the brand*

Because of growing competition and application of the marketing concept – which leads companies to make exactly what 'the market' is asking for – many products look similar today. Still, thanks to trademark legislation (such as the Benelux Trademarks Act), a company can legally protect its well-designed brand against imitation by competitors through registration. As pointed out previously in section 7, protection can be granted for different regions in the world, giving the brand registered trademark status.

To protect its exclusive rights to a particular brand, a firm should first make sure that its own brand is not an infringement on any other brand that has already been registered with, for example, the Benelux Trademarks Office or the US Patent and Trademark Office. In case

MARKETING MISTAKE
Automobile Brand Names

The company that imports Fiats into the Netherlands advised its Italian parent not to name its top of the line model Fiat *Croma* in Europe, but in vain. The Fiat *Croma* – reminding consumers of a similarly named brand of margarine in the Netherlands – was launched but not well received, and the importer suffered as a result. Other car manufacturers have avoided such blunders by enlisting the expert assistance of brand name agencies. For example, Volkswagen was advised not to sell its Vento model on the British market as a *Diago*. The name would have evoked memories of the controversial goal by Diego Maradona in the 1986 World Cup quarterfinals, which caused the English team to be eliminated from the World Cup in Mexico. The Citroën *Evasion* was re-branded in the UK as the Citroën Synergie, because English consumers might regard the Evasion as a car for people who try to avoid paying taxes ('tax evasion'). And in Germany, Rolls-Royce decided to rename its Silver Mist model Silver Shadow, because in German the word 'Mist' means manure or garbage.

Many companies that have decided on a brand name without the help of professional name-searchers have ended up regretting their blunders. Mitsubishi Motors, for example, had to change the name of the Mitsubishi *Pajero* in Spain

© Rolls-Royce Motor Cars LTD

when it discovered that in Spanish the word *pajero* has inappropriate connotations. Its competitor, Toyota, made a similar mistake in France with the Toyota *MR2* which – phonetically – is almost indistinguishable from a French expletive. The Chevrolet *Nova* is another classic example. The car was not very successful in Spanish-speaking countries, because in Spanish 'no va' means 'it doesn't go'! It's difficult to think of a worse name for a new car...

of any conflict, a court will decide if consumers are likely to be confused, mistaken or deceived about the source of the product or service.

Even if a company's brand is protected by law, it still must keep its brand name from becoming a *generic term* used by the public to refer to the general product category. This is most likely to happen to a brand for a completely new product that catches on right away. If the brand name becomes such a generic term, the product has essentially become 'brandless' again – since as a generic term the brand has little strategic value and cannot be protected anymore as an exclusive brand name. This is what happened with linoleum, nylon, vaseline, escalator, zipper, walkman and aspirin (originally a brand name registered by Bayer); while brands such as Chocomel, Maggi, Jeep and Luxaflex are still in danger of becoming generic names on the European market. To prevent its brand name from becoming a generic term referring to the whole product class, the company should always spell the name with a capital letter and include the ® (registered trademark) symbol immediately following the brand name. The word 'brand' is sometimes added after the trademark symbol (i.e. Kleenex® Brand Tissue).

Also, by advertising its brand on a regular basis (and emphasizing that the brand name is an adjective, rather than a noun), a company can try to prevent the public from using its brand name for competitive products. In doing so, a company can preserve the distinctive power of the brand and avert any attempts to have the registration of the brand declared null and void.

In order to be protectable, a brand name must be distinctive. If it is purely descriptive or suggestive of a certain product feature (such as Wash 'n Shine), it is a weak brand name, and difficult to protect. The product's label must also explicitly state which company manufactures the product.

A trademark may be more than just the brand name – such as Red Bull – or a brand mark. The law allows companies to trademark other aspects of their products. Any feature that serves to *distinguish* or identify a particular product, such as a name, term, design, symbol, distinctive shape or colour is considered to be part of the *brand* and can be protected.

Hence, even a product's packaging and design could be trademarked. Because these product attributes may also be central to a product's marketing success, we will now explore them in more detail.

7.7 PRODUCT DESIGN AND PACKAGING

A key question in marketing a product is how it comes across to consumers. Their first impression may be influenced not only by the product's design and styling, but also by the packaging in which it is offered. For that reason, product design and packaging are closely related.

7.7.1 Design and styling

Most consumers choose between competing products based on their (subjective) perceptions of the product's benefits, physical appearance and other sought-after features. Firms that meet the buyers' expectations and develop an attractive product, tend to be more successful than those ignoring customers' needs and wants. Therefore, a critical task of marketing-oriented firms in developing a new product is to find out what their customers want. In particular, its managers pay close attention to product design, or how the product is conceived and produced, from a technical and commercial point of view, as well as from the consumer's perspective.

An important aspect of design is the physical appearance of the product or styling. In addition to being useful and *functional* – in terms of serving the purpose for which it is bought (for instance, saving time) – a product should also be *attractive*. Products that are both practical and aesthetically pleasing are the ones consumers prefer. Since all of the senses may play a role in assessing the attractiveness of a product, designers may focus on the product's colour, fragrance and taste in its development.

Another relevant factor in the buyers' brand choice is product features, specific design characteristics that enable a product to perform certain tasks. Examples could be a product's safety, comfort and user-friendliness. Although many companies concentrate on a product's design to improve its performance, make it easier to use and reduce the manufacturing cost, in general, the more features a product has, the higher its price (along with its perceived quality). Since a high price may be a barrier to sales in developing markets, some companies use reverse engineering; this is the process of disassembling a competitor's product piece by piece to take a close look at its components and get clues about the production process, with the objective of making a stripped-down product at reduced costs. It is clear that a well-planned product design is essential for all products, including low-priced items.

In mature markets, product design and styling decisions are vital because a prestigious, upscale design may be just what the target market wants. To illustrate, many people are willing to pay high prices for Bang & Olufsen's sleekly styled flat TVs and sound systems. This has enabled B&O, a relatively small Danish company, to carve out a place for itself between the international giants that dominate the global television and audio markets.

7.7.2 Packaging functions

Since how a product is packaged can have a major impact on consumers' buying decisions, packaging – just like design and styling – is a crucial component of a company's product strategy. A **package** is the wrapper or container for a product, used to protect, promote, transport and identify a product; it usually includes a *label*, which is a product description printed on the package.

Packaging, the first thing customers see in a store, even before they see the actual product, is more important to consumers than you might think. Many shoppers, for example, refuse to accept products in damaged packaging. In fact, the package is one of the most noticeable product attributes that influence the customer's perception – and therefore their brand choice. Because of the significant role it plays in the initial communication process, packaging is a valuable marketing instrument.

Manufacturers spend a great deal of money on packaging, often more than on advertising and marketing research combined. In the food products industry, the packaging costs, including materials, typically make up over 25 per cent of the total cost of the product (ex factory). Considering that this percentage is even higher for such items as liquid detergents, toiletries and pharmaceutical products, it is worthwhile analyzing the main functions of packaging.

Traditionally, on a functional level, a package was thought of as a container with largely a *technical* function. Packaging had to have utility for both consumers and intermediaries in the distribution channel. Its main objective was to divide the product up into smaller quantities (bags of sugar and flour), to protect it from damage and moisture during transportation and storage in warehouses (fruit and vegetables) and to prevent premature spoilage (barrels of herring, vacuum packed fresh meats). Packaging made it easier to keep inventory and reduced shipping and storage costs. In this product-oriented period, managers concentrated on these *primary functions* of packaging. The consumer's preferences were barely considered.

The **packaging functions** were expanded with the arrival of fully automatic packaging methods and self-service supermarkets. Now, customers could examine and compare each product at their convenience. Consequently, the emphasis in packaging shifted to *communication functions* that had previously been part of the sales assistant's job. The package and the label on it had to catch the buyer's attention in a crowded marketplace, prominently identify the brand and clearly describe and promote the product's features.

Today, marketers view packaging as an important strategic tool and pay considerable attention to its *commercial functions*. In addition to its primary function, they now examine the extent to which technological developments in packaging can create a longer product life and protect the product better, while taking up less space on retailers' shelves (think of the round can used for Pringles potato chips). Innovative packaging can also make the product easier to use, as illustrated by a motor oil container with a convenient built-in spout for pouring. All in all, companies tend to concentrate their efforts in developing packaging on four marketing functions that are related to the presentation of the product: providing product information, creating an image, product differentiation and stimulating consumption.

Product information

More than half of all purchases made in supermarkets are decided on while consumers are in the store. Therefore, companies selling consumer goods make sure their packaging and labelling attract consumer attention and convey important information about the product straight from the store shelves. For maximum marketing effectiveness, a label should be an integral part of the package. The basic details provided on product labels, however, are partly dependent on government regulations, which vary by country.

The label usually identifies the name of the product, the brand, the name and the address of the manufacturer, distributor or importer, the net contents, the country of origin, the ingredients and nutritional values. Other legally required product information displayed on the packaging are directions on how to use the product, storage instructions and the expiry date. Companies that design customer-oriented labels make sure that the average purchaser will have no difficulty understanding what is printed on the package.

Informational labelling not only helps savvy consumers make good product choices, but should also make useful information available to intermediaries in the channel of distribution. The Universal Product Code (UPC) – a numerical barcode printed on packages that can be read by optical scanner systems and processed by computers – offers companies a wealth of information that may help them cut costs, improve inventory control, track sales and develop effective marketing strategies.

Symbolic image

Like a product's brand name, a package should boost the brand's image and communicate its value. Just as a fine liqueur requires a bottle that is different from one used for table wine, expensive perfumes are packaged in crystal bottles, not because crystal will protect the perfume better than plain glass, but because the package relays the message that this product is of high quality. Serving as a communication link between the seller and the buyer, a quality package signals a quality product.

Like the product's brand image, packaging evokes certain feelings in the consumer. The marketer must ensure that the image expressed by the product's package (luxurious, modern, innovative, etc.) is consistent with the social-symbolic image conveyed by the product itself.

Product differentiation

Often the package is the primary vehicle used to differentiate a product from its competition. When a consumer rushes through a supermarket containing thousands of items, the package must catch their eye, hold their attention and create a clear perception in their mind. Ideally, a package stimulates some form of interaction between the consumer and the product or brand. Playing an important role in the company's product differentiation strategy, packaging can be used to reinforce the brand's positioning. It can also help the firm target a particular customer segment.

Stimulate consumption

Companies have been very successful in developing packages that help sell the product and increase its consumption. As previously discussed, marketers may use packaging to differentiate their products, suggesting new uses or providing extra convenience for their customers. This often stimulates the product's consumption. For instance, packaging was the innovative force behind successful new products such as microwaveable popcorn and hand soap pumps. These new kinds of packaging changed the products in the buyers' perception and helped companies to penetrate new markets. Larger packages (such as two litre bottles of Coke and margarine in 500 gm tubs) not only tend to increase consumption, but also partially shift the stock function from manufacturers to retailers and consumers. Incidentally, single-portion packs (such as individual servings of powdered milk for coffee) may also lead to an increase in sales or revenues.

In conclusion, a product's consumption usually increases if packaging makes the product more *user-friendly*, as do aerosol cans of whipped cream and small bottles (or cans) of soft drinks. Packaging can also be effectively used to announce a temporary price cut or another kind of promotional offer – primarily to stimulate sales. Consumer response to packaging, however, can vary by country. For instance, most of the tennis balls sold in Europe come four to a can. Americans, on the other hand, prefer a three-pack and Japanese consumers a two-pack.[10] Therefore, it is vital for global companies to research the differences between foreign markets before making decisions about packaging.

7.8 MARKETING OF SERVICES

For decades, marketing literature devoted relatively little attention to services marketing. Most marketing executives and authors traditionally focused on products and, therefore, assumed that services should be marketed in much the same way. Although this certainly is not true for all services, that misconception limited research on developing optimal strategies to market services effectively. Another reason for the limited focus on services might have been that services are not as concrete as products. While a product is a tangible object, a **service** is an intangible – and almost instantly perishable – activity that gives users a certain level of satisfaction, but that does not involve ownership and cannot be stored. However, while services lack physical substance, to customers they are just as important as products.

Therefore, the relative lack of attention paid to the marketing of services was not justified – especially since in developing and mature markets, service industries are important to the economy and vital in creating job opportunities. In many industrialized nations, the service sector accounts for 50 – 75 per cent of the gross domestic product (GDP). Also, the majority of start-up companies are service businesses. In short, the global service economy is booming, and service employment continues to grow.

It comes as no surprise that today more attention than ever is devoted to **services marketing**, defined as systematically stimulating sales of 'intangible activities' by facilitating the exchange process between service providers and buyers. In fact, the use of marketing techniques by telecommunication companies, banks, insurance companies, law firms, health care organizations and other service firms is the fastest growing area in marketing. While in the past, many service companies completely ignored marketing, now their managers are embracing it and appreciate its proven ability to help them meet their objectives.

In the last section of this chapter on product strategy and services marketing, we begin by defining what is meant by a service. Next, we will assess the importance of the service sector. Finally, we will explore how service organizations can increase their productivity.

7.8.1 Characteristics of a service

Services involve all kinds of activities. Getting a haircut, going to the doctor, enjoying a drink at the neighbourhood café, having your car repaired, getting advice about a mortgage and buying travel insurance are all examples of consumption (and simultaneously, production) in the service industry. Instead of supplying a tangible product to meet the customer's needs, service organizations concentrate on the various benefits that they offer or activities that take place while interacting with the individuals or organizations for which they are providing the service.

A better understanding of services can be gained if a product is seen as a noun and a service as a derivative of the verb *to serve*. From that perspective, a product is a tangible object or device, whereas a service is an intangible 'product' involving a deed, a performance or an effort that cannot be physically possessed.[11] Products, such as a can of Red Bull or a mobile telephone, are produced, sold and then consumed or used. Services, on the other hand, are often sold, produced and consumed simultaneously.

The differences between products and services can be best summarized by considering the unique characteristics of services. In addition to their *intangibility*, services have three other characteristics that differentiate them from products. These are the *inseparability* of production and consumption (buyers are dependent on sellers), *perishability* (a service cannot be inventoried) and *heterogeneity* (performance standards are difficult to maintain). These characteristics require customer-oriented companies to develop special marketing programmes for services.

Intangibility

As previously emphasized, unlike products, services are **intangible**. Therefore, potential buyers cannot physically examine, touch or taste a service before making a purchase decision. This makes it difficult for them to objectively evaluate services beforehand.

Customers can see and try out a product such as a bicycle before buying it, but this is not the case in purchasing a service like an airline trip. Similarly, students cannot touch the education that they get by attending classes. The intangible benefit of studying is to become more knowledgeable and develop certain skills (such as the ability to write a marketing plan), but knowledge and practical skills are not something individuals can physically possess. As a final illustration, someone who buys a ticket to see a movie, actually purchases access to an intangible experience which is difficult to evaluate, especially in advance. The opinions of film critics and friends, who each have their own expectations and perceptions, are not necessarily a good indication of the movie's quality. After the show, the customer leaves the cinema with an expired ticket and their own memories of the (hopefully positive) experience. Their overall impression is probably influenced by the customer-orientation and attitudes of the theatre's employees, the quality of the movie theatre and the behaviour of the other customers watching the same movie.

As is apparent from these examples, most products and services consist of a combination of tangible and intangible elements. Therefore, it is not always possible to make a clear distinction between goods and services. This is illustrated by the **services continuum** (or *product-service continuum*) shown in Figure 7.8,[12] which classifies products according to their tangibility.

Pure goods (if they exsist at all), such as salt and soft drinks, are at one end of the continuum, while pure services such as education, consulting and other service-dominant activities are at the other. This framework can graphically put marketing opportunities into proper perspective. Of course, most products and services are 'hybrid' in nature since practically every manufacturing company offers services with its products (for example, financing with a car purchase) whereas service providers offer some products as well (such as drinks during a

FIGURE 7.8 The product-service continuum

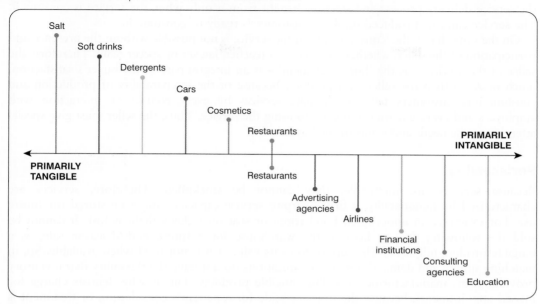

flight). In between the two extremes on the continuum, all consumer and business products contain a combination of tangible and intangible features. Marketers, in developing their promotional strategies, realize that a consumer's preference for a certain company can be based on tangible items (for instance, in a fast-food restaurant, on the food itself, such as a Whopper or Big Mac) or on intangible benefits (such as on the family orientation, speed, service or convenience). The key decision for a restaurant in plotting its promotional strategy might be, 'What do we stress in our advertising, the quality of our food or our friendly service? What is the basis of our true competitive advantage?'

A product's position on the product-service continuum has significant implications for the company's marketing and promotion strategy. Companies marketing tangible goods, such as cars, typically emphasize intangible aspects like status or adventure in their positioning strategies. On the other hand, firms that offer *services* try to 'tangibilize' these by associating their services with tangible items or symbols. For example, airlines, in advertising their business class services, tend to show comfortable seats, a friendly cabin crew and delicious meals to get the message across, reducing their potential customer's uncertainty about the service quality.

In conclusion, the more a marketing offering is characterized by intangible features, the more difficult it is to apply the usual marketing tools developed and tested for products. Intangible services require different marketing techniques if they are to be sold successfully.

Inseparability of production and consumption

After purchasing a tangible product, the buyer can take it home and has complete control over the product. In contrast, the purchase of a service does not involve transfer of ownership. Services are subject to inseparability. This means that services are produced and received at the same time and are inseparable from the service provider.

Usually, a service marketer doesn't produce anything until a consumer buys the service and informs the provider what they want. For example, when a consumer goes for a haircut, the stylist cuts their hair then and there. The customer has considerable input into the service delivery process and starts to benefit from it only when the service is consumed. The service can't be produced until the customer is ready to consume it.

On the other hand, the 'consumption' of the service is not possible without the presence and participation of the seller, whether the seller is a teacher, lawyer or soccer team. Therefore, the seller of the service – as the 'human element' – is an integral part of the buyer's satisfaction, much more so than the seller of a product. Because of the inseparability of production and consumption, customers tend to evaluate services by every contact or interaction with employees and every experience related to using the service. Thus, the seller must give special attention to the needs and wants of the buyer.

Perishability

Because services are intangible, they cannot be stockpiled. Therefore, services are characterized by **perishability**: a firm's surplus service capacity cannot be stored for future use. For example, an unoccupied hotel room or seat on today's flight is lost. It cannot be sold the following day, or kept in the warehouse for a future end-of-season sale, as a tangible product might be. The service loses its value if it is not used when available. So, in matching supply and demand, service organizations do not have the flexibility that inventory provides firms manufacturing or selling tangible products. This is why dentists charge for missed appointments, because the time set aside for a patient's consultation or treatment is lost if that patient does not show up.

The demand for services is rarely evenly distributed over time. As a result, service providers often have excess capacity during quiet periods and insufficient capacity during peak periods. Because wide fluctuations in demand cannot be smoothed over with inventory, service providers must be concerned with peak load and excess capacity. Their best option is to find ways of managing supply and demand for their services in order to create a better match. Movie theatres try to influence demand through differential pricing. They offer matinée rates to shift some demand to off-peak times, just like telephone companies charge lower rates for long-distance calls at night and at weekends. The services supply can also be managed by hiring part-time employees. A restaurant, for instance, will hire extra waitresses to work during peak dining hours. Nevertheless, because of the fluctuation in demand, the customer does not always get value for money at times of high demand, when delays, lines of customers and a lack of personal attention are all too common.

Heterogeneity

Because *people* play a central role in providing services, quality levels vary with each person's capabilities and day-to-day job performance. Therefore, it is difficult to maintain uniform performance standards for services. The quality of service varies not only between firms in the same industry (compare the output of different advertising agencies), but also from one transaction to another by the same service provider. One employee may be more knowledgeable or better trained than another. Further, the service a single employee provides can vary from customer to customer, day to day or even hour to hour, depending on their mindset, energy level and mood at a particular moment.

Heterogeneity, or variation in quality, usually increases as the degree of labour intensiveness increases. In order to ensure that it consistently meets customer service standards, a service provider must carefully select, train and supervise its employees. Many of the skills required in the human-intensive service industry can be learned. Staff members can also be motivated through incentive bonuses and awards (such as 'employee of the month'). Generally, employees who are given more responsibility tend to increase their efforts and commitment.

A company can measure and control service quality by monitoring customers' satisfaction. Many hotels and restaurants conduct opinion surveys, while airlines ask passengers to evaluate their services. As a result, the quality of the service can be standardized and the reliability improved by developing routine, detailed procedures for the various tasks (such as in fast-food preparation). Mechanizing the process may also enhance consistency, as banks have accomplished by installing automated teller machines. Similarly, airlines have improved their service quality through online reservation systems and Internet or self-service check-in procedures.

7.8.2 Importance of the service sector

The economies of most industrialized nations have, slowly but surely, become less manufacturing-based and more service-based. The number of jobs in the service sector has grown much faster than even the fastest growing industries in the production sector. The increased employment opportunities in service industries have especially benefited the female work force; in most European countries, more than half of all newly created jobs for women are in service-related jobs.

The most important long-range reason the service sector has grown so rapidly in Western nations has been the creation of a large middle class with a substantial amount of money available for discretionary spending. A service is just what the name implies: a job or activity purchased by one person from another that the buyer cannot or does not want to perform. For many years most services were limited to professional services – doctors, dentists and lawyers – and to domestic help. As our economy became more affluent, new services developed, including those of beauticians, pet hotels, catering services and personal trainers.

A second reason for the expansion of the service industry is that the number of households has increased at a greater rate than the population. Smaller households mean fewer people to help with household tasks and usually more disposable income. Also, because there are an increasing number of dual income households, the working partners have neither the time nor the inclination to do many of the things around the house that their parents did. As a result, many of them use service organizations to clean their houses, do their hair, maintain the garden or care for their pre-school children.

The last reason for the increasing amount spent on services is that the price of services has grown much faster than the price of products. Why? Because wage increases are more easily offset by productivity increases in the manufacturing sector than in the service sector. This also explains why certain types of services – such as traditional shoe and watch repair companies – gradually become unaffordable and disappear. Yet at the same time, new marketing opportunities open up in the service economy, especially those in which labour-saving technologies and self-service play a greater role.

7.8.3 Increasing productivity

As previously mentioned, the service sector has been the fastest growing component of the economy over the past decades. The obstacle that could slow growth of the service sector in the 21st century is the ever increasing cost of labour. Already, people are simply priced out of the market for many services. The solution to this problem is obvious, but difficult to implement – to increase the productivity of the service sector labour force.

The traditional way to increase productivity in a business is to invest more capital and provide better training for employees. To some extent, both approaches have been used in the service sector.[13] For example, fast food restaurant chains, which offer a mix of products (hamburgers) and services (quick meals), have spent a great deal of money on increasing the scale of their operations and on equipment needed to prepare food quickly and inexpensively. These firms offer extensive training programmes at their home offices for franchise owners and at individual store sites for franchise employees. This reduces the cost per item and increases profit margins.

Railway companies and movie theatres have adopted similar strategies – investing in high speed or double-decker trains and showing many films in a single building with a central box office and lobby. Other service organizations use various marketing techniques to change consumer behaviour, thereby increasing productivity indirectly. Three such techniques are modifying the timing of demand, involving the customer and changing buyer expectations.

Modifying the timing of demand

The fact that service providers cannot inventory their services creates a dilemma. If an organization has insufficient capacity, it will lose customers and buyers will be dissatisfied. If on the other hand it employs enough people and invests sufficient capital to handle peak demand, it will simultaneously undermine its profitability, because it will still have the same high overheads during off-peak periods. A sensible alternative to increased spending is to influence the customers' consumption patterns, specifically, to modify the timing of demand.

A more even spread of demand has a positive effect on managing a business as well as on the service quality. For example, the postal service in most countries encourages consumers to mail their Christmas cards earlier. Also, flexitime (flexible working hours) relieves pressure on the public transportation system during rush hour, and has resulted in a significant increase in usage during more lightly travelled periods. This shift in demand can also be accomplished through differential pricing. Some restaurants offer lower prices ('early-bird'-specials) to encourage dining before peak hours, while tourist resorts, too, try to develop non-peak demand by offering attractive rates in quiet periods.

Involving the customer

For some businesses, it is possible to increase productivity by having the consumer play a more active role in the purchase of products and the performance of services. The underlying idea is that if some of the required work is transferred to the buyer, the company saves time and money that can be spent on more productive activities. In doctors' surgeries, for example, patients are usually asked to fill out their own medical records. Also, many European supermarkets have customers weigh their own fruit and vegetables and stick the price label on the bag, or let them scan and bag their own groceries.

Changing buyer expectations

In addition to managing demand and involving the customer more in the actual delivery of the service, it may be possible, through the effective use of marketing communications, to convince the buyers to expect less service from the organization. The result is often a substantial increase in productivity. For example, fast food restaurants have been able to convince their patrons to order and pick up their meals at the counter and to clear the tables before they leave the restaurant. The consumer benefits from fast service and relatively low prices.

Other companies have been able to reduce the service buyers expect, and at the same time provide additional benefits to their customers. Examples include express counters at some hotels and car rental companies. Customers fill in the necessary forms themselves – without clerical assistance – and, as a result, spend less time waiting in line. However, in order to prevent eliminating a portion of the service that buyers really value and possibly losing customers to a competitor, the firm should first determine, through marketing research, what aspects of the services consumers consider non-essential and are willing to give up in exchange for certain benefits.

SUMMARY

1 Definition of a product

A product is much more than a physical item. In marketing the *augmented* product, the degree of success greatly depends on its intangible, added features, such as the warranty, available credit, speed of delivery and service quality. Product attributes or features that are derived by the consumer, including the brand image, the status acquired through ownership and the convenience of using the actual product, all contribute to the customers' satisfaction with the overall product. To compete successfully in the market, companies should, in their external communication, emphasize the customers' possible reasons for buying the product (the complete bundle of benefits) rather than the plain product and its physical features, no matter how great the product or service may be.

2 Product classifications

While business-to-business products and services are sold to commercial enterprises and government organizations for resale or for use in the production of other goods and services, consumer goods are sold to individuals – as ultimate consumers – and households for their personal consumption. Depending on the amount of time and effort the consumer is willing to spend on the buying decision and on the frequency of purchase, consumer goods can be classified as *convenience products* (bought frequently with minimal effort), *shopping products* (which are carefully compared in terms of price, quality and style prior to purchase) and *specialty products* (with such a high consumer involvement and brand loyalty that buyers are willing to make a special effort to obtain them). Finally, products unknown to the potential buyer or products of which the consumer is aware, but does not actively seek, are called *unsought products*. Although these product classifications have important implications for marketing strategy development, it is not always possible to generalize about the four categories. How a product is classified in a particular purchase depends on the perception, attitudes and buying behaviour of the individual customer.

3 Product mix decisions

A company's product portfolio, product mix or *assortment* consists of all of the product lines and items it carries. To optimize the product portfolio,

we first need to analyze and decide on several dimensions of the product mix: the assortment's width (the number of product lines), length (the total number of products that a company offers in its product mix or in a product line), depth (the number of product items – including brands, types, models and sizes – in a product line), consistency (the link between the lines in the product mix) and height (the average price level). By dividing the products up into the core and the peripheral assortment (in line with the 20/80 rule), we are in a better position to make decisions about reorganizing or expanding the product portfolio. A product line can be extended through *line stretching* (trading up or trading down) or *line filling* (adding items within the existing product lines and prices ranges). If a company applies its established brand name to a new product in a different product class, it follows a strategy of *brand extension*. This, too, is a frequently used strategy in business.

4 Product life cycle

The product life cycle can be a helpful planning and forecasting tool in developing and proactively adapting marketing strategies. Many successful products move through five stages in their life cycles: introduction, rapid growth, turbulence, maturity and decline. Each stage generates different profit margins and requires unique marketing strategies. The product life cycle is most applicable at the level of the product type or form. Product life cycles can often be extended by pursuing the strategies of increasing usage by current users, suggesting variations on uses for the product, creating new users and finding new uses for the product. Many companies try to extend a product's life in the maturity stage, creating a PLC with a scalloped pattern. If the product is revitalized in the decline stage, a cycle-recycle pattern is typical.

5 Product and service quality

To influence consumers' choice of brand, many manufacturers emphasize the *quality* of their products in advertising and promotion. Some companies apply the concept of Six Sigma to try to create products of near perfect quality. However, as marketing-oriented managers know, quality is a subjective concept that includes both technical quality (does the product do what it is supposed to do?) and consumer quality (does it satisfy the needs of consumers, given their expectations?). Other elements of the product that may be effective marketing tools in today's competitive corporate marketplace are the *warranty* – which spells out what the seller will do if the product is defective or does not perform properly – and the *service* provided, during the purchase but also pre- and post-purchase. Customer service includes such things as identifying buyers' needs, technical advice, on-time delivery, maintenance and repairs. In judging service quality, consumers use criteria related to tangibles, responsiveness, empathy, assurance and reliability. Since consumers consider an increasing number of product attributes *dissatisfiers*, many companies focus on *relationship marketing* to provide their customers with added value. Many products are differentiated through this social dimension, as well as through mass customization and one-to-one marketing.

6   Brand equity

One of the ways in which companies develop relationships with their target markets is through their *branding strategy*. Therefore, having a strong brand in the market is a major asset to a company, the value of which is referred to as brand equity. A brand is a name, term, symbol, design or combination of these elements that identifies products and services and distinguishes them from competitors' products. The primary functions of branding are to identify the seller, to create a product image, to stimulate repeat purchases and to facilitate new product introductions. The competition is fierce and conflicts occur frequently: manufacturers (with their premium and standard brands) and distributors fight over control of a brand's distribution channel in the 'battle of the brands'. To be most effective, manufacturers should decide whether to use individual brands or a blanket family brand name strategy for their products. A good brand name must be distinctive and appropriate for the product, communicate the product's benefits, and be easy to pronounce and remember. Current legislation enables companies to protect not only their brand names and brand marks, but also their products' distinctive shape and packaging.

7   Design and packaging

Consumers without a particular brand preference usually base their buying decisions on the visual appearance of the product and its packaging. *Product design* concerns the styling, aesthetics and function of a product. Design involves the product's look and feel, as well as ease of assembly, installation and, of course, use. Thus, an optimal product design is not based solely on technical criteria (the product's features that allow it to perform certain tasks), but also on consumers' perceptions and preferences, including the aesthetic appeal. Aesthetics start with the product's *packaging*. In addition to containing and protecting the product, the most important functions of packaging are to serve as a vehicle for information about the product, to enhance its brand image, to differentiate the product and to stimulate consumption. All of these are important objectives of the product strategy.

8   Services marketing

While a product is a physical object or device, a service is an intangible – and almost instantly perishable – activity that gives users a certain level of satisfaction, but does not involve ownership. In addition to *intangibility*, three other distinguishing characteristics of a service are that buyers are dependent on sellers (*inseparability* of production and consumption), a service cannot be inventoried (*perishability*), and performance standards are difficult to maintain (*heterogeneity*).

The economy has grown increasingly service-based, as the service industry continues to expand. This is due to the growing purchasing power of consumers, the greater number of households and the increase in the price of services. Productivity in the service sector, in some cases, can be increased through the traditional approach of providing more capital and training per employee. Another option is to influence consumer behaviour by managing demand, involving the customer in performing the service and lowering buyer expectations. These challenges make services marketing a fascinating field.

DISCUSSION QUESTIONS

1   A product can be defined in different ways, based on its features or attributes. Indicate what you would call the various elements of a PC and define the types of products resulting from this classification.

2   The founder of Revlon, Charles Revson, was quoted in Chapter 1 as saying, 'In the factory we make cosmetics, in the store we sell hope!' Comment on this statement in light of our definition of a product.

3   In this chapter we made a distinction between the 'core product', the 'actual product' and the 'augmented product'. Does this mean that marketers try to make products, that are actually the same, appear different? What does the consumer stand to gain from these distinctions? And what are the risks of this approach for the marketer?

4   Describe the various product attributes for a fragrance such as AXE Body Spray or Chanel No. 5.

5   Comment on the following statement. 'Because a service is not tangible, it cannot be a branded product.'

6   Most experts agree that not all products pass through the same life cycle. Why, then, is it important to study the product life cycle?

7   What would a brand with national distribution that is not clearly preferred by a group of consumers be called? Give a few examples of these kinds of brands and explain what purpose they serve.

8   Two of the reasons for using individual brands are 'to protect existing products' and 'to stimulate internal competition'. Aren't these two reasons in conflict with each other? Explain your answer.

9   Comment on the following statement. 'When developing a packaging policy, companies should assess their short-term and long-term costs and benefits in light of the environmental and safety aspects.'

10 Do you think that packaging will be more important to the marketing manager ten years from now than it is today?

CHAPTER 8
NEW PRODUCT DEVELOPMENT

LEARNING GOALS

After studying this chapter you will be able to:

1	Recognize what is new about a 'new' product
2	Understand what motivates companies to develop new products
3	Outline the development process for new products
4	Identify various types of new product management organizations
5	Explain why new products succeed or fail
6	Discuss the implications of the adoption process for strategy development

8.1 What is a new product?

8.2 Reasons for product development

8.3 Developing new products

8.4 Organizing new product development

8.5 Why new products succeed or fail

8.6 Diffusion of innovations

Find your own angle

Discover your creative side with the new EOS 60D.
The vari-angle screen and Basic+ features give you
the freedom to reflect your mood and capture
images just as you see them.
canon.co.uk/EOS60D

EOS
60D

Canon

you can

Firms primarily develop new products and services to replace old ones that customers have tired of using. Since products become obsolete faster than ever, companies must continually renew the product mix to boost revenues and profits and to increase market share.

Managers often complain that competitors are introducing new products that they could have thought of themselves. A promising product idea or proposal may be floating around in the organization for some time, without action being taken to push the idea to the next level. In fact, there is seldom a lack of ideas in most organizations. The key to success in innovation, however, lies in the company's ability to identify the best new product ideas and to effectively develop and launch the products and services based on these ideas. This chapter in *Marketing: A Global Perspective* offers practical guidelines for new product and services development.

MARKETING IN ACTION
Reverse Innovation From Emerging Markets

For decades, global companies have flourished by making relatively high-priced products for prosperous consumers in the West. Meanwhile, these multinationals often offloaded their production surpluses – typically outdated stock from the previous season – in developing economies at discounted prices, instead of also developing entry-level products to cater for the needs of low-income buyers. Thus, innovation used to *trickle down* from rich nations to emerging markets.

But the flow of new products can also go the other way. Today, corporations such as *Nestlé*, *Nokia* and *Philips* realize that it may be more profitable to create cheap products specifically for the developing world. Then, after successfully penetrating these mass markets, they can make additional profit by offering virtually the same items – as bargains – to price-sensitive buyers in richer nations. This new strategy – called *trickle-up* or *reverse innovation* – transforms the traditional product development method: instead of innovation coming from Europe or the United States and then descending to emerging markets, the process is reversed. To successfully shift their resources to emerging markets and sell products in developing as well as developed nations, marketers must get out of their comfort zone and come up with strategies for largely identical products tailored to buyers – consumers or companies – with different levels of purchasing power.

© Emmanuel R Lacoste / Shutterstock

Marketers must get out of their comfort zone to 'trickle up' innovations from emerging to developed markets

In business-to-business marketing, one reason why companies in the West are purchasing simplified products that suppliers originally designed for the developing world is that – with recession-era budgets – they are more cost-conscious than ever. General Electric's management identified this marketing opportunity when it began selling a lightweight, battery-powered model of an electrocardiograph (ECG) machine – initially developed for healthcare providers in China and India – in the US. With a retail price of $500 – a fraction of the price of much larger machines with similar high-tech features – this field model turned out to be perfect to meet the needs of first responders in industrialized countries. The smaller and cheaper machine will be pitched to a new target market of medical professionals – primary-care doctors, rural clinics and visiting nurses – who need an affordable device they can easily carry around.

In addition to gaining market share worldwide, *GE Healthcare* also benefits from lower product development costs. Instead of spending millions of dollars and taking several years to develop a new portable ECG device, the company managed to cut its investment by 90 per cent and launch the machine in industrialized nations within months. It simply enhanced the Chinese model by adding some accessories, such as USB ports and Ethernet (a type of local area network) to upload and transfer patients' medical data. For GE, this reverse innovation approach rapidly reduced the cost of doing business.

Managers looking for reverse innovation opportunities in consumer markets should not waste any time either. By successfully developing inexpensive products for emerging markets and then quickly repackaging them (with or without adaptations) for more advanced markets, they may stop local startups that are trying to create a 'first mover' advantage in developing countries and then compete with them head-on after entering the European or US market. More and more companies in the West are relying on trickle-up innovation, motivated by the effective introduction of developing-world products in African and Asian markets as well as the changing purchasing behaviour of buyers in industrialized countries. Nokia, for instance, conducted extensive marketing research to find out how consumers in Morocco and Ghana share their mobile phones so others can listen in on interesting phone conversations. This enabled the Finnish corporation to not only create an improved handset for the African market, but also to install better speakers in smart phones targeted at European consumers who like to share their favourite songs and videos with friends.

There are numerous other examples of companies that are now marketing innovations intended for emerging markets to price-conscious consumers in advanced economies. Swiss multinational *Nestlé* gained so many new customers in India and Pakistan for its Maggi dried noodles – priced at 15 eurocents per single-serve package – that it repositioned this low-fat product as an inexpensive health food in the New Zealand and Australian market. *Levi's* success with its inexpensive Denizen

brand in India and China prompted the company to start selling the same jeans in its home market. Denizen jeans now sell for $18 to $30 in the US, about one-third to one-half the price of a pair of Levi's in that country. And *Procter & Gamble* successfully offered its Vick's honey cough syrup, made for the Mexican market, as a basic cold-remedy product to American and European consumers.

So what's the downside of reverse innovation for firms pursuing this strategy? The greatest risk is *cannibalization*: customers buying the new, lower-priced product as a substitute for the company's more expensive brand (with a higher profit margin) that they used to buy. This fear of a cheap new product 'stealing' sales of an established one was the main reason for Philips Electronics, after installing inexpensive, solar-powered LED lighting centres in African countries (South Africa, Egypt, Kenya, Ghana and Morocco), to not launch this product in the West. A second risk is that potential buyers in advanced markets may worry that cheap products designed for emerging markets could lack the quality and features they need, which, to them, is even more crucial than a decent price. Therefore, marketers should make sure that new products, no matter at what price they are offered, meet the needs and wants of the target market.

Most firms that systematically develop innovations for emerging markets are still at the beginning of the cycle. Economists predict that over the next two decades, 75 per cent of the world's economic growth will be generated by the more than 130 developing countries. Without doubt, this high level of economic growth will create huge marketing opportunities for companies with *reverse innovation* strategies across the globe.[1]

Of all of the decisions for which marketers are responsible, those related to the development and introduction of new products and services are probably the most critical. The successful launch of a new product has a positive effect on the company's *competitive position* and its long-term *profitability*. Both of these are of strategic importance to the firm.

In the corporate world, it is hard to predict the future of a new product. Even after it has been successfully introduced, it may be difficult to determine who its buyers are, how they perceive the new product or service and how the competition will respond. On the other hand, companies that accept the financial risks involved in new product development and do launch a successful innovation, can increase not only the size of the market in which they operate, but also their own market shares and profits. At the end of the day, increasing market share and profitability are important marketing objectives for any firm.

In this chapter, we will first examine what we mean by a 'new' product. We will also look at the main reasons for the development of new products and services. Next, we will analyze the product development procedure as it takes place in business, as well as the best way to organize and manage this process. Finally, we will identify the main reasons new products fail or succeed and explore the adoption of innovations by different groups of buyers in society.

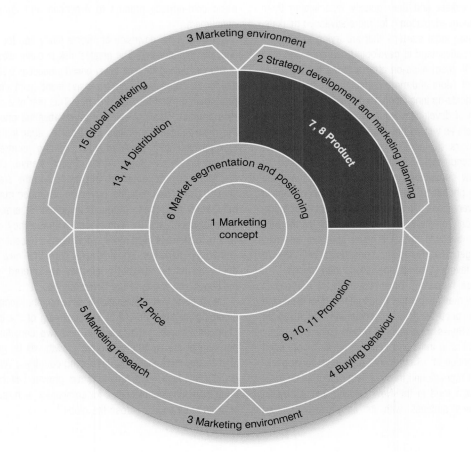

8.1 WHAT IS A NEW PRODUCT?

The dictionary defines innovation as 'a creation resulting from study and experimentation'. Others describe innovation as 'the introduction of something *new*'. Every year, countless new products and services are introduced to the market, but not each is equally new. How *new* a product really is strongly affects how the developing company handles the product. If, for instance, a product is considered as radically new, it will go through a more extensive test marketing and fine-tuning procedure than a product that is no more than an improved version of an existing one. Also, in the case of a breakthrough innovation, the company's marketing strategy must be carefully tailored to the customer's learning process and new consumption pattern.

8.1.1 Types of new products

Relatively few products and services launched by companies each year are *entirely* new. In fact, the term 'new' is not easily defined, because it has several meanings. For example, when the taste of Coca-Cola Light (called Diet Coke outside of Europe) was changed several years ago, sales of the new product increased considerably. But should this soft drink with the new flavour actually be considered a new product? Or, is it simply a product modification, because the change, although it is a significant improvement, is limited to just one of the (tangible and intangible) elements of an existing product?

When trying to define a new product we can take different perspectives. The consulting firm Booz Allen Hamilton, which has studied thousands of new product introductions, categorizes them based on whether the product is new for the *company*, new for the *consumer* or new for *both*. In the first case (new for the company), managers devote far more attention to developing, testing and introducing the product than when it is only new for *consumers* (meaning that customers are not yet familiar with the product when it is introduced). Then again, a product that is new to the company may just be a *me-too product*, meaning that it definitely is not *new to the world*. Still, how new a product is depends very much on whether we are taking the point of view of the customer or the marketer. This is apparent from the classification in Table 8.1.

A product innovation is the only new product type that is fundamentally new to both the company and consumers. These breakthrough products are at the very beginning of the product life cycle and, if successful, may lead to an entirely new industry. The first microcomputer, generating the then flourishing personal computer industry, is a classic example of this. Less than 10 per cent of all new products introduced by companies are true innovations. Yet they can, despite the high risks in introducing them, result in a higher return on investment than any other category of new products.

TABLE 8.1 Classification of new products

New product type	Description	Example
Product innovation	A new to the world product that provides a new way of satisfying needs and wants and creates a whole new product category.	iPad
Me-too product	A new-to-the-company product that is already sold by other firms	TomTom navigation system
Product line addition	A line extension or a flanker brand, added to the company's existing line of products in a particular category	Senseo Vienna; Pulsar
Product modification	An improved version of one of the firm's current products that replaces the original product	Microsoft Windows 8
Repositioned product	A product intentionally positioned or marketed in a different way to create a new image in the minds of the target market or, alternatively, retargeted for a new use	Johnson & Johnson's baby powder; Cialis

A *me-too* or, as it is sometimes called, *new category product* is an item that is new to the company, but not to the marketplace, as it is already sold by other firms. Introducing this 'new-to-the-company' product usually involves less risk than a new product innovation, even though consumers may prefer the established brand. However, since competitors have already been marketing a comparable product for some time, the company, in launching its imitation product, can at least try to avoid any mistakes these competitors made. Its goal should be to develop a 'creative imitation' of the leading product, ideally with features above and beyond those of the original and clearly positioned for the most likely buyers in the company's target market.

Most new products introduced to the market are *product line extensions*, which are new, but closely related variations of a firm's current products added to its product line under the same brand name (for example, Senseo Vienna coffee pads, Cherry Coke and the Gillette Fusion razor blades). Another form of product line addition is a **flanker brand**, a new item introduced under a new brand name into a product category in which the company already sells products (for example, Pulsar watches sold by Casio, or Ralston Purina's introduction of Pro Plan dry dog food).

More than one-third of all new products launched by companies are simply *product modifications*, or improvements to their current products, such as the new iPhone or the new model E-Class of Mercedes. A product modification differs from a line extension in that the original product does not remain in the product line. Product modifications may be either *functional* modifications (redesigned products that are safer, more convenient or effective), *quality* modifications (using better materials that make the product more durable or dependable) or *aesthetic* modifications (improving the product's sensory appeal by changing how it looks, tastes, smells, sounds or feels). By launching product modifications, companies try to build stronger relationships with their customers.

Finally, a *repositioned product* or 'repositioning' is a deliberate attempt by the marketer to change the positioning of their brand or to create a new target market by suggesting a new use or application for the product. A classic example is Johnson & Johnson's baby powder, repositioned to appeal to adults. More recently, Cadillac has been repositioning its latest models to appeal to a younger and more performance-oriented target market in Europe.

8.1.2 *How innovation affects consumers*

Innovation for the sake of innovation is pointless. Before a company develops and introduces a new product, it should assess how it might affect their customers' consumption patterns. Only then will it be able to plot an effective marketing strategy that increases the likelihood prospective buyers will accept and use the new product.

The key question is how the product is new from the potential buyer's perspective. If we define a new product as one which either performs a new function or provides a major improvement over existing products, then how *noticeable* is the new function or improvement? For instance, it is easier to sell a new model of a mobile phone or digital camera that is cheaper than the previous model, smaller in size, attractively designed with a large screen and remarkably easy to use, than it is to market a new product with functional improvements, additional features and benefits that are invisible or unknown to consumers (such as a new MP3 player). In the latter case, it may be better to emphasize the potential uses and *benefits* of the new portable music player in the promotion strategy, than to highlight the technical details of the product innovation.

The initial success of the *Smart* car in some European countries, for example, is perhaps due to the fact that customers perceived it as a fairly ordinary car, although Daimler considered it a radical innovation (with a new platform, different distribution channel and unique customer service). If the company had explicitly listed all of the innovative elements of the *Smart*, the vehicle might not even have survived the introduction stage of its product life cycle. Because many consumers prefer to opt for something that is reliably familiar rather than a truly innovative product, particularly in periods of economic decline, the threshold should always be made as low as possible when launching an innovation. Therefore, in its marketing communication strategy, the company should focus on selected practical improvements (those that provide greater customer satisfaction) rather than emphasizing the fact that its product is a 'completely new innovation'.

As outlined in Table 8.2, we can broadly classify new products based on how difficult it will be for consumers to accept and learn to use the product.[2] The least degree of learning is required for new products based on **continuous innovation**. This is typically an improvement of an existing product that requires virtually no adjustment on the part of the customer. Since buyers don't have to be 'taught' how to use the new product or service, the company can simply focus on creating awareness and making sure it is available wherever the customer expects it to be sold.

For products incorporating **dynamically continuous innovation**, only minor changes in consumer behaviour are needed to use the new product. Successful marketing of such a new item basically involves communicating the product's benefits to buyers and instructing them on how to use it or integrate it into the daily routine. Finally, when launching a product based on **discontinuous innovation** – an innovative product with which the prospects are unfamiliar – the firm realizes that consumers need to make significant behavioural adjustments in using it. The appropriate marketing strategy entails educating customers about this completely new product to help them adapt to a new consumption pattern.

TABLE 8.2 Classification of new products based their impact on consumer behaviour

Low ← Effect on required consumer learning and on consumer behaviour → High

Type of innovation	Continuous innovation	Dynamically continuous innovation	Discontinuous innovation
Impact	Consumers do not have to change their attitudes or behaviour	Consumers need to adapt their behaviour and consumption patterns slightly, to learn to use the new product	Consumers go through an extensive learning process and behavioural changes in order to use the new product
Examples	Gillette's five-bladed Fusion razor; car with hybrid engine	Digital camera; harddisk recorder; sonic electric toothbrush	Email; iPhone
Marketing objectives and strategy	Maximize consumer awareness and availability in retail channels	Clear positioning and clarification of product benefits through marketing communication	Stimulate consumers' learning process through demonstrations, personal selling, samples and no-risk trial offer

BHP is a UK-based specialist content marketing agency founded in 1991 that endeavours to help clients connect with SMEs through intelligent use of business content, understanding the needs of small businesses and providing support through the series of 'Donut' websites.

A 'new product' can be a product or a service; the next revolutionary computer chip, or a new holiday package put together by a travel agent. The point is, it is *new*, so it is often risky. This perspective will not help you generate the ideas for completely new products, or recognize a winner when you see one. It focuses on the next stage - turning an idea into a product, once you have decided to go ahead with it.

To begin with, ask yourself: Can you complete it? Apart from having the right idea in the first place, there are three essential ingredients for successful new product development. Firstly, You need the relevant **skills**. For instance, if you are developing a new food product, having a technician create the right look and taste is only the start. Other issues include sourcing ingredients, the mass production process, quality control, packaging, customer trials, costing and pricing, and so on. You may need to include several people from outside your business.

Secondly, you need to commit sufficient *resources*. If you can only afford a half-hearted attempt, do not begin. Without the critical mass of people, time and money invested, your project will be doomed. If you commit too many resources, the rest of your business may suffer. You may need finance.

Thirdly, you need *personal commitment* to the success of the project. Though teamwork is important, in a smaller business it is often the owner-manager who must drive the project. In practice, most new product development is incremental - improving on an existing product. Compared with starting a product from scratch, this is relatively straightforward.

While a good product idea is no guarantee of success, a bad product idea is a guarantee of failure

Identify major risks early on, so you can decide if the overall risk is worth the potential reward. Analyze all the *market risks*. Establish the likely volume of sales, and the marketing and sales cost of achieving each sale. Is your target market growing or shrinking? Determine any foreseeable changes in your market that could affect the success of your product launch - such as new product safety legislation. Are there any competing products already in the market that may block your route to entry? What are the strengths and weaknesses of the product? Can you offer something different and unique? The killer blow for a new product will often be something you have not even considered.

Analyze the *technical risks*. Do you need to invest in new equipment or technology to make the production possible? It is extremely helpful to have a *working prototype* to test. This need not be an expensive process. For mechanical devices you may need both a 'works-like model' and a 'looks-like model'. If you are improving on an existing product, you may only need to model the new features. Start with a simple prototype such as a drawing. Good feedback at this stage can save time and money. Potential customers, suppliers and members of the development team can give extremely valuable feedback once they see what the product is and how it works.

Avoid being the pioneer who has to learn the hard way. Look for *evidence* of what others have achieved before you. Look at recent developments in related products. Visit trade shows to get ideas of forthcoming products and trends before they hit the market. Work out how to *reduce each risk* to an acceptable level. Can your new design be patented or protected in some other way?

While a good product idea is no guarantee of success, a bad product idea is a guarantee of failure. Here are some of the fatal flaws:

→ You cannot sell at the **price or volume** necessary to make a profit – UK shoe manufacturers face serious price competition from firms at home and abroad. Even the most stylish new line may have to be discounted.

→ Your product can easily be **copied** – You may invest heavily to develop a new type of service and build up a market for it. Competitors can launch 'me-too' services at lower prices, as they have not incurred all the costs.

→ You lack **market power** – A new piece of software may be the best in the market, but it could be doomed to failure if you lack an effective route to market.

→ Your product is **over-ambitious** – A new methane car would require breakthroughs on several fronts - engineering the car itself, persuading petrol stations to offer methane fuel, persuading consumers to buy the car and persuading someone to finance the project in the first place.

You need to know the *what*, *when* and *how much* of your new product before you can turn your idea into a project. Make sure you have a **unique selling proposition** ('USP') - a reason for customers to choose your product over a rival's. www.marketingdonut.co.uk[3]

New product innovations can only become successful if consumers perceive them as *relevant*. Procter & Gamble found out about this when it introduced *Dryel* on the European market. This was a unique product that allowed consumers to clean their 'dry clean only' clothes (such as suits and silk blouses) in a tumble dryer. The product was safe and worked well from a technical point of view, but as an innovation it failed. Consumers simply were not used to putting these types of clothes into either their washer or dryer, or just did not understand what the product could do for them and left it on the shelf.

8.2 REASONS FOR PRODUCT DEVELOPMENT

Many firms are constantly developing new products, brands and product modifications. They are working on a portfolio of new products so that at any point in time, they have a variety of prototypes in different stages of development. They get most of their revenues from products that did not even exist in any shape or form ten years earlier. Since product life cycles are getting shorter and profit goals may be missed without the help of new products, new product development is so prevalent that sooner or later, most managers are likely to be involved in developing or marketing new products. This forces even conservative managers to establish procedures to search for opportunities for new products and evaluate them systematically. We will first explore the primary reasons for new product development and then focus on the *make-or-buy* decision for product innovations.

8.2.1 Why firms introduce new products

Managers are always looking for something unique or creative to make a company stand out. 'Innovation is seeing what everyone sees, but *doing what nobody else does*', says Cor Stutterheim, former CEO of Logica, the company that invented text messaging (SMS) and multimedia messaging (MMS).[4] However, this need to stand out in the market by developing and launching new products and services is not a goal in itself, especially considering the risks involved. The driving force behind new product development is trying to maximize the firm's *return on investment*. Research has shown that on average, new products account for 40 per cent of a company's profits. Without their contribution, it may be impossible to realize the profit objectives spelled out in the business plan. However, as we will see, there are other, more specific reasons for new product development in business.

Sales growth objectives

Many corporations establish sales growth objectives of over 10 per cent per year. Although the marketing department can conceivably achieve these ambitious business objectives by selling more of the firm's current products and services, it is often easier to acquire new sales by introducing new products. This was a major reason that Philips, which already controlled a large part of the television market, introduced LCD television sets to the European market.

Striving for product innovations to increase sales especially makes sense in a saturated market. As an illustration, the introduction of the iPad and other brands of tablets took place at a time when most households already owned a PC or laptop.

Excess capacity

A second reason why companies introduce new products is to utilize excess capacity, either in production, distribution or in the R&D department. Whether production facilities are used at 70 per cent or 100 per cent capacity, the firm still has to cover such *fixed expenses* as depreciation, insurance premiums, plant security and other costs that remain stable in the short run, regardless of any variation in production. Therefore, a new product idea that might not otherwise seem lucrative to the firm may represent an interesting opportunity to offset the fixed overhead costs.

Completion of the product line

A third motive to introduce a new product is to complete the company's existing product line. By adding new items to its product assortment on a regular basis, a company kills two birds with one stone: it takes advantage of marketing opportunities by serving new market segments (*niches*) and increases its customers' tendency to buy the brand. In other words, adding a new product often boosts the sale of existing products in the company's product portfolio.

Government regulations

Stricter government regulations sometimes make it necessary to adapt existing products or develop new ones. The now compulsory safety features in many countries on bicycles (such as reflective tyres) and cars (airbags, a third rear light) are obvious examples. Government measures can also indirectly lead to innovations and marketing opportunities. A classic example – companies that make toothpaste did not start adding fluoride to the products they sell in Europe until government measures banned the fluoridation of drinking water.

Competition

A company's competitors always pose a threat. A specific action – or just the threat of such an action – frequently motivates a business to innovate (for example, to improve its packaging) or to introduce a new product. To illustrate, Unilever's main reason for launching *Robijn*, a detergent for delicate fabrics, was Procter & Gamble's strategic attempt to claim the fine fabric detergent market for itself with *Dreft*. Similarly, Nestlé Purina brought Gourmet (single serve portions of cat food) onto the market after its competitor

Mars had built up the segment of luxury products for cats with its Sheba brand (cat food in foil trays). In jumping into the market, a 'me-too' company realizes that it made a mistake by not recognizing the potential of a product, but at least it does not want to compound its error by staying out of the market. Furthermore, there is always a chance that a great me-too product will end up becoming the market leader.

Companies launching **substitute products** – products that are viewed by the user as alternatives for other products – may also threaten competition. Mobile telephones have made pay phones obsolete, while SUVs have replaced station wagons and are now increasingly being replaced themselves by crossover vehicles. Finally, a firm may choose to enter a market to prevent a competitor from exploiting the market first. In this case, it is the threat of a competitive action, rather than a specific past action, that prompts the firm to act.

Changing needs and wants

Here's one of the most pressing reasons for companies to innovate. A recent study by *Accenture* estimated that the average firm loses half of its customers within about five years of attracting them. That's because their customers' needs and wants continue to change over time. Innovation is not only a good way to attract new buyers, but also an effective way to keep current customers loyal as consumers and the environment change.

Many firms launch new products in response to demographic trends (such as households becoming smaller), changing *lifestyles* (more leisure time) and similar developments that affect the needs and wants of certain groups of consumers. A company's effort to satisfy the evolving customer needs and preferences is the most marketing-oriented motive for product innovation. For example, many new products cater to the increasing consumer interest in health (Becel Pro-Active), convenience (Edet Wipe & Clean kitchen towels), flexibility (Apple notebooks), safety (TomTom portable GPS car navigation systems) and quality (Purina ONE dog food).

New technology

In many firms, the **Research & Development** department (R&D) is constantly working to achieve technological breakthroughs. Philips, which owns more than 100 000 patents, spends more than three billion euros per year on R&D. However, new technologies also create opportunities for innovation in less *technology-driven* organizations. This may lead to improved new product development (for example, the innovative application of microchips or the use of environmentally friendly packaging) as well as more efficient production methods (robotics) and marketing techniques (Internet shopping).

8.2.2 *Make or buy?*

Once a company decides to introduce a new product or service to the market, there are two strategic options. One is to develop the product internally (which we will explore shortly). The second is to either acquire a patent, licence or established brand, or to buy out a firm that is already making the product or delivering the service. In other words, a **make-or-buy** decision is essentially the choice between doing it yourself and getting someone else to do it. Research shows that the main motive behind approximately one-third of all mergers and takeovers is the immediate acquisition of specific products or services. Hence, quite a few companies prefer to 'buy' rather than 'make' a new product. Of course, the 'buy' option is not always available to companies, since European Union officials, as well as the US Federal Trade Commission, have ruled that any merger of two businesses resulting in significantly reduced competition is a violation of antitrust laws. There are three additional factors that

TABLE 8.3 Internal product development versus takeover or merger

Consideration	Internal development	Acquisition
Profitability	Greater profit potential	Quicker profits
Risk	More risk	Less risk
Know-how	No overlap	Synergy / Possible duplication

should be considered in a *make-or-buy* decision. As outlined in Table 8.3, these are the potential profitability, risk and management know-how.

Profitability

Compared to internal development, a merger or acquisition typically yields the business *quicker* profits, because the product is already under production or on the market. As a result, the firm does not have to undertake such time-consuming activities as plant construction, sales force training and test marketing. Instead, the product can be sold immediately. If there is a high profit margin on the new product, this will immediately increase the company's revenues. For example, Unilever was able to boost its profits considerably after its acquisitions in the skincare and cosmetics industries, which have higher profit margins than its food products and detergent businesses.

On the other hand, the potential return on investment (or ROI) is *greater* if the product is developed internally, because the company is able to keep the entrepreneurial rewards – for taking the initiative and commercial risk – for itself. If one firm purchases another in order to acquire a successful product, it pays the market value for the business, which will have been enhanced due to prior success of the product in question. Therefore, the so-called entrepreneurial return from the new product remains with the original owners of the acquired business.

Risk

Typically, less risk is involved with a new product acquired through merger than with a product developed internally. Even the most innovative companies may have to examine dozens of new product ideas before developing one new product. In addition, as many as half of all new products never generate a satisfactory return.

Although focused and decision-oriented marketing research will limit the risk involved in developing a product internally, such risk is further reduced when a product is part of an acquisition. The acquiring firm has the opportunity to carefully examine how the product has been received by the market. For example, Nestlé, which already marketed Friskies pet foods, was able to evaluate the European market position of *Felix* and *Bonzo* products before it took over Spillers, the company that owned these brands. Management assumed that if a product has a decent market share, it will likely continue to do well in the near future.

Know-how

An important consideration for a company facing a *make-or-buy decision* is the potential for synergy, the possibility of increasing the efficiency and effectiveness of its operation by carrying out activities jointly rather than separately. Some key questions to be asked in the acquisition decision are whether the company will benefit from an expanded product assortment, a united market approach, joint purchasing of raw materials, an improved product development process and the unique management expertise after a merger.

One advantage of a merger or takeover is that it often provides the acquiring firm with the management and personnel skills that it needs. When Procter & Gamble took over *Iams*, the maker of one of the world's most expensive pet foods, it suddenly owned the fastest growing company in Europe's top segment of pet foods sold in specialty stores, with a reputable management that was able to compete successfully in a market with major brands like *Royal Canin* (of Mars) and *Hills* (of Colgate Palmolive). In fact, the objective of a merger may not be so much to gain a particular product, as it is to obtain the services of experienced executives.

Unfortunately, in some cases the added personnel may lead to unnecessary duplication. For example, if both organizations have a marketing director, the firm now has two, one of whom, regardless of their qualifications, may have to be terminated. Generally, little duplication will result if the product is acquired through merger, but maintained as a separate division with its own manufacturing and marketing personnel. On the other hand, duplication of personnel is likely to occur if the acquired product is fully integrated with the rest of the firm's products. Obviously, there will be no duplication at all if the new product is developed internally.

8.3 DEVELOPING NEW PRODUCTS

Although the development and marketing of new products is no easy task, a company's future may well depend on it. In fact, research shows that management's 'lack of drive to innovate' is one of the three major reasons for failure in business. To increase their chances of success – and at the same time keep the high costs of creating new products under control – many companies split up their product development into seven phases. As illustrated in Figure 8.1, the **product development process** – the sequence of activities a company uses to transform product ideas into marketable products and services – starts with formulating a new product strategy and ends with the introduction or commercialization of the product.

Executives who are most successful in developing new products plan the entire process carefully. To make sure they get the necessary support and financial backing from their organizations, they first examine or (re)define the company's mission, objectives and overall strategy. Next, they assess the role of new products. How committed is the firm to innovation, and what seem to be the most lucrative opportunities for new product development? Once they have completed this initial analysis – which may also result in guidelines for a comprehensive product strategy – they proceed with the first stage of the product development process. The entire process can take a long time. For example, from the initial idea to the final product being introduced in the stores, the development of Blue Band Culinesse – a liquid cooking margarine made by *Unilever* – took more than two years!

8.3.1 New product strategy development

A firm's new product strategy is part of its overall marketing strategy. Thus, the **new product strategy** should link the firm's product development process with the objectives of the marketing department, as well as, indirectly, with the goals of the business unit and the corporation. Without clear objectives and a well-planned product strategy, new product development is unnecessarily risky. Putting a set of objectives and strategies down on paper is the first step, if for no other reason than to be able to identify – with the right criteria – the best ideas for new products.

FIGURE 8.1 Model of the product development process

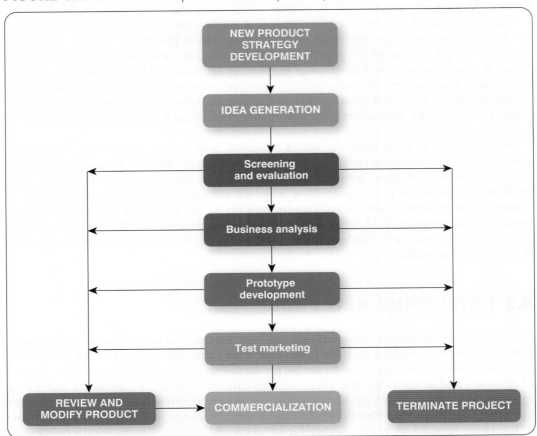

Objectives

What is the company's goal in taking on the challenge of new product development? The main reason for its commitment of resources may be to increase its sales and profits, but, as we have seen, there may also be other motives, such as the need to utilize excess capacity.

Because the company's objectives depend not only on its strategy but also on the environment in which it operates, it makes sense to conduct a SWOT analysis, since this provides insight into the organization's strengths and weaknesses *and* relevant opportunities and threats. Rather than simply generating a list of new product ideas, this phase should produce an analysis of interesting markets for which the company might be able to develop successful products, as well as a clear indication of the strategic role these products could play.

The strategic role of a new product can be both *external* (such as penetrating a new market or defending the company's market share) and *internal* (for instance, using excess capacity or sustaining the company's reputation as an innovative organization). These kinds of motives establish a context for the new product development and may lead to an offensive or a defensive strategy.

Proactive and reactive strategies

Product development strategies can be proactive or reactive. A company with a *proactive strategy* focuses on anticipating future events: it implements strategic changes in its policies because it expects significant developments, trends or other changes in its environment. This kind of company is constantly searching for new marketing opportunities. It invests in R&D and consumer research (as Philips and Unilever do), encourages an entrepreneurial spirit among its managers and tries to take over companies with promising products. The objective of this proactive strategy is to stimulate and initiate changes.

A company with a *reactive strategy* adopts a defensive approach. It only implements reactive changes in response to events that have already taken place in the environment. This type of firm tends to make *me-too products*. Of course, it may still keep track of buyer preferences in order to come up with products that are possibly better than those of competitors.

8.3.2 *Idea generation*

The idea generation or exploration phase is the stage in the product development process during which the company searches for innovative ideas. Since these ideas represent the company's future, management must do everything it can to encourage the flow of new product ideas. Large corporations may count very much on their own research departments or units in the way that, for example, *Philips* relies on Philips Research (often called 'NatLab'). But this company also tries to get consumers involved in the product development process early on. 'We need to know what the consumer thinks, what gets them excited or turns them off,' says a Philips executive.

Philips has had its fair share of unsuccessful product launches. Video 2000, CD-i and DCC all performed well and were high-quality products, but none of them attracted a mass market. Marketing manager Wieger Deknatel knows why. 'In the past, we often came up with new products that were based on our technical capabilities, instead of consumer needs. This kind of *technology-push* has now been replaced by a *consumer-pull* strategy. After all, we are no longer confined by technology. But we can't say that about consumer needs. I was at a conference in the States the other day and heard a marketing professor express it perfectly: "We have all the technology in the world to do what we want. *What do we want?*" That's really the question that Philips is focusing on right now.'[5]

New product ideas also come from a variety of other sources, including intermediaries, the marketing department, sales representatives and other co-workers. Salespeople who frequently interact with customers learn what people do or do not like about the current products and how they can be improved. A firm should, therefore, consider establishing formal lines of communication between the sales force and the new product planning staff, so that new product ideas can easily travel up the organization. It also makes sense to read trade journals, attend trade shows, visit competitors' websites, watch new products that are

The unsuccessful Video 2000 launched by Philips

© SSPL / Getty

being test marketed and analyze these on a regular basis. Finally, companies may use *brainstorming* and other techniques to stimulate staff creativity and to systematically activate the generation of ideas.

8.3.3 *Screening and evaluation*

The model in Figure 8.1 shows that after generating as many ideas as possible, the company decides in each subsequent stage which ideas should be filtered out and which should be given the green light for continued development. During this screening stage, about 80 per cent of new product ideas are eliminated. Ideas that are not feasible or not compatible with the company's mission or long-term objectives (as established during the first phase), end up in the trash can. The remaining ideas are examined more closely. Management must decide what criteria will be used in evaluating ideas and what role consumer research should play in the screening stage.

Screening criteria

What criteria do companies use to *screen* new product or service ideas? Research shows that the main criterion is the expected *return on investment*. Managers also consider the size and growth of the *market* for the new product and the potential *positioning* strategies to make the product acceptable and unique in the customers' perception.[6] The lack of any 'hard' data about the technical and commercial feasibility of products at this stage forces analysts – even in large companies – to make the initial selection of promising ideas in a rather subjective manner.

Concept test

The second step in the screening and evaluation stage is to conduct a *concept test*. Because the product does not yet exist, marketing researchers describe the proposed product in detail (the way the consumer would see it when buying or using it) and, if possible, include a drawing or picture of the package and label. The company then presents this *product concept* to consumers who are part of the target market to assess how potential customers react and to determine whether they are pleased or critical. This gives the company an insight into the potential market and the product features that consumers like best. Sometimes this is done during a separate concept development phase in which product ideas are analyzed to identify features that should be incorporated in a new product.

Concept tests are not always foolproof. Products and services that consumers are not interested in during research, may indeed become quite successful. For instance, the initial concepts for fax machines, CNN and mobile phones were not well received because potential users could not see the benefits of these advanced new products and services. Marketers, who often develop a sixth sense for determining what types of products the market is likely to accept, moved ahead, regardless, with great success.

8.3.4 *Business analysis*

In the business analysis stage, the company tries to determine if each of the proposed products or services that has survived the previous phase, will be profitable to the firm. This stage forces the analyst to make some assumptions about the product's expected revenues and costs. Although these are only estimates, which makes some people sceptical, the alternative of not trying to determine a product's potential profitability before developing a prototype and conducting test marketing, would be careless. Ultimately, not every product that is technically feasible, should, from a commercial perspective, actually be developed and launched. Two ways to perform a business analysis are to draw up a *pro forma* income statement or to conduct a market share study.

Pro forma income statement

To develop a *pro forma income statement* we need to estimate the expected revenues, as well as the production and marketing costs at various levels of production and sales. In a well-run company, (internal) cost data are typically stored in a marketing information system (MIS). If not, the firm's accounting department can provide this information, unless the proposed production will utilize completely new technology.

Making a realistic forecast of the revenues, unfortunately, is much more difficult. When developing capital goods or durable consumer goods we may use an opinion survey, in which a group of executives or sales representatives is polled regarding their future sales expectations. Another option is using the *direct questioning technique* – which involves directly asking potential customers how much they think they will order in a given period. Even with these techniques, though, predicting the sales and the life cycle of a new product is quite risky.

Market share projection

If it is not possible to make an accurate sales forecast, the market share approach can be useful, particularly if competitors have already launched a similar product. Market share analysis involves linking a product's break-even point to the existing industry sales for the product. The break-even point is defined here as the quantity of unit sales at which the product's total revenue is equal to its total costs. In other words, it is the point at which the incoming revenue from the product or service pays all fixed and variable expenses, but does not generate any profit for the company. We then relate this break-even quantity (for example, one thousand items) to the current sales of the product type throughout the industry (for example, five thousand products). As a rule of thumb, the higher the industry market share required for the product to break even (in this example, 20 per cent), the less likely it is that the new product will succeed.

One limitation of market share projection is that it requires an existing product to serve as a basis for comparison. Therefore, in developing a truly new product, market share analysis is unreliable. Another problem is that this conservative technique assumes the product will gain a share of only the current market, and that all sales are at the expense of competitors. Often, however, new products will lead to an expansion of the market and greater sales throughout the industry, thereby increasing profits for all competitors.

8.3.5 Prototype development

Until now, the product was little more than an idea on paper. But in this stage, the company makes a prototype: the first concrete test model able to perform all of the technical functions. Developing a demonstrable physical product requires committing significant financial resources. Typically, prototype development, with all of its technical complexities, requires about three times as much money and time as the screening and business analysis stages combined. Nevertheless, the company must determine whether it can manufacture the product at an acceptable cost level and whether it is able to develop the required technology.

The prototype development phase is most likely to succeed if the company adopts a *market-oriented* approach. Actual consumer behaviour – and *not* a technically improved product – should be the primary criterion in this phase. If the company only tests its prototype under objective laboratory conditions, it runs the risk of miscalculating user acceptance, as the following example illustrates.

Philips – a company that spends 7 per cent of its sales on R&D – developed a new iron that was twenty-five grams lighter than the previous model. However, when the company subsequently did research to find out how women actually ironed their laundry, it discovered that rather than lifting the iron and allowing the heat of the appliance to do the work, many women kept pressing the iron onto the article of clothing with a great deal of force. This made lighter irons, from the consumer's perspective, irrelevant.

In a laboratory, researchers may not notice crucial characteristics of consumer behaviour. Therefore, laboratory tests should be correlated with consumer tests. The R&D staff should be provided detailed information about the product concept, the potential customers, the desired product benefits and the importance of these benefits to consumers.

Once a prototype is developed, the firm will need to make the necessary decisions about packaging, branding and the rest of the marketing mix. After all, a customer's perception of a product's quality and value is not only dependent on the physical object, but also on brand image and other intangible features. These decisions about the marketing mix can be modified later, depending on the results of test marketing.

8.3.6 *Test marketing*

At this point, most new product ideas have already been eliminated. The remaining products need to be test marketed. **Test marketing** refers to the introduction of a trial version of the new product on a small scale, but supported by a complete marketing campaign, in a limited area (the *test market*) with a population that is representative of the selected target market in order to assess the effectiveness of the marketing strategy and the commercial viability of the product.

Sometimes companies skip the test marketing phase altogether and simply launch the product. This may be feasible if the firm is already familiar with the market, if the brand name is well known, if the budget does not allow for market testing or if a competitor is about to introduce a similar product. Another option is to restrict the product's trial launch to a single chain of supermarkets or drug stores. This is known as a *mini test market*. Scaled-down test marketing still allows the company to assess the effectiveness of different shelf positions or in-store materials in terms of their effect on consumer purchases. On the basis of the test marketing results, the firm not only decides which product to market, but also how it should be marketed. This reduces the risk of failure.

A key question at this stage is who should perform the test marketing – an external agency (for the most objective data) or the company's own marketing research department. Using in-house personnel reduces the risk of leaking test marketing plans, information that could be used by competitors to disrupt the findings or develop a me-too product.

Developing, test marketing and commercializing a new product may be quite time consuming. Take Nespresso, an almost instant espresso that is made by machine from a little capsule of coffee. Nestlé started working on the technology in 1970 and filed its first patent in 1976. It was another decade before it was ready to start selling Nespresso pods and machines. Thereafter the business lost money for a decade. But now it is one of Nestlé's fastest-growing products. Sales have been increasing by 30 per cent annually (even though Nespresso is a premium brand) to about €3 billion in 2010. Consumers are, presumably, making coffee at home and trading down from more expensive coffees sold by the likes of Starbucks. 'It took off very, very slowly,' says Nestlé CEO Paul Bulcke. 'It was 20 years of conviction that got us there.'[7]

8.3.7 *Commercialization*

Only about half of the products that are test marketed result in market introduction with a full-scale marketing campaign in this final stage of the product development process. Often they are only launched after they have been adapted based on the test marketing results. The remaining products are abandoned.

Today, companies are more systematic and efficient than ever in how they approach new product development and identify lucrative marketing opportunities. Studies show that several decades ago, companies still needed around 60 new product ideas in order to launch one successful new product. Now, this number has dropped to less than seven ideas. This significant improvement is the result of more companies now including a strategy development phase at the start of the process to help them find promising areas for new product development. Better concept testing and test marketing techniques also contribute to a more effective new product development process.

Some people think that during the commercialization or *introduction* phase, all a marketer can do is hope for the best. This is not the case. Marketers usually complete or revise – in light of the test marketing findings – a detailed plan that outlines who should do what, as well as how, where and when it should be done. For instance, the company may have to open up new plants and produce enough inventory to supply the wholesalers or dealers in the distribution channel. Also, advertising and promotion strategies should be outlined for the year ahead, and sales representatives must be trained so they can communicate the benefits of the products and services offered, relative to those of competitors.

Some new products are initially introduced in only one area of the country or market and then, if successful, are sold in other submarkets. Such a **roll-out strategy** enables marketers to monitor the product's sales and avoid the risk of exceeding the production or marketing capacity of the organization. The analysis focuses on questions like: Which segments of the market are buying the product? How are retailers and other middlemen reacting to the product launch? And what counter-moves are competitors making? When all is said and done, the commercialization phase may be spread out over a period of two or more years and may involve several marketing strategy (and product) modifications before the product is launched in other regions or countries.

8.4 ORGANIZING NEW PRODUCT DEVELOPMENT

Peter Drucker, the late management guru, argued that the two main reasons for a company's existence are innovation and marketing. He said that if a firm does not innovate, it will not be an effective organization and cannot be successful over time. In a recent Booz Allen Hamilton study, for which fifty top managers of major companies were interviewed, 90 per cent stated that innovation was critical to realizing their strategic objectives. Yet most of these senior executives were only marginally satisfied with how their companies' current innovation and new product development was organized, and only half of the improvement efforts met their expectations.[8]

Most companies follow the systematic approach outlined in our model of the product development process (Figure 8.1) when evaluating and managing new product opportunities. Yet in many firms, new product development efforts run into problems. Because each and every new product idea has to go through all of the phases step by step, it often takes a long time to convert promising ideas into a finished product that can be commercialized. Also, in many cases there are no clear company *objectives* for innovation. Even if the objectives are spelled out, they are not always translated into concrete *management tasks* as part of a marketing action plan.[9]

PROFESSOR'S PERSPECTIVE
David Chalcraft (University of Westminster, UK)

David Chalcraft is a professional marketer enjoying a varied marketing-related career in industry, business and latterly, lecturing within higher education. A long period in the oil industry, working for major international petroleum organizations in a range of marketing roles, has been followed by a number of years working as a marketing advisor, both within a marketing consultancy and as a freelance consultant. This role is now combined with an urge to pass on the fruits of his experience to the next generation of marketers and business people studying at the University of Westminster.

There are several well-known models for new product and service development (NP&SD) which clearly outline the key steps to be undertaken in a logical way. These serve many organizations well in helping to ensure that good ideas are taken forward and resources are focused in the most cost effective way. However, this approach is not always appropriate in all situations or for all organizations. Another approach is the 'ready, fire, aim' concept that takes the key steps of the conventional NP&SD process and re-models them to meet particular demands.

Advance Fuels (Retail) Ltd (AFR) runs a highly innovative fuelling facility targeted at heavy users of diesel, such as the black cabs serving Heathrow airport in London. The brain-child of entrepreneurs Bradley Reed and Mike Nairn, it is an example of 'dynamically continuous innovation' in that it requires only slight changes in behaviour by its customers yet offers significant benefits over established competitors. It runs unmanned, 24 hours a day, seven days a week. For users it offers two major advantages over its competitors. Firstly, a very customer-centric service tailored to their needs; and secondly the cleanest fuel available, leading to improved mileage, reduced maintenance costs and lowered vehicle emissions – all very important issues to this clientele.

A chance conversation between the partners led to the identifying of an opportunity to shake up what traditionally has been a mature, slow growing market. Lacking the resources to follow a conventional, formally structured new service development process they chose to adopt a 'consumer-pull' approach and focus on heavily involving the customers and other key stakeholders right from the start in an effort to move through idea generation, screening and evaluation quickly but thoroughly. This meant a long period of discussion with cab operating companies and individual drivers (both rather conservative groups). Additionally, it was vital to have key stakeholders on board. Their endorsement of the fuel would be critical to encouraging the target groups to start using the service. To deliver this, a process of dialogue and extensive laboratory testing was undertaken to prove the value of the fuel so that it could be recommended by the major manufacturers of cabs and cab engines. At the same time detailed negotiations were taking place with the owners of the land on which the site is situated to ensure that their needs also were being met. A thorough business analysis indicated that the likely level of market demand, set against the level of investment required, would be profitable in what is a notoriously low margin business.

'Ready, fire, aim' implies launching before testing when experimentation is unfeasible

AFR then combined the stages of prototype development and test marking in the building of their first site: a real case of 'putting your money where your mouth is'. This bold approach focuses on the most important form of product and service development feedback – feedback from actual customers based on 'real life' use of the service and the fuel. This customer-focused approach speeds up and shortens the learning curve when proving the worth of a new product or service. This seemingly counter-intuitive approach of launching before testing is completed can work well when, although the basic proposition is sound, the finer details of the offer are unclear and cost, time or the nature of the product/service make prolonged experimentation unfeasible. Although the site is unmanned, the partners are regularly physically in attendance or on the phone talking to the customers, taking feedback and resolving problems on a daily basis, 24 hours a day. The result is a level of service that is regularly being refined and developed to ensure customer expectations are met. What's more some very strong client relationships are being forged at the same time.

The next step is to move to full commercialization of the service at key sites across London and farther afield secure in the knowledge that the ready, fire, aim approach to this new service development has not only covered the key steps outlined in the classic model of NP&SD but delivered a service that already is proven, offers an unrivalled range of benefits and is valued by the most important single stakeholder group: the customers.[10]

A common problem in new product development is that the process is split up into distinct parts that are then allocated to different departments in the company for completion. This makes it difficult to *coordinate* the total process. Usually, the managers charged with responsibility for the various tasks are already quite busy. They have to stay on top of their own jobs and tend to regard the additional work related to new product development as less important than their routine duties. This presents a major challenge in a world where new products are rapidly replacing older ones and where, in many branches of industry, more than half of the products currently offered were not even part of any business plan just five years ago!

To avoid such problems, more and more companies are now creating *venture teams* to better organize their innovation and new product development efforts. Though new product development can be structured in many ways, we will first focus on venture teams – as an effective form of *project organization* – and then examine alternative ways to manage product development.

8.4.1 *Venture teams*

A **venture team** is a tightly structured, independent group of people from different departments or functional areas of the enterprise. The team members are usually relieved of their normal tasks and responsibilities for as long as they are associated with the project. In this way, venture teams differ from other types of committees in the company. The underlying objective is to temporarily free a multidisciplinary group of talented, enthusiastic managers from daily operating problems and bureaucratic hurdles, so they can spend all their time on the new product. The task of this organizationally separate team (usually flexible in its life span) is to evaluate new product ideas and – if a product appears to have profit potential – to carry it through to commercialization, without strict deadlines. This tends to create an entrepreneurial spirit, especially if the venture team members are allowed to share in the profits of the product once it reaches the market.

The multidisciplinary project teams that *Unilever* sets up for developing food products for health-conscious consumers are an example of venture teams. Marketers work closely with R&D managers, medical specialists and legal experts in a team separate from the permanent departmental, functional, or divisional structure of the organization. With the active support of top management, this type of collaboration expedites the product development process considerably.

8.4.2 *Alternatives to venture teams*

Truly enterprising venture teams are market oriented, rather than product oriented, and they look for opportunities with above-average growth potential. As a result, their members must often address complex questions, such as: What business are we in? What unsatisfied consumer needs could we, as a company, meet? The characteristic flexibility of a venture team to respond to the ever-changing needs of the market is hard to copy under any other management system.

Yet, venture teams have disadvantages too. They are expensive because their members are usually well paid, and they require staff assistance and supporting facilities. It may also be hard to find the right individual to lead the team, since entrepreneurial managers – who are scarce in large companies – must be persuaded, with their bosses' permission, to temporarily leave their jobs and join the venture team. Finally, venture teams may become so emotionally involved with a new product idea that they may not be able to recognize its flaws and may be unwilling to drop it before it reaches the final stage in the product development process.[11]

Therefore, some firms, particularly if they have not grown to the point of having lost their entrepreneurial spirit, prefer a more *permanent* organizational structure to support new product development. The most widely used alternatives to venture teams are new product managers and new product committees.

New product managers

A new product manager performs more or less the same functions as a *product manager* in the sense that a single person coordinates all of the company's efforts for a (new) product. Johnson & Johnson and General Electric are among the many corporations using this new product management system.

The *new product manager* is responsible for developing the new product concept, as well as for outlining an effective launch or roll-out strategy. Of course, this strategy is usually planned in consultation with the marketing department. Once the new product is available in stores, the new product manager's task is complete and responsibility for the commercial success of the new product – including implementing the marketing strategy and monitoring its performance – is officially turned over to the marketing department.

New product committees

Like a venture team, a *new product committee* is multidisciplinary. It is usually made up of the CEO of the firm along with managers from the departments involved in the development of a new product or service. For example, at Agfa-Gevaert – a Belgium-based multinational that develops, produces and distributes digital imaging systems and IT-solutions – a typical new product committee consists of co-workers from the marketing, production, R&D and quality control departments. Because it brings together people with different backgrounds to work on a common challenge, the committee is often successful in encouraging brainstorming sessions within the organization and also serves as an effective system of organizational communication. Another advantage of using new product committees is that the responsibility for the work involved in evaluating new products is fairly distributed. For example, various subcommittees are charged with the tasks of compiling financial analyses and identifying potential marketing problems, and, eventually, writing a report for the overall new product committee.

There are also *disadvantages* to working with new product committees. Without formal authority within the organizational structure, the participants are not always motivated to get the work done. They may take a long time to make decisions, because the committee members can only work part-time for the committee. Also, in their decision-making they sometimes pay more attention to the consequences for their own departments than to overall company interests. As a result, their decisions are often 'committee compromises' that completely satisfy no one. At Agfa-Gevaert, for example, each committee member still has to answer to their own supervisor or manager, who also has the right to suspend decisions made by the committee if they are not convinced that the decisions are prudent.

If a company decides to use new product committees, it may benefit from observing the following guidelines:

→ Management should spell out the committee's responsibilities and make sure that they are understood.

→ The committee should have a formal agenda and minutes of the proceedings.

→ A strong leader, such as the company's president or a senior department head, should be appointed to chair the committee.

→ Representatives of all departments should be included on the committee, but it must be kept small enough to be manageable.[12]

8.4.3 *Speeding up new product development*

Why does it take a Japanese electronics company only nine months to develop a new product, while its European competitors, on average, require twice as much time to get a similar item ready for production? The answer is that Japanese firms look upon fast product development as an essential weapon in the competitive battle. Since the life cycle of many products is getting shorter, the Japanese have systematically accelerated new product development.

European firms often take far too long to introduce their new products. As a result, they miss out on the 'honeymoon' phase in which they could get the highest profit margins and greatest market share. In fact, studies indicate that if a company launches a product six months too late, in the next five years this product will generate about 30 per cent less profit than a product that is brought to the market on time, even if the development budget is exceeded by 50 per cent!

Most European companies could cut the time they spend on developing a new product by half, if they focused on that goal. This, in turn, would reduce R&D costs tremendously. By being the first one to launch a new product, the firm can set the technical standard itself *and* charge a relatively high price. This *first-mover advantage* also allows the company to quickly recoup its development costs. Research shows that there are at least six ways for companies to speed up the product development process:[13]

1 *Start early.* Give the go-ahead for product development before there is an obvious consumer demand. Apple is a good example. It identified the potential market for the iPod early on and was the first to develop this type of MP3 player, just as Sony was first – based on intuition and a unique vision – with the Walkman and the Discman two decades earlier.

2 *Outsource part of the process.* Focus on the essential, strategic aspects of new product development and leave the rest of the process to experts outside of the company. This may be a tough decision for any manager who looks at a new product or service as 'their baby'.

3 *Use internal competition.* Get two development teams within the same firm to compete with each other. This approach (often used in the computer industry) is expensive, but quite lucrative if it speeds up the product's introduction.

4 *Make stages overlap.* Start working on the next stage of the product development process before the previous phase has been completed, even if the specifications have not yet been finalized. This is a classic way to hasten lead times, but it requires excellent internal communication.

5 *Use other people's ideas.* To accelerate new product development, adopt valuable and practical solutions that others have provided. It is faster to imitate than to innovate!

6 *Assemble the right team.* A great team should include both perfectionists and people with an eye for the market. For example, Philips tries to speed up the development of new products by assigning executives who convey the wishes of the various product divisions to the R&D department. The company also collaborates with external partners, such as Douwe Egberts, Nike and Unilever. 'We can now develop a new generation of televisions in six to seven months. In the past, it would have taken years,' says a Philips executive. 'Our research is getting more efficient and effective every day.'[14]

Every company should carefully weigh the advantages and disadvantages of different ways of organizing new product development. The best form of new product management not only depends on its compatibility with the existing organizational structure, but also on the skills of the company's managers, time constraints and the available financial resources or budget for the project. While there is no such thing as a recipe for new product development, one thing is certain: with the increasing global competition in business, a well-planned strategy that speeds up the product development process is essential.

8.5 WHY NEW PRODUCTS SUCCEED OR FAIL

Although firms now manage the product development process better than ever before, many new products and services fail. Research shows that the failure rate for new products that make it into the stores is greater than 30 per cent. This is a high number when you consider that approximately half of the products reaching the test marketing phase are never introduced to the market, and that the vast majority of new product ideas have already been eliminated prior to test marketing. In other words, companies invest millions of euros on products and services that never turn a profit!

There are no standard definitions of successful products and failed products. Some argue that a new product can only be called successful if it meets the original expectations of the firm's management in virtually every respect. If not, it will probably be defined as a failure.[15] This could mean that the firm still makes a profit, but that it does not achieve its profitability objectives, or, even worse, that it takes years to recover its R&D and marketing costs. Of course, in calculating profitability we should also measure and consider the effect of the new product or service on sales of the rest of the product mix. To learn from the product development strategies of others and reduce the risk of introducing a new product or service that fails, let's examine the most common reasons for product success and product failure.

8.5.1 *Successful introductions*

Researchers have identified at least five factors that strongly influence whether a new product or service will be a success.

Customer orientation

A new product has to satisfy customers' needs and wants. After all, consumers only buy products that they perceive as useful or attractive. Marketing research should indicate the extent to which this is the case.

To illustrate, as European consumers became increasingly interested in healthier and more convenient ways to cook, bake and fry food, Unilever introduced liquid versions of its

MARKETING TOPPER
Alfa Romeo: Italy's Next Global Luxury Brand?

No matter where carmakers are based, offering an attractive luxury model is a crucial element of their marketing strategy. VW has Audi, GM has Cadillac, Toyota has Lexus and – after selling Volvo, Land Rover and Jaguar to Chinese investors – Ford's upscale ambitions are riding on Lincoln again. Greater profits are the key motive for carmakers' strategic focus on luxury automobiles: their mark-up is usually five times higher than those of mainstream vehicles that appeal to a much broader market. In addition, luxury car brand names tend to have a positive effect on sales of 'regular' cars produced and sold by the same company.

To illustrate the importance of luxury car brands, VW's top management recently expressed an interest in acquiring Alfa Romeo – an automobile brand now owned by Italian carmaker Fiat – because it believes that Volkswagen has the most expertise and experience in marketing luxury brands. Granted, Volkswagen has proved itself managing the ten brands it already owns, from the basic Skoda and VW to the upscale Lamborghini and Bentley. But without doubt, the main motive for the attempt to acquire Alfa is its profit potential. Volkswagen's luxury-priced Audi, for instance, accounts for nearly half of the company's earnings. Imagine what a new Alfa Romeo luxury sedan or sports coupe and a two-seater sports car that could rival BMW's hot-selling models would do for VW's profits, which are already notably higher than those of any other automaker in the world.

Unfortunately for VW, Fiat has no intention of selling the Alfa Romeo brand to a competitor. This sporty Italian brand has not been available in America since Alfa's exit from the US in 1995. Fiat-Chrysler's chief executive Sergio Marchionne, however, intends to turn the company into a major global player through an ambitious marketing strategy that focuses on re-introducing Alfa Romeo in the American market. The CEO hopes that a successful relaunch of this premium sport brand in the United States will be a catalyst for entering China and other overseas markets as well.

According to Marchionne, the Alfa premium brand is crucial to Fiat-Chrysler's future. Not only will it generate suffi-

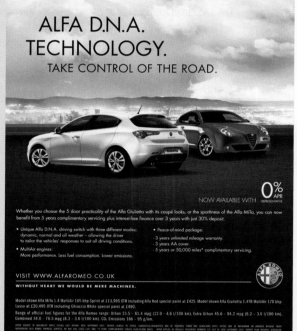

ALFA D.N.A. TECHNOLOGY.
TAKE CONTROL OF THE ROAD.

NOW AVAILABLE WITH 0% APR REPRESENTATIVE

Whether you choose the 5 door practicality of the Alfa Giulietta with its coupé looks, or the sportiness of the Alfa MiTo, you can now benefit from 5 years complimentary servicing plus interest-free finance over 3 years with just 30% deposit.

- Unique Alfa D.N.A. driving switch with three different modes: dynamic, normal and all weather – allowing the driver to tailor the vehicles' responses to suit all driving conditions.
- MultiAir engines: More performance. Less fuel consumption. Lower emissions.
- Peace-of-mind package:
  - 3 years unlimited mileage warranty.
  - 3 years AA cover.
  - 5 years or 50,000 miles* complimentary servicing.

VISIT WWW.ALFAROMEO.CO.UK
WITHOUT HEART WE WOULD BE MERE MACHINES.

ALFA ROMEO

cient profits for the company to increase its investments in Research & Development, but designing and producing new Alfa Romeo luxury car models requires technologies that will also make the company more competitive in marketing high-volume vehicles such as Chrysler, Dodge and Fiat that are primarily targeted at mass markets. Clearly, Fiat-Chrysler's top management intends to match Volkswagen's lucrative strategy for Audi with Fiat's own Alfa Romeo brand.

After a 20-year absence in the US, Alfa is viewed with nostalgic affection

Attaining Marchionne's ambitious marketing goal of increasing Alfa's worldwide sales volume to more than half a million cars by 2014 – including over 80 000 in the United States – is a huge challenge, especially when starting virtually from scratch in the US and China, the world's two biggest car markets. In North America, the new luxury cars will be distributed by Chrysler, and sold by Fiat franchises mostly owned by Chrysler dealerships. A wider range of products will give Fiat dealers more cars to sell. Fiat's top management is convinced that the American market is ready for Alfa Romeo cars, especially since the brand name is not well known over there. While in Europe, Alfa Romeo's brand image has been stained because of its former lineup of second-rate models with quality problems, in the US – after a 20-year absence – the brand still has a great reputation and is viewed with nostalgic affection.

In the early stages of planning Alfa's relaunch in the US, the Italian management insisted on sharing parts between brands in order to reduce costs. This plan was in line with the strategy developed during the Fiat-Chrysler reorganization. Alfa's initial production plans called for cutting costs by sharing Fiat's powertrains and other parts that would cover as much as 65 per cent of the car's value. More recently, however, the CEO decided that Alfa Romeo models would get brand-exclusive engines that rely on technology from Fiat's *Ferrari* and *Maserati* divisions. The key marketing objective is to *differentiate* the upscale Alfa Romeo from Chrysler so as to improve its chances of success in the highly competitive US market.

American car enthusiasts have anxiously been awaiting Alfa Romeo's return to their country. From an engineering perspective, for an upscale sporty vehicle to carry the Alfa Romeo nameplate, it must live up to high quality standards. But at the end of the day, the brand's future will depend on the company's success in *positioning* Alfa Romeo as an exclusive luxury brand that meets the customers' expectations, and – in order to boost the company's profitability – warrants a price level that reflects its perceived value.[16]

Croma (frying fat) and *Blue Band* (margarine) products. Because these liquids – with lower saturated fat and cholesterol content – are healthier and the new packaging is both user friendly (squeezed out of the bottle into the pan) and hygienic (no more greasy, half-used margarine sticks in the refrigerator), the new product launches were successful in this large, high-growth market.

Core business activity

A new product is most likely to succeed if there is a synergy or fit with the company's core business activities (including its R&D, manufacturing and distribution capabilities). This also implies that the firm's management – through marketing research – is familiar with the marketing challenges it is facing.

Since *Unilever* started concentrating on its core activities, it has successfully divided its new product development into three sectors: food (for instance, items to be prepared in the microwave), skin care (such as Fabergé and Elizabeth Arden products) and chemicals (among which are artificial flavours for margarine). This has resulted in many successful new products.

Superior product

Buyers will prefer a new product that, in the consumers' eyes, is better than competing products in terms of quality, unique features or innovativeness. Probably the most important ingredient of success for any new product or service is its ability to provide an important and observable benefit (such as ease of operation, more features, better taste or advanced technology) to a large number of customers in the target market.

At *Nestlé*, every new product must undergo a so-called '60/40+' analysis: at least 60 per cent of those tasting it must prefer it to a rival product or the one it is replacing, plus it must be more nutritious. The company has, for instance, produced a new way of churning its ice cream that produces much smaller ice crystals than the standard method. As a result it still tastes creamy even though it has half the fat.

Stimulating corporate culture

The most successful innovative companies are those whose management encourages employees at all levels to exercise initiative and accept taking risks. Such an entrepreneurial mindset changes the game from minimizing risk to maximizing reward, from fine-tuning marketing to breaking new ground, and from following standard formulas to pushing boundaries.

3M is successful in encouraging initiative because of a corporate culture in which employees' mistakes in product development are quite acceptable. The company's motto is, 'It's better to ask for forgiveness than to ask for permission.'

Well-planned product development process

Firms with the most successful products pay close attention to activities before the actual development starts, including a clear definition of the target market, customers' needs and preferences, and the product concept.

Unilever has increased its capacity for innovation by creating multidisciplinary project teams, maintaining frequent contacts with customers in consumer panels and concentrating on a limited number of brands. Employees who invent something that does not have a fit, or synergy, with Unilever's marketing mix, R&D or manufacturing capabilities are encouraged to develop the idea outside of Unilever. The company has even set up a special fund (Unilever Ventures) to help provide seed capital for these ventures. By investing in innovative young companies, Unilever is able to increase its own R&D efforts for new product development.[17]

8.5.2 *Failed introductions*

Year after year, countless new products and services are introduced, and many fail. Success and failure rates vary from one company to another, but research shows that, in general, consumer products fail more often than business products. We also know that new products and services fail for different reasons, and that there are five major causes of these failures, most of which can be avoided with careful planning. These are a lack of clear product benefit, a poor marketing strategy, quality problems, unanticipated competitive reactions and bad timing.

No clear product benefits

The most common problem in failed introductions is that the product, even though it performs adequately, does not offer any significant advantage over competitive products already well established in the market. Before a new product is launched, management should be able to answer this question. 'What does the new product do differently or better than existing products?' If its benefits are not unique or clear, then the product is unlikely to be a success. Many of the marketing flops described in this book's *Marketing Mistakes* illustrate the lack of 'relative advantage'.

The major reason for development and introduction of products that are not unique or better is insufficient *marketing research* and market analysis. Often, this is the result of unreasonable pressure to match the success of a rival that has recently launched a profitable new product. That could bring about overly optimistic forecasts of market acceptance, leading to rushed and risky marketing decisions. As long as managers themselves try to decide what the marketplace wants, without asking potential buyers about their needs and expectations, companies will continue to struggle with new product failure.

Poor marketing strategy

The marketing strategy for a new product or service must be carefully planned. Sometimes marketers fail to correctly identify and analyze the various market segments and don't know enough about the target market. This may subsequently lead to an inappropriate marketing plan and a poor implementation of the marketing strategy, especially in markets in which the firm has little experience. Lack of an effective marketing effort may cause product failure, not because the product is bad, but because management does not understand the customer service, distribution or promotion requirements of the market. Such a lack of insight could, for example, result in an advertising campaign that does not communicate an effective positioning of the brand or other key components of the message.

An often profitable strategy for a firm in this situation is to form a strategic alliance with another company and closely cooperate in marketing the new product. To illustrate, Philips has been quite successful in the international market by developing and launching products in collaboration with Douwe Egberts (*Senseo*) and Nivea (*CoolSkin*). Companies should also give a new product or service the extra attention it needs after it has been introduced to the market. This does not always happen. Many marketers have a tendency to move on to the next project before the new product is up and running or able to stand on its own. This can be a grave mistake: the marketing strategies of new products almost always require modification once the company has been able to assess the initial reactions of the customers and intermediaries to the product.

Quality problems

Failed product launches are sometimes due to unforeseen product deficiencies (such as design problems) sabotaging the firm's prospects of success. Other products have to be recalled from the market because of teething troubles or technical difficulties in the manufacturing process that affect their quality. Often, it proves difficult to maintain the quality level achieved during the test marketing phase after switching to mass production in order to serve a larger marketplace. Because the company is on a tight schedule (especially if competitors are working on a similar item), there may not be enough time to refine the product or the production process.

Unanticipated competitive reactions

Many of the reasons why new products fail are within a company's control and can be avoided. But this is not the case when it comes to the reactions of competitors. They may cut prices, run a promotional offer, or quickly launch a similar product. Yet, the company should anticipate competitive reactions and incorporate these into its marketing plan; otherwise, its sales forecast may be overly optimistic.

Bad timing

A firm that has not yet established a strong market position for its current products may not be able to concentrate on new product development. Adding new items to a dubious product mix causes customers to have doubts and may undermine the company's financial position. Management first needs to make sure that its existing products achieve full potential, possibly by reducing manufacturing costs and increasing market share. It should also eliminate any weak products. Only then will the firm be in a position to systematically focus on developing new products and be able to invest enough in marketing to make them commercially viable.

Sometimes, companies end up being too slow or too fast in developing a new product or service, leading to a poorly timed and failed introduction. For instance, consumers may postpone a purchase if the economy is heading towards a recession. Or, in an attempt to beat competitors to the market, a firm may launch a new product prematurely by skipping one of the steps (such as test marketing) of the development process.

Occasionally, a company introduces a service or product for which the market is simply not yet ready. However, more often products are launched too late, after the demand has already been satisfied by another company. This problem becomes even more serious as many products must first be approved for sale by government regulatory agencies. Managers also complain that the government often takes too long to grant licences for construction or expansion of production facilities. The slow grinding of the bureaucratic mills may delay the planned introduction of a product by months. This can cause any new product to fail; after all, 'timing is everything'.

8.6 DIFFUSION OF INNOVATIONS

The *product life cycle*, as discussed earlier, shows the distinct stages that a new product passes through from birth (introduction) to death (in the decline stage), with the implication that the product requires a different strategy at each stage to market it effectively to potential buyers. Few consumers buy a new product immediately after it is introduced. Most sales are realized once the product has been on the market for some time. This is how new products are gradually adopted by society over time and over various categories of buyers ('adopters'). This process is known as the *diffusion of innovations*.

The **diffusion process** – the spread of new ideas and products through society and their acceptance by various groups in the target market – can also be analyzed from the buyers' point of view. From this perspective, the key questions marketers should ask are:

→ Exactly how does the *adoption process* take place? What stages do consumers go through before they decide to make a purchase?

→ How long does it take before an individual decides to buy an entirely new product and, from that perspective, what types of buyers (*adopter categories*) can we distinguish?

→ What characteristics or *attributes of innovations* influence their adoption rate, or how quickly the new product or service is accepted by society?

We now examine these points in more detail, starting with an analysis of the adoption process.

8.6.1 The consumer adoption process

Most innovations are not purchased en masse immediately after they are introduced. At launch time, the product development process may have been largely completed, but for the individual consumer, the acceptance or **adoption process** is just beginning. As we know from personal experience, people don't simply go out and buy a new product. Instead, consumers go through a series of attitudinal and behavioural changes that lead to product trial, purchase and adoption – which is when they decide to keep using the product on a regular

MARKETING MISTAKE
Size Matters in Global Marketing

Some exports or overseas marketing efforts fail simply because a product is too large or too small for local use, or is not offered in the right package. Companies that operate internationally will benefit from knowing that in global marketing, one size doesn't fit all.

Many large companies that enjoy global marketing success today have gone through a learning curve. Swedish furniture retailer *IKEA*, for example, has seen its degree of success affected by how well it has adapted – or failed to adapt – the size of its furniture to the new markets it entered. It learned the hard way from early blunders in the United States and Japan. 'American customers were buying vases to drink from, because our glasses were too small,' recalled Goran Carstedt, the former head of IKEA North America. 'Our beds were measured in centimetres, not king, queen and twin. Our sofas were not deep enough, our curtains were too short, and our showroom kitchens didn't fit US-size appliances.'

That was about twenty years ago. Since then, IKEA has not only adapted the sizes of its products for the majority of North American consumers, but also for smaller demographic groups within the US, such as the Latino population. It sent its designers to visit Latino homes, where they learned that most Latino families are relatively large and therefore need larger dining tables and sofas to fit everyone. Conversely, IKEA found that offering a smaller product size was essential for success in Japan. When it first entered the country, the Swedish chain store failed to meet consumer needs and left the Japanese market. Twenty years later, the furniture giant returned with a more successful focus on 'small space living', which is the reality for most Japanese homes.

Sometimes the ideal product size is dependent on personal preference, such as the Chinese consumer's liking of roomier backseats in *automobiles*. Other times, product size preferences are dictated by practical considerations, such as the need for Japanese cars to fit in traditionally small parking spaces. In fact, some car models failed because they were only 30 centimetres too long

for most Japanese parking garages. Differences in product size also apply to food products and beverages in Japan. *Starbucks*, for instance, offers its drinks in smaller cup sizes, while some grocery items are sold in smaller packages in Japan simply because its average household size is smaller as well.

Cultural differences not only affect the size of the packages that companies use in various countries, but also the material, quality and colour of a product's container; these may influence how a product is perceived by potential buyers. To illustrate, *Neerlandia* – a Dutch producer of powdered milk – for years had successfully exported its product to Africa in tin cans. To cut costs, the company switched to alu-packs made of aluminum foil, but this created unexpected challenges. According to Professors Tevfik Dalgic and Ruud Heijblom, customs officials in one African country were suspicious that the new packages contained illegal drugs. When the product – after intense scrutiny by customs – could finally be sold in stores, sales volume went down. Apparently, consumers had been using the empty tin boxes to boil water and prepare food in, and even as building blocks. Hence, Neerlandia discontinued the alu-packs and reintroduced the former reusable tin box packaging.

Another company that struggled when it first tried to sell its product overseas, in Great Britain, was *Campbell's*, the (condensed) soup company. This American company offered the same amount of product in a can half the size of non-condensed competitor products. But since British consumers were not used to buying condensed soups, the smaller Campbell's cans looked like a bad deal next to the larger containers of competing soups.

Preliminary market research can help companies avoid such international marketing mishaps. The British chocolate maker *Cadbury* conducted research to assess consumer perceptions of its purple wrapper in different cultures. As intended, the British saw the colour purple as luxurious; however, the Taiwanese perception of purple caused them to perceive the product as a low quality chocolate. These insights enabled Cadbury to repackage its products for the Taiwanese market with a more appropriate wrapper design.

A simple packaging change had a huge impact on customer perception and sales

Sometimes, even after completing their marketing research, companies would rather not adapt their marketing policies to local customs. Shin Ohkawara, CEO of *Kentucky Fried Chicken* Japan, had to fight KFC's top management to break from its standard American practices as he tried to adapt to the local culture that expects

higher standards of quality and presentation, even from fried foods. Instead of dumping chicken into buckets, KFC Japan now neatly arranges chicken in a single layer, in wide boxes with ribbed, plastic bottoms to minimize grease absorption. This simple packaging change had a huge positive impact on customer perception and sales. 'Compared with the United States, packaging costs us more than twice as much, but we are doing it,' explained Ohkawara, who also insisted on additional quality improvements to make the franchise successful in Japan. It illustrates that managers may need to take bold stands to break from the norm in order to achieve international marketing success.

Package *standardization* can sometimes be an efficient product strategy, but international food marketers should recognize when *localization* is more appropriate. By respecting cultural nuances or preferences and adapting their packaging and presentation, marketers will be better positioned to see their products reach consumers' homes to let them discover for themselves how good the brand really is.[18]

basis. According to Everett Rogers, the *adoption process* (also known as the *response model*) involves five stages – as illustrated in Figure 8.2 – that sometimes take place over an extended period of time.[19]

1 *Awareness*. The consumer first learns of a new product, but lacks full information about it.

2 *Interest*. They become interested in the innovation and starts looking for additional information.

3 *Evaluation*. The potential customer considers the product's benefits and tries to decide if it is worth trying.

4 *Trial*. To see if the product meets their needs, the individual makes a trial purchase or tests the innovation to determine its usefulness.

5 *Adoption* (or *rejection*). The customer decides to become a regular user and adopt the innovation, or (if they are not satisfied with it) to reject it.

Not everyone goes through each stage in the adoption process. Consumers who are initially interested in the product may stop halfway through the process when they find the product unsuitable, in which case there is no **adoption** of the innovation. Others skip a stage to adopt the product (such as a new tablet) more quickly, particularly if there is little risk involved in making the purchase.

FIGURE 8.2 The response model: stages in the product adoption process

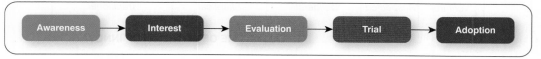

Rejection may occur at any point in time, including in the adoption stage. Also, both adoption and rejection of the product can be temporary or permanent. At any rate, a marketer must have sufficient insight into the adoption process – by consumers as well as by intermediaries – to influence it effectively. This is crucial, because if many consumers do not adopt an innovation, the commercialization of the product is doomed to fail.

8.6.2 Adopter categories

One person will accept an innovation more readily than another. Some people buy a new product as soon as it is hits the stores, since they enjoy being the 'first one on the block' to own it. Others will only buy it after nearly everyone else is using it. Research conducted by Everett Rogers shows that people who purchase a new product within roughly the same period of time after it has been launched, share certain characteristics. Thus, it is possible to group consumers into categories according to their degree of innovativeness. Based on the length of time it takes them to adopt a new product, consumers can be classified into one of five categories. These five **adoption categories** are illustrated in Figure 8.3.

The **adoption curve** shown in the figure represents a normal distribution of the buyers in a potential market over time and illustrates what percentage of the consumer population falls within each of the adoption categories. The categories, based on the buyers' relative time of adoption of innovations, are called innovators, early adopters, early majority, late majority and laggards. Although these may be random categories, this classification has been successfully used in numerous studies. From this research we know, for instance, that by the time the *early majority* get around to buying a particular product for the first time, the *innovators* and *early adopters* are soon to make repeat purchases.

FIGURE 8.3 Distribution of adopter categories in the product diffusion process

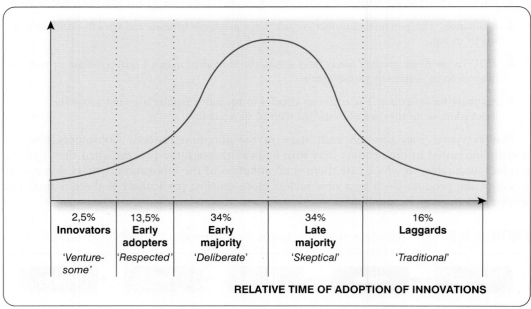

2,5% Innovators	13,5% Early adopters	34% Early majority	34% Late majority	16% Laggards
'Venture-some'	'Respected'	'Deliberate'	'Skeptical'	'Traditional'

RELATIVE TIME OF ADOPTION OF INNOVATIONS

Profile of product adopters

The first 2.5 per cent of the population who buy the innovation are known as the **innovators** or *consumption pioneers*. These individuals are eager to buy new products. For them it is almost an obsession to be first among their friends or colleagues to have something cutting edge. They are usually young, adventurous, well-educated and willing to accept risks. They use multiple information sources, especially the Internet. They also have a relatively high income and can afford to make an occasional 'dud' purchase. Because innovators are the first to adopt a new product, they often set off a *trend*.

The second group, **early adopters**, makes up the next 13.5 per cent of consumers who adopt an innovation. A new product can only be considered a marketing success once it is

© Miguel Medina / AFP / Getty

purchased by both the innovators and early adopters. Yet people in these two categories are actually quite different from one another. Compared with innovators, the early adopters are less cosmopolitan, but better integrated into the social system. With a slightly above-average education, they are often leaders and role models in the community as well as *opinion leaders*: their views and advice are important to the remaining adopter categories! Although early adopters respond to most trends and are relatively quick to buy something new, they are still selective in their purchasing.

Consumers in the third category, the **early majority** (34 per cent of potential adopters), adopt a new product just before the average person. While they are sensitive to new market developments, they are deliberate and cautious in trying new products and services. Early majority adopters compare prices and brands or collect other information before making their carefully considered purchase decisions. They have quite a few informal social contacts in the community and only adopt innovations after their peers have done so.

People in the **late majority** (like the previous category, 34 per cent of the population) are very sceptical of new products and adopt them after the early majority does. They eventually adopt new products because of economic necessity or overwhelming peer pressure. These somewhat older consumers with a below-average social status and income tend to get their information from their relatives and acquaintances rather than from the mass media or Internet.

The **laggards**, the fifth group and comprising 16 per cent of the population, are the last people to accept the innovation. These older, lowest-income consumers have the most local perspective in that they interact primarily with neighbours and friends (with similar values) in their community. They are suspicious of new products and oriented toward the past. When these 'old-fashioned' consumers finally buy the product, it may already have been replaced by a new innovation.

Implications for marketing

How useful is this classification of product adopters for a company's strategy development? The main reason to study the diffusion and adoption of innovations is to be able to develop marketing plans that stimulate and speed up the purchase of newly introduced products and services. The key questions here are which adopter group should receive most attention in marketing our new product, and with what message? These decisions are especially important at the beginning of the product life cycle.

As we saw earlier, marketers who use the product life cycle as a planning tool are at a significant advantage. Figure 8.4 shows the relationship between the product life cycle (shown here with four stages) and the consumer adoption process. To achieve a rapid market penetration for a new product or service, we need to focus our first promotional and sales

FIGURE 8.4 Relationship between the product life cycle and the adoption process

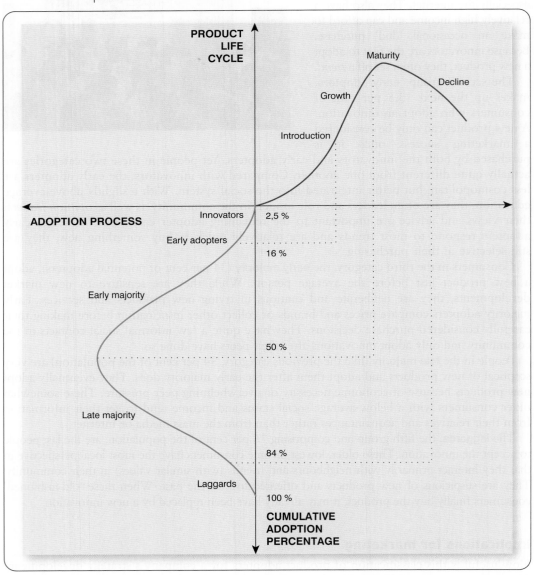

efforts on innovators and early adopters. These consumers begin purchasing a new item early in the diffusion process, building the sales curve that takes the product or service from the introduction stage to the growth stage of the life cycle. We cannot just concentrate on the innovators. Although they are the first to buy the product, they are generally not well enough respected in the community to influence later purchasers through opinion leadership and word of mouth. On the other hand, many segments of society – particularly the early majority, during the growth stage of the product life cycle – look to the early adopters for information and advice about an innovation. That influences their attitudes and behaviour as consumers. Thus, if a company cannot convince early adopters of the merits of the product, its chances of success are greatly reduced.

As the late majority customers adopt the new product or service, it moves from the growth stage into the maturity stage of the life cycle. Marketers should now reinforce their customers' adoption decision and defend against rivals with me-too products. By the time the laggards start buying the product or service, it will be in the maturity or decline stage of the PLC. Marketers may then try to extend the product's life span by encouraging continued purchasing.

The diffusion of innovations model also has valuable implications for the company's promotion and positioning strategies. In the introduction stage, for instance, the firm should effectively promote the product to create awareness of its arrival on the market and its benefits. Innovators and early adopters respond to different types of new product information than early majority, late majority and laggards. The firm should emphasize the product features that will be of most interest to these early purchasers. For example, we know that early adopters rely primarily on impersonal information sources and pay most attention to technical details, scientific information and performance tests. Although followers depend more on word-of-mouth communications, such as the opinions of those who have already bought the product, they are also interested in company-generated promotional information. Hence, marketers should continue to adjust the promotion campaign, as well as the product itself, in order to stimulate patterns of adoption and repeat purchases.

8.6.3 *Product features and rate of adoption*

The **adoption rate** refers to how quickly a new product or service is accepted by society. This differs significantly among innovations. Some new products are accepted only gradually, while others are readily adopted. Frisbees, for instance, moved from the introduction stage to the maturity stage of the product life cycle in less than half a year.

There are five attributes or characteristics of an innovation that determine its speed or rate of adoption. According to Rogers, these are a new product's relative advantage, compatibility, complexity, divisibility (possibility of trial use) and observability.

Relative advantage

In order to be adopted at all, an innovation must look like it is a considerable improvement over current products on the market. An innovation – such as the iPad – that is perceived as being substantially superior to existing products or ideas has a significant **relative advantage**. This relative advantage may involve physical improvements, aesthetic appeal, a lower price, a trusted brand name or greater ease of use, all of which may increase the product's rate of adoption. For marketers, the challenge is to quickly and successfully communicate the benefits or advantages of the new product in comparison to products already available.

© Dudarev Mikhail / Shutterstock

Compatibility

New products are more readily accepted if they are consistent with the experiences, attitudes and needs of potential adopters. For instance, dual income families are more inclined to buy time-saving household appliances than are traditional families. These products are compatible with the lifestyle and values of the buyers.

The perceived compatibility can differ considerably from one country to another. When, on average, 65 per cent of kitchens in Europe were equipped with microwave ovens, this appliance could be found in less than 5 per cent of kitchens in the Netherlands. Apparently, the innovation was in conflict with the existing norms or did not tie in with the lifestyle of Dutch consumers at that time. If a new product is a major change from older ones or does not seem to be in line with the interests of potential customers, educational advertising campaigns and clear instructions can facilitate the transition to the innovation.

Complexity

Simple products tend to be adopted more rapidly than complicated products. The more complex the product is, the greater the efforts required of the marketer (to sell it) and the consumer (to learn to use it).

Marketers should never forget that prospective customers are not as informed about the product or service as they are. An apparently simple design, as well as sales presentations and promotional material can lower the threshold by helping buyers understand how to use the product.

Ease of trial use

New products and services that the consumer is able to try out, or use on a small scale for trial purposes before the purchase, meet with the least resistance. The *divisibility* of a new product refers to the extent to which prospective customers can sample it.

Promotions involving coupons offering discounts on the purchase price or the distribution of free samples are often successful strategies in accelerating the adoption rate, because they enable consumers to reduce or eliminate the risk of financial loss when they try the new product. The possibility of placing trial orders or renting products can also increase the rate of adoption.

Observability

The term observability or *communicability* refers to the degree to which the importance, superior attributes or benefits of an innovation are visible in a tangible form or can be communicated to others. The higher the innovation's observability, the more quickly it will be adopted. For example, the rapid rate of adoption of new fashions and new car models has a lot to do with the high visibility of these products. They reflect the customer's lifestyle and help make a statement to reference groups. For other items, in-store demonstrations, YouTube videos or even websites that reveal the product's superiority may stimulate first-time purchases and adoptions.

How the *lack* of observability of a product's benefits can slow down its adoption rate became apparent to a company that was trying to sell pre-emergent weed killers; these are sprayed on the field before weeds actually develop. Since there was no sign of dead weeds, farmers were not convinced that the new pesticide served any purpose. Therefore, it took years before this innovation was accepted in the farming industry.

SUMMARY

1   New products

For many companies, launching successful new products and services drives their sales growth and future profits. Most new products, including me-too products, line extensions, flanker brands, product modifications and repositioned products, provide a significant improvement over existing products. Others, which are new for the company as well as for customers, perform a new function and – as product innovations – may spawn a completely new industry.

Analyzing a product's newness from the customer's point of view, we can classify new products according to their effects on consumer behaviour. Based on the degree of consumers' efforts in the process of accepting and learning to use the new product or service, a distinction can be made between a continuous innovation (no new behaviour has to be learned), a dynamically continuous innovation (requiring minor changes in behaviour) and a discontinuous innovation (for which consumers need to adopt completely new consumption patterns). All of these types of new products or services require specially tailored marketing strategies.

2   Reasons for product development

Companies introduce new products for a number of reasons: to meet sales objectives, to utilize excess production or distribution capacity or to complete a product line. New products can also be developed in response to government measures, to prevent other firms from gaining a competitive advantage, to cater to changing consumer needs or wants and to make use of new technology. A product acquired externally generates smaller but quicker profits than one developed internally. Other factors affecting a make-or-buy decision – in addition to the likelihood of antitrust litigation – include the risks associated with the product, as well as the management expertise and personnel requirements involved.

3   Developing new products

Many newly introduced products fail. By systematically dividing the product development process into distinct phases, a firm can increase its chances of success. The first step is to spell out the objectives of innovation and to choose between a proactive and a reactive strategy. With a systematic approach, the idea generation stage should yield a large number of proposals for new products and services from many diverse sources. These new product ideas are then screened and evaluated;

the goal is to eliminate as many ideas as possible that are inconsistent with the firm's objectives. To select the best ideas, some firms use consumer concept tests. During the business analysis phase, the economic feasibility of the production process and profitability of the proposed new products or services are assessed. For this purpose, the firm may develop either a *pro forma* income statement or a market share projection.

The objective of the next stage, prototype development, is to create a concrete test model of the product. At this point, the rest of the marketing mix is developed as well, so that the marketing strategy, consumer response and the product's chances of survival can be evaluated in a test market. Finally, test market successes proceed to full commercialization. Before the product is rolled out, this stage involves starting up production, building inventories, shipping to distributors or dealers, recruiting and training a sales force, informing retailers about the product and advertising it to consumers.

4   Organizing the product development process

Companies should be well organized and prepared to evaluate and manage new product opportunities. A venture team is made up of specialists from different departments, who spend all of their time on the new product or service. Venture teams are assembled to recreate an entrepreneurial spirit within the organization by assessing new product ideas and carrying the potentially most lucrative ones through to commercialization. They should be separate from the company's regular organizational structure and report directly to its president or a senior manager. Although a venture team is set up on a temporary basis, its flexible life span may extend over several years.

The down side of venture teams is that they are expensive, and participants may become emotionally involved with the products. It may also be difficult to find the right leader to chair the team. Consequently, some firms prefer to stimulate the innovation process in other ways. The most commonly used alternatives to venture teams include new product managers and new product committees.

5   Reasons for failure or success

Many new products fail. They are taken off the market because the company is unable to recover its development, production and marketing costs or because the product, while perhaps marginally profitable, does not meet the firm's profit, sales or market share objectives. The main reasons for new product failure are that the product has no clear benefits as compared to existing products, a poor marketing strategy, quality issues, failure to anticipate competitors' reactions and bad timing.

A new product or service is most likely to be successful if it satisfies the buyers' needs and wants (preferably in a large, growing market), if there is a synergy or fit with the company's core activities, if the new product is perceivably better than competing products, if it has been developed in an organization with a stimulating and entrepreneurial corporate culture and, finally, if the entire product development process was well organized.

6   The diffusion process

Diffusion of innovations refers to the spread of new ideas, products and services through society and their gradual acceptance by various groups of adopters in the market. Marketing-driven companies focus their promotional, sales and other marketing efforts on two groups of people who buy new products early in the diffusion process: innovators, and early adopters who tend to influence later purchasers through opinion leadership and word of mouth. The other adoption categories in Rogers' classification are the early majority, late majority and laggards.

Most buyers go through an acceptance or adoption process of five stages: awareness, interest, evaluation, trial and adoption. An effective marketing strategy will facilitate potential customers' movement through these phases, from first hearing about a new product or service to its adoption. The adoption rate depends on the product's relative advantage, its compatibility with the consumer's norms and values, its complexity, its divisibility (or ease of trial use) and the observability of the innovation's superiority or benefits to the consumer.

DISCUSSION QUESTIONS

1   A company that makes wheat flour has a large share of the consumer market with several premium brands containing wheat flour. The company is now considering developing a powder that can be mixed with water to make a delicious vegetable sauce. Of course, this product will have to compete with other vegetable sauces on the market. Develop a detailed proposal for a concept test for this new product.

2   A discontinuous innovation involves the introduction of a completely new product. This is a relatively rare phenomenon in business. Give some examples of this kind of innovation and explain why they are so rare. How do you assess the future for new products?

3   Do you think the risk associated with the development of new products will increase during the next ten years? Why or why not?

4   Research shows that only a small percentage of new product ideas come from customers. Isn't this in conflict with the marketing definition presented in Chapter 1, and summarized in six words as 'find a need and fill it'? Explain your answer.

5   In what ways can a company use its customers as a source of new product or service ideas?

6   Test marketing results are often more positive than the actual results achieved after the launch of the same product. How would you explain this?

7   What alternatives are available to a company to eliminate a product or service that has reached the end of its life cycle?

8   Compare and contrast different approaches to organizing the new product development process. As a marketing consultant, which one would you suggest for a family-owned business specializing in making tools? Which one would you recommend for a large multinational corporation?

9   Comment on the following statement. 'In this firm we never worry about a new product that fails because we don't reach our profitability objectives. We only need to worry if we don't recover our production and marketing costs.'

10 What does Everett Rogers' diffusion of innovations theory have to offer the marketing executive?

PART FOUR
PROMOTION
DECISIONS

In Part 4 of this book we explore how companies develop an effective promotional strategy to communicate with their markets. Chapter 9 describes promotion as a communication process. The better we understand this process, the better able we are to set and achieve our communication objectives, whether we use an advertising campaign or one-on-one communication via the Internet. Most organizations try to build relationships with their customers through various forms of marketing communication, including public relations. This applies to both the consumer market and the business-to-business market.

The most widely used marketing communication instruments will be addressed in Part 4. Chapter 9 examines communication strategies and public relations, while Chapter 10 analyzes advertising and sponsorships. Chapter 11 focuses on personal selling, direct marketing and sales promotion.

9 Marketing communication strategies

10 Advertising

11 Sales management

CHAPTER 9
MARKETING COMMUNICATION STRATEGIES

LEARNING GOALS

After studying this chapter you will be able to:

1	Explain what marketing communication is and how the communication process works
2	Apply the two-step flow of communication model when identifying the target audience
3	Formulate sound communication objectives using the AIDA or hierarchy-of-effects model
4	Discuss the advantages and disadvantages of various ways to set the promotional budget
5	Select a company's optimum communication mix
6	Identify the role of public relations in a marketing-driven organization

9.1 What is marketing communication?

9.2 Communication strategy: target audience

9.3 Setting communication objectives

9.4 Establishing the communication budget

9.5 Determining the communication mix

9.6 Public relations

FREE YOURSELF

Image courtesy of The Advertising Archives

A successful marketing strategy demands much more than developing and launching a good product or service. Even if a product is marketed at the right price and sold through the right distribution channels, success is by no means guaranteed. Effective communication with the target market is an essential part of marketing programmes, requiring a carefully developed promotional strategy.

Companies have to select the best communication tools to inform customers of their products and services and to persuade or remind buyers of the benefits they offer. Whether firms rely on advertising, public relations, personal selling, sponsorship or other means of communication such as social media, they must attract people's attention and convey the intended message. Hence, the question is not if an organization should communicate, but how to communicate most effectively. A well-executed promotional strategy can contribute significantly to the realization of marketing goals.

MARKETING IN ACTION
Why Hyundai is Targeting Europe

Most big car companies spend millions of euros on advertising and other forms of marketing communication to promote their brands worldwide. Korean automaker *Hyundai Motor*, however, was lucky enough to get some sensational *free publicity* from an amateur video recorded during the *Frankfurt Motor Show* in Germany. The video fragment, posted on YouTube and viewed nearly two million times across the world, shows Martin Winterkorn, the CEO of *Volkswagen* – one of Hyundai's major European competitors – checking out the adjustable steering column on the Hyundai i30 hatchback model. He was obviously impressed, marvelling how nothing seemed to rattle, before questioning desperately why VW (or *BMW*, for that matter) cannot do this while Hyundai apparently can. With Volkswagen's CEO name-checking the Korean brand as a key competitor, Hyundai's executives, without doubt, realized that their company was on the right track in seizing the global market. Best of all, the publicity's positive effect on Hyundai's brand image could not have been attained through any type of advertising campaign.

This open admiration of a Korean compact car by Volkswagen's top management – on home turf – only reinforces the success of Hyundai's aggressive marketing strategy, not least as the i30 was priced 10 per cent cheaper than the typical VW Golf, at only €15 500. Hyundai, based in Seoul and until recently perceived as inferior to European car companies, has quickly established a reputation of building

high-quality cars sold at much lower prices than its rivals. Because of the outstanding price/quality relationship, Hyundai and its sister company *Kia Motors* now occupy a prestigious second place in the top-ten list of foreign car makers in the US. In fact, Hyundai and Kia combined are selling more than 1.1 million vehicles per year in America, over three times as many as Volkswagen's 325 000 cars; a phenomenal record in one of the world's largest car markets.

> Europe is a top priority because it affects how Hyundai is perceived elsewhere

Having succeeded in America, Hyundai's next goal is to substantially increase its market share in *Europe*. The timing is right, as the recession has made most consumers on the continent more price-conscious than ever. To increase its brand awareness, Hyundai sponsored the *World Cup* with German football legend Jürgen Klinsmann becoming an ambassador for the brand. By expanding or building new plants on the continent, it has also been able to tailor its product line to European car buyers' preferences. Clearly, being successful in Europe is of great importance for the Korean car maker. Its chief operating officer for the region, Allan Rushforth, has pointed out that Europe is a top priority for the company because it affects perception of Hyundai elsewhere.

Hyundai is on a roll in the global car market. Its blend of *reliability*, *value*, *design* and *innovation*, coupled with an exceptional product warranty that effectively communicates the quality level of its vehicles, has resulted in twice as many car sales for the company compared to the previous decade. This growth rate significantly exceeds Volkswagen's 60 per cent growth. It has also

© Mark Fagelson / Alamy

turned Hyundai into one of Volkswagen's key challengers. The German company's larger scale – from its bestselling VW product line to its upscale brand *Audi* – gives it a competitive advantage. But Hyundai's global ambitions will put additional pressure on all European carmakers' brands in the increasingly competitive automobile market, with *Renault*, *Peugeot*, *Citroën*, *Fiat* and *Opel* expected to lose market share.

Meanwhile, Kia is increasing its sales volume in Europe by 15 to 20 per cent per year, while the automobile market as a whole has been shrinking. Kia sales have been rising in spite of the company's annual price increase of 2.5 per cent for the past three years. Hence, even during Europe's debt crisis, Kia has been growing without offering major discounts, focusing instead on its *positioning* strategy built around the vehicles' attractive *design* and longer *warranty*. 'Kia's quality is now comparable with many of the Japanese and European players,' according to KPMG automotive analyst John Leech, allowing the Kia to compete on its brand image and high quality level at a competitive price. By adding a third shift to its factory in the Czech Republic, Kia has been able to reduce production costs more than its competitors and raise its profitability.

Kia has been expanding its *Slovakian* factory to increase production of its Cee'd compact and Sportage, a small sport-utility vehicle. The company is also working on a sportier design to further increase its market share. Paul Philpott, Chief Operating Officer at Kia Motors Europe, believes that Kia has the potential to become a major player in the European market, with annual sales of more than half a million vehicles. He argues that two

things will drive the brand's image: *design* and *marketing*. Kia's design is well received by consumers since the company recruited former top Audi designer Peter Schreyer. However, the carmaker is not planning to compete head-to-head with Europe's luxury car brands. Paul Philpott has made it clear that he doesn't think it is right for Kia to go premium, referring to the brand's positioning and marketing communication strategy.

In Europe, Hyundai's CEO Rushforth hopes to boost sales levels of Hyundai vehicles by a quarter – to half a million cars – before 2014. To make that happen, the company has launched various new models, including the i40 sedan, the three-door Veloster sports coupe, the i30 compact and i40 wagon. These last two models have been designed and branded exclusively to appeal to car buyers in *Europe*. While the Hyundai Sonata, for example, suits the American market, where demand is greater for family sedans, European consumers prefer hatchbacks, crossovers or wagons. The popularity of these models has enabled Hyundai to open factories in the *Czech Republic*, *Russia* and *Turkey*, where it builds cars for the European continent.

Long known primarily as a maker of smaller cars, Hyundai is now adding more upscale cars in Europe, such as the €42 000 ix55 SUV (known as the Veracruz in the US). Industry analysts think that for the time being, most Europeans car buyers are hesitant to spend big on Hyundai's higher-end cars. They argue that consumers will probably trust VW or other established brands more when purchasing upscale models. If Hyundai, however, continues to successfully implement its global marketing strategy, car buyers' *brand loyalty* could change much faster than expected.[1]

Companies communicate with many groups. Usually, consumers are the primary target market for their promotional campaigns. This explains the high advertising budgets in the business world. But there are also other groups that they communicate or maintain relationships with, such as suppliers, distributors and stockholders.

Advertising is just one of the many vehicles companies use in approaching customers. An effective marketing communication or promotion strategy (the second P in the marketing mix) also involves other channels including the Internet and such tools as publicity, public relations, sponsorship, personal selling, direct marketing and sales promotion. These will all be discussed in this part of the book.

Why do we pay so much attention to communication in *Marketing: a Global Perspective*? The information exchange between sellers and buyers is a crucial component of the marketing process. A brand's market value is largely the result of the effect a well-planned marketing communication strategy has on the buyers' attitudes and behaviour. Products are often purchased solely because of a desirable brand name (such as Apple) or a symbolic image

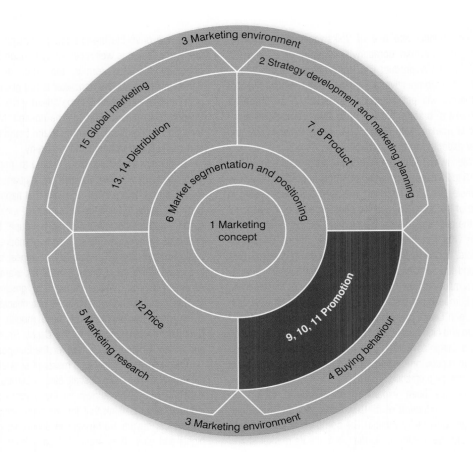

(Coca-Cola). This added value is created through the companies' successful communication efforts. Therefore, commercial mass communication is a virtual necessity in today's business environment, in light of the sheer volume of products and services on the market and the increasing pressures of global competition.

To use a company's promotional tools effectively, we must understand the workings of the communication process in both personal and mass communications. In this chapter we will explore a systematic approach to developing a marketing communication strategy. This includes selecting the target audience, formulating the communication objectives (based on the most widely accepted response hierarchy model) and setting the budget. We will also look at what it takes to develop an effective promotional campaign. The chapter concludes with specific guidelines for choosing the best promotional mix, including the use of public relations.

9.1 WHAT IS MARKETING COMMUNICATION?

Promotion or marketing communication – terms often used interchangeably – refers to the combined tools a company uses to build and maintain favourable relationships by informing or persuading a target audience to view the organization positively, to accept its ideas or to stimulate demand for its products and services.

In strategy development, as outlined in a business or marketing plan, some managers distinguish between promotion and marketing communication. Hence, we will first examine the differences between these two communication tools and identify the activities that are part of a typical promotion or marketing communication mix, as well as their intended effects.

Most organizations use both personal and mass communication. As we will see, each of these options has its advantages and its drawbacks. No matter what strategy we choose, we should have a clear understanding of how communication works. We will therefore analyze this process step-by-step based on a widely used communications model.

9.1.1 *Marketing communication and promotion tools*

Although marketing communication and promotion are related, when examined more closely, the differences between these two terms become apparent. This is illustrated in Figure 9.1.

Some forms of marketing communication are not really considered 'promotion'. This specifically applies to *public relations* (PR), a broad set of communication efforts used to create a favourable image and a positive relationship between the organization and its internal and external stakeholders. Most managers do not consider PR to be part of the promotion mix. However, free publicity, for which public relations departments are usually responsible, is included in the promotion mix.

Conversely, certain forms of *promotion*, such as coupons, savings stamps and other sales promotion devices, are usually not treated as marketing communication activities. Marketing communication efforts are generally intended to maintain long-lasting relationships with customers. *Sales promotion*, on the other hand, involves activities or materials that act as a direct stimulus, providing incentives (such as rebates, sweepstakes, games, free samples, premiums and coupons) to influence consumers' short-term buying behaviour. The fact that sales promotion activities could also have long-term effects and are sometimes used for months or even years, does not alter the primary intention behind the use of this instrument. To clarify this, let's take a closer look at various elements in the communication and promotion mix, based on their definitions, beginning with advertising.

FIGURE 9.1 Marketing communication and promotion tools

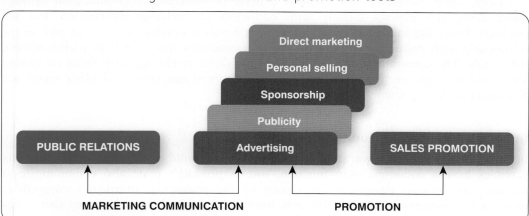

The communication mix

Advertising is essentially the 'mouthpiece' of a business. We define it as any paid form of non-personal communication about products, services, ideas or organizations by an identified sponsor using the mass media to influence the knowledge, attitudes or behaviour of those who are part of a target market.

Publicity, on the other hand, refers to unpaid communications about the company, its products or services that are broadcast or published in news media, but for which media time or space has not been purchased. This commercially significant kind of news is usually based on information a company distributes as a press release to media outlets, in hopes that it will be published or broadcast. Obtaining positive editorial attention in the media is an important objective of the public relations department. This is because a primary function of public relations is to promote mutual understanding between the organization and its target audiences. PR staff work to build up good relationships with various stakeholders (interested parties), mainly by creating a positive image of the organization. This is done through traditional means of publicity, but also through the increasingly widespread use of sponsorship programmes, investments in causes and events to support the company's corporate and marketing objectives. Sponsorship refers to providing financial or other types of support to an organization or individual involved in a particular sports, artistic or similar endeavour, in the hope of acquiring commercial publicity, thereby gaining goodwill or increasing public awareness of the company's name and its brands.

Advertising differs from personal selling in that advertising involves no face-to-face communication or, for that matter, any personal contact between the advertiser and the audience. In personal selling a company sales representative usually makes an oral presentation to a potential buyer with the ultimate objective of selling a product or service. This is part of a process by which the salesperson identifies prospective customers, assesses their needs, presents product information, gets a commitment and then provides follow up to maintain the relationship.

The purpose of sales promotion, too, is to encourage customers to buy the product, now rather than later. This marketing instrument creates a temporary shift in the price/value ratio or relationship of a product or service, either through a limited-time price discount or by enhancing the value ('Limited offer: now 20 per cent more free'), intended to increase sales in the short run. Examples of sales promotion or so-called 'promotions' are displays, coupons, contests, premiums, free samples, demonstrations and participation in exhibitions, fairs or trade shows that stimulate consumers' purchasing and enhances dealers' effectiveness in the firm's distribution channels.

Finally, direct marketing is a two-way process of marketing communication through which companies interact directly with customers to exchange information and sell products. From the marketers' point of view, it involves developing a direct and lasting relationship with customers in order to create transactions that help both parties achieve their goals. The communication methods used for direct marketing often focus on getting an immediate response. However, newsletters, sponsored magazines and other media are also direct marketing communication devices.

Integrated marketing communications

In strategy development we should always keep in mind that other marketing mix variables have a communication function, too. A product's price also communicates a message, as does its design or the colour of the packaging. In today's competitive business environment, the marketing mix must be developed in such a way that it has maximum communication impact and encourages busy, value-conscious consumers to buy. Therefore, more and more firms rely on integrated communication or *integrated marketing communications* (IMC), the strategic integration of several – simultaneously used – media and elements of the communication mix that reinforce each other forming a comprehensive, consistent message to a targeted audience. For most managers, such complex integration poses major challenges.

Stealth, guerrilla, buzz and viral marketing

One characteristic of IMC is that any contact people have with the product, brand or organization is considered to be a part of marketing communication. Products and brand names may be featured in TV shows and movies (*product placement*), in computer games, on T-shirts or even on sports facilities (such as the Philips Arena in Atlanta, for which Philips paid more than $170 million in naming rights). These alternative types of marketing communications and publicity generators are sometimes referred to as stealth marketing, since they are considerably more subtle than advertising and often succeed in reaching audiences bombarded by advertising and sales promotion stimuli who are sceptical about traditional efforts of 'big business' to sell them on a product.

Young consumers can often be effectively reached through guerrilla marketing, marketing activities in which an organization traps consumers with product-related messages or other promotional content in unexpected places. Guerrilla marketing efforts range from putting stickers on tangerines or on the back of concert tickets, to paying people masquerading as fans to chat on the web about one of their favourite CDs. Although guerrilla marketing is an affordable and powerful tactic for small firms with limited budgets, large companies such as Coca-Cola and IBM have also successfully used this innovative approach to promote new products and services. Effective guerrilla marketing often leads to a buzz, which is authentic word-of-mouth generated by real customers who talk to their friends about a product or service.

An alternative to guerrilla marketing is viral marketing. This is an inexpensive method for a company to spread the word ('like the flu') about a product or service by recruiting customers to be its 'sales agents' and offering them an incentive to pass on a message about the company to other consumers. For example, by including the message 'Get Your Free Email at Hotmail.com' at the bottom of each email sent by Hotmail users, the company expanded its global customer base by millions in just a few months, significantly increasing its advertising revenues in the process.[2]

9.1.2 Comparing personal and mass communication

Communication can best be described as the transfer or exchange of information between organizations and people, often in an attempt to influence them. This information transfer can happen through two different channels. The first is through people; this is known as

FIGURE 9.2 A comparison of the most widely used promotion instruments

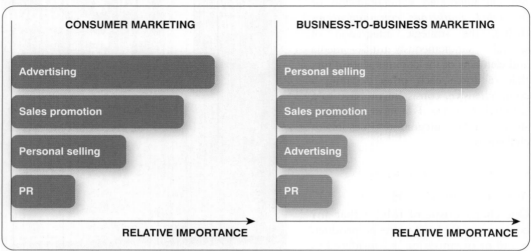

interpersonal or *personal communication*. The other channel of communication is a non-personal one involving the use of sales promotion, publicity or the **mass media**. These are media such as television and national newspapers that can, for a price, reach large target audiences.

Unfortunately, it is not possible to determine exactly who the recipients of a message are. Whenever a mass medium is used, we refer to it as *mass communication*. Since communication from person to person occurs almost exclusively through PR and personal selling, most other forms of promotion can be classified as mass communication.

Relative importance of the various communication instruments to a company will depend on whether it focuses on the consumer market or the industrial market. This is shown in Figure 9.2.

In marketing consumer goods, companies rely primarily on advertising (followed by sales promotion, personal selling and public relations). After all, mass media allows a company to reach a large audience quickly and inexpensively in terms of per contact cost. On the other hand, in business-to-business marketing, the greater part of the marketing communication budget is spent on personal selling. This particularly applies to relatively expensive products, the purchase of which involves considerable risk for buyers. Although advertising is used in the business-to-business market as well, its purpose is primarily to make potential buyers aware of the benefits of new products and to generate requests for a sales representative to call, email or visit. In both markets, the use of the Internet is steadily rising, but this is not always reflected in companies' marketing budgets.

Benefits of personal communication

The primary benefit of personal communication, which allows two-way feedback, is that a more complicated message can be communicated. Compare that to mass communication, in which it is often difficult to get one central idea across. Another advantage is that both the order in which a product's benefits are presented and the complexity of the message can be tailored to the recipient, instead of to the 'average' reader, viewer or listener. This reduces the chance that the information provided is too difficult or too simple and, therefore, insufficiently persuasive.

TABLE 9.1 Advantages and disadvantages of personal and mass communication

	Personal communication	Mass communication
Ability to reach a large audience		
Speed	Low	High
Cost per person reached	High	Low
Influence on the individual		
Ability to attract attention	High	Limited
Consistency of the message	Low	High
Probability of interest and response	High	Low
Accuracy of comprehension	High	Moderate to low
Feedback		
Direction of the message flow	Two-way	One-way
Speed of feedback	High	Low
Accuracy of feedback	High	Low

Feedback

When we compare interpersonal and mass communication, as in Table 9.1[3], it is obvious that many of the pluses and minuses boil down to the differences in feedback. First of all, mass communication allows for one-way feedback only. Another problem is that this feedback of information is not direct, but has to be organized by the sender, usually through market research. Consequently, the feedback may be slow or inaccurate.

Conversely, the advantage of personal selling is that the potential buyer can respond instantly to the sales presentation. This, in turn, enables the seller to request clarification of the response and to react immediately to the buyer's objections, thereby increasing the chance of actually influencing the buyer's attitude and behaviour. However, the cost per contact is much higher than with mass communication.

9.1.3 How does communication work?

Managers sometimes complain that half of their company's promotion budget is wasted, but they are just not sure which half it is. To better understand why a promotional message may be misunderstood or is not received by the prospects at all, we should systematically examine the various elements of the **communication process**. In the macro model of Figure 9.3, communication is portrayed as a process in which a sender or source (e.g. a sales representative or advertiser) tries to deliver a message to a receiver via a certain medium. This receiver, a potential customer, is the target of the communication, or the 'communication object'.

To increase the chances of a message being received, we have to communicate the right signals in the most effective way and at the right time. Thus, the first step is to turn the idea to be communicated into a graphic format or symbolic form, such as words, numbers and images suitable for transmission and having the same meaning for the receiver. This is known as **encoding**. To do this we choose copy (text) and an ambience (such as a candle-lit dinner) that closely matches the intended receiver's way of thinking or field of experience. The message carrying the idea is then transmitted by choosing an appropriate 'message channel' or medium: a communication channel or vehicle, which conveys the message from

FIGURE 9.3 Communication model

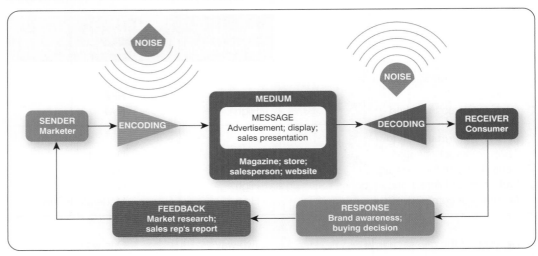

the sender to the receiver. This may be done verbally through a sales representative or through a posting on the Internet, a billboard, a weekly flyer distributed door-to-door or in the case of an advertising campaign, through advertisements in magazines and newspapers read by members of the target market.

The receiver must now *interpret* the message by uncovering the meaning of the symbols. This is called **decoding**. The words and images are 'translated' into certain information.

Image Asset Management

Since the signs and symbols in the message are converted back into ideas and concepts, *decoding* is the mirror image of encoding. Usually, people evaluate not only the message itself, but also the sender. Thus, whether or not the intended message gets across partly depends on the reliability and credibility of the source. The effectiveness of the communication is also influenced by the extent to which the sender and receiver have similar interests or share a common frame of reference ('speak the same language').

The communication process can be distorted by what is known as 'noise'. This is not necessarily sound, like the noise of a passing jet interfering with a salesman's presentation. Noise, any distraction reducing the clarity and effectiveness of the communication, has many sources and may affect all parts of the communication process. It may be caused by the medium, such as a slow Internet connection or the clutter of competing ads and pop-ups on the web. Noise can also come from competing messages or from within the message itself. This is a potential problem when symbols with which the receiver is unfamiliar are used or if those symbols have a different meaning to them than to the sender, possibly as the result of a misunderstanding between the marketer and the advertising agency. All of these cause distortion in the decoding of the message. As a result, the receiver gets a different message than the sender intended.

Once the message has been received and processed, the receiver can react to it. Their *response* can, for example, be a purchase, an increase in brand awareness or an attitude change. Through *feedback* (the element of the response that can be measured) we can find out if the 'message sent' was actually the 'message received' or if the message needs to be adjusted. Feedback takes many forms; it might consist of a smile, a nod or another expression of a listener's interest. It might be a marketing research report, a returned coupon or an online order from a consumer visiting the company's website. Marketing management needs effective feedback in order to identify and correct the causes of ineffective communication. The model discussed here can serve as a useful guideline by indicating where something can go wrong in the marketing communication process.

9.2 COMMUNICATION STRATEGY: TARGET AUDIENCE

A well-planned communication strategy involves a number of steps, as illustrated in Figure 9.4.

This chapter covers the first half of this model. We will start by examining how to identify the target audience, formulate the objectives, set the budget and determine the communication mix. These are four essential steps in developing a communication plan. The rest of the communication strategy involves developing the message, selecting the media to be used in the campaign and measuring the results, followed by making any necessary adjustments or improvements to the communication strategy. These last decisions will be discussed in Chapter 10, when we explore how to develop a company's advertising strategy.

The first step in developing a successful communication programme is to identify the communication target group or target audience. Before we can decide which promotional instruments would be most effective in realizing the communication objectives (still to be defined in detail), we need to think about the market to be targeted. What segments can we identify? Which ones are our target audiences? And, what would be the best way to reach them? Should we employ a pull or a push strategy?

The communication target audience is a specific group of people or organizations to whom the message is addressed. While this would seem to be the same as the company's target market, the communication target audience may extend beyond the target market.

PROFESSOR'S PERSPECTIVE
Don Schultz (Northwestern University, USA)

Don E. Schultz is Professor Emeritus-in-Service of Integrated Marketing Communications at Northwestern University. He has consulted and lectured in Europe, the Middle East, Asia and South America. Schultz is currently an adjunct professor at the Queensland University of Technology in Australia, and a visiting professor at the Cranfield School of Management and at Hull University's School of Business in the UK. He has been a visiting professor at Tsinghua University and Peking University in Beijing, China, and at Hanken, the Swedish School of Economics in Helsinki, Finland.

Doing marketing and communications work outside of your own borders is a tough transition. Following the different structures, systems, rules and regulations can be confusing if you haven't done it before, and not every company that hopes to find the pot of gold at the end of a foreign rainbow is a global giant with unlimited resources.

The approach used by many global newcomers is to pull up the most recent, best looking marketing communication materials that worked in the domestic market, have them translated to the local language, get a few stock photos of the 'locals' and they're good to go. And too many times, they come right back, pockets empty and sales nowhere near projections, without even having learned from the experience abroad.

I've seen it far too often: Take a domestic programme and assume that it will work in another country's economy, culture, language and marketing system. But it doesn't, and few seem to know why. When reviewing the foreign failure, you hear comments like: 'We used the most current marketing and communications thinking. We employed all the attractive communication tools that are in vogue in our own markets. Must be the customers out there in Brazil or India or Russia or Turkey or Indonesia or wherever who didn't understand. Can't be us. We know what we're doing!' They're right. They know what they're doing in Western economies. But often, those skills are simply irrelevant in an emerging market.

What to do? Ask the locals!

If this scenario sounds familiar, it should. It is a combination of my quarter-century of experience trying to help companies – no matter where they are located – go global. Looking back, the 'why did we fail?' problems can be grouped into three broad categories. First of all, South Africa, Egypt or Qatar is not really just like your home country, with only a different language. Stuff we do here often doesn't work over there, primarily because people in emerging markets are just learning to be consumers. They simply don't have the 100-year consumption background that industrialized nations' residents have.

Second, it's easy to assume that people in these markets have similar needs, wants, aspirations and motivations as their counterparts in the West. It takes more effort to really understand emerging-market customers in their own context, and even more work to adapt marketing programmes to the realities of local conditions.

Third, many organizations overlook the basics, things that make those markets different – things the locals know, but you don't. What to do? *Ask the natives*! In particular, 'natives' who have lived and studied overseas and then have to adapt Western concepts and approaches to make them work in their home countries. What they're interested in learning is: what can be used as is, what must be adapted and what should simply be ignored?

At my university, we asked a group of top graduate students from overseas to help us identify the factors that distinguish emerging markets and to develop some guidelines for marketing and communication. They analyzed ten key markets: *South Africa, Morocco, Nigeria, Egypt, Kenya, Qatar, India, China, Indonesia* and *Thailand*. Why those countries? Those are their home countries. Their reviews were extensive, and ranged from analyses of each country's infrastructure and logistical systems to the role of government and bureaucracy in marketing and communication, including media and the development of the Internet. Here are *ten takeaways* that might help any manager faced with developing a *local* programme in a *foreign* country. Many of these factors are not even mentioned in international marketing textbooks.

1. Don't count on local consumer research. It either doesn't exist or is fake.

2. If your company has a local database, it may not be very good. Analytical skills are lacking in many of these markets.

3. Communal – not individualistic – values dominate in emerging markets. Ignore the local culture at your own risk.

4. There are many bureaucratic hurdles, such as paperwork and red tape, for even the simplest decision.

5. High levels of corruption exist and are simply accepted.

6. There is a huge shadow market for almost everything. In some countries, the grey market is as large as the actual marketplace. Tax collection is sporadic and avoiding taxes a national pastime in some markets.

7. There is limited regulation and enforcement of copyrights, patents and other intellectual property rights – and often, little recourse.

8. Print is not dead in many markets, but television still rules for the mass market.

9. Digital and social media are growing quickly and mobile is everywhere.

10. In many countries, you simply can't get from here to there. A lack of infrastructure means much marketing must be local or regional at best.

That's just a glimpse of what these 'natives of somewhere else' say that Western marketers must consider if they really want to succeed in these foreign markets. So here's some good advice to anyone planning an emerging-market strategy: Ask the natives, and look for the ones who know and understand both the native and outsider views of the world.[4]

Organizations not only communicate with customers and those who influence the customers, but also with other stakeholders, such as channel partners, investors and (potential) employees. Therefore, we often make a distinction between the *primary* target audience (the receivers in which we are most interested) and the *secondary* target audience. The latter may be less crucial to the organization, yet can play an important role in achieving the corporate objectives.

An effective promotional strategy can only be developed if we keep the target audience in mind. From this perspective, we will now look more closely at the differences between a pull strategy and a push strategy. After that, we will explore the two-step flow model of communication.

9.2.1 Pull and push strategies

A company can either concentrate its promotional efforts on consumers or on intermediary channel members. This will, of course, affect the communication mix. We therefore distinguish between two different communication strategies, known as a pull and a push strategy. These two approaches are illustrated in Figure 9.5.

FIGURE 9.4 Steps in developing a communication strategy

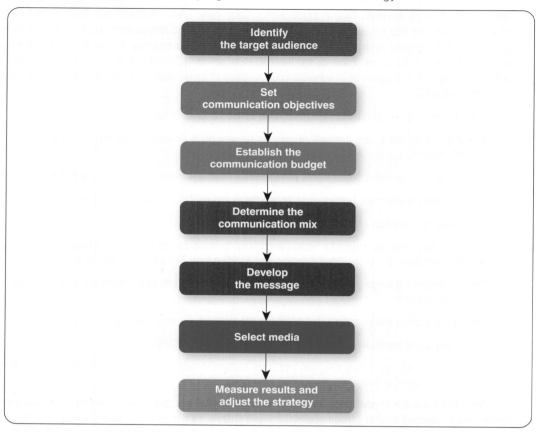

FIGURE 9.5 Pull strategy versus push strategy

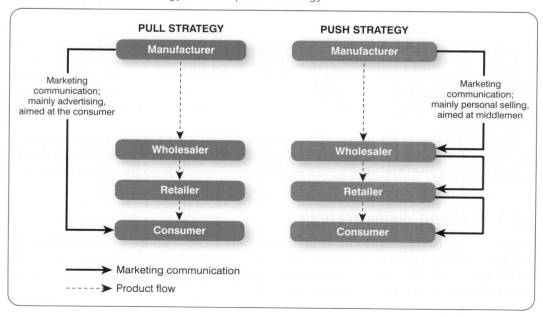

Image Asset Management

A **pull strategy** allows a manufacturer to target ultimate consumers directly – over the heads of distributors, through an advertising campaign – to stimulate demand and encourage buyers to ask for its product or brand at the retail level. This, in turn, puts pressure on the distribution channel. Retailers, facing demand from consumers, will want to carry the product or service and will order it from wholesalers. These middlemen are then 'forced' to place an order with the manufacturer, in effect helping to pull the product through the channel. The product's national advertising campaign is sometimes supported by sales promotion (such as the distribution of free samples) or other elements of the promotional mix to further motivate resellers to provide the product. In today's competitive market, more and more new products find a place on the jam-packed shelves of supermarkets because of the manufacturer's pull strategy.

In contrast, a **push strategy** primarily relies on personal selling through account managers or sales representatives. Here, the manufacturer's objective is to convince the wholesaler – or whatever middleman is at the next level in the distribution channel – to carry and sell the merchandise, by giving them attractive trade discounts or other purchasing incentives. The wholesaler, in turn, pushes the product forward by persuading retailers, usually by offering them cooperative advertising allowances or other types of support, to include the item in their assortments. The retailer then uses advertising, leaflets, displays and other in-store promotional instruments to encourage consumers to buy the product. Of course, a customer-oriented manufacturer or importer using this approach will still keep the ultimate target market (i.e. consumers) in mind when making marketing decisions. The push strategy is widely used for industrial or business products, as well as for consumer goods such as furniture and clothing.

Actually, marketers seldom have to choose exclusively between these two extremes. Instead, the emphasis will be on either a pull or a push strategy. Most manufacturers have both an advertising budget and a sales budget. They use a combination of these marketing instruments to influence various target groups. Ultimately, their marketing communication mix will depend largely on the distribution channels used.

9.2.2 *Two-step flow of communication*

Although companies often use marketing communication just to *inform* or *remind* target markets of a product or service, another frequent goal of communication strategies is to *persuade* potential buyers, trying to influence their attitudes and behaviour. Communication research has resulted in two models of the persuasion process: the 'one-step flow' and 'two-step flow' of communication models.

One-step flow model

Most communication models in the marketing literature are forms of the one-step flow model. This applies to the overall model of the communication process (as earlier shown in Figure 9.3), as well as to the response hierarchy models discussed in the upcoming section 9.3. The 'one step' in the one-step flow model means that the organization or sender *directly* addresses the consumer as the receiver of the message. This classic model is closely linked to the *stimulus-response mechanism* from psychology: it assumes that a mass medium (stimulus) has a strong and direct effect (response) on the target audience.

Two-step flow model

Research has shown that in many cases information or ideas reach the target audience through *opinion leaders*. These are individuals who, because of their expertise in a particular field or knowledge about a product or service category, have a great influence on the attitudes and behaviour of others. Since opinion leaders tend to talk to other consumers about the products or services that interest them, the information transfer in these situations takes place primarily by *word-of-mouth*.

The **two-step flow model** of the communication process, shown in Figure 9.6, reflects this additional step. It suggests that mass media influence on consumer behaviour is limited and that marketing communication should, in fact, be directed towards opinion leaders who will hopefully pass the information they have learned on to the wider public.

Opinion leaders are an important group for marketers. They are not only among the first buyers of a new product, but also play a key role as *gatekeepers* who filter information before passing it on to others. Although information circulated by opinion leaders often influences purchase decisions of other consumers more than advertising and other promotion tools, it is almost impossible for companies to control or influence this form of communication.

Marketers unfortunately find the usefulness of the two-step model limited for other reasons, too. Opinion leaders – with their narrow areas of interest – vary per product

FIGURE 9.6 Two-step flow of communication model

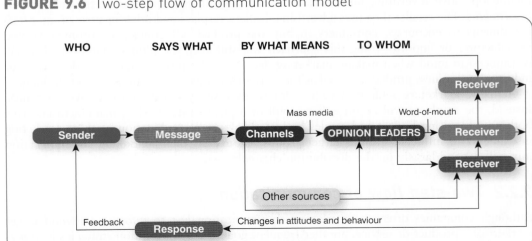

PRACTITIONER'S PERSPECTIVE
John Bissell (Gunderson Partners)

John Bissell is a former managing partner at Gundersen Partners, a marketing consulting and executive recruitment firm.

'In today's Internet world of instant communication and information, consumers from all over the world want – or even *demand* – open, honest and timely two-way communication with the companies that make the products they buy. It didn't used to be that way. For decades, the new product development and marketing success model was a totally impersonal process: Develop a Unique Selling Proposition … translate the USP into effective advertising … run commercials on television … build trial … and wait a couple of years to start making a profit. Except for commissioned market research, there was no real need for corporate management – or even for marketing people – to have any *direct contact* with consumers. Even *retailers*, the only people who did interface with consumers, were excluded from the corporate communication channel, and very few executives ever officially set foot in the stores where their new products were sold.

Consumers demand open and honest communication with companies

A lot of today's CEOs were raised and educated in this inward-directed environment. But they increasingly realize that bland, safe relationships with customers are dead. Today, markets are *conversations*. Brand loyalty is not something that a firm owns. It is built on respect, and largely based on how the company has conducted itself in conversations with the market.

The traditional distinction between manufacturing companies and service companies is rapidly breaking down. To-day's marketers are learning that all companies are in the *customer service* business, whether they like it or not. Be-cause of this trend, there are many international career opportunities for marketing people with service industry experience to make a meaningful contribution to production companies. Besides, managing this *ongoing dialogue* between the company and its customers should no longer be a specialized and separate task of the public relations or customer relations department. This is all about *marketing*. In fact, it's a more crucial component of *brand building* than any advertising or promotion programme.

Encouraging this type of open consumer dialogue is also a great way for marketing people to interact with their consumers, look for ideas on new products and product improvements and detect early warning signs on emerging problems in the company-customer relationship. Of course, the *Internet* is the perfect vehicle to initiate this conversation from anywhere in the world. Smart marketers are seeing the Internet not as a place to sell or advertise, but as a way to provide and *collect information* and open up a highly efficient two-way global *communications channel* with their customers. It can especially be useful in *innovation* and brand building.

I remember someone telling me once that for every complaint letter a firm receives, there are 200 other consumers who are thinking the same way but did not take the time to write. With that in mind, when I was still working at Procter & Gamble, we used to do detailed analyses on the content of the thirty or so 'comments' (P&G-language

for complaint letters, since the company refused to acknowledge that anyone would really complain) received each month on a typical detergent brand.

Guess what? Now brand managers have the pleasure of talking to thousands of these people every month! *Interactive marketing* is a lot more fun and also much more productive than analyzing consumer letters, but you'd better carve out some time on your calendar! Customers across the globe want to talk with you'...[5]

category and, in terms of socio-demographic and psychographic characteristics, differ only slightly from 'followers', making it difficult to identify them. It is also complicated to reach them (there is no 'Opinion Leaders Weekly' magazine to which they all subscribe!). Further, the followers do not rely solely on opinion leaders, but on other sources of information as well. For example, their consumption patterns are also influenced by the 'trickle down' effect from the higher social classes in society. In conclusion, with the limited impact of the mass media on consumer buying behaviour, it is by no means easy to develop an effective marketing communication strategy!

9.3 SETTING COMMUNICATION OBJECTIVES

Decisions about the communication strategy can only be made if we have clearly defined communication goals. Many corporate conflicts related to strategy development and implementation are caused by the lack of operational objectives. Without clear goals, there are neither criteria for decision making nor measurement standards for evaluating the effectiveness of promotional campaigns. Therefore, we should first spell out in detail what we want to accomplish.

It is tempting to express communication or advertising objectives in terms of a desired increase in *sales*. That would also make it easy to later determine the effectiveness of a campaign. However, reaching a sales goal is not necessarily an indication of advertising performance, since other factors also influence sales, including product availability, competition and price. Therefore, a sales target is more of a **marketing objective** than an advertising objective. And of course, advertising is just one of the many available tools to realize marketing objectives.

There is no direct link between sales volume and a single marketing instrument. So, how should we formulate the advertising or **communication objectives**? Although they are derived from the overall marketing goals, it is advisable to express communication objectives in terms of what we want to achieve with the communication campaign as specifically as possible, such as a particular advertising recall, product recognition or brand awareness. An example of expressing an advertising objective as a specific communication task is 'to increase *unaided brand awareness* from 18 per cent to 30 per cent among the primary target audience in the next six weeks.' Other examples of desired 'communication effects' – which may be expressed as objectives – are changing consumers' attitudes towards the brand (for example, when pursuing a repositioning strategy to create an upscale *brand image* in the target market) and stimulating *buying intention* ('To get one in five households to the point where they are planning to purchase the product in the next thirty days'). The relationship between advertising and these variables is much more direct and *measurable* than the relationship between advertising and actual sales. Besides, not every promotional message is intended to make consumers buy something right away.

It is clear that we have to formulate separate objectives for each marketing communications effort, assuming that different programmes are developed for individual brands, models, product lines and, in a global marketing strategy, for different countries and customer groups. In order to better understand how the target audience might react to a marketing communication campaign, in stating the communication objectives, we should look at a logical hierarchy of possible effects of our communication efforts. These consumer reactions or responses generally take place in a set order, with a reinforcing effect (known as a *learning* or *response hierarchy*). Response hierarchies suggest that potential buyers have to be led through a series of steps before they actually purchase a product or service. To effectively use this in our promotional strategy development, we can draw on several **communication models**. These reveal the relationship between communication and the buying decision process. Here, we make a distinction between two categories, the classic response hierarchy models and the non-classic response hierarchy models of the learning process.

9.3.1 *Classic response hierarchy models*

A **classic response hierarchy model** (or *hierarchy of effects model*) suggests that the consumer always passes through certain stages of learning – in a fixed sequence – before making a purchase. First they acquire information or knowledge (*cognition*), followed by appreciation or liking (*affection*) and finally progressing to the willingness to take action (*conation*, or the behaviour stage). Through its communication strategy an organization can influence the consumer's decision-making process by moving them step-by-step further up the ladder from awareness to action. The best-known classic response hierarchy models (also called 'learning models') are the AIDA model (developed by Strong in 1925) and the hierarchy-of-effects model, developed by Lavidge and Steiner. They are essentially very similar.

The AIDA model

The **AIDA model** – often used to help structure sales presentations – describes the steps a person goes through before making a buying decision. As shown in Figure 9.7, the consumer's information processing and decision-making usually involve four stages, leading to a more positive attitude towards the product or an actual purchase. These stages are expressed by the acronym AIDA: attention, interest, desire and action. The exhibit also indicates how a firm can express its promotional objectives in each of these stages.

In purchasing situations in which a buyer goes through this entire process, the marketer first has to capture the potential buyer's attention (for example, through sports sponsorship). Then, a promotional message (such as an advertisement or publicity) should arouse interest in the product or service. At the next stage, the firm should stimulate the desire to own the product or use the service by convincing the consumer of the product's ability to satisfy their needs and wants. The main challenge in marketing remains to actually convert a prospect's willingness to buy into an actual product purchase (for example, through sales promotion).

FIGURE 9.7 The AIDA model

Formula	Stages	Possible objectives
A	Attention	Get noticed
I	Interest	Raise curiosity
D	Desire	Stimulate a craving for the product
A	Action	Make consumers buy

Lavidge and Steiner's hierarchy-of-effects model

The *hierarchy-of-effects model* (or the 'Lavidge-Steiner model') is actually an expanded version of the AIDA model, because it proposes more steps and potential responses. As indicated in Table 9.2, the model identifies six stages in the buyer's adoption process: *awareness, knowledge, liking, preference, conviction* and *purchase*. The first five stages relate to the awareness and attitude formation, which precede any purchase. Advertisers often use this model in setting advertising objectives and choosing effective communication themes in the various stages that the consumer passes through, as well as in measuring their effects.

The hierarchy-of-effects model is also a useful tool in marketing research. The right-hand column of Table 9.2 presents some questions which consumers could be asked in a communication feedback study. At the same time, the questions could be used to determine the level at which consumers are in the hierarchy of communication effects. Clearly, if a

TABLE 9.2 Lavidge -Steiner's hierarchy-of-effects model

Level	Description and task	Possible questions
1 Awareness	Extent to which the consumer knows the product, the brand or its manufacturer. *Brand awareness can be increased by frequently repeating the brand name in a simple advertising message; however, this may take some time.*	a. Unaided recall: what brands of notebooks can you name? b. Aided recall: have you ever heard of Dell notebooks?
2 Knowledge	Does the consumer know what the product has to offer? Exactly how many features are known and what does the target market think about the product? *Transmitting information is the main communication objective at this stage.*	a. How much internal memory does the Dell Inspiron E1405 have? b. Does the Dell Inspiron E1405 have an Intel Core Duo Processor?
3 Liking	Does the consumer have a positive or negative attitude towards the product? *Only with a thorough insight in this can the marketer make any necessary product changes and develop an effective message.*	Please indicate on the following scale how you feel about a Dell notebook: → very positive → somewhat positive → no opinion/ neither positive or negative → somewhat negative → very negative
4 Preference	The extent to which the target market not only likes the product, but actually prefers it over other brands. *A marketing communication strategy can emphasize product performance, price, quality or other characteristics. The preference should be measured before as well as after the campaign.*	If you were going to buy a notebook today, please indicate, by putting a (different) number between 1 and 5 in front of each brand, which brand you prefer most (1) and least (5)? → Toshiba → Lenovo → Dell → Apple → HP
5 Conviction	Consumers could actually prefer a certain product, but – due to circumstances (such as lack of money or conflicting advice) – may not intend to buy it. *The marketer must convince the target audience that the purchase makes sense.*	Could you indicate on a scale of 0 to 100 – on which 0 means: no chance at all and 100 that you are completely sure about it – how great the chance is that you will actually buy a Dell notebook in the next six months?
6 Purchase	Some consumers may be convinced that the product is a 'good buy', but end up delaying its purchase. *The marketer has to persuade the prospects to act through an attractive promotional offer or proposition.*	a. Did you purchase a notebook? b. What brand of notebook did you buy?

marketer directs a promotion campaign for a new product towards a target audience of, for example, a million consumers, a part of this group will drop out at each stage, because not everyone exposed to a medium will carefully read or listen to the message and absorb the information. And even among those who do so and may actually have a need for the product, not everyone will change their attitude or buy the product or service.

A comparison of classic response hierarchy models

The relationship between the AIDA model and the Lavidge-Steiner hierarchy-of-effects model is apparent from the left-hand column of Figure 9.8, where the stages in the models are classified based on the dimensions of knowledge, feeling and behaviour. As discussed in the analysis of attitudes in Chapter 4, when formulating communication objectives, we may attempt to evoke a *cognitive* response (the easiest one to attain), an *affective* response or a *conative* response.

The *cognitive* stage in the response hierarchy addresses the ability of a target audience to process information. Initially, the consumers to be targeted are not familiar with the brand. Thus, the first impression or perception of the brand takes place in this stage. Prospective buyers are made aware of the product and get to know it better. Their cognitive responses consist of the thoughts that occur at this learning stage (essentially awareness, knowledge and comprehension).

In the *affective* stage of consumers' information processing, the product or brand is being evaluated. In this pre-use phase, consumers form a positive or a negative judgement about it. The feelings, emotions or moods aroused as consumers assess the product (or when exposed to another stimulus, such as a TV commercial), are called the affective response (such as interest, liking, conviction).

FIGURE 9.8 Relationship between the classic response hierarchy models

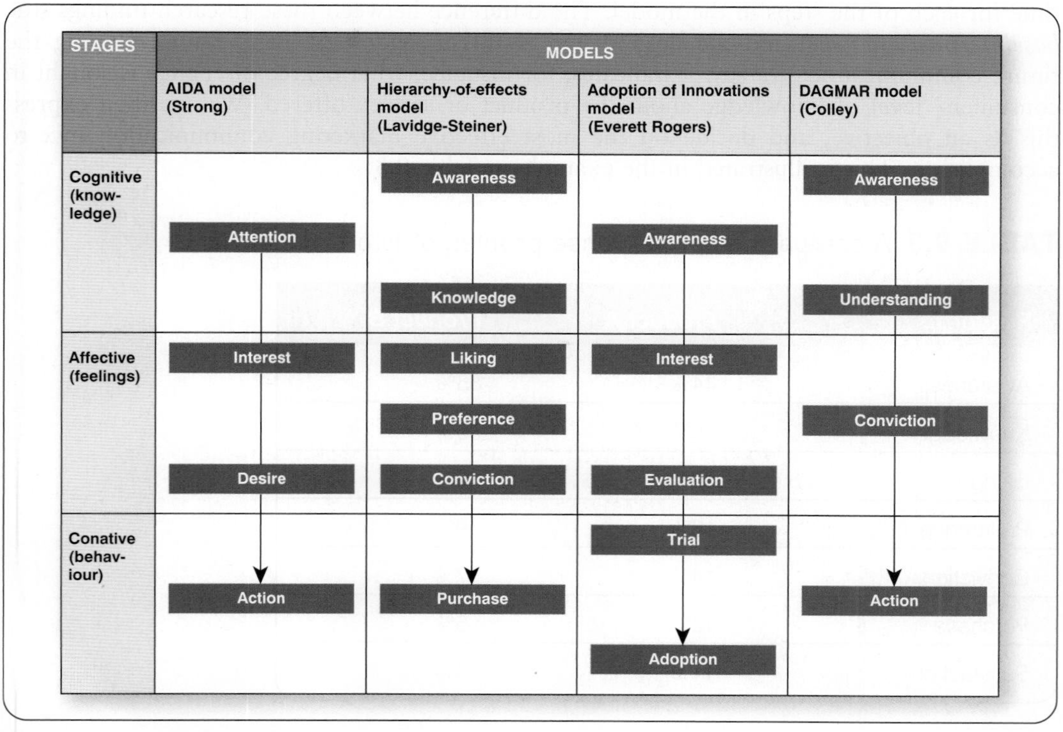

Finally, in the behaviour or *conative* stage, consumers decide how to react. Their experiences and responses may be negative, resulting in a decision not to buy an advertised brand. Alternatively, a positive response may lead to an actual purchase, the intention to buy or, for example, a visit to the dealer resulting in a trial or purchase at a later time. From a marketer's perspective, this is the most difficult stage through which to move a potential buyer.

To complete the overview, in the last two columns of Figure 9.8, two additional classic models of the response process are outlined, on which we will not elaborate here. The *adoption of innovations* model (by Everett Rogers) was already discussed in section 8.6.1. Finally, the *DAGMAR* model (by Colley) will be presented in Chapter 10, where we will look again at defining advertising goals.

9.3.2 *Implications for promotional strategies*

Objectives are only useful if they are correctly formulated. They must always be *concrete*, and *measurable*. Only then can we determine in time whether our objectives have been achieved. Thus, a good promotional objective should precisely define the target audience and specify in quantitative terms (as a desired percentage change, relative to a certain benchmark) what we want to accomplish and within what time period. In addition, the objectives related to the various elements of the communication mix should be *complementary*: they should supplement each other in a logical fashion. We therefore must determine in advance what the roles of advertising, sales promotion, sponsorship, online marketing and other activities should be in realizing the communication objectives and overall marketing goals.

As an aid in defining communication objectives and afterwards measuring the results, we can use one of the *response hierarchy models* just discussed. For example, an objective may be aimed at building awareness, creating interest or getting potential buyers to act. First, through marketing research, we measure the starting position at that particular point in time for each of the steps in the model. The difference between these research findings (the *baseline measurement*) and the desired end results provides the basis for developing the future communication strategy. It indicates, for instance, what degree of change is sought in consumers' level of knowledge about the product or service offered. We can then express this as an objective, and decide on the most effective marketing communication mix to accomplish it. This is illustrated in the example in Table 9.3.

TABLE 9.3 A comparison of response profiles of two products

Response	Product A	Product B
Awareness	44%	85%
Knowledge	35%	55%
Liking	20%	18%
Preference	16%	9%
Conviction	14%	7%
Purchase	12%	5%
Satisfaction	11%	4%

Market research shows that two products have the following profiles on the total target market (equal to 100 per cent).

Here, an extra dimension has been added to the six stages of the *hierarchy-of-effects* model. It expresses the extent to which consumers are *satisfied* with their purchases (an important concern for any marketer wanting to succeed in the long run). The percentages in this overview are cumulative. To illustrate, it means that for product A, 11 per cent of the *entire target market* is satisfied. At the same time, 25 per cent (11 of 44) of the consumers in the target market who are aware of the product are satisfied. This second percentage is much more meaningful; after all, how can you be satisfied or dissatisfied with a product you don't know?

Product B's profile shows that although many consumers know something about the product (55 per cent knowledge), they are not very enthusiastic about it (only 18 per cent liking). Hence, the message or some product attributes definitely need to be changed. In contrast, product A appears to be better liked by consumers, but, unfortunately, few people (only 44 per cent) have heard about it.

One could conclude from this analysis of product A that increasing brand awareness is a much needed communication objective. A national advertising campaign might be an effective **communication instrument** to accomplish this. If, given a different set of circumstances, the number one objective is to increase the number of trial purchases, a more appropriate strategy would be to use sales promotion activities to motivate prospects to try the new product or service.

To measure the results achieved, companies rely on market research. Comments received directly from customers, such as those received through the company's website, also provide a valuable indication of the degree of satisfaction among buyers. Unilever, for example, has created a special department (the Consumer Care Centre in Rotterdam), which annually responds to hundreds of thousands of questions, complaints and suggestions received by telephone, mail and email. Given the huge number of customer comments requiring an immediate response, the department itself has become an important marketing tool for the company.

9.3.3 *Non-classic response hierarchy models*

Research into buying behaviour shows that consumers do not always pass through the cognitive, affective and conative stages in that order. Sometimes, this standard learning or response hierarchy is not automatically followed, particularly in situations where:

→ The consumer is not very involved with the product or purchase. Here, the *low- involvement hierarchy* applies.

→ The available products or services from which the consumer has to choose are perceived to be very similar and the buyer experiences *cognitive dissonance*. Here the dissonance hierarchy applies.

Figure 9.9 reveals the order in which consumers pass through the response hierarchy in those situations. These two alternative hierarchies – as proposed by the *low-involvement theory* and the *dissonance reduction theory* – will now be briefly explained.

Low-involvement hierarchy

Gasoline, laundry detergents and other *low-involvement* products are bought routinely because to consumers, most brands seem to be about the same. In this 'low-involvement decision-making', consumers tend to continue buying a familiar and trusted brand.

FIGURE 9.9 Alternatively ordered response hierarchies

CLASSIC RESPONSE HIERARCHY MODEL	LOW-INVOLVEMENT HIERARCHY	DISSONANCE HIERARCHY
Cognitive (knowledge)	**Cognitive** ├─ Awareness └─ Knowledge (passive)	**Conative** ├─ Awareness └─ Purchase
Affective (attitude)	**Conative** └─ Purchase	**Affective** ├─ Liking ├─ Preference └─ Conviction
Conative (behaviour)	**Affective** ├─ Liking ├─ Preference └─ Conviction	**Cognitive** └─ Knowledge

However, if the consumer does switch to another brand, the most likely order in which they pass through the stages in this so-called *low-involvement hierarchy* are: *cognitive* stage (awareness, with some knowledge of the brand), *conative* stage (purchase) and *affective* stage (liking, preference, conviction). To illustrate, a consumer may have found out about a new brand through advertising or a supermarket promotion, buys the product and then is satisfied when using it. Only afterwards do they change their attitude towards the brand ('I'm glad I tried Dreft. I like it better than my previous brand of detergent.'). Chances are they will then continue to buy the new brand.

As opposed to following the stages in the classic response hierarchy, the buyer *acts* first and only then determines their attitude. The buyer, in effect, takes a risk, as is often the case with relatively simple products. These items are usually in the maturity stage of the product life cycle. In order to influence the consumer's buying decision under these circumstances, firms have to make sure that the brand name has a familiar sound to it (a communication objective) and that the product's quality at least meets that of competing brands. The greatest challenge is to entice the consumer to buy.

Dissonance hierarchy

Characteristic of the *dissonance hierarchy* – also known as *dissonance reduction theory* or the dissonance/attribution model – is the buyer's high involvement with the product or purchase process, coupled with a quick purchase decision. They try to act to the best of their ability. However, the buyer experiences a feeling of anxiety called *cognitive dissonance*, because there is not much difference between competing brands, the differences are hard to see or because they don't know what exactly to look for when making a choice. To get rid of this negative feeling, they are inclined towards dissonance reducing behaviour. One option is to make their attitude consistent with the purchase decision made. They learn to appreciate the product while using it and then start looking for information to justify their decision.

MARKETING MISTAKE
Benecol: Failing Functional Food?

© Chris Pancewicz / Alamy

Do you know what *Benecol* is? For the uninformed, it's a light margarine that can help lower your cholesterol. It was first introduced and test marketed in *Finland* and is now available in 26 countries. With well-substantiated proof of its benefits and a proven track record in Europe, McNeil Consumer Products believed they had a hit on their hands and also introduced the new product in the US, the company's largest and most competitive market. But in spite of a big advertising budget and an extensive public relations campaign during the product's launch, the brand soon went into a downward spiral. What went wrong?

The product's limited success reflects the firm's inability to put itself in the customer's shoes

Much of the product's initial lack of success is related to an ineffective marketing communication strategy, which seems to reflect the company's inability to put itself in the customer's shoes. The first and most obvious problem is the *brand name*. Benecol just doesn't sound appetizing, and to many consumers, it sounds more like a cough medicine than margarine. Apparently, McNeil wanted the brand to sound as if it offered benefits beyond just being low fat. The name is derived from 'Benefits Cholesterol'; hence 'Bene-col', and falls into the category that marketers call 'functional foods'. But the name fails to actually make the product's benefits clear to consumers. Compare that with a similar, but competing product from Unilever's Lipton division, *Take Control*, which, to potential buyers, is a much more direct and meaningful brand name.

The company's *packaging* decisions have not helped the product either. At first, the new margarine from Finland was sold in a package with an illustration of a mountain valley, which seemed to promote country living rather than a healthy lifestyle. Even after changing this, the understated package graphics – with a lime green colour that some people associate with mould in dairy products – did not increase market penetration.

The *pricing* strategy for Benecol Spread may be another obstacle to marketing success. It is priced much higher than other margarines. First introduced as a package of twenty-one individual servings in portion control cups, the product sold for around $5.79 in the US market. This worked out to $14.35 a pound. That was nearly twice as much as a comparable package of Take Control, which was launched at $7.98 a pound. The price difference contributed to a consumer perception of Benecol being an expensive product. And consumer perception is hard to change, even after several price reductions.

Brand name, packaging and price aside, the real problem may be as simple as Benecol being perceived by consumers as *irrelevant* to their needs. For a product like Benecol to catch on (especially with such a high retail price), the benefits must be repeatedly emphasized. But the company failed to do that. And unfortunately for Benecol, most consumers don't worry about their cholesterol level, even when told it's 'too high.' Many people don't visit their physician on a regular basis, and they do not know their cholesterol levels. Without a *perceived need* for the product in the target market, an effective marketing strategy is crucial for the product to survive. But the marketing strategy did not seem to be well planned either.

Before the brand was even established with its *unique selling proposition* (that the product reduces the 'bad' LDL cholesterol), McNeil Consumer Products began introducing new items in other product categories. The margarine had barely reached store shelves when four varieties of Benecol Salad Dressing were launched: Creamy Italian, Thousand Island, Ranch and French Style. Then came Benecol Snack Bars in three flavours: Peanut Crisp, Wild Strawberry and Chocolate Crisp.

History and common sense tell us this *brand extension strategy* was a mistake. Virtually no marketer has ever successfully launched multiple products across product categories simultaneously, or one right after the other. For example, brands like Healthy Choice from ConAgra and

SnackWell's from Nabisco were introduced in one basic category at a time. After *Healthy Choice* had established a position in the healthy frozen meal category, it expanded with more than 300 brand extensions, including packs of hamburger, cereals and ice cream. *SnackWell's* staked out its image and a successful following for low fat or no fat cookies in its manufacturer's area of strength. Only then was it extended into more than 125 other products.

To turn the tide, McNeil's marketers have been promoting the line through *physicians* and other healthcare professionals. But it may be too little too late. Despite a top margin return, supermarkets may not continue to offer the brand shelf space if it gets virtually no promotion at the retail level and continues to show slow sales. It's now up to the consumer to keep the Benecol line alive despite the initial marketing mistakes. Either that, or the company should come up with a more effective marketing strategy to communicate the healthier living benefit. If that doesn't happen, a functional food item from – originally – Finland may disappear from the global marketplace.[6]

This situation often occurs with durable consumer goods in the growth stage, or at the beginning of the maturity stage in the product life cycle. If, for example, a very busy, career-oriented individual wants to buy a smartphone, they may – influenced by the sales person – make a quick decision so they won't have to spend hours comparing the dozens of available cell phones. After the purchase they collect the necessary information (for instance, by reading the instruction manual or visiting the manufacturer's website) and, only then, finds out more about the brand and actually develops a preference for it. Thus, the buyer passes through the cognitive stage at the very end of the learning hierarchy. In conclusion, consumers do not always act rationally and progress through the hierarchy of effects in a logical sequence. Customer-oriented managers should consider these exceptions to the rule when defining marketing communication objectives.

9.4 ESTABLISHING THE COMMUNICATION BUDGET

Once the objectives have been defined, the organization has to decide how much it should spend on marketing communication. This is a difficult decision, as one product or service may need more promotional support than another. Also, the competition and other environmental conditions, such as the industry growth rate and the firm's position in the marketplace, may vary by product and by sector. Moreover, it is not easy to measure the effectiveness of a promotional campaign. Therefore, a rule of thumb for determining the optimal budget for marketing communication is of little use. Yet, advertising expenditures must be allocated like any other business expense.

Theoretically, there is a solution to the problem of setting a budget, as research has shown a link between promotion expenditures and sales. For example, some managers try to track the effects of their advertising campaigns by using a **sales response model**. This model describes

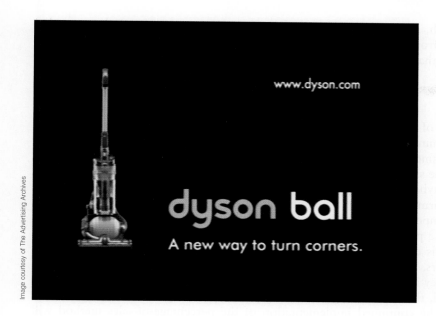

the impact of advertising expenditures on the sales level of an advertised product. It shows, among other things, that an increase in the promotion budget only has a significant effect after a *minimum threshold* has been reached. We also know that the increased effectiveness, after a continued rise in the level of expenditures, starts to drop again at a particular point. In the real world, however, it is not easy to come up with reliable estimates of sales or profits for any given promotion budget. Hence, the return on investment for communication expenditures is not clear, especially because a budget can be spent in different ways.

Many managers therefore apply their own rules and assumptions in budget development. Most assume that a certain degree of repetition of an advertising message is necessary before a campaign has any effect at all. But different methods are used to set the communication budget. The most widely used techniques in business are the percentage-of-sales method, the affordable method, the competitive-parity method and the objective-and-task method.

9.4.1 Percentage-of-sales method

One of the most common ways to establish a promotion budget is to calculate the budget as a percentage of either past or projected sales. If a firm sets the marketing communication budget equal to 5 per cent of the previous year's sales, and sales last year were five million euros, then the budget for the coming year will be 250 000 euros.

To illustrate, Van Melle (producer of *Mentos* and other candy products) tries to keep its budgeting simple by allocating 15 per cent of sales to advertising (almost entirely spent on television commercials). With sales exceeding half a billion euros, this amounts to quite a budget! An alternative to this method is to earmark a percentage of profits for establishing the promotion budget. Still other companies set aside a fixed amount per product (such as per car sold), which ultimately also results in a fixed percentage of sales.

Advantages

The percentage-of-sales method has several advantages. First, it is a clear and *simple* method of budgeting. The amount to be spent on promotion can be seen at a glance. Second, it is a *safe* and affordable method. The firm does not need to worry about overspending, because the maximum budget is in line with its financial resources. Finally, if all major competitors use the same approach, it creates *stability* in the level of promotion within the industry. It prevents competitors from trying to outdo one another with ever higher budgets. Especially in a saturated market that has nearly reached its potential, such an advertising war would be pointless.

Disadvantages

The major drawback of the percentage-of-sales method is that the level of *sales* – with a year's delay – determines the level of promotion, while this should be the other way around. Since the assumed causal sequence of effects is reversed, it's putting the cart before the horse. After all, the sales level is, partially, the result of the promotion expenditures. And if sales lag behind, maybe more (rather than less) should be spent on promotion.

Sometimes, the firm's marketing communication budget needs to be temporarily increased because competitors raise their budgets or because of other developments in the environment. With the percentage-of-sales method, this can only be done if the percentage itself is increased. This decision is not easily made, as in many firms the same percentage has been used for years.

If not enough money is spent on promotion, there's a risk that the company will go into a downward sales spiral, thereby creating a declining promotion budget which in turn results in decreasing sales. The continued implementation of the percentage-of-sales method will then only perpetuate the mistake. Conversely, companies that systematically overspend on promotion will continue to waste money. Nevertheless, given its advantages, the percentage-of-sales method can provide a useful starting point for budget development.

If, despite the drawbacks, this budgeting method is used, it is preferable that a percentage of projected sales be allocated rather than a percentage of last year's sales. In this way, the marketing communication expenditures are tied to current and future activities rather than to those of past years.

9.4.2 Affordable method

Some small firms with limited financial resources and working capital use the affordable or *all-you-can-afford* method in setting the promotion budget. Their marketing communication expenditures are dependent on the available funds. Under this approach, whatever cash is left after budgeting for fixed expenses and a reasonable profit is allocated to promotion. If other expenditures (such as for product development) start demanding a larger share of the firm's resources, this may unfortunately be at the expense of promotion. Similarly, if any cuts have to be made, promotion, being no more than a balancing item, is often the first casualty.

Although this approach may seem safe, a disadvantage is that the budget can vary enormously from one year to the next. More importantly, it is unrelated to the promotional objectives or the firm's other marketing functions, which makes long- term planning impossible. Also, the firm could miss opportunities to generate extra sales because of underspending, or it could easily spend too much, since profitability is not even considered in budgeting. Some small businesses may not have any choice, but – because of the lack of any market orientation – the affordable method is a poor solution to the task of setting the budget.

9.4.3 Competitive-parity method

In industries dominated by a small number of large companies, firms tend to set their communication budgets based on that of the leading competitor, either in absolute amounts or relative to the firms' market shares. To illustrate, if the market leader spends an estimated

4 per cent of sales on advertising, then that ratio of advertising costs to sales is taken as the industry norm. As a result, a firm that, for example, books 20 per cent of total sales in the entire industry, will also be responsible for 20 per cent of the sector's overall promotional spending. The assumption behind this so-called competitive parity or *meeting competition* method is that the industry leader has the most accurate and timely market information and is likely to have set its promotion budget in an optimal way. Also, managers are typically hesitant to depart from the industry norm out of fear that, if they did, it would cause a competitive price or advertising war among competing firms. Most of them prefer the more conservative strategy of maintaining the status quo.

Advantages

The competitive-parity method is easy to implement because it does not require complicated sales forecasts or appraisals of future market conditions. The budget is given, provided that we know (or are able to estimate, based on rivals' annual reports, trade journals and other publications) how much the industry leader spends on promotion. An indirect benefit of this approach is that it forces management to keep track of competitors' marketing activities and to carefully consider their own company's share in the total promotion spending.

A company's *advertising share* plays an important part in the battle for market share. As long as a firm keeps pace with the level of expenditures of its rivals, it will, most likely, prevent them from making inroads into the firm's market share and causing a drastic change in its market position.

Disadvantages

Many of the drawbacks of the percentage-of-sales method also apply to the competitive-parity method. For instance, if the industry as a whole has been spending less on promotion than the optimal level, a large potential market may remain untapped; the opportunity cost of not taking advantage of this may be immense. On the other hand, perhaps all the firms in the industry are overspending, particularly if the industry has reached the maturity stage in its life cycle.

A more fundamental problem with the competitive-parity method is the assumption that the products and services of the competing companies are perceived as identical. The reality is that – although the firms may be selling comparable products or services at comparable prices – the brand images, perceived benefits as well as the types of customers who are loyal to a particular firm may differ substantially. Moreover, a customer's brand preference will not only be influenced by the number of advertisements placed, but also by the choice of media, creative appeal, corporate image, distribution strategy and other key elements of the marketing strategy.

9.4.4 Objective-and-task method

The best but most difficult method of setting the advertising or promotion budget is the *objective-and-task* method. Instead of splitting a particular budget among various promotional instruments – as in the three previously discussed 'top-down' approaches – this budgeting method specifically ties the company's promotional spending to its marketing communication objectives. It is therefore considered a 'build-up' approach. In using the objective-and-task approach, we first determine exactly what communication goals we wish to achieve (the 'objectives'), then, which activities are required to realize them (the 'task') and, as a final step, add up how much those will cost (the budget).

To illustrate, if the marketing plan calls for increasing the brand awareness of our products by 20 per cent we must first establish – through a combination of marketing research, experience and good judgment – what advertising messages have to be communicated, how often and through which media in order to reach that goal. Our marketing communication budget will be based on those analyses and calculations. Ultimately, this budget may still be expressed as a percentage of sales, so it can be compared with previous years' budgets and with the competitors' expenditures. That way, we can also make sure that the budget does not exceed a certain threshold.

The objective-and-task method is conceptually superior to the other approaches because it assumes, unlike the percentage-of-sales method, that the level of brand awareness and sales vary with the level of promotion. It also suggests that the promotion budget is not a consequence of sales, but a means of realizing sales. At the same time, it is the only budgeting method that forces us – after a complete situation analysis – to clearly state our (quantifiable) objectives and then translate them into specific tasks.

Although the objective-and-task approach enables us to develop a promotional plan and budget without the most accurate data on future sales or competitors' activities, we do need insight into the relationships between the promotion activities and consumer attitudes, perceptions and buying behaviour. The in-depth analyses and calculations required for this budgeting method provide much of this insight. But even the most experienced managers are not always able to estimate – in spite of market research – how much and what kind of promotional effort is required to reach each of the agreed-upon objectives. This is because the effectiveness of an advertising campaign is difficult to predict, while the *carry-over effect* of promotion activities from the past cannot always be measured. Because of these uncertainties, marketers sometimes ask for promotion budgets that later turn out to be too high.

9.4.5 *Anti-cyclical budgeting*

When demand for their products or services declines – as in times of **recession** – and cutbacks are necessary, many firms decrease their advertising and promotion budgets. This is often an 'automatic' process, for instance when the budget is set as a fixed percentage of sales (as in the percentage-of-sales method), when there is less money available for promotion (as in the affordable method) or when major competitors scale down their budgets (as in the competitive-parity method of budgeting). Some managers even believe that promotion is useless when customers are spending less, and temporarily cease all promotion efforts.

As advocates of *anti-cyclical budgeting*, other managers, however, argue the opposite. They, too, link the level of their marketing communication spending to fluctuations in the *economic cycle*, but in such a way that in a period of weak economic activity or *recession*, they actually *increase* promotional spending (or, at least, reduce it less than the decrease in sales). In this way, they try to contain any further drop in sales. Conversely, during a period of strong economic growth they reduce their promotion activities, or at least, allow their promotion budget to increase relatively less than sales. Such an approach creates an *inverse* relationship between the level of sales and the marketing communication budget.

This method is not illogical, as research has shown that companies budgeting anti-cyclically during a period of recession saw their market shares rise dramatically and were able to maintain this increase after the recession ended. Hence, in a period of recession – with the right communication budget – it is often easier to increase market share than when economic growth returns.

How to apply it in business

The idea of anti-cyclical budgeting has become somewhat neglected since the rise of the response hierarchy models (including the DAGMAR model, to be discussed in the next chapter). Such models propose that only in exceptional situations is there a *direct*, demonstrable relationship between advertising and sales. Still, many managers continue to utilize anti-cyclical budgeting.

How anti-cyclical budgeting is applied depends on how the communication budget is set in an organization. For example, when a firm uses the percentage-of-sales method, it simply takes a higher percentage during a period of recession. Alternatively, when the objective-and-task method is used, anti-cyclical budgeting involves setting ambitious marketing objectives (such as to maintain sales volume) and translating these into specific promotion tasks and activities, like specifying how much advertising will be needed in which media.

Carry-over effect

Experienced managers know that with the objective-and-task method, it is not easy to figure out how many advertisements are needed to reach the desired level of brand awareness, brand preference or, ultimately, sales. This is mainly due to the carry-over effect, in which past advertising campaigns continue to have an impact today, and current promotion activities will also continue to bear fruit in the future. Realizing that the effect of promotion is going to last beyond a single time period (while, of course, decreasing over time) makes it difficult to estimate or isolate the effect of one single campaign.

Although it is hard to predict how great the carry-over effect of the firm's promotional efforts will be, we can get a head start – and create a competitive advantage – by incorporating an anti-cyclical budgeting approach in a marketing strategy which is aggressive across the board. This may lead to decisions such as combining more advertising with a temporary price cut (especially in slow growth periods), improving product and service quality, introducing new economy-size packaging or other measures to provide *added value* in the customer's perception. Product improvements such as these also have news value and may offer an ideal theme for advertising campaigns and other promotional activities.

9.5 DETERMINING THE COMMUNICATION MIX

Once the marketing communication budget has been established, it has to be allocated to the various promotion instruments in the best possible way. We must, for example, decide if the emphasis in our promotional efforts should be placed on advertising, sponsorship, personal selling, sales promotion, public relations or other marketing communication tools.

Because these options are – to some extent – substitutes for each other, determining the most effective communication mix may prove challenging. We must weigh a variety of factors, including the available budget, the product or service characteristics, the company's goals and the target market. We will see that the choice of instruments is also influenced by the decision to focus on either *theme communication* (sometimes called awareness communication) or *campaign communication* (also called action communication). Finally, we will examine the effectiveness of various marketing communication instruments in bringing about a particular consumer response.

9.5.1 Guidelines for choosing an ideal mix

There are no standard solutions or formulas for developing an effective marketing communications programme. To illustrate, a major global cosmetics brand has successfully acquired a dominant position on the European market by pursuing a *push strategy* for years. Its main emphasis in promotion has been on personal selling and customer consultations in retail stores, rather than on advertising. Yet, when this company recently started investing in

MARKETING TOPPER
Exporting the Magic of London Taxis

London is well known for its traditional 'black cab'. Much like the red telephone boxes, the iconic taxi has become synonymous with England's capital city. Yet in recent years its territory has grown, and passengers are just as likely to hail a 'London' taxi on the other side of the world. Indeed, *Saudi Arabia, Bahrain, Kuwait, Lebanon* and the *United Arab Emirates* are just a few of the countries in which you can catch such a black cab these days. Recently, Baku, *Azerbaijan*'s capital, nestled on the coast of the Caspian Sea, added thousands of these cabs to its fleet, a departure from the 20 000 – often unlicensed – Ladas previously still in operation from the bygone Soviet-era. There is one obvious visual distinction separating the new Azerbaijani taxis with their London cousins: they are painted violet, as personally requested by the country's president. What prompted the oil-rich nation to suddenly buy these British taxis?

It's a long shot, but the answer may well rest with the annual *Eurovision Song Contest*, a widely watched TV event in which dozens of Western and Eastern European nations participate. The winning country traditionally hosts next year's competition, and thanks to the success of its entry, the Azerbaijani nation found itself presented with this honour. Hosting a large international event invites attention on the global stage and requires solid infrastructure, hence leading to an alliance with British cab manufacturer *Manganese Bronze Holdings*.

> # London-style cabs have an emotional attraction in the Middle East and Eastern Europe

Azerbaijan's investment reflects a wider global trend as the British car maker continues to enter other

Courtesy of Image Asset Management

energy-rich markets. Today, Manganese is selling more taxis overseas than domestically. Obviously, brand image is important, even for nations that only get one chance to make a first impression to travellers who are taking a cab from the airport to their hotel. John Russell, Manganese's chief executive officer, emphasizes that London may well have the world's finest taxi service for travellers, whether arriving for business or pleasure. He recognizes the emotional pull this has on cities aspiring to rival their contemporaries in the region.

The Azerbaijani taxis cost €20 000 each – about half of the price charged in the UK, due to economies of scale and lower vehicle requirements. Besides, each cab driving abroad is also a free form of *promotion* for its manufacturer, justifying the substantial price cut. By 2014, Azerbaijan looks to increase its fleet of London cabs to over 3 000. The breakdown of the Soviet Union, and Azerbaijan's resultant independence, has opened up new possibilities and Manganese is not the only western company to take advantage of the marketing opportunities. The country has attracted investments of up to €30 billion from a range of corporations, such as the Norwegian oil and gas company Statoil, Total and BP. Its capital, with a population of 2.5 million, has become increasingly affluent, and its leaders want a transport system to reflect this.

Matthew Cheyne, International Market Development Director for The London Taxi Company says, 'Baku has set high standards for its transport network system and London Taxis fit in perfectly. The London Taxi Service offers a fully trained driver in an easily recognizable vehicle with a meter so there is a transparent and consistent pricing structure for all types of passengers, something that has never been offered in Baku before'. As 'cabbies' of the state-funded company, Baku Taxi, will attest, the spacious inside is clearly a hit with passengers. Bizarrely, Baku's cabbies could even become stars of the small screen, after interest from a UK television production company.

Even further from home, a *Singapore* based taxi company praises the benefits of the London cab, as 'iconic with its distinctively vintage exterior'. Yet there are more practical connotations which extend beyond image. 'Remarkably engineered, the London Cab taxi features a legendary tight turning circle. Greater maneuverability means easier, safer and convenient operation for both the driver and passengers.'

The London taxi's global success can be attributed in part to a successful *joint venture* between Manganese and Geely Automobile Holdings based in China. Geely acquired 20 per cent of the UK company in exchange for the exclusive rights to market London taxis in Asia and China. Manganese, in turn, purchases body parts and components from Geely to assemble the vehicles in England. In the short run, this business relationship caused serious problems for Manganese as it installed faulty steering boxes in hundreds of taxis that, subsequently, had to be taken off British roads until the affected components in the recalled sedans could be replaced with UK-supplied parts. In the long run, however, the joint venture may enable the company to launch a new taxi model by 2014. The black cab's latest innovation is the introduction of Wi-Fi for passengers. Hopefully, this will allow Manganese to continue to focus on its core business of – in Russell's words – 'marketing the magic of the London taxi' across the world.[7]

national advertising campaigns in combination with the use of social media, and in effect switched to a *pull strategy*, it managed to increase its market share. Most likely, the brand would have remained successful under the old strategy as well. That does not mean, of course, that decisions about the communication mix don't really matter. In this case, however, it appeared that advertising and personal selling were interchangeable and could be effectively substituted in the promotional mix. In the absence of rules of thumb, we will review some factors that can provide guidance when deciding on the communication mix. These are the company's goals, the target market, product attributes, stage in the product life cycle and the available budget.

Goals

A key question in determining the right marketing communication mix is what we want the campaign to accomplish and how. Depending on our goals or objectives, we can either use theme or campaign communication. When using **theme communication**, advertising, public relations and sponsorship are ideal instruments to create brand awareness and – in the long run – influence the knowledge or attitudes of members of the target market. On the other hand, the purpose of **campaign communication**, sometimes referred to as 'price-offer promotion', is to directly increase sales volume by stimulating (short-term) consumer buying behaviour through sales promotion. The most useful instruments to implement theme and campaign communication are shown in Figure 9.10.[8]

Target market

The nature of the *target market* plays an important role in choosing the right communication mix tools. If the target market is large and, because of its geographical dispersion, difficult to

FIGURE 9.10 Common instruments used in theme and campaign communication

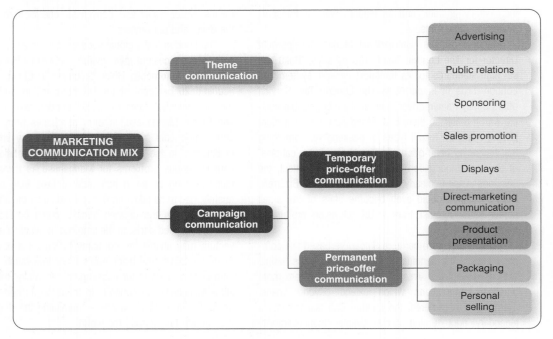

reach, the most economical way to contact prospective customers is by means of *mass communication*. Using personal selling would be far too expensive. Hence, companies such as Heineken and Unilever rely primarily on advertising in the mass media, targeting millions of widespread product users. On the other hand, organizations targeting wholesalers in the business-to-business market are better off using *personal selling*. Through personal contact, these companies are able to tailor their marketing communication efforts to the information needs of those individuals who are involved in purchasing decisions.

Product characteristics

Which communication mix works best depends very much on the main *product attributes* or characteristics. In assessing the type of product to be marketed, we take into account three key factors:

1 *Complexity.* Information about a highly technical product is usually communicated more effectively by a sales force than through an advertisement or a 30 second commercial. A skilled sales person can also demonstrate the product and explain exactly how it meets the buyer's needs.

2 *Risk* involved. Investing in a high priced, durable product may involve both financial and social risks for the buyer. In selling a new generation satellite communication system to a small firm, for example, a well-trained sales representative or consultant showing how the system can be tailored to the customer's needs and wants can make all the difference in persuading the potential buyer.

3 *Service* required. For some products, buyers expect excellent service and personal attention, including the acceptance of a trade-in, any necessary modification and installation of the product, and after-sales service. Here too, personal selling plays an important part in the promotion mix.

In B2B marketing, but also in selling consumer durables (such as home appliances and cars) or services (including banking, medical and legal services), personal contact between the buyer and the seller is essential. The main role of advertising in these cases is to support the tasks of sales people, enabling them to work more efficiently. Advertising can, for example, help to increase brand awareness or establish the company's reputation. This is especially important in the initial stages of consumer buying behaviour, when buyers become aware of their needs and determine their preferences. Personal selling is equally vital to build trust, close the sale, obtain shelf space and provide after-sales service.

Stage in the product life cycle

Just as a firm's promotional objectives vary by the product life cycle stage, the effectiveness of different communication tools and activities for consumer goods changes over the life cycle, too. Even before the launch of a new innovative product, most companies try to get *publicity* to increase potential buyers' awareness and interest.

Especially in the introduction stage, publicity and informative advertising are effective instruments for creating *primary demand*. In addition, *sales promotion* techniques (such as product demonstrations, free samples, coupons and rebates) may be used to stimulate product trials among consumers. At the same time, *personal selling* and trade deals will help the company gain access to distribution channels, obtain shelf space and secure the necessary cooperation of motivated dealers and retailers. As the product or service enters the maturity or decline stage of its life cycle, the firm needs to make sure that the most effective marketing communication tools are used at all times to maximize its profits.

Available budget

A small communication budget will definitely affect marketing strategy development. After all, the available resources will determine what communication mix is feasible, and therefore what promotion instruments can be used to influence consumers' orientation and buying behaviour.

Image Asset Management

FIGURE 9.11 Impact of communication instruments on consumer response

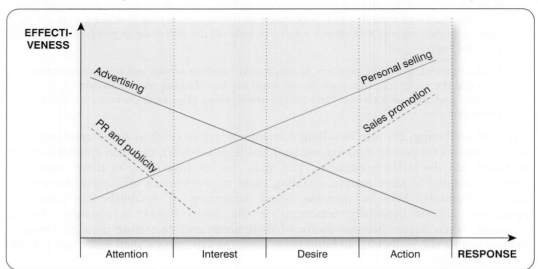

Lack of financial resources often forces companies to use cheaper, less effective methods than would be possible with a higher budget.

9.5.2 *Intended consumer response*

Clearly, each of the instruments in the communication mix will have a different impact on consumers. Therefore, when developing and implementing marketing communication strategies, we must keep in mind what type of consumer reaction we seek. Consumer response can be broken down according to the AIDA model into four steps: attention, interest, desire and action. In Figure 9.11 these stages are linked to various promotional tools that are most effective in creating these types of responses.[9]

As is clear from the graph, advertising is most effective in creating attention and interest, but – except in campaign advertising – usually will not lead to direct action. With personal selling, this pattern is inverted. Public relations and publicity are also useful to help draw attention to something and generate interest. Finally, sales promotion has the greatest impact on getting consumers to actually buy. In the end, a successful marketing strategy calls for a well-planned use of a combination of promotion instruments carefully tailored to the target market.

Recently, consumer preferences for communication tools have changed a great deal. Until recently, personal contact with a sales person or other company representative was clearly preferred by the majority of customers, both in the orientation stage and during the actual purchase. Today, the *Internet* appears to be the channel of choice for consumers seeking information about a product or service. Particularly for companies involved in marketing consumer durables, this shift in consumer preference has a huge impact on what will prove to be an effective communication mix.

9.6 PUBLIC RELATIONS

Public relations is rapidly becoming a critical component of the communication mix in global business. It is brought into play as a vital tool to support the company's advertising, personal selling and sponsoring activities in communicating with the market. Unfortunately, not everyone considers PR to be a *marketing* function. That's because some PR specialists report directly to their company's top management, rather than to the head of the marketing department. In addition, many public relations functions are aimed at other publics or stakeholders than the firm's customers.

This is especially true for *corporate public relations*. Corporate PR may be defined as a broad-based effort to maintain a climate of goodwill for the company's marketers. In business, creating goodwill – for instance by opening dialogues with various groups to defend the company's interests – is typically a top management responsibility. Of course, its ultimate purpose is still to create a solid foundation for the organization's marketing efforts. This is accomplished by building sound, long- term relationships with all stakeholders (usually through initiating two-way communication) and by influencing the perceptions and attitudes of consumers and other publics. That's where PR comes in.

Since corporate public relations activity often addresses social responsibility and corporate image issues, much of corporate PR boils down to image building. Image building refers to the company's efforts to gain public understanding or acceptance and to create a positive image of the corporation in the eyes of the public and other groups through various forms of marketing communication. The company's *desired* identity, however, may be quite different from its *actual* corporate identity in the target market's perception or in public opinion. Thus, the message may not always be getting across properly. To avoid that, the company should strive for *integrated marketing communication* (IMC), in which, as previously discussed, all messages and communication tools are strategically integrated so that they reinforce each other in producing a consistent message to the target audience. This creates added value or synergy in the firm's marketing communication. It is clear that marketing and public relations overlap in many ways, and an increasing number of experts consider PR to be a key part of a company's communication function.

Marketing PR – conducted at a lower level in the organization – focuses solely on the company's brands. It supports the firm's products and services. Because marketing public relations is, without a doubt, part of marketing communication, it is usually the marketing or product manager's responsibility. They may try, for example, to obtain free *publicity* for a new product or service in selected mass media. Hence, marketing PR, as compared to corporate public relations, is more targeted, and usually aimed at customers, intermediaries and

other stakeholders that directly influence marketing results. Of course, managers at all levels should make sure that these public relations activities, too, fit into the company's overall marketing strategy.

9.6.1 *Public relations functions*

As we have seen, *public relations* involves a wide range of marketing communication activities in order to systematically create a positive image of the organization and its strategy, and to improve the company's relationship with its publics. The 'public' in public relations refers to all stakeholders who have the potential for affecting or being affected by the organization. These publics may include customers, employees, stockholders, suppliers, the financial community, labour groups, activists, the media, government officials as well as the community in which the organization operates. The word *systematic* in the definition underlines the importance of carefully planning the public relations tasks or functions. With such an approach, all types of issues become routine operations and even unexpected events, such as a product recall (when defective or contaminated products are returned to the supplier), can be dealt with in line with a blueprint for action (as *crisis public relations* or 'crisis management' should).

There can only be a good relationship between the organization and its publics if there is open, two-way communication. In providing and seeking information, PR staff members generally keep a close eye on relevant developments in society – including the positions of labour unions, government agencies and pressure groups – enabling them to respond effectively to their publics. Their efforts are aimed at stakeholders both inside the organization (internal publics) and outside (external publics).

Internal publics

Internal publics consist of the company's personnel (including management) and their family members, as well as former employees and the Board of Directors. These groups are all kept informed of the enterprise's activities in order to increase their efficiency, motivation and involvement. As ambassadors of goodwill, they may share the news with other publics, helping – via word-of-mouth communication – to build relationships with external audiences.

Much of the internal communication about the organization's practices is concerned with displaying its *corporate identity* or 'personality'. The employees should feel comfortable with how the organization presents itself and will hopefully reflect the corporate identity in their own behaviour and attitudes. This will make it more likely that the firm's strategies are adopted and implemented by motivated employees. Their involvement is particularly important in customer- oriented campaigns, the success of which depends on the commitment of all company personnel.

Common internal communication media include personnel magazines, company bulletins, newsletters, email, notice boards and brochures. Company tours, video presentations, exhibitions, complaint boards and receptions with company executives are also popular public relations tools.

External publics

The *external publics* on which PR focuses include customers, intermediaries, suppliers, trade organizations and shareholders. Each is an important contributor to the survival and wellbeing of the organization. Other outside stakeholder audiences are consumer organizations, pressure groups, labour unions, job applicants and even – within the context of public opinion – the entire population.

Public relations functions in this area include new product publicity, product placement, media relations, government lobbying, event sponsorships, speech writing or advising executives on the firm's positions with respect to public issues, and other external corporate communications. Communicating a positive image to the public is often accomplished through corporate advertising. Such a campaign may be used to call attention to the company's involvement with the community or a successful effort to prevent environmental damage. An alternative to corporate advertising is free media exposure through press releases, leading to publicity. Messages communicated through publicity are more believable because they are coming from an objective source, as compared to advertising that is controlled and paid for by the company. If used to enhance the company's credibility or to raise awareness of its new products and services, publicity also benefits the company's sales representatives.

If necessary, the public relations officer must defend the organization against unexpected and unfavourable publicity resulting from environmental pollution, an unsafe product, exceptional profits, controversial behaviour of employees or some other negative event or crisis. To reduce the adverse impact of damaging news coverage, a constructive PR strategy requires the organization to clarify its position, take immediate steps to correct the problem (if the accusations are justified) and explain the measures it has taken as objectively as possible.

Besides mass media and the company's own websites, other external PR functions used to create and maintain a positive image for the organization are participating in career fairs in education, organizing company visits or excursions and holding meetings with suppliers, distributors, consumers and shareholders (to present the annual report).

9.6.2 *Planning the PR strategy*

Since public relations has become a widely used tool in companies, the nature of the work has become broader and deeper. The greater *depth* is reflected in the more systematic approach to strategy development in the profession; this has, as a side effect, also advanced the integration of PR and the marketing discipline. We will explore a systematic approach to PR at the end of this chapter. But first, we'll take a closer look at how the *broadening* of public relations has led to the emergence of several specializations in the field.

Specializations in public relations

Exactly what tasks a PR manager performs will largely depend on the nature and size of the organization. In a small firm, the president or CEO will do much of the PR work. But if the company is so vast that it has a dedicated department or manager for public relations, then the PR manager will usually represent the company on committees and at press conferences (or at least advise management on these activities). By maintaining contacts with various publics, they will try to build mutual trust and understanding, which should also benefit the organization. All in all, the PR manager will be responsible for a considerable part of the *corporate public relations* functions discussed above.

The larger the organization, the more room (and need!) there is for specialization. Separate departments or people can dedicate themselves to functions such as *internal communication*, public information and *financial public relations*. This provides more time for top management to concentrate on public affairs (PA). Public affairs is a strategic management function concerned with the relationship between the organization and its external environment, involving the analysis of societal developments, political decision-making and public opinion affecting the company and, in particular, focuses on the resulting opportunities and threats.

Much of the work in the area of public affairs revolves around lobbying, or trying to put pressure on government officials to influence legislation and regulation, and drawing attention to the interests of the company or industry. An increasing number of companies have specialists on the payroll for lobbying or seek help from consultants before making their cases to legislators.

A systematic approach to PR

An interesting development is the recent advances made in the public relations field, reflected in the professional methods of well-trained PR specialists. Like marketers, they take a systematic approach to analysis, planning, implementation and control, as illustrated in Figure 9.12.

To develop a successful public relations strategy, we begin with a thorough *analysis* of the status quo, preferably by conducting a situation analysis. We investigate how its various publics perceive the organization and how an unfavourable image (or any other problem) came about. By putting both this information and important characteristics of stakeholders in a database, they can be directly linked to each other.

In the second stage – of *planning* and strategy development – we establish how the organization would like to be perceived, whether that is feasible and how we can achieve this. What specific public relations objectives would we like to realize in the framework of

FIGURE 9.12 A systematic approach to public relations

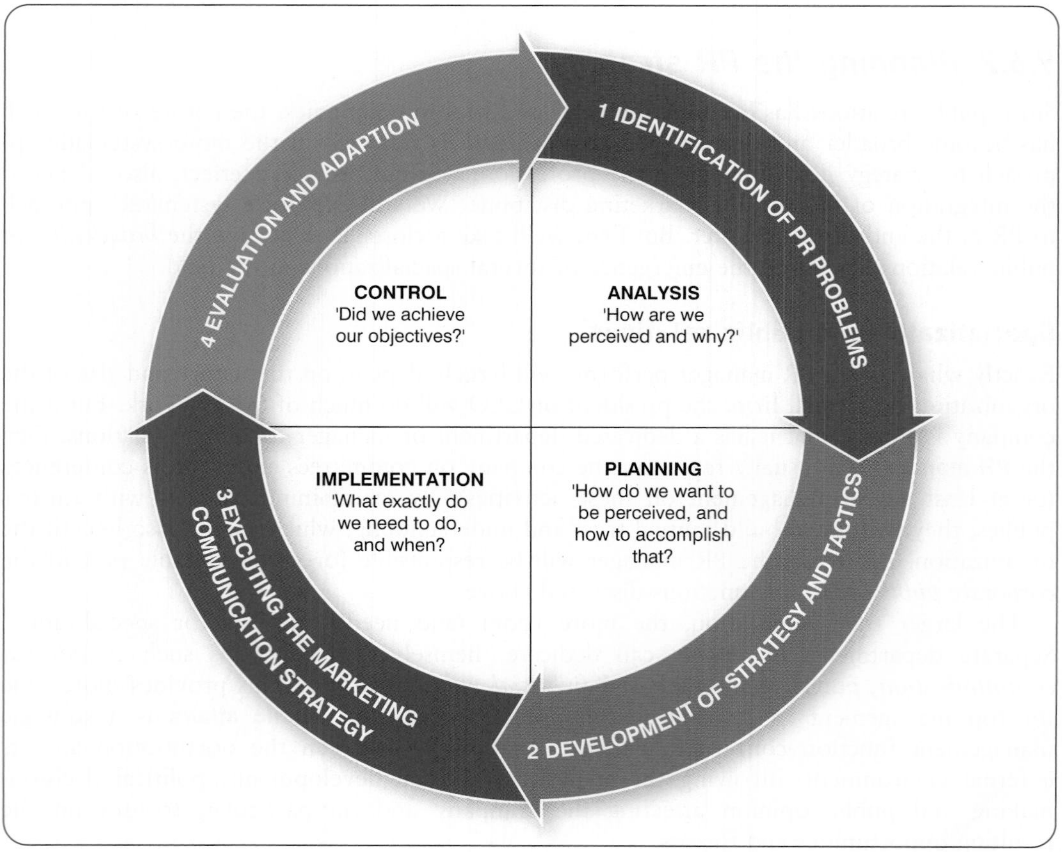

the marketing communication strategy? Each objective, along with the appropriate strategy, should be presented in detail in the public relations plan.

The last two steps – *implementation* and *control* – are concerned with strategy execution. Here we monitor and analyze the effect of the planned activities and campaigns on customers and other stakeholders. If it appears that the target audience does not react as expected or the plans are not feasible for another reason, we may have to adapt the strategy or tactics in the (final) control phase. One of the great advantages of this systematic approach is that it leads to closer cooperation between public relations managers and others in the organization.

SUMMARY

1   Marketing communication or promotion

Marketing communication is the process by which an organization delivers a message – converted into words and images – through the mass media or other message channels to a target audience. The receivers then decode the signs and symbols in the message. Feedback should indicate whether the message (despite any noise) has been correctly interpreted and has led to the intended response. Through their marketing communication or promotion strategies, companies try to build relationships with their customers and other stakeholders. They accomplish this by using the right combination of promotional tools (the 'promotional mix'), including advertising, sales promotion, personal selling, sponsorship, public relations, publicity and direct marketing. The ultimate objective of marketing communication is to inform and remind buyers in the target market of a product or service, to persuade them or to influence their opinions in order to achieve the desired response.

If a mass medium – one that essentially anyone can receive – is used to reach a large audience, it is referred to as mass communication. However, if the number of potential buyers is limited, interpersonal communication is more efficient: the feedback enables the marketer to immediately adjust or clarify his message and to respond directly to any buyer objections.

2   Identifying the target audience

An effective marketing communications strategy can only be developed with the exact target audience in mind. Depending on whether we focus primarily on ultimate consumers or on intermediaries at the next level in the distribution channel, the emphasis will be on a *pull* or a *push* strategy. Advertising campaigns are an efficient marketing tool in a pull strategy, whereas a motivated sales force plays a major role in a push strategy.

According to the two-step flow model of the communication process, a marketer should try to reach the opinion leaders. They, in turn, pass the information on to the wider public and, through word-of-mouth, influence the purchase decisions of other consumers more than the mass media ever could.

3   Communication objectives and models

Developing a promotional strategy begins with spelling out the *objectives*. These should not be expressed in terms of desired sales volume, but stated in terms of clear, detailed tasks we want to accomplish with our marketing communication efforts, such as a particular change in brand awareness, brand image or consumer attitudes. Classic *response hierarchy models* may be helpful in defining specific goals as measurable communication effects. These information processing models describe the cognitive and affective stages that potential buyers pass through before they ultimately decide to purchase a product or service (in the conative or behavioural stage). In plotting communication strategies, marketing-oriented managers use the AIDA model or rely on the hierarchy-of-effects model developed by Lavidge and Steiner. The Lavidge and Steiner communication model proposes six steps: awareness, knowledge, liking, preference, conviction and purchase. Companies may need several advertisements, each focusing on achieving a single step in this hierarchy. Sometimes customers pass through the stages in the learning hierarchy in a different order than might be expected based on rational consumer behaviour. Two non-classic response hierarchy models with different sequences of steps are the low-involvement hierarchy and the dissonance hierarchy.

4   Budgeting methods

Of all the possible ways of setting the advertising or promotion budget, the objective-and-task method is conceptually the best. Here we first determine what objectives we wish – and, as an organization, are reasonably able – to achieve, and then which specific marketing communication tasks (and what budget) will be required to reach these goals. This method recognizes, for example, that an advertising message will have to be repeated a number of times before it has any noticeable effect. In most firms, however, the percentage-of-sales approach is more likely to be used than a build-up approach like the objective-and-task method or, for that matter, than other top-down approaches such as the competitive-parity or the affordable method of budgeting.

Companies using anti-cyclical budgeting spend more on promotion when sales slow down, and relatively less when sales pick up again. This *inverse* relationship between sales volume and the marketing communication budget tends to increase market share, especially in periods of slow economic growth. Since the carry-over effect of promotion expenditures makes it difficult to predict the effect of a single advertising campaign, establishing the budget remains a challenge in business.

5 Communication mix

To some extent, advertising, personal selling, public relations, promotion or the use of social media through the Internet and other message channels can be used interchangeably. However, in determining the optimum communication mix, results-oriented marketers should take into account their specific goals, the nature of the target market, the product characteristics, the stage in the product life cycle and the available budget. *Awareness communication* is often used to influence consumers' knowledge level or attitudes and to add value by attaching a psychological surplus to the brand. In the long run, this tends to increase consumers' willingness to buy. Advertising, public relations and sponsorship are excellent communication tools for this.

Conversely, sales promotion, displays, direct marketing and other forms of *action communication* are most effective in directly influencing consumer buying behaviour, often resulting in sales increases. Ultimately, the communication mix we choose very much depends on the consumer response we are seeking.

6 Public relations and marketing

An important tool in any company's communication mix is public relations. The target audience for *public relations* activities includes company employees, customers, stockholders, intermediaries, suppliers and other publics or stakeholders. Therefore, PR serves both an internal function (such as motivating employees) and an external function (for example, creating a positive image). Successful organizations take a systematic approach to the analysis, planning, implementation and control of their marketing communication efforts, including public relations.

DISCUSSION QUESTIONS

1   Managers would like to know the return on their investment in marketing communication. Yet, they usually do not express the company's communication objectives in terms of sales or profits. Why is it generally better not to formulate marketing communication objectives in terms of the desired additional sales or profit? Describe a situation in which it would be possible to express a company's promotional goals in terms of sales.

2   A large Mercedes dealer has grown so much that the organization has both a marketing and a public relations department. This highly profitable company is now considering becoming a major sponsor of a popular soccer team as well as a local zoo. Which department do you think took the initiative for these sponsoring activities and who are the target audiences?

3   Describe the AIDA model and its implications for a company's marketing communication strategy.

4   Comment on the following statement: 'Marketing communication is rather useless and makes products unnecessarily expensive'.

5   What is the relationship between a marketing communication and a positioning strategy?

6   How can the effectiveness of anti-cyclical budgeting be increased? Give some examples.

7   Explain the concept of integrated marketing communication. How can this approach be justified, knowing that some companies spend millions of euros on advertising their brands to create a high-quality image, while they also set budgets to run sales promotion campaigns, allowing their customers to buy the same products for a lower price?

8   Comment on the following statement: 'Advertising and other forms of communication should reflect the norms, values and lifestyles of consumers in the target market'.

9   What are the main causes of some companies' poor performance in the area of public relations?

10 How can an organization measure the results of its public relations efforts? Suggest several methods.

CHAPTER 10
ADVERTISING

LEARNING GOALS

After studying this chapter you will be able to:

1	Understand advertising's role in business and in society
2	Distinguish between different types of advertising
3	Explain how to formulate proper advertising objectives
4	Describe the importance of a well-planned advertising strategy
5	Identify the major steps in developing an advertising campaign
6	Compare various media evaluation and selection techniques
7	Discuss how the advertising effort can be evaluated
8	Recognize the role of sponsorships in marketing communication

10.1 The role of advertising
10.2 Types of advertising
10.3 Advertising planning
10.4 Advertising strategies
10.5 Developing the advertising campaign
10.6 Media selection
10.7 Measuring advertising effectiveness
10.8 Sponsorships

Advertising and other forms of marketing communication play a key role in marketing. They help to create an exchange between a company and its customers, build a sound reputation for the firm and promote lasting relationships with customers. An effective advertising and positioning strategy can convince buyers of the quality of a product or service, and thus positively influence buying decisions, repeat purchases and brand loyalty.

Advertising adds value, not just for suppliers but for buyers, too. It gives buyers crucial information to make the right purchasing decisions. This can save them time, money and effort. The importance of advertising is obvious, when you realize that worldwide, over 400 billion euros is spent on it every year; a huge amount to help achieve the objectives of countless organizations as well as their customers.

To make sure that the marketing communication budget is spent well, we must be able to develop effective advertising campaigns. In this chapter we will explore this challenge, as well as other promotional mix decisions.

MARKETING IN ACTION
Sesame Street in Africa

Sesame Street, the popular children's show now running into its fifth decade and featuring an imaginary street in New York, USA, has arrived in *South Africa* and, more recently, in *Nigeria*, fully adapted to its new audience. The two muppets from the famous US show, Big Bird and Cookie Monster, have a new, cute friend in Africa: *Kami* – the world's first *HIV-positive* Sesame Street character – a lovable five-year-old muppet girl with golden hair who enjoys sharing stories about her exciting life with others. She is also playing a key role in South Africa's and Nigeria's war against AIDS.

Takalani Sesame ('Be happy Sesame' in Venda), South Africa's version of Sesame Street, has been shown on the *South African Broadcasting Corp*. network for over a decade. Under the creative direction of its US originator (Sesame Workshop), and co-produced by local partners, the South African version uses homegrown characters and situations to educate while entertaining young children throughout the country. The much-loved television programme is broadcast weekly in all the official languages spoken in South Africa – Afrikaans, English, Venda, Zulu, Swazi, Xhosa, Ndebele, Sesotho, Northern Sotho, Tsonga and Tswana – and is watched by millions of children.

The popular TV show helps children to enjoy South Africa's multiracial culture

Takalani Sesame, in which former Secretary-General of the United Nations *Kofi Annan* and Archbishop *Desmond Tutu* have made guest appearances, teaches kids basic skills and rules of behaviour. This uniquely South African

interpretation of the Sesame model engages children and their parents while promoting basic school readiness, literacy, mathematical ability as well as health and hygiene. In addition, the programme explains the nature of South Africa's multiracial culture and tries to help children enjoy it.

Although its target audience is very young children (three to seven years of age, but older kids watch the show too), Takalani Sesame doesn't shy away from the big issues in South Africa. A major challenge for the show is to effectively address the problem of HIV, a medical condition that one in ten South African people – including a quarter of a million children – have to live with every day. Millions of orphans have lost their parents to AIDS. By discussing in the programme what it means to be HIV-positive or what to do when someone you know has AIDS, the people making the television programme want to help reduce the stigma associated with the disease. By not ignoring the topic or handling the disease as taboo, HIV or AIDS patients are less likely to be treated as social outcasts in the future.

The show's popular and fun-loving character *Kami* (meaning 'acceptance' in the Tswana language) has very little in common with the label often put on sufferers of HIV. Instead, on the screen she comes across as a cheerful and healthy HIV-positive character. Kami provides valuable insights into what it means to have HIV or AIDS. She encourages kids to talk to each other about how people suffering from the disease are rejected and become socially isolated, and even discusses death. And since Kami is such a warm character (not to mention emotionally more mature and smarter than a typical five-year-old child), she has a significant influence on South African children of all ages.

Another remarkable adaptation of the Sesame Street TV show is targeted at children in *Nigeria*. Here, in West Africa, the programme is called *Sesame Square*. Besides Kami, the show – for its lighter side – stars *Zobi*, a furry, blue, energetic cab driver whose upsetting adventures motivate children to try to avoid the troublesome issues he's getting involved in. Zobi is the Nigerian version of *Cookie Monster*, and – since Nigerian kids don't have access to cookies – he has an uncontrollable craving for yams, a staple food in the Nigerian diet. In a country with a population of over 150 million people – about half under the age of 14 – the programme typically addresses the huge problems that most Nigerians have to deal with. These include diseases such as AIDS and malaria, but also social issues such as discrimination against specific religions or female citizens. Of course, on the sunny side, Sesame Square also features a positive view of living in Nigeria.

According to Sesame Workshop's senior director of international projects Naila Farouky, the programme's emphasis continues to be on health and hygiene issues. To illustrate, in a recent episode Zobi was caught in a hilarious situation, struggling to get out of a mosquito net after waking up. While it was a funny show, the underlying message is that a mosquito net is essential in not getting infected with malaria. A priceless lesson in Africa, where every hour, more than 75 children die of malaria. In addition, there are over 250 000 HIV-positive children in Nigeria alone, according to the National Agency for Control of AIDS. However, Sesame Square and Takalani Sesame do not only address social and health issues, but also focus on learning skills such as reading, writing, calculating and other forms of pre-school education, all with a very entertaining twist. That's probably what makes Sesame such a popular children's television programme on the African continent.[1]

Advertising is an integral part of our lives. As consumers, each of us normally sees or hears more than a thousand advertising messages a day from businesses wanting to tell or sell us something. Whether we are aware of it or not, these messages influence our opinions or buying decisions. Therefore, advertising is a driving force in the economy. We define **advertising** as any paid form of non-personal communication about products, services, ideas or organizations by an identified sponsor using the mass media to influence the knowledge, attitudes or behaviour of those who are part of a target market.

For many companies this prominent form of mass communication is essential to increasing sales and market share. They must spend their advertising budgets wisely to compete successfully. As emphasized in the previous chapter, every marketing communication decision should be carefully weighed, with the characteristics and needs of the target audience always in mind.

The most important decisions we will explore in this chapter are determining the *advertising objectives,* developing an advertising strategy and a campaign with an effective *message,* choosing the best *media* and, finally, *measuring* the effects of advertising in order to evaluate and potentially adjust the strategy. It is important to have a clear understanding of this entire process to make the best decisions when selecting an advertising agency and to give meaningful feedback during the development of the advertising campaign.

In this chapter we will also focus on *sponsorships* as a useful supplement to the firm's advertising strategy. We will analyze both the function of sponsorship in the communication mix and the objectives that organizations hope to achieve.

Before examining the major steps in planning the advertising effort, we will look at advertising's role in the economy and in business. We will also compare different types of advertising.

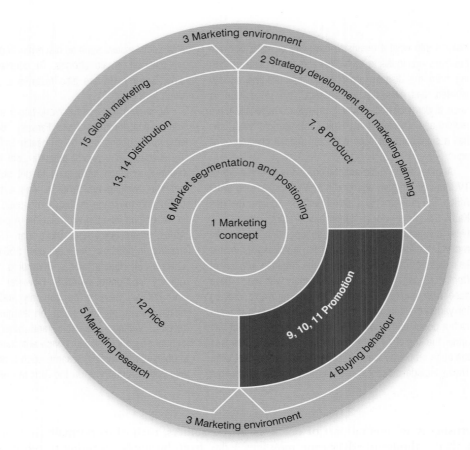

10.1 THE ROLE OF ADVERTISING

When you tell someone that you are studying marketing or work in the field of marketing, the response is often something like, 'Marketing? That's primarily selling and advertising, isn't it?' Apparently, advertising, as one of the most visible elements of marketing, is viewed by some as marketing's rough equivalent. In reality, however, the role of advertising, although of major importance, is rather limited, despite the vast sums of money spent on it. To gain a better understanding of advertising, we will consider its *influence* on society and examine its *place* in corporate strategy.

10.1.1 Influence on society

Many overestimate the influence of advertising. Some think that advertising can persuade people to buy products and services that they don't really need. But, as our analysis of consumer behaviour has already made clear, there are many factors that affect purchasing behaviour. Others consider advertising to be a waste of money. Almost everyone is sometimes bored or annoyed by advertising and most TV viewers surf from channel to channel during the commercial breaks.

Despite the fact that advertising is often criticised, there are also many consumers who see the benefits of this form of mass communication. They consider advertising a useful source of information on existing or new products and services. The advocates also realize that advertising revenues are used to finance TV programmes and to keep the subscription prices of their newspapers and magazines at reasonable rates. But there are other advantages, too. Advertising enables the development of mass markets that promote economic growth and lead to economies of scale in production and distribution. Also, it lowers the cost of personal selling, because many buyers are already aware of the product's value before buying it. This keeps prices down. Moreover, manufacturers whose names are associated with the advertised brands are more inclined to maintain high quality standards. This benefits everyone. Finally, many non-profit organizations, including charities, colleges, universities and government agencies, take advantage of advertising. As a result, these institutions have become more customer-oriented.

The positive effect of advertising on society as a whole does not mean that every organization will benefit equally from using this marketing instrument. Some firms advertise even though the revenue generated is not in proportion to the cost. To avoid wasting money, we must know how to develop an advertising campaign that will produce the intended effect.

10.1.2 *Place in the organizational structure*

Although advertising is used by many companies to promote brands, introduce new products and change the corporate image, in the marketing discipline it plays a less prominent role than most people think, because advertising is just one instrument in the overall marketing communication mix. Furthermore, the communication mix is largely determined by the marketing plan and the overall business plan. Figure 10.1 illustrates the hierarchical position of advertising in corporate communication strategy.

As we can see, the corporate plan or *business plan* provides the starting point for advertising planning. The *marketing plan* is derived from the business plan. Naturally, the strategic marketing decisions in that plan (dealing, for instance, with the target market, distribution channels and budgets) will have major implications for the company's communication policy.

This communication policy is developed further in the marketing *communication plan*. The marketer now has to decide which instruments (such as public relations, advertising, sponsorship, personal selling, direct marketing or sales promotion) will be included in the communication strategy as well as the objectives of these instruments. Weighing all of the options, they will select a communication mix in which the elements reinforce each other to form a comprehensive, consistent message to the target audience. As we know, the best results will be achieved when the company's marketing communication is fully *integrated*.

FIGURE 10.1 Hierarchical position of advertising

Carla Fourie is a marketing strategist at Twenty3Media, based in Cape Town. This marketing agency specializes in creating and implementing marketing strategies for businesses of various sizes, with a client base stretching over South Africa and Namibia. Fourie has extensive experience in both traditional and online marketing and in developing result-oriented marketing strategies that take into account the client's business goals and marketing budget. In the following perspective, she discusses the role of advertising in South African firms.

Advertising plays an important and substantial role in marketing strategies across the world. Companies depend on advertising to generate awareness for their products and services, create a desire within the target market and consequently increase leads and sales for the business.

An advertising strategy forms a key component of the marketing strategy that should be well-planned. Not only should the creative messages of a campaign be properly crafted and scrutinized, the business must also ensure that each ad is in line with the organization's positioning strategy. Most large corporations appoint advertising agencies to take care of the advertising section of their marketing strategy, but unfortunately most small and medium firms don't have the budget to hire an advertising agency or even a marketing consultant for that matter.

Nonetheless, an advertising strategy – whether developed in-house or outsourced to an agency – should be based on the marketing goals of the business's marketing strategy. For example, is the objective of an advertising campaign to strengthen a brand's reputation through increased awareness in the target market or is the goal to drive leads and sales for a specific product?

Once the advertising objectives are formulated and the ad campaign's creative approach is determined, management should decide what marketing communication channels to use. For example, a radio ad's content will be vastly different from that of a print ad. In addition, there are many advertising platforms to consider. From print to outdoor, broadcast and online, management must ensure that it selects the platform (or platforms) most relevant to its target market. If your business sells car engine oil and you're advertising in a women's monthly magazine, your marketing message will probably not reach your target market and consequently your marketing budget is wasted.

In terms of budgeting, online advertising is more cost-effective than using traditional advertising media like print, radio and television. Regardless of the media selection, to maximize its effectiveness, the advertising campaign should be memorable. Today's consumer is exposed to so much advertising that the ads should aim to create a *buzz* among the target group, inspiring the target audience to share the message with friends.

Creative and innovative campaigns can differentiate you from competitors

An example of a South African company that promotes new products by creating a buzz is *rubybox*, which allows women to test beauty products before buying. For a nominal fee, each subscriber receives a 'rubybox' every month filled with sample-sized beauty products. Once consumers have used them, they can also buy full-sized beauty products through the company's website. *Rubybox* created a cheeky online ad with a touch of mischievous humour and posted it on *YouTube*. Within two weeks, the ad went viral and reached nearly 40 000 views, generating lots of buzz across social networks like *Facebook* and *Twitter*. As the video was only released online, the company managed to keep its advertising costs low. Thus, creativity and innovation can go a long way to make a marketing communication budget stretch.

The fast food takeaway chain *Nando's* features another South African brand that provides great ads that generate buzz. The key to success to these ads is that they are topical (related to a big local news event) and that the punch line always ties back to the company's products. Its marketing budget allows for advertisements in the country's top newspapers and commercials on television stations that generate buzz online through sharing and commenting on social media sites like Facebook and Twitter. Its most recent broadcast advertising campaign is called '25 Reasons We Love South Africa' in celebration of Nando's 25th anniversary. Each ad focuses on one reason why we love South Africa – but with a tongue-in-cheek twist; a clever campaign that presents Nando's as an innovative and cheeky brand.

The outcomes achieved by both Nando's and rubybox illustrate that no matter the size of your marketing budget, you can create memorable and successful advertising campaigns. While many factors will influence the success of a campaign, creativity and innovation can set you miles apart from the competition.[2]

Finally, based on the communication plan, we develop the advertising plan. Strategic advertising planning consists of several steps. These include selecting the advertising target audience, formulating the advertising objectives, setting the advertising budget (discussed in the previous chapter) and developing the advertising strategy. The advertising plan also includes information regarding the selection of various media for the campaign, and measurement of the results.

10.2 TYPES OF ADVERTISING

Depending on its marketing strategy and goals, an organization may use different types of advertising. To provide an overview of the various types, they are classified on the basis of the *communication process*; the process by which a *sender* tries to deliver a *message* to a *target audience* or receiver through a certain *medium*. Table 10.1 shows the classification.

TABLE 10.1 Classification of advertising based on the mass communication model

Sender	Target audience	Message	Medium
Product advertising	Consumer advertising	Informative advertising	Broadcast advertising
Collective advertising	Business advertising	Institutional advertising	Print advertising
Retail advertising	Professional advertising	Selective advertising	Point-of-purchase advertising
Cooperative advertising	Trade advertising	Generic advertising	Direct advertising
Combination advertising		Theme advertising	Direct mail advertising
Non-commercial advertising		Campaign advertising	Email advertising
		Comparative advertising	Opt-in email

10.2.1 *Classified by sender*

When analyzing the communication process using the mass communication model discussed in the previous chapter, the *sender* or source of the message is the first element to consider. Viewed from the sender's perspective, advertising can be broken down into manufacturers' or product advertising, collective advertising, retail advertising, cooperative advertising, combination advertising and non-commercial advertising.

Product advertising

Many of the ads to which we are exposed daily are forms of national consumer advertising from well-known manufacturers, like Sony, Apple and Procter & Gamble. This is known as *manufacturers' advertising* or product advertising. Most companies advertise their brands, goods or services to make consumers aware of their product range and to inform them about new or improved products. They also try to create brand loyalty by suggesting new uses for their products and by promoting outstanding features and benefits of new products or services. To illustrate, Microsoft has been employing product advertising campaigns to launch more user-friendly, repositioned software products (such as Windows 8) and to persuade consumers to buy the upgrade.

Collective advertising

Sometimes manufacturers or dealers use national advertising to stimulate *primary demand*, or demand for a product category (such as chicken) rather than for a specific brand. This joint advertising by competitors in the same sector is called collective advertising. Examples of collective advertising campaigns – often born of necessity, during periods of declining demand – are those for bread, pork, wool, flowers, milk and movie theatres. When such campaigns are paid for by organizations at the same level of the supply chain, it is called *horizontal* collective advertising. If this type of advertising is used to stimulate interest or demand for a product or service in the introduction stage of its life cycle, it is referred to as pioneer advertising.

Retail and cooperative advertising

Retailers are another major source of advertising messages. The main objective of retail advertising is to bring as many customers as possible into the store. What they buy there is not as important as the fact that they *are* there. Despite their different goals and interests, the retailer and the manufacturer sometimes share the cost of a *joint* advertisement or advertising campaign; this is known as cooperative or co-op advertising. Because these companies operate at different levels of the supply chain, this is a form of *vertical* collective advertising. The costs are shared on a percentage basis; a fifty-fifty arrangement is common.

One benefit of co-op advertising to the manufacturer is that the retailer will be more likely to promote their products. This creates a form of cooperation at the local level, at a lower cost than an advertising campaign paid for by the manufacturer alone. The retailer or dealer enjoys the same advantage. They also reap the rewards of a professionally developed advertising campaign, which may enhance the prestige and image of the store.

Cooperative advertising, however, does have some *disadvantages*. The manufacturer must spend more time and money to gain the cooperation of retailers, yet they may have little control over the content of local ads. A drawback for the retailer is that a national advertisement is not necessarily ideal for local use, particularly if the manufacturer gets more attention than the store.

Combination advertising

If two or more companies who are not selling the same products but have a common interest share the costs of an advertising campaign, this is referred to as **combination advertising**. Examples include the advertisements of retailer associations intended to attract more visitors to a shopping centre: the participating stores are not each other's direct competitors. Because they are cooperating at the same level in the supply chain, this is a form of *horizontal* combination advertising.

This also applies, for example, to the combined advertising of a manufacturer of washing machines and a producer of detergents.

A similar type of cooperation between organizations at different levels in the supply chain is called *vertical* combination advertising. A cooperative advertising campaign between a manufacturer and a retailer to promote a particular brand serves as one example.

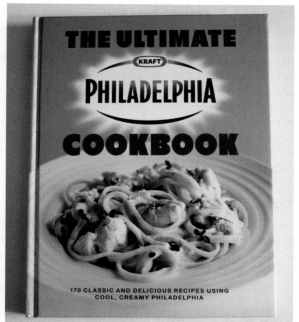

Non-commercial advertising

Advertising is not limited to commercial messages designed to promote products, services or ideas with the intention of making a profit. Organizations such as government agencies, civic groups, charitable institutions, political and religious organizations increasingly use **non-commercial advertising** to create a positive attitude toward certain (often ideological) matters. An example is **public service advertising**, donated by the advertising industry to promote activities for social good. Environmental protection as promoted by the World Wildlife Fund, and the government's drug and alcohol abuse prevention campaigns are examples of public service advertising that encourages positive social change.

10.2.2 *Classified by target audience*

Advertising may be aimed at a consumer audience, but can also be targeted at organizational buyers (business advertising) and intermediaries in the distribution channel (trade advertising).

Consumer advertising

Consumer advertising refers to all advertising targeted at the consumer. It is aimed at individuals who buy products and services for their own use or for their household members. Various advertising media may be used for this. Of those, **webvertising** (advertising through Internet websites) is gaining ground most rapidly. Other widely used media in consumer advertising are newspapers, magazines, radio, TV and billboards in outdoor advertising.

Business advertising

Business advertising is targeted at organizations and people who buy or specify products and services for use in business. A large proportion consists of industrial advertising, aimed at those who buy or influence the purchase of industrial goods and services. Or, business advertising may be targeted at organizations in the services sector, such as schools, hospitals and care facilities, with or without profit motive. Since organizational buying behaviour is typically a group process, the advertiser must tailor the message to multiple parties involved in the purchasing decision. Business advertising also includes professional advertising, with a target audience of licenced or accredited individuals (such as doctors, lawyers and accountants) who practise in their respective fields under a set of professional standards or a code of ethics.

Trade advertising

The objective of *trade advertising* is to communicate with members of a distribution channel. It is directed at wholesalers, retailers and agents who buy the advertised products for resale to their customers, or other channel members who provide support in the marketing process. Trade advertising has an important function, but is often underestimated because it is less visible than advertising in mass media for the wider public.

10.2.3 *Classified by message*

The type of advertising message a company develops depends on the purpose of the campaign. In terms of the *message*, we make a distinction between informative, institutional, selective and generic advertising. Another classification, discussed earlier, is theme versus campaign advertising. A final option is to develop a comparative advertising campaign.

Informative advertising

If a company primarily wants to pass on factual, usually verifiable information about a product or how it is used, appealing to rational rather than emotional motives, it employs *informational* or informative advertising. This is more common in trade advertising than in consumer advertising. Trade ads often feature a detailed description of the product along with suggestions on how to present it attractively in a retail setting. The ads are supplemented by displays, price discounts, contests and other trade promotional tools to persuade the retailer to carry the product or to provide more shelf space.

Industrial advertising, which is directed at buyers already familiar with the product category, also fundamentally differs in content from consumer advertising. Instead of focusing on expressive product characteristics (symbolic features like brand image that help consumers express their personalities or lifestyles), industrial ads emphasize instrumental product characteristics, such as technical or functional features of the product or service. Thus, the message in business advertising is more informative.

Institutional advertising

While historically, advertising was mainly product-oriented, now that most companies market a variety of products, many are committed to institutional or *corporate advertising*. Unlike product advertising, which is intended to stimulate purchases or 'sell products', institutional advertising is designed to influence attitudes. It is aimed at the general public (sometimes investors, potential employees and other stakeholders) and promotes the organization's ideas and role in the community as a corporate citizen, regardless of its products or services. Institutional ads usually address broad image issues, such as the customer orientation of the employees, in order to create goodwill and build a favourable image. Therefore, it is sometimes referred to as *corporate image advertising*.

A special form of institutional advertising is advocacy advertising, used by corporations to react to criticism or to express views on controversial issues. The company may express its position on such issues as the government's international trade policy, anti-smoking regulations, tax rates or its own recycling efforts. Often, advocacy advertising not only benefits society, but also helps to create a positive corporate image.

Selective versus generic advertising

Advertising has various purposes, as we have seen. Still, most advertising messages are developed to directly influence demand. In this effort, we make a distinction between selective and generic advertising.

Selective advertising seeks to affect the demand for a particular brand of product or service by promoting its unique or differentiating characteristics. On the other hand, generic advertising concentrates on the customer benefits that apply to all brands in a product category, instead of benefits that are unique to specific brands. These ads, which are directed toward *primary demand*, are designed to stimulate demand for the whole product category.

Theme versus campaign advertising

As discussed in section 9.5.1, there is a big difference between using theme or awareness advertising and campaign or action advertising in the marketing communication mix. To increase familiarity with the product's name and package, or to enhance its brand image companies use theme advertising. In other words, this form of advertising is used to increase the knowledge or influence the attitudes of the target audience. Marketers of national brands, for instance, try to add value and build a positive brand image by emphasizing the occasion or pleasant 'atmosphere' in which the product is used or by positioning the brand strategically.

Theme advertising is more about sowing than reaping: it affects the consumers' future buying behaviour. Most retailers, however, prefer campaign advertising. This is advertising intended to bring about immediate action on the part of the reader or viewer, and get them to buy the product right away. Usually, temporary price discounts or other sales promotion efforts announced in the ad help to increase sales in the short run.

The effect of this type of advertising is easier to measure than that of theme advertising. Some managers claim that through campaign advertising, they effectively 'buy' turnover (and market share), whereas with theme advertising they 'buy' consumers.

Comparative advertising

Although comparing products and services is an essential part of the decision-making process for most buyers, advertising campaigns in most countries do not reflect that. Yet, more and more marketers have started using comparative advertising, in which two or more brands are compared based on one or more product characteristics. In most countries this is legal, provided that the qualities or features of competing brands are not misrepresented. Unfortunately, many business people are confused about what is and is not permitted – especially in Europe – and, because of legal implications, stay away from comparative claims in their advertising. Consequently, an effective instrument to compete head-on is left unused in most companies' commercial tool boxes.[3] Comparative advertising is most common for new products being launched against strong competitors and for products that are experiencing sluggish growth or a loss of market share.

10.2.4 *Classified by medium*

Manufacturers and retailers advertise in both *national* and *local* media. They use radio and TV commercials, referred to as broadcast advertising, and advertisements in local and national newspapers and magazines, called print advertising. Often a combination of national, regional and local media is used. Many franchise organizations, including McDonald's, rely on national media to increase brand awareness and enhance the brand image, and on media near the location of the business for local promotions, such as temporary discounts and special offers.

For many retailers the *store* itself is the most important communication vehicle. The other media used should support and enhance the store image. Grocery chains prefer to use newspapers, allowing them the flexibility of advertising fresh produce and announcing price changes through this medium without delay. In-store promotion and advertising (such as signs, wall posters, shelf 'talkers' and other materials in the outlet where a product is sold) is known as point-of-purchase advertising.

Direct advertising is frequently used in promotional campaigns: here the advertising vehicle, such as a *sponsored magazine*, is also the medium. Direct mail advertising is advertising, usually addressed personally, that is sent through the mail. Although the cost per contact of this type of advertising is relatively high, the content of the message can be tailored to the *prospect*. As a result, direct mail gets more attention than advertising in the mass media. We will return to this when we examine direct marketing in the next chapter.

Finally, the Internet is increasingly used as a medium that is less expensive, less cluttered and often more effective than traditional media. Company websites and online advertising have all the capabilities of direct mail at a fraction of the cost and are used by more and more companies to communicate interactively with the target audience.

The most important growth area in online advertising is individually targeted emails, not mass-oriented banner ads or pop-ups. Using the Internet, commercial messages are sent via email. A large part of marketing-related email is permission granted or opt-in email. In other words, a customer grants the marketer permission to send him messages on certain topics. In Europe, email advertising is regulated to a great extent. European Union countries require firms to let customers know what data are being collected and retained, explain to them how the data will be used in the future, and give customers the opportunity to opt-out of the process. Still, the Internet is a medium on which consumers spend more time than with traditional media, and it is the only medium where they are just one click away from a purchase.[4]

An example of a UK advertising campaign devised by PRG to promote local authority grants and loans to improve privately owned homes. The ads were placed in regional newspapers and bus shelters and helped Eastbourne Borough Council achieve previously unattainable grant-distribution targets.

PROFESSOR'S PERSPECTIVE
Mihalis Kavaratzis (University of
Leicester, UK)

Dr Kavaratzis lectures in the UK, having previously held the post of Associate Professor of Marketing and Tourism at the International Business School in Budapest, Hungary. He studied in his native Greece, and Scotland, before completing a PhD at the University of Groningen, the Netherlands. Kavaratzis has widely published on brand management. His research interests include the effects of place branding campaigns on the social and cultural mosaic of contemporary cities. In this perspective he discusses the power of the brand.

In boardrooms across the globe, managers often discuss the role of the company's brands in their marketing strategies. These are useful discussions, especially when they disagree on what the brand really stands for. Some consider the brand equal to the product it refers to, others treat the brand as the name or logo, while still others describe brands as relationships or as experiences. From a managerial perspective, brands are important marketing tools because they differentiate the company's products, create unique associations in people's minds and provide strategic objectives for management. From the point of view of consumers and the society, brands can be perceived as signs that create and circulate a particular meaning, making them cultural phenomena. They can also be seen as media or interfaces that allow interactions and relationships to develop.

Brands have both a *functional* and a *symbolic* dimension. The functional dimension refers to 'what the brand does' while the symbolic dimension refers to 'what the brand means'. The two are connected but are far from identical. To an extent, the functional power of a brand stems from the product it is associated with. In this sense, the functionality of the brand is built through product development. The symbolic power of a brand stems from the 'narrative' associated with it. In this sense, the symbolism of brands is built through marketing communication. *Advertising* is crucial in this process of 'narrating the brand' but it is only one of the many channels. Also, keep in mind that the power of brands goes beyond an actual purchase. To illustrate, the brand *Ferrari* symbolizes different things to different people although most of them do not own a Ferrari (or, perhaps, precisely because of that).

How attractive a brand is to consumers largely depends on the brand's meaning to themselves and the people they interact with. They may use the brand as a form of self-expression by underscoring their values or lifestyle. Thus, brands only 'come alive' through consumers. The challenge for marketers is to combine the functional and symbolic power of brands and to base the brand's strategic objectives on consumer-oriented insights. A common tactic is building brand associations through a variety of sensory stimuli such as taste, shape, texture, colour or music, all of which can be emphasized in the company's marketing communication. The careful crafting of appealing and suggestive brand names can also lead to higher brand recall. Another brand strategy is celebrity endorsement, which transfers values and meanings from the celebrity to the brand (and vice versa). On the more symbolic side, brands might try to offer feelings of warmth and comfort, such as those found in human relationships, or use consumers' nostalgia from their childhood. Nowadays, as consumers become more and more brand-savvy, a mixture of tactics is necessary.

The Red Bull Air Race adds the aura of an
adventurous, fun lifestyle to the brand

Offering the brand to consumers as an experience is such an integrating approach, which focuses on staging a wider and compelling brand experience through communications, events and the product itself. For instance, *Red Bull* energy drink has successfully used this integrated tactic with clever advertisements, staging of intriguing events in clubs, using promotional material as evidence of the drink's experience and sponsoring events such as the Red Bull Air Race, which add to the brand the 'aura' of an adventurous, unconventional and fun lifestyle. At the end of the day, the objective is to offer a unique and memorable experience to consumers who will associate it with the brand and – if successful – will support the brand through purchase or positive word-of-mouth. In other words, what contemporary branding is all about is understanding how people form the brand in their minds and how they relate to it. That allows marketers to develop effective advertising campaigns that create brand equity and givers customers a reason to remain loyal to the brand.[5]

10.3 ADVERTISING PLANNING

Marketers use advertising to achieve three main objectives: to inform, to persuade and to remind. They use *informative advertising* to create initial demand for new products or services by announcing their availability or informing potential buyers of specific features. They also increase the demand for their current products by using *persuasive advertising*, to convince prospects that the company's products meet their wants and needs better than competitors' products. Finally, marketers employ *reminder advertising* to reinforce their previous advertising messages and to keep the brand name foremost in consumers' minds. These three objectives are often pursued simultaneously. Many advertisements not only provide *information*, but also *influence* the attitudes and buying behaviour of the target audience. Clearly, companies rely on advertising to increase sales or profit, as well as to realize other important goals.

As a rule, the best results will be achieved if we take a systematic approach, outlined in a strategic *advertising plan*. This approach involves several steps. First, based on a market *analysis*, we formulate long-term goals, which specify the contributions advertising is expected to make in achieving the overall company objectives. After translating these goals into more specific short-term objectives, we decide on what *means* should be used (such as what message and which media) and how – in the control stage – we will measure the results of our advertising efforts. Finally, we calculate the required budget for achieving these advertising objectives and determine whether they are feasible.

We will first look at setting advertising objectives. By now, it should be apparent that the work of advertising practitioners

© Lenscap / Alamy

requires much more than just creativity and artistic skills. As with solving any other problem in marketing, a step-by-step approach to planning and decision making is necessary to achieve great results.

10.3.1 Establishing advertising objectives

Advertisements as the public sees them, particularly those broadcast by large companies, are the result of the combined efforts of many people from different functional areas of the organization. Marketing research experts identify market needs and develop a profile of target customers. Product managers, financial managers and sales personnel set the advertising budget, allocate it, establish the product line and choose the appropriate channels of distribution. Artists and copywriters design the advertising message. Media planners and account executives make media and scheduling decisions, while various other specialists, too, may be involved in managing the advertising effort.

The input from these experts provides all types of information, such as marketing research numbers, market analyses and product data. But exactly what the advertising effort is expected to accomplish often remains vague. The lack of operational objectives makes it difficult to assess afterwards what effect the advertising campaign actually had. In order to determine criteria for decision making and measurement standards for evaluating the advertising effort, we should first establish the advertising objectives, not just in terms of marketing communication, but also in relation to implementation of the rest of the marketing strategy.

Market control

Advertising is just one element in the communication mix. It is not an end in itself. However, advertising is useful in *helping* to achieve certain marketing objectives. If, for instance, a firm's priority in a particular year is to increase demand for its product, an advertising campaign could be developed to increase sales per customer. Another goal might be to attract new customers who have never bought the product or brand before. If consumers using competing brands do, indeed, switch to the advertised brand, the advertising has a so-called substitution effect. Other options for the company would be to introduce a new product or updated model, and to expand the distribution network for its product line. Advertising can play a supporting role in these marketing activities, too. Finally, companies frequently consider maintaining current sales levels as a marketing goal. This could be accomplished through increasing customers' brand loyalty, again by using effective advertising.

All things considered, companies invest a lot of money in theme advertising, thereby creating a bond between the buyer and the brand. This relationship increases the probability of repeat purchases and contributes to a higher sales volume. In this sense, advertising's function is to gain a greater degree of *market control*.

Advertising and the marketing mix

Although the advertising function is subordinate to the company's overall marketing strategy, advertising is an essential strategic tool for helping achieve the marketing objectives. For each of the marketing mix variables, the marketer must decide what advertising should accomplish. Since advertising objectives also guide campaign development, marketers should define them as specifically as possible. In fact, the advertiser can only determine whether their advertising worked if the objectives are stated in measurable terms and specify a time frame. If, for example, the objective of advertising is to increase brand awareness among consumers, the marketer should state both the current level of awareness – as a benchmark – and the desired increase in brand awareness as a result of the advertising campaign.

In the area of *product strategy*, advertising is a means of facilitating the launch of a new product. An advertising campaign can make buyers aware of the introduction itself, as well as of the important *features* of products and services. If a product has unique qualities that would make a good **advertising appeal** (such as a reason for someone to buy the product), the company may even focus its message on this one basic theme. The advertising appeal chosen for the campaign is called a **unique selling proposition** (USP); it often becomes the campaign slogan or jingle. A USP will only be effective if it features a unique strength of the advertised product or service that is important to the customer and cannot be easily copied by the competition. It can then be used – as a cornerstone in the company's positioning strategy – to create a readily identifiable image for the product.

Advertising is also an important tool in the company's *pricing strategy*, because it can be used to communicate changes in the price of a product. Special offers, introductory discounts and end-of-season discounts more effectively attract potential buyers when advertised. Its likely effect on the demand curve will be discussed in Chapter 12.

Finally, advertising supports the firm's *distribution strategy*. For example, when pursuing a pull strategy, advertising can help move products through the distribution channel by stimulating demand for them. Often, manufacturers use cooperative advertising to persuade middlemen to put more push behind the product, or to encourage retailers to advertise in order to identify themselves as local outlets where consumers can find the product. In conclusion, advertising reminds current users of the product, it attracts potential users and it may even increase demand by suggesting alternative uses for the product.

10.3.2 *DAGMAR model*

As applies to objectives for all types of marketing communication, advertising objectives should not be expressed in terms of product sales. Instead, the objectives should be directly related to the communication effect or response desired from the advertising campaign. A proper objective should:

→ Describe exactly *what* we want to accomplish in terms of changing people's knowledge, attitudes or behaviour.

→ Identify a *target audience*.

→ Stipulate a time *period*.

Examples of proper advertising objectives are: 'Create brand preference for our product among at least 30 per cent of single college students between the ages of 18 and 25 before the end of June' and 'Persuade one member of each fifth household in Amsterdam to visit the new department store between the 15th of November and the 5th of December'. The link between advertising and these variables (generating brand awareness or brand preference, creating interest or desire or getting consumers to act) is much more direct than the relationship between advertising and an increase in sales.

A tool used widely by marketers in advertising planning – including setting objectives – is the DAGMAR model. DAGMAR is an acronym for *Defining Advertising Goals for Measured Advertising Results*. As discussed in Chapter 9 (and outlined in Figure 9.8), this hierarchy-of-effects model is based on the premise that the consumer passes through the stages of *awareness, understanding, conviction* and *action*. Thus, the DAGMAR model provides criteria for setting objectives. Advertising's job is to lead the consumer step-by-step to the purchasing decision. In fact, different ads can make the consumer aware of the product's existence, provide them with more information, convince them of the product's benefits as compared to other brands and, finally, persuade them to make the purchase.

How to apply the DAGMAR model

The practical value of the DAGMAR model is that it expresses advertising objectives as explicit, psychologically defined effects and measures advertising performance in terms of these effects. The implementation of DAGMA involves several steps. First, we assess the market, focusing on the availability of similar products and their positioning, the advertising messages used by competitors and predominant buyer motives. Next, we analyze the market position of our product on a hierarchy of-effects scale. How aware are prospective buyers of the product to be advertised? What exactly do they know about it? What are their attitudes toward the product and toward competing brands? And how do customers use the product? If it is not already known, we should also investigate how the product's price, design, ease-of-use, warranty, customer service and other attributes influence the buying decision.

"Will it be sunny in Paris this weekend?"

You speak. Siri helps. Say hello to the most amazing iPhone yet.

 iPhone 4 s   vodafone

Image courtesy of The Advertising Archives

Such an analysis provides an objective overview of what the product has to offer, revealing – from the consumer's point of view – its shortcomings as well as its strengths, relative to other brands. This information, combined with the company's intention to base its marketing communication goals on the response hierarchy concept, allows management to formulate specific advertising objectives for the target audience. These objectives form the basis of the campaign and will also provide the criteria that can be used later to determine whether the goal was indeed achieved.

A systematic approach to advertising efforts is especially important when dealing with the advertising agency. The DAGMAR model is a useful planning tool because it directs the creative effort, facilitates the elaboration of measurable goals and, finally, allows the integration of behavioural science theory into advertising management. Whatever methods or models are used in advertising planning, setting objectives should always be one of the first steps.

10.4 ADVERTISING STRATEGIES

Once the advertising objectives have been established, we need to work out a strategy to achieve them. When setting objectives, we were mostly concerned with the intended *effect* of the message on the consumer (such as increased brand awareness). In developing an advertising strategy, the key issue is to determine *what message* should be communicated to attain this effect. We could, for example, show what values the brand represents, what that means to the consumer and why they should therefore buy the product.

At the outset, a major decision to be made is how to communicate the *positioning*. The advertising strategy is usually driven by the positioning required to make sure that the ads are consistent with how the firm wants its products and services to be perceived. An effective positioning strategy will place the brand in a unique and preferred position in the prospect's mind. A consistent brand image is crucial, because, due to the great number of ads and commercials, consumers let most messages pass them by. If the advertisement does not immediately clarify what the brand stands for, the message will probably not make an impression. To break through the clutter, the ad must stand out in an engaging way.

There are so many *me-too products* on the market today that few brands have a truly Unique Selling Proposition (USP). If these me-too products also adopt a 'me-too positioning', their chances of success will be diminished. Therefore, every organization should strive to create distinctive advertising. A clever advertising strategy offers no guarantee of success, however, without a well-planned strategy, failure is certain.

It is clear that the choice of advertising strategy will largely depend on the objectives to be realized. Two marketing communication experts, Van Raaij and Floor, have classified the most widely adopted advertising strategies in the corporate world into four categories.[6] These are closely related to the stages in the *product life cycle*. To a great extent, the potential effectiveness of advertising depends on management's recognition of a product or service's stage in the product life cycle, and on its skill in adjusting the thrust of the advertising effort accordingly.

10.4.1 Introduction stage

Stimulating primary demand not only requires ample funding, but also involves considerable risk, because in the introduction stage, consumers do not yet know the generic product. Advertising is especially important in creating awareness of and developing interest in the new product. *Pioneering advertisements* tell consumers about the product, what it can do and where it is available. As the product type gains acceptance and consumers are becoming familiar with it, advertising's job is to stimulate selective demand by informing consumers about the brand and its benefits.

In order to make consumers aware of what a new type of product has to offer them, the advertising campaign should communicate the basic product features. Most importantly, the *functional characteristics* should be emphasized to the targeted innovators. For instance, advertising may, preferably in objective terms, explain the basic attributes of the product (e.g. traditional, natural, strong, environmentally-friendly, technologically advanced) or its *effect* (healing, nutritious, efficient, timesaving or sophisticated). To illustrate, Reebok once spent a major portion of its advertising budget on explaining how its pump technology created a custom fit for its Reebok Pump shoes.

In subsequent advertising, the *affective characteristics*, those which might influence a consumer's feelings or emotions, may be highlighted, such as the product's *appearance* (robust, tough, distinguished, simple design). These features are not always measurable, but will likely enhance the brand image. Another advertising strategy is to focus on the product's relative competitive value in the marketplace. For example, the advertiser may underline the functional or practical benefits of buying or using the product, related to its *cost* (inexpensive, valuable, economical) or its actual *use* (safe, reliable, easy to operate). Ads are often informative, while sales promotion (such as coupons, rebates or free samples) may be used to generate product trial, and trade deals to gain access to the product's distribution channels.

Although a national advertising campaign for the introduction of a completely new product requires a large budget, the first-mover advantage may result in the advertiser becoming the market leader. This automatically creates goodwill. Competing brands cannot later easily undermine that position by presenting themselves as 'better', because they will not have the credibility of the original product.

10.4.2 Market growth stage

In the growth stage of the life cycle, the target market is already familiar with the main features of the product. However, as more and more apparently similar new brands are introduced, the company constantly must defend itself against rivals' attacks. Ads become more persuasive and less informative. The brand has to be effectively *positioned* relative to the newcomers on the mass market to develop or maintain a strong brand preference. This requires a strategic decision regarding which functional attributes should be highlighted to stimulate selective demand. Entering the growth stage may also have an impact on the other components of the marketing communication mix, such as on the use of personal selling (to hold and increase distribution) and sales promotion (to provide an incentive to buy or create brand loyalty).

One way to show how the brand differs from competing brands is to focus on *distinctive product attributes* in advertising. Now that the features that were initially communicated have probably become standard for the entire product category, they can no longer be linked exclusively to the innovating company's brand. To differentiate the brand, a claim previously made by no other market rival is required. Note that it does not necessarily have to involve product characteristics unique to the brand. As long as the company is the first to highlight these attributes in its campaign, the brand can effectively claim them as its own. Think of *Volvo*, which for many decades has successfully positioned itself as the safest car, or Nike, known for its products for serious athletes.

A second advertising option in the market growth stage is to add *affective product attributes* to the positioning of a brand that was launched with a campaign revolving around instrumental (or functional) characteristics. As some of the illustrations in this book show, many marketers attempt to give their established brand more of an emotional value over time. To illustrate, Kellogg's campaign for Smart Start cereal originated with an emphasis on informing consumers about its ingredients that lower cholesterol and blood pressure. More recently, however, its ads feature the product's great flavour ('See how tasty intelligent can be').

10.4.3 Market maturity stage

In the maturity stage of the life cycle, the total market will soon be saturated. Increased sales are only possible at the expense of other brands. Therefore, advertising's task is to further increase brand loyalty and to make present buyers less receptive to competitors' offers. There are various strategies for this.

An approach often taken is to increase – through brand name advertising – the *unaided brand awareness*, particularly as many consumers give little thought to what they are buying when shopping. They simply choose the best-known brand. The brand that is most frequently advertised – in the most creative way – is likely to retain present customers.

An effective *retentive advertising* strategy (one which reminds users to buy the product) is to differentiate the brand by pointing out a product characteristic where the brand's *performance* is superior. Take, for example, some laundry detergent ads. This will reinforce consumers' brand choice and help retain wholesaler and retailer support. An alternative strategy, particularly when there are very few product differences, is to communicate that the brand offers the same performance at a *lower* price. However, the inherent risk of relying on such value-based advertising is that competitors will reduce their prices, resulting in a price war. Another danger of this strategy is that it may increase buyers' sensitivity to price and encourage them to make price comparisons.

A final option is to attract new buyers by announcing something 'new' in an ad. This could be a temporary price cut, a special deal (for instance a two-for-one offer) or a product improvement. If this solves a consumer's problem, they will consider switching brands. Marketers of cameras, snacks and gasoline often adopt this advertising strategy.

10.4.4 *Market decline stage*

If the marketer decides not to 'milk' a product in its final stage of the life cycle by keeping the costs down, there are few remaining advertising options. One of these last options is to suggest a new use for the product. An example is an advertising campaign for cheese, offering suggestions for using cheese as a snack or in a wide range of dishes. A related approach is to stimulate an increase in the frequency of consumption. Various campaigns for chicken, eggs and meat have successfully applied this strategy. Alternatively, an advertising campaign can try to attract a *new target market*. The revival of the bicycle industry, for example, is partly the result of an advertising strategy that appeals to a mature consumer segment.

Eventually, a marketing strategy may be pursued to phase out the product profitably. While this usually involves a cut in promotional costs, some advertising may be continued to retain current buyers and remind them that the product or service is still available.

10.5 DEVELOPING THE ADVERTISING CAMPAIGN

Most ads are not developed separately, but are part of a broader campaign. An **advertising campaign** is a collection of different but related advertisements or commercials based on a single theme, which appear in different media as part of an advertising plan designed to meet an organization's advertising objectives. With the objectives set and the strategy – within the budgetary constraints – outlined, we are now ready to develop the advertising campaign. This has to be done in a systematic fashion.

Many campaigns result in a misuse of funding because the message is barely noticed or fails to impact its target audience. Generally, this is due to how the advertising strategy is 'translated' into the *creative concept*, or how the message is communicated to the target market. The creative strategy combines the 'what should be said' (as outlined in the advertising strategy) with the 'how it is said' (spelled out and illustrated in the creative concept). In other words, the advertising message actually takes shape through the creative strategy, which leads to a creative concept.

Once everyone agrees on the advertising strategy, a *briefing* has to be prepared before work can begin on developing the creative concept. Figure 10.2 illustrates the stages in this process. Although the advertiser or 'client' usually leaves the development and execution of the creative concept to the advertising agency, the first step in the development of the advertising campaign is the briefing to the advertising agency.[7]

10.5.1 *Briefing*

As soon as an advertising agency is hired, it must be properly informed about the company's viewpoint, wishes and other matters related to the campaign. The client's instructions to the advertising agency are known as a **briefing**.

Essentially neither the advertising agency nor the advertiser can plan or execute a solid campaign without a good briefing. The briefing specifies what message the advertising campaign

FIGURE 10.2 Steps in developing an advertising campaign

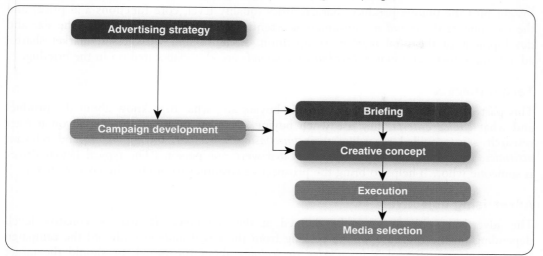

should get across. Without specific instructions the agency could literally develop dozens of campaigns with as many themes. With a well-prepared briefing, the copywriters and other contributors in the agency will know exactly what is expected of them. This allows them to develop a creative concept that presents the advertiser's brand in the most favourable light and persuades prospective buyers to consider purchasing the product or service, provided that is the campaign's goal. At the same time, the advertising briefing provides the client with a frame of reference against which the agency's concept proposals will later be evaluated.

A complete briefing will contain both marketing and advertising components. As a rule, the briefing will include necessary background information on the product and the market, a description of the target market, the advertising objectives and – perhaps most important for the creative director, copywriter and art director – the proposition. Also included are the company's guidelines for the copy and artwork, the media preferences, advertising budget and timetable.

The new, improved SFG20 standard maintenance specification for building engineering services. Now including Customiser Compliance and Service Model to prioritise and customise your building maintenance regime.

New criticality ratings enable streamlined budget and project management. With bespoke maintenance models for specific building types and live technical updates to prevent over-maintenance of assets and ensure compliance, clients, consultants and contractors are more in control than ever.

Customise. Prioritise. Lead the way.

For a product order form go to www.sfg20.co.uk/subscribe or call 01768 860405
SFG20 is published by B&ES Publications.

 **SFG20**

© PRG Ltd

A recent advertising campaign devised by PRG to launch two new components to SFG20 – the industry standard building maintenance tool for the building engineering services sector. The ads appeared in trade magazines and on trade websites targeting facilities managers, building contractors and consulting engineers.

Product and market

Insight into the unique product characteristics (quality level, core functions and price) and the meaning of the *brand* to consumers is essential to its positioning strategy. The size and development of the total *market* (competition, strengths and weaknesses, market shares, advertising efforts) and major *distribution channels* are also elaborated on in the briefing.

Target market

This part of the briefing explains who the buyers are, what they know about the product and what *choice criteria* they use when buying. Detailed information – based on market research – is provided regarding their *purchasing behaviour*, buying *habits* and relevant *attitudes*. Describing the target market as if it were one person ('The typical Jaguar driver is someone who…') helps to bring the prospective customer to life for the creative team.

Advertising objectives

The advertising objectives can be defined at the cognitive, affective or conative level, depending on the response we are seeking from the target audience. Should the campaign focus on affecting people's *knowledge* or *feelings* about the brand, or should the target audience be spurred into *action*? And how does this fit in with the rest of the marketing and communication strategy?

In addition to these *descriptive* elements, this part of the briefing also includes a *task-related* component, expressing the client's expectations with respect to the communication effect or other impact of the advertising campaign. This provides a yardstick by which to measure the effectiveness of the campaign and evaluate the advertising agency's work at a later stage.

Proposition

The *advertising platform* or proposition is a brief description of the product's major benefits to the buyer that the advertiser – as selling points – might include in their advertisements. It is also referred to as the *advertising theme* or *advertising appeal*. A particular ad may include one or more of these major ideas from the proposition. Usually, the same selling points are used throughout the campaign, providing continuity over time and hopefully resulting in a significant impact on the target market.

As a key component of the briefing, the proposition should consist of concepts that are important to the product's users and that motivate them to purchase the product. Those could be *functional* ('instrumental') product characteristics (such as the design or technology used), or *symbolic* ('expressive') features (such as the brand personality). Essentially, the proposition is the translation of the advertising strategy (which describes in marketing terms the best selling points to be used in approaching the target market) into 'plain consumer language'. Hence, the proposition tells the potential customer in their own vocabulary what we 'promise' them and why they should buy the product. Although the proposition describes the basic or unique selling points, it does not indicate how to effectively present them in a creative advertising campaign. That is the advertising agency's task.

Since the proposition is the foundation on which to build the advertising message and plays a crucial role in developing a consistent brand image, it should not be frequently changed. It should also be kept short and simple. One or two sentences containing just one major appeal or reason to buy, is usually sufficient. Its purpose, after all, is to identify one clear message or emotional impression that the consumer is likely to retain from the ad after being exposed to it. An advertising campaign (such as *Philips'* campaign with the theme 'Sense and Simplicity') is most effective when the ad's content (*what* we want to say) and its form (*how* we say it) are perfectly aligned.

Unfortunately, many propositions fail to meet these criteria. Some are too long and include various types of arguments, without a clear choice being made. It is difficult for the creative team to extract the essence of the proposition if the decisive selling point is 'hidden' somewhere in the text. Even worse are propositions formulated from the advertiser's rather than the customer's point of view, and propositions so general that any competitor could use the same argument.

Guidelines for copy and design

In order to find out what type of campaign the client has in mind, the advertising agency needs some clear *guidelines* for the copy and art direction. The briefing might specify, for instance, that the television commercial should demonstrate the product's major benefit for maximum impact, that, in addition to a logical appeal, a less rational benefit should be emphasized to create added value, that a particular jingle should be used at the end of the spot and that the ads must be compatible with a more extensive global campaign.

Media preferences

The media selection and the creative concept are so closely linked that these decisions must be considered simultaneously. The creative concept will indicate what type of media should be used for the campaign to be most effective. If, however, the use of certain media would exceed the budget, this information must be communicated to the creative team as part of the briefing.

Budget and media scheduling

Specifying the available budget will prevent unnecessary work and frustration. If, for example, the budget is not sufficient to allow messages to be placed on blimps, airplanes' trailing banners, hot-air balloons and scoreboards at soccer games, the advertising agency may consider less expensive advertising vehicles, such as the brand name appearing on T-shirts, in printed programmes of rock concerts, on grocery carts in supermarkets or inlaid in store flooring.

The briefing should also specify media scheduling, setting the timing and sequence for the advertisements that are part of the campaign. The media planner can only take submission deadlines for radio and television stations into account if they know when the first commercial must be broadcast. Generally, media scheduling is influenced by the consumer's purchase frequency (products with a short repurchase cycle require consistent media schedules throughout the year), the sales pattern (advertising may be increased – or decreased – during periods of peak sales) and competitors' activities (small companies may temporarily stop advertising when large competitors boost their advertising). Finally, advertisers must be concerned about the 'forgetting rate', or the speed with which buyers forget the brand if they are not exposed to advertising.

10.5.2 *Creative concept*

Once the briefing is completed, work on concept development can begin. The advertising agency now tries to think of that one big idea – consisting of words, images, tone and style – which communicates the proposition most effectively. Thus, concept development is a fundamental step in the process of turning the proposition into a creative idea (concept), which serves as a cornerstone of the ad.

Advertising agencies' account executives often apply a rule of thumb in creating effective advertising, namely 'Sell the sizzle, not the steak'. The point is that advertising should sell the intangible benefits of using a product, rather than the tangible features or attributes. A benefit addresses the consumer's question, 'What's in it for me'? If these benefits are important to the consumer, they may be a major input in selecting an advertising appeal or USP for a campaign, such as convenience, environmental consciousness, love, health or fun. These appeals are broad enough to allow the agency to devise a number of subthemes to be used in a campaign or promotional activity.

There are several possible approaches to creating attention-getting or memorable advertising. Some products can attract the target audience's attention simply by explaining its benefits (for example, a diesel engine's fuel economy), how it works (the *iPhone*'s built-in HD video editing feature) or what ingredients it contains (retinoids in skin care products). This is known as an *explanation concept*.

Alternatively, the ad can show what the product or service can do for the consumer (designer clothing providing recognition or status) or for those around them (life insurance taking care of dependents' future needs). This so-called *effect concept* is also used in commercials for deodorant or ads for cars. Another way for advertising to create added value is by suggesting a link between the product (such as perfume) and something else (romance, sex appeal). This *association concept* has worked well for Marlboro, advertising its masculine Marlboro man (linking its brand to feelings of freedom and adventure, brought to life by the rugged, horseback-riding cowboy). Finally, if a brand has a distinctive benefit, it may be compared with competing products – whether those are identified by name or not (*comparison concept*). This seems to be *Procter & Gamble*'s favourite approach in advertising its brands.[8]

10.5.3 *Execution*

After the client has approved the creative concept presented to them, the advertising agency can begin *executing* the message. This requires decisions on both the *artwork* (the layout and illustrations) and the *copy* (the verbal part of the ad, including the headline, body copy and signature, which is the advertiser's name and logo). It is important for the:

→ *Headline* to attract the attention of the target audience, while inspiring prospects to read on.

→ *Illustrations* to convey the right atmosphere as well as factual information, if needed.

→ *Body copy* to be credible in communicating the necessary information.

The ad may also have a tagline or slogan, a catchy phrase relating to the marketing message. Many consumers hearing a slogan immediately think of the product and can even sing along with the accompanying jingle. Often, they remember effective *slogans* long after they are no longer used in advertising. Examples of memorable slogans are 'Just do it.' (*Nike*), 'Come to think of it, I'll have a *Heineken*', 'Probably the best lager in the world' (*Carlsberg*), 'Vorsprung durch Technik' (*Audi*), 'Have it your way' (*Burger King*) and 'Sense and Simplicity' (*Philips*).

Technical development of the advertising (such as the artwork and typography) requires extensive planning, coordination and attention to detail. Among the companies and individuals helping to design the campaign may be production companies, commercial artists, media companies and printers. All in all, the campaign development may take months. Some of this time will be spent on media selection and advertising research. Both of these topics will be discussed in the following sections.

MARKETING TOPPER
Dos Equis: Heineken's Star in the US

Heineken beer was the first foreign brew to be sold in the United States after Prohibition ended in 1933. Its *first mover advantage* and great advertising campaigns (such as 'Come to think of it – I'll have a Heineken') contributed to the brand's status of the best-selling imported beer in America for decades. In the1990s, however, Corona became the No. 1 imported beer. It primarily appealed to young people who prefer a lighter tasting beer and who were probably inspired by commercials that associate this Mexican brand with a wild and wonderful life with plenty of parties. More recently, Heineken lost some market share to Belgium's Stella Artois. Now, Heineken is counting on its own beer brand from Mexico to boost its US standing: *Dos Equis*.

The Dutch brewing company became the legal owner of Dos Equis, Tecate and other brands after its €5 billion acquisition of Fomento Económico Mexicano SAB's beer unit. The fastest growing premium Mexican beer in the US is crucial to Heineken's plans to revive its fortunes in North America. What makes Dos Equis such an attractive brand is that it is a popular beer in a *broad segment* of the population, as opposed to other imported or microbrew brands that just appeal to a niche segment. Heineken executives seem to agree. 'The brand has proven resilience in today's economy and has potential for continued double digit growth for many years to come,' according to VP Marketing, Colin Westcott Pitt. 'Dos Equis is our shining star in the US,' says John Nicolson, the head of Heineken's Americas unit at the brewery company's headquarters in Amsterdam. 'We've got to be *young*. We don't want to be part of the past.'

Heineken International BV is happy to make room on store shelves for its Mexican brand. Sales of Dos Equis – named after the two Xs on its label – are up 22 per cent at a time when the Heineken brand's sales declined by 1 per cent and other imported beer sales by an average of 4 per cent. At the core of Dos Equis's success is effective marketing and advertising. That includes its 'Most Interesting Man in the World' ad campaign, featuring stories of one worldly man's experiences. The commercials'

catch phrase is 'I don't always drink beer, but when I do, I prefer Dos Equis.'

The Dos Equis adverts have gained a cult following on YouTube and Facebook

The unconventional TV adverts, which won a Titanium Lions award at the advertising industry's Cannes Lions International Festival of Creativity, show the sophisticated man as a dare devil acting recklessly in a range of bizarre situations. These include skydiving while sitting in a kayak and armwrestling with previous political leaders such as Churchill, Stalin and Mao. The spots have gained a cult following on *YouTube* and *Facebook*. The social media *buzz* has made Dos Equis into a popular brand, especially among beer drinkers in their early twenties. Industry analysts agree that the increase in Dos Equis sales can largely be attributed to its high quality advertising campaign.

The Americas, including the US and Brazil, are Heineken's second-biggest market after Western Europe, accounting for nearly 25 per cent of the brewer's overall sales. But Dos Equis is responsible for only a small part of the Dutch brewer's sales revenues in the United States. The Mexican brew represents just 0.6 per cent of the US beer market volume, as compared to the Heineken brand's 2.2 per cent. Still, Heineken Lager is increasingly thought of as a drink for older drinkers. It's been downsizing its distribution outlets in the US after it became too universal during the 1990s, 'losing its aura of exclusivity', according to Nicolson.

Now, the brewing company is trying to regain lost ground by repositioning the Heineken brand to make it more attractive to young drinkers who are financially well off. At the same time, the company is *pushing* its brand more aggressively in bars and restaurants. Its new television commercials, which depict a young guy living it up at parties and in restaurants, look more like a campaign for designer brand clothes or an expensive perfume than for an imported beer. 'The new, much edgier global ad campaigns for Heineken appear to be working to arrest the decline,' says industry analyst Trevor Stirling. The Heineken brand, which entered into a global partnership with Facebook to collaborate on digital campaigns, already has well over five million 'Likes.'

For now, Heineken, the world's most international brewer that accounts for 18 per cent of the consolidated volume of beer sold globally, is benefiting from its repositioning strategy. Still, industry analyst Anthony Bucalo doesn't think that the Heineken brand itself will show much *long-term* improvement. 'A lot of the big brands have about 25-year *life cycles* where – after peaking out – they start declining. Heineken hit that point in the middle of the last decade,' he says. 'They can stabilize the business, but the future of Heineken USA is in the Dos Equis brand.'[9]

10.6 MEDIA SELECTION

Selecting appropriate media to convey an advertiser's message to its target audience is crucial to campaign development. Media types to be utilized, such as *visual* media (newspapers, magazines, direct mail, outdoors), *auditory* media (radio) or *audiovisual* media (TV, Internet), should be determined at an early stage, so that they can be considered in plotting the creative strategy. But, allocation of the advertising budget across individual *media vehicles* (which specific news magazines, TV programmes, etc.) is usually decided after making the creative decisions. The advertising agency's media planner (or media expert) makes these choices based on certain *criteria* and includes them in a *media plan*.

10.6.1 *The media plan*

There is no such thing as a perfect advertising medium. Media selection is dependent on such factors as the target audience, product type, media objectives, available budget and the costs of the alternative media. The advertising agency's media planner is responsible for getting the message to the target audience in an optimal and cost-effective way through the appropriate media.

In the media plan – part of the advertising plan – they define the *media objectives* and present the strategy to achieve them. This media plan includes budget details, a description of the optimal media mix (media types as well as individual media vehicles) and the *media scheduling* (the timing and sequence of a series of ads, specifically outlining the use of colour and format in the ads). The media plan will show – based on media research findings – the best opportunities to reach the target audience and how the message will actually be conveyed to the target market.

Media objectives

The media objectives are derived from the marketing communication and advertising objectives. Thus, the media to be chosen must contribute to realizing these previously defined overall goals. An important consideration in setting media objectives is the primary target market we want to reach through advertising. But what we really focus on in the media selection, is the (media) target audience – the segment targeted by a particular medium. This target audience does not always coincide with the 'marketing' target market, in terms of their characteristics or location. The target audience, for instance, may be smaller (limited to the southern part of the country) or larger (involving potential buyers as well as influencers of the purchase). Obviously, the target audience should be described based on the results of media research.

In addition to describing *whom* we want to reach, the objectives must also spell out *what* we want to accomplish (in terms of the stages in a hierarchy-of-effects model), within the limitations of the media budget. Selecting the right media is complicated, because we have to stretch the budget to cover the number of people we want to reach as well as the number of times we want to reach this audience.

Reach refers to the number of different people or households exposed at least once during a specific period (usually four weeks) to either the medium ('medium reach') or to the advertisement in that medium ('advertisement reach'). Frequency refers to the number of times a person is exposed to a particular medium or advertisement within a given time frame. Since most consumers need several (at least three) exposures to a message to comprehend it and link it to a particular brand, these numbers will have an impact on the media types and vehicles selected.

Media types

The medium is the message. This statement by Canadian communication theorist Marshall McLuhan makes sense. In marketing, the selected medium is often as important as the content and format of the advertising message. Advertisers can choose between various media types that are all quite different. Audio-visual media (such as websites) are excellent for messages in which the product is demonstrated, and visual media (magazines) is best for messages with high information content. Also, some media enjoy a higher level of reader loyalty or status than others, and therefore add more value. Table 10.2 provides an overview of the pros and cons of some major advertising media.

10.6.2 Criteria for selecting media

Which media are best capable of carrying a message to the company's target audience depends on three factors: the medium's communication capability, the reach, and the cost of each medium. These are the three selection criteria media planners most commonly use in evaluating the available media forms and the alternatives, or vehicles, within each medium.

Communication capability

The communication capability of a medium refers to its effectiveness in conveying a particular type of message. The medium's impact depends partly on its *technical features*, such as the reproduction quality of colour graphics, its lack of clutter and the number of advertising versus editorial pages. For complex information, magazines from which ads can be clipped and saved are generally more suitable than radio and TV with their short exposure time and perishable messages.

TABLE 10.2 Advantages and disadvantages of major advertising media

Media types	Advantages	Disadvantages
Newspapers	Ads reach large audience Excellent coverage of regional and local markets Ads can be placed and changed on short notice Frequent publication possible Reader can save complex message for future reference	High cost of national coverage Difficult to reach specific target audience Short life span of ad Poor reproduction quality Often superficially read
Magazines	Can target specific market segments High-quality colour Credible source for target audience Long advertising life (week/month) High pass-along rate Noise caused by many other ads	Too expensive for regional coverage Long lead times reduce flexibility Medium cluttered with other ads Limited demonstration capabilities
Sponsored magazines	Can target a selective audience Increases customer loyalty Accessible for third party advertising	Relatively high production cost Difficult, time-consuming publishing process Visual only
Free circulation newspapers	High reach because of free circulation Geographic segmentation through regional editions Relatively low cost	Limited attention-getting and communication capabilities High 'waste' Only published on certain days
Television	Involves multiple senses (sight and hearing) High impact because of use of motion Reaches large (national) audience Entertainment carryover and 'forced' encounter Prestigious form of advertising	High cost and limited availability Viewers switch stations to avoid commercials Short exposure time due to high costs Fewer (young) people are watching television Difficult to target narrow audience segments Perishable message in a cluttered medium
Radio	Wide reach, including drivers and workers Fairly low cost Captive audience before and after news broadcasts	Difficult to communicate complex information Limited attention because of other activities while listening Requires high frequency of message repetition to achieve comprehension and retention
Movie theatre	Allows for geographic segmentation Commercials can entertain viewers and create excitement	High 'noise' level distracting audience Short exposure time
Outdoor	Little competition due to limited availability High reach and repeat exposure at reasonable cost Geographic selectivity with message located close to point of purchase	Not appreciated in countryside and controversial in many towns Even short and simple message may not attract readers' full attention Difficult to target specific group and to measure the audience
Direct mail	Circulation (little waste) controlled by advertiser Complex or creative message can be personalised Hidden from competitors Easy to measure effectiveness	High cost per contact Perceived as junk mail Mailbox clutter
Internet	Enables company to track customers and build databases Interactive ad with link to advertiser's website allows for immediate response Creative possibilities in fast growing medium at moderate cost	Not everyone uses the Internet Effectiveness is difficult to measure Consumer concerns about privacy and security

Advertisers who want to incorporate current events in their messages tend to choose daily newspapers with short lead times for placing ads. Alternatively, if they need interactive ads with audio and video capabilities, they probably turn to Internet advertising.

The *context* of the medium (both the editorial content and the type of advertising it contains) also has an impact on its communication capability. An authoritative medium can actually increase an advertisement's credibility. To illustrate, an ad for an exclusive ski trip will probably have optimum effect in a special winter sports feature of a well-respected news magazine. To maximize its effectiveness, an ad should always fit the medium.

A final consideration is the *contact situation*, the circumstances under which the consumer comes into contact with the medium. Cinema advertising, for instance, is usually viewed in a relaxed setting. And while the morning edition of a newspaper may only be quickly scanned before leaving for work, a particular market segment will consult a TV guide almost daily. The advertiser should also consider whether the medium will be read, seen or heard for entertainment and distraction, or specifically to find information. Finally, media to which the consumer has a strong *loyalty* will be considered more attentively and completely than an insert in a newspaper.

Reach

A second criterion for evaluating the available advertising media is the medium reach, or number of people who encounter or have been exposed to the medium (often expressed as a percentage of the total number of people that could have been reached). For print media, this figure generally differs from the *circulation* (the number of copies of an issue distributed), because some publications are not looked at (or not even taken out of the protective packaging), while others may be shared and read by several people.

In their analyses, advertisers and advertising executives further classify a medium's reach. Total reach refers to the number of people (or percentage of the total that could have been reached) that may have been exposed to the medium; they will have seen at least one issue in a particular year. If, for example, 7.5 million people have at some time (in a given year) read *Cosmopolitan*, this constitutes the 'total reach' in that year.

The reach per issue may differ significantly. Magazines with an attractive cover, for example, may sell more than a typical issue through over-the-counter sales. Other magazines may be kept and looked at (again) at a later time. Therefore, in media planning we generally consider the average reach. This is the number of individuals during the publication interval (such as a week for weekly periodicals) who may see any given issue of the medium. The survey question might be, 'Have you read an issue of *Cosmopolitan* in the past week'? For TV advertising, the average reach is the average number of people that would view the commercial at the (different) times that it is broadcast during or in between programmes.

Sometimes it is crucial that an advertisement is seen shortly after the medium's publication date. For example, a Valentine's Day special offer would become pointless if seen after Valentine's Day. The advertiser is then interested in the current reach. This is the number of people within a publication interval who see an issue intended for that period ('Have you read this week's *Cosmopolitan*?').

Magazine subscribers do not read every issue. By using a medium several times, we can increase the *cumulative reach* or unduplicated reach, which refers to the total number of people exposed to an ad a single time. When someone views an advertising message for the second time, it is known as duplicated reach.

For an advertiser, the sheer number of people reached is generally less important than the percentage of the target audience that a particular medium reaches. This is known as the *target market reach* or coverage. Let's assume that *Cosmopolitan* is read by 115 000 fashion-conscious young people in Belgium. The target market for Cosmopolitan is comprised of a total of 780 000 people in that country. *Cosmopolitan*'s coverage of fashion-conscious young people is, therefore, 115 000 divided by 780 000 = 14.7 per cent. The rest of the reach, which falls outside the target market, is referred to as *waste*.

Media costs

As we have just seen, when analyzing media, advertisers are interested in evaluating the degree to which the target market will see an advertisement in a specific medium (often referred to as *advertising exposure*). Apart from the reach and communication capability of the medium, the media costs are also often used as a criterion in selecting media. With a small budget, the choice of media will be immediately restricted by the *absolute costs* per medium. The *cost per contact* will be a major factor in the media strategy. Media costs are always calculated in terms of cost per thousand, or CPM (M is the Roman numeral for 1 000). Cost per thousand refers to the cost of reaching 1 000 individuals or households in the target audience with the advertising message in a particular medium. CPM allows media planners to compare the relative cost effectiveness of different media vehicles that have different exposure rates.

An example of the calculation of cost per thousand (CPM) will help clarify some of these terms. Suppose that a trade journal has a *circulation* (print run) of 6 000. Since each subscriber to the journal passes it on to, on the average, one other person, the *medium reach* is 12 000. If 10 000 of these people are part of the advertiser's target market and the cost of a half-page ad is €1 250, then the *cost per thousand* is: €1 250 / 10 = €125. This number reflects the cost to deliver a message to 1 000 people.

From these numbers we are not able to deduce how many individuals will actually view the ad and interpret the message correctly, let alone if it influences their buying behaviour. Furthermore, in companies or families where more than one magazine is read, the target audience may be exposed to the message several times. Just like a greater reach, this greater *frequency* may be desirable, because some ads contain more information than consumers can digest in a single exposure, even if they do pay close attention to the details.

When reach (expressed as a percentage of the total market) is multiplied by frequency, we obtain a commonly used number in advertising, called gross rating points (GRP). By comparing the GRP number of a magazine to the GRP of placing an ad on a billboard or on television, we can assess the effectiveness of alternative media vehicles. Regardless, in order to obtain the appropriate number of GRPs to realize the objectives of an advertising campaign, the media planner must balance – within the cost constraints – both reach and frequency. For that, they must decide what is more important, reach (exposing more people fewer times) or frequency (exposing fewer people more times). That decision will certainly affect their media choice.

10.7 MEASURING ADVERTISING EFFECTIVENESS

With so many media and advertisements competing for the potential buyer's attention, advertisers need to closely examine the target audience's response to their messages. Generally, the more costly the production and execution of an advertising campaign, the more research is conducted to help maximize the company's campaign's effectiveness. Some research designed to evaluate the results of advertising is difficult and expensive. But without an assessment strategy, the advertiser cannot determine if its advertising makes a contribution to realizing the marketing goals or whether its investment in a campaign has a decent return.

Since marketing research companies conduct *media research* on a regular basis, advertisers usually have no problem deciding where to place their ads and determining the size of the audience. There is literally an entire industry of organizations in business to conduct and share media research. Measuring the effects of advertising, however, is more complicated: whether a particular message attracts attention, is interpreted correctly and is remembered by consumers, may be evaluated in various ways and at different stages in the development or execution of a campaign. The type of advertising research that focuses on the effect of a message – before, during or after a campaign – is known as a copy test.

An evaluation of advertising effectiveness may involve both *pretesting* (the testing of audience reactions while the advertisement's copy, illustrations and layout are being developed, sometimes referred to as 'copy testing'), and *posttesting* (during or after the campaign, when the advertising has been produced in final form). In addition, media may be rated on how well they deliver the advertiser's message. Whatever testing method is used, it should certainly include an assessment of the extent to which the (previously defined) advertising objectives have been attained. In order to do that, *baseline measures* (such as the level of awareness of a new service) should be taken before the start of an advertising campaign and compared with measurements afterwards so that the results of the campaign can be verified.

10.7.1 *Pretesting*

A pretest may be conducted before the ad is published or broadcast to decide which version of an advertisement is best or to determine if a particular ad communicates the intended message. The advertiser wants to make sure that there are no unforeseen communication barriers. Pretesting gives management an opportunity to assess the effectiveness of a particular element of a message and make any necessary adjustments while work on the ad or the campaign continues.

Pretests can either be conducted early during campaign development – in the concept stage, when only rough copy of the advertisement is available – or in a later stage, when the creative team is already working on the ad layout and design.

Common objectives of a pretest are:

→ To determine if an advertising message grabs people's attention, evokes interest, is well understood or elicits any other intended communication effects.

→ To select the most effective version of a number of proposed ads or commercials.

→ To decide on the best sequence and frequency of the campaign ads. Various testing procedures are available for print and broadcast ads at this early stage. Here we will look at some of the methods most widely used by marketing researchers.

Portfolio test

Consumers are asked to look through a portfolio or loose-leaf binder containing the test ad as well as other ads. Afterwards, they are asked to record their impressions on several evaluative scales in a questionnaire to measure which of the ads attracted their attention, was most informative or most likely to change their attitudes. Sometimes the ad is included in a *dummy magazine*, after which a memory test is used to ascertain which ads consumers remember seeing and what they think was in them. This is known as a *recall test*.

Consumer jury

This 'jury test' is similar to the portfolio test, although the test ad is not hidden in between other advertisements. Here, a panel of potential buyers of the advertised product is asked what drew their attention to the ad and is asked to rate how they like it. This research can also be conducted through *focus group interviews*, in which consumers are probed more extensively about the ad.

Theatre test

Consumers are invited to watch new movies or test television shows in which commercials have been inserted. They then fill out a questionnaire to submit their opinions about the ads. A less costly way to obtain this information is through a *trailer test*, in which people are invited into a trailer, located in a shopping centre parking lot, where they are asked for their reactions to some advertisements.

10.7.2 Posttesting

In a posttest, advertising copy is evaluated after it has been published in a medium to measure the communication effect. Posttesting can help to determine:

→ Whether the advertising did have the intended effect.

→ When a theme becomes boring and should be replaced.

→ What the exact medium and advertising reach is.

The type of research we choose will depend on the objective of the advertising to be tested. If the objective was to change consumers' attitudes, a different type of research is required than with an objective such as 'increasing the number of showroom visitors by 20 per cent'.

Earlier, when we made a distinction between measuring the communication effect and the *sales effect*, we noted that an increase in sales (essentially a 'behavioural effect' of advertising) was not an appropriate criterion to evaluate a campaign, simply because sales are also affected by environmental variables, such as competition, the economy and the *carry-over effect* of advertising. Therefore, an increase in sales can only be ascribed to advertising in situations such as a short-lived campaign (for example, when announcing a price discount on Friday only), ads by mail order companies or special offers on company websites where the response can be directly measured through the number of orders or inquiries received (*inquiry test*). In other situations, an appropriate posttesting approach to measure the effect of advertising on sales is the so-called *sales test*. Sales tests allow a producer, distributor or researcher to manipulate an advertising variable (such as an ad's copy or frequency) and measure subsequent sales effects by keeping track of data collected through checkout scanners in stores.

However, since it is difficult to measure the direct effects of advertising on sales, most marketers assess print ads according to how well consumers can remember them. Posttest research methods based on memory include recall tests and recognition tests. Recall may be measured through aided or unaided recall methods. In an *aided recall* test, subjects are provided with a list of brands, products, company names or part of an advertisement and asked which ones they remember seeing and actually read. In an *unaided recall* test, on the other hand, the respondents are asked which ads they have seen recently. They are not provided with any clues to help them remember. A typical research question might be, 'Which of the advertisements that you saw yesterday, do you remember?' Finally, in a recognition test, the research subjects are shown the advertisement in question and asked if they recognize it. Only if they do, are they asked additional questions to find out what part of the ad they actually read.

MARKETING MISTAKE
Ambush Marketing: Hijacking the Olympics

One of the perks for professional athletes is the abundance of 'freebies' – complimentary goods, from sportswear to gadgets – provided at major tournaments. When London hosted the 2012 Olympic Games, this was no exception. The 10 000 competitors who descended upon Stratford's Olympic Village were given complimentary condoms from the market-leading brand, *Durex*, owned by the British company Reckitt Benckiser. But this multinational consumer goods company did not publicly broadcast its Olympic connection, despite the games' historic draw as a marketing jackpot amongst top global brands like *Samsung*, *Adidas*, *Coca Cola*, *BP* and *BMW*.

The reason for missing out on this great marketing communication opportunity lay with restrictions imposed by the London Organizing Committee of the Olympic Games (LOCOG) against non-official sponsors associating themselves with the tournament; unlike Reckitt Benckiser's direct rivals, Procter & Gamble, who contributed to the £1 billion (€1.25 billion) collectively paid to become official sponsors. In safeguarding their partners' investments, LOCOG took a tough stance on unauthorized brands illicitly attaching themselves to the event via *guerrilla* tactics, or, more typically, *ambush marketing* – a marketing strategy through which an advertiser with a competing brand (not an official sponsor) associates itself with a big sporting event while avoiding the sponsorship fee.

Why companies should wish to align themselves with the Olympics in the first place is obvious, not least because it makes commercial sense. Paul Deighton, LOCOG's CEO cited 'the ultimate feel-good association', tapping into a wider theme of the core values that the Olympics represents: aspiration, dedication, fighting spirit, being the best and beating the competition – all positive qualities attached to the brand through official sponsorship. In real terms, the internationally televised and reported event presents an advantageous and exclusive platform to project the company, ahead of its rivals, while helping to recruit young talent and inspire the existing workforce.

© AFP / Getty

Smart marketers have to think creatively to bypass the strict impositions

Many world sporting occasions are targeted by ambush marketing, the soccer *World Cup* and *UEFA Champions League* being other major examples. Smart marketers have to think creatively, and often mischievously, to bypass the strict impositions. When the credit card *Visa* sponsored the 1992 Winter Games, competitor *American Express* cheekily opted for the tagline you 'don't need a visa' to enjoy the games. Meanwhile, the 2010 World Cup witnessed a stunt by Dutch brewer *Bavaria*, involving thirty-six scantily-clad glamour models in orange, garnering wide publicity at a Holland-Denmark game, much to the annoyance of official sponsors, *Budweiser*. Ambush marketing has become a mainstay of major sporting events to rival the official sponsors.

The zero-tolerance actions of LOCOG (sanctioned by the UK's Parliament), although specific to the London games, have set a precedent for future events on the world stage and could have a significant impact on marketing at the Rio de Janeiro games of 2016. Restrictions were placed on advertising near the stadiums, in response to previous years like Atlanta 1996, when *Nike* plastered its famous tick logo across the city, angering official sponsor, *Adidas*. Even key word combinations involving 'London', '2012' and 'summer' were prohibited in advertising, with penalties potentially exceeding €25 000. As one commentator, Blayney Stuart, of the UK's Chartered Institute of Marketing, suggested, 'This is a new development in the history of marketing – that previously acceptable commercial practices can now be faced with criminal charges because a powerful organizer doesn't approve.'

LOCOG's justification for its strict stance was that unauthorized promotions have a negative impact on the Games through companies profiting without financial investment. In London 2012, the grey area of defining exactly what constitutes a breach presented a challenge of ingenuity, practically inviting covert marketing techniques from those who dared. Gambling site Paddy Power took full advantage of the ambiguity with the slogan, 'Official sponsor of the largest athletics event in London this year!' followed immediately by: 'There you go, we said it (Ahem, London France that is)'. The controversial, tongue-in-cheek statement was technically truthful, even if in reality referring to an egg and spoon race held in the lesser-known London in France!

Yet this case raises an additional key issue, as demonstrated by another enterprise which fell foul of the British Olympic team – US hip-hop mogul, Dr Dre, and his brand of luxury 'Beats' headphones. Having received a free pair, many athletes were seen wearing the distinctive, desirable headphones in their warm-up routines shortly before competing, and some even 'tweeted' about them, leading to a crackdown by their superiors for illicit endorsement. Following the old adage that all publicity is good publicity, by drawing attention to the offence, arguably this episode had an adverse affect in the resultant publicity, appearing in newspapers and trending online. Indeed, as a review by data analysts Nielsen found prior to a World Cup event, ambush campaigns by brands such as *Bavaria*, *Nike* and *Carlsberg* effectively eclipsed those of the official sponsors, through smarter, innovative ideas and the ensuing buzz amongst the press and social media. As Blayney Stuart noted, 'The irony is that the more you try to clamp down on it, the more coverage it gets'.

Hopefully, future Olympics organizing committees will use a more subtle approach than the World Cup officials during the ambush campaign that smuggled in the 36 Dutch students. They were all ejected from the stadium, with some facing arrest and put in jail; an unfortunate outcome for them, yet a huge marketing coup in raising awareness of the previously little known *Bavaria* brand. Furthermore, whereas clampdowns can be made in the real world, it is very difficult to police the Internet, which has fast become the greatest tool of communication. As commentators such as German sports lawyer André Soldner have attested, ambush and guerrilla marketing is unlikely to disappear for good, despite the risks involved. Ultimately, the imposition of more restrictions will simply demand more ingenuity and creativity from guerrilla marketers in overcoming the legal boundaries they face.[10]

10.8 SPONSORSHIPS

Although most people have a positive impression of sponsorship, it is definitely not charity. Sponsors, for example, never remain anonymous. On the contrary, their intention is to increase company or brand name awareness. In addition, the parties enter into a contractual agreement requiring them to meet certain performance standards.

In Chapter 9, *sponsorship* was defined as providing financial or other support to an organization or an individual involved in a particular athletic, artistic or other social endeavour with the intent of receiving commercial publicity to increase the public's awareness of the company's name and its brands, or to gain goodwill. More specifically, the *sponsor* usually provides funding, products (such as branded t-shirts, ball caps or other novelty items), marketing experience (e.g. how to secure free publicity) or other services, such as management consultancy. In return, the *sponsored* organization helps to attain the marketing communication objectives of its 'benefactor'. It sometimes carries the name of its sponsor, provides space for billboards or a reception area (like a skybox in a stadium), tries to get media exposure for the sponsor (for example by wearing a branded cap or holding a can of Coke during an award ceremony) or will grant the sponsor rights to use a logo (such as the Olympic rings). This also provides the company with an opportunity to integrate the sponsorship activities into other marketing communication activities, such as advertising campaigns. At the end of this chapter we will explore the objectives of sponsoring events, developing sponsorship strategies and evaluating their effectiveness.

10.8.1 *Objectives*

Worldwide, companies spend over €25 billion per year on sponsorships. One reason for the popularity of sponsorships is that companies can avoid the *clutter* of advertising in media and, instead, generate publicity by associating their names with special events and achievements. To reach the target audience, they must stand out from their competitors, both in terms of their message and the way in which they try to get it noticed. Sponsorship is in line with consumers' changing *media habits*, which have become less dependent on and, therefore, less receptive to television and other traditional media.

Sponsorship also offers opportunities for *creative* media use. It creates a *platform* for advertising and public relations, while in-store merchandising, sweepstakes and other promotions can be linked to a sponsored event to gain additional publicity.

Yet another advantage of sponsorship is that a company can approach consumers without putting any (perceived) pressure on them, which they sometimes feel when exposed to personal selling, advertising or other tools from the company's promotion mix. This enhances communication, especially when trying to improve the company's image. The consumer's *positive feelings*, emotions or passion when attending a sponsored concert, art exhibition or sports event – like a tennis or golf tournament or soccer game – may actually transfer to the brand. At the same time, the company can entertain its sponsors, outstanding employees and most valuable clients during these events and give them special treatment to enhance these relationships.

Sponsoring special events and causes also makes it possible for organizations to *target* specific geographic or behavioural segments. Those would be much harder to reach in a cost-effective way through an advertising campaign. Finally, sponsorship is an ideal marketing communication tool for producers of cigarettes and alcoholic beverages as it enables them to circumnavigate the government's *advertising ban* on these products.

While all of these are important reasons for companies to spend part of their marketing communication budgets on sponsorships, the most frequently stated sponsoring objectives in business are:

→ *To increase brand awareness.* Many forms of sponsorship (such as shirt sponsoring for soccer teams or sponsorship of the World Cup) create prolonged exposure to a company or brand name. This tends to increase name recognition and recall. That, in turn, facilitates the introduction of new products and services under the existing brand name.

→ *To enhance brand image.* Companies usually select sponsorship events that match or enhance the brand image or corporate reputation that they want to convey. Banks and investment companies, for instance, may sponsor classical music concerts to reinforce or improve their image as solid and dependable organizations. Brands can also be repositioned through sponsorship. Heineken associates its name with many events for young people to help create brand preference in this target market.

→ *To create goodwill.* Many perceive sponsorship of worthy causes, charities or other non-profit organizations as proof of good corporate citizenship. It helps companies to create goodwill and gain the approval of employees, stockholders, distributors, consumers and many other stakeholders.

10.8.2 *Sponsorship strategies and assessment*

In providing financial support to an event in exchange for being associated with it, a company essentially acquires access to the event's audience as well as the positive image associated with the event. Because the sponsor's support of an event like le Tour de France presents an obvious benefit to this annual bicycle race and its participants, it is usually perceived more positively than advertising or other forms of marketing communication. Whether the event or activity is an exposition, convention, art festival or sporting event, the sponsor should make sure that it enhances its corporate image and that its audience is compatible with the target market of the company's brand.

That also applies to small firms, which – through sponsorships – are able to compete locally against larger competitors with large marketing communication budgets. To protect their investment, and benefit most, they should be willing to fight ambush marketing. Ambush marketing is a practice by which a company that is *not* an official sponsor of an event or organization tries to associate itself with the event through its own ads, for instance by showing a rock group on concert tour that another company is sponsoring. Ambush marketing is not an uncommon practice in the corporate world. Dutch brewer *Bavaria*, for instance, was accused by FIFA of organizing an ambush marketing stunt that led to 36 women wearing skimpy, orange dresses – paid for by Bavaria – being ejected from Soccer City by South African police during the *Heineken*-sponsored 2010 World Cup.

There are many other sponsorship strategies worth pursuing. Some companies spend a portion of their marketing communication budget on *cause-related marketing*. This is a special type of sponsorship in which a company affiliates itself with a charity and raises money by donating a certain percentage of the purchase price of particular items to that non-profit organization. Other companies buy the *naming rights* of sports arenas. For example, *Philips* acquired the naming rights to the $250 million Philips Arena, a multi-purpose sports and entertainment complex in downtown Atlanta. It paid a record $170 million over 20 years for that privilege, making the name serve as an enduring ad for the sponsor.

Many sponsors try to measure the effects of their sponsorship investments. Most of them try to calculate the value of the media coverage by determining the number of seconds their company or brand name is visible in TV programmes. This is then translated into the amount of money it would take the company to get this exposure through buying advertising time on that particular programme. Although this is certainly not a perfect method to measure the effect of sponsorships, it is better than no estimate at all of return-on-investment.

SUMMARY

1 Role of advertising

The role of *advertising* in an organization is addressed in the advertising plan, but is also partly determined by the strategic marketing decisions discussed in the communication plan, the marketing plan and the business plan. These plans should describe how a company would benefit from using this marketing instrument as part of its overall strategy. Although the influence of advertising in society is not as significant as commonly believed, many advertisers increase their budgets on an annual basis. The importance of advertising in achieving companies' objectives is evidenced by the fact that worldwide, over 400 billion euros is spent on it year after year.

2 Types of advertising

The various types of advertising can be classified according to the elements in the communication process – by *sender* (as in product advertising and cooperative advertising), by receiver or *target audience* (business advertising, trade advertising), by *message* (institutional advertising, theme advertising) and by *medium* (point-of-purchase advertising, direct advertising). With theme or awareness advertising, the advertiser tries to add value to the product by increasing brand awareness or improving brand image, thereby influencing the attitudes of the target audience. In the long term this increases consumers' willingness to buy.

However, campaign or action advertising, which often includes short-term price discounts, influences consumer behaviour more immediately and usually results in a temporary increase in sales.

3 Defining advertising goals

Advertising is not an end in itself, but can help to attain marketing objectives (such as to gain greater market control). An advertising effort begins with establishing goals or objectives. These objectives provide the basis for management decision making and evaluating the effectiveness of advertising. *Advertising objectives* should be expressed not in terms of increased product sales, but must be directly related to the communication effect or response desired from the advertising campaign.

Examples are a specific increase in product recognition, recall, brand awareness or a change in buyer attitudes. The DAGMAR model ('*D*efining *A*dvertising *G*oals for *M*easured *A*dvertising *R*esults') provides guidelines for setting appropriate objectives, assuming that advertising's job is to lead the consumer step-by-step to the purchasing decision. This hierarchy-of-effects model suggests that the consumer passes through the stages of *awareness, understanding, conviction* and *action*.

The DAGMAR approach is a useful planning tool, because it gives direction to the advertising agency's creative effort and provides criteria for evaluating campaign proposals as well as measuring advertising performance.

4 Advertising strategies

In developing advertisements, the key question is what message the advertiser should get across to achieve the effect, as outlined in the advertising objectives. To break through the clutter, an ad must stand out in an attractive way. For maximum impact, it is also essential to present a consistent brand image, in line with the company's positioning strategy. Both the advertising objective and message – featuring functional or affective product attributes – change over the product life cycle. Products and services in the introduction or market growth stage require a different advertising strategy than those in the market maturity or decline stage.

5 Campaign development

If we look at the advertising strategy as the *what* in the communication process ('What message should be communicated?'), then the creative concept embodies *how* the message is conveyed.

In a briefing, the advertiser or client typically outlines the content or theme of the message (as specified in the proposition), after which the advertising agency, which is responsible for the creative strategy, works with the company to develop the advertising campaign. The advertising message may, for example, associate or compare the product with something else.

This depends on the proposition that is part of the briefing to the advertising agency. The client also incorporates relevant background information and guidelines for the media selection in the briefing.

6 Selecting media

Once the campaign has been developed, the advertising agency's media planner must choose the appropriate mix of media to reach the company's target audience in a cost-effective way. In the *media plan* they define the media objectives and present the strategy to achieve them. Which media types and vehicles are best capable of carrying the message to the target audience depends on three factors: the communication capability, reach and cost of each medium.

7   **Evaluating the advertising effort**

With today's emphasis on the bottom-line in the corporate arena, the evaluation of advertising effectiveness is more important than ever. Whether a particular message attracts attention, is interpreted as intended and is remembered by consumers, may be measured in various ways and at different stages in the development or execution of a campaign. A pretest may be conducted before the ad is published or broadcast. At this early stage, the most widely used testing methods are portfolio tests, (consumer) jury tests and theatre tests. In a posttest, advertising copy is evaluated after it has been shown to the target audience to measure the communication effect. Posttest research methods based on memory include aided and unaided recall tests as well as recognition tests. Whatever testing procedure is used, it must include an assessment of the extent to which the advertising objectives were attained.

8   **Sponsorship**

Sponsoring events is becoming increasingly popular in business. Sponsorships are especially effective since consumers tend to associate their enjoyment of pleasant events with the sponsor, which in turn creates brand preference and loyalty. The most common sponsoring objectives are to increase brand awareness, to improve brand image and to create goodwill among stakeholders. To assess the results of sponsorship, some companies try to link their expenditures to an increase in brand awareness or sales. Others simply calculate the seconds or minutes of airtime during which the name is visible and convert that number into how much they would pay for this media coverage in advertising euros.

DISCUSSION QUESTIONS

1   One of the best-selling brands of premium vodka is Ketel One. It is priced substantially higher than most other brands of vodka, while very little is spent on advertising and other forms of marketing communication.
    a. How do you think this product has managed to gain a considerable market share in the premium liquor segment?
    b. Would you advise the company's management to expand its market share by increasing the advertising budget? Explain your reasons.
    c. One of advertising's main functions is to increase market control. Explain what this means.

2   What does the DAGMAR model involve and how useful is it in developing an advertising strategy?

3   What is the best way to assess the effect of an advertising campaign?

4   What are the advantages and disadvantages of the various methods used in business to set the marketing communication or advertising budget?

5   Creating an advertising message is teamwork, and includes efforts of both a copywriter and art director. Elaborate on the functions of 'copy' and 'art' in advertising.

6   In developing an advertising plan, the advertiser often has to make a fundamental choice between theme and campaign advertising. Compare these two approaches, including an example, and explain under which circumstances theme advertising or campaign advertising may be preferred.

7   How do marketers decide which media to use in their advertising campaigns?

8   How can companies measure the effectiveness of their advertising – both before and after a campaign – and what are the limitations of these methods?

9   Some managers look at advertising as a necessary expense in order to inform their target market, while others believe that advertising adds value to a product. What might be the added value of advertising?

10 Why are companies spending an increasing part of their marketing communication budget on sponsorships?

CHAPTER 11
SALES MANAGEMENT

LEARNING GOALS

After studying this chapter you will be able to:

1	Identify various types of sales jobs with different responsibilities
2	Discuss the basic steps in the personal selling process
3	Apply the 'management by objectives' method in managing the sales force
4	Describe several ways of allocating the sales force to sales accounts
5	Understand how companies recruit, select, train, motivate and compensate salespeople
6	Outline the most important direct marketing techniques
7	Explain how promotions may influence buying behaviour

11.1 Importance of personal selling
11.2 The selling process
11.3 Sales management and objectives
11.4 Sales force structure
11.5 Building and managing the sales force
11.6 Direct marketing
11.7 Sales promotion

Two major tasks of marketing-oriented managers are to find customers and to retain them for the company. There was a time when the number one priority in business was simply to find customers. Salespeople spent most of their time looking for new buyers. As soon as they found one, they moved on to secure the next prospect. And typically, they would leave the order follow-up – including providing post-sale service – to their co-workers in the back office.

Today, the emphasis in business is on retaining customers, especially profitable ones. Since the cost of attracting a new customer is, on average, about five times as high as retaining an existing one, every effort is made to keep customers satisfied. Loyal customers are no longer taken for granted. This new approach calls for sales representatives – who are responsible for maintaining external contacts – to play a key role in the firm's customer orientation. It is their task to build lasting relationships with buyers and to satisfy their wants and needs to the greatest extent possible. This is not always easy, as the chapter will show. But, it is certainly worth the effort: nothing is more important for a company than a satisfied and loyal customer!

MARKETING IN ACTION
The CMO's Global Challenge

One thing is certain for all people who follow the path to become a Chief Marketing Officer (CMO); they will be faced with many challenges and trials on a day-to-day basis! First of all, access to information has given consumers more power in their relationships with companies. This development continues to affect marketing's role in business. Plus, there has been a dramatic increase in the range of media choices, including social media. This broader array makes it more difficult for marketers to decide how to best reach the target market. Finally, the pressure to show a high return on marketing investment and to align marketing expenditures with both corporate strategy and sales revenue has made the Chief Marketer's job that much tougher. Thus, it's no wonder that most CMOs only stay with the same company for less than three years. One might ask what *skills* are required to become an effective global CMO. Indeed, in today's competitive global market, these leaders are continuously pushed to perform and beat their rivals.

Anxious to find out why it is an attractive job, Marc de Swaan Arens – a former global marketer and now a consultant to companies such as Unilever, Sony and Cadbury – asked global CMOs what motivates them to excel in their business and what essential talents make this possible. They all agreed on at least one thing: a company's highest ranking marketer should be as skillful in right-brain thinking (being intuitive and thoughtful) as in left-brain thinking (being analytical and logical). As *brand champions*, CMOs may take on the role of creatively focused poets or passionate artists. But as *leaders* who are responsible for financial growth, they must be numbers-driven, and skilled in creating and managing a complex organization that can work globally. Great marketers are managers who realize that both types of capabilities are essential. Therefore, these leaders don't hesitate to ask for assistance in performing tasks that they may be less competent at.

> Great marketers realize that both right-brain and left-brain thinking skills are essential

Rob Malcolm, retired President of Global Marketing, Sales, and Innovation at Diageo – the world's largest premium alcoholic beverages company based in London – offers another valuable perspective. It reflects his experience at Diageo, where he was in charge of more than 70 brands in 170 countries with an annual marketing budget of €2 billion. He points out that the Chief Marketing Officer, in addition to the marketing function, also has a *leadership function*. Their leadership role can range from just being a facilitator to being a builder or advocate of the brand to being a strategic partner to the CEO.

Defining the right leadership role and getting senior management's agreement is the first challenge for the CMO. The successful Chief Marketer will not only be a *strategic* partner in the C-suite, but will become the driver of the corporate strategy, increasingly defining the vision for the future. To become this, the CMO must earn the trust of the others in the C-suite, especially

the Chief Financial Officer, the Chief Sales Officer and the Chief Information Officer.

Regarding the *marketing function* role, the CMO must become the voice of the *customer* inside the company, ensuring that the customer's needs are represented in all corporate decision making. They must be the advocate of the brand throughout the organization, demonstrating the impact various decisions will have on building or hurting the brand. They should also be the firm's external *radar*, monitoring and reporting competitive activities, changes in customer buying behaviour and other external factors that could impact the firm's performance. Malcolm describes this function as 'relentlessly scanning for opportunity' to find 'transformational insights for future growth.'

The successful CMO will use this environmental scanning to be the champion of *innovation* and new product development through deep customer understanding. It is important to have the ability to *experiment*; Malcolm suggests that a fixed percentage of the budget be dedicated to experimentation (it was 15 per cent at Diageo). All things considered, the CMO must become the architect of the future. Most CMOs – just like sales professionals – consider interacting with customers across the globe as a key element to success, and so a passion for empathizing and identifying with the consumer is fundamentally crucial.

Finally, the CMO must be performance driven, documenting the return on marketing investments. To accomplish this, they should develop a General Manager mentality. This, of course, requires knowing the numbers, and knowing how marketing delivers *value*.

Looking ahead, some things will remain the same. Influencing consumer insights will continue to be critical. Brands will still matter and it will continue to be important to build trust in your brand. Content will remain king, and delivering a superior value proposition will always be important to the market.

However, many things will be different. There will be nowhere to hide; with increased transparency, everyone will know much faster when things are not working. Managers must acknowledge that they don't have full control anymore; consumers are in control. And increasingly, CMOs are 'always on' in today's 24/7 world.

To be successful in the future, CMOs must set the example in the organization and improve their digital and technological skills, social media expertise and financial capabilities. Success will also require experimentation, learning, documenting the learning and reapplying it. Ultimately, CMOs should not be right-brained or left-brained. They will have to become 'whole-brained' marketers. Most importantly, the Chief Marketer should have one foot on the ground and one foot stepping into the future. Bring it on![1]

Salespeople are, in many respects, the 'unsung heroes' of marketing. For many organizations, success in marketing depends largely on sales professionals' skills in matching the company's products and services with customers' needs and, of even greater importance, in bringing about ownership transfer. As some salespeople like to say, 'Nothing happens until a sale is made'. Although this is not completely true, as many other marketing activities contribute to the firm's success, it is fair to say that if the product or service is not sold, most of the firm's other efforts have been in vain. Thus, formulating personal selling strategy and managing the sales force that implements it are not only challenging but critical tasks.

Personal selling is a highly distinctive form of promotion (one of the Ps in the marketing mix). Like other forms, it is basically marketing communication. But unlike most others, it is *two-way* rather than one-way communication. Thus, personal selling involves social behaviour, with both the salesperson and the prospect influencing each other by what they say and do. The outcome of each sales situation depends significantly on the success both parties have in communicating with each other and in reaching a common understanding of their needs and objectives. In most cases, this two-way communication and direct feedback leads to faster results.

This chapter is important not only because selling is crucial to the company's success, but also because there are more high-paying professional positions in sales than in any other area of marketing. Furthermore, many young men and women who eventually move into

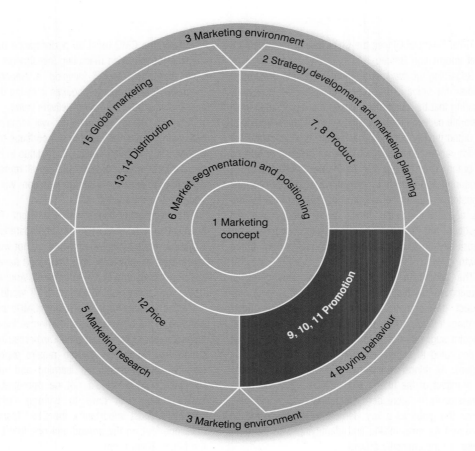

marketing management positions begin their careers in sales. In this chapter we will first make a distinction between various types of sales jobs. After examining their relative tasks we will analyze the selling process, step-by-step. Next, we'll review the organizational structure and management of the sales team. For instance, how large should the sales force be? How do we determine the best size for sales territories? Do salespeople perform better on commission or on a straight salary?

We finish the chapter with an overview of direct marketing and sales promotion, which are clearly related to personal selling. In *direct marketing,* we also try to approach customers in the target market in as personal a way as possible and build long-lasting relationships with them. And although in *sales promotion* we generally use our resources in the short term to break down any barriers to making a purchase, we can also develop themed and other promotions to underline the brand image and support the sales function. Before examining direct marketing and sales promotion in more detail, we will explore personal selling.

11.1 IMPORTANCE OF PERSONAL SELLING

Some people don't have a high regard for salespeople. They think of selling as an undesirable profession lacking in status and creativity. They depict salesmen as slick, high-pressure fast-talkers with dubious ethics. In doing so, they stereotype the role of the salesperson in a negative, inaccurate and often unfair manner. Unfortunately, this biased image has tainted the sales profession to the point that many students are not interested in pursuing careers in sales, or even in marketing. What they may not realize is that countless market-driven companies rely heavily on the revenues generated by the sales force. And while there are undoubtedly salespeople who are pushy or have questionable ethics, there are a great many more highly professional sales representatives who act responsibly and want to ensure that customers purchase needed and affordable products.

Since personal selling occurs through divergent communication channels, types of sales jobs vary considerably. The nature of sales positions also varies from one firm to another because differences in sales strategies and objectives cause salespeople to vary their emphasis on specific tasks. Let's look at different types of sales jobs, as well as the primary tasks and responsibilities of sales professionals.

Image Asset Management

11.1.1 *Types of sales jobs*

Most companies use different kinds of sales personnel. Based on the functions that salespeople perform and the amount of selling and creativity required for these tasks, we can distinguish between several types of personal selling. From that perspective, salespeople may be classified into three categories: order takers, order getters and sales support personnel. Although some companies use just one of these types of personal selling, others use a combination of all three.

Order taking

Someone who processes routine orders and reorders through the Internet or over the phone, or who handles transactions initiated by the customer in a retail store, is an order taker. Because order taking does not involve much creative selling, this type of sales job is usually the lowest-paying sales position. Order takers' most important responsibility is to perpetuate an ongoing relationship with existing customers and seek repeat sales. In spite of the routine nature of their work, their responsibilities should not be undervalued: in the absence of order takers, customers might not have an ample product supply when it is needed and may well buy their products and services from a competitor. With the increased application of the marketing concept in customer service-oriented companies, the role of order takers is also changing from simply facilitating routine transactions that customers initiate, to identifying and solving problems in order to better meet customers' needs.

There are two types of order takers: inside and outside order takers. Typically, *inside order takers* are retail salespeople ('over-the-counter selling') or salespeople who work in sales offices and receive orders by mail, telephone ('inbound telemarketing') and the Internet. Hence, they may be working at the retail, wholesale or producer level. As more and more consumers and business people order through the Internet, the role of inside order takers will continue to change.

In contrast, *outside* or *field order takers* visit customers and replenish inventory stocks of wholesalers, retailers or other resellers ('field selling'). They could be route sellers (delivering products like soft drinks from trucks while collecting return bottles) or also assist – as merchandisers – in arranging promotional materials and in-store displays. The recent development of computer technologies, such as scanners and hand held computers, designed to facilitate the inventory control and order-tracking functions performed by outside order takers has enhanced their efficiency and productivity. Yet, their function essentially has not changed.

Order getting

The order getter is a more traditional salesperson who identifies potential customers, gives them necessary information, persuades them to buy and then closes the sale. They are also responsible for providing after-sales service. This task is sometimes referred to as *creative selling*. The order getter's job requires a high degree of customer empathy, professionalism and creativity, especially when dealing with highly technical products (such as computer systems) or services (such as designing software). Similar to order takers, these sales professionals may work as inside or as outside order getters. Order getters may focus on either current clients, who previously purchased from the company, or on new customers, in which case their job is to locate prospects and convert them into buyers ('new-business sales').

When a *new-business salesperson* builds and maintains a long-term relationship with an important customer, they often continue to service that customer or 'account' as the primary contact. They are then referred to as an account manager. Many businesses strive to increase their order getters' productivity through team selling. Typically, a selling team is a combination of a sales representative, a product manager, a *technical specialist* (responsible for product demonstrations and the setup of complex equipment) and possibly other functional experts, who cooperate in developing products, services and programmes to identify and satisfy the prospects' needs. This is a form of *relationship* or *consultative selling*, which focuses on developing mutual trust and maintaining a long-term relationship between buyer and seller. This is accomplished through a systematic process that emphasizes personalization and empathy in interactions with clients.

Sales support

While support salespeople do not attempt to get orders themselves, in business-to-business marketing they greatly facilitate the selling process. Their job is to help identify prospective customers, to create goodwill, to educate buyers and to provide the best possible service after the sale. The most common types of customer sales support personnel are missionary salespeople, sales engineers and trade salespeople.

The missionary salesperson – often called a *detail person* or *detail rep* – is usually employed by a manufacturer, to assist its customers in selling to their own customers. To illustrate, missionaries may visit retailers to encourage them to buy certain products from wholesalers, who are the producers' direct customers. Pharmaceutical manufacturers often use detail reps to call on hospitals and professional people such as physicians and dentists to acquaint them with new drugs, leave samples and establish potential for future sales.

A **sales engineer** or industrial rep is also someone who does not actually sell products and services, but who has considerable technical expertise and specializes in identifying customer needs and in analyzing and solving customer problems. Sales engineers are viewed as consultants and often work for producers of technical equipment or chemicals. Finally, **trade salespeople** typically help the manufacturers' customers build up their volume by providing promotional help. They may assist customers with their selling efforts by setting up in-store displays, rearranging shelf space and conducting demonstrations. Usually, a trade salesperson is an order taker as well as a support person.

11.1.2 Multiple roles of salespeople

Personal selling is a powerful, but relatively expensive marketing instrument. The average cost of a sales call is over €150, while some sales calls may cost the firm hundreds of euros. Other communication tools, such as advertising, are less expensive per contact. Therefore sales personnel must be used selectively. The use of personal selling in a company's marketing strategy is especially appropriate:

→ In a small business market with a limited number of buyers who purchase in large quantities, or in a *geographically concentrated* market which allows the sales representative to visit many customers per day. This lowers the cost per visit.

→ In selling products and services requiring considerable attention or *modification*. When offering customized products or services that require client education, salespeople are a critical link between the company and its customers.

→ When a *long-lasting relationship* between the firm and its customers is called for. A customer who is about to make a long-term commitment to a supplier (for instance, when purchasing a custom-made computer system) tends to value a professional relationship with the company's representative as a partner in this mutual venture.

In these and many other situations, salespeople perform multiple roles that have a significant impact on the overall success of the company. We will now briefly review some major roles of salespeople, as illustrated in Figure 11.1.

Introduce products

A personal selling effort is essential in persuading prospective customers to try or purchase a new product. Particularly when considering the purchase of complicated or custom-designed

FIGURE 11.1 Key tasks of sales representatives

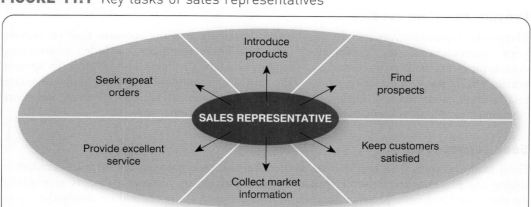

products, buyers may need technical advice and assistance. Since salespeople are on the front line, they often have insight into their customers' strategies and future plans and may be able to suggest how the new product or service can help achieve those objectives. In cooperation with sales support people, they may then be well positioned to solicit new product purchases.

Additionally, in consumer goods marketing, suppliers with limited advertising budgets often use a *push strategy* to convince intermediaries in the distribution channel of the potential turnover and profitability of a new product. Here, too, personal selling is a must.

Find new prospects

Of all promotion mix elements, personal selling is the most precise and allows companies to identify the best prospective customers on which to focus their sales efforts. Other promotional methods are targeted at groups of people or firms, some of which may never become promising sales prospects. By continually seeking out and obtaining new potential customers and developing relationships with them, sales representatives can acquire additional shelf space at the expense of the competition. They can also assist customers in promoting or selling the product line. Ultimately this will lead to more intensive distribution for the company's products and an increase in its market share.

Keep customers satisfied

Salespeople are at the heart of building relationships. Applying the concept of *relationship selling*, sales professionals try to create a trusting partnership with their clients by maximizing customer satisfaction through listening, advising and educating them, as well as by properly handling any complaints. Meeting customers' expectations and maintaining a close relationship with them is critical to long-term success and will help increase customer loyalty. This certainly applies in a saturated market with products in the mature stage of the life cycle.

Collect market information

Marketing-oriented companies are creating effective procedures for both providing and collecting relevant market information on a regular basis. Salespeople have the greatest freedom to adjust a message to satisfy their customers' information needs. Since personal selling involves face-to-face interaction with customers, salespeople (acting as the 'eyes and ears' of the company) obtain immediate feedback. This may help the marketer monitor changing buyer needs and wants, develop new products and services, adjust promotional strategies, assess current and future competition and keep track of other important developments in the marketplace.

Provide excellent service

Many sales representatives spend more time on 'servicing' existing accounts than on making sales presentations to prospective buyers. These services include maintaining communications with new customers, helping to adapt products and services to specific needs, arranging – or assisting with – the customer's employee training and enhancing relationships with existing clients. A salesperson's ability to identify, analyze and solve customers' problems contributes to providing excellent customer service.

Seek repeat orders

Even manufacturers who only sell to wholesalers use their sales forces to assist retailers in selling the products to consumers. Sales representativess or account managers give advice on the most favourable product presentation for the stores' shelves and on display set up to make sure that the product captures the customers' attention. By providing promotional help and assisting retailers to build up their volume, salespeople produce sales revenue through repeat orders and contribute to higher profits for both the manufacturer and the intermediaries in the distribution channel.

11.2 THE SELLING PROCESS

Occasionally, someone is said to be a 'born salesman'. A successful salesperson's style, determination and systematic approach are not acquired at birth. Salespeople consciously develop these qualities by adopting a positive attitude, obtaining the proper education and relentlessly pursuing their goals. They know that – as shown in Figure 11.2 – selling a product or service involves three phases: *preparation, persuasion* and *transaction*.

In fact, anyone can learn the systematic series of steps in the creative selling process and, through training and experience, become proficient in handling the related tasks. As we will see, much of a salesperson's work takes place before the initial interaction between the salesperson and prospective buyer, and it continues after the sale.

11.2.1 Preparation

Before approaching the potential buyer, experienced salespeople spend a great deal of time 'doing their homework'. This preparation phase before the sales call involves two steps. The first is searching for potential customers (*prospecting*) and qualifying them. The second step – called preapproach – is obtaining further background information about the most promising prospects and planning sales interviews with potential customers.

Prospecting

Identifying and developing a list of potential customers is called prospecting. For products and services, such as insurance policies, that are single instance purchases, continual prospecting is essential to sustain sales. Salespeople usually obtain names of prospects from online databases, company sales records, trade association directories, responses to advertisements or websites. Others prefer to use referrals, contacts recommended by current customers, colleagues, suppliers or other individuals, to identify prospects.

In evaluating or *qualifying* prospects, salespeople often distinguish between three types of prospects. A (*sales*) lead is the name of a company or person that may be a possible buyer. A *prospect* is a potential customer who needs or wants the product or service. Finally, a qualified prospect (or 'qualified sales lead') is someone who needs the product, and has the financial means to purchase it as well as authority to make the final purchasing decision.

Most salespeople prefer finding prospects through referrals, rather than by making cold calls. Cold calling involves contacting potential buyers – often marginal prospects – without a prior appointment, or making phone calls to every firm in a directory in an attempt to set up an

FIGURE 11.2 Phases in the selling process

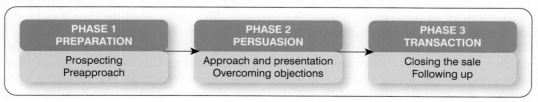

PHASE 1 PREPARATION	PHASE 2 PERSUASION	PHASE 3 TRANSACTION
Prospecting Preapproach	Approach and presentation Overcoming objections	Closing the sale Following up

appointment. Research indicates that one referral is as valuable as ten cold calls. Once the salesperson identifies qualified prospects, they should enter the pertinent information into a database for their own future reference or for use by colleagues who sell non-competing product lines.

Preapproach

Before the sales representative actually contacts a potential buyer, they should collect specific information about the qualified prospect. With this information at hand, they can determine the best approach method, plan their strategy for the sales call and prepare for possible questions, so that they can have a fruitful discussion or information exchange with the prospect. The process of gathering this information is known as the **preapproach**. Sources of financial data and other useful information include Dun & Bradstreet reports, Standard & Poor's 500 Index, the company's annual report and its website. Informal sources, such as non-competing salespeople who have previously dealt with the prospect, may also be helpful.

Many questions need to be addressed at this stage. Who in the organization makes the purchasing decisions? Would it be best to secure an appointment by letter, email or telephone? Is this individual part of a *decision-making unit* (DMU)? At what stage in the purchasing process is the prospect at this time? With which suppliers do they currently do business? What is this person looking for in a product or service? And what is known about the selection or buying criteria used? The more the salesperson knows about the firm's purchasing behaviour and the better they incorporate this information into their sales presentation, the greater their chances of convincing the prospect that they will benefit from the purchase.

11.2.2 *Persuasion*

The second phase, *persuasion*, composes the core of the creative selling process. Just as in advertising, the message has to be communicated in a particular sequence. For this, the previously discussed AIDA model (or another response hierarchy model) can serve as a guideline for planning and making the presentation. Most sales representatives keep a particular model or formula in mind during the approach and presentation. To persuade buyers they also must be prepared to respond to their objections.

Approach and presentation

With the foundation established during the preapproach stage, the salesperson is now ready to contact or 'approach' the prospective buyer. The **approach** is the salesperson's initial contact with the prospect. Knowing, as the saying goes, that 'you never get a second chance to make a good first impression', the approach is critical and must be carefully planned. The salesperson should strive to present themself well, gain the buyer's attention and build interest in the product or service.

At the same time, they will definitely want to learn more about the prospect's needs and objectives. In order to immediately build rapport during this first direct contact, they will probably tell the buyer *who* referred them, or bring up names of common business acquaintances, before they ever mention the product. It is vital that they start building a relationship by adapting to the prospect's social style. Of course, when the time is right, the salesperson makes the transition to the presentation.

Converting a prospect into a customer by stimulating interest and creating a desire for the product is the primary objective of the **sales presentation**. This is the communication component of the selling process, in which the salesperson explains the product's main features and strengths, illustrated by success stories of current users. To get them involved, the salesperson may ask the prospect to hold or use the product or have them participate in a demonstration, just as an automobile salesman will invite a prospective buyer to take a car for a test drive. The seller should not only talk, but also carefully listen during the presentation, because the prospect's questions and reactions provide an opportunity to learn more about their needs and concerns. After all, in a problem-solving role, it is difficult to come up with solutions for customers without listening to what they have to say. And while the salesperson may have prepared a canned presentation, based on recall of memorized information, observing and listening to the prospect allows them to adjust the message to the information needs of the potential buyer. However, they should never overstate any claims about the product offering to maintain their credibility.

Canned presentations are usually based on a response hierarchy model to systematically induce gradual acceptance of the product or service and to prompt the prospect in their decision-making process. For example, using the hierarchy-of-effects or *Lavidge-Steiner model*, the purpose of the sales presentation is to take the prospect through the stages of awareness, knowledge, liking, preference and conviction before they are ready to purchase a product that will meet their needs and add value to the company. In contrast to a canned presentation, a need-satisfaction presentation is more flexible and tailored to address the specific needs and interests of the prospect, rather than being built around general benefits that will hopefully appeal to the prospect. This customized format focuses on problem-solving efforts and contributes significantly to building a relationship between seller and buyer.

Another popular form of presentation is a *features-benefits* framework, which the salesperson may use to discuss the product in terms meaningful to the prospect. To plan such a presentation, they may utilize a matrix known as a sellogram in which product features are related to customer needs. This technique prepares the salesperson to point out the benefits of those features rather than discussing technical specifications. For example, when a customer comments that they are primarily interested in the appearance of a bike, a bicycle seller can present various reasons for buying a particular model (such as its fully welded solid frame, smooth lacquered finish and automatic lighting) and at the same time point out how they satisfy the customer's needs and wants. A well-organized, clear and concise presentation, supported by PowerPoint, audio-visual aids or multimedia presentation materials substantially increases the chances of successfully persuading the prospect to buy.

Overcoming objections

Most prospects will have questions or voice objections during a sales presentation. They may require more detailed information about the product's features and benefits, or may express disagreement or doubt about some of the statements the seller makes. Whether or not the presentation leads to a transaction depends a great deal on how the salesperson responds to these questions and objections. *Objections* are excuses for not making a buying decision or commitment, or simply a polite way of saying 'no thank you'. They may be valid and logical (as in the case of a prohibitively high price or a prospect's doubt about the quality and delivery time) or psychological in nature, as when the purchasing agent resists changing an established routine or hesitates to take the risk of making a unilateral buying decision.

Experienced salespeople know that the objections raised will not necessarily prevent the prospect from buying and certainly do not signal the end of a sales presentation. On the contrary, if anticipated and managed well, these objections provide an opportunity to show the competitive superiority of the product and highlight its price-performance relationship, as well as to gain a more thorough insight into the organization's buying process.

Well-trained sales professionals with excellent listening, communication, problem-solving and negotiation skills may use several techniques to overcome the potential buyer's objections.[2] They may:

→ *Acknowledge the objection and turn it into a reason for buying.*
Suppose the potential customer says, 'The price is too high.' One possible response would be, 'Yes, the price is a bit higher, because we only use the best materials. And look at all the accessories that are included in the purchase price. By the way, did you know that the operating costs are lower than those of other brands?'

→ *Postpone responding.*
Deferring the answer to later in the presentation will reduce the tension. 'I will respond to that in just a minute, but first, let me bring up another point.'

→ *Agree and neutralize.*
Do not deny the objection raised, but show that it is relatively unimportant and discuss a related benefit. 'That's true. Other customers have said the same thing, but they all came to the conclusion that the advantages outweigh the disadvantages. You'll see what I mean as soon as you take it on a test drive.'

→ *Accept the objection.*
Simply accepting a valid objection tends to work better than denying it. Let the prospect express their reservations, search for the reasons behind them and stimulate further discussion. From a long-term perspective, it may even be wise to end the presentation at this point by referring the potential buyer to a reputable competitor.

→ *Deny it.*
If the objection is based on misinformation and is incorrect, meet it head on with a respectful, but firm denial.

→ *Ignore the comment.*
This is useful if the objection is meant to be a distraction or stalling mechanism, but is otherwise not relevant to the purchase decision.

Each of these techniques works best if the salesperson remains calm, says nothing negative (especially about competing products) and has anticipated in the preapproach stage of the selling process what objections the client might raise. Professional salespeople are skilled at placing themselves in the buyer's shoes, and have an excellent feel for timing. They know when to move on to the next phase and gain the prospect's commitment.

11.2.3 Transaction

Since buyers can choose from a number of potential sellers, the sales representative is responsible for gaining the prospect's commitment. So far, the salesperson has done everything possible to maximize the chances of making a successful transaction by showing how the product will satisfy the buyer's needs without pressuring them into making a premature decision. Hopefully, the buyer and seller have identified common interests, created a bond of trust, feel that they could develop a professional alliance and, in short, that the relationship 'clicks'.

A successful relationship between the buyer and the seller requires a firm commitment from both of them. Of course, the sales representative must believe in their own products or services to convey credibility and to persuade the buyer. The buyer, at the same time, should be confident in their dealings with the salesperson. They must be convinced that their decision is well-founded and that they have negotiated effectively to this point. Now, the salesperson enters the *transaction phase*, the final episode in the selling process. It involves two steps: closing the sale and following up.

Closing the sale

The most important part of the personal selling process cannot begin until all of the buyer's objections have been properly addressed. Closing is the stage in the selling process when the salesperson asks the prospect to buy the product or service and obtains a commitment from them. If the objective of the sales call is to schedule a demonstration, then closing involves getting the prospective buyer to commit to a product demonstration. If, on the other hand, the goal is to negotiate a contract, closing means getting the buyer to sign the contract. Often, however, it is difficult to determine exactly *when* the buyer is willing to commit themself. Therefore, closing is the most challenging part of the selling process.

Experienced salespeople watch for certain *signs* from the prospect, such as 'body language' or physical actions indicating their readiness to purchase. For example, the prospective buyer examines the product carefully, nods in agreement as the salesperson summarizes, or begins to read the order form. The salesperson also looks for certain comments ('I think that our maintenance costs will drop with these new machines.') or questions ('When can you make delivery?' or 'Are both of these models available right away?'). If the representative does not immediately respond to these signals by closing the order, they will miss their chance at an open goal. If, on the other hand, the seller is too persistent in trying to get a commitment, the prospect will feel that they are pressured into making a decision and may refuse to commit to anything at all. Therefore, closing the sale is a balancing act between being persuasive and being pushy.

Closing the order remains a matter of timing and can be initiated in various ways. The sales representative may attempt a trial close by asking the buyer, for example, if they prefer model A or model B and then waiting for a response. A trial close typically involves questions about colour preferences, delivery time and similar decisions that buyers must make when purchasing the product. Other representatives like to point out the limited inventory or availability, or refer to an expected price increase. Sometimes they promise a discount as an extra incentive if the order is placed immediately. Finally, the salesperson can again summarize all of the benefits of the purchase that both parties agreed on, and then ask for permission to take an order or trial order.

Following up

While closing is the climax of the salesperson's visit, the selling process is not completed when the order is taken. To make sure that the customer is satisfied and will provide the company with future business, all of the promises regarding delivery, installation, performance and service must be kept. Only then may we count on positive word-of-mouth and repeat sales.

In this follow-up stage, after the order has been implemented, the customer should be visited again to make certain that their expectations have been met. A follow-up visit is also a clear indication that the supplier wants to build a permanent relationship with the customer. With the growing interest in relationship management in the corporate world, salespeople are increasingly motivated to maintain ongoing relationships with customers. In conclusion, there has been a significant shift from a 'transaction-oriented' to a 'relationship-oriented' approach to conducting business in marketing and sales.

11.3 SALES MANAGEMENT AND OBJECTIVES

Not every successful sales professional is willing to accept the added responsibility of managing the sales force. After all, there is quite a difference between being a customer-oriented and fairly independently operating sales representative, solely devoted to selling, and being

MARKETING MISTAKE
Sales versus Marketing – Still at War?

© wfarnas / Shutterstock

In most organizations, Sales and Marketing are distinct activities, and perhaps inevitably friction can arise when the two functions must work in tandem. When the sales volume is lower than expected, Marketing often points the finger at the sales force's unsuccessful implementation of the carefully considered strategies that the marketing department has devised. Sales people, on the other hand, like to complain that Marketing has set the prices too high, and spend a disproportionate share of the budget. They believe that the money would be better spent on increasing the size and quality of the sales force or on higher commissions for successful sales representatives.

Many sales professionals think that marketers do not sufficiently relate to their customer base. Marketers, in turn, will accuse the sales team of shortsightedness, or *marketing myopia*. As they see it, the reps are far too fixated on the experience of the individual customer, lack insight into the overall market and fail to anticipate future developments. Both groups frequently underestimate each other's accomplishments.

> # Sales people and marketers often underestimate each other's accomplishments

The principle reasons why Sales and Marketing don't get along are twofold, largely centring around economic and cultural factors. There is often *economic* tension because the two sides have to split the overall budget assigned to them by top management. First of all, the budget reveals which of the departments yields the most power within the business. Moreover, salespeople tend to disapprove of how much money Marketing spends on three of the four marketing mix variables –

price, promotion and product. Marketers – who usually urge the sales force to 'sell the price' instead of 'selling through price' – set the prices too high, they argue, making it harder for them to negotiate and sell the product or service. Salespeople view promotion expenditures – to create both awareness and interest, in addition to desire for a product – as unnecessary expense, especially when television advertising is involved. And they contest that products don't have the features, style and quality level their customers prefer. Most likely, that's because the sales team's assessment is influenced by individual customers' needs and wants, whereas the marketing department is focused on market demand, or product characteristics that appeal to a broader target market.

While economic tension is common between Sales and Marketing, cultural concerns are even more deep-seated. Culture is closely related to people's values, which may differ between marketers and sales professionals. The distinct nature of each role often demands a different set of skills and attitude towards approach, as reflected by how a typical day is spent: behind a desk, or out in the field. Traditionally Marketers have tended to be more analytical, data-orientated and project focused, owing to a comparatively more formal education than their counterparts. Their key task is to create a *sustainable competitive advantage* for the company. Sales professionals or account managers, on the other hand, devote much of their time to building relationships with current customers and prospects. They know what buyers want and which product features they are most interested in, making them experts in predicting whether or not a product will fly. As the company's frontline group, salespeople are well positioned to gain an intimate understanding of existing customers, to observe the forces at work in an industry and to identify potential new business, all of which may contribute to the company's growth. But their priority is closing sales, and that's how they make a living. Therefore, it is not surprising that these co-workers often have a difficult time coordinating their efforts.

In many organizations, sales and marketing people don't work well together at all. Both groups seem to put more time into complaining than in making a true effort to better communicate with each other. Nevertheless, there's no excuse for a company to not try to improve the working relationship between the two functions. For instance, senior management can help schedule frequent get-togethers between Sales and Marketing to encourage a more structured form of communication. It can also make sure that they are more closely aligned physically, working in the same part of the building. It can alternate jobs, organize shared assignments or provide other opportunities for salespeople and marketers to work together. Product managers, market researchers and other marketers should sometimes join sales representatives as they call on clients, and observe or participate in key account planning meetings. Likewise, sales professionals or account managers can contribute to developing a marketing plan and may want to attend product planning sessions, sharing their insights into customer buying behaviour. This will make both parties more familiar with the other's ways of thinking and acting, and hopefully end the war between Sales and Marketing.[3]

actively involved in **sales management**, the process of planning, organizing, implementing and controlling the personal selling function.

Managing the sales force is the complex and challenging task of directing and coordinating the selling efforts of a group of people who, as a team, are working to achieve certain goals compatible with the company's overall marketing and promotion strategies. Nevertheless, the best salespeople in an organization are very likely to be promoted into positions of greater marketing and management responsibilities. Even those who would rather continue to work in personal selling to build a career in sales will increasingly find themselves involved in the development and implementation of an effective **sales strategy**. Hence, in the next three sections we will explore, as illustrated in Figure 11.3, the most important managerial decisions related to personal selling.

FIGURE 11.3 Components of a sales strategy

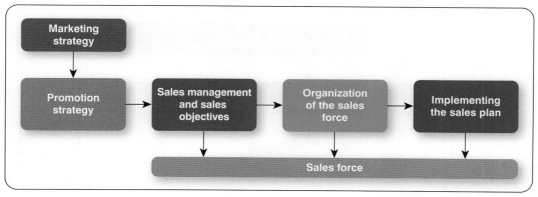

11.3.1 Managing the sales effort

Managing a sales force is not an easy undertaking. After all, sales representatives act as independent business people (although with the protection of working for an organization), do not like close supervision and prefer to spend their time selling. They are attracted to sales not only by the excellent commissions, but also by the flexibility and freedom of a job 'on the road'. Typically, they plan their own schedules, create their own sales strategies and may go several days or even weeks without face-to-face contact with management. For the **sales manager** and their superior, the national or *general sales manager*, this creates the challenging situation of directing the sales force from a distance.

The sales manager must evaluate and motivate individual salespeople who are working in very different competitive environments. Simply imposing specific tasks and assigning **sales objectives** on these independently operating sales representatives offers no guarantee that they will allocate their time for activities and customers in accordance with the marketing goals and overall corporate objectives. In busy periods, for example, the follow-up on previous orders and the acquisition of new customers may get put 'on hold'. Or, when they are very involved with introducing new products or seeking repeat orders from important accounts, they may not devote sufficient time to other duties, such as generating and qualifying leads or following up on recent sales.

Therefore, sales managers spend much of their time organizing and structuring the sales team. The sales manager's function includes determining in detail the most efficient selling process and formally outlining specific procedural guidelines for salespeople to increase their productivity, including, for example, where they might find new prospects, how they should approach prospective customers and what terms they could negotiate in closing a sale with potential buyers. But in order to effectively guide salespeople's performance, sales managers must pay special attention to actively involving salespeople in sales planning and in setting sales targets and other objectives in keeping with the company's overall marketing objectives.

11.3.2 Management by objectives

One system many sales managers have found effective for managing sales forces is **management by objectives** (MBO). Using this method, sales managers and salespeople jointly identify performance goals and strategies for reaching those goals. These shared objectives are then utilized to evaluate the performance of each salesperson. The management by objectives process is illustrated in Figure 11.4.

FIGURE 11.4 Management by objectives

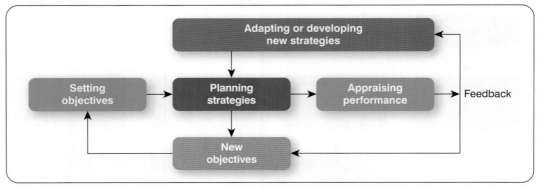

TABLE 11.1 Possible objectives in an MBO system

Responsibility areas	Possible objectives
Sales volume	Increase sales volume by 10 per cent
Gross margin	Keep average gross profit margin of products sold at 10 per cent
Number of calls per day	Increase the number of calls per day to four
Order/call ratio	Increase order/call ratio to 30 per cent
Average order size	Increase average order size to €900 by eliminating certain types of accounts
Expenses and expense ratios	Reduce the cost per call to €80; the cost per order to €160; and the ratio of selling expense to net sales to 20 per cent
New accounts	Generate ten new accounts per year

Setting objectives

In establishing objectives, the first step for the sales manager is to identify areas of responsibility important to the company's marketing objectives. Once these have been isolated for consideration, specific objectives must be set for each area of responsibility. For example, a key responsibility area might be the profit contribution a sales representative must achieve in a given period of time. They may also be held responsible for making a certain number of sales calls, the acquisition of new accounts or generating a designated sales volume. Both the sales manager and the sales representatives must agree on these targets. And like all marketing objectives, they must be stated in clear, precise and measurable terms and include a deadline or specific time frame. Some examples of responsibility areas and possible objectives are presented in Table 11.1.

In addition, salespeople who take part in setting their objectives are generally very motivated to succeed. They know exactly how their performance will be evaluated and fully understand the criteria against which sales performance is being measured. This will prevent misunderstandings between sales management and the sales force and help increase productivity.

One company that has successfully integrated the management by objectives principles into its sales organization is Xerox Netherlands. For most of his fifty experienced district account managers, General Sales Manager Vincent Zoetmulder sets no targets, but expects them to submit a well-considered work programme. 'The only thing I still do, is check to see if their plans are sound and will lead to maximum quality and satisfied customers', he says. 'Other than that, I support my people wherever I can and give them as much freedom as possible performing their jobs.'[4]

Planning strategies

In creating a strategy or set of strategies that enable the salesperson to accomplish their objectives, the sales manager and the salesperson make a good team. The sales manager (sometimes called *sales director*) usually has a broader range of experience and may be able to advise the sales representative about strategies that have worked for other members of the sales force. In contrast to the sales manager's wide scope, sales representatives are intimately knowledgeable of their own sales territories, and can quickly assess whether the suggested strategy is potentially worthwhile. This, in turn, allows them to tailor the sales manager's experience and proposed strategies to their own sales situations.

Performance appraisal

Performance evaluation should be an ongoing process; the sales manager and the salesperson should periodically review progress toward the agreed upon goals. The sales representative may fail to reach their objectives for any of at least four possible reasons:

1 The *objective* is unrealistic. Objectives should be set high enough to pose a challenge, yet not so high that they are unachievable.

2 The *strategy* is ineffective. A poorly formulated sales strategy must be reviewed and adjusted.

3 The *environment* has changed. An economic recession or other uncontrollable environmental force may render a sales objective irrelevant.

4 The *salesperson* is ineffective. Salespeople who are incompetent or don't put full effort into their work, should be given additional training and support, or should be replaced.

Ultimately, achieving sales objectives should not, for the organization, become an end in itself, and salespeople should not be held solely accountable for this function. A salesperson's commitment and other contributions to the sales team effort may also be critical to the company's customer retention and future success.

Integrating MBO with other policies

If *management by objectives* is to be successful, it must be integrated with other corporate policies. Most critically, following a performance appraisal, the required resources should immediately be made available to adjust the strategy, if necessary. Additionally, the application of an MBO system should not conflict with the sales compensation plan. A sales representative who, through their own efforts, meets or exceeds their sales objectives should receive adequate monetary compensation for their performance. If their hard work goes unrecognized, they may become frustrated and lose interest in maintaining their work ethic. Of course, sales contests, sales training programmes and other corporate activities should also be consistent with the management by objectives system.

11.4 SALES FORCE STRUCTURE

Since personal selling is a costly marketing tool, no firm can afford a sales force that is disorganized. To maximize the company's profitability, the sales manager must make sure that the sales territories and sales representatives are well organized and efficient. They face three major decisions regarding sales force design:

1 How should the *sales force* be organized? According to geographical region, product line or customer type?

2 How large should the sales force be? The number of sales representatives deployed will have an impact on market share as well as profit.

3 How large should the *sales territories* be? Too large a territory will result in missed opportunities, while a territory that is too small may not generate sufficient income for a sales representative that is partially compensated through commissions.

PROFESSOR'S PERSPECTIVE
Peter Spier (SKEMA Business School, France)

Courtesy of Peter Spier

Peter Spier is British and has lived in France for some 30 years. He is a seasoned negotiator and trainer, and a faculty member at SKEMA Business School, France, which also has campuses in the USA and China. After a career negotiating in the photographic business, he teaches marketing and negotiation skills to students and professionals from a range of backgrounds. Peter Spier has a doctorate from the University of Oxford and an MBA from ESCP-EAP in Paris.

Before moving into teaching, I worked as sales and marketing manager, first setting up a sales office for a San Francisco-based company in France, then managing an agent network and selling into international markets, for an international photographic agency. These were exciting jobs. In both I experienced the satisfaction of increasing sales and developing markets. In the first job, setting up a new business and developing a new market, and in the second, driving through projects, managing agent and client relationships across borders and across cultures, sharing the pleasure of setting up exhibitions or reportages…. With agents across Europe, I very quickly realized that market dynamics and negotiation styles vary substantially across countries and cultures.

Negotiation styles vary substantially across countries and cultures

As a teacher I try to convey the excitement I felt then to my students. My first post was in a school in Paris that was set up to make sales 'respectable' in a country where it is often seen as marketing's 'poor relation'. In my present school we have developed an MSc in international marketing and business development that insists on the fact that the two go hand-in-hand to drive top-line growth in companies. My students will find jobs in both areas, often spending time in sales before moving on to marketing, as is often the case in large FMCG (fast moving consumer goods) companies. Some will catch the bug and choose to remain in sales. Sales offers a range of possibilities, including working with channel partners in *category management* and *trade marketing* for FMCG goods, or *key account management* in the B2B arena.

And students should be awake to the *opportunities*: companies are keen to recruit good candidates at master's level. Every year we take part in an International sales challenge organized by another French business school. It is there that the French Sales Director for a large global software firm recently commented that when selling Enterprise Resource Planning or ERP solutions (a business management system that includes all facets of a business from planning to manufacturing, through sales and marketing), they need sales people able to grasp the strategic issues of their clients and exchange with the CEO. This is a challenging environment.

In addition to this strategic vision, we develop in our students the *self-confidence* and skills required to become a good sales person. The ability to *listen* and grasp the client's perspective is paramount; but so too are the skills required to *communicate* and defend *value*. The idea that marketing insists on higher prices that sales seeks to bring lower is a false dichotomy. If performance is measured correctly, their objectives can be aligned. Even promotions can be used to consolidate and to build value rather than to undermine it. You just need to know how.

The term *business development* has become a way of 'selling sales'. It encompasses the challenges of understanding markets, working with channel partners and clients. It further includes the notion of recognizing and developing new business opportunities. My present school is situated in Sophia Antipolis, the largest technology park in Europe. Working with entrepreneurs, one quickly realizes that good ideas are not enough for a successful business. The challenge of identifying and reaching the right market is equally important. It is here that business development steps in. But then sales plays its part. Seeing things from the client's point of view is essential. It is this that provides the appropriate arguments – no longer generic, but crafted to the needs and preoccupations of the client, with the agility and creativity to respond to opportunities as they arise.

Drawing on a variety of sources, I also try to develop in my students an awareness of the powers of influence and *persuasion*. *Empathy* and insight are essential. *Emotional intelligence* is an asset. But insights about rational biases and framing – or profiling – bring further interest to the topic. This becomes yet more intriguing when looking at the decision-making processes of organizations, or when the cultural component is added. As an area of study or a potential career, this 'parent pauvre' – or poor relation – is rich indeed![5]

11.4.1 *Organizing the sales force*

Sales managers are responsible for organizing the field sales force. They should decide which representatives should visit what customers to sell the company's products and services. There are several options. The sales territories can by organized by geographic region, by product line, and by customer, market or industry. No one system is best for all firms. In fact, some companies use a combination of methods, or alternatively, organize their sales professionals by marketing function performed (such as account maintenance or account development), or by individual client or account. For instance, most supermarket chains allow only selected account managers to visit their headquarters, while merchandisers service individual local stores.

However, in other industries with smaller or a lesser number of customers the field sales force does, in fact, play an important role in selling products and services. The sales force structure implemented depends on the number and type of prospects or customers and the way they prefer to buy, as well as the number and type of products sold and markets targeted, the competitors and the size of the sales force. Let's now explore the most common methods of organizing the outside sales force, with its advantages and limitations.

Territorial sales force structure

The simplest way to organize the sales force is by region. Management divides the target market into distinct districts or territories. For a global company these could be continents or countries, and for a domestic marketer, states, counties, provinces or cities or parts thereof. This is known as a territorial sales force structure. As illustrated in Figure 11.5, each salesperson is assigned to a particular territory and is expected to sell the company's entire line of products to all interested customers in that region. Typical of this type of sales organization is a hierarchical structure with various levels of sales management positions. For example, the general sales manager may have a number of regional sales managers reporting to them, each of which is supported by several district managers, sales representatives and service merchandisers.

One drawback of this type of sales force structure is that the salesperson's specialized product knowledge may not be adequate in the case of highly technical, complex products. Furthermore, they have to divide their attention over different types of customers and industries, making it difficult to adopt a customer-focused mindset in serving the target market. Advantages of a geographical sales organization are the limited travel time and lower expenses. Also, the sales representative can respond quickly to unexpected measures or

FIGURE 11.5 Territorial sales force structure

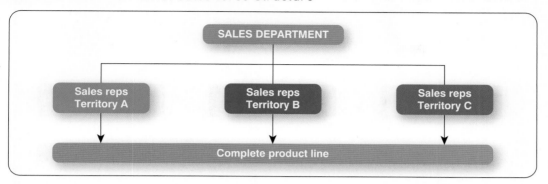

campaigns by local competitors and can effectively tailor their approach to regional customs and preferences. Still, many firms are moving away from using a geographic sales organization as they strive for a greater degree of customer orientation among salespeople.

Product sales force structure

With the increased interest in product management, many companies have adopted a product sales force structure – as shown in Figure 11.6 – by using a separate salesperson or sales force for each product or product line. This type of sales organization is especially appropriate for companies marketing various non-related and highly technical industrial products. To sell these complex products effectively, specialized salespeople need to have in-depth knowledge of the products' technical features and most common market applications. By selling only a limited number of products, they will more easily develop that expertise, enhancing their long-term relationships with customers.

The product line organizational structure is quite costly. Unless the salespeople are able to operate nationwide, multiple sales forces or product specialists, carrying only their 'own' products, may be required for different market regions. Large customers who use several of the supplier's products may be called on by more than one of the company's salespeople. This duplication of selling effort is not only confusing, but also inefficient, both to the seller (extra travel expenses) and to the buyer, whose purchasing agent has to make more time available to meet with different salespeople representing the same supplier.

FIGURE 11.6 Product sales force structure

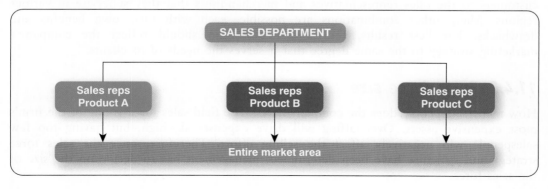

FIGURE 11.7 Organizing sales territories around customers in specific industries

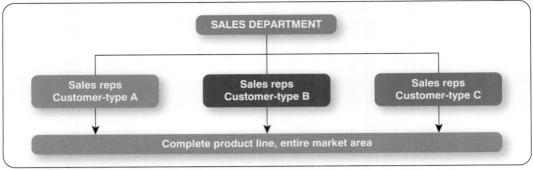

Customer sales force structure

In markets with different types of buyers who have different needs (e.g. specialty stores and supermarket chains), suppliers may organize their sales force around specific classes of customers or industries (here: A, B and C). This is known as a **customer sales force structure**; it is illustrated in Figure 11.7.

Organizing sales territories around clients allows customer-oriented companies to emphasize relationship selling, offer specialized customer support and use different sales force strategies for each major type of customer served. Some suppliers have different salespeople or account managers for their consumer products and their industrial divisions. Other suppliers assign separate sales teams to specific industries, such as the medical community, financial services and retailing. Still others organize their sales force by customer size, assigning salespeople to small, medium and large accounts. Having a senior sales manager focusing on a major national account – often called *key account* – allows them to become an expert and act as a consultant to that client. This approach is consistent with the marketing concept and is appreciated by most customers.

Other methods

There is no ideal sales force structure for all sellers in all situations. In practice, companies offering a wide range of products or services to different types of customers located in a large geographic area often combine several methods of organizing the sales force. Their salespeople may be allocated by product and customer type, by product and territory, by customer and territory or any other combination. Also, the company's General Sales Manager may service a few major accounts themself and leave smaller customers to the sales representatives and merchandisers that they supervise in various regions. Many other combinations are possible, each with their own benefits and drawbacks. For best results, the sales organization should reflect the company's marketing strategy to the same degree that it serves the needs of its clients.

11.4.2 Sales force size

How many salespeople does the company need? The field sales force is one of the firm's most expensive assets. Overstaffing will drive expenses sky-high, but having too few salespeople will negatively affect the selling effort. Therefore, once the sales force strategy and structure have been determined, management has to decide on the size of the sales force.

If the sales force size is less than optimal and must be reconsidered, as it may be following a merger or reorganization, the best method for arriving at a size figure is to use a mathematical or formula-based method. Most sales managers use the **Talley formula** (also known as the *workload approach*), which integrates the number of customers to be visited, the call frequency necessary to service a customer each year and a salesperson's average amount of selling time available per year. Expressed as a formula:

$$\text{Number of sales reps} = \frac{\text{Number of customers served} \times \text{Average call frequency}}{\text{Available selling time per rep}}$$

To illustrate, assume that a company has grouped its clients into different classes based on size, importance and other factors related to the sales effort required to maintain them. In Belgium, the company has 300 Type-B accounts (specialty stores) requiring 12 calls per year and 50 Type-C clients (discounters), requiring six calls a year. The sales force's *workload* – the required number of calls on its accounts per year – in this case is $(300 \times 12) + (50 \times 6) = 3\,600 + 300 = 3\,900$ calls per year. If an average salesperson, after deducting time spent on non-selling activities such as travel, sales meetings and administration, can make four calls a day (750 on an annual basis), the company will need five sales representatives to service its Type-B and Type-C accounts ($3\,900/750 = 5.2$). If the number of prospects increases or any other part of the formula changes, the sales manager can simply recalculate, and adjust the sales force size accordingly.

In deciding sales force size in the example above, management might allocate six rather than five sales representatives to the accounts, considering the company's rate of sales force turnover (defined as the number of salespeople resigned, fired or reallocated per 100 on the sales force). If the firm has a 15 per cent annual turnover, it will probably need an additional sales representative to serve these clients. Every sales force should have some turnover. When there is none, the sales team may be growing stale, with inefficient salespeople staying on because management has failed to replace or reassign them. Management should try to optimize turnover so as to eliminate 'dead wood' and at the same time keep turnover costs as low as possible.

The sales force size should be sufficient to achieve all of the firm's personal selling objectives, among which is generating a certain sales volume. This can be established for the overall sales team, but also expressed as quotas for individual sales representatives. However, sales management should not only set quantitative, but also qualitative objectives – such as building goodwill, or maintaining the intermediaries' cooperation in providing customer service to consumers – which may be more difficult to express in terms of a specific workload.

While the Talley formula is especially useful in estimating the required number of salespeople for new firms or for those entering new markets, in practice the number of sales representativess will usually grow towards the ideal situation. Efficiency is essential in running a business and managers tend to be cost-conscious. They realize, for example, that if a sales representative will cost the company €75 000 a year, in which period they will make 750 sales calls, each call will cost the firm around €100. A customer who is visited ten times a year must, therefore, yield enough return to make these sales calls (amounting to around €1 000) worthwhile. At a gross profit of 25 per cent on sales, this client must spend at least €4 000 a year to warrant regular sales calls. Providing more frequent calls than a customer's sales volume would justify is often based on qualitative considerations, such as the competitive situation, the account's potential growth in the expanding market or the company's distribution strategy and objectives.

11.4.3 *Sales territory allocation*

A sales force's effectiveness depends, in part, on the size of the sales territories, or how sales management divides the existing territories among the firm's sales representatives. The objective, of course, is to maximize the long-term profitability of each representative and the company as a whole by making sure that each salesperson's time is allocated properly to the accounts. There are several key factors that must be considered when making sales territory allocation decisions: territory potential, workload and territory size.

Territory potential and workload

Each territory must have sufficient sales potential for the assigned salesperson to generate an equitable income. In addition, all representatives should feel that their own sales territory offers as much potential as other territories. Therefore, the sales manager should assess the revenue potential of all prospective and current accounts – based on marketing intelligence, as well as salespeople's call reports, invoices and customer feedback – and also estimate how much of the sales representative's time is needed to service each of these accounts. Ultimately, such considerations will lead to a territory division in which no sales representative works harder than their colleagues to earn a comparable income.

As previously discussed, sales territories are established by combining a group of geographic or control units (such as metropolitan areas, provinces, census tracts or zip codes) for which market data are available, allowing sales management to measure their sales potential. The sales manager can then attempt to establish sales territories both with equal sales potential and requiring roughly the same workload. This is difficult, because territories with similar sales potential are not generally equal in geographic size. This means that sales representatives assigned to geographically larger territories must put in more hours to achieve a given sales volume. On the other hand, if sales management forms territories in such a way that each requires equal hours of work to call on all customers, the territories' sales potentials will vary. Sales representatives will then have unequal earning potential (at least, if part of their earnings are derived from sales commissions).

While the sales manager may use commercial programmes or software to develop optimal sales territories and allocate them to individual salespeople in a fair manner, some inequities are difficult to avoid. There are several ways to solve this problem. Some sales managers try to balance income potential and territorial workloads by adjusting the formula used for calculating commissions in certain territories. In addition to using differential commission rates, management may help individual salespeople maximize their territories' sales potential by providing supplemental training or coaching and by ensuring that the sales representatives devote their time to the firm's most profitable accounts. They may also assist in routing and scheduling salespeople by determining the sequence of customer calls, the number of sales calls to be made and the best time to make them. This will maximize selling time and minimize time and money spent on travelling, waiting and lodging.

In order to guarantee that territories remain in balance, the sales manager should periodically review territories where a sales representative exceeds, or fails to meet, quotas for an extended period of time. When quotas are routinely exceeded, the territory potential may be too large, allowing the sales representative to reach quotas with little effort. In such instances, the sales manager can then either add another salesperson to that territory, or raise the quota. If, on the other hand, a sales representative consistently falls short of their quota, the territory may be lacking potential (in which case it should be enlarged to include new prospects) or the sales representative should receive additional sales training so that they are better equipped to increase their number of customers, generate a higher sales volume and build enduring relationships with clients.

Territory size

A territory's ideal size will depend not only on quantitative factors, but on other considerations that influence the work pattern of salespeople. One of them is the nature of the product. For example, a territory should be kept *small* when selling consumer goods with a high turnover, and the salesperson is required to call on each account frequently. Smaller territories are also preferable when there are a large number of retail customers, due to an intensive distribution strategy, when the firm is facing stiff competition that threatens its market share and in situations where the representatives are responsible for tasks other than selling, such as installing the product, training personnel and providing service.

In other cases, the company would be better off keeping its sales territories relatively *large*. For instance, sales of industrial durable goods, which last longer than fast moving consumer goods, do not require frequent repeat visits. This, in turn, allows the salesperson to carry more accounts. The same applies to markets with only a few customers, such as in distribution channels where the firm only conducts business with wholesalers. Larger territories – with sufficient potential sales volume – are also desirable when targeting new, rather than better-established markets or if the firm has an experienced, highly productive sales force which can cope with a sizeable market area.

11.5 BUILDING AND MANAGING THE SALES FORCE

Personal selling is a team effort that calls for thorough planning that ensures salespeople are available whenever and wherever customers need them. It requires a sales plan describing the target market, the sales organization, the sales objectives and practical guidelines for the plan's implementation, including the development and management of a sales force to achieve the objectives. It also requires a *sales man*ager who is a good leader, with strong experience in recruiting, selecting, and training sales representatives who can make a significant contribution to accomplishing the company's goals. Successfully motivating a team of dedicated sales professionals and financially rewarding them for their performance through an attractive compensation plan are also key factors in achieving the sales objectives.

11.5.1 Recruitment, selection and training

Before the company begins an active search for new sales personnel, it must formulate an accurate *job description* – a document describing the objectives and requirements of the sales position and how the salesperson is expected to accomplish them. The job description outlines: (1) specific tasks the salesperson is to perform, (2) the customers to be visited, (3) the types of products and services to be sold, (4) the physical and mental demands of the job and (5) how the salesperson interacts with the inside sales force or other company personnel and to whom they report. The job description can then be converted into a statement of specific job qualifications, such as the knowledge, skills, aptitudes and behavioural characteristics needed to be a successful salesperson in this position. Once management has developed a detailed and exact job description and has sufficient insight into the credentials and skill set needed for the sales position, it is prepared to recruit qualified applicants.

Recruiting salespeople

To develop and maintain an effective sales force, the sales manager must recruit the right type of salesperson. If there are no prospective job candidates from other departments

MARKETING TOPPER
Google's Internet Bus in India

India is one of the fastest growing economies in the world and one of the frontrunners in information technology. But its population of 1.2 billion is still largely *offline*: the Internet has only reached roughly 100 million individuals – about 8 per cent of its citizens. The country's poor infrastructure, high cost of getting an Internet connection and lack of relevant content are often cited as reasons for India's low Internet penetration. Fortunately, progress is being made to overcome these challenges.

For the fast growing number of mobile phone users, India's current mobile networks are now offering extensive data services. And today, an hour of Internet usage costs less than ten rupees. Local content is improving too: the *Hindi Wikipedia*, for instance, exceeds one hundred thousand entries. So why are most of India's citizens still offline? Currently, the primary hurdle to greater use of the Internet in India is the lack of *consumer awareness*.

Here's the good news: *Google India* has been working hard to raise consumer awareness through a unique programme of educating the offline population about the Internet's benefits. To actually take the Internet to the people, the global search company has outfitted a large white web-connected bus to visit – like a giant travelling salesman – different regions all across India, stopping in small towns for a few days at a time and inviting locals into a different world. By allowing India's citizens to go online on one of the six computers in this free 'mobile

cybercafé', Google is offering them the opportunity to *experience* the Internet first hand, often for the first time.

Google's success in India can be duplicated across the globe

The Internet Bus project was created to make India's consumers and students – as well as teachers, business people and government officials – aware of the value and potential *benefits* of the Internet in their everyday lives. From a marketing perspective, it was also initiated to tap into India's huge market, and to learn to develop effective *strategies* for targeting other emerging economies in the world. The India market consists of a broad range of potential new users with different demographic characteristics, literacy levels, application needs and infrastructure challenges. All things considered, if Google can be successful in India, it can have a positive impact anywhere on the globe.

The Google Bus has already travelled more than 50 000 kilometres in India, making stopovers at about 2 000 locations in 150 villages and cities in 11 states since it began its promotional journey a few years ago. In this customized bus, over 1.5 million people grabbed the opportunity to experience the joy of going online. Of these prospects – after talking to Google's representatives – over 100 000 customers have registered to get their own Internet connection. Overall, the number of consumers using the Internet is expected to grow by 300 per cent in the next few years.

The thinking behind Google's demonstration and sales efforts on this subcontinent is to 'get them committed while they're still young' and then try to hold on to the new customers. A significant side benefit for the company is that it gains useful insights into various Internet users' preferences and search behaviour. In the end, the information gathered by this type of research enables Google to develop products and services tailored to the opportunities and preferences of large market segments in nations across the globe. This project is part of a wider global initiative by Google, with similar ventures extending across African countries including *Nigeria*, *Kenya*, *Cameroon* and *Uganda*.

While the Google Internet Bus project was primarily launched with the objective of boosting awareness by introducing India's underprivileged and illiterate masses to the magic of the Internet, Google's managers were pleasantly surprised to see many people from different walks of life step into the bus to find out what the web could do for them. They believe that their efforts will enable Indians to use the power of knowledge and information for economic prosperity. But the Google Bus' success pleases India's prime minister on public information infrastructure as well. In fact, both India's government and Google are like-minded in their commitment to democratizing information, communication, education and entertainment. If both parties continue with the same level of enthusiasm, it is likely that they can make the number of people in India who are 'connected' grow from 100 million to over a billion...[6]

within the company, they must look outside the company to attract a sufficient number of recruits. Qualified candidates may be found through a variety of sources, including employee referrals, participation in job fairs at colleges and universities or through public and private employment agencies or headhunters. Placing classified advertisements in newspapers, trade journals or on specialized websites is another means frequently used to attract experienced salespeople.

The *personnel recruitment ad* is still an important source of applicants. Because highly productive sales representatives are generally already working for another company, the ad must be able to attract the attention of a sales professional who is not actively seeking employment. This is asking a lot of an advertisement. In such an ad, the description of the company's needs and preferences must be tailored to those of the applicants it wants to attract. The personnel ad must, for the most part, be written with the prospective applicant in mind, even though such ads, because of their high visibility to the general public, are often seen as a corporate public relations instrument as much as a recruiting method. Because a company, particularly in its first year, invests heavily in its sales representatives, an efficient recruiting and selection programme that reduces the turnover rate in the sales department is a significant responsibility of the sales manager.

Selecting sales personnel

How managers evaluate and screen salespeople varies from one firm to the next. The selection process should effectively match the job candidate's needs and characteristics (such as their reflectiveness and social skills) with the skills required for the selling tasks (for example, the ability to network and build customer relationships). Which candidate the company selects, also depends on the training it can offer its salespeople. The procedures companies use for selecting sales representatives range from a simple interview in the personnel office as an initial screening method, to multi-stage information gathering systems that include application forms, in-depth interviews with management, psychological tests, reference or background checks and physical examinations. The number and relative sophistication of these screens depend on the resources management is willing to invest in its selection effort. Sales managers also consider how applicants conduct themselves throughout the process. For instance, if someone does not ask for an appointment during the initial contact or for the actual sales job towards the end of the selection process, they may also be reluctant to ask a prospective buyer for a commitment or an order.

Firms usually try to select candidates with ideal personal characteristics for the position. One basic quality every salesperson must possess to be successful is empathy. Empathy is the ability to understand the customer's problems, that is, to see a particular situation as the prospect or customer perceives it. This trait helps the salesperson to anticipate the customer's reaction to a sales presentation and thereby tailor it accordingly, and, if necessary, to make modifications. In addition, experts agree that great salespeople exhibit enthusiasm, a high level of energy, self-confidence, sociability, ambition, flexibility and good organizational skills. Sales representatives must also be resilient and optimistic, because their profession can sometimes be lonely and discouraging. Even the most successful sales professionals occasionally return to the office empty-handed.

Sales training

The best way to increase sales force productivity is to provide in-depth training. Sales force training is an ongoing process for novice and veteran salespeople alike. All sales recruits must undergo initial training in order to learn about the company's products and services, its policies and the competition. Usually, those with little or no selling experience are also required to attend in-house sessions or external seminars on selling techniques and practices, often enhanced by role-playing sessions or other simulations. Informal on-the-job training, in which the sales manager joins sales representativess in the field and offers guidance and constructive criticism, is commonly used to keep seasoned salespeople up-to-date and help polish their negotiation and relationship building skills. Generally, companies with complex products and services offer the most extensive continual training programmes. To save time and money, many organizations with limited budgets now add web-based training to their sales training programmes.

11.5.2 *Sales force motivation and compensation*

A key factor in any individual's personal success is *motivation*, the driving force behind their behaviour in achieving particular goals. Sales managers, generally speaking, spend more time motivating staff than other function managers. We will first examine why salespeople need extra encouragement and, subsequently, the role of sales compensation plans in motivating them.

Motivating sales representatives

Because of the nature of their work, sales representatives have to be constantly motivated. Selling involves problem solving during repeated calls on prospects; this may lead to great successes but also to mental pressure and, unfortunately, frequent rejection. Thus, selling is typically characterized by alternating states of exhilaration and disappointment. In the course of a day, a salesperson may receive one large order and lose two others. Such rapidly cycling 'ups' and 'downs' can, over time, affect motivation. Moreover, it is difficult for most people to 'lose' as openly as a sales representative does when they return to the office empty-handed. In those frustrating times, the understanding and support of the sales manager are extremely important to morale.

Although motivation to perform comes from within, a sales manager may use various methods to build on their sales representatives' drive to achieve their objectives and inspire them to operate at peak performance levels. For some highly productive sales representatives, working hard to beat the set quota and winning sales contests is enough of

a motivator. Others are particularly motivated by a reward system that rein-forces success. Incentive programmes providing gifts, trips, memberships in clubs or honour societies, distinguished salesperson awards and plaques for recognition (such as 'salesperson of the month') are most conducive to both motivating employees and improving customer service.

Extra encouragement and recognition for sales representativess may also be necessary to prevent complacency, or worse still, apathy. Someone calling on the same customers year after year and developing personal, more social relationships with them may come to believe that creative selling is no longer necessary. They may, in fact, be less alert to a customer's changing operating environment and needs than a competitor's sales representative who takes more time to discuss business with a potential client. Finally, sales representativess are distanced from their colleagues much of the time, and, as a result, it is difficult for them to connect with the company's *esprit de corps*. However, if the sales manager can generate enthusiasm among sales representatives for meeting group performance targets and can strengthen feelings of group identification in addition to building sales force morale, there is a good chance that individual sales performances will also improve.

Sales compensation plans

Salespeople like to be rewarded immediately for their performance, particularly when a great deal of effort was involved. Rewarding salespeople for superior performance, however, is only one of the objectives of a remuneration system. Other objectives are to control and direct the sales effort, and to attract (and retain!) effective salespeople.

There are three types of sales compensation plans:

→ *Straight salary* – fixed earnings not based on sales or profit generated.

→ *Variable income* (also known as *straight commission*) – earnings directly tied to the sales or profit generated.

→ *Combination system* – base salary plus an incentive, usually a bonus or commission on sales or profit generated.

In the United States many companies pay the sales staff as 'commissioned salespeople' with variable incomes based solely on commission. However, in most European countries, a straight commission system – because of the minimum wage mandated by law – is only allowed when independent agents, not directly affiliated with the company through a binding employment contract are used. Many European sales representatives, therefore, receive a relatively high base salary, often supplemented by some form of *pro rata* monetary compensation, such as a bonus or profit share. Especially in high-growth industries, these commissions play an important role as an incentive for extra sales efforts and make it possible for a motivated salesperson to earn a six-figure income.

Each compensation system has its advantages and disadvantages. A straight salary plan gives management a large degree of control over how sales representatives spend their time. This is vital when salespeople are also responsible for non-selling activities, either provided to customers (such as consulting, product servicing, inventory maintenance and, of course, relationship building) or to the company (such as training new salespeople, providing marketing intelligence data, finding new prospects or promoting new products). Its primary drawback is that a straight salary does not offer any financial incentive to increase sales.

A straight commission plan provides salespeople with a direct financial incentive to strive for high selling efficiency. However, it may hinder them from providing customer service and also instill considerable insecurity in salespeople because they lack control over some of the variables (such as competitors' moves or an economic recession) that affect sales volume and, thus, their income. Commission programmes may also backfire if salespeople focus on selling the most lucrative products, and ignore those that may satisfy customers' needs, but do not generate high commissions. Therefore, some companies base sales commissions on the number of units sold, regardless of price, or use a sliding scale involving different percentage rates for sales levels generated by different products. This serves to keep the sales representatives motivated while protecting the customers' interests.

The third and most popular method of sales force remuneration – the combination system – tends to be favoured by salespeople as well as their employers because it combines the benefits of salary and commission plans while reducing the potential shortcomings of each. For the salesperson, it offers an incentive to excel, while minimizing extreme swings in earnings. The benefit for the firm is that it has a right to ask the salesperson to perform non-selling duties, since not all compensation is tied directly to sales. Finally, more and more companies are starting to use compensation plans where commissions are not just based on sales volume, but also on criteria such as customer satisfaction and customer retention rates. This reflects a truly customer-oriented approach and stimulates the sales force to build and maintain lasting relationships with their customers: a win-win situation for all parties involved in the selling process.

11.6 DIRECT MARKETING

An increasing number of companies are adopting direct marketing, using the Internet, telephone, direct mail and other media to directly communicate and interact with prospects and customers. Some of these organizations started using this form of marketing primarily to reduce the cost of prospecting or to solicit an immediate response, such as a purchase or a request for information. Other businesses were motivated by the desire to gain more control in the distribution channel by circumventing powerful retailers who often demand a substantial profit margin to carry a product, and may then offer it in stores in a manner inconsistent with the manufacturer's marketing and positioning strategy.

A second group of companies uses direct marketing as an effective tool to build, maintain and improve customer relationships, integrating it into their ongoing *relationship marketing* efforts. As we will see, the objectives of relationship marketing (developing and

PRACTITIONER'S PERSPECTIVE
Simon Kelly (Chief Cohesion Officer at Cohesion)

Simon Kelly is Chief Cohesion Officer at Cohesion and Senior Lecturer at Sheffield Business School. Kelly has worked closely with sales leaders to drive successful growth, in senior marketing positions in Major Global Telecommunications, and in consulting assignments to major TMT (Telecoms, Mobile, Technology) players. Here he offers his perspective on how to create an effective B2B sales and marketing team.

Courtesy of Marsha Kelly

In B2B successful sales teams become valuable to both their own organization and their customers because of their know-how and expertise. It is no longer good enough to be a walking product catalogue for your firm because the customer can already find all this on the Internet. The buying organization is looking for sales people that understand their business and the issues that they face in their specific roles. High performing sales people tend to be *micro marketers*. For one, or a few companies, Account Managers need to create mutual value for their company and the customer by:

→ Deeply understanding the customers industry and their position in it.

→ Specifically understanding key issues affecting customer performance.

→ Articulating how the company can uniquely help the customer organization.

→ Bringing partners to the table that can help solve a broader range of customer issues in greater depth.

→ Creating value propositions for the customer that move the needle for their business.

In the words of my old Managing Director, 'This sounds simple, but it ain't easy'. The Account Manager in this 'sense and respond' model needs to be able to turn around to the rest of their organization and be confident that it can deliver a solution that works for the customer. This is about much more than just speaking the customer 'industry' language, although it is the starting point.

High performing sales people tend to be micro marketers

So, if the challenge is to create a team that creates mutual value, what are the implications for sales management and marketing?

Training and education: In my experience, we found that *product portfolio training* was the *hygiene factor* (a motivating factor which may not necessarily stimulate work satisfaction if present in the organization, but can cause negative effects on morale if absent); *sales technique training*, on the other hand, was *table stakes* (the minimum entry requirement in order to function effectively) – in marketing language, we might also refer to these as *dissatisfiers* and *satisfiers*, respectively. The real difference was made by 'winning on value' sessions which helped sales and marketing people understand what value means to customers and how to create mutual value.

Sales people brought along research on customer issues which allowed them to build *value propositions* based on potential solutions to these issues.

The ideal condition for 'winning on value' sessions was gaining deep industry sector understanding. Working with universities that had specialist knowledge in industry sectors – for example, Aberdeen University for Oil – was invaluable here. They would bring expertise from their faculties and from industry to give our Account Managers a platform of knowledge on which to build compelling customer value propositions.

Customer seminars and events: Focusing on key customer issues was essential here. Executives get lots of invites to events that they cannot possibly attend. To cut through this *noise*, the marketing department have to help sales by creating events that are relevant and resonant. We managed to get genuine C Level attendance to intimate seminars by working with university professors and other industry experts to create short provocation papers focused on key business issues. There was very little discussion about what we sold. These sessions were all about the customer. What these sessions did for moving forward large contract negotiations gave us ROI that was off the Richter scale.

Targeting and motivation: Here a move away from the tried-and-trusted product targeting aggregation – or *undifferentiated marketing* – was essential. The customer-centricity we advocated meant that large opportunities were created 'outside-in' – based on customer need – often which they didn't even know about. Overall revenue, sales and profitability targets were essential in this world.

Recruitment: This was about bringing in business people who were, or could be, 'micro marketers'. This type of sales person was a long way removed from the silver tongued extrovert portrayed in most bad training videos. This new business person not only had to deeply understand the customer but also had to be able to align our own teams to develop and deliver the customer solution.

Finding marketers who understood this whole approach was also a challenge as getting some of them to suspend their product obsession was no mean task. The results spoke for themselves. In two organizations I worked in, this approach drove record growth – one incumbent and one challenger.

Today's marketers have to rise to the challenge presented by taking this approach. They must understand the importance of a close link between marketing and sales and appreciate that it is sales personnel who have the daily dialogue with customers. The marketing role is about harnessing customer feedback from sales to keep strategy development real; analyzing and synthesizing this feedback to spot key trends and develop responses; providing sales with insights about customer issues and trends; and finally, facilitating customer events that deepen the understanding of the customer. Successful implementation will drive revenue and sales growth.[7]

maintaining relationships that are beneficial to both parties) and those of direct marketing are closely related. The main difference between these two forms of marketing is that direct marketing includes specific marketing instruments (such as direct-response television advertising and business-to-business direct mail) to achieve the firm's objectives. Organizations using direct marketing adopt a strategy incorporating both *direct* distribution to and communication with the customer. Current technology makes it possible for them – using sophisticated, well-maintained computer databases – to approach carefully targeted individual consumers or market segments with customized, highly personalized marketing strategies. This method of communication has proven to be an excellent way to build and enhance long-lasting and lucrative relationships with customers.

We will first explore what direct marketing and the related strategy of database marketing entail. We will then examine the marketing tools and media most commonly used to maintain contact with customers. Finally, the growth and evolution of direct marketing will be discussed.

11.6.1 What is direct marketing?

The term direct marketing is widely used, and can refer to several different activities. Some people consider it primarily to be an advertising or selling technique, while others view it as a direct distribution method. Still others consider it a direct communication strategy or key element of the firm's marketing communication mix. In reality, direct marketing – as a marketing approach or system – is a combination of these concepts. There are many forms of direct marketing in which different media are used, as is apparent from our definition.

Direct marketing is a custom tailored marketing approach in which the company's objective is to build lasting relationships with carefully targeted individual consumers or buyers in narrowly defined segments and – using detailed customer information from a computerized database and direct communication tools such as the Internet, telephone or direct mail – to generate an immediate, measurable response in the form of an order, a request for further information, or a visit to a store, website or other place of business for the purchase of a product or service.

Advantages of direct marketing

Direct marketing is the fastest growing form of marketing ever. It involves many different marketing methods utilizing various media, such as direct mail, catalogues, direct selling, infomercials, direct-response television advertising and, of course, Internet marketing. There are several reasons for direct marketing's growing popularity, both among consumers and businesses.

Consumers' life styles are changing, and many of them have become interested in convenient and dependable ways to shop. A great deal of product information is now readily available through the Internet. Saving travelling time and money, consumers – using a credit card or other available payment method – can shop from their homes or offices, and have their selected products delivered right to the front door. Two-worker families, for whom direct purchasing has become an appealing alternative to fighting traffic and going to the mall or even the supermarket, especially appreciate this convenience.

For companies, direct marketing represents an *inexpensive* way to reach their markets. Suppliers increasingly sell products and services through their websites, or rely on direct mail and telephone marketing to touch base with buyers at the right moment. With the high cost of personal selling, direct marketing offers a low-cost alternative to establish and maintain contacts with customers.

In today's fragmented markets, direct marketing also allows businesses to reach a narrow, carefully selected *target market*. They avoid the wasted resources of appealing to mass audiences through a 'shotgun approach'. Knowing the target audience well, they can personalize their direct marketing communication efforts and tailor their offers to the needs and wants of their prospects ('rifle approach'). At the same time, very large audiences, impossible to reach through other channels, can be tapped through e-commerce. Even small or start-up businesses can now focus on the international market using well-designed websites.

Since direct marketing typically involves *two-way* communication, it is an interactive form of marketing. Marketers can now create one-on-one interactions. For instance, communicating by telephone and through websites, a company like Dell is able to customize its products based on direct responses from buyers. Some even refer to direct marketing as *direct-response marketing*. The bottom line is that its results are measurable, allowing management to assess the extent to which it has reached its marketing communication objectives by calculating, for example, the number of requests for information or actual purchases during a campaign.

Finally, advanced technology equips companies to construct complex, detailed customer databases and manipulate the data – using predictive models – to establish relationships between these data and the intended marketing results. Database information – used to create personalized marketing communications that appeal to individual consumers in the database – is not only useful in obtaining orders from specific buyers, but also in creating long-term customer *relationships*. This has made direct marketing a valuable marketing tool in an era when companies are no longer simply seeking a single sale or transaction, but are striving to retain their customers in lasting, mutually beneficial relationships.

Database marketing

Not too long ago, customer 'lists' or databases were primarily used by catalogue and mail order companies that sent bulk mailings to their customers. That has changed. Today, it is important for any customer-oriented organization to develop a sound customer database. And for companies engaged in direct marketing campaigns, an extensive database of current and potential customers is even more critical. Many firms committed to building direct relationships with their customers want to learn as much as possible about customers and potential buyers, and use that information to their advantage. That's where database marketing comes in. Essentially, database marketing is identical to direct marketing, with the exception that it specifically requires use of a database, as pointed out in the following definition.

Database marketing is the use of computer database technologies to systematically collect, store and analyze information about individual customers in order to develop customized marketing activities, converting customers into active buyers and possibly building profitable long-term exchange relationships with them. Lists of up-to-date information may be based on customers' electronic bank transfers, credit card transaction records, responses from previous direct mail campaigns or, in industry, trade show registration or other records that identify certain groups of customers or prospects. Business-to-business lists may also include data on companies' annual sales volume, purchasing history and names of the members of its Decision Making Unit.

Customer databases may be quite large. While they are often compiled internally by the company's marketers, databases can also be purchased or rented from specialized list providers for use on a one-time basis. Some research firms sell customer databases ranging from thousands to millions of consumers who, for example, have recently retired, moved or share other characteristics that make them potential buyers of particular products and services.

Armed with a database containing valuable information about the target market, a company can develop a direct marketing strategy that will lead to lower costs per order than a strategy in which the market is targeted through traditional mass media. In fact, a major advantage of a well-planned database marketing campaign is that the campaign's *reach* and *coverage* ('target market reach') will coincide almost exactly. Furthermore, the *response* from the target audience will be relatively high, since database marketing allows the firm to target more precisely and adjust its message to individual customer needs and preferences.

Customer names and addresses are just one component of the *database*. A functional database may also provide data on demographics, consumption patterns, shopping habits, brand and media preferences and lifestyles. An analysis of these data may show, for example, when consumers should replace certain products they own or exactly when various contracts or subscriptions expire. Marketers may then approach these customers in advance with, as in the case of subscription goods and services (such as magazines or mobile phone contracts), a discount or another attractive offer to convert a trial subscription or expiring contract into a permanent or new one. This type of transaction is called a conversion. Direct marketers also keep a record of the responses that each campaign generates and determine which prospects should be approached again.

The raw data that marketers collect – no matter how timely, relevant, unbiased and accessible they are – have only marginal value without more thorough evaluation. The lists of prospects or buyers, combined with customers' consumption profiles and other data, must be compiled and organized properly to create meaningful information on which managers can base direct marketing decisions. This requires an upfront investment of time and money, but it is worth the effort. List management, which includes evaluations of past campaigns to determine how the available information can be organized and used more effectively in future communications with customers, results in lower costs per order in direct marketing.

11.6.2 *Direct marketing forms*

Two major direct marketing forms are personal selling and online marketing. Personal selling was discussed in the first part of this chapter, while online marketing will be explored in Chapter 14, which covers retailing. In this section, we will examine several other forms of direct marketing, including direct mail, telephone marketing and direct response television advertising. Each of these interactive media allows for two-way communication between the supplier and buyer and provides a measurable response.

Direct mail

Direct mail refers to any advertising message that is addressed with either the recipient's name and street address or street address only and sent by mail or other form of private delivery service to a prospect in the target market. The format can range from a simple postcard or leaflet with a special offer or an announcement, to a letter or a package containing a sales letter, a promotional brochure, sometimes a sample, a CD or DVD and typically a response card. The 'statement stuffers' included in other mail, such as bank or credit card statements or packages from catalogue companies, are another form of direct mail. Usually the sender will try to evoke a response by making a temporary offer or by offering a free gift with an order.

Using a carefully compiled, selective mailing list and a personalized message designed to fit the prospective buyer's specific needs, a company will effectively reach better and more prospects through direct mail than with any form of advertising. If direct mailers use statistical techniques to analyze customers' past purchases, financial information and lifestyles or other psychographic data, they can deliver personalized messages and appeal to a narrow target audience with great precision. Messages can either be sent through regular mail or by email, fax or voicemail.

Included in the direct mail category are catalogue and mail order companies. Catalogues are usually designed for highly segmented markets. To millions of consumers, ordering from catalogues offers a convenient and attractive alternative to in-store shopping. Among the biggest threats to traditional catalogue marketing are competing retailers' websites. Today, many catalogues are web-only. In response to this trend, most companies originally known for their printed catalogues have established web catalogues and now also conduct business via the Internet. The Internet is the fastest growing direct mail vehicle, and many companies have experienced phenomenal successes through web development. In fact, Dell can largely attribute its number two ranking in PC sales to its direct marketing campaigns on the Internet.

Business-to-business commerce also uses each of these direct mail tactics. Like other promotional tools, direct mail is rarely used alone, and is often a supplement to other direct marketing forms. It provides an excellent way to maintain contact with B2B customers between salespeople's calls. Like advertising, it can help develop the product awareness or acceptance that increases purchase probabilities when buyers are contacted by the company's salespeople. When the number of prospects in the organizational market is small, each can be sent an individually designed message, thus increasing the potential impact. Other advantages of direct mail, in comparison to other media, are that – since circulation is controlled by the sender – there is little waste and the message remains hidden from competitors.

Telephone marketing

Another important system for direct marketing is telephone marketing: many companies use the phone as an interactive marketing instrument to systematically approach target markets and to initiate, develop and enhance relationships with customers. Although telephone marketing is less costly than personal selling, it is much more expensive than direct mail and advertising. In terms of expenditures and sales generated, however, telephone marketing is the leading direct marketing communications technique.[8]

Some confuse this form of direct marketing communication with telemarketing or teleselling, a practice which – due to the intrusive nature of the telephone and consumers' objections to unsolicited telephone sales calls – has acquired a bad image in the consumer market. Consumers often complain that telemarketers are pushy, use misleading selling techniques and invade their privacy at home. Consumer organizations in many countries have reacted by warning consumers to be cautious regarding telemarketing, while lawmakers all over the world have responded with legislation that restricts telemarketing calls to certain hours of the day and to consumers not registered on a 'do not call' list. The implication for marketers is that, to be accepted as legitimate business people, they should not call on consumers who indicate they will not accept telephone solicitation.

The majority of telephone marketing efforts take place in the organizational market. In fact, business-to-business marketers are responsible for more than half of all telephone marketing sales. Marketers use *outbound* telephone marketing to actively solicit prospects and sell directly to consumers and businesses. *Inbound* toll-free numbers, on the other hand, are frequently used to receive orders from catalogues, direct mail and advertisements, but also to provide information and handle complaints from customers in the follow-up stage of the selling process. In general, the telephone is a useful tool to support and strengthen the effectiveness of traditional marketing methods and to enhance the relationships with clients through personal contact. It can help improve customer service, and is used to collect marketing data and dispense information, for example to announce the opening of a new store or to introduce a new product or service. Especially in B2B marketing, it is, from the customer's perspective, an effective marketing method and a preferred way to interact with suppliers.

Other direct marketing media

A sponsored magazine is a direct mail medium effective in conveying information to customers and in enhancing the relationship between a business and its customers. Distributed free of charge, this type of consumer magazine typically consists of editorial articles and other features, such as announcements of newly introduced products and advertising by third parties. It may also serve as a catalogue that presents an overview of the entire product mix. Sponsored magazines are also known as *house organs*, a broader category which includes printed or electronic newsletters, stockholder reports and dealer publications.

Television and radio – better known for their role in mass advertising – are also used as direct marketing media. A popular format is the infomercial, an extended television commercial for a single product presented in a television show format. It usually lasts 30 minutes, mixes information and entertainment and often features products like cosmetics, fitness equipment and small kitchen appliances. It includes a direct-response telephone number, generating immediate feedback and providing a quick and effective way to measure results and develop a customer database. The term direct response advertising refers to any medium used to elicit an immediate response from a target audience. By definition, it includes a communication mechanism such as a phone number to call, a coupon to be mailed or an online address to get in touch with the seller. Regular 60-second TV spots, which persuasively describe a product and urge consumers to call a toll-tree number to order, are a common alternative to infomercials.

Direct response advertising is only one form of direct response television marketing. The other form is television home shopping, a TV programme or cable channel that presents products to television viewers, encouraging them to call a toll-free number and order the products featured in the programme. As with infomercials, this form of direct marketing allows marketers to build a database and immediately assess the results of their marketing efforts.

11.6.3 Evolution of direct marketing

For many firms today, direct marketing is more than a supplementary marketing channel. They use direct marketing through the Internet as their primary way to approach prospective buyers and customers. Many of them, including Dell Computers and Amazon.com, began as direct marketers only, and have grown very rapidly as a result.

In addition to using a high-quality database, companies should integrate their direct marketing activities into the overall marketing communication strategy. They can increase response rates significantly if they develop a carefully coordinated campaign involving several media, such as direct mail, a website, a toll-free phone number and telemarketing, all used simultaneously.

Such an approach, known as integrated direct marketing, may well double or triple the usual response rate of a regular mailing.[9] Other trends in the evolution of direct marketing are outlined in Table 11.2. In conclusion, direct marketing via interactive media is a rapidly growing marketing strategy and will continue to present lucrative marketing opportunities for firms committed to building lasting relationships with their customers.

TABLE 11.2 Evolution of direct marketing

Subject	From	To
Emphasis on	Prospects	Customers
Objective of marketing activities	Customer acquisition	Customer retention
Focus	Transactions	Relationships
Time horizon	Short-term	Long-term
Marketing expenditures are	Costs	Investments in the customer
Communication with customers	Indirect	Direct
Measurement of success	Consumer promotion	Customer
Customer viewed as	Member of the target market	An individual
Involvement with customers	Marketing or Sales department	Entire organization
Marketers' – task	Persuade	Persuade and listen
Managerial mindset	Make and sell	Sense and respond
Marketing process	Action-reaction (response)	Interaction (dialogue)
Database used for	Personalizing messages	Customized offer (one-to-one marketing)

11.7 SALES PROMOTION

Because of cut-throat industry rivalry, many companies systematically pursue every conceivable competitive marketing edge. Firms rely not only on advertising, public relations, sponsorships, personal selling and direct marketing, but also use *sales promotion* (often called *promotions*) to increase the effectiveness of their marketing communication efforts.

Promotions are becoming an increasingly important element of the promotional mix for one major reason. These marketing expenditures deliver immediate sales results. Thus, companies spend a large part of their marketing communication budgets on sales promotions, including discount coupons, sweepstakes, point-of-purchase displays, free samples and mail-in rebates. All of these are tools or programmes developed by marketers to create interest in certain products or services and to encourage consumers (as well as intermediaries in the distribution channel) to order or buy immediately. The final section of this chapter is devoted to sales promotion, concentrating on types of promotions that can successfully influence buying behaviour. We will also examine current trends in sales promotion.

11.7.1 *Objectives of sales promotion*

Most managers view **sales promotion** as a set of direct incentives to temporarily increase the basic value of a product relative to comparable products on the market, thereby encouraging distribution channel members to step up their selling efforts and consumers to buy the product. To help increase sales, a sales promotion campaign can add a dimension to each element of the marketing mix. For instance, the price/value relationship of a product may, from the buyer's perspective, be augmented in the short-term by offering:

→ Extra product – for instance, a bonus pack containing a larger quantity or extra units.

→ A service – a loyalty programme that rewards customers making repeat purchases (with merchandise or future upgrades).

→ A discount – a savings coupon affixed directly to the package.

→ A chance to win something of value by entering a contest or sweepstakes.

These techniques may all help pull the product through the distribution channel by conveying a sense of urgency to purchase before the promotion is discontinued.

Theme promotions

Traditionally, sales promotion techniques were intended as short-term incentives designed to generate immediate consumer purchases. Marketers used promotions as supplements to the other components of a firm's promotional mix. Promotions were primarily forms of campaign or *action* communication.

However, today – with more ads than ever and fewer differences between competing brands – the focus of sales promotion has changed from short-term objectives (such as an immediate buying response) to long-term goals (creating brand equity or brand loyalty). Marketers increasingly develop *theme* promotions that add something tangible to their communication efforts. For example, they may offer a well-chosen premium that adds to the affective value of their brand, or develop a loyalty programme to encourage repeat purchases, build a loyal customer base and enhance the company's reputation. This, in effect, brings sales promotion into the mainstream of the marketing plan. A hotel chain's frequent-stay programme to help the company attract loyal guests is one example. If these types of promotions mesh well with the company's theme advertising campaign, they may even be able to influence the consumer's attitude towards the brand, leading to a *long-term* change in their buying behaviour. Such strong and lasting influence would be impossible using less sophisticated forms of sales promotion, such as a coupon offering a one-time only price discount.

Horizontal and vertical promotions

When establishing the objectives of promotion campaigns, we make a distinction between horizontal and vertical promotions. *Horizontal promotions* are designed to increase sales by attracting new customers. These may be individuals who have never tried the product before (in which case there is a *market expansion*), or people who usually buy competing brands. In both cases, the group of buyers is *expanded*, increasing the brand's sales volume. To achieve this objective of stimulating product trial, we could use sales promotion techniques that reduce consumer cost and risk, such as free samples, coupons or rebates.

If, on the other hand, we target our current customers with a sales promotion campaign to induce them to buy more of their favourite brand, then this is referred to as a *vertical promotion*. The objective of this strategy could be twofold:

→ To increase consumer inventory and consumption. Promotions like a buy one, get one free special (also referred to as a *deal*) may motivate consumers to buy more than they normally would. This short-term price reduction builds up the stock on the consumers' kitchen shelves, which tends to lead to greater consumption of the product on hand.

→ To encourage repurchase and increase brand loyalty. Loyalty programmes, also known as frequency marketing programmes, help create repeat-purchase patterns, which are crucial for the product's long-term success and survival.

Other promotions to keep existing customers and to reinforce or maintain their purchase patterns for the product or service include airlines' frequent flyer programmes, on-package coupons for future discounts (on pizzas, for example), special price incentives (for instance, to convert a trial magazine subscription into a permanent one) and redemption programmes or bonus points that consumers receive for every euro they spend on products (such as Shell's *Air Miles* in Europe). A secondary objective of this type of promotion is to neutralize competitors' promotions, as is common in the mobile phone market, when consumers are offered a new cell phone and other incentives to encourage them to renew contracts, rather than switching to a competing service provider with comparable offerings.

Consumer sales promotions are also commonly used to spur impulse purchases, to boost brand awareness, to increase sales of complementary products (such as Gillette's Fusion razor blades after offering a rebate for the razor), to allow price flexibility (in appealing to a price-conscious market segment), to emphasize novelty or to suggest new uses of the product. Sales promotion objectives related to channel members are often demand-oriented as well. They include increasing sales, gaining distribution, obtaining sufficient shelf space, receiving cooperation in sales promotion efforts and creating dealer enthusiasm.

We will now make a more refined distinction between campaigns aimed at consumers (consumer promotions) and channel members (trade promotions), including the sales staff (sales force promotions). Then we will examine the most noteworthy trends in the use of sales promotion.

11.7.2 Consumer promotions

Not only do retailers target consumers with sales promotion campaigns; manufacturers design similar promotion campaigns to alter consumer buying behaviour. Consumer promotions initiated by retailers usually attempt to attract customers to specific stores, whereas

TABLE 11.3 Consumer promotions: objectives, strategies and activities

Objectives	Possible strategy	Sales promotion activities
Attract new users	Encourage trial purchases	Samples, refunds, premiums
Increase product usage	Suggest new applications and consumption patterns	Product demonstrations, bonus packs, point-of-purchase displays
Retain current customers	Fight competitive brands by offering incentives to stock up	Bonus packs, coupons, club promotions
Launch a new brand	Reduce potential buyer's risk perception	Price-offs, samples, demonstrations
Enhance brand image	Reinforce theme advertising message through integrated communication	Event sponsorship, contests, loyalty programmes

those developed by manufacturers often promote established brands or introduce new products. Especially when faced with stiff competition, marketers try to increase sales by providing direct incentives.

Table 11.3 outlines consumer promotions' main objectives, along with possible strategies and sales promotion techniques to achieve them. A marketer rarely uses them all. Their choice of consumer promotions depends on such factors as the target audience, the company's overall marketing strategy, the available marketing communication budget and the actual product or service. We will now consider the most commonly used consumer promotions.[10]

Price promotions

One of the most frequently used types of sales promotion is a price promotion or *price deal*, a temporary reduction from a previously established price, which may take the form of a price pack deal, a coupon or a rebate. Price promotions change the value equation and are used to prompt new users to try an established brand, to encourage current users to buy more of the product, or to help launch a new brand or an improved product.

A *cents-off deal* or price pack deal offers a brand at less than the regular price, or, alternatively, offers buyers an extra quantity through the package itself (for example, 'now 25 per cent more'). This type of price promotion can be implemented quickly and is easy to communicate through, for example, a sticker on the package or label that indicates the savings off the product's regular price. Moreover, the impact of price pack deals is easily measured. Some manufacturers offer a reduced price only once a year to avoid tarnishing the quality image of their national brands. If the distribution strategy allows it, the temporary price discount will be targeted only towards the most price-sensitive segment of the market. In fact, a major drawback of short-term price reductions is that they attract more 'bargain hunters' than regular buyers. Although they are often intended to increase trial among potential customers or to retaliate against rivals' actions, they don't change market shares permanently. Furthermore, existing users may stockpile goods on the kitchen shelves by buying the product sooner than they normally would or by purchasing extra quantities. As a result of such stockpiling, future sales may fall off.

To prevent stockpiling, many companies prefer to use **rebates** or *cash refund offers*. After sending in one or more 'proofs of purchase' (often the Universal Product Code), the receipt and a rebate form, the customer receives a one-time cash refund (part of the purchase price) by mail or, in European countries, typically as a direct deposit to a bank account. This particular form of consumer sales promotion is used only by manufacturers; retailers are not involved in the process. Manufacturers' rebate costs may be limited by several factors, such as a rebate offered on a low-priced item or low **redemption** rates due to buyers forgetting to send in the request or missing the deadline for submission. This so-called slippage is less likely to occur if refunds are substantial (as with a car purchase) or if the information for the rebate can be submitted online.

A final form of price promotion is **coupons**. These are certificates, usually with an expiration date, for money off the purchase price of selected products. Typically, coupons are distributed by mail, printed in newspaper or magazine ads or on packages and labels. They are also printed at the checkout on the back of cash-register receipts or can be downloaded from the Internet. Coupons are designed either to attract new users or to encourage past users to make repeat purchases. They are also an effective brand-switching incentive. Although coupons are the most widely used consumer sales promotion technique in the United States, consumers in other cultures don't accept couponing to the same extent as American consumers. Although the number of coupons distributed and redeemed has been declining recently, online couponing – the distribution of coupons on the Internet – is still expanding.

Samples

Sampling refers to the free distribution of a small quantity of a product – usually in the early stages of its life cycle – in an attempt to demonstrate a product's value or use and to encourage future purchase. It draws increased attention to a brand and actually puts the product in the consumer's hands. The use of free **samples** to gain retail distribution and to persuade potential customers to try new products is widespread among manufacturers of food, household products and personal care and grooming products, particularly for new brands or products with characteristics that are difficult to describe in advertisements. This sales promotion method decreases the consumer's perception of risk by allowing product trial before buying a full-size version.

Samples may be delivered door-to-door or mailed. Sampling can also be accomplished by demonstrating or distributing the product at a retail store, or by attaching a sample to

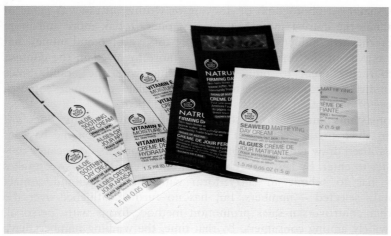

Image Asset Management

another product (*on-pack*), either with a product from the same manufacturer (*cross sampling*) or from another company (*joint promotion*). To be an effective promotional device, samples should be given to as many people as possible. Not surprisingly, therefore, free samples can be an expensive form of promotion. Also, sampling is effective only if the product distributed is actually superior to competitive products already on the market and if the consumer is able to perceive the superiority without much difficulty.

Premiums

Premiums are items offered at no cost or at a considerable saving over the retail price with purchases of other products. They are generally effective in encouraging consumers to try a new product or a different brand, as long as the premium is related to the product it accompanies. Other objectives of premiums are to increase consumption, create goodwill, enhance the product's image or broaden the customer base by persuading non-users to switch brands.

There are three types of premiums. The first is a *free premium*, an item that the consumer receives after buying the product. This is often a *free-in-the-mail premium*, an item mailed to the consumer in exchange for some proof (such as a UPC code) that the promoted product has been purchased. Or it may be a *with-pack premium*, which accompanies the product inside the package ('in-pack'), is attached to the package ('on-pack') or is placed near the product ('near-pack').

A second type of premium is called a self-liquidating premium, because the consumer is offered the opportunity to purchase the premium below the regular retail price, usually equal to the seller's cost for the product. The third, and final, type of premium is known as a *reusable container premium*, because the product's package is the premium. In Europe, for instance, manufacturers of marmalade, chocolate or hazelnut spread (such as *Nutella*) sell some of their products in glass jars that are reusable as drinking glasses. While the use of premiums in promotional campaigns has increased considerably in recent years, the most successful premiums appear to be those that are easily recognizable and, in a creative way, suit the target audience as well as the product's brand image.

Contests, sweepstakes and games

Marketers design contests and sweepstakes to generate interest in their products or services, often in an attempt to encourage consumers to switch brands. In a contest, consumers can win prizes based on their creative or analytical skills in completing a task such as solving a puzzle, creating a slogan, making a photograph or drawing or writing an essay. A panel of judges is assigned to evaluate the entries and select the best ones. Today, more and more companies turn to the Internet to conduct contests, not only to save time and money, but also to get consumers – as part of the online experience – more involved in the contest, and, by doing so, encouraging them to build a relationship with the brand. Since governments in most countries impose legal restrictions to regulate consumer contests, many firms use the services of promotion specialists in organizing them.

The condition that contestants must perform some type of creative activity, does *not* apply to sweepstakes, in which prizes – like in a lottery – are awarded on the basis of chance alone. Sweepstakes often draw ten times more entries than contests do because they take less time and are easier to enter. By law, a purchase cannot be required for sweepstakes entry. A consumer only has to submit an entry form with their name and contact information or – randomly selected – numbers, but has no further influence over the outcome. In this somewhat controversial sales promotion method, forms with 'personal' numbers are distributed widely among consumers. By that time, the winning numbers have already been drawn, but will be announced later. In practice, only a fraction of the prize money is claimed, therefore the winnings announced often greatly exceed the actual funds disbursed. Global marketers should realize that sweepstakes are banned in several European countries and are regulated in most nations to ensure that the chances of winning are clearly communicated and to guarantee that the prizes are actually awarded.

Games are similar to sweepstakes, but typically cover a longer period of time. They usually require participants to collect something, such as missing letters or numbers in bottle caps, every time they buy a product. Since collecting multiple pieces may be necessary to help them win a prize, a game tends to stimulate repeat purchases.

Frequency programmes

Many companies have developed incentive programmes to reward loyal customers for making multiple or repeat purchases. These are known as frequency programmes or loyalty marketing programmes. Airlines' frequent flier programmes offering free tickets – or an upgrade to a business class seat – to passengers who have travelled a particular distance with the same airline or its partners are common examples. Other service companies, such as hotels and car rental agencies, offer similar frequent-user incentives. For these firms, frequency programmes are an effective marketing tool to fight the trend of declining brand loyalty among price-conscious consumers.

Many people carry several loyalty cards that, when used regularly, reward them with redeemable points. To illustrate, frequent shopper or 'bonus' cards offered by many supermarkets and chain stores are widely used by consumers to get discounts on products that vary weekly. At the same time, the companies issuing these cards can obtain valuable information from their registered customers that allows them to build long-term, mutually beneficial relationships with customers by sending them emails or letters with coupons and information of interest. In short, frequency programmes allow marketing-oriented companies to target their key customers effectively with incentives or tailored offers that reward them for their loyalty.

11.7.3 Trade promotions

As opposed to consumer promotions, which are designed to generate sufficient demand to *pull* a product through the distribution channel, successful trade promotions *push* the product through the channel. Trade promotions are sales promotion campaigns aimed at retailers, wholesalers, agents or other middlemen that encourage them to carry the manufacturer's products and promote them effectively. Most manufacturers spend more money on trade promotion than on consumer promotion tools. Common trade promotion objectives are to help resellers gain or maintain distribution, to increase order size and increase reseller inventory, to influence resellers to promote the product or to offer a price discount, to allow special displays for the product or to do whatever it takes to increase sales. Some supermarket chains are presented with more than a hundred promotions a week! Which promotions retailers decide to support not only depends on how attractive the consumer samples or premiums are, but also on the discounts or other incentives offered to management for participating in the campaign.

There are two distinct forms of trade-oriented sales promotions. Selling-in activities influence resellers to carry specific products, pay close attention to them and keep larger quantities in stock. Incentives such as giving the reseller free product for each unit ordered, providing in-store assistance to set up an effective product display or offering a holiday trip or other such perks for ordering specific quantities are all intended to gain the retailer's support.

On the other hand, the objective of selling-out activities is to increase the retailers' turnover. Using marketing tools such as flyers, window posters, displays and other supporting store material, suppliers can help to improve the retailers' sales results. These activities are also known as *merchandising*. Another sales promotion method commonly used is assistance in training the reseller's sales force to increase its sales performance.

For both selling-in and selling-out activities, some of the sales promotions just reviewed as consumer promotions are also used as trade promotions. In addition, discounts to increase inventory levels and trade allowances (such as slotting fees or cash payments made to retailers for access to shelf space in stores for special shelf locations or displays) are also widely used. In the remainder of this section, we will examine POP displays and trade shows as unique trade promotions.

Point-of-purchase displays

Due to the lack of flexibility in floor space, retailers need variable, attention-getting elements in their stores. Attractive displays, also known as *point-of-purchase* (POP) displays, help retailers to direct shoppers' attention to a particular product. Almost any product can be promoted successfully by means of floor-stand or end-aisle displays. Typically provided by the manufacturer at no charge to the retailer, displays highlight the product and offer information, and stimulate product purchases. Widely used forms of point-of-purchase promotions are banners, racks and exhibits placed in retail stores, but also in-store audio messages to increase sales of a particular brand. Signs attached to store shelves ('shelf signs') and extensions of store shelves to draw attention to the featured product ('shelf extenders') are other examples of such displays. Since the majority of retail purchase decisions are made in-store, these POP promotions can be very effective.

Displays are not always intended to entice consumers to make *impulse purchases* – unplanned, spur-of-the-moment purchases. They are increasingly used for product demonstration and to provide information that cannot be communicated in media advertising. The increasing number of audio-visual demonstrations in department stores and home improvement stores illustrates their effectiveness and popularity. If displays can be placed on a counter, they can even be used in small stores with limited space; these are referred to as *counter displays*.

Sales from displays are almost always higher than from the shelves. Supermarket sales are no exception; the sales volume of a product placed in a display often increases by more than a thousand per cent. Manufacturers – as providers of trade promotions – are therefore willing to pay retailers to present their products in a display at a prime POP location, such as close to the cash register. Other organizations, such as banks, travel agencies and even government agencies are now also increasingly using displays as a source of information or to increase sales.

Trade shows

A trade show – one of the earliest forms of sales promotion – is an event, usually lasting several days, at which marketers exhibit and demonstrate their products to current and prospective buyers who represent resellers and other members of the distribution channel. These exhibitions are usually organized by industry trade associations to take place during their annual meetings or conventions.

In Europe, companies involved in business-to-business marketing on average spend more than 25 per cent of their marketing communication budgets on trade show activities. This expenditure is even greater than in the US, where thousands of trade shows and conventions are conducted annually. Manufacturers view these as an excellent opportunity to launch new or improved products for a target audience of channel members eager to learn about the latest developments in their particular industry. Hence, trade show exhibits can be a very effective means of communication with the target market at relatively low cost.

In addition to introducing new products and services, companies typically participate in trade shows to promote or enhance their corporate image, to train sales personnel, to take product orders and to test the market for a prototype product, gather feedback and conduct other types of marketing research. Additional selling and non-selling functions of trade shows include identifying prospects, recruiting dealers or salespeople, servicing present customers and collecting information about rivals' new products and services.

Trade shows also provide an effective forum to influence those members of an organization's buying centre who are involved in the decision-making process for major purchases. Since each of these managers needs information in their own specialized field, a supplier can, by having various experts attend the trade show, provide the potential customer with any and all required information at the event. One of the company's executives can also make themselves available to meet with potential customers. Most importantly, trade show participants should not only set explicit marketing communication objectives related to their attendance before the show starts, but should also follow up soon after the show ends by communicating with interested visitors to hopefully begin cultivating a long-term relationship.

Sales force promotions

A third target group for promotion activities – generally considered a critical part of trade promotions – is the company's own sales force. These promotions, known as **sales force promotions**, are usually incentives to encourage salespeople to improve their sales performance by acquiring new customers, providing better service, introducing new products or making an effort to sell the entire product line. The most widely used sales promotion tools are *bonuses* (for instance on sales volume or number of new accounts) and *sales contests*, with prizes such as money, gifts and trips for the most successful salespeople. In addition, sales meetings may be held at luxury resorts to celebrate reaching certain targets and to create a team spirit within the sales force.

Service-oriented companies such as hotel chains sometimes rely on sales promotions to keep all of their employees motivated. For instance, many firms provide cash prizes for the 'employee of the month' to publicly recognize this individual's accomplishments and to spark excitement among all of the co-workers.

11.7.4 *Current trends in sales promotion*

'Advertising makes marriages – promotions keep them exciting.' This statement illustrates that while sales promotions may only have a modest effect on buying behaviour, they can still influence brand loyalty. Although promotions have always been an important marketing tool, there have been some interesting changes in the ways they are used. The most striking trends are toward ever increasing expenditures, growth in tailored promotions and the combined use of promotions and direct marketing techniques.

Higher expenditures

Since sales promotion includes various types of activities, it is not easy to determine how much money companies spend on this endeavour. However, most experts agree that every year, more money is spent on sales promotion than on advertising, especially by companies marketing fast moving consumer goods.

The primary reason for the growing use of sales promotion is that many consumer goods companies are operating in *mature markets*. There are limits to the number of bags of potato chips and coffee that people are willing to buy. Since it is increasingly difficult to create *distinctive* advertising for products that, from a functional perspective barely differ, unique promotions can usher a brand to the forefront of the market. Therefore, *product managers* like to work with large promotion budgets, particularly if their product is likely to become obsolete quickly due to a *short life cycle*. Moreover, in order to move upward within the organization, these managers must achieve a significant increase in sales volume and profit within a short period of time. This can be accomplished through attractive (but costly) promotions.

The competitive battle at retail level is also intensifying because of the increasing power of large and expanding retail chains, which tend to give priority to marketing their own store brands. Since there is only so much shelf space they can allocate to any given product category, manufacturers are forced to provide more sales promotion in support of their brands than they would under more favourable conditions. This, too, has resulted in high sales promotion expenditures.

Advertising agencies often complain that in many of these consumer goods companies, theme or awareness advertising is treated as a 'stepchild'. Money is only allocated to it if there is any money left over after funding the sales promotion campaigns. Clearly, this approach to decision making is not always based on careful consideration of the long-term strategy.

A major downside to these growing promotional expenditures is that consumers are being conditioned to frequent sales promotion campaigns. Special incentives and deals lead to forward buying by consumers as well as distributors: they buy more than they need in the near future, to carry them through to the next time a reduced price is being offered, when they can again stock up at low prices. Thus, an increased emphasis on promotions may lead to short-term increases in sales volume, while decreasing profits.

Tailor-made promotions

With more and more chain stores now organizing promotions around their private labels and store brands, there are fewer opportunities for manufacturers of national brands to conduct large-scale sales promotion campaigns requiring retailers' involvement. To ensure the cooperation of chain stores in their promotions, national brand manufacturers are increasingly offering retailers exclusive, custom-designed promotions. Hence, there has been a shift away from standardized national campaigns towards single use, tailor-made promotions. This reflects the growing power of retailers who, among other things, try to reinforce their store image and ambience through promotions that tie in best with their own positioning and target markets.

Initially, retailers asked their suppliers for custom-designed promotions closely matching their target audience or store image. Many manufacturers responded favourably to this. If asked, they could provide fun, spectacular or discount-related promotions that, even though sometimes inconsistent with their brand image, resulted in a substantial sales volume. This approach became more difficult when chain store organizations began developing their own promotions and subsequently invited manufacturers to take part in them. After all, a particular barbecue promotion, contest or loyalty programme does not always necessarily match the positioning of the manufacturer's barbeque sauce brand.

Unfortunately, this trend has led to a greater number of small-scale, tailor-made promotions. This, in turn, increases the likelihood of making huge, costly mistakes. Even large companies and agencies that are specialized in sales promotion may experience difficulties because each promotion is tailor-made and used only once. Mistakes caused by lack of experience may turn into financial disasters and damage relationships with customers.

Direct marketing techniques

A third trend in the development of sales promotion campaigns is the increasing use of *direct marketing techniques* in executing promotions. Contacting only selected prospects may well involve additional costs but increases the response rate (which is usually relatively low with promotions). A high-quality database also limits the so-called *subsidizing* of buyers who participate in a promotion but would have purchased the product anyway – with or without the sales promotion campaign.

In conclusion, we noted that despite the higher expenditures on promotions, large-scale, undifferentiated sales promotion campaigns are not as commonplace as they once were. The successful use of sales promotion requires a careful selection of the target audience and the well-planned use of effective promotion techniques.

SUMMARY

1   Personal selling

Personal selling, as a cornerstone of the company's promotion strategy, plays a significant role in the organization's overall marketing effort. The stereotypical image of an aggressive salesperson putting their foot between the door is steadily being replaced by that of a more professional salesperson: a customer-oriented team player who sells products that meet the clients' real needs and who works hard to keep the customers satisfied. Sales professionals' tasks vary, depending on whether they are order takers (such as merchandisers), order getters (such as account managers) or sales support personnel (such as sales engineers). Sales representatives may play multiple roles. Some help to introduce new products and find new prospects. Others spend much of their time collecting market information, providing excellent service and seeking repeat orders. And all of them are responsible for customer satisfaction. Effective sales professionals view their mission as one of maintaining long-term relationships with their customers, not of achieving the highest possible sales figures.

2   Creative selling process

No two sales professionals use exactly the same selling techniques. Yet, most salespeople go through a systematic process as they sell their products and services. This selling process consists of three phases: preparation, persuasion and transaction. The preparation phase takes place before potential buyers are contacted and consists of two stages. Prospecting involves the search for and qualification of potential customers. In the preapproach stage, further information is collected on prospects to determine the best way to approach them. In the persuasion phase, the seller approaches the potential customer for the first time. During the sales presentation, the sales representative tries to convert them into a customer by delivering the message and creating a desire for the product or service. The transaction phase involves two steps: closing the sale and following up. Thus, after getting a commitment from the prospect, the sales professional must make sure that the customer is fully satisfied, improving the odds that they will become loyal to the supplier.

3   Management by objectives

A successful sales manager focuses not only on sales volume targets, but also on the entire selling process and strategy that drive their sales organization to realize these and other objectives. Salespeople are increasingly involved in the development of sales plans, which specify in detail what must be accomplished. Through the *management by objectives* method, sales managers and members of the sales team jointly identify performance goals and plot or improve the sales strategies for reaching those goals. The sales representatives' personal involvement in setting objectives, planning strategies and appraising performance motivates them to perform at high levels.

4   Organizing and managing sales territories

The most common methods of organizing the sales team are by geographical region (territorial sales force structure), by product line (product sales force structure) and by market or customer type. This last option – the customer sales force structure – is the most marketing-oriented approach. Since the sales force is an expensive marketing tool, the sales manager has to determine the optimal sales force size. The required number of sales representatives may be calculated with the Talley formula, which integrates the number of customers served, the average call frequency and the available selling time per representative. This method is also known as the workload approach. The effectiveness of the sales team partly depends on management's sales territory allocation decisions. Sales territories should have equal sales and income potential and require about the same amount of work for the representatives assigned to them. A sales territory's ideal size also depends on the nature of the product, the channel of distribution, the stage of market development, the desired intensity of market coverage, the strength of the competition and the quality of the company's sales force.

5   Developing a sales force

Since the quality of a sales force can make or break a company, recruiting and selecting successful salespeople is one of the sales manager's greatest challenges. In many organizations, recruitment is continuous in order to attract the best applicants. It starts with an accurate job description, translated into a statement of job qualifications. The selection procedure is designed to satisfy the firm's needs, such as finding individuals with specific knowledge and skills or reducing the sales force turnover rate. Once they are hired, training is essential to the success of sales representatives. Sales training is also provided to experienced salespeople in an ongoing effort to sharpen their selling, relationship building and negotiation skills. Selling is often a high-pressure job, involving repeated calls on customers with varying degrees of success. Therefore, well-designed incentive programmes and sales contests involving gifts and awards providing recognition for performance are necessary to both motivate sales representatives and improve customer service. Compensation, too, is a key factor in increasing sales force motivation, satisfaction and retention. Other common objectives of a sales compensation plan – involving straight salary, straight commission or a combined salary-incentive plan – are to reward salespeople for superior performance, to control and direct the sales effort, and to attract and develop effective salespeople.

6   Direct marketing

The fastest growing form of marketing is direct marketing. It is a custom tailored marketing approach in which the company's objective is to build lasting relationships with carefully targeted individual consumers or buyers in narrowly defined segments. The cornerstone of direct marketing is a well-maintained customer database. Using detailed customer information from this computerized database and interactive media such as direct mail, the telephone and Internet, the direct marketer attempts to generate an immediate and measurable response in the form of an order, a request for further information, or a visit to a store, website or other place of business for the purchase of a product or service. Sponsored magazines, infomercials and direct response advertising are other direct communication tools effective in conveying information to selected potential buyers.

A direct marketing strategy can be used both in the consumer and in the business-to-business market. For example, direct mail, as a supplement to other direct marketing forms, provides an excellent way to maintain contact with B2B customers between salespeople's calls. Each of the prospects can be sent an individually designed message, thus increasing the potential impact. Overall, direct marketing is a rapidly growing marketing strategy and will continue to present lucrative marketing opportunities for firms committed to building lasting relationships with their customers.

7   Promotions

Most consumers love sales promotions. While advertising offers consumers a *reason* to buy, promotions offer them an extra *incentive* for action. Traditionally, sales promotion techniques were only intended as short-term incentives designed to generate immediate consumer purchases. Today, however, marketers also develop *theme* promotions that add value to the brand, help build a base of loyal customers and enhance the firm's reputation.

Sales promotions are either directed at ultimate consumers (consumer promotions) or members of the distribution channel (trade promotions). Consumer promotions include price promotions (price pack deals, rebates and coupons), samples, premiums, contests, sweepstakes and frequency programmes. Trade promotions consist of point-of-purchase displays, trade shows and sales force promotions. Among the most important current trends in promotions are a significant increase in sales promotion spending, the shift away from standardized national promotions to tailor-made campaigns for retailers and the use of direct marketing techniques in sales promotion to increase response.

DISCUSSION QUESTIONS

1   Explain the role of ethical behaviour in personal selling.

2   Describe personal selling in your own words. Is this consistent with the image held by the general public of a salesperson?

3   From a company's point of view, what are the main advantages and disadvantages of personal selling as compared to mass communication?

4   What is the relationship between the transaction phase in the selling process and the term cognitive dissonance, as discussed in Chapter 4?

5   Explain the process of management by objectives. Is this a good tool for sales managers? Why or why not?

6   Comment on the idea of the 'born salesman', which leads some people to believe that they would not be able to have a successful career in sales.

7   Describe some factors that have contributed to the strong development of direct marketing and others that have slowed its further growth.

8   Give a description of the ideal direct marketing product.

9   What types of sales promotion tools would you use for the following products: canned soup, industrial lubricants, gardening equipment and home furnishings?

10   If promotions primarily have short-term effects, why is so much money spent on them?

PART FIVE
PRICING DECISIONS

Part 5 of this book examines companies' pricing strategies and price determination. Price is a unique marketing tool. It is the single most flexible element of a firm's marketing mix, and can be altered more rapidly than the product, promotion or distribution strategy. In addition, price setting does not require the investments or resources needed for developing new products, advertising campaigns or distribution channels. Thus, one of the most effective ways to maximize profits is to make the right pricing decisions.

Many variables affect price, which in turn influences the company's sales volume and profits. Every price change that affects sales will typically result in competitors adapting their own prices. In this respect, price is an essential weapon in the competitive battle. Moreover, pricing is becoming increasingly important due to the impact of the Internet, which makes pricing information widely available anytime, anywhere.

Marketers try to create solid price/quality relationships for their products and services. In determining prices, they keep a finger on the pulse of market changes, including demand, their own costs and the competition. Making the right pricing decisions is a complex and crucial marketing task. Perhaps no other marketing instrument receives as much attention and criticism from customers as does pricing!

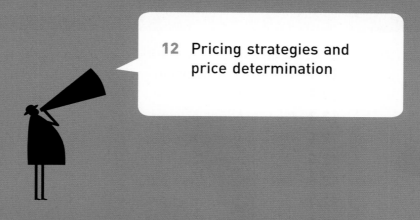

12 Pricing strategies and price determination

CHAPTER 12
PRICING STRATEGIES AND PRICE DETERMINATION

LEARNING GOALS

After studying this chapter you will be able to:

1	Explain the significance of price to customers and its relationship to other marketing variables
2	Understand the role of the pricing mechanism and the meaning of the demand curve
3	Compare two opposite pricing strategies for new products
4	Systematically develop a pricing strategy, including pricing objectives
5	Identify the most widely used types of discounts and allowances
6	Discuss common cost-based approaches to pricing and their advantages, constraints and risks
7	Understand the concepts of demand-oriented pricing and price elasticity of demand
8	Recognize the nature of price competition in different types of market structures

© Makushin Alexey / Shutterstock

Without prices there can be no marketing. Products may be offered in various markets, but ownership transfer will, in fact, occur only when buyers and sellers agree on prices. Thus, a company's pricing policy has a major impact on its sales volume and its profits. Consumers will not purchase a product, if they think the price is too high. If, on the other hand, the price is set too low, the firm will potentially miss out on profit. Therefore, no other feature of the product receives as much attention – from both buyer and seller – as its price.

Some managers are inclined to lower their prices as soon as sales decrease. A price cut, however, has only a temporary effect. It is decidedly preferable for price to play a *strategic* role in company policy. Insight and a well-planned marketing strategy are essential. The model for pricing decisions considered in this chapter provides a useful framework for strategy development.

MARKETING IN ACTION
The Value Proposition in Multichannel Retailing

It might be a retailer's worst nightmare: a consumer stands before a wall of flat-screen TVs, contemplates a purchase and pulls out a smartphone to see if a better deal is available elsewhere. This increasingly common sight may heighten retailers' fears that they are caught in an inevitable race to the bottom on price. Yet while price competition is tough, our consumer research and client experience show that *perceptions of value* still matter in the ever-more-complex multichannel-retailing environment. Retailers can employ proven tactics to shape perceptions and take advantage of the fact that consumers care about more than just the price tag when they buy.

> Consumers love low prices, but retailers shouldn't overlook how shoppers perceive value online and in stores

A recent survey we conducted[1] shows that price is just one of a range of factors consumers take into account when buying products: they also consider the degree of trust they have in a retailer, its product assortment, and their previous buying experiences (Exhibit 12.1). So even in the most competitive product categories, such as consumer electronics, retailers can look beyond price and actively shape perceptions of the value they offer. None of this happens by chance; retailers can implement strategic moves to get credit for superior value.

Consider, for example, how consumers view leading sellers of women's apparel in the United States (Exhibit 12.2). While *actual* average prices at Kohl's and JCPenney are similar (the *x*-axis), consumers clearly *perceive* Kohl's as offering

lower prices (the *y*-axis). Amazon.com – which typically has among the lowest prices in categories such as consumer electronics – charges more for similar types of apparel than Kohl's and JCPenney do, yet retains a 'halo' of value among the consumers we surveyed.

In our experience working with dozens of offline, online and multichannel retailers, we've found that they can use certain pricing moves to play the value card. The first is identifying key value items – products that have the greatest impact on value perceptions. In consumer electronics, for example, flat-screen TVs and computer hard drives are hot-ticket products that draw customers to stores or websites. Second, these items must be priced competitively to create a public perception that a retailer offers good value, and discounts on them can be recouped with higher prices on less visible products. Finally, prices should be the same no matter which retail channels a consumer uses: stores, the web or catalogues.

Retailers also can carefully craft product assortments in ways that influence value perceptions. For instance, in categories with clear 'good,' 'better' and 'best' ranges – such as flat-screen TVs – retailers can display models side by side, attract consumers with hot prices on good models, and then encourage trading up by clearly articulating the features and benefits of the better and best

EXHIBIT 12.1 Consumers consider more than price in deciding whether to purchase a product.

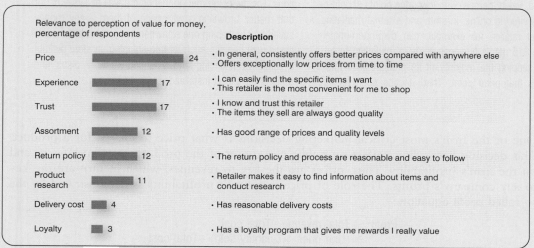

Relevance to perception of value for money, percentage of respondents

		Description
Price	24	• In general, consistently offers better prices compared with anywhere else • Offers exceptionally low prices from time to time
Experience	17	• I can easily find the specific items I want • This retailer is the most convenient for me to shop
Trust	17	• I know and trust this retailer • The items they sell are always good quality
Assortment	12	• Has good range of prices and quality levels
Return policy	12	• The return policy and process are reasonable and easy to follow
Product research	11	• Retailer makes it easy to find information about items and conduct research
Delivery cost	4	• Has reasonable delivery costs
Loyalty	3	• Has a loyalty program that gives me rewards I really value

Source: Q4 2010 McKinsey survey of 6 000 US consumers on multichannel pricing and price checks of >1 100 items across 20 retailers

EXHIBIT 12.2 There is a gap between what US retailers charge for women's apparel and how their prices are perceived

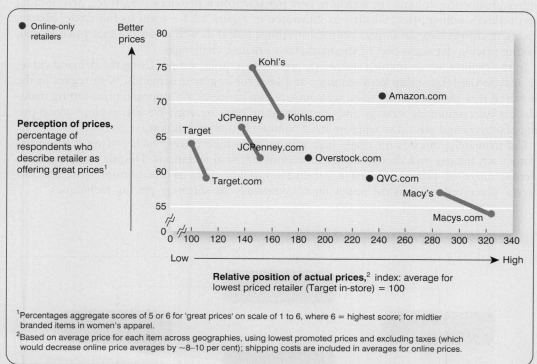

Relative position of actual prices,[2] index: average for lowest priced retailer (Target in-store) = 100

[1]Percentages aggregate scores of 5 or 6 for 'great prices' on scale of 1 to 6, where 6 = highest score; for midtier branded items in women's apparel.

[2]Based on average price for each item across geographies, using lowest promoted prices and excluding taxes (which would decrease online price averages by ~8–10 per cent); shipping costs are included in averages for online prices.

Source: Q4 2010 McKinsey survey of 6 000 US consumers on multichannel pricing and price checks of >1 100 items across 20 retailers

options. This strategy has proved to be as effective on-line as it is in stores.

Second, value 'heroes' with low price points should be *overrepresented* in online, in-store and external marketing. An apparel retailer, for example, can disproportionately showcase $15 men's business shirts in marketing materials while keeping the majority of its product assortment well above that price point. Third, tactics such as free shipping, in-store pickup, generous return policies and price-match guarantees are critical drivers of value perceptions. For the consumer pondering the wall of TVs – or, for that matter, browsing a web page of them – any money saved by purchasing one elsewhere may seem trivial compared with benefits such as free shipping, in-store pickup, a range of financing and extended-warranty plans and options for expert installation.[1]

One of the firm's most critical marketing decisions is what price to charge for a product. This decision has a direct effect on public perception of the product, on who buys it, and on the firm's profitability. Thus, prices are the key to revenues, which in turn are the key to any company's profits. The role of price in a firm's profitability is demonstrated by the so-called **profit equation**:

$$\text{Profit} = \text{Total revenue} - \text{Total cost}$$
$$= (\text{Unit price} \times \text{Quantity sold}) - \text{Total cost}$$

For a given quantity, a higher price will result in higher revenues for the company. However, price also affects the quantity sold, as we will see when analyzing the demand curve later in this chapter; thus, a higher price may reduce sales volume. Moreover, the quantity sold will usually affect the company's costs because of *economies of scale* associated with a higher production volume. In addition, cost per unit often provides a basis for determining the product's selling price, which – as illustrated in Figure 12.1 – takes us full circle. Hence, pricing decisions have an impact on total revenues (sales) as well as on the unit price (costs), making pricing decisions one of the marketer's greatest challenges.

In the chapter, we examine a *systematic* approach to price setting. Using the demand curve, we analyze the relationship between price and sales (or customer demand). With regard to the launch of new products or services, we compare two diametrically opposed price-setting methods: the price skimming strategy and the penetration price strategy. We also explore which pricing objectives and price discounts are most commonly used in business.

Unfortunately, there is no single best way to determine prices; each pricing method has distinct advantages and disadvantages in various decision situations. Despite the sometimes narrow range of prices between a product's variable costs as the bottom limit and the buyers' perceived value as the upper limit, companies use different pricing techniques.

FIGURE 12.1 Price setting and its implications

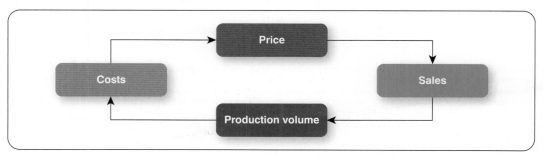

The simplest and most common approach to setting prices is based on cost. In addition to *cost-oriented* pricing strategies, we will also look at *demand-oriented* pricing. The latter approach revolves around the question of how much the product is worth to the buyer. Since a product's value is subjective and may vary from one person or target market to another (depending, for example, on the consumer's income level and available substitutes), the buyer's price sensitivity must be assessed.

With insight into the prices that buyers are willing to pay as well as the costs of manufacturing and marketing the product, the price ceiling and the price floor become apparent. However, neither demand-oriented nor cost-oriented pricing takes into account the pricing strategies of major competitors. In practice, competitors' prices are often a key factor in price determination. Therefore, we will also explore *competition-oriented* pricing and in this context, make a distinction between an oligopoly, monopolistic competition and other market forms that affect price setting. We close Chapter 12 with an analysis of competitive bidding in the B2B market.

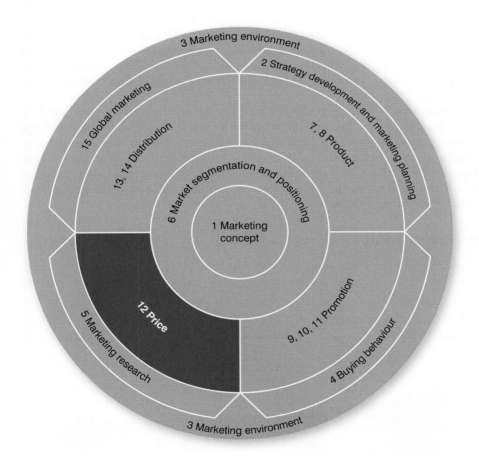

12.1 THE PRICING DECISION

Because of the many factors to be considered, pricing decisions can be complex. There is often uncertainty about customers', distributors' and competitors' reactions to price. Still, as with other marketing decisions, the customer is the ideal place to start in **price setting**, as they are the dominant influence on price. The key question is how much money the product or service is worth to the buyer. From a marketing perspective it would be best to view price setting as the art of 'translating' the product's *value* in the eyes of the customer into the amount of money they are willing to pay. As explained in Chapter 7, this is not just about the *physical* product, but the total 'package' or bundle of benefits that consumers buy, including the *augmented* product's intangible features (such as its brand image and warranty).

For example, if a product, from the target market's perspective, is worth no more than 15 euros, then that amount establishes the current ceiling for the possible prices we could charge. The lower limit or bottom will be determined by the costs. In this way, a range of amounts can be identified between the *perceived* value and the costs, from which we should select the best price. As we will see, other considerations also play a role in price setting.

In any case, price decisions are influenced by various assumptions, such as economic projections and the assessment of purchasing power development. If these estimates are incorrect, the established price may not be the best possible price. The price level will also be influenced by other elements of the marketing mix (such as the product's quality level and distribution channels) and by such factors as the seller's inventory level, fluctuations in demand and degree of market saturation. All of these critical issues must be incorporated in the pricing strategy.

How is price determined? What forces do we take into account in making a pricing decision? In order to develop an effective **pricing policy** we should – in addition to demand and cost considerations – take into account the corporate and marketing strategy, competition, other components of the product mix, the resellers' interests and any legal and ethical constraints. Figure 12.2 shows that each step in the pricing decision reduces the range of feasible prices for the product to the point where, from the small set of remaining price options, we select the best alternative.

12.1.1 Perceived value

In setting the optimum price for our products, we must have an understanding of the needs and wants, spending behaviour and purchasing habits of the prospective buyers we are

FIGURE 12.2 A multistage approach to pricing

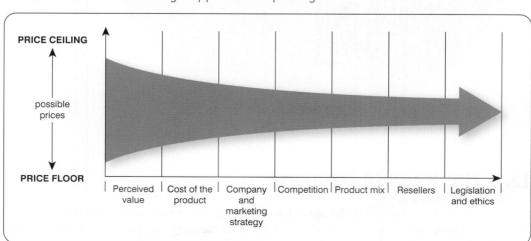

targeting. We should also examine their *perception* of the product's value, relative to its price. After all, the **price** is the *exchange value* of the product, expressed in terms of the amount of money the buyer is willing to pay in return for the desired product or service. This amount is not necessarily in direct proportion to the costs. Diet-conscious consumers, for example, are willing to pay more for low-fat margarine (in effect a mixture of margarine and water) than for real margarine!

Understanding consumers' **value perception** and deciding on the product's intended image are essential in determining the price ceiling, especially in pursuing a price discrimination strategy. **Price discrimination** refers to charging different buyers (for example, customers in different regions or purchasing at different points in time) different prices for the same quantity and quality of products or services. Hence, these prices are not based on differences in cost, but on differences in customers' price sensitivity. For example, a prestige product developed for high-income customers may merit a higher price than a comparable or somewhat lower-quality version targeted to a larger, more price-sensitive group of consumers. Similarly, by charging lower telephone rates during non-peak hours, telephone companies influence consumer demand and maximize total revenue.

Image courtesy of The Advertising Archives

12.1.2 *Cost of the product*

Business executives regularly assess the cost of their products. Under normal conditions, they avoid selling them at too low a profit margin or below cost. **Loss leaders**, products that are sold at a lower than usual markup for the purpose of increasing store traffic, are an exception. The retailer hopes that the loss of the regular markup on these products will be made up by the profits on other items that customers also buy once they are in the store. Pricing at less than **cost**, however, is not a common strategy.

For effective pricing decisions, understanding the nature of different types of costs is crucial. A **variable cost**, such as the cost of raw materials, is a cost that varies directly with the number of units produced and marketed. By contrast, **fixed costs**, often called *overhead* costs, tend to remain stable at any production level. They include rent, lease payments and insurance premiums.

Variable costs tend to impose a price floor on a product's eventual selling price. Unless the company is able to cover its full costs in the long run and its variable costs in the short run, it will have to discontinue production. Because there is usually little we can do to change a product's variable costs, in price setting we might reconsider how we should allocate our fixed costs (such as management salaries) to different products, as these costs are not directly related to the manufacture of any single item. Since the allocation of these overhead costs may be arbitrary, a change in the accounting system may make a particular price level or strategy feasible. On the other hand, when considering a new product, we may estimate all relevant costs – direct variable, overhead, administrative and selling – and then apply a higher-than-normal markup to reflect the extra risk involved in launching a new product.

12.1.3 *Company and marketing strategy*

The pricing strategy must be consistent with the company's objectives and marketing strategy. To illustrate, a company strategy that calls for targeting an upscale market segment justifies *prestige pricing*: a relatively high price that lends an air of exclusivity to high-end products appealing to status-conscious consumers. If, on the other hand, the company intends to increase its market share, it may be necessary to lower prices as a key component of a repositioning strategy. The more clearly the corporate objectives and marketing strategy are spelled out, the more capable we are of developing an effective pricing strategy to achieve the intended results.

12.1.4 *Competition*

How will the product's price affect competitors? When launching a new product, a high introductory price may encourage other companies, attracted by the high returns, to introduce a similar product. In contrast, a low price – with a modest profit margin – will make competitors less inclined to enter the market.

In the case of existing products, we must consider the effect of a price change on other companies in (or even outside of) the industry. If we initiate a price change, will competitors raise prices, lower prices or hold the line on prices? In an *oligopoly* – an industry with a small number of sellers, such as the beer, tobacco, music production and aircraft industries, the decisions of one firm influence, and are influenced by, the decisions of others. We can expect that most companies will follow a price reduction by the **price leader**, but not necessarily a price increase. If the competitors do not follow suit, the company initiating the price hike may see its customers switch to other suppliers. Typically, in oligopolistic markets, the less a product is differentiated from its competitors, the more likely competitors will adopt a *follow-the-leader approach* and conform to a price change.

Sometimes companies compete not only with identical products or services, but also with substitutes. For example, in response to the increased prices of new and previously owned aircraft, *NetJets Europe* is promoting fractional jet ownership as an alternative to buying planes. It targets companies whose executives travel periodically and encourages them to join other firms in buying shares in a new jet, saving money in the process.

12.1.5 Product mix

An important consideration in pricing decisions is whether the proposed price is likely to have a positive or negative effect on the sales of the other items in the firm's product mix. Occasionally, a company deliberately keeps the price of its main product low to attract customers. For instance, in many restaurants food generates only a small profit, while the highest profit margin is on soft drinks, wine and desserts.

The impact of a product's price on sales of closely related items should certainly be examined for **complementary products**. These are products sold or used jointly with other products, such as printers and ink cartridges or razors and blades. Gillette, for example, sells the Fusion Power and Venus Breeze razors at less than cost but makes considerable profits on the sales of the cartridges that are part of this shaving system.

12.1.6 Resellers

The end users' value perception greatly influences pricing decisions. Most products, however, are supplied to resellers (wholesalers and retailers) before they are made available to final consumers. Therefore, in setting the price we must also take into account the sometimes conflicting interests of the **middlemen** or *intermediaries*. Retail organizations, for instance, may refuse to carry products with an insufficient profit margin.

Price negotiations between the supplier and distributors usually begin with the normal trade **margins** for the product. If the manufacturer or importer wants the reseller to provide extra benefits, such as free installation or service, the manufacturer may have to offer the reseller a higher-than-average margin. The promotion strategy, too, influences margins. For example, chewing gum manufacturers who advertise their own brands offer retailers a lower profit margin than, say, TV set producers. The relatively high **gross margin** for electronics retailers includes a supplier contribution to their promotion and service costs. Manufacturers also consider the price structure of the retailer's product assortment and the need to pursue an independent pricing strategy in strengthening their competitive position in the marketplace, as in the case of discount chains.

12.1.7 Legislation and ethics

Pricing policies of manufacturers and retailers must conform to national laws and regulations as well as to ethical expectations of customers and society in general. A variety of legal and regulatory constraints affects companies' pricing decisions. Generally, legislation is intended to protect competition among firms within markets as well as the rights of consumers. Many countries have laws designed to protect the 'general interest' by prohibiting price fixing, **cartels** or other contracts or conspiracies that restrain trade. They may also put restrictions on *price discrimination* that can inhibit competition among resellers. In addition, they have outlawed **predatory pricing**, a practice where one company tries to drive out competitors by temporarily pricing at such a low level that rivals cannot match their cuts and still profit.

As pointed out in Chapter 3, the law only defines minimally acceptable behaviour. Firms must not only meet the minimum legal standards, but should also conduct business – including price setting – on the basis of their own *ethical* standards. What price increase, for example, is acceptable when demand exceeds supply, and supply must be rationed to prevent shortages? Even price increases in situations where the value customers receive merits higher prices may be resented by buyers, or viewed as unethical. Nor is it ethically responsible to mislead consumers in advertisements with price promotions. Oftentimes, ethical codes of conduct offer managers a clear guideline. Nevertheless, in practice, difficult decisions still may have to be made, in which each person has to decide for themself – based on personal standards of ethics – where the boundaries of acceptability lie.

12.2 DEMAND CURVE

The price determines not only the firm's sales volume (in units), but also its sales revenue (expressed as money). **Revenue** is the per unit price multiplied by the number of units sold. The marketer must set a price for their product that generates enough revenue to cover the costs of producing and marketing it, and to allow for a satisfactory profit. The higher the product's price and profit margin are, the more the firm is willing to produce. But products with high profit margins may also attract new suppliers to the market.

Thus, price affects both demand and supply. If the price is high, there is relatively little demand, but because of the profit motive, plenty of supply. This, in turn, increases competition. It also creates a downward pressure on prices, as a result of which more consumers will buy the product. The demand will therefore go up. For companies, however, the price decrease – due to the more intense competition – will lead to lower margins and eventually to a reduction in market supply. This phenomenon is called the *price mechanism*.

12.2.1 Price mechanism

The **price mechanism** described above is one of the main forces at work in the economic system. From a macro-economic perspective, the price mechanism performs three vital functions:

→ *Comparison.* The price level and price fluctuations allow buyers and suppliers to compare the value and potential scarcity of various products.

→ *Stimulation and reduction.* The price of a product may stimulate production by suppliers or reduce consumption by its users. Since most markets are dynamic, capable of adjusting rapidly to the price or quantity of goods available, price will balance supply and demand, unless the **market mechanism** is distorted by government subsidies or price guarantees (as with some agricultural products). Artificially low prices may result in secondary markets, like online auctions.

→ *Rationing.* The price mechanism largely determines who makes certain purchases. As a product becomes more expensive, fewer people are able to buy it. Thus, scarce products are rationed in society through pricing decisions.

To gain a better understanding – from a marketing perspective – of the effect of price on the quantity demanded of a product, we can project it in the form of a graph using the demand curve. The **demand curve** shows the maximum number of products that customers will buy in a market during a period of time at various prices if all other factors remain the same. We will first look at movement along the demand curve and then at shifts of the demand curve.

12.2.2 *Movement along the demand curve*

For most products and services, demand is a function of price: demand increases as price decreases, and *vice versa*. Thus, an inverse relationship exists between price and demand. Since the typical demand curve slopes downward and to the right, the tendency of demand to vary inversely with price is called a movement along the demand curve. Figure 12.3 shows this relationship. As price is reduced from €8 to €6.75, the quantity demanded increases along the demand curve from four units to six units.

A price drop from €10 to €2 per unit in our example makes sales rise drastically from two units to 16 units. The demand curve slopes downward because, as the price decreases, new buyers begin to purchase the product and, in some cases, the current users begin to buy more of it. Incidentally, the graphical representation of demand – rather than being a straight line graph – is slightly curved, because continually dropping prices do not lead to proportional increases in demand. Slowly but surely, the market becomes saturated, causing purchases to tail off.

In some cases demand will increase, not drop, when prices go up, depending on customers' perceptions of the product's value at a certain price. Therefore, when a company raises its price, customer demand may go up as well. For instance, consumers interested in prestige products might find a more expensive designer purse or luxury car more desirable.

12.2.3 *Shifts of the demand curve*

Something quite different from a movement along the demand curve is a *shift* of the entire demand curve. Such shifts are not caused by price changes, but by one of the more fundamental forces behind the growth in demand, such as a change in consumer preferences, a more effective advertising campaign or the introduction of a new product to the market.

Figure 12.4 illustrates both an upward and a downward shift in demand. With an upward (or positive) *shift of the demand curve* (a shift to the right), the company can expect to sell a larger number of products at each price level. Assuming the upward shift in the diagram

FIGURE 12.3 A typical demand curve

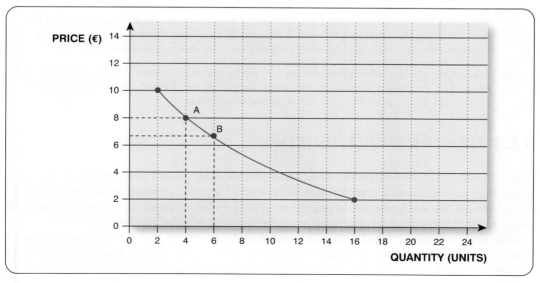

FIGURE 12.4 Shifts in demand

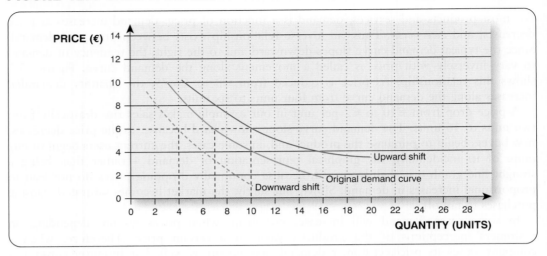

below, the company can expect to sell ten units at a price of €6 each, whereas with the original demand curve it could expect to sell only seven units at that same price. An example of an *upward* shift in demand is the demand curve for ice cream that shifts to the right when the weather gets warm; at the same price, the demand for ice cream goes up.

A downward (or negative) shift of the demand curve has the opposite effect. In the graph of Figure 12.4, at a selling price of €6, demand drops to four units. In other words, the demand curve moves to the left. The main forces underlying shifts in demand are changes in:

→ *Consumer tastes*: As consumers tired of drinking the once popular Bacardi Breezer, Bacardi lost sales as the demand curve shifted downward.

→ *Market size*: the greater the decrease in the number of consumers, the more the demand curve shifts to the left. To illustrate, a decline in the birth rate has caused a negative shift in the demand for baby care products such as baby shampoo, prompting Johnson & Johnson to reposition these products for greater adult use.

→ *Consumer income*: as consumers' real income or purchasing power increases, demand for most products also increases, whereas a decrease in consumer purchasing power has the opposite effect (leading, for example, to lower car sales during a recession).

→ *Availability of substitutes*: given the laws of supply and demand, the introduction of a similar product to the market usually causes a negative shift in the demand curve of the existing product, as does a price decrease for comparable substitutes.

12.3 NEW PRODUCT PRICING

The only time a marketer has the freedom to decide how much to charge for a product is when they are launching a completely new product. The more distinctive the product is, the more options the company has in pricing it. If it is a *discontinuous innovation* – that is to say, a revolutionary new product without close substitutes – the marketer can choose from a wide range of prices. This holds true especially if they expect the new product's uniqueness to last for some time. Most new products, however, no matter how distinctive they are in the introduction stage of the product life cycle, have only a limited period free from

PROFESSOR'S PERSPECTIVE
Ken Bernhardt (Georgia State University, USA)

Ken Bernhardt, Regents Professor of Marketing and Special Assistant to the Dean at Georgia State University, has published extensively on marketing and consumer behaviour. He is former Chairman of the American Marketing Association and former President of the Association for Consumer Research. He has consulted for many businesses, including Kimberly-Clark, Chick-fil-A and UPS.

Pricing is one of the most important decisions marketers face, yet very few companies have a person or team of people who are responsible for that function. There are people with clear responsibility for product design and development, sales, advertising and promotion and distribution, but no one for pricing.

When there is an individual responsible for pricing, it is often someone from the finance department rather than the marketing department, which is where pricing decisions belong. As a result, prices are often set by default by the sales force. This is the last place that prices should be set because sales people typically are rewarded by volume and good sales people know that a lowered price will generate more volume. Unfortunately this often results in significantly less profit. Another suboptimal way to set prices is based on costs. With some help from a long-time friend, Jay Klompmaker, a pricing guru and professor emeritus at the University of North Carolina, let me explain six rules for successful pricing.

Rule No. 1: *Base your price on perceived value*: more prices are better than fewer prices.

Value can be determined only by customers, and different customers have different perceived value. Marketers understand the concept of market segmentation when it comes to product development and advertising, but tend to ignore segmentation in pricing. Averages will kill you in pricing. Therefore, there should be a wide range of prices charged, or a wide price band. A price band is the ratio of the highest price charged to the lowest price charged. Most companies have too narrow a price band, which means that they are undercharging some customers, thus leaving money on the table, and have too high a price for others, thus leaving potential volume on the table. As an example of an organization with too narrow a band, consider a performing arts organization with prices ranging from $27 down to $20 (or a price band of 1.35). They are probably under-pricing the best seats for Saturday nights (and are sold out) and over-pricing the worst seats for Tuesday night (thus ending up with plenty of empty, unsold seats).

Rule No. 2: Ask this of your customers: *Pay for what you get*.

Give customers what they want and don't be afraid to charge them for it once they get it; nothing more and nothing less. This requires a clear understanding of what customers want and what they are willing to pay for it. Often those customers a company thinks are its best customers are not very profitable. They may chew up a significant amount of costly technical support, sales support, R&D or design assistance, demand extra services like frequent deliveries, require carrying of extra inventory and are constantly demanding volume discounts and beating you up on price. It may turn out that small-volume customers who pay high prices are the most profitable. Changing your mix of customers over time can be one way of raising average prices and increasing profitability.

Rule No. 3: *Raising prices across the board is not smart*; it often leaves both volume and margin on the table.

Companies with high margins benefit more from added volume gained through price cutting and vice versa; companies with low margins benefit more from increased margins (through price increases).

Price is the last thing that should be discussed, not the first thing

Rule No. 4: *Prices need to be sold, not just set.*

It is important to first build value, then communicate value ('sell the value') and finally capture the value through the price. The best way to sell value is by talking about product quality, service quality and product innovation. Price is the last thing that should be discussed, not the first thing. Product and service quality rather than price is what drives market share. Price changes are matched by competitors too easily; leaving a little on the table also will help perceived value and your customers will love you for it.

Rule No. 5: *Make price cutting difficult.*

When sales people ask for a price cut, change the terminology. Have them ask for a profit cut instead. For example, if your margin is 20 per cent and a sales person is asking for a 5 per cent price cut for a customer, have them ask instead for a 25 per cent cut in profit. That will reduce the pressure to reduce prices.

Rule No. 6: *Manage price by putting someone in charge* and develop good customer, competitor and cost information.

Establish measures of success for price determination and base rewards on these measures for the development and implementation of pricing strategies that help an organization to stay competitive.[2]

competition. And once the initial or **introductory price** has been announced, it may be difficult to change. A price increase by the supplier often leads to resistance in the distribution channel, while a price reduction is not always passed on to the end user. Therefore, price decisions for new products must be made very carefully, based on market research that provides an understanding of the likely buyers and competitive response.

When a product is new to the market and there is no established industry price norm, consumers do not know what the product is worth. They cannot easily compare it with something that already exists. The manufacturer, however, has more information. For one thing, they know their production costs. They also know their investment in Research & Development and must recover this expenditure as well. Moreover, market research may provide an indication of the **price limits** within which the product can be sold.

What is considered an acceptable price level will depend both on the customer and on the type of product. Some innovations may be positioned as **prestige products** or *status products*. Because these appeal to status-conscious consumers, their price – especially when the company uses a *selective distribution* strategy – should be relatively high. Other products are targeted at the mass market, where a low price is much more important than top quality. Using an *intensive distribution* strategy, the firm may be able to sell a large volume of these products. In between these two market segments, there is often a third target market of consumers who seek 'value for money'. They are looking for a product of acceptable quality at a reasonable price.

When introducing an entirely new product, we must first determine into which of these three *price zones* the product best fits. Only then can we select an appropriate pricing strategy. There are two diametrically opposed options in new product pricing: a price skimming strategy and a penetration pricing strategy. Each has its advantages and disadvantages.

12.3.1 *Price skimming strategy*

Price skimming is a strategy of introducing a new product at an artificially high price. This is a price level that the market will not be able to sustain in the long run. Price skimming (or *market-skimming pricing*) gets its name from the expression 'skimming the cream off the top'. The company first appeals to early adopters who are willing to pay a premium for the privilege of being among the first owners of an innovative product with unique benefits. Then over time, the price is gradually lowered to attract successive customer segments that are more price sensitive. A skimming strategy works best for new types of durable consumer goods, such as high-tech cellular phones, from which **prestige buyers** derive status.

To see how price skimming works, take a look at Figure 12.5, which shows a demand curve that could lead to pursuing a price skimming strategy.

Assume in this case that the market price of the new product is expected to stabilize at €300. But before the competition introduces a similar product, our firm, by adopting a price skimming strategy, is able to sell a number of units at a much higher price. For example, the firm succeeds in selling a thousand units (of an initial production run of 6 500 units) at a price of €600 each, and then 3 000 (4 000 − 1 000) units for €400 each. As competition develops and the market becomes saturated, the company further reduces the price to the expected equilibrium level of €300 in order to appeal to a broader market. The total revenues are:

$$(1\,000 \times €600) + (3\,000 \times €400) + (2\,500 \times €300) =$$
$$€600\,000 + €1\,200\,000 + €750\,000 = €2\,550\,000$$

Had the price immediately been set at €300, sales would have amounted to only 6 500 × €300 = €1 950 000. The difference between these amounts (€600 000) constitutes the extra revenue earned by the company that successfully pursues a price skimming strategy. Economists call this the **consumer surplus**.

FIGURE 12.5 Price skimming strategy

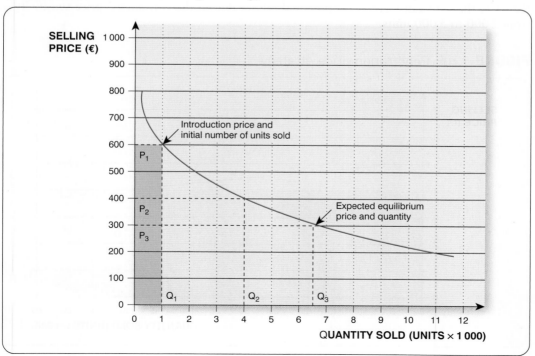

A price skimming strategy – often used in combination with a *product differentiation* strategy – provides several benefits. It makes it possible for companies to *segment* the market according to price sensitivity, or acceptable cost to consumers. The initial cash flow allows the firm to recover development costs quickly, freeing funds for reinvestment in other projects. Usually, the shorter the payback period for a new product, the less risk is involved. Simultaneously, if the firm's production capacity is limited, a skimming price can help restrict demand to within the company's production capability. Not surprisingly, the greatest problem with price skimming is that it attracts competition into the industry. The above-average return will invite rivals to introduce similar products. For example, Philips, after introducing its first widescreen TV at a price of almost €5 000, within a year faced competition from the Finnish company Nokia, which offered its TVs for much less, driving down the market price.

12.3.2 *Penetration price strategy*

A **penetration price strategy** is the opposite of price skimming. A company using this strategy introduces a new product at a very low price to speed up its market acceptance and drive sales upward. It expects to gain a large market share quickly by selling a ginormous number of products to a price-sensitive mass market. Penetration pricing is often used to launch staple goods. For instance, when a greatly improved or new type of laundry detergent is introduced, few people are willing to pay a premium to be among its first users. The manufacturer then introduces the product at a price the market can support long-term, hoping to expand demand for the product. In short, near future profits are sacrificed for lasting growth.

Figure 12.6 shows a demand curve of a product with an *elastic* demand, where consumers are sensitive to price changes. Here, the marketer's best strategy may be to use a penetration price. The slope of the demand curve (established on the basis of market research) indicates that, although the company could initially charge more than the expected market price of €4, there is little incentive to do so. By charging only €4 rather than €6, the firm can increase its potential sales – due to the consumers' price sensitivity – from 2 000 to 5 000 units.

FIGURE 12.6 Penetration price strategy

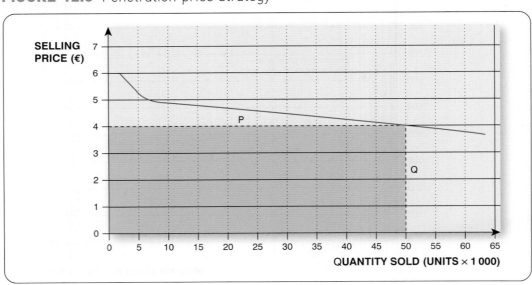

TABLE 12.1 Penetration pricing compared to price skimming

Penetration Pricing	Price Skimming
Consumers are highly price sensitive (elastic demand)	Consumers are not price sensitive (inelastic demand)
Strong competition is expected soon after the product launch	Product is unique, without many substitutes
Large sales volume will lead to lower costs per unit (economies of scale)	Elite market allows high introductory prices and segmentation based on price sensitivity
Objective is to maximize market share, while expanding demand	Objective is to maximize sales revenues and profits across segments

Rather than using a high introductory price, the company prices low to *penetrate* the market and move quickly from the introduction to the growth stage of the product life cycle. As the comparison in Table 12.1 illustrates, a low price only makes sense if consumers are price sensitive (resulting in more market growth) and potential competitors could easily enter the market. Penetration pricing will then act as a barrier to entry, deterring rivals with me-too products. Since there is little opportunity for new competitors to make a high return on investment, they may decide to pursue more lucrative marketing opportunities instead.

Of course, the manufacturer must have sufficient production and distribution capacity to meet the large demand. Also, the strategy works best if the variable costs make up only a minor part of the selling price. A good example is easyJet, a low-fare airline that gained a large market share in its territory – and at the same time, increased the overall size of the European market – through penetration pricing. Other requirements for this pricing strategy are a sound financial position and a relatively long product life cycle, since it will take some time to recoup the product's development costs. On the other hand, a major advantage of penetration pricing is that a higher production and sales volume enable the manufacturer to achieve economies of scale and reduce unit costs substantially, often by 30 to 50 per cent.

A drawback of penetration pricing is that the company is denied additional profits that could be generated by selling to consumers who might pay a much higher price, especially for a durable product. It is, therefore, important to determine the size of this segment. If research shows that many people are willing to pay a premium, the company should consider adopting a skimming strategy before building sales momentum by attracting as many buyers as possible to the market.

12.4 PRICING OBJECTIVES

While most companies adjust prices every year, studies show that very few do so based on a systematic pricing strategy review. Managers often make price changes and other pricing decisions without assessing how these fit into the company's overall marketing and pricing strategy. In fact, many firms don't even have a basic pricing strategy and do not conduct any serious pricing research to develop one.[3] Although their managers may have a tacit understanding of the firm's pricing strategy, they do not include explicit pricing objectives in their marketing plans.

Yet, price setting has a major impact on sales and profitability, and therefore on the continuity of the business. Thus, pricing plays a strategic role in a firm's marketing policy. In developing or reviewing that policy, we must carefully decide on the *pricing objectives*, indicating what we want to achieve through pricing. In this section, we will first examine a systematic approach to pricing products or services and then explore the most widely employed pricing objectives.

12.4.1 *A model for pricing decisions*

Pricing decisions should be made systematically. The model in Figure 12.7 demonstrates the steps involved in this decision-making process. The process begins with the formulation of the corporate mission statement, which in turn dictates the *corporate goals*. These goals then become the basis for determining the marketing objectives. As discussed in Chapter 2, the mission is expressed in terms sufficiently broad that they allow the company to adjust with the changing needs and preferences of its customers. In contrast, the *marketing objectives* are much more specific. They are typically stated in terms of particular markets and products, specifying criteria such as the expected market share and the firm's sales or profit objectives.

Once the marketing objectives have been defined, *marketing programmes* are developed for each product. This step involves relating product decisions to distribution, promotion and pricing, in order to create an integrated marketing mix. As the programme evolves, we must also decide on the firm's *pricing objectives*, which should be stated in detail and include the time frame for achieving them. We must make sure that the pricing objectives support the company's marketing objectives and overall goals because pricing objectives, in turn, influence decisions in finance, production, accounting and other functional areas.

The pricing objectives guide the development of the company's pricing strategy and tactics. The **pricing strategy** provides the framework through which we translate our

FIGURE 12.7 A model for pricing decisions

pricing objectives into actual market pricing tactics. An example of a pricing strategy is a price skimming strategy for a new product. In addition to the introductory price and general price level, the price strategy may address the desired price stability or price competition. *Pricing tactics* determine how the firm should establish its price. Tactics specify which activities (such as offering price promotions) will best achieve the stated objectives. In the final step of the pricing model, the firm *implements* its pricing decisions. That process will be discussed later on in this chapter.

Our model for pricing decisions also has several *feedback* loops. After a price is implemented and the market has reacted, we must decide if the set price makes it possible for the firm to meet its pricing objectives. If not, we may wish to recycle through the pricing strategy and tactical decisions, adjust them as we see fit and establish new prices. Sometimes the feedback may indicate that there are no problems with the pricing strategy's execution, but that the pricing objectives are simply no longer feasible, prompting changes in both the marketing objectives and marketing programme.

12.4.2 *General pricing objectives*

In business, pricing objectives are formulated in various ways. Since the pricing strategy should be consistent with the overall company strategy, some managers will derive their pricing objectives straight from the *corporate goals*. For example, the pricing objectives may be expressed in terms of the planned organizational growth or profitability. In other companies, pricing objectives are directly derived from the marketing objectives and are stated in terms of the desired revenues or market share. We refer to these as *general* or *derived* pricing objectives.

To illustrate, if an organization's *corporate goal* is to become the leading producer in the European market, and its *marketing objective* is to substantially increase its market penetration in all member states of the European Union, it might formulate its pricing objectives in terms of lowering prices to increase brand loyalty and providing major discounts to maximize sales. However, increases in brand loyalty and sales are not necessarily the sole result of the company's pricing strategy, since other factors – such as product availability, efficient distribution, an attractive advertising campaign, superior customer service and the use of other marketing mix variables – also affect the company's performance in the competitive market. Therefore, increasing brand loyalty and sales are more appropriate marketing objectives than pricing objectives.

In conclusion, it is ill advised to express pricing objectives in terms of general or derived criteria such as the desired profitability, market share, brand loyalty or sales volume. Instead, an effective pricing strategy includes specific, *bona fide* pricing objectives to provide guidance in price setting and enable management to measure the effectiveness of a particular price in, for example, creating awareness and positioning the product as offering value for money.

12.4.3 *Specific pricing objectives*

Although many firms use the general or derived pricing objectives discussed above, in a marketing plan pricing objectives are better expressed as specifically as possible in terms of what we want to achieve with price setting. Therefore, many truly marketing-oriented organizations prefer to formulate their pricing objectives in terms of (the desired changes in) *price perception*.

Consumers' price perception reflects how they view or experience a price, for instance, whether it is too high or too low. Although any perception or evaluation of price is subjective, it may very well determine what the consumer will or will not buy. This is known as their 'price behaviour'. When measuring consumer price perception (as is done through Nielsen panel research), a distinction is drawn between its three components, i.e. the price *awareness*, *acceptance* and *sensitivity*.

Price awareness refers to the degree of consumer knowledge about the prices of alternative products and services that they are interested in buying. Do consumers think, for example, that the cell phone rates charged by T-Mobile are higher or lower than those of its competitors? Price awareness is routinely measured through market research.

By concurrently measuring **price acceptance**, the marketing researcher can also discover if consumers think the prices charged are reasonable. Do customers believe, for example, that the recent price decrease by their cell phone provider, prompted by competition, is sufficiently attractive for them to stay with their present provider, or do they consider the price still too high? A company's insight into the **price thresholds** – the highest and lowest prices that buyers are willing to pay for a particular product or service – might trigger a price adjustment by the company.

Finally, **price sensitivity** indicates the extent to which consumers will react to small price changes. For example, will customers make longer or more frequent phone calls if rates are lowered by 10 per cent? We will return to this issue in section 12.7, when looking into the price elasticity of demand.

12.4.4 *Pricing objectives in practice*

Information on the pricing policies of European companies is scarce. Managers safeguard their pricing objectives as classified information. Several studies have shown that many firms establish multiple pricing objectives. In some cases one predominant goal is pursued in combination with several either long- or short-term supplementary pricing objectives. For example, a company may wish to 'achieve a market share of 25 per cent within three years and obtain at least a 12 per cent return on investment next year by offering products at a highly competitive price'. Although not all of these are specific pricing objectives, they are not unusual in business. We will now explore the most common pricing objectives that companies set for themselves. As outlined in Table 12.2, these can be classified as *profitability* objectives, *sales-related* objectives and *competitive effect* objectives.

TABLE 12.2 Pricing objectives

Type of objective	Purpose	Example
Specific (measurable) pricing objectives	Influence price perception	Adjust price of mobile phone service to match consumer expectations
Profitability objectives	Target return on investment Profit maximization Gross profit margin	Set prices to allow a 15 per cent return on investment in newly developed products
Sales-related objectives	Target market share Sales maximization	Lower prices by 10 per cent to yield a 7 per cent increase in market share
Competitive effect objectives	Meeting competition Value pricing	Reduce price of music downloads to compete with Apple's iTunes

Target return on investment

Some social critics believe that companies price their products and services so as to make as much profit as possible. However, research shows that most firms – in addition to their other objectives – are more interested in a *satisfactory* return or profit (large enough to survive and to attract investors or satisfy market analysts) than a maximum return. Moreover, *profit maximization* requires complete understanding of the company's cost and demand relationships, which may be hard to assess, especially in multi-product companies. Therefore, prices are seldom set only to ensure profit maximization.

The most common pricing objective in business is to achieve a *target return on investment* (typically around 15 per cent after taxes). Since not all cost and revenue data needed to forecast the ROI are known when determining prices, this pricing objective is usually reached by trial and error. Other companies use comparable objectives, such as a target *return on assets* or *return on sales*. Corporations that are market leaders, such as Shell and Unilever, set pricing objectives to meet specific targets for profit returns. These companies are usually the *price leaders* in their industries; smaller competitors will adapt their prices accordingly.

Gross profit margin

Many companies, particularly those engaged in commerce, price to achieve specific targets for a gross profit margin per unit. This gross margin or *markup* – a percentage added to the purchase price or cost price of an item – should generate the profit contribution the firm is seeking. The gross margin – the amount that is left after the cost of goods sold is deducted from sales revenues – is typically expressed as a percentage of revenues. The margin may be increased by lowering the cost of goods sold, raising prices or both.

When determining their products' selling prices, some firms add a fixed percentage to their costs. Others use percentages that differ by product category. Supermarkets, for instance, may add a larger markup to their margin generators (less price sensitive items, such as shoe polish) than to the rest of the product assortment. This cost-based price setting method (to which we will return later) is known as *markup pricing*. Many companies that use target ROI pricing for new products, use cost-plus or markup pricing for their existing products.

Target market share

Many marketing-oriented companies pursue a pricing strategy with a market share objective. Their goal is to maintain or increase their share of a particular market. To gain a target market share, they may offer discounts, especially when industry sales are stable or declining. If buyers are price sensitive, the reduced price will translate into increased sales. But if the sales volume doesn't increase enough to make revenues rise as well, profits will suffer. However, if the main goal is to acquire a particular market share, then the potential for a lower return is of little significance and is an accepted risk.

While many firms specifically price to gain or increase market share, most companies consider market share a means to other ends. It can serve as a springboard to higher sales – or even *sales maximization* – or, through lower unit costs, to higher profits. A company striving only to maximize sales ignores profits, competitors and the rest of the marketing environment, as long as sales are increasing. Other companies, especially large ones, may price their products to limit their market share, thereby avoiding litigation based on violation of antitrust or other such competitive practice legislation.

Meeting competition

Companies adopting competition-oriented pricing – in which they simply match competitors' prices – do not really have a pricing strategy of their own. In effect, they let established industry price leaders make the pricing decisions for their industry. They then meet the market price, at least for their products not holding a leadership position. In case of price changes, they may either match their competitors' price moves or consistently charge somewhat higher or lower prices than their rivals. The primary advantage of meeting price cuts is that it will eliminate a competitive advantage. It may also prevent a price war, with prices spiralling downward in successive rounds of price cuts actuated by competitors to maintain their unit sales or market share.

Price stabilization and value pricing

Many companies endeavour to keep their prices relatively stable. Just as they keep prices from rising to 'what the market will bear' during strong economic conditions, they avoid price reductions during an economic downturn to prevent a price war. Whether operating on the consumer or on the business market, they regard price stabilization as highly desirable. Realizing that their customers differ in price sensitivity, they may launch lower priced products to appeal to the most price-sensitive buyers, while adding new features to their current products, without lowering price, for value-conscious customers.

Marketing-oriented managers know that in a competitive market, buyer behaviour is not just driven by low prices, but by overall product value. For many buyers, specific product characteristics or *attributes* are as important as price in making purchasing decisions. To appeal to this segment, many customer-driven companies have adopted a strategy of value pricing (also called value-based pricing), and compete on the basis of a superior price/quality relationship. Through research, they determine which features their customers want in the products and services they buy, as well as the value of these attributes to the customers. Thus, their price setting starts with their customers' perceived value. These firms do not necessarily charge the lowest prices in the product category. Instead, they offer just the right combination of quality and good service at a fair price. A common way to adopt a value pricing strategy is to offer lower-priced versions of products and services with an established brand name, such as the McDonald's value menu and the Holiday Inn Express budget hotels.

Ikea, for example, owes much of its success in the global furniture and household accessory market to its strategy of value pricing. The Swedish retailer attracts millions of value-conscious customers who realize that the quality level of its low-priced products is comparable to that of more expensive brands. In the fast moving consumer goods sector, Procter & Gamble was able to adopt a value pricing strategy for its Pampers, Ariel, Head & Shoulders and other national brands by re-engineering its manufacturing and distribution system to become a low-cost producer while maintaining a high quality level. Dell implemented a value pricing strategy by providing features in its notebooks not found in competitors' products, effectively contending for a share of the rapidly expanding low-price segment of the computer market.

To exercise more control over future success, small and medium-sized firms having little or no sway over industry prices should provide something special to the market that their larger competitors cannot. By instilling interest in specific product features or benefits that their target market would value, they may successfully pursue a strategy of non-price competition. Instead of emphasizing low prices, they could focus on the creative use of other marketing instruments. Ultimately, offering benefits such as unique product features, better accessibility, a superior warranty or outstanding customer service may result in greater customer loyalty than a marketing strategy only emphasizing low prices.

PRACTITIONER'S PERSPECTIVE
Rick Wartzman (The Drucker Institute)

Rick Wartzman, previously White House Correspondent at The Wall Street Journal, *is now an Irvine Senior Fellow of the New America Foundation, a public policy think tank. He is also the Director of The Drucker Institute at Claremont Graduate University. Peter F. Drucker, who wrote dozens of books and countless articles, was hailed by* Businessweek *as 'the most enduring management thinker of our time'. He influenced everyone from Winston Churchill to Bill Gates.*

Peter Drucker loved music – Haydn and Beethoven, Mozart and Mahler. If the late management philosopher was still around, he would undoubtedly be grabbed by the newest offering from an altogether different sort of act: the British rock band *Radiohead*. Not its synthesizer-driven sound. Drucker, rather, would be struck by Radiohead's bold focus on something that far too many businesses overlook: *pricing*. If effectively tied to an overall marketing strategy, it can be a powerful tool in helping an enterprise seize opportunities. Radiohead boldly focused on something that too many businesses overlook: pricing.

Radiohead focused on something that far too many businesses overlook: pricing

When Radiohead launched *In Rainbows*, it allowed consumers to download the album and – here's the twist – pay whatever they thought it was worth, including nothing at all. Properly pricing a product is no easy exercise. It involves a complex bit of calculus that takes into account not only a business' up-front investment but also the ongoing costs it expects to incur (as it moves down the learning curve and, presumably, becomes more efficient); the position of its competitors; and the crucial interplay between price and volume. Furthermore, it requires a degree of self-restraint. 'The first and easily the most common sin among businesses', Drucker argued, 'is the worship of high profit margins and of *premium pricing*.'

Historically, many companies ignored these factors. They set the price of something simply by adding up their expenses and then slathering on top as much profit as they thought the market would bear. As Drucker pointed out, such 'cost-driven pricing' was backward. He ultimately concluded that, 'the only thing that works is price-driven costing' (also known as *backward pricing*) – figuring out what customers believe a product or service is worth and then designing the item accordingly. 'Cost-driven pricing is the reason there is no American consumer-electronics industry,' Drucker asserted in an article he wrote more than two decades ago. 'It had the technology and the products. But it operated on cost-led pricing – and the Japanese practiced price-led costing.'

What Radiohead has done is take things to an even more sophisticated level. In effect, the band has embraced to the extreme the idea of *value-based pri*cing, often called *demand-oriented pricing*: charging customers what you believe they're willing to pay, given the benefits provided them. In the business-to-business market, in particular, this means establishing different prices for different consumers for the very same product, based on its value to each. Since word of Radiohead's pricing plan broke, reactions have ranged from disinterest to near fury, with some predicting that the band's take-it-to-the-people approach would help hasten the demise of the big record labels. I'm far from convinced that the release of this one album, in and of itself, will prove ruinous for the industry. But I would bet on this: It's bound to help the band enhance its own bottom line.

Thomas Nagle, co-author of the classic *The Strategy and Tactics of Pricing*, is also impressed by Radiohead's savvy. Twenty years ago, when the first edition of his book was published, he cited the wisdom of musicians who charged relatively little for concerts because these live performances were what drove record sales – then the most lucrative part of the business. Now, he says, 'the world has flipped.' By pricing *In Rainbows* so flexibly, Radiohead may well attract new fans that will fill its concerts, which are the real money machines of music today. Consumers are often willing to pay for something, even if they can get it for free, as long as they perceive that it's a fair deal. And sure enough, research shows that Radiohead fans plunked down, on average, €7 for their digital copy of In Rainbows – right in line with what Apple's iTunes charges for most albums. All of which, of course, validates a page right out of the Drucker songbook: 'What the customer sees, thinks, believes and wants, at any given time, must be accepted by management as an objective fact and must be taken as seriously as the reports of the salesperson, the tests of the engineer or the figures of the accountant.'[4]

12.5 PRICING METHODS

Although companies may be able to change their prices quickly to deal with unexpected developments such as a competitive move, frequent price adjustment may not be the best course of action. After all, price is a strategic marketing tool. A company's optimum price level is closely related to its positioning strategy and long-term goals, such as the quality reputation and profitability it wants to achieve. Numerous successive changes in list prices can impede obtaining these objectives, damage the company's long-term performance and cause confusion among both resellers and consumers. Instead, a better strategy may be to adjust the company's pricing approach to the current economic conditions and customer price perceptions, either by adopting a value pricing strategy, or by influencing customer buyer behaviour through discounts and allowances that reduce the final amount the customer pays.

We will now analyze how channel members can maintain their control over prices and effectively appeal to the target market. First, we will consider the importance of a stable base price in the business-to-business market. Next, we will explore the types of discounts from the list price and the allowances that suppliers may offer their customers. Finally, we examine the most commonly used methods for setting *transfer prices*.

12.5.1 *Base price*

Just as manufacturers benefit from price stability, intermediaries in the trade channel function best with the margin stability provided by steady prices. In developing their own marketing strategies, wholesalers and retailers alike rely on their suppliers' consistent pricing policies to help them regulate their own prices and profit margins. Thus, for all organizations in the distribution channel, stable prices are the basis for an effective pricing policy.

In the business market, most products have an established base price (also called *list price*), which is the general, publicly announced price for which the company expects to sell the product. In the case of completely new products, the introductory base price level is correlated with the company's overall pricing strategy: it will either price the new product above the market (price skimming) or below the market (penetration pricing). For established products, of course, the base price level is partly dependent on the prices charged by competitors.

Many products in business-to-business transactions, however, are not sold at the base price. Buyers may be able to negotiate a *discount* – or reduction from the base price – from the supplier, depending on quantities purchased and the time of year. Also, from a tactical perspective, the supplier may fine-tune its prices in some markets to respond to temporary changes in the level of demand or competition. Moreover, the actual prices are partly dependent on the influence or control of the other distribution channel members. Retailers, for example, can gain greater control over prices by linking their resale support to the profit margins allowed by the supplier, by carrying competing products in their product range, and by stimulating demand for their store brands so that their customers become loyal to them rather than to the manufacturer.

Manufacturers, on the other hand, can increase their control over prices by not offering their products to discount retail chains, by allowing the resellers adequate profit margins, by creating a strong brand image that justifies high prices and, if possible, by pre-marking prices on their packaging. A *recommended retail price* or, as it is often called, Manufacturer's Suggested Retail Price (MSRP) – whether or not printed on the package – provides retailers the option of selling the item at that price. The relatively high profit margin compensates specialty stores for the product line depth and high level of customer service they offer. At the same time, large retail chains and discount stores may offer the product at a lower price and still make a profit because of their higher turnover and economies of scale.

Sometimes, a supplier suggests a relatively high resale price in an attempt to advance resellers' cooperation. If they want retailers to aggressively promote the product, the supplier may set a high base price that allows resellers to secure above-average mark-ups. However, for a product to compete successfully at a price above the market, it must either be so strongly differentiated that consumers consider it superior to other brands, or resellers must enthusiastically and heavily promote it.

12.5.2 *Discounts and allowances*

Setting prices for companies that buy products for resale, manufacturing purposes or use within their own organization is different from setting prices for consumers. In business markets, it is customary for suppliers to quote a product's list price, and then refer to any available discounts and allowances that reduce the final price for the potential buyer. These price reductions influence customer buying behaviour and are typically offered for volume purchases, off-season buying and early invoice payments. Discounts are also offered to intermediaries for performing certain marketing functions in the channel. When properly coordinated with the overall pricing strategy, price discounting can help a company build or maintain long-term relationships with its customers and reinforce its competitive position.

Quantity discounts

Price reductions granted for large-volume orders are known as quantity discounts. Depending on the firm, the order size may be calculated in monetary terms (such as in euros or dollars) or in numbers of units purchased. The purpose of a quantity discount is to induce customers to buy more products than they otherwise would. The main justification for the discount is that it costs the seller less per unit to sell a large order than a small one. A large order, for instance, requires no more paperwork than a small one, nor does it take up much more of a salesperson's time. In addition, the seller can pass transportation and inventory cost savings on to the buyer.

Quantity discounts can be either cumulative or non-cumulative. Cumulative quantity discounts are based on the quantity a customer buys over a period of time, usually one year. The greater the cumulative amount purchased, the greater the discount. Although the seller does not reap the economies of scale in production, marketing and order handling realized when a customer buys all items at once, cumulative discounts encourage repeat buying. They therefore serve to tie the customer to the supplier.

Non-cumulative quantity discounts are based on the size of an individual purchase. Each sale is independent, and the size of the discount, if any, is computed on the number of items ordered at one particular time. Non-cumulative quantity discounts encourage large individual purchase orders, but do not build customer loyalty to the same extent as cumulative discounts.

Seasonal discounts

A discount from the regular list price to buyers that purchase products or services out of season is a seasonal discount. By getting price-sensitive resellers to stock up on a product ahead of its selling season, manufacturers (for example, of snow boards or ice skates) with sales volume varying greatly over the year can iron out the peaks and valleys in their production and marketing activities. In addition to smoothing out the sales pattern, a seasonal discount pushes inventory from the seller to the customer who buys early. It can also help service marketers like hotels, airlines and cruise lines increase off-season demand.

Cash discounts

It is a common practice in many industries to offer channel members and organizational buyers reductions in price in exchange for prompt payment. These price cuts are called cash discounts. An invoice reading 'net 30 days' means that the entire amount due must be paid within thirty days. By contrast, many invoices read 2/10, net 30, which means that the seller is offering the buyer a 2 per cent discount if the bill is paid in full within ten days. If the customer does not make payment within the ten-day period, the entire balance is due within thirty days without a discount. If the invoice is not paid within thirty days, the company may charge interest.

From a marketing perspective, a company may offer cash discounts for at least two reasons. First, it may want to encourage the prompt payment of bills, since accounts receivable are an expense and a collection problem for many organizations. Second, competitors' pricing policies in the industry may be such that the firm cannot afford *not* to offer cash discounts.

Functional discounts

A functional discount (also referred to as a *trade discount*) is a reduction of the list price granted by a manufacturer to middlemen for handling distribution-related services or functions in the trade channel that would otherwise be the manufacturer's responsibility. These marketing functions may include customer inquiry response, sales promotion, warehousing, financing, transportation, installation and repair. An important criterion for the manufacturer in determining both the price and the trade discount is what margin they are willing to offer the intermediaries. The functional discount should allow resellers to set prices that offset the cost incurred in performing these functions, while generating an acceptable profit. If the discount is inadequate, few resellers may be willing to carry the product.

Functional discounts for resellers vary from one industry to another. Therefore, they are quite similar across brands of a particular type of product or service. Not only do they depend on the nature and length of the trade channel, but also on a reseller's position in that channel and the marketing activities they are expected to perform at that level. For example, an import agent – operating a large-scale business – will be allowed a lower margin than a full-service wholesaler or retailer.

Allowances

Like discounts, allowances help a firm influence customer buying behaviour without formally reducing the list price of a product or service. Allowances are pricing adjustments that *indirectly* lower the price a reseller or other customer pays in exchange for taking some action, such as participating in a sales support programme, promoting a product or buying a product during a certain time period. Three important types of allowances are trade-in allowances, promotional allowances and rebates.

Trade-in allowances are price reductions granted to buyers for turning in a used product when purchasing a new one. Since these allowances are part of the payment on the new product, they encourage the prospect to make a purchase. A seller can reduce the price the buyer has to pay significantly without changing the list price by raising the value given on the trade-in item. Trade-ins are quite common in the aircraft industry as well as in the consumer market for automobiles.

Promotional allowances (also known as *trade allowances*) are used to reward resellers for promoting products to customers through advertising, personal selling, displays or other promotions. These incentives are attempts to integrate promotional strategies within the channels of distribution. Without changing list prices or trade discounts, dealers are offered cash payments or given free products for participating in advertising and sales support programmes developed to increase sales. As a pricing tool, a promotional allowance is like a functional discount; for example, the producer may pay half the cost of an advertisement that a retailer runs to promote their product. Most retailers pass on a portion of these savings to consumers.

Finally, rebates are refunds of a portion of the purchase price to customers who buy a particular product during a specific period. They are used for products ranging from cars and computers to cameras and canned foods. Rebates don't affect list prices, but stimulate customers to buy when marketers want to sell, such as during periods of slow sales. They are also used to give consumers a reason to try a new product, at least if they are willing to fill out a form, mail it in and wait several weeks to receive a check in the mail or, more typically in Europe, a direct deposit in their bank account. For manufacturers, the advantage of a rebate over a simple price reduction is that this temporary incentive can be granted and eliminated without changing the basic price structure. And while consumers may resent a price being restored to the original, higher level after a temporary price reduction, they often appreciate the opportunity to buy a product if they will be refunded part of its purchase price.

12.5.3 *Transfer pricing*

Many corporations sell products or services from one of their divisions or subsidiaries to another. Although these internal transactions are usually not paid for with funds, the organization still must determine the price of the goods transferred in terms of the revenues (to the supplying business unit) and costs (to the buying business unit). The most commonly used methods for setting transfer prices are the market price system and the cost-based system.

Market price

Typically, if a market price for the transferred product exists, it is used as the company's internal transfer price (sometimes less a small discount to reflect the lack of sales effort and other expenses). This system has several advantages. The division's profit on the product represents its real economic contribution or *added value*, making it possible to compare the division with similar independent suppliers.

In addition, the division's management is under the same cost-control pressure as its independent competitors. And finally, management does not waste time negotiating a transfer price, since the price charged is based on the market price.

Cost-based price

If a market price does not exist or cannot be estimated, the product's transfer price is usually based on its cost. Under this approach, known as *cost-based transfer pricing*, management decides how cost should be calculated and what profit margin will be allowed. To prevent inefficiencies in the selling division from being passed on to the buying division in the form of high prices, the transfer price is calculated using standard costs per unit, provided by the company's accountants. If the seller's actual production cost is higher than the standard cost, the seller must sustain the loss, unless external factors – such as unanticipated cost increases for raw material or currency exchange rates – have significantly increased costs per unit.

Two alternatives for calculating the transfer price based on *standard full cost* (what it would cost to produce the goods at full plant capacity) are *actual full cost* (calculated by dividing all fixed and variable costs for a period by the number of units produced) or *cost plus investment* (calculated at full cost plus the cost of a portion of the selling division's assets used for internal needs). Which transfer pricing method the organization uses depends on its business strategy and the nature of the divisions' interaction. Management must make sure that the transfer price is fair to each business unit involved in the transaction.

If the corporation's selling unit markets the product to external customers, then the *profit margin* for internal sales should be the same as for external sales. When the business unit does not sell outside the company, however, the mark-up should be based on the average gross margin or typical mark-up in the industry, or on the profitability of similar products made by other divisions. In international transactions, tax considerations may also play a role in setting transfer prices.

In today's global marketplace, transfer pricing is a difficult but critically important strategic pricing problem for many companies. To evaluate the performance of a strategic business unit's management when most of its sales are internal requires that the transfer price be as realistic as possible. Only then can the company determine just how effective the division's managers are and whether it should continue to manufacture and sell the product or deliver the service.

12.6 COST-ORIENTED PRICING

Firms can chose from several approaches in setting their selling prices. The most widely used approaches, as Figure 12.8 illustrates, are cost-, demand- and competition-oriented pricing. Other executives prefer to employ a combination of these methods, called *combination pricing*.[5]

Many companies establish the price of their products based on costs. Using this approach, known as cost-oriented pricing, the buyers' reactions to price and the prices

FIGURE 12.8 Alternative approaches to price determination

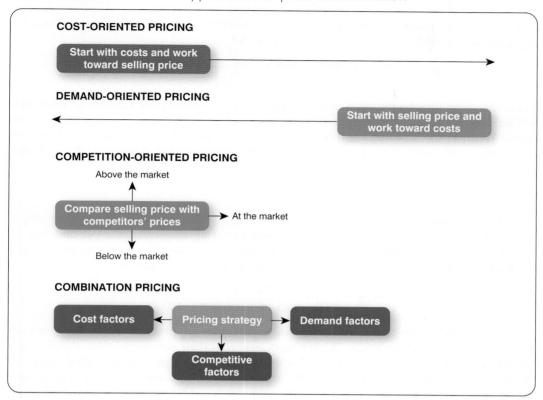

charged by competitors are of secondary importance, yet most marketers try to estimate the likely impact of a cost-derived price on product demand. Two types of cost-oriented pricing are commonly used in business: cost-plus pricing and variable cost pricing. Additional means of determining price include the break-even analysis and the target return pricing technique. We will now examine each of these pricing procedures.

12.6.1 Cost-plus pricing

The most frequently used form of price setting in business is *cost-based pricing*. This is a method of determining the selling price of a product or service whereby cost is increased by a predetermined percentage of these costs to provide a profit margin. This method is straightforward and easy to use, since managers usually know their costs of doing business or can calculate them with great accuracy. In addition, there is no need to estimate elasticity of demand or competitors' reactions to prices. Two common forms of cost-based pricing are cost-plus and mark-up pricing.

Cost-plus pricing

Cost-plus pricing is price setting by thinking like an accountant: price equals cost plus overhead plus a reasonable, predetermined profit. In setting prices with cost-plus pricing (sometimes called *incremental-cost pricing*), management tries to allocate only those costs directly attributable to a specific product or output. First, the seller's costs are calculated – either during a project or, more typically, when it is completed – after which a specific amount (or percentage of the cost) is added to the seller's cost to establish the price. This is a common approach in pricing custom-made equipment or projects in which production costs are hard to predict, as happens when raw material prices fluctuate. The formula for cost-plus pricing is:

$$\text{Price} = \frac{\text{Total fixed costs} + \text{total variable costs} + \text{projected profit}}{\text{Units produced}}$$

Thus, the steps for computing a cost-plus price are to estimate the number of units that will be produced, calculate the total fixed and variable costs and add a desired profit to costs. A major shortcoming of this approach is that profit is expressed in relation to costs rather than sales, and price is determined without taking consumer demand into consideration.

Mark-up pricing

In cases where some costs, such as overheads, are difficult to determine, mark-up pricing is preferred. A company using mark-up pricing sets prices by calculating the per-unit cost of manufacturing (or purchasing) products and then determining the mark-up percentages needed to cover selling costs and profit. The formula for mark-up pricing is:

$$\text{Price} = \frac{\text{Product cost}}{(100 - \text{mark-up percentage}) : 100}$$

Wholesalers and retailers that sell many different types of products often use mark-up pricing to establish selling prices. Rather than analyzing their operating costs, they use the per unit cost of buying the product and add a predetermined percentage, called mark-up, to the cost of the product for profit and for expenses not otherwise taken into consideration. The total then determines the selling price. This approach is also applied by trading companies, bars and restaurants. It would be difficult and time consuming for these firms to determine the 'correct' price for each of their products. Therefore, they use standard mark-ups (stated in terms of the selling price) for broad product categories to determine (gross) profit.

Although the percentage mark-up in retail stores varies from one product category to another, the same percentage tends to be used in determining prices within a single product category. This turns pricing into a routine task that can be performed quickly. For example, a department store might set its mark-up on men's clothing at 50 per cent over cost, the mark-up on women's clothing at 70 per cent and the mark-up on jewellery as high as 125 per cent. Mark-ups by product category vary due to differences in competition, buyers' price sensitivity, product turnover and the risks associated with selling each type of product.

How mark-up prices are calculated

The mark-up is typically stated as a percentage of the selling price, although it may also be expressed as a percentage of the cost. To illustrate, assume that a retailer purchases a shirt for €30, adds €15 to the cost and then prices it at €45. The mark-up of €15 is either the percentage of the selling price, 33 1/3 per cent (€15 : €45), or the percentage of the cost, 50 per cent (€15 : €30).

In the above case, the cost figure used in calculating the mark-up is the direct cost of acquiring the product. Direct costs are costs incurred solely for a particular product. However, the retailer's cost accountant might show that in addition to the amount that the retailer must pay the manufacturer for the shirt, which is the variable cost, there are also fixed costs (such as storage costs) that must allocated to each shirt. At a certain production or sales level, these costs are constant per unit. Since direct costs include both variable and fixed costs, the constant (or fixed) costs must be added to the variable costs in order to determine the direct costs (also called traceable or attributable costs) of a product. In addition, there are overhead or indirect costs (such as salaries for sales personnel) that are more difficult to estimate on a per product basis, but can be allocated to each shirt through a mark-up for indirect costs. This mark-up must be high enough to allow the retailer (or other firm) to pay the overhead costs associated with selling the product. As shown in the example on mark-up pricing below, a final mark-up is added on top of this to provide a particular profit margin and to establish the selling price.

Calculation of a product's selling price:

Variable costs	€ 30.00
Constant ('fixed') costs	€ 10.00 +
Direct costs	€ 40.00
Mark-up for indirect costs (overhead) 5 per cent	€ 2.00 +
Total costs per unit	€ 42.00
Mark-up for a profit margin of 25 per cent of cost	€ 10.50 +
Selling price	€ 52.50

Mark-up chain

Regardless of the company's raw materials purchasing price and production cost, when determining a profit margin or selling price to middlemen, management should realize that the selling price to the ultimate consumer depends on the mark-ups of intermediaries in the distribution channel. This is demonstrated in Table 12.3, which shows a *mark-up chain* for a product when mark-up is expressed as a percentage of the selling price at each level in the supply chain.

In this example, the total cost of manufacturing each unit of the product is €40. Assuming a 25 per cent mark-up of the selling price to achieve profit objectives, the manufacturer would have to charge €53.33 (€40 × 100/75). This, in turn, becomes the cost of the product to the wholesaler. As a result of the 25 per cent mark-up at the manufacturing level, the 30 per cent mark-up at the wholesale level and the 40 per cent mark-up at the retail level, at the end of this chain, the retail price has risen to €126.98.

TABLE 12.3 A typical mark-up chain

Price Components	Manufacturer	Wholesaler	Retailer
COST	€ 40.00 (75%)	€ 53.33 (70%)	€ 76.19 (60%)
MARK-UP	€ 13.33 (25%)	€ 22.86 (30%)	€ 50.79 (40%)
SELLING PRICE	€ 53.33* (100%)	€ 76.19 (100%)	€ 126.98 (100%)

*To calculate the manufacturer's selling price, assume that .75x = €40, where x = the selling price for the manufacturer.

Problems with mark-up pricing

The mechanical application of mark-up pricing results in three major problems. The first problem with calculating selling prices based on the same general mark-up percentage is that real overheads may vary significantly from one product to the next. To illustrate, men's suits usually command a higher mark-up than dress shirts, since it takes more of the salesperson's time to sell a suit than a shirt. Moreover, once the suit is sold, stores generally pay for the cost of alterations; another cost not incurred by selling a shirt. Allocation of overheads is difficult and may result in inaccurate selling prices.

A second, more fundamental problem with a uniform mark-up percentage is that this pricing approach is in no way market-oriented. Mark-up pricing does not factor in demand for the product or competitors' pricing strategies. This may result in some products being underpriced and others overpriced. Consequently, a firm misses the opportunity to make additional profits from high demand items, while also possibly losing sales of products that might benefit from a lower mark-up. Customers may buy these from a competitor charging less.

The third problem with applying the same mark-up to all products is that a high mark-up may actually reduce total profits. Suppose that a product's selling price, with a profit margin of €2, results in sales of 10 000 units. With that mark-up, the profit contribution is €20 000. If, however, a mark-up of €1 would lead to a sales volume of 50 000 units, the profit contribution could be €50 000. Thus, a lower profit margin per unit can generate a higher overall *profit contribution*.

Therefore, marketers always attempt to assess whether a high mark-up may reduce profits by slowing the firm's stock turnover. **Stock turnover** is defined as the number of times the company's average inventory is sold in one year. If, for example, the value of the inventory at hand averages €50 000 and annual sales are €1 000 000, then the company 'turns' or sells its inventory 20 times per year (€1 000 000 : €50 000).

Table 12.4 shows the relationship between sales, stock turnover, mark-up and profit for two retailers, each with a different pricing strategy.

Store B has a higher mark-up (40 per cent) than store A; this has reduced sales to €3 000 000 and the stock turnover rate to three times per year. Although the gross profit (€1 200 000) is higher than Store A's, the firm's actual profit (€900 000) is less than Store A's because of the extra cost of carrying inventory (interest and insurance payments and inventory maintenance). The bottom line is that a company should monitor the effect of mark-up adjustments on the stock turnover rate in order to achieve the best possible profit position.

TABLE 12.4 Relationship between sales, stock turnover, mark-up and profit for two stores

Factors	Store A	Store B
SALES	€ 5 500 000	€ 3 000 000
MARK-UP (AS A PERCENTAGE OF SALES)	20%	40%
GROSS PROFIT	€ 1 100 000	€ 1 200 000
AVERAGE INVENTORY	€ 550 000	€ 1 000 000
STOCK TURNOVER RATE	10 X PER YEAR	3 X PER YEAR
INVENTORY COSTS (30%)	€ 165 000	€ 300 000
PROFIT LESS INVENTORY COSTS	€ 935 000	€ 900 000
PROFIT (AS A PERCENTAGE OF SALES)	17%	30%

To counter the drawbacks associated with mark-up pricing, many firms, as previously discussed, use cost-plus pricing by applying different mark-up percentages, not only by product category, but for individual items or brands within product lines as well. The company then adjusts these 'flexible mark-up percentages' based on buyers' price sensitivity, competition, the real cost of selling the item and anticipated turnover rates.

12.6.2 *Variable-cost pricing*

Marketers often find that a product's likely market price is not high enough to cover the to-tal cost of manufacture or acquisition. Should an item be produced or not? In the long run, a product must generate enough revenue to at least equal its production or acquisition costs. In the short run, however, a firm using variable-cost pricing (also called *direct-costing*) can profitably produce some items that are priced below their total cost. The price is then based on the variable costs, without the overhead or fixed costs being directly allocated to these products.

Especially when a company, operating at normal capacity and with a full order portfolio, receives an extra, incidental order, such as from a customer overseas, it may charge a price based only on the extra production and sales costs incurred in supplying the product. This is sometimes referred to as the *differential cost*. The selling price then includes the direct cost plus a mark-up for profit. In the long term, this pricing strategy is feasible only if all of the company's fixed costs are covered by its regular sales at higher prices.

Contribution margin

In the short run, a firm using a variable-cost pricing approach should only produce and sell a product when the revenue generated by the product is greater than its total variable costs. Revenue in excess of variable costs is known as the contribution margin. It is used to absorb part of the company's total fixed costs as well as to provide a profit.

To illustrate the use of variable-cost pricing, Table 12.5 presents revenue and cost data for a watch company producing and marketing three types of watches. The total fixed costs are €280 000. These costs are allocated to the product types based on a formula that assigns the overhead to the production of these three items.

The total profits at this time total €260 000. Clearly, the firm must consider ending the production of product type III immediately. Not only is it losing money on the product (€60 000), but the variable costs for this model are greater than its revenue, resulting in a

TABLE 12.5 Variable cost pricing for three products

	Product Range		
	Type I	*Type II*	*Type III*
Revenue	€ 650 000	€ 300 000	€ 400 000
Variable costs	€ 200 000	€ 200 000	€ 410 000
Contribution margin	€ 450 000	€ 100 000	(€ 10 000)
Fixed costs	€ 100 000	€ 130 000	(€ 50 000
Profit	€ 350 000	(€ 30 000)	(€ 60 000)

negative contribution margin of €10 000. Although by discontinuing type III the other two products will have to absorb its fixed costs (€50 000), the firm still saves €10 000. The result is that total profit increases from €260 000 to €270 000 (€350 000 − €30 000 − €50 000).

While the firm might also consider discontinuing type II, it probably will not do so. Although the company appears to be losing money on this product, the revenue it generates is greater than its direct variable costs. Its contribution margin of €100 000 helps cover the company's fixed costs. If type II were also taken out of production, all the fixed costs (€280 000) would have to be covered by product type I, thereby reducing the firm's total profits to €170 000 (€350 000 − €180 000). Therefore, in the short run, as long as a product's revenue is greater than its variable cost, production should continue.

There may also be other reasons to continue making and selling a product below total cost. For instance, if a product is new on the market, the company may have anticipated the losses and be willing to continue production because of the product's potential profits. Or the product may occupy an important position in the firm's product line. Thus, if discontinuing production of one product would mean that its dealers are less willing to carry the other products, the company may well decide to keep making it. In the long run, however, a company must cover all of its costs in order to survive and prosper.

Constraints and risks of variable-cost pricing

The major risk associated with variable-cost pricing – in the case of customers negotiating to obtain prices that do not cover the manufacturer's total costs – is that it could cause the market to deteriorate. Occasionally, the strategy may even trigger a price war, resulting in reduced profits for all companies in the industry. Once prices have been lowered, they cannot always be brought back up to previous levels. And, if other customers learn of preferential pricing granted to particular buyers, increased pressure is brought to bear on the supplier to lower its prices.

The manufacturer in the example in Table 12.5 can only continue to supply product type II at a loss, because the gross margin on type I is relatively high. However, competitors who only produce a type II model will not be able to continue to sell this product very long at a competitive price that does not cover the total costs.

An extreme form of selling products far below the average market price is called dumping. In case of excess capacity, the price charged may even be below cost. Because companies have an interest in preventing price wars in the domestic market, dumping usually takes place in foreign markets.

12.6.3 Break-even analysis

With a cost-oriented approach to pricing, the demand for a product or service is generally not taken into account. Nonetheless, many managers try to estimate what will happen to their profit if, at a particular selling price, sales begin to rise or fall. The best way to examine the relationship between total revenue (at a given price) and total cost at various levels of output in order to determine break-even analysis profitability is by conducting a break-even analysis. It involves calculating the number of units that must be sold at a certain price for the firm to cover costs and, hence, break even. Such an analysis also enables the marketer to estimate the impact of various prices on the company's profit position.

A break-even analysis will reveal the break-even point, where total revenues equal total costs; thus, the break-even point for a product is defined as the number of units sold at which product revenues match total product costs. At sales in excess of the break-even point, the company begins to earn a profit. The break-even point is calculated using the following formula:

$$\text{Break-even point (in units)} = \frac{\text{total fixed costs}}{\text{unit selling price} - \text{unit variable costs}}$$

Consider the case of a product with an €80 selling price, variable costs of €30 per unit, and associated fixed costs of €10 000. The break-even point for this product is calculated as follows:

$$\text{Break-even point} = \frac{€10\,000}{€80 - €30} = 200 \text{ units}$$

Viewing this relationship in another way, if the company sells 200 of these products at a margin of €50 per unit (selling price – variable costs per unit), it would generate €10 000 in revenues, just enough to cover the product's fixed costs, and therefore incur no loss.

Figure 12.9 graphically depicts the break-even relationships. The fixed-cost line is horizontal, indicating that fixed costs do not change with the level of production. Variable costs, which increase as the level of production rises, are added to the fixed costs. The total cost line is the sum of total variable costs and total fixed costs. Finally, the total-revenue curve is the price per unit multiplied by the number of units sold. The higher the price, the steeper the angle of the revenue curve. The intersection of the total revenue curve and the total cost line shows the break-even point – in this example, at 200 units (the break-even sales volume) and at a total revenue of €16 000 (€80 × 200 units).

Flexible break-even analysis

A break-even analysis tells the company how many units of a product it must sell for total product revenues to equal total product costs, but not whether that number of units will actually sell at the specified price. Break-even analysis gives no indication of the correct unit price in terms of demand, competition and other market factors, only the break-even sales volume for a particular price. This limitation can be partially overcome through a

FIGURE 12.9 Break-even analysis

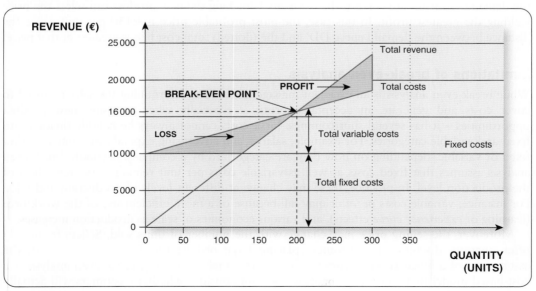

FIGURE 12.10 Flexible break-even analysis

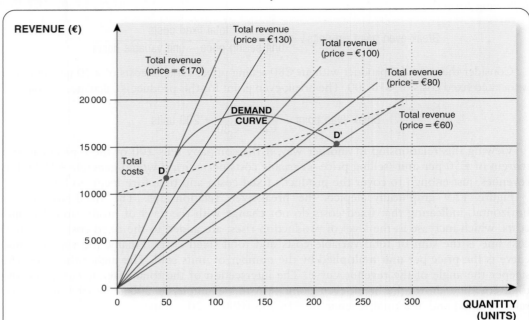

flexible break-even analysis. Under this approach, we draw a series of total revenue curves, each based on a different price for the product. On the basis of experience or market research studies, we then estimate the expected sales volume for the product at each price and the total costs at that production level. Finally, these estimate points are connected to form a demand curve showing how total revenue varies with price.

Figure 12.10 uses the data in Figure 12.9 to demonstrate flexible break-even analysis. The graph shows for each of a series of price alternatives the cost-revenue relationship. Assuming the demand estimates are correct, the company launching the new product can select the price yielding the greatest profit. In this case, the most profitable price is €130 per unit, since the distance between the demand curve DD' and the (dotted) total-cost line is greatest at that price.

Limitations of break-even analysis

While break-even analysis is an excellent managerial tool for determining the sales required to cover costs and generate an acceptable profit – especially when assessing new product opportunities – it has several shortcomings. First, costs cannot always be handily divided into fixed and variable categories. For example, salaries and advertising expenditures may be either fixed or variable, depending on how they are categorized by a company. Secondly, break-even analysis assumes that fixed costs as well as variable costs per unit remain static, regardless of the production level. In practice, these may change at different levels of production and sales. For instance, variable costs per unit may fall because of a more efficient use of the workforce (learning or *experience curve* effects), and various economies of scale as production increases.

Moreover, the selling price may change with the number of units sold. Sellers frequently offer quantity discounts to customers placing large orders; this is inconsistent with the assumption of a linear revenue curve in break-even analysis. Finally, break-even analysis is a cost-based model that ignores demand. It does not consider whether customers will actually buy the product or service at the specified price and in the quantities required to break even or generate a profit. Obviously, this information would significantly affect the company's pricing decisions. Therefore, the marketer's task is to go beyond considering only cost factors and to also consider pricing from the customer's perspective in making decisions.

12.6.4 *Target-return pricing*

When considering the introduction of a new product, marketers may have to determine whether they will be able to price the product high enough to provide a specified or *target* return on investment (ROI). If the product cannot be priced sufficiently high to achieve this rate of return on investment, management may decide against a product launch. From experience, however, managers at Shell, DuPont, General Motors and other companies that use *target-return-on-investment pricing* generally know what selling prices are feasible.

Target return pricing can be implemented in conjunction with break-even analysis. The first steps are to estimate the amount of capital required to manufacture the product and to specify a required rate of return. This rate can then be converted into monetary terms, such as euros or dollars and added to the fixed cost figure in the numerator of the break-even formula.

To illustrate, again assume that the selling price of a product is €80, variable costs per unit are €30, and total fixed costs are €10 000. If the required investment is €20 000 and the company wants a 25 per cent return on investment, this amounts to a €5 000 return (€20 000 × 25 per cent) before taxes. The target-return break-even point is calculated as follows:

$$\text{Target-return break-even point} = \frac{\text{fixed costs} + \text{required return}}{\text{price} - \text{variable costs per unit}} = \frac{\text{€10 000} + \text{€5 000}}{\text{€80} - \text{€30}} = 300 \text{ units}$$

Note that 300 units is not the break-even point, but the number of units that the firm must sell in order to achieve the desired 25 per cent return on investment. Figure 12.11 diagrams

FIGURE 12.11 Target-return break-even analysis

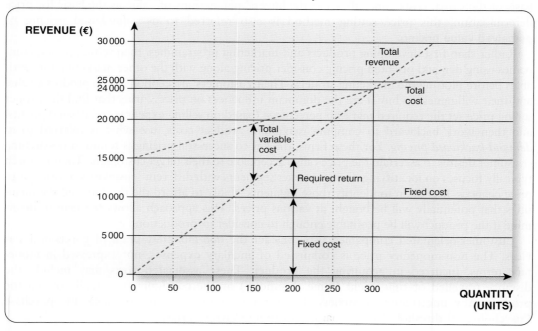

this target-return break-even analysis. Any sales over and above 300 units would contribute to profits in excess of the 25 per cent return on investment. If less than 300 products were sold, the company would be falling short of its target return objective.

The net change in total cost that results from producing and marketing one additional unit is known as **marginal cost**. Because these additional costs involve the variable cost of one extra product, the marginal cost is generally expressed per product unit. If we express both the change in fixed cost and variable cost per unit, then the average fixed cost per unit declines as production goes up, while the variable cost per unit initially decreases but rises again later. Therefore, this cost curve usually takes a U shape. The initial economies of scale in manufacturing and purchasing resulting from increased production give way to inefficiencies as, for example, production space becomes overcrowded and employees can no longer handle the greater quantity requirements.

Returning to our target-return break-even point example, the next step in the analysis is to decide whether the target figure of 300 units is realistic, given a selling price of €80 and current demand conditions. The firm may have to lower the selling price, thereby increasing the number of products that must be sold before the firm reaches its return objective of €5 000. Having an understanding of buyer behaviour and demand-oriented pricing is therefore essential.

12.7 DEMAND-ORIENTED PRICING

Although cost calculations – as a price setting component – are important for managers responsible for planning and budgeting, buyers are rarely interested in how companies determine costs and establish profit margin targets for their products and services. Of more concern to consumers is whether a product's price is within range of what they are willing to spend. This perceived value influences consumers' buying decisions and consequently overall demand. Therefore, a growing number of firms employ **demand-oriented pricing**; they try to set prices at the level that intended buyers are willing to pay, rather than on the basis of their own costs. Since they use the buyers' perceptions of value as the basis for price determination, this price setting method is also referred to as value-based pricing or **perceived-value pricing**.

Rather than first developing products and marketing programmes, then setting prices, companies using demand-oriented pricing consider pricing along with the other marketing mix variables before plotting the marketing strategy. Their customers' perception of the product's value and their willingness to buy it are the dominant influences on price. Firms that find the proper selling price set the required mark-up percentage (based on selling expenses and desired profits) and then work backward to compute maximum product costs, use what is referred to as *demand-backward pricing*. For these firms, the key to successful pricing is found in researching consumer desires to ascertain the price range acceptable to their target customers. Their research typically focuses on identifying distinct market segments with different sensitivities to price or to price changes. It goes on to identify those segments' ability to afford the product and the quantities that potentially will be bought at various prices. This approach allows the firm to determine if the product will be profitable enough to consider its production.

Customer-orientated companies also consider the **non-monetary price** of goods and services. The non-monetary price is comprised of ancillary expenses, not expressed in monetary terms, incurred in acquiring the product. These associated costs may include the distance travelled or time spent ('time threshold') by the consumer to actually obtain the product. Any uncertainty or anxiety the customer must overcome to make the purchase ('psychological threshold') is also a form of non-monetary price.

MARKETING MISTAKE
Buick's Reintroduction in China

Achieving brand loyalty from their customer base is something that all successful marketers will aspire to. For many brands it is the key to their survival, particularly as more and more products compete for space on shelves, and ultimately, to fill shoppers' baskets. However, critics have questioned whether brand loyalty is a cultural phenomenon and hence whether it varies from country to country. Taking China as a case in point, some business people argue that Chinese consumers are not loyal to brands; they will buy brand A on one occasion, then brand B or C on their next shopping trip. Marketing managers claim that it is difficult to be successful in a market without predictable buying behaviour.

Although consumers in China tend to change preferred brands more often than their counterparts in the West, it has little to do with their cultural background. A more likely reason for the relatively low brand loyalty is that consumers in this emerging market have more options available to them than they were accustomed to before. Moreover, foreign companies targeting these buyers often do so without much insight into their needs, wants and purchasing behaviour. In reality, as long as they meet their expectations, many consumers in China continue to buy the same brands they trust.

To illustrate, more than two out of three luxury watches bought in China carry the same brand name: Omega. Also, there are more than two thousand Kentucky Fried Chicken restaurants in the country that cater to customers who appreciate KFC and apparently remain loyal to the brand. These Western corporations are successful because they learned as much as they could about their customers' needs and preferences, adapted their marketing strategy and carefully positioned their brand. Also, they primarily appeal to young consumers, realizing that these will likely be their most loyal customers in the future. In contrast, companies that don't really know their target market and use marketing strategies that are not tailored to buyers' specific needs will not be able to retain customers and may lose them to more customer-focused rivals.

China's foreign passenger car sales provide an illustration of the market's complexities. In marketing automobiles, brand image is a key factor to success. Consumer perceptions of car brands are particularly crucial in young markets such as China, where eight out of ten cars are sold to individuals who purchase one for the first time. Since the Chinese market for imported passenger cars has only existed for about thirty years, the stereotypes that consumers associate with specific brands are often quite different from those in the West. For example, while Mercedes is perceived as a prestigious brand in most countries, Chinese consumers associate it with a – less glamorous – retired senior citizen life style. And Buick, which is considered anything but an upscale brand in the United States, its country of origin, is looked upon in China as one of the most desirable luxury automobiles.

About 20 years ago, General Motors sought to establish a joint venture for building cars in China. It is significant that local officials insisted that the venture would make Buicks, instead of Chevrolets, as GM had suggested. They pointed out that P'u Yi, China's last emperor, had a Buick in the 1920s, and so did Chinese leaders such as Sun Yat-sen and Zhou Enlai. These historical roots had contributed to Buick's upscale brand image in China. Accordingly, GM executives positioned Buick as a brand for senior executives and other elites. It worked, as it allowed the company to sell Buick luxury cars at even higher prices than those of BMW and Mercedes. Soon, GM sold more Buicks in China than at home: more than 650 000 vehicles shortly after the first Buick car plant started operating in China.

A lower price and diluted brand image caused Buick's market share to dive

When the Chinese automobile market – with 30 per cent annual growth – started to beat the United States in terms of both market size and growth rate, Buick struggled to maintain its market share among first-time buyers. In 2007, the company decided to offer a new basic Buick model with a low sticker price of less than €10 000. At first, when tens of thousands of young consumers in China bought these new inexpensive Buicks, sales volume took off. But soon, the damage of the diluted brand image had its effect on sales: General Motors had to offer rebates and other price concessions in order to attract price-conscious buyers and move its cars off the lot.

Buick made a classic error of failing to establish to the market what its name tag represented. As a result, sales tumbled. Affluent consumers and corporate executives refused to drive or to be chauffeured in a luxury car with a brand name that was now associated with 'cheap'.

At the same time, price sensitive individuals and families who had purchased the new low-end Buick model were increasingly dissatisfied with the substandard quality level of their vehicle.

As soon as General Motors' management became aware of the damage done to Buick's reputation as a result of its marketing mishap, it implemented a remodelling programme and marketing campaign to correct the situation. This strategy was successful, and soon, the company's double-digit sales growth rates resumed. Buick is now selling well over half a million vehicles per year in China, which is about three times as much as it sells in the US. Hence, in spite of temporarily diluting its brand, Buick's luxury cars have not lost their attractiveness to China's increasingly savvy consumers.[6]

Naturally, demand-oriented pricing is feasible only if we manage to correctly assess the product demand at particular prices. To better understand the nature of demand, we now look at customers' price sensitivity or the 'price elasticity of demand' and other types of demand elasticity.

12.7.1 *Price elasticity of demand*

Let's assume you run your own business and, facing increased competition, have just decided to lower prices. Sales will typically increase, but what effect will the change in demand have on total revenue? Will total revenue increase, stay the same or – due to the lower price – decrease? This question can be answered only if we know the slope, or elasticity, of the product's demand curve, allowing us to predict how much change in customer buying we can expect at each price along the demand curve. Price elasticity of demand measures the degree to which customers are sensitive to changes in price. It is formally defined as the percentage change in quantity demanded relative to a given percentage change in price. In a sense, the word elasticity indicates that changes in price usually cause demand to stretch or retract like a rubber band. If reducing the price of a product results in sales of enough additional units to increase total revenue for that product, then the demand for that product is said to be price elastic.

Price elastic demand curve

Graph A in Figure 12.12 shows a price elastic demand curve. When the selling price of the product is lowered from €10 to €5, total revenue increases from €50 (€10 × 5 units) to €125 (€5 × 25 units). Despite a price reduction, the company increased total revenue because the percentage increase in quantity demanded was greater than the percentage decrease in price. The market for this product appears to be very price sensitive; in other words, there is a price elastic demand. Conversely, assuming the same price elasticity of demand, if the company increased the price of the product from €5 to €10, total revenue would decline. Thus, as a businessperson you would, generally speaking, not be in favour of such a price increase. Elastic demand prevails in the automobile and home furnishings industries, and has contributed to the success of companies such as *Hyundai* and *Ikea*.

FIGURE 12.12 Three types of price elasticity of demand

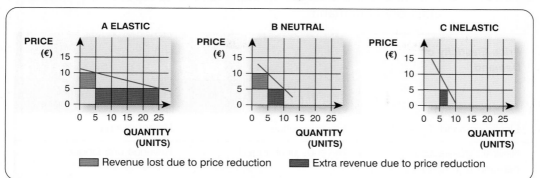

If the demand curve in the graph is completely horizontal, the product is said to have *perfectly* or *totally elastic demand*. The individual firm then has no control over prices. The market price and the demand curve for the company coincide. As we will see later, this is typical for *pure competition*, such as in the agricultural market.

The demand curve for a product is characterized by unitary elasticity when a change in price has no effect on total revenue. Looking at the unitary elastic demand curve in Figure 12.12B, we see that total product revenue at a selling price of €10 per unit is equal to total revenue at €5 per unit. In other words, the percentage decline in price was offset exactly by the percentage increase in the number of units sold. By cutting the price in half, sales (in units) will double, but the firm gains nothing in terms of revenue.

Price inelastic demand curve

When a price change has little or no effect on the quantity that consumers are willing to buy, we have a case of price inelastic demand. A price reduction will then result in a decrease in revenue. An inelastic demand curve is shown in Figure 12.12C. When the price is reduced from €10 to €5, the number of units sold increases from five to only seven. Therefore, the percentage reduction in price was not offset by a corresponding increase in the quantity demanded.

Similarly, under inelastic demand conditions, a price increase generates greater total revenue, since the reduction in the number of units sold is more than compensated for by the higher price received for each unit sold. In the short run, the demand for necessities – such as gasoline, electricity and even cigarettes – is inelastic because consumers have strong needs for them and cannot significantly cut back on buying these products when prices rise. This is one reason that the government heavily taxes some of these items. In fact, customers are less sensitive to the price of any product or service they see as a necessity. To illustrate, research in the hotel industry has shown that demand for hotel rooms is inelastic, regardless of whether they are in luxury or budget hotels.

Measuring price elasticity

The likely effects of price fluctuations on sales revenues – depending on the degree of price elasticity – are summarized in Table 12.6.

The left-hand column shows the degree of price elasticity of demand. Bear in mind that price elasticity of demand is a ratio representing the percentage change in the quantity of a product or service demanded as a result of a price change of 1 per cent.

TABLE 12.6 Effects of price changes on sales revenues depending on price elasticity of demand

Price Elasticity of Demand	Price Change	
	Price increase	Price cut
Elastic demand ($E_p < -1$)	Lower revenue	Higher revenue
Neutral ('iso-elastic') demand ($E_p = -1$)	Revenue unchanged	Revenue unchanged
Inelastic demand ($0 < E_p < -1$)	Higher revenue	Lower revenue

Price elasticity of demand (Ep) over the range of a demand curve can be measured by using the following formula:

$$E_p = \frac{\% \text{ change in quantity demanded } (q)}{\% \text{ change in price } (p)} = \frac{\frac{\Delta q}{q}}{\frac{\Delta p}{p}}$$

Because the two variables (price and quantity demanded) generally change in opposite directions, price elasticity of demand – expressed as the price elasticity coefficient – is usually a negative number: price cuts lead to a greater demand, and price increases to a smaller demand. However, for simplicity reasons and by convention, elasticity numbers are sometimes shown as positive numbers. Regardless, depending on the results of the computation, price elasticity of demand may assume three forms: elastic, inelastic and, between these two, unitary demand.

When price elasticity is equal to –1, demand is *unitary*. This means that the percentage change in price is identical to the percentage change in quantity demanded so that sales revenue remains static. The minus sign verifies the inverse relationship between price and demand. A price elasticity that is less than –1 (such as –3) indicates an *elastic* demand. For example, a 2 per cent decrease in price that results in a 6 per cent increase in demand (thereby actually increasing sales revenue), yields a price elasticity of – 3. This indicates a price sensitive product. Finally, a price change that leads to a relatively small change in demand indicates an *inelastic* demand, with a price elasticity coefficient of between 0 and –1.

To illustrate, assume that the selling price of a product is lowered from €5 to €4.75. As a result, sales increase from 100 000 to 104 000 units. The price elasticity of demand is:

$$E_p = \frac{\frac{4\,000}{100\,000} \times 100}{\frac{-0.25}{5.00} \times 100} = \frac{4\%}{-5\%} = -0.8$$

Because the price elasticity is between 0 and –1, demand is inelastic. With an elasticity coefficient of –0.8, if price is lowered by 5 per cent, demand will increase by 4 per cent (0.8×5). Thus total revenue will fall.

Influences on the price elasticity of demand

Because revenues depend on price and demand, we must anticipate how customers are likely to react to price changes. Several factors affect a product's sensitivity to price. The first one is the availability of substitutes. A product's demand curve becomes more elastic if substitutes are easily obtained – that is, when a product or service faces more competition. A Kingston flash memory stick, for example, has many substitutes and is more price elastic than a prestigious product or unique service, such as a Ferrari or a liver transplant. Because today's buyers can easily find and assess comparable product alternatives by shopping online, the elasticity of a product's demand is greatly increased.

The effect of a price increase on *primary demand* (for the entire product category, such as laundry detergent) will differ from the effect on *selective demand* (for a specific brand, such as Dreft). Primary demand is generally inelastic, while selective demand is elastic. Hence, while the total market for laundry soap may be inappreciably affected by a general price increase, consumers – even though they may feel some loyalty for a particular brand – will probably switch to a competing brand if the price of their favourite brand increases more than other brands. Only unique products in the market can feasibly be priced higher.

The second factor underlying the price elasticity of demand is the price of a product relative to the consumer's purchasing power. Big-ticket items, especially those requiring a high percentage of a buyer's disposable income or budget (such as cars) are more price sensitive than inexpensive ones, such as salt or chewing gum. A limited number of food products for which consumers know the prices, such as milk and coffee are the exception. Since consumers use these to compare prices at supermarkets, these items are price elastic and, therefore, price sensitive. Demand for big-ticket items is also elastic because these are typically durable products that consumers have the option of repairing instead of replacing, thus extending the product's useful life.

A variety of additional factors may affect price elasticity of demand. For instance, buyers are less sensitive to price when they're facing only a minor price change – below a threshold level – or when part of the cost is shared with another party. Another factor determining price elasticity is consumers' time perspective. Price sensitivity tends to be less in the short run than in the long run if it takes consumers a while to adapt their behaviour (for example, to use less energy), to explore other possibilities or find a new, less expensive supplier.

Image Asset Management

Finally, price elasticity varies by market segment because not all consumers are equally price-conscious. Buyers can be divided into segments such as price shoppers, convenience shoppers, status seekers and brand-loyal customers. Since price elasticity is important for marketers because of its relationship to total revenue, they should measure price sensitivity for various targeted segments and under different marketing conditions.

Evaluation of price elasticity

Price elasticity of demand is difficult to determine, since it typically varies throughout the range of feasible prices for a product or service. Therefore, we must always specify the relevant price range or proposed price increase when describing the elasticity of demand for a particular item. In practice, elasticity is not easily measured; this is not because the mathematics of elasticity are obscure but because of the difficulty of estimating the shape of the demand curve for most products. Only large corporations systematically gather the necessary information about demand and prices to gain insight into the slope of the demand curve.

Although many marketers rely on *managerial judgment*, intuition and experience in isolating the effect of price on demand, others use analytical models and statistical techniques to predict how a product's price level influences demand. For instance, some use regression analysis to establish the relationship between sales and price over time. Other research methods used to measure the demand curve are *customer surveys* in which the buyer's intention to purchase at various prices is measured, and *test marketing* or laboratory experiments in which prices are varied to determine how price changes affect sales. Although each of these approaches may prove useful in a particular situation, none provides an error-free solution.

Even with the problems of estimation, elasticity is still one of the most important and useful concepts that economics has given marketers. We do not need to know the exact numerical price elasticity of demand in order to incorporate this concept into the planning process. While there may be some error in assessment, getting consensus estimates from several managers familiar with the market can provide a better understanding of the demand curve. If the demand for the product is elastic, every effort should be made to ensure that the final price is competitive. On the other hand, if demand is inelastic – knowing it is probably impossible to maximize product revenue simply by increasing its price – we should try to compete on the basis of *non-price factors*, such as an attractive company website, superior customer service and a unique brand image or other marketing tools that add value for customers.

12.7.2 Income elasticity of demand

Another significant influence on product demand is the buyer's income. Consumers' disposable income (personal income less taxes paid) and particularly their discretionary income – the money in the hands of consumers after they pay taxes and buy necessities – has a great impact on luxury purchases. Just as the price elasticity of demand indicates how responsive demand is to a change in price, income elasticity of demand (also called *income sensitivity of demand*) demonstrates the relationship between an increase in consumers' disposable income and the corresponding change in consumption. The formula for income elasticity is:

$$E_y = \frac{\%\ \text{change in quantity demand}}{\%\ \text{change in disposable income}}$$

This formula is subject to Engel's Law, named after Ernst Engel, who researched how consumers changed their spending habits as their incomes increased. His studies have been supported by later research. Engel found that as family income rises, the percentage of income spent on:

→ Primary needs (food, utilities such as electricity and other necessities) declines.

→ Housing and household items remains relatively constant.

→ Most other categories (such as clothing, transportation, health care, recreation and savings) increases.

Engel's Law is graphically represented in Figure 12.13, which shows the relationship between income (Y) and expenditures (price × quantity demanded) for specific products or product categories.

Product 1 satisfies a primary need. The so-called *Engel curve* shows that at a higher family income, the increase in expenditure on the product abates. At an income level of €60 000 the saturation point has been reached. Since the expenditure on this particular product even decreases as income continues to rise, analysts sometimes refer to this type of product as an **inferior product** (a term which, incidentally, has nothing to do with the quality of the product).

How do we compute the income elasticity of demand? Focusing on the steep part of the curve between parts A and B for Product 2, the income elasticity of demand is:

$$E_y = \frac{\Delta q(\%)}{\Delta y\ (\%)} = \frac{\frac{5-3}{3} \times 100\%}{\frac{37-30}{30} \times 100\%} = \frac{66.6\%}{23.3\%} = +2.8$$

Since any outcome greater than 1 indicates an income sensitive product, there is clearly a high degree of income elasticity in this section of the demand curve for Product 2. However, between points B and C the curve is income inelastic, as the following computation shows.

$$E_y = \frac{\frac{6.5-5}{5} \times 100\%}{\frac{55-37}{37} \times 100\%} = \frac{30}{48.6} = +0.62$$

FIGURE 12.13 The Engel curve

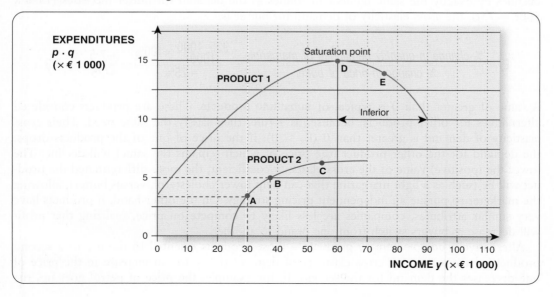

The demand curve for Product 1 shows a negative income elasticity of demand between points D and E.

$$E_y = \frac{\frac{13.5-14.5}{14.5} \times 100\%}{\frac{75-60}{60} \times 100\%} = \frac{-69}{25} = -0.28$$

By definition, *inferior products* have a *negative* income elasticity ($E_y < 0$). Research on income changes shows there are two additional product categories. The first one is referred to as **essential products**. As a percentage, consumer spending on these products (that usually satisfy *primary needs*) generally increases at a slower rate than the consumer's income. The income elasticity of demand for these products is therefore positive with a value of between 0 and 1 ($0 < E_y < 1$). The second category involves so-called **luxury products**, such as advanced digital cameras and other durable consumer goods. Since the proportion of income spent on these luxury products increases as consumer income rises, they are characterized by a high income elasticity of demand ($E_y > 1$).

12.7.3 *Cross elasticity of demand*

Demand for a particular item may also be affected by changes in the price of another product. This phenomenon is called **cross elasticity of demand**. The formula for cross elasticity of demand is:

$$E_x = \frac{\% \text{ change in quantity demanded of Product A}}{\% \text{ change in price of Product B}}$$

When products are part of a line of similar products (such as various brands of detergents) and are close *substitutes* for each other, a rise in the price of one will increase the demand for the other. Or, conversely, a decrease in the price of one product will increase the demand for it and simultaneously decrease the demand for the other product.

To illustrate, suppose a particular group of people consumes 500 tonnes of butter and 1000 tonnes of margarine. If the price of butter were to be lowered by 25 per cent, its consumption would increase by 15 per cent. If we assume that the demand for margarine declines by exactly the same number of tonnes as the demand for butter increases (15% x 500t = 75t), the cross elasticity of demand for butter is:

$$E_x = \frac{\% \text{ change in quantity demanded of margarine}}{\% \text{ change in price of butter}} = \frac{\frac{925-1000}{1000} \times 100\%}{-25\%} = \frac{-7.5}{-25} = +0.3$$

A value of greater than 0 is typical of **substitute products**. These are products considered alternatives for other products, because, as a rule, they satisfy the same need. Their cross elasticity of demand is greater than 0 ($E_x > 0$): if the price of one of the products drops, the demand for the other product (the price of which remains the same) will decline. The lower the (positive) value of the cross elasticity coefficient, the more differentiated the product will be (such as a light margarine that can help lower cholesterol, versus butter), allowing the marketer to pursue an independent pricing strategy. On the other hand, if products have very similar attributes, companies are less likely to compete on price, realizing that profit will decrease as buyers switch from one brand to another.

Alternatively, **complementary products** – those products essential to the use of a second product – have a negative cross elasticity of demand ($E_x < 0$): an increase in the price of one decreases the demand for the second. If, for example, the price of petrol goes up, the demand for SUVs will eventually decrease. Finally, products for which a price change of one does not affect the demand for the other have a neutral relationship and are called **indifferent goods**. They have a cross elasticity of demand of 0 ($E_x = 0$).

With the concept of elasticity of demand in mind, let us first turn to *price lining* and then to two other types of demand-oriented pricing: price differentiation and psychological pricing.

12.7.4 *Price lining*

As emphasized in the discussion of the product portfolio in Chapter 7, an effective pricing strategy must consider the relationships among all of the products and services a company offers. After all, most customers compare the products available in terms of price and quality. Therefore, price lining is a useful strategy, particularly in retailing. **Price lining** is the practice of offering a product line with several items at a limited number of prices, called *price points*. This requires market-driven decisions on the lowest- and the highest-priced product in the merchandise line and on the price differentials for all other products in the line. A well-balanced price range allows customers to narrow the decision-making process, by first deciding on how much to spend for a product and then by selecting only from those products offered at that particular price point.

Sometimes, manufacturers develop products for different price points. In other instances, the price of an item may bear little relationship to its cost. All of the products may have been purchased at the same cost and then, depending on the item's style, colour and anticipated demand, marked up at different percentages to arrive at specific price points. The company is primarily interested in covering the total cost of the entire product line, making a reasonable profit and competing successfully with other sellers.

The buyers' perceptions of the entire merchandise line, however, are the marketer's main concern in price lining, and these are greatly affected by the lowest- and highest-priced items in the line. A bottom price that is set too low may cheapen the entire line's image, whereas too high a price at the top may cause consumers to consider the line as being priced above the mass market. Yet, the various price points must be spaced far enough apart for consumers to note differences among product versions. Also, the **price gaps** must be associated with the perceived differences in the value of the products or services offered. Otherwise, customers might view the price floor as the 'right' price and assume there are no quality differences among models. If well chosen, the price points help the marketer to define important product features that differentiate the products and assist the consumer in deciding whether to spend more or less within the range of acceptable prices. If the price difference between two successive quality levels is small enough, some customers may be inclined to buy the more expensive item. This increases the firm's profits, provided that the difference in costs is smaller than the price difference.

To clarify the principle of price lining, assume that a retail chain is offering five brands of digital cameras with a product mix of 13 different models. Rather than setting 13 different prices – an inefficient and non-transparent pricing policy – the marketer establishes, based on market research, an acceptable price range for this product line (that is, a price floor and ceiling) and a third distinct price point in between these two. As the graph in Figure 12.14 illustrates, they choose price points of €79, €119 and €199.

One assumption underlying price lining is that demand is elastic at each of the selected price points but inelastic between these price points. In practice, as long as the selected prices are attractive, customers will not react to small price changes. In the example above, the retailer believes that the prices of €199, €119 and €79 are the most suitable prices for the digital cameras and that a reduction to, for example, €145, €109 and €75 will not result in increased purchases. However, the consumer does react to the price gap between €129 and €119. The demand curve is very elastic between these two price points.

FIGURE 12.14 Price lining for an assortment of digital cameras

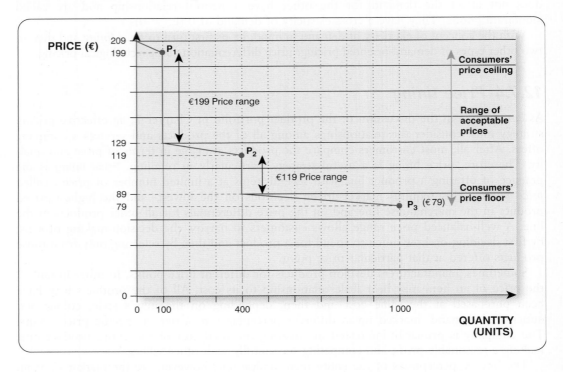

Taking a look at Figure 12.14 again, the graph indicates that at a price of €79, a total of 1 000 cameras would be sold. The consumer perceives a price level of €89 as being considerably higher. Between €89 and €119, consumer demand remains constant at 400 units, because buyers do not perceive any real differences in this price range. To maximize sales revenue, the retailer would be advised to set the price point P2 at €119. At the prices selected, the firm will sell 100 cameras at €199, 300 at €119 and 600 at €79. Total revenue is higher than if they were to offer the digital cameras only at €79, even though they would still sell 1 000 of them.

Generally, as we move up the product line, the price differentials should get larger, because here consumer demand becomes more inelastic. Another rule of thumb in price lining is that as costs rise, the ratio between the price points must remain approximately the same, in order to maintain the existing relative price differences. With a cost increase of 25 per cent, for example, the new selling prices, if possible, would have to be around €99, €149 and €249.

Price lining is a strategy certainly worth considering, since it has benefits for both prospective buyers and sellers. Consumers are less confused if offered a variety of merchandise at each established price allowing comparisons between different quality options available within a certain price range. For sellers, price lining is a proven strategy to maximize profits. Since they cannot charge each individual customer the maximum price they are willing to pay, a practical alternative is to set a limited number of price points that are close to the top of the range of prices deemed acceptable by the buyer. Sellers can also appeal to several market segments and trade up buyers within the established price range. Finally, price lining allows sellers to simplify purchasing, maintain a smaller inventory, discourage the entry of new competitors in the distribution channel and increase overall sales.

12.7.5 *Price differentiation*

A company may offer a lower price to some customers than it does to others. Although the physical product may be the same, the price adjustment is justified and reflects cost differences in customer type, location, time of delivery or some product features. This type of diverse, demand-oriented pricing is called price differentiation. It is also known as *differential* or *differentiated pricing*. It involves the sale of a product or service at different prices that do not reflect a proportional difference in costs. Price differentiation is sometimes referred to as *price discrimination*, although conceptually, there is a distinction between the two terms.

Price discrimination is defined as the practice of charging different buyers different prices for the exact same quality and quantity of goods. Contrary to price differentiation, where transactions may involve different products, price discrimination involves the sale of commodities 'of like grade and quality' at different prices. Because price discrimination is illegal in many countries and under various circumstances, it can become a complicated legal issue, especially for international marketers. In the US market, for example, it is illegal for suppliers to offer different retailers different prices without economic justification, particularly if this would lessen or hurt competition. But this type of price discrimination is not illegal when the buyers are consumers (who do not compete with each other), or when the sale on the business market involves services, rather than products. For the most part, only price differences that substantially lessen competition on the market or create a monopoly are considered unlawful. Although discounting in general enhances a company's sales, obvious price discrimination could result in negative reactions from customers.

In most countries price discrimination within a distribution channel is allowed if the price differences are justified by costs (with economies of scale justifying a quantity discount), and if non-competing buyers are involved, with no apparent harm to competition. Price differentials to different customers are also legal if matching a competitor's lower prices or meeting other changing market conditions (such as the obsolescence of seasonal products or rising energy costs) and, of course, if the goods are physically different. Finally, special discounts are permissible if they are made available to all competing resellers, large and small, on a proportionate basis. Under these conditions, the pricing strategy is referred to as segmented or differentiated pricing.

A differentiated pricing strategy is not for every company, even if it doesn't stray into the area of illegal price discrimination. But it may be a lucrative option when the market consists of several distinct market segments with different elasticities of demand. A company can then sell the product at a high price in target markets characterized by inelastic demand and at a lower price in markets characterized by elastic demand, as long as those buyers are not able to resell their

Offering slightly different products (such as a 'limited edition' collection and a regular product line) at substantially different prices is a form of price differentiation

Image Asset Management

purchases to buyers in the higher-priced segment. Successfully catering to separate segments will also prevent *cannibalization*, which would occur when a new, lower priced product 'steals' some of the sales of the established product.

Price differentiation can take several forms and is usually based on one of the following factors: customer-type, product-form, location or timing.

Customer-type pricing

Some people are simply better than others at negotiating price. This alone can make a big difference in how much they pay for a product or service. Also, different prices may be charged to different segments or groups of customers. Children, students and older adults, for example, usually pay less for event, museum and theatre tickets and for public transportation.

Product-form pricing

Price differentiation is product-based when the firm sells two slightly different products at substantially different prices. Typically, the price difference is not justifiable on the basis of cost. Consider the prices of the 1.7oz. and 3.4oz. bottles of Chanel No. 5 fragrance, where the price difference between the two bottles (€60 and €87) is disproportionate to their respective costs.

Location-based pricing

A firm may charge different prices for different locations, even though the cost of offering each location is the same. Theatre tickets are an excellent illustration: a seat close to the stage is priced higher than a seat at the back of the theatre, despite the fact that installation and maintenance costs are the same for all seats. Bottles of wine priced differently, depending on whether they are purchased in a liquor store or a restaurant, are another example.

Time pricing

Price differentiation based on time is feasible if demand for a product varies over the business cycle – by the season, by the day or even the time of day. Christmas decorations sold at a premium in December are marked down heavily during January, just as unsold ski clothing is usually available at greatly reduced prices in spring. Hotels that fill their rooms with business clients on weekdays charge less on weekends to maintain full occupancy, and some phone companies offer lower rates in the evenings than during the day.

Price differentiation or differentiated pricing goes by many names. It is sometimes called *revenue management* or *yield management*. By constantly adjusting the prices and number of seats allocated to different fares airlines apply this system to maximize revenues. Analysts predict a substantial expansion in differentiated pricing practices as the field of electronic data processing rapidly advances. Corporate websites, or commerce servers, recognize customers and may charge them based on their purchasing history. The 'clickstream' navigated by a customer can be used to classify that individual as price sensitive and direct the potential buyer to 'specials' or lower prices being offered on the site. Thus, as yield management becomes more sophisticated, developing effective pricing options is also becoming more complex and a greater challenge for marketers.

12.7.6 Psychological pricing

Not all consumers perceive and react to price in the same way. People's tastes and preferences will forever differ. Similarly, what is an everyday purchase for one person may bring about a more prestigious life style for another along with the means to make a public statement about their lifestyle choices. Companies using psychological pricing consider non-economic or psychological factors in price determination and try to influence a customer's perception of a product's price to make it more attractive. Two common applications of psychological pricing are prestige pricing and odd pricing.

Prestige pricing

Some products are primarily purchased for status reasons. *Status products* are only appealing to prestige buyers if they remain beyond the reach of the general public. Therefore, companies using prestige pricing set prices at an artificially high level to convey prestige or a quality image, hoping that the prestige price will attract quality- or status-conscious buyers. This tends to work best when consumers cannot easily evaluate the quality differences between available products and will therefore associate a higher price with higher quality. For prestige pricing to be effective, the product also has to be visible to others who judge the individual by it, or at least have an opinion about the purchase. Product categories in which selected products are typically prestige priced include fragrances, jewellery, liquor and automobiles. Even some appliances such as Viking gas ranges, Sub-Zero refrigerators and Dyson vacuum cleaners are prestige priced.

As discussed in section 12.2.2, the typical demand curve is downward sloping, meaning that a price reduction is generally accompanied by an increase in demand. By contrast, the demand curve associated with prestige pricing is *backward bending* or 'contrary'. This is known as a *backward-bending* or contrary demand curve.

As the example in Figure 12.15 illustrates, up to a selling price of €5, price increases initially result in more purchases. Above that price, however, product demand slackens and the curve bends backward, indicating a decline in sales. An example of a product that may sell worse at lower prices than at higher ones is wine bought in supermarkets. It is a product with large quality differences impossible to assess in the store without the price tag or the label. Wine buyers will often associate a low price with low quality, and would rather shop in a liquor store with a larger product assortment, if they intend to spend more

MARQUE THE OCCASION.

To celebrate the forthcoming wedding of HRH Prince William of Wales and Miss Catherine Middleton, a very special Royal Edition of the BMW M3 Coupé will be available at BMW Dealerships throughout the country from today, and for this month only. The majestic Royal Edition is available in three colours – Regal Red, Bridal White and Imperial Blue. It is resplendently upholstered in Windsor White Dakota leather and adorned with our commemorative 'Will' emblem. For more information, call 0800 777 120 or contact pauline.yorlegg@bmw.co.uk

THE NEW BMW M3 ROYAL EDITION.

BMW M.

Official fuel economy figures for the BMW M3 Coupé: Urban 16.0 – 17.8 mpg (17.7 – 15.9 l/100 km). Extra Urban 30.4 – 33.2 mpg (9.3 – 8.5 l/100 km). Combined 22.8 – 25.2 mpg (12.4 – 11.2 l/100 km). CO₂ emissions 290 – 263 g/km.

FIGURE 12.15 Contrary demand curve associated with prestige pricing

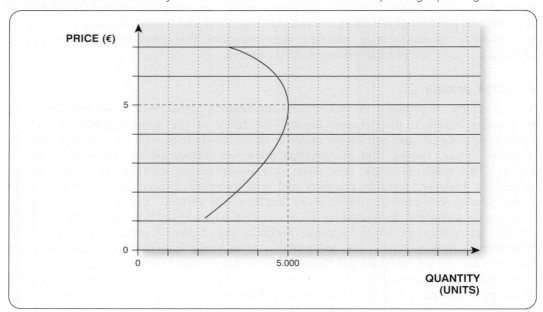

than €5 per bottle. Especially if consumers are not familiar with the product and consider the purchase important (for instance as a gift item), they want to limit the purchasing risk and tend to view price as a *quality indicator*.

Odd pricing

Using odd pricing, often called odd-even pricing, companies set prices at odd numbers just below round numbers. Why? Marketers assume that there is a different psychological response to odd prices like €1.99, €19.95 and €499 than to even prices. Consumers may get the impression that the company carefully considers its prices and sets them as low as possible. They may also think that odd prices represent discounts, perceiving a price of €38.95 as a price reduction from €40. The precision associated with the price implies a bargain.

Even very small price differences can have a huge impact. For instance, think about the price of €199.95 for a new model cell phone. While the actual price is only 5 cents less than €200, many consumers will view the price in the €100 to €200 range instead of in the €200 plus range. Odd prices may also help shoppers stay within budget and still purchase the best product available within their price limits.

A consumer willing to spend no more than €60 for a shirt will be interested in a €59.95 shirt and, because it is within the intended price range, may be as eager to purchase it as a €52 shirt. Thus, in odd pricing, the psychological difference is usually much greater than the absolute price difference between the odd price and the round number.

Figure 12.16 shows the demand curve for a product being offered for an odd price and a rounded amount. If the firm were to charge the odd price of €1.95 – just under the price threshold – it could expect to sell 140 units. If, however, the firm raised its price to the even amount of €2.00, it would sell only 90 units.

Between the two price points of €1.95 and €2, the demand curve is very *elastic*. What is also striking in this example is that raising the price from €2.00 to €2.95 would result in

FIGURE 12.16 Demand curve under odd-even pricing

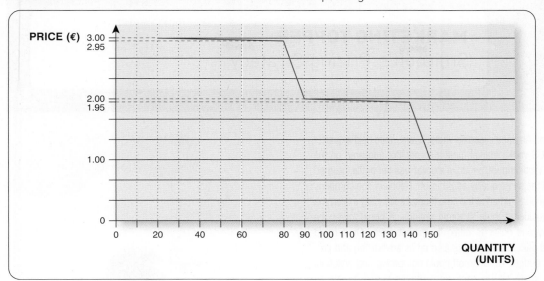

lost sales of only ten units. The demand curve is very *inelastic* between the even and the much higher odd price; consumers are almost as willing to pay €2.95 as €2 for the product!

Although research shows that consumers are more likely to make a purchase if a price ends in 9, there are some times when even prices are the standard in effective marketing. Marketers often use even prices to give a service or product an upscale or exclusive image, knowing that these even prices may influence a consumer to view the product as a premium brand. Therefore, even prices are sometimes essential in pricing a product or service. If a physician were to charge €59.99 for a consult, the consumer might think the medical care was substandard.

12.8 COMPETITION-ORIENTED PRICING

Of all marketing decisions, those related to price are most likely to prompt an immediate reaction from competitors. Price is the most easily matched competitive marketing variable, and many firms closely monitor rivals' prices, especially in mature markets where demand is inelastic. Therefore, most marketers depend on *non-price competition*, such as better product design and advertising. By shifting the demand curve to the right, they hope to sell more product at any given price. In reality, however, competitive forces in many industries are so strong that marketers are not able to set their own prices. When a company uses its major competitors' prices rather than cost or demand considerations as its principal basis for price setting, it follows a strategy of **competition-oriented pricing**.

A company pursuing a competition-based pricing strategy does not readily respond to changes in costs or demand unless such changes also affect competitors' prices. Firms can, in fact, avoid competing on price altogether by meeting the market price – the industry's average price level for similar products – or might utilize the market price as a reference point for their own pricing. This form of competition-oriented pricing, which reflects the tendency of companies to price at or near industry averages, is called **going-rate pricing**. The firm may charge the same as competitors ('at the market'), more than competitors ('above the market') or less ('below the market').

MARKETING TOPPER
Smirnoff's Pricing Strategy

Smirnoff, America's leading vodka brand, once held a quarter of the US vodka market, until a competitor appeared on the scene. Wolfschmidt, priced at a dollar less per bottle, claimed to have the same quality as Smirnoff. Heublein, the company that owned Smirnoff at the time found itself facing a dilemma and considered three strategic options. It could *lower* the price by one dollar to retain its market share. Or, it could keep its price the *same*, but step up its advertising and promotion budget. Or, Smirnoff could do *nothing* and watch its market share fall. In each case, profits would tumble as Smirnoff seemed to face a no-win situation.

© Santanor / Shutterstock

Through its price increase and positioning, Smirnoff became the elite brand

The marketers at Smirnoff thought of a fourth – now classic – strategy. The company *raised* the price of Smirnoff by a dollar! It then launched a new brand, *Relska*, to compete with Wolfschmidt. Finally, a third brand, *Popov*, was introduced, at a price even lower than Wolfschmidt. Through this positioning strategy, Smirnoff became the elite brand and Wolfschmidt an ordinary brand. Heublein saw its profits greatly increase as a result of effectively marketing three brands that were more or less the same in both taste and production costs, but differed dramatically in branding concepts and perceived quality. This is but one classic example of how price – as an indicator of perceived quality – can play a predominant role in a company's marketing strategy.[7]

Some companies, when products in their industry are homogeneous, deliberately price 'at market' through a strategy of **me-too pricing**. In services marketing, this is typical for online travel services such as Expedia and CheapTickets, as well as for airlines that often charge comparable fares on the same routes. Cosmetics companies, such as Revlon, also tend to price their products at market, thereby providing a reference price for competitors that choose a strategy of above- or below-market pricing. A watch manufacturer like Rolex, following a premium pricing strategy, proudly emphasizes that it makes one of the most expensive watches available on the market. Manufacturers of prestigious global clothing brands such as Prada and Dolce & Gabbana, also deliberately set premium prices for their products. Whether or not they can successfully do so depends on customer loyalty, brand image and other marketing mix variables that affect their competitive positioning in the market.

Conversely, if companies with more efficient organizations, superior production technology or greater economies of scale use below-market pricing, they follow a **discount pricing** strategy. Discount retailers such as Aldi and Wal-Mart successfully appeal to price-conscious consumers by setting prices considerably below those of other chain stores. Below-market pricing also exists in business-to-business marketing and has, for example, greatly contributed to the success of Texas-based Dell. Below-market pricing is not without risks, though, as it may force other firms to lower prices in order to sell enough merchandise to survive. As more firms match the reduced prices, it may affect the entire industry. If the lower prices do not attract new buyers and expand the market enough to compensate for the loss of per-unit revenue, the price cuts will leave all competitors in the industry with less revenue.

Despite the pitfalls of competition-oriented pricing, it is a common strategy because it is simple and requires no detailed cost per unit data, insight into demand curves or measurement of demand elasticity. Managers assume that the market price represents the collective wisdom of all companies in the industry in determining a price fair to buyers that also yields a reasonable return to sellers.

Additionally, pricing at the market level does not disrupt competition or lead to aggressive retaliations, particularly if companies matching each other's prices emphasize marketing tools other than price to develop areas of distinctive competence and attract buyers with a successful *differentiation* strategy.

As with demand-oriented pricing, companies using competition-oriented pricing pursue a **backward pricing** strategy. Taking into consideration the country's Value Added Tax (VAT) and retailer and wholesaler mark-ups, the manufacturer must work backward from the proper retail selling price to determine its own ex-factory price. As is apparent from the following example, the manufacturer's selling price is considerably lower than the price consumers are charged:

Unipak, an importer of a Korean brand of LCD TVset with a built-in hard-disk DVDrecorder, wants its most popular model to sell in retail stores for €25 less than a model offered by its main competitor, which sells for €499. Thus, Unipak is shooting for a retail price of €474 (including 21 per cent VAT). Taking into account a retail margin of 40 per cent and a wholesale margin of 20 per cent, the company – utilizing competition-oriented pricing – can now determine its own selling price by working backward from the target retail price.

→ The selling price of the retailer, excluding 21 per cent VAT, is 100/121 x €474 = €392.

→ The retailer's margin amounts to 40 per cent of €392 = €157.

→ The price to the retailer is therefore €392 – €157 = €235. This amount is also the wholesaler's selling price.

→ With a 20 per cent wholesale margin of €235 the price to the wholesaler is €235 – €47 = €188. This amount is also the importer's selling price. If the importer wants to make a profit, they must keep their own cost below €188.

If the appropriate retailer and wholesaler mark-ups are stated as a percentage of cost, rather than as a percentage of the selling price, the calculation is similar. The retailer's selling price of €474 (€392 excluding VAT) is then 140 per cent, or 140/100 x their purchase price. The price to the retailer is 100/140 x €392 = €280. This amount equals the wholesaler's selling price, which is 120 per cent of the wholesaler's cost. The ideal selling price for the importer, using the backward pricing approach, turns out to be 100/120 x €280 = €233.

12.8.1 Competition and market structures

Competitors (whether from the same industry or not) tend to have a great impact on the firm's marketing strategy and the rewards the company reaps from it. As pointed out in Chapter 3, competition is not just limited to other brands of the same type of product that consumers consider direct substitutes. Buyers have other options, too. In the continuous battle for market share we should put ourselves in the customer's shoes and consider the various forms of competition from their viewpoint. In addition to *brand competition* (for example, between JVC and Panasonic), a company may be facing *product competition*, i.e. between different types of products within the same product category, such as between a camcorder with a built-in 60 GB hard drive and a HD camcorder using MiniDV tapes. A company must also take into account *generic competition* against a completely different product line that is nonetheless able to satisfy the same consumer need. An example might be an early adopter's choice between an Xpress satellite radio with a car kit and a TomTom touch screen portable GPS that plays MP3s and audio books.

The extent to which a company can set its own prices also depends on the type of competitive market in which it operates. This, in turn, is predicated on the number of firms in the industry competing with each other to meet the demand. Economists generally identify three *market forms*:

→ A monopoly, with one seller.

→ An oligopoly, with few sellers.

→ A polypoly, with many sellers.

If we also take into account the distinction between heterogeneous and homogenous products, we can identify four market structures: monopoly, oligopoly and the two forms of polypoly: monopolistic competition (sometimes called 'heterogeneous polypoly') and pure competition ('homogeneous polypoly').

Comparing these types of markets – as in Table 12.7 – we note that the consumer's power increases and the seller's power declines as the market displays fewer features of a monopoly. It becomes apparent that the type of competition a company faces greatly influences the extent of price competition which, in turn, has major implications for the necessary level of product differentiation and the importance of promotion in stimulating demand, as well as for other marketing tasks. A manager must recognize the type of market structure in which they operate to be fully aware of the options for developing price and non-price strategies. We will now examine the four types of market structures, starting with a monopoly.

TABLE 12.7 Distinguishing features of the four market structures

Characteristics	Market Structures			
	Monopoly	Oligopoly (heterogeneous)	Monopolistic competition	Pure competition
Number of competitors	One seller	Few	Many	A very large number
Example	Natural gas company	Automotive industry	Most national brands	Agricultural products
Product type	Unique product (no substitutes)	Predominantly heterogeneous (highly differentiated in buyers' perception)	Product differentiation with numerous substitutes	Homogeneous
Promotion	Low level of importance	Essential element of marketing mix	Important	Not important
Relation with distribution channel	Producer may be able to dictate terms	Considerable influence	Some influence	Little or no influence
Extent of price competition	None: sole seller sets price	Some, although sellers try to avoid price competition	Competition over range of prices	Almost none: market sets price
Price elasticity of demand	Depending on need for product, elastic or inelastic	Kinked demand curve; inelastic below kink, elastic above	Depending on uniqueness of product, elastic or inelastic	Totally elastic
Competitive advantage	No direct competitors	Non-price elements of the marketing mix	Potentially each of the marketing mix instruments	None: products are identical
Ease of entry into industry by new firms	Regulated by government	Difficult	Somewhat difficult	Easy
Primary task of marketing	Increase demand for the product class	Differentiate the product in other areas than price	Differentiate product from competitors in any possible way	Garantee sufficient and timely delivery at the market price

Increasing power of consumers

Declining power of sellers →

12.8.2 *Monopoly*

In a pure **monopoly**, a single organization wholly provides a particular product or service in the regional or domestic market. This could be a firm with a *patent*, giving it exclusive rights to offer the product or, more often, a public utility such as local cable or water company. Typically, marketing is of minor concern in a monopolistic structure, since the company is government regulated and without direct competition. Hence, its managers do not have to consider any rivals when setting prices, although they may have to follow strict government imposed pricing guidelines. Microsoft, for instance, with its more than 80 per cent share of the PC operating system market, has been fined by the European Union for unfair pricing practices, which, in turn, forced management to reconsider its pricing strategies in the business-to-business market.

Left unregulated, a monopoly might not only communicate poorly with customers and provide little or no customer service, but, most importantly, can set high prices. The **supply curve** of such a monopoly will be identical to the (overall) demand curve, since the supply curve shows the number of products that could be sold at various prices. Because there is only one supplier, the organization can unilaterally determine whether to offer a limited number of the product at a high price or a larger number at a low price. Total revenue, of course, will vary for each price/quantity combination.

A regulated monopoly is forced at least to cap prices and offer reasonable customer service. It may even promote its mission as being in the public interest. Some former 'absolute' monopolies (such as telephone and power companies, as well as postal services) have become deregulated, stimulating price competition in those markets. Other monopolies face increased competition from firms offering product or service substitutes that meet the same customer needs. Thus, they must devote more resources to innovation and to ensuring consumer satisfaction. Needless to say, all of this is beneficial to the customer.

12.8.3 *Oligopoly*

Quite a few managers operate in an oligopolistic market, or **oligopoly**. This is a common in-dustry structure in which a few companies control the lion's share of the market. A quantita-tive measure used to determine the existence of an oligopoly is the *four-firm concentration ratio*: the market share of the four largest companies in the industry. An oligopoly is defined as a market with a four-firm concentration ratio higher than 40 per cent. Examples include capital-intensive industries such as the cell phone service providers, and the entertainment, steel and automobile industries. While no single seller controls any of these markets, each one is familiar with the strategy of its rivals and may respond as much to competitive pres-sures as to the needs of the marketplace. For firms marketing standardized products – com-modities such as cement, oil or fertiliser – an oligopoly results in inflexible prices, as none of the competitors can charge more than the prevailing price.

Depending on whether the products are standardized or differentiated, we make a distinction between two types of oligopolies. In a *pure* or **undifferentiated oligopoly**, which produces and markets commodities (such as aluminium), the preference of buyers – who see no differences between the products offered – will be driven by such considerations as price or the quality of customer service. If all competitors offer the same price and service, a firm can only gain a competitive advantage by reducing its costs. In such a market the competitors, who are more or less dependent on each other, are so easily swayed by price competition, that if one of them – as a *price leader* – is the first to announce price changes, the others in the industry tend to quickly follow. This market structure, however, is not widespread.

Since most companies are striving for a protected market segment by emphasizing differences in product quality, features, design, packaging or brand image (such as in marketing cars, jetliners and laptops), pure oligopolies commonly develop into differentiated oligopolies. If a company succeeds in attracting loyal customers who favour one of the product attributes perceived by consumers to be superior, this competitor is in a better position to develop an independent pricing strategy and even charge a premium price. To illustrate, companies marketing detergents, gasoline and even electricity have differentiated their products effectively to create a loyal customer base that prefers their brand, even if it is more expensive than comparable products. Nonetheless, the freedom to set prices in an oligopoly is, by definition, limited.

Kinked demand curve

The characteristic price rigidity of oligopolistic competition can be explained by the theory that the firm reacts one way when a competitor reduces prices and another way when a competitor raises prices. That is, oligopolistic firms tend to follow a price reduction, so as not to lose sales to the firm that initiated the reduction. On the other hand, they tend not to necessarily match a price increase because, by maintaining their current price, they may be able to pick up customers lost by the firm initiating the price increase. As a result, oligopolistic firms learn to administer their prices in a rigid manner; each firm knows that it is more profitable to agree tacitly on a common industry price than to modify price repeatedly.

This price inflexibility leads to what economists call a kinked demand curve, illustrated in Figure 12.17. How is this characteristic reflected in the demand and supply curves in oligopolistic markets? In an oligopolistic market, an individual company's demand curve has a 'kink' at the present market price, caused by the inflexibility of price. Economists refer to this as a kinked demand curve, or, from an individual supplier's perspective, a kinked supply curve. These curves are portrayed in Figure 12.17.

FIGURE 12.17 Kinked supply curve in an oligopolistic market structure

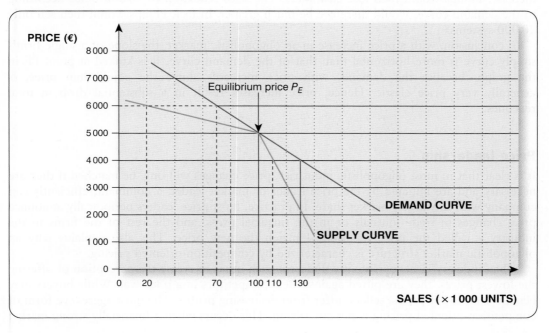

The difference between the overall market's demand curve and the individual company's kinked supply curve is that in the supply curve, the reactions of competitors to price changes are taken into account. Since a single competitor has a great impact on total industry sales, its rivals will likely match any competitor's price cut to prevent it from gaining additional sales.

Point PE in the graph is the long-term equilibrium price. The supply curve is kinked at this point because, for price increases above the equilibrium price, demand tends to be very elastic. That is, price increases result in declining product revenues, assuming, of course, that the company's rivals hold the line on prices.

Contrastingly, for prices lower than the equilibrium price, demand tends to be inelastic; price reductions do not increase revenues – and in fact, will probably reduce total industry revenues – because competitors also lower their prices. Thus, (pure) oligopolistic markets are characterized by a high degree of *price rigidity*: prices tend to remain – in a sense, inflexibly – at the equilibrium price or 'market price'. The following example will illustrate this.

Suppose that in the oligopolistic consumer hi-tech electronics market, Philips – as illustrated in the graph of Figure 12.17 – is currently selling 100 000 home theatres (a widescreen plasma TV and digital satellite receiver, including a Dolby Pro-Logic audio home entertainment system) at a price of €5 000. The demand curve shows that the company could sell 130 000 units by reducing its price to €4 000. Revenue would then increase by €20 000 000 to €520 000 000, while the company – due to a 30 per cent increase in sales – could achieve major economies of scale. However, its competitors would quickly follow such a price reduction of 20 per cent to prevent losing sales. Philips would therefore see its sales rise not to 130 000, but only to 110 000 units. As the curves in Figure 12.17 show, with a price reduction the slope of the supply curve is much steeper than that of the demand curve at a price below the market price (and is therefore more price inelastic).

If on the other hand, Philips were to increase its price (for example, to €6 000), its competitors would, most likely, either not react or would implement a smaller price increase. Philips would then lose customers. The sales reduction to 70 000 units, according to the demand curve, would therefore be much greater. In fact, Philips would then sell only 20 000 systems.

In conclusion, with a price increase in an oligopolistic market, the slope of a single firm's supply curve is more horizontal than that of the demand curve. It is kinked at point PE in the graph, because the demand, with price increases above the equilibrium price, is generally very price elastic. Hence, price increases result in a substantial drop in total revenues.

Price leadership

It is clear that in most oligopolistic industries, price changes will only be matched if they are necessary and are initiated by the price leader or market leader, a dominant, efficiently run company with the largest market share. In practice, most price leaders periodically announce price changes in trade journals or in the financial press, and the rest of the firms in the industry – called the price followers – match the new price. This also explains why an oligopolistic market structure is characterized by competition-oriented pricing.

When industry rivals persistently undercut each other to create the perception of offering the lowest prices, they are pitted against their competitors in a price war. While buyers may benefit from lower prices, sellers suffer from decreasing profits. The most aggressive form of competition-oriented pricing is put-out pricing. This occurs when a financially strong market leader drastically lowers its price to force smaller competitors with less financial stamina out of the market. The price may be so low that it does not even cover variable costs and therefore results in a loss. The strategy is financed by profits earned on other products or by other company divisions. Companies lacking profitable product ranges or financial reserves will not survive and often withdraw from the market before going bankrupt. Aggressive price wars – like those between airlines on selected routes – are therefore only temporary in nature.

A related strategy is **stay-out pricing**, in which the price is (temporarily) set so low that other suppliers do not even try to enter the market. The low price often barely covers the costs. Thus, the limited opportunities for making a profit will make the market unattractive to potential newcomers.

A price strategy intended to prevent new competitors from entering the market, is only feasible if the price leader also has the lowest production costs. Hence *Unilever* painstakingly streamlines its operations to improve efficiency and foster innovation. 'I'm convinced that if we allow our margarine production costs to go up, our US competitor Kraft will enter our market', explains the company's CEO. 'They have a huge market share in the United States right now, but not in Europe. Only by continuing to be the *least expensive* and most *innovative* competitor are we able to maintain our position of price leader. If we slacken either effort, we will be overtaken.'[8]

A *stay-out pricing* strategy is most effective in situations requiring a substantial capital investment upon entering the market; the low price level makes it difficult to get a satisfactory return on investment and therefore increases the barrier to entry. After the – usually temporary – threat of new rivals has subsided, the price leader (often the only supplier) can increase its price to a profitable level again without the imminent threat of new competition.

12.8.4 *Monopolistic competition*

The most common market form is **monopolistic competition**. Examples are national brands of food products as well as the apparel and shoe industries. Here, market entry is fairly easy, and firms generally compete with products that are similar, but not identical. Because sellers can differentiate their products by means other than price, many compete on non-price factors. To illustrate, the products may differ in terms of ingredients, quality, design, packaging or just advertising and distribution approaches. Marketers use these features to attempt to create their own 'monopoly' in the competitive fight; therefore, this market form is usually called monopolistic competition.

The marketer's greatest challenge is to successfully tailor the product to the buyers' preferences and to position it so that it appeals to a broad consumer base. The seller that succeeds in this, will have their own declining supply curve. It then has the choice of asking a higher price and selling less, or lowering the price and increasing sales. The greater the distinctiveness of the brand and the higher the brand loyalty, the more a company can charge for its product, relative to the competition. But the amount of the price premium cannot exceed the average price by much or the firm loses market share, as some fringe buyers switch to lower-priced substitutes.

Under monopolistic competition, a marketer has greater price setting flexibility than under oligopolistic competition. With the larger number of competitors, a price change by one affects each of the others only slightly. For instance, if one firm cuts the price, it may sell more, while each of its rivals loses very little business. Therefore, instant retaliation by competitors and price wars are less likely under monopolistic competition than in other competitive settings.

12.8.5 *Pure competition*

In a market characterized by pure competition, there are so many buyers and sellers that none of them is powerful enough to control or even significantly influence price. The forces of supply and demand determine the prevailing market price. Since all products are much alike, buyers have little or no preference for a particular supplier. Pure competition also assumes that all buyers are informed about all sellers' prices, and that there are no artificial restraints on prices, such as price fixing by the government, or price control by individual companies, trade associations or other concerns.

The markets that come closest to this market structure are stock and commodities exchanges and agricultural markets. For example, the Aalsmeer Flower Auction in the Netherlands sets the world price for flowers and plants by bringing supply and demand together by means of the auction clock – a process through which large and small batches of flowers are sold within fractions of seconds for a total of more than 20 million flowers per day. This type of market is *transparent* to both parties: both buyers and sellers can easily see what products are being offered and how differences in quality lead to different prices.

In a market with pure competition there is no reason for a supplier to charge less than its competitors, since its entire production volume can be sold at the (higher) market price. Also, a price cut may not be economically feasible, since pure competition tends to lead to low prices that just meet costs. A lower price than the current market price would lead to a loss, and if a firm *did* cut the price, competitors would immediately match it. Charging a price above the market price would not make sense either, since this would result in customers going to a competitor. Hence, a supplier can only increase its profit through production or distribution cost reductions.

As Figure 12.18 demonstrates, each individual supplier has a *horizontal supply curve*. This means that the market price for a supplier is given and that, theoretically, it could sell any quantity at that constant price. Even without having a marketing strategy in place, its sales volume is limited only by its own production capacity.

FIGURE 12.18 Horizontal supply curve in a market characterized by pure competition

It is clear that no company could compete either through price cutting or, for that matter, by offering a better product, because, theoretically, product differentiation is non-existent in pure competition. Due to the lack of distinctive product advantages and the fact that the fully informed buyers purchase solely on a price basis, it would prove futile to advertise the product. Thus, under pure competition no marketing controllables exist, and marketing strategies are not required.

Even though, in this chapter, we have explored cost-, demand- and competition-oriented pricing separately, in practice, components of these three approaches are often integrated into what is called combination pricing. A *cost-oriented* approach is used to analyze the costs of doing business – including examining break-even quantities and profit margins – and to establish a price floor. A *demand-oriented* approach helps marketers determine the prices customers in various market segments are willing to pay, as well as the ceiling prices for intermediaries in the distribution channel. This approach relies on customer perceptions of value to drive pricing decisions. By examining the price elasticity of demand, managers can better predict the effect of price changes. Finally, companies will use a *competition-oriented* approach to assess their rivals' prices and use the market price as the principal basis for price setting. Clearly, there is no single best way to determine prices, but it is the combination of these three methods that allows companies to determine the optimum price and realize their pricing objectives.

12.8.6 *Competitive bidding*

In some industries, the buyers rather than the sellers of a product or service hold a dominant market position. This is often the case in industrial markets (such as the oil exploration market) in which there are few buyers (such as petroleum companies) of a particular type of equipment (such as drilling rigs). Marketers who want to pursue these organizational customers are often asked by a potential buyer to submit bids specifying the price on proposed purchases or contracts. Private companies, as well as government agencies use this competitive bidding system (or, from the buyers perspective, tendering) to encourage suppliers to sell at the lowest possible price. A sale is finalized when the sealed bids are opened and the contract is awarded to the lowest bidder.

To start a round of competitive bidding, the potential buyer may circulate a request for proposal (RFP), in which vendors are asked to compete for an order. At this stage, the buyer's most important procurement task is to develop an accurate description and specifications of the product or service that the organization wants to buy. This may require the assistance of the company's technical staff, such as designers and engineers. Often, suppliers meet with the potential customer to determine their exact needs and to persuade them that they should be placed on the 'qualified bidder' list; this is a list of vendors that a buyer believes can provide the specified product or service. Suppliers are asked to compete for an order by showing how they will meet the product specifications, the service requirements and other criteria. After the bids are received, the buyer evaluates each marketer's package and price and then accepts the bid that best fits the requirements and budget.

The government, too, makes regular use of public tendering, requesting sealed bids to get the best price for large projects. If there are just a few suppliers or quick delivery is required, private tendering is the best purchasing procedure. Here – without any public announcement – a limited number of favoured suppliers, instead of all interested vendors, are invited to take part in a tendering procedure. The terms of the contract are sometimes negotiated, emerging through offers and counter-offers in negotiations between the buyer and the seller. When the potential customer's requirements or the marketer's expertise are unique, negotiated pricing helps both sides agree to an acceptable price for a non-standard product or service. On the other hand, when purchasing standard items, price is often the only variable by which the buyer can differentiate among suppliers. In the final section of this chapter, we examine how most suppliers draw up competitive bids, as well as the various factors affecting these bids.

Maximizing expected profit

Although several highly sophisticated bidding models have been developed, most can be reduced to the basic premise that the supplier is trying to maximize expected profit; that is, the amount of profit that they would receive on average from a particular bid. This is called the expected profit method. To implement this decision rule, the seller must estimate the profit associated with a number of potential bids, as well as the probability of winning the contract with each of the bids.

Sealed bid pricing is not an easy task for the vendor. First, the bidding company must calculate the costs of providing the service or product. Then, they must set a price relative to the prices they expect their rivals to submit. This price must cover costs, generate an acceptable return, and be low enough to be selected by the buyer. Thus, the seller must attempt to assess the chances of winning a contract at various prices, determine the potential profit under different bidding outcomes, and select projects for which the cost of preparing and submitting a bid is justified. The lower their own bid is, the greater the chance that competitors' prices will be higher and that the contract will be awarded to them. At a low submitted price, however, the profit on the contract will also be low. The optimum price is, therefore, a difficult decision, especially since the company should only submit bids that will not harm its position if awarded the contract. Table 12.8 illustrates how a supplier can use the expected-profit decision rule to formulate a bid while maximizing profit.

Suppose that a contractor has calculated a project's cost to be €29 500. They now consider submitting seven bids between €30 000 and €60 000. Notice in Table 12.8 that as the bid increases, profit also increases from €500 to €30 500. Raising the bid does not result in additional costs, only increased profits. The third column in the table lists the subjective probability of the supplier winning the contract at each of the bid prices. These probabilities of selection are determined based on what the supplier knows about the buyer and general competitive practices in the industry. Finally, the expected profit for each bid is calculated by multiplying the probability of winning the contract by the profit associated with that bid.

In this example, a successful bid of €30 000 results in a profit of €500, but because the chance of winning the contract is about 80 per cent, the expected profit is €400 (0.80 x €500). Usually, the supplier submits the bid with the highest expected profit. A bid of €45 000 for the contract yields a profit of €5 425. Bids higher than this amount result in much lower probabilities and, therefore, lower expected profits, too.

TABLE 12.8 Alternative bid prices and expected profits in competitive bidding

Bid	Profit	Probability of selection	Expected profit
€ 30 000	€ 500	80%	€ 400
€ 35 000	€ 5 500	70%	€ 3 850
€ 40 000	€ 10 500	50%	€ 5 250
€ 45 000	€ 15 500	35%	€ 5 425
€ 50 000	€ 20 500	25%	€ 5 125
€ 55 000	€ 25 500	15%	€ 3 825
€ 60 000	€ 30 500	10%	€ 3 050

Reasons for lower bid prices

The expected-profit decision rule only works when the seller bids on a number of projects simultaneously. The supplier does not expect to win all of these contracts; in fact, most sellers bid on more projects than they could reasonably undertake because of the low probability of winning all of them. Three additional considerations may cause a supplier to put in a bid that does not yield the highest expected profit: company objectives, excess capacity and follow-up bid opportunities.

The *objectives* of a company may range from profit maximization to survival until more profitable business conditions develop. The expected profit decision rule leads to profit maximization. However, if the firm pursues another objective – such as increasing market share – it may price very close to its variable cost, without being able to contribute to overhead. In the situation presented in Table 12.8, this firm might bid less than €30 000 in order to win the contract.

A company with *excess production capacity* may decide against putting in a bid with the highest expected profit in favour of the bid with a much greater probability of winning. After all, any amount in excess of the variable costs will make a contribution to overhead. In this case, the supplier, wanting to utilize excess capacity, might choose a bid of €35 000, since the probability of winning the contract with this bid (0.70) is twice as high as the chance of being awarded the contract with the €45 000 bid.

A final reason for submitting a bid that does not represent the highest expected profit is the prospect of *follow-up bid opportunities*. Often, the recipient of an important contract will have much better chances of winning larger and more profitable contracts with customers in the future. Even a bid that only covers variable costs may maximize long-term profits. Similarly, new sellers, seeking an opportunity to demonstrate their skills, may decide to bid low in order to win contracts and get their feet wet in the industry.

SUMMARY

1   Setting the price

Price is the element of the marketing mix most easily and quickly changed, without substantial investment. Accurate pricing is also one of the most effective ways for a firm to become more profitable. This makes pricing one of the most important marketing decisions. A customer orientation plays a key role in price determination. As we've seen, the selling price reflects the *value* that customers are willing to exchange for a desired product. This determines the upper limit of the range of possible prices. The lower limit depends on the product's *cost*.

Other considerations in pricing decisions are the company's strategy and objectives, competition, the effect on the product mix, the resellers' interests and finally legislation or ethics. The selling price is a major *marketing tool*, because it will influence sales – and therefore the firm's production volume. This in turn will affect the company's cost per unit, which again is one of the inputs in price determination, thus completing the circle. Hence, pricing is one of the most critical decisions in marketing strategy development.

2   Price mechanism and demand curve

The price of products and services affects both demand and supply. For example, a high price – with a large profit margin – may lead to many suppliers in the market, even if the total demand is limited. Due to increasing competition, prices will fall, causing demand to go up. The lower profit margins, however, also lead to a reduction in supply. As a result, prices can rise again; the cycle then repeats itself. This *price mechanism* is one of the driving forces of the economy: it measures the relative value of goods, making it possible to compare products with one another. It also stimulates or curbs production, and rations scarce products.

The *demand curve* provides a clear under-standing of the relationship between price and demand. The demand curve for a particular product graphically illustrates how customer demand responds to a series of possible prices. Movement along the demand curve is the result of a price change: in a downward sloping demand curve, demand increases as the price decreases. On the other hand, a shift in the demand curve (either upward or downward) is the result of more fundamental market forces, such as changes in consumer tastes, income, the market size or availability of substitutes.

3   Pricing new products

In new product pricing, the innovating marketer's primary considerations in choosing between price skimming and penetration pricing are how quickly competitors can launch their own versions of the new product and the effect of their entry into the market. For a new product with a large potential market – one that is likely to attract competitors soon after the product's introduction – *penetration pricing* is usually the most appropriate strategy. The low selling price helps the firm to penetrate the market and gain a large market share quickly. It also tends to discourage potential competitors by making the market appear less attractive than with a price skimming strategy. Conditions for a penetration pricing strategy include sufficient production and distribution capacity, a sound financial position and a long product life cycle.

With a *price skimming* approach, the marketer charges the highest price that early adopters, who most want the product, are willing to pay. This allows management to 'skim the cream' from the target market – especially if the product is perceived as having unique advantages – and then reduce the price over time to appeal to the next most lucrative segments. A successful skimming strategy enables the company to recover its product development costs quickly and maximize profits across seg-ments. Of course, a high introductory price, which often generates greater initial profits than would a lower price, will also encourage competitors to enter the market.

4   Pricing objectives

Using a systematic decision-making approach, the pricing objectives indicate what we intend to achieve through price setting. The pricing strategy, in turn, provides the framework within which we translate our pricing objectives into the actual market pricing tactics. In a business or marketing plan, pricing objectives should be formulated as *specifically* as possible, in such a way that there is a direct and measurable relationship with the price. Market-driven firms often express their pricing objectives in terms of *price perception*, such as a desired change in price awareness or price acceptance.

Among large companies, the most common pric-ing objectives are profitability objectives, including target return on investment, profit maximization and a desired gross profit margin. Other common pricing objectives are sales-related objectives, such as target market share and sales maximization, and competitive effect objectives, such as meeting competition and value pricing.

5 Control over prices

In business transactions, few customers pay list price for merchandise. Most buyers get a discount – or reduction from the base price – from the supplier. The actual prices resellers pay depend both on the functions they perform in the channel of distribution and on their degree of control over prices. Retailers, for example, gain greater control over prices by linking their resale support to the profit margins granted by the supplier, by carrying competing products, and by creating loyalty for their own store brands. Manufacturers can increase their control over prices by allowing the resellers adequate profit margins, by creating a strong national brand image that justifies high prices and by printing a recommended retail price on their packaging.

By offering *discounts*, manufacturers can influence their customers' buying and marketing behaviour. These price cuts are typically offered to middlemen for volume purchases (either cumulative or noncumulative quantity discounts), off-season buying (seasonal discounts), early payment of invoices (cash discounts) and for handling distribution-related functions in the trade channel that otherwise would be performed by the manufacturer (trade or functional discounts). When properly coordinated with their overall pricing strategy, price discounting can help a firm to build long-term relationships with customers and improve its competitive position. Like discounts, *allowances* help a company influence customer buying behaviour without formally reducing the list price of a product or service. Allowances are pricing adjustments that indirectly lower the price that a reseller or other customer pays in exchange for taking some action, such as participating in a programme, promoting a product or purchasing during a particular time period. The most widely used types are trade-in allowances, promotional allowances and rebates.

Corporations within which products are sold from one division to another must set the price of the goods transferred in terms of the revenues and costs to their business units. The *transfer price* can be based either on the product's market price or on its actual production costs per unit.

6 Cost-based price determination

The three major dimensions on which prices of products and services can be based are cost, demand and competition. The simplest and most commonly used method of price setting is cost-oriented pricing. With *cost-plus pricing*, management tries to allocate only those costs directly attributable to a specific product or output. The seller's costs are calculated, and this amount or a specific percentage of it is added to the item's production cost to establish its price. When costs, such as overheads, are difficult to determine, firms use *mark-up pricing* to establish a selling price.

Variable-cost pricing – or direct costing – enables a firm to temporarily price below its full costs but still to contribute to overhead and profit. The product's price is based on the variable costs only. The difference between the variable costs and the selling price is called the contribution margin. A major risk of using variable-cost pricing is that it may trigger a price war, resulting in reduced profits for all companies in the industry.

Break-even analysis is a means of determining the number of products or services that must be sold at a given price to generate sufficient revenue to equal total costs. Only sales above the break-even point will lead to profit. If we also take into account the expected demand for the product at various prices, a flexible break-even analysis is a useful tool. A break-even analysis may well be combined with another pricing method, *target return-on-investment pricing*. This allows marketers to determine a new product's price level to achieve a desired or target return on investment.

7 Demand-oriented pricing

The opposite of the cost-oriented price determination is demand-oriented pricing, also referred to as *perceived-value* or *value-based pricing*. Using this strategy, companies set prices at a level that the intended buyers are willing to pay, and then deduct their own as well as the resellers' customary profit margins. Correctly assessing consumers' interest in a product at different price levels requires an insight into the buyer's price sensitivity, making price elasticity of demand a fundamental concept in demand-oriented pricing.

The *price elasticity of demand* indicates the sensitivity of buyers to price changes in terms of the quantities they will purchase, and thus how responsive demand will be to a price increase or decrease. For instance, a price change that leads to a relatively small change in demand indicates an inelastic demand. Typically, buyers are less price sensitive when there are few substitute products, or when the total expenditure for the product is low relative to their income. *Income elasticity of demand* shows the relationship between an increase in consumers' disposable income and the corresponding change in consumption. Lastly, demand for a product may also be affected by another product's change in price. This phenomenon is called *cross elasticity of demand*.

When a firm establishes a series of prices for a type of product, it creates a price line. *Price lining* requires two determinations: the floor and ceiling of the price range are established, and a limited number of price points are set for the various items within that range. The same product can often be sold to buyers under more than one price. *Price discrimination* is the practice of charging different buyers different prices for goods of like grade and quality. The most common forms of *price differentiation* are based on customer type (e.g. student discounts), product form (gift packages), location (seating in concert hall) and time (post-season sale). Setting the right price is part science, part art. In using *psychological pricing*, firms take into consideration the psychology of prices and not just the economics. With some prestige products, the higher the price, the more consumers are willing to buy the product. Consumers are also more inclined to buy a product with an odd-numbered price than with an even-numbered price, especially if the amount is just under a particular threshold. No wonder so many companies have adopted an odd-even pricing strategy.

8   Competition-oriented pricing

When a company uses its competitors' prices as the primary basis for price setting, it follows a strategy of competition-oriented pricing. Marketers have the option of pricing at the market (me-too pricing), above the market (premium pricing) or below the market (discount pricing).

Based on the number of sellers and the type of product, companies operate and set prices in four types of market structures: monopoly, oligopoly, monopolistic competition and pure competition. In an *oligopoly*, a few large suppliers account for a high percentage of the market, so every seller is highly sensitive to the marketing actions taken by its competitors, including pricing. Price cuts are usually copied by competitors, but price increases only if the market leader takes the initiative. This explains the price stability on this type of market as well as the shape of this (kinked) supply curve. The most common market form, which typifies retailing, is *monopolistic competition*. The marketer's main challenge here is to keep the brand distinctive and to appeal to a target market of loyal buyers through an effective product positioning strategy.

In the B2B market, several suppliers – through *competitive bidding* – may independently submit bids to a potential buyer for a specific product or service. The bidding company must take the cost of providing the service or product into account as well as the prices its rivals are expected to submit. All companies use the expected profit decision rule, recognizing that as the bid price increases, the potential profit also increases but the probability of its winning the contract decreases.

DISCUSSION QUESTIONS

1   Apple was the first American company to launch a touch-screen smart phone on the global market. Prior to its introduction in the United States, market research indicated that a significant group of consumers would be willing to pay a high price for this new mobile phone if they could own it immediately after its introduction. Therefore, Apple decided to launch the iPhone at a high selling price. It intended to lower the price as competitors began introducing similar products.
a. What pricing strategy was Apple pursuing, and what are its main advantages and disadvantages for the company? Under what type of competitive structure do firms tend to use this type of strategy?
b. What alternative pricing strategy could Apple pursue for this new product, and why do you think the company decided against that strategy?

2   When formulating pricing objectives, would you prefer to express them in terms of sales growth or an increase in market share? Explain your answer.

3   Fully explain why price is a unique element of the marketing mix.

4   To what extent do the product life cycle stages influence pricing decisions? Give examples.

5   Assume that a company sells its products on both the business market and the consumer market. Which of these two types of buyers is in a stronger position? How does the price setting process differ in these two markets?

6   Explain the benefits and risks of price differentiation and give some practical examples of this strategy that you have encountered as a consumer.

7 What is the use of a break-even analysis for a marketer in deciding whether or not to develop a new product?

8 What type of firm with a cost-oriented pricing strategy generally prefers to use cost-plus pricing rather than target-return pricing?

9 What is the difference between elastic and inelastic demand, and what factors affect a product's price sensitivity?

10 Comment on the following quote: 'If the price elasticity of the demand for your product is inelastic, your price is probably too low.'

PART SIX
DISTRIBUTION DECISIONS

German cars, American tablets and Dutch beer have one thing in common. They are for sale virtually everywhere. The availability of such brands as BMW, iPad and Heineken to consumers in most countries is not accidental. Rather, it is part of the carefully planned distribution strategies of their producers and resellers.

In Part 6 of this book we focus on the remaining P in the marketing mix – Place or distribution. Once again, we take the supplier's perspective because this company must make decisions about how to get its products into the customers' hands at a reasonable cost. Among the marketer's main considerations are the extent of market coverage and the selection of distribution intermediaries. Since retailers play a key role in the distribution process, both through their stores and online, we will explore retail marketing as well as Internet retailing. The Internet and global distribution networks have opened world markets to any company. Ultimately, companies can only continue to grow if their managers understand the international market's unique characteristics and develop an effective global marketing strategy.

13   Distribution

14   Retailing

15   Global marketing

CHAPTER 13
DISTRIBUTION

LEARNING GOALS

After studying this chapter you will be able to:

1	Explain which factors influence a marketer's choice of distribution channels
2	Distinguish between intensive, selective and exclusive distribution strategies
3	Discuss useful criteria for selecting and evaluating marketing intermediaries
4	Identify major trends in wholesaling
5	Understand the objectives and management of physical distribution

13.1 Importance of marketing channels

13.2 Target market coverage

13.3 Channel leadership and management

13.4 Wholesaling

13.5 Marketing logistics

Every company must determine how best to deliver its products or services to its customers. Most companies use distributors, which perform various distribution functions. Involving such intermediaries as trading companies, wholesalers and retailers in selling products to the final users requires considerable management attention.

No single marketing activity generates more conflict than distribution. This is largely because companies must frequently work side by side with other organizations in the marketing channel, sometimes with those having opposing interests. A manufacturer, for instance, typically wants to maximize sales of their own product, whereas the retailer may be more interested in offering customers a wide array of competing brands.

How do products and services move through channels of distribution? What functions do the intermediaries perform, and which parties have most power? What is the influence of e-commerce on conventional distribution channels and marketing strategies? How do suppliers decide in what channels and stores to offer their products? Do the resellers' profit margins increase the price of products and services to an unreasonable extent? These are but a few of the critical questions we will explore in this chapter.

MARKETING IN ACTION
Zara's Global Stretch: One Size Fits All?

Image Asset Management

In a competitive industry where ordering products months in advance is common, the ability to react rapidly to changing trends and consumer preferences has transformed a European company into one of the world's biggest clothing retailers. Thanks to this unrivalled capability for delivering the goods (or 'instant fashion' as it has been dubbed), Zara, the clothing wing of Spain's Inditex, has beaten the odds to become a leading international brand. Recently, Zara's value was estimated at a staggering €32 billion; impressive for a company founded on a mere €30! Its designs have even attracted a blossoming style icon, the UK's Duchess of Cambridge, who was spotted in a £49.95 blue dress from Zara shortly after her globally televised royal wedding. Meanwhile Harvard Business School has praised the company in a recent study for putting the customer-focused approach to operations.

The fashion giant's marketing success is based on the *vertical integration* of design, 'just-in-time' production, delivery and sales through a fast-expanding chain of trendy stores offering affordable fashion in hot demand regionally. This achievement comes at a time when low-cost Chinese imports increasingly challenge the European fashion business. And although – when it comes to marketing inexpensive fashion products in the casual wear retail sector – speed is vital, the 'one size fits all' principle does not apply. Instead, Zara relies on one of the most successful logistics operations on the globe to match supply with demand.

About three hundred young designers, most of them recruited straight from the world's best design schools, work at the company's headquarters in La Coruña in Galicia, a relatively deprived area in the north of Spain. The designers keep in regular touch with Zara store managers – who hold frequent staff meetings to discuss local trends – to determine the bestsellers and customer preferences. The garments are then produced, mostly in Spain, Portugal and Morocco, which Inditex calls its 'proximity'. The logistical efficiency allows Zara more flexibility. The chosen textiles are prepared domestically, then transported to local co-operatives, where the clothes are stitched together. Finally, the finished products are shipped across Europe and globally by truck or plane. Limited batches prevent any unnecessary surplus stock and increase customers' perceived exclusivity of the items. When lines are sold out, they are substituted rapidly with fresh alternatives instead of 'more of the same' stock. It's the ultimate marketing technique to attract frequent shoppers to the stores. European customers, in fact, visit Zara stores an average of seventeen times a year, nearly six times as much as other fashion stores.

> Zara spends less than 0.3 per cent of sales revenues on advertising to keep its retail prices low

To put this into perspective, Hennes & Mauritz (H&M) of Sweden launches about 3 000 new items per year; Zara, meanwhile, produces around 11 000 – nearly four times this. A new Zara product is delivered to stores within five weeks after its design; for a new version of an existing model, the required time is reduced to only fourteen days. No casual fashion chain can beat that! No wonder that Zara store managers check their tablets or laptops each day to find out the new models being offered; at the end of the day, they only buy the products that they think their customers will like best. Thanks to this effective method of fine-tuning the new product development process, all store managers actually influence the designs that the company will introduce. It also prevents Zara from having to discount slow-selling products, as is common among other retailers. And by spending only about 10 per cent of what most competitors spend on IT, and less than 0.3 per cent of sales revenues on advertising (as opposed to an average of 4 per cent spent by its rivals), Zara manages to keep its retail prices low.

Today, only about one-third of the company's production – mostly basic products – is outsourced to Asia. Hence, the company is not affected as much by Asia's rising costs. But Zara still is a global company: it has over five thousand stores in about eighty nations, 60 per cent of them in Europe. Zara's marketing approach, sometimes referred to as an *oil stain strategy*, involves opening a few test stores in a new country first, to develop a better insight into local consumers, before further penetrating that particular market. It should be noted, however, that Zara sells the same products in various countries for different prices. The same products will cost nearly twice as much in Western Europe as in Japan, for example. Experts wonder how much longer Zara can continue to do this, especially now that it is increasing its *online* sales across the world.

As Zara continues to expand in Africa, Latin America and Australia, it has become the first global retailer to sell fashion products developed especially for the seasons of the southern hemisphere. Management realizes that consumers in these markets follow fashion trends as much as buyers in the west, and would resent being offered the previous year's products.

In conclusion, the clothing company that breaks all the rules – garnering the respect of both royalty and academia – owes this feat largely to its rapid response, anywhere in the world; new fashion designs from sketch pad to store racks within a month. Inditex accomplishes this by listening to the customer and keeping a tight grip on every link in its supply chain, right down to using in-store staff as a barometer for trends. The company even boasts green credentials, utilizing a combination of wind and solar power, recycled cardboard boxes and bicycles in warehouses, to help bring their products to market. More than anything else, Zara has proved that it is possible – and lucrative – to mass market cheap, fast and ethical fashion in a stylish way to maximize consumer satisfaction and customer loyalty.[1]

The concept of distribution is commonly associated with moving products from point A to point B, from the manufacturer to the customer. And that is, in fact, physical distribution, with transportation, warehousing, order processing and inventory management being the core activities. Distribution, as one of the four elements of the marketing mix, entails much more than that. A company has to decide which distribution channels (including the Internet) are most suitable for delivering its products and which retailers – such as supermarkets or specialty stores – are best to engage for that purpose. These are strategic decisions that at the same time require making a fundamental choice between intensive, selective or exclusive distribution. Distribution decisions may also involve considering the option of an alliance with other organizations, such as through a franchising arrangement.

The efficiency of its distribution channel is often what separates a successful company from an unsuccessful one. A common misconception among managers is that if a company makes a needed product, that product will automatically spread throughout the marketplace and land in the hands of the consumer. Most companies soon come to the realization that they must spend as much time working on distribution strategy as they do on any other strategic component. Distribution planning is further complicated by the fact that the marketing channel consists of several independent organizations that do not always follow the manufacturer's lead with respect to every promotion, pricing or distribution decision. We will now first examine the meaning of a distribution channel and what functions it should perform.

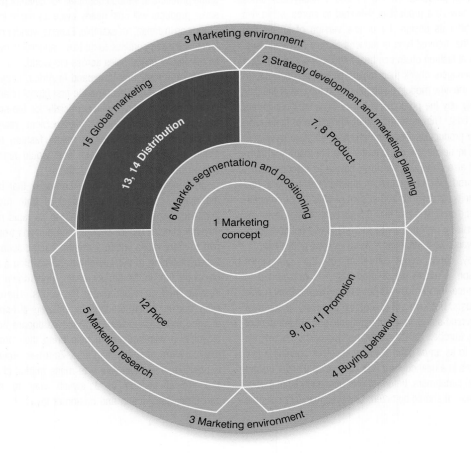

13.1 IMPORTANCE OF MARKETING CHANNELS

Because marketing channels determine where and how customers buy, establishing the right distribution structure is of great importance. Other components of the marketing mix can often be easily changed. Companies can add or drop items from their product mix, raise or lower prices, and adjust advertising campaigns without fundamentally changing the way they do business. But making major changes in a company's distribution strategy is much more complicated, since other organizations, such as wholesalers and retailers, may play important roles in the distribution channel.

In today's global business environment characterized by mounting competition, an efficient and well-planned distribution system is a vital part of a company's marketing strategy. Managers realize that many of the crucial distribution tasks are most efficiently performed by specialized intermediaries. Hence, they need to determine which tasks to delegate and how to organize the marketing channels without losing control of the distribution function. This requires strategic – and often difficult – decisions about the types of channels that will best meet their own objectives as well as their customers' needs. As a result, many executives spend more time planning and executing distribution decisions than on any other element of the marketing strategy.

13.1.1 What is a distribution channel?

While an appealing design, creative promotion and an attractive price may encourage consumers to buy a product, these marketing efforts are useless if customers cannot purchase the product when and where they prefer. That's where the marketing or distribution channel enters the equation. The **distribution channel** is a network of independent organizations that, combined, perform all of the activities necessary to link producers and end customers. Products sell better when buyers can obtain them conveniently. The distribution channel allows the seller to locate and supply the users of its merchandise, and helps the buyer to find and obtain the products or services they seek.

While channels of distribution are often thought of as static networks, in fact they are quite dynamic. This is evidenced in two major ways. First, *new* channels are continually being established. To illustrate, products such as laptops and MP3 players are increasingly being sold at department stores, drugstores, discounters and through outlets or marketing channels other than specialty stores. And new automobiles, traditionally only sold at dealerships, are now also being offered through the Internet. Secondly, organizations typically *modify* the structure of the existing channels if doing so improves their efficiency. A new channel of distribution may be created – or an existing one improved – if it helps sellers and buyers to increase their efficiency or effectiveness in the exchange process.

From the producer's perspective, an effective **distribution strategy** involves the analysis, planning, implementation and control of the activities that make the right products available to the target market at the right time, at the right place and at the lowest possible cost. As our definition of the distribution channel suggests, the organizations that constitute the channel must continuously cooperate to accomplish the members' distribution objectives. Even though the physical products may not change during the distribution process, they have to be offered and delivered in quantities and combinations that the customer wants. If the distribution channel is functioning properly, the buyers – consumers and organizational users alike – should have no difficulty in finding the products and services they need.

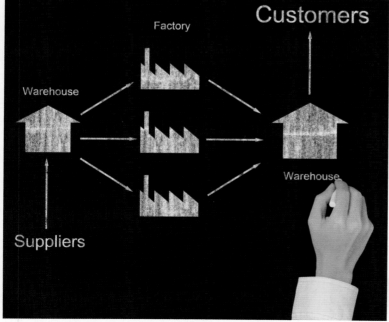

Distribution intermediaries (also called *middlemen* or *resellers*) play a major role in the marketing of goods and services. Intermediaries, functioning as exporters, brokerage firms, importers, agents, wholesalers and retailers, are organizations or individuals that operate between the producer and consumer in a channel of distribution. The cost of their services impacts the prices customers are charged. Most of the intermediaries' functions cannot be eliminated, but they can be shifted from one channel member to another. Therefore, it is imperative for producers to assess the intermediaries' performance periodically to ensure that they are properly executing their tasks. As we will see in the next few sections, there are different types of distribution channels and intermediaries that perform a variety of functions.

13.1.2 Types of distribution channels

Since a product can take many routes to get from seller to buyer, marketers must find the most efficient course. The shape or form that a distribution channel takes is known as the channel structure. It consists of all firms and institutions (including producers and final customers) involved in selling, buying, transferring title and performing related functions. Figure 13.1 depicts some of the most widely used channels in the consumer market. These channels vary in the number of levels, referred to as the channel length.

There are two basic types of channels. A direct channel of distribution (a zero-level channel) entails the movement of products and services from producers to consumers without the use of independent intermediaries. Many manufacturers, such as Dell, are very successful in selling directly to final consumers through the Internet. Producers or service providers that sell to consumers at company-owned outlets, for instance BP-owned gas stations, also use a direct channel. The other examples of channels in Figure 13.1, as we see, involve one, two or three levels.

These are called indirect channels. Possible intermediaries include independent retailers, wholesalers and agents. Most manufacturers use these longer channels of distribution because they are not large enough themselves, for example, to own their own retail outlets, or they feel that independent intermediaries can distribute their merchandise more efficiently. One drawback of using intermediaries is that the producer gives up some

FIGURE 13.1 Channels of distribution in consumer markets

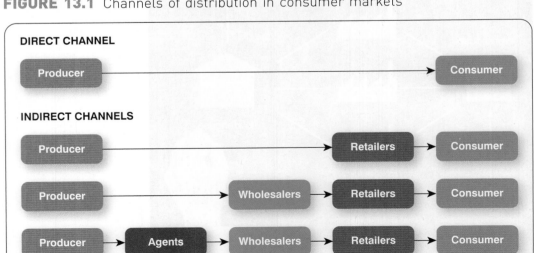

TABLE 13.1 Factors influencing the choice between a long or short distribution channel

	Long distribution channel	*Short distribution channel*
Market factors	Large market (consumers) Geographically dispersed High purchase frequency (small orders) Sales support and servicing not important	Small market (business users) Geographically concentrated Low purchase frequency (large orders) Sales support and servicing crucial
Product factors	Durable products Low-priced products Simple products (standardized) High variable costs	Perishable products High-priced products Technically complex products (customized) High fixed costs
Organizational factors	Channel control not required Narrow product line Limited resources	Channel control crucial Broad product line Sufficient resources

control of the distribution process and, with it, some control over customer service and other important functions.

In the industrial or organizational market, short channels of distribution prevail. These transactions often deal with high-priced merchandise with greater profit margins, which allow the producer to use its own sales force. Also, custom-made products are not even manufactured until ordered, and distributors may lack the required technical knowledge to handle these transactions. Finally, these goods may require frequent service and direct contact between the manufacturer and buyer. Direct delivery is also common in the services sector, where it is obviously not possible to keep inventory. The most important factors influencing the choice between a long or short distribution channel are summarized in Table 13.1.

Many companies, rather than using a single-channel strategy, reach several market segments with a single product (or similar products under different brand names) through multiple distribution channels. By using dual distribution, also called a multichannel distribution system, firms can expand their market coverage, lower marketing costs and offer greater opportunities for customization, which could all help increase sales. Banks and travel organizations, for instance, reach their customers over the Internet, through retail offices and by telephone, while Acer laptops are for sale through various dealers, retail stores, direct mail and websites.

A special form of multichannel system is the so-called hybrid system, in which the channel members perform complementary tasks for the same customer, instead of for different segments. An example of a hybrid system is shown in Figure 13.2. The producer uses their own sales force to approach prospects and clients - including Customers 1 and 2 in the chart - in order to present the product and close the sale. Customer 2 in the chart enjoys the benefits of a hybrid system, in which an Export Management Company - as the producer's partner - takes care of financing the transaction and installation of the product, while an independent export agent is, on behalf of the producer, is in charge of providing post-sale service. In today's competitive market environment, for many firms hybrid systems or other forms of multi-channel marketing are a necessity, not a choice. This is apparent as we examine the major functions that distribution channels perform.

FIGURE 13.2 A hybrid channel system

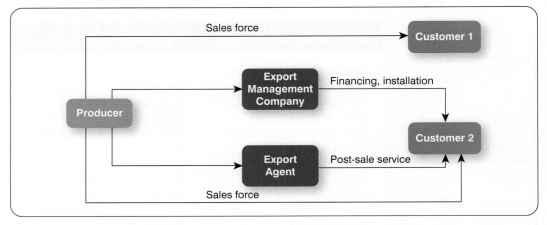

13.1.3 *Distribution channels create utility*

To facilitate the exchange process, channels of distribution create place utility (by offering products in places where customers shop), time utility (making products available when buyers want them) and possession utility (by providing ownership or arrangements that give customers the right to use the product, such as a lease or rental agreement). Creating these types of utility (through such activities as transportation, inventory control and financing) is only possible with an effective – and integrated – marketing mix. This requires cooperation between channel members as well as a careful coordination of product, price, promotion and distribution decisions. If these are lacking, sales will suffer. A consumer who can't find their favourite brand of beer on the supermarket shelf because it is sold out, may go to another store. The first store loses the sale and, more significantly, risks losing future business from that customer.

It is especially important that the company's promotion programme be coordinated with its distribution programme. There is nothing more frustrating to a marketing manager than discovering that a well developed sales promotion campaign for a particular product has stimulated demand that the company is unable to meet because of early stockouts and poor inventory planning. On the other hand, physically moving the product to the market without adequate promotional support will result in excess inventories, which could force the firm to reduce the price of its product.

In some cases, distribution considerations may actually dictate the type of product a company develops and how it prices and promotes the item. Companies such as Unilever and Procter & Gamble make excellent products that are well advertised and competitively priced. However, one of the major factors that separate these companies from their smaller competitors is the size and effectiveness of their distribution networks. Therefore, when these corporations are considering a new product, they make sure it is compatible with their current distribution system and will get the necessary support from intermediaries.

13.1.4 *Distribution channels increase efficiency*

Consumers may not always recognize the value that intermediaries in the marketing channel create. Manufacturers, however, are definitely aware that these middlemen make selling products and services more efficient by reducing the number of sales contacts needed to reach the target market. Larger retailers and wholesalers accomplish this, first of all, by *breaking bulk*: they buy large quantities (containers, pallets or cases) of products from many manufacturers but sell only a few or even one at a time to many different buyers.

The second way that intermediaries provide value and increase efficiency in the flow of products and services is by *creating assortments* that reduce the number of transactions. This occurs by offering a wide variety of products in one location, enabling consumers to conveniently buy many different items from one store or seller at a time. These two functions, in bridging the gap between the limited variety of products offered by individual producers and the limited quantity of a wide assortment of products demanded by consumers at the same location, are also referred to as the *collective* and the *distributive* function.

The reduction in the number of transactions through the use of intermediaries is illustrated in Figure 13.3. This simplified example of how a channel of distribution works shows a system with three producers and five consumers. Without a retail intermediary, the producers would each have to make five contacts to reach all of the buyers in the target market. This would require a total of fifteen contacts or transactions. When a retailer acts as an intermediary, each producer only has to make one contact, which reduces the number of transactions to eight. Clearly, this is a more efficient way to distribute products.

In addition to reducing the number of contacts, an intermediary may increase the efficiency of the channel through their marketing experience, specialization and economies of scale. This set of skills and characteristics allows intermediaries to add value by efficiently performing three fundamental functions.

The first one is the so-called *transactional function* that entails buying, selling and risk taking. Intermediaries accept the risk of not selling the products they stock. Channel intermediaries also perform a *logistical function* that involves assorting, storing, sorting and transporting of merchandise. Finally, they carry out a variety of *facilitating functions* in the marketing channel that make products and services more attractive to buyers, for example by grading, offering customer service and extending credit. At the same time, they assist manufacturers, for example through providing maintenance contracts and repair services for the products they carry. All of these functions help create a more efficient distribution process.

Some critics or companies suggest that by eliminating wholesalers, import agents or other middlemen consumer prices may be lowered. We have all seen the advertising claim 'we sell directly to consumers and pass the savings on to you', implying that customers pay less because of a manufacturer's direct delivery to the consumer. Obviously, intermediaries

FIGURE 13.3 How distribution channel intermediaries reduce the number of transactions

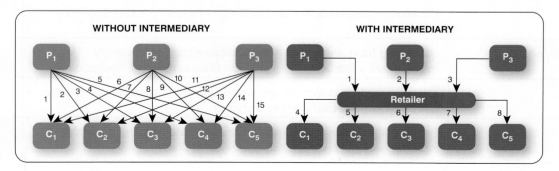

that cost more than they add value by contributing to the marketing process are doomed to be eliminated. However, the services that the eliminated intermediary provided now have to be performed by another party, and this does not necessarily lead to a competitive advantage: the consumer still has to pay for them. In fact, the efficiency in the channel may actually be improved by adding an extra link to the supply chain. Still, an increasing number of buyers prefer to bypass retailers and purchase through companies' websites. In many product categories, consumers spend billions of euros on items bought through the Internet, much of it at the expense of transactions through conventional distribution channels. In addition to its convenience, they value the ability to directly and instantaneously communicate with customer-oriented suppliers through online retailing.

13.1.5 Distribution channels create a supply chain

As a product moves down the distribution channel from producers to consumers, it changes hands more than once as independent channel members perform various key tasks, also referred to as **distribution functions**. Many of these require special skills. Six of the most important functions of the channel of distribution are summarized in Table 13.2: they include transactional functions (relationship building and promotion), logistical functions (sorting and inventory control) and facilitating functions (financing, and research and marketing information).

In order to bridge the place, time and possession gaps that separate products and services from potential buyers, the functions to be performed in the channel go beyond the flow of physical products. Some functions, such as promotion, product and title flows, make up a *forward flow* of activity from the seller to the buyer. For example, the manufacturer may send salespeople to call on wholesalers and retailers while simultaneously advertising directly to consumers. Other functions, such as ordering and payment, provide a *backward flow* from buyers to the seller. A third category of

TABLE 13.2 Key functions performed in distribution channels

Distribution function	Description
Relationship building	All marketing activities related to selling, service and maintaining long-term customer relationships
Promotion	Stimulating demand through advertising, sales promotion and personal selling to offer information and service to customers
Sorting	Purchasing in large quantities and breaking into smaller amounts desired by customers
Inventory control	Maintaining adequate stock – through transportation and inventory management – in order to keep products close to their final destination
Financing	Extending credit to customers and providing financial support to suppliers by placing orders and paying invoices on time
Research and marketing information	Providing information and market feedback to customers and suppliers, including relevant trends and competitive conditions

FIGURE 13.4 Typical flows in the marketing channel

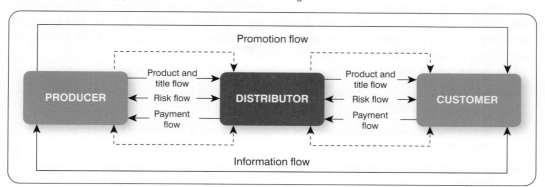

functions (including negotiation, finance, information and risk taking) occurs in both directions. The product may move very well through the channel, but if the other flows are not planned properly, the channel will fail to perform as a whole. Five important flows are illustrated in Figure 13.4.

13.1.6 *Value chain*

Traditional marketing channels consist of producers, wholesalers, retailers and customers. Manufacturers do not only maintain relationships with their customers, but also with suppliers and intermediaries. When the facilitating institutions such as shipping companies, banks, communication companies and other firms that indirectly contribute to marketing exchanges, are also considered in the joint effort of all channel members, the marketing channel is referred to as a supply chain, also called a value chain. First portrayed by Michael Porter in his book *Competitive Advantage*, the value chain serves as a means for companies to identify ways to create, communicate and deliver more customer value on every activity the company performs. Upstream management focuses on managing raw materials, inbound logistics and warehouse and storage facilities. Downstream management, in contrast, focuses on managing finished product storage, outbound logistics, marketing and sales, and customer service.

A supply chain is the complete sequence of suppliers and activities that contribute to the creation and delivery of products and services. It begins with the raw materials used in the production process, proceeds to the actual manufacturing activities and ends with the delivery of finished products through the distribution channel to the buyers. It includes all activities that increase the perceived value of the purchase to the buyer. Obviously, logistical management plays a vital role in the supply chain to make sure that customers get what they need at the time that they want it. Thus, a major function of the distribution channel is the combined effort of all of its members to form a supply chain that can serve customers as efficiently as possible by creating a competitive advantage. The cooperation between the company and its suppliers, distributors and ultimately customers who partner with each other to enhance the performance of the entire system and to provide buyers with the highest possible value results in a so-called value delivery network.

As Michael Porter has highlighted, the value chain identifies nine strategic activities the company can engage in that affect both sides of the value chain: benefits and costs. These *value-creating activities* include five *primary* activities and four *support* activities, which are discussed below.[2]

The five primary activities in the supply or value chain are *inbound logistics* (sourcing raw materials for production), *operations* (converting raw materials into final products), *outbound logistics* (transporting and distributing the final products to the marketplace), *marketing and sales* (communicating the value proposition to the marketplace) and *service* (supporting customers during and after the sale).

The four support activities are:

→ *firm infrastructure*: how the company is set up for doing business (are the internal processes aligned and efficient?).

→ *human resource management*: how the company ensures it has the right people in place, trains them and keeps them.

→ *technology development*: how the company embraces technology usage for the customers' benefit.

→ *procurement*: how the company deals with vendors and quality issues.

Through supply chain management, the channel members form long-term partnerships in an effort to minimize transportation, inventory, administrative and handling costs by eliminating inefficiencies; at the same time, they strive to improve customer service and maximize customer value in each activity they perform through innovation and a customer orientation. Technological developments – resulting in tools such as bar codes, electronic billing, buying order verification and image processing – have stimulated integrated information sharing among channel members and have created increasingly sophisticated systems of supply chain management.

13.2 TARGET MARKET COVERAGE

Whether an organization decides to use one or multiple distribution channels to reach its target market, its choice of intermediaries or retail stores may greatly affect sales and profitability. Some companies need only one location to reach their markets and customer segments, while others need thousands of retail outlets. The decisions about the type and number of intermediaries are *strategic* decisions, since the firm enters into a long-term agreement with channel institutions on which it becomes partially dependent. Managers who select ineffective marketing channels and intermediaries are likely to face serious problems. The number of outlets used to distribute a product or service in a particular market is called distribution intensity. Optimal distribution intensity should ensure adequate *market coverage in* the target market.

In developing the channel for the best coverage of the target market, we should first determine the composition of the potential customer base. And we must examine their purchasing patterns – what, when, how and where they buy – bearing in mind that consumers' buying habits are quite different from those of industrial or business customers. Of course, in selecting the best marketing channels and intermediaries, we should also consider the product's characteristics and its stage in the life cycle. Products and services that are high-priced, technically complex and require customization should be sold through a shorter, more direct distribution channel – through a direct sales force – than inexpensive, simple products. To employ and successfully manage a direct sales force, however, the manufacturer must have the necessary financial and marketing resources.

The product life cycle is relevant because as products become more mature and markets more saturated, different channels are used than those most appropriate for the product's initial launch. Digital cameras and cell phones, for example, are no longer offered only

PROFESSOR'S PERSPECTIVE
Uchenna Uzo (Lagos Business School, Nigeria)

Uchenna Uzo is a Professor of Marketing at the Lagos Business School, *Nigeria. His research interests focus on sales and channel management. He has consulted for organizations in the creative industry and continues to consult for small and medium scale enterprises. He is a member of the American Marketing Association and a fellow of the Scandinavian Consortium for Organizational Research. He teaches courses in Sales and Marketing at the university.*

Marketing channels – the routes to market used to sell products and services to consumers and business buyers – are major sources of competitive advantage. Marketing channels are not mere conduits for delivery of goods and services. In many marketing courses, students are taught about building competitive advantage. However, most of these courses emphasize product or service differentiation alone. Yet channels can become major differentiating assets for firms, especially in the face of *global* changes in consumer behaviour. In Africa, consumers are gradually transiting from purchasing in informal retail outlets to purchasing in more organized retail outlets. For instance, Nigeria's retail industry that was originally focused on selling in open market spaces with a bargaining culture for determining prices has recently witnessed an increased presence of international chains such as *Shoprite* (owned by Retail Supermarket Nigeria Limited) and *Spar* (owned by Artee Industries Ltd). In addition, telecoms giants like *Bharti Airtel* and *MTN Nigeria* are developing customer solutions that will position them as both B2C and B2B companies in the competitive landscape of the African continent.

These trends suggest that organizations need to pay more attention to the *strategic* issues behind channel design, channel experiences and channel relationships. Different buyers require different routes to market and different sellers to serve them. The *channel design* process needs to be managed carefully. A good example of a well managed channel design process is that of *Iroko Partners* (Africa's *Netflix* and online platform for distributing Nollywood movies). Under the leadership of the CEO, Jason Njoku, the company has pioneered an innovative form of channel design. Iroko Partners became the first *online* movie distribution company to secure exclusive rights to distribute movies made by Nollywood (Africa's largest movie producer and the world's second largest producer after India). Prior to Iroko's entry, movies made in the Nigerian movie industry (Nollywood) were produced and sold directly to customers on DVDs without cinema screenings. By engaging in intense negotiations with movie sellers, Iroko established a formidable online distribution model that offered a win-win proposition to the sellers, movie consumers and Iroko. One lesson from the Iroko experience is that consumers, retailers and wholesalers all need to be involved in the channel design process.

Apple enjoys a high level of brand loyalty because channel experiences are well managed

Another important fact about marketing channels is that *channel experiences* greatly influence buyers' purchase decisions. For example, thousands of *Apple* customers are ready to spend hours in long queues outside *retail stores* in order to buy their latest Apple products. Apple has secured a high level of brand loyalty because channel experiences are well managed. An important message to manufacturers is that they need to pay attention to branding points of sale in order to communicate the right image and the right experience.

Finally, *channel relationships* matter. Well managed relationships can help companies secure a larger market share in highly fragmented market settings. For example, *Coca-Cola Nigeria PLC* managed to secure 50 per cent share of the bottled water market in Nigeria by establishing robust channel *partnerships* with its distributors nationwide. Coca-Cola Nigeria offered incentives such as branded wholesale outlets and commission based targets to strengthen their channel relationships. A major take away from the Coca-Cola experience is that manufacturers have to ensure that they do *not compete* with their channel partners for end users. Managing marketing channels is hard work, but well managed channels secure competitive advantages.[3]

through specialty stores, but are available in a wide range of channels and outlets and through websites that reach millions of consumers. Additional factors affecting the intensity of distribution will be discussed later. In deciding on the type and number of intermediaries to use at each channel level, there are three possible strategies: intensive distribution, selective distribution and exclusive distribution.

13.2.1 *Intensive distribution*

In an **intensive distribution** strategy, the product or service is made available to buyers through as many outlets as possible, in effect all suitable wholesalers and retail stores willing to stock and sell the product. This strategy tends to increase sales, if for no other reason than that the customer will be widely exposed to the product. It also maximizes convenience and impulse buying of the product.

An intensive distribution strategy is usually chosen for *convenience products* such as candy, snacks and soft drinks that are quickly consumed, frequently replaced and have a wide appeal across a broad group of buyers. They are products, as discussed in Chapter 7, that a consumer is unwilling to make a special effort to find, or even to compare prices and quality. For most brand-name convenience products, intensive distribution is necessary because if a consumer's favourite brand is not available on the shelves, they are more likely to buy a different brand than to go to another store to find it. For similar reasons, suppliers in the business market use intensive distribution for office products that have a high replacement rate and require almost no sales effort or service. Here, too, there is a direct relationship between product availability and sales volume.

While an intensive distribution strategy may increase market coverage and sales volume, an overly aggressive promotional effort may hurt long-term performance. Products with low margins might not generate sufficient profit to advertise extensively and to employ a sales force able to service the large number of intermediaries required to supply the market. If, as a result of sales promotion, retailers get involved in aggressive competition and possibly a price war, their profits will decline, making it harder for the manufacturer to get them to push the product. This is one disadvantage of intensive distribution, as is less overall control using mass distribution in a long distribution channel. Intensive distribution, however, does not mean that there is no need for the producer to use any form of selection. For instance, stores with a low sales volume may sometimes be excluded from the distribution network. Overall, however, intensive distribution makes most national brands available in more than 90 per cent of the retail outlets that carry these types of products.

13.2.2 Selective distribution

Selective distribution, as the name implies, is the level of distribution at which a product is sold by a number of retailers but not by all potential retailers in a market area. Instead, the manufacturer selects a limited number of outlets to handle its line based on factors such as customer service levels provided by the distributor, the distributor's credit rating and other requirements. Products are typically only distributed through retail outlets where sales volume, order size and inventory turnover yield sufficient profit. Marginal retailers are avoided.

Since there are fewer intermediaries to call on, the manufacturer can decrease their marketing costs. Selective distribution also fosters close relationships with the channel members, enabling the supplier to increase cooperation and maintain control. It is easier, for instance, to make the retailers follow specific rules for advertising and displaying the products in their stores. And because there is no intense competition between dealers, price cutting can be prevented. In fact, manufacturers often pursue a selective distribution strategy to help them build a superior brand image and, in turn, charge a premium price.

With all of its advantages, selective distribution is the most widely used distribution strategy. Many business products are sold on a selective basis to maximize control over the distribution process. On the consumer market, selective distribution is especially appropriate for *shopping products* such as most apparel items, cameras, household appliances, electronic equipment and other durable products, where after-the-sale service is essential. Consumers are willing to spend a significant amount of time comparing alternatives before they buy these items, which are much more expensive than convenience products. At this level of distribution intensity, retailers are motivated to sell the products but don't have the same incentive as with an exclusive sales territory.

13.2.3 Exclusive distribution

Exclusive distribution is the extreme opposite of intensive distribution because a single retail outlet in a particular market – or a strictly limited number of select dealers in a trading area – is allowed to sell the company's products. Since buyers may have to search or travel far to purchase the product, an exclusive distribution strategy is only suitable for *specialty products* (such as Patek Philippe watches), possibly some shopping goods (with a low purchase frequency) and, in business-to-business marketing, for high-priced industrial equipment. It is not appropriate for convenience products or for products that consumers consider ordinary, since this will obviously result in lost sales.

Exclusive distribution arrangements can create a considerable marketing advantage for manufacturers by assuring that only outstanding resellers – with a reputation consistent with their product's own brand image – represent their products. For example, a cosmetics company such as Shiseido allows just a few high-end retailers to sell its products. Not placing their products in drug stores helps the firm maintain an image of quality and prestige for its brand. If the products were more widely available, they would lose the aura of exclusivity that attracts buyers in the target market.

This distribution strategy is typically used for expensive items, for products that require extensive after-sale service, or in markets with only a small number of buyers. Manufacturers may also use exclusive distribution to maintain control over the service level by requiring dealers to carry a full inventory, take part in promotional programmes and train their sales consultants to offer active sales support and superior customer service. In return, resellers receive relatively high profit margins and are guaranteed an exclusive sales territory.

FIGURE 13.5 Relationship between buying behaviour, product type and level of distribution intensity

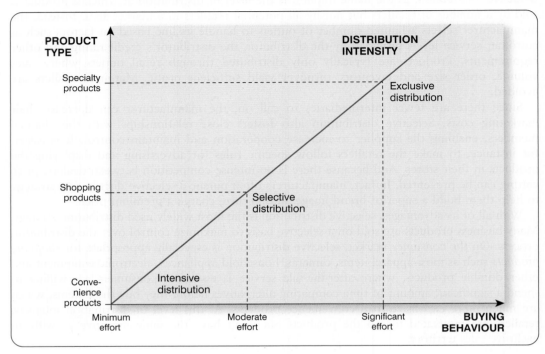

Exclusive distribution generally limits distribution costs since the manufacturer services a smaller number of accounts. It also tends to create a harmonious relationship between the middleman and the manufacturer, because each feels a part of the other's organization. That cooperation is essential if the product is to succeed.

As part of an exclusive distribution strategy for high-priced products, marketers may try to enforce an **exclusive dealing** arrangement, which prohibits a retailer from handling competing products. This will increase the retailer's dedication to the manufacturer's products. Exclusive dealing arrangements are often used in the distribution of automobiles and various brands of women's designer apparel.

As illustrated in Figure 13.5, there is a relationship between the type of product (convenience, shopping and specialty products) and the willingness of consumers to make a special effort to buy them (shown on the horizontal axis). This combination of factors provides guidelines in opting for a strategy of intensive, selective or exclusive distribution.

13.2.4 Optimal level of distribution intensity

The most important determinant of the optimal level of a product's distribution intensity is where consumers *expect* it to be sold. For instance, if consumers expect to find a product only at exclusive specialty stores in large cities, then the manufacturer would not want to have it carried by drugstores. This applies to most specialty products, which are characterized by strong brand loyalty and for which the consumer is willing to make a special purchasing effort. These products should be distributed selectively or exclusively. In contrast, convenience products such as milk or dishwasher soap, with relatively little brand loyalty, should be made available through as many retail outlets as possible. They require intensive distribution because, given the consumer expectations and buying behaviour, the manufacturer simply cannot count on consumers going out of their way to purchase the product.

Another important influence on the intensity of distribution is the manufacturer's need or desire to *control* the marketing strategy – such as the product's price, brand image and level of customer service, as determined by the elements of the marketing mix. Some questions to be considered include: How often is the product or service purchased? How is it used? What are its service requirements? Will a change in consumer preference for a particular design affect sales? Each of these considerations has an impact on distribution intensity. To illustrate, a home theatre system or washing machine for which the dealer is normally required to maintain a service department, is generally sold via selective distribution. Intensive distribution would not be appropriate because the number of retailers capable of servicing the product is limited; exclusive distribution would not be suitable because of insufficient brand loyalty. Expensive watches, also requiring the retailer to retain a service department, are usually distributed exclusively through well-established stores. A community of 500 000 rarely has more than three authorized Rolex watch retailers, while it may have as many as 50 Seiko dealers.

The price the manufacturer charges middlemen often determines what type of distribution outlets will carry the product. The higher the retailer's profit margin, the more ancillary product services they can be expected to perform. Retailers with exclusive distribution rights for a given product usually expect to have a high profit margin on each unit sold in order to offset the costs of employing well-trained salespeople and maintaining service facilities. However, products distributed intensively in supermarkets have a much smaller mark-up because customers usually do not need the assistance of salespeople to make the purchase.

Finally, promotion and channel decisions also affect each other. In the case of intensive distribution, the retailer is expected to do little more than provide display or shelf space for the product. Any mass-media advertising, therefore, is usually paid for by the manufacturer with a strategy to pull the product through the marketing channel by creating demand for it. To illustrate, some retailers prefer not to sell cigarettes since they are not very profitable. However, retailers who do not carry cigarettes realize that consumers may go elsewhere to purchase not only the cigarettes, but also other, more profitable items. In contrast, the margins for products distributed exclusively are high enough for the retailer to provide sales support, as well as some local advertising. Because of the important role played by channel members, we will now look at the process of selecting and working with them.

13.3 CHANNEL LEADERSHIP AND MANAGEMENT

Developing an effective distribution channel strategy requires a number of crucial decisions. Who should lead the marketing channel, and what can this company do to increase efficiency? What criteria should managers use to decide which intermediaries to include in the distribution channel? How can channel conflicts be avoided or resolved? And finally, what factors should the channel captain consider in evaluating the performance of independent intermediaries in the supply chain? Let's explore these questions in our analysis of channel leadership and management.

13.3.1 Who should lead the marketing channel?

The fastest way to penetrate a new market is to gain access to a distribution channel with sufficient target market coverage through an agreement with an established intermediary. Since a firm's channel partners are an extension of its own marketing operations, they should be selected carefully to ensure that they are customer-oriented and have enough product knowledge to serve the market well. Firms constantly seek out better ways to get their products into the customers' hands. In designing an effective channel system, they carefully analyze customer needs, establish channel objectives in light of the customer service level desired by the target market and evaluate the distribution alternatives.

Since products and services should be made available wherever customers expect to find them, marketers often use multiple channels, providing buyers a choice of various outlets. So, it isn't unusual for consumer products supplied through different types of distribution channels to be sold by retail institutions in direct or indirect competition. Think, for example, of a hair care brand sold through salons, drug stores and supermarkets. Figure 13.6 illustrates how different types of marketing channels (such as a short and a long distribution channel) may overlap.

The extent to which overlapping channels cause fierce price competition or other undesirable conflicts often depends on the *channel captain* or channel leader. This is a channel member with enough *power* to control others in the distribution channel, and one likely to influence their strategies.

MARKETING MISTAKE
Benetton's Colours Start to Fade?

Once the envy of all fashion retailers, Benetton has become a shadow of its former self, losing its allure as consumers flock to rival brands. In its glamorous heyday, it boasted its own basketball team, an Italian rugby club and a Formula One racing team. Legendary racing-driver Michael Schumacher won his first ever championship in 1994 in a Benetton car. These former glories now seem a world away and it is telling that the Italian family who founded the company in 1965 – and who are still majority shareholders – shifted focus towards their other interests, in luxury hotels, sports equipment and roadside restaurants, rather than the Benetton clothing brand.

Part of the problem is that Benetton continues to produce in-house clothing lines, alternating ranges too infrequently. Unfortunately, this outdated business model generates disappointing results compared to competitors *Zara* and *H&M*, that react quickly to the latest catwalk trends with 'instant fashion' reproductions at attractive prices. Benetton Group meanwhile has lagged behind the styles of the past decade. Previously perceived as an 'edgy' brand, most young consumers now view Benetton as old-fashioned, attracting a more mature demographic. Instead they shop at Abercrombie and other stylish retailers they see as being more current.

In the past ten years, sales revenues have barely increased by 2 per cent, totalling roughly €2 billion. It doesn't look like its fortunes are set to improve: the Italian clothier has been pretty much deserted by the most important fashion retailers in Europe. Compare that to the Zara and Bershka chains – owned by Inditex of Spain – that led to a rise in sales of 600 per cent to more than €14 billion, or H&M (Sweden's Hennes & Mauritz) that nearly increased its sales volume four times over to €10 billion. Both companies expect an annual sales increase of at least 6 per cent in the coming years.

While Zara and H&M run the majority of their own stores, Benetton predominantly adopts a franchise model, selling most of its goods at a wholesale price under half of the price generated through retail. Since most outlets are not run by Benetton directly, it has proved difficult to adjust product rotation according to demand. Benetton has lacked the immediate interaction from actual shoppers, failing to connect and react quickly enough to consumer dissatisfaction and empty stores, which eventually made numerous franchisees quit to look for more lucrative business opportunities.

This disappointing slump in Benetton's fortunes is in marked contrast to the 1980s, when its sensationalist ad campaigns sent shockwaves through the industry. Promotions featured intentionally provocative imagery (and certainly risqué to contemporary audiences) including death row murderers and breaking religious and racial taboos. This roused much excitement amongst press and shoppers, leading to a significant exposure and profits for the brand. Yet from an international presence of over 7 000 outlets in the mid-1990s, the once controversial and exciting label gradually became outmoded.

Benetton needs an awareness of cultural differences in other territories to adapt marketing strategies accordingly. Advertising campaigns showing the Chinese Premier kissing US President Barack Obama, for example, while acceptable in Western cities, would not necessarily be approved of in China. Besides, a business model and marketing techniques that were appropriate in the 1980s would need significant adaptation in order to penetrate emerging BRICS countries. Zara and H&M

made the transition to truly global brands; something Benetton failed to accomplish to the same degree of success.

To firmly control the supply chain, Benetton's European competitors are vertically integrated

The main issue is that Benetton's key competitors use a *vertical-integration* model, allowing them to firmly command all activities in the supply chain, from concept, through production and into the shops. This has enabled Zara and H&M fast relocation of manufacturing to countries where garments can be produced at a lower cost. In contrast, Benetton's model, necessitating larger overheads, simply cannot compete. Four recent top management transitions have not improved performance either. Moreover, roughly 50 per cent of its sales volume is generated domestically. With doubts concerning the Italian economy, it is a tough time to be so reliant upon a single, and potentially unstable, market. Indeed, Italy's recession has especially affected the middle class – the very people who traditionally have tended to shop at Benetton.

More positively, the company still has a presence in over 100 countries, suggesting there are still markets where Benetton may find room to thrive with the right strategies. Furthermore, recent restructuring at Benetton will save nearly €100 million in reduced costs for raw materials. In addition, an injection of about half this amount in a Serbian factory should improve roll-out efficiency of new lines, while reducing manufacturing outlay. However, more than half of Benetton's revenue is taken away by costs, significantly more than its rival brands, meaning much smaller profit margins.

It's crucial for Benetton to prove that it is able to control cost inflation and to make sure that it won't lose further ground against competitors, through critically monitoring quality and demand, and adopting a faster response to changing consumer tastes. This may well be Benetton's biggest challenge in the next few years.[4]

Let's now look at some key sources of power in the channel, at the need for a channel leader to have a differential advantage, and at vertical marketing systems that reduce the chances of channel conflicts.

Channel power

Channel power is the ability of one channel member to cause another channel member to act in ways it otherwise would not have acted. Manufacturers use both incentives (for example,

FIGURE 13.6 Overlapping marketing channels

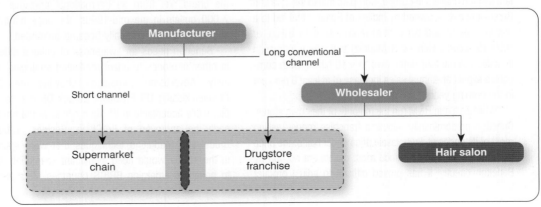

Image Asset Management

sales contests or cooperative advertising allowances) and sanctions (such as a threat to delay delivery or end the relationship) to gain intermediaries' cooperation. At the same time, the channel captain should continue to emphasize that all channel members are partners in a joint effort to meet the needs and wants of the product's final users.

The primary sources of power in the channel are economic power and position power. Economic power manifests itself in the concentration of capital resources. Companies with strong financial resources are able to conduct ongoing, in-depth marketing research, employ the most highly experienced management team and best allocate advertising budgets to create brand or store loyalty. For example, Unilever, a national brand behemoth, owe their leading market position in some product categories to substantial investments in new product development, as well as the profit margins and incentives they provide resellers in the channel to gain their support.

Position power, on the other hand, stems from the location of the company in the channel. In particular, those companies closest to the customer and controlling access to the mass market enjoy a favourable position. Many large retail organizations have more power in the distribution channel than wholesalers or manufacturers. In fact, national supermarket chains with high sales volumes derive their channel power from a combination of economic and position power. One reason supermarket chains in Europe and the United States have gained channel power relative to manufacturers is their well-planned use of private labels to position their stores in the market.

Differential advantage

A powerful position in a distribution channel is not necessarily permanent. Until the 1970s, for example, major manufacturers such as Unilever controlled marketing channels that supplied fast moving consumer goods in many European countries. With products in strong demand, these channel leaders could exercise control by offering or withholding their products from particular intermediaries, and did not hesitate to use their power to impose pricing and other conditions on retailers before supplying them. At that time, they were the only organizations in the channel in a position to develop full marketing programmes, complete with new product development and introduction, national advertising campaigns for premium brands and the selection of wholesalers and retailers.

The manufacturers' channel leadership began to slip when new laws made *vertical price fixing* illegal, their products matured and competitors began to develop similar products. The power at that point shifted to retailers, which were then better situated to pick and choose among the manufacturers and the product lines they would handle. Most supermarket chains also developed distributor brands (*store brands*) and offered these to customers at lower prices, thereby increasing their loyalty to the store. Since even the largest manufacturers were not able or willing to establish their own retail outlets, they had to cooperate with channel intermediaries if all of their products were to reach the marketplace.

There is no obvious or definitive answer to the question of who should lead the marketing channel. Yet, it is important that one organization assumes a leadership role so that products can be most efficiently brought to the marketplace. Generally, the company with the greatest differential advantage will become the leader. A firm's differential advantage – also called distinctive competence – is an advantage that is unique to an organization, has obvious value for customers and is difficult to match by a competitor.[5] The manufacturer's distinctive advantage is founded on being better than others at developing and producing the goods demanded by society, while retail organizations have the distinct knowledge and resources to effectively deliver those products to the market. In marketing channels, a differential advantage is often temporary and can only be maintained through continued innovation. It only becomes a permanent or sustainable competitive advantage when competitors cannot duplicate the benefits of another channel member's value-creating strategy.

Vertical marketing systems

A marketing channel performs best if conflict can be avoided through dynamic leadership by one of the channel members. In the past, however, many distribution channels did not have a strong channel captain that assigned roles and managed conflict. These so-called conventional distribution channels were fairly loose networks in which organizations such as manufacturers, wholesalers, retailers and sometimes brokers and agents worked independently of each other. The relationships between these separate businesses were limited to simply selling to and buying from each other. Although there were occasional power struggles as each firm tried to maximize its own profits – even if this reduced profits for the system as a whole – most conventional channels were still successful in accomplishing the common goals of creating demand, limiting costs and increasing customer satisfaction.

Recently, however, an improved system of providing leadership and managing channel relationships has emerged. It is called a vertical marketing system (VMS) – a professionally managed and centrally coordinated network of channel relationships designed for maximum efficiency and market impact. The producer, wholesaler or retailer can control a VMS, but they act as a unified system. One of them, the channel captain, either owns the other channel members, has contracts with them or wields influence so powerful that they all cooperate. The three major types of vertical marketing systems – corporate, contractual and administered – are shown in Figure 13.7.

Today, most consumer products are sold through a vertical marketing system. The word *vertical* refers to the 'downstream' flow of goods, or 'down the channel' from manufacturer to consumer.

A corporate system is a VMS in which one company owns and controls other channel members at a different level of the distribution channel. Levi Strauss, for example, not only makes jeans but also markets them through its own Levi's® Stores. This is an example of forward integration, in which a manufacturer operates its own retail stores or distribution

FIGURE 13.7 Types of vertical marketing systems

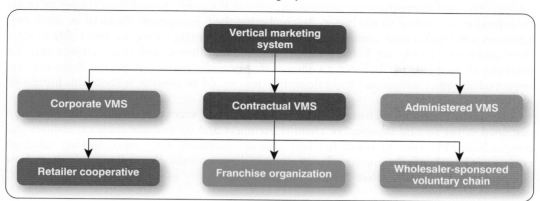

centres. An alternative way of forming a corporate vertical marketing system is through backward integration. It occurs when a retailer acquires a manufacturer or a manufacturer buys a raw material supplier thereby gaining control over an input in the distribution or production process upstream in the channel. Here, too, the objective is to improve the efficiency and effectiveness of the channel.

The most common form of VMS, a contractual system, is one controlled and coordinated by formal contracts, as opposed to ownership. Independent firms at different levels in the channel sign a formal agreement that specifies each member's rights and responsibilities and indicates how they will participate. There are three popular forms of contractual arrangement. One is a *retail-sponsored* cooperative in which retailers establish a wholesaling operation to help them compete effectively with large corporate chains. Each retailer is required to buy a certain percentage of merchandise from the wholesaler in which they own shares. The members typically have a common store name and store brand.

A second type of contractual VMS is a *franchise*. In this organization, the parent company, or franchisor, grants the franchisee the right to sell certain products or services under an established name and to operate according to specific marketing guidelines. They also provide marketing research, promotional, purchasing and other support services. In this huge growth industry, numerous companies distribute their goods and services – with minimal financial risk while maintaining quality control – through systems of franchised dealers. Among the many examples in the global market are McDonald's restaurants, Holiday Inn hotels and Coca-Cola bottlers.

Finally, a *wholesaler-sponsored voluntary chain* involves a wholesaler strengthening its independent retail customers by developing a contractual relationship with them. As the channel leader, the wholesaler negotiates prices and delivery to fulfil the needs of the retailers downstream in the channel. By adopting a common name, standardizing buying and inventory control methods and coordinating promotional programmes, retailers can achieve economies of scale allowing them to better compete with large chain organizations.

In an administered system, a large, dominant channel member uses its power to coordinate the channel at the successive stages of production and distribution. This could be a manufacturer such as Unilever gaining cooperation from retailers (in providing shelf space and participating in sales promotion) during a new product launch. Another case in point would be a large retailer such as Ikea using its purchasing power to influence certain manufacturers in the type of products they make and their delivery policies.

A vertical marketing system should not be confused with a **horizontal marketing system**, in which companies (competitors or non-competitors) at the same channel level cooperate to get their product or service to the buyer. By combining their production, financial or marketing resources – through a joint venture or other type of arrangement – they are better able to serve their customers. KLM, Air France, Delta, Aeroflot, Northwest and other airlines are, for example, all members of SkyTeam, an alliance that provides passengers greater flight options, improved customer service and more flexibility than would be possible without this horizontal marketing system.

Since many distribution channels lack these forms of alliances, the producer has to make a sustained effort to find prospective channel members and to evaluate their capabilities and compatibility. In order to select the best channel members, they must develop selection criteria and evaluate the intermediaries against these criteria. We will now look at how companies systematically select channel members.

13.3.2 Selecting channel members

The evaluation and selection of resellers is most relevant to the firm if it pursues a strategy of selective or exclusive distribution. After all, with intensive distribution, the manufacturer tries to persuade as many acceptable retailers as possible to carry the product – often in multiple distribution channels – to reach all of the users in the market. Limited distribution, on the other hand, requires manufacturers to make more carefully considered distribution choices.

Since a marketing orientation involves taking the customer's viewpoint, the *market segments* targeted by the company influence the evaluation of channel alternatives. The selected channel members must be compatible with the customers' buying behaviour and expectations of the target market. First of all, is the company targeting organizational customers or ultimate consumers? How do the buyers prefer to access the product? What channel member functions do customers in each segment value? For example, do some buyers need fast delivery and are they willing to pay for it? Which available or new channel members are best able to meet the customers' requirements?

The more a company knows about the buying habits and other characteristics of its customers (Where are they located? How do they buy? What appeals to them?), the better it can decide on the types of intermediaries to use. In practice the decision of which intermediaries to include in the channel of distribution is also influenced by the company's characteristics (such as its financial and human resources) and goals, as well as competitors' distribution strategies and other forces in the market environment. The product's characteristics and the distributors' availability and willingness to carry the products or offer the services must also be taken into consideration.

Company characteristics

The company's own financial and personnel resources may limit the range of distribution network options. A manufacturer with limited capital and marketing expertise may be forced to use intermediaries to sell the product, even if direct marketing would be more profitable. On the other hand, the greater the firm's resources, the more control it has over how the product is marketed. It can use its own sales force and is able to exercise more control over resellers through the use of special promotion campaigns, displays and mass advertising.

The selection of appropriate distribution channels is also influenced by the extent to which it helps the company realize its overall goals and objectives. If a company's goal is to maximize profitability (instead of, for example, increasing market share or entering new markets), the firm may estimate for each channel option both the sales volume potential and costs of channel usage, and then compare their potential contributions to long-term profit.

Competition

How do competing firms distribute their products or services? Do they use intensive, selective or exclusive distribution? Do they employ outside intermediaries or do they perform the distribution function solely with their own personnel? These are key questions not because the competition is always right, but because the company may have to change its distribution policies in response to a competitor's change in distribution practices. This competitor could be at the same level in the distribution channel (for example, another manufacturer), at a different level (a wholesaler) or in a different distribution channel (such as the Internet). In addition, the selection of distribution channels and channel members could be affected by environmental factors such as economic, technological, political, legal and ecological forces.

Product characteristics

The channels and partners a firm decides to use are very much related to the characteristics of its products. Convenience, shopping and specialty products are sold in different stores and, therefore, through different channels. But the selection of channel members is also influenced by a reseller's skill at offering technically complex products or by perishable items' need for special handling. Moreover, the product's desired image may make it best suited for sale in specialty stores or other upscale retail outlets. Finally, as Table 13.3 shows, the channel design may have to be adapted as the product moves through the various stages in the product life cycle.

Availability of distributors

The selection of channel members is a two-way street. In many markets, the large, powerful retail organizations are in the driver's seat when it comes to selecting merchandise (thereby, specific manufacturers' brands) they will carry. Manufacturers may have to present a

TABLE 13.3 Distribution strategy changes during the product life cycle

Characteristics	Introduction	Growth	Maturity	Decline
Number of channel members	Few (exclusive)	Several (selective)	Many (intensive)	Few (exclusive)
Added value by channel	Very high	Medium	Low	Very low
Profit margins	High	Medium	Low	Very low
Strategic priority	Market penetration	Market expansion	Market share	Efficiency
Examples of channel alternatives used	• Direct sales force • Discounters	• Specialty stores • Company website	• Internet • Specialty stores	• Franchisees • Direct mail

convincing case that selling their products will be lucrative for resellers. Prospective intermediaries that don't have faith in a product will not be willing to sell it. Or if they already carry a competitive product with a strong sales record, they may be reluctant to jeopardize the relationship with their current supplier by starting to sell a competing brand.

Assuming the manufacturer does have a high quality product, how can it persuade the best distributors to carry the merchandise? To secure the services of quality channel members, they may offer incentives, or (usually financial) inducements to encourage distributors to sell the product or service. Frequently, the incentives are based on the distributor's performance. As an example, the manufacturer may provide grants or cooperative advertising programmes to supplement a distributor's own advertising initiatives, or offer sales promotion assistance in the form of free promotional literature and point-of-purchase displays. Alternatively, they may provide a training programme for the distributor's sales force, or free consulting advice in the areas of purchasing, inventory control, order handling and financial management. These incentive plans are an increasingly common component of the manufacturer's *trade relations mix*. A manufacturer unsuccessful in attracting a distributor can either try to sell the product directly or engage a qualified reseller with less immediate potential.

Selection criteria

In making the final selection of suitable channel intermediaries, the manufacturer is likely already to have a preference for certain organizations and people based on their personal judgment and current contacts. However, in order to objectively evaluate one potential channel member against another, the manufacturer should assess each prospective distributor in relation to a uniform set of criteria.

Useful *selection criteria* for prospective distributors include their cooperativeness, existing product line assortment, growth potential, number of years in business, clientele, service reputation and compatibility with the target market. Each must also be financially strong enough to commit the resources required to maintain necessary inventory levels or sales programmes, and to extend credit to their accounts (as is expected of wholesalers). A Dun & Bradstreet credit rating is the usual source for determining a distributor's financial condition. Other frequently used selection criteria include the size and quality of the sales force (formal training, experience, commitment and customer service), inventory and warehouse practices (willingness to carry sufficient inventory, location of the distribution centres, handling of returns and speed of delivery), and the expertise or reputation of management (especially as it relates to the marketing strategy and sales objectives).

13.3.3 Channel conflict

Some managers feel that any form of conflict among channel members is dysfunctional and inefficient. Others, by contrast, feel that a lack of conflict breeds complacency, making it more difficult for the system to adopt innovations. The fact remains that regardless of management opinions on the subject or how carefully the intermediaries have been selected, conflict is not uncommon within a distribution channel. The channel members differ significantly in terms of their channel positions, strategies, the tasks they perform and their profit objectives. These conflicting interests may lead to a channel conflict: a situation in which one channel member's behaviour is at odds with the interests of another and prevents it from achieving its objectives. In this clash of strategies and goals between the supply chain members, three types of channel conflict may arise: horizontal, multi-channel and vertical conflict.

Horizontal conflict takes place between intermediaries at the same level in a marketing channel. An example is competition between two or more wholesalers or two or more retailers, such as different supermarkets selling similar products or even identical brands at different prices. A frequent source of horizontal conflict is a company's increased distribution intensity in a particular region. A Subway franchisee, for instance, may oppose a new Subway restaurant opening up close to their own and complain about it to the franchisor.

If channel conflict happens because a manufacturer, due to its dual distribution strategy, sells through different types of retailers in the same market area – for instance supermarkets and drugstores – the clash is regarded as a *multi-channel conflict*. Such conflict is often the result of one of the types of distribution outlets, typically a discounter, selling the product at a lower price, or getting more favourable terms from the manufacturer because of its high volume purchases.

While most people in a free market society consider horizontal or multi-channel conflict healthy competition, the same does not necessarily apply to a vertical channel conflict. *Vertical conflict* develops among members at different levels of the same marketing channel, such as between a manufacturer and a wholesaler over issues like inventory policies, the level of promotional support or wholesale margins. Vertical conflicts, too, are often caused by a producer's dual distribution strategies. One illustration might be a manufacturer that creates competition by giving consumers the option of direct online purchasing through its own website, resulting in a conflict with its traditional bricks-and-mortar retailers. Conflict can also appear when a channel member altogether bypasses an intermediary – typically a wholesaler – and sells or buys products directly. This bypassing of intermediaries is called **disintermediation**. The term is also used to describe the appearance, often through e-commerce, of completely new types of intermediaries that displace traditional resellers.

Focusing on vertical conflict, we will now analyze the most common sources of channel conflict and methods of resolving them.

Sources of conflict

The most significant sources of conflict in the channel of distribution are channel members' incompatible goals and lack of clarity or disagreement in assigning roles. While all channel members may accept some general *goals*, such as delivering the product or service at a competitive price to the customer, each firm in the supply chain also has its own goals that depend on the unique problems and opportunities it faces. Unfortunately, the goals of individual channel members often are incompatible. The manufacturer may wish to expand the sales of a new product while the retailer refuses to invest the capital required to sell additional products. In the practice known as **full-line forcing**, for instance, a manufacturer may require retailers to carry its full product line, including those products retailers find slow-moving or unprofitable. This approach can be used to a manufacturer's advantage in expanding its product line; however, retailers, pursuing short-term profitability, sometimes prefer to carry only the more desirable, established products. Requiring middlemen to carry a full product line is most likely to occur when resellers are dependent on the manufacturer in a particular product category.

Another frequent cause of channel conflict is uncertainty about each company's *roles*. This usually happens when a channel member does not perform as expected or when the parties cannot agree on the assignment of roles ('who does what?'). For example, do manufacturers have the right to use their own sales forces to sell to large buyers, leaving just the smaller accounts to intermediaries, or to enforce territorial restrictions, dictating where a wholesaler can sell products? Can the manufacturer require intermediaries not to sell competitive products (*exclusive dealing*) even if such sales are essential to their business? Other **role conflicts** typically have to do with marketing research (what market information the producer and the intermediaries should share) and desired inventory levels (how many items retailers are required keep in stock).

Solutions to channel conflict

Sometimes a conflict seems so difficult to resolve that the frustrated parties simply discontinue their working relationship. This resolution often leads to reduced profits for both parties as well as to dissatisfied customers, who must now find new ways to obtain the merchandise they want. When long-term service commitments are involved, the situation becomes even more complex.

There are at least two legal remedies to avoid severing a business relationship. One is to resolve the conflict through *litigation*, by which a fair and impartial court determines whether one of the parties has been harmed and, if so, what remedial or punitive action should be taken. Although litigation leads to a final public decision, it is expensive and time consuming. In addition, the firms involved in the dispute often find it difficult to work together again after a tough court battle, especially if media coverage of the legal action further damages the business relationship. Therefore, most firms prefer the alternative of arbitration.

Arbitration is a process of negotiation and conflict resolution involving a third party brought into the dispute to act as an impartial hearing judge. When the two parties present their arguments, this expert person or arbitrator not only determines which party is at fault, but also stipulates specific actions each party must take to resolve the dispute. Since both parties have agreed prior to entering into arbitration to accept the verdict, arbitration is an effective way of solving conflicts in the marketing channel.

13.3.4 Evaluation and control of distributors

Suppliers must regularly evaluate the performance of the independent resellers in their distribution channels. They need to assess how effective these middlemen have been in realizing their distribution objectives. Armed with this information, they are able to adjust their distribution strategies as deemed necessary. Sales performance is, by far, the single most important consideration in evaluating distributors. Other assessment criteria include inventory management and warehouse procedures, distributors' willingness to participate in promotional activities and their contribution to achieving a satisfactory service level.

Sales performance

A supplier always prefers to work with a distributor that consistently meets its sales objectives. In evaluating sales performance, suppliers generally make a comparative analysis of each distributor's current sales volume to its sales in previous time periods, such as the prior year or quarter. This analysis of historical sales data – broken down by product or product class, and by type of customer or customer industry – is widely used in assessing channel member performance.

Distributors may also be evaluated by comparing their actual sales figures against the previously established **sales quotas**, sales objectives or goals that can be expressed in units sold, total revenues or market share. Quotas can be set for a line of merchandise or even for individual products. In evaluating any particular distributor, it is useful to look at how successful the other distributors have been in meeting their quotas. This information also helps the manufacturer determine if realistic sales objectives were set.

Yet another assessment used by suppliers is a comparison of the sales performance of each individual reseller with that of other resellers. This can be accomplished in a number of ways. One technique is to compute the average sales volume for all the firm's distributors and then compare each distributor's performance to the 'average' distributor. This comparison can be made using a variety of sales data, including total sales, sales by product type and rate of sales growth. A second approach is to compare a distributor's sales performance with the average performance of the supplier's best distributors – usually those in the top 10 per cent. Most companies using these techniques break down the data into sales regions. Distributing the results of this analysis to its own sales force helps the supplier's salespeople identify the distributors in their sales region that may need additional support.

Other evaluation factors

Suppliers are not inclined to spend much time evaluating the sales performance of distributors that meet or exceed their sales quota. This, however, may be a mistake; an assessment of other important factors could alert the supplier to potential problems or help even top performing resellers increase sales. Evaluating channel member performance requires attention to the same key factors a supplier looks at when selecting a new distributor. These *functional* areas include a distributor's financial position (can they, for example, maintain inventory at the required level?), their sales force (do they employ enough well-trained sales people to successfully sell the product or service?), the professional relationships with other channel members (do they work effectively with other firms in the supply chain?), their customer orientation (do they keep up with changing customer preferences?) and expected future developments (how well will this reseller perform in the future?). These last two criteria, especially, should be carefully considered, since customers and technological developments often drive major changes in marketing channels, as we have seen with e-commerce in both consumer and organizational markets.

Control of the distribution channel

From a management point of view, distribution is both a controllable marketing instrument and an environmental factor. A manager's tasks include deciding on the distribution intensity, determining the optimal length of the marketing channel and selecting distributors. Less controllable, however, are the channel structure, the balance of power within the supply chain and the resellers' behaviour. Ultimately, the degree of control a manufacturer can exert over distributors strongly depends on its *power* in the channel.

Suppliers pursue various strategies to increase their control of the distribution channel. Some adopt a selective or *exclusive distribution* strategy, hoping that the resellers will value the relationship with the supplier and, as loyal partners in the distribution system, be more willing to cooperate with any reasonable requests. In the business market, for instance, this may help to persuade channel members that it is in their best interest to adopt the suggested price schedule. The supplier can reinforce its pricing by advertising the product or featuring it on their own website at a specified price or by attaching a price ticket to the product at the time it is produced. Still, suppliers cannot legally force resellers to accept a particular pricing strategy.

Other suppliers try to control their resellers' activities through the type and amount of *promotional assistance* they provide. If they want a reseller to advertise the product, they may offer them a cooperative advertising allowance. They can also provide intermediaries with brochures, displays and other promotional layout materials, designed by professional marketing communication agencies, to present their products or services in the best possible light and control how they are represented to the consumer.

Finally, suppliers can try to strengthen their ties with resellers by offering assistance in customer service, credit practices, inventory control procedures or even by providing more rapid delivery from their own distribution centres. They can reinforce efficient and dependable actions on the part of intermediaries by rewarding them with special discounts or performance bonuses. In marketing channels characterized by intense competition and continuous information-technology innovation, these strategies may help suppliers to secure the intermediaries' future *loyalty*.

MARKETING TOPPER
Keeping Up with Africa's Middle Class

From 'soap to soup', demand for consumer products in Africa is growing exponentially. In large part, this is due to Africa's growing middle class. According to the African Development Bank, this 'middle class' (Africans who earn between €1.50 and €15 per day) is quickly expanding. In 2010, the African middle class was about one-third of the country's population (roughly 300 million potential consumers), but it is projected to more than triple to one billion consumers in about 50 years. That translates into higher laundry soap sales for the Anglo-Dutch multinational *Unilever*, more children's milk powder sales for the Swiss multinational *Nestlé*, and increasing yogurt sales for French multinational *Danone*. Unilever, Nestlé and Danone are among the many global companies that realize the importance of marketing to the African continent as they chart their growth strategies over the next decade. Nestlé, for example, expects almost half of its sales to come from emerging markets in the next few years, with African markets a major part of that segment.

Thus, for companies around the world, Africa's attractiveness is increasing. The continent has survived the global downturn well, and its economy is growing faster than most non-BRIC emerging markets (the acronym BRIC was first used in 2001 to express the broader shift in economic growth toward emerging markets and originally included Brazil, Russia, India and China; it was renamed BRICS after South Africa was incorporated). No wonder that this enormous growth opportunity is attracting a huge number of global companies. A significant percentage of the world's top 50 consumer packaged goods companies already maintain a presence there, and companies from emerging markets are trying to enlarge their footprint there as well.

Marketing to this unique and expanding market will require a more thorough understanding of the landscape, considering that this substantial continent is a medley of various cultures and languages. Hence, mar-

keters must decide how to best alter products and marketing strategies to suit the differing consumers' needs. It will also require tailoring products to the specific needs of African consumers who are very price-sensitive. Multinationals that want to benefit from this growing economy are already offering products in small, affordable packages, which are quite attractive to many African consumers, especially those living in rural areas.

Fast growing companies that bypass traditional distribution channels and create more innovative ones (such as informal retail channels) realize that they need a completely different type of sales force than they use in industrialized markets. As they enlarge their presence in a country, they may have to recruit and train workers locally in order to generate a workforce that better fits their needs. They also have come up with creative solutions to deal with challenges in an emerging market's infrastructure, and to make sure that they get reliable transportation and utility services.

Before selecting an appropriate *entry strategy* for the African market, there are some other important issues and features of emerging economies to consider. The first one is the decision of *what countries* to enter and where to grow. Most companies choose to first enter 'economically robust' countries such as South Africa, Nigeria, Kenya and Egypt. Within those nations, they often settle down in large, established city markets before moving into smaller towns. But in most emerging markets in Africa, the key to success is to remain flexible enough to seize opportunities as they arise, such as acquiring businesses that are offered for sale because they are privatized.

A second decision involves whether to *partner* with or *acquire* local companies with the right complementary capabilities. Partnering can help secure loyal customers, provide crucial access to distribution channels or supplier networks and obtain production facilities. It may also enable the company to gain a competitive advantage by aligning with strong local brands. In a region with higher risks for acquisitions, it may be wise to start with smaller companies, purchasing a majority stake in a joint venture and creating clauses that allow easy exit if necessary. Working with local experts and conducting research to analyze the market and the available financial data will allow management to reduce the risk and make the best possible choices.

The last decision is *what products* or brands to sell in Africa. Some companies, instead of offering local products or brands to gain ground, prefer to market existing products, if that appears to be a lucrative growth opportunity. Unilever chose to educate Nigerian consumers about the merits of twice-daily teeth brushing, effectively growing the markets for its established brands of toothpaste and toothbrushes at the same time.

South Africa may be the next best place on Earth to explore growth opportunities

Entering or expanding a business in Africa may seem difficult because of the continent's diverse nature. But Africa, and in particular, South Africa, may not be much more challenging than most other emerging markets. In fact, because growth in other developing markets appears to be slowing down, South Africa may be the 'next best place on Earth' to explore new growth opportunities.

It certainly was a lucrative opportunity for the world's largest retailer, *Walmart*, which has been eager to expand its international footprint as its domestic growth possibilities in the United States become more saturated. It acquired a 51 per cent stake in *Massmart*, a company with a strong presence of wholesale and retail stores in South Africa and in 13 other countries in Africa. At the end of the day, the partnership will enhance Massmart's ability to reach more middle-class consumers in Africa, will provide a starting point for Walmart to increase its presence in a fast-growing emerging market and will likely signal to other foreign companies the accessibility of African markets. For South African price-conscious consumers, this may translate into lower prices, as few retailers in the world could hope to compete with Walmart's well-known strengths in volume-based low pricing and logistics of suppliers and distribution.[6]

13.4 WHOLESALING

In many countries, wholesalers are the weakest link in the supply chain, and they face the constant threat of being eliminated. Yet, as an extension of the producer's sales force, wholesalers provide a wide range of essential services to both producers and retailers.

The term **wholesaling** refers to all transactions in which products or services are bought for resale, used in making other products or for general business operations. Wholesalers do not sell to ultimate consumers. Because wholesalers sell to retailers as well as to manufacturers and other wholesalers, and some products are sold several times at the wholesale level, in most economies wholesaling constitutes a larger sector than retailing.

Do wholesalers play a useful role in distributing products and services to consumers? Would the prices of products be lowered if the wholesaler were taken out of the equation? To give a balanced answer to these questions, we will explore the marketing functions performed by

wholesalers, examine why the wholesaling intermediary's position has been weakened and will learn how wholesalers may secure their position in the distribution channel in spite of the rapidly changing market. We conclude that only a market-oriented approach will lead to success.

13.4.1 *What is a wholesaler?*

There is no universally accepted definition of a wholesaler. That is because many different types of intermediaries engage in wholesaling activities. Some handle broad lines of products and provide retailers a wide range of services. Other wholesalers specialize in selling only to manufacturers and other wholesalers. Still others never actually own or take physical possession of the goods they sell.

For our purposes, a **wholesaler** is defined as a firm that specializes in assisting producers to sell products to other wholesalers, importers, retailers or businesses that, in turn, sell the products to ultimate consumers or use them to produce something else. Wholesalers (often called *distributors*) sell large quantities of merchandise but a defining feature is that they do not deal directly with ultimate consumers. However, they are not necessarily large organizations. When a greengrocer supplies a local restaurant with asparagus, it is acting as a wholesaler.

Wholesaling intermediaries, a broader category than wholesalers, includes not only wholesalers, but also brokers, import brokers and agents that conduct important wholesaling activities but do not take title to the products they sell.

Wholesalers perform various key services for other firms in the distribution channel. Acting as adjuncts to the manufacturer's own sales force, they provide trained sales people who sell directly to retailers. This, in turn, allows producers and service companies to sell locally without contacting customers. By purchasing products in large quantities and holding them in inventory, they reduce the producer's warehousing and physical distribution costs. They build the assortments their customers want and are able to quickly deliver them at a relatively low cost, even to small resellers.

Wholesalers may offer financing for manufacturers by prompt payment of invoices and to retailers and other buyers by extending credit. They provide marketing and research support in the distribution channel by keeping manufacturers up to date on market developments and opportunities, and by communicating the suppliers' promotional plans to other channel members. By bearing the cost of theft, damage and inventory obsolescence, they absorb some risks otherwise taken by the manufacturer. Most importantly, wholesalers enable manufacturers to concentrate on producing goods and developing services that satisfy customers' needs and wants. It is clear that wholesalers are a crucial link in the distribution process, providing managerial assistance and optimal customer service while increasing supply chain efficiency.

13.4.2 *Types of wholesaling*

Wholesalers can be classified into three broad categories: manufacturer-owned wholesalers, merchant wholesalers and agents and brokers. As we will see, these various intermediaries differ in terms of who owns the wholesaler and who owns the products they sell.

Manufacturer-owned wholesalers

Some manufacturers establish a separate business unit in which they set up their own wholesaling operation, referred to as a manufacturer-owned wholesaler. This allows them to maintain total control over how the products are sold, while focusing on production.

Distributing directly through company-owned facilities makes sense when other intermediaries cannot effectively handle the product line. Such a situation may arise if the products need special attention (such as technical assistance), are perishable or have a high value per unit, which would require a substantial investment on the part of the intermediary. Manufacturer's wholesalers are also used when they are more economical than dealing with an independent wholesaler, for instance when there are few, geographically concentrated customers, or when orders are large. The final reason for manufacturers to operate their own wholesaling facilities is that they are unable to locate a good wholesaler to carry their products. Many wholesalers, for example, refuse to sell directly competing products.

There are two types of manufacturer-owned wholesalers: sales branches (also called *sales outlets*) and sales offices. A sales branch is a wholesale outlet that stocks and sells products to nearby customers. It is located away from the factory, typically where high-volume customers are concentrated and demand is high. Here, the manufacturer essentially performs all of the wholesaling functions, including providing sophisticated managerial assistance to clients, which include business buyers, retailers and other wholesalers.

A much more common form of wholly-owned wholesaling facility is a sales office. Unlike branches, sales offices carry no inventory but serve as a base for sales representatives who call on customers in the region. When a sale is made, the merchandise is delivered directly from the manufacturer to the buyer. Located close to the company's customers, sales offices help limit selling costs and support customer service.

Merchant wholesalers

Many producers have found that it is more lucrative to use merchant wholesalers than their own sales branches to sell to business buyers and retailers. Merchant wholesalers are independently owned firms that purchase goods from manufacturers for resale to other channel members. A manufacturer is likely to use these middlemen when it is not economically feasible to use its own sales force to sell directly to business users. To illustrate, a manufacturer's distribution and selling costs to reach 1 500 business users will be much lower if it sells to 15 merchant wholesalers, each with 100 accounts, than if the manufacturer uses its own sales people to call on 1 500 customers. In fact, merchant wholesalers constitute the majority of companies engaged in wholesaling activities in organizational markets.

Depending on the number of functions they perform, merchant wholesalers are classified as either full-service or limited-service wholesalers. Full-service wholesalers take title and possession of the products they sell and provide a full range of services to their customers. Many employ a sales force, store inventory, offer financing, make deliveries and provide management assistance. In the business-goods market, some full-service wholesalers – usually called industrial distributors – sell machinery, business tools and supplies to manufacturers. Yet other full-service wholesalers sell to retailers, carrying either several merchandise lines or an extensive assortment of a single product line.

A **service merchandiser** is a full-service wholesaler that markets specialized lines of primarily non-food items to grocery retailers. Because they provide the racks or shelves on which merchandise is displayed, this type of wholesaler is sometimes known as a rack jobber. The service merchandiser supplies products with high profit margins, such as magazines or health and beauty aids, which are not usually considered part of the regular food store assortment. Delivery drivers periodically check displays, replenish the stock and keep inventory records. Service merchandisers assume risk by retaining title to the products. The only responsibility of the retailer, who receives a percentage of sales revenues, is to provide space for the merchandise and to collect the money for items that are sold. The economic rationale for service merchandisers is that they permit supermarkets to carry a wider variety of merchandise than they could handle if they relied only on their own marketing expertise.

Limited-service merchant wholesalers also take title to the merchandise they sell, but do not offer a complete line of marketing services to their customers. They specialize in just a few functions. Manufacturers perform the remaining functions or pass them on to other intermediaries or to customers. Because limited-service merchant wholesalers usually do not deliver products, carry inventory, extend credit or provide marketing information, the mark-up on the merchandise they sell is lower. Three common types of limited-service merchant wholesalers are drop shippers, truck wholesalers and cash-and-carry wholesalers.

Drop shippers, also known as *desk jobbers*, negotiate sales but never take physical possession of the goods. Instead, they forward orders from buyers to manufacturers who ship directly to a location specified by the customer. The products sold by drop shippers are bulky goods, such as building materials, for which there is a substantial economic advantage in avoiding the extra handling cost of transporting the merchandise to the wholesaler prior to its delivery to the customer.

Truck wholesalers, sometimes called *truck jobbers*, use their trucks as warehouses for merchandise they get on consignment from a large full-service wholesaler. Dealing primarily with small retailers, restaurants, hotels and hospitals, they sell and deliver semi-perishable and perishable food items such as fruit, cheeses and bakery products directly from the back of their trucks. Although they provide many of the services of full-service wholesalers, they do not extend credit to their customers.

Cash-and-carry wholesalers perform most wholesaling functions except for financing and delivery. Instead, their customers must go to the warehouse, pay for the merchandise and carry it away themselves. Small retailers, caterers and business customers that are too small for other wholesalers to call on or businesses that need to quickly replenish their stock may use these wholesalers. Cash-and carry wholesalers – such as Makro – are commonplace in Europe and South America, and they specialize in such product categories as groceries, office supplies, clothing and seasonals.

Agents and brokers

Agents and brokers, another category of independent wholesalers, facilitate the buying and selling of goods and services. They may or may not take possession of the products they handle, but unlike merchant wholesalers, they never take title; that is, they do not accept legal ownership of merchandise. They are compensated by either a commission or brokerage fee, which is generally based on the product's selling price, whereas merchant wholesalers make their profits from sales of the products they own.

Sometimes called *functional middlemen*, agents and brokers perform only a limited number of services, one of which is related to the transfer of title. Their chief function is helping to bring buyers and sellers together for a sale and to assist in negotiation. They typically specialize in certain products or types of customers, often have long-standing relationships with prospective buyers and know their markets well.

The most common type of agent wholesaler is the manufacturer's agent. This independent person or small business usually markets several related, but non-competing, product lines in a specific geographic area, and is paid a percentage commission on each sale they facilitate. Since manufacturer's agents – often called *manufacturer's representatives* – take the place of the manufacturer's sales force, they have no authority over price and distribution decisions. These reps are most active in business supplies, clothing, furniture and food products. Because they represent a number of manufacturers and spread their fixed cost over several products, manufacturer's agents can survive and prosper in a market not large or developed enough to warrant a full-time company salesperson.

Selling agents – including export/import agents – have more authority than manufacturer's agents. They handle all of the manufacturer's output, have no territorial restrictions and act as the firm's independent marketing department. They control prices, promotion and terms of sale. Selling agents are often used by small producers that are not interested in the selling function or have difficulty maintaining a marketing department. They are often found in the textile, industrial equipment, metal and chemical industries. Because selling agents control prices, they have the tendency to reduce the price to expedite the sale. Although this can be disastrous for producers, it has little impact on selling agents, whose revenue is a function of total sales, not profit.

Unlike agents, brokers have no continuous relationship with the seller or buyer. They assist in negotiating a contract between two parties, are paid a fee when the transaction is completed by the client who hired them, and then move on to another project. They perform fewer functions than other intermediaries. Familiar examples are real estate brokers, insurance brokers, mortgage brokers and food brokers. Manufacturers that want to get their products into international marketing channels often work through *export brokers* that specialize in matching exporters with foreign buyers.

Finally, in product categories such as used automobiles, antiques, livestock, flowers, fruit and other agricultural products, auction companies (also called auction houses) are crucial in bringing buyers and sellers together. These are products for which inspection of the goods by potential buyers is important. Typically, the seller or the seller's agent brings products to the auction company, where buyers are invited to bid on them. The selling price of the merchandise, sold to the highest bidder, is dependent on supply and demand, which may change quickly.

Online auction companies, which use the Internet to connect buyers and sellers, have an increasingly strong impact on wholesaling. Online auction sites such as eBay offer computers, electronics, equipment and other capital assets, office supplies, airline tickets and many other products in large quantities at wholesale. A growing number of online auction houses specialize in selling surplus goods for companies around the world. Sellers benefit by receiving a fair market price for these products, while buyers enjoy getting bargains without having to spend much time on researching the market to find an attractive deal. With improving technology and the explosive growth of the Web, online auctions will likely spread rapidly in wholesaling.

13.4.3 *The future of wholesaling*

In the last twenty years, wholesaling has changed significantly. On the one hand, there has been a trend toward *vertical integration*, in which manufacturers strive to own or control their intermediaries. On the other hand, *power* in the marketing channel continues to shift toward large retailers that buy directly from manufacturers. As a result, many independent wholesalers, caught in the crossfire between manufacturers and retailers, have been eliminated.

The remaining wholesalers are trying to defend their place in the supply chain as they face increased competition from distribution and transportation companies that are expanding their scope by providing services traditionally offered by wholesalers. But perhaps the biggest threat to the wholesaling industry is the growth of the *Internet*, which allows sellers and buyers to interact directly while bypassing wholesalers altogether.

In response to the direct-buying programmes of large organizational and retail buyers, new sources of competition in the distribution channel, more demanding business customers and the advance of new technologies, what can wholesalers do to survive and thrive in the marketplace? Prosperous wholesalers are developing strategies to turn the challenges they face into successfully pursued marketing opportunities.

Market-driven wholesalers understand that they can add value and strengthen the relationships with other channel members by increasing the efficiency and effectiveness of the entire supply chain. And they realize that they can only accomplish this if they continuously improve their services, trim their costs and use the Internet to their advantage. Some wholesalers – striving for economies of scale – have grown by acquiring other wholesalers, or by expanding into retailing, for instance by opening up *hypermarkets* (sometimes called 'wholesale clubs') that appeal to cost-conscious consumers. Others are partnering with suppliers and customers, in ways such as through *franchising* programmes, to reinforce their market position, or are moving into international markets, establishing a sales force abroad to acquire new accounts. This trend toward creating larger companies and strategic alliances in order to increase efficiency and strengthen the wholesaler's market position is likely to continue in the future.

Rather than acting simply as order-takers with limited services such as financing, transportation and storage, more wholesalers are adding value as a channel partners by assuming functions previously performed by their customers. They now assist in store design and employee training or provide other services that help streamline product movement and increase their customers' productivity throughout the distribution channel. Wholesalers have also become more flexible in providing these services, offering principal clients customized pricing, tailored logistics programmes and even adapted products (in terms of quantities or packages) to meet the changing needs of the customers, final users and suppliers. This is quite a departure from their previous approach of offering standardized products in stores or through catalogues and the Internet. Whatever steps they take, all measures should become integral parts of a carefully planned marketing strategy.

The first step in developing an effective marketing strategy is to define the target market. What type of retail organization (or other type of buyer) does the wholesaler target and which customer service needs should they satisfy? What product mix would be most profitable in targeting this market segment? A **wholesaler owned brand** with an attractive price-quality relationship may add value to products and enhance the *relationship marketing* strategy.

The wholesaler's pricing strategy should be more creative than simply adding a 20 per cent mark-up to the product's cost. Temporary discounts on certain items to attract new customers, in combination with attractive financing options, may increase future revenues. By developing automated warehouses and sophisticated materials-handling systems as part of a well-planned distribution strategy, costs may be further cut and long-term profitability increased.

An integrated promotion strategy may further strengthen the wholesaler's competitive advantage. Personal selling should not be considered order taking, but an opportunity to help solve customers' problems and to build a mutually satisfactory business relationship. Trade advertising should not only be designed to inform and persuade buyers, but should also contribute to building the desired corporate identity. Further, sponsorship, publicity and other components of an integrated marketing communication programme can help build greater awareness of the wholesaler's activities and mission. In conclusion, an efficiently operating wholesale organization with a carefully developed marketing strategy can secure its competitive advantage, help develop customer loyalty and thus protect its position in the market place.

PRACTITIONER'S PERSPECTIVE
Julian Glover (6x6 Creative Ltd, UK)

Julian Glover is a Marketing Manager at DSH, chartered accountants and business advisors, based in Kent, UK, and Managing Director of 6x6 Creative Ltd. His interests include tactical marketing and strategic marketing planning. He also lectures at Canterbury Christ Church University on various aspects of marketing including branding, direct marketing and the fundamentals of marketing, to both undergraduate and post-graduate students.

Over recent years, *distribution* has grown in importance in the marketing mix to become an important differentiator for a business or organization. It is a tool that the marketing practitioner can use to gain significant *competitive advantage*.

The principle reason for this is the adoption and adaptation of technology. Every aspect of the *supply chain* – from procurement to distribution – has been touched to a greater or lesser extent by technology. *Consumers* are now in a commanding position, in many cases able to pick and choose the distribution channel that suits *them* rather than the supplier. Businesses have been forced to introduce new channels, or change existing ones to become shorter and more flexible. Many companies' marketing operations have risen to embrace and exploit these changes and nowhere has this been more visible than in retail marketing. *Tesco Stores*, in the UK, is a prime example of an organization that has changed its distribution channels to give its customers greater control and choice. By contrast, the demise of *Comet Electrical Stores* – and many other companies – has demonstrated the cost of a failure to adapt.

Marketing practitioners across a broad spectrum of businesses and organizations, not only in the B2C sector but also the B2B and G2C sectors, have been forced to adopt and adapt to new distribution methods. As a result of customers demanding greater *choice* and *flexibility* of distribution channels, marketing practitioners have to acquire new skills and knowledge to meet their demands.

The range and role of the new methods of distribution as well as their advantages are described elsewhere in this textbook. For the practicing marketer, these changes and their related benefits have affected them in numerous ways.

Firstly, if marketers ever felt they had the luxury of *time*, this has been stolen from them. A distribution system that once could be measured in days is now measured in seconds or even milliseconds. Where once consumers queued around the block for hours, or even days to be the first to buy that sought-after product, they can now buy online at virtually the same instance it becomes available; the only delays being those imposed by Internet connections and servers. This means that marketers have to move quickly to ensure that their product offering continually fits with consumers' demands. It requires them to not only be more *responsive*, but to also look ahead and *plan* more effectively. They now need to communicate and work far more closely with other departments such as production and logistics to create *shorter*, *faster* supply chains. The success of such a strategy is clearly shown by retailers like *Zara* (as seen in the *Marketing-in-Action* case).

The introduction of new and adaptation of existing distribution channels has required marketers to acquire, learn and exploit new *skills*. Traditionally, marketers learnt the practicalities of their trade effectively 'on the job', where skills such as retail management and promotions were passed down like some latter day apprenticeship. Today, marketing practitioners need to continually acquire and master new skills, learn to keep up to date with contemporary *technology* and be able to *anticipate* future applications and developments. For example, only a few years ago, mobile phone *apps* were viewed by many marketers merely as an interesting novelty. Today there are few large organizations and businesses that have not exploited the app. As a result, many marketers have found themselves on a very steep learning curve to be able to introduce and integrate apps into their distribution portfolio. The same applies for *social media*. The marketing media is crammed full of seminars and workshops promising to help marketers master *Facebook* and *Twitter as business tools*.

Pressure is also now coming from *within* the organization. Once upon a time, marketing practitioners considered the competition to be the enemy, but many are now fighting a new enemy – the finance department! Every new distribution channel, every app, every interactive website comes at a cost and marketing professionals are finding that not only are they under pressure to keep pace with the competition, they are being forced to do so within ever tighter *budgets*. Many marketers now talk of 'robbing Peter to pay Paul'. Catalogue shopping store *Argos*'s decision to close a number of its retail outlets in favour of online business – or, for that matter, *Newsweek*'s recent initiative to stop publishing its print edition and go all digital – highlight the type of decisions being made. In addition, the fiscal squeeze has seen *recruitment* and *outsourcing* budgets cut and like so many others, many marketing practitioners are being required to take on new *roles* and skills over and above their existing workloads.

There is no doubt that for professional marketing practitioners, the availability of new and exciting distribution channels offers them significant competitive advantages, but only if they can adopt them quickly and effectively into their strategic plans. But for some marketers, time and budgets are against them right now, and it could be a cold and bleak future.[7]

13.5 MARKETING LOGISTICS

Marketing logistics, also called *logistics* or *physical distribution*, is the vital link between a company and its customers. It encompasses a broad range of activities pertaining to delivery – getting the right number of products to the right place at the right time at the lowest total cost. Logistics (a military term that refers to the maintenance of material and personnel) includes such functions as order processing, warehousing, materials handling, inventory control and transportation. In a business context, it may also involve packaging, private trucking fleet operations, customer service, and plant, warehouse or store location planning.

Although logistics or physical distribution activities have traditionally been thought of strictly as cost centres, they can sometimes be major revenue generators. Outstanding service, dependability and speed of delivery that increase customer satisfaction may be more important managerial considerations than costs. When properly integrated with the overall marketing effort, logistics can be a powerful tool in positively differentiating the firm from its competitors.

As Figure 13.8 shows, there is more to logistics than transportation. While distinguishing between the flow of goods and the flow of information, the diagram illustrates that logistics management consists of two basic activities: materials management and physical distribution management.

Materials management entails the analysis, planning, implementation and evaluation of activities to cost-effectively expedite the flow of raw materials and related information from suppliers to the factory for a streamlined production process. This *inbound distribution* precedes the actual production process. Once the goods have been manufactured, **physical distribution management** focuses on planning and coordinating the warehousing, inventory control and transportation of the finished product from the producer to the resellers and, eventually, to customers. Here, too, information management is an important

FIGURE 13.8 The logistics process

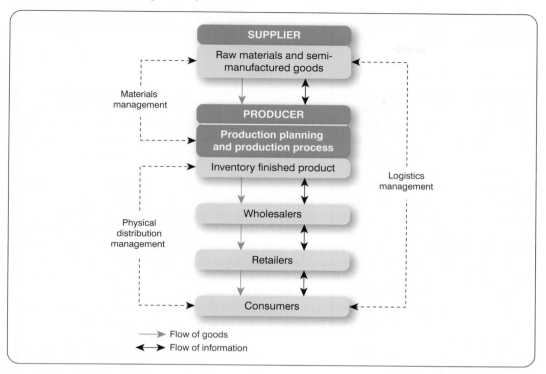

aspect of the *outbound distribution* process. In this final section of the chapter, we will explore the key functions in logistics and the importance of an integrated logistics approach.

13.5.1 Key activities in logistics

Marketing and logistics are closely related if for no other reason than that merchandise sold by the marketing department is delivered to the customer through the physical distribution system. For most firms, the goal of physical distribution is to enhance customer service while minimizing costs and transit time. Obviously, these goals are difficult to realize in equal measure. Providing great customer service by maintaining large inventories and offering rapid transportation will increase costs. Therefore, logistics managers try to strike a balance between containing costs and increasing service levels.

Although most managers realize that limiting the number of warehouses, minimizing inventory levels and shipping in bulk will save money, not all have insight into the exact cost data and analyses critical to logistics expenditure evaluation. One reason is that responsibility within the organization for managing the physical flow of goods is often fragmented. Each department, while moving the product through its part of the overall production and distribution system, tries to increase the efficiency of its operations. The problem with this approach, however, is that it makes it difficult for the firm to develop a truly company-wide, integrated marketing logistics system. Management is often best able to simultaneously increase efficiency and customer service by properly coordinating the related tasks, perhaps by appointing a logistics specialist. But regardless of where responsibility lies, creating an efficient logistics system while maintaining superior service and rapid product delivery requires appropriate decisions in each of the three key functions of logistics: order processing, inventory management and transportation of raw materials and finished products.

Order processing

Order processing refers to activities that take place between the time a customer's purchase order is received and the time a product has shipped, including the handling of all paperwork associated with the sale. Although order processing is a basic logistics activity, it directly affects customer satisfaction. Accurate and timely order processing ensures that customers receive what they order, when they need it, that they are accurately billed and get the service they expect.

The processing of an order happens in three stages: order entry, order handling and order delivery. *Order entry* begins when the company's salespeople or customers place a purchase order via mail, telephone, fax, email, an extranet or the Internet. Electronic ordering is less time consuming than a manual, paper-based ordering system and, consequently, reduces costs. Therefore, most firms use *electronic data interchange* (EDI), a software-based system, to integrate their order processing data with inventory, production, accounting and transportation. The advantage is that the data, which are shared throughout the firm and linked to other information, only need to be entered into the system once.

After the order has been entered into the firm's database, *order handling* requires several steps. First, the order is transmitted to a warehouse to verify product availability, and to the credit department to check the prices, terms and buyer's credit rating. Next, an order confirmation is sent, while all documentation for the order (for example, the *bill of lading*) is prepared. If the item is out of stock, the customer is offered a substitute; alternatively, a *backorder* is created or the order is scheduled for production. In the *order delivery* stage, finally, the order – assembled and packed for shipment – is scheduled for delivery by a carrier. An invoice is sent to the customer, inventory records are adjusted, and the order is delivered. The order documentation then becomes part of the customer's file of transactions with the seller.

Inventory management

In addition to controlling order processing and transportation, a logistics manager must also regulate their company's inventory. *Inventory management* includes warehousing, materials handling and inventory control. The primary rationale for carrying inventories is that it is not physically or economically feasible to handle each sale on a custom order basis. Inventory management allows companies to maintain adequate assortments of products to meet different customers' needs and to serve as a buffer against fluctuations in supply and demand. Inventory is also maintained to protect the firm against unexpected events such as strikes and shortages, to attain production efficiencies or to negotiate purchasing and transportation discounts. Finally, carrying inventory may provide a hedge against suppliers' price increases.

Warehousing – the design and operation of facilities for storing and moving goods – is not generally regarded as one of the critical factors in marketing logistics. However, this is a mistake. Since a company's investment in inventory often represents a large portion of its total assets, inventory and warehousing decisions have a significant impact on physical distribution costs and the quality of customer service. Warehouses are not only used to store products, but also to prepare them for shipment, coordinate shipments, and transport orders to customers.

A company has three basic warehousing alternatives: private warehouses, public warehouses and distribution centres. A *private warehouse*, either owned or leased, is appropriate when the firm needs to store a large amount of goods regularly to meet customers' needs. It can be custom designed or selected on the basis of the company's specific needs, and it gives the firm greater control over the movement of its merchandise. *Public warehouses*, on the contrary, are rented and serve a wide variety of customers that pay only for the amount of space used. They are a good alternative for firms without the resources or desire to operate their own facilities or those that need maximum flexibility due to seasonal or unpredictable demand for their products. *Distribution centres* are large, highly automated warehouses serving regional markets. These businesses receive goods from suppliers and factories, regroup them into orders and ship them to customers quickly. Since the focus is on movement of goods rather than storage, a distribution centre's main activity is often described as 'throughput'. With the rising volume of online buying, an increasing number of distribution centres specialize in *e-commerce*: they are designed to pick and ship individual items to consumers in a large geographic area, rather than to distribute a large quantity of a particular product on pallets in truckloads or rail shipments to retail stores (as illustrated in Figure 13.9).

Materials handling is the movement of inventory (product, parts or raw materials) into, within and out of the warehouse, or between warehouses and manufacturing facilities. Since the physical handling of goods can be time-consuming and costly – as it can lead to damage, theft or

FIGURE 13.9 Example of a distribution centre

waste – most firms use automated systems to move goods quickly with minimal handling. In this area of logistics, the use of technology is widespread. Materials handling efficiency is commonly enhanced by using means such as *bar coding*, which allows an item to be identified by a computer-coded bar pattern, electronically controlled vehicles that transport pallets, cases or products by following a preset route embedded in the floor, and even computerized robots that stack, load and unload cases and containers in distribution centres.

Inventory control is another key area in logistics; it involves trying to maintain the lowest level of inventory that will still enable the company to meet customer needs and avoid incurring additional costs for carrying excess stock. In many industries, inventory carrying costs, including the costs of financing, insurance and lost goods, exceed 25 per cent of the value of the inventory per year. Therefore, inventory decisions have a great impact on a firm's operating costs and profitability. To enhance their decision making, marketers have developed two methods for streamlining inventory management: just-in-time and quick-response inventory control systems.

A just-in-time (JIT) inventory system applies primarily to the materials-handling part of logistics. With the JIT system, a purchasing company limits the amount of inventory it keeps on hand, relying instead on its suppliers' fast, on-time delivery. When parts are needed for production, they arrive on the factory floor 'just in time', meaning exactly when needed. By ordering more often and in smaller amounts, less capital is tied up in storage facilities and inventory of raw materials and parts. More importantly, JIT may provide companies a competitive advantage through the flexibility to stop production of slow-selling products in favour of those for which there is an increased demand. A JIT system can only be used in industries where demand forecasting is reliable. In the automobile industry, for instance, many parts suppliers have located their production and distribution facilities near automobile manufacturers to provide fast service – such as delivering additional supplies as they're needed – at relatively low cost. In retailing, the JIT method is known as the quick-response (QR) inventory system. Suppliers, aided by collaborative computer systems, provide retailers with merchandise by restocking according to current sales. Through this inventory control system, they help reduce retail inventory while providing a merchandise assortment that is in line with the actual buying patterns of consumers.

Transportation

For most companies, transportation is the largest physical distribution expense. Overall, this logistics activity typically accounts for 5 to 10 per cent of the price of products, a percentage likely to increase with the rising price of oil. Logistics managers must select the best mode of transportation, both for moving raw materials and parts from suppliers to point of production, and for moving finished products to point of sale or consumption. Their options are the five major modes of transportation: railroads, trucks, airways, water transportation and pipelines.

From a marketing logistics perspective, the principal issue facing management in selecting the optimum mode of transportation is to meet customer-service demands. Beyond that, there are several important assessment criteria. These include *costs* (the rate charged by the carrier), *dependability* (reliability in delivering goods on schedule), and *speed of delivery* (the time required for pick-up, handling, transport and delivery). *Special handling* requirements (such as refrigeration and temperature control) and *traceability* (how easily a shipment can be located and transferred) are also important in selecting the best means of transport.

With the increased use of containers that can be loaded on trains, ships, trucks and planes, a single shipment may involve a combination of modes of transportation. This combination of transportation forms is called *intermodal* shipping. One common example is loaded trailer cars that travel 'piggyback' on railcars.

13.5.2 *Strategic issues in physical distribution*

In many industries, the key activities in logistics or physical distribution – order processing, inventory management and transportation – account for roughly half of all marketing costs. Whichever channel member or intermediary performs these functions, they are costly and greatly affect customer satisfaction. Hence, they are of strategic importance to marketers at all levels in the distribution channel. The significance of physical distribution should be carefully contemplated and its requirements incorporated in developing the *marketing mix*.

Marketers should, for instance, consider how a particular product design or packaging affects the ability to stack, move, store or track an item, and how line extensions (such as offering multiple styles and models of a product) may complicate warehousing and transportation. In addition, marketing communication campaigns should be coordinated with logistics functions to ensure that the featured products are widely available to potential buyers. And in pricing, quantity discounts may be offered to stimulate large purchases, which will, in turn, lower warehousing costs. At the same time, prices should be set in such a way that they balance supply and demand. Marketing-oriented companies assess all relevant characteristics of the market segments they are targeting and develop an effective logistics system to make sure that they can efficiently deliver the right amount of products to the right place at the right time at the lowest possible overall cost.

Maintaining outstanding customer service while trying to curtail logistics costs requires management to first define priorities and acceptable performance for the quality of customer service it wants to provide, and then decide how to accomplish these goals by moving goods at the lowest total cost. In meeting these challenges, the company should avoid **suboptimization**, which occurs when managers of different logistics activities try to minimize their individual department's costs without considering the impact on the firm's overall expenses or optimal profitability. By accepting relatively high costs in one logistics function (such as moving goods in a partially loaded truck), a firm may reduce its total physical distribution costs or significantly increase customer satisfaction (perhaps through expeditious delivery of needed merchandise), which will help build customer relationships and increase long-term profitability.

Since decreasing costs in one area may raise costs in another, physical distribution should be viewed as a system rather than a number of unrelated activities. Any decision concerning a particular element of the physical distribution system must be made in terms of its impact on the other elements of the system as well as on the system as a whole. This so-called **total cost approach** to physical distribution – referring to all costs incurred in accomplishing the customer-service objectives of the physical distribution system – shifts the emphasis from reducing the separate costs of individual activities to minimizing overall distribution costs. The method calls for analyzing the costs of all distribution options, even those considered expensive or impractical. To illustrate, if a firm wants to increase the number of warehouses, it should weigh this cost against order processing, inventory and transportation expenses. In the end, all distribution costs should be weighed against customer service standards.

High-quality customer service – a crucial ingredient in building long-term customer relationships – is the ultimate goal of all logistics activities. In order to profitably satisfy customer requirements, management should research customer needs and wants and determine how marketing logistics may be used to provide the optimal level of quality service. Customer requirements may vary from timely communication about orders and convenient deliveries to accurate billing and affordable after-sale support. Once the customer needs are analyzed, the logistics manager can develop a set of service standards, measure the company's performance in providing what buyers expect and track its progress in delivering any desirable improvements in customer service.

SUMMARY

1 Choice and functions of distribution channels

A *distribution channel*, or simply a marketing channel, is an organized network of independent firms that, in combination, perform all of the activities required to link producers with end customers in order to accomplish the marketing task. For the partners involved, providing customer satisfaction should be the driving force behind marketing channel decisions. Therefore, buyers' behaviour and preferences are important concerns of the distribution channel members.

Channels of distribution permit sellers to locate and supply the users of their merchandise, and allow buyers to find and obtain the products they desire. Since new distribution channels are continually established and existing systems modified, they are dynamic and useful networks. The intermediaries minimize the number of necessary contacts or transactions, and further add value by performing transactional, logistical and facilitating functions in the marketing channel that benefit both sellers and buyers. Since these functions are more basic than the organizations currently responsible for them, a key question is which distribution channel members are in the best position to perform the various channel functions. Although they can be shifted among channel members, these functions use up scarce resources and can often be performed most efficiently through specialization. This will keep consumer prices low.

There are two types of channels: direct channels (without independent intermediaries) and indirect channels, which may include wholesalers, retailers or other resellers. Through multichannel distribution, such as a hybrid system in which the channel members perform complementary tasks for the same customer, companies can expand market coverage while lowering costs.

Distribution channels perform several important functions. First of all, they create place, time and possession utility to facilitate the exchange process. They also increase *efficiency* by reducing the number of sales contacts needed to reach the target market and by using intermediaries that are specialized in such tasks as breaking bulk and creating assortments. Finally, by creating a carefully managed *supply chain* – the complete sequence of suppliers and activities that contribute to the creation and delivery of products and services – and forming long-term partnerships among its members, distribution channels help improve customer service and maximize customer value in all activities performed.

2 Level of distribution intensity

Marketers typically choose one of three levels of target market coverage: intensive, selective or exclusive distribution. This decision involves determining how many intermediaries to use. Intensive distribution entails placing the products in as many outlets as possible. It is used to achieve mass-market selling, as is common for most national brands found in supermarkets. Selective distribution uses more than a few but less than all of the middlemen who are willing to carry a product. It is an appropriate strategy for shopping products and some specialty products. The most restrictive form of market coverage is exclusive distribution. This involves using a single reseller in a geographic area. The optimal level of distribution intensity depends on consumer expectations and willingness to take the time and effort to buy a particular product or service. Another key consideration is the overall marketing strategy used to sell the product or service.

3 Channel power and management

Manufacturers tend to use independent channel intermediaries – or middlemen – because they lack the capital and expertise to perform all distribution functions themselves. The channel member that leads the marketing channel is a function of its economic and position power. The channel member with enough power to control the others in the distribution channel and to influence their strategies is called the channel leader or channel captain. Generally, the company with the greatest differential advantage will become the leader. A differential advantage is usually temporary and can only be maintained through continued innovation. As opposed to conventional distribution channels, which are fairly loose networks in which manufacturers, wholesalers, retailers and other organizations work independently of each other, vertical marketing systems are centrally coordinated, highly integrated operations that work together to better serve the ultimate consumer. The three major types of vertical marketing systems are the corporate, contractual and administered VMS.

In *selecting* the best distribution channel and most suitable middlemen, the company must first consider the target customers' buying habits and expectations. Knowing who they are, where they are located, how they prefer to buy and what exactly appeals to these buyers makes it easier to decide on the types of outlets and distributors to use. Next, management should decide what characteristics distinguish the better middlemen. In selecting appropriate resellers and developing an effective strategy, the company should analyze its internal resources and goals and the competitors' distribution practices, as well as other market environmental forces. The product's characteristics and stage in the life cycle, and the distributors' availability and willingness to sell the merchandise should also be considered. Some key selection criteria in choosing specific intermediaries include the current product lines, growth potential and service reputation of the potential distributors, their credit and financial situation, their sales strength, their inventory and warehouse practices and their management abilities.

A *channel conflict* involves goal-impeding behaviour by at least one of the firms in the supply chain. Differences in goals may lead to three types of channel conflict: a horizontal conflict (between intermediaries at the same channel level), a multi-channel conflict (between different types of resellers) and a vertical conflict (among members at different levels of a particular marketing channel). One example of a vertical conflict, know as disintermediation, occurs when a channel member bypasses a wholesaler or another intermediary. The most common sources of conflict in channels of distribution are incompatible goals and unclear roles of channel members. Other channel conflicts involve the communication of market research data and desired inventory levels. Although a dispute between channel members can be resolved through litigation, most firms prefer to work out their differences through arbitration.

Manufacturers must periodically assess how effective their resellers have been in achieving the distribution objectives. The single most important criterion in the *evaluation* of distributors is sales performance. When evaluating sales performance, most suppliers use historical sales trends, the distributor's success in meeting sales quotas and comparisons with other distributors' sales data. Other evaluation criteria include a distributor's financial position, how many well-trained sales people it employs, its interaction with other channel members, its customer orientation and whether it is expected to perform well in the future. To increase their control of the marketing channel, some suppliers adopt a selective distribution strategy, provide promotional materials and funds or offer assistance in such areas as customer service. These strategies help to develop a closer relationship with resellers and to secure their loyalty.

4 **Developments in wholesaling**

Wholesalers are companies that assist manufacturers in selling products and services to retailers, other wholesalers or businesses that, in turn, sell these to ultimate consumers or use them to produce something else. They perform various key services in the distribution channel, but primarily serve as an extension of a manufacturer's sales force by selling directly to other firms. There are three categories of wholesaling intermediaries: manufacturer-owned wholesalers (such as sales branches and sales offices), merchant wholesalers (including various types of full-service and limited-service wholesalers) and, finally, agents and brokers that do not take title to the merchandise they sell.

Although independent wholesalers are caught in the crossfire between increasingly powerful manufacturers and retailers, are facing more competition from other intermediaries that are providing services traditionally offered by wholesalers, and are often bypassed by sellers and buyers who deal directly through the Internet, many marketing-oriented wholesalers have managed to improve customer service, cut costs and use the Internet to their advantage. By developing a well-planned marketing strategy and increasing the efficiency and effectiveness of the entire marketing channel, they can add value and protect their position in the supply chain.

5 **Logistics management**

An effective marketing logistics strategy can give a firm a competitive edge in the marketplace. Delivering the right product to the right place at the right time at the lowest total cost is a key ingredient in building long-term customer satisfaction. Logistics management entails both materials management (organizing the flow of raw materials and parts to the factory) and physical distribution management (getting the finished product into customers' hands). A company's physical distribution capabilities can serve as an effective sales tool for its marketing department.

Logistics includes three interrelated tasks: order processing, inventory management (which includes warehousing, materials handling and inventory control) and transportation. These are of strategic importance to all channel members and should be considered and coordinated in developing the marketing mix. To provide the highest level of customer service at the lowest price, logistics managers should think in terms of total cost. The total cost approach requires that all decisions concerning one element in the physical distribution system be made in terms of their effects on the total system. This allows management to weigh distribution cost trade-offs, which occur when cost increases in one area lead to cost decreases in other areas. Finally, it should consider the costs of potential sales losses from lower performance levels. At the end of the day, companies can improve customer relationships by setting specific service standards in marketing logistics and measuring their performance to ensure they provide what customers expect.

DISCUSSION QUESTIONS

1   Why is the firm's distribution strategy so vital to its marketing efforts? Is it more important than the other elements of the marketing strategy?

2   How would you describe the difference between a distribution channel and a supply chain?

3   What are the advantages and disadvantages of exclusive distribution from the manufacturer's point of view?

4   What are the most important marketing functions of the distribution channel?

5   Describe the various types of vertical marketing systems and explain their advantages as compared to conventional distribution channels.

6   Why do some wholesalers face the threat of elimination while others do not? Is a shorter distribution channel beneficial to the retailer?

7   Should a company that is targeting four different markets use more than one distribution channel? Discuss the pros and cons of various options.

8   What are the major sources of conflict in marketing channels?

9   What criteria should be used to assess how well a company's logistics department is performing?

10   What is meant by the 'total cost approach' to physical distribution? Give an example of total cost thinking.

CHAPTER 14
RETAILING

LEARNING GOALS

After studying this chapter you will be able to:

1	**Understand the many faces of retailing**
2	**Identify the major types of retailers**
3	**Explain how the Internet has changed the way consumers buy products**
4	**Recognize why franchising is a win-win marketing system for all parties**
5	**Describe the importance of major account management**
6	**Develop a well-planned retail store positioning strategy**

Retailing is the most familiar part of marketing to the average person; yet, it is often misunderstood. While retailers are the most visible and accessible distribution channel member to ultimate consumers, many people do not realize that these are often professionally managed organizations that implement carefully planned marketing strategies. Retailers have become quite sophisticated in such areas as purchasing, inventory control and advertising. Hence, one of the most exciting aspects of the retailing industry – a large employer – is that it provides a wide variety of opportunities for business students and marketing specialists with an entrepreneurial interest.

Most retailing transactions are conducted in stores. Yet, new forms of distribution channels and retailing continually emerge. As more consumers start shopping online, for instance, electronic commerce in retailing holds increasing potential. In fact, retailing is the primary driving force behind the breakthrough of e-commerce. Still, despite the popularity of e-commerce, traditional retailers continue to attract a large segment of consumers who want to see, touch and test products before buying them, appreciate real-life customer service and enjoy their shopping experience in actual stores. In order to compete successfully, these 'bricks and mortar' retailers must adapt their strategy and develop new services to meet the changing demands of savvier consumers, including those who use the Internet to decide what to buy. In this chapter, we will explore the changing retailing landscape. The more we know about current trends and concepts in retailing, the better equipped we are to develop successful retailing strategies.

MARKETING IN ACTION
How IKEA offers Value for Money

Swedish firm IKEA operates about 350 stores in more than 40 countries, and achieves over 25 billion euros in sales per year. Founder Ingvar Kamprad has catapulted his company from a tiny mail order catalogue business to the largest furniture retailer in the world by constantly innovating with the customer's purse in mind. IKEA's democratic design philosophy is embodied in its vision statement:

At IKEA, our vision is to create a better everyday life for the many people. Our business idea supports this vision by offering a wide range of well-designed, functional home furnishing products at prices so low that as many people as possible will be able to afford them.

Mr. Kamprad and his 'co-workers' incorporate this frugal, egalitarian philosophy into all aspects of the business. IKEA regularly stages *Anti-Bureaucracy Weeks* during which executives work on the shop floor and man the cash registers. Executives are also expected to fly economy class, stay in cheap accommodation and cut costs wherever possible.

The company integrates its founder's thrifty sensibilities into its design process as well. Mr. Kamprad says, 'Anyone can design a desk that will cost 5 000 kronor, but only the highly skilled can design a good, functional desk that will cost 100 kronor.' To achieve the lowest price possible without sacrificing style or quality, the IKEA design team takes a novel and innovative approach to their work. While most companies first create a product, find a manufacturer and then decide on the price, IKEA reverses the paradigm, doing the exact opposite.

Members of IKEA's Product Strategy Council scour the globe to find new trends in home décor, and use a product grid (matching up product types with price points) to detect holes in the product line. After deciding on a new product concept, the Council checks competitors' prices, talks with suppliers about production costs and selects the best and most cost-efficient building materials. The Council then sets a target price of at least 30-50 per cent below the competition. Now that a price has been determined, the IKEA design team can begin sketching out a product.

Image Asset Management

The design team is charged with creating a stylish product while staying within the stringent design requirements dictated by the Council. The task of designing each product to be easily assembled and to fit into IKEA's signature flat packaging adds an extra dimension of challenge to the design process. IKEA's flat packaging design is an innovation that saves the company millions in shipping costs, and allows the customer to easily transport the product. And, since the customer has to assemble nearly every product IKEA sells, additional cost savings are realized and are ultimately passed on to the consumer. Considering all the factors involved in designing such products, it is understandable that this process can sometimes take years.

The emphasis on cost cutting continues even after the product has been designed and introduced into stores. IKEA's proud goal is to decrease prices by 2 to 3 per cent per year. Executives boast that over a six-year time span they lowered the price of the popular Klippan sofa from 354 euros to just 202 euros. While the idea of decreasing already low prices may sound ridiculous in today's business world, IKEA can focus on this objective because it is a privately owned company and, therefore, is not accountable to stockholders.

Not only has IKEA reversed the design process, but it has also stripped away the 'sacred cows' of the furniture retailing category by eliminating attributes that other specialty retailers consider necessary to compete. IKEA has done away with high-touch sales consultants, enormous product selections, door-to-door delivery services and furniture built to last a lifetime.

As a part of this so-called *reverse positioning* strategy, IKEA has supplemented its stripped-down *value proposition* with benefits never before associated with low-end furniture retailers. The most visible innovation that has come to symbolize IKEA is its one-of-a-kind *shopping experience*. Visitors to IKEA enter a gigantic showroom organized into model rooms that offer the customer a treasure trove of design ideas and consequently serve as a form of *up-selling* for IKEA. A customer might, for instance, go to IKEA to look at a couch, but when they see how well that couch goes with a particular rug they may be inclined to buy both. IKEA has just gently up-sold the customer, but they still leave the store feeling happy about their purchase.

> IKEA's unique mix of store attributes makes customers think that visiting the store is an outing

Another trait that signifies the IKEA *shopping experience* is its characteristic serpentine *pathway* that keeps customers moving efficiently throughout the store, enticing them to view each and every item. In fact, IKEA wants its visitors to linger and goes to great lengths to make them feel comfortable. The store offers a free daycare centre for children complete with indoor playground, a café featuring a variety of Swedish delights and the hands-off staff make shoppers feel at ease perusing the showroom. In some respects IKEA can even be compared to a casino, considering there are no windows in the store, very few exits and the senses are bombarded by low priced, yet stylish items that seem to pop up around every corner. In the end, IKEA's unique mix of store attributes makes customers think that visiting the store is more of an outing than a chore.

Without a doubt, IKEA has become a worldwide home décor titan of unparalleled proportion. Retail industry analyst Richard Talbot summed up the IKEA phenomenon best by saying, 'They're so dominant in that particular field that they really are a *category killer*.' IKEA's creative business model has become so effective and so indomitable that, at this point, the only question left to ask is, 'What will they think of next?'[1]

The search for a great product, for some, is half the fun. Millions of consumers have embraced the 'shop till you drop' philosophy, and find shopping to be an exciting part of their lives. At the same time, by efficiently marketing merchandise for the consumers' personal use, retailers enhance the quality of the daily lives of countless consumers who do not enjoy spending time in stores. The function of offering products in small quantities suitable for household consumption is actually reflected in the word retailing, which is derived from the French verb *retailler*, meaning to cut up.

Retailers range from small 'mom-and-pop' stores to giant chains generating billions of euros in sales each year. To cope with changing consumer needs and the invasion of new rivals with innovative retail formats, most retailers have adopted a customer orientation as a crucial step in effectively managing their businesses. Realizing that they are in a strategic position in the marketing channel, they not only try to build long-term relationships with customers, but also develop partnerships with manufacturers and middlemen. And some retailers are more successful than others. To understand why, we will take an in-depth look at marketing strategies in the rapidly changing retailing environment.

In this chapter, we will first explore the role of retailing in society and the most popular types of retail institutions. We will also examine the phenomenal growth of online retailing and the great variety of retailing strategies pursued in the marketplace. This includes franchising, a retailing form that continues to grow in popularity. As we will see, among the retailer's most important decisions are their choices of the target market and the retail format to best satisfy customers' needs. From that perspective, the last section of the chapter examines the most challenging issues and decisions retailers face as they try to create value for customers.

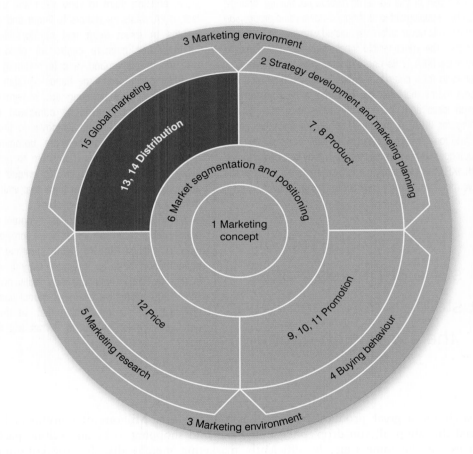

14.1 THE ROLE OF RETAILING

Retailing is big business and an important marketing activity. It is also a dynamic industry in which numerous retail establishments are locked in a fierce competitive battle, to the benefit of both consumers and employees. In most nations, the retail sector accounts for more than one out of every ten jobs.

By definition, **retailing** includes all activities involved in selling products and services directly to ultimate consumers for their personal, family or household use. Retailers are the only channel intermediaries that are in direct contact with final consumers. Since a typical shopper does not interact with manufacturers or wholesalers, to consumers, retailers represent the distribution channel. Because they make decisions regarding store locations, merchandise selections, the quality of sales personnel, store layout and customer service policies, retailers may influence the buyer's image of the products offered even more than the actual manufacturers. We will now explore the importance and evolution of retailing in society.

FIGURE 14.1 Key functions of retailers

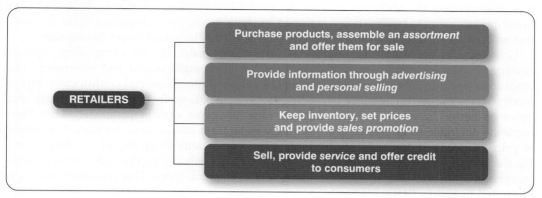

14.1.1 *Importance of retailing*

A retail store is much more than just a place to buy a product. Marketing-oriented retailers attract customers by adding value to the merchandise through their location, the available product assortment, store image and customer service. They also enhance the value of products by helping consumers make product selections and by making shopping more enjoyable and convenient. Ultimately, consumers are often more interested in the shopping experience than in the actual products or services they buy. It is clear that the retailer's task extends far beyond purchasing products for the purpose of reselling them to final consumers. Some of the key functions performed by retailers are summarized in Figure 14.1.

The first key function – assembling assortments of products and services from various suppliers to sell – is often referred to as **sorting**. It includes a retailer's strategic decisions about the appropriate depth and width of the assortment. In addition to the marketing functions outlined in Figure 14.1, the retailer also gives feedback to manufacturers and other channel members, thus providing them with marketing research support. Retailers are able to do this because of their unique position: they act as both marketers and customers in distribution channels. They can easily pass information gained from their consumers on to producers and the wholesalers from which they buy.

Retailing is also a major force in the global economy. Although most retailers are quite small, a few giant organizations dominate the industry. Regardless of the size of an individual retailer, retail organizations as a whole employ many people and – in supplying products and services to the ultimate consumer – generate a large sum of money in annual revenues. The retailing industry includes an increasing number of service retailers, providing useful services that fuel the economy. Among these are hotels, restaurants, banks, fitness clubs, tourist attractions, repair shops and health care services.

14.1.2 *The wheel of retailing*

Retailing, like every other aspect of marketing, never stands still. New types of retail stores are introduced, grow in popularity, and then – after reaching the decline stage of the *retail life cycle* – disappear over the years. The **wheel of retailing** hypothesis offers an interesting explanation for these changes. According to this theory, new types of retailers that try to fill niches in the retailing environment enter the market as low-margin, low-status discounters. The companies' low prices, which typically result from reducing customer services or other cost-cutting measures (such as locating in low-rent areas), allow them to compete effectively and take market share away from conventional retailers. This soon attracts imitators. Competition also increases because the established retailers often react by introducing lower priced items (a *trading-down* strategy), starting a price war, acquiring other discounters or even by cutting back on the facilities and decor in their own stores (*downgrading*).

Gradually, as the new discounters try to increase sales by attracting more upscale customers, their operations and facilities become more sophisticated and expensive. The innovators begin to offer more services (such as delivery, alterations and credit), carry higher quality merchandise (for instance by adding an in-store bakery, fresh produce or meat), and move to better locations, forcing them to raise prices to remain profitable. They then become vulnerable to competition from a new generation of low-price retailers that appeal to price-conscious shoppers left behind as existing retailers move up the wheel. After entering the market with minimum services, the innovators eventually go through a similar metamorphosis in their *trading-up* phase as the wheel of retailing turns. This evolution process is illustrated in Figure 14.2.

Retailers in several industries seem to have followed the evolutionary cycle suggested by the wheel of retailing. Hotels, for instance, undercut by budget hotels or motels, have added amenities such as restaurants, fitness centres or spas. In doing so, they

FIGURE 14.2 The wheel of retailing model

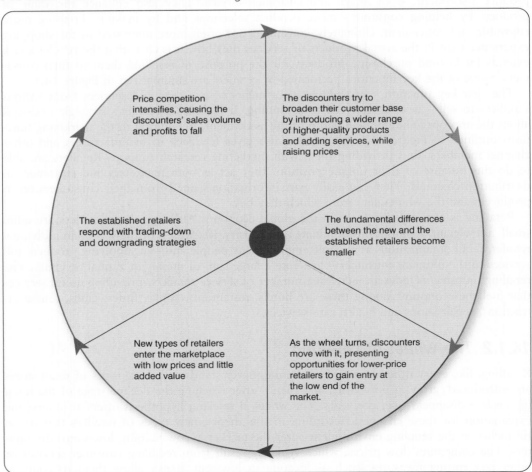

become targets for less expensive hotel chains, unless they pursue distinct pricing and marketing strategies targeted at the low-end, medium, and high-end market segments.

By way of illustration, *InterContinental Hotels*, rather than becoming vulnerable to low-price competition by constantly upgrading its hotel rooms, has developed various hotel formats that appeal to different target markets. These include *Holiday Inn Express* (targeted at in-and-out travellers who prefer low prices over amenities), *Holiday Inn* (aimed at the middle-class market and providing higher-cost features such as a swimming pool, restaurant, lounge and conference rooms), *Staybridge Suites* (an all-suite hotel for guests looking for an extended-stay hotel for business, relocation or leisure) and *Crowne Plaza* (offering premium accommodation for business and leisure travellers who want a high level of service and facilities). Knowing that travellers have different lodging needs at different occasions, the holding company has tied its various formats together with the same 'Priority Club' loyalty programme.

Likewise, supermarkets have been challenged by discount stores, which, in turn, have been undercut by warehouse clubs or superstores offering more product choices and lower prices. These superstores, however, which originally offered very basic, no-frills merchandising, have now added higher levels of customer service. They have also increased their mark-ups. Much the same has happened to factory outlet stores and even complete outlet malls. These are moving upscale from their bargain-basement origins as warehouses for manufacturers' imperfect or excess products, now offering better atmospherics and more services such as expert sales help and generous return policies. With their operating costs increasing and with regular stores becoming more competitive, there are now few differences in the outlets' prices and regular stores' sale prices.

The wheel of retailing helps us better understand the successful strategies of innovative retailers who discover ways to offer better and lower-priced merchandise to consumers. It also makes us aware that their winning strategies may only pay off until a creative, new type of low-cost retail institution comes along to appeal to price-conscious shoppers. But the wheel does not explain all forms of retailing. Some retailers, for example, start off with a **low-margin retailing strategy** but never trade up. They hang on to their success as discount stores going after a particular niche in the market. Other retailers, such as upscale specialty stores, start out at the market's high end with a **service retailing strategy**, and then may or may not pursue a trading-down strategy. Retailers in all market segments, however, realize that, with the wheel of retailing turning and such retailing venues as online retailing becoming more popular, they may have to adjust their strategies to survive and prosper.

14.2 TYPES OF RETAIL OPERATIONS

The field of retailing covers a lot of ground, from local sidewalk vendors to upscale shopping centres, giant superstores and global corporate websites. The seemingly endless variety of retail operations in most countries can be classified along several dimensions. A fundamental distinction is that between store-based and non-store-based formats. *Store-based retailers* operate from a fixed location, and customers visit the store to select products or services. Alternatively, *non-store-based retailers* use means such as direct marketing, vending machines or the Internet to reach consumers at home, at work or any place except a store. Store-based formats can be further classified by location, distinguishing between isolated stores and those located along with other stores in a *shopping centre*. In this section, we will focus on three kinds of retail operations: the major types of retail stores, non-store retailing and shopping centres.

MARKETING MISTAKE
Wal-Mart Flunks German

American super-retailer Wal-Mart is widely considered one of the most powerful companies in the world. Curiously, the discount retailer's first venture into the European market turned out to be a massive setback. How could such a prosperous company and retail industry leader not succeed in Germany? The answers lie in both a lack of market research, and Wal-Mart's failure to adapt to the local culture. Upon close inspection it becomes evident that Wal-Mart pursued a fundamentally flawed internationalization strategy due to its ignorance of key features of the extremely competitive German retail market.

In an attempt to perpetuate sizzling growth rates, Wal-Mart began expanding aggressively into markets outside the United States. Germany, the largest retail market in Europe, seemed like a perfect launching point into the lucrative European market. Upon entering the German market over two decades ago, Wal-Mart acquired 21 *Wertkauf* outlets and 74 *Interspar* retail stores, immediately making it the fourth largest retailer in Germany. Despite moving quickly and aggressively into the German market, Wal-Mart reportedly never turned a profit. Finally, after eight years of heavy losses, the company decided to exit Germany by selling its stores to German retailer *Metro* at a bargain basement price.

So what happened to Wal-Mart in Germany? The first ill-fated executive decision was acquiring the Interspar chain. While the smaller Wertkauf was considered a very strong chain, Interspar was a struggling brand with many outdated and poorly located stores. And, due to stringent building regulations, Wal-Mart never built a new store in Germany, sharply constricting its expansion. Nor could Wal-Mart strike an agreement to purchase another discount retailer to fuel its growth in Germany. Since the company didn't expand past its original 95 stores, it was unable to garner sufficient economies of scale to compete with the much larger discount retail chains operating in Germany. In effect Wal-Mart was never able to consistently offer low prices while maintaining its profit margins, and therefore could not follow through on its slogan of 'everyday low prices.'

Wal-Mart thought the labour unions were communists

Adapting its business model to mesh with the German culture proved to be another stumbling block for Wal-Mart. Famous for its confrontational relationship with unions, the company continued this trend by exhibiting a lack of cooperation with Germany's powerful labour unions.

Wal-Mart refused to formally acknowledge the outcome of the sector-specific centralized wage-bargaining process (the standard procedure for determining wages in Germany). To the company's complete surprise, the union retaliated by organizing walkouts at 30 stores throughout the country – resulting not only in lost sales, but also in bad publicity for 'union-bashing' Wal-Mart. Hans-Martin Poschmann, secretary of the Verdi union, summed up the relationship by saying 'Wal-Mart did not understand that in Germany, companies and unions are closely connected… They thought we were communists.'

Wal-Mart also brought in American executives to run the German operation, and closed one of its acquired chain's headquarters. Each of these actions both angered the German public, and hindered the firm in better understanding the German market. Those same executive managers asked for unlimited access to suppliers' factory floors, being either unaware or unconcerned that Wal-Mart played a minor role in and had limited buyer's power on the German market. Needless to say, the vast majority of suppliers did not oblige.

Within the company Wal-Mart attempted to instill its 'cultish' corporate values into its new German employees instead of tailoring them to meet German preferences and attitudes. This is particularly true of the famous *ten-Foot Rule* ('three-Metre Rule' in metric Germany) and the institution of the *greeter*. Wal-Mart's sales associates are encouraged to take this pledge: 'I promise that whenever I come within ten feet of a customer, I will look them in the eye, greet them and ask if I can help them.' Both practices were largely abolished after shoppers, unaware of the role the customs played in Wal-Mart's service concept, had repeatedly complained that they had been harassed by strangers on store premises. Wal-Mart's overly familiar style of customer service indeed appealed to neither its German employees nor its customers.

Wal-Mart's failure in Germany has taught them many valuable lessons as they expand throughout the world, the most important of which is to adapt its business model to fit the culture of its host country. Company spokeswoman Elizabeth Keck summarized the German debacle by saying 'We literally bought two chains and said, "Hey, we are in Germany. Isn't this great?" It is a good, important lesson, a turning point. Germany is an example of our naïveté.'

Wal-Mart's CEO Mike Duke also commented on Wal-Mart's failure in Germany and its lessons for management. 'Although Wal-Mart is a global corporation', he says, 'we serve consumers locally and definitely must learn to respect and appreciate their preferences'. This is especially important in continuing to enter Africa's sub-Saharan countries, in which Wal-Mart identified opportunities to serve millions of new customers. Meeting consumers' unique needs is also key to success in *South Africa* (where the company collaborates with *Massmart*, which has operations in 15 nations) and in large emerging markets with a growing middle class, including Brazil (and other Latin American nations), India and China. When you are shopping one of China's Wal-Mart stores, Mike Duke argues, it feels like being in a Wal-Mart, but yet, you'll see live fish in the seafood department because, 'that's how Chinese consumers prefer to buy their fresh fish.' And, incidentally, adapting the products and services to foreign customers' real needs and wants also happens to be the most effective strategy for Wal-Mart to get a grip on overseas markets…[2]

14.2.1 Major types of retail stores

The highly competitive nature of retail distribution makes for tremendous variety and frequent change in types of retail stores and retailing methods. Periodically, new types of retail formats appear on the retail scene, and those that succeed have an impact on established retail stores, which, to survive, must modify their way of doing business.

Retail stores can be classified based on several characteristics, including product lines, relative prices and the service level offered. Classifying retail stores according to their product assortment or **merchandise mix** – the total set of all product lines and products offered for sale by a retailer – requires assessing the degree of depth and breadth in the product lines. In retailing, *depth* refers to the number of offerings available to a consumer, and *breadth* refers to the variety of products carried. To illustrate, a department store has a wide product mix (breadth) compared to a specialty store that only sells flowers (depth). Other types of retail stores, based on their product assortments, are convenience stores, supermarkets and hypermarkets. Their retail strategies are summarized in Table 14.1, at the end of this paragraph. Determining what to sell is one of the retailer's most important strategic decisions (comparable to selecting its target market), and strongly affects its identity and success. If the retailer's merchandise mix is too limited, it may not attract enough customers to survive. If, on the other hand, it is too broad, the retailer may be perceived as a 'Jack-of-all-trades, master of none'.

Another way to classify retailers is by the *relative prices* charged. Although most retailers avoid aggressive price competition and adhere to standard pricing, there are other options. One is offering higher-quality products or services at premium prices. A second option is to charge relatively low prices for regular merchandise and private labels. Such a strategy is commonplace among discount stores, factory outlets and warehouse clubs.

Finally, retailers may be classified by the *level of service* they perform for their customers. Stores can be categorized as full-service (such as department stores offering specialty goods and providing individualized customer assistance), limited-service (such as variety stores that carry merchandise for which consumers require little assistance) and self-service (such as supermarkets in which customers make their product selection with no assistance). In this section of the chapter, we will first compare the most common types of retail stores.

Specialty stores

Specialty stores are relatively small-scale stores offering a great deal of product depth within a narrow range of product lines. Often, they sell only one type of product, such as women's shoes, clothing, fish or jewellery. Specialization may take the form of offering *consumption-related* items (such as a party shop selling wine, cheese, nuts and French bread) or may be based on appealing to a *specific consumer segment* (as a health food store caters to health conscious individuals). In each category, some stores owe their success to a form of *superspecialization*. A bookstore might, as an example, specialize in children's books or a sporting goods store sell only scuba diving equipment.

Although some specialty stores (such as The Body Shop) are chain outlets, they are usually owner-managed businesses. Successful specialty stores compete effectively against department or discount stores because they have a better understanding of their local target market's needs and are able to more readily adjust to changing market conditions. Many consumers prefer shopping at these stores – regardless of the somewhat higher prices – because they don't have to search through racks of unrelated products and are likely to be advised about a tailored assortment by informed salespeople.

Convenience stores

A convenience store is a small shop, located in or near a residential area that carries a limited assortment of food products and high-turnover convenience goods. It usually has longer hours than supermarkets, but charges higher prices on comparable products. This retailing format is growing in part because Shell, BP and Texaco, along with most major oil companies, have been converting many of their gasoline stations into attractive convenience stores. Consumers – who appreciate the extended hours of operation, fast service and convenient locations – use convenience stores to buy fill-in items like candy, cigarettes, fast food, soft drinks and magazines.

Supermarkets

Supermarkets are large, departmentalized food stores that carry a limited range of non-food products. The supermarket retailing concept was developed many decades ago when food retailers realized that a large-scale operation would let them combine self-service, impulse buying, low prices, volume sales and one-stop grocery shopping. In addition to being conveniently located, it is important that a supermarket's prices are seen as competitive and its meat and produce departments – one means by which a supermarket can differentiate itself from competitors – are viewed as offering superior quality.

Although supermarkets are arranged by departments for maximum efficiency in stocking and handling products, they have central checkout facilities. They must operate efficiently because net profits after taxes may be less than 1 per cent of sales. To enhance the merchandise selection and improve profit potential, supermarkets are offering increasingly more non-food convenience products including household utensils, beauty items, health-related products and other pharmacy items. This practice of a single retailer selling unrelated lines of merchandise is called **scrambled merchandising**. As long as the margins on food items remain low, supermarkets will continue to expand into higher margin non-food items, as well as homemade meal replacements (prepared, ready-to-eat food) to compete with takeaway and fast food restaurants.

Hypermarkets

As stores try to satisfy increasing consumer demand for one-stop shopping for food and household products, much larger stores called **hypermarkets** or *superstores* are replacing conventional supermarkets. These huge establishments, originally introduced in Europe by the French firm *Carrefour*, are at least twice the size of supermarkets. In addition to a wide selection of grocery and general merchandise products at discount prices, they offer various services. Hypermarkets may, for instance, feature pharmacies, restaurants, beauty salons, optical shops and bank branches. This strategy is based on the notion that offering customers everything at the same location will eliminate the need for them to shop elsewhere.

Although governments of some European countries attempt to discourage this innovation in discount retailing to protect the interests of established retailers, superstores are successful across Europe, South America and the Arab subcontinent (including the *United Arab Emirates*), where big retail stores are still a novelty. They are less popular in the United States. Although US consumers need the variety, convenience and service offered by superstores, they find shopping in them overly time consuming, and they have other options for cross shopping. These include **supercentres**, a combination of a supermarket and discount department store that is not as mammoth as a hypermarket. One major organization banking its future on this new retailing format is Wal-Mart. The company, which is pushing to expand aggressively into the international retailing market, is planning to add hundreds of new Wal-Mart Supercenters in the coming years. Meanwhile, supermarket chains strive to increase efficiency in an attempt to match the supercentres' low prices.

Department stores

A **department store** is a large, service-oriented retail institution that carries a wide product mix of shopping and specialty goods, and offers a deep selection in product categories such as apparel, cosmetics, jewellery and household products. To streamline marketing efforts and the store's internal management, related product lines are organized into separate departments, resembling specialty stores. Customers make purchases and pay within each department – sometimes called **shop in the shop** – rather than at a central checkout area. Department stores built a prestigious reputation by offering many services, such as delivery, store credit cards, giftwrapping, liberal return privileges and personal selling assistance. Providing superior customer service allows department stores to sell more distinctive, higher margin merchandise.

Department stores are strategically located in attractive urban areas or occupy **anchor positions** in shopping malls. Since they generate a great deal of customer traffic, their placement at opposite ends or at the midpoint of a shopping centre creates pedestrian traffic

© Yuri Arcurs / Shutterstock

throughout the entire shopping facility. Expensive locations, frequently leaseholds, result in higher operating costs that force department stores to charge at least, and sometimes more than, competitive prices. With consumers becoming more cost-conscious, the future of department stores is unclear.

Although department stores remain consumers' favourite place to shop in some countries, in Europe and the United States they struggle to succeed. Squeezed by hypermarkets and discount stores at one end of the price spectrum and by attractive specialty stores at the other, department stores must adapt to the rapidly changing market. Some have pruned their product mix and closed unprofitable departments, such as electronics and furniture. Many department stores have gone upscale. Still others are expanding opening hours and invest in renovating stores to better serve their customers' needs.

Discount stores

Discount department stores, often called *discounters* or **discount stores**, are an offshoot of department stores. Like traditional department stores, they carry various product lines, but at lower prices. Their lower mark-ups are made possible by offering limited customer services, having fewer upscale facilities with more products displayed on the sales floor and more emphasis on self-service, with customers wheeling shopping carts. Primary examples of these 'full-line discount stores' are Target and Wal-Mart.

In Europe and Latin America, a smaller and popular version of this type of retail store, the **variety store**, targets the mass market with an extensive range of low-priced products. This scaled-down adaptation of a department store in a low-service setting may also carry a limited assortment of high-turnover grocery products. Well-known examples of this retail format include Woolworth's (Great Britain), HEMA (The Netherlands) and Monoprix (France). In the US, discount stores or hybrid combinations of variety stores and drugstores, such as Walgreen's, have replaced most variety stores.

A more recent adaptation of the discount store, rapidly growing in the US, is the **warehouse club**, or *wholesale club*. At clubs such as Costco and Sam's club, the way merchandise is displayed, usually in a bare-bones building, in boxes or on pallets, reinforces the retailer's bargain image among price-conscious customers. This members-only establishment combines cash-and-carry wholesaling (for small retailers that buy products for resale or for business use) with discount retailing (for consumers employed by government agencies,

TABLE 14.1 Types of stores and retail strategies

Type of store	Assortment	Prices	Service level
Speciality store	Narrow width, extensive depth	Competitive to above average	Average to excellent
Convenience store	Medium width, low depth	Above average	Average
Supermarket	Food: wide and deep Non-food: narrow width and low depth	Average	Average
Hypermarket	Extensive width and medium depth	Competitive to low	Average
Department store	Extensive width and depth	Average to above average	Good to excellent
Discount store	Extensive width and depth	Low	Slightly below average
Category killer	Narrow width, extensive depth	Very low	Average

banks, hospitals or schools). Instead of paying an annual membership fee as business customers do, individual consumers pay about 5 per cent more on each product purchased at a membership warehouse club. By focusing on product categories like fresh produce and meat, the club channel is an increasingly competitive threat to supermarkets.

There are many other forms of low-price retailing gaining market share. The best-known examples are *warehouse-style food chains* (such as *Aldi*, a German low-margin discounter with over 7 000 stores worldwide) and factory outlet stores. **Factory outlet stores** are operated by a manufacturer of a national brand – such as HUGO BOSS – and typically dispose of surplus stock or clearance merchandise. Two other types of low-price retailers popular with consumers are off-price specialty chains and warehouse showrooms. An *off-price specialty chain* buys surplus fashion-oriented products from several manufacturers. It then sells these brand-name family apparel and home fashion products in its stores at low prices, as, for example, Marshalls and its sister company T.K. Maxx do in the US. A *warehouse showroom* – such as *Ikea* – is a large retail store, usually located in a low-cost building, with substantial on-premises inventory and limited service.

From a product assortment perspective, the Swedish home furnishings store Ikea is also an example of a limited-line store. A **limited-line store** offers an extensive assortment of models within one product line or a few related lines. This type of retail operation targets price-conscious consumers who want to select from complete lines when buying certain products.

Category killers

Category killers are a special type of limited-line store. By offering, at low prices, a huge selection of products in a single product line (such as sporting goods, toys, office supplies or electronics), these stores dominate their narrow merchandise segments. Considered the ultimate in specialty stores, the category killer is named for its marketing strategy's intent.

Its objective is to expand rapidly and 'kill' the competition by offering so many low-priced products within the line that customers find it impossible to leave empty-handed. Examples of specialty chains based on the category-killer concept are Foot Locker, Toys"R"Us, Staples and MediaMarkt. These category-dominant retailers increase customer satisfaction by featuring stores that make shopping easy and, with everyday low prices, save consumers time by eliminating the need for comparison shopping.

Although the specialty discount store format has been quite successful, category killers are facing increased competition from warehouse clubs and other discount stores pursuing an aggressive cost cutting strategy across many product lines. Internet companies that are able to offer an unlimited selection of products at competitive prices delivered overnight, directly to the customer's door are, however, their greatest threat. This clearly illustrates how, in today's dynamic retail market, even category killers are vulnerable to cut-throat competition from aggressive rivals.

14.2.2 Non-store retailing

While most retailing transactions still occur in stores or some other concrete structure, retail's physical restrictions are beginning to disappear. In the past few years, the non-store retailing growth rate has far exceeded that of in-store retailing. Any method a company uses to create an exchange without requiring a customer to visit a store is considered **non-store retailing**. Today, consumers wanting to avoid the stress of shopping in malls or the crowds in stores have a range of non-store alternatives, some as simple as placing a phone or online order.

There are advantages and disadvantages associated with non-store retailing. To consumers, the prime benefit is the opportunity to select and buy products at their own convenience, twenty-four hours a day, seven days a week. The merchandise can then be delivered directly to the customer's home address. Consumers that are busy or dislike shopping, or those with few store choices, perhaps because they do not drive or are disabled, find delivery an especially attractive service. Disadvantages include the limited assortments of some non-store retailers and the inability to test a product or have it altered before it is delivered.

The major forms of non-store retailing are direct marketing (discussed earlier in this book), direct selling, network marketing, street peddling, automatic vending and online retailing. Since online retailing is the newest and fastest growing form of non-store retailing, we will explore this method separately, in the next section of this chapter. The other retailing activities that occur outside a retail outlet will be discussed here. We'll start with direct selling.

Direct selling

Traditionally called *door-to-door selling*, **direct selling** is the marketing of products and services to ultimate consumers through personal interactions and sales presentations at home or in the workplace. As pointed out in Chapter 11, direct selling also includes phone solicitations initiated by the retailer.

Companies such as Avon, Mary Kay, Herbalife and Electrolux all offer personalized service in face-to-face encounters with consumers across the world. This type of non-store retailing works best for products that require a lot of information to sell or to use, such as nutritional supplements or cosmetics. Direct retailers' sales, however, have recently declined as retail chains began to offer comparable products at discount prices. The growing number of dual-career households lowered the number of potential buyers at home, posing a dilemma for direct sales and resulting in strategic adaptations. Rather than using a cold-canvass approach, with salespeople knocking on doors or calling people to find customers, direct sellers began identifying prospects through the Internet, telephone, mail or shopping mall intercepts and making appointments with them. They now also rely on referrals, in which past buyers recommend prospects to a salesperson.

Although some direct sellers, such as Avon, have started to present products and to take orders at offices during lunch hours or breaks, most direct sales are still made in consumers' living rooms. Some firms owe their success to the **party plan** system, originally popularized by Tupperware, in which a direct seller attends a get-together at a host customer's home to demonstrate products and take orders. Because of the friendly party ambience at these home shopping parties, consumers often order products they would not purchase in a regular store.

The direct selling industry is still facing major limitations. As a result of fraudulent business practices by some firms in the past, direct selling has a negative image among consumers. Also, with commissions for salespeople running up to 50 per cent of the sales price and, on top of that, a high sales force turnover, it is an expensive form of retailing. To pursue new opportunities, direct sellers are expanding into promising foreign markets, such as China, Argentina and Mexico. It is in countries without efficient distribution channels or where consumers need to be educated about new products and services where direct selling will likely continue to grow.

Network marketing

A special form of direct selling is **network marketing**, also known as *multilevel marketing*. This is a strategy used by direct selling companies in which a so-called master distributor persuades other individuals to join the organization as independent agents and then resells the company's merchandise to these distributors who eventually make sales to consumers. The master distributor receives commissions on all the products sold by the people they recruited, and works constantly to motivate them.

The best-known multilevel network company is Amway (also called Quixtar in the US), whose millions of independent distributors operate in nearly one hundred countries. Its product lines include personal care products, jewellery, electronics, water purifiers and insurance. Since the distributors also sell merchandise during personal encounters with consumers and at home shopping parties, the difference between this and traditional direct selling is not the selling method but the fact that network marketing provides the successful (master) distributor with two sources of income.

Although more than half of Amway's agents do not make any money, an investigation found that Amway does not qualify as a pyramid scheme. A **pyramid scheme** is an illegal network in which the initial distributors profit by selling merchandise to other distributors, with most of the products never reaching the ultimate consumer.

Street peddling

While most nations in the Western world have developed from being largely dependent on street peddlers selling their merchandise door-to-door to more efficient distribution systems through supermarkets, superstores and indoor shopping malls, in many countries **street peddling** is still a common form of non-store retailing. In both isolated villages and major cities all over the world, peddlers continue to play an important role in providing services and getting products into consumers' hands. They include individuals selling snacks and food items from pushcarts in the streets or temporary stalls set up in open markets, to professional peddlers selling merchandise to consumers from their vans or trucks. The products they sell range from produce, meat and cheeses to inexpensive watches, T-shirts and household items. Although they are banned in some cities, often due to lobbying by established retailers who pay higher taxes and overhead expenses, other communities recognize and support their crucial role in attracting shoppers and tourists.

Automatic vending

More than two thousand years ago, Hero of Alexandria introduced the world's first vending machines in Egyptian temples to dispense sacred water for five-drachm coins. Today, millions of coin or credit card operated vending machines offer a variety of convenience goods, with beverages, food, snacks and candy accounting for over 80 per cent of sales. These vending machines, which eliminate the need for salespeople, can be placed in non-traditional locations and allow 24-hour sales, making it possible to meet customers' needs when and where stores cannot. Because of this convenience, consumers using vending machines are willing to pay more for certain products than their usual price in a retail store. This compensates for the high equipment depreciation expenses, the costs of the location lease and the frequent servicing and repairs due to stock-outs, breakdowns and vandalism.

Although most vending machines have been limited to small, routinely purchased products such as cigarettes, candy and coffee that consumers like to buy at the nearest available location and use in close proximity to the machine itself, retailers increasingly recognize the potential of this underused marketing tool. Among the most interesting innovations are state-of-the-art vending machines, which dispense everything from office supplies and disposable cameras (refrigerated to protect the film) to life insurance policies at airports. New opportunities to sell via automatic vending depend on the target market's needs and preferences, which vary by country. For instance, Levi's jeans were once sold through vending machines in France, movie soundtracks and boxer shorts in the United States and everything from underwear to fresh sushi in Japan.

14.2.3 Shopping centres

As any commercial real estate agent will tell you, the three most important factors in retailing are 'location, location, location'. A favourable location is of great importance. Because it dictates the limited geographic trading area from which the retail store attracts customers, location becomes a decisive factor in profitability, growth and even the survival of the business. The retailer is making an investment that will reduce its future adaptability. Of all components of the retail strategy, store location is the least flexible. Even prices, promotional campaigns and product assortments are more easily changed.

When selecting a site location, retailers use several criteria. They consider the location of the company's target market within the trading area, the potential customers' characteristics, the area's economic growth potential and the degree of competition. Merchants prefer compatibility with other retailers in the surrounding environment since stores that complement each other attract more customers. Retailers must evaluate ease of movement to and from the site, assessing such factors as the availability of public transportation, number of parking spaces and pedestrian traffic. Additionally, they gauge site characteristics, such as the size and visibility of the lot or building and the rental, leasing or ownership terms.

A retailer can choose to locate in a free-standing building, a central business district or a planned shopping centre. Large, well-known retailers (for example, Ikea or major car dealers) often prefer an isolated, *free-standing building* along main roads since they are destination stores. A **destination store** is a store with an established image and an attractive product assortment that consumers deliberately visit. An increasing number of retailers decide not to locate in a pedestrian mall because of the greater visibility of a free-standing store and the opportunity to expand rapidly without having to wait for new shopping centres to be developed.

Another option for retailers is to locate in a central business district, better known as a *downtown shopping area*. These traditional – but often unplanned – business districts, which feature a variety of department and specialty stores, are a central part of the retail landscape in cities and towns around the world. Often closely situated to cultural activities, they are essential in drawing tourists to cities like London, New York, Paris, Dubai and Amsterdam.

A final popular option for retailers is to locate in a centrally owned and managed **planned shopping centre**. A planned shopping centre is a group of retail stores, designed, coordinated and marketed to shoppers in a geographic trade area in order to satisfy specific customers' needs. The main difference between a central business district and a shopping centre is that the shopping centre is planned to have a **balanced tenancy** – so that the stores complement each other in the variety and quality of their merchandise – and to provide ample parking space. We will now explore the pros and cons, and the various types of shopping centres.

Advantages of shopping centres

Shopping centres, with their wide range of product offerings, are designed to attract shoppers. They are truly synergistic retail operations: there is so much merchandise on display that many more people are drawn to the shopping centre than would otherwise visit any of the stores if they were free-standing. Anchor stores are strategically located so that pedestrians must pass many small stores in order to go from one anchor store to the next. As a result, these smaller stores, usually without much drawing power of their own, benefit from the increased foot traffic.

Projecting a cohesive image, shopping centres are attractive in structure and appearance. The ambient temperature is regulated year round, within individual stores and in the enclosed walkways connecting stores. Using natural light, plants, fountains, art and background music, a shopping centre or mall creates a pleasant and clean shopping environment, often in contrast to stores located in the traditional central business districts.

Shopping centres may also provide retail organizations with market segmentation choices, since they target different socio-economic groups. Some malls are aimed at bargain-oriented customers, while others attract less price-conscious or upscale consumers. Regardless, the tenants share the costs of joint promotional campaigns and benefit from cooperative programmes and community events designed to attract shoppers to the centre. By working together to promote these activities, the retailers can generate a great deal more excitement and interest among consumers than if they operated alone.

Disadvantages of shopping centres

Locating in a shopping centre has several disadvantages. The first concern for many businesses is high rent, which eats into profits. Some retailers also fear that stores located in a mall may lose some of their identity because of lease restrictions on the merchandise they may sell. Other merchants (such as restaurants) dislike the restricted hours of operation.

A more serious problem for a retailer is to be located in a shopping centre that does not have the proper mix of stores. Under those circumstances, the common promotion campaign may not attract enough shoppers, or there may be too much direct competition. If there are too many shoe stores, for example, each shoe store will have a difficult time surviving. An additional drawback for small merchants may be that anchor stores dominate the tenants' association. Finally, retailers in shopping centres may be hurt by the trend that many of today's consumers have less time for shopping, so they select more convenient free-standing stores or neighbourhood centres for their shopping needs.

Types of shopping centres

There are three basic types of shopping centres. The smallest type is the **neighbourhood shopping centre** (sometimes called *strip centre*), consisting of ten to fifteen stores. It provides for the sale of convenience products (food, drugs and sundries) and personal services that meet the daily needs of an immediate neighbourhood trade area. The major tenant usually is a supermarket, which serves as an anchor store to a number of smaller specialty stores. This kind of centre provides convenient shopping for consumers who live within a few minutes' commute. Most neighbourhood centres do not sponsor regular coordinated shopping centre events, but rely heavily on personal contacts and the convenience of the centre to compete against the larger malls.

Community shopping centres are designed to serve approximately five times the number of people that a neighbourhood centre serves. They draw consumers looking for shopping and specialty goods not available in neighbourhood centres. In addition to a supermarket or a drugstore, the community centre includes a small department or discount store as well as from ten to fifteen smaller specialty shops. The attraction of the community centre is its greater depth of merchandise and its convenient location. It is likely to have several major centre events each year – such as art exhibits and outdoor sales – in order to generate publicity and attract customers.

Regional shopping centres or *malls* attract large numbers of shoppers willing to drive significant distances to find products and services not available in their home towns. They often have two or three large department stores and – with more than 100 specialty stores – the widest product mixes and deepest product lines of all shopping centres. They provide general merchandise, apparel, furniture, home furnishings and many personal and professional services. Typically, shopping malls are regional shopping centres. With a target market of more than 150 000 consumers, this type of centre sponsors events on almost a weekly basis to draw customers.

Retail experts in some countries view regional shopping centres as being out of touch with the needs of the aging population. Traditional shopping malls are indeed rapidly losing favour among consumers. To replace malls in a saturated market, several new types of *non-traditional shopping centres* have emerged that appeal to different market segments. One type of non-traditional shopping centre is the previously discussed **factory outlet mall**. These malls feature discount and manufacturer-owned factory outlet stores selling excess merchandise, although some also offer upscale merchandise.

Another type of non-traditional shopping centre is the so-called **power centre**. This shopping centre does not include a traditional anchor department store. A power centre is usually located near a regional mall and brings together category killers and off-price stores. As previously mentioned in our discussion of discount stores, off-price retailers are stores that purchase manufacturers' overruns, returns, seconds and off-season products for resale to consumers at steep discounts (up to 50 per cent less than department stores). Examples of American off-price retailers that offer limited lines of national-brand and designer merchandise are Burlington Coat Factory, Marshalls and (in Europe) T.K. Maxx.

Finally, the newest generation of shopping centres is known as the lifestyle centre. This open-air retailing format appeals to upper-income consumers who dislike the mall. It offers a combination of an outdoor urban shopping area and a neighbourhood park landscaped with decorative fountains, plazas, park benches and stages for live concerts or other entertainment. It features upscale stores, restaurants and movie theatres in an appealing outdoor environment as well as luxury apartments, condominiums, townhouses and office parks. Especially now that high-income consumers transfer more of their shopping to the Internet, retail developers continue to explore alternatives to traditional shopping malls and e-commerce. To affluent consumers, among the most appealing options are lifestyle centres that combine shopping with relaxation or entertainment.

14.3 ONLINE MARKETING

Over the span of just a few years, the Internet has experienced exponential growth; along with that growth, its user base has expanded dramatically. Worldwide, more than one and a half billion people regularly go online, at home, work, school or at a public access site. Because the Internet allows managers to more effectively communicate with customers and prospects, e-marketing plays an increasingly important role in strategic planning and developing marketing strategies.

The extraordinary growth of Internet use and online information services has created exciting opportunities for marketers to build long-term relationships with customers. It also allows firms to target new markets more precisely, and even to tap into previously inaccessible markets. These opportunities have spurred most customer-oriented retailers to establish websites for corporate publicity, promotion of products or services and online sales.

In this section, we will first consider the significance of e-commerce, particularly for retailers. Then, we will look at the key benefits of Internet retailing for both merchants and consumers. Finally, we will analyze the cornerstones of a successful e-marketing strategy.

14.3.1 Overview of e-commerce

Internet retailing may well be the greatest innovation in retailing since, over 25 years ago, stores began using electronic scanners and computers at checkout counters to read bar codes on products. Today, these devices are not only used to retrieve prices, but also generate data that helps retailers make a variety of marketing decisions about inventory control, allocation of shelf space and even advertising.

The Internet has changed the retailing industry in an even more spectacular and fundamental way. Although *Internet retailing* – also called online retailing, electronic retailing or simply e-retailing – in many countries still accounts for only a small percentage of total retail sales, it has become an important part of many retailers' strategies. In this section, we will come to understand this development by studying the meaning of e-commerce and many of the related business activities that take place through Internet applications (such as email campaigns and virtual shopping carts) or other digital technologies.

PROFESSOR'S PERSPECTIVE
Elmira Bogoviyeva (KIMEP University, Kazakhstan)

Elmira Bogoviyeva is Assistant Professor at KIMEP University, Kazakhstan, having taken an MPhil at Maastricht School of Management (Netherlands) and a PhD at the University of Mississippi (USA)

The retailing industry in developing countries is considerably different from what consumers in the developed world have got used to.

Retail formats vary a lot. Traditional forms coexist with new. Unorganized selling can be observed ubiquitously. In countries like India, China or Thailand, thousands and thousands of people make their living by reselling convenience goods like tea, personal hygiene products and socks. On the streets you can meet women and men selling freshly made meals, produce from their own piece of land and hand crafts. Markets are thriving. You can walk hundreds of metres or even kilometres through the aisles of food, apparel, shoes, textiles, furniture and carpets. 'Mom and pop' stores are abundant in CIS countries ('Commonwealth of Independent States', an organization, formed during the breakup of the Soviet Union, whose participating countries are former Soviet Republics, including Russia, Kazakhstan, Ukraine, Azerbaijan, Georgia and Armenia). These are former first floor apartments turned into small convenience stores. Consumers with busy lifestyles plan their shopping trips, visit discount centres, 'cash & carry' stores or hypermarkets to buy food items and some other household items for a week or two ahead. They buy in bulk and enjoy prices 20 or 25 per cent lower than in the supermarket near their apartment.

Consumers in CIS countries are learning a new way of spending their leisure time: shopping!

While visits to shopping centres in developed countries decline as consumers transition to online stores, people in the developing world are learning a new way of spending their leisure time – shopping. Shopping malls grow like mushrooms in the centre and at outskirts of the cities. Some individuals visit modern trading centres because of the selection of branded boutiques gathered in one place. Others appreciate the levels of service and atmosphere. Youngsters enjoy cinema theatres and food courts. While moms are shopping, fathers with kids enjoy new movies in cinema theatre or entertainment centres. Growing middle class representatives in the city of Sao Paulo, Brazil prefer a shopping centre called Cidade Jardim not for luxury brands only, but because it is safe to shop there.

Competition is intensifying. The consolidation of retail space among fewer companies is progressing. Retailers think of new ways to get traffic to their stores. 'Sale' works like a magic word as budgeting consumers come to shop for apparel and other high involvement goods only a during a discount period. Shopping centres attract busy professionals by arranging 'nights of discounts' and concert programmes during national holidays.

Atmosphere, variety, entertainment, experience – these are magic words for managers of malls. Blockbusters and game arcades are not enough any more. Shopping centres in a cold climate are built with a water park right under the roof. Companies producing children's clothing create fairylands, childhood development centres, where kids enjoy painting, practise national crafts and make pancakes.

The diversity of retail formats corresponds to the multiplicity of groups of consumers in developing countries that vary in terms of personal income, social class and purchasing habits. Some consumers earn a dollar per day and spend it as soon as they earn it. Others can afford frivolous fashion shopping trips to Milan, Paris and London. One thing remains universal: a person from a developing country appreciates the 'personal touch' and the more and better the attention to the consumer, the higher the chances of a retailer seeing a client come back.[3]

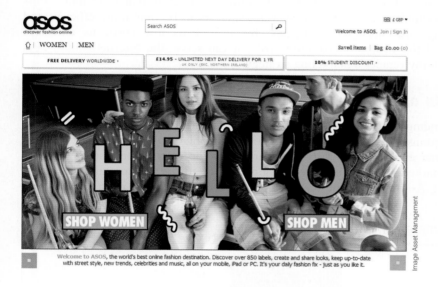

Welcome to ASOS, the world's best online fashion destination. Discover over 850 labels, create and share looks, keep up-to-date with street style, new trends, celebrities and music, all on your mobile, iPad or PC. It's your daily fashion fix - just as you like it.

Image Asset Management

E-commerce refers to a company's efforts to facilitate its online merchandise sales by using marketing principles to guide prospective buyers to a website. There are two types of company websites: corporate and marketing websites. A corporate website – which virtually every business has – is designed to make information available about the company and its offerings. Its primary goal is not to sell products or services, but to increase the company's visibility and create customer goodwill. By contrast, the objective of a *marketing website* is to provide convenient shopping experiences. An effective marketing website engages visitors in interactions that will move them closer to a store visit, demonstration or actual purchase.

Electronic marketing or **e-marketing** is the means by which e-commerce is achieved. It comprises any marketing activity conducted through the Internet, from buyer analysis to providing post-purchase customer service. E-marketing, by definition, includes the strategic process of positioning, pricing, promoting and distributing products and services to specific target markets over the Internet. **E-retailing** is an integral component of e-marketing: the e-marketing efforts directed towards ultimate consumers.

A further distinction may be drawn between e-marketing and online marketing. Although closely related, electronic marketing is a broader term than online marketing. While **online marketing**, also called *Internet marketing*, always involves an interactive computer system to connect sellers and buyers electronically, *e-marketing* encompasses additional digital technologies, such as DVDs, instant messaging, videoconferencing and interactive store kiosks. Eventually, the *e* may be left out of all definitions discussed here when a greater proportion of business contacts and transactions is conducted through digital technologies.

Meanwhile, several categories of retailers are flourishing in this ever-changing market. Countless bricks-and-mortar retailers have become brick-and-click firms: they operate as traditional stores but, as *multichannel* retailers, also have a significant web presence. Their customers appreciate having the option of either the hands-on buying experience in a store, with its immediate gratification, or the convenience of shopping on the Internet. A smaller number of firms, such as eBay and Amazon.com, have become successful as pure-click companies (also called *click-only* firms or *dot-coms*); these Internet-only retailers limit themselves to conducting business online, making the Internet the core of their marketing strategies. A pure-click company – without a storefront – remains a popular format for new companies, especially for *Internet-niche* retailers that specialize in offering specific products to designated consumer segments around the globe.

Whatever lies in store for Internet marketing's future, it is clear that e-retailing offers many attractive opportunities for marketing-driven managers to become more efficient and effective in reaching customers and prospects. Because of its low costs, its extensive geographic reach and the variety of marketing roles it can serve, the Internet should be a major component of any retailer's marketing strategy.

14.3.2 *Benefits of Internet retailing*

The Internet is changing the way companies develop and implement marketing strategies. Online marketing promises exciting new opportunities for retailers to effectively reach buyers in the virtual Internet environment. This departure from the conventional strategies of a bricks-and-mortar marketing environment offers a myriad of advantages to marketers of the twenty-first century. As illustrated in Figure 14.3, Internet retailing's main benefits are

FIGURE 14.3 Benefits of online retailing

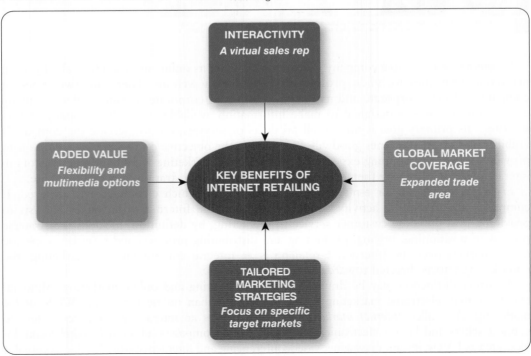

increased Interactive communication between the firm and consumers, an expanded trade area for potentially global market coverage, tailored marketing strategies and added value.

Interactivity

While advertising, sales promotion and most other forms of marketing communication are unidirectional (from the firm to its target audience), the Internet can be utilized interactively: from the firm to the customer, as well as from the customer to the firm. When visitors to a website communicate their needs or desires directly to an online retailer, the firm can interact with these potential buyers in real time. Two-way or reciprocal communication is established instantaneously, just as it would be through a salesperson, but at a much lower cost to the company than maintaining a sales force. As soon as a consumer clicks on an area of the website to learn more about a product's features and price, the company can provide them with details they need to make an informed purchase decision. The customer, however, controls the type and amount of information they receive from the seller. This approach to buyer-seller communication is called interactive marketing.

The exchange of information through websites is by no means limited to consumers indicating their buying preferences and companies providing the specifications of products that fit those criteria. Because they have access to a feedback mechanism, consumers can also voice complaints to a company's management, or ask specific questions. In fact, an astonishing amount of information is available online from a variety of sources. Using the Internet as a low-cost communication channel, customers can easily acquire detailed information about other products and services, including independent reviews of competing brands and blog (or 'weblog') opinions, such as those found on Facebook and other web communities or online social networks.

The ability to interact directly with consumers through the Internet motivates many marketers – as 'virtual sales representatives' – to be innovative in attracting prospective buyers to their websites. These efforts tend to boost competition for the consumers' attention and keeps rivals on their toes. Thus, successful e-retailers not only generate traffic for their own websites, but also may have a positive influence on industry performance as a whole.

Global market coverage

As a result of the Internet's low entry costs and the continuous improvement of search engines such as Google, even small retailers with limited resources can expand their trade area – the region where prospective customers are located – from a few city blocks to potentially the entire globe. Despite the higher distribution costs, a global retailing website may lead to lucrative marketing opportunities. Because retailers can reach so many potential buyers via the Internet, they may even successfully grow a specialized retail business for collectibles or niche products (for instance, exclusive wines, exotic hot sauces, halal Belgian chocolates and fly-fishing tackle) that would be significantly less profitable if limited by geographic boundaries.

Tailored marketing strategies

Online retailers are better able to develop a tailored marketing strategy for a particular target market than traditional bricks-and-mortar firms. By adapting the marketing mix to the needs and preferences of a certain type of customer and by contacting this market segment through targeted emails, they can effectively focus on specific target markets. An entertaining and visually appealing website or an attractive offer in an email message may encourage customers to pass promotional information on to others, which will help the retailer create an effective viral marketing campaign.

Added value

Internet usage benefits both businesses and their customers. For marketers, the Internet offers an array of advanced multimedia options, especially now that more consumers than ever before are converting to broadband or other high-speed connections. Thus, many web-sites now feature streaming video and photo galleries, including 3-D pictures of products that can be rotated 360 degrees. The flexibility of this dynamic medium also allows retailers to quickly adjust prices, advertising content or other elements of the marketing mix. At the same time, Internet retailing reduces expenses by eliminating the need for costly retail facili-ties and in-store sales people. Some products, like digitized music and software sold via the Web, can be downloaded when ordered, totally doing away with shipping costs. Because of more efficient communication between online firms and their suppliers, inventory and other operating costs may be lowered as well.

Customers, too, stand to gain from online retailers' rapid response and expanded customer service capabilities. Being able to buy a wide variety of products 24 hours a day, seven days a week, from any location with Internet access when most traditional stores are closed, benefits both online sellers and buyers. While consumers may not get the instant gratification that comes with a store purchase, they may still enjoy the online experience with retailers who have enhanced their websites with interactive or experiential activities. Examples are apparel stores that use virtual models to assist customers with clothing selections and automobile manufac-turers that allow potential buyers to build a personalized virtual vehicle by selecting their favour-ite features, colours and options. A number of retailers, such as Amazon, add value to the shopping experience by featuring product reviews. Others furnish price comparisons between competing offers (Expedia and other online travel agencies) or provide suggestions to individual customers based on their past purchases.

14.3.3 *Cornerstones of e-marketing*

Internet retailing has exploded for one major reason: many consumers find online shopping a convenient, and often less costly, way of buying what they need. Without leaving home, a customer can search the Web for the best vendor or lowest price, order the product and then have it delivered the next day right to their front doorstep. Online shoppers value the in-home privacy and the convenience of 24-hour access to a wide selection of merchandise available for comparison shopping.

Retailers, however, recognize that with millions of webpages accessible to online shoppers, simply having a website does not guarantee that anyone will visit it or buy anything. After all, the Web is a so-called pull medium, whereby users determine which webpages they view and in what order. Because retailers have no control over who visits their sites, getting and keeping consumers' attention requires marketers to go the extra mile in effectively communicating the value and benefits of their products before viewers lose interest and look elsewhere.

Developing a successful e-marketing strategy involves making clear, informed choices about a website's objectives, its target audience, its main features and, finally, how it will be managed. As Figure 14.4 illustrates, these decisions and activities are the four cornerstones of a well-planned e-marketing strategy.

Objectives

Developing an effective e-marketing strategy first requires setting qualitative and quantitative objectives that articulate what we want to accomplish. For example, will we use the Internet primarily to reduce cost, or to help generate sales? Manufacturers may realize cost reduc-tions by using the Internet as an alternative distribution channel for a particular market

FIGURE 14.4 Cornerstones of an e-marketing strategy

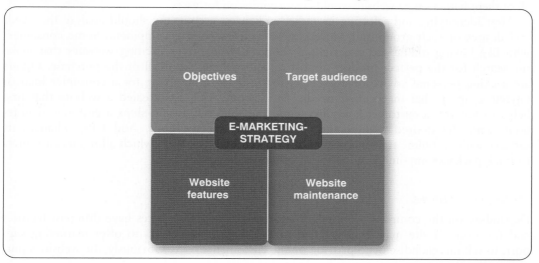

segment while eliminating middlemen. And in their daily operations they can even help streamline retailers' purchasing and inventory management functions by providing customers, through a password-protected website, invoices and order status information. Retailers may try to reduce costs by using the Internet to supplement their traditional customer service, shifting some of the call centre's data entry workload to the consumer.

Another company objective in pursuing an e-marketing strategy is to increase sales. Two types of websites – informational and shopping sites – may contribute to this goal. For instance, a retailer can promote its products or services – as well as its image – by advertising on Google, Yahoo! and other major search engines, or by featuring a product or promotional message on its own website. On such an informational site, consumers may also be able to assess financing options or request a price quote, but cannot actually place orders. By contrast, a shopping site's key marketing role – as an 'electronic storefront' – is to generate sales. A well designed website with the right graphics, colours, message and navigational features may help create a positive shopping experience for customers and persuade them to place online orders. A favourable consumer response is most likely with a strategy of mass customization, which allows online customers to individualize a mass-market product or service at a reasonable price. Ultimately, an attractive website gives the company a competitive edge by stimulating repeat purchases and customer loyalty.

From a marketing control perspective, management's most frequent downfall in developing an e-marketing strategy is failing to spell out clear choices. Without formulating specific objectives it is impossible to measure the extent to which the objectives are being met, and it becomes more difficult to make any necessary strategy adjustments.

Target audience

Websites can be designed for different market segments. Potential target audiences include the general public, customers, retailers, suppliers, investors, (potential) employees and other stakeholders. The nature of the target audience strongly influences the type of website, its layout and navigational features. The website's content and use of language should be in line with the expectations of the typical visitor. The least user-friendly websites tend to be those aimed at multiple parties. Recognizing this, Unilever developed a 'web portal' for each of its target audiences. This corporation's stakeholders and target markets are so diverse, that trying to address the needs of all of them with a single website would create confusion for users.

After identifying and selecting its target audiences, a company should analyze the needs and desires of each group and address these in its website development. Some consumers who like buying online are experiential shoppers who prefer exciting websites that make the search for the perfect product almost as enjoyable as the thrill of the purchase. Others are seeking personal advice or assistance, for instance in applying for a consumer loan or buying a laptop that meets their needs. To illustrate, Dell has created a website that first helps to identify a customer's requirements, and then builds and ships a customized notebook with the desired components, features and specifications. And UPS enhances its services with an online tracking system, distributed over the Web, which allows its customers to track packages anytime from point of origin to destination.

Website features

Depending on the company's objectives and target market, websites have different features and functions. A site may be developed to exchange information, to offer marketing support, to sell merchandise or to provide online customer service. Obviously, the website's purpose will influence its design and development.

Many organizations use a specialized web design company to develop, host and maintain their websites. Web designers must be carefully briefed to ensure that the site incorporates the right content and necessary bells and whistles to fully integrate with the retailers' overall marketing communication strategy and with any existing 'brick and click' stores it operates. Customers expect to find the same brands and products, whether they shop in the company's stores or online. Hence, retailers often have in-store kiosks to give customers the option of ordering products not found on the shelves. Conversely, Wal-Mart has been working on a real-time inventory feature on its website with information that helps customers decide whether to go to a particular store or to buy online.

A frequent problem for online retailers is that many visitors, soon after they get to 'checkout', abandon their shopping carts without completing the purchase, usually to compare prices or shipping and handling charges at other sites. Many never return to the site.[4] Some firms deal with this matter by displaying an overview of competitors' prices or including a link to a comparison engine. Others try to simplify and improve their websites, since poor site design is a major reason for abandoned online transactions. Research shows that many online shoppers complain about incomplete product information, poor site navigation and a time-consuming checkout process.

Customer-oriented managers treat their website as a constantly changing billboard that must attract and sustain consumers' attention and convert viewers to buyers. In designing a website, they especially pay attention to such features as a memorable domain name and an easy-to-navigate homepage that – as the gateway to the organization – projects a brand image, provides useful information and directs visitors, through planned links, to other relevant pages of the site. The site content should include information on the mission and company background, the products or services, an online shopping cart and customer service. Other important website features are shopping tools (such as a secure payment mechanism and a system for the buyer to register to gain access to premium areas and simplified purchasing), use of multimedia (graphics, photos, animations, video clips), electronic data interchange to facilitate the exchange of information among company personnel and with channel members, and a feedback link so that online visitors can communicate with someone within the company who will respond promptly to customer questions and complaints.

Website maintenance

In the ever-changing environment of the Internet, a company's e-marketing strategy may have to be modified periodically in order to remain effective. Especially for an Internet merchant, managing and maintaining a website is essential in continuously meeting consumers' expectations. This includes deciding on the optimal scale of online activities in light of the firm's marketing strategy, allocating the necessary budget to maintain and service the website, and assessing its strengths and weaknesses.

Experienced online marketers regularly evaluate their e-marketing strategy to make sure that the stated objectives – in terms of sales, customer service, brand image and other measures – are being achieved and to determine what changes are in order. They track daily site traffic, sales revenues, how long visitors stay on the site, repeat purchases and the costs per transaction. In evaluating the quality of their website, they also assess the average download time, ease of navigability, creativity, informational value, simplicity of buying and printability of the website's pages. Internet usage among consumers will undoubtedly continue to grow. The future is bright for merchants who, in taking advantage of the enormous potential of e-marketing, use a systematic approach in developing, assessing and improving websites to attract customers who like to buy products and services on the spot.

14.4 FRANCHISING

In the first part of this chapter, we have analyzed different ways in which retailers sell their merchandise to consumers. We will now examine how retailers themselves purchase products for resale and how this may influence their marketing efforts. The way a retailer buys products – and particularly the choice of suppliers – depends largely on whether it is independent, belongs to a chain or is part of a vertical marketing system. We will first review these different forms of ownership and then focus on franchising, a major, fast-growing force in the competitive retail market. Then, let's explore the most common types of franchise arrangements, as well as the pros and cons of franchising, from both the franchiser's and the franchisee's perspective.

14.4.1 Forms of ownership

A useful way to classify retailers is by type of ownership. There are three general forms of retail ownership – independent, corporate chain and contractual system. Of these three, the most prevalent is the independent retailer. An independent retailer owns and operates a single store that is not affiliated with other retailers. In many countries, the majority of retail establishments (including those staffed by the owners and their family members) are run by independents. Examples include small outlets such as clothing stores, restaurants, bakeries, florists and other neighbourhood shops. This relatively great number of independent businesses is the result of ease of entry into the market, since many kinds of retailing require little capital investment and few technical skills. Although independent retailers often fail within a few years due to intense competition, poor management and insufficient funding, those that survive despite their size usually provide outstanding personal service, sell products not offered by their competitors or have a location advantage.

A second form of ownership, the retail chain or **corporate chain**, is a group of stores, commonly owned and controlled, that sells the same merchandise line. It typically has centralized purchasing and decision making. Although some retail chains have only a few units, most consist of a large number of stores, giving them the buying power to negotiate with suppliers and obtain volume discounts. Chain stores also have more efficient inventory

MARKETING TOPPER
Abercrombie's Retail Theatre in Europe

About twenty years ago, American retailers such as Gap and Talbots entered the European market as part of an ambitious expansion strategy. Unfortunately, high rents, tough regulations and a lack of demand killed their ambition to further invade this region of the globe. Within a few years, both Gap and Talbots closed their stores and all but left the continent altogether.

Luckily for them, today's European business environment is very different. American casual clothes and styles – such as rolled-up jean shorts, worn-looking Oxfords, tailored sweatpants and even flip-flops – are increasingly popular among European teenagers who are turned off by the traditional clothes – think knotted scarves and Chanel jackets – favoured by their parents. Whether they're living in Paris, Rome or Amsterdam, teens aspire to wear the same kind of clothes as their idols featured in American movies and TV shows such as Vampire Diaries, Gossip Girl and Glee. And they are excited to now have the opportunity to check these clothes out in a store located in their own country.

This consumer enthusiasm explains why US retailers such as Gap and Tony Burch have opened stores in Italy, Michael Kors, Banana Republic and Tommy Hilfiger in France and Victoria's Secret in Great Britain, its first store outside of America. It also explains why frequently, hundreds of young people are anxiously waiting outside of the recently opened Abercrombie & Fitch shop on the Champs-Elysées in Paris for their turn to enter and go on a fulfilling shopping spree. In nations where – not too long ago – people were demonstrating against globalization in front of a McDonald's or other symbols of US global expansion, a young generation is eager to spend their savings in trendy American fashion shops. And today, one of the companies to benefit most from consumers' changed perceptions of American fashion retailers is Abercrombie & Fitch.

One reason why Abercrombie has turned into a global brand is, without doubt, the Internet. The web has not only abridged the language barrier, but also

© Kumar Sriskandan / Alamy

increased consumer awareness of US retailers' brands and products. In addition, it has made young consumers more cosmopolitan and, as global citizens, reduced their loyalty to European apparel brands. However, an awareness of the customs, payment systems and consumer laws specific to that country is key for American retailers such as Abercrombie trying to break into Europe. This was highlighted at a recent international summit on e-commerce hosted in Barcelona with a focus specifically on how to penetrate into foreign markets.

For retailers with an abundance of stores in the saturated American casual fashion market, overseas shops generate high revenues and profits. In Europe, where clothes are more expensive than in the US, there is no need for frequent sales and high discounts to move well-liked brand-name products. Opening more European locations is especially lucrative for retail chains because – in contrast to the Asian market – neither the store nor the American garments themselves need to be adapted to go well with European customers.

But there's another reason why it's a bigger challenge for Abercrombie & Fitch to be successful in Asia than in Europe. When the company recently opened a flagship store in Hong Kong, Shaun Rein of the China Market Research Group argued that the company could become a victim of the 'middle class image trap': its clothes are rather expensive for Chinese consumers, while its brand name has little status appeal. Most Chinese middle class consumers prefer to either 'trade up' to prestigious brands or to buy low-priced clothes from fast fashion merchants (such as Zara and H&M), but shy away from presenting themselves as middle class folks. Therefore, apparel retailers such as Abercrombie & Fitch, Banana Republic, Gap and Marks & Spencer struggle to gain market share in the Chinese market.

The absence of premium US clothing brands on the European market has forced consumers to shop online

To European consumers, on the other hand, American fashion is particularly attractive because US clothing brands – that young buyers are fond of – have been absent from the European retail market for many years. This has forced potential buyers to shop online (still less common than in the US), for which they pay high import duties and shipping charges, or to personally travel to 'the States' to shop for Abercrombie and other fashionable brands. This last option has enhanced American brands' status appeal.

To encourage consumers to actually visit its bricks-and-mortar stores in Europe, Abercrombie has gone the extra mile to create an overwhelming shopping experience. As part of its 'retail theatre' approach, Abercrombie brought along a hundred young American men to Paris, who – as models – positioned themselves outside the new store to attract screaming teenage girls looking for eye candy or a 'Kodak moment'. That is, until strong-minded police officers – referring to legislation that outlaws semi-nudity on this prestigious shopping boulevard – forced the masculine models to either put on a shirt or leave. Inside the store, Abercrombie's signature scent Fierce is pumped all over the place to create the sensuous disco-like shopping environment the retail chain is well-known for. Greeters welcome each customer with the same expression, in this case 'Hi, what's up?', pronounced with an obvious French accent, making the attention even more special. With this marketing strategy, no wonder that Abercrombie stores in Europe – since the moment they opened their doors – continue to attract huge crowds of adolescents, eager to 'shop until they drop', and then show off the expensive clothes to their friends.[5]

management and cost control systems, and gain economies in advertising or sales promotion, which in turn allows them to underprice independent retailers. Corporate chains are strongest in supermarkets, department stores, shoe stores and electronics stores, among others.

A *contractual system* – sometimes called an 'association of independents' – refers to independently owned stores that, by contractual arrangement, band together to function like a chain in order to gain some of the benefits of a large-scale operation. Chapter 13 discusses three kinds of contractual vertical marketing systems. The first system, a *retail-sponsored cooperative* or simply **retail cooperative**, is a group of retailers that establishes a central buying organization (at the wholesale level) and adopts a common store name to conduct joint promotion campaigns to help them compete with chains. The second type is a *wholesaler-sponsored voluntary chain* or **voluntary chain** in which a wholesaler formally agrees with a group of independent retailers to use a common name and to participate in bulk buying. A chain typically develops a private label brand and engages in joint merchandising.

The third – and fastest growing – form of contractual retail organization is the *franchise*. As the remainder of this section will demonstrate, the key difference between a **franchise organization** and the other two types of contractual systems (retail cooperative and voluntary chain) is that the franchise is based on a unique (often patented) product or service, a well-known trade name and a systematic way of conducting business.

The popular fast food chain Subway is an example of business-format franchising

Image Asset Management

14.4.2 *Types of franchise arrangements*

A **franchise** was earlier defined as a contractual arrangement between a parent company or franchiser (a service organization, manufacturer or wholesaler) and a number of franchisees (independent businesspeople) who buy the right to own and operate – in accordance with strict guidelines – one or more units in the franchise organization to sell certain products or services under an established trade name. The franchisee pays an initial, one-time franchise fee to obtain the rights to a franchise, as well as monthly royalty fees, usually in the range of 3 to 8 per cent of gross revenues. In return, the franchisee can call upon the marketing and operating assistance of the franchiser. They typically get help in finding a good location, benefits from participating in cooperative buying and advertising and receives management training.

There are two basic forms of franchising. The first is product-distribution franchising, such as a Volvo dealership or a Shell service station, a franchise arrangement in which the franchisee sells certain products provided by a producer or wholesaler. Another example is a Coca-Cola bottler who is licenced to bottle and distribute the company's soft drinks to retailers in a particular region. This is also referred to as 'trade name franchising'.

The second basic form of franchising is **business-format franchising**, such as in the case of Holiday Inn and Subway. Here, the franchiser sells franchisees the right to use its format or approach to doing business and provides step-by-step operational and decision making guidelines. This form of franchising has quickly spread in the past few decades throughout the hospitality and fast-food industries, especially in Europe and the US; it is sometimes referred to as 'retail franchising'.

The franchiser can occupy any position in the marketing channel. A franchise formed by an automobile manufacturer with its dealerships, for instance, is termed a manufacturer-retailer franchise. A wholesaler, such as a soft drink bottling company, may be engaged in a franchise agreement with the beverage's producer. This type of franchise would be considered a manufacturer-wholesaler franchise. A franchiser could also be a wholesaler with a franchise system for a chain of drug stores (a wholesaler- retailer franchise) or, finally, a service company with a unique approach to performing a service, such as in the hotel or car rental business. This kind of franchise arrangement – called a service-sponsored franchise – is the fastest growing type of franchise in the Western world.

14.4.3 *Advantages and disadvantages of franchising*

Many franchise organizations have a unique business format, product or service that was successful locally at a time when the originating company lacked sufficient capital to expand its own retail outlets. That's where franchising came in. Franchising offered a mechanism for such companies to grow beyond local boundaries.

Franchising works best if the product, service or approach to doing business stands out from the crowd and catches on in the market. The company should also aggressively promote the franchise name. Such promotion helps in recruiting a group of highly motivated franchisees willing to work long, hard hours – a central ingredient of a successful retail franchise. In addition, the franchiser must have a system in place to exercise strict control over the presentation and delivery of merchandise in the franchisees' outlets. After all, the chain's overall brand image and recognition, as well as the continued success of the format, depend on consistency among outlets in marketing high quality products and services. The key word here is 'consistency'.

Franchising is an ideal commercial alliance, because it combines the benefits of a corporate chain (professional retail management) with those of a small or medium-sized firm (flexibility and personal commitment of independent business people). While there are several distinct advantages to franchising, there are also a few disadvantages. Often what seems to be an advantage to one of the parties in the contract is a disadvantage to the other. Table 14.2 outlines this situation. We will look at franchising first from the franchiser's perspective, then from the franchisee's viewpoint.

TABLE 14.2 Advantages and disadvantages of franchising for both parties

Franchiser's perspective	Franchisee's perspective
Advantages	Advantages
1. Rapid expansion	1 Opportunity to become an entrepreneur in an established business
2. Limited investment	2 Help in obtaining bank financing
3. Several sources of revenue	3 Training and managerial advice provided
4. Motivated franchisees	4 Franchiser's reputation increases sales
5 Less risk	5. No personnel problems
Disadvantages	Disadvantages
1 Little control over franchisees	1 High start-up costs
2 Profit sharing with franchisees	2 Percentage of gross receipts paid to franchiser
3 Lack of attractive retail locations	3 No adaptation to local market conditions
	4 Too much control by franchiser
	5 Contract written to benefit franchiser

Franchiser's perspective

Franchising offers the franchiser the opportunity to establish a national or even international presence for a locally proven business format. The primary advantage for the franchiser is that this form of alliance allows them to expand distribution of their product or service with the funds provided by the sale of franchises. They can continue to grow without major capital expenditure, as the franchisee is expected to invest all the money to build (or lease) and to equip the facility. Several revenue sources can be built into the franchise contract to ensure a constant stream of income, including an initial fee to obtain the franchise, a percentage of gross operating revenues and profits from selling the required supplies to the franchisee.

In the franchisee, the franchiser has a motivated, locally oriented representative who knows the target market well. Since this person is responsible for hiring their own local staff, most of the personnel problems of a wholly owned chain simply do not exist for the franchiser. Finally, a franchiser has more control over how their product is marketed and promoted at the retail level than a manufacturer that sells its products through completely independent dealers or retailers. This may benefit both parties, since an established franchising company can afford to hire experienced professionals to develop an effective marketing strategy and retail operating system.

Still, one disadvantage to the franchiser is that they lose a measure of control over franchised operations. If the franchisee does not maintain the facility properly, it reflects poorly on the entire organization. Or if the franchisee chooses to limit operating hours and loses sales, there may be little the franchiser can do about it. Another disadvantage is that the franchiser gives up potential profits by franchising rather than operating as a chain. This does not, however, apply to every business, since some diligent franchisees make more money for the franchisers than they could make for themselves. A final drawback is that it is increasingly difficult in saturated markets to acquire lucrative retail locations for new outlets. This may present difficulties for new franchise companies that need a large and prominent enough location to gain brand awareness and consumer confidence.

Franchisee's perspective

The franchisee's major advantage is that, while remaining 'their own boss', they are assisted by the franchiser in establishing the business. This may include site location recommendations, help in obtaining bank financing and instruction in day-to-day business operations. Once the franchisee is in business, the franchiser may sponsor training programmes for the owner's employees at the franchiser's headquarters and provide on-site consulting services to the franchise owner. This may explain why, despite risk being a factor in any business, franchises have a better track record than start-ups. The franchisee also benefits a great deal from a franchiser's reputation and Internet presence. When people travel, they may not know anything about the Holiday Inn in Edinburgh, but they are familiar with Holiday Inn's international reputation. As a result, they are more likely to reserve a room there than at an independently operated hotel.

A significant problem for some franchisees is raising the capital required to begin operations. Once they are successful, a considerable portion of the operation's gross receipts is channelled back to the franchiser. This may lead to conflicts, particularly when the franchisee believes that the franchiser does not understand unique local conditions and the franchise agreement does not allow them to adjust the marketing strategy to meet the needs of the local market. Finally, many franchising contracts have been written primarily for the benefit of the franchiser: they clearly define the franchisee's obligations, but are ambiguous about the corresponding responsibilities of the franchiser. Therefore, a potential franchisee might want to use a checklist – such as the one in Table 14.3 – to assess various franchise opportunities.

TABLE 14.3 Franchisee checklist: a franchiser's responsibilities and conditions

> → A tried, successful business format
>
> → A strategy providing future growth opportunities for franchisees
>
> → A marketing communication and advertising plan
>
> → Training and managerial advice tailored to each franchisee's needs
>
> → A fair and convincing win-win contract between the two parties
>
> → A sound company reputation without legal conflicts
>
> → Territorial restrictions: no competition within the franchise
>
> → Reasonable exit conditions for franchisees
>
> → Personal contacts and mutual trust

14.5 KEY ACCOUNT MANAGEMENT

In many industries, the growing channel power of retail organizations has made manufacturers increasingly dependent on resellers. Large-scale retailers are frequently taking on the role of channel captain within distribution networks. Because they are constantly evaluating new products and lines to make sure that they mesh with the store image and product range, manufacturers must take retailers' needs and preferences into account. Thus, in addition to consumer marketing, manufacturers also pursue a *trade marketing strategy*, often called a *push strategy*.

Realizing that a clear insight into retailers' marketing strategies may increase the likelihood of their products being carried by those retailers, most manufacturers develop separate in-house programmes tailored to major retail accounts – that is, their important, large-volume customers. In this section, we will explore the significance of key account management and the role of the key account manager. Depending on which retailers they target, manufacturers pursue either a price or a service-oriented distribution strategy.

14.5.1 *Dual target market approach*

The terms **key account management** or *major account management* are widely used to describe a company's management of its large customers. Some prefer the terms *strategic*, *national* or *global* account management. Regardless of the phraseology, a **key account** is defined as a large account that receives special treatment from a vendor's marketing or sales executives. Since these large customers represent the lion's share of a company's sales volume and profit, they are vital to sellers. Therefore, the account is too important to be serviced only by a territorial sales representative. Another characteristic of major customers is the complexity of the buying process, as people in different geographic areas may be involved in a purchase. Even at a single site, retail executives from various functional areas may participate in a major buying decision. They are often called upon to devise custom-made products or packaging, price concessions and special promotions or other services.

Obviously, there is a need for close organizational coordination both within the seller's company and between buyer and seller. The national or **key account manager** coordinates the sales efforts directed toward a major retail account. To prevent chaos, large retail organizations avoid direct contacts with a supplier's individual departments (marketing, sales, credit, distribution). Because these retailers also wish to limit dealings with salespeople from different territories, who may want different contracts for each site, they appreciate the assistance a key account manager provides.

Effective coordination of a manufacturer's marketing and sales efforts is particularly crucial because the manufacturer should tailor its marketing mix both to the ultimate consumer and large retail customers. Figure 14.5 illustrates this so-called **dual target market** approach and demonstrates the relationship between a product management and a key account management strategy.

Key account managers create formal or strategic relationships with major retailers in order to pursue mutual goals, such as increasing sales and profits. Each of these relationships is founded on the account manager's intimate knowledge of the industry, the company and the customers' needs, as well as on trust, commitment and cooperation. Many companies have created separate divisions or sales forces to sell to key accounts. Their key account managers' goal is to maintain and penetrate the existing accounts, rather than to generate new customers. They focus on meeting their major customers' needs by effectively coordinating and implementing the strategies developed by the marketing or product managers and sales executives within their own organization. Others use top executives – with the authority to make decisions about prices and the allocation of manufacturing facilities – to call on key accounts, while employing the regular sales force to service the retail customers' field or branch offices and stores.

Finally, some corporations use global account management to interact with buyers. **Global account management** is a sales force structure that coordinates product and service

FIGURE 14.5 Key account management and product management in a dual target market approach

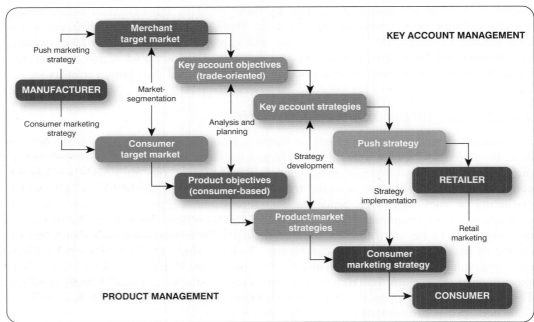

delivery across the globe to various subsidiaries of multinational customers. Corporations using global account management typically employ several sales teams operating abroad, each dedicated to a single, global customer. The company can then provide uniform pricing to a particular retail organization worldwide, making adjustments only for differing transportation fees and tariffs. Many suppliers have adopted this system because customers have demanded it.

One thing is certain. Suppliers inclined toward myopic thinking ('How do I get my products on the retailers' shelves?') rather than thinking from the merchant's perspective ('How could this product help the retailer attract loyal customers and increase their sales volume and profits?') are falling short on the account management front. They will not gain the retailer's confidence. That's why nearly all national brand manufacturers have introduced a key account management system.

14.5.2 Low margin and service retailing strategies

Consumers with relatively high disposable income can spend more on non-essentials. They may, for example, buy premium brand shopping products from *specialty retailers* to support a lifestyle that reflects a particular self-image. For this type of fun shopping prices are of minor importance. When buying convenience products, however, the same consumers may value *price shopping* and *shopping efficiency.*

Many consumers grocery shop as inexpensively and quickly as possible and, at the same time, buy other products from retailers offering premium brands and services that add value to the shopping experience. This buyer tendency has spawned different types of retail stores that focus on these two distinct preferences. Some retailers – in particular discounters – pursue a low margin retailing strategy, while others practise a service retailing strategy. Manufacturers that sell to these different store types often build their strategies around these different retailing formats by pursuing either a price distribution strategy (aimed at low-margin retailers) or a service distribution strategy (aimed at resellers with a service retailing strategy). Thus, depending on the types of products sold and the customer service preferences, retailers offer different levels of service.

Self-service retailers appeal to consumers who are willing to perform many functions themselves. These retailers have eliminated most, if not all, non-essential customer services. They keep their prices for convenience products low by running a low-margin, low-cost, high-volume, self-service operation. Examples are warehouse stores and discounters such as Aldi. Self-service operations, however, have been increasingly implemented by airlines (self-service kiosks at airports), hotels (express check-out) and superspecialty stores or category killers such as MediaMarkt that carry nationally branded, fast moving shopping products.

Full-service retailers, such as upscale department stores and specialty stores, offer personalized attention and a variety of services that add value to the customer's shopping experience. They typically carry distinctive products and may provide services such as interior design assistance, delivery and installation. Their higher overhead and operating costs are passed along to customers in the form of higher prices.

Finally, limited-service retailers provide a moderate number of services (such as gift wrapping and merchandise return privileges) and more sales assistance than self-service outlets, but not as many services as full-service retailers. They typically carry shopping products. While salespeople are available in departments such as jewellery and electronics, consumers are responsible for the majority of shopping activities.

PRACTITIONER'S PERSPECTIVE
Andreas Schaaf (BMW India)

Andreas Schaaf is President of BMW India. He joined BMW in 1996. Schaaf was previously head of product and price planning for Asia-Pacific, Africa and Eastern Europe, head of market development and Vice President Sales and Marketing for BMW South Korea.

Since we entered the Indian passenger car market about five years ago, the luxury car segment has had a phenomenal growth. By 2020, we expect this segment to reach an annual sales volume of 150 000 cars, which is ten times its current size. If that happens, India will be among the top ten countries in the world for the BMW Group. And with India becoming the fourth largest car market in the world in a few years, the premium segment will continue to grow.

There are a few things that have helped us be different – the product, marketing, dealership network and the spirit of the employees. The BMW brand is highly attractive for people with a modern perspective. The fact that BMW is aimed at a target market that drives the future of India has definitely helped us. We are perceived as a dynamic, sporty, innovative and *aesthetic brand*, and hence we've have done well with a younger target market. The average age of the BMW buyer in India is 40 years.

Instead of having a huge advertising budget, we develop more touch points where people can have a *personal* connect with the brand. For example, if you walk into a BMW dealership today, you will see that the place is sophisticated and you will be treated very well. We conduct innovative marketing activities – professional golf tournaments, wine tasting sessions, events with fashion designers – that have helped us get close to the customer.

We have spent a lot of time creating a unique *spirit* within the company. To give you an example, we became number one in 2009, but the next ten months we were trailing our biggest competitor, Mercedes-Benz. Instead of losing faith, the group came together – not only at the corporate level but also at the plant, financial services arm and at the dealer network level. The fact that people are *emotionally* connected within the organization has made a huge contribution to our success. In the meantime, BMW toppled Mercedes-Benz again to become the numero uno luxury car maker of India.

We recently launched our *financing* arm in India to service the credit needs of retail customers, fleet owners and dealers. India is a strong financing market and 80 per cent of the cars that we sell are financed. The financing option plays a very crucial part in the buying process, and that is the reason we set up the BMW Finance service. Going ahead, I think this will help us create finance products that are made to measure. Also, it is all about speed – today if we want to create a finance product, we can do it very quickly since it is within the company and you can immediately receive feedback for it.

In deciding on *dealers* and their locations, whernever you put a person who is eager to develop a market, there will be success. The top down approach doesn't really work. We do not have company owned dealerships, but *retail partners*. It is wrong to assume that a company that is very strong in design and manufacturing of premium cars should also be the best in selling those cars. Selling a premium car requires a good network. Hence, the fundamental belief at BMW is to leave the selling to the retail people who have a local connect. We call them the local heroes.

We have what we call the *one-global-brand-approach* and that is our strength. I don't think it would make sense for a global company to design a specific car only for the Indian market. Every localization would weaken the fundamental positioning of the brand. We have minor adaptations for the Indian road and weather conditions. This includes a higher suspension as ground clearance in India is low, and different intake filters as the air in the country is more polluted. These are minor changes to guarantee that products are running without any fault.

If you enter a new market with a small target group, you first build a premium image for the brand

The launch of the X1 model — the least expensive car in our portfolio — was an important part of our product strategy. If you look at our *product portfolio* in India, we had covered the entire range except the entry level. But when you enter a new market, the business does not start with entry models. Our experience shows if you enter a market which has a relatively small target group, you first need to build a *premium image* for the brand through the high-end models. Still, we think the X1 is the perfect car for the Indian market since — as a sport utility vehicle — it has the required ground clearance. But this is not the end so far as launches in the segment are concerned. As the market grows and fragmentation continues, we will launch products across other segments as well.

We also started our own *used-car* business. In terms of brand equity, there are two aspects. In the new-car business, you need to have your discount level in control as that can impact your brand reputation. Also, the used-car business does not dilute your *brand equity*; it tends to do the opposite. If you run the used-car business in a professional way, it will help increase value for your customer as the resale value goes up. It will allow a *new* set of people to experience the brand for the first time, and eventually they might buy a new car. We are developing premium-used car operation centres, where cars will be sold out of the dealerships. These will not be sold out of the parking lot or the basement, but out of a 100 per cent dedicated floor in the showroom. It will have a great atmosphere — with the same standard as a new car dealership.

As far as our *global plans* are concerned, BMW has a special focus on BRIC countries, of which India is a part. Macroeconomic factors indicate that India will emerge the strongest among the BRIC countries. We are relatively small in India today, but the future belongs to India, and the whole company shares this vision. My goal is to establish the foundation for the future organization.[6]

14.6 RETAIL MARKETING

In today's mature market, retailing is in transition. Retailers of the 21st century don't simply find the best products, put them on the store shelves and hope that customers will come in and buy the merchandise. Like manufacturers, they develop a strategic plan, focusing on questions such as: What is our core business? What is our target market? Which companies are we competing against? And, how do we differ from our competitors? The answers to these questions are vital, especially now that many retailers engage in *scrambled merchandising* to generate more traffic and convert stores into one-stop shopping centres. In doing so, they have supplemented their offerings with products and services that are neither related to each other nor to the retailer's original business. Scrambled merchandising may blur a store's image in the consumer's mind, making it difficult for the retailer to be successful in highly competitive markets.

To succeed, retailers should carefully plan how they will compete. They must define and select a target market and tailor the retailing mix to the target customers' tastes in order to achieve the company's objectives. Retailing objectives may include creating a more upscale store image, higher sales of specific product lines or increased customer satisfaction. The strategies retailers use to reach these objectives may include updating décor, developing a new advertising campaign or adjusting product assortments, price and service levels.

By definition, the term **retail marketing** encompasses the broad spectrum of retailers' marketing activities, including:

→ analyzing competitors and the target customers' profile and shopping behaviour.

→ developing a *store format* and positioning strategy to attract and serve the target market.

→ using a consistent, integrated *retailing mix* to gain customer loyalty.

Since strategic planning and market segmentation have been examined in previous chapters, we begin by analyzing the elements of a store format and will investigate how retailers can develop a distinctive store image and ambience. We will also consider the retailing mix and explore current trends in retailing.

Dell, realizing the limitations of its business model to reach all consumers, opened a chain of kiosks in shopping malls across the USA, Canada, Australia, Hong Kong and Singapore, but then shut down over 150 kiosks in US malls and airports after getting its products on the shelves of retail stores such as Wal-Mart, Staples and Best Buy.

14.6.1 Store image: positioning the retail store

In an era when consumers have many choices of what to buy and where to find it – including websites and television shopping channels – retailers must go beyond offering quality products at fair prices. They also must position their stores effectively to gain a competitive advantage over other retail outlets that are trying to attract the same shoppers. Above all, they must give the consumer a reason to frequent the store. Here, the key to success is creating an effective *store format*. The *store concept* or **store format** is the foundation of any retail business. It reflects the retailer's strategic choice to appeal to a carefully selected target market of customers with specific needs and shopping expectations. The store format's building blocks are the selected *target market* (Who do we want as our customers?), the *product assortment* (Do the merchandise and services offered match the customer's expectations?) and the *market positioning* (How can we differentiate the store from others in the shopper's mind?).

A successful positioning strategy requires the retail organization or store to have an identity, or *store image*, that has added value and clear advantages over its competitors. In the next few paragraphs, we will examine the importance of store image as well as an effective image-building procedure.

The importance of store image

Even before entering a store, consumers have certain expectations. They will most likely expect low prices in a discount store, for instance, and personal attention in a specialty store. After an actual visit, customers formulate certain impressions of the store based on its format. The combination of consumer expectations and impressions creates a **store image**.

While a store image is partially a function of the store format, it also has an emotional or psychological dimension. Some consumers are attracted to a store because it has a warm, trustworthy atmosphere; others may view the same store as old-fashioned and unpleasant. Research shows that customers tend to portray a store in the same terms (such as elegant or tacky) they might use in describing a person. The point is that it is impossible to objectively define a store image. Marketers may work to develop a 'personality' for a store, but ultimately, it is customer perception that defines the image.

Although a store's location, merchandise, pricing, services, promotional campaigns and reputation each contribute to its image – the functional and psychological picture in a consumer's mind – retail stores project their personalities extensively through atmospherics. **Atmospherics** – the physical elements of a store's design – is the use of floor layout, fixtures, lighting, sounds, scents and other design elements to influence consumers' perceptions and make the store 'feel right'. These components of the in-store environment appeal to consumers' emotions, encourage browsing and are likely to lead to more frequent and larger purchases.

Image-building procedure

There are no sure ways to create a positive store image; each situation must be analyzed as unique. However, retailers have come to rely on a systematic, multi-step procedure proven to work. Retailers first identify store image characteristics that potential customers find most important. These factors vary widely from store to store. Characteristics customers seek in a fast food restaurant, for instance, include the quality and taste of the food, the friendliness, appearance and efficiency of the employees, the restaurant's cleanliness, layout and atmosphere and the prices on the menu. Table 14.4 presents ten common factors that determine store image.

After identifying the image elements perceived by the public as crucial, the second step is to determine how the store ranks in terms of these factors, as well as how competing stores match up to them. This ranking and comparison is important, if for no other reason than that it provides a database against which the final plan to build or change the store's image will later be judged for effectiveness.

The next step is to decide what image the store should have. For instance, does the retailer want to stand out for its reasonable prices or its excellent customer service? This decision should be based on a SWOT analysis. At this point, the retailer must recognize that the store cannot be all things to all people. A positive image in one segment may actually be an unfavourable image in another. In considering their strengths and in choosing an ideal overall image, the retailer may assign points (such as a number between 1 and 10) to each element of the desired image.

TABLE 14.4 Ten store image attributes

Store image factors	Description
Merchandise mix	Selection or assortment of products and services offered, their quality, style and guarantees.
Services mix	Overall customer service provided by sales clerks, presence of self-service, credit policies, delivery service, ease of merchandise return.
Price level	The store's price level relative to competitors, the added value, sales promotion and special offers.
Clientele	Social class appeal, customer self-image congruency and store personnel.
Physical facilities	Lighting, air conditioning, lavatories, store layout, aisle placement and width, elevators, carpeting and architecture.
Convenience	Store location, parking facilities and other factors that make shopping easier.
Promotion	Advertising, premium and store brand strategies, house style, sales promotions including displays and loyalty programmes.
Store ambience	Furniture, colours and atmosphere-congeniality, which is the customer's feeling of warmth, acceptance or ease.
Institutional factors	Reputation, reliability and the conservative-modern projection of the store.
Post-purchase satisfaction	Customer's satisfaction with the store and the purchase, including the merchandise in use, returns and adjustments.

The retailer is now ready to formulate a plan for overhauling its image. Experienced retailers know that a new or better image is easier to advance if concrete changes in décor or operating practices accompany the image change. After implementing the plan to support the new image, the last step is to monitor the results of the image transformation effort. The retailer should conduct surveys of customers to find out how they evaluate the store on the important store image attributes, and compare this assessment with the targeted scores for the ideal image. Such performance monitoring helps the retailer to determine whether the image building project has been effective and, if not, what elements of the retailing mix should be adjusted to further modify the store's image.

14.6.2 *Retailing mix*

While the store format represents the retailer's strategic choice to appeal to the target market, the **retailing mix** brings the *tactical* use of the marketing tools into play. Retailers should carefully consider this mix, and decisions should always be made with the consumer in mind. Since consumers shop for various reasons – to look for a specific product, to find out more about new items or just to enjoy the shopping experience – retailers cannot simply fill shelf space with merchandise. They must select and promote the desired products, train salespeople to better assist customers and use all available marketing strategies that will make shopping convenient or enjoyable and that will increase store patronage. As Figure 14.6 illustrates, the retailing mix consists of six Ps: the four marketing mix variables plus Personnel and Presentation. Let's look at them now from a retailer's perspective.

Product

The first component of the retailing mix is the *product*, in retailing also referred to as the product assortment or merchandise mix. In developing product strategy, retailers must decide which products and brands to carry, taking into account the variety or *product mix width* (the number of product lines offered), and the *product line length* or depth (the number of brands and products in each line).

FIGURE 14.6 Retailing mix: the six Ps

Stores carrying tens of thousands of products certainly provide consumers with choice. But because retail space is limited, a major consideration in product selection is *market appropriateness*: To what extent do products appeal to the store's target market? To manage the product assortment, retail organizations often use an approach called category management. In order to maximize sales volume and profits in each product category (such as pet food in supermarkets), a single person is given responsibility for selecting all products that the target customer may view as substitutes for a comparable item. Other retailers rely on data mining to decide which products to carry and at what price, what mark-downs to offer and what advertising campaigns might prove effective with the target audience. In addition to market research, merchandise selection may be based on fashion trends, past sales, customer enquiries and competitive conditions. On the supply side, product availability and supplier reliability are also important selection criteria.

It is not easy for retailers to distinguish themselves from other stores through the products they offer, since competitors often sell the same popular brands. Therefore, a retail organization usually offers products that others don't carry, such as *store brands* and national brands on which it holds exclusive distribution rights. Additionally, retailers may offer specific items that enhance the store image (such as innovative or prestige products), niche products (such as diet or vegetarian food) and seasonal items (offered only at certain times of year). The downside to offering a wider assortment is that it may complicate inventory management. The challenge then becomes keeping ample supplies of hot-selling items in stock while deciding when and how to promote or discount slow-moving products.

Promotion

Whether a retailer wants to attract new shoppers or build a relationship with current customers, they can choose from a variety of promotion tools, including advertising, sales promotion, personal selling, direct marketing and public relations. Most stores also use websites to provide information and sell products directly. To most effectively position the store in consumers' minds, retailers should implement an *integrated marketing communication* strategy.

While intriguing national retail advertising can reinforce a chain's image positioning, much of retailers' advertising is carried out at the local level to provide information about the store's location, merchandise and special sales. In a competitive market, the use of sales promotion tools such as coupons, displays, frequent shopper reward programmes, in-store demonstrations and food sampling can mean the difference between flat sales or increasing each shopper's average purchase. Not only do promotions draw more customers into the store, but they also inform consumers about new or improved products. Though they may attract business, price promotions rarely retain customers. Personal selling efforts tend to be more effective in creating store loyalty. Consumers appreciate well-trained salespeople who greet shoppers, help them find the right merchandise and professionally handle complaints.

Price

For retailers, prices can be a powerful competitive tool and customer draw. The retailer's ultimate goal is to sell a product or service, and attractive prices are crucial to stimulating sales. But too many retailers fail because they focus on price alone to differentiate themselves from the competition. Instead, the pricing strategy should be coordinated with the other elements of the retailing mix as well as the target market and desired store image.

In most markets, successful retailers are found at all price ranges, from low to high. While discount retailers and mass merchandisers sell products in large volumes at ultra low prices to appeal to bargain hunters, some leading specialty stores offer premium quality brands without discounts. In spite of low sales volume, their high mark-ups result in a profitable business. For tactical reasons, they may occasionally have storewide sales or offer mark-downs on some products to serve as loss leaders or traffic builders. But the overall combination of high prices, high quality merchandise, excellent personal service and an attractive store ambience offers their customers added value.

Place

The founder of the world's largest retailer, Wal-Mart, often claimed that retailing is a simple business with only three basic tasks: to attract consumers into the store, to convert them into paying customers and to operate as efficiently as possible, so as to reduce costs. Although this statement may sound simplistic, it in fact summarizes the strategies that all retailers must implement. Place or distribution, the fourth retailing mix variable, is instrumental in helping to accomplish these tasks, and will significantly affect a store's growth and profitability.

Since convenience is a vital ingredient to success in retailing, selecting the best possible store location may well be the most important aspect of the retailer's place decisions. A bad location is difficult for even the best retailer to overcome. The chosen location must be accessible to the targeted customers in an area that is consistent with the retailer's positioning. In selecting a store location, merchants analyze the demographic characteristics – such as the income level – and purchasing behaviour of consumers in the surrounding area. They also investigate local regulations and evaluate the competition and transportation patterns. In a dynamic market, retailers realize that as a result of changes in population trends, consumer buying behaviour, the location of other stores and real-estate availability or values, a perfect location today may be a poor location tomorrow. Therefore, they need to continually monitor the retailing environment.

Personnel

Customer service, in a nutshell, is all the activities that enhance the quality and value customers receive while shopping and buying merchandise. It is the number one goal of any store's floor staff. Retail employees should strengthen the store image, and they greatly influence customer satisfaction. But, in reality, shoppers are often displeased with the service quality they receive from store personnel. Research shows that retail customers often complain about long lines at the checkout, associates who are nowhere to be found when they are needed, out-of-stock products and salespeople who are not knowledgeable about the store's policies or products.

Although retailers know the importance of customer service, many fall short of providing or improving it. Some simply don't hire enough people to wait on their customers, while others have trouble attracting and retaining a quality labour force. Regardless, since customers well served are customers retained, providing great customer service is a key success factor in the retailing mix.

A store's atmosphere is greatly enhanced by informed, helpful and enthusiastic personnel and, because they can persuade shoppers to buy, they can contribute to increased sales. Retail personnel are often trained in *suggestion selling*, in which they encourage a customer to supplement the original purchase with a related product (for example, suggesting the addition of a drink when ordering a meal). Another common practice in retailing is trading up, which involves persuading customers to buy a higher-priced product than they intended to buy. As long as store personnel are selling what consumers actually need or want, and offer excellent customer service, they can provide the retailer with a substantial competitive advantage.

Presentation

'Retail is theatre', according to executives charged with deciding how stores should present and position themselves in consumers' minds. They realize that to consumers, shopping may be as much a form of entertainment or social interaction as it is an exercise in buying. Like seasoned stage managers, they ensure that customers entering the retail store experience surroundings replete with visual displays, sounds and other sensory cues presented to maximum effect.

The **presentation** of a retail store – the sixth and final P in the retailing mix – is of strategic importance because it is instrumental in attracting the target market and defining the store image. The key element of any store's presentation is its *atmosphere*, also known as ambience or atmospherics. It is something customers can feel, and it tends to affect their shopping mood, time spent in the store and impulse purchases. Atmospherics, in terms of the overall impression created by the store's physical layout and surroundings or by its décor, include both exterior and interior components.

The store's *exterior* appearance includes its architectural design, entrances, window displays, signs, the surrounding area and traffic flow. Store visibility and the storefront in particular play a key role in attracting shoppers. The interior décor of the store should tempt consumers to linger and to make purchases. Interior atmospheric elements include store layout (the floor space allocated to customers, selling and storage), merchandise presentation, flooring and wall coverings. Aesthetic considerations, those interior sensory cues related to lighting, scent, temperature, background music and colour, contribute to store atmosphere and affect customer behaviour. Research shows, for instance, that bright colours such as red and yellow tend to make customers feel hungrier and eat faster, which increases sales volume in fast food restaurants. In conclusion, retailers should periodically evaluate the atmosphere that their target customers prefer and then adjust the atmospheric features to stimulate the intended consumer awareness and action.

14.6.3 *Recent trends in retailing*

Gone are the days when simply minding the store was the only requirement for running a profitable retail business. Today, more than ever before, a strong consumer orientation is essential for long-term success. Retailers have to search continually for new ways to better serve existing customers and attract new ones. In planning marketing strategies, they must take into account four major trends and respond decisively and effectively to the developments they face. The most prominent rapidly evolving trends in the marketplace are those relating to changing consumer behaviour, technological advances, the emergence of new forms of retailing and global retailing.

Changing shopping behaviour

Consumers no longer want to spend as much time shopping as they once did. Both the number of bricks-and mortar retailers consumers depend on and the number of times they visit those stores per month is in decline. Bustling through daily life, shoppers seek convenient locations and store hours, excellent customer service and a wider variety of premium labour-saving products and services (such as ready-to- eat foods) in stores that provide one-stop shopping. They also demand reasonably priced products, such as store brands.

To adapt to the time constraints, changing lifestyles and shopping preferences of dual-income households and working women, retailers are opening weekends, lengthening hours of operation and offering special services (such as home delivery and installation of consumer electronics). Others establish comprehensive specialty boutiques and use more efficient displays to limit the number of departments a shopper must visit, or they use the store-within-a-store concept to save customers time. Since the Internet offers consumers an attractive alternative to traditional stores, retailers are continually expanding their Web presence.

Technological advances

While technological advances are manifest in every aspect of life, the Internet has clearly uncovered a wealth of marketing opportunity for online merchants. Bricks-and-mortar retailers have also embraced new retail technologies to remain competitive. As previously discussed, many retail organizations are using sophisticated information technology and software systems to process transactions online, order electronically from suppliers around the globe and improve operating efficiency wherever possible.

To illustrate, most retailers rely on scanning systems to reduce checkout time, improve inventory control and reduce spoilage. More and more companies, including airlines, hotels and supermarkets, are turning to self-scanning procedures, allowing consumers to bypass traditional checkout attendants. Others provide means for customers to use cell phones or other wireless devices to order and pay for merchandise. Another trend, seen in many restaurants, is the use of touchpads to enter orders and speed up service. A final illustration of the increasing importance of retail technology is the use of video kiosks in store or non-store locations to present information, process orders or enhance atmospherics.

While most technological advances help retailers save time and money or offer consumers a more satisfying shopping experience, they also create challenges for retail executives in deciding which new technologies to adopt or, at least temporarily, reject. Because the pace of technological developments will not slow, navigating this complex, sometimes baffling environment requires careful and continuous analysis of the anticipated impact of technological breakthroughs on the retail business.

Shorter retail life cycle and new retailing formats

With the changing consumer preferences and intensifying rivalry between retailers, retail life cycles are becoming progressively shorter. The retail life cycle involves four distinct stages – early growth, accelerated development, maturity and decline – that reflect the emergence, growth and decline in market share of new retail forms that present a major departure from other retailing practices. Today, store concepts reach the maturity stage of the life cycle – in which their market share begins to level off – very quickly, making innovation almost mandatory. To illustrate, whereas downtown department stores took as long as 80 years to reach maturity, more recent store formats, such as home improvement centres and factory outlet stores, did so in less than 15 years. The ability of retailers to adapt in dealing with changing markets and institutions is critical. Their main challenge is to postpone the decline stage – in which market share and profit decrease significantly – by appealing to new market segments or by adopting other marketing strategies to fend off competition.

Retailers have developed a wide range of store formats and strategies that offer specific benefits for different market segments. To reach a broader group of consumers and offer them more choice, multichannel retailers have integrated their store, catalogue and Internet operations, becoming click-and-brick marketers. Gas stations that feature convenience stores make shopping simple and convenient for commuters. Other retailers focus on cost control. For instance, fast food chains like NY Pizza and Subway, in their efforts to penetrate the Dutch market, are experimenting with a form of co-branding by allowing the two restaurants to share a single retail space; this format allows them to share common costs and some personnel. Giant retailers such as specialty superstores or category killers are using their buying power to offer substantial price savings to customers, meeting the needs of price-sensitive consumers. Alternatively, some retailers choose to differentiate themselves from competitors with 'entertainment retailing' by sponsoring guest appearances or inviting artists to perform in their stores.

Global expansion of retailers

As the nations and peoples of the world interact more closely, retail organizations are increasingly interested in foreign markets as vehicles for globalization and increasing sales. European retailers such as Carrefour (France), Ikea (Sweden), Benetton (Italy) and Marks and Spencer (UK) are among the leaders in global retailing. At the same time, US companies such as McDonald's, Pizza Hut and Starbucks, with their proven formats and strong brand positioning, have become household names worldwide.

To become globally prominent, retailers must adjust to varying cultural norms. As the vignettes in this book illustrate, some retailers have been more successful in conforming to foreign markets than have others. But with domestic markets becoming saturated and global opportunities still abundant, retailers will continue to pursue global expansion.

SUMMARY

1 The changing retail landscape

Retailers are the critical link between manufacturers and final consumers, and their added value is significant for both parties. The functions they perform include sorting, providing information, keeping inventory, setting prices and providing customer service. Overall, the economy is heavily dependent on the retailing industry, which is one of the largest employers.

The wheel of retailing describes how new types of retailers can gain a competitive foothold by offering customers lower prices than traditional stores, while maintaining profits by reducing or eliminating services. To better serve their customers, these discounters tend to gradually upgrade their products or services, while raising their prices. The cycle continues when new retailers with a low-price appeal enter at the market's low end to challenge established companies that have travelled up the wheel from their stripped-down beginnings. Although there are some exceptions to this theory, marketing experts believe that the wheel pattern is an accurate indicator of future retailing venues and developments.

2 Classifying retail operations

The major types of retail stores include specialty stores, convenience stores, supermarkets, hypermarkets, department stores, discount stores and category killers. Their marketing strategies differ considerably, due to variations in the width and depth of their product assortments, their pricing policies and service levels. Convenience stores, for instance, operate as 'mini-supermarkets', whereas discount stores are self-service, general merchandise stores that offer brand name and private-label products at low prices. New retail formats commonly appear. One such innovation is the superstore or hypermarket, a huge retail outlet that offers both supermarket and discount store shopping in one location. Superstores face increased competition from category killers, a new breed of specialty retailer that concentrates on a particular product category and competes on the basis of extensive product availability and low prices.

Since many consumers want more convenience in shopping, non-store retailing is growing faster today than in-store retailing. Each of the forms of non-store retailing discussed here – direct selling, network marketing, street peddling, automatic vending and online retailing – has its own set of market advantages and limitations. A shopping centre is advantageous to the retailer because it draws large numbers of people. Merchants located in neighbourhood, community and regional shopping centres all benefit from the traffic. However, there are also some problems associated with shopping centres. They are expensive to build and lease, and they offer the individual retailer little control over the immediate environment. Increasingly popular alternatives to these traditional shopping centres are factory outlet malls, power centres and lifestyle centres.

3 Retailing and the Internet

The increasing number of consumers using the Web presents exciting marketing opportunities for numerous companies. With the rapid growth of the Internet as a major distribution channel, merchants who ignore Internet retailing run the risk of missing out on a huge segment of today's market. The main benefits of online retailing for marketers are the increased interactivity in buyer-seller communication, the broad market coverage, the ability to develop tailored marketing strategies for target markets and the unique added value that online retailers can provide. E-marketing has also increased the efficiency of physical distribution, both in business and consumer markets. Electronic order processing via the Internet and the high speed of communication has lowered costs and raised customer satisfaction. In building and maintaining a successful website as part of an e-marketing strategy, managers should make clear choices and decisions on the site's objectives, the target audience, the main features of the website and, finally, how it will be effectively managed.

4 Franchise retailing

Franchising, in which a franchisee uses a franchiser's trade name, products, services and business format in return for several fees, is attractive to both franchisers and franchisees. To a franchiser, this is a way to secure many of the advantages of having their own outlets without having to finance and manage them. Franchise retailing enables them to expand their operations rapidly with only limited capital. For franchisees, an advantage of the franchise system is the opportunity to become a successful entrepreneur in a proven business with access to managerial advice as well as planning and operating assistance from the franchiser. This win-win situation makes franchising a popular system worldwide for rapid expansion.

5   Strategic account management

Manufacturers tailoring their marketing mix to ultimate consumers as well as to important retail customers that purchase large quantities, use a dual target market approach. In addition to following a product management strategy, they are likely to employ key account managers to interact with customers that account for a large share of the company's sales volume. This twofold customer orientation is consistent with the marketing concept. A key account manager is dedicated to coordinating all marketing and sales efforts directed toward major retailers or other customers in the supply chain. Depending on the level of service that retailers provide – levels typical for a low margin retailing strategy or a service distribution strategy – manufacturers and their key account managers will build their marketing strategies around these retailing formats.

6   Store image and retailing mix

A store's image may be its most important asset. Yet, some retailers hardly realize that their store has a certain publicly perceived image, or they hope that customers accept the store as it is. To achieve their company's objectives, however, it is essential for retail executives to carefully develop a positive store image and customize the retailing mix to appeal to the target market. Effectively differentiating the store from competing stores in the minds of customers has several benefits. It will enhance the retailer's competitive advantage and increase customer retention. Loyal customers, in turn, are more likely to forgive the store for errors, such as being out of stock in a product category. Moreover, positioning the store forces the retailer to formulate its objectives, monitor the changing needs and wants of the selected target market and build on its strengths in responding to rivals that may try to imitate the store's successful format.

Selecting the right mix of products and services that help position the store and meet the needs of the targeted customers is only one of the retailer's responsibilities. They have to make the right marketing decisions in other key areas as well. The six Ps of the retailing mix used to create the store format comprise: Product (including the merchandise mix), Promotion (advertising and promotions), Price (mark-ups and special sales), Place (location and hours), Personnel (customer service) and Presentation (store layout and ambience). A well-planned and integrated retailing mix offers consumers a sound value proposition and may provide the business with lucrative opportunities to expand globally.

DISCUSSION QUESTIONS

1   Many retailers have adopted marketing-driven strategies in the past decade. How would you explain this, and what are the underlying reasons?

2   Distinguish among the various marketing strategies employed by the different types of retail stores.

3   Which types of retail operations will experience the greatest sales gains in the near future, and why?

4   What are the advantages and disadvantages of shopping centres from the retailer's perspective?

5   Does the Internet provide useful opportunities for relatively small retailers?

6   Analyze the benefits and disadvantages of retail franchising from the perspective of the franchiser, the franchisee and society.

7   Why do an increasing number of manufacturers rely on key account management these days?

8   Explain the meaning of a store format. How does the retailing mix vary from the marketing mix?

9   What is meant by store image? How can a retailer successfully transform its image?

10   Discuss how retailers can improve customer service by using technology.

CHAPTER 15
GLOBAL MARKETING

LEARNING GOALS

After studying this chapter you will be able to:

1	**Explain the importance of global marketing and how to plan for international expansion**
2	**Assess the international environment influencing business operations abroad**
3	**Develop various strategies for entering new global markets**
4	**Discuss the distinction between a customized and a standardized marketing strategy in developing worldwide marketing programmes**

15.1 International marketing planning

15.2 Global marketing environment

15.3 Market entry strategies abroad

15.4 Customization or globalization?

Global markets abound with opportunities for profit. Managers must develop a global vision, however, not just to identify and capitalize on international marketing opportunities but also to remain competitive in domestic markets. In fact, a company's toughest competition often stems from rivals abroad. Additional revenues aside, companies pursue foreign marketing opportunities to reap benefits that include economies of scale from continued expansion. They also gain fresh insight into buyer behaviour and marketing communication or distribution approaches that can be successfully implemented in the domestic market or abroad.

Today, not only large corporations, but also small start-up firms can conduct business anywhere in the world. Advanced communication tools, global distribution networks and, of course, the Internet have opened world markets to any organization. Its managers may well encounter challenges associated with an unfamiliar culture, diverse laws and regulations or restrictions imposed by the host country's government. Ultimately, managers can only implement effective marketing strategies if they know the marketing fundamentals, have insight into the international market's unique characteristics and develop a global marketing strategy. This chapter provides a foundation for thinking globally and reaching international markets and customers.

MARKETING IN ACTION
Why McDonald's is 'Going Glocal'

Are you familiar with the expression: *not invented here*? It reflects an attitude of managers who refuse to accept a new product or idea that was developed outside of their own organization. It stifles innovation, and is bad for business; especially for a global business.

Take, for example, McDonald's, the world's largest chain of hamburger fast food restaurants currently operating in 120 nations. For decades, it was perceived as an all-American organization. Since businessman Ray Kroc, a franchisee, bought the chain from the McDonald brothers and watched over its worldwide expansion, the restaurants focused on burgers, fries and shakes, no matter where they were located. Even when the corporation started to aggressively expand internationally and opened up hundreds of restaurants overseas, it continued to replicate the menu that was offered in its home territory, the United States. For a long time, any new product that was introduced had always been developed in its American headquarters in Oak Brook, Illinois. In fact, when McDonald's moved into the Spanish and Italian market, it actually shipped the tiles that had to be installed in the restaurants from the US, even though these European countries were known for their own fine ceramics.

© David Levenson / Alamy

> ## McDonald's growth and profits are dependent on how it manages its global expansion

Soon afterwards, the company realized that its traditional management approach was not effective in addressing the challenges that came with global expansion. For one thing, McDonald's *brand image* was suffering, both in the US and abroad. Therefore, the company reorganized to transform its management model. From that moment on, McDonald's has allowed managers of its restaurants in foreign countries to decide for themselves on what strategies should or should not be pursued. This *decentralization* initiative enabled the organization to adopt a successful business model in an era in which McDonald's future growth and profits will be dependent on how it manages its global expansion.

In the international marketing literature, the strategic changes that McDonald's implemented are referred to as *going glocal* (a combination of the terms 'global' and 'local'). It involves finding the right balance between protecting and managing your global brand, and meeting the specific needs and wants of customers in different parts of the world. To make it work, it calls, on the one hand, for explicit rules about the limits of this form of decentralization in order to protect the company's *corporate logo* and *brand equity*, and, on the other hand, the necessary delegation of authority and freedom to let overseas units be managed by the *locals* who are most familiar with the *market* and the *marketing environment*. To illustrate, it enables McDonald's country managers to plot their own *promotional* strategies and to develop *products* and *services* that are tailored to their customers' unique preferences. For McDonald's, it worked as well as it did for *Google*. That company would not have been as successful as it is today if top management would not have required each foreign site and search machine to offer the company's services in the country's language and to adapt the content to the local customs and preferences.

With its new corporate culture, McDonald's – as a global company – has flourished as never before. Instead of just selling standard items from its American menu, it features unique products and services that are tailored to local tastes and preferences. To illustrate, in Holland, McDonald's sells – in addition to the Big Mac, Quarter Pounder and other classic sandwiches – the so-called *McKroket*, a local favourite consisting of a deep-fried patty of beef ragout on a hamburger bun with mustard sauce. In the UK, it offers *Oatso Simple* (porridge oats) as a popular breakfast item. In France, consumers can order a *Croque McDo* (two toasted slices of bread with ham and melted cheese in between), along with a bottle of wine. In India, the *Maharaja Mac* (substituting its signature sandwich, the Big Mac) contains no beef (which isn't eaten for religious reasons), but chicken or lamb. And in South Korea, the *Bulgogi burger* (a pork patty hamburger in soy sauce) is as popular as the *Rice burger* (shredded beef between two rice patties) is in Taiwan. Even McDonald's upscale coffee and cappuccino choices, which were introduced to compete with Starbucks, originated from outside the US: the whole new coffee strategy was developed and tested in Australia, before the products found their way onto McDonald's menus worldwide.

In conclusion, by going *glocal* and giving its foreign restaurants the liberty to make many of their own decisions, McDonald's has created a *corporate culture* and decentralized management system that stimulates *innovation* wherever it occurs. By encouraging the company's local executives to share their most successful new products with colleagues around the world, not only the customers, but also the local restaurants and the McDonald's corporation are benefiting. While implementing dozens of different marketing strategies is not easy, it enabled McDonald's to increase profits and continue to expand around the globe.[1]

The expansion of the European Union to 27 countries, one massive free market spanning eastward from Ireland and Spain to Finland and Greece, not only impacts the economic and political future of Europe, but it entices many companies to take advantage of abundant, new marketing opportunities. Now that Poland, the Czech Republic, Hungary, the Slovak Republic, Slovenia, Lithuania, Latvia, Estonia, Cyprus, Malta, Bulgaria and Romania have joined the EU, and the majority of member countries have adopted its common currency, the euro, international marketers face fewer obstacles to marketing merchandise across national boundaries. Because of the eastward expansion of the European Union, major barriers to the free flow of products, services, labour and capital across these nations' borders have been eliminated. The Treaty of Lisbon will further streamline internal operations and allow the EU to enter into international agreements as a political entity. As the largest economy in the world with over 500 million consumers and a combined GDP (gross domestic product) of €10 trillion, the European Union forms a vast common market.

The European Union's long-term goals are to eliminate all internal trade barriers and stimulate economic growth, making its economy even more competitive and strengthening its position as a political and economic world power. To simplify transactions among member nations, it is working toward standardization of business regulations, import duties and value-added taxes and is trying to eliminate customs checks. Yet, despite the EU making progress toward its economic goals, countries like the United Kingdom, Denmark and Sweden have refused to adopt the euro. Quite a few other barriers and conflicts still divide the member nations. As a result, it may take considerable time for the EU to truly become one deregulated market.

And, although European consumers may have become more homogeneous in their tastes and preferences in the past decade, most of them still value individual cultural heritage and strive to preserve their time-honoured traditions and customs. From that perspective, the EU will never be a 'United States of Europe', as some economists have termed it; pan-European marketing strategies may not be effective as initially hoped. Thus, most firms will not be able to market a single 'Europroduct' for a generic 'Euroconsumer'. With over twenty different languages and distinct national customs, Europe will always be a more diverse continent than, for example, the United States. Regardless of greater uniformity in product standards, the elimination of most tariffs that affect pricing decisions and fewer regulatory restrictions on marketing communication, managers will still be required to develop different marketing strategies to appeal to buyers in different European countries.

While many international marketers are already successfully adjusting marketing mixes for consumers in different countries to reflect differences in needs and wants, others entering these markets for the first time may have questions crucial to strategy development. How, for instance, do economic, political-legal and cultural environments differ from one country to another, and how does that affect marketing strategy? Should we first export our products before considering alternative market entry strategies such as licencing, franchising or joint ventures? And, is it better to standardize our international marketing strategy or to adapt it to each individual foreign market? Since these questions are also relevant for markets outside of Europe and may well influence the success of international marketing strategies, we will examine these issues in this final chapter of *Marketing: A Global Perspective*.

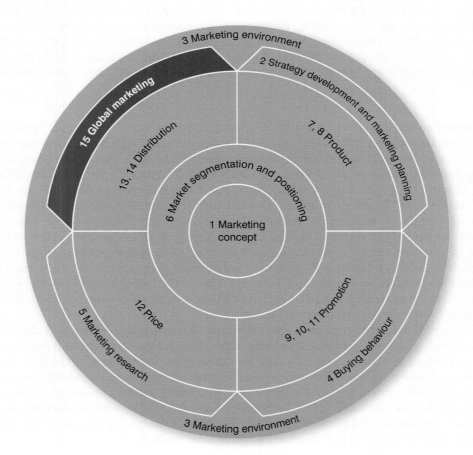

15.1 INTERNATIONAL MARKETING PLANNING

Most companies face ever increasing competition. Should the domestic market become too saturated to offer growth opportunities, executives frequently decide to market across international borders. Some must fend off even more competition as foreign rivals expand into their home markets to steal away market share; this is powerful motivation to internationalize by trading products overseas. At the same time, an increasing number of companies with global ambitions engage in international marketing by systematically identifying and pursuing global marketing opportunities. Nearly every industry and firm in the world is impacted by international competition.

The nature of an organization's involvement in international marketing defines the type of company it is and the strategy it will pursue. In this section, we will first examine the features of international, multinational and global marketing. Then we will explore a systematic approach to planning international marketing activities.

15.1.1 What is global marketing?

Companies conducting business internationally generally transition through several stages: international marketing, multinational marketing and global marketing. How much time they spend in each stage may vary; some organizations move quickly from one stage to the next, while others remain in a particular stage longer.

International marketing

International marketing refers to marketing activities directed at customers outside of the domestic market. Hence, the transactions are planned domestically and implemented across borders. In the early planning stage for international expansion, the company's focus is still on the home market, where the products are typically manufactured. Based on its strengths, the company will seek opportunities to sell its merchandise abroad and – often through export – gain initial market share.

In the early stages of international marketing, many small firms with a limited range of products consider sales to international customers as incidental. Today, however, even small firms – especially those with effective websites – move into new international markets much faster than even a decade ago. Companies may also evolve towards international marketing as a result of doing business with domestic customers having global operations. These customers may request more service or place orders that require the firm to work with their foreign subsidiaries.

drinkaware.co.uk for the facts   Enjoy Responsibly

If Carlsberg did team talks...
englandteamtalk.com

Since the international marketer may be subject to a new set of environmental constraints and often to conflicts resulting from different laws and cultures, they may be required to adapt the product or marketing mix to comply with these legal and cultural standards. The basic principles of marketing still apply, but their implementation and complexity in an international setting may change significantly.

Multinational marketing

For companies actively pursuing business opportunities abroad to succeed, they must adapt to international markets. At this point, international markets are no longer an afterthought, but an integral part of the company's growth strategy. These companies engage in **multinational marketing**.

A *multinational company* is a worldwide player with significant operations and marketing activities outside its home country. AkzoNobel, BP, Volkswagen and Royal Dutch Shell are prominent examples. Although corporate headquarters are typically in the home country, the domestic market accounts for less than half of sales and profits. The multinational company views the world as consisting of unique parts and it markets in each country as a local market-oriented firm would. As a result, it practises decentralized decision-making and customization for these individual markets based on critical differences. Since multinationals usually have as many product variations, brand names and communication strategies as countries in which they operate, they pursue what is known as a *multidomestic marketing strategy*.

Multinationals usually have production or sales units in multiple countries, and, therefore, do not rely on exporting. Instead, management will establish licencing or joint ventures with various organizations abroad. Multinationals not only produce and market in foreign domains, but also conduct research, employ local work forces and develop new products and services worldwide.

Global marketing

A global company views the entire world as its market. But instead of tailoring its marketing mix to fit the unique needs of customers in specific countries, as is typical for multinational marketing, a **global marketing** strategy is an approach to international strategy that advocates marketing a product in essentially the same way – or at least with minimal modifications – in all foreign markets. Thus, marketing strategies are developed for the entire world, focusing on the similarities across national markets instead of the differences between them. Standardization of marketing activities benefits organizations by allowing them to realize economies of scale in production and marketing activities.

A global marketing strategy is used for many business-to-business products (such as HP business servers), luxury products targeted at upscale consumers (Dior) and mass market products (IKEA). Many **global brands** use similar product and marketing communication strategies across multiple countries and cultures, lowering the cost of implementation.

The term *global marketing* is also used to describe the coordination of marketing activities in various geographic markets to effectively fight worldwide competition. Finally, global marketing may simply refer to a company developing marketing activities around the globe in order to pursue several foreign markets.

As a worldwide player, a global company has the greatest geographic scope. It doesn't necessarily have to be a large multinational corporation. In fact, the appeal of serving a global market is so great that a new generation of start-up firms has emerged that market products in different countries immediately instead of gradually moving into foreign markets. These are called *born-global firms*.

Companies that do not take part in the global market should realize that in today's competitive environment, isolation is no longer an option. Most organizations and industries are directly or indirectly impacted by economic, political-legal and cultural developments in the world market. Those that choose not to participate may be forced to react to the international marketplace, and thus are ill-prepared for cut-throat competition from foreign countries.

15.1.2 Strategic planning for international expansion

International marketing and domestic marketing share many characteristics; systematic planning and decision making are essential to effective marketing strategy development in both cases. The differences lie in the questions asked at each stage in the planning process. International marketing's complexity, where risk of failure is high and there are more decisions to be made, further distinguishes it from domestic marketing. Figure 15.1 illustrates differences in the decision making processes.

Internal analysis

After making the decision to internationalize, we must determine which countries offer the best opportunity for success. Because this determination is, in part, dependent on the company's strengths and weaknesses, we first conduct an internal analysis. This analysis evaluates the marketing tools and the human and financial resources at the company's disposal. We also set objectives for developing international activities. In addition, the company should determine if its market expansion strategy entails expansion into a large number of markets or a limited number of markets.

This decision is directly related to another key question of the internal analysis, that being the firm's motivation to internationalize. To help clarify motivation, we may ask several questions. Is the company reacting to declining sales in a saturated domestic market? Does it have excess capacity or overproduction? Are competitive pressures increasing? Is the company trying to limit the risk of dependency on a single market? Or, more proactively, is the goal to generate additional profits through potential economies of scale? Does the business have a technological advantage or unique product not available to potential rivals? The internal analysis should help us determine in subsequent stages of the planning process if there is a good strategic fit between the company's strengths and objectives and the characteristics of the foreign markets under consideration.

Global screening

Screening and analyzing international markets is best conducted in phases. To determine if a market presents solid opportunities, we first evaluate – based on predetermined criteria – the market and the sales potential for each country.

A rough assessment of a foreign market's attractiveness may be based on a brief analysis of *environmental factors* and trends, such as a country's political stability, its distance from

FIGURE 15.1 Stages in strategic planning and decision making for international expansion

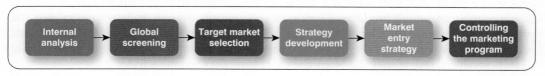

the domestic market and the size and projected growth of the market. To understand size and growth potential, we use generally available (*secondary*) data about the size and composition of the population, including information about income distribution, buying power and demographic trends (such as an increase in the ageing population). We then break the analysis down into factors relating to the product to be launched or the industry. Qualitative criteria play a role as well, including our impression of the country's culture and its implications on how the product will be used, or the explicit desire to establish a subsidiary in a region where many important clients are located.

Target market selection

For the remaining countries on the shortlist, we undertake a more thorough analysis of the market and sales potential. For example, to assess the projected market growth we gather marketing research data (such as surveys of potential buyers) and other information about consumers' current or changing buying habits.

To estimate the sales potential, the portion of the market that we might capture in the long term, we also take a critical look at factors such as consumer *perception* of the product (e.g. brand image and user-friendliness), *competitors* (their strength in the marketplace and how they will respond), the *distribution channel* structure (including the anticipated support from intermediaries) and *consumers* (their willingness and ability to buy a new product that is manufactured abroad).

Once the markets have been analyzed, we decide which segments to target. For that we need information about the preferences, attitudes, consumption patterns and accessibility of various groups of buyers. After entering the foreign market, we may be able to increase the number of target markets.

Strategy development

During this stage, the company develops an effective marketing strategy and adds detail to the objectives formulated during the internal analysis. The objectives are refined to describe the sales objectives for each target market and how fast the international activities should grow. Competition is identified, as are potential allies.

We also design the product, promotion, price and distribution strategies – the *marketing mix* – in this phase. Which products will be used to penetrate the market, and to what extent they should be adapted to the local needs and preferences is now decided. Philips, for example, only turned a profit in Japan after the company adapted its coffee makers to the compact Japanese kitchens and its electric razors to smaller Japanese hands. Other questions relative to the marketing mix include: Which communication media should we use, and what exactly should our message be? What price should we charge to make the product attractive and meet our sales targets? And, which distribution channels will best put our products into the buyers' hands?

The importance of adapting an advertising message to the target market's culture is evidenced by *Clarins*' struggle to interest Chinese male consumers in its personal care products. The typical Chinese man could not relate to the advertising campaign models Clarins used in targeting them. This was a costly mistake. Already nervous that caring about their appearance meant that they were not manly, Chinese males were put off by Clarins' ads. To advertise male grooming products, Clarins chose ethnically diverse, metrosexual models that presented an image with which most Chinese men could not identify. When viewing ads, potential buyers were confused as to why they would want to look like the models using Clarins products and, if they did want the look, how they would achieve it.

Clarins is not alone in portraying its brand in an odd light to consumers abroad. Too many brands launch advertising campaigns centred around preppie blond models lounging on sailboats. In a country where sailboats and the Hamptons are not in the popular imagination, this advertising tack does not work.[2]

Market entry strategy

What is the best way to enter the foreign market? Is it via exporting, or by immediately utilizing licensing agreements, joint ventures or direct investments? In keeping with the expression 'structure follows strategy', the extent to which we modify the organizational structure to implement international marketing strategy is affected by the means of entry into the foreign market. In any case, the organizational structure must be appropriate to the international environment. Many companies first establish an export department, then go on to create an international division (such as a foreign subsidiary to oversee the various activities) and grow towards being a global organization.

Controlling the marketing programme

The last step in the strategic planning process is to monitor and evaluate the results achieved abroad on a regular basis. In order to respond effectively to the international opportunities and to create an ideal framework in which to successfully penetrate the selected markets, it is necessary for the organizational structure, the company culture and the administrative processes to be properly aligned with each other. If the firm is not able to meet its objectives, it can either modify its objectives if it decides they were not realistic or it can adjust its strategy in an effort to meet the established goals.

15.2 GLOBAL MARKETING ENVIRONMENT

International marketing is 'the art of bridging distances', an art that should be mastered before scouting the globe for opportunities. The challenge is more one of bridging the gap between diverse cultures and the differences in the economic and technological forces that affect foreign markets than of bridging physical distances.

A successful international marketing strategy requires a careful environmental analysis, as discussed in Chapter 3. It makes sense that firms operating internationally should consider whether and how to adapt to local conditions in foreign markets. Just as in the domestic market, the strategy should be tailored to uncontrollable variables in the *external environment*. From that perspective, international marketing is in no way unique. However, developments in the global marketing environment tend to have much greater impact on strategy, both in terms of the constraints they impose on business operations and the opportunities they provide for new product or service ideas in untapped markets. That is what makes environmental scanning of foreign markets more complex. And, it makes international marketing – with all it uncertainties and risks – a challenging task for today's manager. In this section, we will consider the economic, political-legal and cultural environments of business and their powerful influence on the development of a company's international marketing strategy.[3]

15.2.1 *Economic environment*

The current world population is estimated at approximately seven billion people, living in over 200 countries. Levels of economic development vary greatly within that population.

PROFESSOR'S PERSPECTIVE
S. Tamer Cavusgil (Georgia State University, USA)

S. Tamer Cavusgil is Executive Director of the Center for International Business Education and Research at Georgia State University's Robinson College of Business in Atlanta. A Fellow of the Academy of International Business, he researches and writes about global business strategy, early internationalization, emerging markets and risk measurement and mitigation in international markets. Cavusgil is the author of more than a dozen books and over 200 refereed journal articles, is founding editor of the Journal of International Marketing and Advances in International Marketing, and serves on the editorial review boards of a dozen professional journals, including the Journal of International Business Studies.

Globalization of markets and competition has transformed the way we do business in a remarkable way over the past three decades. Yet another facet of globalization has been the formation of a global market for *talent*. When multinational enterprises recruit talent, they no longer need to confine their search to a domestic market. Indeed, these companies are sourcing talent everywhere, wherever it is available.

The practice of recruiting human resources from a global talent pool actually represents yet another phase of *offshoring*. As you will recall, manufacturing jobs have been relocated to low labour cost countries since the 1970s. Beginning with the early 1990s, IT applications began their migration to India. Over the past decade, we have witnessed yet another phase. Today offshoring is not just about moving highly codified, transactional work such as credit card processing, claims administration and call centre functions. It is about sourcing talent everywhere. And the talent that is sourced is not only procurement, HR, legal services or engineering services, but also white-collar employees for highly-skilled, high-paying jobs.

Advanced economies no longer have a lock on highly-skilled, high-paying jobs

A recent survey (Duke/Booz Allen Offshoring Research Network Survey) suggests that advanced economies such as the United States and those in Europe no longer have a lock on highly-skilled, high-paying jobs. High-end work such as chip design, financial and legal research, clinical trials management and book editing is now being sourced to countries such as India, China, Hungary, Brazil and the Philippines. What is different about this phase of offshoring is that, while cost-reduction remains a key reason for moving offshore, companies are also seeking to gain access to highly skilled scientific and engineering talent available in these countries. The global mobility of white-collar employees is evident in the ranks of many multinational companies such as Coca-Cola. These companies benefit by tapping top talent from wherever it is available. Often the corporate office draws from the subsidiaries and vice versa.

While recruiting talent on a global scale is not without its challenges, many multinationals are getting better at recognizing and exploiting this opportunity. Many maintain databases of their global talent pool accessible through company intranet. The global talent market also means that companies often have to compete for such talent. For highly skilled individuals in science and engineering, this trend provides opportunities to search for best positions around the globe.

This newest facet of globalization simply implies global access to intellectual capital. Those with critical skills – including those working in marketing and other business disciplines – can now join the global talent pool. It also implies that the graduates of universities around the world who equip themselves with proper skills, knowledge and a cosmopolitan view can expect to find employment opportunities far from their home town.[4]

For this reason, managers thinking of marketing internationally must realize what potential buyers can afford. Manufacturers of expensive products such as designer brand watches and jewellery, or upscale cosmetics would struggle to survive in a nation where most people cannot afford those products. A company will prosper most in an already flourishing economy.

A country's current and potential ability to purchase and consume products and services is influenced by its economic health or economic environment. Thus, an effective way for a company to evaluate the market or the sales potential for its products is to assess that environment. Widely accepted measures of economic performance include a country's stage of economic development, economic infrastructure and purchasing power.

Level of economic development

A nation's level of economic development largely determines its prospects as a host for international business expansion. As illustrated in Figure 15.2, economists make a distinction between three basic levels of economic development.

Less developed countries, such as many nations in Africa and South Asia, have a low standard of living. The economy is agriculturally based. These countries are, in global marketing terms, at 'the bottom of the pyramid'. The people living in agrarian economies grow their own food and barter for other goods. These countries may export raw materials, such as minerals, to industrial nations and are attractive markets for staples and inexpensive products. An increasing number of global companies are trying to develop affordable products to cater to the needs of these low-income people, most of which make less than two euros per day.

FIGURE 15.2 Three levels of economic development

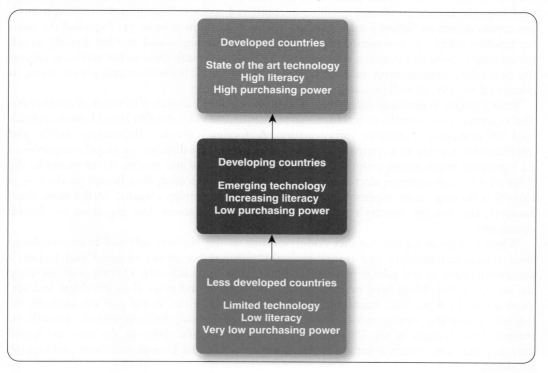

About 80 per cent of the world's population lives in *developing countries*. The economies in developing countries are shifting emphasis from agriculture to industry, and there is a visible middle class, usually consisting of small business entrepreneurs. Because of the large number of skilled workers and potential buyers, these countries attract quite a few international companies. Various countries in Latin America (such as Brazil and Venezuela) and Eastern Europe (Poland, Hungary) fall into this category. This grouping includes the countries of Hong Kong, Singapore, Thailand, South Korea, Malaysia and Indonesia, a cluster of countries referred to as the 'Dragons of Asia' because of its rapid economic growth. These Pacific Rim countries are a powerful, growing market for computers, cell phones and other high-tech products.

Finally, the most highly industrialized nations in the world are the *developed countries*; they include most of Western Europe, the United States, Canada and Japan. These industrialized countries have strong private enterprise, a sophisticated marketing system and – with a large middle class – a huge market potential for products and services.

Economic infrastructure

A country's *economic infrastructure* – the systems of transportation, communication, distribution, banking and public services – is its foundation for modern life and efficient marketing. For this reason, infrastructure is an essential consideration when planning to enter foreign markets and deciding which are best suited to investment.

An underdeveloped infrastructure may constrain a multinational's plans to manufacture and market products or services in certain countries. However, while developing economies may have poor communication and utility networks, they may have enormous, rapidly growing economic potential. Some global cell phone service providers underestimated the potential market for their services in many areas due to those countries' low **gross domestic product** (GDP, i.e. the market value of all products produced by a nation) and limited use of land line telephones. To illustrate, China encountered serious difficulties developing a modern communications industry infrastructure for its 1.3 billion people, yet bypassed the need for landline telephone connections by leapfrogging technologies and moving directly to cell phone usage. Now this country, with one of the highest growth rates in the world, is emerging as a telecommunications megamarket with more than 500 million cell phone users, as compared to only 65 million cars.

Since changes in *exchange rates* (the price of one country's currency in terms of another nation's currency) can complicate international marketing, *currency stability* should also be considered in evaluating economic infrastructure. A foreign currency fluctuating widely and unpredictably relative to a company's home currency makes it difficult for global companies to set consistent prices across countries. It could also affect sales and profits. If, for example, the value of a foreign currency decreases relative to the British pound, then British products – as exports – become more expensive for consumers in that foreign country. At the same time, however, this foreign country's products – as imports – become less expensive for British consumers.

When European Union member countries such as the Netherlands and France replaced their traditional guilders and francs with the euro, stable prices resulted and Europe's competitiveness in the global marketplace increased tremendously. Having one currency, the euro, has simplified how multinational firms market and price their products and services across Europe. Still, economic trends in one part of the world can substantially influence marketing opportunities in another. For instance, high economic growth or interest rate changes in the US may have an impact on the value of the euro on world currency markets, which affects the price, and thus sales of European export and import products.

Purchasing power

For attractive market opportunities to be present, it is not enough for a population to be simply large and growing, as is the case in many developing countries. The economy must provide enough purchasing power for consumers to satisfy their needs and wants. Buying power varies enormously between countries. In analyzing a country's purchasing power, an international marketer of consumer products not only evaluates the average per capita or household income of a nation's consumers, but also the *income distribution*, or how the income is distributed throughout society.

As a rule of thumb, a country's purchasing power grows as the proportion of middle-income households in that nation increases. To illustrate, about two-thirds of Western European households have a purchasing power of at least 20 000 euros per year. Compare that to less established market economies in Southeast Asia where three-quarters of households have an annual purchasing power of less than 5 000 euros. Because of this diversity, marketing success abroad is rarely possible without effectively segmenting each national market and pursuing a market strategy tailored to the needs of the targeted segments.

15.2.2 *Political-legal climate*

Before consumer buying power can be converted into effective demand for products or services abroad, marketers must understand the country's political and legal climate. The diverse political, legal and regulatory forces in foreign countries play a critical role in marketing activities and can present a level of complexity that challenges the most seasoned global marketer. Even the best marketing plans may go awry as a result of unexpected political and regulatory developments and the failure to anticipate them. These forces can seriously disrupt an otherwise successful business venture.

Laws and measures not specifically aimed at international marketing activities can, nonetheless, affect the company's international competitive position. The impact of these regulations can be either negative (minimum wage legislation that increases the production costs of labour-intensive export products) or positive (EU- sponsored subsidies that allow for lower selling prices).

Other laws and regulations are clearly designed to address international marketing issues. They, too, may either obstruct a company's efforts to operate abroad or protect it from adverse activities. International treaties against counterfeiting are one case in point. These treaties have been negotiated to prevent the sale of inferior products, like knock-offs of Prada handbags and Rolex watches, under replica logos. By granting China and Taiwan admission to the World Trade Organization (WTO), governments of western countries expect the practice of imitation and theft to significantly decrease.

The WTO administers international trade and investment accords and can impose trade sanctions. The organization is over 150 members strong and accounts for over 97 per cent of world trade. The WTO's decisions are made by the full membership, and all participating governments must ratify agreements.

The WTO's objective is to facilitate free, fair and predictable trade. Through a series of trade negotiations (known as *rounds*) that set standards for how much countries are allowed to favour their own goods and services, the WTO has become a global referee for trade. With over three-quarters of its membership being from the world's poorer countries, negotiations in recent years have focused on issues concerning these countries and GATT (the WTO's predecessor) agreements giving them special benefits.

One important issue that the WTO tackles is protection of copyright and patent rights. The WTO's TRIPS Agreement (Trade-related Aspects of Intellectual Property Rights) was designed to standardize how intellectual property rights are protected around the world, and to bring them under common international rules. It sets minimum levels of protection that each government must provide for the intellectual property of fellow WTO members. This protection will help firms prevent pirated versions of software, books and music CDs from being sold in other countries. Yet, despite the enactment of such measures, piracy remains a serious problem for many companies, as their profits continue to be eroded by illegal sales.[5]

In addition to evaluating current political and legal environments in foreign markets, the duration of these influences must be assessed. How long will a positive or negative climate remain in place? Three important criteria for this analysis are the country's political stability, the government's trade regulations and the degree of protectionism.

Political stability

Political stability is the extent to which a nation's government is expected to remain strong and unchallenged. Global marketers can never be certain that any country – no matter how strong and well-developed it may be – will always remain politically stable. Increasing unemployment or *nationalism* (a host country's attempt to promote its interests), for example, may lead to tighter restrictions on foreign companies to foster the development of domestic industry at their own expense. From a business perspective, the degree of political stability in a foreign country is strongly related to the government's orientation toward trade with other nations and toward foreign companies in particular.

In assessing political stability, two practical criteria are:

1 Consistent business policies.

→ Do government policies regarding corporate profits, taxes and expansion remain unchanged over time?
and

2 Orderly succession of political power.

→ Is there a systematic process for electing or appointing government officials?

Only when both factors are positive will most companies be able to invest and market in a foreign country, while prospering in the long term. International companies often assign staff members to track political conditions around the globe ('political risk assessment' or PRA), allowing them to continuously evaluate the stability of foreign markets and forecast potential risks. Other firms use external consulting services to evaluate the political risks of their overseas markets.

Business operations can be greatly affected by a government's political actions. When political power suddenly changes hands through manipulation or violence – such as terrorism or war – a corporation may suffer huge losses. As a result of political issues, companies in the Middle East, Africa or in such countries as the former Yugoslavia have lost billions of euros. Even in the absence of violent acts, foreign firms can be the target of demonstrations or suffer other significant setbacks abroad. To respond to public sentiment, the incumbent government may, for example, impose new corporate taxes, block credit or even nationalize companies.

Trade regulations

Countries use a wide range of laws and regulations to influence business practices of companies operating within their national borders. Many are, in effect, trade barriers or commercial restrictions. Japan has formulated more than 10 000 explicit regulations affecting trade. Safety regulations for automobiles, for example, specify that only Japanese parts – meaning no imported products – can be used for repairs or replacements. The Chinese government continues to censor the Internet for the more than 250 million users in that country. There are numerous marketing restrictions in Europe, too. In the Netherlands there is a ban on advertising cigarettes, in Greece on advertising toys and in Sweden no company is allowed to target children in advertisements. In addition, there are literally thousands of rules and regulations dictating how products are made and marketed in EU member states.

Even the European Union's mandatory ISO certification (internationally recognized quality standards) – in affecting business practice – may (potentially) restrict international trade. The ISO (International Organization for Standardization) has two sets of quality standards. The ISO 9000 (or ISO 9001) standards ensure that a company's products and services meet established (technical) quality standards, whereas the ISO 14000 (or ISO 14001) standards set requirements for operations that minimize harm to the environment. As a condition of doing business with them, many European firms require suppliers to be ISO 9000 or ISO 14000 certified. For some companies, this may limit their opportunities for international marketing. For example, although organizations in more than 150 countries participate in both series of quality standards, to date only about 10 per cent of the ISO-certificates issued are held by American firms.

Protectionism

Despite an overall decline in the use of government regulations to limit foreign suppliers' ability to market products and services, many nations still practise **protectionism**, a policy of legal controls that shield domestic businesses and industries from foreign competition. Protectionist policies are primarily imposed to foster the survival and growth of domestic companies. In addition to promoting the domestic industrial development, arguments in favour of protectionism include retaining domestic jobs and limiting economic dependency on other countries.

As Figure 15.3 illustrates, protectionism is typically accomplished through tariffs and quotas. A **tariff** (also called *import tariff* or *duty*) is a tax levied on specific products entering a country. Tariffs raise the price of imported goods, making domestic products seem less expensive and, therefore, more attractive by comparison. Whether tariffs are intended to generate revenue for the government of an importing country (*revenue tariffs*) or to increase the

FIGURE 15.3 Effect of protectionism on world trade

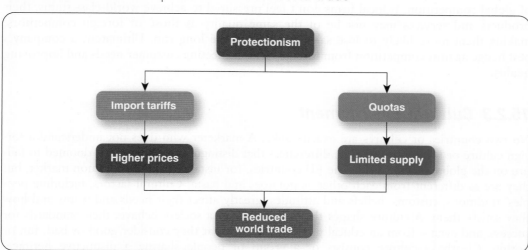

retail price of an imported product to match or exceed the price of a comparable domestic product (protective tariffs, which usually are higher than revenue tariffs), they impede free trade between nations.

In industrialized countries, the average tariff on goods is 4 per cent. Yet the effect of tariffs on consumer prices is substantial. To illustrate, the tariffs and other trade barriers imposed on bananas cost European consumers close to two billion euros a year.

Instead of tariffs, some governments use dumping laws to protect domestic firms from foreign competition. *Dumping* is the practice of selling merchandise in a foreign country at a lower price than it commands in the producer's domestic market, or at a price below its production costs, to gain market share. Companies that engage in dumping are, in many countries, subject to fines. Those fines are distributed to the domestic firms affected by the dumping practices.

In addition to direct taxes on imported products, governments may set more subtle administrative or *non-tariff barriers*. Since the GATT and WTO agreements repealed tariffs on various products, some governments now rely on non-tariff barriers to limit imports or – through export subsidies – stimulate exports. These trade barriers include special permits, customs barriers (such as extensive, mandatory inspections of imports) and quotas.

A quota is a limit on the quantity of a specific product an importing country will accept in a specific time period. One reason that Europeans pay about twice as much for bananas as do American consumers is that Europe set up a quota system and import licence controls to limit the importation of bananas. Although this resulted in demand being greater than supply, the trade barrier was created to support banana growing in former African, Caribbean and Pacific colonies and to restrict imports from Latin America. After the WTO ruled that the European Union's banana import regime unfairly discriminated against Latin American banana growers, countries like Ecuador decided to seek sanctions against the European Union.

Another technique used to protect local producers – and to retaliate against other countries – is the embargo, a government's suspension of trade in a particular product or with a certain country. Embargoes are usually put into place for political, health or religious reasons. To illustrate, The United States prohibits the import of Cuban rum and cigars because of political differences with that country. It also forbids importation of any product containing dog or cat fur due to its stance on animal rights.

While *protectionism* is meant to protect domestic companies against foreign competition, it may have the opposite effect if it prevents domestic marketers from facing the realities of global competition. If local firms don't feel pressured to achieve world-class status, their products and services may not be of the same quality as those of foreign competitors, making them more likely to lose sales and jobs in the long run. Ultimately, a company's best hedge against competition from foreign rivals is meeting customer needs and improving quality.

15.2.3 Cultural environment

No two countries or cultures are exactly alike. A marketer who does not understand a foreign culture or is insensitive to the differences that distinguish each nation is doomed to failure on the global playing field. The EU countries, for instance, share a common market, but they are as different from each other as potatoes and pasta. Cultural factors, including peoples' traditions, customs, beliefs and attitudes, greatly affect their needs and wants and how they satisfy them. A culture shapes the way people in a society behave, their standards for success, and even – from an ethical point of view – what they consider good or bad, fun or boring. Clearly, a culture consists of a group of people sharing a distinctive heritage.

MARKETING TOPPER
Oreo: East Meets West

How did Kraft manage to make the Oreo – America's best-selling cookie – into a marketing success in China, the world's most heavily populated market? By delegating decision-making authority to the *local* managers of its Chinese division. Kraft's executives know that the best way to stimulate an entrepreneurial mindset leading to growth in sales and profits is to tell each overseas business unit to make its own decisions about how to *tailor* the company's products and marketing strategies to its target market.

To illustrate, in *Germany*, Kraft effectively launched *Milka* dark chocolate bars, knowing that German consumers prefer the more bitter taste of this type of chocolate. And since *Russian* consumers appreciate premium instant coffee, Kraft positioned its *Carte Noire* brand of freeze-dried coffee as an upscale product by serving it at events such as fashion shows, film festivals and operas. In fact, Kraft's CEO Irene Rosenfeld has been urging the company's international marketers to remain customer-focused in meeting the local consumers' needs and wants.

Thus, even though the Oreo has been the same tasting sandwich cookie in the US for over one hundred years, sales did not take off in *China* until the product was changed into a variety that tasted less sweet than the American original. Arriving at that reduced-sugar formula took a long period of test marketing in which 20 different prototypes were assessed and compared. The final version is now being offered in a package costing just €0.22, since the original larger package (containing 14 Oreos for 55 cents) was too expensive for most Chinese consumers.

© Jaimie Duplass / Shutterstock

Marketing research also showed Chinese consumers' increasing interest in drinking milk. To take advantage of that trend, Kraft developed a grass roots campaign to introduce consumers in China to the US habit of having cookies with milk. The company recruited and trained 300 students to become official brand ambassadors and give away free cookies – while riding bikes with wheel covers looking like Oreos – to hundreds of thousands of consumers in Beijing. It was a marketing campaign developed by local managers that their American counterparts could not have dreamed up in trying to appeal to Chinese consumers. In addition, Chinese kids were featured in TV spots teaching their parents how to 'twist, lick and dunk' chocolate Oreos, that is, twisting a cookie apart with both hands, licking its cream centre and then dunking both halves into a glass of milk before eating them.

Although sales of Oreo cookies went up, Kraft – that was losing market share in China to its competitor Nestlé – understood it had to go further than just adjusting the round cookies' sugar content and flavour. So in 2006 – ten years

Kraft's grass roots campaign introduced the Chinese to having cookies with milk

after the introduction of Oreo on the Chinese market – Kraft changed the cookie into a long rectangular-shaped product made up of four layers of crispy wafer with a vanilla and chocolate cream filling, all coated in chocolate. Other more recent product innovations for the Chinese market include a hollow tube-like Oreo, so milk can be drunk through it like a straw, in addition to a radical new twist on the traditional cookie, containing a green tea-flavoured filling. It is clear that the new Chinese Oreo, in its many shapes and forms, has very little in common with the all-American version introduced in the late 19th century, leading some commentators to question exactly what constitutes the true 'essence of *Oreoness*'.

Kraft's global marketing strategy has turned out to be quite successful. The new Oreo wafer sticks are not only beating the original round-shaped version in sales, but have also become the number one selling biscuit on the whole Chinese market. They are even outselling HaoChiDian, a popular Chinese brand of biscuit and, due to the success in China, have now been rolled out across other markets like Australia and Canada. By any standard, that is an impressive global marketing achievement.[6]

To cite just one example of cultural differences, soccer (Association football) is the most popular televised sport in Europe and Latin America, and therefore a major marketing opportunity for advertisers, but both viewership and sponsorship lag far behind in the United States, where fans prefer American ('gridiron') football or baseball.

Before entering a foreign country and trying to develop meaningful relationships with customers, a manager should study all aspects of that country's culture. Because cultural values and consumer attitudes vary widely between countries, it is important for marketing executives to closely examine a nation's heritage before introducing a product or service into that country. Successful global companies work hand in glove with market research companies and marketing communication agencies that provide valuable insight into the similarities and differences among consumers in different nations. In developing international marketing campaigns, these agencies often rely on **cross-cultural consumer analysis**. The objective of such analysis is to gain working knowledge of the social values, customs, cultural symbols and use of language in different societies.

Values

Each society has a common set of fundamental *values*, shared by its citizens, which reflect their moral beliefs and are learned through experiences within that culture. These values include freedom, safety, health, love, recognition and family. From these values issue *norms*, or specific rules determining socially acceptable behaviour and distinguishing right from wrong.

Values influence a person's decisions to buy certain products or services. In India, for example, McDonald's offers the chicken based Maharaja Mac (two chicken patties with smoke-flavoured mayo) to replace the beefy Big Mac because the Hindu population regards the cow as a sacred animal. As pointed out in Chapter 3, cultural values also influence consumer perception of brands and, in marketing, affect the type of promotions likely to appeal to the target market.

Customs

Customs are traditional activities or practices that determine what is considered normal and how people are expected to act within a society. Experienced international marketers are well aware that customs differ significantly from one country to another. Without doubt, societal customs hold sway over marketing strategies in foreign markets. For example, multinational companies market food products differently in Italy than in Great Britain, simply because Italians, in general, care more about what they eat than British consumers.

To be effective abroad, global marketers should also be familiar with local *business customs*, particularly if these reflect ethical values that conflict with those of their home countries. Bribery is an example. The custom of giving or taking token business gifts is widely accepted in countries where officials expect this form of compensation in exchange for performing such services as awarding contracts or expediting transactions. These payments – looked upon as a cost of doing business – are not considered unethical in many cultures and are even, in many instances, tax-deductible expenses. However, governments in many of the world's major exporting nations have made it illegal for firms to offer bribes, payoffs or kickbacks to foreign government officials and others to sweeten a deal, regardless of local customs.

Certain culturally-based customs play a crucial role in determining the very framework of business negotiations. To illustrate, both Dutch and American managers in meetings with potential suppliers come straight to the point so that they can get things done quickly. By contrast, the Japanese – especially senior executives – find this kind of behaviour unacceptable. Doing business in Japan often requires long evenings of dining and drinking, and business negotiations do not begin until a comfortable level of familiarity has been established. During negotiations, the Japanese typically adopt a wait-and-see posture and do not further discuss the offer with the other party until they have formulated a response. Western managers who fail to understand this non-verbal behaviour may inadvertently raise their offer several times during those silent stretches on the mistaken assumption that by saying nothing the Japanese are turning down the offer. That failure to understand the Japanese negotiating style of listening in meetings instead of voicing opinions has cost European and American companies dearly.

Cultural symbols

Symbols are another cultural element important to international marketing campaigns. If used correctly, *colours* and numbers can attach positive meaning to a company's offerings making them more attractive to buyers. Or they can lead to marketing problems and even marketing failure if used in a way that evokes negative feelings. Red, for instance, is a popular colour in China, but is not favourably received in Africa. White is the colour of mourning and death in China and Korea, while in many Spanish-speaking countries the colour purple has the same connotation.

Numbers, too, are fraught with symbolism, and they should be used with careful consideration. For example, in Japan, Tiffany & Company packages its glassware and porcelain dinner plates in groups of five (rather than four) pieces, because the Japanese are as superstitious about the number 4 (the Japanese word for four, shi, also means 'death') as some cultures are about the number 13.

Finally, the *country of origin* or manufacture of products may symbolize superior or inferior quality in some countries. Buyers' perceptions of foreign countries can affect their attitudes toward products made there and can influence product adoption and use. That, in turn, may affect the marketing strategies of global companies. In much of Western Europe, for example, German automobiles exemplify outstanding *engineering*, while Korean cars may still be perceived as less expensive, poorly constructed *me-too* versions of other car makes. In the perception of many consumers, the most sophisticated audio equipment is made in Japan, while an American company offers the best mobile phone on the market (Apple iPhone), even though Korea (Samsung, LG) is making quick advances. Ultimately, the extent to which a product's brand image and country of origin influence purchases is very much dependent on a country's cultural characteristics.

Language

Communicating in a foreign language is challenging, whether you're branding a product, translating a slogan, designing a package with product labelling and usage instructions,

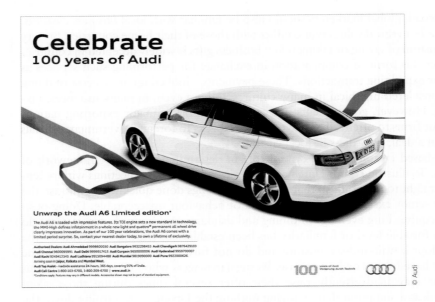

scripting a television commercial or building and maintaining a global website. Brand names or words which are attractive or logical in a person's native tongue may have misleading connotations after translation. A classic example is GM's Nova, a car that was hard to sell in Latin America where the name translates into 'no go'. Undoubtedly, international marketers who speak and write the language of a foreign market and have mastered its many nuances have a distinct competitive advantage. Fluency in foreign languages breaks down many barriers to effective global marketing communication.

The preferred language for communicating with customers is their own language. However, few global marketers speak more than five languages, and, of those they do speak, perhaps only one or two are among the world's five most spoken languages: Mandarin (Chinese), English, Hindustani, Spanish and Russian (rank ordered by number of speakers). In the European Union alone, 23 different languages are spoken. With more than 3 000 languages and dialects spoken around the globe, making sure that marketing messages are properly translated to convey the intended meaning is easier said than done. Language usage can

be especially demanding when selling in multilingual countries such as Belgium (Flemish and French) and Canada (English and French). This challenge is multiplied a hundredfold when marketing in India, a country with twenty different languages and over 200 dialects in which no language – except Hindi – is spoken by more than 10 per cent of the population.

It is clear that a company cannot just translate its marketing message word for word. Most global marketers choose to work with translators who have longstanding experience in the language and with the host country. Many translators use **back translation**, a process that translates writings that have already been translated into a foreign language back into the original language. Ideally, the back-translation should be done by a different translator. Then the forward translation and the back translation are compared for differences, and any errors in translation are corrected. At the end of the day, international managers realize that in order to avoid embarrassing mistakes or confusion, it is essential to work with local people who are familiar with the subtleties of their own language.

Self reference criterion

Managers working or travelling abroad for business purposes understand that values, customs and modes of operation in other cultures differ from those in their home countries. Still, many of them tend to respond to situations based on knowledge they have accumulated over a lifetime, in a way that is closely associated with their own culture. In business, the idea that 'we' differ from 'them' is called the **self-reference criterion** (SRC) – the subconscious reference to one's own cultural values and experiences, or home country frame of reference. Unfortunately, the values, meanings and symbols that relate to our own culture may not have the same relevance to people of other cultures, or may not be perceived as 'correct'.

To illustrate, a company that has successfully launched a new product or service in the domestic market may assume that it will, without adaptation, also be successful in foreign markets. In this example, the self reference criterion refers to the assumption that what works domestically, will also be suitable for the foreign market, and, therefore, there is no need to investigate the possibility – through marketing research – that the product should be altered. This assumption often leads to failure. A better approach for marketers is to adopt the principle of 'When in Rome, do as the Romans do'. Managers should never allow their perception of foreign market needs to be biased by their own cultural experience, and they must adapt accordingly.

Ethnocentric orientation

Most people tend to view their culture – including their own values, customs, symbols, language and attitudes – in a positive light. Many even believe that certain aspects of their culture are superior to those of other cultures. Of course, this is also true of managers. Some not only believe that their own country's culture is better, but also feel that the business strategies developed for marketing in their own country reign supreme. This home country orientation – as a subconscious bias – and belief that the home country's approach to business is superior (and thus can be replicated abroad) is called **ethnocentric orientation**. Since the assumption that one's own culture is, in some way, superior to another can interfere with a successful global marketing approach, marketers should avoid ethnocentrism.

Consumer ethnocentrism applies to consumers who consistently prefer products or people of their own culture over those from other countries. International marketers are aware that these consumers tend to evaluate products and services from other countries critically and prefer not to buy foreign-made products. But managers themselves should not fall into that trap.

Ethnocentric managers stress their home countries' cultural values when marketing abroad, even when such values are irrelevant. Seasoned global managers, on the other hand, take local differences into account, and therefore are more likely to adopt a **geocentric orientation**. This is a management orientation based on the assumption that there are similarities and differences in the world that can be understood and integrated into a global marketing strategy. From this perspective, no country is superior or inferior to another. Geocentric marketers accept the differences between countries and recognize that successful international marketing requires respecting both home- and host-country cultures. They sincerely believe that the whole world is their home market. That attitude has contributed a great deal to the successful global marketing strategies of many companies.

15.3 MARKET ENTRY STRATEGIES ABROAD

Once management has a solid grasp of the global marketing environment, it must decide if it *should* go global. After making a commitment to enter the global marketplace, the next decision is how to do it. Since the entry strategy provides the framework for targeting the market and has long-term implications for all other marketing decisions, it is a critical strategic decision.

Marketers can choose from four major market entry strategies: exporting, licencing, joint ventures and direct investment. Their preferred strategy will depend on three factors: the risk they are willing to take, their (financial) commitment to international marketing and how much control they want to maintain over their global marketing activities. Figure 15.4 illustrates this. Let's examine these market-entry strategies, beginning with the least risky one: exporting.

15.3.1 *Exporting and Licensing*

The simplest way to target a foreign market is through exporting. **Exporting** entails manufacturing products in one country and selling them in another. This entry strategy en-

FIGURE 15.4 Levels of involvement in global marketing

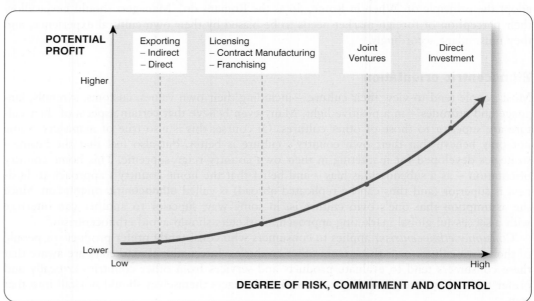

PRACTITIONER'S PERSPECTIVE
Elizabeth L. Ward (Thought Partners Consulting)

The Atlanta Chapter of the American Marketing Association – a professional organization with nearly 40 000 members in over 100 countries – recently asked its Executive Advisory Board to discuss marketing in the next decade and how marketers can prepare for the changes that will be taking place. The members include 21 senior marketers from companies such as AT&T, Chick-fil-A, Coca Cola, Cox, Google and 22 Squared. Elizabeth L. Ward, Principal at Thought Partners Consulting and Board Member and Programming Chair at AMA/Atlanta wrote a white paper based on the insights from these senior marketing leaders, titled '20/20 in 2020: Toward a New Vision in Marketing.' Ken Bernhardt, Professor of Marketing at Georgia State University, highlighted some of the key findings from this report in one of his marketing columns for Atlanta Business Chronicle.

The white paper *20/20 in 2020: Toward a New Vision in Marketing*, reflecting the insights of senior level marketing executives from over twenty companies, discusses three important themes. These are 1) the changing relationship between brands and consumers, 2) the new demand for personalization ('It's all about me!') and 3) the changing role of marketing in the organization.

Relationship between brands and consumers: The balance of power continues to shift, with consumers gaining increasing influence. Consumers expect a higher level of service and also more immediate response to their demands and feedback. They expect more personalized recognition proportionate to the amount of business they do with the company and the amount of information they give.

Ten years ago marketers 'drove consumers to websites and pushed and pulled them to products marketers wanted them to buy.' Today, consumers want to choose the company they do business with. Increasingly, marketers will need to solicit consumers' willingness to participate and engage them in real dialogue. Relationship building will precede or even replace the sales pitch, and companies will focus on building brand advocates. As Richard Ward, CEO of 22 Squared, put it, 'Consumers want to be recognized and rewarded for being an active participant in the relationship with the brand.'

Rewards will become increasingly personalized, based on each customer's past purchases and expressed interests. Going forward, marketing departments will need to recognize that consumers are co-creators and it will become less clear who reports to whom.

New demand for personalization: In the expectation of receiving a more personalized experience, consumers are willing to share a huge amount of information. But marketers are just starting to figure out how to use that information to deliver truly customized experiences.

Social media, mobile devices and localization are all major forces that are coming together. Mobile devices will become increasingly important as the outstanding customizable device, transmitting where you are and what you are doing at any given moment. As Tom Lowry, director of industry and technology for Google, put it, users will have higher expectations of 'Just for Me' product design. He names Amazon and Netflix as examples of brands that are delivering personalized messages today.

Changing role of marketing: The skill sets needed in marketing and the ways of working will look dramatically different in the next decade. There will be increased accountability for marketing actions. The speed of change is increasing with 'disruptions' in markets happening faster than ever. Therefore marketers will need to retool their planning and decision making practices to enable them to move at faster speeds.

There will no longer be 12 month planning cycles. Decision making must occur lower in the organization because there is not time to go up the decision making ladder. Budgets and resource allocation will have to become more flexible to enable marketers to quickly respond to opportunities and respond to changing consumer needs.

Listening to consumers will become part of everyone's job

Product life cycles will become shorter. Market intelligence will require new tools to keep a constant finger on the pulse of consumers. Listening to consumers will become part of everyone's job. Marketers will need to find the right balance between precision and speed. They will need to form a closer relationship between marketing and IT. Currently there is too much data and too few insights.

Words of Advice for 2020: The final section of the white paper presents the following advice for marketers:

→ Pay close attention to *customer experience*. With products and prices becoming increasingly similar, the total brand experience (and especially customer service) will become the key differentiator. As one board member put it, '*customer service will become the next killer app.*'

→ *Be real* and have nothing to hide. Consumers increasingly have ways of finding out if you are cheating or faking (think 'greenwashing').

→ *Deliver value* to customers by using the information you have gathered from them and they will give you value in return.

→ Focus on the most important ways to *customize*, allowing customers to personalize the products, services and experiences (including method of payment, delivery, data portability and functionality).

→ Rethink organization structure and leadership values to be more *responsive* to the changing needs of the market. As one executive put it, '*everyone is in marketing now.*'

→ *Test. Learn. Repeat.*

All of this sounds like good advice to me. The next decade will have more changes in marketing than any previous decade. It's a great time to be in marketing.[7]

---

ables firms of all sizes to participate in global business. It does not require drastic changes to the product (only minor modifications in labelling or packaging), to the organization, or even to the company's goals. However, it is not the most appreciated entry strategy in host countries because it does not create many new jobs.

Exporting is often associated with small companies. Typically, small businesses account for over 80 per cent of a country's exporters, but only for 20 to 30 per cent of export volume. Large corporations account for the remainder of export sales, and they may be in it for the long run. To illustrate, Swedish furniture manufacturer IKEA has successfully built its entire global marketing strategy around exporting. Its modular furniture that packs flat, is lightweight and must be assembled by consumers themselves can be shipped almost anywhere around the world at limited cost.

Indirect exporting

Often, firms do not have a coherent exporting strategy. They take an opportunistic approach by simply selling surplus products without any specific analysis and targeting or without making a special effort to do so. If a company does not deal directly with foreign buyers but works with an independent intermediary such as an export agent, it is called indirect exporting. This approach requires minimal investment and limits risk, because the exporting company does not need its own sales organization to make contacts abroad.

Indirect exporting may be an appropriate strategy if the exporter has limited funds, if customers are dispersed or difficult to locate and if local customs are unique. However, it is not likely to result in growing management commitment to international markets or increased capabilities in serving them.

Many businesses sell products in domestic markets that eventually are shipped abroad. In some cases, the domestic firm does not even know that its products have left the country. This may happen to small suppliers that sell products to multinationals, which then use them as an input into their international sales. Another example is a small domestic manufacturer that sells to the local buying office of a foreign department store.

Indirect exporters may use different types of intermediaries. **Export agents** bring together sellers and buyers from different countries and collect a commission for arranging sales. **Export merchants** and *export houses* buy products from different companies and then sell them abroad. They are specialists at identifying foreign suppliers and customers and at understanding foreign customers' needs. Two other types of international intermediaries that can help the company with its market-penetration efforts are export management companies and trading companies.

An **export management company** (EMC) is an independent firm that provides most of the services that an in-house export department would. It provides instant information and management expertise to its clients and assists in documentation, financing and transportation. EMCs are used primarily by firms that cannot afford their own export departments.

Export management companies have two primary forms of operation: They either take title to the products and operate internationally on their own account, or they perform services as agents. In fact, an EMC may act as a distributor for one client or transaction (purchasing products from the domestic firm, selling them in its own name and assuming the trading risk) and as an agent for another. When working as an agent, the EMC does not take title to the goods, and is primarily responsible for developing business or sales strategies and establishing new contacts abroad. Since it does not share in the profits from a sale, it depends on high sales volume, on which it charges a commission.

The most useful EMCs in helping client firms in their international marketing efforts are those that have specific expertise in selecting markets because of previous exposure, existing contacts and language capabilities. Unfortunately, some EMCs have taken on too many merchandise lines and thus have not been able to give each client firm the attention that it might have anticipated. For its part, the export management company runs the risk of being too successful – that is, the client firm could capitalize on the markets developed by the EMC and move its own sales force into these markets. Accordingly, EMCs have been careful not to tie themselves too closely to any single manufacturer.

A second type of major intermediary is an international **trading company**, a marketing intermediary that takes title to the products, exports, imports, invests, manufactures and **countertrades** (in which it barters products rather than selling them for cash). The *sogoshosha* of Japan, such as Mitsui and Mitsubishi, are among the best known export trading companies. Trading companies provide a much wider variety of marketing services to the exporting firm than EMCs. These services, as well as their vast market coverage and credit reliability make them attractive to domestic firms interested in selling abroad. The major drawback of trading companies, from the domestic manufacturer's perspective, is the lack of control over whether the companies carry competing products or whether they even push the manufacturer's products at all.

Direct exporting

Under **direct exporting**, the manufacturer themself performs all the necessary export functions, including conducting the required marketing research, contacting local distributors, preparing export documentation and setting prices. Direct exporting typically results in increased sales for the exporter. Whether it yields additional profits depends on whether the incremental revenues are greater than the extra costs associated with running an in-house export operation, overseas sales office or distribution network. Some firms overcome the hurdles of identifying and targeting foreign customers or finding retail space by creating effective websites.

Through direct exporting, the firm cannot only earn a higher return on its investment, but will also exercise greater control over how its merchandise is sold, including which products are emphasized in the selling effort. Management learns the competitive advantages of its products faster and can therefore expand more rapidly. Finally, direct exporting puts the firm in a better position to forge relationships with its trading partners and to gain information about the needs of foreign markets. This can lead to further international growth and success.

Licencing

Managers can avoid both direct involvement and direct investment in the international marketplace through a contractual arrangement called licencing. In a **licencing** agreement, the international company (licencer) gives another firm (the licensee) the right to produce and market its products in return for a fee or royalties. Typically, the firm in the foreign market buys the right to use the company's patent, trademark, copyright or expertise in how to produce and sell a particular product. Coca-Cola, for example, licences bottlers around the globe to produce Coke with the secret-formula-syrup supplied by the Atlanta-based corporation.

Because of the advantages of licencing, many companies have eagerly embraced this form of entry strategy. Since no investment of management time or capital is required, the licence option is available at little risk to small businesses that otherwise would not be able to enter foreign markets. The licensee's market can even be a test market for other international marketing activities.

Even multinational companies with abundant capital may not have the expertise to manufacture and market products overseas. Since the licensee produces the product in its home market, the international company can avoid many of the barriers-to-entry that it might have encountered. Foreign governments may favour licencing agreements over direct investment because licencing brings technology into the country without also bringing large direct foreign investments. As a result, it is often easier to obtain government approval for a licence than for a direct investment. Besides, licencing reduces the risk of **expropriation** – a government takeover of a company's operations – because the licensee is a local company that can provide leverage against government action. Moreover, the royalties are an attractive source of income for companies that provide a return on its investments in Research & Development.

A company's commitment to global business is greater with licencing than with exporting: its products are now produced in more than one country. Still, the licencer does not have full control over how its products are manufactured and sold. If the licensee does a poor job, the company's reputation could be damaged. Also, the more expertise a licencer provides the local company, the greater the probability that they may actually be training their future competition. When the agreement expires, the licensee – rather than renewing the contract – may adapt the product and use the experience they have gained to capture part of the market for themselves. At this point, a licensee may even expand sales efforts to other international markets. The best way of preventing this is to continuously innovate so that the licensee depends on the licencer for product improvements and effective marketing strategies.

There are several variations of licencing. With **contract manufacturing**, a company contracts with a foreign firm to manufacture a designated volume of its product to specification, with the final product carrying the domestic company's name. Reebok, for example, hires Asian contract manufacturers to produce its athletic footwear. If contracting manufacturing or other business activities, such as providing customer service help lines, take place in nations with less expensive supplies and labour, it is referred to as **outsourcing**. This is a controversial business strategy (especially when child labour is utilized abroad) and is sometimes characterized as 'exporting jobs'.

A related option is contract assembly, in which a foreign firm is contracted to assemble – rather than to manufacture – components and parts that have been shipped to that country. Some Dutch coach manufacturers, for instance, have their buses finished and upholstered in Portugal and other countries with lower wages. Similarly, in services industries, a company may supply management know-how or other services to a foreign firm that provides the capital. This form of licencing that is popular in the hospitality industry is called **management contracting**.

Finally, *franchising* is a form of licencing in which the franchiser grants a franchisee, with professional support, the right to use a tried-and-tested formula for success, including its name, products, logo, methods of operation and other elements of the franchiser's business. As discussed in Chapter 14, this is one of the fastest-growing strategies for entering new markets. It is often a partnership between a producer and retailers (such as automobile dealers). Many companies in the service sector (including McDonald's and Marriot) use franchising to quickly expand in foreign markets.

15.3.2 *Joint ventures*

A company that wants to be more committed to an international market than is possible through licencing may consider a collaboration with another organization known as a joint venture. A **joint venture** is formed when a company entering a new market pools its resources with those of a local firm to form a new and separate firm in which they share ownership, risks, control and profits. In addition to sharing the financial burden, the local partner offers the foreign entrant a better insight into the market, the expertise needed to sell the product in the host country, and access to resources such as real estate and vendors. The partners' contributions to the joint venture – which do not necessarily have to be equal – can vary widely and may consist of capital, know-how, technology, plants, equipment and sales organizations.

Some countries strongly encourage – or, like China, legally require – joint ownership of companies entering its domestic markets, although these restrictions are loosening now as a result of WTO negotiations. Over 50 000 joint ventures between Chinese and foreign

A joint venture between Air France, KLM and Delta Air Lines

Courtesy of Image Asset Management

companies have been created to gain access to this huge market. In other nations, too, joint ventures can open up market opportunities that otherwise would not be available. If a company can identify a partner with a common goal, a joint venture may represent the most viable strategy for international expansion.

Potential problems in joint ventures, as in all partnerships, involve implementing the concept and maintaining the relationship. Failures often arise out of conflicts of interest, such as disagreements over how profits should be shared, or about whether earnings should be reinvested into the joint venture. For joint ventures to be successful, the two parties joining forces must maintain effective communication to ensure that they continue to agree on their marketing strategies and objectives.

15.3.3 Direct investment

A final strategy for entering global markets is international **direct investment** in foreign firms, or in production and marketing facilities. This entry strategy represents the ultimate degree of commitment to a foreign market. It requires the highest level of investment – total ownership of the foreign division or subsidiary – and exposes the company to significant risks, especially in politically unstable countries. However, there are also considerable advantages to a direct investment strategy:

→ *Financial* advantages (transport savings, lower costs through cheaper labour and raw materials, tax advantages or government incentives and all profits going to the parent company).

→ A *synergistic* effect if the international company is able to weave its various foreign subsidiaries into an international production and marketing system that is capable of generating greater profits, without local partners that may have conflicting goals.

→ Better *understanding* of local market conditions through a close partnership with local suppliers and distributors.

→ A favourable corporate *image* among customers and other stakeholders because of local commitment and job creation.

→ Full *control* over the foreign operation without conflicts among partners about the strategy pursued, because there are no partners.

Many companies start their international marketing activities with indirect or direct export and, if that entry strategy proves successful, follow a progression in which they move to the increasingly risky strategies – illustrated in Figure 15.4 – as their managers gain confidence in their skills and want more control over their operations abroad.

15.4 CUSTOMIZATION OR GLOBALIZATION?

When a company enters a new foreign market, it must determine if or to what extent it should modify its marketing strategy to fit local market conditions. Does the product need to be adapted? Are existing advertising and sales promotion campaigns applicable to the new market? Would the current pricing strategy be effective in the international market? And should the type of distribution network that the firm uses in the domestic market be replicated abroad? There are no easy answers to any of these questions.[8]

At the beginning of this chapter we noted that internationally operating companies have to make a choice between *multinational* marketing on the one hand and *global* marketing on the other. This actually amounts to choosing between a *customized* marketing strategy

MARKETING MISTAKE
Cross Cultural Blunders

Ever made a cultural blunder when working abroad? You're not alone. Take a look at some examples of cultural disregard in international business that resulted in negative (but often humorous) consequences.

→ An aftershave commercial presented a romantic scene between a man and a woman that also showed the man's dog. It failed in Middle Eastern countries where dogs are considered unclean.

→ An American telephone company tried to sell its products and services to Latinos through a commercial in which a Latino woman tells her husband to call a friend to inform her that the couple would be late for dinner. The commercial bombed, since Latino women don't issue instructions to their husbands, and a man's use of time would not require a call about tardiness.

→ A US telephone company attempted to promote its products and services in Saudi Arabia. Its ad portrayed an executive talking on the phone with their feet propped up on the desk, showing the soles of their shoes – a serious insult in that country!

→ A sales manager in Hong Kong tried to control employees' promptness at work. He insisted they come to work on time instead of arriving fifteen minutes late. They complied, but then left exactly at five o'clock instead of working into the evening, as they had previously done. Much work was left unfinished until the manager relented, and the employees returned to their usual time schedule.

→ A golf ball manufacturer packaged golf balls in packs of four for convenient purchase in Japan. Unfortunately, pronunciation of the word 'four' sounds like the Japanese word for 'death' and items packaged in quantities of four are unpopular.

→ A sales manager should have done their homework before they approved a promotion that compared the Helmsley Palace Hotel in New York to the Taj Mahal – a mausoleum in India...

→ Procter & Gamble used a television commercial in Japan that had been popular in Europe. The ad showed a woman bathing, her husband entering the bathroom and touching her. The Japanese considered this ad an invasion of privacy, inappropriate behaviour and in very poor taste.

Refusing a cup of coffee offered by a Saudi businessman is considered very rude

→ An American business person refused a cup of coffee offered by a Saudi businessman. Such a rejection is considered very rude, and the business negotiations stalled.

→ A Japanese manager in a US company was told to give critical feedback to an American subordinate during a performance evaluation. Japanese, however, use high context language and are uncomfortable giving direct feedback. It took the Japanese manager five tries before they could be direct enough to discuss the poor performance in such a way that the American understood.

→ A European firm printed the 'OK' finger gesture on each page of its Latin American catalogue. In many parts of that region this is considered an obscene gesture. Six months of work were lost because the firm had to reprint all the catalogues.

→ FedEx, in expanding overseas, failed to consider cultural differences: In Spain the workers preferred very late office hours, while in Russia the workers took truck cleaning soap home due to consumer shortages. FedEx finally shut down over 100 European operations after €1.5 billion in losses.

→ Samarin, a Swedish antacid, was advertised in Arabic newspapers by showing only the brand name and three non-adapted images used earlier in Europe. The first picture showed a man who looks ill; in the second one, he drinks a glass of Samarin, while in the third one, he looks healthy and happy. The intended message (Samarin makes you feel better) did not come across because Arabic consumers read from right to left, and saw a healthy person becoming sick after using the product.

and a *standardized* marketing strategy. Customization means tailoring marketing activities to each local market. With such a 'localized' approach, marketers focus on the differences between countries and carefully adapt their product, promotion, pricing and distribution strategies to the unique needs, wants and other characteristics of each foreign target market. That usually results in the highest level of sales. Unilever and other detergent manufacturers, for instance, adapt their products to local water conditions, washing machines, and laundry habits and make other marketing strategy modifications as well.

Under a global or standardized marketing strategy – the second option – the company uses a common marketing plan for all countries in which it operates and implements it with minimal modifications in each market. This approach downplays differences among countries. Its main benefit is cost savings. In essence, the choice between a customized and a standardized approach means choosing between *effectiveness* (higher sales) and *efficiency* (lower costs).

In the UK, the cleaning product Jif was rebranded as Cif in order to standardize with continental Europe

© PSL Images / Alamy

The evaluation of the pros and cons of standardization and customization depends on a prior assessment of the role of international sales or marketing in the firm's overall corporate strategy. If the firm is only interested in exporting as an outlet for excess production capacity, then management should focus on finding international markets that are receptive to products that have already been developed for the domestic market. In contrast, if the company takes international expansion seriously and wants to gain a permanent foothold in new markets abroad, then it should seriously consider customizing its products and marketing strategy to fit the needs of its local markets. With this in mind, we will now explore the benefits and limitations of standardization. Can we effectively market products without making major modifications or other special provisions for the international marketplace? Or is the either-or debate between a customized or a standardized approach to international marketing too simplistic a view of this issue?

15.4.1 *Pros and cons of standardization*

The issue of whether the international marketing mix should be standardized has been debated for many years. Advocates of standardization argue that it results in cost reductions through economies of scale. For example, Nike athletic shoes are standardized worldwide. By offering the same basic product in all of its foreign markets and thereby increasing the size of its production runs, the company can increase its profit margin by taking advantage of cost economies. Also, R&D costs can be spread over a greater number of units. The reduced costs will make the firm's products, whether sold domestically or internationally, more profitable.

Another advantage of standardization lies in the areas of advertising efficiency and customer relations. Using the same advertising theme everywhere will lower the advertising costs per product unit and per potential buyer. Standardized advertising also provides a consistent image of the company's products and brand name across its various markets, thus creating greater brand power. It will reassure consumers who, today, are increasingly mobile and exposed to global media, about the consistent quality and reliability of the product and the sincerity of the advertiser. Marketing or promotion ideas that have proven successful in one country may have universal appeal and work in markets around the world.[9]

With these benefits in mind, many companies have developed *global brands* and standardized global marketing strategies. They assume that worldwide markets, due to better communications and transport facilities, are becoming more homogeneous. To illustrate, 19-year-old students in Amsterdam may want the same products and lifestyles as students in New York or Tokyo. 'Take a look at kids all over the world who wear identical Nikes and jeans, listen to the same music on their iPhones, spend a lot of their time on Facebook and like Big Macs and Coke', they say. Today, the latest fashions and products spread throughout the world at lightning speed via TV and the Internet. The lower production and marketing costs enable companies to offer their customers premium quality and reliable products at lower prices. That compensates buyers for the fact that the standardized products and services with a strong, universal appeal are not perfectly tailored to their unique needs and wants.

But a global marketing strategy does not always work. There are many examples of standardization failures, including *C&A* in Great Britain, *Marks & Spencer* on the European continent and *Levi's* in Asia. The most significant disadvantage of standardization is simply that cultural, economic and political-legal differences make it difficult to send the same message to all countries and to implement a single standardized marketing strategy with the same degree of success everywhere. Marketers and advertisers like to believe in universal needs and appeals. However, time and time again it turns out that the most successful marketing strategies implemented across national boundaries are those that are tailored to the needs and preferences of each targeted customer group. Which is, of course, the very essence of the marketing concept.

15.4.2 *Think globally, but act locally...*

Determining what strategy works best – globalization or customization – is not an all-or-nothing decision. Besides, choosing between these options will not help marketers develop a competitive strategy. Instead, we must decide on the extent to which the marketing mix should be standardized. A totally standardized approach yields cost savings and may be simple to implement, but is not practical because it ignores differences in customer behaviour, needs, marketing systems and laws across the world. Short-term financial and organizational benefits should not be gained at the expense of long-term strategic thinking and marketing-oriented decisions. On the other hand, a totally localized approach provides no competitive advantage in brand recognition, economies of scale or market growth to a multinational company. Thus, management should consider standardization to the degree possible and be responsive to local issues and needs at the same time.

'If you look at it from an organizational perspective, centralized decision-making is much more efficient', says former Proctor & Gamble brand manager Johan Brand. '*Brains* for global strategy development and hands for local marketing execution. But each of the foreign markets may be entirely different! In Europe we often run into local barriers and issues that are hard to tackle at headquarters. These countries require separate marketing policies. That calls for a whole lot of local *hands.*'[10]

The marketer's task is to develop products and services to meet the needs and wants of all buyers in the target markets. A *multinational approach* or **differentiated international marketing strategy**, in which the marketing mixes are tailored to the local conditions in each country, is not always a viable option. Most seasoned international marketing managers prefer **global localization**, also called a *glocal* marketing strategy or simply 'glocalization'. These marketers 'think globally but act locally', seeking a balance between standardization and adaptation. It's an approach in which the firm's corporate strategy provides global strategic direction, and management tries to exploit good strategies, ideas and products on a wider regional basis, while the local units or subsidiaries in each country focus on adapting the strategy to their local markets. Coca-Cola has been using a glocal marketing strategy for

decades. Although the company is widely known for its global brands, such as Coke and Sprite, it has also launched dozens of local brands of other soft drinks, juices, bottled water and iced tea.

An example of *global localization* is Procter & Gamble's initial strategy for Pringles, an originally American brand of potato chips. In an attempt to penetrate the European market, the company first built an exact copy of its Pringles plant in Jackson, Tennessee in the town of Mechelen, Belgium. However, sales in Europe never took off after Pringles' introduction in Europe, most likely because the company had centralized all of its marketing efforts and forgot about local marketing. 'We had only one type of package and the same advertising for all countries', a spokesperson admits. 'It was too static.'

Then, Procter & Gamble decided to invest in the brand and develop local flavours. It developed Salt & Vinegar for the British market (in response to their fondness for fish and chips), Sour Cream Onion for Sweden, low salt Pringles for Japan and Oranjekaas ('orange cheese') for the Dutch market. Some of these have since become standard flavours in various countries, while others were temporarily offered as 'Limited Edition', identified by the hat worn by Mr Pringles on the package.

The advertising campaigns were also adapted for each country. To get a more emotional response to commercials, research was conducted to find out when consumers tend to eat potato chips in different countries. In the Netherlands that turned out to be at parties, when people are relaxing or visiting each other as well as after school time. Italians eat chips before meals, the British when watching football matches on TV and the French at barbecues. That information was incorporated into advertising campaigns. Thanks to its *glocal marketing* strategies, P&G soon succeeded in increasing Pringles sales more than fivefold![11]

15.4.3 Developing a global marketing strategy

In developing a worldwide marketing mix, we should first acquire an in-depth understanding of the company's foreign target markets. Usually, the necessary insight can be obtained through the same marketing research techniques used in the domestic market; Only with relevant and accurate information available the marketing mix can be effectively standardized whenever feasible and tailored for global markets whenever necessary.

International product and promotion strategies

Marketers can choose from among five international product and promotion strategies for a particular foreign market. As Figure 15.5 illustrates, these are straight extension, product adaptation, promotion adaptation, dual adaptation and product invention.

FIGURE 15.5 Global product and promotion strategies

		Product		
		Same product	**Adapt product**	**New product**
Promotion	**Same promotion**	Straight extension	Product adaptation	Product invention
	Adapt promotion	Promotion adaptation	Dual adaptation	

In a **straight extension**, the simplest of the five strategies, the company makes virtually the same product and markets this product with about the same message in the domestic market and abroad. This one-product, one-message approach has worked well for companies such as Levi's, Heineken and Apple. As part of a global marketing strategy, it is an appropriate approach when consumers have about the same needs, wants and uses for the product and the company can sell the product without modifications in brand name, ingredients or packaging.

The strategy of adapting a product or service to meet local preferences or market conditions is called **product adaptation**. This is the most widely used strategy in international marketing. Domestic products often must be modified to meet foreign electrical requirements, laws, language needs and consumer wants. Cosmetics companies, for instance, develop different formulas and colours to satisfy the needs of women with various skin types and preferences. And Shell offers adapted diesel and gasoline blends based on each country's climate and regulations.

A **product invention** strategy, in this context, refers to either creating a totally new product, or drastically changing an existing product for a foreign market to take advantage of a unique marketing opportunity. The Philips wood stove to improve cooking conditions of poor consumers in developing countries is a striking example.

For straight extension and product adaptation strategies, similar promotion messages are used abroad and in the domestic market. However, in a **promotion adaptation** strategy, the basic product remains the same while promotion emphasis is altered. To illustrate, in countries like the Netherlands, bicycles are an important mode of transportation, whereas in the United States, they are mainly used for recreational purposes. Therefore, marketing communication in the US might emphasize escape and fun, as compared to functionality and durability in other countries. Finally, in a **dual adaptation** strategy, companies modify both their product and promotion strategies.

International pricing strategies

Since price setting can critically affect success in overseas markets, global companies face a major challenge in developing an effective pricing strategy as part of their international marketing efforts. A company could charge the same price for its product around the globe, but this uniform price might be too high for less affluent consumers in developing countries. Or it could let their prices depend on what buyers in each country are willing to pay, but that approach would not take actual cost differences between countries into account.

Frequently, prices in international markets are determined by a cost-plus approach, i.e. by adding a certain profit margin to the costs of manufacturing and marketing products. Companies following this approach face a **price escalation** issue. Because costs such as tariffs, shipping and importer or exporter margins can be high for products sent overseas, their prices will be considerably higher than those charged by local competitors for comparable products. Therefore, some firms make smaller or simplified versions of their products for foreign countries that can be sold at reasonable prices.

Finally, international pricing strategies are increasingly influenced by Internet sites that show to what extent companies charge higher or lower prices in various countries. This is forcing some companies that sell their products online to move toward setting uniform prices all around the world.

International distribution strategies

Global distribution networks are complex value chains that often include exporters, importers and other middlemen, as well as different transportation systems. Because these additional intermediaries in marketing channels often add costs, they usually increase a product's final selling price. Therefore, international companies are under constant pressure to shorten distribution channels and make them as efficient as possible.

Physical distribution, too, is a vital aspect of overseas marketing. In developing countries, manufacturers must typically go through many different types of distribution channels – usually longer and less efficient than in the home market – to get their products into the consumers' hands. Global marketers must adapt promptly to these conditions to profit from sales in those markets. They may have to deal with thousands of 'mom-and-pop' stores or small independent wholesalers, some of whom transport products to remote rural areas on bicycles or oxcarts. In addition, the lack of communication and warehousing facilities in some foreign markets makes distribution planning – which is of critical importance in global marketing – a significant challenge for internationally operating companies.

SUMMARY

1 Planning for international marketing

Companies narrowly focused only on the domestic market frequently overlook lucrative opportunities abroad. They may lose sales to competitors because they fail to benefit from the international experience and economies of scale gained from marketing abroad.

Marketing internationally is most effective if we tailor marketing strategies to the local conditions. A multinational corporation operates in each country as a local market-oriented firm would. In contrast, a global marketing approach focuses on customers' similarities across national markets instead of their differences. Standardizing marketing strategies benefits companies by providing economies of scale in production and marketing activities.

Because of the high risk of failure, marketing across borders requires careful planning and strategy development. The initial planning process requires several steps: an internal analysis (identifying the firm's strengths and weaknesses, marketing objectives and number of foreign markets to be entered), global screening (environmental analysis to determine the attractiveness of various markets) and target market selection (assessing the market and sales potential, and the segments in each region to be targeted). The next steps are strategy development and selecting an optimal market entry strategy. Finally, international marketing planning requires implementation and control of the marketing programme.

2 International environmental analysis

International marketing is the art of bridging distances, such as the differences in the economic and technological development between foreign markets and the gap between diverse cultures. Marketing strategies have to be effectively tailored to these uncontrollable factors in the *external environment*. A global environmental analysis starts with a critical assessment of the economic environment, such as the level of economic development, economic infrastructure and purchasing power in various countries. We also anticipate developments in the political-legal climate. What, for example, is the government's attitude toward foreign companies and trade with other nations (political stability)? Are a country's trade regulations an attempt to create trade barriers or commercial restrictions? Does the government of a foreign nation impose protectionist policies such as tariffs, quotas and other administrative barriers?

Finally, in evaluating the cultural environment, many companies rely on a cross-cultural consumer analysis. The objective of such analysis is to gain working knowledge of the social values, customs, cultural symbols and use of language in different societies.

3 Entry strategies for global markets

Once we have decided to enter the global marketplace, the first step is to select an appropriate entry strategy for each chosen market. Companies have four alternative approaches for entering global markets. Many firms start as exporters, then increase their commitment to operating abroad by moving to licencing or joint ventures, and finally make a direct investment in foreign markets. The decision about the extent of commitment involves a trade-off between control and risk. Direct involvement gives management more control over the company's strategy abroad and increases potential profits, but at the same time increases risk if the international operation is not successful.

Exporting entails producing goods in one country and selling them in another, either through an intermediary (indirect export) or an in-house exporting operation. Under *licencing*, a firm offers the right to a patent, trademark or a form of partnership, such as a franchise. In a *joint venture*, a foreign company and a local firm join hands and invest in a local business. Finally, direct investment entails a company investing in and owning a foreign subsidiary or division.

4 Think globally, act locally

The most successful international marketing programmes are those that are carefully tailored to the needs and wants of each foreign target market. Indeed, this is the essence of the marketing concept. Research shows that 'the universal consumer' does not exist. The choice between customization and globalization is often a choice between greater effectiveness and higher efficiency.

A company's primary consideration is how much it will adapt the marketing mix – product, promotion, price and distribution – within each country. Several major options were discussed in this final chapter of Marketing Fundamentals. Experienced international marketers argue that managers should think globally but act locally, seeking a balance between globally standardized strategies and locally adapted marketing mix tactics. Their rule-of-thumb is to standardize marketing programmes whenever possible, and customize them wherever necessary.

DISCUSSION QUESTIONS

1   What are the key similarities and differences between marketing in one's own country and international marketing?

2   Why is the commitment of a company's management important in international marketing?

3   Which key considerations affect a company's entry strategy in a foreign market?

4   Describe the intermediaries' tasks in an indirect market entry strategy.

5   Outline the most important criteria marketers use to decide which foreign markets they should enter.

6   What are the pros and cons of licencing as a possible entry strategy?

7   Why do many companies prefer joint ventures to direct investment for entering foreign markets?

8   What are the differences between a local product or brand, an international product or brand and a global brand? Give an example of each.

9   Describe some major factors that determine which distribution strategy should be used abroad.

10 Which criteria should a company use in deciding whether or not to standardize its international marketing strategy?

GLOSSARY

20/80 rule A principle stating that about 20 per cent of the products that a company offers account for 80 per cent of its total sales.

Abell model Analytical tool to help define a company's business, based on customer segments, customer functions (benefits sought) and technologies.

Absolute price difference In odd pricing, the actual difference between two prices (e.g. €99.95 and €100) is much less than the difference perceived by consumers.

Account Manager Company representative who is the primary contact for an important customer, responsible for providing day-to-day support and maintaining the relationship.

Acquisition The purchase of an organization – including all of its current products – by another one.

Actual product Combination of product and service features that deliver the core benefit to the customer, such as design, quality level, ease of use and brand name.

Additional demand Demand from customers who already own the product and buy another one to use it in addition to the existing product.

Administered system Vertical marketing system in which a large, dominant distribution channel member uses its power to coordinate the production and distribution activities performed by other channel members.

Adoption A consumer's decision to keep using a particular product on a regular basis.

Adoption categories Five categories of consumers based on how long it takes them to adopt a new product: the innovators, early adopters, early majority, late majority and laggards.

Adoption curve A normal distribution of the buyers in a potential market over time, illustrating what percentage of the consumer population falls within each of the adoption categories.

Adoption process A series of attitudinal and behavioural changes consumers go through that lead to product trial, purchase and adoption.

Adoption rate A measure of how quickly a new product or service is accepted by society, as determined by five product characteristics: relative advantage, compatibility, complexity, divisibility and observability.

Advertising Any paid form of non-personal communication about products, services, ideas or organizations by an identified sponsor using the mass media to influence the knowledge, attitudes or behaviour of those who are part of a target market.

Advertising appeal A product's unique qualities, such as a key reason for someone to buy it, that would make effective advertising content and may even be used as a campaign slogan or jingle.

Advertising campaign A collection of different but related advertisements or commercials based on a single theme, which appear in different media as part of an advertising plan designed to meet a company's advertising objectives.

Advisor External consultant who offers a company several alternatives to choose from or who facilitates the purchase decision in some other way.

Advocacy advertising A type of institutional advertising designed to react to criticism or express views on controversial issues.

Affective component A person's emotions and *feelings* about an object; the attitude's 'feeling' component.

Affective response Feelings, emotions or moods (such as interest, liking, conviction) aroused as consumers assess a product or when exposed to marketing stimuli such as commercials.

AIDA model A model that describes the stages (attention, interest, desire, action) a person goes through before making a buying decision.

AIO variables Specific 'activities, interests and opinions' that make up a consumer's lifestyle.

Allowance Price adjustment that – indirectly – lowers a buyer's price in exchange for them trading in a used product, participating in a promotional programme or buying in a period of slow sales.

Ambush marketing A practice by which a company that is not an official sponsor of an event or organization tries to associate itself with the event through its own ads, such as by showing a rock group on a concert tour that another company is sponsoring.

Anchor position Placement of large, well-known retail stores at opposite ends or at the midpoint of a shopping centre, creating pedestrian traffic and serving as an attracting force to draw consumers to the centre.

Anticipatory socialization Adopting the values, standards and consumption pattern of a group someone is eager to join.

Approach The salesperson's – carefully planned and critical – first contact with a prospect.

Arbitration Conflict resolution through negotiation with a third party brought into the dispute to act as an impartial expert or arbitrator.

Aspiration group Reference group of which someone is not a member, but to which they aspire to belong.

Assortment height The average price level of the product items or brands in a company's product mix or in a product line.

Atmospherics A retail store's use of floor layout, lighting, sounds, scents and other design elements that influence consumers' perceptions and make the store feel 'right' (*Ambience*).

Attitude A learned tendency to respond in a consistent way to certain ideas, people, objects or organizations.

Attitude formation Development of a person's attitude toward an object.

Attitude object A product, service, brand, store or person that consumers develop a positive or negative attitude toward.

Attitude research Research on how attitudes develop and how its components should be measured.

Attributes Product characteristics used in evaluating the options in a purchase decision.

Auction company Type of agent that brings buyers and sellers together by selling products, that usually are inspected by potential buyers, to the highest bidder (*Auction house*).

Augmented product Intangible, psychological benefits and service-based features - part of the company's promotion, price or distribution strategy – that make a product more attractive, such as an extended warranty or free home delivery and installation.

Average gross margin The typical mark-up in the industry.

Average reach The number of individuals during the publication interval (such as a week for *Time*) that may see any given issue of the medium.

Back translation The process of – after translating a document into a foreign language – having it translated back by another bilingual person into the original language, enabling a comparison of the two versions for errors.

Backward integration A company forming a corporate vertical marketing system by acquiring one of its suppliers, thus gaining control over an input in the distribution or production process upstream in the channel.

Backward pricing Price-setting strategy in which a company works backward from a product's ideal consumer price to determine its own (ex-factory) price.

Balanced tenancy Different stores in a shopping centre complementing each other in the variety and quality of their merchandise.

Bartering A direct exchange between parties of products or services, without any money changing hands.

Base price The publicly announced price for which the company expects to sell a product (*List price*).

Basic needs Conditions essential for survival, such as the availability of food, water and shelter.

Battle of the brands Fight between manufacturers and retail distributors for power and control of the distribution channel.

BCG portfolio analysis Developed by the Boston Consulting Group, it offers a bird's eye view by placing the company's SBUs (question marks, stars, cash cows and dogs) in a four-cell 'market share / market growth matrix'.

Behavioural segmentation Subdividing the aggregate market into segments based on people's product usage rate, degree of brand loyalty and willingness to buy.

Benchmarking Comparison of your own business performance and strategies with those of other organizations in order to improve them.

Benefit segmentation A form of psychographic segmentation in which markets are defined in terms of the benefits that people seek from the product, and then segmented based on consumer preferences for specific product characteristics (*Benefits-sought segmentation*).

Benelux Trademarks Act Trademark legislation providing legal protection for brands – through registration – against imitation by competitors.

Black box Model of consumer decision making used to identify unperceivable factors – such as consumers' mental processing – that influence their buying behaviour.

Branch of industry A group of organizations within a *sector* with similar production techniques and products (for example, the book industry within the graphic sector).

Brand A name, symbol or design that a company uses to identify its products or services and differentiate them from those of others.

Brand competition Competition between brands of the same product type that are substitutes because they are similar (e.g. Grolsch and Heineken lager beer).

Brand equity The financial and marketing value of a company or brand name, based on its strengths, the customers' attitudes toward the brand and benefits of using the product. Strategic and financial value of a brand to a company based on positive customer attitudes about the brand.

Brand extension Using the existing brand name with an established brand image for new products in a different product category (*Spin-off*).

Brand image Consumer perception of the brand's personality that arouses certain feelings or emotions.

Brand loyalty The degree to which a customer will keep buying the same brand, regardless of modifications in the marketing mix or the alternatives offered by rivals.

Brand mark Element of a brand that cannot be vocalized, such as McDonald's Golden Arches (*Logo*).

Brand name Part of a brand that can be spoken, including letters, words and numbers.

Brand stretching Launching new products or product items under an existing, successful brand name, possibly in new market segments through a line extension or brand extension strategy.

Break-even analysis Analyzing the relationship between total revenue (at a given price) and total cost at various levels of output, in order to calculate the number of units that must be sold at a certain price for the firm to cover costs and, thus, break even.

Break-even point The quantity of units sold at which the product's total revenue is equal to its total costs.

Brick-and-click Multi-channel retailer that has both a retail store and an online store.

Bricks-and-mortar Traditional 'street-side' business – such as a book store – that deals with its customers face to face in a company-owned or rented store or office, and competes with web-based businesses that have lower operating costs and more flexibility.

Briefing The client's instructions to an advertising agency about the company's viewpoint, wishes and other matters related to a campaign.

Broadcast advertising Commercials aired on television or radio, typically called spots.

Broker Individual who assists in negotiating a contract between two parties and is paid a fee when the transaction is completed by the client who hired them.

Build strategy Aggressive growth strategy to increase an SBU's market share by turning a question mark into a star.

Business advertising Advertising targeted at organizations and people who buy products and services for use in business.

Business definition Answer to the question, 'What business are we in?' based on (Abell's) three dimensions: the customers (target markets), their needs (desired benefits) and technologies used to satisfy the needs.

Business-format franchising A form of franchise agreement in which the franchiser sells franchisees the right to use its format or approach to doing business and provides step-by-step operational and decision making guidelines (*Retail franchising*).

Business objectives Goals and targets that a business sets for itself.

Business products Products or industrial goods (e.g. production equipment, materials, supplies, software) sold to organizations that resell them, or use them to make their own products or to provide a service.

Business scope Part of the business definition, describing the extent of the firm's current activities.

Business strategy How an organization – in light of its mission, core competencies and current environment – intends to achieve its long-term objectives.

Business-to-business marketing Marketing to companies to support the resale, use in daily operations or manufacture of other products (*B2B; business, industrial* or *organizational marketing*).

Buyer DMU member in charge of obtaining competitive bids, selecting a supplier (although his superior may negotiate the contract) and setting up delivery schedules.

Buyers' market Market in which supply exceeds demand so that buyers are in a stronger position than suppliers, and resulting in aggressive selling efforts to win over prospects.

Buying power The financial ability of a consumer to purchase products and services.

Buzz Word-of-mouth generated by consumers who talk to their friends about a product or service, often through social media.

Campaign advertising Type of advertising intended to bring about immediate action by the consumer, and get them to buy the product right away.

Campaign communication Use of marketing communication tools (such as sales promotion) with short-term effects, such as increasing sales volume (*Price-offer promotion*).

Canned presentation Presentation based on memorized information about the product's general benefits, to be adjusted to the potential buyer's information needs.

Cannibalization The loss of sales by a company of its established product after launching a new, usually lower priced, version of the product that – since buyers perceive it as a substitute – steals some of the sales of the original item.

Carry-over effect The continuing impact of past advertising and promotion campaigns.

Cartel Group of separate companies that collusively determine prices and production volume in order to maximize mutual profits.

Cash-and-carry wholesaler Wholesaler targeting small retailers, caterers and others that drive to his warehouse, pay for the products and carry it away themselves.

Cash cow SBU with a high market share in a market growing less than 10 per cent per year; its surplus cash flow is used to finance the growth of other SBUs with higher growth potential.

Cash discount Reduction in price offered to business buyers in exchange for a prompt payment.

Cash flow Movement of cash into and out of a company, based on receipts and disbursements.

Category killer A special type of specialty or limited-line store that offers a huge selection of products in a single product line (e.g. electronics) at low prices.

Category management Marketing strategy in which a single person is responsible for an SBU that consists of all products in a product category that the target customers may view as substitutes for a particular item, allowing him to better evaluate buying patterns and new market trends.

Causal research Market research that examines a cause-and-effect relationship (*Experimental research*).

Cause-related marketing Strategic approach to corporate philanthropy through linking the company's products to a social issue, usually by contributing money for each product that consumers buy.

Centralized organization Organization in which most decisions are made by top-level managers who delegate little decision-making authority down the chain of command.

Channel conflict Situation in which one channel member's behaviour is at odds with the interests of another and prevents it from achieving its objectives.

Channel leader Distribution channel member with enough power to control other channel members and to influence their strategies.

Channel length Number of intermediary levels used in the distribution channel.

Channel power The ability of a channel member to make another channel member act in ways it otherwise would not have acted.

Channel structure Shape or form of a distribution channel, consisting of all firms and individuals (including producers and final customers) involved in selling, buying, transferring title and performing related functions.

Choice criteria Product benefits that consumers consider in evaluating and choosing between alternatives.

Classic response hierarchy model Model (such as the AIDA model) suggesting that consumers pass through certain stages of learning – such as cognition, affection and conation – before buying.

Closed-ended question Survey question asking the respondent to choose between a limited number of responses.

Closing Stage in the selling process in which a salesperson asks the prospect for a commitment to buy a product or service.

Co-branding Putting two well-known brand names from different companies on a single product, such as Gillette and Duracell.

Cognition The processes of reasoning, interpretation and mental problem solving without any direct experience.

Cognitive approach Theory about learning, underlining that some insights are gained by analytical *thinking* and *information* processing, enabling better decision making.

Cognitive component A person's *knowledge* and beliefs about a product or another object; the attitude's 'knowing' component.

Cognitive dissonance Unpleasant feeling of doubt about the brand choice after making an important purchase decision (*Buyer's remorse*).

Cognitive response The thoughts that occur at the cognitive stage in the response hierarchy, such as awareness, knowledge and comprehension.

Cold call Method of calling on an unfamiliar company or potential buyer without a prior appointment.

Collective advertising Joint advertising by competitors in the same sector to stimulate *primary demand*, which is demand for the whole product category.

Combination advertising Companies that are not selling the same products but have a common interest – such as retailers in a shopping centre – sharing the costs of an advertising campaign.

Combination pricing Price-setting in which components of the cost-, demand- and competition-oriented pricing strategies are combined.

Commission A fee paid to a salesperson for each sale made, which provides an incentive for extra sales efforts.

Communication Transfer or exchange of information between organizations and people, sometimes in an attempt to influence them.

Communication capability The medium's effectiveness in conveying a particular type of message, depending on its technical features (e.g. colour graphics) and lack of clutter.

Communication instrument Tools such as sales promotion or personal selling to get a message across and achieve other marketing objectives.

Communication mix The particular combination of marketing promotion tools that work together to communicate the marketer's message, achieve marketing objectives and satisfy the target market needs.

Communication model Model that outlines the relationship between various stages in communication and consumer information processing as part of the buying decision process.

Communication objective A company's desired result from a communication campaign, such as a specific level of advertising recall or brand awareness.

Communication plan A four-step process of identifying the target audience, formulating objectives, setting a budget and determining the communication mix.

Communication process A process in which a sender (e.g. an advertiser) tries to deliver a message to a receiver (potential customer) via a certain medium.

Communication strategy Strategy for communicating a desired message to a desired target audience through a medium.

Communication target audience A specific group of people or organizations to whom the message is addressed.

Community shopping centre A type of shopping centre offering shopping and specialty products and designed to draw five times as many people as a neighbourhood centre.

Comparative advertising A type of advertising in which two or more brands are compared, based on important product features.

Compatibility The measure of how well new products fit with the lifestyle and values of consumers.

Competition-oriented pricing Pricing strategy in which a company's competitors' prices rather than demand or cost considerations – are its principal basis for price-setting.

Competitive advantage A company's unique strengths or capabilities (such as superior customer service) that cannot be easily duplicated by rivals, and account for its performance or market position.

Competitive bidding Process in an industrial market in which suppliers submit bids that outline the product specifications, with the contract being awarded to the firm with the best offer and lowest price.

Competitor A rival firm with products that are considered as alternatives by buyers with similar needs.

Complementary products Products sold or used jointly with other products, such as a printer and ink cartridges. A product that is essential to the use of another product may be characterized by a negative cross elasticity of demand, such as petrol, of which a price increase will lower the demand for SUVs.

Conative component A person's intended (and actual) *behaviour* with respect to an object; the attitude's 'doing' component.

Concentrated marketing Targeting strategy in which a firm – with the same marketing mix – focuses on only one or a few markets, hoping to gain a large share of these segments.

Concept development The process of coming up with the central theme of an advertising campaign – consisting of words, images, tone and style – that effectively communicates the proposition.

Concept development phase Stage in new product development during which ideas are analyzed to identify desirable product features.

Confrontation matrix Based on the SWOT analysis, this tool combines a company's internal strengths and weaknesses with external opportunities and threats in order to identify possible strategies.

Consumer advertising Advertising targeted at consumers who buy products for their own use or for household members.

Consumer behaviour Consumers' decision making, information seeking and communication behaviour, influenced by their personal circumstances such as demographic characteristics, lifestyle and situational factors.

Consumer goods Products sold to individuals or households for their personal use or consumption (*Consumer products*).

Consumer marketing An organization's marketing activities directed at the end users of a product.

Consumer surplus The difference between the total amount that consumers are willing to pay and the amount that they actually pay for purchasing the number of units of a new product that they want, which also reflects the extra revenue earned by a company with a *price skimming* strategy.

Consumerism Consumers' empowerment to protect them from unfair business practices and promote information transparency.

Consumption pattern Consumers' buying habits, use and eventual disposal of products.

Contest Company-sponsored competition in which consumers can win prizes by using their creative or analytical skills in completing a task, such as writing a slogan.

Contingency plan Course of action to be followed – as an alternative to the primary marketing plan – in the event of major changes in an existing situation, such as an unanticipated threat or opportunity.

Continuous innovation Improvement to an existing product that requires virtually no adjustment on the part of the customer.

Contract manufacturing Joint venture in which a company contracts with a foreign firm to manufacture a product that it wants to market under its own brand name.

Contractual system Vertical market system, in which independent organizations at different levels in the distribution channel sign a contract (e.g. a franchise arrangement) that spells out each company's rights and responsibilities.

Contrary demand curve A backward bending (instead of downward sloping) demand curve, which is typical for prestige pricing: as the price increases, demand increases (*Backward-bending demand curve*).

Contribution margin Revenue in excess of variable costs, used to absorb (part of) the company's fixed costs as well as to provide a profit.

Control System for evaluating business or marketing results and, if needed, taking corrective action to ensure that the objectives are efficiently realized.

Control group Group of subjects who did not receive the experimental treatment of which the researcher measures the effect on the experimental group, to allow a comparison of the two groups and assess the experimental variable's effect.

Controlled experiment Research method in which the researcher manipulates a test group (*experimental group*) in order to compare the results with those of a *control group* that was not exposed to the treatment.

Convenience products Items that the consumer buys frequently and immediately, with a minimum of shopping effort.

Convenience store A small shop, located in or near a residential area that carries a limited assortment of food products and high-turnover convenience goods.

Conventional distribution channel A rather loose channel network in which companies such as manufacturers, wholesalers, retailers, brokers and agents work independently of each other.

Conversion A type of transaction that converts a trial subscription into a permanent or new one.

Copy test A type of advertising research that focuses on the effect of a message before, during and after a campaign.

Core assortment Products – about 20 per cent of the retailer's merchandise mix – with a high turnover rate.

Core competencies The company's strengths and well-performed activities that its customers appreciate and competitors would find hard to duplicate.

Core product The basic function or (intangible) problem-solving benefits that the product provides, such as satisfying the customer's need for convenience (*Core benefit*).

Corporate advertising Form of advertising designed to communicate a positive image to the public, for example by showcasing its community involvement or sustainability strategy.

Corporate chain A commonly owned and controlled large group of stores with centralized purchasing and decision making that sell the same products (*Retail chain*).

Corporate culture The norms, ideas and values that the members of an *organization* share, which influence the way they think and communicate as well as their relationships and management style.

Corporate identity The company's actual image in the target market's perception or in public opinion.

Corporate system Vertical marketing system in which one company owns and controls other channel members at a different level of the distribution channel.

Cost The amount of money needed to support certain activities, such as producing a product or delivering a service.

Cost focus strategy Niche strategy in which a company (such as Ryanair) charges low prices, made possible by a cost advantage in a narrow target market through reduced expenses.

Cost leadership strategy Generic strategy that involves cutting expenses and reducing prices of standardized products in order to gain market share by appealing to price-sensitive customers.

Cost-oriented pricing Strategy of setting a product's price based on its costs, then adding a mark-up.

Cost per thousand The cost of reaching 1 000 individuals or households in the target audience with the advertising message in a particular medium (*CPM*).

Cost-plus pricing Price-setting based on the accounting principle that a product's price should equal the variable costs and fixed costs per unit, plus a predetermined percentage of those costs to provide a profit margin.

Counterfeiting Copying, imitating or falsifying something in order to defraud or deceive people (*Forging*).

Countertrade Arrangement of the sale of a product in combination with an offsetting transaction, in which a company sells product A to a foreign customer and agrees to buy a certain amount or quantity of product B from another company in the same country, often with some money or credit involved in the deal.

Coupon A certificate, usually with an expiration date, for money off the purchase price at the point of sale.

Coverage The percentage of a target audience that a particular medium reaches (*Target market reach*).

Cross-cultural consumer analysis Analysis to get insight into the social values, customs, cultural symbols and use of language in different societies.

Cross elasticity of demand The demand for a particular product (e.g. butter) is influenced by changes in the price of another product (e.g. margarine).

Culture Set of values, customs, beliefs and symbols that members of a community have developed to shape their behaviour and way of life and help distinguish them from other communities.

Cumulative quantity discount Price reduction based on the quantity a customer buys over a year, designed to create customer loyalty.

Current reach The number of people within a publication interval who see an issue intended for that period.

Customer Ultimate consumer or organization that buys or rents products and services.

Customer loyalty The extent to which a customer makes repeat purchases from a particular supplier or continues to buy the same brand.

Customer sales force structure Sales force organized around specific industries or types of buyers (such as supermarket chains and specialty stores) with different needs.

Customer service Every form of assistance before, during and after the purchase that will make a product more valuable for customers and easier to buy or use.

Customization Tailoring the company's marketing activities to each local market (*Adaptation*).

Customs Traditional activities or practices that determine what people in a society consider normal and how they are supposed to act.

Data mining Use of supercomputers and mathematical tools to sift through an extensive database to identify patterns of buying behaviour or other potentially useful knowledge.

Database The available information about customers and prospects, including demographic data and their past purchases.

Database marketing The use of computer database technologies to systematically collect, store and analyze information about individual customers in order to develop customized marketing activities.

Decentralized organization Organization in which top management delegates much of the decision-making authority to lower levels in the hierarchy.

Decider The person who ultimately selects the product to be bought, even though another DMU member is formally authorized to select the vendor.

Decision making unit Temporary or permanent group of people from different departments of a firm who participate in the purchasing process (*DMU*; *Buying centre*).

Decline Stage of the product life cycle when sales of the whole product class begin to fall rapidly because of the saturated market, changing tastes and new technologies.

Decoding The process of 'translating' or interpreting words and images into certain information.

Degree of urbanization Percentage of the population living in cities.

Delphi method Form of expert research to get insight into uncertain market developments, in which experts submit their forecasts and are then shown those of other experts in subsequent rounds, allowing them to revise their opinion until consensus is reached.

Demand The quantity of products or services that buyers are willing to purchase at various prices at a given time, based on certain wants or needs.

Demand curve Curve that shows the maximum number of products at various prices that customers will buy in a market, if other factors remain the same.

Demand-oriented pricing A price-setting strategy based on the price that buyers are willing to pay, rather than based on the company's costs.

Demarketing Strategy to – temporarily or permanently – reduce total consumer demand ('general demarketing') or the demand of a specific group of buyers ('selective demarketing') for products that are in short supply or may be harmful to society.

Demographic characteristics Personal characteristics such as age, gender, level of education, marital status and income that influence a consumer's buying process.

Demographic factors Characteristics of a human population – such as its size, birth rate and composition – that greatly affect a firm's markets.

Demographic market segmentation Dividing the total market into subgroups based on demographic consumer data such as income, social class, age, stage in the family life cycle, gender, ethnic background and education.

Department store A large, service-oriented retail institution that carries a wide product mix of shopping and specialty goods, and offers a deep selection in product categories – with related product lines organized into separate departments – such as apparel, cosmetics and household products.

Derived demand The demand for an industrial product (e.g. sheet steel) is driven by – or derived from – the demand for related consumer products (e.g. cars).

Descriptive research Research design that focuses on determining how often something occurs or to what extent some situations vary over time, without considering possible relationships between different factors.

Desk research Effort to find out what information is readily available on the topic being researched.

Destination store Store with an established image and an attractive product assortment that consumers deliberately visit.

Differential advantage A company's unique advantage that reflects true value for customers and is not easy to match by a rival (*Distinctive competence*).

Differentiated international marketing strategy A multinational approach in which a company's marketing mixes are tailored to the local conditions in each country it enters.

Differentiated marketing Targeting strategy in which a company tries to reach the entire market (or the greatest possible part of it) by developing a unique, tailored marketing mix for each of the segments it operates in.

Differentiated oligopoly Oligopoly in which companies sell products (such as bicycles) that differ in quality, design and brand image, making them less than perfect substitutes.

Differentiation focus strategy Offering services or products (e.g. Aston Martin) to a limited target market that are significantly different from those of competitors (*Niche strategy*).

Differentiation strategy Charging premium prices for high quality products or unique services that customers perceive as superior to other brands.

Diffusion process The spread of new ideas and products through society and their acceptance by various groups in the target market.

Direct advertising Form of mass promotion sent directly from an advertiser to individual customers through letters, folders or a sponsored magazine.

Direct channel Distribution channel in which products and services are moved from the producer to the consumer intermediaries.

Direct cost The total of variable and fixed costs that – in price-setting – can be attributed to producing or selling a particular product.

Direct exporting Export strategy in which a producer performs all of the export functions, such as marketing research, contacting local distributors, preparing export documentation and setting prices.

Direct investment Entry strategy in which a company makes a large – and sometimes risky – investment in a foreign firm, total ownership of a subsidiary or of production and marketing facilities.

Direct mail An advertising message that is sent directly to a prospect in the target market.

Direct mail advertising A type of advertising, usually addressed personally, that is sent to individual customers through the mail.

Direct marketing A custom tailored marketing approach that allows a company to communicate directly with customers by using detailed customer information from a computerized database and direct communication tools such as interactive consumer websites, email, mobile messaging and direct mail to generate an order or other response. A two-way process of marketing communication through which companies interact directly with customers to exchange information and sell products.

Direct marketing communication A firm's tailored marketing communication efforts that allow it to effectively appeal to a narrow, carefully selected target market (*Rifle approach*).

Direct response advertising Any medium used to get an immediate response from a target audience, eliminating an intermediary in the purchase process.

Direct response television marketing Selling a product directly over the television by urging consumers to call a toll-free number, bypassing standard retail stores.

Direct selling The marketing of products and services to ultimate consumers through personal interactions and sales presentations at home or in the workplace.

Discontinuous innovation Innovation that requires significant behavioural adjustments to use the new product.

Discount pricing Below-market pricing in order to appeal to price-conscious buyers by firms with e.g. better production technology or greater economies of scale.

Discount store Large retail store carrying various product lines at lower prices than department stores, made possible by offering limited customer services (*Discounter*).

Discretionary income What's left of a consumer's income after paying for necessities and taxes, which greatly affects luxury purchases.

Disintermediation Bypassing of established middlemen, or appearance – often through e-commerce – of new types of intermediaries that displace traditional resellers.

Display Presentation device to help retailers directing shoppers' attention to a particular product (*Point of purchase display*).

Disposable income Personal income less taxes paid.

Disposable personal income A consumer's after-tax income available for spending and savings.

Dissatisfier A product's missing features that may be a reason for consumers not to buy it.

Dissonance reducing behaviour A consumer's post-purchase behaviour of, for example, changing his attitude in order to justify a previous action, thus reducing anxiety of potentially having made a poor purchase decision.

Distribution The marketing mix component that is concerned with decisions about making the product available to customers when and where they prefer to buy them, including the selection of distribution channels and intermediaries (*Place*).

Distribution channel A dynamic network of mostly independent organizations that, combined, perform all of the activities necessary to link producers with end customers in order to achieve the marketing task.

Distribution functions Key tasks that intermediaries perform in the channel, such as inventory control, promotion and financing.

Distribution intensity Number of outlets used to distribute a product or service in a particular market.

Distribution strategy Analysis, planning, implementation and control of the activities that make the right products available to the target market at the right time, at the right place and at the lowest possible cost.

Distributor brand Brand that is owned and controlled by a retailer, wholesaler or other type of reseller.

Diversification strategy Increasing sales volume by introducing new products to attract customers in new markets or by acquiring a company not related to the firm's current business.

Divest strategy Strategy to withdraw from the market by selling off business units classified as dogs or question marks.

Dog SBU with a low market share and a modest cash flow in a saturated, low-growth market. A firm may maintain dogs as long as they are profitable.

Downgrading Rare positioning strategy designed to influence the customer's perception through quality and price reductions or changes in store format and ambience.

Downstream management Managing activities in the supply chain that deliver customer value, including storage of finished products, outbound logistics, marketing, sales and customer service.

Drive A strong stimulus that encourages action or motivates someone to reduce a need.

Drop shipper Wholesaler who does not take physical possession of the goods, but forwards orders from his customers to manufacturers who ship directly to the buyer (*Desk jobber*).

Dual adaptation International marketing strategy in which a company modifies both its product and promotion strategies to meet international needs.

Dual distribution Strategy in which a manufacturer uses two types of distribution channels to reach customers.

Dual target market approach A manufacturer's efforts to tailor its marketing strategy not only to the ultimate consumer (through product management), but also to large retail customers (key account management).

Dumping Selling a product (usually in foreign markets) far below the average market price, and – in case of excess capacity – even below cost.

Duplicated reach The total number of people exposed to an ad for the second time.

Durable consumer goods Products (such as bikes) that consumers use for a relatively long period of time.

Dynamically continuous innovation Improvements to an existing product that require only minor adjustments on the part of consumers.

E-commerce A company's efforts to boost online sales by using marketing principles to guide potential buyers to its website.

E-marketing Any marketing activity using digital technologies, such as an interactive computer system as well as DVDs, instant messaging, videoconferencing and interactive store kiosks to achieve e-commerce, such as buyer analysis, pricing, distributing, promoting and positioning products and services to specific target markets over the Internet.

E-retailing The e-marketing efforts directed towards ultimate consumers, a key component of most retailers' strategies (*Electronic retailing*, o*nline retailing*).

Early adopters The second category of consumers who adopt an innovation, generally opinion leaders and role models.

Early majority The third category of consumers adopting an innovation, who are cautious in trying new products and services.

Economic factors Indicators of the economic environment, such as consumer purchasing power, inflation, interest rates, exports, unemployment and the retail price index.

Economies of scale Cost savings as a result of producing or selling a larger number of units.

Effective demand Total number of products currently sold or – in the case of durable goods – purchased by customers in the past.

Effectiveness The extent to which one succeeds in meeting the stated targets.

Efficiency The cost of the resources used, relative to the results.

Embargo A government's suspension of trade in a particular product or with a certain country for economic, political or health reasons.

Emergency goods Products purchased when the consumer urgently needs the item, such as an umbrella during a downpour.

Empathy The ability to understand the customer's problems and to see a particular situation as the prospect or customer perceives it.

Encoding The process of turning an idea into a graphic format or symbolic form.

Engel's Law Research findings named after Ernst Engel, showing how consumers change their spending habits as their incomes increase.

Environmental analysis Monitoring and evaluating the company's external environment to identify opportunities and threats.

Environmental diagnosis Evaluation of the significance of opportunities and threats disclosed by an environmental analysis.

Environmental factors External, non-controllable forces and developments that may affect a firm's market position and marketing strategy.

Environmental scanning Collecting information about relevant elements of a company's environment.

Essential products Products, such as food, for which consumer spending – as a percentage – increases at a slower rate than the consumer's income.

Ethics Someone's moral principles, values and personal standards (a deeply rooted sense of what's right or wrong) that affect his actions and decisions.

Ethnic pattern Attitudinal and behavioural characteristics of members of an ethnic group – that is a minority in a larger society – having racial, religious, linguistic, cultural or other traits in common.

Ethnocentric orientation The belief that the home country's approach to business is superior, and – as a subconscious bias – should be replicated abroad.

Evaluation Assessing the extent to which the marketing objectives are being accomplished.

Evoked set The (limited) number of brands that someone considers in making a purchase decision.

Excess capacity When actual output is less than what is achievable, occurring in production when demand for a product is less than what a company could supply.

Exchange The transfer of products, services, money or other items of value between buyer and seller.

Exchange objects Products, money or intangible items of worth (such as services, information or status) that are exchanged in a marketing transaction.

Exchange transaction A transfer of something of value between a buyer and a seller – underlying all marketing activities – so that both parties' needs are met.

Exclusive dealing Form of exclusive distribution that prohibits a reseller from carrying competing brands.

Exclusive distribution Distribution strategy in which only a single outlet – or a limited number of select dealers in a trading area – is allowed to sell the company's (specialty) products.

Expected profit method Decision rule in bidding in which a supplier tries to maximize his expected profit by estimating the profit associated with several potential bids as well as the probability of winning the contract with each of these bids.

Experience curve Decrease in variable costs per unit – based on the learning effect – as the company gains experience in producing and selling the product (*Learning curve*).

Experimental group Randomly selected group of subjects in an experiment who receive an experimental treatment in order to measure and compare the effect with the control group.

Experimental research Form of causal research in which the researcher systematically manipulates and controls an independent variable (e.g. price) and measures its effect on the dependent variable (e.g. buying behaviour), under tightly controlled conditions.

Experimental variable *Independent variable* (such as price discounts or commercials) that are systematically varied in order to measure any changes in the elements that the researcher wants to examine.

Expert research Exploratory research to tap the knowledge and opinions of people who are – often professionally – familiar with the problem under investigation (*Expert opinion* or *experience survey*).

Exploration phase Stage in new product development during which the company searches for innovative ideas.

Exploratory research Small-scale study to obtain a tentative explanation of a problem or to identify additional problems for investigation.

Export agent Intermediary that brings together sellers and buyers from different countries and gets a commission for arranging sales.

Export management company Independent firm, offering services that an in-house export department would, such as providing information, management expertise, financing and transportation (*EMC*).

Export merchant Intermediary that buys – and takes title to – products from different suppliers and then sells them abroad.

Exporting Manufacturing products in one country and selling them in another.

Expressive product characteristics Symbolic product features – such as the emotional meaning of a brand – that meet the buyer's need to express his lifestyle (e.g. status) or personality (e.g. ambition), often used as a positioning theme.

Expropriation Government takeover of a company's operations, usually without any compensation to the owners.

Extended demand The sum total of the *initial* demand plus the *additional* demand for a particular product during a period of time.

Extensive problem solving A consumer's broad and thorough analysis of information when making a major buying decision.

External environment Influences and groups originating outside the organization in the macro- and meso-environment that are *uncontrollable*, but influence its strategy and performance.

External search A consumer's information-gathering about a product or service, using personal, public, commercial or experiential sources before making a purchase decision.

External source A source of secondary data (e.g. industry sales figures) outside of the organization, such as reports sold by Nielsen or available through the Internet.

Eye camera Instrument used in a laboratory situation to record eye movements.

Factory outlet mall Non-traditional shopping centre with discount and factory outlet stores selling excess merchandise, with some offering upscale merchandise.

Factory outlet store Retail store operated by a manufacturer of a national brand to dispose of surplus stock or clearance merchandise.

Family Independent household of two or more people living together based on marriage, blood relationships, cohabitation or adoption.

Family brand Selling multiple products under the umbrella of a single brand name (*Umbrella brand*).

Family branding strategy Strategy – common in the automobile industry – to give products in the same product line a single brand name, making it easier to launch new models that benefit from the brand's reputation.

Family life-cycle The phases through which a traditional family progresses – from getting married and childbirth to the empty nest, retirement and a partner's death – each one affecting the family's needs and buying behaviour.

Fast moving consumer goods Products that consumers buy frequently and, like other *convenience products*, have a relatively low profit margin (*FMCG*).

Field experiment Experiment conducted in a realistic environment in order to capture cause-and-effect relationships.

Fixed cost A cost – such as insurance premiums – that remains stable at any production level (*Overhead costs*).

Flanker brand New item introduced under a new brand name into a product category in which the company already sells products.

Flexible break-even analysis A variation of break-even analysis that shows the cost-revenue relationships for each of a series of price alternatives for a new product, enabling the company to set a price that yields the greatest profit.

Focus group Motivation research setting in which eight to twelve people meet with a *moderator* to discuss a subject.

Follow-up Post-purchase communication with a customer to ensure that their expectations have been met.

Forward buying Customers or retailers buying more of a product than they need in order to carry them through to the next time a reduced price is being offered.

Forward integration A company acquiring another firm – such as a wholesaler, retailer or other reseller downstream in the distribution channel – to gain more control and improve efficiency.

Franchise Contractual arrangement between a parent company or franchiser and a number of franchisees who, as independent businesspeople, buy the right to own and operate – in accordance with strict guidelines – one or more units in the franchise organization to sell certain products or services under an established trade name.

Franchise organization The various companies that – within a franchise system – work together to achieve their goals.

Frequency The number of times a person is exposed to a particular medium or advertisement within a given time frame.

Frequency programme Incentive programme that rewards loyal customers for making multiple or repeat purchases (*Loyalty programme*).

Full-line forcing A manufacturer requiring retailers to carry their full product line, including slow-moving or less profitable items.

Full-service wholesaler Wholesaler who takes title and possession of the products they sell and provides a full range of services – including managerial assistance – to their customers.

Fun shopping Consumer buying behaviour focusing on an enjoyable shopping experience, in which prices are of minor importance.

Functional discount A list price reduction that a manufacturer grants to intermediaries for their handling of distribution-related tasks, such as warehousing, installation and customer service (*Trade discount*).

Galvanometer Instrument used in a laboratory situation to detect changes in the electrical resistance of the skin ('galvanic skin response') in order to measure a subject's emotions.

Games A type of sweepstakes that covers an extended period of time, requiring participants to, for example, collect numbers in bottle caps, every time they buy a product.

Gatekeeper Contact person (such as a purchasing agent or secretary) who controls the flow of information to other buying centre members.

General Electric portfolio analysis Multi-factor portfolio model in which business units are classified in a nine-block matrix based on their market attractiveness (including market growth, competition, profit margin) and competitive position (market share, brand image, customer loyalty, etc.)(*Market attractiveness-competitive position matrix*).

Generic advertising Advertising highlighting customer benefits that apply to all brands in a product category, rather than those that are unique to specific brands.

Generic brand Plainly packaged, lowest priced product, identified only by a generic class (such as 'tea') or product characteristics.

Generic competition Competition between alternative product lines (such as beer, wine and whisky) that may satisfy the same consumer need.

Generic need satisfaction The notion that a company's market and competition should be defined by overall customer experience instead of specific products or services; thus, a movie theatre competes with night clubs, restaurants and other establishments with a similar recreational function.

Generic strategy Marketing approach to gain a competitive advantage in an industry through a cost leadership, a differentiation or a focus strategy.

Geocentric orientation Management perspective that there are similarities and differences in the world that should be respected in strategy development, and that no country is superior or inferior to another.

Geodemographic segmentation Segmentation of consumers based on a combination of geographic and demographic data by clustering potential customers in neighbourhoods or zip code areas based on consumer behaviour and lifestyle data.

Geographic segmentation Segmenting business and consumer markets based on geographic criteria, such as nations, provinces, cities, neighbourhoods, market size, population density or climate in order to better tailor the marketing strategy to the preferences in various regions.

Global account management Sales force structure that coordinates product and service delivery across the globe to various subsidiaries of multinational customers.

Global brand A brand that is marketed in several countries under the same name and with similar, centrally coordinated marketing strategies.

Global localization Finding a balance between *standardization* and *adaptation* by thinking globally (providing global strategic direction by exploiting good strategies on a wider regional basis) but acting locally (adapting the strategy to local markets) (*Global marketing strategy; globalization*).

Global marketing Strategy by a global company that views the entire world as its market, focuses on *similarities* instead of differences between markets and tries to market each product in the same way – with minimal modifications – in all foreign markets. *Global marketing* may also refer to developing marketing activities around the globe, or to the *coordination* of marketing activities in various foreign markets.

Going-rate pricing Form of competition-oriented pricing in which a company tends to price at or near industry averages.

Green marketing Developing or modifying and marketing products that are environmentally safe, which may include changing the production process, packaging and promotion strategies.

Gross domestic product The market value of all products that a nation produces (*GDP*).

Gross margin Price minus cost of goods sold, or the difference between revenue and cost before accounting for certain other costs (*Gross profit margin*).

Gross rating points A measure of the effectiveness of alternative media vehicles, calculated by multiplying reach (expressed as a percentage of the total market) by frequency (*GRP*).

Growth Stage of the product life cycle in which sales grow at an increasing rate, and faster than ever (*Rapid growth stage*).

Growth strategy Strategy that aims to expand a firm's market share – even at the expense of short-term profits – through increased sales to current users or by targeting new users.

Guarantee The assurance that a product is as represented and will provide the expected performance.

Guerrilla marketing Marketing activities in which an organization traps consumers with product-related messages or other promotional content in unexpected places.

Harvest strategy Strategy to maximize short-term cash flow – at the expense of market share – by minimizing marketing investments for a dog or question mark (*Milking*).

Heavy user A consumer who uses a considerably larger amount of a particular product than the average level of consumption of all buyers of this product.

Heterogeneity Characteristic that a service varies in quality, making it difficult to consistently meet customer expectations.

Heterogeneous products Products such as clothing and cars that buyers perceive as being different from one another.

Hierarchy of needs Maslow's classification of human needs, from the most pressing (physiological needs) to the least pressing (self-actualization).

Hierarchy of objectives Ranking of goals in order of importance, reflecting the company's priorities.

High involvement The high degree of importance that a consumer perceives a product to have for him personally.

Hold strategy Investment strategy to maintain an SBU's market share, for example when defending a cash cow's current market position.

Homogeneous products Products that buyers view as identical, such as milk, sugar, bananas and metals, making price their primary choice criterion.

Horizontal marketing system A system in which companies at the same distribution channel level cooperate – and combine their production, financial or marketing resources – to get their products or services to the buyer.

Household Basic residential unit (such as spouses or roommates) in which economic production and consumption are organized and carried out.

Hybrid system Special form of multichannel distribution system in which different channel members perform complementary tasks for the same customer, such as one intermediary demonstrating new products and another one providing post-sale service.

Hypermarket Huge retail outlet that offers both supermarket and discount store shopping in one location (*Superstore*).

Hypothesis Statement about the expected relationship between two or more variables or a future development that needs to be tested or verified through research before deciding how to solve a problem or deal with the circumstances.

Ideal self concept Someone's perception and attitudes about the person they would be like if they were perfect or ideal.

Image Someone's perception of a product, brand or an organization, which – from a marketing perspective – should overrule the reality of the situation.

Image building A company's public relations efforts to gain public understanding or acceptance and to create a desired image in the eyes of the public and other groups.

Implementation The process of converting a plan into action through executing detailed marketing action plans.

Impulse goods Convenience products bought without pre-planning or careful decision-making, such as a pack of chewing gum at the store's checkout.

Impulse purchase A consumer's unplanned, spur of the moment purchase after noticing a product online or in a store.

Incentive Reward for a specific behaviour, such as discounts for customers participating in promotions.

Income elasticity of demand Relationship between an increase in the consumer's disposable income and the corresponding change in consumption (*Income sensitivity of demand*).

Independent variable Variable (a *cause*, such as competitors' prices) of which the value has an effect on the value of the dependent variable (the *result*, such as sales).

Indifferent goods Products for which a price change of one does not affect the demand for another.

Indirect channel Distribution channel in which the producer depends on at least one intermediary to get his products into the buyer's hands.

Indirect costs Costs (such as salaries) that are not directly tied to a product, but that can be allocated to it through a particular mark-up per unit (*Overhead*).

Indirect exporting A type of exporting in which a company does not deal directly with foreign buyers, but works with an independent intermediary such as an export agent.

Individual brand A unique brand name for each product in a portfolio.

Industrial advertising Advertising aimed at those who buy or influence the purchase of industrial goods and services.

Inferior product Products – characterized by a negative income elasticity – for which expenditure decreases as consumer income increases.

Influencer DMU member who affects the purchase decision by helping to define the technical specifications or by providing information for evaluating the options.

Infomercial An extended television commercial for a single product presented in a television show format.

Informative advertising Advertising developed to pass on factual and verifiable information about a product or how it is used, appealing to rational rather than emotional motives (*Informational advertising*).

Initial demand Demand from first-time buyers who have never purchased the product before.

Initiator Role in the DMU of someone who sets off the buying process by being the first one to recognize that the company needs to make a particular purchase.

Innovation A creation resulting from study and experimentation, leading to the introduction of something new.

Innovators The first category of consumer adopting an innovation: generally young, adventurous risk-takers (*Consumption pioneers*).

Inseparability Characteristic that services are produced and received at the same time and cannot be separated from the service provider.

Inside sales force Professional sales performed remotely and not face-to-face with the customer to support the traditional field sales force (*Remote sales; Virtual sales*).

Institutional advertising A type of advertising designed to influence attitudes of stakeholders, rather than to sell products.

In-store test Field experiment (e.g. A.C. Nielsen's *Controlled Store Test*) involving similar retail stores – split up into an *experimental* and a *control group* – in which a researcher measures consumer acceptance of new packaging, displays or another *treatment variable* and the effect on turnover or another *dependent* *variable* by comparing sales volume of the two groups of stores.

Instrumental product characteristics Product features (such as the design or technology used) that – since they satisfy the buyer's functional needs – are sometimes used in the positioning strategy. Functional or technical features of a product or service.

Intangible Part of a product (or service) that potential buyers cannot physically examine, touch or taste before making a purchase decision.

Integrated communication The strategic integration of several simultaneously used media and other elements of the communication mix that reinforce each other, forming a comprehensive, consistent message to a targeted audience (*Integrated marketing communications; IMC*).

Integrated direct marketing A marketing campaign involving several media, such as direct mail, a website, a toll-free phone number and telemarketing, all used simultaneously.

Intellectual property rights Legal agreement that gives the holder or creator exclusive rights and protection of e.g. copyrights or patents, and helps prevent pirated versions of software, books and music being sold in other countries.

Intensive distribution Distribution strategy in which a (convenience) product is sold in as many outlets as possible, maximizing impulse buying of the product.

Interactive marketing Buyer-seller communication system over the Internet in which a buyer specifies what product he is interested in (thus controlling the information that he wants to receive), and the seller immediately sends that information.

Interactive media Media – such as direct mail, telephone marketing and direct response television advertising – that allow for two-way communication between the firm and the buyer and provide a measurable response.

Intermediary Independent organizations or individuals – functioning as exporters, importers, agents, wholesalers and retailers – that operate between the producer and consumer in a channel of distribution (*Middleman, reseller*); Middleman, such as a distributor, marketing research or logistics company that operates as a link between producer and consumers and provides services to facilitate transactions.

Internal communication Communication inside a company, often designed to display the corporate identity or personality to employees in order to influence their attitudes and behaviour.

Internal environment A company's functional areas or departments – including the organizational structure and corporate culture – and its available resources (financial, commercial, technical, natural and human) that it may use to achieve its objectives.

Internal marketing Marketing activities directed at individuals or departments within the organization to encourage cooperation and ensure that all co-workers are well trained and motivated to satisfy customers.

Internal search A consumer subconsciously scanning their memory to see what they already know about a product or service.

Internal source Secondary data (e.g. sales analyses) on file within the researcher's own company (e.g. the sales department).

International marketing Marketing activities directed at customers outside of the domestic market, while the firm primarily focuses on the domestic market.

Intranet Internal communications network that links the company's employees, departments and databases through Internet technology.

Introduction stage First stage of the product life cycle, in which most consumers are not even aware of the product and its potential uses.

Introductory price The price at which a company introduces a new product.

Inventory control Trying to maintain the lowest level of inventory that will still enable the firm to meet customer needs and avoid incurring additional costs for carrying excess stock.

Investment strategy Strategy to increase or maintain a business unit's market share or to create a more balanced portfolio. Four options are to build, hold, harvest or divest.

ISO 9000 standard Certification for production and service facilities – as determined by the International Organization for Standardization – enabling a company to meet high quality standards.

Joint venture Alliance in which a company entering a new market pools its resources with those of a local firm to form a new, separate firm in which they share ownership, risks, control and profits.

Just-in-time Inventory management system that limits the amount of inventory a company needs to hold by relying instead on suppliers' fast, on-time delivery of materials and parts in the exact quantities that are needed for production (*JIT, quick-response, QR*).

Key account A large account that receives special treatment from a vendor's marketing or sales executives.

Key account management Management of a company's most important customers (*Major* or *national account management*).

Key account manager The person responsible for coordinating the company's sales efforts directed toward a major retail account so that this customer can limit their interaction with the company's sales people in different territories.

Kinked supply curve An individual supplier's perspective of a kinked demand curve, with the kink at the current market price caused by the inflexibility of price in an oligopoly.

Label Integral part of the package that identifies the product's name, brand, manufacturer, net contents, country of origin, ingredients and nutritional values.

Laboratory experiment Experiment in which respondents are asked to perform a particular activity in an artificial setting, with the researcher controlling all relevant variables and manipulating others that relate to the marketing decision to be made.

Laggards The sixth and last category of consumers who adopt an innovation, often older, low-income and 'old-fashioned' consumers.

Late majority The fourth category of consumers adopting an innovation, who are usually sceptical of new products.

Lavidge-Steiner model Expanded version of the AIDA model that identifies six stages in the buyers' adoption process: awareness, knowledge, liking, preference, conviction and purchase (*Hierarchy-of-effects model*).

Lead The identification of a person or company that may be a potential buyer.

Learning How somebody – through information processing, reasoning and practice – gains knowledge and may change their attitude or behaviour.

Licencing Agreement in which the (international) company gives another firm (the licensee) the right to produce and market its products in return for a fee or royalties.

Lifestyle A way of living, characterized by someone's activities, interests and opinions.

Lifestyle centre A combination of an outdoor urban shopping area and a neighbourhood park landscaped with fountains, plazas, park benches and stages for live concerts, featuring upscale stores, restaurants and theatres as well as luxury condominiums, townhouses and office parks.

Lifestyle segmentation Market segmentation based on how groups of people – given their underlying values, attitudes, opinions and behaviour patterns – conduct their lives.

Lifetime value Present value of the profit a company anticipates making from an individual customer who buys the company's products over an average lifetime.

Light user Consumer who uses significantly less of a particular product in a certain time period than the average level of consumption of all buyers of that product.

Limited-line store Retail store that offers an extensive assortment of models within one product line or (such as Ikea) a few related lines and targets price-conscious consumers.

Limited problem solving The restricted effort and time spent by a consumer when buying products that he is already familiar with.

Limited-service merchant wholesaler Wholesaler – such as a drop shipper, truck wholesaler or cash-and-carry wholesaler – who takes title to the merchandise they sell, but performs only a limited number of functions for their customers.

Line extension Using the existing brand name for new product items in the same product line, such as introducing new flavours, ingredients or package sizes.

Line-filling Expanding the product line by adding more items within the existing range of products and prices.

List management Selling mailing lists, evaluating past direct marketing campaigns to determine how the available information can be used more effectively in future communications with customers, and updating the list database of customers in order to decrease costs per order.

Lobbying Influencing government officials to create legislation to enact, defeat or change certain laws, or to conduct other activities to protect a company's interests; The process of trying to influence decisions made by government officials, such as legislators or members of regulatory agencies.

Logistics management A company's management of materials and of the physical distribution of its products to the customers.

Loss leader Product sold at a lower than usual markup in order to increase store traffic.

Low-involvement The low degree of importance that a consumer perceives an inexpensive, frequently purchased product to have for themself.

Low margin retailing strategy Retailing strategy that offers products at discount prices and a low level of customer service, targeting a target market of price-conscious consumers, and resulting in low profit margins for the retailer.

Luxury products Products with a high income elasticity of demand, meaning that the proportion of income spent on these luxury products increases as consumer income rises.

Macroenvironmental factors Outside forces (e.g. the economic climate) that a firm can neither control nor influence, but do affect its strategies and performance.

Macromarketing Role of the marketing system in distributing goods and services to society to ensure that its scarce resources will satisfy people's needs as effectively as possible.

Make-or-buy The choice between developing a product internally or obtaining an established product by acquiring an existing company.

Management by objectives A sales management approach in which sales managers and sales people jointly develop strategies and set performance goals for reaching those goals, which are then used to evaluate each salesperson's performance (*MBO*).

Management contracting Form of licencing management and organizational expertise in the form of services, such as in the hospitality industry.

Manufacturer brand Brand owned by the product's maker, sold and advertised nationwide (*National brand*).

Manufacturer-owned wholesaler Wholesaling operation – such as a *sales branch* or *sales office* – set up by a manufacturer to maintain total control over how his products are sold.

Manufacturer's agent Independent agent who represents several manufacturers and sells related, but non-competing product lines for a commission on the price (over which he has no authority) of each product sold (*Manufacturer's representative*).

Manufacturer's suggested retail price The price – recommended by the manufacturer – that retailers may choose to sell a product for (*MSRP*).

Margin The difference between the total unit costs for an item and the selling price.

Margin generator A less price sensitive product to which retailers – using mark-up pricing – may add a large profit margin.

Margin stability Situation in which intermediaries enjoy consistent profit margins on products over time.

Marginal cost The net change in total cost that results from manufacturing and marketing one additional unit.

Mark-up The difference between the merchandise cost and the retail price of a product, usually expressed as a percentage of the retail price.

Mark-up pricing Pricing a product by calculating the per-unit cost of manufacturing or purchasing it, and then adding a mark-up percentage to cover its selling costs and profit.

Market From a marketing perspective: customers – a group of potential buyers or organizations with needs and wants that a company can satisfy by providing certain products or services. The term *market* may also refer to the quantity of goods sold in a specific period.

Market arena A market, broadly defined, in which companies compete – regardless of the industry in which they operate – that satisfy the same need or whose products fulfill the same function.

Market development strategy Identifying new (e.g. demographic or export) markets, or new uses for current products (as in yoghurt garlic sauce).

Market leader A company holding the largest share of a certain market segment, thanks to economies of scale in production, promotion and distribution.

Market mechanism The role of a free market – not distorted by government subsidies – in allocating resources in a society and decisions about which quantities of products and services will be produced and distributed.

Market orientation Business philosophy in which companies consider not only customers, but also intermediaries and competitors in making decisions at all levels of the organization.

Market-pull Strategy in which changing customer needs or preferences trigger a search for technological innovation that leads to better products (*Demand-pull*).

Market research plan Description of the methods and techniques that will be used to ensure that the research is carried out in an objective and unbiased manner.

Market segment Group of customers with distinct needs, wants and other common characteristics that may be approached with a tailored marketing strategy (*Segment*).

Market segmentation Dividing the total heterogeneous market for a product – based on demographic, geographic, psychographic or behavioural criteria – into smaller, homogeneous market segments of buyers who have similar needs and wants or respond in the same way to a distinct marketing strategy (*Segmentation*).

Market share The percentage of the total market or of total industry sales of a product held by a company.

Market share objective The company's goal to increase or maintain its share of a market.

Market stretching Extending a product's life cycle in the PLC's maturity stage by tapping new markets or through product improvements.

Marketing Developing, pricing, promoting and distributing products, services or ideas that are tailored to the market; this process includes all activities that create value and systematically lead to increased sales or another desired response, establish a good reputation and ongoing relationships with customers, so that all stakeholders achieve their objectives.

Marketing audit A systematic, critical and impartial review and appraisal of the total marketing operation.

Marketing concept A market-driven management mindset and business practice of 'making what customers want', based on the company's fundamental goal of satisfying customer needs while meeting its objectives.

Marketing control A four-step process of 1) setting specific marketing goals, 2) measuring progress toward realizing these goals, 3) comparing the actual results with the goals and 4) taking corrective action, when necessary.

Marketing Decision Support System Coordinated set of data, tools and techniques, complemented by analysis and interactive software that allows managers to access MIS data and conduct their own analyses (*MDSS*).

Marketing ethics A marketer's principles and ethical standards that guide his marketing decisions and behaviour.

Marketing information system Combination of people, equipment and procedures to collect, sort, analyze, evaluate and communicate relevant and timely information to marketing decision makers (*MIS*).

Marketing intelligence system System through which publicly available information about consumers, competitors and developments in the marketing environment is gathered, processed and made available as an input into the MIS.

Marketing logistics Broad range of activities related to the delivery of a company's products, such as order processing, warehousing, materials handling, inventory control and transportation (*Logistics, physical distribution*).

Marketing management The analysis, planning, implementation and constant evaluation of all activities to ensure that a company's products and services are tailored to the needs and wants of potential customers.

Marketing manager Executive responsible for analyzing, planning, implementing and controlling the company's marketing activities (such as customer service and social media use) and for coordinating these with other departments' marketing-related activities (such as product repair, shipping and warehousing).

Marketing mix Combination of four controllable marketing variables – product, promotion, price and place (or distribution) – developed to appeal to a particular target market.

Marketing myopia A shortsighted management's tendency to narrowly define its business in terms of its products instead of broader benefits that customers seek, often resulting in missed marketing opportunities.

Marketing objective A company's intended results from its marketing efforts.

Marketing organization Structure for making and implementing decisions about the marketing mix, for example through a product management system.

Marketing plan Managerial document that analyzes the marketing situation – including opportunities and threats – and specifies how the organization intends to use its resources and marketing tools to implement the marketing strategy and achieve its formulated objectives for a product line, brand or the entire business.

Marketing proposition A carefully tailored marketing mix to target a specific market segment upon market entry.

Marketing research The systematic and objective gathering, analyzing and interpreting of data that help marketers explore opportunities and make better marketing decisions.

Marketing research process Systematic approach to developing and executing marketing research, which includes defining the problem and research objectives, the research plan, secondary data and exploratory research, refining the research design, primary data collection and, finally, analyzing, interpreting and presenting the research results.

Marketing strategy Part of the business strategy that describes how the company – within its business definition – intends to achieve its long-term marketing objectives, including implications for deciding on target markets, marketing mix variables and positioning.

Marketing tactics Blueprint for action – based on the marketing mix – detailing which measures must be taken when, to meet the short-term objectives.

Mass customization The use of flexible computer-aided manufacturing systems allowing marketers to offer individually tailored products to a large number of customers cost-effectively.

Mass media Media channels such as television or print media that are able to reach a large target audience.

Materials handling The movement of inventory (product, parts or raw materials) into, within and out of the warehouse or between warehouses and manufacturing facilities.

Materials management Management of activities to expedite the flow of raw materials and related information from suppliers to the factory for a streamlined production process.

Maturity Stage of the product life cycle in which sales peak and prices, along with profits, keep falling.

Me-too pricing Competition-oriented pricing strategy in which companies with homogeneous products deliberately price 'at market'.

Me-too product Imitation version of a successful product, launched by a competitor.

Media Television, radio, newspapers, magazines, direct mail advertising, billboards and other mass media or communication channels through which an advertiser gets their message across to their target audience.

Media plan Part of the advertising plan that defines the media objectives and presents the strategy to achieve them, including details about the budget, the optimal media mix and media scheduling.

Media planner Person responsible for getting the message to the target audience in an optimal and cost-effective way through the appropriate media.

Media scheduling Plan that specifies the timing and sequence for the advertisements of a campaign, as influenced by purchase frequency, sales pattern and competition.

Media types Visual media (newspapers, magazines, direct mail, outdoors), auditory media (radio) or audiovisual medial (TV, Internet).

Medium reach The number of people who encounter or have been exposed to the medium, often expressed as a percentage of the total number of people that could have been reached.

Membership reference group Reference group in which a consumer participates, influencing their attitudes and purchase decisions.

Merchandise mix Total set of all product lines and products that a retailer offers for sale.

Merchandiser Sales representative responsible for arranging promotional materials and in-store displays for retailers.

Merchant wholesaler Independently owned firm that purchases goods from manufacturers for resale to other channel members they do business with.

Merger Combination of two or more organizations for the purpose of pooling resources.

Mesoenvironmental factors The firm's immediate external environment in which it interacts with customers, suppliers, intermediaries, competitors and public groups that, while uncontrollable, can be influenced.

Mesomarketing All activities developed by collaborating organizations within a *supply chain* or *sector* to match supply and demand, meet a certain need and realize their shared marketing objectives.

Microenvironmental factors Departments (e.g. production) and resources (e.g. financial means) that are part of the organization, but outside of the marketing department (*Internal environmental factors*).

Micromarketing The marketing activities of an individual organization.

Middlemen Independent companies in the supply chain that link producers and ultimate consumers (or industrial users), such as wholesalers, retailers and other resellers (*Intermediaries*).

Mission A company's overall purpose, basic values and distinctive competencies to guide its decision-making in serving customers and answering the fundamental question: 'What business are we in?'

Mission statement Formal description of a company's mission to direct its growth, usually listing its products or services, target markets, *core competencies* and the technologies it should master.

Missionary salesperson Manufacturer's representative who promotes goodwill by providing detailed product information and assisting the company's customers in selling to their own customers (*Detail person, detail rep*).

Modified re-buy Re-evaluation of available options by a (dissatisfied) company that has bought the product before, but now modified the product specifications or intends to assess new suppliers.

Monopolistic competition The most common market form, in which firms compete with products that are similar – but not identical – and market entry is fairly easy.

Monopoly Regional or domestic market in which there is only one organization (such as a utility company) to provide a particular service or product, often with government-imposed pricing guidelines.

Motivation Someone's reasons (needs, wants, goals, forces, etc.) to act in a particular way (*Motive*).

Motivation research *Qualitative* research conducted to gain insight into consumers' (subconscious) motives, mindset and behaviour, for example when purchasing products.

Multichannel distribution system The use of two or more distribution channels by a seller in order to expand market coverage, lower marketing costs and offer greater opportunities for customization, all contributing to higher sales.

Multinational marketing Conducting marketing activities in foreign markets – that account for more than half of sales and profits – by a multinational company that views the world as a set of unique countries, and markets in each one as a local market-oriented firm would.

Multiple sourcing System through which a company buys from several suppliers in order to reduce its costs and dependency on any one supplier.

Mystery shopper Researcher posing as a normal customer, gathering observational data about store appearance and cleanliness, types of products displayed, quality of service and employees' interaction with customers.

Need A deficiency that a consumer experiences when his physical or emotional balance is disturbed, prompting him to fill this void.

Need competition Rivalry between different kinds of needs on which the consumer is willing to spend money (e.g. exotic cruise versus remodelling the home).

Need-satisfaction presentation Flexible and tailored presentation to address the specific needs and interests of the prospect.

Neighbourhood shopping centre The smallest type of shopping centre with a supermarket to provide convenient shopping for consumers who live within a few minutes' commute (*Strip centre*).

Network marketing A special form of direct selling in which a 'master distributor' recruits independent agents, resells the company's merchandise to these distributors and makes a commission on their sales to consumers (*Multilevel marketing*).

New product strategy Sequence of activities to transform product ideas into marketable products and linking this process with the goals of the marketing department, business unit and corporation.

New task Buying situation in which the company is a first-time buyer of a product, requiring more information and often an extended buying centre to reduce the risk.

Niche strategy A company that – as a 'nicher' – concentrates on only one market segment that is of minor interest to major rivals, hoping to avoid a competitive fight.

Noise Any distraction reducing the clarity and effectiveness of the communication.

Non-commercial advertising Advertising to create a positive attitude toward certain – often ideological – matters by non-profit organizations such as government agencies, civic groups, charitable institutions and political organizations.

Non-cumulative quantity discount Price reduction based on the size of an individual purchase order.

Non-durable consumer products Consumer packaged goods (for example, shampoo) or products with a life cycle of less than three years, such as clothes.

Non-monetary price The cost to a customer (other than money) to acquire the product, such as the distance travelled and time spent on shopping, as well as the risk that the product will not provide the expected benefits.

Non-price competition Marketing strategy emphasizing benefits other than a low price, such as unique product features, a better warranty or outstanding customer service.

Non-profit marketing Strategy of organizations with charitable or other public service goals that, without seeking profits, strive to satisfy customers' needs and maintain market share (*not-for-profit marketing*).

Non-response Failure to obtain information from some elements of the population that were selected for the sample because of their incorrect addresses, unwillingness to participate or inability to answer certain questions, undermining the *representativeness* of the survey and possibly the *reliability* of the research results.

Non-store retailing Any method a company uses to create an exchange without requiring a customer to visit a store, such as online sales.

Objective The results the organization wants to achieve; in order to motivate and provide guidelines to managers, objectives should be specific, measurable, attainable, realistic and time-bound.

Observation Method of data collection through which someone's behaviour is recorded, without questioning them and usually without them even being aware of the process.

Odd pricing Strategy of setting prices at odd numbers just below round numbers to bring about a favourable psychological response from the customer (*Odd-even pricing*).

Off-price retailer Stores that purchase manufacturers' overruns, returns, seconds and off-season products for resale to consumers at about half the price of department stores.

Oligopoly Industry structure in which only a few companies control most of the market.

One-to-one marketing Customized marketing strategy to create long-term relationships with individual customers.

Online auction company Online auction (with a site such as eBay) that offers products – often surplus goods in large quantities at wholesale (*Virtual auction*).

Online database Computerized files of information available from online commercial sources or elsewhere through the Internet, accessed via PC, laptop, tablet or other mobile devices.

Online marketing Using an interactive computer system to connect sellers and buyers electronically (*Internet marketing*).

Open-ended question Survey question that a respondent can answer as they wish, with their answer recorded word for word.

Opinion leader A person who influences other people's views and buying behaviour or to whom others turn for information and advice.

Opportunities External events or trends that a company could possibly exploit to its advantage.

Opt-in email Email messages for which a customer has granted a marketer permission to send them on certain topics.

Order getter Traditional salesperson who contacts existing and potential customers to give them relevant information, persuade them to buy and close the sale.

Order processing Activities taking place between the time a customer's purchase order is received and the time a product has shipped.

Order taker Salesperson who processes routine orders through the Internet or over the phone and does not engage in creative selling or persuasion.

Organization Framework through which employees are assigned to certain jobs and their activities coordinated in order to execute plans and realize the objectives.

Organizational buying behaviour Behaviour associated with a group of people purchasing on behalf of an organization.

Outside sales force Salespeople who go out into the field to meet with potential customers face-to-face.

Outsourcing Controversial strategy in which a company contracts manufacturing or another activity, such as providing customer-service help lines, in nations with less expensive supplies and labour.

Overhead costs Costs remaining stable regardless of any variation in production level.

Package Wrapper or container for a product, used to protect, promote, transport and identify the product.

Packaging One of the most noticeable product attributes that influence the buyer's perception and brand choice.

Packaging functions Combination of communication and commercial objectives, such as providing product information, creating an image, product differentiation and stimulating consumption.

Party plan A retailing strategy in which a direct seller, such as Tupperware, attends a get-together at a host customer's home to demonstrate products and take orders.

Penetration price strategy The introduction of a new product at a very low price to speed up market acceptance and discourage potential competitors.

Penetration strategy Boosting market share by selling more of the firm's existing products to current customers (e.g. through promoting new uses) or by attracting new customers within the current target market (*market penetration strategy*).

Perceived value pricing A price-setting strategy based on the buyer's perception of value (*Value-based pricing*).

Perception The process whereby people collect (through any of their five senses), organize and personally interpret information to give meaning to the world around them.

Perceptual map A graph showing how (potential) customers perceive competing brands in a product category along two or more dimensions (e.g. cheap/inexpensive and progressive/conservative), usually important product attributes (*Product positioning map*).

Peripheral assortment Products – about 80 per cent of the retailer's merchandise mix – with a low turnover rate, but high profit margin.

Perishability Characteristic that a service cannot be stored for future use and loses its value if not used when available.

Personal interview Face-to-face interview between the market research company's interviewer and the respondent.

Personal selling A salesperson identifying prospective customers, assessing their needs, presenting product information face-to-face, persuading the customer to make a purchase and following up to maintain the relationship.

Personality An individual's experiences and psychological characteristics that make them unique, leading to a consistent pattern of responses in handling perceived reality.

Personality characteristics Someone's tendency to respond in a consistent and characteristic (e.g. ambitious or aggressive) way to stimuli from their environment as a way of coping with perceived reality.

Physical distribution management Management that focuses on planning and coordinating the warehousing, inventory control and transportation of the finished product from the producer to resellers and customers.

Physical factors Environmental or ecological factors that managers consider when deciding about using scarce natural resources or limiting noise, air, water and soil pollution.

Pilot survey Preliminary study to test a questionnaire before proceeding with a full-scale market research investigation.

Pioneer advertising Collective advertising used to stimulate interest or demand for a product in the introduction stage of its life cycle.

Place utility The added value by making a product available wherever consumers want it.

Planned shopping centre Group of retail stores designed, coordinated and marketed – with a balanced tenancy – to shoppers in a geographic trade area in order to satisfy specific customers' needs.

Point-of-purchase advertising In-store advertising and promotional materials such as wall posters, signs and displays.

Political-legal factors Government policies, laws and regulations that affect marketing practice.

Political stability The extent to which a country's government is expected to remain strong and unchallenged, ensuring an orderly succession of political power.

Population All individuals with the characteristics in which the researcher is interested (e.g. all iPhone 5 owners in the UK) and therefore are part of the group that is studied.

Portfolio analysis Evaluation and comparison of an organization's SBUs, used to allocate corporate resources and guide strategic planning.

Positioning Creating a clear, powerful and consistent image for the company's products – relative to those of competitors – that should occupy a prominent position in the customer's mind.

Posttest An evaluation of the effectiveness of advertising copy after it has been published to measure the communication effect.

Potential demand The number of products *over and above* current sales that suppliers could sell between them, assuming they have an optimal marketing mix.

Potential market Estimate of a product's maximum possible sales in the entire market if all suppliers would have an optimal marketing strategy; in other words, the effective demand plus the potential demand (*Market potential*).

Power centre Shopping centre near a regional mall without a traditional anchor department store, but with several category killers and off-price stores.

PR manager A dedicated person who represents his company on committees and press conferences, trying to build mutual trust and understanding with external stakeholders.

Preapproach Collecting and analyzing background information about a potential buyer before approaching him.

Predatory pricing Trying to drive out a competitor by temporarily pricing at such a low level that the rival can't match the price cut and still profit.

Premium Item offered at no cost or at a considerable saving over the retail price with the purchase of another product.

Premium brand Manufacturer owned, widely available brand with the highest perceived quality and price.

Presentation One of the Ps in the retailing mix – which includes the store's ambience and which is key in attracting the target market and defining the store image.

Prestige buyer Buyer who is willing to pay high prices for high quality products and services, from which he derives status.

Prestige price Artificially high price level for a product to convey prestige or a quality image.

Prestige product Product positioned and perceived as a high quality item, justifying a high price based on its added value to status-conscious buyers (*Status product*).

Pretest An evaluation of the effectiveness of a particular advertisement – or an element of the message – before it has been published.

Price A product's exchange value, expressed in terms of how much money the buyer is willing to pay in return for the desired product.

Price acceptance Extent to which buyers consider the price charged for a product reasonable.

Price awareness Consumer knowledge about the price of the product or service they consider buying and of the alternatives.

Price differentiation Demand-oriented pricing strategy in which a product is offered at different prices that do not reflect proportional cost differences in, for example, time of delivery, location or product features (*Differential* or *differentiated pricing*).

Price discrimination Charging different buyers different prices for the exact same quantity and quality of product or services.

Price elastic demand Demand that increases as the price of a product goes down, and decreases as the price goes up.

Price elasticity of demand The extent to which customers in a particular market are sensitive to price changes.

Price escalation A substantial increase in prices of products offered in foreign markets due to a cost-plus approach involving costs such as shipping, tariffs, exporter and importer margins.

Price follower A company that matches any price change made by the price leader in the industry.

Price gap The difference between the price points in a *price lining* strategy, which should be spaced far enough for consumers to note differences among the product versions.

Price inelastic demand Situation in which a price change has no effect on the quantity bought, meaning that a price cut will lead to a decrease in revenue.

Price leader The company that, in a competitive market, is usually the first one to change the price.

Price limit The maximum and minimum amounts of money for which a product can be sold.

Price lining Offering a product line with numerous items (e.g. clothes) at a limited number of prices, called price points.

Price mechanism Force in the economic system that typically sends the price up when demand is greater than supply, and down when supply is greater than demand.

Price pack deal Promotion that offers a brand at less than the regular price, or offers buyers an extra quantity ('Now 25% more') through the package itself (*Cents-off deal*).

Price perception How customers experience or view a product's price, including whether it is too high or low.

Price/quality ratio Measure to assess whether a product offers value for money.

Price rigidity Situation in an oligopolistic market in which companies follow a price decrease by a competitor, but not necessarily a price increase, resulting in a kinked demand curve.

Price sensitivity The extent to which consumers respond to a small price change.

Price-setting The art of 'translating' the product's value in the eyes of the customer into the amount of money he is willing to pay.

Price skimming Introducing a new product at an artificially high price that the market will not sustain in the long run.

Price stability Situation in which the prices in an industry or economy remain steady over time.

Price threshold The highest and lowest prices that buyers are willing to pay for a particular product or service; it may also refer to the minimum order amount at which free shipping or a quantity discount applies.

Price war Intense market competition in which competitors – in successive rounds of price cuts – fight for market share.

Pricing objective Specific pricing goal derived from marketing objectives, often stated in terms of desired revenues or market share.

Pricing policy Strategy to determine the price that a company will charge for its products and services, which has a major impact on its sales volume and profits.

Pricing strategy Part of the marketing strategy that provides the framework within which the company translates its pricing objectives into a market price.

Primary data Data collected through 'field research' for the research study at hand.

Primary demand The total demand for a new product type that the pioneering firm can beneficially stimulate by convincing the target market to use the type of product, rather than its own brand.

Primary group Group – such as immediate family or co-workers – with whom someone interacts frequently and informally.

Print advertising An advertisement on printed paper such as in a newspaper, magazine, newsletters or fliers.

Private label Brand exclusively produced for a chain store or voluntary chain and priced lower than other brands.

Private tendering Competitive bidding process in which a limited number of favoured suppliers are invited to take part in a tendering procedure.

Product A combination of tangible and intangible characteristics that enable an object or service to satisfy a customer need.

Product adaptation Modifying a product or service to meet foreign (language) requirements, laws, consumer needs and preferences, without changing the promotion strategy.

Product advertising Advertising to make consumers aware of their brands, goods or services and to inform them of new or improved products (*Manufacturers' advertising*).

Product attributes A mix of tangible and intangible product features, functions and benefits that affect customers' brand choice.

Product class Group of products that are homogeneous or perceived as substitutes for each other in terms of meeting a consumer need.

Product competition Competition between different types of products within a particular product category (such as between lager, malt and bock beer).

Product concept Management orientation that focuses on improving product quality, while regarding marketing as unnecessary and assuming that 'a good product will sell itself'.

Product design The form or structure of a product.

Product development process The sequence of activities a company uses to transform product ideas into marketable products and services.

Product development strategy Growth strategy (in the product-market expansion matrix) in which the firm introduces a new – or substantially modified – product to reach new buyers in the currently serviced market.

Product differentiation *In the context of a product range*: Offering several products that differ in style, quality, price or another product attribute, primarily to attract buyers who are looking for variation (*Differentiation*).

Product differentiation *In the context of a product mix*: Offering various products that differ in styling, quality, price or other features from the company's other offerings in order to appeal to buyers looking for variety (*Differentiation*).

Product features Specific design characteristics that enable a product to perform certain tasks.

Product information Legally required data on a package, including storage instructions and expiration date.

Product innovation A new product type that is fundamentally new to both company and consumers.

Product invention Creating a completely new product (or drastically changing an existing one) for a foreign market, to take advantage of a marketing opportunity.

Product item A product type listed as a distinct offering with an article number in the company's catalogue or on its website.

Product life cycle Graphic visualization of the stages that a new product passes through over time – from birth to death – in the marketplace (*PLC*).

Product line Group of closely related items in the company's product mix that meet the same needs, appeal to the same types of customers or use the same distribution channels.

Product line depth The number of items (brands, types, models, sizes) in a product line.

Product line extension Adding a (closely) related product to the current product line – in order to satisfy a different customer need – through a trading-up, trading-down, line filling or brand extension strategy.

Product line pricing Pricing products in the company's product assortment that are consumption-related (such as wine and cheese) or complementary in their use (computer hardware and software) in relation to one another.

Product manager Marketer who develops and implements the strategic and annual plans for a particular product or product line.

Product-market combination One of the units in which the organization is split up for implementing its strategic decisions to focus – with specific products – on groups of prospects with particular needs.

Product-market-technology combination A business unit's strategic choice of products marketed, customers served and technologies utilized to satisfy market needs.

Product mix The collection of products that a manufacturer offers, including its product lines, product types and brands; also referred to as *product assortment* by resellers.

Product mix consistency The extent of similarity between the products a company offers.

Product mix length The total number of items that a company sells.

Product mix pricing strategy Pricing the company's products in its product lines or assortment so as to maximize profits on the total product mix.

Product mix width The number of product lines that a company sells: the more product lines, the wider the product mix.

Product modification A change to one of the tangible or intangible elements of an existing product.

Product quality The combined features of a product that affect its ability to meet the customers' wants and needs.

Product recall Efforts to have defective or contaminated products returned to the company that sold them.

Product sales force structure Sales force structure in which a separate sales force or salesperson is used for each product line, brand or product.

Product type Individual product (e.g. Gillette's Fusion razor) that – because of certain product attributes – differs from other types (Gillette Mach3) of the same product.

Production concept Business philosophy that emphasizes an efficient production process designed to maximize product output and reduce cost, often at the expense of meeting marketplace needs.

Professional advertising Advertising targeted at licenced or accredited individuals, such as doctors, lawyers or accountants.

Profit equation Mathematical formula that demonstrates the relationship between unit price, quantity sold, total cost and profit.

Profit margin Measure of how much out of each euro of sales a company keeps in earnings, expressed as a percentage.

Projective technique Research technique in which the subject is shown a photograph, drawing, story or a list of words and asked to react, giving the researcher insight into his personality, values, needs and (buying) motives without his realizing it (*Indirect questioning technique*).

Promotion adaptation International marketing strategy in which the basic product remains the same, while the promotion campaign emphasis is changed.

Promotional allowance Incentive from the manufacturer to reward resellers for promoting products through displays, advertising and other activities (*Trade allowance*).

Prospecting Developing a list of potential customers from online data bases, company sales records and responses to ads or websites.

Protectionism A policy of legal controls protecting domestic companies from foreign competition in order to help domestic firms, save jobs, promote national industrial development and limit economic dependency on other countries.

Prototype The first concrete test model of a product able to perform all of the technical functions.

Psychographic market segmentation Dividing markets into segments based on consumers' lifestyles, attitudes, interests and personality characteristics.

Psychographics Analysis of people's lifestyles to identify the motives for buying and using certain products and services.

Psychological pricing Demand-oriented pricing in which consideration is given to the buyers' perception of a price (as in a *prestige price* and *odd pricing*).

Public affairs A strategic management function concerned with the relationship between the organization and its external environment, involving the analysis of societal developments, political decision-making and public opinion affecting the company.

Public group Individuals, companies, the government, investors and other groups that may influence – and are affected by – how a firm achieves its objectives.

Public information Information which is free and accessible to the public.

Public relations Activities to promote mutual understanding between the organization and its target audiences.

Public relations plan Detailed plan that outlines the strategy to achieve the company's PR objectives.

Public relations tasks A company's carefully planned activities to create a positive image of the organization and its strategy and to improve the relationship with its publics (such as customers, employees, stockholders, banks, the media and government).

Public service advertising Advertising donated by the advertising industry to promote activities for social good.

Public tendering Competitive bidding by the government, which requests sealed bids to get the best price for large projects.

Publicity Unpaid communications about the company, its products or services that are broadcast or published.

Pull strategy Strategy through which a manufacturer targets ultimate consumers directly – over the heads of the middlemen – through advertising and social media to stimulate consumer demand and encourage buyers to ask for its product at the retail level.

Pupillometer Instrument used in a laboratory situation to measure changes in the size of the eye's pupil.

Purchasing motivation Driving force behind a person's buying decisions, rooted in a negative (e.g. solving problems) or positive (e.g. sensory fulfillment) stimulus.

Pure-click Internet-only retailer that only conducts business online, but is better able to develop a tailored marketing strategy for its target markets than traditional bricks-and-mortar firms (*Click-only firm*, *dot-com*).

Pure competition A market in which there are so many buyers and sellers of homogeneous products that none of them is powerful enough to influence price, which is set by the forces of supply and demand.

Push strategy Pushing a product down the distribution channel by relying on personal selling and offering attractive trade discounts and other purchasing incentives to intermediaries.

Put-out pricing A strong market leader's attempt to force smaller competitors with less financial stamina out of the market by drastically lowering their price.

Pyramid scheme Illegal network in which the initial distributors profit by selling merchandise to other distributors, with most of the products never reaching the ultimate consumer.

Qualitative research Flexible, small-scale study seeking in-depth, open-ended responses, of which the results are indications that cannot be generalized or quantified.

Quality management Analysis, planning, implementation and control of all activities that consistently improve the technical quality of the firm's production process and products.

Quantitative research Marketing research with an emphasis on data that can be statistically analyzed to verify a hypothesis and develop scientifically meaningful, numerical conclusions.

Quantity discount Price reductions that buyers receive for large-volume orders.

Question mark SBU with a low market share in a fast-growing market. Because of its negative cash flow, marketers must decide whether to invest in this SBU in order to increase its market share (*Problem child*).

Quick Response Just-in-time method used in retailing by arranging for suppliers to provide retailers with merchandise by restocking according to current sales (*QR*).

Quota A limit on the quantity of a particular product that a country will import per year.

Random sample Sample in which everyone in the population has an equal chance of being selected.

Rationalization Emphasizing a product's merits and dismissing its drawbacks by a consumer in order to reduce his cognitive dissonance.

Reach The number of different people or households exposed at least once in a certain period to a particular medium or to an advertisement in that medium.

Reactive change Changes in response to events that have already taken place in the environment.

Real self concept A person's self-image in terms of how he actually is (*Actual self*).

Rebate A partial refund of the original payment for a product from the producer (*Cash refund offer*); Cash refund of a part of the purchase price by the seller to the buyer of a product.

Recall A marketing research test that measures – through aided or unaided recall tests – how well consumers can remember a given media message. For example, consumers might be asked which advertisements they saw yesterday.

Recession A slowdown in economic activity that generally occurs after a widespread drop in consumer and business spending.

Recognition test A marketing research test based on memory in which consumers are presented with an advertisement and asked if they recognize it.

Redemption The rate at which buyers participate in rebates.

Reference group Group of people having a substantial influence over an individual's attitudes and behaviour.

Reference person A person that someone chooses as a basis for self-appraisal or as a 'point of reference' in determining their own preferences, beliefs and behaviour.

Referral Recommendation to speak to a new prospect – someone who may need or want the product – by current customers, colleagues, suppliers or others.

Reflex A type of psychological need, such as the urge to belong to a group.

Regional shopping centre Large shopping centre with at least three department stores and 100 specialty stores that attract many shoppers willing to drive a great distance to find products and services not available in their home towns (*Mall*).

Regression analysis Statistical technique to find a causal relationship between two variables, e.g. to predict how a product's price affects demand over time.

Relationship Ongoing interaction with a customer, resulting in long-term satisfaction and loyalty.

Relationship building Developing and maintaining long-term relationships with buyers, in an effort to turn them into loyal customers.

Relationship management The management of ongoing relationships with customers in order to meet their long-term needs.

Relationship marketing Strategy that focuses on developing long-term relationships with customers – to earn and retain their business – as well as with distributors, suppliers and society at large.

Relative advantage The perception of an innovation, such as the iPad, as being substantially superior to existing products or ideas.

Repeat purchase The subsequent purchase of a product after the buyer's first purchase, indicating that they are becoming brand loyal and frequently used as a measure of customer satisfaction.

Replacement demand Demand from those who already own the product, but purchase a new one to replace it.

Repositioning Attempt to create a new image in the customer's mind for an existing brand through a combination of advertising and other marketing activities.

Research and Development A company's department that aims to discover solutions to problems or create new products and knowledge (*R&D*).

Research Design Proposal specifying the marketing research questions, the data collection method (including the sample and research instrument), how the responses will be analyzed and the study's constraints.

Reseller A wholesaler, retailer or other intermediary that buys and resells products at a profit without any further processing.

Retail cooperative A group of retailers with a central buying organization (at the wholesale level) and a common store name to conduct joint promotion campaigns to help them compete with chains.

Retail life cycle The emergence, growth and decline in market share of new retail forms that can be categorized into four stages: early growth, accelerated development, maturity and decline.

Retail marketing Marketing strategy of a retail company, including the analysis of customers and competitors as well as the use of a store format and *retailing mix* to create loyal customers; a broad range of marketing activities, including analyzing competitors and customers' shopping behaviour, developing a store format and positioning strategy to attract and serve the target market, and using a consistent, integrated retailing mix to gain customer loyalty.

Retailing All activities involved in selling products and services directly to ultimate consumers for their personal, family or household use.

Retailing mix The six Ps of the retailing mix used to create the store format and develop a positive store image: the Product, Promotion, Price, Place, Personnel and Presentation that a retailer can combine in different ways to attract consumers.

Retrenchment strategy Strategy in the PLC's decline stage in which a company pulls out of unattractive market segments, but can profitably continue to serve customers who still want the product.

Return on investment A measure of profitability that indicates whether or not a company is using its resources in an efficient manner (*ROI*).

Revenue The per unit price multiplied by the number of units sold.

Revenues Income that a company receives from normal business activities.

Reverse engineering Disassembling a competitor's product to analyze its components and production process, in order to make a new product at reduced costs.

Role conflict Friction in a distribution channel due to inadequate performance of channel members or disagreement on the assigned of roles ('Who does what?').

Roll-out strategy The initial introduction of a new product in only one area of the country or market before it is offered in other submarkets as well.

Route seller A type of field order taker who visits customers directly to replenish the inventories of retailers and wholesalers.

Routine problem solving A consumer's rapid decision making when buying a frequently purchased product out of habit.

Safety stock Extra inventory that a company keeps on hand as a safety cushion in case the demand for a product exceeds the sales forecast.

Sales branch Manufacturer-owned wholesale outlet, located away from the factory, which stocks and sells products to nearby, high-volume customers.

Sales engineer Someone with technical expertise – often viewed as a consultant – who does not sell products but helps to identify customer needs and solve problems by providing technical support.

Sales force promotions Incentives to encourage sales people to improve their performance by acquiring new customers, providing better service or introducing new products.

Sales management The process of planning, organizing, implementing and controlling the personal selling function.

Sales manager Management position that involves coordinating, evaluating and motivating the efforts of multiple salespeople in order to increase their productivity.

Sales objective Specific sales goal of a company or individual to be achieved over a certain period of time.

Sales office Common form of manufacturer-owned wholesaling facility that carries no inventory, but serves as a base for sales reps who call on customers in the region.

Sales plan Plan that describes the target market, sales organization, sales objectives, strategies for achieving the objectives, resources needed and practical guidelines for the plan's implementation.

Sales presentation Stage of the selling process in which the salesperson creates an interest or desire for the product by explaining its main features and strengths, illustrated by success stories of current users.

Sales promotion A set of direct incentives to temporarily increase the basic value of a product relative to comparable products on the market, stimulating consumers to buy it; A marketing instrument that creates a temporary shift in the price/value ratio of a product or service in order to encourage customers to buy a product.

Sales quota Sales objective or goal that a salesperson, distributor or branch office manager is expected to meet in a period of time, expressed in units sold, total revenues or market share.

Sales response model Model that describes the impact of advertising expenditures on the sales level of an advertised product.

Sales strategy Systematic approach to managing the company's sales efforts, including setting and achieving sales objectives, organizing the sales force and executing the sales plan to meet customers' needs.

Sample Segment of the population selected for marketing research in such a way that it represents the overall population, allowing the research results to be generalized to the entire population.

Sample The free distribution of a small quantity of a product, usually in the early stages of its life cycle.

Satisfier The features of a product that, from a customer's point of view, significantly improve its quality and are reasons to buy it.

Scanning Use of barcodes to identify products in a distribution system or to create a database of sales per store, enabling automated inventory management as an input for strategy development.

Scenario Description of a likely outcome of possible developments at some point in the future in light of the company's current decisions.

Scrambled merchandising The sale of items not usually associated with a retail establishment's primary lines in order to generate more traffic (*Scrambled retailing*); A retailer offering products that are not related to the store's main product lines, such as a supermarket selling cosmetics and other nonfood items.

Screening Stage in the new product development during which ideas that are not feasible are eliminated.

Seasonal discount Discount from the list price for buying a product out of season.

Secondary data Pre-existing data that have been collected for another purpose at an earlier time.

Secondary group Formal group – such as trade union or professional organization – with whom a person interacts occasionally.

Sector Horizontal section or link in the *supply chain*, made up of companies that perform the same function in the production or trade of a certain product (for example, the detergent industry).

Segmentation conditions Requirements for effective market segmentation, such as the measurability, size and accessibility of the segments and the feasibility of the strategy.

Segmentation criteria Consumer characteristics – such as demographic, geographic, psychographic or behavioural variables – that can be used to subdivide the aggregate market into more homogeneous subsets of buyers or market segments.

Selective advertising A type of advertising which seeks to affect the demand for a particular *brand* of product or service by promoting its unique characteristics.

Selective attention A person's ability to screen out most information that he is not interested in.

Selective demand Demand for a specific brand, rather than a type of product.

Selective distortion People tend to see only what they want to see and hear what they want to hear, consistent with their beliefs (*Selective interpretation*).

Selective distribution Level of distribution at which a (shopping) product is sold in a limited number of outlets, and not by all potential retailers in a market area.

Selective exposure Someone's efforts to avoid most of the messages and other excessive stimuli in his environment.

Selective retention People's tendency to only remember the information that is relevant to their current problem or decision.

Self-concept How a person sees themselves, and how they believe others perceive them (*Self-image*).

Self-liquidating premium A premium that the consumer pays for – including the handling fees – by purchasing it below the regular retail price.

Self-reference criterion Subconscious reference to your own (home country) cultural values and experiences, when evaluating an issue.

Sellers' market Market in which demand exceeds supply, giving sellers an advantage over customers.

Selling agent Agent who handles the manufacturer's entire output without territorial restrictions and – since he acts as the firm's independent marketing department controls prices, promotion and terms of sale.

Selling concept Market approach in which a company's emphasis is on the selling function ('selling what we make') instead of other marketing activities.

Selling-in activities Promotions to stimulate resellers to carry specific products and keep large quantities in stock.

Selling-out activities Manufacturers providing marketing tools such as flyers, window posters, displays and other supporting store material, designed to increase the retailers' turnover.

Sellogram Matrix – to structure a sales presentation – in which specific product features (quality, durability, etc.) are related to certain customer needs in order to appeal to a particular prospect.

Semi-structured interview Interview in which the majority of the questions are open-ended, with the interviewer writing down the answers as they are given.

Sentence completion Projective technique, in which the respondent is asked to complete a list of sentences with the first words that come to mind (e.g. 'People who drive a Jaguar are…').

Service An intangible activity that gives users a certain level of satisfaction, but that does not involve ownership and cannot be stored.

Service merchandiser Full-service wholesaler who markets specialized lines of primarily non-food products to grocery retailers, providing the racks on which the merchandise is displayed (*Rack jobber*).

Service retailing strategy Strategy by retailers – such as upscale specialty stores – that involves having a narrow assortment of high priced, quality products with an emphasis on a high level of service; Retailing strategy that offers products at premium prices and a high level of customer service, resulting in high profit margins for the retailer.

Services continuum Spectrum, ranging from primarily tangible to primarily intangible to identify a product or service based on this combination of attributes (*Product-service continuum*).

Services marketing Systematically stimulating sales of 'intangible activities' by facilitating the exchange process between service providers and buyers.

Shop in the shop Department store layout in which customers make purchases and pay within each department, rather than at a central checkout area.

Shopping products Products for which the consumer typically compares the quality, price and style of a few alternatives before buying them, such as cameras or clothing.

Single-channel strategy Strategy in which a manufacturer uses only one type of distribution channel to market its products.

Situational influences Factors typically related to when, where and how a consumer shops that influence his buying behaviour.

Six Sigma A quality management system designed to satisfy customers by achieving quality through a systematic process of developing near-perfect products and services.

Slogan A catchy phrase relating to the marketing message, such as 'Just do it.' by Nike.

Slotting fee Cash payment made to a retailer for access to shelf space in stores, for special shelf locations or placing displays (*Slotting allowance*).

Social class Relatively permanent and homogeneous group of individuals or families sharing similar values, interests, lifestyles and behaviour.

Social responsibility An organization's commitment to maximize its positive and to minimize its negative impact on society.

Social status Prestige relating to being an accepted member of a social class.

Socialization Incorporation of typical values, norms and symbols by those who learn about a culture.

Societal marketing concept Extension of the *marketing concept* in which management considers the broader societal consequences of its production and marketing activities and tries to balance the long-term interests of the consumer, the company and society as a whole.

Sociocultural factors Customs, values and behavioural norms that consumers learn and that influence their lifestyle and consumption habits.

Sorting Assembling a range of products from various suppliers that a retailer wants to sell, reflecting their decision about the appropriate depth and width of the product assortment.

Specialization Offering a narrow variety of merchandise mix (such as health food) while appealing to a specific consumer segment (e.g. health conscious consumers).

Specialty products High-involvement products (such as parachutes) or services (such as child care) for which consumers are willing to make a special effort.

Specialty store Relatively small-scale store offering a narrow range of product lines with a great deal of product depth.

Split-run test Comparing the effectiveness of two advertisements by placing them in different parts of the print run of a magazine, followed by a recall study.

Sponsored magazine A direct mail medium, distributed free of charge and typically consisting of editorial articles about new products as well as advertising, that is effective in passing on information to customers and in enhancing the relationship with them.

Sponsoring objectives Key reasons for companies to spend money on sponsorships, such as to increase brand awareness, enhance brand image and create goodwill.

Sponsorship A company providing financial or other support to an organization or individual involved in a particular sports, artistic or similar endeavour, hoping to acquire commercial publicity.

Standard brand Manufacturer owned brand with a smaller market share and somewhat lower quality and price than a premium brand.

Standardized marketing strategy Strategy in which the company uses a common marketing plan for all countries in which it operates, and implements it with minimal modifications in each market (*Global marketing*).

Staples Homogeneous convenience products, such as sugar, often bought on the basis of price.

Star SBU with a large market share in a high-growth market; it has a modest cash flow since most of its profits are spent on marketing to protect its market share and finance further growth.

Stay-out pricing Pricing strategy in which the price is temporarily set so low that other suppliers do not even try to enter the market.

Stealth marketing Alternative types of marketing communication – such as product placement – and publicity generators designed to approach the consumer in a more subtle way than traditional advertising.

Stimulus-response model Notion that we learn through experiences – based on stimuli – triggering us to develop certain habits in our behaviour or response (such as buying).

Stock turnover The number of times a company's average inventory is sold per year.

Store format The retail store's product assortment and market positioning that reflects the retailer's strategic choice to appeal to a carefully selected target market of customers with specific needs and shopping expectations (*Store concept*).

Store image How a store is defined in a shopper's mind, based on its physical characteristics, retailing mix and a combination of the customer's expectations and impressions.

Storytelling Questionnaire method of data collection in which the respondent is shown a drawing, picture or cartoon, about which he is asked to tell a story, or to elaborate on his own experiences as a consumer.

Straight extension Making the same product and marketing it with about the same message in the domestic market and abroad.

Straight re-buy Routine purchase of standard products (such as office supplies or maintenance services) that a company needs on a regular basis.

Strategic alliance Agreement between two organizations to work together in achieving a common objective or meeting an important business need while remaining independent.

Strategic business unit A self-contained business or part of a diversified company (such as a subsidiary, product line or brand) with its own management, set of competitors and a distinct strategy (*SBU*).

Strategic group Group of competitors with common strategic features (e.g. location, size), strengths (product range, distribution intensity) and strategies (growth strategies, positioning).

Strategic planning Development of a long-term plan to effectively use the company's resources – within the constraints of its *mission* and *business definition* – in order to maintain a strategic fit between its objectives and the market opportunities.

Strategic profile Snapshot of a company's 'big-picture' strategy – including its target markets and products – outlined at the highest organizational level.

Strategy The courses of action through which – in what markets and with what resources – a company intends to realize its marketing goals (such as an increased market share) in the next two to five years.

Stratified random sample After dividing the population into mutually exclusive subsets or 'strata' (e.g. male and female students), the respondents from each stratum are selected randomly in proportion to their percentage of the population, allowing the research results to be generalized to the whole population.

Street peddling Individuals selling snacks and food items from pushcarts in the streets, temporary stalls set up in open markets or from their vans or trucks.

Strengths A company's capabilities that may help it realize its objectives.

Structured interview Interview in which the closed-ended questions as well as their order are determined in advance and the applicable answers simply need to be ticked or circled by respondents.

Styling The physical appearance of a product that, from a marketing perspective, should be both functional and attractive.

Subculture Part of a culture whose members subscribe to the cultural mores of the overall society, yet also share beliefs, customs and consumption patterns that set them apart.

Sub-optimization Lack of cooperation between departments, resulting in less than the best possible outcome; Situation that occurs when managers try to minimize the costs of their own department or activities (such as logistics) without considering the impact on the company's overall expenses or profitability.

Substitute Product or service that can easily replace a similar product or service.

Substitute products Products that are considered by the user as alternatives for each other since they satisfy the same need.

Supercentre A combination of a supermarket and discount department store that is not as mammoth as a hypermarket.

Supermarket Large food store that carries a limited range of non-food products, combining self-service, low prices, volume sales and one-stop grocery shopping.

Supplier marketing A buyer's proactive approach throughout the purchasing process in strategically 'managing' suppliers to reduce the cost of products and services bought (*Procurement marketing*).

Supply chain The series of people and organizations – from the manufacturer to the consumer – involved in the production, distribution and consumption of products and services; The complete sequence of suppliers and activities that contribute to the creation and delivery of products and services (*Value chain*).

Supply chain management Management of a network of interconnected companies that – as partners in the supply chain – are involved in creating and delivering products to customers, from the point of origin to consumption.

Supply curve Graph showing how much of a product is expected to be offered to the market and at what price(s), which in a monopolistic market structure will be identical to the overall d*emand curve*.

Support sales people Staff who facilitate the selling process by identifying prospective customers, creating goodwill, educating buyers and providing service after the sale.

Survey Systematic data collection by asking a group of people a series of questions online or through mail questionnaires, personal or telephone interviews about products or services, their opinions, attitudes and buying behaviour.

Sustainable competitive advantage A company's permanent differential advantage, since competitors cannot duplicate the benefits of its value-creating strategy.

Sweepstakes Company-sponsored lottery that awards prizes on the basis of chance alone.

SWOT analysis An analysis – as the groundwork of strategic planning – that identifies a company's *strengths*, *weaknesses*, *opportunities* and *threats* in order to assess the implications (*situation analysis*).

Synergy Attempt to increase the efficiency and effectiveness of an operation by carrying out activities jointly rather than separately.

Tactic A company's actions to implement the broader strategy and meet its short-term objectives (one year or less).

Tailor-made promotions Exclusive, customized promotions offered by a national brand manufacturer to ensure the cooperation of retail chain stores.

Talley formula Formula used to calculate how many sales reps a firm needs, which integrates the number of customers to be visited, the call frequency necessary to service a customer each year and a salesperson's average amount of selling time available per year (*Workload approach*).

Target audience The segment of consumers or businesses targeted by a particular medium.

Target market The selected market segments on which a company focuses its marketing efforts.

Target market selection Choosing the segment(s) of buyers that the company defines as its market, and for which it develops specific marketing activities.

Tariff A tax on specific products entering a country, which raises their price and stimulates the purchase of – less expensive – domestic products (*Import tariff*, *duty*).

Team selling A form of consultative selling in which several experts – typically sales, marketing and technical specialists – work together in developing and presenting products and services to key decision makers of a buying organization.

Technological factors Technology-related influences on a company's external environment, such as new ways to increase efficiency or solve problems.

Technology push Strategy in which technological breakthroughs (e.g. in space exploration) motivate product developers to look for suitable applications in consumer markets.

Telemarketing Making unsolicited telephone sales calls that – due to the intrusive nature of this practice – has acquired a bad image in the consumer market (*Teleselling*).

Telephone interview Market research interview as part of a telephone survey, usually conducted through computer-assisted telephone interviewing (CATI).

Telephone marketing Direct marketing system in which the phone is used as an interactive marketing instrument to systematically approach target markets and to develop and enhance relationships with customers.

Television home shopping TV programme or cable channel that presents products to television viewers, encouraging them to call a toll-free number and order the products featured in the programme.

Tendering Competitive bidding from the buyer's perspective, wherein a buyer requests bid proposals from multiple suppliers in order to obtain the lowest price.

Territorial sales force structure A type of sales force structure in which the target market is divided into distinct districts or territories to sell the entire product assortment to all interested buyers in that region.

Test market Limited geographical area, representative for the overall market, in which marketers launch a new product in order to assess its commercial feasibility and marketing mix.

Test marketing Introduction of a trial version of a new product on a small scale.

Testimonial advertising Ads or commercials in which celebrities, experts or other consumers endorse a brand or discuss their own positive experiences with a product.

Theme advertising Type of advertising used to increase familiarity with the product's name and package or to enhance its brand image.

Theme communication Use of marketing communication tools (such as advertising, PR and sponsorship) with long-term effects, such as creating brand awareness and influencing the prospects' attitudes.

Threats Trends or forces in the environment that may – unless the firm effectively reacts to them – negatively affect its revenues and profits.

Time utility The added value by making a product available to consumers when desired.

Total cost approach In a physical distribution system, total cost refers to all costs incurred in achieving the customer-service objectives, which shifts the emphasis from reducing the separate costs of individual activities to minimizing overall distribution costs.

Total demand The sum total of the *extended* demand plus the *replacement* demand.

Total reach The number of people that may have been exposed to a particular medium at some time in a given year.

Trade-in allowance Price reduction granted to customers for turning in a used product when buying a new one.

Trade marketing Marketing strategy aimed at intermediaries such as retailers that carry the products or consider including them in their product range.

Trade organization Organization – representing a group of businesses – that promotes collaboration, standardization or education within an industry.

Trade promotions Sales promotion campaigns aimed at retailers, wholesalers, agents or other middlemen that encourage them to carry the manufacturer's products and promote them effectively.

Trade salespeople Staff who help the manufacturers' customers build up their volume by providing promotional help, for example in setting up store displays and rearranging shelf space.

Trade show Event at which marketers exhibit and demonstrate their products to other members of the distribution channel.

Trademark A distinctive sign – legally registered and protected – that a company uses to help identify and distinguish its products.

Trading company Marketing intermediary that takes title to products, exports, imports or produces them, invests and countertrades.

Trading-down Lengthening the product line with a lower priced, lower quality product to reach a larger target market (*Down-market stretch*).

Trading up Product assortment strategy that involves lengthening the product line with a higher priced, better quality product to meet the needs of the high end of the market (*Up-market stretch*).

Transfer price The price internally charged when a product is sold from one branch, division or subsidiary of a company to another one.

Trend Pattern of a phenomenon over time (e.g. the growing number of households) that is part of the external environment and may lead to marketing opportunities.

Trial close Selling technique in which the salesperson asks a question (such as 'What colour do you prefer?') that would usually be asked after the purchase decision.

Truck wholesaler Wholesaler who sells perishable food items – that they get on consignment from a large wholesaler – directly from the back of their truck to small retailers, restaurants and hotels (*Truck jobber*).

Turbulence Stage of the product life cycle in which most consumers are aware of the product and – as strong competitors are fighting for market share – sales continue to grow, but at a decreasing rate.

Two-step flow model Model that includes an additional step in the communication process in which companies should target opinion leaders, who then pass the desired information on to the wider public.

Ultimate consumer Individual – not always the buyer – who uses or consumes the product (*End user*).

Uncontrolled experiment Experiment (such as a test market) in which the researcher does not intervene, but simply measures the outcome of a certain factor, determining how independent variables (e.g. current prices) affect a dependent variable (e.g. sales) (*Quasi-experiment*).

Undifferentiated marketing Targeting strategy used when a company goes after the whole market with the same product and a marketing strategy with mass appeal, hoping to achieve economies of scale and keep costs at a minimum.

Undifferentiated oligopoly Oligopoly in which companies sell standardized commodities (such as aluminum), making buyers focus on price and customer service (*Pure oligopoly*).

Unduplicated reach The total number of people exposed to an ad a single time (*Cumulative reach*).

Unique selling proposition A product's unique strength that is important to customers and cannot be easily copied by competitors (*USP*).

Unitary elasticity The demand curve for a market reflecting the fact that a change in price has no effect on total revenue.

Universal product code Numerical barcode printed on packages that can be read by optical scanner systems and processed by computers, providing a wealth of information. (*UPC*).

Unsought products Products of which consumers either aren't aware, don't want to think about or suddenly discover they need in order to solve an unexpected problem.

Unstructured interview Interview in which the interviewer has a checklist of discussion points and continues his questioning until he has sufficient insight into the respondent's motives or reasoning (*In-depth interview*).

Upgrading Positioning strategy designed to influence the customer's perception through quality improvements, price increases or enhancement of the store format.

Upstream management Managing raw materials, inbound logistics, warehouse facilities and similar activities that add value in the supply chain.

User One of the most important people in the buying process, because his feedback on the product's performance will play a key role in future purchasing decisions.

Utility The extent to which a product or service satisfies the needs and wants of a consumer or an organization.

Value delivery network Teamwork by a company and its suppliers, distributors and customers, partnering with each other to enhance the performance of the entire system and provide buyers with the highest possible value.

Value perception A customer's perceived ratio of the price paid for a product to the quality or worth he received in return.

Value pricing Strategy to compete on a superior price/quality ratio, rather than the lowest price (*Value-based pricing*).

Values The beliefs, preferences and prejudices that influence someone's world view.

Variable cost A cost – such as of raw materials – that varies directly with the number of units produced and marketed.

Variable-cost pricing Pricing a product based on its variable costs, without fixed costs or overhead being directly allocated to a particular product (*Direct-costing*).

Variety store Small version of a department store, but offering fewer services and targeting the mass market with an extensive range of low-priced products.

Vendor rating Systematically evaluating and ranking current or potential suppliers based on their experience, quality level, location, customer service and other criteria.

Venture team Multidisciplinary team from different functional departments temporarily assembled to develop a new product.

Vertical marketing system A professionally managed and centrally coordinated network of channel relationships designed for maximum efficiency and market impact (*VMS*).

Viral marketing Inexpensive way for a company to spread the word about its products or services by offering customers an incentive to pass on a message about the company to other consumers.

Vision Short statement As a supplement to the mission statement-of what management wants the company to achieve in the future.

Voluntary chain A retail organization in which a wholesaler formally agrees with a group of independent retailers to use a common (brand) name, and to participate in bulk buying and joint merchandising.

Warehouse club Adaptation of a discount store in which products are offered in bulk and displayed in boxes or on pallets (*Wholesale club*).

Warehousing The design and operation of facilities for storing and moving goods.

Warranty Written statement of how the seller will compensate a buyer for any shortcoming in a product due to production errors or faulty materials within a certain period after being purchased.

Weaknesses Internal constraints that could obstruct a firm's ability to reach its goals.

Webvertising Advertising through Internet websites.

Wheel of retailing Model that describes how new types of retailers with low prices gradually – through upgrading – add value, providing opportunities for innovative stripped-down retailers

to enter the market and challenge established companies.

Wholesale intermediary Category of intermediaries that includes wholesalers as well as brokers, import brokers and agents that conduct wholesaling activities without taking title to the products they sell.

Wholesaler Company that helps producers to sell products to other wholesalers, importers, retailers or firms that, in turn, market these products to ultimate consumers or use them in their own business (*Distributor*).

Wholesaler owned brand Brand exclusively offered and promoted by retail stores that have a strategic alliance or other close business relationship with a wholesale organization.

Wholesaling All transactions in which products or services are bought for resale (not to ultimate consumers), for use in making other products or for general business operations.

Word association The respondent is presented with a list of product features or brand names and, after each one, is asked to say the first word they think of.

Word-of-mouth People sharing information about products or promotions with friends, primarily through social media.

World Trade Organization International agency that promotes and regulates trade between member countries, oversees global trade agreements and resolves conflicts when they occur (*WTO*).

CHAPTER NOTES

CHAPTER 1

1. Based on: '5 ways L'Oréal plans to increase market share', *Business Week.com*, March 27, 2012; *Sustainability Factsheet*, L'Oréal, April 2, 2011.
2. 'French wine industry ponders shift in marketing strategy', *French 24 International News*, June 23, 2011; Jeffery T. Iverson, 'Kiwi Cuvée: The Next Generation of French Wines', *Time World*, http://www.time.com/time/world/article/0,8599,195 4571,00.html, January 18, 2010; 'France loses wine title to Italy', *The Connexion*, June 14, 2011.
3. Adapted from: Charles W. Lamb, Jr., Joseph F. Hair, Jr. and Carl McDaniel, *Marketing*, Thomson, 7th edition, 2004, p. 10. © 2004 Cengage Learning. Used with permission.
4. See also: Philip Kotler and Gary Armstrong, *Principles of Marketing*, Upper Saddle River, NJ: Prentice Hall, 10th edition, 2004, p. 14.
5. Adapted from: Willian G. Nickels and Marian Burk Wood, *Marketing. Relationships, Quality, Value*, New York, NY: Worth Publishers, 1997, p. 6.
6. Adapted from: Paul Gremmen, 'Op de knieën voor de klant', *Adformatie*, 38, September 18, 2003, pp. 32–35.
7. Adapted from: Luberto van Buiten, 'De Engineered Jeans zijn heel belangrijk geweest', *MarketingTribune*, December 20, 2002, pp. 50–52.
8. Robert C. Blattberg, Gary Getz and Jacqueline S. Thomas, *Customer Equity*, Boston Massachusetts: Harvard Business School Press, 2001; adapted from: William O. Bearden, Thomas N. Ingram and Raymond W. LaForge, *Marketing: Principles and Perspectives*, McGraw Hill, 4th edition, 2004, pp. 5–6.
9. Laetitia Radder for Cengage Learning EMEA.

CHAPTER 2

1. Based on: Beth Kowitt, 'Why McDonald's wins in any economy', *Fortune*, September 5, 2011; Dave Carpenter, 'McDonald's profit climbs 27% on worldwide sales', *USA Today*, 2007; Danya Proud *et al*, 'McDonald's Announces Commitment to Offer Improved Nutrition Choices,' *McDonald's Press Release*, July 26, 2011.
2. The strategy seminar was organized by the Nyenrode University in Breukelen, the Netherlands. See also: Leo van Sister, 'De nieuwe concurrentie', *Adformatie*, January 30, 2003, p. 44.
3. http://www.usa.philips.com/about/company/index. page; 'Strenge meester Boonstra berispt Philips-top', *NRC Handelsblad*, April 19, 1997, p. 21.
4. Adapted from: Charles W. L. Hill and Gareth R. Jones, *Strategic Management: An Integrated Approach*, 4th edition. Boston: Houghton Mifflin, 1998, pp. 37–38; Roger A. Kerin *et al*, *Marketing*, 7th edition. McGraw-Hill Irwin, 2003, p. 42. © McGraw-Hill. Reproduced with permission.
5. Bronislaw J. Verhage and Eric Waarts, 'Marketing planning for improved performance: A Comparative Analysis', *International Marketing Review*, Vol. 5, No. 2, Summer 1988, pp. 20–30; 'Global brands must focus, simplify and adapt, says Bain & Co.', http://blog.freedmaninternational.com, September 30, 2011.
6. Karin Bosveld *et al*, 'Oude merken, jonge marketeers: Beddenfabrikant Auping wordt steeds meer inrichter', *Tijdschrift voor Marketing*, June 2002, p. 14–15.
7. Adapted from Keith Hammonds, 'De Grote Ideeën van Michael Porter', *Fast Company*; see also: *Next!*, May 2001, pp. 38–41.
8. Adapted from: Mike Ackermans, 'Marketing-approach Unilever blijft al met al succesvol', *Tijdschrift voor Marketing*, April 1987, pp. 10–21. The analysis is based on interviews with former Unilever marketers.
9. For an in-depth overview of marketing planning and strategy development, see Bronis Verhage, *Strategische Marketing: Analyse, planning & praktijk*, Leiden: Stenfert Kroese, 1986.
10. Based on a presentation at the ECR-conference in Paris in June, 2005 and adapted from: Elsbeth

Eilander, 'Dieter gelooft in co-existentie', *Tijdschrift voor Marketing*, June 2005, p. 4.

11. Based on an interview with C. K. Prahalad during a congress organized by the Association for Strategic Policy-Making (Vereniging voor Strategische Beleidsvorming (VSB)). See also: Ben Greif en Michiel van Nieuwstadt, 'Op naar Azië', *NRC Handelsblad*, February 12, 1997, p. 17.

12. Marcus Thompson and Shona Sinclair for Cengage Learning EMEA.

13. Quinty Danko, 'Topmanagers van buiten zijn een ramp', *Intermediair*, January 10, 2002, pp. 29–31; Rinske Hillen, 'Passie binnen de regels', *Baak!*, June/July 2002, pp. 6–7.

14. Adapted from: Benson P. Shapiro, 'Can Marketing and Manufacturing co-exist?', *Harvard Business Review*, September-October 1977, pp. 104–114.

CHAPTER 3

1. Tom Mulier, 'Nestlé's Recipe for Juggling Volatile Commodity Costs', *Bloomberg Businessweek*, March 27, 2011, pp. 29–30; Shelley DeBois, 'How Big Chocolate plans to save its cocoa supply', management.fortune.cnn.com, February 7, 2012.

2. Quote based on an interview by Frenk van Empel, 'Managers zijn niet wendbaar genoeg', *NRC Handelsblad*, September 13, 1996, p. 15.

3. In the United States this is known as 'paralysis by analysis'. See also: O. C. Ferrell *et al*, *Marketing Strategy*, The Dryden Press, 1999, pp. 31–32.

4. Matthew Lynn, 'How Nokia Fell from Grace', *www.businessweek.com*, September 15, 2010; Rauha, 'Bloggers increasingly influence Nokia's share price', *maemo.org*, July 18, 2011; Tim Worstall, 'The Fall of Nokia: Apple, Google's Android and Samsung to Blame', Forbes, July 29, 2011; Ben Rooney, 'Nokia, a Top-100 Brand No More', *The Wall Street Journal*, May 22, 2012; Scott Moritz and Adam Ewing, 'AT&T Set to Sell First Nokia Windows 8 Phone in US', *www.businessweek.com*, October 4, 2012.

5. Pete Engardio, 'Beyond the Green Corporation', *BusinessWeek*, January 29, 2007, pp.50–64; 'Why Going Green Can Mean Big Money for Fast-Food Chains,' *Time*, Sonia van Gilder Cooke, April 9, 2012; 'Can Going Green Make Walmart Cool?' Kerry A. Dolan, Forbes, May 16, 2011; 'Evaluating the ROI in Going "Green"' Tom Bruursema, June 19, 2012, www.environmentalleader.com; 'From Fringe to Mainstream: Companies Integrate CSR Initiatives into Everyday Business', May 23, 2012, Knowledge@Wharton; 'Business sees Green in

Going Green', *CNN*, Kevin Voigt, December 21, 2006, CNN.com

6. Bart Jungmann en Sheila Sitalsing, 'Dominante snelle jongerencultuur verdwijnt', *de Volkskrant*, July 5, 2003.

7. Bas Kist, 'Stimorol verwant', *Adformatie*, 30 August 2001, p. 13; Bas Kist, 'Merkenrecht: belangrijke ontwikkelingen voor marketeers', *Tijdschrift voor Marketing*, February 2002, pp. 42–44.

8. Pascal Jacobs, 'Lobbyen in Brussel', *Management Team*, June 1, 2002, pp. 34–38.

9. Part of the material in this chapter on environmentally and socially responsible corporate behaviour is adapted from: Thomas C. Kinnear, Kenneth L. Bernhardt and Kathleen A. Krentler, *Principles of Marketing*, HarperCollins Publishers, 4th edition, 1995, pp. 59, 61, 65.

10. Andrew Weir for Cengage Learning EMEA.

11. Ir. J.M.H. van Engelshoven during a talk he gave as the director of the Koninklijke/Shell Groep at a congress on ethics and enterprise organized by the University of Groningen. See also: 'Ethiek stelt bedrijven voor dilemmas', *NRC Handelsblad*, May 12, 1990, p. 21.

12. Adapted from: Roger Kerin *et al.*, *Marketing*, McGraw-Hill Irwin, 8th edition, 2006, p. 100. © McGraw-Hill. Used with permission.

13. Philip J. Rosenberger III and Bronis J. Verhage, 'The Power and the Glory: A Mini-Case On Switching Off Unilever's Power', *Proceedings*, 1996, Australian Marketing Educators Conference, 1996, pp. 23–25.

14. Adapted from: Fred Sengers, 'Word verantwoord voor het te laat is', based on interviews with Ronald Jeurissen and Johan Wempe, president of MVO Nederland (CSR Netherlands Centre of Expertise), *MarketingTribune*, February 22, 2005, pp. 52–53.

15. Parts of this paragraph are adapted from: Archie B. Carroll, 'The Pyramid of Corporate Social Responsibility: Toward the Moral Management of Organizational Stakeholders', *Business Horizons*, July/August 1991, p. 42; William M. Pride and O. C. Ferrell, *Marketing. Concepts and Strategies*, Houghton Mifflin Company, 2006, pp. 91, 110; Kurschner, '5 Ways Ethical Busine$$ Creates Fatter Profit$', *Business Ethics*, March/April 1996, p. 24.

16. Parts of this paragraph are adapted from: Margaret A. Stroup *et al,* 'Doing Good, Doing Better: Two Views of Social Responsibility', *Business Horizons*, March-April 1987, p. 23; William M. Pride and O. C. Ferrell, *Marketing*, Boston: Houghton Mifflin

Company, tenth edition, 1997, pp. 65–66; Bronis J. Verhage and Karl E. Henion II, 'International Marketers Should Consider the Ecological Aspects of a Culture When Going Abroad', *Proceedings', American Marketing Association*, Chicago, 1986; *Business Horizons*, July/August 1991; 'Good Guys Finish First', *Business Ethics*, March/April 1995, p. 13.

CHAPTER 4

1. Adapted from: Bill Johnson, 'The CEO of Heinz on Powering Growth in Emerging Markets', http://hbr.org/2011/10, October 2011; Kasey Feigenbaum, Justin White, Elliott Matticks, 'H.J. Heinz Inc: Industry Analysis', Furman University, 2011.

2. Adapted from: E.J. McCarthy and W.D. Perrault, Jr., *Basic marketing: A managerial approach*, Irwin, 10th edition,1990, p. 170.

3. Fred Krijnen, 'Bedreigde huwelijken en de werking van de wasmachine', *Adformatie*, March 1, 2001, pp. 36–38.

4. John A. Howard and Jagdish N. Sheth, *The Theory of Buyer Behaviour*, New York: Wiley, 1969, pp. 27–28.

5. Adapted from: Marnix de Bruyne, 'Een slogan "voor altijd"', *NieuwsTribune*, May 8, 1997, pp. 40–41.

6. Adapted from: Russell Belk, 'Situational Variables and Consumer Behaviour', *Journal of Consumer Research*, December 1975, p. 157-163; Vickie Clift, 'Who's Influencing Your Customer's Decisions?', *Marketing News*, February 27, 1995, p. 33; Marsha L. Richins and Bronis J. Verhage, 'Cross-Cultural Differences in Consumer Attitudes and Their Implications for Complaint Management', *International Journal of Research in Marketing*, Vol. 2, 1985, pp. 197–206.

7. Ken Bernhardt, 'To the Point', *State of Business*, Georgia State University, Spring 2005, p.31. Reprinted with permission of Ken Bernhardt.

8. John A. Howard, 'Learning and Consumer Behaviour,' in *Perspectives in Consumer Behaviour*, Revised, edited by Harold H. Kassarjian and Thomas S. Robertson, Glenview, Ill.: Scott, Foresman and Company, pp. 75–86.

9. Piet Levy, '10 minutes with… Diana Oreck', *Marketingnews*, October 30, 2010. Reprinted with permission of American Marketing Association.

10. Kinnear, Bernhardt and Krentler, op.cit., p. 195 © 1995. Printed and electronically reproduced by permission of Pearson Education, Inc., Upper Saddle River, New Jersey.

11. Robert T. Green, Bronis J. Verhage *et al,* 'Societal Development and Family Purchasing Roles: A Cross-National Study', *Journal of Consumer Research*, Vol. 9, No. 4, March 1983, pp. 436–442. Abstract published in *Journal of Marketing*, Fall 1983, p. 137. A study conducted for Sanoma Uitgevers in 2002 shows that the percentage of decisions made jointly in Dutch households is constantly increasing; see also the interview with Professor Fred Bronner in: Paul Gremmen, 'Reclame voor het hele gezin', *Adformatie*, October 2, 2003, pp. 28–30.

12. Adapted from: Nate Boaz, John Murnane and Kevin Nuffer, 'The basics of business-to-business sales success', *Marketing & Sales Practice*, May 2010. Boaz and Murnane are associate principals in McKinsey's Atlanta office, where Nuffer is a consultant.

13. Adapted from: Michael D. Hutt and Thomas Speh, 'Business-to-business Marketing', in: K. Douglas Hoffman, *Marketing Principles and Best Practices*, Thomson, 2006, p. 219 Used with permission of Michael Hutt.; Adapted from Patrick J. Robinson, Charles W. Faris, and Yoram Wind, *Industrial Buying and Creative Marketing*, Boston: Allyn & Bacon, 1967.

14. Based on a quantitative study conducted among one hundred companies. See Irene Fetter-Grotendorst and Rebecca van Eijlt, 'Wie kent nu echt zijn klant?', *Tijdschrift voor Marketing*, November 2001, pp. 24–27.

CHAPTER 5

1. Damian Kulash Jr., 'The New Rock-Star Paradigm', *The Wall Street Journal*, December 17, 2010; 'Amanda Palmer on raising $1 000 000 on Kickstarter: "Never take people's loyalty for granted"', *NME Online*, June 4, 2012.

2. Revealed by the *NIPO Business Monitor*. See also, 'Marktonderzoek in het Nederlandse bedrijfsleven', *Tijdschrift voor Marketing*, September 1995, pp. 52–53.

3. Adapted from: Theo Loth, 'Philips gaat klant bij naam noemen', *Adformatie*, February 2004, p. 64.

4. Based on: Elisabeth A. Sullivan, 'The future of research lies in accessing customer feedback in all of the various ways that consumers communicate', *Marketingnews*, June 30, 2011, p. 78. Reprinted with permission of American Marketing Association.

5. Adapted from: Missers, *Tijdschrift voor Marketing*, October 2005, p. 73.

6. Jessica Lichy for Cengage Learning EMEA.
7. Ryan Flinn, 'The Big Business of Sifting Through Social Media Data', *Bloomberg Businessweek*, October 31, 2010, pp. 20–22; Bronis J. Verhage, 'Coca-Cola: When a Crisis Affects Your Image', *The State of Business*, GSU: Office of External Affairs, Vol. XII, No. 3, Fall 1999, pp. 7-8; Andrew Hampp, 'Gap to Scrap New Logo, Return to Old Design', *adage.com*, October 10, 2010; 'We hear you! How companies respond to user feedback', *South Source*, November 2012.
8. Bronis J. Verhage and Philip J. Rosenberger, 'The Power and The Glory: A Mini-Case on Switching Off Unilever's Power', *Australian Marketing Educator's Conference*, 1996, pp. 23–25.
9. Quote taken from an interview with Stef Gans published in *Tijdschrift voor Marketing* and also in Quinty Danko, 'Soepmaker gaat kruidenieren', *Intermediair*, August 8, 2002.

CHAPTER 6

1. Source: Janet Marrissey, 'The Milennials Check In', *The New York Times*, March 13, 2012; 'The Milennials Check In', www.connectedhotel.net March 17, 2012; Erin Dostal, 'Ritz-Carlton Company Hotel company launches mobile app', *Direct Marketing News*, 1 March 2012, http://www.dmnews.com/ritz-carlton-hotel-company-launches-mobile-app/article/239200/
2. Adapted from: Thomas C. Kinnear, Kenneth L. Bernhardt and Kathleen A. Krentler, *Principles of Marketing*, New York, N.Y., HarperCollins Publishers, 4th edition, 1995, p. 148.
3. Adapted from: Philip Bueters, 'De allerarmsten als markt', *FEM Business*, March 4, 2006, p. 42, http://www.design.philips.com/about/design/designnews/newvaluebydesign/helping400million_people_give_up_smoking.page.
4. See for example: Bronis J. Verhage, 'Energiebesparing als Sociale Marketingstrategie: Implicaties voor het Overheidsbeleid', *Economisch Statistische Berichten*, vol. 64. No. 3232, November 28, 1979, pp. 1249–1253.
5. Based on an interview by Piet Levy, '10 minutes with Eric Paquette', *Marketingnews*, November 30, 2010, pp. 28–29. Reprinted with permission of American Marketing Association.
6. Marsha L. Richins and Bronis J. Verhage: 'Assertiveness and Aggression in Marketplace Exchanges: Testing Measure Equivalence', *Journal of Cross-Cultural Psychology*, Vol. 18, No. 1, March 1987, pp. 93–105.

7. Adapted from: Karin Bosveld, 'Marketingprof V. Kumar: marketingmythen doorgeprikt', *Tijdschrift voor Marketing*, April 2004, pp. 34–36.
8. See also: Hoffman *et al.*, *Marketing Principles and Best Practices*, Thomson, 3rd edition, 2004, p. 245.
9. Edwin Visser: 'Het nieuwe designdenken', *MarketingTribune*, January 13, 2004, pp. 12–14.
10. Paul Groothengel: 'Drukte rond de kaarttafel', *Tijdschrift voor Marketing*, April 2001, pp. 74–75.
11. Adapted from: Jyoti Thottam, 'The Little Car That Couldn't', *Time*, October 24, 2011; Ann Marie Kerwin, 'A world of inspirational problem-solving, savvy brands and smart marketing', *Advertising Age*, June 14, 2010; Taruna Sondarva, 'Indian Automotive Industry: Emerging Global Auto Hub', www.ikonmarket.com, September 2011.
12. Paul van der Kwast, 'Heineken poetst flets merk op', *Intermediair*, September 6, 2001, p. 17; 'Gemaksflesje Heineken slaat aan', *Distrifood* (Extra), May 24, 2003, p 7.

CHAPTER 7

1. Adapted from: Kirsten Korosec, 'The Red Devils' Brand Offensive', *Marketingnews*, September 30, 2010, pp. 14-18 Reprinted with permission of American Marketing Association.; www.manutdrcb.com
2. Gary Armstrong and Philip Kotler, *Marketing: An Introduction*, Prentice Hall, 8th edition, pp. 200–201. © 2007. Printed and electronically reproduced by permission of Pearson Education, Inc., Upper Saddle River, New Jersey.
3. A. Salmin Amin, 'PepsiCo CMO Amin On How To Build A Billion-Dollar Brand', *Forbes*, January 26, 2012. Used with permission of PepsiCo.
4. Based on: Chris Reiter, 'BMW's Mini: Little, But She Is Fierce!', *Bloomberg Businessweek*, February 12, 2012; Frances Perraudin, 'From Four Wheels to Two: Has Mini Gone Too Far?', *Time*, September 29, 2010; Tim Higgins, 'Daimler's Smart Starts US Marketing Campaign to Improve Model's Image', Bloomberg Businessweek, September 23, 2011.
5. Adapted from Theodore Levitt, 'Exploit the Product Life Cycle', *Harvard Business Review*, November-December 1965, pp. 81–94.
6. Adapted from General Electric's Website: www.ge.com: 'What is Six Sigma?', May, 2006.
7. Adapted from: Martin Christopher *et al*. *Relationship Marketing*, Oxford, U.K: Butterworth Heinemann, 1991, p. 70-71; D.A. Garvin, 'Competing on the Eight Dimensions of Quality,

Harvard Business Review, November-December, 1987, pp. 101–109; William G. Nickels and Marian Burk Wood, *Marketing. Relationships, Quality, Value*, New York, N.Y.: Worth Publishers, 1997, p. 323.

8. Madéle Tait for Cengage Learning EMEA.
9. Bronis J. Verhage, Ugur Yavas, Robert T. Green and Eser Borak: 'The Perceived Risk – Brand Loyalty Relationship: An International Perspective', *Journal of Global Marketing*, vol. 3, no. 3, 1990, pp. 7–22.
10. Thomas C. Kinnear, Kenneth L. Bernhardt and Kathleen A. Krentler, *Principles of Marketing*, New York, N.Y.: HarperCollins Publishers, 4th edition, 1995, p. 203.
11. Leonard L. Berry and A. Parasuraman, *Marketing Services: Competing Through Quality*, New York: Free Press, 1991, p. 5; part of this paragraph is adapted from William H. Cunningham and Isabella C.M. Cunningham, *Marketing. A Managerial Approach*, Cincinnati, South-Western Publishing Company.
12. G. Lynn Shostack, 'Breaking Free from Product Marketing', *Journal of Marketing*, April 1977, p. 76. Reprinted with permission of American Marketing Association.
13. This section is adapted from Christopher H. Lovelock and Robert F. Young, 'Marketing Potential of Improving Productivity in Service Industries', in Pierre Eiglier *et al., Marketing Consumer Services: New Insights*, Cambridge, Mass.: Marketing Science Institute, 1977, pp. 111–118.

CHAPTER 8

1. Adapted from Reena Jana, 'Inspiration from Emerging Economies', *Businessweek*, March 23 & 30, 2009, pp. 38–41; Natalie Zmuda, 'P&G, Levi's, GE innovate by thinking in reverse', *Advertising Age*, June 12, 2011; 'Philips to install 100 solar-powered lighting centres across Africa', *ledsmagazine.com*, August 20, 2012.
2. Thomas Robertson, 'The Process of Innovation and Diffusion of Innovation', *Journal of Marketing*, January 1967, p. 15; Bronislaw J. Verhage, 'The Diffusion of Energy Conservation Measures: Implications for an Effective Communications Strategy', *Proceedings*, Sixth Annual Seminar on Advertising and Public Policy, ESSEC, Cerge-Pontoise, France, 1980.
3. Adapted from 'New product development', *The Marketing Donut,* http://www.marketingdonut.co.uk/marketing/market-research/new-product-research/new-product-development; Reproduced with kind permission of BHP Information Solutions Ltd.
4. 'Marketeer zoekt altijd iets unieks', *MarketingTribune*, December 16, 2003, p. 53.
5. Mirjam Hulsebos, 'Consumentenbehoeften als beperkende factor', *Tijdschrift voor Marketing*, May 2000, pp. 10–13.
6. Bronislaw J.Verhage, Ph. Waalewijn en A. J. van Weele, 'Het ontwikkelen van ideeën voor nieuwe producten: aanzet tot innovatie', *Bedrijfskunde*, 2, 1980, pp. 153–161.
7. 'Nestlé – The Unrepentant Chocolatier', *The Economist*, October 29, 2009.
8. Ken Bernhardt, 'Marketing Innovation: Creating Competitive Advantage', *Atlanta Business Chronicle*, January 27, 2006.
9. Bronislaw J. Verhage, Ph. Waalewijn en A.J. van Weele, 'Het ontwikkelen van ideeën voor nieuwe producten: aanzet tot innovatie', *Bedrijfskunde*, 2, 1980, pp. 153–161.
10. David Chalcraft for Cengage Learning EMEA.
11. David S. Hopkins, 'Options in New Product Organization', New York: The Conference Board, 1974, pp. 42–43.
12. *Ibid.,* pp. 44–45.
13. R.G. Cooper and U. de Bretani, 'Criteria for Screening Industrial Products', *Industrial Marketing Management*, Vol. 13, 1984, p. 149-156; Booz, Allen & Hamilton, 1982, *op. cit.*; 'Most New Products Start with a Bang. End up as a Bomb', *Marketing News*, March 27, 1987, p. 36.
14. 'Philips wil ontwikkeling van producten versnellen', *NRC Handelsblad*, March 29, 1989, p. 11.
15. David Hopkins, 'New Product Winners and Losers', New York: The Conference Board, 1980.
16. Adapted from Tommaso Ebhardt, 'Fiat Takes Alfa Romeo for a US Test Drive', *Bloomberg Businessweek*, April 24, 2011, pp. 19-20; Jason Siu, 'Alfa Romeo Giulia to Target BMW 3-Series', www.autoguide.com/auto-news/2012/08/; Christina Rogers and Gilles Castonguay, 'Alfa Romeo Plots a Return to America', *The Wall Street Journal*, September 24, 2012; Christina Rogers and Gilles Castonguay, 'Fiat Counts on Chrysler for Help with US Alfa Launch', *The Wall Street Journal*, September 24, 2012.
17. Jaap van Ede, *op. cit.*; see also: Bronis Verhage and Philip Rosenberger III, 'The Power and the Glory: A Mini-Case on Switching Off Unilever's Power', *Proceedings, 1996 Australian Marketing Educators Conference*, 1996. pp. 23–35.

18. Based on Adam Wooten, 'Size matters in global product marketing', *Deseret News*, May 20, 2011, and 'Cultural tastes affect international food packaging', *Deseret News*, June 17, 2011.

19. Parts of this section are adapted from: Everett M. Rogers, *'Diffusion of Innovations'*, New York: The Free Press, 3rd edition, 1983.

CHAPTER 9

1. Chris Reiter, 'The Contender', *Bloomberg Businessweek*, January 30, 2012, pp. 21-22; Alan Ohnsman and Sookyung Seo, 'How Kia is Rapping Its Way Into America's Heart', *Bloomberg Businessweek*, November 29, 2010, pp. 23-24; Jorn Madslien, 'Kia grows in shrinking European market', www.bbc.co.uk/news/business, March 14, 2012.

2. For a discussion and interesting examples of new ways of appealing to customers, see: Michael R. Solomon, Greg W. Marshall and Elnora W. Stuart, *Marketing. Real People, Real Choices*, Upper Saddle, NJ: Pearson Prentice Hall, 4th edition, 2006, pp. 370–371.

3. Adapted from: J.F. Engel, M.R. Warshaw, and T.C. Kinnear, *Promotional Strategy*, 7th edition, Irwin, 1991, p. 78. © McGraw-Hill. Used with permission.

4. Based on: Don E. Schultz, 'Ask a Native', *Marketingnews*, May 30, 2011, p. 11. Reprinted with permission of American Marketing Association.

5. Adapted from: John Bissell, 'Customers Want To Talk With You', *Brandweek*, September 11, 2000. p. 42. © Wright's Media. Used with permission.

6. Adapted from: Robert M. McMath, 'Spread Alert', www.failuremag.com/arch_mcmath_benecol.html. Reprinted with permission of Failure Magazine LLC.

7. Steve Rothwell and Zulfugar Agayev, 'London Taxis Next Stop: Azerbaijan', *Bloomberg Businessweek*, March 19, 2012; www.london-taxis.com, 2012; Singapore Limousine Taxi Cab, http://www.limousinecab.com/; Jason Deign, 'Ride to the future in a London cab', *The Network: Cisco's Technology News Site*, July 22, 2012, http://newsroom.cisco.com/feature/970105/Ride-to-the-Future-in-a-London-Cab; Paul Sonne, 'Azerbaijan Hails London Taxis to Upgrade Its Unlicensed Fleet', *The Wall Street Journal*, 15 May 2012 http://online.wsj.com/article/SB10001424052702304192704577440408046828 2556.html; 'Manganese Bronze taxi steering fault solution found', *BBC News Online*, November 15, 2012, http://www.bbc.co.uk/news/uk-england-coventry-warwickshire-20349949

8. Adapted from: Ko Floor and Fred van Raaij, *Marketingcommunicatiestrategie*, Leiden, Stenfert Kroese, 1989, p.14. Used with permission of Noordhoff Uitgevers bv, The Netherlands.

9. Adapted from: Thomas E. Kinnear, Kenneth L. Bernhardt and Kathleen A. Krentler, *Principles of Marketing*, 4th edition, pp. 482–483. © 1995. Printed and electronically reproduced by permission of Pearson Education, Inc., Upper Saddle River, New Jersey.

CHAPTER 10

1. Adapted from: George Webster, 'HIV-positive muppet to star in Nigeria's "Sesame Street"', www.cnn.com/2010?SHOWBIZ/TV/10.06/sesame.street.nigeria, October 6, 2010; www.time.com, September 22, 2002.

2. Carla Fourie for Cengage Learning EMEA.

3. Bronis J. Verhage, 'Niets beter dan vergelijkende reclame', *Intermediair*, vol. 18, nr. 29, July 23, 1982, pp. 1–7.

4. For an interesting discussion of online advertising, see Terrence A. Shimp, in K. Douglas Hoffman, *Marketing Principles and Best Practices*, Thomson South-Western, 3rd edition, 2006, pp. 452–455.

5. Mihalis Kavaratzis for Cengage Learning EMEA.

6. This section is based on: Drs J.M.G. Floor en Prof. Dr W.F. van Raaij, *Marketingcommunicatiestrategie*, Leiden: Stenfert Kroese, 1989, pp. 180–199. Used with permission of Noordhoff Uitgevers bv, The Netherlands.

7. Adapted from: Floor en Van Raaij, *op.cit.*, Ibid, pp. 218-239.

8. Adapted from: F.F.O Holzhauer, in J. Roomer (red.), *Handboek Reclame*, Deventer: Kluwer, 7.3.0.1–26.

9. Adapted from: Clementine Fletcher, 'Heineken's Most Interesting Saviour', *Bloomberg Businessweek*, January 9, 2012; 'Dos Equis Most Interesting Saviour of Heineken', *Bloomberg News*, December 20, 2011; 'Dos Equis Named Beer Brand of the Year', *BusinessWire*, October 27, 2011.

10. Matthew Boyle, 'Top Secret: Durex's Olympic Condoms', *Bloomberg Businessweek*, March 5, 2012, pp. 27-28; Vanessa Kortekaas, 'Olympic sponsors seek podium for brands', *Financial Times*, September 3-4, 2011, p. 12; http://careers.guardian.co.uk/careers-blog/could-ambush-marketing-help-you-find-a-job; Jessica Dane, '"Ambush Marketing" keeps LOCOG on its toes',

MSN UK, July 25, 2012 http://sport.uk.msn.com/olympics-2012/inside-track/blogpost.aspx?post=d06adab5-4c44-481b-9efc-8b2a9632027b; 'London Eye: Dr Dre beats the brand ban – for a while', *The Independent* August 3, 2012.

CHAPTER 11

1. Based on: Marc de Swaan Arons, 'Winning in Global Marketing', www.forbes.com, July 1, 2010; Ken Bernhardt, 'The CMO of the Future', *Atlanta Business Chronicle*, June 3, 2011; Ken Bernhardt, 'CMO's Unprepared for Changes in Marketing', *Atlanta Business Chronicle*, December 2, 2010. Used with permission of Ken Bernhardt.
2. Adapted from: Charles M. Futrell, *Fundamentals of Selling*, McGraw-Hill, 8th edition, 2004, Chapter 12; Roger A. Kerin, *et al., Marketing*, McGraw-Hill Irwin, 8th edition, 2006, pp. 537–538.
3. Adapted from Philip Kotler, Neil Rackham, and Suj Krihnaswamy, 'Ending the War Between Sales and Marketing', *Harvard Business Review*, July-August 2006, pp. 68–78; Maryanne Hancock, Homayoun Hatami, and Sunil Rayan, 'Using your sales force to jump-start growth', *Marketing & Sales Practice*, April 2011.
4. Adapted from: Martijn Vissers, 'Van dozenschuiver tot dienstverlener', *Adformatie*, December 6, 2001, p. 53; Luberto van Buiten, 'Van keiharde verkoop naar advies', *MarketingTribune*, May 6, 2003, pp. 22–23.
5. Peter Spier for Cengage Learning EMEA.
6. Based on: L.M., 'Hailing the Google bus', *The Economist*, October 11, 2011; Dulue Mbachu, 'Google Invests in African Internet Expansion for Future Revenue', www.bloomberg.com, May 4, 2011; 'Google Internet awareness bus arrives on 40-day tour', *The Times of India*, September 27, 2011; 'Google Bus Brings Internet to Rural India', www.neatorama.com/2011/10/09/, October 9, 2011; 'Google. The Internet Bus Project', www.google.co.in/intl/en/landing/internetbus/, July 2012.
7. Simon Kelly for Cengage Learning EMEA.
8. Part of this section is adapted from: William O. Bearden, Thomas N. Ingram, Raymond W. LaForge, *Marketing. Principles & Perspectives*, McGraw-Hill Irwin, 4th edition, 2004, pp. 481–491.
9. This section is partly based on an interesting discussion on integrated direct marketing in: Philip Kotler and Gary Armstrong, *Principles of Marketing*, Pearson Prentice Hall, 11th edition, 2006, pp. 515–516.

10. Adapted from: Ko Floor and Fred van Raaij, *Marketingcommunicatiestrategie*, Leiden: Stenfert Kroese, 1989, pp. 480–499. Used with permission of Noordhoff Uitgevers bv, The Netherlands.

CHAPTER 12

1. Jeffrey Helbling, Josh Leibowitz, and Aaron Rettaliata, 'The value proposition in multichannel retailing', McKinsey Quarterly (Source: Marketing and Sales Practice), May 2011.
2. Ken Bernhardt, 'Use Pricing Strategies to Stay Competitive', *Atlanta Business Chronicle*, September 22, 2006. Reprinted with permission of Ken Bernhardt. Also see: Harvard Business School's Working Knowledge Newsletter (http://hbswk.hbs.edu/item/3107.html) and The McKinsey Quarterly (http://mckinseyquarterly.com/article_abstract_visitor.aspx?ar=1841&L2=16&L3=19).
3. Based on McKinsey's Pricing Benchmark Survey; Kent Monroe and Jennifer Cox, 'Pricing Practices that Endanger Profits', *Marketing Management*, September/October 2001, pp. 42–46.
4. Rick Wartzman, 'Drucker on…Radiohead?', *The Drucker Difference*, October 11, 2007. Reprinted with permission of the YGS Group.
5. Adapted from: Joel R. Evans and Barry Berman, *Marketing. Marketing in the 21st century*, Thomson, 10th edition, 2007, p. 638.
6. Adapted from: Shaun Rein, 'The key to successful branding in China', *BusinessWeek Online*, September 26, 2007; 'Buick Highlights Brand's Modern Transformation', *http://media.gm.com*, May 11, 2010; Paul A. Eisenstein, 'Buick may owe its survival to China', www.msnbc.cm/id/37361381/ns/business-autos/, May 27, 2010; Andrew Jacobs and Adam Century, 'In China, Buick's for the Chic', *The New York Times*, November 15, 2011, p. B1.
7. Adapted from: Philip Kotler and Gary Armstrong, *Principles of Marketing*, Pearson Prentice Hall, 11th edition, 2006, p. 339.
8. Adapted from: Gérard Brockhoff and Bart Verweij, 'Het (on)gelijk van de prijsvechter', *MarketingTribune*, November 4, 2003, pp. 38–39.

CHAPTER 13

1. Adapted from: 'Inditex: The future of fast fashion', www.economist.com/node/4086117, June 16, 2005; 'Global stretch. When will Zara hit its limits?', *The Economist*, March 10, 2011; 'Fast fashion: Zara in India', *Forbes*, July 29, 2010; Marion Hume,

'The secrets of Zara's success', *The Telegraph*, 22 June 2011, http://fashion.telegraph.co.uk/news-features/TMG8589217/The-secrets-of-Zaras-success.html#

2. Michael E. Porter, *Competitive Advantage: Creating and Sustaining Superior Performance*, The Free Press, a division of Simon & Schuster Adult Publishing Group, 1988.

3. Uchenna Uzo for Cengage Learning EMEA.

4. Armorel Kenna, 'Benetton: A Must-Have Becomes a Has-Been', *Bloomberg Businessweek*, March 20, 2011; Assif Shameen, 'The Rise and Dramatic Fall of Benetton', *The Edge Financial Daily*, March 20, 2012, http://www.theedgemalaysia.com/in-the-financial-daily/210663-the-rise-and-dramatic-fall-of-benetton.html; Christopher Emsden, 'Benetton Profit Declines, Sales Steady; Sees Tough Year Ahead', *The Wall Street Journal*, January 31, 2012, http://online.wsj.com/article/BT-CO-20120131-710169.html

5. Based on *Dictionary of Marketing Terms*, American Marketing Association, www.marketingpower.com 2008.

6. Matthew Meacham and other Bain & Company partners, 'Growing With Africa's Consumers', *Forbes*, April 4, 2012; 'The Beast in the Bush', *The Economist*, February 17, 2011; Walmart in South Africa: 503 Laid Off Workers Reinstated as Condition of Merger, www.huffingtonpost.com, March 16, 2012; 'Consumer Goods in Africa: A Continent Goes Shopping', *The Economist*, August 18, 2012; 'By Foot, By Bike, by Taxi, Nestle Expands', *The Wall Street Journal*, Devon Maylie, December 1, 2011; 'Big Boxes for Boks', *The Economist*, June 2, 2011; 'The African Consumer Market', *African Development Bank*, http://www.afdb.org/en/blogs/afdb-championing-inclusive-growth-across-africa/post/the-african-consumer-market-8901

7. Julian Glover for Cengage Learning EMEA.

CHAPTER 14

1. Partially based on: Youngme Moon, 'IKEA Invades America', *Harvard Business School*, Case 9-504-094, 2004; Kerry Capell, 'How the Swedish Retailer became a Global Cult Brand', *Business Week*, November 14, 2005, p. 96; Lianne George, 'It's Swedish For Invincible', *Maclean's*, August 14–21, 2006, pp. 33–36.

2. Adapted from: Andreas Knorr and Andreas Arndt, 'Why did Wal-Mart fail in Germany?', *Institut fur Weltwirtschaft und Internationales Management*, Bremen, Germany, Band 24, June 2003; M. Lander and M. Barbaro, 'Walmart Finds That Its Formula Doesn't Fit Every Country', *The New York Times*, August 6, 2006; 'Charlie Rose talks to Mike Duke', *Bloomberg Businessweek*, December 10, 2010, p. 30.

3. Elmira Bogoviyeva for Cengage Learning.

4. This section is adapted from Evans and Berman, *op.cit.*, pp. 195–198.

5. Stephanie Clifford and Liz Alderman, 'American Retailers Try Again in Europe', www.nytimes.com/2011/06/16/business/global/16retail.html, June 15, 2011; 'US e-retailers get tips for succeeding in EU markets', *Fibre2Fashion*, June 11, 2012, http://www.fibre2fashion.com/news/apparel-news/newsdetails.aspx?news_id=112125; Katie Hunt, 'High Street fashion brands look to China for profits', *BBC News Business*, July 15, 2012, http://www.bbc.co.uk/news/business-18607684

6. Preeti Khicha, 'Dr Andreas Schaaf, India President, BMW', *Business Standard*, January 17, 2011, http://www.business-standard.com/india/news/qa-dr-andreas-schaaf-india-president-bmw/421946/ Used with permission.

CHAPTER 15

1. Adapted from: Peter Gumbel, 'Big Mac's Local Flavour', *Fortune*, May 5, 2008, pp. 114–119.

2. Shaun Rein, *op.cit.*, 2007

3. Parts of this paragraph are adapted from: Roger A. Kerin *et al.*, *Marketing*, McGraw-Hill Irwin, 7th edition, 2004, pp. 183–191.

4. Based on: S. Tamer Cavusgil, 'Offshoring of Talent', *State of Business Online*, Georgia State University, Robinson College of Business, Vol. XXII No. 1, Spring 2010. Used with permission of S. Tamer Cavusgil.

5. http://www.wto.org/english/thewto_e/whatis_e/tif_e/agrm7_e.htm

6. Adapted from: Julie Jargon, 'Kraft Reformulates Oreo, Scores in China', *The Wall Street Journal*, May 1, 2008; 'Kraft flavours Oreo with banana, green tea and mango to appeal to world', *Chicago Tribune*, May 7, 2012 http://articles.chicagotribune.com/2012-05-07/business/chi-kraft-flavors-oreo-with-banana-green-tea-mango-to-appeal-to-world-20120507_1_green-tea-oreos-kraft; Robert Smith, 'Rethinking The Oreo For Chinese Consumers', *National Public Radio*, January 27, 2012 http://www.npr.org/blogs/money/2012/01/27/145918343/rethinking-the-oreo-for-chinese-consumers

7. Adapted from: Ken Bernhardt, 'Toward a New Vision of Marketing', *Atlanta Business Chronicle*, April 1, 2011. Used with permission of Ken Bernhardt; Jo Ann Herald, 'Marketing 20/20. Are you Ready for It?,' *State of Business Online*, Georgia State University, Robinson College of Business, Vol. XXIII No. 2, Fall 2011.

8. Bronis J. Verhage *et al.* 'Will A Global Marketing Strategy Work?', *Journal of the Academy of Marketing Science*, Vol. 23, No. 2, 1989, pp. 68–78.

9. Bronis J. Verhage, Ugur Yavas and Robert T. Green, 'Global Consumer Segmentation versus Local Market Orientation', *Management International Review*, Vol. 32, No. 3, 1992, pp. 265–272.

10. Adapted from Jaap van Sandijk, 'Er wordt niet meer gecommuniceerd', *Tijdschrift voor Marketing*, June 2001, p. 12.

11. Adapted from Paul Gremmen, 'Met nieuwe smaken een zoutje communiceren', *Adformatie*, April 17, 2003, p. 44.

INDEX